SAFIRE'S
POLITICAL
DICTIONARY

SAFIRE'S
POLITICAL
DICTIONARY

An Enlarged, Up-to-Date Edition
of *The New Language*
of Politics

BY

WILLIAM
SAFIRE

BALLANTINE BOOKS · NEW YORK

For Mark

Introduction
to the First Edition
1968

The new, old, and constantly changing language of politics is a lexicon of conflict and drama, of ridicule and reproach, of pleading and persuasion. Color and bite permeate a language designed to rally many men, to destroy some, and to change the minds of others.

Part of it is the private argot politicians use in talking to other insiders, when they *take him to the mountaintop* and wonder if the *smell of magnolias* will cause a *bullet vote*. Another part is the language about politics, from *smoke filled room* and *whistlestopping* to a *passion for anonymity*. Finally, there is the public language used by political figures, from a needling *barefoot boy from Wall Street* to an evocative *just and lasting peace*.

This is a dictionary of the words and phrases that have misled millions, blackened reputations, held out false hopes, oversimplified ideas to appeal to the lowest common denominator, shouted down inquiry, and replaced searching debate with stereotypes that trigger approval or hatred.

This is also a dictionary that shows how the choice of a word or metaphor can reveal sensitivity and genius, crystallize a mood and turn it to action; some political language captures the essence of an abstraction and makes it understandable to millions.

The language of politics is vivid. *Gutfighters* with an *instinct for the jugular* and *hatchetmen* adept at *nut-cutting* prowl the political jungle. An anonymous voice becomes a *voice from the sewer*, a bigot an *apostle of hate*, a pessimist a *prophet of gloom and doom*, a censor a *bookburner;* men who enter the political arena with *foot-in-mouth disease* leave in a *hail of dead cats.*

The best of the phrases in politics paint word pictures: you can see the *man on the wedding cake;* you can almost feel the *wave of the future.* And the lexicon delights in disaster: *landslides, prairie fires, tidal waves,* and *avalanches* are the goals of *whirlwind campaigns.* Politicians pray that *lightning may strike.*

The language dips into the Bible for *all things to all men, Eleventh Commandment, fight the good fight,* and *Armageddon;* turns to church terms for *party faithful, party elders, bleeding heart,* and *gray eminence;* to poetry for Shakespeare's *strange bedfellows,* Wordsworth's *Happy Warrior,* T.S. Eliot's *wasteland;* to the American Indian for *sachem, mugwump, muckeymucks,* and *off the reservation;* to horseracing for *dark horse, running mate, front runner, bolt, shoo-in;* and to the military for *campaign, camps, boom, spoils, rally, regular, hundred days, man on horseback, war horse,* and *old fogy,* as well as wargaming words like *escalation, counterforce,* and other products of *Foggy Bottom* and the *think tanks.*

It encompasses the jargon of the news media *(off the record, authoritative sources, backgrounder, dope story, leak, plant, not for attribution)* and the language of the civil rights movement *(black power, white power structure, Freedom Now, backlash, We Shall Overcome, soul, tokenism, Uncle Tom, Jim Crow, segregation, stand in the doorway)*

The political zoo offers most metaphors of all. *Doves* and *hawks* fly in its aviary, along with emblematic *bald eagles,* as *lame ducks eat crow* on the *rubber-chicken circuit* and all look warily at the *floo-floo bird,* lowest in the *pecking order.* The menagerie features the familiar *elephant* and *donkey,* with a big cage for *tigers (Tammany* and *paper)* who enjoy *twisting the lion's tail.* The *mossback* ignores the racket of the *watchdog committees* and the *bird dogs* and *kennel dogs* yapping at the *fat cats,* who in turn hunger for a *red herring* and long to hear *shrimps whistle.* The willing *gopher* and the *coon,* whose skin is a prize for presidential walls, shudder at the ominous silence from the *dinosaur wing,* where *copperheads* slither and *gerrymanders* abound. In the candidates' stable, the *dark horse,* the *wheel horse,* and the *stalking horse* are hitched in a *troika,* as the old *war horse* awaits the *man on horseback.*

NOT IN THIS DICTIONARY

As defined here, the language of politics does not include much of the language of government. If a word has a good definition available in most dictionaries, this is not the place to look for it. "Amendment" is not here, though *rider* is; "assistant majority leader" is not, but *whip* is; "vice president" is not, though *Throttlebottom* and *heartbeat away from the presidency* are; "president" is not, but *loneliest job in the world* and *presidential initials* are; "diplomat" is not, but *shirtsleeve diplomat, striped-pants diplomat,* and *cookie pusher* are.

In the same way, this dictionary concerns itself not with the historical event, but with the language that comes out of it: there is no "Marshall Plan," "Point Four Program," or "Monroe Doctrine" here, though there is an entry on *doctrines;* no "Atlantic Charter," but an entry on *four freedoms;* no "Geneva conference," but entries on *summitry* and *spirit of;* no "Army-McCarthy hearings," but entries on *point of order* and *junketeering gumshoes;* no "government agencies," but an entry on *alphabet agencies* and *acronyms.* The *Bay of Pigs* is included because of its use of *fiasco,* and the Cuban missile crisis of 1962 is listed under *eyeball to eyeball.*

OLD PHRASE, NEW CONTEXT

A linguistic view of history offers a few insights. Promises and appeals to Negroes and whites took the shape of slogans like *vote yourself a farm, forty acres and a mule, three acres and a cow, the full dinner pail,* and *black power.* For diplomats, there is a lesson in Kennedy's choice of *quarantine* to describe a blockade, taken from the preconditioning of the word by FDR before World War II; in the same way, McKinley used the revered *manifest destiny* to justify his acquisition of Hawaii.

Most of the seemingly "new" language is surprisingly old: Henry IV's *chicken in every pot,* Al Smith's cooing *doves* and Thomas Jefferson's *war hawk* accusation, Henry Clay's struggle against the *can't win* theme, Alf Landon's borrowing of *New Frontier* from Henry Wallace, Teddy Roosevelt's blast at the *lunatic fringe,* all are old and have been used as new.

There is the longevity of the terms *advice and consent, vox populi,* Aristotle's *political animal* and Bacon's *presidential timber,* and the use of *Hottentots* as a symbol of underdeveloped nations. There is a sisters-under-the-skin relationship between Louis XIV's *L'état c'est moi* and Frank Hague's *I am the law,* and subtle differences between a *kitchen cabinet,* a *brain trust,* and a *privy council.*

Some words are freshly minted: in the thirties, *boondoggle* and *gobbledegook* were neologisms that stayed with us; in the sixties, *clout, crunch,* and *charisma* took on new political meaning.

The political language is constantly changing: *gutter flyer* replaces *roorback, angry young men* edges aside *young Turks, swing voter* takes over for *floater, opportunist* for *trimmer, plum* for *persimmon, smokescreen* for *cuttlefish,* henchman for *fugelman.* See OBSOLETE TERMS. But some die and are born again: *snollygoster* and *mossback* were Harry Truman favorites, and *Philippic* makes an occasional reappearance.

Phrases are sharpened in use; longer statements by Jefferson and Cleveland became "few die and none resign" and *public office is a public trust.* Bismarck's "iron and blood" wound up as "blood and iron," and Churchill's "blood, toil, tears and sweat" (with a long history of its own) was popularized as "blood, sweat and tears."

CHORUS COINAGE, PHANTOM COINAGE

Sometimes a word or phrase pops into the political language spontaneously, without an individual coiner. "As Maine Goes, So Goes the Nation" was a well-known slogan; when only Maine and Vermont went for Landon in 1936, it was natural for hundreds of politicians to say "As Maine goes, so goes Vermont" in a chorus coinage.

More mysterious, however, is the phantom coinage: a word like *backlash,* more apt than *backfire* or *boomerang* or *reaction,* subtly carrying the slavemasters' whip, appears to have entered the language by osmosis. It was quickly accepted because it filled a linguistic need. The coinage of *medicare,* also dwelt on at length here, is included because it shows how the right word will triumph over governmental obstacles. The coiner of *medicare* was neither famous nor had an important national forum: his word grew slowly and inexorably until it could not be stopped. So did *infrastructure,* despite Churchill's scorn.

BOOSTING

Frontlash, coined in full view of a television audience, is an example of the word that takes a ride on another word. The technique of "boosting"—changing a word or phrase slightly to add irony or a fresh meaning—is as old as phrasemaking: some abolitionsts in 1850 called themselves the Know Somethings, provided an antonym for the Know Nothings; John Birchers today blast the "America

Last" philosophy of their enemies. When Adlai Stevenson suggested the Republican slogan should be "Throw the Rascals In," or Richard Nixon accused Lyndon Johnson of launching a "war on prosperity," they were boosting—playing on familiar phrases. This is a useful device for making a point, and the strength of a phrase can often be determined by how many *turnarounds* have been given it. Allan Nevins' *too little and too late,* for example, went through "enough and on time" to "too much too soon," and is not dead yet.

In this way, Lyndon Johnson made *let us continue* an early theme of his administration, boosting on John Kennedy's "let us begin"; *peacenik* and *Vietnik* (see -NIK) grew out of *beatnik;* "scrambled eggheads" appeared as a refinement of the original word, and FDR talked of a "sixth column" of gossips and defeatists. Every current phrase offers ammunition for boosting: *black power* spawned dozens of other powers, including "blackboard power" for militant teachers.

Since the weight of a word can tip political balances, politicians are wise to concern themselves with usage. In his final campaign FDR said, "This Administration has made mistakes. That I freely *assert.* And I hope my friends of the press will not change that to *admit.*" Sherman Adams, searching for the right word to characterize his dealings with industrialist Bernard Goldfine, rejected "unwise" and "wrong" to select "imprudent." Harry Truman used *red herring* with impunity, as Al Smith did before him, until he agreed to its use in a communist context, when suddenly it became a terrible *blooper.*

DISPUTES

When two distinguished sources say the other is "in error," which do you believe? When the conflicting sources are books, there is recourse to other sources, original letters, or manuscripts. A reference in the *winds of change* entry is made to Milton, as quoted in Bartlett's: "Though all the winds of doctrine were let loose to play upon the earth, so Truth be in the field, we do ingloriously by licensing and prohibiting to misdoubt her strength." But the *Oxford Dictionary of Quotations* substitutes "injuriously" for ingloriously. Who's right? A check of the original text gives the nod to "injuriously."

But when flesh-and-blood eyewitnesses disagree, there is no resolving the claims. When Professor Raymond Moley and Judge Samuel Rosenman each state flatly that he gave *New Deal* to Franklin Roosevelt to coin, citing date and place, the historian has to throw up his hands. Both Professor Moley and Judge Rosenman were responsive to the author's queries on a number of items, and I am grateful to them; the reader can see what each source says and make his own decision. Similarly, there were conflicting credits given to the coinage of *New Frontier;* in that case, however, the author was given enough background to suggest a judgment.

The reader will find no gleeful "Hah! He was wrong" comments from the author regarding inaccurate entries in venerable sources about political sayings. The reason is that new information is constantly turning up showing earlier uses. Harold Ickes is credited with *government by crony,* which he used four days after it had appeared in an Arthur Krock column credited to a "press gallery wit," who Krock now admits was himself. That makes Krock the coiner—until somebody comes up with an earlier use. There are also varying reports on the context of Dean Rusk's *eyeball to eyeball* remark, two of which are reported under that entry.

PRESIDENTS AND THEIR PHRASES

The memories of an era can be evoked by a look at its inventory of political phrases. Some are coined by a President, some by his cabinet, others coined for use against him. Here is a balance sheet of phrases by Administration, with popularizations included under coinages. First, FDR:

coinages	descriptions	attacks
forgotten man	alphabet agencies	clear it with Sidney
economic royalist	brain trust	traitor to his class
again and again and again	pump-priming	that man in the White
New Deal	hundred days	House
Good Neighbor Policy	nine old men	indispensable man
rendezvous with destiny	voice from the sewer	spend and spend
four freedoms	dollar-a-year man	court-packing
day of infamy		boondoggle
Happy Warrior		
fireside chat		
arsenal of democracy		
iffy question		
Martin, Barton and Fish		
nothing to fear but fear itself		
one third of a nation		
quarantine the aggressor		
my friends		

The Roosevelt era's phrase record offers a sharp contrast with Harry Truman's:

coinages	descriptions	attacks
do-nothing 80th Congress	Marshall Plan	five percenter
give 'em hell, Harry	Truman Doctrine	government by crony
red herring	Point Four program	influence peddler
Fair Deal		had enough?
		soft on communism

The Eisenhower years included many from Dulles and Wilson:

coinages	descriptions	attacks
domino theory	new look	security in prison
spirit of	Eisenhower doctrine	brinkmanship
modern Republicanism		Eisenhower syntax
atoms for peace		what's good for General
open skies proposal		Motors
engage in personalities		bird dog . . . kennel
I shall go to Korea		dog
bigger bang for a buck		
agonizing reappraisal		

coinages

unleash Chiang
massive retaliation
curl your hair

Of these, the last five coinages were used for attacks.

A different pattern appears for John F. Kennedy:

coinages	*descriptions*	*attacks*
New Frontier	Irish Mafia	managed news
profiles in courage	Bailey Memorandum	absentee Senator
Ask not . . .	Kennedy Round	
Alliance for Progress		
I am a Berliner		

The balance sheet for Lyndon Johnson:

coinages	*descriptions*	*attacks*
Great Society	Johnson Treatment	credibility gap
war on poverty	smell of magnolias	big-Daddyism
creative federalism		Macbird
coonskin on the wall		
Let us continue		
nervous Nellies		
press the flesh		
chronic campaigner		
no wider war		

Like Truman's red herring remark, however, three of Johnson's coinages have been used against him: *coonskin on the wall* and *nervous Nellies* became attack phrases used by his critics, and *press the flesh* was used as an example of crassness or corniness.

FDR's thirteen-year span, as might be expected, produced more phrases than any of the other, shorter administrations. The quality and staying power of the coinages and popularizations of FDR stands out over his four successors as well. There are at least six landmark catch phrases of FDR *(New Deal, Good Neighbor, four freedoms, day of infamy, fireside chat, nothing to fear but fear itself)* as against one for Truman *(do-nothing Congress),* three for Eisenhower, two of which were Dulles' *(domino theory, agonizing reappraisal, massive retaliation),* two for Kennedy *(New Frontier, Ask not),* and two for Johnson *(Great Society, war on poverty).*

Major phrases associated with candidates who lost in this period include Wendell Willkie's *One World, loyal opposition,* and *campaign oratory,* with *barefoot boy from Wall Street* against him; Dewey's *time for a change* with *idiot engineer* and *man on a wedding cake* against him; Stevenson's *dinosaur wing, talk sense to the American people, numbers game, nuclear proliferation,* with *egghead* against him; Nixon's *kitchen debate, Checkers speech,* and *cloth coat,* with the last two also used against him; and Goldwater's *defoliate, extremism in defense of liberty,* and *no-win* all of which were also used against him in addition to *trigger-happy, nuts and kooks,* and *little ladies in tennis shoes.*

The most popular target for phrases in the postwar period was Senator Joseph

McCarthy, who popularized *I have in my hand, security risk,* and *point of order,* and was hit with *guilt by association, character assassin, McCarthyism, big lie,* and *junketeering gumshoes.*

There was a relatively arid period in the twenties. Hoover coined *rugged individualism* and *noble experiment,* with *chicken in every pot* and *prosperity just around the corner* thrown at him; Al Smith came up with good uses for *baloney, Santa Claus, laundry ticket,* and *lulu;* Coolidge's "the business of America is business" is generally forgotten, though he can be credited with *against sin;* Harding coined *normalcy,* and was associated with *smoke-filled room.*

Woodrow Wilson and Theodore Roosevelt, however, were great phrasemakers. Wilson coined *New Freedom, little group of wilful men, too proud to fight, watchful waiting, open covenants, peace without victory, make the world safe for democracy,* and *self-determination of nations,* with *war to end wars* unduly credited to him.

Compare the type of Wilson phrases with the type of Theodore Roosevelt's: *lunatic fringe* and *hat in the ring,* in active political usage today; *bully pulpit, stand at Armageddon, big stick, malefactors of great wealth, pussyfooting, weasel words, mollycoddle, muckraker, parlor pink, Square Deal,* and *100% American.*

The other giants of political coinage were Abraham Lincoln *(just and lasting peace, malice toward none, don't swap horses,* possibly *presidential bug,* and *you can't beat somebody with nobody,* and just about every other line of the *Gettysburg address),* Thomas Jefferson *(entangling alliances, few die and none resign, life, liberty and the pursuit of happiness),* and English Conservative Edmund Burke who coined such necessary words as *colonial, diplomacy, electioneer, federalism,* and *municipality.* Winston Churchill's *blood, sweat, and tears, pumpernickel principality, sheep in sheep's clothing,* crowned by *iron curtain*—which, alongside Herbert Bayard Swope's *cold war,* was the major postwar coinage—carried on the Burke tradition.

Though political phrases are most often coined by politicians, they are also the province of journalists (William Allen White's *tinhorn politician,* Arthur Krock's *government by crony,* Walter Lippmann's *Atlantic community*), professors (Raymond Moley's possible coinage of *New Deal,* Allan Nevins' sure coinage of *too little and too late,* John Kenneth Galbraith's *affluent society*), judges *(curse of bigness, clear and present danger, with all deliberate speed),* generals *(unconditional surrender, no substitute for victory, vote as you shot),* and voices in a crowd *(give 'em hell, Harry!* and *tell it like it is!).*

Candidates have often provided the material for the opposition. This may be done by the candidates' supporters (a Blaine supporter coined *Rum, Romanism, and Rebellion,* which was used effectively against Blaine) or by the candidate himself (Barry Goldwater's *defoliate* flowered throughout his campaign). In turn, candidates have been given ammunition by their opponents: *whistlestopping,* which characterized the Truman 1948 campaign, was first used as a term of derision by Senator Robert Taft.

Hidden Entries

Every lexicographer is faced with the problem of writing entries he knows nobody is ever going to look up. He puts them in anyway, hoping a browsing reader will trip over them. Some of these, like *son of a bitch* and *baloney,* have had interesting political usage even though they are not political expressions. Others are *great, political use of,* as well as *black, wall,* and *new.* Speech constructions are also hidden entries, and the reader is directed to *"I See" construction* for a brief history of visionary statements, *contrapuntal phrases* and *turnarounds* for a brief look at how to make a phrase more memorable, as well as *Gettysburg address* for a look at poetic use of images and repetition of words.

Phrases are entered the way they are most often remembered or quoted and not necessarily the way they were spoken. "The only thing we have to fear is fear itself," for example, is entered as *nothing to fear but fear itself.*

Euphemisms are hidden in an entry by themselves, but clichés are tagged as such when they appear individually. *Madison Avenue techniques* are always "high-powered," images are always "projected," there are *gaps* for everything and the cliché that bounds along most merrily on election-night television is *tantamount to election.*

Words used to describe language have their own problems of fuzzy usage. *Jargon,* as used herein, is synonymous with *cliché* and *bromide,* as is illustrated in the *Pentagonese* entry; *argot* is used when a word in a specialized vocabulary has not been abused; *lingo,* which used to be quite close to *argot,* is now used loosely as being synonymous with *language, tongue, lexicon,* and *vocabulary. Cant,* however, preserves its meaning as slang used by insiders with intent to confuse outsiders, as in *strike a blow for freedom,* except when it refers to unintentional repetition as illustrated in the entry *cant.*

RESEARCH

The author is a former reporter, a practicing public relations man, and a part-time politician—and not an expert in linguistics. Amateur linguists and semanticists tend to come up with fanciful speculations on origins and as a rule this has been avoided (with the exception of *nitty-gritty* and *waffle,* which were too much fun to resist). When the author ventured to suggest *flip-flop* was onomatopoeic, a Random House editor sent the entry back with a little slip that asked "onomatopoeic of what?" and that little pretension was killed.

Those who guided, checked, and argued with me at Random House were Robert Loomis, Laurence Urdang, and Thomas Hill Long. My own chief researcher was Sally Cutting, and typists were Trees Landewé and Michelle Séjourné. The copy editing was done by Carol Levine. For titles of source books, see the bibliography in the back.

There are political expressions in this dictionary not available in any other —*Hymie's Ferryboat, lightweight, power brokers, $K_1 C_2$, the Hill, heft, waxworks, yellow dog Democrats, rubber-chicken circuit,* and many others. These are by way of a return on the investment of time made by many professional linguists who answered my queries, among them James Macris of *American Speech* and I. Willis Russell of the University of Alabama.

I am especially grateful to those active in politics who contributed expressions and helped with definitions, though I stand responsible for the accuracy of all. Among these were John A. Wells, Ray Schafer, John Trubin, John J. Gilhooley, Roy M. Goodman, Harry J. O'Donnell, and Charles McWhorter.

One research difficulty was the problem of making notes on expressions used at small political meetings. In confidential gatherings, a man who pulls out a pencil and paper is looked at askance, and I would often have to prove that I had just written down something like *"gopher*—one willing to 'go for' coffee."

In a very few instances, there was no modern public usage of a well-turned political or historical phrase available; rather than let the item slip for lack of currency, I would pass these on to friends in both parties who were in a position to suggest them to public figures. When the phrase was used and quoted in a newspaper, I could then complete the entry; that was the only scholarly cheating involved.

SOMETHING BORROWED

A prime purpose of this book is to make readily available the words that worked for politicians. By showing from what these words were derived (or on what analogy they were coined), I hope to have removed a certain guilt about borrowing in phrase making. The political subdivision of the English language has been in business too long for almost any phrase to be totally original; some of the best are twists of others. The many quotations herein, necessary to show usage, are also possible springboards for better usage. The best entries are those put together from the words of others that will suggest more apt words from others to come. Winston Churchill, as he wrote of fighting on the beaches, in the hills, and in the streets of wartime England, was familiar with Clemenceau's defiance in 1918: "I shall fight in front of Paris, within Paris, behind Paris." An apt quotation may make a point, but an apt alteration of a good phrase makes a speech and helps in the making of a leader.

Introduction
to the Second Edition
1972

Suppose, only four years ago, a political figure had this to say: "Despite the *instant analysis* and the *effete snobs,* the *silent majority* supports *Vietnamization,* and the steady *winding down* has allowed our allies to *hack it.* On the domestic side, though, the *game plan* could use a little *benign neglect.*"

Nobody would have known what he was talking about; these phrases all entered our lives between 1968 and 1972. To say nearly the same thing, using phrases coined before 1968, our political cliché expert might have tried this: "Despite the *sensation-seeking commentators* and the *eggheads,* the *Great Unwashed* buys the theory of '*let Asians fight Asians,*' and the steady *descalation* has enabled our allies to win the *hearts and minds of the people.* On the domestic side, though, *jawboning* got lost in a *hail of dead cats.*"

Much flavor, and some precision, is lost in the translation; the political language adapts to shifting circumstances with the coinage and acceptance of new phrases to define current events and moods. While *Great Unwashed* was derisive, *silent majority* is respectful; while *egghead* was not originally intended to be mocking, *effete snob* was so intended, and *jawboning* was only a small part of the economic *game plan.*

New phrases gain acceptance to fill a political-linguistic need, when the old phrases are over-used or miss the mark.

COINAGES, DESCRIPTIONS, ATTACKS

First, an inventory. Here are the major coinages or popularizations by the Administration during the Nixon years:

black capitalism	New Federalism
bring us together	Nixon Doctrine
effete snobs	old wine in new bottles
game plan	radic-lib
hack it	silent majority
instant analysis	strict constructionist
lift of a driving dream	Vietnamization
linkage	workfare
nattering nabobs of negativism	

Here are the descriptive phrases that came from outside the Administration that gained currency in that span:

heartland	machismo
household word	Middle America

new politics
psephology
quality of life
reordering of priorities

social issue
winding down
women's lib

And here are the phrases that were most often used in attacks on the Administration in the Nixon years:

benign neglect
Nixonomics
Southern strategy

The paucity of attack phrases in comparison to the coinages and descriptions should come as no surprise, since this has been the case in the three previous administrations. *Credibility gap* was the only major attack on Johnson; *managed news* was the most that could be managed against Kennedy, and *brinkmanship* was the remembered dig at Eisenhower. One has to go back to the Truman years for a bumper crop: *five percenter, government by crony, influence peddler, mess in Washington, had enough?,* and *soft on communism.* Although *credibility gap* continued in use against Nixon, it had lost its freshness as a phrase; *benign neglect* was used against the administration for a time then faded; *Nixonomics* never really caught on. Only *Southern strategy,* refurbished after its use against Senator Goldwater, remained in active use as an accusation of regional favoritism.

THE LINGUISTIC COUNTERATTACK

Two points become apparent from a look at the inventory of coinages and descriptions. First, a need existed to describe a significant and ordinarily inarticulate group of voters. *Silent majority* was certainly the major coinage of President Nixon. *Middle America,* minted by columnist Joseph Kraft, was also used to characterize these "forgotten Americans." And *heartland,* an old geopolitical word used by Eisenhower and popularized by columnist Kevin Phillips in the late sixties, is another approach to the same constituency.

Second, not since the presence of John Foster Dulles in the Eisenhower years (with *agonizing reappraisal, massive retaliation,* and *brinkmanship*) did a figure other than the President become responsible for well-known words and phrases. Vice President Agnew is represented here with *effete snobs, nattering nabobs of negativism, household word, radic-libs,* and *instant analysis.* Oddly, no attack word was coined for use against him.

Both the focus on the *silent majority* and the attention paid to the Vice President are evidence of a larger trend: linguistically, the past four years have been enlivened by a counterattack of the political right. In 1968, the "new politics" dominated the neologistic scene: *participatory democracy, power to the people,* and *reordering priorities* bestrode the stage, with *quality of life* in the wings. Since that time, scorn has been heaped on *limousine liberals,* concern has been expressed about the *social issue,* and approbation has been given *strict constructionists.*

LIKELY TO LAST

Like vintage wine, some political phrases take a long time to mature into clichés. *Quality of life* was a Stevenson phrase that waited fifteen years for an interest in the environment to ripen it; *heartland* was an Eisenhower word later applied to a Nixon following, and *Southern strategy* was coined in the late fifties to become most useful a decade later. On the other hand, some phrases take hold quickly and as rapidly turn to vinegar—*reordering priorities* is a case in point. To close out the metaphor, *old wine in new bottles,* with its Biblical origin, can be expected to come into vogue from time to time, never powerfully enough to wear out its welcome.

Which of the major coinages of the Nixon years will last? Not *Vietnamization,* certainly—if ever a word was created to drop out of the language after its usefulness ended, that is it. *Bring Us Together,* perhaps, if the theme is reinforced in later years. The *Nixon Doctrine* will probably do better than the Truman Doctrine but not nearly so well as the Monroe Doctrine. The *lift of a driving dream* has had a hard time getting off the ground, but the *full generation of peace,* in time, might take hold.

Silent majority is, of course, fixed in the political language already as firmly as Eisenhower's *domino theory* or Truman's *do-nothing Congress,* almost of the magnitude of FDR's *fireside chat* and *four freedoms. Hardhat* is another word of this era that fills a linguistic vacuum and is likely to last. I am not as sanguine about *black capitalism* as a phrase; the labeling of welfare reform as *workfare* may yet make it to *Medicare* status if it is enshrined in legislation.

Perhaps by choice, the Nixon Administration will be the second in the past six that does not have a monicker of its own—no *New Deal, Fair Deal, New Frontier, Great Society.* Eisenhower did not have a name for his time; the last Republican administration to have a handle was Teddy Roosevelt's, which had two—the *New Nationalism* and the *Square Deal.*

Had Nixon wanted at the outset to call his administration the New Whatever, he could have done so—made official and repeated often enough, a title would have stuck. President Nixon was tempted by "new road," but chose to change the pace of the last couple of Administrations and go without a title, which would have given cartoonists and metaphor-hungry journalists a handy target for criticism. After *New Frontier* and *Great Society,* it was felt, another promissory slogan would have been met with some scorn. Instead, the President let an intellectual designation, *New Federalism,* have a brief run; it served a modest purpose. He tried out the *New American Revolution* in early 1971, which did not take, and he did not try to drive it home; his heart was in *full generation of peace,* a phrase of Nehru's, and later in the *new prosperity.* Labor's George Meany helped the latter along, asking "What was the matter with the old prosperity?" and providing a nice opening for the reply: "War and Inflation."

POOR IS BACK WITH US

A laudable resistance to euphemism appears to be setting in. Although the kind of mind that, a century ago, could label the Civil War "the late unpleasantness" remains with us, blasts at verbal bobbing and weaving have been loud and effective in recent years.

Culturally deprived and *disadvantaged* are crumbling, except for isolated outposts in academia, and *poor* is once again acceptable as a word, if not a state; chalk one up for straight talk. *Job action,* for workers who cannot legally strike, is labeled *strike* by headline writers now; another victory. When a national conference was held in 1971 to discuss the problems of the aging, *elderly, sunset years,* and *senior citizen* were shunned, and the conference was called, of all things, the White House Conference on the Aging.

Sugar-coating is still with us: A government foreign affairs writer may call a poor country *have-not, underdeveloped,* or even *poor,* but the final copy always reads *developing nation. No-knock,* however, is a standoff; the Attorney General would have preferred *quick entry,* and the people on the other side of the door refer to it as *bust-in.*

Incursion, as applied to the action in Cambodia in 1970 was much criticized as a euphemism for *invasion*—unfairly so, in this writer's opinion. An invasion had already taken place by the North Vietnamese, and our forces were invited in; invasion would have been the wrong word, while incursion, with its connotation of limited foray of short duration, was apt.

But no defense is offered here for the phrase "protective reaction," euphemism's high-water mark of recent years. An attack on positions that fired upon unarmed aircraft might well be called for, but they are better called what they are—an attack, or bombing sortie.

This Second Edition contains not only phrases minted since 1968, but fills in gaps left in the earlier work. *Rainmaker* and *rabbi* are here, along with *Three-Eye League, bedsheet ballot, hatched, street smarts, low profile,* and *true believer;* China watchers will be satisfied with the inclusion of *hundred flowers* and *Great Leap Forward.* The *revolution of rising expectations* belongs in the language of politics, as do *yahoo, sick man of Europe,* and *jawboning;* I have belatedly caught up with them.

The most glaring omission up to now has been *Founding Fathers,* a classic political Americanism that one might have thought dated back to the early nineteenth century; the coiner turned out to be Warren G. Harding. (The 1920s were a productive era for American slang; *gang* and *gangster,* which originally had comradely political overtones, as in Harding's "Ohio gang," gained their new primary meanings of underworld association.)

In the four years between editions, some new evidence on old coinages turned up: Stewart Alsop was probably responsible for *Irish Mafia,* and Joseph Alsop is credited by Barry Goldwater with *Southern strategy.* Reporter David Wise and an unidentified headline writer collaborated on *credibility gap,* Irish politician Thomas Jones coined *passion for anonymity,* economist Walter Heller came up with *Quadriad,* broadcaster Eric Sevareid suggested *quality of life* to Adlai Stevenson, and Judge Joseph Proskauer wrote *Happy Warrior* into FDR's nominating speech for Al Smith. For these and other helpful corrections and suggestions, I am indebted to historians Eric Goldman and Sir Denis Brogan, writer Richard Hanser (the *Founding Father* detective) and reporters Gene Gleason and Paul Hoffman.

INSIDE WRITING OUT

For a lexicographer, inside an administration is a good place to be. You can ask an associate when he first started to use *game plan* and the Defense Department will go to some lengths to help you dig up the first use of *Vietnamization*. Newsmen use their jargon on you as they ask for help in doing *thumbsuckers* and *ticktocks,* or play the game of *rule out.*

Judge Samuel Rosenman, who wrote many of FDR's speeches, reviewed the first edition of this book in 1968. The following year, when I began to work at the White House, I asked him to come to Washington to visit the present generation of writers. In accepting the invitation he wrote:

"Your presence down there on the speechwriting team reminds me of a funny, but true, incident. President Roosevelt was fond of smoked sturgeon, and I used to send him some on occasion. Of course I bought the sturgeon from the 'Sturgeon King,' Barney Greengrass [in New York]. Barney was very proud of this; and whenever I came into his store for any purpose he would talk about it in a loud voice, especially if there were a lot of customers present. Out of a sense of protocol, he would never refer explicitly to the President by name but always as 'that fellow.' Of course everybody in the store knew whom he meant.

"One day, during a period when the President was out fishing on Vincent Astor's yacht, whose galley probably contained none of Barney's specialties, I came into the store. The place was packed with customers. As soon as he saw me he called out in a stentorian basso: 'Hello, Judge, I see that *that fellow* is out catching his own sturgeon.'

"And so I thought: You are now out making your own political language. I hope it will be voluminous enough to produce a second, amplified edition."

The political language added in this second edition does not include many phrases I had a hand in shaping, but like many writers before me, I have found the White House to be both a center of action and a superb observation post.

Introduction
to the Third Edition

THE GOLDEN AGE

If you were looking at a chart of neologisms over the past century, checking for new peaks of word coinage the way a doctor reads an electrocardiogram or a polygraph operator looks for surges of activity on a lie-detector chart, you would be struck by the peaks reached in the years 1973 and 1974. Politicians and historians will deal with that period in their own ways, but to lexicographers, the era of the Watergate vocabulary was a Golden Age of Political Coinage.

Some of the expressions fixed in the public tongue in those days were nonce words—"shredder" has already lost its sinister connotation—but a survey of Watergate lingo makes the point that this time had no precedent in its political linguistic fecundity:

at this point in time	hardball
big enchilada	inoperative
cover-up	laundering
CREEP	nobody drowned at Watergate
deep-six	plumbers
dirty tricks	Saturday night massacre
enemies list	smoking gun
executive privilege	stonewalling
firestorm	twisting slowly, slowly in the wind
-gate construction	

This list ignores the phrases that had already been part of the colloquial tongue ("break-in," "caper," "paper the file," "team player"); locutions unfamiliar to laymen but which had lives in the law ("obstruction of justice," "abuse of power," "misprision of a felony"); and phrases that seemed unforgettable for the nonce but now have become frozen in time ("third-rate burglary," "sinister force," "expletive deleted," "Deep Throat," "Huston plan," "candyass," "limited, hangout route"). The list includes some phrases that have a long history in American slang: DIRTY TRICKS had nineteenth-century usage and was recently applied to the CIA's covert operations before assuming its current political meaning of foul play, or the extreme of HARDBALL; DEEP-SIX was naval slang, meaning to jettison after the call of six fathoms; LAUNDERING and COVER-UP were familiar to con men; and INOPERATIVE was used in an important Lincoln statement. A legal phrase, EXECUTIVE PRIVILEGE, was rooted in the Eisenhower years.

But the Watergate investigation leading to the resignation of President Nixon not only popularized expressions that had been little known, but spawned new language likely to be used for generations: COVER-UP, loosely applied to any obstruction of justice (or used by any reporter denied access to information), is a political charge that now carries weight; STONEWALLING, an Australian cricket term given new meaning as refusal to comment, seems here in politics to stay; and TWISTING SLOWLY, SLOWLY IN THE WIND is likely to be used whenever Presidents let their nominees go without support.

FORD'S LINGUISTIC DECENTRALIZATION

The rush of coinages followed a time of average manufacture of neologisms in the Nixon years. After the period that produced GAME PLAN and SILENT MAJORITY (described in the introduction to the second edition), that Administration went on to produce TILT, WORK ETHIC, UP TO SPEED, WATCH WHAT WE DO, and PLAY IN PEORIA. And the Watergate coinage was followed by a two-year linguistic silence: Gerald Ford's presidency was unique in this century for not producing a single memorable phrase. "Our long, national nightmare is over" was received with relief but not recognition; Mr. Ford's most newsworthy action, the pardon of his predecessor, contained no phrase that became part of the political language. His "WIN button"—for "Whip Inflation Now"—was derided and soon forgotten. Reflecting his caretaker presidency, Mr. Ford's language provided a time for lexicographers to digest the tumult of the 1973-74 period and to prepare for a return to normal phrase production.

However, during the decline of Nixon and the subsequent service of President Ford, a new producer of coinage came forward: Henry Kissinger and his circle of articulate aides at the National Security Council and the State Department gave us QUIET DIPLOMACY, SHUTTLE DIPLOMACY, BACK CHANNEL, BARGAINING CHIP and STEP BY STEP.

These American terms coincided with the emergence of additions to the foreign diplomatic vocabulary. The foreign affairs lexicon of the sixties—DÉTENTE, LINKAGE, "era of confrontation"—was supplemented by the popularization in the seventies of HISTORIC COMPROMISE, DEVOLUTION, HEGEMONY, EUROCOMMUNISM, the old French TERRORISME, and the ancient English MOST FAVORED NATION; NEUTRALIST withered and THIRD WORLD took its place.

At a time when the White House was less of a focal point of power, the vocabulary of other power centers reached the general discourse. In the federal bureaucracy, PERKS and DOUBLE DIPPING were discussed by WHISTLEBLOWERS who resented SANITIZED files and the flow of JUICE by bureaucrats adept at CYA (covering your ass); what used to be HONEST GRAFT now became the "revolving door." In the Congress, the BOARD OF EDUCATION became more widely known as the place where the House leadership used to lean on young members who no longer put up with such domineering instruction. SUNSHINE LAWS and SUNSET LEGISLATION were the talk of the Hill, and "staffers" either used or denounced the Harvard-MIT complex known as the CHARLES RIVER GANG.

Another power center with its own lingo was the MEDIA (formerly the press), home of "media hype" and MEDIA EVENTS (formerly "pseudo-events"), which hung the -GATE CONSTRUCTION on every suspected scandal (Koreagate, Lancegate). SOURCES were quoted and LIDS were observed, as what used to be known as the FOURTH ESTATE strove to avoid what newsmagazine insiders acronymed MEGOS (my eyes glaze over).

Thus has the fount of new phrases and comfortable clichés become decentralized. Arms control provides its SALT lexicon: NUKE is a verb, and YIELD a noun; FRATRICIDE, the first capital crime in the Bible, is now the unintended explosion of a brother missile. Economics is no longer the "dismal science" in argot: the FREE LUNCH has been denied, the DOUBLE DIGIT is raised, and the SNAKE IS IN THE TUNNEL.

In the intelligence community (the word COMMUNITY has replaced ESTABLISHMENT), the inside argot has come in from the cold: from BIGOT LIST to BLACK BAG JOB, from SYNECDOCHE to FLUTTERING, the spookspeak has been frequently translated in Senate hearings and popularized in novels. (MOLE was a fiction writer's term for what the professionals called "penetration"; now the professionals use MOLE.)

THE CARTER START

As Jimmy Carter came into office, the White House resumed its normal role of phrasemaking, at about the pace of the beginning of the Eisenhower Administration. In his campaign, Mr. Carter's best-known phrases were "Why not the best?" (the title of his book), ETHNIC PURITY, lust in my heart, you can depend on it, I'll never lie to you, I don't intend to lose, DISGRACE TO THE HUMAN RACE (the tax system), and ZERO-BASE BUDGETING. In office, he sought to instill a "new spirit" in several speeches, but that did not catch on; his revival of William James's MORAL EQUIVALENT OF WAR did better, and his unintended paraphrase of John F. Kennedy's LIFE IS UNFAIR attracted attention.

The most significant phrase in the beginning of Mr. Carter's Administration was HUMAN RIGHTS, an idea he adopted after its reintroduction in the midseventies by Daniel Patrick Moynihan and Ronald Reagan; that phrase had been rooted in France and the U.S. in the late eighteenth century, and was given a modern assist from Eleanor Roosevelt at the United Nations in 1948. Toward midterm, TAX REVOLT was popularized, riding in from the surf of California, as was ONE-HOUSE VETO. The most colorful Carter usage was the THREE-MARTINI LUNCH, a coinage of Florida Governor Reubin Askew, used by George McGovern in his 1972 campaign. Carter's phrases reflect his nonrhetorical engineering training ("adequate," "competent," "disharmonious," and "incompatible" are favored adjectives) and his preference for the question-and-answer discourse rather than the written address. And BORN AGAIN gained a new, nonreligious meaning.

LOVE'S LABOR NOT LOST

This tome is now approaching 450,000 words, with 1,600 terms defined in about 1,200 entries. Since the second edition, the lexicographer has again undergone metamorphosis. From a public relations man in the early sixties—see FLACK, SELLING CANDIDATES LIKE SOAP, MADISON AVENUE TECHNIQUES—to a

White House aide in the early seventies—see SPEECHWRITER, GHOST, and creations like NATTERING NABOBS OF NEGATIVISM, WORKFARE and (gulp) CREEP—to a columnist for the *New York Times* today (see PUNDIT, THUMB-SUCKER).

In each incarnation I have kept a hand in the development of this labor of love, collecting citations for new words, digging further into the origins of other entries, filling in gaps of words that should have been covered in the beginning. Therefore, the latest version contains BEANBAG (which politics ain't) and BLOVIATE (not a Warren Harding invention, as widely assumed, but an Americanism dating to the mid-nineteenth century); DISH THE WHIGS (useful to those who hate ME-TOO ers) and ROORBACK (the predecessor to "last-minute smear"); Nazi expressions like NIGHT OF THE LONG KNIVES, and FINAL SOLUTION, as well as HOLOCAUST, which was not used in its current meaning until the sixties.

The latest edition follows the emergence of the latest isms—RACISM, ELITISM, SEXISM—and tracks the origin of PIE IN THE SKY to labor legend Joe Hill. The lexicographer has often tried to get the answers from original sources (reliable, authoritative, and anonymous): the foreign service officer who coined SALT is in these pages with his reminiscence, as is the German economics professor who put the SNAKE IN THE TUNNEL, along with a recollection sent along by the old FDR hand who was there when his luncheon partner coined "they never go back to POCATELLO."

As a newspaper columnist, I have become more opinionated and polemical in my writing, but partisanship stops at the dictionary's edge: as a lexicographer, I have tried—God, how I've tried—to remain nonpartisan. Although the practice of politics pits Democrat against Republican, liberal versus conservative, the tough-minded against the tender-hearted, the study of politics divides the house differently; into the politically active and the politically inert. That is why politically active people of all persuasions, and certain ex-colleagues of unfortunate convictions, have responded willingly to queries about who coined what and when.

Some nit-picking correspondents (from Shakespeare's "thou flea! thou nit!") like George Johnson, Paul Hoffman, Richard Hanser, Irwin Safir, and William Dougherty have helped this work shake out some of its errors, and their continuing criticism is sought; reviewers like linguist Mario Pei and Sir Denis Brogan, reviewing the two earlier editions in *Encounter*, have helped set this work straight. At the dictionaries, David Guralnik at Webster's *New World* was always responsive, and Anne Soukhanov at Merriam-Webster made available that organization's incomparable citation file on several entries; while at *American Heritage*, Alma Graham went to considerable trouble digging up derivations. (One of the delights of lexicography is the way people in this commercial, competitive field feel it their responsibility to respond to scholarly inquiry.) At the libraries, Joseph Ross and his cohort at the Library of Congress have plowed through original sources to come up with WINDFALL PROFIT, FINAL SOLUTION, CONFLICT OF INTEREST, and AFFIRMATIVE ACTION; at the *New York Times* Washington bureau, Kathie Wellde and chief librarian Sunday Orme have run down leads and employed the computerized Information Bank to find what human minds cannot remember. On legal terms, Justice Potter Stewart found CHILLING EFFECT at my request WITH ALL DELIBERATE SPEED, and slanguist Stuart Berg Flexner responded generously with what dictionaries and computers did not know. At Random House, editor Robert Loomis has believed in this project for twelve years, and copyeditor Barbara Willson caught more mistakes than I care to acknowledge.

Normal political differences and tensions were suspended; in tracking the etymology of political language, we are all lexicographers. And even blunders can help. For an example of the way mistakes lead to new discoveries, take THUNDER ON THE LEFT. In my *New York Times* column I misattributed the phrase to G. K. Chesterton; a reader wrote in to point out a 1925 book with that title by Christopher Morley. I ran a correction, which caused a retired professor to write in with another correction: he sent a page from the 11th edition of *Bartlett's Quotations* that cited the first use of THUNDER ON THE LEFT in a 1640 tract by "Sir Eustace Peachtree." Grimly, I ran another correction, which brought a letter from a Kit Morley fan who was able to prove that Mr. Morley, while one of the editors of *Bartlett's* in the forties, perpetrated a small hoax: he playfully attributed his own phrase to a nonexistent sage of three centuries ago. It's all straightened out in here, thanks to that series of forward fumbles.

THE DISAPPEARING ART

In studying the derivation of political phrases, the lexicographer digging through early drafts of famous speeches can pick up on insight on the evolution of speechwriting. The craft of ghosting is hardly new—President James Madison, for example, wrote the speeches given by his Secretary of State—but the willingness of some of the greatest orators to accept suggestions from colleagues is rarely considered. One reason the political speech is a declining art today is that most modern politicians turn to speechwriters for the complete job, and do not collaborate closely in the preparation of the expression of what is—or should be—in their own minds.

In researching MUSICAL METAPHORS, I stumbled across the derivation of Lincoln's "the mystic chords of memory," which illustrates the way a political leader can take a thought contributed by an aide and shape it to his own style.

The Civil War had not yet begun. In his draft of his first inaugural address, President-elect Lincoln had planned to conclude with a message to his "dissatisfied friends" in the South that the choice of "peace or the sword" was IN YOUR HANDS, and not in his. William Seward, whom Lincoln had beaten for the Republican nomination and after the election had appointed Secretary of State, suggested in a letter that this note of defiance be tempered with "a note of fraternal affection," and submitted language for the penultimate paragraphs:

> I close. We are not, we must not be, aliens or enemies, but fellow countrymen and brethren. Although passion has strained our bonds of affection too hardly, they must not, I am sure they will not, be broken. The mystic chords which, proceeding from so many battlefields and so many patriot graves, pass through all the hearts and all hearths in this broad continent of ours, will yet again harmonize in their ancient music when breathed upon by the guardian angel of the nation.

Lincoln accepted Seward's idea of seeking to evoke the sentimental ties that could help bind the nation together, and he used Seward's musical metaphor as well. But he rewrote the suggested passage, lifting it from oratory to poetry:

I am loath to close. We are not enemies, but friends. We must not be enemies. Though passion may have strained, it must not break our bonds of affection. The mystic chords of memory, stretching from every battlefield and patriot grave, to every living heart and hearthstone, all over this broad land, will yet swell the chorus of the Union, when again touched, as they surely will be, by the better angels of our nature.

Do users of political language today make that kind of effort to persuade and inspire? I think not. If they did, would it work? Styles change with the times, and Seward's florid style may seem excessive to us now, but Lincoln's improvement produced a soaring simplicity that I believe has what we now call impact.

In using the BULLY PULPIT of the White House in this century, Theodore Roosevelt tried strenuously, and often succeeded; Taft did not try; Wilson succeeded; Harding failed; Coolidge and Hoover did not try; FDR succeeded; Truman did not try; Eisenhower succeeded only in his farewell; Kennedy succeeded; Johnson and Nixon tried and sometimes succeeded; Ford went out of his way not to try; and Carter seems not to be trying.

Oratorical success does not ensure political success, as can be seen, but those among us who love the political language—and realize what it can to do uplift and lead—hold out the hope that it helps.

SAFIRE'S
POLITICAL
DICTIONARY

ABOMINABLE NO-MAN sobriquet of Sherman Adams, Eisenhower's chief of staff, who took on the onus of unpleasantness produced by the President's negative decisions.

By becoming the "no-man," the flinty former New Hampshire governor assumed the role of lightning rod for resentment that would ordinarily have been directed at the Chief Executive. Critics said Adams usurped a portion of the presidential decision-making power by "insulating" Eisenhower. Friends said he permitted himself to be a scapegoat: "the yesses come from Eisenhower, the no's from Sherman Adams."

The phrase is a play on the "Abominable Snowman of the Himalayas," legendary monster whose tracks are "found" and shuddered at by occasional mountain climbers.

See PALACE GUARD; GRAY EMINENCE; I NEED HIM.

ABOVE POLITICS a stance taken most often by generals and businessmen dissociating themselves from partisan strife, often in the hope of attracting political support from opposing sides.

Nonpartisan connotes no controversy at all; *above politics* implies that partisanship exists and there is an individual above it. Applied to issues and not to individuals, however, *nonpartisan* and *above politics* are synonymous.

Politicians occasionally place themselves above politics when they feel they no longer need political allies, when they are ready to become elder statesmen, or when they have reached a point described by Francis Bacon in 1612 in his essay "In Great Place": "All rising to great place is by a winding stair; and if there be factions, it is good to side a man's self whilst he is in the rising, and to balance himself when he is placed."

Among U.S. Presidents, Eisenhower was one of the few able to place himself above politics on many occasions. Another military hero, Admiral George Dewey, was less successful. When asked his party affiliation, the hero of Manila Bay smiled: "I am a sailor. A sailor has no politics." To his amazement, he soon found himself with no support from either political party.

See BIPARTISAN; NONPARTISAN; PARTISAN; WATER'S EDGE.

ABUSE OF POWER, *see* **ARROGANCE OF POWER.**

ACADEMIC FREEDOM the right of scholars and students to conduct their studies and express their findings or opinions free of institutional, political, or sectarian control.

Who first used the phrase is uncertain, but it has been a rallying cry for many decades; it is one of those ideas to which few will admit opposition.

The magazine *World's Work* wrote in 1901: "Every right-thinking man will stand firmly for academic freedom of thought."

Each era has had its own kind of controversy. Early in the history of American higher education, churches dominated the campus and the degree of their control was occasionally an issue (and still is, as in the 1966 faculty strike at St. John's University, a Roman Catholic institution in New York). The development of land-grant universities also made state politics a factor, and one which still crops up. New Jersey's 1965 gubernatorial campaign had its most contentious moments when the Republicans made a major issue of a Marxist professor at Rutgers, The State University, who had argued against United States involvement in Vietnam and added he "hoped" the other side would win. The Republicans demanded his ouster. Richard Hughes, the Democratic incumbent, supported the professor on the grounds of academic freedom. Hughes was resoundingly reelected.

Nationally, academic freedom became a subject of argument during the McCarthy-influenced 1950s. There was pressure not only against leftists, liberals, and dissenters in general, but also against the presence of their books in publicly sponsored libraries. In 1953 President Dwight Eisenhower, speaking at Dartmouth, made his widely quoted response: "Don't join the BOOK BURNERS. Don't think you are going to conceal faults by concealing evidence that they ever existed." In the sixties, the passions of the McCarthy period had cooled, but the academic freedom controversy found its central forum at the University of California's Berkeley campus. See NONSTUDENT.

In 1967 the brouhaha was over the Central Intelligence Agency's subsidization of student groups. After the first round of investigations, Senator Richard Russell, chairman of the Armed Services Committee, said, "all this clamor about impairing academic freedom . . . is a lot of hogwash."

ACCOMMODATION compromise; relaxation of international tensions after a conciliatory, usually unilateral gesture.

Woodrow Wilson used the word in its present political sense in his "Peace Without Victory" speech early in 1917: "Difficult and delicate as these questions are, they must be faced with the utmost candor and decided with a spirit of real accommodation if peace is to come with healing in its wings, and come to stay."

When labor leader John L. Lewis split with American Federation of Labor chieftain William Green in 1935 to form the Committee (later Congress) of Industrial Organizations, Arthur Krock wrote in the *New York Times:* "After all, as Huck Finn realized when he heard the Child of Calamity and the other braggart on the raft tell what they would do to each other—and didn't—the most-publicized impasses are those which are surest accommodated. Yet this one looks less soluble in an era of realignments." Ultimately, the AFL and CIO reached their "accommodation."

In 1951 Dr. Edward Corwin wrote in the *New Republic* that Congress and President Truman, in the midst of a constitutional dispute over sending troops to Europe to serve in the North Atlantic Treaty Organization, should undertake "a decent consultation and accommodation of views."

As PEACEFUL COEXISTENCE began to be talked of during the post-Stalin era, the terms *accommodation, recon-*

ciliation, realignment and DÉTENTE became popular in many liberal journals, and the SOFT ON COMMUNISM attack lost some of its appeal.

The proponents of a policy of accommodation are quite serious, but the word was introduced to the political vocabulary by a comic writer, Artemus Ward (Charles Farrar Browne), in 1866: "My pollertics, like my religion, being of an exceedin' accommodatin' character. . . ."

See DOVES.

ACCOUNTABILITY, *see* OVERSIGHT; SIGN OFF ON.

ACRONYMS, POLITICAL

words formed from the initials of agencies, programs or phrases.

Military acronyms have led the way. *A.W.O.L.* (Absent Without Leave) is a much-used Army term. *Snafu* (in bowdlerized form, "Situation Normal: All Fouled Up") was used by U.S. Secretary of State Dean Acheson on a visit to England in 1952 to apologize for an administrative error: "It is only as the result of what in the United States is known as a *snafu* that you were not consulted about it." (Churchill pronounced it snay-foo.) Derivatives were *fubb* (Fouled Up Beyond Belief) and *tuifu* (The Ultimate In Foul-Ups). *WAVEs, WACs,* and *WRENs* became well-known words, as did *radar* and *sonar.* Troops of the Republic of Korea soon were known as *ROKs.*

VEEP was first applied to Vice President Alben Barkley and then came to mean the vice president of any organization.

UNIVAC (Universal Automatic Computer) became a familiar friend on election night. When President Eisenhower spoke to ACTION (American Committee to Improve Our Neighborhoods), he wondered which

came first—the initials or the name.

Former Secretary of Defense Robert A. Lovett ("the Bald Eagle of Foggy Bottom") told the National Institute of Social Sciences in 1952 that he frankly advocated the use of what he termed "initialese." Time was saved by referring to the Commander in Chief, Far East, as CINCFE, and to his counterpart in Europe as CINCEUR. CINCUS (Commander in Chief, U.S. Fleet) was shudderingly dropped when naval officers pronounced the acronym. As for his own position as Secretary of Defense, the initialese was SECDEF rather than the more obvious S.O.D. "S.O.D. was abandoned," Lovett explained, "because it would require the most careful enunciation in order not to be excessively accurate as a description of the Secretary of Defense."

Often political acronyms are designed to be humorous. "MOM and POP briefings," reported Scripps-Howard in 1967, "are all the rage at Peace Corps Headquarters here. These are acronyms for 'Memo on Marriage' and 'Policy on Pregnancy.' " However, the War on Poverty lent itself to an ethnic slur.

During the Nixon Administration, top-secret studies were labeled "National Security Study Memoranda" and called by an awkward acronym, NSSM, pronounced "Nissim." When Zbigniew Brzezinski took over as National Security Adviser in the Carter Administration, he wanted all vestiges of Kissingerese removed; accordingly, the word "Presidential" was substituted for "National Security" in these memos: Presidential Study Memorandum. However, after one day of "PISSIMs," the name was further changed to "Presidential *Review* Memoranda," and became known throughout the Carter Administration as more prim PRMs.

The last word on acronyms belongs to a cartoon in *Punch* (September 28, 1977), showing two angry people marching under a banner titled "COCOA—Council to Outlaw Contrived and Outrageous Acronyms."

See MEGO; GULAG; CREEP; RIF; SALT.

ACTIVIST as a noun, a person willing to work for a cause, to take direct action to accomplish or dramatize its aims; as an adjective, the attitude of that person.

At the turn of the twentieth century, *activist* was the name of a philosophy of realism, akin to "pragmatist," assuming the active existence of everything. By 1920 the adjective's meaning changed to a description of a policy of energetic action; German intellectuals called political engagement *Aktivismus.*

Activist as a noun, with its current meaning, was set forth in 1954 by Arthur Koestler, in *Invisible Writing:* "He was not a politician but a propagandist, not a 'theoretician' but an 'activist.' "

The word seems to have replaced *agitator,* which is now a quaint derogation of a labor organizer. This word came into popularity when a high-level committee of English army officers was organized in 1647 to kidnap King Charles I, called "the Adjutators" (from adjutant, or assistant); the Presbyterians promptly nicknamed them the Agitators, as shakers-up of the status quo. In 1842 "the Agitator" was the sobriquet of Daniel O'Connell, advocate of Irish freedom.

In modern times, organized labor has not given up on the word. Lane Kirkland, Secretary-Treasurer of the AFL-CIO, told his convention in 1977: "The founders of the American labor movement left us all with one central theme and doctrine: 'Agitate,

Educate, Organize.' " Mr. Kirkland, in the same speech, defined "militancy" as "an attention-getting device most successfully and easily employed by spearing one's colleagues for the titillation of the press."

Militant is a calibration more active than "activist." In England in the thirties, the word was often applied to labor leaders holding out for high wage demands; by 1960, London's *Economist* was describing "a 'more-militant-than-thou' attitude" on the part of some trade union leaders. In the late sixties the word became popular in the U.S. as a label, usually intended to be perjorative, but not taken that way by those so described, for a demonstrator with "non-negotiable demands." Most of the time, "militant" implied a lack of reasonableness: ironically, militants usually displayed a distaste for anything military, whether National Guard troops or military service in Vietnam.

Professor Leopold Labedz, in the 1977 *Fontana Dictionary of Modern Thought,* held that *militant* "refers properly to the degree of radicalism in a person's politics" and *activist* merely to "the degree of involvement in politics," but such a nice distinction is rarely made in current American political use.

In the vocabulary of verbal representation, an *advocate* is a persuasive spokesman, and has a positive connotation, as in the title assumed by Ralph Nader, "consumer advocate"; an *apologist* is a propagandist, once meaning an explicator of God's word but now only used to mean a slavish mouthpiece; a *spokesman* or *spokeswoman* or *spokesperson* is a neutral term for one who presents a point of view for another, often on television.

In the lexicon of activism, an *activist* is one who presses for the idea of direct action; a *lobbyist* is a derogatory description of a paid activist on the other side; a *supporter* is a less active member of the troops, giving rise to the vogue term "supportive"; a *demonstrator* or *protester* is one who participates in street action and may be derogated as a *rioter;* a *dissident* is a heroic description of a demonstrator, noisier than a *dissenter;* and a *militant* is a fierce and uncompromising believer in a cause who—when endowed with leadership qualities—can be called a *firebrand.* Both *rabble-rouser* and *agent provocateur* are obsolescent.

ADAMANT FOR DRIFT, *see* **LOYAL OPPOSITION.**

ADMINISTRATION regime; the government of a specific leader.

European and United States usage differ on this word. In Europe, "government" is used to describe a particular leader's time in power; the Callaghan government replaced the Wilson government. When, as in France, a government "falls," only the leadership falls—the structure of government, of course, continues.

In the U.S., the word *administration* is used to designate the term of a president, while *government* is used to mean the ongoing constitutional organization. "Administration officials" and "administration policy" are U.S. government men and policies, but the use of the temporary word stresses the temporary tenure of U.S. elected officials.

Regime is the loosest word of the three and can be used for the power-span of an individual ("the Brezhnev regime") or a mode of government *(l'ancien régime).* This is a European word, however; in the U.S. it is mainly applied to foreign governments or eras. Thus, Englishmen in 1978 thought of "the Carter govern-

ment" in the U.S., and Americans talked of "the Callaghan administration" in Great Britain, each applying his own usage to the other's political system; both, however, referred to a "Gaullist regime," as did the French. In U.S. usage, *regime* is slightly pejorative; Senator George McGovern derogated the Saigon government in 1972 as "the Thieu regime."

A second use of "administration" is in subcabinet-level government agencies, as "National Recovery Administration," "Federal Housing Administration." In recent years there has been a tendency to substitute *agency* for *administration* in these titles. A *commission* differs from an administration or agency in that it is a quasi-judicial board; an *authority* is an organization set up by legislative act, one step removed from political influence or likelihood of change as an administration (in its first, overall sense) changes.

ADVANCE MAN one who arranges for publicity, protocol, transportation, speaking schedules, conferences with local government officials, and all the details smoothing the way for a political figure.

Preparations for a campaign trip are known as "advancing." Members of the advance party usually move into a city three or four days ahead of the candidate. At least one professional writer is on hand to draft "local inserts" for the candidate's speeches. He might prepare specific data on how the regional economy was suffering under the opposition administration, or scan local newspapers for issues on which the candidate might comment. Such a writer would also develop a humorous introduction that would have special meaning for local voters or politicians.

Advance men work with local

party leaders to plan the schedule, determine the motorcade route, decide on platform sites and seating, help get the crowds to turn out, handle police and press, distribute press kits, flags, buttons and banners, and arrange for "spontaneous" hand-lettered signs, etc.

President Dwight D. Eisenhower's advance man at the Republican convention in San Francisco in 1956 was the resourceful Tom Stephens, who, in this note to Sherman Adams, concerned himself with the probable weather:

> If the President arrived some time between 8:30 and 9:30 at night I believe it would be most helpful to him. While it is not cold here in the evening, it does get cool, and if you will look at the weather reports for the last couple of years, which I am enclosing, you will find that it has never gone below 50 degrees and seldom over 60 degrees between 8:30 and 9:30 around the 22nd, 23rd or 24th of August.

There are all kinds of "advance men" in politics, from those who attend to relatively small but important details to those who influence policy. And the advance man will occasionally make news himself: Eisenhower press secretary James Hagerty, advancing a presidential trip to Japan (that never took place), found himself in the center of riots and left-wing demonstrations.

A sign frequently displayed in rooms where experienced advance men teach the trade to neophytes reads: "If you arrive with the candidate, you're not advancing."

The predecessor phrase of "advance man" appears to have been "advance agent"; in 1897, the circus term was politically applied by Tennessee Congressman H. R. Gibson who lauded "that great priest and apostle of protection, and that great

advance agent of prosperity, William McKinley." See BANDWAGON.

In the special lingo of advance men, *newsies* (which include *wires, reels,* and *stills*) and *staffers* make up the *caravan* following *the man.* Sometimes included are *surrogates,* a half-dozen VIPs who can speak for the candidate before, after, or instead of a personal appearance. The advance staff can schedule, or *pencil in,* a hasty *dropby,* or a *visual,* which is a *photo opportunity,* even if this means *lunching him out,* or denying the candidate a midday meal; ears are cocked at the rally for the *wrap-up,* or standard peroration, which is the signal for a mad dash to buses to beat the crowd out of the hall.

In 1973, during the Watergate investigation, the term "black advance" was used to describe the darker side of advance work. Presidential aide Richard Moore, acting as an investigative counsel, drafted a memo dated March 22, 1973, detailing what he found in interviews with aides Dwight Chapin and Gordon Strachan regarding the disruptive activities of Donald Segretti: "They made reference to Dick Tuck [a Democratic prankster] and cited the kind of harassment of the campaign activities of opposition candidates which Tuck has engaged in over the years. At one point, Strachan described the type of activity as 'black advance,' a term used in political campaigning to describe the planning of measures to harass the opposition or to detect and guard against harassment by the opposition." Segretti served a jail term for campaign infractions, and Chapin (who advanced the 1972 Nixon trip to China) was sentenced for perjury; suddenly, political advance work learned its limits.

ADVICE AND CONSENT the phrase in the U.S. Constitution (Art.

II, sec. 2) enabling the Senate to act as a check on the appointive and treaty-making powers of the president.

This ancient phrase was popularized in 1959 when it was used as the title of a novel by Allen Drury, later made into a motion picture. The title was *Advise and Consent*—not *advice*—taken from Senate Rule 38: "the final question on every nomination shall be, 'Will the Senate advise and consent to this nomination?' "

However, most earlier expressions of the phrase used the noun "advice" rather than the verb "advise." In current use, the verb is preferred and automatically changes the companion word, "consent," from a noun to a verb. A frequent play on the phrase, especially after Senate opposition to the Vietnam war became outspoken, is "advise and dissent."

In its original form, advice and consent is one of the oldest English phrases in current political use. In A.D. 759 King Sigiraed gave lands to Bishop Eardwulf "with the advice and consent of my principal men." In 1184, Henry II issued the Forest Assize "by the advice and consent of the archbishops, bishops, barons, earls, and nobles of England," and Henry III ascended the throne "by the common advice and consent of the said king and the magnates."

The English colonies in America preserved the phrase and the concept, with the executive acting "by and with the advice and consent" of whatever the legislative body happened to be named. The old statute book of North Carolina began with the phrase: "Be it enacted by his Excellency Gabriel Johnson, Esq., Governor, by and with the advice and consent of His Majesty's Council and General Assembly . . ."

At the 1787 Constitutional Convention, it was natural for the English-trained lawyers to use the phrase in describing the action of the Senate to review appointments: "He [the President] shall nominate, and by and with the advice and consent of the Senate shall appoint ambassadors, other public ministers, and consuls, etc."

The "advice" function soon atrophied and was merged into "consent," and though the phrase survives intact, in practice its meaning has been halved: the Senate checks, but usually does not share, the presidential power of appointment. See BLUE SLIP.

An omission in the Constitution led to a century-long battle between the executive and legislative arms of the U.S. government: Need the President seek the advice and consent of the Senate in the removal of appointed officials? Though Jefferson grumbled about the offices packed with Federalists when he came to power in 1800 ("few die and none resign"), he displaced only 39; Andrew Jackson, when the Senate refused to amend the civil-service laws to make places for his followers, proceeded to replace more than a thousand political appointees in his first year and the Senate did not take up the strong President's gauntlet. See SPOILS SYSTEM.

Weaker Presidents followed Jackson, however, and "senatorial courtesy" soon encroached on both powers of appointing and removing. See PERSONALLY OBNOXIOUS. The Tenure of Office Act of 1867 seized enormous power from Andrew Johnson's hands by limiting removal of public officials to reasons of "misconduct or crime." Only slightly modified, the law rankled Presidents Grant, Hayes and Garfield, but not until 1887 was a President—Grover Cleveland—able to have the act repealed and permanently wrest the power of consent from the Senate. Said Cleveland to the Senate: ". . . my duty to the Chief Magistracy which I must preserve unimpaired in all its dignity and vigor compels me to refuse compliance . . ."

The most dramatic case of the Senate's withholding advice and consent was its rejection of the League of Nations, despite Woodrow Wilson's pleas; this is inaccurately identified with the LITTLE GROUP OF WILFUL MEN. During the Eisenhower Administration, the refusal to confirm the appointment of Admiral Lewis Straus as Secretary of Commerce was a surprising defeat. In 1969, the Senate rejection of Supreme Court nominees Clement Haynsworth and G. Harrold Carswell was widely interpreted as a reassertion of the "advice" function, as was the 1977 resistance to the Carter nomination of Theodore Sorensen to be Director of Central Intelligence, which caused him to withdraw.

AFFIRMATIVE ACTION, *see* QUOTAS.

AFFLUENT SOCIETY   the current economic condition of the U.S.: rich and booming, with undertones of unrest from those not participating in the affluence.

The publisher's blurb on a recent reprint of John Kenneth Galbraith's 1958 book reads, *"The Affluent Society* has added a new phrase to our language." It has. Positioned between Walter Lippmann's *The Good Society* and Lyndon Johnson's GREAT SOCIETY, Galbraith's phrase was taken up by critics of America's effort to come to grips with poverty at home. Yet his theme was not pessimistic:

The affluent country which conducts its affairs in accordance with rules of another and poorer age also foregoes opportunities. . . . The problems of an affluent world, which does not understand itself, may be serious, and they can needlessly threaten the affluence itself. But they are not likely to be as serious as those of a poor world where the simple exigencies of poverty preclude the luxury of misunderstanding but where, also and alas, no solutions are to be had.

Just as "austerity" was the vogue word in England after 1945, "affluence" took the lead in 1958. "The Conservatives turned 'austerity' into a dirty word," wrote British author John Montgomery, "the Socialists said that 'affluence' was an upper-class word and that in any case Britain was not really affluent."

The most typical use of the phrase was made by Dr. Martin Luther King, Jr., in a 1963 letter written to ministers from a Birmingham jail: ". . . when you see the vast majority of your twenty million Negro brothers smothering in an air-tight cage of poverty in the midst of an affluent society . . . then you will understand why we find it difficult to wait."

AGAIN AND AGAIN AND AGAIN an oratorical device of FDR's.

During the 1940 campaign, Wendell Willkie's charge that FDR was leading the nation into war annoyed the President and worried his advisors. Bronx boss Ed Flynn wired his demand that Roosevelt reassure the public that he was not going to send Americans into foreign wars.

"But how often do they expect me to say that?" Roosevelt asked Harry Hopkins and speechwriter Robert E. Sherwood. "It's in the Democratic platform and I've repeated it a hundred times."

"Evidently," said Sherwood, "you've got to say it again—and again —and again."

Roosevelt liked the phrase, especially since his own pronunciation of "again" was distinctive in U.S. speech, rhyming with "rain" rather than "when." The sentence, "Your boys are not going to be sent into any foreign wars," was written, and Judge Samuel Rosenman wanted to add, as FDR had often before, "except in case of attack." Roosevelt disagreed: "If we're attacked it's no longer a foreign war." This was a mistake that he was later to regret.

In a famous Boston speech (see MARTIN, BARTON, AND FISH) the President said: "I have said this before, but I shall say it again and again and again: Your boys are not going to be sent into any foreign wars."

Four years later, in the campaign against Republican Thomas E. Dewey, FDR found himself on the defensive because he had not used the "except" clause Rosenman had recommended. The President turned a minus to a plus by repeating the phrase originally associated with the statement: "I am sure that any real American would have chosen, as this government did, to fight when our own soil was made the object of a sneak attack. As for myself, under the same circumstances, I would choose to do the same thing again, and again, and again." The crowd, remembering, roared its approval.

The phrase continued to reverberate after Roosevelt's death in 1945. The *Chicago Tribune,* an arch-foe of FDR, recalled it in 1948 while lambasting somebody else: "The Great I Am, old Again and Again and Again himself, couldn't possibly have done a better job of bunking the American people. . . ."

AGAINST SIN, *see* **RUNNING AGAINST HOOVER.**

AGEISM, *see* **SEXISM.**

AGITPROP obvious propaganda. In a 1977 theater review in *Time,* T. E. Kalem wrote of a play by Bertolt Brecht: "One word of joyous warning. In *Happy End,* Brecht has dropped agitprop. The show has no redeeming social value save delight."

The word is a *Time* favorite. In 1935 the newsmagazine reported: "Far more serious, far more earnest is the Depression-born movement of workers' theaters which are currently putting on 'agit-prop' (agitational propaganda) plays in 300 U.S. cities."

Like "apparatchik" (bureaucrat), the word has a nicely sinister foreign tone and is frequently used in newsmagazine description of political propaganda, in the U.S. and abroad. It comes from *agitatsiya propaganda,* a department of the Central Committee of the Communist Party in the Soviet Union dealing with political persuasion. Still hyphenated in many dictionaries, it has lost its hyphen in current journalistic use.

AGONIZING REAPPRAISAL reassessment; phrase used by U.S. Secretary of State John Foster Dulles in December 1953, hinting at a possible change in American policy toward its European allies.

By "agonizing reappraisal" Dulles meant that any basic change in American foreign policy that would weaken the position of American allies in Europe would be very painful to the U.S.; however, since the U.S. had growing commitments in Asia, Africa, and Latin America, it might have to shift its area of primary concern from the European continent to one of the other major areas of East-West conflict. He told the National Press Club: "When I was in Paris last week, I said that . . . the United States would have to undertake an agonizing reappraisal of basic foreign policy in relation to Europe. This statement, I thought, represented a self-evident truth."

The mouth-filling nature of the phrase has kept it in the political language long after its specific Europe–to–Far East meaning died. In 1965, Yale professor and leading "dove" (see DOVES) Staughton Lynd called presidential adviser McGeorge Bundy "that unagonized reappraiser."

Trying to persuade Israel to offer more concessions in his SHUTTLE DI-PLOMACY, Secretary of State Henry Kissinger called for a "reassessment" of U.S. support, a word Jimmy Carter exploited in a 1976 debate with President Ford.

For other Dulles coinages, see BRINKMANSHIP; MASSIVE RETALIA-TION.

AIDE-MÉMOIRE, *see* **POSITION PAPER.**

ALARMIST   one who attempts to arouse fear; sometimes a person who is easily frightened himself and transmits his panic to others.

The word has been used many times in American history, especially prior to and during wartime. Of French origin *(alarmiste),* the word was coined during the French Revolution. It is attributed to Bertrand de Barère de Vieuzac, French lawyer and revolutionist who defended the Terror. It was used in England in 1794 by the Irish dramatist and orator, Richard Brinsley Sheridan, in a speech in Parliament: "Will the train of newly titled alarmists . . . thank him for remarking to us how profitable his panic has been to themselves, and how expensive to the country?"

In the U.S. the word was employed in 1840 by Representative White of Kentucky, quoted in the *Congressional Globe:* "Sir, open and bold usurpations never alarm me. I fear no danger of the perpetuity of this government, from the assaults of the manly tyrant or despot. I can look with some forbearance upon the unjust pretensions to power, asserted and defended upon principle yet, whilst I protest, I am no alarmist."

The word is current. "Alarmist cries about the lack of civilian control of the military," said Truman's Secretary of Defense Robert Lovett, ". . . deal with a strawman issue."

The retaliatory words are usually "smug" and "complacent," using the symbol of an ostrich with its head in the sand.

ALIENATION   disengagement and withdrawal from a society felt to be so oppressively paternal and centralized as to be suffocating to the individual. The word was popular as part of the terminology of the New Left.

The "Establishment"—especially the "Liberal Establishment"—is the foundation of the "power structure" (see WHITE POWER STRUCTURE), the shibboleth of New Leftese. A rejection of centralized, remote government, and a hatred of Big Brother in business, university, and political life caused the new radical to disengage.

Historians of "The Movement" Paul Jacobs and Saul Landau explain that " 'Alienation' was used to describe the society's effects on its citizens, and American society was seen as the source of injustice and suffering everywhere."

In current use the word has broadened to a general sense of malaise and helplessness. Irving Howe, editor of *Dissent* and a critic of the new radicals, wrote that "alienation is not some metaphysical equivalent of the bubonic plague which constitutes an irrevocable doom; it is the powerlessness deriving from human failure to act. . . . Each time the civil rights movement brings some previously mute Negroes into active political life, each time a trade union extends its power of decision within a factory, the boundaries of alienation are shrunk."

Although alienation became a byword of the New Left, it was also frequently used in self-description by members of the New Left's sworn enemy, the "Intellectual Establishment." University of Toronto Professor Lewis Feuer comments:

> In the new parlance an Establishment Intellectual ceases to be an "intellectual" since, to be an "intellectual," he must have one characteristic above all: He must regard himself as "alienated" from the community, "alienated" from the workings of representative democracy, "alienated" from what he wants to call the "System." There have been men of great intellectual power in American Government— Jefferson, Adams, Franklin, to name a few—but they were not "intellectuals" because they were involved actively in public affairs and responsibilities from their earliest mature years.

The meaning of the word to the general public was summarized by comedian Bob Hope who, throughout the forties, used a standard gag line whenever things became too complicated or subtle: "Where does an alien go to register?"

Conservatives, hard-liners, and silent majoritarians have long considered the word alien to their taste, or the sort of language used by alienists, or "shrinks." *Washington Post* columnist Roger Rosenblatt caught

this distinction in a July 1978 piece about the cultural differences of Democrats and Republicans, providing this table to show the different terms used for the same things:

DEMOCRATS	REPUBLICANS
total	corporate
influence	clout
truth	bottom line
disturbed	sloshed
innovations	software
alienated	jerk
hostile	jerk
defensive	jerk
sensitive	jerk
chairperson	"chairperson"

ALL DELIBERATE SPEED, *see* **WITH ALL DELIBERATE SPEED.**

ALLIANCE FOR PROGRESS the name of John F. Kennedy's Latin American policy, first used by him in a campaign speech at Tampa, Florida, in October 1960.

Speechwriter Richard Goodwin recalls that the phrase was born while he was riding in a campaign bus rolling through Texas in September 1960. Trying to think of the words which would express for Kennedy what GOOD NEIGHBOR POLICY had expressed for Franklin D. Roosevelt, Goodwin's eye caught the title of a Spanish-language magazine left on the bus in Arizona: *Alianza.*

Kennedy agreed that "alliance" should be part of the phrase; but alliance for what? Goodwin telephoned Karl Meyer, one of the editors of the *Washington Post,* for suggestions. Meyer, in turn, called Ernesto Betancourt, a Cuban who had broken with Fidel Castro and was working for the Pan American Union in Washington. "Betancourt said to Meyer," Goodwin informs the author, "that it should be Alliance for something, and proposed several alternatives including 'development,' 'freedom,' 'progress,' etc., from which the final version was selected."

Ted Sorensen offers a slightly different version: "I suggested 'Alianza,' assuming that it had broader meaning than 'alliance' because it was the name of an insurance cooperative organized by some of our Mexican-American supporters in Arizona. A Cuban refugee and Latin America expert in Washington, Ernesto Betancourt, suggested through Goodwin the addition of 'para el progreso' (although for some time we mistakenly dropped the 'el'). The candidate liked it—and the Alliance for Progress was born."

In his Tampa speech Kennedy outlined the Alliance, which included "unequivocal support to democracy" and opposition to dictatorship; provision of "long-term development funds, essential to a growing economy"; stabilization of the prices of the principal commodity exports; aid to programs of land reform; stimulus to private investment and encouragement of private business "through mixing capital with local capital, training local inhabitants for skilled jobs, and making maximum use of local labor."

The Alliance for Progress was launched officially on March 13, 1961, before the Latin American diplomatic corps assembled for the occasion in the White House.

"I have called on all people of the hemisphere," said President Kennedy, "to join in a new Alliance for Progress—*Alianza para Progreso* —a vast cooperative effort, unparalleled in magnitude and nobility of purpose, to satisfy the basic needs of the American people for homes, work and land, health and schools. . . . Let us once again transform the American continent into a vast crucible of revolutionary ideas and efforts."

Any grand title lends itself to ridicule. Asked Senator Everett Dirksen in 1967: "Where is the Alliance? Where is the Progress?"

ALLITERATION repetition of the same consonant or sound in consecutive words; a device, when used obviously, to coin a slogan or catch phrase; when used subtly, to create a mood rather than a phrase.

"Apt alliteration's artful aid," a 1763 turn of phrase by Charles Churchill always used in discussing alliteration, has been neatly disposed of in Fowler's *Usage:* "not as good an example of alliteration as it looks, since only the first two a's have the same value."

When a Member of Parliament made a snide reference to "fancy franchises," Benjamin Disraeli replied: "Alliteration tickles the ear and is a very popular form of language among savages . . . but it is not an argument in legislation."

The careful culling of consonants to pack a punch in politics has long been in U.S. common use, for good and evil. An early Ku Klux Klan slogan: "Kill the Kikes, Koons, and Katholics." In the 1876 campaign: "Hayes, Hard Money and Hard Times."

In the twenties, politicians tried to emulate the alliterative success of Warren G. Harding, who made history with "not heroics but healing, not nostrums but NORMALCY, not revolution but restoration, not agitation but adjustment, not surgery but serenity, not the dramatic but the dispassionate, not experiment but equipoise, not submergence in internationality but sustainment in triumphant nationality."

In 1952 Adlai Stevenson, stung by the "Korea, Communism and Corruption" slogan of the Republicans (see K_1C_2), attacked all the alliterative phrases: ". . . each of the following words will appear at least once: crime, corruption and cronies; bossism, blundering and bungling; stupidity and socialism . . ."

"Words can do more than convey policy," John F. Kennedy wrote in 1961, using alliteration to show what he meant: "They can also convey and create a mood, an attitude, an atmosphere—or an awakening."

President Johnson, whose corniness of style offended many intellectuals, addressed a joint session of Congress five days after the Kennedy assassination and used alliteration subtly and effectively: "I profoundly hope that the tragedy and the torment of these terrible days will bind us together . . ."

Vice President Agnew, campaigning in 1970 to elect Republican congressmen, used "pusillanimous pussyfooters" and "vicars of vacillation" against Democrats, reaching a crescendo with NATTERING NABOBS OF NEGATIVISM. In so doing, he made alliteration a campaign issue, but the technique was contagious—Senator George McGovern denounced the Vice President's "foaming fusillades."

ALL-OUT WAR, *see* **TOTAL WAR.**

ALL THINGS TO ALL MEN
deliberate ambivalence; two-facedness.

The phrase is used against a politician who makes conflicting promises in an effort to win an election or gain political advantage. But it can also be used to describe public speculation about an unknown quantity. Jonathan Daniels, former press secretary to President Roosevelt, wrote of the reaction to Harry Truman's ascension to the presidency when Roosevelt died: "He seemed all things to all men and all men including New Dealers and anti-New Dealers, Roosevelt friends and Roosevelt enemies, old friends and new ones, Pendergast politicians, Truman committee members, the eager and the ambitious, seemed to expect that he would be all things to them."

Deliberately seeking to be all things to all men is universally condemned but widely practiced; oddly, the phrase is related to concepts like "beauty is in the eye of the beholder" and "a face only a mother could love." In a work of art, varying interpretations of the same object is a mark of greatness; in diplomacy, a studied ambiguity is often admired; but in politics, a man who seeks to be all things to all men runs the risk of being nothing to anybody, and the practitioner can be attacked as "fuzzy" or for being "tall in the STRADDLE."

In 1826 Benjamin Disraeli entitled a chapter of his novel *Vivian Grey* "All Things To All Men," using the phrase in its current sense.

The duplicity in being all things to all men is readily admitted by the Christian saint who coined the term and perfected the art. In I Corinthians 9:20, Paul the Apostle says: "And unto the Jews I became as a Jew, that I might gain the Jews . . ." On that principle he ordered the circumcision of Timothy, to recommend his ministry to the Jews, despite Christianity's substitution of baptism for circumcision as a religious rite. He continues two verses later: "To the weak became I as weak, that I might gain the weak: I am made all things to all men,

that I might by all means save some."
He justifies the means by the end in
10:32–33: "Give none offense, neither
to the Jews, nor to the Gentiles, nor
to the Church of God: even as I please
all men in all things, not seeking mine
own profit, but the profit of many,
that they may be saved."

The technique of being all things to
all men has an effect not only on the
voter but often on the candidate. "No
man, for any considerable period,"
Nathaniel Hawthorne wrote, "can
wear one face to himself, and another
to the multitude, without finally getting bewildered as to which may be
the true."

ALPHABET AGENCIES term
used to describe, and mildly derogate,
the succession of new agencies
created by the early Franklin D.
Roosevelt Administration.

New administrations, authorities,
and corps appeared in sudden profusion in 1933: NRA (National Recovery Administration), TVA (Tennessee Valley Authority), CCC (Civilian
Conservation Corps), and AAA (Agricultural Adjustment Administration) were among the best-known.

The term was originally "alphabetical agencies," used in this manner by
Bronx Democratic boss Ed Flynn: "A
small informal committee was
formed, however, consisting of
[James] Farley, [Frank] Walker,
[Louis] Howe and myself. We were
primarily interested in taking care of
the original group of people who had
started out with us in the campaign
prior to the convention in Chicago.
This group became known as the
'FRBC': 'For Roosevelt Before Chicago.' Perhaps this was the first of the
New Deal alphabetical agencies."

The alphabet-agency phrase gave
color to the charge of excessive bureaucracy. Democrat Al Smith, dis-

enchanted with Roosevelt, described
the government as "submerged in a
bowl of alphabet soup," and Republican campaigners at their 1936 convention carried an Alfred Landon
banner that read "UP WITH ALF—
DOWN WITH THE ALPHABET!"

Of course, the use of initials in describing government acts and agencies did not originate with the New
Deal. In World War I, Great Britain's
Defence of the Realm Act was called
DORA, and the American Expeditionary Force was the AEF. In Germany in the twenties, *National-
sozialistische* was shortened to Nazi,
and in Russia the *Obyedinennoe
Gosudarstvennoe Politicheskoe Upra-
vlenie* (United Government Political
Administration) was known as the
OGPU. See ACRONYMS, POLITICAL.

Today, with a variety of government agencies operative and accepted, the phrase conveys mild
amusement but the political sting is
gone.

**ALWAYS FALLING, NEVER
FALLEN,** *see* **ADMINISTRA-
TION; SPLINTER GROUPS; BU-
REAUCRACY.**

AMATEURS professional politician's scornful word for citizens
inexperienced in political campaigns
and who show up near election time
only, but without whom most campaigns would be doomed.

The obvious difference between an
amateur and a professional in politics
is the degree of experience. More important, however, is the willingness to
work in what politicians call "the
vineyards" on a year-round basis,
without the glamour and excitement
of a campaign.

Amateurs should not be confused
with VOLUNTEERS, lower-level cam-

paign workers who are recruited for canvassing, poll-watching, letter-writing, coffee-klatsch-giving, and clerical work. In a professional politician's eyes, amateurs include those top-level businessmen, labor leaders, attorneys, advertising and public relations people who are highly paid and highly successful in their own fields. Many have excellent political judgment and skills beyond most political pros; their enthusiasm and the transient nature of their politicking are their strengths, because they can speak their minds freely. Moreover, they are unaware of obstacles that the professional knows exist; through sheer ignorance of previous failure amateurs sometimes scale heights no sensible pol would ever attempt.

On the other hand, many of these high-level amateurs enter politics with a distaste for the pros, or "hacks" (see HACK) as they call them, and reject out of hand the experience and sensitivity leaders have to the often useful TROOPS.

Because there are a great many more amateurs than pros, the public image of the amateur is that of a fresh-faced, civic-minded citizen out to do battle for a cause he believes in, versus the cigar-chomping image of the political professional. For this reason, many candidates call themselves "amateurs." Adlai Stevenson kept referring to himself and his close associates as "amateurs" long after he and they had acquired solid professional standing. In the seventies, the wisest politicians were the "anti-politicians."

The appearance of being an amateur, then, is something to be coveted; the act of doing political work amateurishly is something to be avoided. "An important maxim to remember is 'Don't be an amateur,' " said Henry

Cabot Lodge in 1951, when he was the unofficial campaign manager for Eisenhower in battle against the "pros" behind Robert Taft. "The job of being a professional politician, in spite of the odium which some persons have falsely attached to it, is a high and difficult one," Lodge continued. In that instance, as in others, amateurs acting professionally, in tandem with pros, were able to capture the nomination.

See VOLUNTEERS; for antonyms, OLD PRO; PROFESSIONAL.

AMERICAN BOYS orator's reference to American troops, now with a corny or chauvinistic connotation.

"We want to get the boys out of the trenches," said Henry Ford in 1915, explaining the purpose of his Ford Peace Ship. He did not add, Gilbert Seldes insists, "by Christmas," nor was he referring to "American boys" who were not yet fighting. Nevertheless, the idea of "getting the boys home by Christmas" has become a phrase used in every U.S. war since.

Isolationist Senator Burton K. Wheeler, on January 12, 1941, infuriated FDR by stating, "The lend-lease-give program . . . will plow under every fourth American boy." Roosevelt called this remark "the rottenest thing that has been said in public life in my generation."

In the Korean War, General Douglas MacArthur, dismissed by President Harry Truman, told a Senate investigating committee in May of 1951: "You can't just say 'Let that war go on indefinitely while I prepare for some other war,' unless you pay for it by the thousands and thousands and thousands of American boys."

Secretary of State John Foster Dulles made what Sherman Adams termed "an unfortunate blunder" in using the term during Senate testimony on the "Eisenhower Doctrine" in 1957. Senator Wayne Morse wanted to know why England and France were not brought into the U.S. stand in the Middle East so that "American boys won't have to fight alone." Dulles replied: "If I were an American boy, as you term it, I'd rather not have a French and a British soldier beside me, one on my right and one on my left." He regretted the undiplomatic remark immediately.

Lyndon Johnson probably regretted a "boys" statement made during the 1964 campaign that came back to haunt him. Urging a policy of restraint in Vietnam, on August 12 the President attacked those pressing for escalation: "They call upon us to supply American boys to do the job that Asian boys should do."

The use of "boys," rather than "men" or "troops," is obviously used to play on the emotions of parents; the word stresses the youth of the troops, thereby seeking to increase the public's desire to protect them from bloody warfare. The word is so obviously loaded, however, that there has been a tendency in recent years to steer away from its use for fear of appearing demagogic.

Without the word "American," the word "boys" acquires a different political meaning. The boys are "the boys in the backroom"—the political bosses, a usage still current that can be traced at least as far back as 1879: "Stalwartism," [see STALWART] wrote *The Nation*, ". . . includes indifference or hostility to civil-service reform, and a willingness to let 'the boys' have a good time with the offices."

AMERICAN DREAM the ideal of freedom and opportunity that motivated the Founding Fathers; the spiritual strength of the nation.

Compared with the AMERICAN WAY OF LIFE or AMERICANISM, the American Dream is much less often satirized or considered corny. The American System is considered the skeleton and the American Dream the soul of the American body politic. The phrase has not crossed the usage line from sacred to sacrosanct.

In 1893 Katherine Lee Bates wrote in *American the Beautiful* of a "patriot dream that sees beyond the years." In 1960 the poet Archibald MacLeish, debating "national purpose," said: "There are those, I know, who will reply that the liberation of humanity, the freedom of man and mind, is nothing but a dream. They are right. It is. It is the American dream."

The American Dream, to some, stresses opportunity. Historian Matthew Josephson wrote of Thomas Alva Edison: "The rise of the former trainboy and tramp telegrapher from rags to riches was an enactment of the American Dream."

Negro writer Louis Lomax applied it to equality: "It is the segregationists who are wielding the iron pipes and unleashing the savage dogs . . . if the law-abiding rather than the lawbreakers must cease and desist, then the American promise is but a cruel joke on humanity and the American dream dissolves to the most God-awful nightmare."

Both novelist Norman Mailer and playwright Edward Albee have attacked the phrase in titles. Richard Cornuelle, before becoming executive director of the National Association of Manufacturers, wrote a book in 1965 about the "private sector" called *Reclaiming the American Dream*. In it he said: "We wanted, from the beginning, a free society, free in the sense that every man was his own supervisor and the architect of his own ambitions. . . . We wanted as well, with equal fervor, a good society—a humane, responsible society in which helping hands reached out to people in honest distress. . . . For a long time it seemed that the free society and the good society could be realized together in America. This, I think, was the American dream."

The phrase defies definition as much as it invites discussion. As a force behind government philosophy, it seems to be interpreted by most users as a combination of freedom and opportunity with growing overtones of social justice. In the personal sense, its present meaning can be inferred from Richard Nixon's words accepting the Republican nomination in 1960: "I can only say tonight to you that I believe in the American dream because I have seen it come true in my own life."

See "I HAVE A DREAM"; LIFT OF A DRIVING DREAM; VISION OF AMERICA; "I SEE" CONSTRUCTION.

AMERICANISM   a patriotic political philosophy, sometimes abused by chauvinists; also, a word or phrase peculiarly American.

Theodore Roosevelt popularized "Americanism" in 1909 as "a question of principle, of purpose, of idealism, of character; it is not a matter of birthplace or creed or line of descent." It was Roosevelt who introduced or propagated the phrases "100% American" and "hyphenated American," and he often returned to this theme: "Americanism means the virtues of courage, honor, justice, truth, sincerity and hardihood—the virtues that made America."

The KNOW-NOTHINGS of the 1840s and 1850s used the word Americanism with a different meaning. They were opposed, for example, to waves of immigration and especially to Irish Catholics. Progressives, however, used the word in the opposite sense— to urge assimilation of immigrants into the U.S. social system.

Editor William Allen White wrote of the McKinley-Bryan campaign of 1896: "The election will sustain Americanism or it will plant Socialism." Huey P. Long, U.S. Senator and Governor of Louisiana, frequently accused of secret ambitions to become a dictator, once said that "if fascism comes to America it would be in a program of Americanism." See UN-AMERICAN.

In its linguistic sense, the word *Americanism* was first used in 1781 by John Witherspoon, a signer of the Declaration of Independence and president of the College of New Jersey, which became Princeton University:

> The first class I call Americanisms, by which I understand an use of phrases or terms, or a construction of sentences, even among people of rank and education, different from the use of the same terms or phrases, or the construction of similar sentences in Great Britain. It does not follow, from a man's using these, that he is ignorant, or his discourse upon the whole inelegant; nay, it does not follow in every case that the terms or the phrases used are worse in themselves, but merely that they are of American and not of English growth. The word *Americanism,* which I have coined for the purpose, is exactly similar in its formation and significance to the word *Scotticism.*

H. L. Mencken, in *The American Language,* wrote: "The first American colonists had perforce to invent Americanisms, if only to describe the unfamiliar landscape and weather, flora and fauna confronting them."

AMERICAN SYSTEM the private enterprise system; occasionally used as a euphemism for capitalism.

"Let the thirteen states," wrote Alexander Hamilton in the *Federalist* Number II, ". . . concur in erecting one great American system, superior to the control of all transatlantic force . . ." Twenty years later Jefferson wrote: "The history of the last twenty years has been a sufficient lesson for us all to depend for necessaries on ourselves alone; and I hope that twenty years more will place the American hemisphere under a system of its own . . ."

In 1824 Henry Clay applied the phrase in a speech defending the protective tariff of that year. To the Kentucky senator, the "American system" meant nationwide economic improvements combined with high tariffs that would reduce America's dependence on imports and expand its domestic market. Hamilton, Jefferson, and Clay used "American system" as a contrast to and defense against the European economy and polity. In the twentieth century the phrase lost its protective-tariff meaning and has been used in the sense of a political and economic philosophy of life. As Herbert Hoover said in 1945: "The American system of life is unique in the world . . . our American system also holds to economic freedom . . . we have proved the American system by raising the standards of life higher than any nation on earth." FDR, accused by Hoover of replacing this system with "regimentation," referred in 1936 to "the American system of private enterprise and economic democracy."

In a 1929 interview, underworld overlord Al Capone used the phrase in the current sense: "Don't get the idea that I'm one of these goddam radicals. Don't get the idea that I'm knocking the American system."

For more modern usages, see SYSTEM, THE, and PROCESS, THE.

AMERICAN WAY OF LIFE phrase now used mainly in FOURTH OF JULY oratory; earlier, a patriotic characterization of the free enterprise system. Often shortened to "the American Way."

One of the Alf Landon slogans in the campaign of 1936 was "Save the American Way of Life," an appeal against the then-radical measures of the New Deal. Telephone operators at the switchboard of the *Chicago Tribune* answered calls with "only— more days to Save the American Way of Life."

Writing in the *New York Times* in 1958, American diplomat and motion-picture executive Eric Johnston felt the phrase was a euphemism and attacked it head-on: "And the word is capitalism. We are too mealy-mouthed. We fear the word capitalism is unpopular. So we talk about the 'free enterprise system' and run to cover in the folds of the flag talk about the American Way of Life."

In *The Republican Establishment,* Stephen Hess and David Broder described the subjective reaction to the phrase in 1967: "Like Romney, there is in Nixon a small-town or Western accent on 'the American way' and 'the things that made America great' that seems stodgy to some and pleasantly nostalgic to others."

"Life style," a 1929 coinage of psychologist Alfred Adler, is a current substitute for "way of life."

ANGRY YOUNG MEN a dissatisfied, impatient group of younger people in a party.

When John F. Kennedy achieved his nomination in 1960, he sought to heal the wounds within the party, especially those of older Democrats like Truman and Averell Harriman, who would have preferred Symington or Stevenson. The nominee explained why he wanted Harriman to second his nomination: "It will be useful for me to have someone who serves as a link to the Roosevelt and Truman administrations; also an older man. I don't want the Convention to think we're just a collection of angry young men."

The "anger" in the phrase was popularized by British dramatist John Osborne, whose 1956 play *Look Back in Anger* articulated a restlessness and disgust, a rebellion against the "old boy" philosophy prevalent in British politics and business, where young men were trained for careers that they later rejected or that the "Establishment" did not permit them to pursue. After the general use of this phrase began to wane, the political lexicon made "angry young men" its own.

Earlier, in 1951, the religious philosopher Leslie Allen Paul had entitled his autobiography *Angry Young Man,* but it was Jimmy Porter, the hero of Osborne's play, and Lucky Jim, the hero of Kingsley Amis' novel of that name, who became the prototypes of angry young men. The phrase crystallized a mood. Wrote critic Kenneth Allsop: "It was as if the pintable ball that many young people feel themselves to be today, ricocheting in lunatic movement, had hit the right peg. Lights flashed. Bells rang. Overnight 'angry' became the code word."

Allsop went on to define the phrase with some eloquence:

> The phrase Angry Young Man carries multiple overtones which might be listed as irreverence, stridency, impatience with tradition, vigour, vulgarity, sulky resentment against the cultivated and a hard-boiled muscling-in on culture, adventurousness, self-pity, deliberate disengagement from politics, fascist ambitions, schizophrenia, rude dislike of anything phoney or fey, a broad sense of humour but low on wit, a general intellectual nihilism, honesty, a neurotic discontent and a defeated, reconciled acquiescence that is the last flimsy shelter against complete despondency—a wildly ill-assorted agglomeration of credos which, although without any overall coherence, do belong to this incoherent period of social upheaval.

"Don't clap too hard, we're in a very old building," goes one Osborne passage. "Yes, very old. What about *that?* (*Pointing to Britannia*) What about her, eh—Madam with the helmet on? I reckon she's sagging a bit if you ask me."

In America, the phrase for a time eclipsed YOUNG TURKS, with which it is synonymous.

ANIMAL, *see* POLITICAL ANIMAL; BIRD DOGS.

ANNUIT COEPTIS, *see* UNITED WE STAND.

ANTITHESIS, *see* CONTRAPUNTAL PHRASES.

ANTI-WASHINGTON, *see* RUNNING AGAINST HOOVER.

APARTHEID, *see* SEGREGATION.

APOSTLE OF HATE   one who espouses bigotry; a racist.

In the post–Civil War era, those who revived bitter memories of the war to advance their own political fortunes were accused of preaching a "gospel of hate." See BLOODY SHIRT.

In 1876 *Harper's Magazine* rejected the use of the phrase: "... anybody in this centennial year ... who does not confine himself to rejoicing over our happy reunion, but looks to see the facts, is [called] an apostle of hate, delighting to dabble his fingers in the gore of the bloody shirt."

At the 1950 convention of the Congress of Industrial Organizations held in Cleveland five years before the union's merger with the American Federation of Labor, the leaders of most of the member unions delivered attacks on the Communists in their ranks. Philip Murray, who was to become the first president of the merged AFL-CIO, called the Communists "apostles of hate" who lied "out of the pits of their dirty bellies." He was primarily attacking the Communists who had seized control of the United Electrical, Radio and Machine Workers Union.

Lyndon B. Johnson, in his speech to a joint session of Congress on November 27, 1963, five days after the assassination of President John F. Kennedy, made a moving plea for unity in dealing with racial bigotry and intolerance:

The time has come for Americans of all races and creeds and political beliefs to understand and to respect one another. So let us put an end to the teaching and preaching of hate and evil and violence. Let us turn away from the fanatics of the far left and the far right, from the apostles of bitterness and bigotry, from those defiant of law and those who pour venom into our nation's bloodstream.

See RACISM.

APPEASEMENT a policy of acceding to the demands of aggressors, which often leads to more demands and greater concessions; an attack word against those opposing intervention in the affairs of another country.

The word was first used in its pejorative political sense by Philip Henry Kerr, Marquess of Lothian, in a letter to the *Times* of London in 1934, objecting to "a limitation of armaments by political appeasement." The word had no negative implications for British Prime Minister Neville Chamberlain. When President Franklin D. Roosevelt wanted to call an international conference in Washington on peaceful relations (an idea of Sumner Welles's), Secretary of State Cordell Hull urged him to check it out first with Chamberlain. The British leader, whose tightly rolled umbrella became the symbol of appeasement in the thirties (see UMBRELLA SYMBOL), wrote the President that such a plan would undermine his own efforts at what he termed "a measure of appeasement" of Italy and Germany.

At the Munich conference on September 29, 1938, the Sudetenland and all vital Czechoslovakian fortresses were yielded to Germany. Chamberlain proclaimed "PEACE FOR OUR TIME" on his return, as Winston Churchill warned: "Britain and France had to choose between war and dishonour. They chose dishonour. They will have war."

Fowler's *Modern English Usage* includes appeasement in a group of "worsened words" whose meaning has gained a new stigma: collaborator, imperialism, colonialism, and academic. "There is no hint in the *OED* definitions of anything discreditable or humiliating about the word [appeasement]. No one thought any the worse of Aeneas for letting Cerberus [dog guarding the gates of Hades] have his usual sop."

The *Domesday Dictionary* gives an appropriately horrible example of the nature of appeasement in this selection from Leonardo da Vinci: "Of the beaver one reads that when it is pursued, knowing this is to be on account of the virtue of its testicles for medicinal uses, not being able to flee any farther it stops and in order to be at peace with its pursuers bites off its testicles with its sharp teeth and leaves them to its enemies."

But Churchill, the man most identified as a foe of appeasement (see MUNICH, ANOTHER; IRON CURTAIN), made these remarks to the House of Commons in 1950:

> It [no appeasement] is a good slogan for the country . . . however . . . it requires to be more precisely defined. What we really mean, I think, is no appeasement through weakness or fear. Appeasement in itself may be good or bad according to circumstances. Appeasement from weakness and fear is alike futile and fatal. Appeasement from strength is magnanimous and noble and might be the surest and perhaps the only path to world peace.

ARENA   place of political combat for the clash of ideologies and personalities.

The original Latin sense of arena is "a sandy place," the center of an amphitheater where sand was scattered to absorb the blood of gladiators.

Henry Clay of Kentucky, a three-time loser for the presidency, wrote in 1837 of being "again forced into the presidential arena"; William Jennings Bryan, destined to be a three-time loser, used the exact words sixty years later. Supreme Court Justice Charles Evans Hughes, asked to run against Woodrow Wilson in 1916, declared: "One who has accepted a seat on the Supreme Court has closed behind him the door of political ambition. It is such a man's duty to refuse any proposal to serve in the presidency, and no patriotic citizen would urge him to cast off the judicial ermine in order to enter political arena." Yet, he ran, lost, served as Harding's and Coolidge's Secretary of State, and was appointed Chief Justice by Hoover.

A representative assembly, wrote John Stuart Mill in *Considerations on Representative Government* in 1861, has a responsibility "to be at once the nation's Committee of Grievances and its Congress of Opinions; an arena in which not only the general opinion of the nation, but that of every section of it, and, as far as possible, of every eminent individual whom it contains, can produce itself in full light and challenge discussion; where every person in the country may count upon finding somebody who speaks his mind as well or better than he could speak it himself . . ."

The word's use has been broadened in recent years to include all political and ideological spheres. President Lyndon Johnson defined Asia as "the crucial arena of man's striving for independence and order." President Eisenhower passed along to friends a copy of a quotation of Theodore Roosevelt's that returned the metaphor to the gladiator's blood-smeared pit:

> It is not the Critic who counts, not the one who points out how the strong man stumbled or how the doer of deeds might have done them better.
>
> The credit belongs to the man who is actually in the arena, whose face is marred with sweat and dust and blood; who strives valiantly; who errs and comes short again and again; who knows the great enthusiasms, the great devotions, and spends himself in a worthy cause; who, if he wins, knows the triumph of high achievement; and who, if he fails, at least fails while daring greatly, so that his place shall never

be with those cold and timid souls who know neither victory nor defeat.

After his defeat in 1960, Richard Nixon sent reprints of his "Man in the Arena" quotation to hundreds of his friends; since that time, supporters of candidates who have lost elections have frequently sent it to their leaders in lieu of a condolence letter.

"Politics," wrote John F. Kennedy in *Profiles in Courage,* "merely furnishes one arena which imposes special tests of courage. In whatever arena of life one may meet the challenge of courage, whatever may be the sacrifices he faces if he follows his conscience—the loss of his friends, his fortune, his contentment, even the esteem of his fellow men—each must decide for himself the course he will follow."

See HAT IN THE RING.

ARMAGEDDON a great, final conflict between the forces of good and evil.

The term was popularized in a political sense by Theodore Roosevelt in 1912. At the time he formed the Bull Moose party so that he could run as an independent candidate for president, thus effectively splitting the Republican ranks (which supported Roosevelt's handpicked choice as successor, William Howard Taft) and enabling Democrat Woodrow Wilson to win. At the Bull Moose party's Chicago convention on August 5, 1912, amid singing of "Onward, Christian Soldiers" and other stirring hymns, "Teddy" thundered: "We stand at Armageddon, and we battle for the Lord!"

The reference, of course, was Biblical; in Revelation, chapter XVI, we read that at a place called Armageddon "there were voices, and thunders and lightnings; and there was a great earthquake, such as was not since men were upon the earth . . . and every island fled away, and the mountains were not found . . . and there fell upon men a great hail out of heaven . . ." Babylon was destroyed, Satan was cast into Hell, and "they were judged every man according to their works."

Geographically, the place is probably the mount of Megiddo, where the Canaanites fought and Josiah was slain; the associations of the spot are suitably warlike.

With the development of nuclear power, the possibility of total annihilation loomed larger. The word was thus used more and more often to describe World War III, and was the title of a novel by Leon Uris about the threat of war in Berlin. General Douglas MacArthur, accepting the Japanese surrender on the deck of the battleship *Missouri* in Tokyo Bay, September 2, 1945, used the word in its current sense, a battleground that would mean the end of civilization: "Military alliances, balances of power, leagues of nations, all in turn failed, leaving the only path to be by way of the crucible of war. The utter destructiveness of war now blocks out this alternative. We have had our last chance. If we will not devise some greater and more equitable system, Armageddon will be at our door."

ARMCHAIR STRATEGIST one who pontificates about world events; a sofa sophist.

The phrase is similar to PARK-BENCH ORATOR, though the armchair strategist might be less inclined to take public positions. The similar phrase *Monday morning quarterback* implies carping criticism with the advantage of hindsight, but an armchair strategist might be enthusiastic as well as critical.

The armchair is a place of comfort from which to make discomfiting remarks; it can also be used as a symbol for laziness. Architect Frank Lloyd Wright claimed in 1938 that "armchair education" was the reason Americans did not realize how discredited their culture was in the eyes of the world.

Wrote *New York Times* correspondent Max Frankel in 1967:

> In most wars, the armchairs are full of generals refighting every battle, recasting every strategy, second-guessing every field commander. But Vietnam, being different in virtually every other sense as well, has also produced a new kind of kibitzer—the armchair diplomat. The galleries in this war are crowded mostly with mediators who second-guess, not the warriors but the negotiators, and spin many an intricate design not for winning the war but for ending it.

ARROGANCE OF POWER the theme of a school of criticism of U.S. foreign policy in the 1960s, questioning the basis of U.S. intervention in some conflicts abroad.

Senator J. William Fulbright of Arkansas, a Democrat, an intellectual, and the chairman of the Senate Foreign Relations Committee, had already raised questions about U.S. foreign policy for some time, as in his speech and book on "old myths and new realities." In 1966, he gave a series of lectures sponsored by the Johns Hopkins School of Advanced International Studies. One of them was entitled *The Arrogance of Power,* as was his subsequent book containing the same material.

Fulbright was skeptical about more than U.S. involvement in Vietnam and the Dominican Republic. He cast doubt on the validity of the nation's general posture in foreign affairs: "For lack of a clear and precise understanding of exactly what these motives [for going to war] are, I refer to them as the 'arrogance of power'—as a psychological need that nations seem to have . . . to prove that they are bigger, better or stronger than other nations." At another point, he elaborated: "One wonders how much the American commitment to Vietnamese freedom is also a commitment to American pride—the two seem to have become part of the same package."

In the debate over Vietnam, Fulbright was far from alone in thinking the U.S. was overextended in its foreign commitments. Many writers and academicians—and even a few retired generals, such as James Gavin and David Shoup—agreed that the U.S. had become too deeply involved. Martin Luther King, Jr., said in 1967:

> . . . honesty impels me to admit that our power has often made us arrogant. We feel that our money can do anything. We arrogantly feel that we have everything to teach other nations and nothing to learn from them. We often arrogantly feel that we have some divine, messianic mission to police the whole world. We are arrogant in not allowing young nations to go through the same growing pains, turbulence and revolution that characterizes our history . . .

In many of the attacks on Fulbright from both parties, the word "arrogant" was seized upon, as in this comment from Democrat James Farley: "It is arrogant indeed for a Senator to indict the character of the American people in time of war, or in the terms used by their enemy."

The phrase spawned other book titles: *The Limits of Power* by Eugene McCarthy, *The Abuse of Power* by Theodore Draper, *LBJ: The Exercise of Power* by Rowland Evans and Robert Novak, and *The Accountability of*

Power by Walter Mondale, and may have had a hand in Stokely Carmichael's BLACK POWER.

Fulbright might have picked up the phrase from John F. Kennedy, who said in 1963: ". . . when power leads a man towards arrogance, poetry reminds him of his limitations . . ."

See POWER CORRUPTS.

ARSENAL OF DEMOCRACY
the role of the U.S. in supplying munitions to the nations opposing the Axis powers in World War II.

The phrase was coined by Jean Monnet, French ambassador to the United States, in a conversation with Supreme Court Justice Felix Frankfurter. Monnet was describing what would be the most effective assistance the U.S. could provide in the struggle against tyranny.

Frankfurter, struck by the forcefulness of the phrase, told Monnet it was precisely the sort that should be given world currency by President Roosevelt. He asked Monnet not to use it again, lest some other statesman pick it up. The Monnet phrase also came to the attention of John J. McCloy, an Assistant Secretary of War, and it was submitted in a draft speech sent by General Edward S. Greenbaum, executive officer of Undersecretary of War Robert Patterson, to FDR speechwriter Samuel I. Rosenman.

Roosevelt used it on December 29, 1940: "We must be the great arsenal of democracy. For us this is an emergency as serious as war itself. We must apply ourselves to our task with the same resolution, the same sense of urgency, the same spirit of patriotism and sacrifice we would show if we were at war."

ART OF THE POSSIBLE   a frequent definition of politics stressing the need for compromise, asking not

"what must be done" but "what can be done."

Political figures, under fire for falling short of attaining lofty goals promised in campaigns, often fall back on the phrase, "the art of the possible," as a useful defense. It emphasizes the practical nature of political rule, with its built-in checks and balances.

Ironically, the source is rarely quoted: the Chancellor of Prussia, Otto von Bismarck (1815–1898), defined politics as "the doctrine of the possible, the attainable . . . the art of the next best."

Adlai Stevenson called Lyndon Johnson "a master of the art of the possible in politics," citing Johnson's own stated philosophy on the subject: "Frequently in life I have had to settle for progress short of perfection. I have done so because—despite cynics—I believe that half a loaf is better than none. But my acceptance has always been conditioned upon the premise that the half-loaf is a step toward the full loaf—and that if I go on working, the day of the full loaf will come."

For another definition, see WHO GETS WHAT, WHEN, AND HOW.

AS IS WELL KNOWN, *see* REPORTEDLY.

ASK NOT, *see* CONTRAPUNTAL PHRASES.

ATLANTIC COMMUNITY   defined variously as "the Western world," the members of the North Atlantic Treaty Organization, or in its most limited sense, the U.S., Great Britain, and Canada.

Walter Lippmann popularized and possibly coined the expression in his book, *U.S. War Aims,* published in 1944. According to Lippmann, the Atlantic community includes not merely the U.S., the United Kingdom and France, but all of the South American and Central American nations, Mexico, Canada and Cuba, Spain, Portugal, Italy, Greece, Switzerland, Belgium, the Netherlands, Eire and Iceland, the Union of South Africa, Australia, New Zealand and the Philippines.

In May 1945, *Fortune* magazine commented: "If her rehabilitation results in prosperity, western Europe will merge with what Walter Lippmann, for lack of a better word, baptized the Atlantic Community."

The use of "community" in the sense of a group of nations with mutual interests can be traced to 1888, when English statesman Henry Molyneux, Earl of Carnarvon, made the prophetic observation: "We are part of the community of Europe, and we must do our duty as such."

AT THAT POINT IN TIME   a circumlocution for "then," carrying a spurious specificity.

In the mid-sixties, "at that point in time" and "in point of fact" were academic-bureaucratic vogue phrases. In a 1968 memo to his political colleagues, the author urged the Nixon campaign to eschew such words as "at that point in time," "exacerbate" and "eschew."

As the televised Watergate hearings began, young bureaucrats of the Nixon Administration's campaign committee (see CREEP) popularized the phrase, which is a combination of "at that point" and "at that time" and seemed more precise than the other vogue term "in that time frame."

But Raven McDavid of the University of Chicago wrote to *American Speech Magazine:* "Since the beginning of the Watergate extravaganza, academicians have amused themselves with the recurrent phrase *at*

that point in time . . . however, much as it embarrasses me, it seems clear that the burrocrats [the misspelling was intentional] were following the lead of the intellectuals." He provided three citations, one from a 1970 *Daedalus,* an early 1973 use in the *American Anthropologist,* and a 1963 selection from Cleanth Brooks' literary criticism of William Faulkner: "he takes us back to a point in time three years before Isaac's act of renunciation."

But the phrase was closely associated with Watergate language, and was used ironically by minority counsel Fred Thompson as the title of his book on the hearings. In 1977 a *Washington Star* editorialist was complaining about the disuse into which the plain words "now" and "then" had fallen. "Even as 'at this (or that) point in time' became an ungainly scrub for now or then, there was the sudden, curious intrusion of 'presently.' In the old days it meant 'in a short while' but now, we take it, means 'at this point in time' or, if you will pardon the expression, now."

$Au H_2O = 1964$ bumper-strip slogan advocating Barry Goldwater for President in 1964.

Much earlier Goldwater support came from young conservatives on college campuses; in all likelihood, a politically minded chemistry student came up with the formula Au (symbol for gold)H_2O (water) equals victory in 1964.

Anti-Goldwater people, pressing the TRIGGER-HAPPY charge, countered with bumper-strips or snipes reading "Au H_2O + 1964 = ⚥ "

For a similar symbol, see K_1C_2.

AUSTERITY, *see* **AFFLUENT SOCIETY.**

AUTARKIC adj., economically viable; in noun form, as "autarky," a nation able to claim self-sufficiency.

This word is most often confused with its homonym, "autarchy," which means autocratic or totalitarian rule. Autarky with a "k" is a nation able to take care of itself, its state of economic affairs brought about by a policy aimed at avoiding dependency on neighboring nations.

The word is old: Samuel Ward in *Balme from Gilead* wrote in 1617 of "the autarchie and selfe-sufficiencie of God." The spelling changed in the late seventeenth century to separate the word from its autocratic confuser.

The connotation of the word changed from good (self-sufficient) to bad (isolationist, selfish), especially during the early sixties, when "declarations of interdependence" became the vogue. In the seventies the word was frequently used in the foreign economic policy addresses of Henry Kissinger.

AUTHORITARIAN, *see* **TOTALITARIAN.**

AUTHORITATIVE SOURCES the screen behind which a political figure airs his views without being directly quoted or identified.

Authoritative sources, informed circles, and *a source close to* are all signals that a BACKGROUNDER has taken place.

The single most authoritative source is called the *highest authority.* He is the President of the United States wearing a beard and dark glasses.

See BACKGROUNDER; NOT FOR ATTRIBUTION; OFF THE RECORD; LEAK; DOPE STORY; SOURCES.

AUTOMOBILE METAPHOR frequently used economic word-picture.

The metaphor first appeared very soon after the introduction of the automobile; in 1907, *Emporia Gazette* editor William Allen White referred to Indiana Senator (and highly regarded orator) Albert Beveridge as "a geared-up speedster, a show car." Woodrow Wilson was reported to have said "the way to stop financial joy-riding is to arrest the chauffeur, not the automobile."

Adlai Stevenson, in the 1952 presidential campaign, used the metaphor to describe what he felt was a schism in the Republican party: "It is an ancient political vehicle, held together by soft soap and hunger, and with front-seat drivers and back-seat drivers contradicting each other in a bedlam of voices, shouting 'go right' and 'go left' at the same time. I don't envy the driver and I don't think the American people will care to ride in his bus very far."

The metaphor was used in an economic context by Richard M. Nixon in a 1965 speech to the National Association of Manufacturers:

This Administration has adopted a completely contradictory policy in dealing with the threat of inflation. It has tried to replace the market's law of supply and demand with Johnson's law of Comply and Expand: Business complies and government expands. But a policy that requires business to slam on the price brakes while government steps on the spending accelerator will in the end only produce a collision—and the family budget will be the casualty.

AVAILABILITY candidate potential; one who has all of the generally accepted qualifications for public office and would offend no significant voting bloc or region. Derogatory when used to describe overeagerness on the part of an unannounced candidate.

Harold J. Laski, the British political philosopher, wrote: "Out of all this complexity [of preconvention maneuvering] there has emerged the doctrine of 'availability.' The party needs a candidate who, positively, will make the widest appeal and, negatively, will offend the least proportion of the electorate. . . . He ought not to possess any nostrum which can be represented as extreme."

Warren G. Harding, the darkhorse candidate who became the Republican nominee for the presidency in 1920 after Governor Frank Lowden of Illinois and General Leonard Wood deadlocked the convention, was considered eminently available, ultimately offering "not nostrums but normalcy." He was a senator who had offended no one, from a large midwest state, personable, handsome, and in accord with the prevailing conservative Republican philosophy.

Hubert H. Humphrey was one of many possible vice-presidential candidates considered by Lyndon B. Johnson in 1964. When newsmen asked him almost daily whether he was in the running, Humphrey would say: "Nobody has to woo me. I'm old reliable, available Hubert." He added: "I'm like the girl next door—always available but you don't necessarily think about marriage."

In courtship, "available" is several cuts below "eligible" in terms of attractiveness; an available girl is one not often dated. In Al Capp's "L'il Abner" comic strip, a character named Available Jones was constantly ready—for a small fee—to go anywhere and do anything. The pejorative sense appeared as early as 1837, in the *Baltimore Commercial Transcript:* "The New York papers are discussing whether the most talented, or the most available man, shall be reelected as candidate for the next presidency."

Incumbent first-term Presidents traditionally seek to disguise their obvious availability to create suspense. William McKinley stated a position of qualified availability which has been restated often: "The question of my acquiescence will be based absolutely upon whether the call of duty appears to me clear and well-defined."

The best play on the word came around the time of its earliest political use. Scorning the selection of William Henry Harrison and John Tyler by the Whigs in 1840 without even the pretense of a party platform, Senator Thomas Hart Benton of Missouri said, "Availability was the only ability sought by the Whigs."

See JOB SEEKS THE MAN.

AVALANCHE staggering ballot majority; thunderous downpour of votes.

Avalanche, like *landslide* and *tidal wave,* are words of natural disaster applied to political disaster. Early use, especially in the "Log Cabin and Hard Cider" campaign of 1840 of Harrison against Van Buren, applied to large crowd turnouts: "It was another of those glorious and enthusiastic Avalanches of the people," said a Harrison handout, "that distinguish this contest from any other in our National History." Later the word came to mean votes rather than people, and the New York *Tribune* wrote in 1888 of the Vermont Democrats being "buried under an avalanche of Republican ballots." This is the use that is current today.

Avalanche refers specifically to votes; *landslide* refers to an election as well as to votes. An election in which the popular-vote differential is not large, but the electoral-vote difference is considerable, is a landslide without an avalanche.

See DISASTER METAPHORS.

AVERAGE MAN, *see* **JOHN Q. PUBLIC; COMMON MAN, CENTURY OF THE.**

AWESOME BURDEN, *see* **LONELIEST JOB.**

AXIS an alliance of powers; specifically, the Axis Powers (Rome, Berlin, later Tokyo just before and during World War II).

The word comes from the imaginary line that can be drawn through a body, and around which that body could revolve. In its political context, the phrase is attributed to Benito Mussolini who said in 1936 that the German-Italian agreement was "an axis round which all European states, animated by the will to collaboration and peace can also assemble." In 1937, he added: "We have forced the axis to Berlin and Rome. That is the beginning of European consolidation."

The Rome-Berlin axis, around which Europe presumably was to revolve, became a familiar phrase in 1938; the *New York Times* wrote, "There was a triangle in 1914—Berlin-Vienna-Rome. There is an axis in 1938—Berlin-Rome." *Newsweek* added: "Central Europe regards the Rome-Berlin axis as an artificial structure."

Adolf Hitler made reference to the axis in his Sportspalast speech in Berlin while the Munich Pact was being negotiated, as he assured the world he had no more territorial demands: "This relation [between Germany and Italy] has long left a sphere of clear economic and political expediency and over treaties and alliances has turned into a real, strong union of hearts. Here an axis was formed represented by two peoples . . ."

With the entry of Japan into the war, the "axis" lost its metaphoric meaning as the alliance became—as it had been in the first World War—a triangle. But the Axis Powers were the opponents of the Allied Powers; "axis" for a generation meant only "Hitler-Mussolini-Tojo," and has only recently begun to regain its original meaning of any two powers in alliance, as in "a London-Washington axis."

When the link between two cities is a function of geography or trade rather than political alliance, the word "corridor" is preferred, unless a new name is devised; the "Boston-Washington corridor" is sometimes called "Boswash."

B

BACKBENCHER a congressman of low seniority; a steadfast supporter of party leaders.

In Great Britain's House of Commons, where this expression originated, a backbencher is one who goes down the line in regular support of the party leadership at the front bench of the House.

As the expression is used in the U.S., the "party regularity" emphasis is dropped, and the "low seniority" aspect is emphasized. In discussing the dark-horse possibilities of freshman Senator Charles Percy, *U.S. News & World Report,* wrote in 1967: "Senator John F. Kennedy of Massachusetts was still a 'backbencher' in 1960 when he took the Democratic nomination away from older and more experienced figures in his party."

See SHADOW CABINET.

BACK CHANNEL a secret or informal method at passing "sensitive" information, circumventing normal procedures.

At U.S. embassies around the world, the Central Intelligence Agency has long maintained a secret communications network designed to by-pass normal State Department cable traffic. This is called "the back channel."

Such an officially unofficial, or discreet, mode is often useful in diplomacy. For example, when the government of Italy did not want Lieutenant General Vernon Walters to be President Nixon's official translator on a state visit to that country (because the Italians suspected General Walters of having financed a right-wing coup attempt with CIA funds), this request was passed by presidential advance men to the CIA in Rome, and back to CIA headquarters in Washington, rather than through regular diplomatic channels.

When National Security Adviser Henry Kissinger called a Nixon speechwriter into his office to discuss a presidential announcement of the failure of secret Paris negotiations with the North Vietnamese, he introduced the subject with a dramatic: "We have had a back channel in Paris."

Thanks to the Kissinger usage in matters other than the particular CIA back channel at embassies, the phrase became national security jargon for any clandestine method of reporting. In the White House in 1971 and later, a "series check" was the classified term for a method of monitoring embarrassing political information gathered by the National Security Agency in the process of eavesdropping on international communications. These data, of political rather than national security significance (such as a foreign leader's personal opinion of a traveling U.S. official) were screened out of the intelligence system and not passed to the CIA. Such reports entered a "back channel" in the White House, with distribution limited to the National Security Adviser, his deputy, and sometimes the President.

The phrase is now used to describe any alternative routing. In 1977, after Mr. Kissinger had left office, the *Washington Post* wrote: "Soviet Ambassador Anatoly Dobrynin confers often on the phone with Kissinger— a 'back channel' arrangement that reportedly has annoyed some at the White House."

BACKER political supporter, especially a financial contributor.

One who will talk about you admiringly is a *fan;* one who will ring doorbells for you is a *worker,* or one of the TROOPS; one who believes in a cause is an *adherent;* one who will put his money where his vote is, is a *backer*— in substantial sums, a FAT CAT. A general term covering all these activities is a *supporter,* or a (name of candidate) *man.* The collective term is *following.*

According to William Riordan in 1905, George Washington Plunkitt of Tammany Hall explained how to begin to get backers: "I had a cousin, a young man who didn't take any particular interest in politics. I went to him and said: 'Tommy, I'm goin' to be a politician, and I want to get a followin'; can I count on you?' He said, 'Sure, George.' That's how I started in business. I got a marketable commodity—one vote."

BACKGROUNDER a press conference, or interview with a single reporter, where the information is on the record but the news source cannot be revealed precisely. See NOT FOR ATTRIBUTION; THUMBSUCKER; DOPE STORY; SOURCES.

Theodore Sorensen explained the John F. Kennedy rationale for backgrounders:

During his Christmas holiday in Palm Beach, both in 1961 and 1962, he invited the two dozen or so regular White House correspondents accompanying him to a free-wheeling three-to-four hour "backgrounder" . . . dividing each session into domestic and foreign affairs discussions. Year-end "think pieces" (which would have been written anyway, he reasoned) were in this way better informed of views attributable to "the highest authority" or "sources close to the administration." Although these phrases deceived no one in the know, it made for a freer and fuller exchange than would have been true of a regular press conference or a larger background group in Washington.

If the technique of the backgrounder is overused, the news media will be overloaded with phrases like "a spokesman said," "a source close to the White House revealed," "political circles are buzzing with the rumor that," etc. This leaves the impression that the top official concerned does not wish to stand up and be counted, which is true enough, but it is not the impression he wants to leave at all. During the 1966 dispute between the Kennedy family and the publishers of William Manchester's book, *The Death of a President,* there were daily Kennedy family backgrounders throughout the crucial week before serialization, causing columnist Murray Kempton to comment: "One always departs with his gratitude for a Kennedy backgrounder somewhat diluted by the wish that it hadn't left the foreground so foggy."

In December 1971 the *Washington Post* decided this technique was being abused; editor Benjamin Bradlee said "the public has suffered from this collusion between the government and the press." Particularly offensive was the "deep backgrounder" in which no source at all could be given. Presidential press secretary Ronald Ziegler promptly agreed: ". . . over the years, to some degree, government has misused backgrounders." Newsmen were cautious in their criticism, however, lest the pendulum swing back too far; the abolition of backgrounders would dry up important sources of news, especially in the foreign policy area.

A cartoon in *Frontier* magazine showed a dais of faceless men with a faceless master of ceremonies speaking at a podium labeled "Washington Press Banquet" and saying: "It's an honor this evening to present the nation's Highest Authority, who will be introduced by a Spokesman Close to the President, following remarks by a Highly Placed Official and A Usually Reliable Source . . ."

When a reporter files a story from a region or city not recently covered, he sometimes reports on the background of events in that area, but that is properly called a *situationer* and not a "backgrounder."

BACKLASH   civil rights recoil: the reaction by whites against Negro advancement when its implications— especially in job competition—hit close to home.

For eighty-three days—from February 10 to June 19, 1964—the Senate debated the Civil Rights bill passed by the House. During that time, "backlash" was given political meaning.

American Speech magazine has provided two leads as to its first use. This sentence appeared in the *Nation's Business* magazine (April 1964): "This sensitivity for such pocketbook issues has politicians of both parties jittery over the possible backlash from civil rights developments." Tait Trussell, managing editor of the business magazine, tracked down the writer of the line, John Gibson. "I talked to John about the source of the word 'backlash,' " Trussell writes of the author. "He believes it was used by Richard Scammon, the director of the Census. However, both John and I seem to recall that the word was being bandied about elsewhere at the time."

Scammon's recollection: "Maybe Oliver Quayle started it; maybe I did. But most likely it just crept into conversations from several sources, like the 'As Maine Goes, so goes Vermont' phrase of election night, 1936."

The second lead was in the *New York Times,* on April 9, 1964. Reporter Earl Mazo wrote: "In the immediate aftermath of the Wisconsin voting it is obvious that a backlash against the current civil-rights drive has materialized." Mazo responded to a query: "I remember using it, of course, but my mind is hazy as to how it came about. I know I was reaching for a word more vivid than 'reaction' that meant reaction. I believe, in that regard, I occasionally used the words 'boomerang' and 'backfire.' I have no idea, Bill, whether I had heard or seen 'backlash' elsewhere before using it myself."

The reason for dragging the reader up and down these blind alleys is to illustrate the "phantom coinage" phenomenon, when a word or phrase seeps into the language without a single source, apparently by osmosis.

However, until another researcher comes up with earlier usage, credit for the word's popularization belongs to Washington columnists Rowland Evans and Robert Novak. After the Birmingham, Alabama, riots in the summer of 1963, President

Kennedy's depressed-areas bill was defeated in the House. In the June 16, 1963, *New York Herald Tribune,* Evans and Novak wrote that this defeat was due to other causes and was not "the first backlash of civil rights turmoil." The columnists used the word frequently afterward, and—like Walter Lippmann with Herbert Bayard Swope's COLD WAR and the Alsops with EGGHEAD and PECKING ORDER—were the popularizers.

Mr. Novak tells the author they took the word from a usage earlier that summer of 1963 by economist Eliot Janeway, which Mr. Janeway corroborates. He had been discussing the impact of automation on white and Negro workers, and pointed out that in any economic downturn there was likely to be a breakup in the long-time political alliance between civil rights groups and labor unions, as white workers "lashed back" at Negro competition for the remaining jobs.

Writing in *Look* in September 1964, Fletcher Knebel gave one derivation of the term: " 'This Thing' was the now famous backlash, a word long used by sports fishermen. The angler casts his lure, watches it fly in a silver arc across the water. Suddenly the lure stops and whips backward toward the fisherman, while a snarl of line fouls his reel. . . . Transferred to the world of politics, the white backlash aptly describes the resentment of many white Americans to the speed of the great Negro revolution, which has been gathering momentum since the first rash of sit-ins in early 1960."

An angrier definition was provided by Brad Cleaveland of the University of California's Free Speech Movement: ". . . the phrase 'white backlash' is the simplest way to say 'the bigotry of the majority' . . . the real meaning of 'white backlash' is 'Don't bug me nigger . . . you're buggin' me with that civil disobedience . . . now stop that or we'll show you who has the tear gas, cattle prods, and shotguns!!!' "

The word was used frequently in the 1964 presidential campaign; a SILENT VOTE motivated by the white backlash was supposed to materialize, but never did to the extent some expected. "For every backlash the Democrats lose," said Lyndon Johnson, "we pick up three frontlash."

Like the killing of Lee Harvey Oswald by Jack Ruby, the coinage of "frontlash" was committed in front of millions. During the television coverage of the Democratic National Convention on August 26, 1964, Dr. Aaron Henry of the Mississippi Freedom delegation objected to the use of backlash to define a minority reaction against a majority trend in his state. Since most of the white population of Mississippi was anti-Negro, he pointed out, it would have to be called a "forward lash."

CBS commentator Roger Mudd repeated the word as "frontlash" and asked fellow commentator Eric Sevareid what he thought of it. Sevareid changed the meaning to refer to those moderate and liberal Republican voters who would desert the party ranks because of Senator Goldwater's conservatism. After President Johnson had accepted the nomination, an NBC newsman asked him what he thought of the effect of the backlash, and the President replied that the term had been overused, suggesting greater use of "what you people call the frontlash . . . that isn't my word, it's yours." Apparently the President had been watching CBS two days before, or had been briefed on the word's use; understandably, the NBC reporters had not, and NBC commentator David Brinkley, following the interview with the President, credited the coinage to Johnson.

BACKUP CANDIDATE, see FALL-BACK POSITION; DARK HORSE.

BAFFLEGAB jargon providing more obfuscation than enlightenment, as is often found in government reports and other official statements.

Bafflegab began appearing in newspapers and conversation in the early 1950's. In a 1952 newspaper interview, Milton Smith, then assistant general counsel of the U.S. Chamber of Commerce, claimed authorship. Smith explained: "I decided we needed a new and catchy word to describe the utter incomprehensibility, ambiguity, verbosity and complexity of government regulations." Before hitting on *bafflegab,* Smith said, he considered "burobabble" and "gabbalia."

Smith's contribution surfaces from time to time, as in a 1967 column by Sylvia Porter, the economics writer. She relegated to "this year's batch of bafflegab" such phrases as "healthy slowdown" and "rolling readjustment." Other euphemisms for recession include "crabwise movement," "high-level stagnation," "period of basic readjustment," and "minislump."

Time magazine in 1968 published a "baffle-gab thesaurus" (unnecessarily hyphenating the word) based on a Royal Canadian Air Force collection of fuzzy phraseology. A ringing, three-word phrase, guaranteed to impress, can be assembled from the spare parts in each of these three categories:

A	B	C
0) Integrated	Management	Options
1) Total	Organizational	Flexibility
2) Systematized	Monitored	Capability
3) Parallel	Reciprocal	Mobility
4) Functional	Digital	Programming
5) Responsive	Logistical	Concept
6) Optional	Transitional	Time-Phase
7) Synchronized	Incremental	Projection
8) Compatible	Third-Generation	Hardware
9) Balanced	Policy	Contingency

In popular usage, *bafflegab* runs behind GOBBLEDYGOOK and OFFICIALESE. Also see PENTAGONESE; ECONOMIC JARGON; CIA-ESE.

BAGMAN intermediary in a political payoff; one who carries the bribe from the beneficiary of a corrupt deal to the grafter. Not to be confused with "black bag job" (see CIA-ESE).

The courts have decided that the word is libelous. Harlem Congressman Adam Clayton Powell described Mrs. Esther James as a "bagwoman" in the policy racket, but chose to make the charge outside the libel-proof halls of Congress. The woman sued for libel and was awarded damages. The congressman spent years avoiding payment and ducking service of subpoenas, requiring him to reside outside his district and country, ultimately followed by House exclusion.

In the administration of Mayor William O'Dwyer of New York, a minor officeholder named James Moran was widely reputed to be the bagman, and went tight-lipped to prison. Newsmen Norton Mockridge and Robert Prall wrote in *The Big Fix:* "Nobody believed, either, that Jim Moran kept all the money he collected. For many years he had been known as a bagman, which in political jargon, is literally the man who carries the bag or boodle for somebody higher up. And the bagman never gets to keep the big money."

Another, more recent, use of bagman is as the military officer who follows the President, carrying the "football." See FOOTBALL, POLITICAL.

BAILEY MEMORANDUM
document alleged to have been written by John Bailey, Connecticut Democratic State Chairman (later National Chairman), demonstrating how useful a Catholic could be on the national ticket.

The Bailey Memorandum was used in an attempt to gain the 1956 vice-presidential nomination for John F. Kennedy, who lost to Senator Estes Kefauver. Contrary to the belief at the time, the document was written by Theodore Sorensen, Kennedy's closest aide.

The sixteen-page memorandum of statistics, quotations, analyses, and arguments sought to answer Democratic fears of "anti-Catholic" votes by raising hopes of recapturing a greater share of the votes of Catholics, especially among conservatives in urban areas who had voted for Eisenhower in 1952. The memo held that a vice-presidential nominee of the Catholic faith would do more to swing states with large electoral-vote totals into the Democratic column than any non-Catholic candidate from the south or farm belt.

When the word of the document spread to newsmen and politicians, Kennedy arranged Bailey's assertion of authorship to avoid being accused of personally injecting a religious issue.

The memorandum controversy again mushroomed during the 1960 presidential election when Republicans reprinted it as an example of a blatant appeal to "Catholic voting blocs." Kennedy, fearing a "Protestant bloc," instructed his aides not to talk publicly in terms of Catholic voting strength.

Sorensen wrote in 1965: "The Bailey Memorandum oversimplified, overgeneralized and overextended its premise in order to reach an impressive conclusion." Many Republicans sadly disagreed.

BALANCED TICKET
a slate of candidates nominated so as to appeal to as many voter groups as possible. Typical considerations in balancing a ticket: the nominees' geographic origin, race or religion, type of experience, position on specific issues, and COLORATION.

In American presidential politics, the home state of the candidates for President and Vice President was, historically, the weightiest item on the scale. More than local chauvinism was involved; whether the issue was slavery or free silver, tariffs or manifest destiny, sectional interests came into play. As national politics grew more complicated—and sophisticated—so did the question of balance. Joe Martin, former House Republican Leader, recalled his 1940 sales presentation to Wendell Willkie on behalf of Senator Charles McNary as a vice-presidential candidate. "You are known as a utilities man; McNary has sided with the public power boys. You're supposed to represent big business interests; McNary was the sponsor of the McNary-Haugen farm bill. You aren't supposed to know much about the legislative process; McNary is a master of it. I think you'd make a perfect team." Neither Willkie nor McNary liked the other's politics, but in the spirit of balance they ran together.

The phrase has even been applied to foreign politics where no election in the American sense is involved. In 1962, Averell Harriman of New York, then Assistant Secretary of State for Far Eastern Affairs, was attempting to establish a coalition government for Laos that would both bring stability to that country and satisfy the great and interested powers. His controversial solution: a TROIKA consisting of rightists, neutralists and pro-Communists. President John Kennedy defended Harriman's efforts, saying: "He's putting together a New York State balanced ticket."

Geographical balance is always sought on a presidential ticket, but it is useless. In 17 out of 24 national elections since the Civil War, vice-presidential candidates on the losing ticket failed to carry their home states. Within recent years, Henry Wallace could not deliver Iowa for Roosevelt in 1940, Estes Kefauver failed to swing Tennessee for Stevenson in 1956, Earl Warren did not carry California for Dewey in 1948, and Henry Cabot Lodge lost Massachusetts to Kennedy in 1960.

In local politics, balance is struck between religion, national origin, and, more recently, race. Most big cities remain not-very-melted pots in which as many lumps as possible must be appealed to. Edward Costikyan, the former leader of Tammany Hall, spoke for the politicians' consensus when he defended the practice of giving the public a *"representative* representation." In *Behind Closed Doors,* Costikyan recalled the apocryphal DREAM TICKET for the Upper West Side of Manhattan when that section was a prosperous ghetto: "one reform Jew, one orthodox Jew and one agnostic Jew."

BALANCE OF POWER the theory that peace is best ensured when rival groups are equal in strength.

An object of international diplomacy for centuries, the term was in use as early as 1700. Alexander Pope wrote a poem entitled "The Balance of Europe" in 1715: "Now Europe's balanc'd, neither side prevails;/For nothing's left in either of the scales." The British, in particular, sought to apply it to maintain a relatively durable peace from 1871 to 1914, with a balance between the Triple Alliance (Germany, Austria, Italy) and the Triple Entente (Britain, France, Russia).

In the U.S., political writers often use the expression to discuss the CHECKS AND BALANCES among the states of the Union or the three branches of government. "Every project," wrote John Adams in 1789, "has been found to be no better than committing the lamb to the custody of the wolf, except that one which is called a balance of power." Before the Civil War, it referred to a balance between the slave-holding and the free states.

The phrase is also applied to disputes among the branches of the government. Franklin D. Roosevelt said in 1937, while discussing his plan to pack the Supreme Court (see NINE OLD MEN), that over the last half-century "the balance of power between the three great branches of the Federal Government has been tipped out of balance by the courts in direct contradiction of the high purposes of the framers of the Constitution."

Occasionally it has been scorned as a shaky way of keeping peace. Thus, Winston Churchill, in his famed Fulton, Missouri, IRON CURTAIN speech in 1946, declared that if the English-speaking Commonwealth joined forces with the U.S., "there will be no quivering, precarious balance of power to offer its temptation to ambition or adventure. On the contrary, there will be an overwhelming assurance of security." In his 1961 inaugural, John F. Kennedy called on both sides in the Cold War to "join in creating a new endeavor—not a new balance of power, but a new world of law, where the strong are just and the weak secure and the peace preserved."

Kennedy later came to see the balance of power as the only real way of minimizing the temptation to adventure, as Churchill put it. During the Cuban missile crisis, Kennedy said: "If we suffer a major defeat, if they suffer a major defeat, it may change the balance of power." Such a change, he said, "also increases possibly the chance of war."

With the advent of nuclear weaponry, another phrase is often used in place of balance of power—"balance of terror," coined by Canadian Prime Minister Lester Pearson in 1955.

BALD EAGLE   the national symbol of the United States; frequent nickname of baldheaded political leaders.

Though references to bald eagles can be traced to 1836, the first patriotic reference is found in the June 19, 1873, *Newton Kansan:* "Let patriots everywhere . . . prepare to do the clean thing by Uncle Sam and his baldheaded eagle."

The bald eagle has been on the Great Seal of the United States since 1782, an olive branch with thirteen olives in its right claw, thirteen arrows in the left (after the thirteen original colonies), and a banner in its beak saying "E Pluribus Unum" (From Many, One). It can be found on the back of every dollar bill. Kennedy aide Ted Sorensen used it metaphorically in 1963: "How does a President choose, for example, in a moment of crisis, between the olive branch of peace (clutched in the right talon of the eagle on his Seal) and the arrows of war (which are clutched in the left)?"

The symbol has also been called "the spread eagle" because of its outstretched wings. The *North American Review* after the Civil War defined "spread-eaglism" as "a compound of exaggeration, effrontery, bombast, mixed metaphors, platitudes, defiant threats thrown at the world, and irreverent appeals to the Supreme Being."

Of course, the "bird of Washington" is only white-headed, not bald; but James M. Husted was cited by Charles Ledyard Norton in 1890 as "the Bald Eagle of Westchester County"; Robert A. Lovett, Secretary of Defense under Truman and a State Department veteran, was the "Bald Eagle of Foggy Bottom" (see FOGGY BOTTOM).

The bald eagle on the Presidential Seal has had a curious history. Heraldic custom calls for eagles on coats of arms to be facing to the right, so that the bird will be facing forward, toward the flagstaff, when flown on a flag ahead of marching troops. During the Administration of President Rutherford B. Hayes, when the Presidential Seal originated, a designer became confused copying the Great Seal of the United States, and turned the presidential eagle's head to the left—looking backward, as it were, while the nation marched ahead.

This national embarrassment could have continued without rectification were it not for President Franklin Roosevelt's concern about the number of stars on the Commander in Chief's flag. As a White House release of October 25, 1945 delicately put it: "It seemed inappropriate to President Roosevelt for the flag of the Commander in Chief to have only four stars when there were five stars in the flags of Fleet Admirals and Generals of the Army, grades which had been created in December 1944."

As this oversight was being corrected, Arthur E. DuBois, chief of the Heraldic Section of the Office of the Quartermaster General of the Army, pounced on the wrong-headed eagle that had been troubling heraldic specialists for years. He designed a new Presidential Coat of Arms, Seal and Flag, with the bald eagle facing toward the right. In heraldry, that is the "direction of honor," which has no ideological right-left significance but has to do with the way the eagle is facing on the flag of honorably marching troops (and, presumably, is why a hostess seats her guest of honor on her right, and why diplomatic protocol calls for guests at a State dinner to speak first to the dinner partner on the right).

The new flag and seal were completed after President Roosevelt's death. President Truman, who unfurled it for the first time publicly on October 25, 1945, called attention to a more important symbolic change. "Now raise that flag up, there," he said to his military aide, General Harry Vaughan, who was holding the previously used presidential flag. "This flag here—in President Wilson's time there were two flags for the President, an Army flag with a red star and a Navy flag for the President with a blue star. President Wilson ordered a single flag for the President, and this was the result of that [*General Vaughan displays flag*] with the white eagle facing toward the arrows, which is the sinister side of the heraldic form, and no color." "This new flag [*to General Vaughan*] if you will raise that one up, now you will see— you can see the difference. . . . This new flag faces the eagle toward the staff which is looking to the front all the time when you are on the march, and also has him looking at the olive branches for peace, instead of the ar-

rows for war; and taking the 4 stars out of the corner and putting 48 stars around the Presidential seal."

In the abbreviated version of this story told to visitors on White House tours, President Roosevelt is said to have had the seal changed so that the eagle would be facing the olive branch of peace rather than the arrows of war. That is true as far as it goes, but it was Harry Truman who caught the war-to-peace significance of the turning of the head of the American eagle.

See **PARTY EMBLEMS; UNCLE SAM.**

BALKANIZATION, *see* **VIETNAMIZATION.**

BALLBUSTER, *see* **NUT-CUTTING.**

BALLOT-BOX STUFFING vote fraud; originally, the illegal insertion of paper votes into the ballot box, with or without the connivance of local election officials.

The practice flourished in the days of Boss Tweed and the heyday of Tammany Hall in New York City. With the introduction of voting machines the practice was curtailed, however, leaving the phrase to mean any attempt to falsify the vote count.

Both practice and phrase appear to have started in San Francisco just after the Gold Rush. An advanced form of ballot-box stuffing was described in the House of Representatives in 1882 by Benjamin Butterworth of Ohio:

> They had been accustomed to have a box so constructed that the lid would pull out in a groove part of the way, and on election morning pulling the lid part way back, so the bottom of the box could be seen, the judge, or one of them, would say, "You see there is nothing in the box." The box would be closed, and

the balloting proceed. True, the box would appear to be empty, while under the lid in the top of the box two or three hundred tickets would be fastened. The box being shut with a thud, the tickets would fall down.

Some historians say that ballot-box stuffing in New York City may have cost James G. Blaine, Republican, the presidency of the United States in 1884. Blaine lost New York State by a margin of 1,143 votes for Grover Cleveland, the Democratic candidate, out of more than 1,100,000 cast. In the Electoral College, Cleveland obtained 219 votes to 182 for Blaine; had Blaine received New York's 36 electoral votes, he would have been elected. According to Henry L. Stoddard, editor and publisher of the *New York Evening Mail,* Tammany politicians arranged for "Battle Ax" Paddy Gleason in Long Island City and John Y. McKane in Coney Island to stuff the ballot boxes to make up Cleveland's 1,143 vote margin of victory.

In the Kennedy-Nixon campaign of 1960, Nixon campaign chairman Leonard Hall was incensed at what he considered flagrant ballot-box stuffing in Texas, some other parts of the South, and particularly Cook County, Illinois. Since a switch of these narrowly won states would have swung the election to Nixon, Hall urged that Nixon declare the election "stolen" and dispute the result, which Nixon declined to do.

In the January 16, 1966, *New York Post,* writer Paul Hoffman recounted the classic story about ballot-box stuffing, updating it to make his central figure "Uncle Dan" O'Connell, a veteran political leader of Albany: " 'Uncle Dan,' President Johnson, and Lady Bird were sailing down the Potomac all alone when their boat sprang a leak. Each grabbed for the

lone life preserver. 'Let's settle this the American way, by secret ballot,' suggested the President. Uncle Dan won it the Albany way . . . his vote was 17 to 2."

See CEMETERY VOTE.

BALLYHOO   as a verb, to create enthusiasm; to promote colorfully; to "beat the drums"; to tout. As a noun, the material of such efforts.

"Last of the professions on the Midway," wrote *World's Work* in 1901, "are those of the 'barker,' 'ballyhooer' and 'spieler.' " The circus origin now applies to stunts, "pseudoevents," and exploitation, both commercial and political, using more modern techniques. Warned FDR in his second fireside chat: "We cannot ballyhoo our way to prosperity." The *Atlantic Monthly* in March 1948 wrote of candidates that are "ballyhooed, pushed, yelled, screamed and in every way propagandized into the consciousness of the voters."

Wilfred Funk believes the word is traceable to the village of Ballyhooly, in Cork County, Ireland, where, according to the March 1934 *Congressional Record,* "residents engage in a most strenuous debate . . . and from the violence of those debates has sprung forth a word known in the English language as ballyhoo."

Eric Partridge agrees: "In Erse, *bally* (or *bal*) means 'a dwelling, a village' and it occurs in scores of Celtic place-names. The precise relationship to this glorified village is uncertain: but American colloquial and slangy speech is 'full of' references to Irish joviality and noisy high-spirits."

A synonym is HOOPLA, which politicians regard as a necessary evil to generate artificial fervor that hopefully ignites genuine fervor. See BANDWAGON. An early edition of *Bartlett's Quotations* indicates "hoopla" as having been a driver's hurrying-up to his horse, a meaning that survives in the political sense of a stimulus to excitement.

BALONEY nonsense, malarkey; stronger than blarney, more politically palatable than unprintable expletives.

"No matter how thin you slice it," said Alfred E. Smith in 1936, "it's still baloney."

It was one of the New York governor's favorite words. Ten years before, when he was asked by a cameraman at a cornerstone-laying ceremony to actually lay a brick for the movies, he had snarled, "That's just baloney. Everybody knows I can't lay bricks." Expressing his opposition to FDR's rumored plan to take the U.S. dollar off the gold standard in 1933, he was widely quoted as saying, "I am for gold dollars as against baloney dollars."

This was not the last baloney attack on New Dealers. Clare Boothe Luce, ridiculing Vice President Henry Wallace's foreign policy proposals in 1943 (see HOTTENTOTS, MILK FOR), used the Smith construction with a new twist: "Much of what Mr. Wallace calls his global thinking is, no matter how you slice it, still Globaloney."

President Harry Truman picked it up again in 1948, to ridicule Thomas E. Dewey's unity campaign: "In the old days, Al Smith would have said: 'That's baloney.' Today, the Happy Warrior would say: 'That's a lot of hooey.' And if that rhymes with anything it's not my fault . . ."

As early as 1943, George Allen wrote to General Eisenhower: "How does it feel to be a candidate?" In his memoirs, Eisenhower recalled his answer: "Baloney!"

When a colleague of Winston Churchill stated in 1953 that "economic planning is baloney," the British statesman was called upon to explain his associate's remark in the House of Commons. Majestically, he evaded the question with "I should prefer to have an agreed definition of the meaning of 'baloney' before I attempted to deal with such a topic."

The word, in its political usage, is current and used in the best circles. James Reston, Washington correspondent of the *New York Times* wrote in 1964: "More harm is done by swallowing political baloney in this country than by swallowing arsenic or smoking reefers."

The word is spelled baloney, bolony, balony, bologna, and in various other ways, but no matter how you spell it . . .

See SALAMI TACTICS.

BANDWAGON a movement appealing to the herd instinct of politicians and voters to be on the winning side in any contest.

The word was used in P. T. Barnum's *Life,* published in 1855, to describe a difficult chapter in the life of the circus: "At Vicksburg we sold all our land conveyances excepting four horses and the 'bandwagon.' "

The humor magazine *Puck* in 1884 depicted Chester Arthur driving a bandwagon carrying other presidential hopefuls, and in 1896 it published a similar cartoon showing a McKinley bandwagon.

Songs have also helped popularize the notion of bandwagons. A song published in 1851, written by W. Loftin Hargrave, titled "Wait for the Wagon, A New Ethiopian Song and Melody," was still a favorite in 1900.

In 1900, too, the Prohibitionists helped popularize a temperance song called "The Prohibition Bandwagon," with the words:

And our friends who vote for gin,
Will all scramble to jump in,
When we get our big bandwagon,
some sweet day.

From 1902 onward the word became well established in American political terminology. In Albert Shaw's cartoon history of Theodore Roosevelt's career, a wagon is shown with Roosevelt's friends making musical noises in his favor but the main character—Senator Thomas C. Platt —is shown running after the wagon frantically trying to jump aboard, with a whip in his hand indicating that he would like to be in the driver's seat.

Most extensive use of a real bandwagon in modern times was the "Eisenhower-Nixon Bandwagon" of 1952, a project conceived by Arthur Gray, Jr., and C. Langhorne Washburn. Three 25-ton trailer trucks, each with a three-man crew, "advanced" Eisenhower appearances throughout the campaign. Each gaily decorated truck contained helium tanks for barrage balloons, twelve "Ike" dresses in sizes ten and twelve with parasols and hats, thousands of buttons and pieces of literature, Navy bosun's whistles, and a jeep with a loudspeaker.

In 29 cities over 32 days, the bandwagon rolled ahead of the candidates to organize parades and major receptions, giving a colorful focal point to local activity. Each night, the campaigners set up what they called an "Ethereal Nocturnal Splendor": powerful searchlights played on the barrage balloons with their "Ike" signs, a sight which could be seen from ten miles away. After taking office, President Eisenhower kept one of the bosun's whistles from the bandwagon in the Oval Office as a memento.

The expression is in use in Great Britain as well. Wrote the *Daily Mirror* in 1966, establishing its independent position: "The *Mirror* . . . does not jump on bandwagons . . . it isn't, never has been, and never will be, a tin can tied to a political party's tail."

BANNER DISTRICT the voting unit in which a party or candidate makes a better showing than anywhere else in a single election; also, the section of a larger constituency in which a politician or party has the strongest support.

Crediting an area with banner status was common practice in political reportage and speechmaking during much of the nineteenth century. Political usage seems to have originated in the 1840 presidential election in which the incumbent Democrat, Martin Van Buren, was challenged by William Harrison, a Whig. In the course of the colorful "Log Cabin and Hard Cider" campaign, a Whig group in Louisiana promised a banner to the state giving the most impressive vote to Harrison. The subsequent controversy over which state won outlived Harrison—who died of pneumonia one month after being inaugurated— and helped popularize the phrase.

Historically, a commander's banner or standard served as a rallying point and symbol of success to come. Much of this meaning has been preserved whether banner is used as a noun or adjective in a figurative sense. Politically, the term has acquired an antique flavor; STANDARD-BEARER, however, is still current. See MILITARY METAPHORS.

BAN THE BOMB, *see* **BETTER RED THAN DEAD.**

BAREFOOT BOY FROM WALL STREET description of Republican presidential candidate Wendell L. Willkie by FDR's Interior Secretary, Harold L. Ickes. Ickes derided a "humble" image of the Indianan by reminding voters of Willkie's success in finance.

Ickes, "the old curmudgeon" (see CURMUDGEON), laced into Willkie soon after the candidate's 1940 acceptance speech. The Secretary characterized the Republican candidate as "the rich man's Roosevelt; the simple, barefoot Wall Street lawyer," which later was shortened to "the barefoot boy from Wall Street." He added later that the candidate was a "one-spur leather puller who does not even pretend to know anything about the West." Ickes was a master at the art of colorful insult (see MAN ON THE WEDDING CAKE; INVECTIVE, POLITICAL), and occasionally was himself on the receiving end: Governor Huey Long called him "the Chicago chinch bug."

BARGAIN AND CORRUPTION, *see* **KINGMAKER.**

BARGAINING CHIP a prospective concession; an arms program justified on the theory that it can be used as a device to induce an adversary to give up an equivalent strategic weapon.

This is now SALT lingo, popularized by members of the National Security Council staff during the early seventies, when Henry Kissinger was National Security Adviser, later adopted by congressmen and writers on the Strategic Arms Limitation Talks. Some diplomatic reporters tell the author they first heard the phrase in the mid-sixties.

In the April 1973 issue of the *Friends' Committee Washington Newsletter,* the term was used instead of its predecessor, "trade-off": "Regarding the SALT negotiations, 14 Republican congressmen appealed to President Nixon to go slow on the 'bargaining chip' idea, calling for re-

straint in development of weapons such as the B-1 bomber and the Trident submarine at this time." In the *New York Times Magazine* a year later, the term was again defined: "Bargaining from strength calls for arms programs that can serve as 'bargaining chips' to trade for concessions that the other side might not otherwise make . . . The pursuit of hedges and chips brings about an intensification of the arms race just to keep 'bargaining-chip gaps' from developing."

The phrase evokes the metaphor of high-stakes poker and was a favored Kissingerism, along with "STEP BY STEP," "QUIET DIPLOMACY" and "SHUTTLE DIPLOMACY." As such, it was attacked as a "foolish approach" by Jimmy Carter in his 1976 campaign. On July 6 Charles Mohr of the *New York Times* reported: "Mr. Carter argued against the possibility of a limited nuclear war and the 'bargaining chips' approach to nuclear negotiations—both central tenets of the [Ford] Administration. These considerations have provided the main justification for building new systems of nuclear weapons."

In the Spring 1977 *Political Science Quarterly,* Robert Bresler and Robert Gray wrote: "The bargaining chip, like the DOMINO THEORY of the 50s and 60s, has become one of the most voguish ideas in the field of weapons development. Yet the concept is perhaps as old as arms competition itself. . . . Bargaining chips that enhance trust, signal a desire not to let technology get out of hand, and are kept clear of projected force postures, may, in the final analysis, be the only ones we should play."

From these excerpts it is apparent that the phrase has a useful appeal to those seeking to build more weapons systems, and is an annoying catch phrase for opponents to overcome. But its gambling origin is obscure: a poker chip, for example, is not used in bargaining. The author hopes a reader will supply the basis for the metaphor (negotiating point? bargaining counter?) for the next edition.

See SALT LEXICON.

BARNBURNERS   persons demonstrating uncompromising determination, even at risk of total loss; practitioners of the art of the impossible.

The word originally designated the antislavery wing of the Democratic party in New York State in the 1840s led by Martin Van Buren and his son, John. The name was devised by the "Hunkers," a Democratic opposition faction, to ridicule Van Buren's radical approach "in the manner of the Dutch farmer who burned his barn to destroy the rats."

The Barnburners played an important role in the presidential election of 1848. They bolted from the Democratic National Convention and joined the Free-Soilers; their combined vote swung the election to Whig Zachary Taylor. The antislavery views led them into the Republican party in the mid-1850s.

The term *Barnburners* is not in current use, but the concept reappears from time to time. A letter sent to President Hoover after his term of office included an affirmative appraisal of his policies: "We are grateful during your occupancy of the White House you never got the idea of burning down the temple of our fathers in order to destroy a few cockroaches in the basement."

Warning of the danger of MCCARTHYISM in meeting the threat of Communist subversion, Adlai Stevenson said in 1952: "We must take care not to burn down the barn to kill the rats."

A *Washington Post* editorial on January 6, 1977, continued the use into recent times: "Canadian radicals and barn-burners of various denominations have titillated themselves for years with talk of resorting to arms in Quebec."

The expression can be traced to a sermon by Thomas Adams in 1629: "The empiric to cure the fever, destroys the patient; so the wise man, to burn the mice, set fire to his barn."

BARNSTORM   to take an extended electioneering trip with many brief stops.

Barnstorming has been widely used at least since the nineteenth century, deriving from the old custom of using a barn for performances by itinerant players; because politicking was something of a rural amusement, the transfer was simple and logical. The term has since been supplemented by "whistlestop." See WHISTLESTOPPING.

Although politicians rarely speak in barns any longer, the usage persists. In October 1944, for instance, the *Chicago Daily News* wrote: "President Roosevelt indignantly denies that his New York and Chicago barnstorming trips violate his pledge not to campaign in the usual sense." Samuel Rosenman later explained that under pressure from Thomas Dewey's strong campaign, "the President soon began to realize that it was necessary for him to get out and fight hard. He also realized that it was up to him to prove that he could stand the physical and mental rigors of a political campaign."

The term can also be used more loosely, as in *Time* magazine in 1947: "Barnstorming Presidential Candidate Harold Stassen whirled through Belgium in one day."

See NONPOLITICAL TRIP; CHATAUQUA CIRCUIT.

BAY OF PIGS FIASCO the abortive invasion of Cuba in 1961 by U.S. supported anti-Castro refugees.

Few phrases of recent coinage are so powerfully fused together as "Bay of Pigs" and "fiasco." The invasion is never referred to as the Bay of Pigs *disaster,* or the Bay of Pigs *tragedy* or *failure, flop, botch,* or even *snafu.* Always *fiasco,* of the same root as "flask," often of wine, which probably caused *fiasco* to gain its connotation of a drunken, ridiculous attempt to accomplish a pretentious feat that falls flat on its face.

The criticism of Kennedy following the invasion attempt soon after his inauguration was vicious: "Caroline is a cute kid, but we shouldn't let her plan any more invasions." But no matter whether the comment came from critics or Kennedy supporters (said Theodore Sorensen: "The Bay of Pigs fiasco had its influence"), the use of "fiasco" was universal. Substituting another word would be as jarring to the ear as saying "the *attack* of the Light Brigade."

In politics and in other fields, a "Bay of Pigs" now means a monumental flop with an overtone of ultimate redemption (as Kennedy redeemed himself in the confrontation with Khrushchev over Cuba a year after the Bay of Pigs, uh, fiasco). Broadway showman David Merrick closed a show in 1966 called *Breakfast at Tiffany's* before opening night, at a loss of $450,000, with the remark: "It's my Bay of Pigs."

BEANBAG what politics ain't. "His early experience," wrote Finley Peter Dunne of his creation, saloonkeeping philosopher Mr. **DOOLEY**, "gave him wisdom in discussing public affairs. 'Politics,' he says, 'ain't beanbag. 'Tis a man's game; an' women, childher, an' pro-hybitionists'd do well to keep out iv it.' "

The above quotation is taken from the preface to *Mr. Dooley in Peace and War,* published in 1898; it had been used earlier by Dunne, on October 5, 1895, in an essay in the *Chicago Evening Post.*

A beanbag is a cloth bag partly filled with beans (or, more recently, with plastic beads), easily catchable, used in a children's game of the same name. In Mr. Dooley's use, the child's play made a dramatic comparison with a man's game, and has been used for that purpose ever since (though the "man's game" has recently been replaced by **HARDBALL**).

"Carter's flaw as a political leader," wrote Jack Germond and Jules Witcover in a column that appeared in the *Washington Star* on September 14, 1977, "has always been his massive self-assurance, his total confidence that no one would believe him capable of political knavery or personal weakness. But in the Bert Lance case, what was in question was his sophistication. And, as Mr. Dooley told us long ago, politics ain't beanbag."

BEATNIK, see -NIK SUFFIX.

BEDSHEET BALLOT a ballot with a lengthy list of candidates, often confusing to voters.

This phrase is most often used pejoratively, as if an attempt is being made to bamboozle voters with complexity; in modern times, it has frequently been used in connection with voting in primaries for delegates to a convention.

A synonym is "blanket ballot"; both phrases use the analogy of bedcoverings to evoke a picture of an enormous piece of paper, capable of handling a bewildering multiplicity of names or propositions.

BEFORE APRIL 9TH MEN, *see* CUFFLINKS GANG; ALPHABET AGENCIES.

BELLWETHER a trend-setter; or, a district with a history of reflecting a nationwide vote; or, a STALKING HORSE.

In 1878 *Harper's Weekly* said the unthinking crowd would "follow the bellwether over any wall and into any pasture, but the independent sheep would not."

Literally, a wether is a male sheep; the leading sheep of the flock sometimes wears a bell.

The Judas-goat or stalking-horse meaning remains: Cabell Phillips, after describing the machinations within the Democratic party to dump Henry Wallace from the vice presidency in 1944, wrote that James Byrnes felt indignant because the party leadership "had deceived him and used him as a bellwether to undermine Wallace and to create an opening for Truman."

The trend-setting meaning is taking over, however. John Kennedy, fighting to hold down prices in 1961, described the steel industry as "a bellwether, as well as a major element in industrial costs."

BENIGN NEGLECT a suggestion to allow tensions to ease, interpreted as a plot to abandon the civil rights movement.

Nixon's urban affairs adviser, Daniel Patrick Moynihan, had a predilection for transmitting his advice in long and literate memoranda. On occasion, the President directed that Moynihan memos be circulated to Cabinet members, who then passed copies throughout their departments.

On March 2, 1970, this casual method of transmission backfired.

"The time may have come," wrote Moynihan, "when the issue of race could benefit from a period of 'benign neglect.' "

In context, Moynihan's meaning was that Negroes would profit if extremists on both sides of the race issue were to lower their voices. But, as *Newsweek* wrote, "to black leaders and their allies, 'neglect'—benign or malign—seemed precisely to describe everything the Administration was and was not doing about race. And they responded with a fury . . ."

Moynihan was quoting the Earl of Durham, who wrote Queen Victoria in 1839 that Canada had done so well "through a period of benign neglect" by the mother country that she ought to be granted self-government.

The oxymoronic overtone of the phrase made it memorable, but the mischief that its misinterpretation could cause made it a tempting morsel to leak to the *New York Times.*

The leak twisted the meaning of Moynihan's advice and hurt him in the liberal community. It did not damage him within the Administration; as the *New Republic*'s John Osborne wrote, "The insiders judged the incident to be an example of how outsiders misjudge insiders and fail to comprehend the intricacies of Presidential counseling and communications."

Columnist Max Lerner could not resist observing "If anything, he might have used Holmes' 'intelligent neglect.' "

Mr. Moynihan, as a Democratic Senator from New York, could take heart, however, in seeing the phrase used in 1978—without reference to him and in the sense it was originally intended—by a *New York Times* editorialist in January 1978: "Early this month, the Carter Administration abandoned its 'benign neglect' of the dollar."

BERLIN WALL, *see* **WALL, POLITICAL USE OF.**

BEST MAN, THE   object of a convention choice; claim by all candidates on the basis of qualifications.

Like ARENA and HAT IN THE RING, the phrase is closely associated with boxing, when the referee concludes his instructions to the fighters with "and may the best man win."

The phrase was used as the title of a play by Gore Vidal, later a motion picture, about the selection of a presidential candidate.

In 1964, when President Lyndon Johnson was faced with the choice of a running mate, proponents of Hubert H. Humphrey used a subtle slogan to soft-sell their candidate: "The Next Best Man."

BETTER RED THAN DEAD
slogan of the British nuclear disarmament movement.

English philosopher Bertrand Russell wrote in 1958 that if "no alternative remains except communist domination or the extinction of the human race, the former alternative is the lesser of the two evils." This was sloganized into "Better Red Than Dead" and became part of the "Ban the Bomb" demonstrations.

John F. Kennedy, speaking at the University of Washington in 1961, took note of the phrase: "It is a curious fact that each of these two extreme opposites resembles the other. Each believes that we have only two choices: appeasement or war, suicide or surrender, humiliation or holocaust, to be either Red or dead."

An obvious turnaround was used by British author Stanley Reynolds in 1964, in a book urging an anti-Communist crusade entitled *Better Dead Than Red.* This effectively sabotaged the slogan; after a while, most people did not know which slogan came first or who was for what. Thermonuclear thinker Herman Kahn (see UNTHINKABLE THOUGHTS) wrote:

> If somebody says, "I would rather be Red than dead," he is a coward, and I think properly an object of contempt and scorn. But if somebody says, "I would rather have everybody Red than everybody dead," he is taking a reasonable position with which I agree.
> While I would rather have everybody Red than everybody dead, we must not allow a situation to develop in which such a choice is the only one we have.

BETWEEN A ROCK AND A HARD PLACE, *see* **ROCK AND A HARD PLACE.**

BIG APPLE   New York City.

In his 1938 book, *Hi De Ho,* bandleader Cab Calloway defined "apple" as "the big town, the main stem, Harlem." In a 1976 conversation with the author, Mr. Calloway explained further that "The Big Apple"—the name of a Harlem night club in the midthirties—was a mecca for jazz musicians. A dance which *Life* magazine in 1937 called "a loose-hipped, freehand combination of 'truckin' and the square dance" was named "The Big Apple," an appelation taken from the night club, according to Calloway.

Robert Gold, author of *Jazz Talk,* published in 1975, points to a 1966 speculation in *Record Research* as the likely etymology: "My suspicion [is] that *Big Apple* is a transliteration of the older Mexican idiom *'manzana principale'* for the main square of the town or the downtown area."

However, American Dialect Society Publication #16 (November 1951) says that "big apple" comes from "racetrack argot: in big time racing, New York City had a tradition of high purses, excellent tracks, fine horses." Why race-track people would use the phrase "big apple" was unexplained, unless the fruit was a reward for a horse.

The evidence seems strongest that Mr. Calloway is on the right track: the phrase was black-English jazz talk originating in the mid-thirties. Mr. Gold also cites *Dan Burley's Original Handbook of Harlem Jive,* published in 1944, defining "apple" as "the earth, the universe, this planet. Any place that's large. A big Northern city." Evidently the apple is the symbol of the earth, and by synecdoche, New York is taken to be that center—and thus the "big" apple.

In the mid-seventies, with New York City in great financial difficulty, the Convention and Visitors Bureau made an attempt to "sell" the city by popularizing the phrase as the city symbol, which seemed more apt than its predecessor, FUN CITY.

BIG CASINO   the center ring, grand arena, place of major action.

Ronald Reagan introduced this gaming expression to politics, referring in 1974 to the race for the presidency as "the big casino." A casino was originally a public dancing and meeting hall, later a place for gambling; the word is also used for a card game.

Wendell Rawls Jr. wrote in the *New York Times* of January 29, 1978, that a Republican candidate for governor of Pennsylvania, Richard Thornburgh, had "helped remove a complacent Federal prosecutor in Philadelphia and encouraged the replacement, Mr. [David] Marston, to look upon the city as

the 'big casino' of political crime." See CARD METAPHORS.

BIG CHARACTER POSTERS, *see* **GRAFFITI; SNIPE.**

BIG DADDY, *see* **GREAT WHITE FATHER.**

BIG ENCHILADA   the top man, or main target; in Watergate terminology, former Attorney General John Mitchell.

An enchilada is a Spanish-American word for a tortilla enclosing chopped meat, topped with a chili-flavored sauce (the root of the en*chil*ada is chili).

"I coined the phrase," former White House aide John Ehrlichman informed the author from his incarceration in 1977. "I've cooked my own enchiladas for years. My California upbringing. Could have said 'big fish,' or 'top dog' or 'big cheese,' I guess."

The phrase was heard on the March 27, 1973, Nixon tape in connection with giving the President's pursuers a substantial prize, in the hope they would be satisfied. Of John Mitchell, H. R. Haldeman said, "He is as high up as they've got," and Ehrlichman replied "He's the Big Enchilada."

The popular food is also used as a synecdoche for the world, or "the entire situation," similar to "the whole ball of wax." After the election victory of Jimmy Carter in 1976, former California Governor Ronald Reagan said that the Democrats, long in control of Congress, would no longer be able to share responsibility for difficulties with Republicans. "For the first time," Reagan said, "the Democrats can not fuzz up the issue by blaming the White House. They've got the whole enchilada now."

BIGGER BANG FOR A BUCK more efficient use of defense appropriations, relying largely on nuclear deterrents.

Secretary of State John Foster Dulles laid down the policy of MASSIVE RETALIATION in 1954 and told the Council on Foreign Relations this policy "permits of a selection of military means instead of multiplication of means. As a result, it is now possible to get, and share, more basic security at less cost."

Defense Secretary Charles W. Wilson promptly dubbed the policy the NEW LOOK (after a fashion phrase describing lower hemlines) and said it would provide "a bigger bang for a buck."

Historian and naval expert Samuel Eliot Morison analyzed it this way: "to strengthen American retaliatory power, to 'get a bigger bang for a buck' as the phrase ran, the defense department built up a long-range 'strategic' air force, with a stockpile of atomic bombs, but neglected both navy and ground forces."

Ultimately, the doctrine of massive retaliation was modified to allow for "brushfire wars" or LIMITED WARS and defense budgets allotted more to ground and naval forces, presumably a smaller bang for a buck but useful when smaller bangs avoid nuclear wars. President Kennedy summed up his approach to the budgetary problem during his Administration with a similar counterphrase: "There is no discount price on defense."

BIG GOVERNMENT an attack phrase on centralized federal authority and massive taxation and expenditure.

The phrase probably stemmed from "Big Business," which also spawned "Big Labor" (both usually capitalized) but the concern about the size and power of the federal authority began with the birth of the nation. Reformer Samuel Tilden, fighting Boss William Marcy Tweed in New York, harked back to the problems of Thomas Jefferson in 1801: "a grasping centralism, absorbing all functions from the local authorities, and assuming to control the industries of individuals by largesses to favored classes from the public treasury . . . were then, as now, characteristics of the period." Tilden called for a return to Jefferson's way: "He repressed the meddling of government in the concerns of private business."

But the rise of populism (see POPULIST) and the advent of the trustbusters showed that the public felt that "bigness" was a greater threat from business than from government. Lawyer Louis Brandeis inveighed against the CURSE OF BIGNESS in business. He was countered later with William Howard Taft's statement: "Mere size is no sin." As a Supreme Court Justice, Brandeis kept up his campaign against bigness in both business and government. When the Court unanimously decided to strike down the National Industrial Recovery Act in 1935—Black Monday, New Dealers called it—Brandeis warned Roosevelt aide Thomas Corcoran: "Tell the President we're not going to let this government centralize everything."

"Maybe it's unfortunate," wrote an editor of the *New Republic,* "but about the only counterweight the little man has to Big Business is Big Government." Republicans and conservative Democrats sharply disagree. Thomas E. Dewey stated the case against Big Government in 1950: "All-powerful, central government, like dictatorships, can continue only by growing larger and larger. It can never retrench without admitting failure. By absorbing more than half of all the taxing power of the nation, the federal government now deprives the states and local governments of the capacity to support the programs they should conduct . . . it offers them in exchange the counterfeit currency of federal subsidy."

Dwight Eisenhower deplored what he called "the whole-hog mentality," which "leans toward the creation of a more extensive and stifling monopoly than this country has ever seen . . . you don't need more supergovernment."

Republican House Minority Leader Gerald Ford, in 1966, blamed it all on the Democrats, labeling them "the party of Big Business, of Big Government, of Big Spending, of Big Deficits, of Big Cost of Living, of Big Labor Trouble, of Big Home Foreclosures, of Big Scandals, of Big Riots in the Streets and of Big Promises."

"The truth about big government," said John F. Kennedy in 1962, "is the truth about any other great activity: it is complex. Certainly it is true that size brings dangers, but it is also true that size also can bring benefits."

BIG LIE   a falsehood of such magnitude and audacity that it is bound to have an effect on public opinion even if it is not given credence by a majority; a propaganda technique identified with Adolf Hitler.

Hitler wrote in *Mein Kampf:*

The size of the lie is a definite factor in causing it to be believed, for the vast masses of a nation are in the depths of their hearts more easily deceived than they are consciously and intentionally bad. The primitive simplicity of their minds renders them a more easy prey to a big lie than a small one, for they themselves often tell little lies but would be ashamed to tell big ones. . . .

Something therefore always re-

mains and sticks from the most impudent lies, a fact which all bodies and individuals concerned with the art of lying in this world know only too well, and hence they stop at nothing to achieve this end.

In the U.S. during the 1950s, Senator Joseph R. McCarthy's critics accused him of using the big lie technique to intimidate his opponents in and out of the Senate. An example is this editorial in the *St. Louis Post-Dispatch* of 1951: "Gloomy Washington prophets are forecasting a period of 'the big lie,' of the furtive informer, of the character assassin, of inquisition, eavesdropping, smear and distrust. They lump the whole under the term MCCARTHYISM."

A Senate committee headed by Millard Tydings of Maryland, following a four-month investigation of McCarthy's charges that there were 81 card-carrying Communists in the State Department, castigated him in terms rarely used about a Senate member: "We are constrained to call the charges, and the methods used to give them ostensible validity, what they truly are: a fraud and a hoax perpetrated on the Senate and the United States and the American people. They represent perhaps the most nefarious campaign of half truths and untruth in the history of this Republic . . . the totalitarian technique of the 'big lie' on a sustained basis." McCarthy's efforts helped defeat Senator Tydings in the next election.

Social scientists in the mass communications field have found that the size of a requested opinion or behavior change is important in the degree of change effected. Herbert Adelson, of Opinion Research Corporation, observes: "The more extreme the opinion change that the communicator asks for, the more actual change he is likely to get . . . communications that advocate a greater amount of change from an audience's view in fact produce a greater amount of change than communications that advocate a position that is not much different from the position that the audience already holds."

BIGOT, *see* **REDNECK; REVERSE BIGOTRY.**

BIG STICK, *see* **DETERRENT.**

BIG TENT   the theory that a political party is a spacious home for debate, and not a cozy bungalow that permits only a narrow political ideology.

TRUE BELIEVERS hold that a political party must "stand for principle" and not muddy up its philosophy with ME TOO ideas held by the opposition.

On the contrary, say the advocates of the Big Tent: there is plenty of room for divergence of opinion within any party, which should be a device for getting into power. They point to Jefferson's statement "Not every difference of opinion is a difference of principle."

After his 1976 defeat, Gerald Ford called a meeting of Republican leaders John Connally, Ronald Reagan and Nelson Rockefeller and said pointedly: "The Republican tent is big enough to encompass the four individuals who were here today."

The phrase is derived from the circus; the big tent has several arenas which can put on separate shows.

BIGWIG   party leader; humorous or sardonic reference to the higherups.

Probably derived from the British law courts, where persons of importance (judges, barristers) wear large white wigs. Charles Dickens referred to them, defending a man "spoken of

by the bigwigs with extreme condescension."

In current political use, the term is most often included in a phrase like "all the party bigwigs were there"; it is used often by reporters but rarely by politicians. In the mid-seventies the word achieved vogue as "biggies," and was extended to "ad biggies" and "media biggies."

See MUCKEY-MUCKS.

BIPARTISAN   *bipartisan* means interparty cooperation on a matter that is essentially political; NONPARTISAN means interparty cooperation on matters nonpolitical.

In bipartisanship, politicians set aside differences to work together on political matters; in nonpartisanship, politicians work together as individuals, as in philanthropic, patriotic or civil causes.

"Bipartisanship" in foreign affairs is most closely associated with Senator Arthur Vandenberg, Michigan Republican, an outspoken isolationist of the thirties. A month after the German invasion of Poland, he was saying: "This so-called war is nothing but about 25 people and propaganda." World War II and a trip to blitzed London changed his thinking, and the ranking Republican in the Senate Foreign Relations Committee made a dramatic speech in 1945 that laid the groundwork for foreign-affairs bipartisanship: "I do not believe that any nation hereafter can immunize itself by its own exclusive action. . . . I want maximum American cooperation. . . . I want a new dignity and a new authority for international law. I think American self-interest requires it."

The Vandenberg switch shattered nascent postwar isolationism and the United Nations Charter was approved with only two senatorial votes against it, a far cry from the furor over the League of Nations after World War I. Vandenberg was hailed by most of the U.S. press for his new stand. At the birth of the Truman Doctrine, which aided the Greeks and Turks in combating internal Communism, "Vandenberg," wrote Truman later, "championed this program in a truly bipartisan manner." But the senator was nagged by his own worry about bipartisanship being carried dangerously far. "To me," he wrote a constituent in 1950, " 'bipartisan foreign policy' means a mutual effort under our indispensable two-party system to unite our official voice at the water's edge so that America speaks with maximum authority. . . . It does not involve the remotest surrender of free debate in determining our position. On the contrary, frank cooperation and free debate are indispensable to ultimate unity."

Within a few months, Vandenberg was asking if "bipartisanship meant more Chinas and more Hisses and more messes with Russian bombs hanging over us," a position not all that far from Robert Taft's blast at "the wreckage that is our Far Eastern policy." Thomas E. Dewey, whose own internationalist position insured bipartisanship in foreign affairs in the 1944 wartime campaign, reasserted the need for such a united front in war but qualified his position with, "I am not prepared to assert that, in a normal, peaceful world, foreign policy should always be bipartisan."

The tension underlying any bipartisanship in foreign policy can never really be relieved: on one hand is the need for a single American voice to the world, on the other hand a need for self-examination and criticism that is the obligation of LOYAL OPPOSITION. In fact, what goes under the heading of bipartisanship is usually a coalition of like-minded men in both parties; Dwight Eisenhower found that Democratic votes put across his foreign policy and foreign-aid programs no fewer than 48 times in 1953.

Vandenberg, often called the "architect of the bipartisan foreign policy," preferred a different word: unpartisan. Presumably, this meant nonpartisan, but experience has shown that foreign policy in times short of all-out war must include "dissent."

See ABOVE POLITICS; PARTISAN; NONPARTISAN; WATER'S EDGE.

BI-POLAR, see POLARIZATION.

BIRCHER a member or supporter of the John Birch Society, best known and probably most active of the ultraconservative, militantly anticommunist splinter groups.

Secrecy is a Birch tenet and the society has done little to publicize itself as an organization. After its founding in 1958, it was more or less discovered gradually by a number of journalists, particularly after the writings of retired candy manufacturer Robert Welch, Jr., founder of the society, became known. Among other things, Welch called Dwight Eisenhower a willing tool of the Communist conspiracy. Welch and his followers are often identified as being on the RADICAL RIGHT, or in Alan Barth's phrase, "rampageous right."

On the derivation of the title, at least, there is no argument. Captain John Birch was an otherwise obscure USAF officer killed by Chinese Communists in 1945, and is sometimes referred to as "the first casualty of the Cold War." The Chinese Red forces were nominally our allies against the Japanese, and his murder, according to the Society, was hushed up by Communist agents in the U.S.

Arthur M. Schlesinger, Jr., describes the Birch Society's mood as "one of longing for a dream world of no communism, no overseas entanglements, no United Nations, no federal government, no Negroes or foreigners—a world in which Chief Justice Warren would be impeached, Cuba invaded, the graduated income tax repealed, fluoridation of drinking water stopped and the import of Polish hams forbidden."

A question often asked of Republican candidates in the sixties was "Do you accept or reject support of the Birchers?" In the 1962 California gubernatorial primary, Richard Nixon specifically rejected them; he won the nomination and lost the election. In 1966, Ronald Reagan refused to take this position, holding that people who supported him bought his views, not he theirs. Reagan—who carefully applied State Chairman Gaylord Parkinson's ELEVENTH COMMANDMENT, which states, "Thou shalt not speak ill of fellow Republicans"—won by close to a million votes, though there is no telling how much of this was the effect of the Bircher straddle.

BIRD DOG . . . KENNEL DOG
one who works to earn his keep (bird dog), rather than one who depends on others (kennel dog).

In 1954, pockets of serious unemployment were distressing the Eisenhower Administration; in Flint, Michigan, 22 percent of the labor force was idle. When Secretary of Defense Charles E. Wilson held a press conference in nearby Detroit, he was asked why his department did not allocate more defense contracts to depressed areas. Wilson suggested that unemployed workers would do better to move to those areas where labor shortages existed, and in reaching for a metaphor came up with the political blooper of the year: "I've always liked bird dogs rather than kennel dogs myself. You know, one who will get out and hunt for food rather than sit on his fanny and yell."

Coming just before an off-year election, the remark was seized upon as an example of a heartless Administration run by unfeeling big businessmen. Union leaders said that workingmen "wear no leash and will not be muzzled." Wilson promptly apologized: "I admit that I made a mistake . . . by bringing up those bird dogs at the same time I was talking about people." See FOOT-IN-MOUTH DISEASE. But the damage was done; other Administration officials were told to keep silent. In his memoirs Sherman Adams wrote: "Learned that the newspapers had [been] expecting me to say something about Wilson and his dogs. Remembering the President's advice, I did not miss that opportunity to keep my mouth shut."

For another Wilson remark that was turned against the Administration, see WHAT'S GOOD FOR GENERAL MOTORS. The former president of GM had an aptitude for raising the hackles of some of his listeners with his turn of phrase. He once told a Senate committee: "The trouble with you men is that you don't understand the problem." Referring to U.S. senators as "you men"—as if they were a group of his employees—did not sit well.

Wilson's bird-dog remark recalls other canine roots in political terminology. A "still hunt"—a method of hunting stealthily, with the dogs muted—was adopted by Tilden supporters in 1876, who boasted that their man conducted a secret "still hunt" of Boss Tweed.

Davy Crockett said: "Are the people like my hounds, that bark when I tell them, and leave off when I stamp my foot at them?" The idea of a dog trailing at his master's heels was probably the derivation of WARDHEELER, and Petroleum V. Nasby used the simile in 1866: "The bold shivelrous Southner . . . and the Dimokrat uv the North foller'n, like a puppy dog, at his heels, takin sich fat things ez he cood snap up."

Speaker Champ Clark of Missouri, whose presidential hopes were sabotaged by Wilson-supporter William Jennings Bryan at the 1912 Democratic convention, was plagued by an old song:

Ev'ry time I come to town
The boys keep kickin' my dog aroun';
Makes no difference if he is a houn',
They gotta quit kickin' my dog aroun'.

In British politics, Harold Wilson received a bad press in 1966 when he mocked Conservative leader Edward Heath's Common Market efforts as "rolling on his back like a spaniel at any kind gesture from the French." Perhaps the most effective use of a canine simile was by Winston Churchill, after being invited by the Chamberlain cabinet to meet German Ambassador Joachim von Ribbentrop: "I suppose they asked me to show him that, if they couldn't bark themselves, they kept a dog who could bark and might bite."

"Bird-dog," used as a verb, has an entirely different meaning: to hunt down, or ferret out, facts, or to follow through on a project until it is successfully completed. Usage: "I don't want this bogged down in red tape— bird-dog it and tell me when it's done." See HONCHO.

For Chinese Communist use of "running dogs," see FELLOW TRAVELER. For another snarling simile, see POLITICAL ANIMAL.

BIRD METAPHORS, *see* FLOO-FLOO BIRD; PECKING ORDER; WAR HAWKS.

BITE THE BULLET   commit to a difficult course of action; make a tough decision.

Lyndon Johnson popularized— and simultaneously stigmatized—the phrase by using it in connection with the hard decisions of the Vietnam war. Criticizing Congress for inaction on a bill to raise taxes, President Johnson said on May 3, 1968: "But I think the time has come for all the members of Congress to be responsible and, even in an election year, to bite the bullet and stand up and do what ought to be done for their country."

In 1975 President Ford said: "Some have said that instead of asking Congress and the nation to bite the bullet, I have offered only a marshmallow," adding that the Congress "wouldn't even chew that marshmallow."

Mr. Ford's metaphoric extension caused Columnist David Braaten of the *Washington Star* to analyze "that recent favorite of literary gourmets, the bite-size bullet" in these terms: "Originally, one bit a bullet to distract oneself from the pain of drastic surgery when no anesthetic was available. It supposedly kept the patient from biting his tongue, or screaming so loud the surgeon was unsettled. From that simple beginning, bullet-biting has come to be used in the quite opposite sense of taking one's medicine. It has replaced the bitter pill as something to be swallowed . . ."

The author queried *American Heritage* on the etymology; Oliver Jensen (perhaps influenced by Rudyard Kipling's "The Soldiers and Sailors Too") gave this first impression: "I think I have always misunderstood the phrase, thinking it had something to do with an old style of bullet that had to have something bitten off it to free the powder for the spark—indicating, so to speak, that you were making the crucial decision to be ready to shoot. But I begin to lose faith in that theory now." Mr. Jensen wrote to Civil War historian Bruce Catton, who sent him this reply:

I can't give you a definite quotation, but it most certainly comes from before the Civil War; I believe it originated with the British army as early as the 18th Century. Here is how it came into being:

It dated from pre-anesthetic days, when a wounded soldier in a field hospital had to have a painful operation, usually the amputation of a limb. (What with the saw and everything, having that done without chloroform, either or morphine would obviously be pretty agonizing). When they were ready to go, the afflicted soldier (who was either strapped down or held firmly in place by two or three husky comrades) would be given a round, soft-lead bullet and told to bite on it. This would help him to get through the ordeal without screaming; the fact that the bullet was of soft lead would make it possible for him to clamp down hard without breaking his teeth. So—to "bite the bullet" meant to endure something extremely bad with suitable stoicism and without making unmanly outcries.

This could not be Civil War in origin. First place, in most cases they had anesthetics in that war. They did have to bite the *cartridge*—not the bullet—when loading those muzzle-loading rifles. The bullet was a cylindro-conoidal bit of lead with a tube of paper attached to the base; paper was full of powder, with the lower end crimped. To load his rifle, the soldier bit off the crimped paper, poured the powder down the barrel, rammed the bullet down after it, and was all ready to operate.

The ammunition-munching metaphor, after a flurry of use in the late sixties, has settled into a political language that needs alternatives to "make difficult decisions." An unnamed member of President Carter's Cabinet was quoted in 1978 by *New York Times* Washington correspondent Hedrick Smith as observing of Mr. Carter: "He's still not ready to admit that some of these things—like 4 percent unemployment and 4 percent inflation and a balanced budget—are irreconcilable. It's terribly painful for him . . . There's a reluctance on his part to bite the bullet and make the hard choices."

BLACK, POLITICAL USE OF

Negro civil rights militants reintroduced the term "black," meaning Negro, in the sixties. A century before, BLACK REPUBLICAN had been used to describe the party of abolition and reconstruction, but in the twentieth century the word was used in its racial sense to describe African natives and as a racial slur to imply that American Negroes were close to their ancestors "in the jungle."

To avoid giving offense, white writers and politicians have referred to blacks as: *Negroes, colored people, nonwhites* (a statistician's word including Puerto Ricans, Mexicans, Chinese, American Indians, etc., but politically a euphemism for Negroes) and most euphemistic of all, *minority group.* When a politician speaks of minority groups, he is mainly concerned with blacks; when he speaks of ethnic groups, he is usually speaking of Jews, occasionally of Italian, German, or other nationality groups.

Negroes have never used the counter-term "majority group" to apply to whites, choosing recently "WHITE

POWER STRUCTURE" and the slang terms "whitey," "honkie," and "Mister Charlie" (see CHARLIE). When comparing Negroes and whites, white is not capitalized, Caucasian usually is.

As Negro racial pride increased, black civil rights leaders frequently compared "white men and black men" and looked on marketers of skin-whitening and hair-straightening products with disdain. Martin Luther King, Jr., launched a poster campaign around the slogan "Black is beautiful" in 1967. White usage of "black" lagged until the emergence of "BLACK POWER" as a slogan in 1966.

Political leaders opposing integration prefer "separation of races" to the harsher term "SEGREGATION"; some politicians go to the extreme of substituting "indigenous" for "native" whenever it appears, though none has gone so far as to say "my indigenous land."

The fear of an unintentional racial slur is real. When New Jersey Governor Richard Hughes held an angry press conference during the 1967 riot in Newark, he said, "We have determined that the line between a jungle assault on law and order may as well be drawn here as anywhere else in America," later repeating his condemnation of "jungle law." Wrote the *New York Post:* "While gubernatorial assistants tried to explain that Hughes was referring to 'the law of the jungle' as opposed to 'civil order,' and meant no racist connotations, the damage had been done."

In 1970, semanticist (later California Senator) S. I. Hayakawa quoted a letter written in 1928 by W. E. B. DuBois to a young man who wanted to stop the use of the word Negro:

Historically, of course, your dislike of the word Negro is easily explained: "Negroes" among your grandfathers meant black folk; "colored" people were mulattoes. The mulattoes hated and despised the blacks and were insulted if called "Negroes." But we are not insulted —not you and I. We are quite as proud of our black ancestors as our white. And perhaps a little prouder. . . . Your real work as a Negro lies in two directions: First, to let the world know what there is fine and genuine about the Negro race. And secondly, to see that there is nothing about that race that is worth contempt; your contempt, my contempt, or the contempt of the wide, wide world.

In a 1974 *Psychology Today* article about bigotry in language, Paul Chance listed a few phrases in which "black" is used positively: Black Beauty, black belt (karate), black gold (oil), black tie, black soil, black pearls. "White," which is usually used metaphorically for "good," has some reverse connotations: white trash, whitewash, white flag, white feather, white slave, white elephant.

Cartoonist Jules Feiffer, alert to language changes (see DISADVANTAGED), pictured a bearded Negro intellectual in 1967 describing the ring-around-the-Rosie of the political use of the word: "As a matter of racial pride we want to be called 'blacks.' Which has replaced the term 'Afro-American'—Which replaced 'Negroes'—Which replaced 'colored people'—Which replaced 'darkies'—Which replaced 'blacks.' "

BLACK CAPITALISM a 1968 campaign phrase pledging government encouragement to Negroes starting their own businesses.

In the middle of his primary campaign, Richard Nixon felt the need to address at some length—and in a positive tone—the problem of racial division in America. In two radio addresses, the first on April 25, 1968, entitled "Bridges to Human Dignity," he outlined his desire to go beyond programs "that feed the stomach and starve the soul."

In the first six drafts of the April 25 speech, one of the ideas he put forward was "black entrepreneurship." Ray Price, the writer working most closely with the candidate on the development of the speech, felt this phrase was awkward and sought an alternative.

In the radio studio where the speech was to be recorded, the author recalled the New York Stock Exchange's recapture of the word "capitalism" from Communist terminology in their "people's capitalism" advertising campaign. Three alternatives — black entrepreneurship, black enterprise, and black capitalism—were suggested to the candidate, who chose the last.

"A third bridge," he said, "is the development of black capitalism. By providing technical assistance and loan guarantees, by opening new capital sources, we can help Negroes to start new businesses in the ghetto and to expand existing ones."

The phrase and the idea received some attention, which posed a problem for Democratic candidate Hubert Humphrey when he later advocated a similar program. After the campaign, one of the Humphrey writers told this writer "we couldn't use Nixon's phrase, black capitalism, so we had to go with black entrepreneurship, which is a mouthful, and is hell to fit into a headline."

BLACK HATS villains; "heavies."

The extension of the Western-movie metaphor to politics is most pronounced when a simplistic "us-against-them" mood dominates the political scene. The users of the phrase are conscious of the satire implicit in its usage: in the shades-of-gray real world of political compromise, few hats are all-black, and all-white hats soon become scuff-marked.

A related phrase is "good guys," easy to spot in a six-gun epic, which writer Jimmy Breslin appropriated for a book title about the Watergate affair: *How the Good Guys Finally Won.*

Elliot Richardson, who as Nixon Attorney General was regarded by many as a white hat in a black-hatted White House, used the phrase in a talk to business leaders in 1977: "Isolated in the corporate fortress, too many businessmen have cast their argument in terms of the traditional interests—profit and capital for investment. But these are the terms of the black hats. They translate, of course, into jobs, prices, consumer satisfaction—even, given responsible political decision-making, into satisfaction of collective wants and ultimately the improved 'quality of life.' But these are all terms which have been expropriated by those now confidently postured in white hats."

See WHITE HATS.

BLACKLIST, *see* **GUILT BY ASSOCIATION.**

BLACK POWER a deliberately ambiguous Negro slogan, meaning antiwhite rebellion to some, the use of political and economic "muscle" to others.

The phrase was used in June 1966 by Stokely Carmichael, then head of the Student Nonviolent Coordinating Committee (SNCC), on the occasion of a SNCC-organized march through Mississippi. It appeared in the *New York Times* on June 18, 1966, in a report that Carmichael was teaching marchers the use of the slogan.

Two weeks before, on May 30, Harlem Congressman Adam Clayton Powell used the phrase in a speech to students at Howard University: "To demand these God-given rights is to seek black power . . ." There may be other previous uses in the black community, but the phrase was made famous in a dramatic context by Carmichael.

Dr. Nathan Hare, Carmichael's sociology professor at Howard University, called the slogan not anti-white, but "anti-antiblack." He added: " 'Power' is the ability to influence another person—even against his will, if necessary . . . 'black power' means the exercise by black people of influence on the forces which oppress us. . . . Assimilation has not worked. . . . As Malcolm X [the late Black Muslim leader] said, 'we've been praying when we should have been preying, or playing when we should be flaying—you know, skinning alive.' "

Floyd McKissick, head of the Congress of Racial Equality (CORE), told Senator Robert Kennedy in 1967: "I believe that black power will be accepted just like Irish power has been accepted." This was using the phrase in its non-violent, political-power sense, and liberal columnist Max Lerner argued its fallacy: ". . . while the Irish and the Jews . . . acted as political appeal groups, they never raised the slogans of 'Irish Power' or 'Jewish power,' nor implied hatred for the majority groups. Nor did they ever scorn to share power with non-Irish or non-Jews, even in the big cities where they were heavily represented."

James Farmer, former head of CORE, tried to moderate the expression: "Black power, whatever the coiners of this slogan mean, to me means shared power—otherwise it leads to an illusion."

To the Black Muslims, Black Panthers, and other extremist groups, the phrase was a rallying cry for guerrilla warfare. When riots erupted in several cities in the summer of 1967, the phrase's more ominous side became apparent.

H. "Rap" Brown, Carmichael's successor at SNCC, began to arouse audiences with his extension of black power to "get you some guns." In Jacksonville, Florida, Governor Claude Kirk showed up unexpectedly at a Brown appearance, appealed to "the Negro pride aspect of black power," drawing the line "at any talk of guns."

In July 1967, the *New York Times* analyzed the meaning of the phrase:

> Many believe the slogan means only that Negroes should take pride in their race and organize themselves for political and economic action. Others view it as an antiwhite rallying cry. Still others see it as a sort of para-military slogan that leads to riots and rebellion . . . the very ambiguity of the phrase is its major strength as a rallying cry for Negroes.

The slogan was important enough to be quoted in a Supreme Court decision a year after its coinage. The Court upheld (5 to 4) the contempt conviction of Dr. Martin Luther King, Jr., for defying a court injunction against a march he led in Alabama. The dissent was written by Justice William Brennan: "We cannot permit fears of 'riots' and 'civil disobedience' generated by slogans like black power to divert our attention from what is here at stake—arming the state courts with the power to punish as a 'contempt' what they otherwise could not punish at all."

Along with "escalate" (see ESCA-

LATION), black power became one of the major coinages of the sixties. A rhyming variation was "flower power," a slogan of the hippies who used flowers as a symbol of love. "Power" was used as the phrase-making device for a variety of groups, including "teacher power" or "blackboard power" for militant educators.

BLACK REPUBLICAN used as a political imprecation by Southerners and some northern Democrats before and during the Civil War in an attempt to label the new Republican party as fanatically pro-Negro.

Stephen Douglas, who was to be Lincoln's chief antagonist six years later, began denouncing "black Republicans" as early as 1854, when what was to become the Grand Old Party had barely hatched. Other orators used it as well. By 1855–56, when the Republicans and abolitionists generally took **"BLEEDING KANSAS"** as a war chant, Democrats and pro-slavery interests answered with "black Republicans." The *Lancaster* (Ohio) *Eagle* in 1855 condemned "black Republicans with their woolly heads."

By 1860 it was so common a curse that candidate Abraham Lincoln devoted part of his address at Cooper Union in New York City to rebuttal. He repeated his party's opposition to slavery but argued that illiterate slaves were largely unaware of the party's stance. Thus, the party could not be responsible for unrest and violence among Negroes. Lincoln said that to dramatize their case, enemies of the new party defined black Republicanism as "insurrection, blood and thunder among the slaves."

Lincoln's defense did no good. He was nominated for the presidency three months after the Cooper Union speech, and in the acrimonious campaign that followed, Lincoln heard himself often attacked as a black Republican. Jefferson Davis used the term in private correspondence.

The phrase might have been adapted from one used in Europe earlier—red republicans—to describe radicals in the revolutionary movements of the 1840s. In this country, many considered the overthrow of slavery just as radical as many Europeans viewed the death of monarchy.

White officer John Pershing led the 10th Negro Cavalry during the Spanish-American War. Because of his service with Negro troops, he acquired the nickname "Black Jack."

Although no longer used seriously in modern American politics—indeed the Republicans' big problem has been to retrieve Negro support—black Republicanism is still employed occasionally in a bantering way. Joe Martin, the former House Republican leader, recalled requesting of Franklin Roosevelt a new federal road for Massachusetts. Roosevelt promptly instructed an aide to call the appropriate official "and tell him I am sending down a black Republican and I want . . . to give him a road."

BLANKET BALLOT, *see* **BED-SHEET BALLOT.**

BLEEDING HEARTS an ultraconservative view of ultraliberals, as those whose "hearts bleed" for the poor, who are "suckers" for every "sob story," and who place tax burdens on all in a mistaken effort to cure social ills.

The liberal who is so labeled considers the one who calls him a "bleeding heart" to be reactionary. See **DINOSAUR WING; RADICAL RIGHT; MOSSBACK.** The conservative who urges a cutback of welfare programs often prefaces his remarks with, "This will be met with cries of anguish from the bleeding hearts, but . . .".

The expression was popularized in the thirties by columnist Westbrook Pegler. See INVECTIVE, POLITICAL. Its origin may be the Order of the Bleeding Heart, a semireligious order of the Middle Ages honoring the Virgin Mary, whose "heart was pierced with many sorrows."

England's *New Statesman* in 1966 showed a cartoon of President Lyndon Johnson in a Christmas sleigh, captioned with a vitriolic poem:

Bedecked with olive branch, he showers
*   blessings on Hanoi:*
The gift of an ephemeral life for every
*   girl and boy.*
But do not judge him harshly if he scat-
*   ters fire and germ,*
You have to steel your bleeding heart to
*   clinch a second term. . . .*

See LIBERAL.

BLEEDING KANSAS   the guerrilla skirmishing, rioting, and other disorders that shook ante-bellum Kansas as proslavery and antislavery factions competed for control.

Which newspaper or political orator first referred to "bleeding Kansas" is unknown, but the phrase appeared in many headlines and speeches when the fighting became serious in 1855–56. Both sides were guilty of atrocities, which included a minor massacre perpetrated by John Brown. In the propaganda war, however, it was the abolitionists who used "bleeding Kansas" as a war cry across the North, especially during the 1856 elections.

Kansas's agony was not the first case of civil strife to be called "bleeding." In the seventeenth century, for instance, it was "bleeding Ireland."

The usage has remained largely historic, although bleeding Kansas can be used to describe a minor conflict that presages a much larger one involving roughly the same issues. Historian Samuel Eliot Morison juxtaposes bleeding Kansas and the subsequent Civil War with the Spanish Civil War and the subsequent World War II.

Wrote John Gunther in *Inside U.S.A.* in 1947: "Does 'Bleeding Kansas' still bleed? Will it still rise to fight injustice? I asked this question generally, and one answer I got was, 'Oh, we still have a hemorrhage once in a while.' "

BLITZ, *see* **DEWEY BLITZ.**

BLOC   a group of citizens or organizations gathered to promote some special interest, as "the farm bloc."

The French popularized the term, applying it to those temporary and shifting combinations of parties in the Chamber of Deputies during the Third Republic. Clemenceau's *Bloc des Gauches,* formed after the Dreyfus Affair, was one example, and Poincaré's *Bloc National,* formed in 1919, was another.

In the U.S., the term has been used to convey the idea of selfish interests as well as special ones. Conferring with his advisers soon after his election to the presidency in 1920, Warren G. Harding asked the question that every one of his successors has had to confront since then: "What shall we do about the farm bloc?"

Adlai Stevenson, during his 1952 presidential campaign, deplored another kind of bloc: ". . . the myth of monolithic voting—the idea that all the votes in a bloc go one way or the other in response to the candidate's willingness to go along with the official positions of the bloc." In a similar vein, John F. Kennedy said during his dramatic confrontation with the Greater Houston Ministerial Association in 1960 that he believed in an America "where there is no Catholic vote, no anti-Catholic vote, no bloc voting of any kind." See BAILEY MEMORANDUM. As the Vietnam war grew, its opponents coalesced into what was called the "Peace Bloc."

For Americans, the word long had another association—in the phrase, "Sino-Soviet bloc," similar to an earlier use of Rome-Berlin AXIS. With the growing split between Moscow and Peking, however, many experts urged abandonment of the phrase as an inaccurate oversimplification. As historian Arthur Schlesinger, Jr., wrote in a memo to the State Department in 1963, when he was serving as a White House aide: "In view of what is going on currently in Moscow, could not the Department bring itself to abolish the usage, 'Sino-Soviet bloc'? The relationship of that phrase to reality grows more tenuous all the time."

BLOCKADE, *see* **QUARANTINE.**

BLOCKS OF FIVE, *see* **SWING VOTER.**

BLOODBATH a feared extermination of allies.

During the Vietnam war, one of the reasons advanced for the U.S. to continue supporting the South Vietnamese forces was that a pull-out of Americans would lead to a "bloodbath"—the killings of tens of thousands of American allies by the North Vietnamese. The word was popularized by California Governor Ronald Reagan.

After the Vietnam war ended, the predicted bloodbath did not material-

ize in South Vietnam, but it did in Cambodia, where an estimated million citizens died after the Khmer Rouge took over in Phnom Penh.

The word is a political extention of "massacre," and is a calque of the German *Blutbad.* According to Eric Partridge, German soldiers called the 1916 Battle of the Somme "the bloodbath," and it was adopted by Allied soldiers in World War I to describe any engagement in which casualties were heavy.

BLOODY SHIRT waved or shaken rhetorically for nearly three decades after the Civil War; an appeal to old wartime emotions to equate Democrats with the Confederacy, and the South with warmongering.

Even before the war, the political antecedents of radical Republicans used the bloody shirt, both literally and in oratory, as a call for retribution. Abolitionist James Baird Weaver recounted how in the 1850s he acquired the stained and shredded linen of a preacher who had been flogged for inflaming slaves. "I waved it before the crowds," said Weaver, "and bellowed: 'under this bloody shirt we propose to march to victory.' "

The term came into wide use in the 1860s and '70s. Both Democrats and moderate Republicans who sought a conciliatory policy used it when attempting to debunk wilder statements of the hard-peace Republicans. Horace Greeley had been a Union man and an abolitionist, but in 1872, when he broke with the Republicans to run for President as an independent, he denounced his former friends for "waving the bloody shirt." Four years later Republican Senator John Logan of Illinois said in a typical speech: "It has come to be a saying . . . that we are shaking the bloody shirt if we call attention to brutal wholesale murder of colored Republicans. . . . When Democrats will stop staining the shirt with blood, we will quit shaking it."

The association of an "ensanguined garment" with vengeance and a debt of blood is ancient. In Shakespeare's *Julius Caesar,* Marc Antony whipped up the fury of his fellow Romans by waving his murdered leader's toga. Gibbon mentions that when the Caliph Othman of Damascus was murdered in A.D. 656, his stained clothes were displayed. It appears in literature and in history—in Scotland (a 1603 massacre by the Clan MacGregor), Corsica, France, and eighteenth-century America, where Patrick Henry displayed a victim's clothing in a court case. Abraham Lincoln was said to have employed a similar trick in an Illinois murder trial where he was assisting the district attorney, saying, ". . . it is better to wave the bloody shirt than to waive justice."

Commenting on American politics in 1880, *Punch* magazine wrote of candidate James G. Blaine:

There was an old stalwart named Blaine,
Who hailed from the region of Maine.
When he felt badly hurt
He would cry "Bloody Shirt"—
And slay over the already slain.

In 1942, writer Carey McWilliams characterized anti-Orientalism on the West Coast—resulting in the imprisonment of American citizens of Japanese descent during World War II—as "California's Bloody Shirt."

BLOOPER an exploitable mistake; a slip of the tongue, or unthinking comment, that can be seized upon by the opposition.

A *blooper* is worse than a *goof,* more adult than a *boo-boo,* not as se-rious as a *blunder,* equivalent to a *gaffe.* Repeated commission of any results in a description of having FOOT-IN-MOUTH DISEASE.

Nelson Rockefeller was asked, as he campaigned for re-election as New York governor in 1966, about his campaign promise of 1962 not to raise taxes. His seemingly casual reply was the result of many strategy meetings of aides, who worried about how to meet the most serious opposition charge. The decision was to admit it had been a mistake. Said Rockefeller: "That was the biggest blooper I ever made."

Blooper is a recent coinage, probably adapted from radio announcers' slang for a spoonerism or slip of the tongue. ("Ladies and gentlemen," said NBC's Harry Von Zell, "the President of the United States, Hoobert Heever.") But the act of blooping has been in politics since the game, science, business, or art began. "Hancock the Superb"—General Winfield Scott Hancock—had a good chance to beat James Garfield in 1880. When asked about tariffs, he replied "The tariff is a local issue," and was pleased that he did not get embroiled in the issue. "The Republicans, however," wrote editor Henry Stoddard, "made much ado about a soldier's ignorance of economics. Hancock's long dream of the Presidency dissolved in these five inopportune but truthful words." Stoddard suggested that it was only a blooper.

Winners' bloopers are seldom remembered; losers' bloopers gain in importance with the years. In the Truman-Dewey campaign of 1948, Truman's whistlestop appearances were seldom on time and Democratic scheduling was less than airtight. See WHISTLESTOPPING. But the Dewey "Victory Special" campaign train rolled on with awesome efficiency, schedules met, speech texts promptly available. At one of the local stops, the Dewey train suddenly jerked away from the station, such a change from the usual smooth start that the candidate exclaimed: "What's the matter with that idiot engineer?"

"This turned out to be a magnificent blooper," wrote Cabell Phillips of the *New York Times*. "In the skilled hands of the Democratic propagandists, it became overnight a jeering anti-Dewey slogan in railroad roundhouses and Union halls all across the country."

A recent British example: in the General Election of 1964, Conservative Prime Minister Sir Alec Douglas-Home faced a tough interrogation on BBC television. In answering a question about a proposed supplement for older pensioners, Sir Alec used the word "donation." Labor supporters of Harold Wilson seized the usage, cartoonists illustrated it, and it was used throughout the campaign to exploit the apparently patrician attitude of the Conservatives.

A recent American example: In the summer of 1971 Senator Ed Muskie told a group of black leaders that he did not believe the American electorate was ready yet for a black on the national ticket. Wrote Milton Viorst, a liberal columnist: "Judged by the conventional political code of conduct, Muskie committed a blooper, perhaps a serious one."

On the international scene, diplomatic errors may be serious (see MIS-CALCULATION) or amusing, as when U.S. Ambassador to the UN, Warren Austin, hoped during the 1948 war in Palestine that the Jews and the Arabs would settle their differences "like good Christians."

BLOVIATE   to orate pompously. Warren G. Harding popularized this word; his biographer, Francis Russel, claimed it was an old Ohio term meaning "to loaf," and, as Harding said, "The world has no use for a loafer." Perhaps Harding used "bloviation" in that sense; however, it soon became applied to his own oratory, and today is best remembered as a description of Harding's forensic fatuousness.

In fact, the word has had that empty-oratory meaning for more than a century. In its October 23, 1909, edition, *Literary Digest* derided a proposal to create a separate state of Southern California by quoting a *Louisville Courier-Journal* suggestion to make Los Angeles a state, an arrangement "which would rid California of a maximum of bluster and bloviation and a minimum of territory."

This meaning of "bloviate" was cited by Albert Barrère and Charles G. Leland in their 1889 *Dictionary of Slang, Jargon and Cant:* "Bloviate (American): a made up or 'factitious' word, which has been used since 1850, and is perhaps older. It is irregularly used to signify verbosity, wandering from the subject, and idle or inflated oratory or blowing, by which word it was probably suggested, being partially influenced by 'deviate.' "

In current usage, that definition stands. The derivation, as Barrère and Leland suggest, is from "blow," which has an old slang meaning of loud and empty talk, and is also the root of the related "blowhard."

BLOWBACK, *see* **CIA-ESE.**

BLUE BOOK, *see* **WHITE PAPER.**

BLUE RIBBON PANEL   a jury or committee chosen on the basis of intelligence or special experience to investigate particularly complex or important matters.

Denoting exclusivity, the term comes from the ribbons worn by members of the Order of the Garter in Great Britain, and the *cordon bleu* of the ancient order of *St. Esprit* in France, as well as from the ribbons awarded to prize-winners, animal and human alike. Though properly applied to juries, "blue ribbon panel" has become something of a cliché for any government-appointed committee. Practically every major investigative or reform group, from the postwar Hoover Commission that recommended sweeping reforms in the U.S. executive branch, to Lyndon Johnson's commission on the draft, has been described in the press as a blue-ribbon panel.

Columnist Art Buchwald spoofed the phrase in 1967: "While Art Buchwald is taking a few days off, a blue ribbon panel has selected some of his articles from the past . . ."

BLUE SLIP   an individual senator's approval of a presidential nomination, the lack of which, in some cases, results in withdrawal of a nomination.

The "blue slip" is the currency of SENATORIAL COURTESY. If a senator objects to a nomination the President has made, he can cast a blackball by simply not returning the approval forms sent out by the Majority Leader. If the appointee is from the senator's state, and if the senator and the appointee, or the senator and the President, are in the same party, the likelihood of a further Senate consideration is small.

Here is the text of a blue slip, 1978 vintage, from the Committee on the Judiciary, Senator James Eastland (D-Miss.) chairman:

"Dear Senator: Will you kindly give me, for the use of the Committee, your opinion and information concerning the nomination of [blank]. Under a rule of the Committee, unless a reply is received from you within a week from this date, it will be assumed that you have no objection to this nomination. Respectfully . . ."

The second sentence is understood by sender and recipient to be the opposite of the truth. If the blue slip is not returned, a committee secretary calls the senator who has not returned it, to make sure the slip did not get lost in the mail; if the senator's office says, simply, that the senator has not yet acted upon it, the blackball has been cast and the nominee has been "blue-slipped."

See PATRONAGE; PERSONALLY OBNOXIOUS.

BOARD OF EDUCATION   a House of Representatives leadership group that gathers on occasion to persuade less senior members of the leadership's wisdom.

In a profile of the new Speaker of the House in 1962, the *New York Times* headline read: "Rayburn's 'Board of Education' Keeps Role Under McCormack." Citing evidence that John McCormack of Massachusetts was a conservative on preserving traditions, the January 29 story pointed out: "The latest is his decision to continue the 'Board of Education.' Under Speaker Rayburn, the group—partly social, partly political and entirely private—met about sundown in an out-of-the-way room on the ground floor of the Capitol . . . Under Speaker McCormack, the same room is used, and the same customs, including the pouring of bourbon and scotch, are maintained." Members included Representative Carl Albert (who succeeded McCormack as Speaker) and Lewis

Deschler, parliamentarian of the House. "The only new member," wrote the *Times* reporter, introducing a future Speaker, "as far as nonmembers have been able to determine, is Rep. Thomas P. O'Neill of Massachusetts. He is a longtime close friend and political associate of Speaker McCormack." See STRIKE A BLOW FOR FREEDOM.

BODY POLITIC any group governed by any means; a governmental system, with the word "body" used in the same sense of "body of laws" or "body of facts."

An early use occurred in Thomas Hobbes's *Leviathan,* published in 1651: "Of systems subordinate, some are political and some private. Political (otherwise called bodies politic and persons in law) are those which are made by authority from the sovereign power of the Commonwealth."

The metaphor linking the human anatomy to the system of government can be found in Plato's *Republic.* In Jean-Jacques Rousseau's *Discourse on Political Economy,* the metaphoric use was extended: "The body politic, taken individually may be considered as an organised, living body, resembling that of a man. The sovereign power represents the head; the laws and customs are the brain . . . commerce, industry and agriculture are the mouth and stomach . . . the public income is the blood . . . the citizens are the body and the members, which make the machine live, move and work. . . ." Rousseau held that "the body politic, therefore, is also a moral being possessed of a will." In *Social Contract* he wondered, "Has the body politic an organ to declare its will?" and warned, "The body politic, like the human body, begins to die from its birth, and bears in itself the causes of its own destruction." (In other

translations, the famous phrase reads "seeds of its own destruction.")

The comparison to the human body offered many American politicians an opportunity to be eloquent. James Garfield, a future President speaking just after the Civil War, pressed for the Negro's right to vote: ". . . the inequality of rights before the law, which is now a part of our system, is more dangerous to us than to the black man whom it disenfranchises. It is like a foreign substance in the body, a thorn in the flesh; it will wound and disease the body politic."

In more recent times, the phrase has been used metaphorically by some, straight by others. Chief Justice Charles Evans Hughes said: "In the great enterprise of making democracy workable we are all partners. One member of our body politic cannot say to another: 'I have no need of thee.' " Dwight Eisenhower helped his audience by defining it: "As we see difficulties and defects in the body politic, in the social order, we must never attempt before our own consciences to dodge our own responsibilities."

Columbia University, conferring its Doctorate of Laws on Adlai Stevenson in 1954, took an extreme metaphoric route: "Physician extraordinary to the body politic, skilled in diagnosis, bold in prognosis, forthright in prescription, buoyant of bedside manner . . ."

Franklin Roosevelt discarded the phrase and used the idea. "A nation, like a person, has a body," he said in his Third Inaugural Address in 1941, which must be fed and housed and clothed in accordance with American standards, and "a nation, like a person, has a mind" which must be kept informed and be understanding. Finally, "a nation, like a person, has something deeper, something more permanent, something larger than the sum of its parts. It is that something that matters most to its future. . . . It is a thing for which we find it difficult —even impossible—to hit upon a single simple word. And yet, we all understand what it is: the spirit . . . the faith of America . . ." Like Rousseau, FDR found in the body politic "a moral being possessed of a will."

BOLT to desert one's party or faction; as a noun, the act of such desertion.

Bolt is venerable in political usage, going back deep into the 19th century, and possibly further, which isn't surprising because the term goes to the heart of party politics: the never-ending cycle of sundering and solidifying loyalties. In 1884 the *Boston Journal* posed this definition: "a bolter's one . . . who can't command and won't obey." That, of course, spoke for the viewpoint of PARTY LOYALTY. Many have upheld the primacy of personal principle. Raymond Moley, who bolted the Democratic party after the 1936 election of Franklin Roosevelt, gave the classic reply: "I was frequently asked why I left the Democratic party. My answer was that the Democratic party had left me."

The term has kept its original meaning, as well as its currency, perhaps because there is no real difference between its political or figurative sense and its literal or physical meaning (the horse bolted out of control). Harry Truman, discussing the defection in 1948 of the Progressives on the left and the Dixiecrats on the right, said, "I was confronted not with one major defection in the Democratic party but with two bolts . . ." A more colloquial term, dropped into the political vocabulary in 1936 by Alfred E. Smith when he publicly broke with

Roosevelt, is to TAKE A WALK. "Red" Barber, then the broadcaster for the Brooklyn Dodgers, was able to tie baseball, domestic politics, and the Cold War together during the United Nations' early years when the Russian delegation, led by Andrei Gromyko, occasionally bolted, or took a walk. Barber would say of a recipient of a base on balls: "He's taking a Gromyko."

In British political usage, "to bolt a bill" is to pass it without close consideration, which in American usage is "railroad it through."

For other horse-racing metaphors in politics, see DARK HORSE; SHOO-IN; FRONT RUNNER. For a milder form of bolting, see OFF THE RESERVATION; for organized bolting, see SPLINTER GROUP and DIXIECRAT.

BOMBING PAUSE a temporary cessation of bombing to determine whether the opponent wishes to negotiate; a concession to create an atmosphere for negotiation.

The phrase was probably introduced into debate about the war in Vietnam by Canadian Prime Minister Lester Pearson, in a speech in Philadelphia on April 2, 1965. Pearson, who as Canada's Minister of External Affairs had won a Nobel Peace Prize, suggested that President Johnson ought to order a "pause" in bombing North Vietnam, which might bring about peace talks.

The phrase gave focus, and the sponsor gave weight, to much previous pressure from what was called the "Peace Bloc" to halt the bombing. On May 13, 1965, the first "bombing pause" began, lasted for six days, and was followed by longer and shorter pauses in subsequent years. DOVES said the pauses were too temporary and too short; "hawks" (see WAR HAWKS) said the pauses were a show of weakness, allowing the North Vietnamese to regroup and resupply.

"Pause" is a word with a curious history in politics. President James Buchanan remarked on the eve of the Civil War, "Let us pause at this momentous point and afford the people an opportunity for reflection"—by which he meant a general election that would relieve him of responsibility.

German propagandists in 1941 described the lull in fighting after the Nazi conquest of Crete as a "creative pause." *Time* magazine in 1942 referred to any cessation of hostilities as the "creative pauses of Adolf Hitler." The phrase was an ominous one, implying a build-up of power for a fresh attack (and offering a good excuse for inactivity).

The word hurt the Conservatives in the 1964 general elections in Great Britain. Chancellor of the Exchequer Selwyn Lloyd, in an effort to meet Britain's balance-of-trade crisis, said of wages and salaries: "There must be a pause until productivity has caught up." The "pay pause" was used by Labour to attack the government; after Labour had won, the "pause" went into effect and became known as a "freeze."

In a book by Richard V. Allen on peaceful coexistence, published by the American Bar Association, the Russian word *peredyshka* is defined: "Breathing Space (Peredyshka)—Period of rest in which forces are regrouped in preparation for another offensive against the West, which usually occurs after a Communist advance has been halted and the 'enemy' has become alert to further Communist aggression; a period designed to relax the enemy's defenses so as to facilitate the next offensive. 'Peredyshka' means 'pause.' "

BOMFOG   a high-sounding, glittering generality.

The word comes from reporters' shorthand covering Governor Nelson Rockefeller's speeches in his 1964 campaign against Barry Goldwater in the New Hampshire primary, which resulted in an upset victory in New Hampshire for Henry Cabot Lodge.

Nancy Shea, of Rockefeller's staff, informs the author:

Bomfog was originated by Hy Sheffer who was at one time the Governor's stenotypist. Hy told me he started using it in the late 1959–60 national effort. Since the Governor used the phrase "the brotherhood of man under the fatherhood of God," so often, Hy began to simplify it on the stenotype machine. *Bomfog* took only two strokes on the machine compared to several more strokes for the whole phrase. The reporters traveling with the Governor's party picked it up and made it famous.

"Brotherhood of man, fatherhood of God" is part of the Rockefeller family credo, a speech by John D. Rockefeller, Jr., etched in marble near the statue of Prometheus in New York's Rockefeller Center: "These are the principles upon which alone a new world recognizing the brotherhood of man and the fatherhood of God can be established."

The initials had an appeal as a political word because it seemed to combine "bombast" with "fog," or amorphous oratory. Its use is no longer limited to critics of Nelson Rockefeller.

BONELESS WONDER, *see* **INVECTIVE, POLITICAL.**

BOODLE   graft; illicit profit derived from holding public office, usually in the form of bribes; more loosely, loot of any type.

This durable word of several meanings came into wide political use in New York during the early 1880s, when the construction of the Brooklyn Bridge was hotly debated. A number of publications used the term around the same time and with the same meaning. Typical was *Puck*'s Dooley-esque spoof in 1883, quoting an unnamed alderman: "They say there's a power of boodle in the building av it; so yous needn't bother about what they'll do wid it." The following year the *New York World* said of the lobbyists' activities: "It has been a double-barrelled shotgun of boodle."

Boodle went national in the presidential election of 1884 and was used most tellingly against James G. Blaine, the unsuccessful Republican candidate. When he attended a Delmonico's dinner in his honor—given by some of the country's richest men —the newspapers dubbed the event the "boodle banquet." A Thomas Nast cartoon depicted Blaine defending "Fort Boodle." Benjamin Harrison, the Republican nominee four years later, absorbed similar attacks, but won anyway. Said the *New York Times* when Harrison took Indiana: "There seems to be no good reason to doubt that boodle and bulldozing have carried the state for Harrison."

As the 1948 Republican convention, Illinois Governor Dwight Green lambasted the Democrats as an alliance of "bosses, boodle, buncombe and blarney."

Although the word's etymology is perfectly proper (it comes from the Dutch *boedel*, meaning property), its American use seems always to have had a larcenous or facetious connotation. At least three decades before it became synonymous with political swag, it was used to denote counterfeit money. Although GRAFT, *fix*, *payoff*, and *bribe* are more frequently used words, *boodle* is still current. "Each time there was a payment," wrote *Life* magazine in a 1968 story on organized crime in New York, "there was this ritual cutting up of the boodle."

In an era of electronic eavesdropping, another synonym is a "wordless word": in lieu of the question "Can he be bribed?" the potential briber says nothing but rubs his thumb against his index and middle finger and raises his eyebrows.

See REACHABLE; LITTLE TIN BOX.

BOOKBURNERS censors; self-appointed guardians of what may and may not be read; anti-intellectuals.

The burning of books considered offensive to the group in power had often occurred in the Middle Ages, but "bookburning" became a political word on the evening of May 10, 1933, less than five months after Hitler came to power. William L. Shirer described the scene in Berlin:

At about midnight a torch light parade of thousands of students ended at a square on Unter den Linden opposite the University of Berlin. Torches were put to a huge pile of books that had been gathered there, and as the flames enveloped them more books were thrown on the fire until some twenty thousand had been consumed. Similar scenes took place in several other cities. The book burning had begun.

Propaganda Minister Joseph Goebbels addressed the students in the light of the pyre: "The soul of the German people can express itself. These flames not only illuminate the final end of an old era; they also light up the new." (See NIGHT OF THE LONG KNIVES.)

FDR, in a message to the American Booksellers Association in 1942, wrote: "We all know that books burn —yet we have the greater knowledge

that books cannot be killed by fire.
. . . in this war, we know, books are
weapons."

Senator Joseph McCarthy, investigating the State Department's predecessor to the U.S. Information
Agency, sent two of his assistants,
Roy M. Cohn and G. David Schine,
abroad to investigate alleged inefficiency and cases of doubtful loyalty.
Their tour (see JUNKETEERING
GUMSHOES) aroused controversy;
subsequently the State Department
excluded "the works of all Communist authors" from U.S. libraries
abroad. One news report chose the
slanted word "burned" rather than
"removed," evoking memories of the
Nazi experience.

President Eisenhower, who refused
to ENGAGE IN PERSONALITIES, made
this observation on the campus of
Dartmouth College: "Don't join the
bookburners! Don't think you are
going to conceal faults by concealing
evidence that they ever existed. Don't
be afraid to go in your library and
read every book as long as that document does not offend your own ideas
of decency. That should be the only
censorship."

History's first recorded bookburning was ordered by the first emperor
of the Ch'in dynasty in China around
220 B.C. The emperor, who was responsible for the completion of the
Great Wall, not merely burned books
but also buried alive a few hundred
scholars in pits mainly to suppress
Confucianism. In China "bookburning and scholar pitting" has become a
familiar phrase.

BOOM (BOOMLET)   a well-publicized movement to promote a political candidate.

Booms may be artificially induced,
but those that have voter appeal often
turn into the real thing. The word

gained political currency in the late
1870s when it was used to describe
the noise and hullabaloo associated
with the growing sentiment for General Ulysses S. Grant for another Republican presidential nomination. An
1879 story in the *San Diego Daily
Union*: "Mr. McCullagh, editor of
the *St. Louis Globe-Democrat*, who
first applied the word 'boom' to the
Grant movement, says he used the
term in the sense that it is applied to
a sudden and irresistible rise in a
river. He wanted a term to imply that
the Grant movement was sweeping
everything before it, and he chose the
word 'boom.' "

The magazine *Puck* speculated in
1879 about the origin of the phrase:
"Lately has been added to our American political vocabulary the word
'boom,' which sprang up nobody
knows where, and means nobody
knows exactly what. The term may
have arisen from the system of booming great rafts of logs on our rivers; or
the term may refer to the boom which
is spread out from the mast to extend
the canvas to the favoring breeze. Our
opinion is that it is the 'boom' of cannon which has given rise to the
phrase." A year later *Puck* posed the
question that puzzles practical politicians to this day: "Can a boom once
boomed be reboomed, or does it boom
itself out at the first boom?"

A boomlet is a boom that makes
only a plaintive, popping sound.
Boomlets are started for candidates
with little real hope of achieving a
nomination. Generally they die out
and the man for whom the boomlet
was launched throws his support to
someone else, possibly in return for a
place on the ticket—which might
have been the reason for the boomlet
all along.

An economic boom is similar in
meaning to a political boom: both are

off and running, though there is less connotation of manipulation in an economic boom.

BOOM AND BUST severe cyclical movement of an economy; apparent prosperity followed by extreme depression; a manic-depressive economy.

The phrase always means something to be shunned. In his 1948 State of the Union message, President Harry Truman used the familiar phrase calling for a comprehensive anti-inflation program "to protect our economy against the evils of boom and bust."

Eisenhower economic adviser Arthur Burns said in 1960: "The American people have of late been more conscious of the business cycle, more sensitive to every wrinkle of economic curves, more alert to the need for contracyclical action on the part of government, than ever before in our history." Unfortunately for the Republicans, economic expansion programs were not pressed at that time and the 1960 election was held in the midst of an economic slump.

The NEW ECONOMICS of John Maynard Keynes did much to encourage the public to believe that government action could indeed eliminate the wide swings of boom and bust. Walter Heller, economic adviser to Presidents Kennedy and Johnson, held that economists had to go beyond contracyclical planning. "Policy thinking," he wrote in criticism of the Eisenhower years, "had been centered more on minimizing the fluctuations of the business cycle than on realizing the economy's great and growing potential."

Steady economic growth, relieved of sharp movements in either direction, became the goal of the new economists. Kennedy aide Theodore Sorensen characterized a long-faced conclave of the Council of Economic Advisors in 1961 with: "There they are, contemplating the dangers of an upturn!"

BOOMERANG a political statement or policy that unexpectedly damages its perpetrator; a disastrous reaction.

In the 1936 presidential campaign, many companies printed flyers for insertion into pay envelopes opposing Roosevelt's Social Security program. "The whole campaign of propaganda turned out to be a boomerang," wrote Samuel Rosenman. "There may have been a time . . . as in the Bryan campaigns, when the workers of the nation, either willingly or unwillingly, took political advice from their employers; by 1936 they were voting on their own."

The derivation of boomerang is familiar: the crescent-shaped hunting weapon used by Australian natives. When hurled, it comes back to the thrower. The metaphor was probably introduced by poet Oliver Wendell Holmes in 1845: "Like the strange missile which the Australian throws /Your verbal boomerang slaps you on the nose." Cartoonist Thomas Nast used it politically in 1877 against Carl Schurz, who made a politically unwise protest against the sale of arms to France. Nast showed Schurz firing a gun which explodes in his face, with the caption: "Carl's Boomerang. Little Children Should Not Investigate (French) Firearms."

In political usage, the word differs from BLOOPER, *blunder, goof, fluff,* and *gaffe,* which are more slips of the tongue than errors in judgment; a boomerang connotes a conscious policy willingly undertaken that turns out to be mistaken because of the unexpected adverse reaction.

Defense Secretary Charles E. Wilson, victim of several bloopers (see **BIRD DOGS; WHAT'S GOOD FOR GENERAL MOTORS . . .**), learned late in his career to be more careful of his statements. Treading carefully in a 1957 press conference, he ducked a question by observing, "I somehow feel there's a boomerang loose in the room."

In 1967 Alan Otten wrote an article titled "The Grating Society" and observed: "Slogans are an established ingredient of political public relations. Probably they are initially helpful in selling a program. But they have a way of wearing out their welcome, even boomeranging. They begin to sound contrived or corny; they provide a rallying cry for a program's foes as well as friends."

For a boomerang with racial overtones, see **BACKLASH.**

BOONDOGGLE   any project on which government funds are wasted through inefficiency or political favoritism; originally a make-work project, using government funds to stimulate the economy.

When New York City's Board of Aldermen (now City Council) was investigating relief payments in 1935, they discovered money was being spent for the teaching of tap dancing, manipulation of shadow puppets, and the geographical distribution of safety pins. One Robert Marshall told the aldermen he was paid for teaching "boon doggles."

The word livened up the hearings, and Marshall explained to the *New York Times:* "Boon doggles is simply a term applied back in the pioneer days to what we call gadgets today . . . no, it is not named for Daniel Boone . . . it is spelled differently."

H. L. Mencken tracked the phrase back into scouting, as the name given

to the braided leather lanyard worn by Boy Scouts. The *Chicago Tribune* wrote that "to the cowboy it meant the making of saddle trappings out of odds and ends of leather, and they boon doggled when there was nothing else to do on the ranch."

Brewer's *Dictionary of Phrase and Fable* gives as the derivation the identical word in Scottish—*boondoggle*—which is a marble given as a gift without the recipient's having worked for it.

The word has lost its Depression-born connotation of keeping the idle busy with government funds, though it always implied waste of money. Now the word is used in attacks on government bureaucracy on all levels, and has acquired a new connotation of favoritism. The Defense Department's "TFX" bomber program was denounced as a "huge boondoggle," and in 1966, a full-page advertisement appeared in the *New York Times* attacking a proposal for the construction of government-owned merchant ships as "a $2 billion government-aerospace boondoggle."

The word "boon" means gift, or favor, and might have played a role in the word's formation; "doggle," however, appears to be the operative verb and can be used to make the term more specific. For example, when the American Legion in 1966 pressed for an expansion of national cemeteries to include all Vietnam veterans and their families, the *New Republic* headlined their comment: "The Gravedoggle."

BORING FROM WITHIN   infiltration of a group or society by agents dedicated to its overthrow; a **FIFTH COLUMN.**

Communists have long been accused of using a technique of takeover borrowed from nature: a tree-destroying beetle embeds its eggs as deeply as it can in a notch in the tree's bark, and the hatching insect instinctively bores its way through the wood.

In *Suite 3505,* published in 1967, Goldwater organizer F. Clifton White wrote about "how Communist agents and their dupes incessantly bore from within in their untiring efforts to destroy our democratic society . . ." Nelson Rockefeller, in 1963, accused the Goldwater men of doing exactly the same within the Republican party, in his first MAINSTREAM statement: ". . . the vociferous and well-drilled extremist elements boring within the party utterly reject these fundamental principles of our heritage."

A "borer" is an obsolete term for political lobbyist; the *Cincinnati National Republican* wrote in 1923 that Pennsylvanians "have applied to each other the elegant appellations of logrollers and borers . . ."

The accusation has not been limited to Communists and extremists. *Chicago Tribune* publisher Robert McCormick, America's leading Britain-hater in the forties, explained his estimate of the reason behind Rhodes scholarships: "The infamous Cecil Rhodes conceived the plan to give free education to Americans in Oxford and make them into English cells, boring from within."

BORN AGAIN in its new political sense, freshly convinced; or, newly returned to the fold.

"Born again" is a phrase central to evangelical Christianity, meaning a spiritual experience resulting in a commitment to Christ. Convicted White House counsel Charles Colson used the phrase in that sense as the title of his 1976 bestseller. When Jimmy Carter became a serious contender for the Democratic presiden-

tial nomination, questions were raised about his religiosity: he freely asserted that he was a "born-again Christian" and his sister, Ruth Stapleton, was an eminent evangelist. This strong assertion of religious belief was regarded by some politicians as a negative, since it was met with suspicion by some voters and with guilt by others.

But the threat of "too much religion" in the candidate turned out to be a political old wives' tale, similar to the shibboleth that no Catholic could run successfully for President, which persisted until John Kennedy won.

The phrase "born-again," however, was taken into the political terminology: Democrats returning to the party were hailed as "born-again Democrats," and liberals reluctant to make difficult spending decisions that required new taxation were dubbed "born-again conservatives."

The phrase is now used in politics with no religious meaning, but with an ironic Carteresque connotation, to mean "newborn" or suddenly converted. Anthony Lake, who was a member of the National Security Council staff in the late sixties and who broke with Henry Kissinger in 1970 to become an outspoken DOVE, became a top policy planner in the Carter State Department. In 1978 the State Department found it necessary to dissociate itself from some of the extremely dovish positions taken by UN Ambassador Andrew Young; although continuing to espouse noninvolvement, Lake "put some daylight" between himself and Young. This led to his being identified by columnists Evans and Novak in June 1978 as a "born-again hawk."

In its theological sense of "being born of God" or becoming a child of God, the phrase first appeared in English in John Wyclif's 1382 translation of the Bible: "But a man schal be born agen."

BOSS, BOSSISM party leader who may not hold public office himself but who, through his control of the party organization, exerts great power over those of his party who do; bossism is a political system so organized. Both terms are almost always used in a pejorative sense.

"Bosses" and "bossism" had their first major impact on the lexicon in the mid-nineteenth century, as big-city political organizations came into vogue. There were many political bosses of course, both urban and rural, but William Marcy Tweed of New York's Democratic party became nationally notorious as "Boss Tweed." A statement generally attributed to him sums up the boss's credo: "You may elect whichever candidates you please to office, if you allow me to select the candidates." He also stole still-uncounted millions in public funds, although recent research disputes this. Upon entering prison he gave his occupation as "statesman."

Few bosses before or since have equaled Tweed in either avarice or self-esteem. But they have played a crucial part in American politics, both in their function of building strong party organizations on the county, city, and state level, and as a recurrent election issue and target for reformers.

Just as the nation is a federal union, each major American party is really a collection of state and local party organizations. The men who tend the machinery get as their principal wage —unless they personally hold public office—power. This power is tangible in the form of PATRONAGE, influence on nominations for great and small posts, and such matters as where a

new road is to be built. But one thing that leaders of this kind rarely obtain is a good public face. Regardless of their honesty, they are often thought of as the gross, evil, Tweed type or as the insatiable tiger clawing over his victims' bodies, as Thomas Nast drew the TAMMANY TIGER in Tweed's day.

The relatively unknown Woodrow Wilson was nominated for governor of New Jersey in 1910 largely through the efforts of boss James Smith of Newark and the state's lesser Democratic captains. Even before he took office, Wilson cooled toward Smith and, as James MacGregor Burns tells it, pictured Smith "not as he really was—a run-of-the-mill party boss— but as evil personified, a party despot, a symbol of corruption and predatory control. . . . Frantically Smith charged Wilson with dishonesty . . . but few would take the word of a boss over the word of a high-minded professor."

There have been many other such instances. Mayor Robert Wagner of New York won nomination for a third term (and then re-election) on a beat-the-boss platform. The irony was that the principal boss, Tammany's Carmine De Sapio, had himself come to power as something of a reformer, had liberalized Tammany's internal practices, and had been a much-valued ally of Wagner's for years. The moral was clear: De Sapio was stripped of power by the very processes he introduced. At the same time in neighboring Bronx County, the late Charles Buckley retained power until his death although he lost his congressional seat to the reformers. Buckley, unlike De Sapio, had never sanctioned the direct election of local party officials.

Since World War II, it has often been said that bosses and tightly held political machines are in such bad health that only political coroners should care. Ed Flynn, a Buckley predecessor in the Bronx, wrote the apologia in his 1947 book, *You're the Boss.* Harry Truman said sarcastically in 1959: "When a leader is in the Democratic Party, he's a boss; when he's in the Republican Party, he's a leader."

BOY SCOUT a naïve politician; one with a head-in-the-clouds approach to government.

"Boy Scout" is a derisive comment, made by cynical reporters or politicians, about those who do not bear the scars of compromise.

The best definition is Disraeli's remark about Gladstone: ". . . honest in the most odious sense of the word." An early political use was by Frank Kent of the *Baltimore Sun,* describing the parade of planners and Ph.D.s into the new Roosevelt Administration in 1933: "Boy Scouts in the White House . . . a government by Pink Pollyannas, first-name slingers, mothers' little helpers."

At a ball given by New York newspaper reporters soon after the election of John Lindsay as mayor, the new mayor was played onstage by a reporter (Edward O'Neill of the *Daily News*) in a Boy Scout uniform. After Michigan Governor George Romney visited New York's City Hall, Lindsay confided to associates: "You know, they call me a Boy Scout. If I am, Romney's an Eagle Scout."

In *The Arrogance of Power* (1967), Senate Foreign Relations Committee chairman J. William Fulbright used Boy Scouts in a story illustrating America's misplaced missionary zeal: "I am reminded of the three Boy Scouts who reported to their scoutmaster that as their good deed for the day they had helped an old lady to cross the street. 'That's fine,' said the

scoutmaster, 'but why did it take three of you?' 'Well,' they explained, 'she didn't want to go.' "

Politicians who make an important point about integrity in government during their campaigns, or who frequently use the word "reform," are often tagged with the title of the current comic-strip or television hero (Lindsay, for example, was often called "Batman"). Another similar appellation is "Mr. Clean," the name of a household detergent. *Newsweek* wrote of Ronald Reagan in November 1967: "At times as governor he comes on like Mr. Clean and Captain Nice rolled into one." A month later, when a kickback scandal embarrassed the Lindsay administration, columnist William F. Buckley Jr. wrote: "It is always piquant when it turns out that Mr. Clean never bathes." See MR. NICE GUY.

The political derogation of Boy Scout had its effect; in 1977 the Boy Scouts of America changed its venerable name to "Scouting/USA."

BOYS IN THE BACKROOM, *see* AMERICAN BOYS.

BRAHMIN aloof elite; a social, intellectual, or political aristocracy which manipulates power from non-elective positions.

The Brahmans of India were members of the highest Hindu caste, at the other end of the scale from the "untouchables"; Brahmanism is the word for the often-attacked but never really removed caste system in that country.

When the word arrived in Boston in the late nineteenth century, the spelling was changed. Oliver Wendell Holmes was the importer of the word in *Elsie Venner:* "He comes of the Brahmin caste of New England. This is the harmless, inoffensive, untitled aristocracy referred to, and which

many readers will at once acknowledge."

Irish politicians in Boston took the
"harmless" and "inoffensive" out of
the word and used it as an epithet.
Boston Mayor James M. Curley's biographer headed one chapter "The
Boston Brahmin-baiter" and quoted a
Curley-watcher as saying: "Jim can
make the term 'blue blood' sound like
the vilest epithet known to man. He
shows the people why it would be a
catastrophe to permit the 'Brahmins,'
as he terms the wealthy and socially
prominent, to obtain a foothold in
politics."

"The Brahmins today," wrote John
Gunther in 1947, "make a wonder-
fully close-knit archaic group, which
nothing in the United States quite rivals. Harvard and trusteeships; the
world placidly revolving around Back
Bay; the Apley-Pulham spirit; aridity
and charm and a Bloomsbury cultiva-
tion; above all, profound family inter-
weavings."

The term is no longer limited to
Boston; Brahmins are everywhere,
raising money and pulling strings,
being occasionally denounced as part
of the EASTERN ESTABLISHMENT by
those who are not "in." But a Brahmin is a power, and it is no longer
considered an insult to be called one.

BRAIN DRAIN   the siphoning of
scientific and technical talent from
one country to another, or from one
academic institution to another.

The phrase probably originated in
1963 in British newspapers concerned
with an exodus of English scientists
drawn to the U.S. by the higher salaries of U.S. corporations and universities.

One U.S. company—American
Gauge and Machine Co. of Chicago
—attacked the subject head-on with
an advertisement in a London news-

paper headed "Brain Drain—or the
Chance of a Lifetime." The company
sought a foundry manager, four
draftsmen, and three machine-shop
foremen.

Britons were most indignant when
this kind of raid was made on their
educated professional class. A government committee warned that "this
deliberate and planned recruitment
should not be allowed to go too far
without remedial action." Labour
party chairman John Boyd claimed
that the brain drain had brought a
windfall savings of $1 billion in edu-
cation and training costs to the U.S.

Trying to smooth over this international irritant, Vice President Hubert
Humphrey sought to emphasize one
facet of the problem: the students
who come to the U.S. with the expectation of returning home with training, but who remain here instead.
"There are thousands of young scientists and engineers working in the
United States who came to learn, but
stayed here to earn," he said in 1966.
"These are precious human resources
[the developing countries] cannot
afford to lose. We can help by working with the developing countries to
insure that too high a percentage of
their students do not come to the
United States to acquire skills which
have no relation to the priorities at
home."

But England was no "developing
country," and the English were concerned with what they considered the
outright piracy of home-trained
brainpower. Lyndon Johnson appointed an Inter-Agency Council on
International Education and Cultural
Affairs in 1965; after two years of
study, the Council reported "some
brain drain" but said it posed "no serious threat" to other countries.

However, a *New York Times* dispatch by John Darnton from Lagos,

Nigeria, on October 31, 1976, described "the 'brain drain' of developing nations, a new class of émigrés who are not political refugees, but self-exiles . . . They concentrate in fields of study that would be useful back home, and then they discover that there is a ready market for their skills in the industrial countries—and a much more pleasant existence."

When the Soviet Union suffered a grain shortage in 1972 and 1973, its wheat purchases from the West—which was not aware of the Russian shortfall—was later termed "The Great Grain Robbery," a play on "train robbery," as well as "the grain drain."

BRAIN TRUST ˙ a group of advisers to a candidate or incumbent, prized more for their expertise in particular fields and intimacy with their patron than for their official position or rank.

Sperber and Trittschuh found its first use in academic circles: "If I went up before that brain trust in the faculty room once more . . ." wrote George Fitch in *At Good Old Siwash* in 1911. In 1928 *Time* headlined an article on a meeting of the American Council on Learned Societies "Brain Trust." To speculate: this could have been a play on "beef trust," which in the early 1900s meant a monopoly on meat but later was a jocular reference to hefty chorines.

The press popularized *brain trust* during the 1930s and the BBC imported the phrase as the title for a British equivalent of an American radio program, "Information Please." The BBC show followed the original American usage—*brains trust*—but the cumbersome *s* fell by the verbal wayside in the United States.

The phrase was first applied to the group of university professors whose brains Franklin Roosevelt picked and trusted during the 1932 presidential campaign. Raymond Moley, one of the original "brain trusters," says that James Kieran, a *New York Times* reporter, coined the phrase. But Samuel Rosenman, who advised Roosevelt to recruit academic help, contends that Louis Howe, Roosevelt's earliest close adviser, used the term derisively in a conversation with the chief. Rosenman says Roosevelt himself then used it at a press conference. In any event, it caught on and stuck through the New Deal and beyond with little change in meaning. Roosevelt himself had preferred calling the original group his "privy council." Critics called it, among other things, "the Professoriat."

See KITCHEN CABINET, IRISH MAFIA and PALACE GUARD for other views of advisers, and EGGHEAD for a derogation of intellectuals.

BRAINWASH to change drastically someone's outlook and opinion pattern; to convince thoroughly, usually through nefarious means.

In current political use, totally committed supporters of an opponent's point of view are derided as "brainwashed"; that is, it is a waste of time to try to convince them of another cause. It is a scare word used in political argument, a frequent warning against being converted. When the American Medical Association chose Dr. Edward Roland Ennis to "answer" President Kennedy on the subject of MEDICARE, the doctor claimed that "the American public is in danger of being blitzed, brainwashed and bandwagoned into swallowing the idea that the King-Anderson Bill is the only proposal . . ."

The word first began to appear in 1950 to describe the technique of mental and physical torture and concentrated indoctrination cf prisoners of war held in Communist countries. "In the newly authoritarian countries," wrote the *American Journal of Psychiatry* in February 1951, "the term 'brainwashing' is born to indicate this systematic breaking down of old loyalties and paternal ties." Wrote the *New York Times* in March: "In totalitarian countries the term 'brainwashing' has been coined to describe what happens when resistance fighters are transformed into meek collaborators . . . [Cardinal] Mindszenty was spiritually softened until he became putty in the hands of his persecutors."

The word—a translation from a Chinese term for "thought reform"—gained currency during prisoner-of-war exchanges at the conclusion of the Korean conflict. Americans were shocked when 21 U.S. soldiers expressed a wish not to be repatriated. Subsequently, a new code of conduct for U.S. armed services personnel was issued to clarify a prisoner's responsibilities under the inducements and threats of "brainwashing." (For a 1941 use by Chinese leader, see Theodore H. White's memoir under CONSCIOUSNESS-RAISING.)

Michigan Governor George Romney's use of the term, in September 1967, illustrated its power. "When I came back from Vietnam [in 1965]," he told a TV interviewer, "I had just had the greatest brainwashing that anybody can get when you go over to Vietnam . . . not only by the generals but also by the diplomatic corps over there, and they do a very thorough job . . ." He had intended to imply that the reason for his change of position about the war in 1967 was that he had been misled two years before. But Romney's use of "brainwash" was in his campaign manager, Len Hall's

words, "not a plus"; ally Jacob Javits called it "inartistic"; Eugene McCarthy said "a light rinse would have been sufficient"; and the *Chicago Daily News* used several current synonyms as they asked whether the U.S. "can afford as its leader a man who, whatever his positive virtues, is subject to being cozened, flim-flammed and taken into camp." See BLOOPER.

BRASS COLLAR DEMOCRAT one who slavishly follows the party line; used mainly in the southern U.S.

Reader's Digest editor Earl Mazo, in a 1972 letter to the author disclaiming coinage of BACKLASH, referred to "brass collar Democrat" as his favorite bit of political slang. A possible allusion is to those newly freed Negroes in Reconstruction days who did not vote Republican. An early slang dictionary (Barrère and Leland, 1895) defines "Big Dog with the Brass Collar" as a leader, now shortened to "top dog." See YELLOW DOG DEMOCRAT.

BREAD-AND-BUTTER   ISSUE a POCKETBOOK ISSUE, one that affects voters' personal budgets.

Bread and butter, the staff of life slightly greased, had a stronger political meaning in 1840 when an Ohio politician named John Brough switched his vote on a bill with the explanation: "I have my bread and butter to look after." Earlier, Washington Irving had referred to these "little, beardless bread-and-butter politicians." The phrase is obviously related to "knowing which side your bread is buttered on."

"The Bread and Butter Brigade" was the derisive term applied to the appointees of President Andrew Johnson. Senator Zachary Chandler of Michigan lashed into Johnson in

1867: "[These offices] were filled by Mr. Lincoln with good, responsible, reliable Union Republicans. [They] were removed by Andrew Johnson to make place for unreliable, irresponsible Copperheads in most cases, or bread-and-butter men, who are worse." Theodore Roosevelt, in his Bull Moose campaign, wrote: "They represent the bread-and-butter politicians and the office holders. And we stand for the future."

Bread-and-butter politician fell into disuse in recent years, and when the phrase reappeared as *bread-and-butter issue*, the pejorative meaning had disappeared. It is still in current political use, though its meaning is more usually expressed as *pocketbook issue*, or one that hits the voter where it hurts. Neither is as strong as the PARAMOUNT ISSUE phrase of the late nineteenth century, or the GUT ISSUE of today.

BREAK ALL THE CHINA carry out an order regardless of obstacles.

" 'Break all the china in this building,' " counsel Charles Colson wrote that President Richard Nixon told him, " 'but have an order for me to sign on my desk Monday morning.' "

This favorite Nixon locution was probably based on "a bull in a china shop" and was taken by some aides to mean "cut through the red tape and usual objections," by other aides to mean "march over a cliff."

The phrase is occasionally used without reference to the Nixon period to describe a bureaucratic shaker-upper, with a connotation of insensitivity: "Criticism of [Director of Central Intelligence Stansfield] Turner as a breaker of china in his own agency," wrote columnists Evans and Novak in December 1977, "is hurting him in the administration."

BREZHNEV DOCTRINE, *see* **DOCTRINES.**

BRIDGE BUILDING measures to reduce the tensions and dangers of the cold war, both between the United States and the Soviet Union and, more generally, between any peoples of differing ideologies.

The bridge as a symbol of peaceful intercourse has a long history; "bridging the bloody chasm" was a phrase used by post–Civil War leaders. Its applications to American foreign policy came into wide use after Lyndon Johnson became President in 1963. In his first State of the Union message, Johnson said: "We must develop with our allies new means of bridging the gap between east and west." He and other officials repeated the phrase often enough—although with variations—to give it wide currency. Senator William Fulbright phrased it this way: "Bridges can be built across the chasm of ideology."

The expression reflected the specific and limited agreements sought, and sometimes achieved, during the Eisenhower, Kennedy, and Johnson Administrations. The partial nuclear test-ban treaty of 1963, the consular treaty ratified in 1967, increased trade relations with Eastern Europe, and other measures were significant, but they hardly constituted a general settlement.

Newspaper use of the phrase without explanation indicated its general acceptance, as when the *New York Times* said in 1967: "The Senate Foreign Relations Committee advanced the Administration's East-West bridge-building program today by approving the United States–Soviet consular treaty." Like so many political terms, bridge building can be overused, as Soviet Premier Nikita Khrushchev pointed out: "Politicians are the same all over. They promise to build a bridge even where there is no river."

Foreign relations applications of the metaphor declined after the Johnson Administration left office. But Richard Nixon, in the campaign of 1968, titled two of his key speeches "Bridges to Human Dignity" and used the phrase from time to time in his Administration to describe welfare reform and BLACK CAPITALISM.

After the 1969 episode at the Chappaquiddick bridge involving Senator Edward Kennedy, the bridge metaphor gained a tragic connotation and was temporarily dropped from political discourse.

BRING US TOGETHER   a closing-ranks theme used by President-elect Nixon on the day after the election, which critics later interpreted as a promise and frequently derided.

"I saw many signs in this campaign," said Richard Nixon on the morning after he had been elected President. "Some of them were not friendly and some were very friendly. But the one that touched me the most was one that I saw in Deshler, Ohio, at the end of a long day of whistle-stopping, a little town, I suppose five times the population was there in the dusk, almost impossible to see—but a teenager held up a sign, 'Bring Us Together.' And that will be the great objective of this Administration at the outset, to bring the American people together. This will be an open Administration, open to new ideas, open to men and women of both parties, open to the critics as well as those who support us. We want to bridge the generation gap. We want to bridge the gap between the races. We want to bring America together."

It was Richard Moore, a California communications lawyer, culling "local color" items for the candidate on the campaign trail, who got off the train in Deshler to mingle with the crowd listening to Nixon speak from the rear platform. He spotted a girl with the sign, hand-lettered and obviously not produced by the local Republican organization, and called it to the candidate's attention.

Nixon first used the phrase at the conclusion of a Madison Square Garden speech in New York City on October 31, 1968, recollecting it as "Bring us together again."

This phrase, briefly used and relatively unnoticed, was not used again in the campaign's final weekend. National unity was not the dominant theme of either candidate, as the country was so torn at the time that such a theme would have been received with scorn. (The initial Democratic posters, "United with Humphrey," were quickly scrapped.)

On Election Day, flying from California to New York aboard the *Tricia,* while the nation's citizens voted below, and frustrated at having no writing assignment after months of heavy production, the author drafted a victory statement. To have sent it to the candidate would have been an invitation to bad luck, so it was passed to Communications Director Herb Klein, who was sure to be around Nixon before he went before the cameras the next day. (No concession statement was drafted by anybody.)

Just before taking the Waldorf-Astoria elevator down to the press room, Nixon glanced at the draft. The "Bring Us Together" suggestion registered.

The *New York Times* headed the transcript "Statement by Nixon Pledging to 'Bring American Together,' " and the Inaugural Committee promptly made it the theme of their festivities. Several Nixon staff aides, this writer included, objected to this, pointing out that while "Bring Us Together" was appropriate for a victory statement, the need for unity should not suddenly be placed ahead of the need for progress; also, the phrase was a call *to* a candidate rather than a call *from* a President. The solution was "Forward Together," which served as the inaugural slogan, but which did not catch on.

The *Times* had sent a reporter and photographer to Deshler to find the little girl; they came up with Vicki Lane and a picture of the sign. The reporter quoted her as saying she saw it lying on the ground and held it up when Nixon was speaking. Since there was no reason to doubt her claim, she was brought to Washington with her family for the inaugural.

As might have been expected, whenever President Nixon took an action that aroused sharp differences of opinion, a common critical refrain was "He promised to bring us together." The phrase was used in this sarcastic sense as the title of a book by Leon Panetta and Peter Gall, once again proving that a phrase with an emotional charge can charge both ways.

BRINKMANSHIP a national security policy dictating that the nation be willing to risk large-scale—or even total—war in order to force an adversary to back down during a confrontation; when used derisively by the policy makers' critics, a reckless gamble or hollow bluff.

During the 1956 presidential campaign, Democrats led by Adlai Stevenson accused the Eisenhower Administration, and particularly Secretary of State John Foster Dulles, of "brinkmanship."

Dulles coined only part of the term

in an interview with correspondent James Shepley published by *Life* in January 1956. Said Dulles: "The ability to get to the verge without getting into the war is the necessary art. If you cannot master it, you inevitably get into war. If you try to run away from it, if you are scared to go to the brink, you are lost." Citing the 1953 Korean peace-talk crisis and the 1954 threats of major war over Formosa and Indochina, Dulles said: "We walked to the brink and we looked it in the face."

The Republicans won the election, but the debate over brinkmanship went on, keeping alive the new term. Even Sherman Adams, Eisenhower's White House aide, questioned Dulles' argument. "I doubt," Adams wrote after leaving office, "that Eisenhower was as close to the brink of war in any of these three crises as Dulles made him out to be."

The metaphor depicting nations falling into war as if plunging over the edge, or brink, of a cliff is old and much used. In 1850 Henry Clay, appealing in the U.S. Senate for amity between North and South over the slavery issue, said, "Solemnly I ask you to pause at the edge of the precipice."

Adding the *-manship* to construct a "facetious formation" is contemporary. Fowler's *Dictionary of Modern English Usage* (2nd edition) compares *brinkmanship* with earlier Stephen Potterisms such as *one-upmanship* and *gamesmanship*. However, Fowler's takes brinkmanship seriously as a word, if not a foreign policy, on the grounds that it is a necessary addition to the vocabulary. Webster's *New International Dictionary* (3rd edition) also accepts it as standard English rather than slang. John Kennedy referred to "the brink" after his 1961 meeting in Vienna with

Nikita Khrushchev and went to the brink the following year during the Cuban missile confrontation. See EYEBALL TO EYEBALL.

At the 1964 Republican convention in San Francisco, some hawkish Goldwater placard carriers waved the slogan "Better brinkmanship than chickenship."

BROKERED CONVENTION a party convention at which many key delegations are committed to FAVOR-ITE SONS, thus cutting down the first-ballot strength of the serious contenders for the nomination, and resulting in bloc bargaining.

Such a convention is dominated by factional party leaders and favorite sons, who deal directly or through "neutral leaders" (see POWER BROKERS) and throw their delegate strength to one or another candidate in return for promised positions on the ticket or in the cabinet, or simply to be with the winner.

The opposite of a *brokered convention* is an OPEN CONVENTION in which individual delegates are free to vote their personal choice. In a *locked-up* or *rigged convention,* the outcome is rarely in doubt, as when an incumbent president is a candidate for renomination or when one candidate is known to "have the tickets" or majority of delegates.

Most conventions are brokered to some degree; only when two or more candidates show real strength and when no STAMPEDE can be started does a genuine brokered convention take place.

By 1972, the proliferation of primaries and erosion of the "unit rule" made brokerage more difficult, though not impossible.

BROTHER JONATHAN early symbol for the U.S.

George Washington referred to his adviser Jonathan Trumbull, governor of Connecticut, as "brother Jonathan" recalling the second book of Samuel in the Old Testament. He may have taken this from the 1787 play *The Contrast,* by Royall Tyler, in which a character named "brother Jonathan" is portrayed as a Yankee trader.

Since a nation needs a symbol for its citizens collectively, or its average man—as the British have "John Bull" and the French "Marianne"— "brother Jonathan" became the first appellation of the typical American.

James Russell Lowell contrasted Englishmen and Americans in 1848 in this way: "To move John you must make your fulcrum of solid beef and pudding; an abstract idea will do for Jonathan."

Rarely used now, the phrase has been replaced by UNCLE SAM.

BROUHAHA, *see* **UNFLAPPA-BLE.**

BROWN DERBY SYMBOL, *see* **TAKE A WALK.**

BUCK STOPS HERE, THE the motto of President Harry S. Truman, who kept a sign with these words on his desk.

The motto meant that the presidency was, in Calvin Coolidge's words, "the place of last resort." It was especially appropriate for Truman, who had to make some momentous decisions: to drop the first atomic bomb; to order U.S. forces to South Korea; to fire General Douglas MacArthur.

Arthur Schlesinger, Jr., writing about John F. Kennedy, observed that "the Constitution made it clear where the buck stopped," and quoted Kennedy as saying: "The President bears the burden of the responsibility. . . . The advisers may move on to new advice." In a BBC interview soon after taking office, Kennedy said, "President Truman used to have a sign on this desk which said: 'The buck stops here'—these matters which involve national security and our national strength finally come to rest here."

Truman's close association with "the buck stops here" led to its present use as a synonym for final responsibility. Tom Wicker wrote in the *New York Times* in 1967: "Thus, in heightening the pressure on Hanoi, Lyndon Johnson is increasing it on himself as well. He makes the choices, and he knows where the buck stops."

The motto comes from the phrase "passing the buck," which is a poker-playing expression. See CARD META-PHORS. The buck was a marker to show who next had the deal; the buck could be passed by someone who did not want the responsibility of dealing to the man on his left. (The marker was occasionally a silver dollar, which, by the way, is how the dollar became known as a buck.)

The motto was adopted by President Jimmy Carter, who placed a small sign with those words on a table near his desk in the Oval Office.

BUG   as a verb, to eavesdrop by means of a concealed transmitter; as a noun, the tiny device used for that purpose.

"Does it have the bug?" That was a question asked by campaign managers of their advertising and printing aides, to make sure that the "union bug"—the oval emblem of the printers' union—was on all campaign literature.

This innocent meaning has been replaced by the more sinister slang meaning of "electronic eavesdrop-

ping." According to Stuart Berg Flexner, since 1889 a "bug" was a card stuck by a gambler to the underside of the gambling table, to be substituted when profitable for a card in hand; the concealed-item meaning was switched over to the little microphone-transmitters, which bore some resemblance to an insect of the same name.

Another slang meaning, the verb "to bug", means "to annoy"; when Attorney General John Mitchell spoke at a press dinner in 1970, he said facetiously, "If you quit bugging me, I'll quit bugging you." The quip, containing both senses of the term, turned out to be the opposite of prophetic.

See TAPS AND BUGS.

BULLET VOTE   one in which the voter enters the booth determined to pull the lever for one candidate and no other on the same or any competing ticket.

Such a vote is based on personal magnetism and voter service within the district rather than ideology. According to *New York Herald Tribune* reporter Tom O'Hara, left-wing New York Congressman Vito Marcantonio claimed a large portion of his support came from "bullet votes." Voters with no interest in the candidates for other offices (and who probably would not have voted at all) lined up to cast their ballots for their favorite congressman. As a result, Marcantonio's total in the forties bulged beyond the others on his ticket. After voting for Marcantonio, many voters then left the American Labor party line to choose Republican or Democratic candidates for other offices, or else cast no other votes for other offices at all. When they cast other votes on other lines, they became *split-ticket voters* (see SPLIT TICKET);

when they cast no other votes they were considered *bullet voters.*

Political leaders may plan bullet voting campaigns in runoffs or in at-large elections. When a voter has a selection of six out of twelve candidates to vote for, or when there are weights assigned to his first, second, and third choices, he may be directed to choose only one, giving no assistance to any other candidate running.

BULLY PULPIT   active use of the presidency's prestige and high visibility to inspire or moralize.

Theodore Roosevelt, a President of expansive character, took an unrestricted view of his job. In the many controversies during his two administrations, he never hesitated to take his case directly to the people from a presidency he called a "bully pulpit."

The image of the White House as a pulpit with the whole nation as congregation—linked with the zesty adjective "bully," meaning first-rate, or admirable—has been frequently used ever since. It has special pertinence in the seemingly endless analysis of active Presidents, or those who take the largest possible view of their office and powers, versus the more restrained chief executives. James MacGregor Burns, discussing the influences that helped form Franklin Roosevelt's political views, says: "T.R. and Wilson were both moral leaders . . . who used the presidency as a pulpit." FDR used the theme in 1932, calling the presidency "preeminently a place of moral leadership."

Douglass Cater recalls that John Kennedy liked to quote the "bully pulpit" phrase. "Among the multitudinous roles a president must fill," says Cater, "his greatest challenge and greatest power must be a blending of those of poet and preacher." In *A Thousand Days,* his memoir of the Kennedy Administration, Arthur M. Schlesinger, Jr., entitled one chapter "The Bully Pulpit."

Early in his presidency, Jimmy Carter used the forum of the White House to exercise some moral suasion on members of his staff: "Those of you who are living in sin, I hope you get married. Those of you who have left your spouses, come back home. Those of you who don't know your children's names, get to know them." Despite this first public use of the White House as a bully pulpit for the edification of the President's staff, it had little discernible effect on the "preacher's choir."

BUNK   pretentious nonsense; claptrap; a long-winded oration meant for hometown consumption.

"Religion is all bunk," declared Thomas Alva Edison.

"History is bunk," stated his friend Henry Ford.

Bunk is an Americanism with a history almost as rich and colorful as "OK." It is a shortening of *bunkum,* which is an altered shortening of *Buncombe,* a county in North Carolina that made up part of the district represented by Felix Walker, who sat in the House of Representatives in 1820. Walker interrupted a debate on the Missouri Compromise with a long, dull, irrelevant speech, apologizing to his impatient colleagues with the statement "I'm talking for Buncombe." In 1828, according to *Niles Weekly Register,* "talking to (or for) Buncombe" was well known. The *Wilmington* (N.C.) *Commercial* referred in 1849 to "the Buncombe politicians—those who go for re-election merely," and British author Thomas Carlyle showed that the expression traveled the Atlantic with its meaning intact: "A parliament speaking through reporters to Buncombe and the twenty seven millions, mostly fools."

The word was clipped to "bunk" toward the end of the nineteenth century, and in George Ade's *More Fables in Slang,* published in 1900, it appeared as "he surmised that the Bunk was about to be handed to him." In 1923 William E. Woodward wrote a book titled *Bunk,* and introduced the verb, to *de*bunk. A school of historians were named "debunkers" for the way they tore down the myths other historians had built up. "Hokum," according to the *OED,* is a blend of hocus-pocus and bunkum.

Another verb occasionally used is "to bunko" or "to be buncoed," which means to be cheated or swindled. The well-meaning politician from Buncombe is not the villain here; more likely, the evil meaning comes from the Spanish *banco,* or game of cards. Senator Frank Brandegee of Connecticut, one of the anti-Wilson LITTLE GROUP OF WILFUL MEN, said in the League of Nations debate: "I am not to be buncoed by any oleaginous lingo about 'humanity' or 'men everywhere.' "

BUREAUCRACY administrative agencies of government (or large private institutions) manned for the most part by career personnel and characterized by rigid adherence to rules and established procedure; almost always used in a derogatory sense.

Bureaucratic is a nineteenth-century label that has stuck for a phenomenon that goes back at least to ancient Rome and old Cathay. King or president, mayor or mandarin, every ruler needs help running things. The first echelon below the top has typically been a kind of aristocracy, whether by appointment, heredity, or election. Below that comes the civil service, or bureaucracy.

In impact on both vocabulary and life, the bureaucracy looms ever larger as the functions of government multiply. The bureaucracy is supposed to administer laws and policies framed by its superiors, but often the manner of administration looms more important than the policy handed down. "The executive bureaucrat," wrote sociologist C. Wright Mills, "becomes not only the center of decision but also the arena within which major conflicts of power are resolved or denied resolution."

The term comes from *bureau,* the French word for office, and was commonly applied to government agencies. After Napoleon's reign, a relatively permanent and quasi-autonomous civil service took firm hold in France and is generally credited with maintaining government functions through the upheavals at the top that make up so much of French history ("always falling, never fallen"). But the French system also produced the evils generally ascribed to bureaucracy. "Wherever possible," said sociologist Max Weber, "political democracy strives to shorten the term of office by election and recall. . . . Thereby democracy inevitably comes into conflict with the bureaucratic tendencies which, by its fight against notable (i.e., patrician) rule, democracy has produced."

A bureaucrat is a self-stopper. But the criticism of public servants, as they call themselves, is often politically inspired: Alben Barkley, in the 1948 Democratic convention keynote address, said "a bureaucrat is a Democrat who holds a job a Republican wants."

Bureaucrats speak *bureaucratese,* which is often called GOBBLEDYGOOK, BAFFLEGAB, PENTAGONESE, or BUZZ WORDS. Adjectives most frequently associated with bureaucracy's noun are "entrenched", "swollen," and "bloated." A favored form of communication is "touching base." When they cannot be reached, they are "in the field." For their most frequent method of self-protection, see COVER YOUR ASS.

BURNING QUESTION, *see* **TOPIC A; PARAMOUNT ISSUE.**

BUSINESS AS USUAL complacency; unconcern for imminent danger: or, determination to carry on despite danger.

Winston Churchill, speaking at the Guildhall in London in the opening days of World War I, said, "The maxim of the British people is 'Business as usual.'" This carried the same kind of bravery-in-adversity message that he restated more eloquently in the early days of World War II.

In the generation between the wars, however, the meaning of the phrase changed radically. During the Depression "no business as usual" was a wry slogan. As war approached again, a "business-as-usual policy" was denounced as unworthy of a people aware of the unusual requirements of a wartime economy. Traces of the previous defiant meaning lingered on, however; during the Battle of Britain, with London under almost constant bombardment, a small sign in the Piccadilly window of A. A. Julius, jeweler, read: "Business as Usual."

In current use, the phrase is synonymous with complacency. The 1962 "Port Huron Statement" of Students for a Democratic Society derogated the "familiar campus" as "a place of commitment to business-as-usual, getting ahead, playing it cool." Richard Neustadt in *Presidential Power* (1960) characterized the Truman-Eisenhower years as "emergencies in policy with politics as usual."

BUSING TO ACHIEVE RACIAL BALANCE the phrase that became the battleground between forces believing in the primary of the "neighborhood school" versus those who held that physical transportation of students was necessary to break down segregation.

The most controversy-laden CODE WORD of the late sixties and early seventies was "busing." (The spelling with one *s*, which looks as if it could rhyme with "confusing," triumphed over "bussing," which is synonymous with "kissing"). To many supporters of desegregation in theory, busing meant carrying the battle for civil rights into their own neighborhoods, and affected their own children; some activists felt cognitive dissonance at that point, and many parents who had been lukewarm about desegregation felt the abandonment of the tradition of keeping children in schools close to their residences was a serious mistake.

The crucial part of the phrase was "racial balance." In the legislative history of Title IV of the 1964 Civil Rights Act, the phrase first appeared (as "racial imbalance") in a message from President John F. Kennedy of June 19, 1963, recommending federal technical and financial assistance to schools which were "engaged in the process of meeting the educational problems flowing from desegregation or racial imbalance . . ."

In the House hearings on this bill, Congressman William Cramer (R-Fla.) tried to get witnesses to define "racial imbalance" with no success; accordingly, the House on January 31, 1964, adopted an amendment he submitted to provide that any definition of "desegregation" in the Civil Rights Act "shall not mean the assignment of students to public schools in order to overcome racial imbalance."

In the Senate, Hubert Humphrey (D-Minn.)—after an 83-day debate had made clear that "busing to achieving racial balance" would have to be sacrificed if any civil rights bill was to be passed—said on June 4 that the amendments dealing with busing "preclude an inference that the title confers new authority to deal with 'racial imbalance' in schools, and should serve to soothe fears that Title IV might be read to empower the Federal Government to order the busing of children around a city in order to achieve a certain racial balance or mix in schools."

The Supreme Court, in *Swann* v. *Charlotte-Mecklenburg Board of Education,* held in 1971 that this language limiting the Civil Rights Act foreclosed the granting of new powers to the courts to redress *de facto* segregation (caused by residential patterns), but did not withdraw from the courts "their historic equitable remedial powers" to strike down *de jure* segregation (caused by discriminatory action by state authorities).

In most of the political debate on the issue of busing, only the most dedicated civil rights activists defended the idea of transporting students to overcome the segregation brought about by living patterns. Changing *de facto* segregation was described as "integration," while most public opinion preferred "desegregation," which stopped short of "busing to achieve racial balance."

A litmus test of the political leanings of the speaker could be found in the adjective used to describe busing. Liberals used "involuntary busing"; conservatives or anti-busing liberals preferred "forced busing."

The word first came into the language with the double-*s* spelling, and was usually associated with military transport: "They were instructed in march-discipline," wrote Rudyard Kipling in 1923, ". . . as well as bussing and de-bussing against time into motor-buses."

See SEGREGATION; SEPARATE BUT EQUAL.

BUTTONHOLE to stop a moving delegate, engage his attention, and press for the support of a candidate or cause; in more general terms, to electioneer.

The verb is colorful because it describes the act of holding on to the persuadee's button, lapel, or any grabbable part of his clothing. The *OED* reports a pre-political usage: "Charles Lamb, being buttonheld one day by Coleridge . . . cut off the button."

The word was adopted by politicians in the mid-nineteenth century. Mark Twain, in *The Gilded Age,* recorded a friend who "bussed and 'buttonholed' Congressmen in the interest of the Columbia River scheme."

In recent years, the word is being limited in application to delegates on a convention floor. In the raucous 1940 Republican convention that nominated Wendell Willkie, the Willkie supporters who overflowed onto the convention floor (see PACKING THE GALLERIES) caused the head of the New Hampshire delegation to shout into the microphone: "Mr. Chairman! I call the attention of the chair to the fact that many people are in the aisles and buttonholing delegates, who have no right to be on the floor of the convention." The chairman's gavel cut off the buttonholers.

A related phrase is "nickel-and-diming," the pursuit of support down to the small change of personal persuasion of individual delegates by the candidate. Gerald Ford's press secretary, Ron Nessen, wrote in his 1978 memoir *It Sure Looks Different from the Inside* of the 1976 Republican delegate hunt:

> Ford . . . appealed to individual uncommitted delegates by phone. He invited many delegates to the White House. . . . it was called "nickel-and-diming," trying to win the necessary delegates one by one . . .

> A joke went around illustrating how some uncommitted delegates played hard-to-get. It seems one delegate from New Jersey received a phone call from the President inviting him to a reception and state banquet for Queen Elizabeth at the White House. There was a long pause of indecision and then, according to the gag, the delegate asked Ford, "What's for dinner?"

BUTTONS, CAMPAIGN a device for a shy voter to communicate his preference; one of the few "absolute musts" in a campaign budget that managers agree is largely a waste of money; a stimulus to enthusiasm of workers.

When the wearing of campaign buttons was spoken of as inelegant in 1900, Congressman E. L. Hamilton of Michigan angrily rose to his feet in the House of Representatives. "The wearing of a campaign button is a harmless sort of decoration," he began, "but a social condition that dictates to a man what kind of a button he shall wear approaches a condition of tyranny, and makes a man want to stick campaign buttons all over him, and protect his privilege with a Gatling gun!"

With the freedom to wear buttons given this First Amendment umbrella, their use proliferated. Button manufacturers like Emanuel Ress

("The Button King") recalled an upsurge in 1940 ("Eleanor Start Packing —The Willkies are Coming," "No Third Term," "Two Good Terms Deserve Another").

Rhyme has always been important to button-makers. "I Like Ike" appeared on buttons manufactured in 1947 (as Eisenhower began to be spoken of as a possible Democratic nominee); "Who Else But Nelse" (Rockefeller), "Madly for Adlai" (Stevenson), "All the Way with LBJ" (Johnson), "Who but Hubert" (Humphrey), and "The Grin Will Win" (Carter) followed.

The style of button showing the candidate's picture and name with some patriotic symbol was replaced by the picture-plus-slogan button in the forties, and gradually the use of pictures on buttons has declined. In 1964, anti-Goldwater forces sported "Extremism in the Pursuit of Vice is No Virtue." When General Eisenhower told that convention to beware of "sensation-seeking columnists," button men within three hours turned out "Sensation Seeking Press" buttons for reporters, along with "Stamp Out Huntley-Brinkley."

In the 1965 John Lindsay campaign for mayor of New York, Adam Mark Lawrence came in with "a great idea for a Lindsay button," which was a button with the copy "Lindsay button." This was followed by buttons that simply said "Button" ("for the sort of people who like to call their dog 'dog' ").

Gold lapel pins and cufflinks, advanced forms of buttonry, are often used as fund-raising devices. "The most successful 'button,' " wrote Ted Sorensen, "was a tie clasp in the form of Kennedy's old PT boat. It became a popular badge for Kennedy supporters and a fast-selling item in the

'Dollars for Democrats' drive." See CUFFLINKS GANG.

There was a tendency in the mid-sixties to use campaign buttons when there was no political campaign. Many carried a social rather than political message: "Make Love Not War," "I Am A Human Being: Do Not Fold, Spindle or Mutilate," "Turn On, Tune In, Drop Out." A wide variety of gag buttons were sold: "Support Mental Health Or I'll Kill You," "Kill a Commie for Christ," "Leisure Suits Make You Sterile," etc.

Many hardened political operatives who would never be caught wearing any button cannot resist one sold at the end of campaigns: "Good Job, Kid . . . Now Get Lost."

BUZZWORD   jargon; or, a vague vogue word intended to trigger a stereotyped response.

A buzzword can be a CODE WORD that appeals to the emotions. When President Carter, angered at the congressional mangling of his energy proposals in October 1977, lashed the oil-industry lobbyists in tones reminiscent of Harry Truman, American Gas Association president George Lawrence replied, "While buzzwords like 'war profiteers' and 'rob' and 'ripoff' might prove successful in inflaming public opinion, they cannot substitute for the production incentives so flagrantly lacking in the Administration's energy plan."

The more common meaning of "buzzword" comes from the derivation of "buzz" as a verbalized hum or hiss: a sense-dulling bit of jargon that puts the outsider to sleep. In a 1974 book, *Buzzwords,* Robert Kirk Mueller defined the word on the cover as "words, phrases or zingo-lingo used by an ingroup, a cult, or the cognoscenti for rapid communication

within the group . . . it refers also to the verbal, intellectual one-upmanship of the cant, slang, jargon, argot and pseudo-tribal language, used by relatively small groups for their own benefit and to help isolate the group from the hoi polloi . . . a sort of pro's prose." He credits the word's coinage to Professor Ralph Hower of Harvard, who "used the label *buzzwords* for those phrases that have a pleasant buzzing sound in your ears while you roll them on your tongue and that may overwhelm you into believing you know what you're talking about when you don't."

Some buzzwords listed in that book are "conceptual framework" (a grand-design favorite of Henry Kissinger's); "going toes up" or "going down the tubes" (to fail); "junior angel" (euphemism for the euphemism "senior citizen"). For others, see PENTAGONESE; BAFFLEGAB; GOBBLEDYGOOK; CIA-ESE.

BY-ELECTION   an election in a locality between general elections.

This is British usage; Americans prefer "special election" to describe a race that takes place when an incumbent dies or resigns. "By-electioneering" is campaigning by or for candidates during these times, and it is interpreted as a test for the popularity of the party in power.

BYZANTINE   Machiavellian; characterized by scheming, double-crossing, backbiting and similarly nefarious behavior often attributed to the denizens of the center of power; or, labyrinthine, arcane, mysteriously complex.

The word was probably introduced to politics by Theodore Roosevelt about 1916, criticizing President Woodrow Wilson as a "Byzantine logothete." Since a logothete in

Byzantium was an accountant, or collector of revenues (from the Greek "to put to account"), former President Roosevelt was derogating President Wilson as one who fiddled with a pencil while World War I called for American intervention.

But "Byzantine" in that phrase only located the main word, which was "logothete"; the Machiavellian nature of the word "Byzantine" did not appear until later.

Arthur Koestler was fond of using this word to describe intricate political workings: "In the old days people often smiled at the Byzantine structure of the Spanish Army," he wrote in 1937, adding in another work eight years later: "The antidote to Eastern Byzantinism is Western revolutionary humanism." That Koestler use is the meaning in Britain today; the 1972 supplement to the *OED* defines the word as "the spirit of Byzantine politics. Hence, intricate, complicated; inflexible, rigid, unyielding."

A different, if related, meaning prevails in the U.S. "Was French party politics," Peter Braestrup wrote in the *New York Times* in 1966, "with its Byzantine maneuvers and its feuding factions, really en route to a transformation?" To most U.S. political writers, the synonym for Byzantine is "devious."

To a churchman, "Byzantinism" has an altogether different meaning: the denial of religious freedom, or the belief that the civil power controls the spiritual power.

The adjective comes from the city of Byzantium, later Constantinople, now Istanbul, which became the capital of the Roman Empire around A.D. 330, and for seven hundred years was the main repository of Roman and Greek civilization.

However, the court of the emperor —usually named Constantine—was marked by rivalries, duplicity and violence, giving the city and the word a bad name today. In fairness, it should be pointed out that this moral decay notwithstanding, the empire was enlarged, civilization spread despite the Visigoths and Vandals, and Russia was converted to Christianity. Notes the *Columbia Encyclopedia,* looking for the brighter side of the maneuvering: "In the unceasing struggle between the great landowners and the small peasantry, most of the emperors favored the peasants. Economic prosperity was paralleled by a new golden age in science, philosophy and architecture." For the complete story of the fall, see Gibbon.

CABAL group hatching a dark political plot; always carries a sinister connotation.

Derived from the Hebrew word *qabbalah,* the mystical interpretation of Scripture said to be handed down to the rabbis by Moses, the word was popularized in the Middle Ages by "Cabalists," a splinter movement in Judaism protesting against religious formalism. The system degenerated into occult formulas and medieval magic.

An inner group of advisors to Charles II of England was known as the "Cabal," legend has it, because the initials of their last names— Chudleigh, Ashley, Buckingham, Arlington, and Lauderdale—formed the word.

John Quincy Adams wrote in his diary of 1821: "I would take no one step to advance or promote pretensions to the Presidency. If that office was to be the prize of cabal and intrigue, of purchasing newspapers, bribing by appointments, or bargaining for foreign missions, I had no ticket in that lottery."

George Brinton McClellan Harvey, editor of *Harper's Weekly,* used the term to describe the group of "irreconcilables" (including Senators Lodge, Brandegee and McCormack) who opposed Woodrow Wilson's League of Nations just after World War I.

William Allen White of the *Emporia Gazette* believed a cabal was responsible for Warren Gamaliel Harding's nomination during the 1920 Republican National Convention. He wrote: "Oil controlled the convention of 1920. It worked through the 'Senate cabal' whose members were so busy hating Wilson that they became easy victims of the greed for oil."

Former President Dwight D. Eisenhower refused to join what he termed a cabal organized prior to the 1964 Republican convention. Refuting newspaper statements claiming he was supporting Governor William Scranton of Pennsylvania for the presidential nomination, the General informed Governor Scranton that he would be no part of a "stop Goldwater" movement forming within party ranks: the movement promptly collapsed.

CAESARISM, *see* **ELEPHANT, REPUBLICAN.**

CALCULATED RISK action taken when inaction or an alternate course offer greater possibilities of danger; a step soberly taken after the likely consequences have been assessed.

This is believed to be a World War II phrase of Army Air Force origin; risks of possible bomber losses were calculated before missions were decided upon. A play by Joseph Hayes, *Calculated Risk,* appeared on Broadway in 1961. Mrs. Omar Bradley told the author in 1978 that the phrase was coined by her husband in a wartime briefing.

Whenever a political figure takes a chancy step, he often labels it a "calculated risk," indicating he fully understands what he is likely to suffer. In a sense, it is a pre-alibi statement.

Humorist James Thurber, writing in *Punch,* put it this way: "I have made some study of the smoke-screen phrases of the political terminologists, and they have to be described rather than defined. Calculated Risk, then, goes like this: 'We have every hope and assurance that the plan will be successful, but if it doesn't work we knew all the time it wouldn't and said so.' "

"With what he [President Kennedy] privately acknowledged to be a 'calculated risk,' " wrote Ted Sorensen, "he named a panel of conservative private enterprise skeptics to review his 1963 AID request. That panel, under General Lucius Clay, recommended cuts while strongly defending the program. [Appropriations Subcommittee Chairman Otto] Passman and Company ignored the defense, accepted the cuts and made still more cuts—and Kennedy's gamble backfired."

CAMELOT   an idealization of the Administration of President John F. Kennedy; now usually used in irony.

Camelot, in the legend of King Arthur, was the city that was home to the Knights of the Round Table. A Lerner-Loewe musical drama of that title starring Richard Burton and Julie Andrews was popular on Broadway at the beginning of the Kennedy Administration, and its evocation of excellence, hope, taste and high courage was seized upon as symptomatic of the idealism of the "new generation" to whom the torch had been passed in Washington, D.C.

Satirist Vic Gold defined the word in 1969 as "mythical U.S. Liberal era" when all men were equal, all women were beautiful, witty, wellgroomed, and *Republicans knew their place.* See also **GOVERNMENT-IN-EXILE.**

CHARISMA was much spoken of at the time, but the years brought a sober reassessment. "Lyndon Johnson suffered to the end," wrote Russell Baker in 1974, after the Nixon resignation, "from the suspicion that he lacked both 'charisma' and 'style,' and often seemed deluded by the notion that but for their lack he could have raised a higher 'Camelot.' " Deriding the public relations style of the Nixon men and alluding to the development of this kind of "p.r." in the Kennedy days, Baker observed: "Politicians will not revive 'Camelot' for a while now. Every disaster has its bright side."

In the seventies, especially after the revelations of the Senate Select Committee on Intelligence in 1975, the political fashion was to denigrate the "false hopes" of the Kennedy years, and to use the term "Camelot" in so doing. "Camelittle" was one disparagement, and when a woman friend of President Kennedy was revealed to have been simultaneously seeing a Chicago mobster, *Newsweek* headlined the story "Cloud over Camelot."

The vision of the seat of government as a citadel of hope will probably reappear one day, possibly with the Camelot connotation, because it is so deeply rooted in the American self-image. "The eyes of all people are upon us," John Winthrop said in 1630, at the founding of the Massachusetts Bay Colony. ". . . we shall be made a story and a byword throughout the world . . . we shall be a City upon a Hill."

CAMPAIGN as a noun, the term is applied to virtually all phases of an effort to win any kind of election, but most particularly the phase involving open, active electioneering; as a verb, to strive for a political nomination or office.

This term has been part of American politics at least since the turn of the nineteenth century. In Massachusetts, John Quincy Adams observed that the 1816 "parliamentary campaign hitherto has been consumed in one laborious effort to suppress the reformers." To provincial journals far inland, the term was already familiar.

"Campaign" comes from the French word for open, level country and evolved from there into the military vocabulary, where it was first used to denote the amount of time an army was kept in the field, and later a particular military operation. In seventeenth-century England, the term was extended to politics and usually meant a session of a legislative body. The meaning further changed in transatlantic passage and has since expanded in meaning as the business of getting elected to public office has grown more complex. But the idea that politics is a form of combat remains. See ARENA. When he accepted the Democratic nomination for president in 1932, Franklin Roosevelt told the convention: "This is more than a political campaign. It is a call to arms."

For other political terms with military origins, see ON THE POINT and MILITARY METAPHORS.

CAMPAIGN ORATORY exaggerated charges, promises, or claims made during the heat of a campaign, expected by the speaker to be taken with a grain of salt, to be deprecated and softened after the campaign is over.

Thomas Macaulay once observed: "The object of oratory alone is not truth, but persuasion." Theodore Roosevelt told Henry L. Stimson, in regard to William Howard Taft's campaigning: "Darn it, Harry, a campaign speech is a poster, not an etching!" Stimson got the point, and later wrote: "A man's campaign speeches are no proper subject for the study of a friendly biographer." Theodore Sorensen agreed: "John Kennedy would not want to be measured solely by the speeches we ground out day and night across the country—and neither would I . . . some, particularly near the close, were overly caustic and captious in their criticism of Nixon."

Arthur Schlesinger, Jr., made the same point: "[Kennedy] began by appearing to adopt the thesis that the State Department should have listened to its pro-Batista ambassadors and recognized the revolution as a communist conspiracy from the outset. This differed markedly from his interpretation in *The Strategy of Peace.* Doubtless it was campaign oratory."

The phrase was firmly fixed in the political lexicon by Wendell Willkie during the campaign of 1940. His hoarse voice had rasped: ". . . if the present Administration is restored to power for a third term our democratic system will not outlast another four years." And "on the basis of his past performance with pledges to the people, you may expect war by April, 1941 if he [FDR] is elected." After his defeat, Willkie traveled to England, held long talks with Winston Churchill, and returned to the U.S. to urge that the U.S. send Britain all available bombers. In Lend-Lease hearings, Senator Gerald P. Nye (R-N.D.) asked how he could square that position with his earlier charges against

FDR. Willkie took a long pause in his testimony, grinned and shrugged: "It was just a bit of campaign oratory."

Representative Joseph P. Martin, then Republican National Chairman, recalls: "Republicans in Congress were particularly incensed . . . it undermined all the criticism that had been made of the President's foreign policy in the campaign."

Just as there is an unwritten law that takes for granted campaign exaggerations, there is also an unwritten law that a candidate may not afterward disown his campaign statements and leave his supporters in exposed positions.

CAMPAIGN PROMISES pledges made by a candidate to gain certain things for his constituents after election.

This is probably the oldest form of politicking since elections began. Said a sign on a first-century Roman wall: "Genialis urges the election of Bruttius Balbus as duovir [commission member]. He will protect the treasury." A candidate's promises, like a party platform, are rarely taken as literal commitments. Often they seem part of a game in which candidates out-promise each other, accuse each other of making rash promises and cite the opposition's unfulfilled promises left over from previous elections.

Occasionally a particular promise takes on major—even historic—importance. One such was Dwight Eisenhower's pledge to go to Korea if elected in 1952. But for the most part, Bernard Baruch's admonition seems valid. "Vote for the man who promises least," said Baruch. "He'll be the least disappointing."

The classic campaign-promise story is recounted by Senator Russell Long (D-La.) about his uncle, Gover-

nor Earl Long. He had promised voters the right to elect their local sheriffs, but once in office, went in the opposite direction. When a delegation came to "Uncle Earl's" office to protest, Senator Long tells the author, "Uncle Earl told his right-hand man, 'I don't want to see 'em—you see 'em.' His aide said, 'What'll I tell 'em?' And Uncle Earl said, right out, 'Tell 'em I lied!' "

CAMPAIGN SONGS ditties using the candidates' names, usually putting words to melodies already popular and whipped up for use at rallies, conventions and similar events; occasionally, a tune and set of lyrics adopted whole as a candidate's theme.

Although few major campaigns run their course today without producing a song or two, political music had its zenith in the nineteenth century, when not only was one's candidate boosted, but the opposition roundly and rhythmically knocked. William Henry Harrison became famous in the Indian battle of Tippecanoe, Indiana Territory, in 1811. Thus the song when he ran for President against the more citified Martin Van Buren in 1840: "Old Tip he wears a homespun coat./He has no ruffled shirt-wirt;/But Mat he has a golden plate,/And he's a little squirt-wirt-wirt." Said a contemporary journalist: "It was a ceaseless torrent of [Whig] music. . . . If a Democrat tried to speak, argue or answer . . . he was only saluted with a fresh deluge." When Harrison's grandson Benjamin ran in 1888, the Republicans sang: "Yes, Grandfather's hat fits Ben—fits Ben;/ He wears it with dignified grace, oh yes!"

The "Battle Hymn of the Republic" provided music for songs both pro and con. The opposition in 1872 sang: "We'll hang Horace Greeley to a sour apple tree . . ." Four years later, the Republican supporters of Rutherford Hayes and William Wheeler offered this chorus: "Glory, glory Hayes and Wheeler./As we go voting on." Candidates generally grin and bear the songs invented for them. Growled U. S. Grant: "I know but two tunes; one of them is Yankee Doodle and the other isn't."

Ring Lardner wrote a number called "Teddy, You're a Bear" in honor of Bull Mooser Theodore Roosevelt. Some of the most famous campaign songs of the twentieth century were Al Smith's theme, "Sidewalks of New York," FDR's "Happy Days Are Here Again" and Eisenhower's "I Like Ike" by Irving Berlin. The rousing tune of "Hello, Dolly" became "Hello, Lyndon" for political purposes in 1964; when Goldwater enthusiasts tried "Hello, Barry," producer David Merrick, a Democrat, threatened to sue.

Political headquarters are deluged with campaign songs to this day. In the 1961 New York mayoralty campaign, a songwriter came up with "Lefkowitz, Gilhooley and Fino," an original ditty which when translated and sung in Spanish for the city's Puerto Rican residents was astonishing in its lack of impact.

CAMPAIGN TRAIL, *see* **STUMP; HUSTINGS.**

CAMPAIGN TRAIN a caravan on rails, containing candidate, political advisers, press, local candidates, and supporters, with an aura of "going to the people."

There are no free train rides for candidates, including Presidents who are campaigning. The Interstate Commerce Commission in the Taft Administration laid down the rule to stop "deadheading" by politicians. This rule was bent slightly in the case of Presidents requiring Secret Service accompaniment, after Calvin Coolidge decided to save some money by traveling to the Black Hills of South Dakota as a drawing-room passenger.

FDR, not especially remembered for his railroad campaigning, covered more than 350,000 miles in 399 railroad trips during his presidency, many on campaign jaunts. "On his trips," wrote White House correspondent Charles Hurd, "Roosevelt normally had to buy from six to eight tickets—for himself, Mrs. Roosevelt or other family members, and for two or three actual staff members. Newspapers were billed for the transportation of their representatives. The Treasury Department paid for the Secret Service agents. . . . Thus in pinchpenny luxury the President toured the country in what was euphemistically described as 'The Presidential Special Train.' "

Thomas E. Dewey called his campaign train "The Victory Special," and it was the scene of a grievous error (See **BLOOPER**); Harry Truman popularized a new political word (See **WHISTLESTOPPING**) in his 21,000-mile, 300-speech **GIVE 'EM HELL** campaign of 1948; Barry Goldwater named his train the *"Baa Hozhnilne"* (Navaho for "To Win Over"), and Lyndon Johnson, campaigning for Vice President in 1960, cut a swath through the South in his "Corn Pone Special."

The pressures of life on a campaign train were described by **PERENNIAL CANDIDATE** Harold Stassen, explaining why General Eisenhower in 1952 allowed himself to be persuaded to remove a statement about General George Marshall from a speech in an area friendly to Senator Joseph McCarthy. "It's easy to judge harshly," Stassen said, "sitting back here in New York and not knowing the pressures that go on inside that insane campaign train. You are trapped there. There are just a few people near you whom you trust. You don't have a chance to get out in the clean air and think things through. ... And when all of them around you gang up, to insist you do this or that, it is just about impossible to fight back."

A campaign train, in an era of television and jet airplanes, symbolizes the old virtues of face-to-face personal campaigning, of "life on the campaign trail," of "being out on the hustings." A candidate seeking votes in this manner shows he is trying, proves that he is a real campaigner; since television crews accompany the train, the "whistlestop" audiences are not really small. In modern times, the campaign train has become a useful, expensive "prop" or backdrop for speeches.

CAMP DAVID, *see* **SPIRIT OF.**

CANDIDATE *"a* candidate" is an office seeker, often the object of scorn; *"the* candidate" is the party's chosen standard-bearer, cherished and adulated by his supporters, a worrisome threat to opponents.

Candidates for high office come in all sizes, from James Madison (five feet four inches, 100 pounds) to Abraham Lincoln (six feet four inches) to William Howard Taft (332 pounds); from not too many backgrounds (25 out of 38 Presidents were lawyers, 5 soldiers, 4 lifelong politicians, 2 engineers, 1 editor); and with a good education (only 9 Presidents never attended college; of the 28 who did, 9 were Phi Beta Kappa).

The word comes from the Latin *candidatus,* wearer of a white toga, which the Roman office seekers always wore as a symbol of purity. The same root gave the language "candor" and "incandescence," qualities that candidates occasionally have.

Candidates have a variety of styles and methods of campaigning (see WHISTLESTOPPING; FRONT-PORCH CAMPAIGN; WHIRLWIND CAMPAIGN, even WHISPERING CAMPAIGN) and surround themselves in different ways (see BRAIN TRUST; PALACE GUARD).

Few candidates will confess that they hate the idea of meeting people (see PRESSING THE FLESH) or attending dinners (see RUBBER-CHICKEN CIRCUIT). All claim to find campaigning exhilarating and a "great opportunity to meet the people"; some actually find it so. Many have to grit their teeth to crack a smile and some would rather shake a fist than shake a hand.

In Shakespeare's *Coriolanus,* the proud Roman general becomes a candidate for consul and must submit to the indignity of soliciting votes from common citizens. He puts on the white toga and asks a citizen: "Well then, I pray, your price of the consulship?" The imperious general is startled by the citizen's mild, perceptive reply: "The price is to ask it kindly."

Candidates may be *undeclared* (example: Edmund Muskie in 1971) or DARK HORSE (James Polk in 1844, Wendell Willkie in 1940); perennial (see PERENNIAL CANDIDATE); they may be *reluctant,* as Adlai Stevenson was described in 1952, or *captive* (see CAPTIVE CANDIDATE), as Stevenson called Eisenhower in 1952; they may style themselves as *unbossed* candidates or *no-deal* candidates, or be styled by their opponents as "the candidate of the *far right* (or the *far left*)." In current use an *undeclared* candidate needs only a formal announcement, at which point he becomes an *avowed* candidate.

At a Republican governors conference in 1967, Nelson Rockefeller declined to hold a press conference because, as he said, "I am not a candidate." When reporters complained that another noncandidate, Ronald Reagan, had held a press conference earlier that week, Rockefeller smiled and said, "Well, he's a different kind of not-a-candidate."

CANINE METAPHORS, *see* **BIRD DOG; CHECKERS SPEECH; FALA SPEECH.**

CANNIBALISM, *see* **IDEOLOGY.**

CANT favorite words of public figures.

Eighteenth-century English theologian William Paley observed: "There is such a thing as a peculiar word or phrase cleaving, as it were, to the memory of a writer or speaker, and presenting itself to his utterance at every turn. When we observe this, we call it a cant word or cant phrase."

A word that keeps popping up in Thomas Jefferson's writings is "boisterous": "Timid men . . . prefer the calm of despotism to the boisterous sea of liberty." "The whole commerce between master and slave is a perpetual exercise of the most boisterous passions." And Theodore Roosevelt, exponent of "the strenuous life," used the word "strenuous" repeatedly.

Adlai Stevenson had an addiction for "felicitous"; his friend, Arthur Schlesinger, Jr., turns often to "odious." John F. Kennedy used "vigor" so often and with such a distinctive Boston accent ("vigah") that it became the butt of jokes; Dwight Eisenhower harped on "deeds"; Lyndon Johnson probably used "must" more often than any other President (thirty-one times in his 1964 message to Congress alone); and Richard Nixon liked to say "let me make one thing perfectly clear" until it became too much of a trademark. Jimmy Carter lays great stress on his aversion to "disharmoniousness" and "incompatibility."

CAN'T-WIN TECHNIQUE a method of pouring cold water on a hot candidacy; an appeal to delegates to set aside affection and loyalty and even their judgment of ability, to concentrate on the man with "winability," the best chance to win.

"Perhaps the most important single influence in the decision of the delegates," observed Thomas E. Dewey in 1950, "is whether they believe a candidate can win if he is nominated."

Henry Clay was among the first to find that out. As a national figure in 1840 and as leader of one of the Whig factions opposing Martin Van Buren and the Jacksonian Democrats, the senator from Kentucky had considerable delegate strength. Thurlow Weed of New York, a powerful behind-the-scenes political figure, decided on the anti-Clay strategy: "Clay can't win." To undermine Clay's support, Weed organized a "triangular correspondence": men professing to be Clay supporters wrote to other state leaders hoping they were having better luck drumming up Clay support than the writer. The men who received the letters were also in on the plot: they in turn showed the letters to genuine Clay supporters with a sorrowful "we like him, but Clay can't win." It worked.

In more recent times, Ohio Senator Robert A. Taft—"Mr. Republican" —lost the nomination to Willkie in 1940, let Ohio John Bricker make the race in 1944 (on the Dewey ticket), lost to Dewey in 1948, and lost his last chance to Eisenhower in 1952.

Taft had been given a taste of the "Taft can't win" treatment in 1948, and tried to bury it forever in a landslide senatorial victory in 1950. He carried Ohio by 430,000 votes that year, in the teeth of vigorous labor opposition; despite the impressive demonstration, he was met in the 1952 convention with the same headshaking—"Taft can't win."

What is called today a "loser image" is a hard thing to shake, and has roots deep in the convention system. "While there are doubts as to my fitness for President," muttered one of the earliest Republicans, Horace Greeley, "nobody seems to deny that I would make a capital beaten candidate."

To be accused of being "one of life's losers" is a hard charge to shake off, especially in a field where the graceful acceptance of defeat is not widely admired. ("Show me a good loser, and I'll show you a loser" was a saying attributed to Henry Kissinger in 1974.) Only election victory can dispose of a loser image; curiously, a triumph over a "can't win" charge in gaining a nomination is itself a long step toward establishing "winability." Richard Nixon showed that in his comeback of 1968; he was later accused of being a "sore winner."

CANUCKS   French Canadians.
In the primary campaign of 1972, Democratic Senator Edmund Muskie of Maine, campaigning in the snows of New Hampshire, was hit by a charge scrawled in a letter to the *Manchester Union Leader* that the candidate, while in Florida, had laughed at a description of French-Canadians as "Canucks."

The "Canuck letter" is now judged to have been spurious, and the Florida incident denied; a White House aide was charged with the DIRTY TRICK, and denied it. But the Canuck charge, along with printed derogation of his wife, brought a reaction from Muskie that was seen as excessively tearful and cost him much support.

The author, in a *New York Times* column, used "Canuck" in passing and received an objection from a fellow writer who said it was a racial or national slur. A query to the *Régie de la Langue Française* in Quebec brought this response from Jacques Robichaud, Secretary:

French-Canadians do not use the word "Canuck." English-speaking Canadians use it sparingly in familiar speech, for example: "The Vancouver Canuck Hockey Team." I am personally unaware that the use of this word by Canadians of either language offends Canadians of French descent.

I must therefore refer you back to the original or present general users of the word. As mentioned in the excerpt from a *Canadian Encyclopedia* attached to your letter, those who have coined this expression were thus referring to English-speaking Canadians originally. It is quite likely that, as a result of the migration of some one and a half million French-Canadians to the New England States in the second half of the 19th Century, the word "Canuck" became primarily associated with them during that period. Today, as suggested in that same encyclopedia, the word refers to any Canadian of either French or English ancestry.

In the final analysis, the context in which a word is used is the only, the real guide as to whether or not it is derogatory.

The Prime Minister of Canada, Pierre Trudeau, also queried, also responded in 1977:

As with all slang, and especially that of nationality, the implications of the word vary a great deal according to the context and the intent of the speaker or writer. Opinion also varies as to who exactly is designated by the word Canuck. Many Canadians feel it refers to all Canadians, some believe it is Eastern Canadians, others that it is French Canadians, while the majority have rarely heard it used in any context. Although much less widely used than the word "Yankee," its connotations have more or less the same range. We have a hockey team called the Vancouver Canucks, as you have a baseball team called the New York Yankees. "Johnny Canuck" was the personification of an English Canadian war hero in a comic strip. The Yankee of "I'm a Yankee doodle dandy . . ." is not the same as 'Yankee, go home.' Thus, you can see that the question you have posed is not easily answered. Whether or not you committed an ethnic slur would depend entirely on the way the word was used.

You asked more precisely about French Canadians' attitude to this word. Personally, I have never heard it used pejoratively in connection with French Canadians, nor have I ever heard or read the term being used by French Canadians.

These comments are not intended as an official definition but rather as my own feelings in this regard. I think that in closing I might mention that, to me, a slang term applied to a nationality by a person of a different nationality could, under certain conditions, be construed as a slur.

Mitford Mathews, editor of the *Dictionary of Americanisms,* wrote in *American Speech* magazine in 1974 that he suspected the word came from the South Sea Island *kanakas,* as reported by Richard Henry Dana in his 1840 *Two Years Before the Mast.* He cites M. Schele de Vere's 1872 entry in *Americanisms: the English of the New World: "Canacks, Canucks* and *K'nucks* are slang terms by which the Canadians are known in the United States and among themselves." Mr. Mathews adds: "If *Canack* instead of *Canuck* had become the current spelling, we might have been spared any puzzlement about its source. It is clearly the shortened form of *Kanaka."*

CANVASS as a verb, to determine the degree of support for a candidate, and sometimes in so doing, to solicit support for the candidate; as a noun, an election or a survey.

The meaning of this word is in the process of changing. The root may be the Old French *canabasser,* to scrutinize, or literally to sift through canvas. For many years, the political meaning of the noun *canvass* was the final scrutiny of an election count, resulting in certification or if necessary re-count. Lord Bryce used this meaning in 1888. "If all the returns have not been received, the canvass must be postponed." The noun also used to mean "election," as in Theodore Roosevelt's use in a boast to Henry Cabot Lodge that he had made "a rattling canvass, with heavy inroads into the Democratic vote."

Within recent years, a second meaning for both noun and verb has been developing: finding out voter sentiment before the votes are cast. Pollsters canvass voters to find out their attitudes. The third—and newest—meaning carries over some of the polling connotation: "canvassers" in current usage are supporters of a candidate who survey other voters with the intent of persuading the doubtful and making sure the "committed" get a reminder telephone call to turn out on Election Day. Frances Costikyan, a Manhattan district leader and wife of the former leader of Tammany

Hall, describes some of the techniques of canvassing:

> . . . canvassing in person is infinitely more effective than a telephone campaign. As any salesman can tell you, it is much harder for people to say "no" face to face. A personal visit gives the voter a chance to size up the worker, to ask questions that bother him in a quiet conversational tone. . . . Most captains have discovered that those who live in the lower floors of the walk-ups (which are the slightly more expensive apartments) and the lower floors of the high-rise buildings (which are the slightly less expensive apartments) are much easier people to talk to. The very poor on the top floors of the walk-ups and the very rich on the top floors of the elevator buildings are too reluctant to commit themselves to anything as public or "controversial" as politics, or too uninterested, to be bothered with us.

A British canvasser is a "knocker-up."

CAPITALISM, see **AMERICAN WAY OF LIFE; FREE ENTERPRISE.**

CAPTIVE CANDIDATE one who is under the domination of others; an attack phrase used when the opponent is too well liked for direct assault.

The phrase came into prominence during the 1952 presidential campaign. Republicans first attacked Adlai Stevenson as being "the captive of the big-city bosses," particularly Jake Arvey of Chicago. Stevenson took up the phrase and turned it around:

> They describe me as a "captive" candidate. They say I am the "captive" of the big city bosses, and then of the CIO, and then of the Dixiecrats, and then of Wall Street, and then of an organization called

A.D.A. . . . I had no idea I was so popular, and I hope I can bear this multiple courtship and captivity with becoming modesty . . . meanwhile, it's not too uncomfortable to be captured by most everybody—except the Republican Old Guard!

After General Eisenhower had won the 1952 Republican nomination in Chicago and had a unity meeting with his opponent, Senator Robert A. Taft (see **SURRENDER ON MORNINGSIDE HEIGHTS**), Democrats pressed hard on the "captive" idea, since it was difficult to attack Eisenhower directly. "I am beginning to wonder who won at Chicago," said Stevenson. "Perhaps there is a six-star general somewhere in the Republican party."

The phrase harks back to images of Harding manipulated by the predatory men around him; it has been used on all levels of politics when a popular candidate offers little chance for an attack.

CARD-CARRYING committed; firmly a member of; dedicated.

The phrase gained currency in the thirties, used to differentiate "hardcore" Communist party members from **FELLOW TRAVELERS,** "leftwingers," and others without actual membership who sympathized with Communist party aims.

Senator Joseph McCarthy revived the phrase in the early fifties with his charge that there were "card-carrying Communists" in the State Department.

The phrase was adopted, in a jocular way, to describe dedicated, **ROCK-RIBBED** Republicans; ". . . one Chicago newspaperman last week characterized him [Robert A. Taft]," wrote a *New York Times* reporter in 1952, "as a 'card-carrying Republican.' " Syndicated columnist William

S. White wrote in 1967 of Richard Nixon that "he is still Mr. Republican to the regular and, so to speak, card-carrying Republicans." The new use cannot be applied to liberals, but can be used to describe conservatives, because of the sharpness of the contrast.

A candidate who has suffered through defeats or has labored for the party is said to have "paid his dues."

CARD METAPHORS
"The bizarre world of cards," wrote Ely Culbertson, bridge expert active in public affairs, is "a world of pure power politics where rewards and punishments were meted out immediately. A deck of cards was built like the purest of hierarchies, with every card a master to those below it, a lackey to those above it. And there were 'masses'—long suits—which always asserted themselves in the end, triumphing over the kings and aces."

Because of the play of power in card games, the metaphor has been applied to politics for centuries. A German poet in 1521 talked of rearranging the affairs of men by "shuffling the cards in a better way," and Thomas Hobbes, in his *Leviathan* (1651) wrote: ". . . there is no honour military but by war, nor any such hope to mend an ill game, as by causing a new shuffle."

In U.S. politics, John Quincy Adams referred to Henry Clay, a renowned poker player, as "a gamester in politics as well as cards." A poker player a century later, Warren G. Harding, explained his own selection as a candidate in the SMOKE-FILLED ROOM in these terms: "We drew to a pair of deuces and filled."

FDR pointed to Mark Twain's *Connecticut Yankee* as the source of the best-known card metaphor, "new deal": ". . . in a country where only six people out of a thousand have any

voice in the government," says Twain's Yankee, "what the 994 dupes need is a new deal." But the phrase was used in a political context throughout the nineteenth century. See NEW DEAL; SQUARE DEAL.

Cardplaying, while not the sport of kings, has often been the recreation of Presidents. Dwight Eisenhower enjoyed bridge, especially with General Alfred Gruenther as his partner; Harry Truman enjoyed poker-playing with his friends, who were promptly labeled "poker-table cronies"; poker, for some reason, connotes gambling more than bridge. A slight dispute exists about the outcome of a poker game played by Truman, Winston Churchill, and others on the train home from Fulton, Mo., in 1946 after Churchill's "iron curtain" speech. "Churchill took [Truman] for a few shillings on the train ride," wrote *Washington Post* correspondent Edward Folliard. "Truman didn't find out until the game was over that old Winston had learned the rudiments in the Boer War." Clark Clifford, who was there, recalls the game differently: "Churchill was rather an indifferent poker player, and had such a rough time that night that the President cautioned those in the game the next day to 'go easy on old Winnie, boys. I don't think he's in our league.' "

Terms like "ace in the hole," a "fast shuffle," "dealing from the bottom of the deck," "up his sleeve," "call a bluff," etc., are all card expressions used as commonly in politics as in everyday speech. "Wheeler-dealer," however, seems limited to big business and national politics, and Lyndon Johnson was attacked by Michigan Governor George Romney in 1967 as he compared the New Deal and Fair Deal with "the Fast Deal."

When President Carter's National

Security Adviser, Zbigniew Brzezinski, picked up a term several Washington columnists were using in 1978 to describe the leverage on the Soviets of a move toward Peking, Soviet leader Leonid I. Brezhnev charged that "attempts are being made lately in the U.S.A., at a higher level and in a rather cynical form, to play the 'Chinese card' against the USSR."

See STAND PAT; BUCK STOPS HERE, THE; GO-IT-ALONE; SLEEPER; FINESSE; BIG CASINO.

CARETAKER one placed in power only to protect the position for another; a seatwarmer.

Despondent Democratic leaders in 1948, certain that Truman could not defeat Dewey, insisted that Senator Alben W. Barkley go on the Truman ticket as vice-presidential nominee, so that—in Arthur Krock's words—"he would be in a position to act as 'caretaker' of the Democratic organization during four and perhaps eight years out of power."

When John F. Kennedy was elected President, Governor Foster Furcolo of Massachusetts appointed Benjamin Smith II to replace him as senator; columnists pointed out that it was common knowledge that Smith was acting as "caretaker" of the seat to be sought later by Ted Kennedy.

Meanwhile, the same word was used to needle President Johnson, as the President who would simply warm the seat of power until another Kennedy (Robert) could run for the office. By quickly adopting his own style and asserting the "LBJ brand" of leadership, he dispensed with the notion that he would ever be a "caretaker president." The word was used to disparage Gerald Ford in 1976.

CARPETBAGGER an outlander moving into a new area to seek political power at the expense of the native politicians.

The term "carpetbagger" gained wide currency in the South during the Reconstruction period. With the help of federal troops and discriminatory laws, Northerners of the period were able to control many public offices. English writer George Rose in 1868 described "what the Southerners call carpetbaggers, men traveling with little luggage and less character, making political capital out of the present state of affairs." Congressman S. S. Cox of New York said in 1875, "The carpetbagger had little to go on and much to get. He made out of Negro credulity a living and he made the Negro his prey. He began as a sharper and was reconstructed into a statesman."

The carpetbag was a symbol of the man who traveled light, and hence of the man on the make. Before the Civil War, a carpetbagger was an itinerant banker with meager assets who operated in sparsely settled areas. Even during Reconstruction, the term began to be applied outside the South to any nonnative politician. Representative James Brooks found it necessary to defend himself in 1868 with this statement: "I was born in the State of Maine and went to New York with a trunk 30 years ago. I did not go there three months ago with a carpet bag." In 1964, another New Englander went to New York and found himself accused of being a carpetbagger. Robert Kennedy was so freshly arrived in the state when he ran for senator that he was repeatedly spoofed: one gag had him appearing before an audience of New Yorkers saying, "Fellow New Yorkites . . ." and another had him asking, "Where *are* the Bronx?" He won anyway.

Alan Otten, chief of the *Wall Street Journal*'s Washington bureau, wrote on April 29, 1970, about the decline of the carpetbagger issue. One case in point was young Jay Rockefeller, who campaigned in 1968 for secretary of state of West Virginia, not exactly known as Rockefeller family territory. To blunt the charge, the candidate told audiences of a phone call he made to advise his uncle Nelson of his intention to introduce Robert Kennedy at a Charleston rally. "There was a long pause at my uncle's end of the line, so I asked him whether he had anything against the senator. There was another long pause at my uncle's end of the line, till finally he said, 'Well, you know he *is* a carpetbagger.' And then there was a long pause at my end of the line."

Otten concluded: "Jay Rockefeller won handily, and perhaps this disarming anecdote helped. Or perhaps people are not quite so concerned any more about voting for men who weren't born and bred right in the locality. . . . In short, 'carpetbagger' just doesn't seem as dirty a word as it once was."

CATHOLIC CANDIDATE, *see* **BAILEY MEMORANDUM.**

CATCHWORD a word that crystallizes an issue, sparks a response; a technique condemned by those not imaginative enough to master it.

"Normalcy" was a *catchword;* "not nostrums but normalcy" a *catch phrase;* "back to normalcy" a *slogan.*

Catchwords and catch phrases can be dead serious, as FDR's use of DAY OF INFAMY and STAB IN THE BACK illustrates; they may take a popular expression and give it political application: "YOU NEVER HAD IT SO GOOD," "HAD ENOUGH?" Or they may build upon previous phrases, as Lyndon Johnson's "LET US CON-

TINUE" was built upon John F. Kennedy's "Let Us Begin."

At their best, catch phrases used as slogans summarize and dramatize a genuine appeal, the way "Vote As You Shot" did for Civil War veterans. At their worst, they are plain silly— "We Polked You in 1844, We Shall Pierce You in 1852" tried too hard.

A slogan need not contain a catchword to be effective, as "He Can Do More for Massachusetts" proved for two Kennedys, and a catchword need not be sloganized with a verb (see LE-BENSRAUM).

Catch phrases rely heavily on alliteration ("Burn, Baby, Burn!"; "Tippecanoe and Tyler, Too"; "Rum, Romanism and Rebellion") and both catch phrases and slogans often make use of rhyme ("All the Way with LBJ"; "I Like Ike"; "Jim Crow Must Go"). For a more thorough analysis of these techniques, see SLOGAN and ALLITERATION.

At the turn of the century, Epiphanius Wilson wrote:

To make the effect of an oration lasting in the memory of the hearers it is good to use some telling phrase or catchword in which the point of the contention is summarized or suggested. Unlettered people carry all their knowledge or wisdom in short rhymes and proverbs, which are delightful even to the most cultivated as being portable, racy, and seasoned with a kind of wit. As models of this sort of watchword we may point to the "Peace with honor" of Beaconsfield, the "toujours l'audace" [always to dare] of Danton, "the Cross of Gold" of W. J. Bryan, the "Plumed Knight" of Ingersoll, and the "iridescent dream" of Ingalls.

The word "catchword" comes from printing. To make reading easier, John de Spira in 1469 printed at the foot of each page the first word

of the next page, a boon to those who read aloud to their families. This was called the catchword; the main entry words in a dictionary were also printed in bold type or capital letters to catch the eye, as "catchword" is at the start of this entry. In the theater, it has occasionally been used as a substitute for "cue."

The greatness of a catchword or catch phrase is often its ambivalence, leaving it open to controversial interpretations for years. "A good catchword," said Wendell L. Willkie in a 1938 Town Hall debate, "can obscure analysis for fifty years." (For one obscure analysis, see ONE WORLD; also MAN IN THE STREET.)

CAUCUS a closed meeting of party policy makers, originally to nominate candidates and now, more typically, to agree on a legislative program; as a verb, so to meet.

In the early days of the Republic, party machinery was rudimentary and even presidential nominations were decided in small meetings, usually of a party's congressional delegation. What is a partisan's chief duty? an Ohio paper asked rhetorically: "To obey the decrees of King Caucus." It was common to ascribe monarchical attributes to powerful institutions: King Cotton controlled the South's agricultural economy and the first King Cong was not an ape, but the Continental Congress.

Andrew Jackson helped start the convention system that took the caucus down several notches in importance, although small groups can sometimes still control a convention. The term itself seems to be genuinely American, deriving from an Indian word meaning "elder," or "counselor." John Adams in 1763 noted the existence of a discussion group in

Boston called the Caucus Club.

See SACHEM.

CELL a secret unit of political activity, taking direction from a central authority but not directly connected to other units.

The word is closely identified with the Communist party; exposés of membership in "Communist cells" were frequent in the thirties and forties, culminating in the Chambers-Hiss confrontation of 1948.

Stephen Shadegg, an early Goldwater supporter, discussed the value of a cellular political structure in *How to Win an Election*. He pointed to Mao Tse-tung's statement "Give me just two or three men in a village and I will take the village" and adapted "The Cell Group" to Barry Goldwater's 1952 and 1958 Senate campaigns:

> The individuals we enlisted became a secret weapon possessing strength, mobility, and real impact. They were able to infiltrate centers of opposition support, keep us informed of opposition tactics, disseminate information, enlist other supporters, and to do all these things completely unnoticed by the opposition. . . . Mao Tse-tung might have been able to take a village with just two or three men. I have learned that to guarantee success in the political effort it is desirable to have three to five per cent of the voting population enlisted in the Cell Group.

The cell imparts a sense of conspiracy to its members, a greater receptivity to ideological discipline, and a direct organizational control from the top to workers at the grassroots. See BORING FROM WITHIN.

CEMETERY VOTE specifically, a fraudulent vote cast in the name of a voter who has died, but who continues to be listed on the registration rolls; generally, any example of BAL-LOT-BOX STUFFING.

It is a collective phrase, similar to "suburban vote" or "upstate vote." Politicians will jokingly say, "He's out jotting down the names from the tombstones." Vote fraud was long treated lightly by many politicians; "Vote early and often" is a familiar phrase on Election Day.

Franklin D. Roosevelt was elected governor of New York in 1928 by a margin of 25,000 votes out of a total of 4,235,000. On election night he told Samuel Rosenman, "I have an idea that some of the boys upstate are up to their old tricks of delaying the vote and stealing as many as they can from us." Worried about the "cemetery vote" and illegal tampering with the results of voting machines, he put in a call to several sheriffs in upstate counties. "This is Franklin Roosevelt," he said, ". . . the returns from your county are coming in mighty slowly, and I don't like it. . . . If you need assistance to keep order or to see that the vote is counted right, call me here at the Biltmore Hotel and I shall ask Governor Smith to authorize the State Troopers to assist you."

Rosenman points out that this was pure bluff: "There was really little that Roosevelt could do if those instructions were not followed, especially if he were not elected. But it worked—the returns began to come in more quickly. And they were better."

Few modern get-out-the-vote campaigns can compare with the results of the drive in New York in 1844. There were 41,000 people qualified to vote that year. Allowing for those who were ill that day, the turnout was heartwarming—55,000. "The dead filled in for the sick," explained Bruce Felknor of the Fair Campaign Practices Committee.

In the 1964 presidential campaign, Lyndon Johnson was under severe attack regarding previous vote-stealing episodes that both worked for him and against him. The old cemetery-vote joke, traceable back to Rutherford B. Hayes, was used again. Little boy is asked why he is crying. "For my poor dead father," he replies. "But your father's been dead for ten years." Sobbing, the boy answers, "Last night he came back to vote for Lyndon Johnson and he never came to see me."

Warren Moscow, in *Politics in the Empire State,* tells of Hudson Valley political boss Lou Payne, who admitted that he sometimes voted tombstones, but added, "We never vote a man unless he would have voted our way if he were still alive. We respect a man's convictions."

CENSURE, *see* **VOTE OF CONFIDENCE; QUOTED OUT OF CONTEXT.**

CENTER OF POWER, *see* **POWER BROKER; OVAL OFFICE.**

CENTRALIZED GOVERNMENT, *see* **BIG GOVERNMENT; CREEPING SOCIALISM.**

CENTRIST an ideological position between extremes within a party; a member of a center party; or one closely attuned to the thinking of the majority.

Colloquial definition is MIDDLE-OF-THE-ROADER, comfortable with the CONSENSUS, in the MAINSTREAM. Sometimes mistakenly used to mean a believer in centralized government.

During the Truman Administration, political scientist Julius Turner wrote: "Only a Democrat who rejects a part of the Fair Deal can carry Kansas, and only a Republican who moderates the Republican platform can carry Massachusetts."

Centrist is of relatively recent political coinage, and is gaining in use as a more sophisticated self-definition than middle-of-the-roader. A similar phrase is *the vital center,* coined in 1949 by Arthur Schlesinger, Jr., as the place for pragmatic liberals to be.

The phrase is now used to define the area where the swing voter lies and where the big decisions are made; a politician who is a centrist can attract both mildly liberal and mildly conservative votes, and can develop a pattern of positions that encompass points on both sides of an ideological fence. But Clinton Rossiter holds that a concern for this kind of centrism need not stultify debate between parties: "The unwritten laws of American politics command that the differences between the parties be relatively few and modest, but it does not follow that those differences also be obscure. Let the parties compete for the millions of Americans in the vital center by offering alternatives that do not wrench our minds too violently in one direction or the other, but let them also offer us alternatives that can be clearly grasped."

See OPPORTUNIST.

CENTURY OF THE COMMON MAN, *see* **COMMON MAN, CENTURY OF THE.**

CHAMELEON ON PLAID, *see* **UNHOLY ALLIANCE.**

CHANGING HORSES, *see* **DON'T CHANGE HORSES.**

CHANNELS, *see* **RED TAPE.**

CHARACTER ASSASSIN one who wages political warfare by seeking to destroy his adversary's reputation, usually by scurrilous means.

The phrase, or variations of it, is probably as old as the tactic—that is, ancient—but it was most recently in vogue during the early 1950s, when Senator Joseph McCarthy's red-hunting forays brought down game of many hues. Besides calling the Communists-in-government issue a RED-HERRING, Harry Truman, in a 1950 speech to the American Legion, denounced "scandal mongers and character assassins." Although McCarthy was a fellow Republican, Dwight Eisenhower later criticized those who "assassinate you or your character from behind." See PHILIPPIC. Toward the end of McCarthy's period of influence, his feud with the Army itself became the subject of a congressional investigation. Joseph N. Welch, an attorney retained by the congressional committee, was shocked when the senator related how a young lawyer in Welch's firm had belonged to a tainted organization. At a poignant moment of the televised hearings, Welch replied, "Let us not assassinate this lad further, Senator. Have you no sense of decency, sir? At long last, have you left no sense of decency?"

The congressional committee has often been a forum for character assassination. Courtroom rules of evidence do not apply. Defamation laws offer no protection because nothing said during official proceedings is actionable. Thus as early as 1876 one member of Congress complained of critics who "say that our committees of investigation are intended to strike down some loyal men, or assassinate character." The Democratic senators who began probing the Teapot Dome situation soon after the death of Warren G. Harding were described by the *New York Tribune* as "the Montana scandalmongers," by the *New York*

Post as "mud-gunners," and by the *New York Times* as "assassins of character." Over the years, their stock rose as Harding's fell.

CHARISMA political sex appeal, that "certain something" that campaign managers look for: a combination of attractiveness, charm, and sincerity that turns a candidate into The Candidate.

Charisma is the ancient Greek word for gift (and is pronounced with a *k*). In theology, it is defined as a grace, such as the power to heal or to prophesy.

In medieval Byzantium, charisma referred to those in a state of maniacal passion—berserk or drugged or in a convulsive fit—who were maintained as a kind of weapon in warfare to inspire loyal troops and frighten the opposition. Earlier in history, charismatic ascetics and "holy men," relying on begging for support, troubled the early Christians; St. Paul's warning "If a man does not work, neither shall he eat" was directed against the alarming spread of charismatic missionaries.

Charisma (the "gift") determined the fate of Chinese monarchs. If war, flood, or famine afflicted the land, it was a sign that the monarch did not possess the charismatic virtue, that he was not indeed a "son of Heaven." Max Weber, in a chapter on charismatic authority in *The Theory of Social and Economic Organization,* wrote: "The term 'charisma' will be applied to a certain quality of an individual personality by virtue of which he is set apart from ordinary men and treated as endowed with supernatural, superhuman, or at least specifically exceptional powers or qualities."

A politician with charisma can build a personal following outside his party, while developing special attachments within his party. Both Roosevelts had it, Eisenhower had it, Kennedy had it. It is less spiritual than "vision" and more elemental than "style."

In 1967 a group of celebrities tried to define charisma for writer Leon Harris in *This Week.* "The person I think who had the most was Malcolm," said Lena Horne, speaking of Malcolm X, the assassinated Black Muslim leader. "I never met him and yet I felt him and still feel him. Malcolm had the thing and Stokely Carmichael hasn't."

Thomas P. F. Hoving, director of the Metropolitan Museum of Art, said:

> The man with the most charisma I ever saw, is Muñoz Marín of Puerto Rico. The minute he walks into the room, you feel it whether you know who he is or not. The same is true of Picasso, of Haile Selassie, and de Gaulle and Chiang. Pope John had it and Pope Paul doesn't. Khrushchev had it and Stalin didn't.

Columnist Stewart Alsop, covering Ted Kennedy's Massachusetts campaign for the Senate in 1962, spoke of the candidate's charisma to a woman reporter, and reported her reply: "Charisma, hell. It's just plain old sex appeal."

CHARLES RIVER GANG a jocular derogation of the academic-political-scientific "community" in Boston.

Both Harvard College and the Massachusetts Institute of Technology have, in recent generations, been the source of valued counsel to Administrations in Washington, D.C.—most often, but by no means exclusively, Democratic. In the mid-seventies the power of this intellectual-technological establishment was recognized by hard-liners on the staff of the Senate Armed Services Committee who dubbed it "the Charles River Gang."

The Charles River, about 47 miles long, has an estuary which separates Boston from Cambridge.

CHARLIE   name used to designate the letter *C;* also, black nickname for whites.

Three uses of "Charlie" have been prevalent in recent years.

1. "Checkpoint Charlie," in Berlin, is the key point of interchange between the American and Soviet sectors. It was named as part of the normal Army use of words to designate letters clearly, as Able, Baker, Charlie, Dog, etc. The significance of this particular checkpoint, plus the alliteration, made the name famous.

2. Members of the armed forces in Vietnam referred to the Viet Cong as "VC" or "C," which naturally became "Victor Charlie," or simply "Charlie." Correspondent Kuno Knoebl wrote a book in 1967 called *Victor Charlie: The Face of War in Vietnam.*

3. In the lexicon of the civil rights movement, "Mr. Charlie" was a derisive nickname for the white man. Author James Baldwin used the phrase in one of his most important works, *Blues for Mr. Charlie.* There appears to be no connection with the letter *C* in this use, although there might have been a derivation from "white Charley," the name for right-wing Whig party members. The *Congressional Globe* of 1842 reported: "There seems to me as much prospect of the ultra-Whigs—the 'White Charlies'—coalescing with the Democrats, as there is of Tyler and his friends."

Other common men's names that have acquired special meanings include George (for good), Jack (I'm all right), and Sam (for UNCLE SAM), a nickname given members of the American, or KNOW-NOTHING, party.

CHARLIE REGAN   a straw man used to absorb resentment in political campaigns.

Every headquarters must turn down a certain number of well-meaning volunteers without offending them. Horrible campaign songs, meaningless slogans, and painful pamphlets are submitted, and must be rejected in a way that will not diminish enthusiasm. At other times, strategic delays are necessary. That is why this phrase is so often heard: "I'll give you a firm go-ahead just as soon as Regan gets back."

Charlie Regan never does get back, for he is the little man who isn't there. He is a fiction, a secret known only to the three or four people at the helm of the campaign. He has a place on the Table of Organization, in a little box near the top, but off to the side (title: "General Campaign Coordination and Liaison"), a desk, a telephone, a listing in the mimeographed directory at headquarters. He has a raincoat, which is sometimes draped over his chair, sometimes neatly hung up.

But there is no Charlie Regan. Whenever anybody calls, he is "down at the printer's." Somehow, being down at a political printer's shop implies exploration of the Mindanao Deep: nobody questions its importance or total inaccessibility.

At the end of the campaign, like all the other top headquarters personnel, Charlie Regan receives a spiritually uplifting letter from the candidate, win or lose. ("Have I ever met Regan? I just can't visualize him." "Oh, you've been in a dozen meetings with him, the little balding guy with the cigar." "Sure, I remember now.")

Countless public officials throughout America think they owe a favor to a man named Charlie Regan, and countless frustrated candidates blame their losses entirely on him.

James Hagerty, White House press secretary under Eisenhower, tells the author, "Our Charlie Regan went by the name of Frank Pierce."

The device might have been derived from "George Spelvin," the name a hungry actor adopts as a pseudonym when he accepts a role so minor that playing it under his own name would hurt his reputation, or the name an impecunious producer uses in a program when the same actor is playing two parts.

CHAUTAUQUA CIRCUIT old-fashioned BARNSTORMING; speaking to culturally active groups in small towns.

On the shores of Lake Chautauqua, New York, Methodist clergyman John Vincent and Lewis Miller called an assembly in the summer of 1874 to promote Bible study in Sunday School. In a few years a permanent summer camp was formed which led to home-study courses in a variety of subjects. The institution was widely imitated, and after 1900, a "traveling Chautauqua" was begun—a series of lectures and concerts held in tents around the country—which lasted until the Depression.

The word came to connote grass roots intellectualism and mobile spee-chifying. In *The Economist* in 1931, the capitalization was dropped as the word became generic: "The Chequers [the Prime Minister's residence] conversations proved to be the first of a series of statesmen's chautauquas in the capitals of Europe." While in Britain the word has a Sunday-School flavor, in the U.S. the meaning is more political. "It seems only fitting,"

wrote the *Atlantic* about Hubert Humphrey in 1968, "that the boy from behind the drug counter in Huron, South Dakota, should wow a Chamber of Commerce convention, that the Chautauqua tent and Grange hall Populist can make a Deep Southern audience jump to its feet."

The word is evocative of a bygone era, campaigning to listening audiences with neither the tedium of the RUBBER-CHICKEN CIRCUIT nor the phoniness of the MEDIA EVENT.

CHAUVINISM, *see* **WOMEN'S LIB; SUPERPATRIOT.**

CHECKERS SPEECH the address Richard Nixon gave on nationwide television to defend himself against charges that he was the beneficiary of a "secret" political fund; now, any such emotionally charged speech.

During the 1952 campaign the Republicans were having a field day with Truman Administration scandals when word got out of the existence of a "secret Nixon fund," as the Democratic *New York Post* called it. The reaction was noisy—and even included demands that Nixon resign his candidacy. Dwight Eisenhower at first appeared to give Nixon little support. Nixon decided on a television rebuttal, and in a 30-minute speech successfully explained that the collection was neither secret nor sinister, but an open and well-audited fund to pay legitimate political expenses such as travel costs. The reaction from both the country and Eisenhower was favorable.

In the course of the speech, however, Nixon tugged at a few heartstrings. He pointed out that he was too poor for his wife to have anything but a cloth coat. He also admitted his family had accepted a present—a cocker spaniel puppy named Checkers. "And you know," he went on, "the kids, like all kids, loved the dog, and I just want to say this, right now, that regardless of what they say about it, we are going to keep it."

In his 1962 book, *Six Crises,* Nixon wrote: "It was labeled as the 'Checkers speech,' as though the mention of my dog was the only thing that saved my career. Many of the critics glided over the fact that the fund was thoroughly explained, my personal finances laid bare, and an admittedly emotional but honest appeal made for public support."

But many felt that Nixon's approach was overly emotional and corny. Wrote Nixon later:

A distinguished political science professor, after making a thorough study of the 1960 election, stated his considered judgment that if it had not been for the fund broadcast I would have been elected President of the United States. It was a neat theory, brilliantly supported by facts and figures, but like most classroom theoreticians he had not faced up to the hard reality of the alternative. If it hadn't been for that broadcast, I would never have been around to run for the presidency.

Nixon took the idea of injecting Checkers into his speech from Franklin Roosevelt's FALA SPEECH of 1944. The Republicans accused FDR of sending a destroyer to fetch his Scots terrier. Roosevelt did more than deny the charge; he turned it around to make it seem a libel on a poor dumb animal. Fala, he concluded, "has not been the same dog since."

Great men do well to have small dogs. Thomas E. Dewey's Great Dane did not help project his master as a warm human being; Winston Churchill's brown poodle, Rufus, was the kind of endearing small animal that appeals to the public.

CHECKS AND BALANCES the limitations on the powers of each branch of government—and on the government as a whole—provided for in the federal and state constitutions.

The federal Constitution's authors feared concentrations of power of all kinds, from monarchism to mob rule. During the nationwide debate over creating a federal union in the 1780s, "checks and balances" emerged as the Federalists' prescription for protecting all sectors of the pluralistic American society.

The term was probably coined by seventeenth-century British political philosopher James Harrington. Among the early users was James Madison, one of the great Federalist advocates, as when during the ratification fight he explained how the landed gentry's rights would be protected: ". . . our government ought to secure the permanent interests of the country against innovation. Landholders ought to have a share in the government, to support these invaluable interests, and to balance and check the other [numerically larger groups]."

This explained the government's diversity. The House of Representatives was popularly elected but the Senate was not. The President could veto congressional action, but only Congress could appropriate funds for him to spend. Federal judges depended on the President for appointment and on Congress for money, but the judges serve for life.

Because it describes simply a fundamental and enduring principle of the American system, "checks and balances" has survived as a term, too. It appears frequently in the statements of judges, politicians and historians. James MacGregor Burns described the "system of checks and balances that would use man's essential human nature—his interests, his passions, his ambitions—to control itself."

CHICKEN IN EVERY POT   an easily attackable Republican slogan created and exploited by Democrats.

King Henry IV of France (1553–1610) was easily the champion phrasemaker of his era. He was responsible for "the white plume" or "plumed knight" expression used by supporters of James Blaine in the late nineteenth century; he coined "Le Grand Dessein," the "great design" for world peace that Franklin Roosevelt appropriated (see GRAND DESIGN); and as a result of his statement *"Je veux qu'il n'y ait si pauvre paysan en moi royaume qu'il n'ait tous les diamanches sa poule au pot"* ("I wish that there would not be a peasant so poor in all my realm who would not have a chicken in his pot every Sunday"), he was given the sobriquet of *le Roi de la poule au pot* ("King of the chicken in the pot").

Herbert Hoover never said it. He did say, on October 22, 1928, "The slogan of progress is changing from the 'FULL DINNER PAIL' to the full garage." The former President's secretary wrote to quote-collector George Seldes in 1958: "No one has ever been able to find, in Mr. Hoover's speeches or writings, of which a very careful file has been kept over the years, the expression 'a chicken in every pot.' Mr. Hoover also never promised or even expressed his hope of two cars in every garage."

The repopularization of the phrase, and Hoover's supposed connection with it, can be traced to a Republican campaign flyer of 1928 titled "A Chicken In Every Pot." Democratic candidate Al Smith, in a Boston campaign speech, held up the flyer and quoted from it:

"Republican prosperity has reduced hours and increased earning capacity." And then it goes on to say Republican prosperity has put a chicken in every pot and a car in every backyard to boot. . . . Here's another good one for you. "Republican efficiency has filled the working-man's dinner pail and his gasoline tank besides, and placed the whole nation in the silk stocking class." . . . Now just draw on your imagination for a moment, and see if you can in your mind's eye picture a man working at $17.50 a week going out to a chicken dinner in his own automobile with silk socks on.

By 1932, reminders of promises of prosperity were particularly embarrassing to Republicans; Hoover's passing reference to a "full garage" was combined with Smith's characterization of the Hoover campaign flyer to manufacture a Hoover promise: "A chicken in every pot and two cars in every garage."

Democratic campaigners do not let it die. In 1960 John F. Kennedy misquoted the phony quotation in Bristol, Tennessee: "It is my understanding that the last candidate for the presidency to visit this community in a presidential year was Herbert Hoover in 1928. President Hoover initiated on the occasion of his visit the slogan 'Two chickens for every pot,' and it is no accident that no presidential candidate has ever dared come back to this community since."

Comedian Dick Gregory played on a more recent meaning of "pot" with this turnaround in 1972: "A chicken in every pot will probably not be revived as a campaign slogan. With the eighteen-year-old vote now in effect, some folks feel the new battle cry is more likely to be 'some pot in every chicken.'"

CHILLING EFFECT an action or situation that inhibits free speech, or threatens to intimidate or dispirit the press.

Justice William Brennan, author of the Supreme Court's 1965 opinion in *Dombrowski* v. *Pfister* (380 U.S. 479), popularized the phrase in its current meaning. A civil rights group in Louisiana protested that the state's Subversive Activities and Communist Control Law subjected its members to harassment by local authorities. Instead of deciding on the basis of bad-faith harassment, the Court found intimidation inherent in "the existence of a penal statute susceptible of sweeping and improper application . . . the chilling effect upon the exercise of First Amendment rights may derive from the fact of the prosecution, unaffected by the prospects of its success or failure."

"Chilling effect" made its next appearance in 1967, in *Walker* v. *City of Birmingham,* this time in a dissent by Justice Brennan to a majority opinion written by Justice Potter Stewart. Since the lexicographer heard that the phrase might have stemmed from Justice Stewart's decision, a letter to that jurist elicited this letter from Justice Brennan to Justice Stewart dated March 7, 1974, describing the derivation:

There is a note in 69 Columbia Law Review 808–842 (1969) entitled "The Chilling Effect in Constitutional Law." That Note traces the concept of "chilling effect" to a concurring opinion by Felix Frankfurter in *Wieman* v. *Updegraff,* 344 U.S. 183, 195 (1952) where Felix, joined by Bill Douglas, said of a teacher's loyalty oath:

"Such unwarranted inhibition upon the free spirit of teachers affects not only those who, like the appellants, are immediately before the Court. It has an unmistakable

tendency to *chill* that free play of the spirit which all teachers ought especially to cultivate and practice; it makes for caution and timidity in their associations by potential teachers."

. . . Frankly, I have no recollection of bottoming the phrase on Felix's *Wieman* opinion nor upon the opinions of lower courts dating back to 1939 and cited in footnote 2 of the Law Review Note. I would suppose that the Note would help meet Mr. Safire's desire for its history.

And so it does, showing how the term "chilling" had been used since 1939 in cases regarding judicially regulated sales. The metaphor can be traced to the sixteenth century to mean "to affect as with cold": the *OED* cites Hooker's *Ecclesiastical Politics* with "chilleth . . . all warmth of zeal." According to the *Columbia Law Review,* the author of this article, written in 1969, was New York attorney Herbert T. Weinstein, and his conclusions in that piece show how the Court has used Brennan's phrase to extend the First Amendment:

At first blush, the doctrine seems merely to indicate a rational relationship between constitutionally protected conduct and the law sought to be held unconstitutional. But if this is the function of the chilling doctrine, the words "deters" and "inhibits" would serve as well as the word "chills." It appears, however, that the Court uses the chilling doctrine for more far-reaching purposes. First it uses the doctrine to justify activism in restricting and eliminating laws which proscribe protected conduct. Here the chilling effect reverses the usual presumption of federalism that federal courts should defer to state courts and open their doors only when state judicial and administrative procedures have been exhausted.

The second function of the chilling effect doctrine is to indicate the abridgement of a constitutional right. Here the chilling effect appears to emphasize a presumption in favor of the protected conduct and against the state regulation which deters it.

In current political, rather than legal, use, the phrase is used by newsmen who complain that others—not themselves—might be intimidated by "leak-plugging" efforts of government officials. (See PLUMBERS.)

CHINA LOBBY attack phrase used against those urging support of Chiang Kai-shek against Mao Tse-tung, and later pressing for aid to Chiang on Taiwan.

In February 1946 a mission to China headed by General George Marshall had arranged for a cease-fire and a coalition government, which began to break up within three months. General Patrick Hurley, in an angry resignation from his ambassadorial post, warned that "subversives" in the State Department were secretly plotting a Communist victory. "Around the country," wrote Cabell Phillips in *The Truman Presidency,* "a 'China lobby' was forming, controlled largely by zealots of the right beating the gongs of public opinion to 'save' China."

General Marshall returned from his mission in January 1947, and American aid to the Chiang government soon began to dry up. Friends of Chiang in the U.S. bitterly criticized this decision, and President Truman in July 1947 sent General Albert Wedemeyer to China for another look. Wedemeyer filed an ambivalent report, which the Truman Administration suppressed, further whipping up the attacks of Chiang's American supporters.

After Chiang retreated from the mainland to Taiwan, the efforts of the "China lobby" were directed to his support on Formosa and the rejection of any attempt to replace the Chiang government in the UN by the Communist Chinese.

Finley Peter Dunne's "Mr. Dooley" (see DOOLEY, MR.) expressed a skepticism toward the Chinese government that existed among many Americans well before the turn of the twentieth century:

"He's th' Chinee ministher," said Mr. Dooley, "an' his business is f'r to supply fresh hand-laundhried misinformation to the sicrety iv state. . . .

"Th' Westhren civilization, Hinnissy—that's us—is a pretty good liar, but he's a kind iv rough-an'-tumble at it. . . . How in th' wurruld can we compete with a counthry where ivry lab'rer's cottage projooces lies so delicate that th' workment iv th' West can't undherstand thim? We make our lies be machinery; they tur-rn out theirs be hand. . . .

"They can't hurt us with their lies," said Mr. Hennessy of our Western civilization. "We have th' guns an' we'll bate thim yet."

"Yes," said Mr. Dooley, "an' 'twill be like a man who's had his house desthroyed be a cyclone gettin' up an' kickin' at th' air."

During the Eisenhower Administration, Senate Minority Leader William Knowland of California was often attacked as a captive of the "China lobby" and was labeled "the Senator from Formosa." When mainland China replaced Taiwan in the UN in 1971, and Richard Nixon paid his presidential visit to Peking in 1972, the influence of the China lobby was seen to have been overrated. When President Nixon arranged for "liaison offices" in Peking and Washington, the name of the "China lobby" began to change to "supporters of Taiwan"; the vogue phrase became "normalization of relations" with the PRC, which President Carter pledged to carry forward in his campaign, based on the Nixon-Mao "Shanghai Communiqué," that 1972 agreement cleverly recognized that Chinese on both sides of the Formosa Straits agreed there was but "one China."

By the mid-seventies, another "lobby"—again carrying the pejorative connotation of manipulation—was spoken of in the U.S. This was the "Israel lobby," which gained much attention when the Chairman of the Joint Chiefs of Staff, General George Brown, said in 1976 that Jewish groups made their influence felt on U.S. policy makers, who considered the defense of Israel "a burden." In Great Britain the "Israel lobby" is called, even more pejoratively, "the Jewish lobby," as in this *Financial Times* usage in 1977: "In Washington, the 'Jewish lobby' has already reacted powerfully and angrily." The phrases that most distressed supporters of Israel in 1977 and 1978 were "imposed solution" (forced upon Israelis by the U.S.) and "legitimate rights" (code words for demands for an independent Arab state on the Jordan River's west bank).

By mid-1978, as Egyptian and Saudi Arabian embassies in Washington became more sophisticated in dealing with U.S. public opinion, hiring lobbyists for that purpose, a counterphrase began to appear: the "Arab lobby."

CHINA WATCHERS   outside observers of political customs inside Communist China; sifters of official statements for hidden meanings.

This phrase is probably derived from "bird watching" with its connotation of intense concentration, intricate analysis and observation from a distance. It has replaced OLD CHINA HANDS—reporters and businessmen who made their careers in the Far East before the rise of Communism there.

A new synonym for China watcher is "Pekingologist," coined on the analogy of KREMLINOLOGIST—those who make their living trying to decipher the puzzles of Soviet government. The creed of the China watcher, Kremlinologist and Pekingologist was summed up by Winston Churchill's description of the Soviet Union: "It is a riddle wrapped in a mystery inside an enigma."

Reuters News Service filed a dispatch from Peking with a helpful glossary of baffling expressions that have appeared in the official press since the "cultural revolution" in 1966:

proletarian revolutionary line: the ideology and policies of Chairman Mao vs.

bourgeois reactionary line: the ideas and policies of Mao Tse-tung's opponents.

three-family village: three writers, Teng To, Wu Han and Liao Mosha, who held important posts in the former Peking Municipal Council and Communist party committee.

four-family inn (sometimes called *four-cadre shop*): four dismissed members of the Party's Central Committee secretariat, Peng Chen, Lu Ting-yi, Lo Jui-ching and Yang Shang-kun.

four olds: old ideas, cultures, customs and habits.

black gangsters: usually applied to people in the literary, cultural and propaganda fields charged with anti-Maoism, but sometimes a description of dissident party officials.

poisonous weeds: writings by the black gangsters.

the red ocean is a big plot: a slogan accusing those who paint walls red of doing so not out of revolutionary ardor but to prevent others from putting up posters.

In 1976 the most frequently used phrase in China was "the gang of four," used to center villainy on Chiang Ching (Mao's widow) and her ultraradical followers. Hua Kuo-feng, Mao's successor, attributed the phrase to an admonishment Mao supposedly directed at his wife and her political colleagues: "Don't be a gang of four."

"China watching" is a construction that has been borrowed for use to describe any group of analysts who laboriously pick over the movements of their subject for hidden meanings—thus, "Bobby watchers" (Kennedy), "Johnson watchers," etc.

CHOICE, NOT AN ECHO attack on "me-tooism" (see ME TOO), a call for a division of parties along ideological lines.

"We think the American people want a clear-cut choice," said Peter O'Donnell, chairman of the Draft Goldwater Committee in April 1963, "between the New Frontier of the Kennedys and Republican principles."

On January 3, 1964, candidate Goldwater announced: "I will offer a choice, not an echo. This will not be an engagement of personalities. It will be an engagement of principles."

Phyllis Schlafly chose the phrase for her best-selling paperback book *A Choice Not An Echo,* published soon afterward; this was called (by Democrats) one of the "three dirty books" of the campaign. The others were *None Dare Call It Treason* by John Stormer and *A Texan Looks at Lyndon* by J. Evetts Haley.

At the 1964 Republican convention, Pennsylvania Governor William Scranton, taking the liberal baton after Nelson Rockefeller's defeat in the California primary, played on the phrase: "I have come here to offer our party a choice. I reject the echo we have thus far been handed . . . the echo of fear, or reaction . . . the echo from the Never Never Land that puts our nation backward to a lesser place in the world of free men."

The Goldwater strategy relied on the presence of a strong SILENT VOTE that had stayed home up to now because Republicans had not drawn a sharp ideological line with Willkie, Dewey or Nixon. The desire for such a reconstruction (called a restructuring in some circles) of the two-party system has not been limited to conservatives. Felix Frankfurter, explaining his vote for third-party candidate Robert La Follette in 1924, quoted English observer James Bryce's comparison of the two American parties: "Both have certainly war cries, organizations, interests enlisted in their support. But those interests are in the main getting or keeping the patronage of the government. Distinctive tenets and policies, points of political doctrine and points of political practice have all but vanished."

FDR flirted with the idea in conversations after the 1940 campaign with Wendell Willkie. Moderates of both parties, however, point out that such a polarization would result in the "left" winning most of the time, and the danger of a drastic wrench when conservatives, through the popularity of an individual or war or depression, finally turned the tables.

See TWO-PARTY SYSTEM; BIG TENT; IDEOLOGY; TRUE BELIEVER.

CHRISTMAS TREE BILLS, *see*
RIDER.

CHRONIC CAMPAIGNER characterization of Richard Nixon by
President Lyndon Johnson, in angry
rebuttal to a Nixon analysis of Vietnam policy.

In the 1966 congressional campaign, former Vice President Richard
Nixon was the foremost campaigner
for Republican candidates nationally.
He carried the attack to President
Johnson, who pursued the same strategy he had used so successfully two
years earlier on Barry Goldwater: to
remain above the battle. With the
polls showing his popularity dropping, Johnson chose to make a dramatic trip to Southeast Asia, including a visit to U.S. troops in Vietnam,
two weeks before election. Nixon held
his fire during the President's trip, but
on Johnson's return put out a closely
reasoned, critical analysis of the Manila Communiqué issued by Johnson
and the Southeast Asia leaders.

The *New York Times* decided to
run the text of the Nixon critique,
which gave it national importance;
the next morning, at the President's
news conference, Johnson startled his
audience by losing his temper. He
called Nixon "a chronic campaigner"
who was "playing politics with
peace."

Johnson's "chronic campaigner"
phrase focused national attention on
Nixon's role in the campaign and
gave him a superb opportunity to
counter with almost presidential
calm.

A similar attack, though less emotional, was made by John Quincy
Adams on Henry Clay: "His opposition to Monroe and myself arises
out of a disappointed ambition, a
determination to run down the administration and become president

by hook or crook in 1824."
See **PERENNIAL CANDIDATE.**

CIA, *see* **INVISIBLE GOVERN-
MENT; DIRTY TRICKS, DE-
PARTMENT OF.**

CIA-ESE spookspeak; the language of the intelligence community
(formerly the intelligence establishment), selected from a glossary compiled in 1976 by the Senate Select
Committee to Study Governmental
Operations with Respect to Intelligence Activities:

asset: Any resource—a person,
group, relationship, instrument, installation or supply—at the disposition of an intelligence agency for
use in an operational or support
role. The term is normally applied
to a person who is contributing to
a CIA clandestine mission, but is
not a fully controlled agent of CIA.

backstopping: A CIA term for providing appropriate verification and
support of cover arrangements for
an agent or asset in anticipation of
inquiries or other actions which
might test the credibility of his or
its cover.

bigot lists: Using the term bigot in the
sense of "narrow," this is a restrictive list of persons who have access
to a particular and highly sensitive
class of information.

black bag job: Warrantless surreptitious entry, especially an entry conducted for purposes other than microphone installation, such as
physical search and seizure or
photographing of documents.

bug: A concealed listening device or
microphone, or other audiosurveillance device; also, to install the
means for audiosurveillance of a
subject or target.

code word: A word which has been

assigned a classification and a classified meaning to safeguard intentions and information regarding a planned operation.

cover: A protective guise used by a person, organization or installation to prevent identification with clandestine activities and to conceal the true affiliation of personnel and the true sponsorship of their activities.

covert action: Any clandestine activity designed to influence foreign governments, events, organizations, or persons in support of United States foreign policy. Covert action may include political and economic action, propaganda and paramilitary activities.

cut-out: A CIA term referring to a person who is used to conceal contact between members of a clandestine activity or organization.

double agent: A person engaging in clandestine activity for two or more intelligence or security services who provides information to one service about the other, or about each service to the other, and who is wittingly or unwittingly manipulated by one service against the other.

executive action: This term is generally an euphemism for assassination, and was used by the CIA to describe a program aimed at overthrowing certain foreign leaders, by assassinating them if necessary.

informant: A person who wittingly or unwittingly provides information to an agent, a clandestine service or police. In reporting such information, this person will often be cited as the source.

informer: One who intentionally discloses information about other persons or activities to police or a security service (such as the FBI), usually for a financial reward.

notionals: Fictitious, private commercial entities which exist on paper only. They serve as the ostensible employer of intelligence personnel, or as the ostensible sponsor of certain activities in support of clandestine operations. (Not to be confused with "nationals," citizens of a given country.)

plumbing: A term referring to the development of assets or services supporting the clandestine operations of CIA field stations—such as safe houses, unaccountable funds, investigative persons, surveillance teams.

proprietaries: A term used by CIA to designate ostensibly private commercial entities capable of doing business which are established and controlled by intelligence services to conceal governmental affiliation of intelligence personnel and/or governmental sponsorship of certain activities in support of clandestine operations.

safe house: An innocent-appearing house or premises established by an intelligence organization for conducting clandestine or covert activity in relative security.

sanitize: The deletion or revision of a report or document so as to prevent identification of the intelligence sources and methods that contributed to or are dealt with in the report.

sheep dipping: The utilization of a military instrument (e.g., an airplane) or officer in clandestine operations, usually in a civilian capacity or under civilian cover, although the instrument or officer will covertly retain its or his military ownership or standing. The term is also applied to the placement of individuals in organizations or groups in which they can become active in order to establish credentials so that they can be used to collect information of intelligence interest on similar groups.

source: A person, thing or activity which provides intelligence information. In clandestine activities, the term applies to an agent or asset, normally a foreign national, being used in an intelligence activity for intelligence purposes. In interrogations, it refers to a person who furnishes intelligence information with or without knowledge that the information is being used for intelligence purposes.

sterilize: To remove from material to be used in covert and clandestine actions any marks or devices which can identify it as originating with the sponsoring organization or nation.

target of opportunity: A term describing an entity (e.g., governmental entity, installation, political organization or individual) that becomes available to an intelligence agency or service by chance, and provides the opportunity for the collection of needed information.

United States country team: The senior, in-country, U.S. coordinating and supervising body, headed by the chief of the U.S. diplomatic mission (usually an ambassador) and composed of the senior member of each represented United States department or agency.

watch list: A list of words—such as names, entities or phrases—which can be employed by a computer to select out required information from a mass of data.

Curiously, in the committee report the phrase *plausible denial* was listed but not defined: it is a cover story which enables high government officials to disclaim knowledge of an intelligence activity. (Asked about the oversight committee's oversight, a staffer said merely, "We closed out the report in such a rush we just forgot that definition," which is a plausible denial.)

Another intelligence agency word is *mole,* an operative planted in another country's intelligence community, a specific form of *agent in place.* This is either reportage or coinage by novelist David Cornwall, whose pen name is John Le Carré; whether or not a fictional fancy, "mole" has burrowed its way into intelligence jargon. Former CIA chief Richard Helms tells the author he never heard "mole" used in his tenure; the word used for that most feared prospect was "penetration."

Fluttering is giving a lie-detector test to one's own agents to find out if they are telling the truth. Rudy Maxa wrote in the October 9, 1977, *Washington Post Magazine:* "Investigators for the Church committee learned—but never revealed—that many of the journalists who had cooperated with the CIA were given lie-detector tests. In the spy business that's called 'fluttering,' and some reporters were fluttered more often than regular agency employees to test their loyalty."

Synecdoche is a word also used by intelligence professionals. The word (pronounced sin-EK-do-key) means a rhetorical device that uses a part to stand for the whole, or a small thing to symbolize a big thing: the BIG APPLE, a nickname for New York City, uses an apple as a synecdoche for the world.

The CIA Inspector General in 1967, Lyman Kirkpatrick, said in an internal report dealing with assassination: "The point is that of frequent resort to syncdoche—the mention of a part when the whole is to be understood, or vice versa. Thus, we encounter repeated references to phrases such as 'disposing of Castro,' which may be read in the narrow literal sense of assassinating him, when it is intended that it be read in the broader figurative sense of dislodging the Castro regime.

"Reversing the coin," the CIA man continued, "we find people speaking vaguely of 'doing something about Castro' when it is clear that what they have specifically in mind is killing him."

Another CIA favorite is *blowback,* coined on the analogy of the automotive "blow by" and the electronic "feedback," or perhaps from the wind-shift danger in the use of poison gas. In what was called "psychological warfare" in the fifties, the Soviets pioneered in "disinformation"—falsehoods, widely disseminated, distinguished from "misinformation" by the intent to misinform—and U.S. "black propaganda" has done the same, notably in the emplantation of bogus material in Khrushchev's "secret speech" in 1956 denouncing Joseph Stalin. The danger of such a farrago of lies being picked up by U.S. correspondents abroad and sent back to the U.S. as the truth is called "blowback"; its CIA synonyms are *fallout,* and *domestic replay.*

Family jewels is a jocular CIA phrase for its own most embarrassing secrets. When James Schlesinger was appointed Director of Central Intelligence in 1973, he asked employees to come forward with information about activities "which might be construed to be outside the legislative charter of this agency." Wrote Schlesinger's successor, William Colby, in his 1978 book *Honorable Men:* "Presented to the Director so that he would know about them, they were promptly dubbed by a wag the 'family jewels'; I referred to them as 'our skeletons in the closet.' Among them were the Chaos Operation against the antiwar movement, the surveillance and bug-

ging of American journalists in hope of locating the sources of leaks of sensitive materials, and all the connections with the Watergate conspirators and White House 'plumbers.' " (The phrase "family jewels" has a long time taboo slang use meaning "testicles," which are a source of pride as the source of progeny.)

See **DESTABILIZE**.

CIGARETTE-HOLDER SYMBOL cartoonists' political symbol for Franklin Delano Roosevelt.

Reporters found it an infallible press-conference barometer. Wrote Associated Press White House correspondent Jack Bell, "If the cigarette in his holder was pointed toward the ceiling and his head was thrown back, the news would be good. If he was hunched over his desk and the cigarette pointed downward, look out, somebody was going to get hell."

Jonathan Daniels, a Roosevelt press aide, described Roosevelt's exultation after triumph at the polls in 1936: "His cigarette holder seemed not merely a scepter but a wand."

Other cartoonists' symbols include Churchill's cigar, Senator Joseph McCarthy's "five o'clock shadow," John F. Kennedy's rocking chair, John L. Lewis' eyebrows, Senator Everett Dirksen's "basset" jowls, Lincoln's stovepipe hat, Theodore Roosevelt's teeth, Coolidge's high collar, Grant's cigar stub, Robert F. Kennedy's shock of hair, Hitler's and Stalin's mustaches, Al Smith's brown derby, Gerald Ford's Band-Aid (from bumping his head) and Jimmy Carter's teeth.

CIRCUMLOCUTION, *see* **RED TAPE.**

CITIZEN OF THE WORLD an internationalist as opposed to an isolationist; more loosely, one concerned with universal issues, whether they apply at home or abroad.

Historian Richard Hofstadter credits Woodrow Wilson with being the first major American figure to urge Americans to be "citizens of the world." Both during World War I and the ensuing fight over U.S. membership in the League of Nations, Wilson constantly tried to combat the isolationist argument that European affairs were no concern of this country. Wilson contended that American principles were not "the principles of a province or of a single continent . . . [but] the principles of a liberated mankind."

Neither the sentiment nor the phrase, of course, was original with Wilson. In 1762 Oliver Goldsmith wrote a satire entitled *Citizen of the World* and the phrase was used in the fourth century B.C. by Socrates. American abolitionist William Lloyd Garrison wrote: "My country is the world; my countrymen are mankind." Franklin Roosevelt, who also had problems with isolationists, said in his last inaugural address: "We have learned to be citizens of the world, members of the world community." John Kennedy expanded the phrase still further in a parallel to his famous "ask not" passage when at his inaugural he said, "My fellow citizens of the world, ask not what America will do for you, but what together we can do for the freedom of man."

CITIZENS COMMITTEE   a pseudo-independent organization set up by a political party to provide a "home" for independents and members of the opposition party; in other cases a genuine nonpartisan committee set up for civic action.

During campaigns it is necessary to enlist the enthusiasm and political activity of people who have no interest in year-round partisan political work.

To provide an umbrella for these citizens who "vote for the man and not the party," the device of the citizens committee was created. In addition, all radio and television commercials and newspaper advertisements must carry the name of the political sponsor; it is considered more palatable to use a citizens committee imprimatur on these advertisements than a political party's. The citizens committee often raises its own money by subdividing itself into "Lawyers for (candidate)," "Professors for (candidate)," "Businessmen for (candidate)," etc. The money raised is then spent at the direction of the party chairman or campaign manager, although there is occasionally some friction between the professionals and the citizens' groups. See AMATEURS.

There is a communist governmental counterpart to this American political technique. In an article on Yugoslavian Marxism, C. P. McVicker writes: ". . . new institutions were created which do serve to bring the ordinary Yugoslav into local government affairs. 'Citizens' councils' are permanent or *ad hoc* bodies of local citizens whose experience and talents make them especially well qualified to advise their people's committee in the various specific areas of its competence."

See VOLUNTEERS; CREEP.

CITY HALL, *see* **GO FIGHT CITY HALL.**

CIVIL DISOBEDIENCE   a doctrine requiring the individual to act against the law, accepting the law's punishment, if he believes the law is morally wrong or politically unjust.

English utilitarian philosopher Jeremy Bentham expressed the position clearly: that it was "allowable to, if not incumbent on, every man . . . to enter into measures of resistance

... when ... the probable mischiefs of resistance (speaking with respect to the community in general) appear less to him than the probable mischiefs of obedience."

In the Declaration of Independence, Thomas Jefferson carried the thought to its political extreme: "... that whenever any Form of Government becomes destructive of these Ends it is the Right of the People to alter or abolish it, and to institute new Government . . ."

Political philosophers have long held that a "natural law" or HIGHER LAW exists that has precedence over the man-made laws, and when these come in conflict the individual has the duty to disobey and resist the man-made laws. But this means that the law may be legally disobeyed, a contradiction in terms that has led to bloody dispute. William Seward of New York said in 1850: "There is a higher law than the Constitution," and his words became an abolitionist rallying cry.

The phrase "civil disobedience" was popularized in the U.S. by Henry David Thoreau's 1848 essay of that title, and in India by Mohandas K. Gandhi in his long battle against British rule. In recent years, it has become one of the cornerstones of the civil rights movement and was expressed eloquently by the Rev. Martin Luther King, Jr., in his "Letter from a Birmingham Jail":

I submit that an individual who breaks a law that conscience tells him is unjust, and willingly accepts the penalty by staying in jail to arouse the conscience of the community over its injustice, is in reality expressing the very highest respect for law.

Of course there is nothing new about this kind of civil disobedience. . . . It was practiced superbly by the early Christians. . . .

We can never forget that everything Hitler did in Germany was "legal" and everything the Hungarian freedom fighters did in Hungary was "illegal." . . .

The noble connotation of the phrase was undermined somewhat in 1967 by the violence of the LONG HOT SUMMER. Civil disobedience was abruptly equated with "race riot" by some, but current usage continues to carry a nonviolent overtone.

Wrote Stewart Alsop in *Newsweek* in 1971: " 'Civil disobedience'—a euphemism for breaking those laws in which the law breaker does not believe—has become both respectable and relatively safe. The civil-rights movement of the early sixties began to make it respectable, and the increasing unpopularity of the Vietnam war has helped to make it safe as well as respectable."

CIVILIAN REVIEW describing a semijudicial board made up of citizens who are not police officers, to investigate complaints made against the police.

"Police brutality" was one of the earliest and most impassioned phrases of the civil rights movement. Photographs of police dogs being loosed on black demonstrators caused a national revulsion that lent impetus to the movement; it also lent credibility to unfair charges of brutality against police officers enforcing the law.

In an effort to lessen racial tensions, several cities adopted civilian review boards to assure minorities of an independent control of police activities. In New York City, the issue of civilian review was put to the voters in 1966, with the concept enthusiastically endorsed by Senators Javits and Kennedy and Mayor John Lindsay. The proposal was overwhelmingly defeated. The police had argued that their own civil liberties were being violated by such a board. However, the vote was attributed to **BACKLASH** by the civil rights groups.

CIVIL RIGHTS   those rights guaranteed to an individual as a member of society; most often applied to the movement for black equality.

Civil rights refers to positive legal prerogatives—the right to equal treatment before the law, the right to vote, the right to share equally with other citizens in such benefits as jobs, housing, education, and public accommodations. In their *Cyclopedia of American Government* (1914), A. C. McLaughlin and A. B. Hart defined civil rights as "those which belong to the individual as a result of his membership in organized society, that is, as a subject of civil government."

The term is sometimes substituted for *civil liberties,* which refers to more negative rights—that is, those things an individual is legally free to do without government interference. Spelled out in the Constitution and the Bill of Rights, the more notable civil liberties include freedom of speech, press, assembly and religion, and protection against unreasonable searches and seizures.

Virtually interchangeable with civil rights is the seldom-used *civic rights,* though the latter is somewhat broader. At the 1924 Democratic convention, for example, liberals who wanted to condemn the Ku Klux Klan for its discrimination against Jews and Catholics as well as Negroes, introduced a plank opposing any attempts "to limit the civic rights of any citizen or body of citizens because of religion, birthplace or racial origin." The plank was narrowly defeated by Southern Democratic votes, and the issue has been a bitterly divisive one in the Democratic party ever since.

"Civil rights," however, is a term more closely associated with the Negro's struggle for equal treatment since the Civil War (though for a time it was used often by labor union organizers). In 1875, Congress passed a Civil Rights Act outlawing discrimination in public accommodations. By 1883, a reaction had set in, and the Supreme Court found key sections of the act unconstitutional. Not until 1957 was another Civil Rights Act passed.

See **SEPARATE BUT EQUAL; WE SHALL OVERCOME; FREEDOM RIDERS; HUMAN RIGHTS.**

CLEAN SWEEP   a smashing, across-the-board victory; a wide-ranging change of officeholders.

In current usage, *landslide* refers more often to a great individual victory; *avalanche* refers to a great number of votes; *clean sweep* refers to a wide party victory with many successful candidates belonging to a single party.

The phrase stems from the expression "a new broom sweeps clean," an English proverb traceable to 1546. In Andrew Jackson's presidential campaigns, "Old Hickory" promised that his hickory broom would sweep out the "Augean stables" of corruption—specifically the "corrupt bargain" of John Quincy Adams and Henry Clay. In 1840 Clay was quoted as saying, "General Jackson was a bold and fearless reaper carrying a wide row, but he did not gather the whole harvest; he left some gleanings to his faithful successor, and he seems resolved to sweep clean the field of power."

Soon after Jackson's inauguration, the phrase's meaning changed. The **SPOILS SYSTEM** entered American politics and a "clean sweep" came to mean a total change of appointive officeholders. In the twentieth century, however, the meaning reverted to its original sense of broad party victory.

CLEAR IT WITH SIDNEY a statement of FDR's used by his critics to illustrate how strongly the President was dominated by organized labor.

Arthur Krock reported in the *New York Times* on July 25, 1944, that Roosevelt had said "Clear everything with Sidney" in connection with the choice of a Vice President in 1944. (The choice turned out to be Harry Truman to replace Henry Wallace. Others being considered at the time were James Byrnes, William O. Douglas, Sam Rayburn, Paul McNutt, Scott Lucas, Alben Barkley, and John G. Winant.)

"Sidney" was Sidney Hillman, head of the Political Action Committee of the CIO, a Roosevelt adviser. The remark was officially denied, but in a book published fourteen years later James F. Byrnes said the remark was made between July 15 and 17, 1944.

Hillman strongly urged that Wallace be kept on the ticket, but it never "cleared" FDR. Truman was Hillman's second choice. The attack on Hillman, Samuel Rosenman felt, "was obviously an unvarnished, unabashed appeal to anti-Jewish prejudices. . . . The President did not try to defend Sidney Hillman, or say that there was no truth to the charge that things had to be 'cleared with Sidney.' Instead, he carried the attack right to his opponent." Roosevelt's attack came early in the campaign, slamming into religious intolerance in a Boston speech: ". . . big as this country is, there is no room in it for racial or religious intolerance . . . and there is no room for snobbery."

Writing about Hillman a decade later, C. Wright Mills gave the phrase sociological significance, ". . . his awareness of himself as a member of the national elite, and the real and imagined recognition he achieved as a member ('Clear it with Sidney') signaled the larger entrance, after the great expansion of the unions and after the New Deal, of labor leaders into the power elite."

In the Eisenhower Administration, a frequent remark was "Clear it with Sherm" (Sherman Adams, see **ABOMINABLE NO-MAN**). In 1967, a *New York Times* story began: "The 'clear it with Hubert' order was issued by the President at a cabinet meeting last Wednesday."

In current usage, "run it past" is overtaking "clear it with."

CLOAKROOM congressional meeting places just off the Senate and House floors, where congressmen confer, trade, and gossip.

As far back as 1868, English observer George Rose wrote to his countrymen about "a rush to the cloakroom amid the shouts and laughter of the House." The "cloakrooms" of the Capitol came to mean not a place to hang a hat but a place to bargain. "In the quiet councils of committee rooms and cloakrooms," wrote former White House correspondent Charles Hurd in 1965, "they negotiate, compromise and trade their votes."

The sense of trading in the cloakrooms appears to be switching more to a sense of gossiping. "The cloakrooms of Congress resounded with a lurid account," reported the *Chicago Daily News* in 1947, "of what General Eisenhower there proposed as a solution." Congressional cloakrooms are tending to become synonymous with "rumor mill" and "rumor factory."

See LOBBY.

CLOSED SHOP a place of work where only union members may be employed.

The "closed shop"—so called because it excludes unorganized workers from the workshop—goes back to labor troubles in Philadelphia's shoe industry in the early nineteenth century. But it was not really used widely until the early twentieth century. Unionists prefer "union shop," because it sounds less restrictive. As the publication *American Federationist* wrote in 1904: "The object of the union shop is not to create a monopoly of opportunity. *It is not a closed shop.*" But the phrase has stuck. In a 1948 article, for example, the *Chicago Daily News* wrote, "A 'closed shop' violates the fundamental rights of the individual." See RIGHT TO WORK.

CLOSED SOCIETY, *see* **OPEN SOCIETY.**

CLOSING RANKS the act of healing wounds after a battle for nomination and achieving party unity in the general election.

After a particularly bitter primary, there are always those who will speak up for the importance of the two-party system and the need to close ranks. Customarily, the victor in a nomination fight extends the invitation to his previous opposition; many political analysts were astounded at Barry Goldwater's 1964 acceptance speech at the Republican convention, when no such invitation was offered.

Like many other political expressions (see ON THE POINT), this is a MILITARY METAPHOR, referring to the scattering of troops during a skirmish and the subsequent need to close

ranks to become a cohesive fighting force once again.

The act of forcing a smile and supporting the man who defeated you or your candidate is a difficult and humbling experience. Two Republicans who opposed William McKinley's nomination in 1896—Henry Cabot Lodge and Theodore Roosevelt—traveled to Canton, Ohio, where the candidate was conducting his FRONT-PORCH CAMPAIGN and made the necessary obeisances. Statesman John Hay wrote: "Cabot and Teddy have been to Canton to offer their heads to the axe and their tummies to the hari-kari knife."

CLOTH COAT, *see* **CHECKERS SPEECH.**

CLOUD NO BIGGER THAN A MAN'S HAND, *see* **STRAW POLL.**

CLOUT power, or influence.

Clout means political *power* when applied to a candidate or public political personage; it means *influence* when applied to a political leader not in the public eye, a large contributor, or member of a palace guard.

Since it can be used to define both political influence and political power, the word has a fuzzy meaning —because there is a difference between power and influence.

Clout, in its power sense, applies to the ability of an individual or group to put across a program, decide a nomination, sway votes. In its influence sense, clout means the ability to reach and persuade those in power; it is one step removed from the power source.

The political use of the word is believed to have originated in Chicago in the 1940s, taken from the baseball phrase "What a clout!," meaning "a powerful hit" or "a long hard drive."

Another possibility is a derivation

from cloth, or specifically handkerchief. Atcheson Hench in *American Speech* magazine (October 1959), pointed out that a "clouter" was originally a handkerchief thief, the noun "clout" later covering any petty thievery. In current underworld lingo, "to clout heaps" means to steal automobiles. It is a short jump from thievery to political influence; still, most politicians think the word comes from a baseball slugger.

Columnist Irv Kupcinet, in the *Chicago Sun-Times,* December 14, 1958, said: "Defendants in Chicago, as in Los Angeles, are found innocent on the age-old legal premise of 'reasonable doubt'—not, as the judge insinuated, 'reasonable clout.' "

A member of the U.S. Office of Education said mournfully in 1972: "We just don't have the clout we would have with specific legislation, and what we need more than anything else right now is some muscle to get this thing moving." Theodore M. Bernstein, in his word-watching column syndicated by the *New York Times,* provided a nice distinction between "clout" and "muscle": "The two words mean vitually the same thing: power or effectiveness, particularly in the areas of government or business. But . . . there is a shade of difference between the two. The accumulation of *muscle* leads to the possession of *clout.* "

An early citation of this vivid political term was supplied the author by writer Paul Hoffman of New York, who found a use in Harold Gasnell's *Machine Politics,* published in 1937, quoting a Chicago precinct captain: "No one gets anywhere in politics or business on his merits. He has to have the 'clout' from behind."

See JUICE.

CLUB, *see* **INNER CLUB.**

COALITION   a grouping of often disparate political elements into a major party, or of several minor parties into a working majority.

"A political aspirant in the United States," Alexis de Tocqueville wrote, "begins by discovering his own interest, and discovering those other interests which may be collected around and amalgamated with it." According to political scientist James MacGregor Burns, "Tocqueville was describing one of the oldest and simplest acts of politics—the effort of the Greek magistrate or the Roman senator, of the Russian revolutionary or the British squire, to piece together a following big enough to win power in a legislative assembly or a political party or a popular election."

One example is the formation of the Republican party. It drew its strength, as Clinton Rossiter wrote in *Parties and Politics in America,* from "almost every party and group on the American scene—from the Whigs, yes, but also from the Democrats, Free-Soilers, Abolitionists, Know-Nothings, local third parties and, lest we forget, the temperance movement."

This is the essence of U.S.-style coalition. In multiparty nations abroad, a coalition involves the fusion of a number of individual parties into a working majority. West Germany's "Grand Coalition" of the Socialist and Christian Democratic parties is an example. In the U.S., by contrast, the major parties are themselves coalitions, combining liberals, moderates, and conservatives, and helping Democrats and Republicans to avoid extremes. For this reason, most politicians instinctively reject suggestions that U.S. politics be realigned into liberal and conservative parties.

Former NBC News president Richard Wald noted the danger in the decline of coalition politics in a 1978 *Esquire* interview with reporter Richard Reeves: "Old politicians were looking for part of the audience, for a coalition. They were looking at problems and saying, 'Look, this is a common problem for many of you. I'll represent you in dealing with it.' The new politicians are looking for chords. They float above the problems. They strike responsive chords. What they really want to do is cloud men's minds."

Words of praise for coalitions are BIG TENT and "umbrella"; attack phrases are STRANGE BEDFELLOWS and UNHOLY ALLIANCE.

COATTAILS political carrying power; the ability to attract and hold support, not only for oneself but for other members of a ticket.

Congressman Abraham Lincoln popularized the phrase in a speech in the House on July 27, 1848, after the metaphor had been introduced by Alfred Iverson of Georgia:

But the gentleman from Georgia further says, we have deserted all our principles, and taken shelter under General Taylor's military coat tail. . . . Has he no acquaintance with the ample military coat tail of General Jackson? Does he not know that his own party have run the last five Presidential races under that coat tail, and that they are now running the sixth, under the same cover? . . . Mr. Speaker, old horses and military coat tails, or tails of any sort, are not figures of speech, such as I would be the first to introduce into discussions here; but . . .

The military connotation soon fell by the wayside and coattails came to mean an inducement to straight-ticket voting.

In the 1960 presidential campaign, Kennedy supporter Adlai Stevenson said of the Republican nominee,

"Nixon is finding out there are no tails on an Eisenhower jacket." In the 1966 congressional campaign, when Nixon achieved a political comeback stumping the country for congressional candidates, he also found use for the metaphor, attacking Lyndon B. Johnson's sagging popularity: "There is a new fashion sweeping the country: skirts are shorter, pants are tighter and the LBJ coattails are going out of style."

See HYMIE'S FERRYBOAT.

CODE WORDS a charge that particular phrases, innocuous in themselves, are intended to transmit hidden meanings.

Charles P. Taft, chairman of the Fair Campaign Practices Committee, said in 1968:

. . . candidates who would never use the word "nigger" nor any of its slurring variations, are using other terms which apparently carry a similar connotation. They are using the racial shorthand in areas of the country where an outright expression of racism would bring immediate social—and political—ostracism. . . .

These forms suggest rather than state, the campaigner's intent. For instance, instead of saying he is opposed to open housing, the sophisticated racist proclaims, "YOUR HOME IS YOUR CASTLE," and leaves the rest unsaid. We cannot prevent voters from casting ballots based on racist sentiment, but we can spotlight those campaigners who appeal to that sentiment. We can, that is, if we point to an objective study of the understood meanings of the campaign code words—the current shorthand of racial bigotry.

Among the words considered part of the "code" at that time were LAW AND ORDER, CRIME IN THE STREETS, and FORCED BUSING.

Undoubtedly, in many cases the

use of these words was intended to, and did, cloak appeal to racial prejudice. However, they were also often used in good faith to discuss controversial topics, and the "code word" charge could be, and was, used as a smear.

The code is sometimes only in the eye of the beholder. In a few areas, for example, whenever the phrase "Roman Catholic" is used rather than "Catholic," anti-Catholic prejudice is suspected—since "Roman" (as in "Rum, Romanism and Rebellion") is occasionally perceived as a word intended to show domination from abroad.

Wrote Max Lerner in the *New York Post* on September 20, 1972:

Every campaign becomes, at some point, a battle of coded words and ideas . . . in which the issues are somehow scooped out and only the verbal husk remains. [Senator George McGovern's] code words are "precious young lives" and "dying far from home for a corrupt dictatorship." Another is "SPECIAL INTERESTS." . . . The code vocabulary of the Republicans is much longer, richer, more available. Take President Nixon's quick visit to an Italian American festival in Prince George's County, Md. All he had to do was use the words "work" and "family" and everybody got the message. He was talking of the WORK ETHIC as against "getting something for nothing." He was talking of family loyalties as against the uprooted and alienated "kids." "QUOTAS" became a coded signal at the Republican convention. It is working overtime for Nixon among the "ETHNICS," and has become one of the major symbols in the areas of Jewish voters.

Although "code words" are sometimes used to mean "euphemism," most often the phrase is an attempt to impugn the motive of the speaker, by imputing a racist, sexist, anti-youth or anti-intellectual overlay to what may (or may not) be intended.

In the *Wall Street Journal* on July 18, 1977, Irving Kristol objected to to use of biased code words in news broadcasts:

There are "ultraconservatives" on TV news (e.g., Cardinal Lefevre, Senator Jesse Helms) but when was the last time you encountered an "ultraliberal"? Apparently there is no such species. Nor are there any "extremists" to the left of center— only "militants" or "activists." An "extremist" is someone who passionately holds the wrong views, while a "militant" is someone who is immoderately pursuing the "correct" ends.

. . . But the neatest ploy of all is the selective use of the word "controversial"; legislation to regulate the price of natural gas is not controversial. Anita Bryant is "controversial"; leaders of Gay Rights groups are not. This is the subtlest code word of them all. Watch for it.

The language of diplomacy is rife with code words. In the Middle East, the phrase "defensible borders" is taken by Israelis and Arabs to mean not returning much of the land taken by Israel in the 1967 war. The phrase "legitimate rights of the Palestinian people" is seen as a commitment to the "right" to a sovereign state, and its use by President Carter in 1977 angered many supporters of Israel, who would have preferred "legitimate interests" (Mr. Carter countered by saying he did not say "legitimate *national* rights").

To whites in South Africa, "majority rule" is a code phrase for black takeover (see ONE MAN, ONE VOTE); among Eurocommunists, "proletarian internationalism" is shorthand for domination by Moscow.

In 1970 the author, preparing a

speech for President Nixon, slipped up on a diplomatic code word. In Europe, the U.S. and the Soviet Union have been negotiating in a desultory fashion about the removal of each other's troops. The Americans call this Mutual and Balanced Force Reduction (MBFR); the Soviets call it Mutual Force Reduction (MFR). In the speech, the writer left out "and balanced"; Secretary of State William Rogers called to ask that the two words be inserted in the written version of the speech as finally released for publication. The reason is that the U.S. thinks the removal of one American across the Atlantic ocean should be "balanced" by the removal of more than one Russian from nearby Europe—as Secretary Rogers put it, "those two words could mean a couple hundred thousand troops." The dispute continues, and some European countries—wanting to offend neither superpower—referred to the talks in 1978 as "M (B) FR" talks.

In 1977, writing in *The New Yorker* about the victory of Ed Koch in New York City's mayoral race, Andy Logan quoted the mayor-elect as saying, "The code word of my Administration will be 'reality.'" The writer added parenthetically, "'code' word is now itself a kind of code word." The mayor probably intended an up-to-date version of "byword."

COFFEE-KLATSCH CAMPAIGN a method of campaigning in urban areas where the candidate meets small groups of voters at a "coffee hour."

Cocktail parties lend themselves to fund-raising, but less to campaigning with the candidate present; they tend to degenerate into bona fide cocktail parties, noisy, and inattentive. The coffee-klatsch (*Klatsch* is German for

noise, akin to the English "clatter") offers a candidate an opportunity to meet about twenty-five people personally, make a brief talk, and move on. The coffee-klatsch is usually given by one of the voters. It costs the host little and has proven an effective technique for apartment-house dwellers.

The German word, sometimes used in full, is spelled *kaffeeklatsch*—one word, lower case, no hyphen.

COLD WAR nonmilitary conflict; ideological hostilities; now used to indicate outmoded or unwanted policies.

Capitalized, *the* Cold War refers to international tension and jockeying for power between the Soviet Union (and its satellites) and the Western nations; lower case, a cold war is any adversary activity short of open conflict; behind-the-scenes struggle; tension and deadlock beneath the political surface, as "the cold war between the Johnsons and the Kennedys."

The phrase was minted by Herbert Bayard Swope, publicist, three-time winner of the Pulitzer Prize, and occasional speechwriter for elder statesman (and Port Washington, N.Y., neighbor) Bernard Baruch. In 1946, about the time Churchill was speaking of an IRON CURTAIN, Swope used "cold war" in a draft speech for Baruch to describe U.S.-Soviet relations (as contrasted to the recent "hot" or "shooting" war). Baruch felt it was too strong, but used it one year later in a speech at Columbia, South Carolina: "Let us not be deceived—today we are in the midst of a cold war." He repeated the phrase, by that time picked up and popularized by columnist Walter Lippmann, to the Senate War Investigating Committee on October 24, 1948.

Since "cold war," along with "iron curtain," is one of the great coinages of the post–World War II period, its birth deserves a close examination. The late Mr. Swope's secretary, Kathleen Gilmour, provided the author with a file of correspondence on the coinage. From Bernard Baruch to Swope, August 17, 1949:

The first time I ever heard the expression "cold war" was when you first said it some time about June 1946. We decided not to use it at that time. I first used the phrase in April 1947 on the occasion of the presentation of my portrait to South Carolina. This was the first time it was given currency or was publicly uttered so far as I know. Immediately afterward, it was very much commented upon, especially in an editorial in the *New York Daily News*. I then called Mr. [Reuben] Maury and told him I had gotten it from you. Later on, he wrote an editorial giving you credit. In other words, you coined the expression and I gave it currency.

Baruch freely credited Swope with the coinage in several interviews; the probable reason Swope elicited the credit in writing was that Walter Lippmann was being given credit as coiner rather than as disseminator. Lippmann, after a while, mentioned to Swope that he recalled a French expression in the thirties, *la guerre froide*, and on May 10, 1950, Swope wrote Lippmann to set him straight:

The first time the idea of the cold war came to me was probably in '39 or '40 when America was talking about a "shooting" war. I had never heard that sort of qualification. To me "shooting" war was like saying a death murder—rather tautologous, verbose and redundant.

I thought the proper opposite of the so-called hot war was cold war, and I used that adjective in the early '40's in some letters I wrote, before our war.

I may have been subconsciously affected by the term cold pogrom which was used to describe the attitude of the Nazis toward the Jews in the middle '30's. I never heard the French expressions to which you refer.

The description became timely again when the Russians were putting pressure on us for the second front, but I used it first in a little talk I made in '45, just before the war ended. Then in '46 at the time BMB made his speech to the United Nations on the American attitude toward the atomic bomb, I used the phrase in the first draft of his speech that I prepared in March or April. Baruch, Eberstadt and Hancock thought it was too severe to describe our relations with the Russians, even though they had been attenuated for a long time, so it was taken out of the speech.

But the words were put in an important speech which Baruch delivered at the end of '46 or the beginning of '47 at the State Capitol in South Carolina when his portrait was unveiled. . . .

I hope this answers your question. I've always believed that I happened to be the first to use the phrase.

A part of the American political language, the phrase gained international currency when Deputy Premier Nikolai Bulganin used it in his opening speech at the Big Four Conference in Geneva on July 18, 1955. Calling for a lessening of international tensions in accord with the "spirit of Geneva" (see SPIRIT OF), Bulganin spoke of the Soviet "desire for a settlement of the outstanding international problems and for the termination of the 'Cold War.' "

Sir Ernest Gowers, who attributes the phrase to Walter Lippmann in his revision of Fowler's *Modern English Usage*, makes this point on its usage: ". . . the metaphor places politicians in a dilemma when they try to follow it up. Are they to advocate a rise or a fall in the temperature of the cold war? The latter would seem to intensify an already alarming crisis; the former to bring the hot war a stage nearer. This problem has to be dodged by doing violence to the metaphor. *In an atmosphere of 'live and let live' for a generation the cold war may well become less turbulent.*"

The problem appears to have been solved by the use of "a thaw in the Cold War," which indicates a melting of the frozen positions without the increased danger of a hot war.

Currently, "cold warrior" is a term of derogation used by supporters of DÉTENTE. Conservative writer Richard Whalen used "Cold War II" in the mid-seventies to describe a hardening of Soviet attitudes, which froze over in 1978 and caused Mr. Carter's National Security Adviser, Zbigniew Brzezinski, to be labeled by many U.S. "doves" as a "cold warrior."

COLLEGE OF CARDINALS, *see* **POWERHOUSE.**

COLORATION ideological identification based on political associations, record and statements.

This has remained an inside political word because its use has been relatively narrow. When a political team is being set up around a candidate, or a ticket is being balanced (see BAL-ANCED TICKET), consideration is given to coloration: RIGHT WING, LEFT WING, private or public power, EASTERN ESTABLISHMENT, Southern Conservative or other region, known for any beliefs or slogans, etc.

Coloration is purely appearance, not necessarily substance; many times, honest, outspoken men acquire —through region, association, family name—a coloration totally different from their point of view.

"The most striking discovery one makes in examining the Johnson history," wrote Selig Harrison in the *New Republic* in 1960, "is how little he has changed. Unlike Kennedy—whose political coloration is not at all what it was ten years ago—Johnson seems to have been from the beginning more or less what he is today."

COLOR METAPHORS BLACK REPUBLICANS referred to those who supported Negro causes in the mid-nineteenth century, and *black* has been used often to describe Negroes and their supporters. See BLACK, PO-LITICAL USE OF. The Black and Tans were opposed by the Lily-Whites, and BLACK POWER emerged in the 1960s.

White is also most often used racially, with a "white hope" stemming from the attempts of white boxers to defeat Negro champion Jack Johnson. And the word CANDIDATE comes from the Latin "white toga," the color symbolizing purity of motive.

However, issues are not all black and white; *"gray* areas" are known to exist, often providing the best atmosphere for a GRAY EMINENCE like a monk who controls a cardinal who controls a king. The gray uniforms of the Confederate soldiers led to the phrase "the grays and the blues" with blue the Union color.

Blue has a sexual overtone. Blue jokes offend bluenoses, who pass blue laws closing stores on Sundays.

Green is the color of the amateur, the newcomer; the greenhorn was carefully cultivated by big-city machines, which also provided cash, or "long green," or "greenbacks." However, the Green Berets of the U.S. Special Forces gave the color professionalism.

Purple symbolizes royalty. The color also is a sign of apoplexy; insulted politicians turn purple.

Yellow stands for cowardice, and there is no baser charge than having "a yellow streak"; yellow journalism deals in sensationalism, derived from the papers that carried the comic strip "The Yellow Kid"; and the dangers in Asia used to be called "the yellow peril."

Brown, as in Brown Shirt, connotes fascism to some; *orange* is often used in describing atomic explosions, and radical *red* has a separate entry herein.

For "color-blind," see QUOTAS.

COLOSSUS OF THE NORTH, *see* **GOOD NEIGHBOR POLICY.**

COME NOW, AND LET US REA-SON TOGETHER   a Biblical saying identified with Lyndon B. Johnson's CONSENSUS.

Adlai Stevenson, introducing a book of Johnson speeches, wrote: " 'Come now, and let us reason together' is Lyndon Johnson's favorite quotation and his best characterization. I can't recall when I first heard him use these words from Isaiah. But for the thirty years I have known him —as a Congressional secretary, Congressman, Senate Majority leader, Vice President, and now President— reasoning together, face to face, has been his method and his strength."

Arthur Schlesinger, Jr., later wrote of a meeting between Johnson and Philip Graham, then publisher of the *Washington Post* in the hectic days before the 1960 Democratic convention: "Graham had meanwhile arranged to lunch that day with Johnson in the double hope of persuading him to release Stevenson from his neutrality pledge in order to nominate Kennedy and also of persuading Johnson to accept the Vice Presidency. But he found the Senate leader

far from Isaiah and in no mood for reasoning together." The paragraph is footnoted "Isaiah 1:18, L.B.J., *passim.*"

From time to time, when Republicans were attacking Johnson's assumption of the centrist position and difficult-to-assail consensus, they pointed to more of the same Isaiah quotation, a prophet's threat: "If ye be willing and obedient, ye shall eat the good of the land; but if ye refuse and rebel ye shall be devoured with the sword."

The prophet's words were used derisively against memories of the Johnson Administration in the early seventies, but were recalled with affection by Senator Hubert Humphrey in October 1977, as the former Johnson Vice President, dying of cancer, addressed the Senate: "What a wonderful place this is, where we can argue, fight, have different points of view, and still have a great respect for one another and, many times, deep affection . . . now my plea to us is, in the words of Isaiah, as a former President used to say,—and I mean it very sincerely—'Come, let us reason together.' "

COMMITTED   cliché for dedicated, involved, a believer in; opposite of alienated, disengaged.

"Participatory democracy" was a catch phrase of the New Left, meaning citizen involvement in the affairs that affect him: the poor involved in the administration of poverty programs, students in the administration of schools, workers in the management of business. Only in this way, the new radicals held, could ALIENA-TION be overcome and people be given incentive to become "committed." The word was popularized in modern politics by French leftist philosopher Jean-Paul Sartre, who urged *engagement* in a 1946 book: "What counts is total commitment."

The word was also used in the negative, referring to the "uncommitted nations," synonym for NEUTRALISTS or THIRD WORLD. In politics, a commitment meant a pledge or promise (see CONTRACT). In the sixties, however, the new meaning of the word took hold and was especially useful because it did not label the one described to any single political belief.

Russell Baker, the "Observer" of the *New York Times,* imagined a dialogue between a jargon doctor and a man who felt that being described as a "liberal" meant that he was no longer "with it."

"Ideally," said the doctor, "you should have people say of you, 'He is committed.' When that happens, and word gets about that you have 'made a commitment,' your return to a gratifying sense of moral superiority should follow quite rapidly."

"But what am I supposed to get committed to?"

"What a silly question! When you were a liberal, you didn't feel that you had to be liberal about anything in particular, did you? The comfort derived from feeling the word snugly wrapped about you. It is the same with being 'committed.' In political unthink, nothing much changes but the words."

Curiously, in its noun form, the word assumed a conservative cast: "to honor commitments" became a hard-liner's plea.

COMMON MAN, CENTURY OF THE   utopian ideal popularized by Henry A. Wallace in a 1942 speech.

"The century on which we are entering can be and must be the century of the common man," said Wallace, who was FDR's Vice President at the time he made the speech. "Every-

where the common people are on the march."

In the middle third of the century, the "common man" was the subject of some lavish flattery. Even Adolf Hitler sought to embrace him. "National Socialism," said the Nazi dictator, "is the revolution of the common man." But political thinkers soon began recalling that commonness had not always been a cherished value— far from it. "The superior man," Confucius said, "thinks always of virtue; the common man thinks of comfort."

In 1956, former President Herbert Hoover warned that "we are in danger of developing a cult of the Common Man, which means a cult of mediocrity." Essayist Joseph Wood Krutch wrote:

From defending the common man we pass on to exalting him and we find ourselves beginning to imply not merely that he is as good as anybody else but that he is actually better. Instead of demanding only that the common man be given an opportunity to become as uncommon as possible, we make his commonness a virtue and, even in the case of candidates for high office, we sometimes praise them for being nearly indistinguishable from the average man in the street.

To Lyndon Johnson, speaking at the Tufts University commencement in 1963, "it seems no longer adequate to describe this as the Century of the Common Man." For, he explained, a "revolution of education" was underway that was "changing the capabilities of the common man," so much so that the period "should henceforth be known as the Century of the Educated Man."

Still, the idea of the common man has not entirely lost its appeal, particularly for politicians. After Richard Nixon's 1952 CHECKERS SPEECH, Scripps-Howard columnist Robert

Ruark wrote: "Tuesday night the nation saw a little man, squirming his way out of a dilemma, and laying bare his most private hopes, fears and liabilities. This time the common man was a Republican, for a change."

COMMUNISM WITH A HUMAN FACE, *see* EUROCOMMUNISM.

COMMUNIST TERMINOLOGY

There are separate entries in this dictionary for PROLETARIAT, PARTY LINE, PEACEFUL CO-EXISTENCE, and WARS OF NATIONAL LIBERATION. The following smattering of Communist terms is adapted from a glossary prepared by Richard V. Allen in *Peace or Peaceful Co-Existence?*, published by the American Bar Association in 1966.

adventurism: "excess revolutionary zeal" that leads to taking unnecessary risks and increases the possibility of error.

bourgeoisie: originally the middle class, as distinguished from the very wealthy; Lenin later enlarged this group to include all property owners. In current use it can mean all non-Communists.

class enemy: a class that holds political power or which stands between the proletariat and its achievement of power; also, anti-Communists within Communist countries.

class struggle: from Marx and Engels in their "Communist Manifesto"— "The history of all hitherto existing society is the history of class struggles." Communist doctrine holds that classes must seek to destroy each other until the proletariat is victorious.

counterrevolution: opposing an accomplished Communist revolution or seeking to crush a developing Communist revolution.

oppressed peoples: citizens of colonial or nonself-governing areas, as well as those emerging nations which maintain too close ties with their former developers.

For a group of Communist terms about deviation from the party line, see REVISIONISM.

COMMUNITY   a kindly lumping together of related organizations, instilling by euphemism a sense of shared purpose rarely present.

The "defense establishment" was a term used by defenders of expanded budgets for the armed services who were derided by critics of the MILITARY-INDUSTRIAL COMPLEX. However, when "establishment" became pejorative—as in EASTERN ESTABLISHMENT—military people and their supporters began talking (in the early sixties) of the "defense community", probably taken from Walter Lippmann's mid-forties ATLANTIC COMMUNITY.

"Community" had a less cliquish connotation, and had been a favored term of home builders, who had changed "tract developers" to "community developers." Similarly, the term "business leaders" was followed by "the business community" as arbiters of whether an Administration possessed "business confidence."

The "community" euphemism came to the rescue of the beleaguered members of the spying profession in the seventies. The "cloak-and-dagger crowd," also known as the "intelligence establishment" became the "intelligence community." As in real communities, resentments soon developed among people living on different sides of the tracks.

A related word, "set," is always used pejoratively in politics, from the isolationist "Cliveden set" in Great

Britain before World War II to the "Georgetown cocktail party set" in Washington in the sixties and seventies.

COMPACT OF FIFTH AVENUE an agreement between Governor Nelson Rockefeller and Vice President Richard Nixon before the Republican convention in 1960, temporarily healing a breach between liberal and conservative wings in the party on the subjects of civil rights and national defense.

The platform committee, headed by Charles Percy, had drafted a platform acceptable to Republican conservatives and middle-of-the-roaders, but the Rockefeller forces let it be known that—unless the document was changed—they would launch a floor fight. Without informing his Chicago convention staff, Nixon went to Rockefeller's New York apartment; over dinner, he offered the governor the vice-presidential nomination, which was declined, and then the two men went over a draft memo submitted by Rockefeller's staff.

The 14-point "compact" that emerged advocated increased defense expenditures, took a cautiously liberal view on health care for the aged and education, and a forthright civil rights position. When the manifesto was passed on to the delegates in Chicago, many were furious at Rockefeller's "high-handedness," others charged Nixon with a SELLOUT. To many conservatives, this appeared to be the opposite side of the coin minted eight years before between Eisenhower and Taft at the SURRENDER ON MORNINGSIDE HEIGHTS.

In fact, those positions advocated in the compact were on the whole those taken by Nixon before and since; he took personal charge of selling the platform committee on the

changes needed, and the furor died, though Senator Goldwater had branded the compact "the Munich of the Republican party." See MUNICH, ANOTHER. President Eisenhower felt that the defense suggestions were an affront to his administration, although Nixon had removed Rockefeller's proposal that $3 billion in additional defense expenditure was immediately necessary. As with all successful platforms, compromises were made; the term "sit-in," part of the Rockefeller statement, was left out of the final plank, but the plank was strongly enough worded to satisfy the liberals. With the help of Representative Melvin Laird of Wisconsin, an accomplished parliamentarian who took over Charles Percy's chair on the 103-man platform committee, the "compact of Fifth Avenue" reshaped the 1960 platform.

COMSYMP Communist sympathizer; FELLOW TRAVELER.

This was a coinage of Robert Welch, founder of the John Birch Society, who held that the leadership of American corporations, universities, foundations, communications media, and government is riddled with Communists and those who agree with Communist aims.

The word was useful to Birchers because it avoided having to say if any particular person under attack was a Communist party member or not.

See PINKO; BIRCHER.

CONCESSION SPEECH remarks of a candidate in the process of being defeated, recognizing the inevitable loss and permitting the winner to make his victory speech.

The two men with the greatest opportunity to refine Presidential concession speeches reacted quite differently. Henry Clay said, "I would rather be right than be President" (see I'D RATHER BE RIGHT), which had the flavor of sour grapes. William Jennings Bryan, after his third defeat, said, "I am reminded of the drunk who, when he had been thrown down the stairs of a club for the third time, gathered himself up, and said, 'I am on to those people. They don't want me in there.' "

To show that defeat need not mean failure, politicians who lose often turn to the comments of sportsmen. Sportswriter Grantland Rice produced this classic: "For when the One Great Scorer comes to mark against your name, he writes—not that you won or lost—but how you played the game." (Green Bay Packer coach Vince Lombardi, in a succeeding generation, took a harder line: "Winning is not the most important thing about football—it's the only thing.")

Napoleon, after Waterloo, said, "My downfall raises me to infinite heights." Winston Churchill began an aphorism with "In defeat, defiance"; Ernest Hemingway, after a serious air crash in 1954, remarked, "I am a little beat up, but I assure you it is only temporary," a modern version of John Paul Jones's "I've just begun to fight."

Although the speech conceding defeat is as old as politics, the modern concession speech began to come into its own with network radio election coverage and blossomed fully in the atmosphere of television. Rapid reporting and analysis of election returns on election night, with computerized "decisions" by commentators (with propagation of phrases like "probable winner" and "too close to call"), has resulted in the opportunity to have both concession and victory statement on the same night.

The televised concession speech can be poignant (Hubert Humphrey after his West Virginia primary defeat by John F. Kennedy in 1960, with a folk singer strumming a melancholy song) or even nonexistent (Nixon in 1960, with the tide appearing to turn in his favor after midnight, as West Coast results made the race one of the closest in U.S. presidential history, but prompting Kennedy's caustic comment: "No class").

One of the most eloquent of the televised concession speeches was Adlai Stevenson's in 1952; after reading his congratulatory telegram to General Eisenhower, he concluded: "Someone asked me, as I came in, down on the street, how I felt, and I was reminded of a story that a fellow-townsman of ours used to tell—Abraham Lincoln. They asked him how he felt once after an unsuccessful election. He said he felt like a little boy who had stubbed his toe in the dark. He said that he was too old to cry, but it hurt too much to laugh."

CONDITION, NOT A THEORY, see PRACTICAL POLITICS.

CONFLICT OF INTEREST the dilemma of a person trying to serve two masters.

"As a phrase, 'conflict of interest' is a relative newcomer to the American lexicon of wrongdoing," wrote *Newsweek* in January 1969. "But as a political problem, it is as ancient as public servants with private incomes, secret holdings or conveniently placed kin." Senator Daniel Webster's 1832 letter to Bank of the United States president Nicholas Biddle was cited: "I believe my retainer has not been renewed or refreshed as usual." At the time of Webster's dunning, the Senate and the bank were in a battle over the bank's charter.

The phrase was probably born, or at least gained currency, during

World War II. In a letter to the Secretary of War on March 31, 1942, Acting Attorney General Charles Fahy gave an opinion about the suggestion that an Army officer be permitted to maintain liaison with a corporation in which he held stock. "Conflict between the interests of the U.S.," wrote Fahy, "the interests of the corporation and the interests of the Army officer as an officer and stockholder of the corporation are more than likely to arise." The Justice official quoted Section 41 of the Criminal Code and a statute forbidding government employees from accepting salary from outside sources for government work, adding: "Both are intended to prevent a conflict between self-interest and the interests of the government."

The phrase has been adopted in the criminal code: Chapter 11 of Title 18 of the U.S. Code is entitled "Bribery, Graft and Conflicts of Interest."

As the phrase became more current recently, columnist Les Whitten made it the title of a novel in the mid-seventies.

CONSCIOUSNESS-RAISING inciting to enthusiastic involvement; awakening the need for political activity; a recognition of suppressed resentments which call for redress.

"Consciousness," wrote John Locke in his 1690 *Essay on Human Understanding*, "is the perception of what passes in a Man's own mind." That quality of perception—of being awake—is usually involved in the many uses of the word.

Although moral philosophers, and later psychologists, popularized the term, in the mid-twentieth century politicians made it their own. It has early Communist associations; former Moscow correspondents have reported to this lexicographer of its frequent use in ideological discussions in

the fifties, and Theodore H. White, in his 1978 book *In Search of History,* writes of an interview held in 1941, in the Chinese Communist redoubt in Yenan, with P'eng Te-hai, a close ally of Mao Tse-Tung: "The men who came in from the field, he said . . . had to have their minds washed out, had to be remolded in ideology. [See **BRAINWASHING**.] At first he thought this could be done in only three months; he had now learned that a full year was necessary to 'remold the brain' before they could go on to study military matters, or economics, or heal, or administration. His interpreter and I searched for a word better than 'brain remolding' and finally the interpreter came up with the phrase 'raising the level of consciousness.' This was the first time I heard that phrase, which, over the years, moved out of China and on to the streets and fashions of America in the 1960's."

Whether it stemmed from Chinese or Russian use, or another origin, the idea of "raising" the level of consciousness (as distinct from "expanding" consciousness through the use of psychedelic drugs) came into use strongly in the sixties in the U.S., in the civil rights movement and most especially in the women's liberation movement. It may have been influenced by its use in psychology: "encounter groups" and "sensitivity training" also used "consciousness-raising" in their terminology.

By the mid-seventies, the word had been taken over by the women's movement—see **WOMEN'S LIB** and **SEXISM**—and the use by Locke in this entry would be frowned upon.

CONSENSUS a broad agreement which, while not necessarily all-embracing, does embrace enough elements to form a sizable majority.

Though Lyndon B. Johnson put his special brand on the term "consensus," politicians and thinkers have been pondering its uses and abuses for centuries. Some twenty centuries ago, the Roman orator Cicero declared, "The consensus of opinion among all nations, on whatever matter, may be taken for the law of nature." Sir Francis Bacon, in his essay *Of Faction,* wrote: "When factions are carried too high and too violently, it is a sign of weakness in princes, and much to the prejudice both of their authority and business."

Not everybody considers the quest for consensus the best *modus operandi.* Activist liberal advisers urged on John F. Kennedy the "superiority of the politics of combat as against the politics of consensus."

Nonetheless, consensus has its clear uses in a nation as diverse as the U.S. Dwight Eisenhower said in 1954: "If we are to build and maintain the strength required to cope with the problems of this age, we must cooperate one with the other, every section with all others, each group with its neighbors." Four years later, he found himself forced to back down from a proposed reform of the Pentagon because "my personal convictions, no matter how strong, cannot be the final answer. There must be a consensus reached with the Congress, with the people that have the job of operating the services."

Consensus is not total agreement. "When President Johnson speaks about seeking a consensus he is not saying that he expects every one to vote for him and to agree with him," wrote Walter Lippmann. "But he is saying that the great internal problems cannot be solved successfully and satisfactorily until and unless they have the support of a very big majority. In the American political tradition, a very big majority is taken to lie between 60 and 75%. An American consensus is more than a bare 51%." What Johnson was seeking to do, wrote Jack Bell in *The Johnson Treatment,* was to effect cooperation among "the liberals, who believed in big government, the conservatives, who wanted federal power diffused, the representatives of big business, big labor, the minorities most vocally represented by the Negroes and the poverty-stricken." (This would more accurately be termed a coalition.)

After the Republican party's big gains in the 1966 elections, New York's Governor Nelson Rockefeller urged the twenty-five GOP governors to work toward a consensus on their objectives before worrying about picking a candidate for the 1968 presidental race. Michigan's Governor George Romney, flying to Puerto Rico for a meeting with Rockefeller, took umbrage at his host's remark. Consensus? "That is Rockefeller's word," snapped Romney. "I associate it with someone else"—namely Lyndon Johnson—"who hasn't fared too well with leadership." Later Romney and Rockefeller made up, and Romney apologetically explained his outburst by saying, "I was just a little allergic to the previous association of the word."

Even with its connotation of evasiveness, the word is still able to bring about confrontations. The school of political historians who disputed the long-held "conflict" school—which held that the study of U.S. history was in the conflict between institutions and ideas—called itself the "consensus" school.

See COME NOW, AND LET US REASON TOGETHER.

CONSERVATION, *see* **ENVIRON-MENTALIST.**

CONSERVATIVE a defender of the status quo who, when change becomes necessary in tested institutions or practices, prefers that it come slowly, and in moderation.

In modern U.S. politics, as in the past, "conservative" is a term of opprobrium to some, and of veneration to others. Edmund Burke, the early defender and articulator of the conservative philosophy, argued that the only way to preserve political stability was by carefully controlling change and seeking a slow, careful integration of new forces into venerable institutions. In his *Reflections on the Revolution in France,* he wrote: "It is with infinite caution that any man ought to venture upon pulling down an edifice which has answered in any tolerable degree for ages the common purposes of society, or on building it up again without having models and patterns of approved utility before his eyes." Abraham Lincoln called it "adherence to the old and tried, against the new and untried."

The philosophy has had some famous detractors as well. Disraeli, who was to become a Tory Prime Minister, wrote in his sprightly novel *Coningsby:* "Conservatism discards Prescription, shrinks from Principle, disavows Progress; having rejected all respect for antiquity, it offers no redress for the present, and makes no preparation for the future." Lord Bryce was of two minds about it in *The American Commonwealth:* "This conservative spirit, jealously watchful even in small matters, sometimes prevents reforms, but it assures the people an easy mind, and a trust in their future which they feel to be not only a present satisfaction but a reservoir of strength."

The political origin of the word can be traced to the *Sénat Conservateur* in the 1795 French Constitution, and was used in its present English sense by British statesman, later Prime Minister, George Canning in 1820. J. Wilson Croker, in the *Quarterly Review* of January 1830, made the concrete proposal: "We have always been conscientiously attached to what is called the Tory, and which might with more propriety be called the Conservative party." It was soon applied in America to the Whigs, amid some derision: *"The Pennsylvania Reporter,"* wrote the *Ohio Statesman* in 1837, "speaking of a probable change in the name of the opposition, from Whig to 'Conservative,' says the best cognomen they could adopt would be the 'Fast and Loose' party."

Today the more rigid conservative generally opposes virtually all governmental regulation of the economy. He favors local and state action over federal action, and emphasizes fiscal responsibility, most notably in the form of balanced budgets. William Allen White, the Kansas editor, described this type of conservative when he wrote of Charles Evans Hughes as "a businessman's candidate, hovering around the status quo like a sick kitten around a hot brick."

But there exists a less doctrinaire conservative who admits the need for government action in some fields and for steady change in many areas. Instead of fighting a rear-guard action, he seeks to achieve such change within the framework of existing institutions, occasionally changing the institutions when they show need of it.

See **NEOCONSERVATIVE. HIDE-BOUND; ROCK-RIBBED.**

CONTAINMENT policy of limiting the aggressive expansion of Communism by military means, in the hope that its failure to expand will weaken and eventually destroy the Communist system.

In February 1946 George F. Kennan, a little-known scholar of Russian history who was counselor of our embassy in Moscow, wrote an 8,000-word treatise on Russia for his State Department superiors that was to change the course of U.S. foreign policy.

Kennan's memo, later printed in the July 1947 issue of *Foreign Affairs* under the title "The Sources of Soviet Conduct," stated:

> ... Soviet pressure against the free institutions of the western world is something that can be contained by the adroit and vigilant application of counterforce at a series of constantly shifting geographical and political points, corresponding to the shifts and maneuvers of Soviet policy, but which cannot be talked or charmed out of existence. . . .
>
> ... no mystical, Messianic movement—and particularly not that of the Kremlin—can face frustration indefinitely without eventually adjusting itself in one way or another to the logic of that state of affairs.

The policy of containment—to establish "situations of strength" around the world so as to stop Soviet expansion—came to encompass the establishment of U.S. military bases in friendly countries, the Marshall Plan, the Point Four aid to underdeveloped countries, and a rebuilding of U.S. military power.

But containment was essentially a defensive policy with little political appeal. Ultimate victory was decades away. There was no cleancut, decisive end to the problem of aggressive Communism. With the loss of China to the Communists in the late forties, American restlessness with containment increased. In the 1952 presidential campaign, General Eisenhower's

foreign policy adviser, John Foster Dulles, expounded a policy that went beyond containment—LIBERATION OF CAPTIVE PEOPLES. After Eisenhower's victory, Secretary of State Dulles explained it to the Senate Committee on Foreign Relations: ". . . a policy which only aims at containing Russia . . . is bound to fail because a purely defensive policy never wins against an aggressive policy. . . . It is only by keeping alive the hope of liberation . . . that we will end this terrible peril . . ."

When no liberations took place, a general disillusionment set in about "liberation," and in recent years "containment" has had the upper hand. The word and policy has, of course, drawn fire. Said Senator George Aiken of Vermont in 1967 regarding Communist China: "I don't know how you go about containing an idea. I also don't know how you go about containing 700 million people."

Curiously, the appeal of "containment" as a geopolitical philosophy, more than a policy, was undermined in the Administration that might have been expected to espouse it. Earl Ravenal wrote in *Foreign Policy* (Winter 1977–78) that Nixon policies in the early seventies had helped transform the international system from "bipolar confrontation" to a more diffused balance of power. "If Nixon and Kissinger did not quite end 'containment,' at least they devalued it, making it an item of strategy rather than ideology, blurring its once-sharp focus of hostility, and generalizing it into the more neutral concept of international 'stability.' "

CONTRACT   an agreement to deliver a political favor; an accepted political assignment.

The *Dictionary of American Slang* defines "contract" as "a political or business favor; a bribe; the fix. 1958: 'Contract—any favor one policeman says he'll do for another.'—G.Y. Wells, *Station House Slang.*"

In underworld lingo, *contract* is an assignment to a *torpedo* to make a *hit;* that is, a contract to commit a murder. That probably explains the sinister connotation in the nonpolitician's mind when he hears the more innocent use of contract by a politician.

In current political use, the "fix" connotation is disappearing; contract now is used as a legitimate promise to perform, with no bribe implied. A contract is not a "deal"; a deal clearly implies a two-way transaction, while a contract is merely an assignment accepted with no specific return favor demanded.

Sample: "You'll sit me on the dais next to the Governor?" "I'll try." "No—make it a contract." "Okay, it's a contract, you'll sit there."

For an 1893 usage, see DELIVER.

CONTRAPUNTAL PHRASES
a phrase-making technique that uses a repeated rhythm with an inversion or substitution of words for emphasis; rhetorical antithesis.

Good speechwriters reach for contrapuntal phrases. The technique is by no means new. "We have fought side by side to make America free," wrote Alexander Hamilton; "let us hand in hand struggle to make her happy." Gilbert Highet pointed out in an analysis of the Gettysburg Address that Lincoln was especially fond of antithesis: "The world will little note nor long remember what we say here; but it can never forget what they did here."

This contrapuntal description of Harry Truman has been attributed to Speaker Sam Rayburn: "Right on all the big things, wrong on most of the little ones."

FDR in his Four Freedoms speech said, "As men do not live by bread alone, they do not fight by armaments alone." In the contrapuntal use of a single word, the possibility for oratorical error is a danger: when, in 1933, FDR shaped a sentence that read "Hard-headedness will not so easily excuse hard-heartedness," he drew a tiny picture of a head over the first word on the reading copy of the speech, and a heart with an arrow through it over the balance word.

John F. Kennedy used the device more than any other U.S. President. "Let us never negotiate out of fear, but let us never fear to negotiate." "A willingness to resist force, unaccompanied by a willingness to talk, could provoke belligerence—while a willingness to talk, unaccompanied by a willingness to resist force, could invite disaster." "While we shall negotiate freely, we shall not negotiate freedom." And, of course, "Ask not what your country can do for you—ask what you can do for your country."

The "Sorensen style" used by Kennedy did not go unnoticed. Columnist William F. Buckley Jr., writing in 1967 about the Communist world revolution, obliquely referred to a single form of contrapuntal inversion: "And unless we learn how to cope with it, it will—as Theodore Sorensen would put it—cope with us."

"In Ted Sorensen," observed *Washington Star* editorialist Edwin M. Yoder Jr. in February 1978, "Mr. Kennedy had a speechwriter of excellent style with a fondness for antithesis, so that it became a sort of rhetorical tic. Like all the rhetorical devices that we inherit from Latin by way of the 18th Century, antithesis needs a strict sense of occasion. It can be absurdly trivialized: 'Always close the door before you leave, but never leave after you have opened the window.' "

See TURNAROUNDS.

CONTROVERSIAL, *see* **CODE WORDS.**

CONVENTION, *see* **SPONTANEOUS DEMONSTRATION; PACKING THE GALLERIES; VOICE FROM THE SEWER; BROKERED CONVENTION.**

COOKIE PUSHER an effete, or "striped-pants" diplomat; a foreign service pharisee concerned with form rather than substance; opposite of SHIRTSLEEVE DIPLOMAT.

The phrase graphically describes one who attends social teas, and presumably cocktail parties; it was popularized by New York Democratic Congressman John J. Rooney, chairman of the House subcommittee on appropriations that oversees State Department spending. "While I have used the expression 'cookie pusher' many times during my years in the U.S. House of Representatives," Congressman Rooney writes the author, "I cannot at all claim authorship, and I have no idea who it was that coined it."

Adlai Stevenson's biographer, Kenneth S. Davis, says the lifted-pinkie phrase was used against Stevenson and his associates in the Committee to Defend America by Aiding the Allies in 1940: "Nor could [Stevenson] fail to resent being dubbed, with his colleagues, a 'cookie pusher,' a 'professional bleeding heart,' a 'warmonger,' day after day in [Chicago] *Tribune* news and editorial columns . . ."

COOLING THE RHETORIC, *see* **RHETORIC.**

COOLING-OFF PERIOD in labor disputes, a time allowed management and labor to negotiate with neither strikes nor lockouts permitted.

The "cooling-off" period became locked into the political language with the passage of the Taft-Hartley Act of 1947. The law specified that sixty days' notice must be given before a labor contract can be changed or terminated; if no agreement is reached within thirty days, the Federal Mediation and Conciliation Service steps in. When a dispute threatens what the president considers to be the national welfare, he is authorized to seek a court injunction to maintain the status quo for eighty days. At the end of this eighty-day cooling-off period, a strike or lockout is permitted.

The phrase has earlier usage in diplomacy. William Jennings Bryan, Woodrow Wilson's Secretary of State in 1913, took the initiative in providing for a method of arbitration on all international disputes, referring these to a permanent investigating commission. He negotiated agreements with thirty-one nations which became known as "Bryan's 'cooling off' treaties."

President Woodrow Wilson, campaigning for the League of Nations in 1919, used an eloquent metaphor in the last major speech before his stroke:

> With a cooling space of nine months for human passion, not much of it will keep hot. I had a couple of friends who were in the habit of losing their tempers, and when they lost their tempers they were in the habit of using very unparliamentary language. Some of their friends induced them to make a promise that they never would swear inside the town limits. When the impulse next came upon them, they took a street car to go out of town to swear, and by the time they got out of town they did not want to swear. They came back convinced that they were just what they were, a couple of unspeakable fools, and

the habit of getting angry and of swearing suffered great inroads upon it by that experience. Now, illustrating the great by the small, that is true of the passions of nations. It is true of the passions of men however you combine them. Give them space to cool off.

COONSKIN ON THE WALL
symbol of victory; similar to "scalp."

At Cam Ranh Bay in South Vietnam, just before the November 1966 elections in the U.S., President Johnson visited U.S. troops in the field and told them, "I salute you. Come home with that coonskin on the wall."

The expression jarred many members of the President's party, as limited objectives and limited war were the basis of diplomatic feelers, and the President's colorful remark appeared close to the MacArthur NO SUBSTITUTE FOR VICTORY statement.

Commented Walter Lippmann three months later: ". . . Lyndon Johnson is a complicated human being. There are at least two spirits wrestling within him. One is that of the peacemaker and reformer and herald of a better world. The other is that of the primitive frontiersman who wants to nail the coonskin to the wall. . . . It is this second spirit which is now tempting him, and on the outcome of the ordeal depends more than it is pleasant to contemplate."

The hide of the raccoon or opossum has had a long background in American speech, and was the symbol of frontiersman Daniel Boone. Estes Kefauver, senator from Tennessee and Democratic vice-presidential candidate in 1956, wore the coonskin cap for photographers and used it as a symbol on many of his handshaking tours. "The irony of Kefauver," wrote Russell Baker of the *New York Times,* "was that the coonskin cap, by which the country at large knew him, was a fraud. It implied a log cabin rustic bred to the cracker barrel circle, but it concealed one of the authentic eggheads of American politics."

CO-OPT to convert by absorption; or, to subvert by suffocating agreement.

In the dictionaries, "co-opt" as a verb, or "co-optation" as a noun, refers to the election to a group of an outsider by a vote of the membership.

In its new political meaning, however, "to co-opt" is to ensnare the victor. Subtly, the Establishment reaches out for the election winner, or the bureaucracy enfolds its supervisory appointee, and in the guise of wanting to help or offering to educate, takes him over by changing his cultural or political outlook. The absorption of outlook is rarely dramatic; on the contrary, it seems to occur by osmosis, as the "outsider" thinks he is convincing or changing the "insiders."

"Co-opt" was used frequently in discussions about the incoming Carter Administration—held to be "anti-Washington"—by congressional Democrats in 1977.

Both sides of the hyphenated word came from voguish forebears. "Co" has been used frequently in recent years, with "co-host" a popular television term, and "co-equal" taken to mean more equal than the usual equal. OPT is the vogue form for "choose," without its impulsive differential.

In the January 1978 issue of *Foreign Affairs,* Jean-François Revel wrote: "As long as the Western communist parties remain organized according to the so-called schema of 'democratic centralism,' meaning a Politburo, recruited by co-optation

. . . it is ridiculous to think of de-Stalinization."

"If you can't lick 'em, join 'em" is an old political axiom; in the case of "co-opt," the axiom appears to be "If you can't lick 'em, flatter 'em, and they'll join you." For an earlier form of stealing the opposition's clothes, see DISH THE WHIGS.

COPPERHEAD near traitor; DE-FEATIST; spokesman for an unpopular cause.

The copperheads were those Northerners who opposed the Union cause during the Civil War. The copperhead snake is considered by many to be the lowest of a low breed: it strikes without warning, contrasted with the fair-minded, noisy rattlesnake.

The word was used in America preceding the Civil War as a synonym for "sneaky," but in the off-year elections of 1862 it became the epithet for Southern sympathizers in the North. The Lawrence (Kan.) *Republican* surveyed the epithet list: "That faction of the Democracy who sympathize with the rebels are known in Ohio as 'Vallandinghamers,' in Illinois as 'guerrillas,' in Missouri as 'butternuts,' in Kansas as 'jayhawkers,' in Kentucky as 'bushwhackers,' and in Indiana as 'copperheads.' "

The word atrophied after the Civil War resentments died down, though the progressive politicians at the turn of the century were derided as "copper-streaked" by their enemies. Franklin Roosevelt renewed its use in 1938, at the suggestion of Thomas Corcoran, to apply it to those Democrats who wished to drag their feet on New Deal legislation: "Never in our lifetime has such a concerted campaign of defeatism been thrown at the heads of the President and Senators and Congressmen as in the case of this Seventy-Fifth Congress. Never before have we had so many Copperheads—and you will remember that it was the Copperheads who, in the days of the War between the States, tried their best to make Lincoln and his Congress give up the fight . . ."

Roosevelt liked the word and used it again just before World War II as a label for Colonel Charles A. Lindbergh and the America Firsters.

CORDON SANITAIRE, *see* **IRON CURTAIN.**

CORN PONE symbol of folksiness and Southern voter appeal.

Corn pone can be a bread made of corn meal, milk, and eggs; or a cereal whose alternative name is hominy grits; or a cakelike bakery product made of pounded corn, pounded sunflower seeds, and boiled beans. Pone can be a wide variety of products made from corn, and can stir as many heated debates about what it is and how it is made as "egg cream" in New York City.

Governor Huey Long brought it into politics as part of his lighthearted but effective campaign to identify himself with rural voters in Louisiana. He started a debate over the proper method of eating corn pone with pot liquor, a juice that remains in the pot after turnip greens are boiled with a piece of salt pork. "Kingfish" Long solemnly held that the pone should be "dunked" in the pot liquor, and not "crumbled" in and then elegantly eaten with a spoon. Governor Franklin Roosevelt of New York wired the *Atlanta Constitution* that he sided with the "crumblers," and Oklahoma's "Alfalfa Bill" Murray called for a wider investigation to include "poke" salad and hog jowl. The matter reached the Solomon's Temple of Emily Post, who decreed: "When in Rome, do as the Romans do."

Corn pone has come to mean "sweet talk," and gentle persuasion. See SMELL OF MAGNOLIAS. Non-Southerners tend to consider it synonymous with "corny" or "cornball," cloyingly folksy, but in the South there is a more gallant political connotation. In 1960 Lyndon Johnson named his CAMPAIGN TRAIN, which did so much to hold the South for the Kennedy-Johnson ticket, "The Corn Pone Special."

Time magazine in 1968 wrote that the nation's cartoonists had pictured President Johnson as "macaw-beaked, jug-eared and two-gunned, a tragicomic, corn pone character."

CORPORATE STATE, *see* **FASCIST; TRAINS RAN ON TIME.**

CORRIDORS OF POWER, *see* **POWER BROKER.**

COST OF LIVING, *see* **HIGH COST OF LIVING.**

COST-PUSH, *see* **INFLATION.**

COUNTDOWN   period of crisis before a decision or event; the last few days before an election.

The word was popularized as the nation watched televised rocket blast-offs from Cape Canaveral, Fla. and announcers in ominous tones said: "Countdown four minutes, thirty seconds and counting," or "two minutes, twenty seconds and holding," with the last ten seconds counted backward to "Ignition. Blast-off."

In 1959 Majority Leader Lyndon Johnson was quoted as saying "The countdown has begun" in regard to pending legislation; in 1960 General John Medaris wrote a book titled *Countdown for Decision* about the confusion in the missile program; the *New York Times Book Review* headlined a review in 1967 "Countdown for the Minds of Men."

Political headquarters in campaigns managed by John A. Wells (New York mayoralty in 1961, senatorial in 1962, Rockefeller for President in 1964 and for governor in 1966) featured large signs titled "Countdown—Days to Go" with the number of days changed daily, a constant reminder of the number of days left until Election Day.

For a time the word was used in lieu of "roll call" by television commentators (many of whom covered the astronaut blastoffs) as the states were called at national conventions. An AP dispatch in July 1960 said that "they professed to believe that Kennedy would lose support in Indiana, Maryland and Ohio in a second countdown."

Subsequently the word enjoyed considerable popularity; comedians spoke of a child who came home after learning "the New Math" counting "10 . . . 9 . . . 8 . . . 7 . . ." But the word settled into the political language quietly and is now used to describe the last tense moments of a campaign.

COUNTERCULTURE   an amalgam of dropouts, professional dissenters, anti-intellectuals, experimenters with drugs, as well as some thoughtful and literate critics of American society in the sixties.

Drug culture is a critical description; *youth culture* neutral; and *counterculture* usually a self-description. The use of "counter" is superior to "anti" because it carries the connotation of offering an alternative.

The word gained circulation in the late sixties as dissident groups began making use of national holidays and local festivities as foils for their own activities. In 1969 a protest demonstration in Washington, D.C. was called a "counter-Inaugural."

The new word, probably based on counterrevolution and counterintelligence, added prestige as it was adopted by social critics and analysts who prepared "counterbudgets" and the like. By treating disparate anti-Establishment groups and individuals as a new culture, the word dignified what had been thought of mainly as a motley crew, and was embraced by those who would not be caught dead in a silent majority.

British author Kingsley Amis and poet Robert Conquest defined the word in the January 10, 1971 *New York Times Magazine* as "(1) Socially: living off bourgeois society without paying literal or metaphorical taxes to it. (2) Artistically: creativity, which, whether using bourgeois materials (words, pigments, etc.) or other materials or none, does not admit of the elitist application of divisive criteria showing one work to be 'better' than another."

As a selling term, it is effective; some of the best fighters in the ring are counterpunchers.

Here is a brief review of the vocabulary of the counterculture, drawn largely from the research of rock music reviewer Mike Jahn:

bummer: bad experience
bust: arrest
cosmic: significant
down: negative experience
far out: superlative
get into: become interested
gig: occupation
goof on: make fun of
groove on: enjoy
heavy: powerful
off: kill

organic: vital
outasight: fantastic
pig: police
put down: insult
put on: prank
rap: extended conversation
rip off: steal
shuck: phony
spaced: distracted
speed: amphetamines
stoned: high on drugs
strung out: drug casualty
together: well-adjusted
trip: experience
up: positive experience
vibrations: impressions

Most of these words were dropped long ago from counterculture usage, but lingered on in the pitiable efforts of squares to appear "with it."

One of the central expressions of the counterculture is "do your thing," which means "establish your own identity," or "follow your star"; critics of the individualistic life style find this the height of self-indulgence. Unlike most of the rest of counterculture vocabulary, the source of the phrase is specific: Ralph Waldo Emerson, in his *Essay on Self Reliance,* wrote: "If you maintain a dead church, contribute to a dead Bible-Society, vote with a great party either for the government or against it . . . under all these screens, I have difficulty to detect the precise man you are. . . . But do your thing, and I shall know you."

COVER-UP any plan to avoid detection of wrongdoing; or, an act to conceal a mistake; specifically, the conspiracy to obstruct justice in the Watergate case.

Mystery writer Raymond Chandler, in *Black Mask* magazine in 1935, gave a character this line: "I don't have to tell you how a police department looks at that kind of a

cover-up on a murder." The law enforcement slang soon crossed into the
political language, to mean a general
—not necessarily illegal—concealment of the truth. In a telephone conversation with financier Louis Wolf-
son in 1968, Supreme Court Justice
Abe Fortas told his former law client
(who was recording the call) that a
conflict-of-interest charge could be
made if their relationship was mis-
construed: "That your giving me and
my accepting the foundation post was
nothing but a cover-up and that what
was really happening was that I was
taking a gratuity from you . . . and
that is very bad."

In the Watergate case, the charge
of cover-up (usually hyphenated,
though sometimes one word) gained
currency early in the spring of 1973.
On April 30, according to a transcript
of a taped conversation with former
Attorney General John Mitchell in
the Oval Office, President Nixon said:
"I want you all to stonewall it, let
them plead the Fifth Amendment,
cover-up or anything else, if it'll save
it—save the plan."

That transcript was released in the
summer of 1974, and the words were
used on the July 22, 1974, cover of
Newsweek. In an interview with
David Frost in 1977, the former President allowed as how a reasonable
person could construe his actions "as
a cover-up," but denied that the concealment had involved criminal action on his part.

Because of its Watergate connotation, the word is now frequently used
to attach sinister implications to any
attempt to withhold information. To
HANG TOUGH is permissible; to
STONEWALL implies grounds for suspicion; to *cover up,* or to engage in a
cover-up, imputes improper concealment or unlawful obstruction.

COVER YOUR ASS   bureacrat's
method of protecting his posterior
from posterity.

Program planner Richard Sachs, in
recommending this entry, suggested
this definition: "Often abbreviated
CYA. A technique for restoring one's
credibility with one's peers; often
used after losing a campaign or foul-
ing a project. After the disastrous
finale of a campaign I worked on in
1970, one of the top managers made
immediate visits to a number of important personages analyzing the reasons for failure and carefully avoiding
his own contributions to defeat,
which had been formidable. It was
said of him that he was out to 'cover
his ass.' "

Several techniques of ass-covering
can be observed: (1) *papering the file*
is an insertion of exculpatory memoranda to direct blame away from the
paperer in case of a future investigation; (2) *cleaning the file,* or SANITIZ-
ING, the removal of material that
might be blameworthy; (3) getting a
superior to SIGN OFF ON, or *surname*
a memo diffuses responsibility.

In a conversation with General
Alexander Haig in 1974, the author
wanted to know why FBI Director
Hoover had insisted on getting signed
approvals from his superiors, and
memos from his aides, before under-
taking certain wiretappings. General
Haig replied, "You know Hoover, he
was always out to cover his ass."

The phrase is rarely used in print,
but occasionally travels in public
under its initials. Robert Bloom, an
official in the Office of the Comptrol-
ler of the Currency, used it that way
in testimony before a Senate committee investigating the financial affairs
of Bert Lance, which was commented
upon in the *Washington Star*'s editorial of September 14, 1977: "He defended himself strenuously, in that

queer pseudo-tough patois favored by upper-level bureaucrats. At one point he used inelegant but apposite shorthand to explain some of his actions— 'CYA,' which, slightly sanitized, translates as 'Cover Your Aft end.' "

COWBOY   a political rebel, usually one opposed to party discipline.

"Cowboy" never enjoyed the political currency of such synonyms as MAVERICK and MUGWUMP and is only occasionally heard today. Its most famous use was upon the death of President William McKinley. Senator Mark Hanna, the leading Republican strategist while McKinley lived, said of Theodore Roosevelt: "Now look, that damned cowboy is President of the United States!"

It is uncertain precisely how Hanna applied the term because Roosevelt had actually lived and worked in cattle country for a time, and was also considered most unfaithful by orthodox GOP chiefs. In fact, it was their attitude that made him President. He was serving as governor of New York in 1900, assiduously earning the enmity of the Republican organization with his reforms. The vice presidency was vacant and the New York Republican leadership promoted Roosevelt's candidacy, some say to get him out of the state. He won the nomination when men favored by McKinley pulled out. "We did our best," Hanna told McKinley, "but they nominated that madman. Now it's up to you to live."

"Cowboy" took on unpleasant connotations during the American Revolution. Tory irregulars in the New York area were called cowboys while rebel marauders were known as "skinners." The idea of a cowboy being someone unreliable stuck. Senator James G. Blaine in 1879 explained his dislike for "those fellows who are

between the parties," by saying that "they are the cowboys of modern days."

See LONER.

COW-WADDLE, *see* **FILIBUS-TER.**

CRADLE-TO-THE-GRAVE   total security: a phrase used to attack welfare statism.

Cradles and graves are mentioned in the same breath as far back as the early seventeenth century. Joseph Hall, Bishop of Norwich, wrote: "Death borders upon our birth and our cradle stands in the grave."

Poet John Dyer wrote in 1726:

A little rule, a little sway,
A sunbeam in a winter's day,
Is all the proud and mighty have
Between the cradle and the grave.

This was parodied by Samuel Hoffenstein in the 1930s:

Babies haven't any hair; old men's heads
are just as bare;—
Between the cradle and the grave lies a
haircut and a shave.

A 1931 political use was by District Attorney Crain of New York, inveighing against racketeers who "have their hands in everything from the cradle to the grave—from babies' milk to funeral coaches."

Throughout the 1930s, "cradle-to-the-grave" was used to attack the New Deal's social security measures. Democratic candidate Adlai Stevenson referred to these attacks in the campaign of 1952: "Republican leadership has opposed us almost every step of the way and now, while adopting everything and proposing to repeal nothing, at least publicly, their orators still sneer at everything we now have and shout about socialism. They call our lives of pride and dignity 'cradle-to-the-grave rides through the welfare state.' "

Other spoofs have included "womb to tomb," the most extreme being "erection to resurrection."

See WELFARE STATE.

CREATIVE FEDERALISM federal stimulation and encouragement of state and local action to meet human needs, rather than by direct federal action.

Governor Nelson Rockefeller of New York put forth the idea of a modified form of federalism in a series of lectures and a 1964 campaign document (distributed as a paperback book) called *The Future of Federalism.*

The word "federalism," with its Founding Father connotation overshadowing its too-much-centralization connotation, was thus given new currency and next appeared as the "creative federalism" concept of President Johnson. *Fortune* magazine editor Max Ways wrote a piece on the subject in 1966.

Both the phrase and the concept appeared to be a defense against the charge of BIG GOVERNMENT domination of American life; the new, "creative" approach enhances the role of those state and local governments who are willing to undertake responsibilities assumed in recent years by the federal government.

Its proponents considered it an advance into new areas with the localities serving as the cutting edge; critics like Raymond Moley said, "The expression 'creative federalism' . . . serves as an impressive screen to cover the retreat of those who, since the presidency of the first Roosevelt, have urged the projection of federal authority into the areas traditionally reserved to the state and local governments."

As for the phrase, President Johnson took something old (the federalism of Jefferson, Hamilton, Jay, and Madison, resuscitated by Rockefeller) and something new ("creative"). In California in 1966, Ronald Reagan took "creative," added it to the mature "society" from Johnson's Great Society, and came up with "the creative society." Rockefeller then countered with an inaugural speech on "the just society." And so it went.

Federalism itself was coined by British conservative Edmund Burke, who also minted diplomacy, expenditure, municipality, and electioneer.

See NEW FEDERALISM.

CREDIBILITY GAP the chasm that sometimes exists between public office and the public's trust.

The term first came into widespread use in early 1965 when American GIs in South Vietnam began sporting buttons reading "Ambushed at credibility gap." President Johnson actually suffered from a bit of a credibility gap when he came to his office; a long career as Senate majority leader, during which he was known as a master manipulator and a crafty compromiser, was responsible for that.

Only a few weeks after becoming President, he opened the gap wider when he hinted to newsmen that his first budget would probably exceed $102 billion, then produced a budget of under $98 billion. A number of other actions opened it into a yawning abyss (most abysses yawn): the excessive secretiveness and frequent overoptimism surrounding the Vietnam war; his charade in 1964 over his choice of a runningmate, which he insisted was not decided until only minutes before he selected Hubert Humphrey; his scheduling a campaign swing in 1966 on the eve of the election, then canceling it and insisting that he had never really planned the trip at all.

Coinage of the phrase in print probably belongs to an anonymous *New York Herald Tribune* headline writer. On May 23, 1965, reporter David Wise wrote a piece that had the word "credibility" in the same lead with the word "gap" though not tied together. The headline read "Dilemma in 'Credibility Gap.'" The phrase was given currency by *Washington Post* reporter Murray Marder on December 5, 1965, in a story about "growing doubt and cynicism concerning Administration pronouncements. . . . The problem could be called a credibility gap."

In a whimsical mood on the eve of his departure as White House press secretary, Bill Moyers remarked that "the credibility gap . . . is getting so bad we can't even believe our own leaks." In a more somber mood, Moyers defined the gap as "the difference between what the President says and what the people would like him to say or what they think he should say."

Walter Lippmann, a less sympathetic observer, wrote in 1967 that "the credibility gap today is not the result of honest misunderstanding between the President and the press in this complicated world. It is the result of a deliberate policy of artificial manipulation of official news." The *Baltimore Sun*'s Henry L. Trewhitt defined it as "the degree of refusal by the public to accept at face value what the government says and does." *New York Times* columnist James Reston wrote: "The most serious problem in America today is that there is widespread doubt in the public mind about its major leaders and institutions. There is more troubled questioning of the veracity of statements out of the

White House today than at any time in recent memory."

The credibility gap developed into a major political issue and was accordingly seized upon by leading Republican contenders for the 1968 presidential nomination. "For years now," said Michigan's Governor George Romney, "we haven't been told the whole facts, and when you begin to find yourself in the position where you can't have confidence in what those who have a public trust are saying about fateful and vital situations, well, you are really in a tough spot."

"Credibility" has also assumed a more significant meaning in the geopolitics of the postwar world. The "credible deterrent" or "military credibility" refers to the degree to which a country convinces a potential enemy of its strength. See GAP.

CREEP the discredited Nixon campaign committee of 1972.

The story of how "CREEP" came into being was recounted in the author's 1975 book, *Before the Fall: An Inside View of the Pre-Watergate White House:*

> . . . My only real contribution to the committee had been a recommendation to stress Nixon's incumbency in its title. When Jeb Magruder came into my office in late 1971, the President had not yet publicly chosen Agnew as his running mate again. . . . Magruder said, "We can't call it 'Citizens for Nixon-Agnew' because that announces Agnew, and we can't call it 'Citizens for Nixon,' because that will be seen as throwing Agnew overboard, so what do we call the committee?" I remembered the 1966 Rockefeller campaign in New York, when the slogan was "Governor Rockefeller for Governor" . . . and I suggested, simply, the Committee to Re-elect

the President. "That's the best you can do?" Magruder inquired. I started to remind him that I was charging clients $90,000 a year for advice when he was selling pancake makeup for a local cosmetics house, but then I thought for a moment: any acronym problem? You always have to watch that. C, R, P. Democrats would have to try to stick an "A" in there to make fun of it, which would be in bad taste and they wouldn't try that; if you made it C, R, E, P, using the "election" as a non-hyphenated capital, you would have a french pancake, and that's even too effete for snobs. It would be safe, solid, and stress the incumbency. And so CREEP was created.

The CRP was dubbed "CREEP" not by a Democrat, but by Republican National Committee Chairman Robert Dole, who felt the RNC was being shunted aside by the brash young men of the Nixon White House. An early printed reference was in the September 15, 1972, issue of *Life:* "The CRP—or 'CREEP,' as some members of the Republican National Committee call it—occupies five floors of one building and spills across the street onto three floors [of another]." On May 21, 1973, *Time* wrote: "But during the campaign he [Dole] fought many a gallant losing battle with the Committee for the Re-Election of the President; in fact it was he who dubbed it CREEP."

Senator Dole's crack had been aimed at the play on the word "creep," which is taken from a person who gives one "the creeps" or who causes the flesh to crawl—a derogation that can be found in a 1930 James T. Farrell story. But after it was discovered that the Nixon committee had financed the break-in to Democratic headquarters at the Watergate office complex, "CREEP" gained a different and far more sinister connotation—as one who enters by stealth —and what had begun as an intra-party gibe became a weapon in the hands of everyone who was anxious to attack anything associated with the 1972 Nixon victory.

CREEPING SOCIALISM measures increasing the sphere of government activity that are accused of having the cumulative effect of undermining private enterprise.

Republicans during Franklin Roosevelt's New Deal and Harry Truman's Fair Deal frequently used "creeping socialism" to describe Democratic programs, especially in the economic and social welfare areas. Historian Samuel Eliot Morison observed later: "Republican orators played this theme in elections and in Congress. . . . [but] postwar developments, especially under Eisenhower, justify the quip that instead of creeping socialism, galloping capitalism emerged from the New Deal and the war."

Indeed, "creeping socialism" survives as a term not so much because of Republican or conservative affection for it, but because liberals find it an easy target. See Adlai Stevenson's gibe under DINOSAUR WING. Walter Lippmann, for instance, wrote in 1962: "The so-called socialism which is supposed to be creeping up on us is in fact nothing more than the work of making life safe and decent for a mass society collected in great cities." When Dwight Eisenhower used the phrase in 1953 ("in the last 20 years creeping socialism has been striking in the United States"), one of his aides wrote him a memo saying it had been "the hallmark of the Old Guard Republicans" and that modern Republicans should have "their own idiom." Eisenhowever agreed.

The word "socialism" was first

used politically in 1835 in England by followers of Robert Owen.

The word "creeping" is now a jocular form of "incipient," not limited to ideology, and can be applied to any "ism" for a piquant effect. "After all the amateurish, impromptu diplomacy," wrote columnists Evans and Novak in 1978 about President Carter's use of carefully prepared remarks upon returning from his first trip abroad, "it could be a sign of creeping professionalism."

CRIME IN THE STREETS initially, urban crime; later a phrase used to derogate the emphasis of "law and order" as an issue.

For a full discussion of the LAW AND ORDER issue, see that entry. Although the words "law and order" were described for a time in the late sixties as "code words for racism," the severe increase in crime—of special concern to Negro victims in slums—soon erased the pejorative connotation. However, "crime in the streets" was used not so much to describe the situation itself as the political issue arising from it, and this has come to mean "making a political issue out of law enforcement." "Law and order" ceased to be regarded as code words by 1971, while "crime in the streets" retained the political, though not especially racist, connotation.

Language expert Mario Pei offered this interesting sidelight in *Modern Age: A Quarterly Review,* in 1969: " 'Crime in the streets' is a very ancient phenomenon, widespread even in such a world-renowned city as imperial Rome. It gave rise, curiously, to French *crier,* which in turn has become English 'cry.' The root word is *'Quirties!'* 'Citizens!' a cry of distress corresponding to our 'Help!'

used by Romans attacked in the streets."

See CODE WORDS.

CRONYISM, *see* **GOVERNMENT BY CRONY.**

CROSSOVER VOTE a theory that a primary in one party can be affected substantially by the votes of members of an opposition party.

During the 1976 Republican primaries, supporters of President Ford explained several losses in state primaries in this way: in those states with no party-registration requirement, many Democratic voters—who would ultimately vote for the Democratic candidate in November—were "crossing over" to vote for Ronald Reagan in the Republican primaries.

"Among those who described themselves as Republicans," wrote R. W. Apple Jr. in the *New York Times* on May 5, 1976, describing a post-primary poll, "Mr. Reagan and President Ford fought on almost equal terms, but the California conservative swept the Democratic crossover voters and beat the President by about 3 to 2 among the independents."

The crossover theory holds that the crossover voter is fickle, or mischievous, or only interested in voting in the more hotly contested primary, and intends to come "home" to the party in which he is registered later in the general election. The theory was challenged by Michael Barone, writing in the *Washington Post* under the headline "That 'Crossover' Nonsense!" "All but an insignificant number of the people who will vote for Gerald Ford or Ronald Reagan or Jimmy Carter or Morris Udall in Michigan," he argued, "will be people who are quite ready to vote for them in the general election. In that sense, and it is the only one that matters, they will be legitimate Republican and Democratic voters, not mischievous 'crossovers.' The 'crossover' theory is nonsense."

But as the influence of the state primary grows in the selection of presidential candidates, the idea of the crossover vote will be offered as an explanation or an excuse by primary losers, who who will insist they were defeated by a vote that did not really reflect the wishes of regular party members.

See NOVEMBER REPUBLICANS.

CROSSROADS, *see* **WATERSHED.**

CROSS THE STREET, *see* **TAKE A WALK.**

CROWDSMANSHIP, *see* **NUMBERS GAME.**

CRUNCH high-pressure squeeze; a period of tension that becomes a political or economic moment of truth, when participants display courage or cowardice.

The verb *to crunch,* probably of imitative origin (as "the ship crunched through the ice"), was given an extra definition in the mid-sixties. Businessmen, editorialized the *New York Times* in 1967, "will lose their fears of a credit crunch when it becomes clear that we are not headed for another 1966 [credit crisis]."

Squeeze is almost exclusively an economic word for tightening; *pinch,* as in Shakespeare's use of "necessity's sharp pinch," is a generalized type of stress, and *in a pinch* is a time of mild hardship; NUT-CUTTING implies action in a crisis toward an individual; *moment of truth,* with its bullfighting origin, has acquired a literary connotation; the *clutch,* with a baseball derivation, is the decisive moment in

a close contest; the *crunch* is the pressure of a political or economic nutcracker.

The word was given new meaning when it was changed from its familiar verb form. Another example of this is "hurting"; to *hurt* or to *be hurt* means inflicting or receiving physical pain, while *hurting* (Dean Rusk in 1967: "the North Vietnamese are hurting") means to be in political or military difficulties. And when the crunch comes, a lot of fence-sitters find themselves hurting.

CRUSADE a political movement characterized by moral fervor; a word used to endow an effort with a religious-moral tone.

Most Americans today identify the word with Dwight D. Eisenhower, but it has had a long political history. "A crusade against ignorance" was urged by Thomas Jefferson in 1786. "Spend and be spent in an endless crusade," Theodore Roosevelt exhorted his supporters. Franklin D. Roosevelt agreed; on the day of his first inauguration, March 4, 1933, he not only called for a "new deal," but issued "a call to arms . . . a crusade to restore America to its own." Three years later, in a cabinet meeting, FDR talked about prospects for re-election: "We will win easily next year, but we are going to make it a crusade."

FDR's 1940 opponent, Wendell Willkie, took a page from "that man's" book; in his speech accepting the Republican nomination, Willkie pledged: "We go into this campaign as into a crusade . . . on the basis of American liberty, not on the basis of hate, jealousy or personalities."

Eisenhower first used the word, in its traditional moral-military context, in his June 6, 1944, "Order of the Day" to the Allied troops poised to invade Europe: "Soldiers, sailors and airmen of the Allied Expeditionary Force: You are about to embark upon a great crusade, toward which we have striven these many months. . . . The hopes and prayers of liberty-loving people everywhere march with you."

The General entitled his best-selling memoirs *Crusade in Europe,* and it was natural for his political advisers to seize on the word so closely identified with their candidate. Throughout the campaign of 1952 he reiterated the word, perhaps most dramatically in his "I shall go to Korea" speech on October 24: "I do not believe it a presumption for me to call the effort of all those who have enlisted with me—a crusade. I use that word only to signify two facts. First: We are united and devoted to a just cause of the purest meaning to all humankind. Second: We know that—for all the might of our effort—victory can come only with the gift of God's help. In this spirit—humble servants of a proud ideal—we do soberly say: This is a crusade."

That Detroit speech was prepared by Emmet Hughes, and its use of "crusade" was limited to the quest for peace, a narrowing down of its earlier use by Eisenhower to apply to anything on the domestic scene as well. Wrote Hughes later: "I struck from the current vocabulary any use of 'Crusade' on the national scene, and 'liberation' on the world scene. Their presumption seemed to me offensive, and they nowhere appeared in any passage of any speech that I prepared for the rest of the campaign." This attitude might have been in response to Adlai Stevenson's gibes about Eisenhower's oft-repeated dedication to a crusade: "The General has dedicated himself so many times, he must feel like the cornerstone of a public building."

John F. Kennedy used the word in an odd, effective context in 1961: "Let our patriotism be reflected in the creation of confidence in one another, rather than in crusades of suspicion."

British correspondent Alistair Cooke, writing in *The Listener* in 1963, made an astute observation about crusades and Presidents: "All Presidents start out pretending to run a crusade, but after a couple of years they find they are running something much less heroic, much more intractable: namely, the Presidency."

The word's moral fervor is built in; its literal meaning is "taking the cross," coined in the eleventh century to describe the first military expedition by European Christians to recover the Holy Land from the Mohammedans.

C THREE C 3, *see* K_1C_2.

CUFFLINKS GANG a group of supporters of FDR in his run for the vice presidency in 1920, tied together later by the postcampaign gift of gold cufflinks from the candidate.

White House aide Marvin McIntyre wore his cufflinks throughout the thirties, symbol of his membership in the "original" group; later Bronx Democratic boss Ed Flynn echoed the sentiment by forming an FRBC Club (For Roosevelt Before Chicago) of those who supported FDR before the 1932 Chicago convention. Twenty years before, Theodore Roosevelt's manager, Senator Joseph Dixon of Montana, used "Before April 9th Men" to hail Roosevelt supporters who spoke up for him before the April 9, 1912, Illinois primary brightened his chances.

Mementos like the cufflinks are cherished by the recipients as a badge of being an early insider, with presumably some slight prerogative over the Johnny-come-latelies. John F. Kennedy gave his aides a PT-109 tieclasp, which became the highest status symbol of the New Frontier.

Cufflinks and tieclasps, chosen for these gifts because of their high visibility and portability, are customarily presented by winners (Nelson Rockefeller's post-1966 gubernatorial campaign gift was a pair of cufflinks with a tiny "rock of Gibraltar" embedded in each). After the 1952 campaign Vice President Richard Nixon presented "Order of the Hound's Tooth" scrolls to his intimates, suitable for framing, and KITCHEN CABINET scrolls to those who accompanied him to the KITCHEN DEBATE in Moscow in 1959. After his 1960 defeat, Nixon sent a desk memento to one hundred key men: a clay replica of the life cast taken of Abraham Lincoln's right hand. Ironically, most of these were not wrapped securely and arrived broken in the mail, and the aide responsible (author of this dictionary) spent six miserable months apologizing, having new ones made and reshipped to impatient, fuming recipients. After his successful campaigning for congressional candidates in 1966, Nixon aides, who had learned a lesson, sent out unbreakable Churchill crowns to helpers across the nation with a quotation from Churchill about the dangers of appeasement.

CULT OF PERSONALITY promotion of personal adulation, as contrasted with collective leadership.

At a secret session of the Communist Party Congress on February 25, 1956, Party Secretary Nikita Khrushchev rose to denounce Joseph Stalin, startling the world and leading to a drastic revision of Soviet history books. Leaked reports of the meeting, distributed by the CIA, quoted Khrushchev as saying that a "cult of personality" had been promoted by Stalin after Lenin's death, and that Stalin had abused his personal prestige by using it to undermine collective leadership of the Presidium. *Pravda* followed up a month later with: "Stalin's disregard of the principle of collective leadership, and the frequent decisions taken by him personally, led to the distortion of party principles and party democracy, to the violation of revolutionary law, and to repression."

There was criticism in Communist circles in later years of a cult of personality growing up around Khrushchev, and some analysts think this contributed to his own downfall. In the Western world, the phrase is occasionally used in an ironic or joking way.

The idea of extending power through a personality cult, of course, was not original with either Stalin or Khrushchev. Alexander Hamilton, in an 1802 letter, outlined a plan for a "Christian Constitutional Society," appealing to people "through a development of a 'cult' of Washington and benevolent activities." The cult that Hamilton had proposed was formed in 1808—the Washington Benevolent Society—too late to help the sagging Federalists.

Columnist Murray Kempton, writing in 1967 about the first U.S. press conference of Stalin's daughter, Svetlana Alliluyeva, commented: "Of all Russians, the daughter of Joseph Stalin is the one to remind his replacements that the Cult of Personality can no more decently be employed to lay all the guilt on one man than it can be to give him all the credit."

CULTURAL REVOLUTION political and social upheaval in the People's Republic of China, fostered by Mao Tse-tung to forestall bureaucratization and to preserve the purity of the revolution as he knew it.

What troubled Party Chairman Mao when he launched the "Great Proletarian Cultural Revolution" was the growing gap in China between city and village, intellectual and peasant. Instead of devotion to the cause, there were signs of REVISIONISM, "backsliding," and "bureaucratism," along with yearnings for such bourgeois things as comfort, status, and education. As *Toronto Star* correspondent Mark Gayn wrote in the January 1967 issue of *Foreign Affairs,* Mao sought "nothing less than the rejuvenation of a great revolution, the rebirth in middle age of the drive, the passion, the selflessness and the discipline it had in its youth a third of a century ago."

The revolution began in November 1965 when a Shanghai newspaper attacked the deputy mayor of Peking, Wu Han, for writing historical plays rather than modern ones. The following year Mao and his then heir-apparent, Marshal Lin Piao, created the Red Guards as instruments to restore purity. Patterned after the peasant youth movement of Hunan in the late 1920s, the Red Guard movement created a reign of terror with public humiliations of those who opposed Mao, kangaroo trials, beatings, and killings.

The faction described as "antiradical" in the West ultimately made a comeback under Teng Hsaio-ping. After Mao's death a short, fierce struggle took place between the "Shanghai radicals" led by Mao's widow and the successor to Mao, Hua Kuo-feng, who had the army's backing. As a result, the group that had gained power during the Cultural Revolution was arrested and denounced as "the gang of four," while

Teng agreed to serve under Hua. Since Mao was being deified, his works could not be criticized, and the Cultural Revolution has since been treated kindly in Communist rhetoric, although its leading lights and their followers were removed from power.

CURMUDGEON   a likeably irascible old man. In politics, a cantankerous, outspoken older politician with a talent for invective.

FDR's Interior Secretary, Harold Ickes, earned the title "The Old Curmudgeon." More recently, New York Parks Commissioner Robert Moses has often been identified as a curmudgeon, but the word still evokes memories of "Harold the Ick." Among his memorable blasts, he tagged Wendell Willkie as "the simple, BAREFOOT BOY FROM WALL STREET", and is sometimes credited with labeling Thomas E. Dewey as "the little man on the wedding cake"; Alfred Landon was "a strong but silenced man." When Huey Long called Ickes "the Chicago Chinch-Bug," Ickes replied, "The trouble with Senator Long is that he is suffering from halitosis of the intellect. That's presuming Senator Long has an intellect." He denounced opponents of academic freedom as "intellectual Dillingers," proponents of the Liberty League as "vestal virgins," and Governor Talmadge of Georgia as "His Chain Gang Excellency." He intended to deliver a speech about Martin Dies, head of the House Un-American Activities Committee entitled "A Case of Loaded Dies," but Roosevelt restrained him.

A curmudgeon may expect to be attacked in kind. Ickes was described as "the New Deal blackjack squad," "blunderbuss Ickes," and (by Joe Martin) "Comrade Harold L. Ickes,

Overlord of the Interior and Commissar of the P.W.A."

The definition of curmudgeon in most dictionaries as "grasping" and "avaricious" (Samuel Johnson thought it may have come from *coeur méchant*, or wicked heart) does not apply in politics; "irascible" and "cantankerous" are the right adjectives. The curmudgeon is liked because he is a throwback to the days when politicians had fewer advisers telling them to soften their words.

In 1969, *Life* magazine columnist Hugh Sidey referred to publisher John Knight, seventy-five, as "an old curmudgeon." Knight looked up the definition in Webster's *New International Dictionary* (3rd edition) and was distressed to see "a miser; niggard; churl" among other disparagements. Sidey quickly wrote one of Knight's perturbed associates: "Word meanings are fluid, like history. Dictionaries are often inaccurate guides to the moment. William Safire's book, *The New Language of Politics*, . . . says 'Curmudgeon—a likeably irascible old man.' That is precisely how I feel about Mr. Knight. I believe he is a splendid journalist, a delightful skeptic, a wonderful human being. Nothing you wrote changes my opinion of this old curmudgeon."

Knight replied to Sidey: "I guess that calls for a drink" and wrote this author: "I have had a lot of fun with being called a 'curmudgeon' but I much prefer your definition to the one in Webster's."

CURSE OF BIGNESS   an attack phrase on monopoly, unlawful combinations, and the power of large corporations.

Labor unrest and violence shocked the nation in 1911, culminating in the dynamiting of the then antilabor *Los Angeles Times* by three union officials. Boston attorney Louis D. Brandeis (later a Supreme Court Justice) wrote the editor of the magazine *Survey* on December 30, 1911: "Is there not a causal connection between the development of these huge, indomitable trusts and the horrible crimes now under investigation? Is it not irony to speak of equality of opportunity in a country cursed with bigness?"

Brandeis' phrase caused a stir; he used it again as the title of an essay published in *Harper's Weekly:* "The Curse of Bigness."

The classic answer to Brandeis' phrase is one of the few memorable phrases of President William Howard Taft: "Mere size is no sin against the law." Both phrases are used in discussions of antitrust cases; David Lilienthal switched the Brandeis phrase around in the 1950s in discussing the "curse of smallness."

CUTTING EDGE, *see* **ON THE POINT.**

DARK HORSE   a long-shot candidate for nomination, usually the second or third choice of many delegates, whose best chance for selection lies in a deadlock of the leading candidates.

The first "dark horse" appeared at one of the earliest Democratic conventions. Indeed, the choice of James Polk of Tennessee proved the usefulness of political party conventions. An impasse had been reached between former President Martin Van Buren of New York and Lewis Cass of Michigan in the convention held in Baltimore in 1844. On the eighth ballot, with neither leader willing to give way to the other, a compromise of Polk was suggested. He received 44 votes, Cass 114, Van Buren 104, Calhoun and Buchanan 2 each, with 134 needed to nominate. On the ninth ballot, the convention stampeded to the "dark horse." Polk received all 266 votes.

Like most compromise candidates who followed him, Polk was not well-known nationally. "Who's Polk?" became a slogan of the 1844 campaign, in which Polk narrowly defeated the Whigs' Henry Clay. The next dark horse to win was Franklin Pierce, who was not considered as a candidate until the 35th ballot, winning on the 49th. The Democrats' slogan then became "We Polked You in 1844, We'll Pierce You in 1852." He, too, defeated the Whig candidate, General

Winfield Scott. In 1876, Rutherford B. Hayes was another successful dark horse.

In more recent times, Warren Gamaliel Harding of Ohio was the most successful dark horse. Army hero Leonard Wood and Governor Frank Lowden of Illinois deadlocked the Republican convention of 1920 for nine ballots. In a suite on the top floor of Chicago's Blackstone Hotel, party leaders selected Harding, a man with no enemies. See SMOKE-FILLED ROOM.

Wendell Willkie in 1940 began his campaign for the nomination as a dark horse against the favorites, Thomas E. Dewey and Robert A. Taft. William Allen White extended the metaphor in a profile in the *New Republic:* "What sort of man personally is this unknown dark horse who is being groomed in the Augean stables of our plutocracy?" See CLEAN SWEEP.

The phrase was used in a novel by the young Benjamin Disraeli, *The Young Duke,* published in 1831: "A dark horse which had never been thought of, and which the careless St. James had never even observed in the list, rushed past the grandstand in sweeping triumph." In politics, it probably first entered the language after Polk and before Pierce. Hans Sperber and Travis Trittschuh find its first printed reference in a quotation from New York's Hamilton Fish, speaking for Lincoln in 1860: "We want a log-splitter, not a hair-splitter; a flat-boatman, not a flat-statesman; log cabin, coonskin, hard cider, old Abe and dark horse—hurrah!"

Reviewing the first edition of this book in *Encounter* magazine in 1968, historian Sir Denis Brogan added: ". . . in a moment of patriotic pride, I should like to suggest that the most brilliant use of the term 'dark horse' was made by John Morley (known to good Radicals as 'honest John Morley,' no doubt to distinguish him from his colleagues); he called Lord Rosebery (who was as proud of having won the Derby as of having been Prime Minister) 'a dark horse in a loose box.' (The term 'loose box' was also used to describe the special accommodation provided for the mistresses of Edward VII at his coronation in Westminster Abbey in 1902.)"

In 1967, "backup candidate" came into use as a more specific form of dark horse, one that would get the support of a group if its own candidate failed. See FALLBACK POSITION.

Other horse-racing metaphors common to politics are BOLT, SHOO-IN, RUNNING MATE, and FRONT RUNNER. Winners take the reins of government; losers are known as also-rans.

DAY OF INFAMY Franklin Roosevelt's reference to the attack on Pearl Harbor on December 7, 1941, asking for a declaration of war on Japan.

The speech was drafted by Roosevelt himself, without the aid of either Robert E. Sherwood or Samuel Rosenman, his speechwriters at that time. The first draft's first sentence read: "Yesterday, December 7, 1941, a date which will live in world history, the United States was simultaneously and deliberately attacked by naval and air forces of the Empire of Japan." In the second draft, FDR crossed out "world history" and substituted "infamy"; he crossed out "simultaneously" and used "suddenly."

The third draft includes insertions in FDR's handwriting: "Last night Japanese forces attacked Hong Kong. Last night Japanese forces attacked Wake Island. This morning the Japanese attacked Midway Island." While the President was preparing to go to Congress, he added the latest news as it came in. Harry Hopkins suggested a sentence, which Roosevelt approved, expressing confidence that we would "gain the inevitable triumph—so help us God."

"The remarkable thing," wrote Rosenman later, "is that on one of the busiest and most turbulent days of his life he was able to spend so much time and give so much thought to this speech." Secretary of State Cordell Hull had argued for a long speech, detailing the history of Japanese-American relations. Roosevelt said that he would go into detail in a fireside chat the next day, and decided on his own six-minute dramatic message to Congress.

Roosevelt's revision from "world history" to "infamy" is intriguing; the word was aristocratic and little-used (Voltaire had written to a friend in 1760: "I wish that you would crush this infamy"), but the change of the word made the phrase memorable.

DEAD END, POLITICAL the mayoralty of any large city; supposedly a thankless job that makes major enemies and aborts a political career.

When New York Congressman John V. Lindsay was being urged to run for mayor, his friends pointed to the careers of Fiorello La Guardia and Robert Wagner as evidence that the job was "a political dead end." Vice President Hubert Humphrey's rise from mayor of Minneapolis, Minnesota, was dismissed as an exception that proved the rule, but it was not.

Wrote *Newsweek* in 1967: "Democrat Richardson Dilworth won national acclaim during the 1950s as Mayor of Philadelphia only to learn the hard way that City Hall is more often a dead end than a steppingstone for promising political careers."

The phrase is derived from the Sidney Kingsley play *Dead End;* its movie version starred a group of tough-talking young actors who became known as "the Dead End Kids." The title was taken from a traffic sign that indicates no exit at the far end of the street, and was used to symbolize the lack of opportunity available to young men from poor neighborhoods. See DISADVANTAGED.

The vice presidency is occasionally referred to as a political dead end. President Eisenhower in 1956 asked Vice President Richard Nixon whether he felt that a cabinet post would be more helpful in furthering his own career. "The President explained to Nixon," reported Sherman Adams, "that history had shown the vice presidency to be somewhat of a political dead end; no vice president in this century had gone on to the presidency except through accidental succession . . ." But with the accidental succession to power of Harry Truman, Lyndon Johnson, and Gerald Ford, the phrase is rarely used today in relation to the office a HEARTBEAT AWAY FROM THE PRESIDENCY.

See GRAVEYARD; STEPPINGSTONE.

DEAL a political trade of favors or support. When either discovered or imagined, an effective attack word that turns what some consider an honorable arrangement into what others consider a bribe.

In 1824, the "era of good feeling" began to sour when John Quincy Adams made a deal with Henry Clay. Andrew Jackson had won a plurality of the popular and electoral votes, but not a majority, and the election had to be decided in the House of Representatives. Speaker of the House Clay threw his support behind Adams, who then won, and promptly named Clay his Secretary of State. In the 1828 election, Jackson's slogan was "Bargain and Corruption" and he won handily.

After that, deals became something to be denounced by all candidates, especially regarding cabinet posts and other appointments, a point that rarely discouraged campaign managers from dealing in realities. Lincoln wired his convention floor manager in 1860, David Davis: "Make no deals in my name." Davis is reported to have remarked, "Hell, we're here and he's not," and dealt freely with the Blair and Cameron forces. As President, Lincoln fulfilled the promises made by Davis, who was rewarded with a seat on the Supreme Court.

At the Republican convention of 1880, former President U.S. Grant went a little too far in denying a deal. "It was my intention, if nominated and elected, to appoint John Sherman Secretary of the Treasury. Now you may be certain I shall not. Not to be President of the United States would I consent that a bargain should be made." No bargain, no support; James Garfield was nominated.

Probably the most monumental deal in U.S. political history occurred in the disputed election between Rutherford B. Hayes, Republican of Ohio, and Samuel J. Tilden, Democrat of New York, in 1876. Tilden had won a majority of the popular vote and led Hayes in the electoral vote 184 to 165, with 185 the necessary majority. Twenty votes, from "carpetbag" governments in Florida, Louisiana, and South Carolina, as well as one from Oregon, were in dispute. The Republican-controlled Senate and the Democratic-controlled House could not agree on how the disputed votes were to be counted. An electoral commission was appointed, with seven men from each party plus one "independent"—Supreme Court Justice David Davis, the same man who made the convention deals for Lincoln. He resigned in favor of an eighth Republican, who threw the election, predictably, to Hayes.

Why did the Democrats hold still for this decision to substitute a Republican for the independent swing man? Because the Republicans agreed to a simple deal: the election of Hayes, in return for the withdrawal of federal troops from the "carpetbag" states, ending Reconstruction governments and giving the Democrats control of the South. In the long run, the Democrats got the better of the deal.

William Randolph Hearst received the Democratic nomination for governor of New York in 1906 from the hands of Tammany Leader Charles Murphy, whom Hearst papers had attacked a few months before as "The Colossus of Graft" and "The Black Hand." Suspecting a deal, writer Edmund Wetmore put into poetry what Hearst might have said:

"So I lashed him and I thrashed him in my hot reforming zeal,/Then I clasped him to my bosom in a most artistic deal."

More recently, at the 1948 Republican convention, Robert Taft (beaten by Thomas E. Dewey for the nomination) agreed to the vice-presidential nomination of his fellow Ohioan, John Bricker, in return for the pledge of Bricker forces for active support of Taft in 1952 (which was forthcoming, though Taft lost to Eisenhower).

As a noun, "deal" takes its coloration from its adjective: a "square deal" is good and a "fast deal" is bad. Its definition depends on the point of view: what is a "cynical bargain" to your adversary is an "honorable compromise" to you. The late Oklahoma Democratic Senator Robert Kerr, a noted wheeler-dealer, liked to say: "I'm against any deal I'm not in on."

DECISION-MAKING PROCESS the way a political executive makes up his mind; a cliché used by press secretaries to block access to information about the conflicting pressures leading to a decision, or used by reporters to describe whatever inside information they can get about what advice was given.

Author Victor Navasky described his 1971 book, *Kennedy Justice,* as "a series of forays into what is forbiddingly known as the Decision-making Process, a look at how an institution makes up its mind . . ."

In the sense used above, the process is institutional, used to show how the man at the top cannot be totally blamed or credited with his conclusions. In this sense, the phrase has a negative connotation, as a difficult-to-penetrate wall, or bureaucratic maze.

The phrase has been used positively as well in the politics of participation, as "we must involve more of the people in the decision-making process."

A typical fifties usage was by Attorney General William P. Rogers to a Senate judiciary subcommittee on March 6, 1958, about EXECUTIVE PRIVILEGE: "I appreciate the opportunity . . . to present my views as to the extent of the inquiry which can be made by the legislative branch of the Government concerning the decision-making process and documents of the Executive Branch."

The process itself can be amorphous and mysterious, as in President Truman's decision to drop the atom bomb, or formally laid out with options, projected consequences, and recommendations, as in many of the decisions that are made through the present National Security Council system. Or it can represent the workings of one man's mind, little influenced by staff.

There is commercial value to its understanding. "The regulatory process in Washington is influenced by political factors," former Deputy Attorney General Laurence Silberman told reporter Steven Roberts of the *New York Times* in 1978. "It's awfully important to understand the nature of the decision-making process, to know what is decided at what level and by whom."

The cliché most commonly associated with "decision-making process" is "input," a term from computer technology.

See TICK-TOCK; BITE THE BULLET; PROCESS, THE.

DEEDS NOT WORDS a platitudinous attack on platitudes; a demand for specific action instead of verbal or written assurances.

The phrase is most recently identified with Dwight Eisenhower, who used it often in speeches. Returning from his promised trip to Korea after his 1952 election, he told reporters: "We face an enemy whom we cannot hope to impress by words, however eloquent, but only by deeds—executed under circumstances of our own choosing." Before the American Society of Newspaper Editors in 1953, he said: "We welcome every honest act of peace. We care nothing for mere rhetoric. We are only for

sincerity of peaceful purpose attested by deeds." He returned to the theme again and again, as in a UN speech in 1953 after a Bermuda Conference: "These are not idle words or shallow visions. . . . These are deeds of peace."

The phrase can be found in Samuel Butler's "Hudibras," a poem satirizing the Puritans, with these lines written before the execution of King Charles I in 1649: ". . . we must give the world a proof/ Of deeds, not words."

Shakespeare's Richard III said, "Talkers are no good doer"; Hamlet, asked what he was reading, replied, "Words, words, words." British Prime Minister Neville Chamberlain used the word "words" in the same derisive sense in a rebuff to Franklin Roosevelt in 1938: "It is always best and safest to count on nothing from the Americans but words." In 1966, the British Conservative party slogan was "Action not words."

The long form of "deeds not words" was used by President Grover Cleveland: "It is not the mere slothful acceptance of righteous political ideas, but the call to action for their enforcement and application, that tests the endurance and moral courage of men." A common variation on the phrase is "in deed as well as word," as used by Mao Tse-tung: "Whoever sides with the revolutionary people in deed as well as in word is a revolutionary in the full sense."

Word and deed have gone hand in hand throughout history. "Deeds are males, words females are," written by John Davies in 1610, was adopted in Italian by the first Baron Baltimore *(fatti maschii; parole femine)* and is the motto of the State of Maryland. A proverb traced to 1546 goes: "That deede without woords shall driue him to the wall." The Roman Catholic confession, traceable to 1075 in something like its present form, talks of sinning "in thought, word and deed." And Plautus, in *Pseudolus,* written about 190 B.C., said, "Let deeds match words."

DEEP BACKGROUND, *see* **NOT FOR ATTRIBUTION.**

DEEP FREEZE, *see* **INFLUENCE PEDDLER.**

DEEP-SIX to dispose of, with emphasis; to destroy or deliberately lose.

In Watergate testimony on June 25, 1973, former White House counsel John Dean attributed the use of the phrase to John Ehrlichman: "He told me to shred the documents and 'deep-six' the briefcase. I asked him what he meant by 'deep-six.' He leaned back in his chair and said: 'You drive across the river on your way home at night, don't you? Well, when you cross over the bridge on your way home, just toss the briefcase into the river.'"

Before entering prison in 1976, John Ehrlichman disputed Dean's testimony in this interview in the *Washington Post*'s *Potomac Magazine* with reporter Nick Thimmisch: "The specific acts by me were supposed to be the conversations with Dean where he said I told him to get Howard Hunt out of the country, and later to 'deep-six' the contents of Hunt's safe. A conversation with Herbert Kalmbach was the basis of another charge. Those conversations never took place."

"Deep-six" is naval slang. "As an ex-Navy type," Joseph Ross of the Congressional Research Service wrote in answer to the author's query, "I know that this is Navy talk, meaning to jettison. It comes from the leadsman's (fellow who took the soundings) call for six fathoms (36 feet) of depth: 'by the deep six.'" Lexicographer Peter Tamony has supplied a 1927 citation in *A Glossary of Sea Terms,* by Gershom Bradford: "Deep six—overboard."

Thus, to deep-six anything is to throw it overboard with an eye toward making its recovery unlikely. When used as a noun, the phrase is not hyphenated; as a verb, it takes a hyphen, contrary to COVER-UP, which is hyphenated only as a noun.

DEFEATIST attack word against those urging caution, or withdrawal from what they consider indefensible positions.

Defeatism may be a state of mind about a social program, or a specific position (so labeled by the opposition) on a particular policy. In his 1936 campaign, Franklin Roosevelt recalled "the many cruel years" of the "era of tooth and claw" when poverty was accepted by "the defeatist attitude."

Charles A. Lindbergh and the America First group, with their worries about the invincibility of Nazism in Europe in the late thirties, were attacked as "defeatist." Then, as in the sixties, the word was often used in conjunction with "appeasers" (see APPEASEMENT); the word has never again reached the currency it had in the thirties, but it occasionally appears as an attack on the DOVES in U.S. Far Eastern policy.

See COPPERHEAD; NATTERING NABOBS OF NEGATIVISM; PROPHETS OF GLOOM AND DOOM.

DEFOLIATE to expose jungle supply lines with the use of atomic, chemical, or incendiary weapons; one of the words used by Senator Goldwater in the 1964 presidential campaign that damaged him most.

Several times in the course of the presidential primaries of 1964, Barry Goldwater raised the possibility of "defoliating the jungle with low-yield atomic weapons" to interdict supplies to the Viet Cong from North Vietnam. When he repeated the point in a television interview, he added that he did not think it was a course the United States should follow. Democrats who were pressing the TRIGGER-HAPPY charge overlooked the senator's reservation in quoting his statement of the possibility of defoliation, and Goldwater adherents cried foul play and QUOTING OUT OF CONTEXT. However, the senator's previous references to the possibility without the reservation gave the charge credence.

At the Republican convention in San Francisco in 1964, civil rights demonstrators marched in front of the Cow Palace carrying signs that included "Defoliate Goldwater."

As the Vietnam war developed, napalm was used to defoliate areas suspected of covering trails or Viet Cong emplacements. In early 1967 the *Saturday Evening Post* reported the "slogan of the Air Force's flying defoliators: 'Only you can prevent forests.' "

New York Times correspondent Max Frankel used the word in 1967 in the sense of removing "confusing verbiage": "Every day someone is urging one side or the other to escalate or to de-escalate, to de-augment and to disinfiltrate, to pause temporarily or unconditionally and, above all, to negotiate. On paper, at least, it is time to defoliate.... The semantic defoliation might best begin with the genus negotium, the Latin root of 'negotiate,' meaning 'not easy.' "

DELIBERATE SPEED, *see* **WITH ALL DELIBERATE SPEED.**

DELIVER   to make good on a political promise, especially the promise to turn out a vote for a candidate.

"Heaven help the legislator who does not deliver," said Illinois Democratic Senator Paul Douglas, shortly after his defeat by Charles Percy in 1966. He was talking about the PORK BARREL and the need for a legislator to promise and get federal projects built in his state.

The first recorded use of the word in a political sense was in a November 16, 1893, issue of *The Nation:* "No man is so fierce in his Americanism as ... a boss who has 'delivered' the vote of his district as per contract." In that sense, to "deliver the vote" was similar to "deliver the goods," a phrase traceable to 1879. But a pejorative connotation was added when "the vote" did not mean all the votes in an area, but an individual vote or another man's influence. "The basis of the break," wrote the *Brooklyn Union* in 1904, "is said to have been a charge that Shevlin 'delivered' Boss McLaughlin in some deal without the latter's knowledge."

Politicians treat the word with enormous respect, because it touches on the essence of power. "There are no alibis in politics," said Kansas City boss Thomas Pendergast. "The delivery of votes is what counts.... All the ballyhoo and showmanship such as they have at the national conventions is all right. It's a great show. It gives folks a run for their money. It makes everybody feel good. But the man who makes the organization possible is the man who delivers the votes, and he doesn't deliver them by oratory. Politics is a business, just like anything else."

In its broader sense—to keep a political pledge—the word was used in the 1948 presidential campaign. Republican Thomas E. Dewey said,

"The 80th Congress delivered as no other Congress ever did for the future of our country." President Harry Truman quoted that line to his "whistlestop" (see WHISTLESTOPPING) audiences, and punched: "I'll say it delivered. It delivered for the private power lobby. It delivered for the big oil company lobby. It delivered for the railroad lobby. It delivered for the real estate lobby. That's what the Republican candidate calls delivering for the future. Is that the kind of future you want?"

Senate Majority Leader Lyndon Johnson in 1958 used the word (in its deliver-the-vote sense) in international relations. After Johnson's statement on outer space to the UN Political Committee, India's V. K. Krishna Menon commented, "I wish that your country would give as much time to disarming as you give to preparations for arming." Johnson was not intimidated. "Well now, Mr. Ambassador, we're ready," he shot back. "We'll disarm tomorrow. Can you deliver the disarmament of the Communist bloc?"

Deliver is the put-up-or-shut-up word of politics. It calls the bluffs of political leaders and calls to account big-promising candidates. Reporter John Gunther, covering the unpredictable state of Ohio in his 1947 *Inside USA,* wrote: ". . . nobody is ever sure of Ohio. Once the manager of a presidential candidate, arriving in Columbus, asked the local boss if he could 'deliver' Ohio. The legend is that the local boss took a deep protesting breath, curled up his toes, and on the spot died of heart failure."

DEMAGOGUE   one who appeals to greed, fear, and hatred; a spellbinding orator, careless with facts and a danger to rational decision.

This is one of the enduring, slash-ing attack words of politics, in use since the American republic began. John Adams in 1808: "It is to no purpose to declaim against 'demagogues.' . . . Milo was as much an agitator for the patricians as Clodius for the plebeians; and Hamilton was as much a demagogue as Burr."

Being denounced as a demagogue is a sure sign to a speaker that he is making powerful points with some part of the public. In different historical periods, those most often denounced were Ben Butler, William Jennings Bryan, Huey Long, and Senator Joseph McCarthy. Reverend Thomas Dixon's attack on Bryan was typical: "a slobbering, mouthing demagogue, whose patriotism is in his jawbone." At one time, "slobber" was an operative verb for demagogue's noun. When Wilson's Secretary of War Newton Baker appealed for support of the League of Nations by referring to "the closed eyes of soldiers in American uniform who were dying and who whispered to me messages to bring to their mothers," Senator Key Pittman of Nevada replied, "The speaker who spoke before here, with his wild burst of oratory, with tears in his eyes and his brokendown, slobbering body across this rail, is trying to appeal to your sympathies, not to your judgment."

Theodore Roosevelt and William Howard Taft, after their falling-out, exchanged charges of "fathead" and "demagogue." Roosevelt observed in a letter to Henry Cabot Lodge: "When there is a great unrest, partly reasoning and partly utterly unreasoning and unreasonable, it becomes extremely difficult to beat a loudmouthed demagogue, especially if he is a demagogue of great wealth."

The appeal to emotion is not the only hallmark of the demagogue; an appeal to class is often included.

When Democrat Al Smith broke with FDR, he made this point in words reminiscent of the earlier Roosevelt-Taft break: "I will take off my coat and fight to the end against any candidate who persists in any demagogic appeal to the masses of the working people of this country to destroy themselves by setting class against class and rich against poor!"

The word has had its defenders. It is from the Greek *demagogos* (leader of the people), which referred to the popular leaders who appeared in Athens during its period of decay. English journalist George Steevens, writing about the U.S. in 1897, held that "in a free country every politician must be something of a demagogue. Disraeli and Gladstone were both finished demagogues, and until we have two more great demagogues in England, politics will continue to be as dishwater." Muckraker Lincoln Steffens wrote in his autobiography: "I had begun to suspect that, whenever a man in public life was called a demagogue, there was something good in him, something dangerous to the system."

But the popular conception of the word was given most eloquently by a President not known for his eloquence, Calvin Coolidge: ". . . the final approval of the people is given not to demagogues, slavishly pandering to their selfishness, merchandising with the clamor of the hour, but to statesmen, ministering to their welfare, representing their deep, silent, abiding convictions."

The word has retained all of its original sting. Relations between Presidents Truman and Eisenhower permanently cooled when Truman referred to Eisenhower's "I shall go to Korea" statement as "a piece of demagoguery."

The final *g* in the adjective *dema-gogic* is soft; the more difficult-to-pronounce and spell *demagoguery,* with its final *g* hard, is more commonly used in the U.S. than *demagogy,* final *g* soft, which is British usage.

DEMAND-PULL, *see* **INFLATION.**

DEMOCRAT a member of one of the two major U.S. political parties, or "democrat with a small *d*": one who favors strong governmental action for the welfare of the many.

It was under Andrew Jackson that the Democratic party, founded in 1828, began using its present name, but "democrat" was current long before that. "Washington," wrote John Adams scornfully toward the end of the eighteenth century, "appointed a multitude of democrats and jacobins of the deepest dye. I have been more cautious in this respect." Others shared his low esteem. A popular poem in the early days of the Republic was Fessenden's "Democracy Unveiled":

And I'll unmask the democrat,
Your sometimes this thing, sometimes that,
Whose life is one dishonest shuffle,
Lest he perchance the mob should ruffle.

The Federalists sneered at Thomas Jefferson's Republicans as "democrats"—panderers to the mob; they in turn scorned the Federalists as "aristocrats." Still, by 1856 the Middletown (N.Y.) *Banner of Liberty* could write that "the name Democrat has become so honorable that all sorts of isms and new-fangled parties claim the name."

In 1955 Leonard Hall, a former Republican National Chairman, began referring to the "Democrat" rather than the "Democratic" party, a habit begun by Thomas E. Dewey. Hall dropped the "ic," he said, because "I think their claims that they represent the great mass of the people, and we don't, is just a lot of bunk." The University of Virginia's Atcheson L. Hench said of this usage in *American Speech* magazine: "Whether they have meant to imply that the party was no longer democratic, or whether they banked on the harsher sound pattern of the new name; whether they wanted to strengthen the impression that they were speaking for a new Republican party by using a new name for the opposition, or whether they had other reasons, the fact remains that . . . highly influential speakers . . . used the shorter adjective."

Some Democrats suggested retaliating by shortening REPUBLICAN to Publican, but the National Committee overruled them, explaining that Republican "is the name by which our opponents' product is known and mistrusted."

Probably the best-known modern quote involving the word comes from Will Rogers: "I belong to no organized party. I am a Democrat."

Republican Theodore Roosevelt, campaigning in the Deep South, supposedly told the classic why-I'm-a-Democrat story. When asked why he was a Democrat, a Southerner replied, "Because my father was a Democrat and my grandfather was a Democrat." A Northerner countered, "What if your father was a horse thief and your grandfather was a horse thief, what would you have been then?" The Southerner's reply: "In that case, I guess I'd have been a Republican."

DEMONSTRATION, see MARCH.

DENIABILITY, see SIGN OFF ON.

DEPRESSION PARTY recurrent Democratic attack against the Republican party since the 1932 campaign; considered demagogic now, often compared to the Republican charge that Democrats are the WAR PARTY.

After Herbert Hoover had been defeated largely by the "Depression party" charge, some Republicans in 1933 sought to attach the Depression label on the Democrats. The feeble effort was devastated by FDR: ". . . although I rubbed my eyes when I read it, we have been told that it was not a Republican depression but a Democratic depression. . . . Now, there is an old and somewhat lugubrious adage that says: 'Never speak of rope in the house of a man who has been hanged.' In the same way, if I were a Republican leader speaking to a mixed audience, the last word in the whole dictionary that I think I would use is that word 'depression.' "

Harry Truman took up the Depression party charge in his GIVE 'EM HELL campaign of 1948, especially relating it to the DO-NOTHING CONGRESS: "The Republican party has shown in the Congress of the last two years that the leopard does not change its spots. It is still the party of the Harding-Coolidge boom and Hoover depression."

Republican Dwight Eisenhower deplored what he felt was an outmoded and unfair attack on his party. In his memoirs he wrote: "For more than twenty years economic depression had been the skeleton in the Republican closet, locked in by demagogues. In many minds [in 1954] the suspicion lurked that this problem might once again prove to be the party's undoing."

See RUNNING AGAINST HOOVER.

DEPTH POLLING motivation research; pollsters' questions that go beyond voting intention.

A man's current attitudes and opinions, studied alongside his previous voting behavior and his social and ethnic background, helps behavioral scientists predict the way he will vote and—more important—what political appeals may get him to vote another way.

"Depth polling" has been adopted as the operative phrase by some political communications experts because "motivation research" has acquired such a bad image. The latter phrase, used by Dr. Ernest Dichter and others, excoriated by author Vance Packard in *The Hidden Persuaders,* led to criticism like this by Professor (later Senator) S. I. Hayakawa, a leading linguist: "Motivation researchers are those harlot social scientists who, in impressive psycho-analytic and/or sociological jargon, tell their clients what their clients want to hear, namely, that appeals to human irrationality are likely to be far more profitable than appeals to rationality."

Polling pioneer Dr. Elmo Roper answered the author's query: "The phrase which is usually used is 'polling in depth' and what that means is nothing more than a check to learn the difference in attitude by various sub-groups in the population and even more particularly, *why* they hold whatever attitude they do hold. As a matter of fact, the first term applied generally to this type of probe was 'depth interview.' Apparently the newspapers insist on the word 'poll,' and 'depth interview' became 'polling in depth.' "

Dr. George Gallup responded as well, also resisting depth polling, the phrase used by laymen: "Usually the expression is 'interviewing in depth'

—or this may be shortened to 'depth interviewing.' This term goes back to 1935. Dr. Paul Lazarsfeld introduced this concept into American research. It typically refers to the long cross-examination of a person with many questions to get at his thinking on a given issue. Today many persons use the term 'depth interviewing' when they have asked more than a few questions on the same subject."

Three levels of polling are currently used, occasionally by the same pollsters: STRAW POLLS or *nose counts; issues polls,* indicating voter feelings about specific issues; and *depth polls.* See POLLSTER.

When a pollster's forecast is accurate, it is not news; when it is wrong, the words of Jesus to the Pharisees (Matthew 16:3) are recalled: "O ye hypocrites, ye can discern the face of the sky; but can ye not discern the signs of the times?"

DESERVING DEMOCRATS party workers worthy of patronage reward.

Three-time candidate William Jennings Bryan, when he became Woodrow Wilson's Secretary of State, tried to take care of a few old friends. He wrote to the receiver-general of the Dominican Republic, Walter W. Vick, on August 20, 1913, asking if he could find some places in the customs administration of that country. Bryan's letter contained the phrase in the following question: "Can you let me know what positions you have at your disposal with which to reward deserving Democrats?"

The letter was indiscreet; Republicans denounced it as an attempted extension of the SPOILS SYSTEM into the administration of a foreign country under U.S. domination.

Democrat Felix Frankfurter explained in 1924 why he was bolting to vote for a third party: "The Republican party is frankly standpat—things are all right. To the Democrats, also, things are all right, only those who administer them are not. What the country needs is 'honest' Democrats and, doubtless, William J. Bryan would add, 'deserving Democrats.' "

The phrase has long ago lost its sting and is now used affectionately; Republicans appeal to "discerning Democrats" for crossover support.

DESTABILIZE euphemism for "overthrow."

Director of Central Intelligence William Colby disclosed to a congressional committee in April 1974 that the CIA had spent $8 million in Chile between 1970 and 1973 in an effort to make it difficult for Marxist Salvatore Allende Gossens to govern.

"The goal of the clandestine CIA activities," wrote Seymour M. Hersh in the *New York Times* on September 8, 1974, " . . . was to 'destabilize' the Marxist government . . . "

Since the word was a freshly coined euphemism, and since it appeared to conflict with sworn testimony by Secretary of State Kissinger that "the CIA had nothing to do with the coup," the term was used with savagery and glee by critics of covert U.S. activities.

Curiously, the word was used again, in a positive sense, early in the Carter Administration. U.S. Ambassador to the UN Andrew Young (see **POINT MAN**) discussed Cuban intervention in Africa as possibly proving to be a "stabilizing force." As Cuban troop strength grew in Africa in 1978, critics of the Carter foreign policy used "stabilizing force" against the Carter men, much as critics of Mr.

Kissinger had used "destabilization" against him.

See **CIA-ESE**.

DÉTENTE an improvement in relations between nations, warmer than accommodation, cooler than rapprochement.

Woven through the history of the post–World War II period is the word *détente,* or such rough equivalents as *thaw,* **ACCOMMODATION,** *normalization of relations,* or *opening to the East.* When President Eisenhower met the Soviet Union's dual leaders, Nikolai Bulganin and Nikita Khrushchev, at Geneva in July 1955, he told them, "We have come to find a basis for accommodation which will make life safer and happier not only for the nations we represent but for the people elsewhere."

The thaw begun at Geneva later froze over; during the Cuban missile crisis of 1962, President Kennedy wrote Khrushchev: "If your letter signifies that you are prepared to discuss a detente affecting NATO and the Warsaw Pact, we are quite prepared to consider with our allies any useful proposals." In his *Kennedy,* Ted Sorensen described the subsequent search for areas of agreement as "the emerging detente." He added: "The breathing spell had become a pause, the pause was becoming a detente and no one could foresee what further changes lay ahead."

Ahead lay the escalation of the war in Vietnam; not until 1971, with the progress of arms-limitation talks and the announcement of a visit to mainland China, did détente become an active possibility.

The heyday of "détente," in policy and in usage, was in 1972 and 1973, as U.S. and Soviet leaders held summit conferences and launched arms-control agreements. After the Nixon resignation, President Ford found both policy and word becoming a burden, as hard-liners previously kept at bay by Nixon attacked détente as a SELLOUT, GIVEAWAY, and a "one-way street." Henry Kissinger's policy was described as "like going to a wife-swapping party and coming home alone."

The Soviet Union resented the attack on the word, rightly interpreting it as an attack on the Brezhnev policies. On January 4, 1976, *Pravda* denounced those in the U.S. who were critical of "one-way advantages" won by the Soviets. "Some people with weak nerves," said the Soviet official organ, "losing self-control, are even speaking in extremes. The pseudo-oracle William Safire, who spread himself across the pages of the *New York Times* on New Year's Eve, croaked: 'Détente is dead. The second cold war has begun.' "

President Carter in 1977 tried to take some of the onus off the now-controversial word by defining it in a Notre Dame speech as "progress toward peace." In a *Foreign Affairs* piece (December 1977) gutsily titled "Russia, America and Détente," former Ford State Department counselor Helmut Sonnenfeldt wrote: "Some of our debates about Soviet policy have tended to turn more on the definition of the labels that have been attached to it than on substance. 'CONTAINMENT,' 'COLD WAR,' 'an era of negotiation,' 'détente' . . . all caught elements of the complex realities . . . but over time they came to obscure rather than illuminate them."

The word has had its tongue-in-cheek defenders. David Braaten of the *Washington Star* wrote in 1973: "In the world of clichés, it is always comforting to have a reliable, steady favorite like détente." Pointing to its use in Bizet's eighteenth-century translation of Herodotus about a period preceding the Spartan sack of Athens, and to its resuscitation by *New York Sun* editorialist Mortimer Lovelace rhapsodizing the Locarno Pact in the twenties, Braaten added: "It meets all the requirements: it is French, and therefore impossible for Americans to pronounce with any degree of certainty; it is short enough to fit in a one-column headline, should that unfortunate necessity arise, yet full-bodied enough to add solidity and a sense of importance to a four-column head-cum-kicker; its meaning is only hazily grasped by its users, and, perhaps most important of all, it means nothing whatever to the reader."

Strangely, a cousin of "détente" is rarely used, except among diplomats: *démarche* means "step forward," or improvement of relations, and cliché-makers can hope that its day will come.

DETERRENT a military force or weapons system whose strength, real or feigned, is capable of forestalling an enemy attack by the threat of devastating retaliation.

"The major deterrent is in a man's mind," wrote Admiral Arleigh Burke in 1960. "The major deterrent in the future is going to be not only what we have, but what we do, what we are willing to do, what they think we will do. Stamina, guts, standing up for the things that we say—those are deterrents."

The concept of preparedness as a deterrent is an old one. In his first annual address to both houses of Congress, George Washington said in 1790: "To be prepared for war is one of the most effectual means of preserving peace." James Monroe, for one, argued otherwise. "Preparation for war," he said in 1818, "is a constant stimulus to suspicion and ill-will." But many agreed with Washington. "Speak softly and carry a big stick," Theodore Roosevelt said in 1901. "You will go far."

In 1940, FDR defended the draft by saying: "Your boys are not going to be sent into any foreign wars. They are going into training to form a force so strong that, by its very existence, it will keep the threat of war far away from our shores." (See AGAIN AND AGAIN AND AGAIN.)

Nuclear weapons were believed by many to be the most powerful deterrent of all against a major war. Though they did not prevent minor wars, they kept them from "escalating" into major conflicts. "What has really happened," Walter Lippmann wrote of the Korean truce in 1953, "is that both sides and all concerned have been held within a condition of mutual deterrent."

Israeli Foreign Minister Abba Eban gave a new wrinkle to the definition in 1966 after his country attacked a Jordanian town in an effort to halt Arab terrorism. He called it "demonstrative deterrence"; a year later the Israelis preferred "pre-emptive strike." This was, however, short of PREVENTIVE WAR—an idea put forward as a means of preventing China from growing too menacing. See MASSIVE RETALIATION; DOOMSDAY MACHINE; SALT (LEXICON).

DEVIATIONISM, *see* **REVISIONISM.**

DEVOLUTION   transfer of power from a central government to a region or locality; sometimes used as a euphemism for secession or separation.

In a general sense, *devolution* is a synonym for "power sharing," a movement that grew popular in the sixties and seventies as charges of "bureaucracy" were often leveled at centralized authority.

Frequent use of the word began in connection with HOME RULE in Ireland, and extended to the calls for "more local say" to outright independence, from Scotland to Quebec. Most early citations in the seventies are from the *Times Literary Supplement.*

In 1975 the *Wall Street Journal* described British Prime Minister Harold Wilson's moves to meet Scottish demands: "The government policy is called 'devolution'—the decentralizing of many government powers and functions." In 1976 columnist C. L. Sulzberger of the *New York Times* wrote: "Arguments over 'devolution' versus local 'nationalism' rage in non-English sections of the United Kingdom including Scotland, Wales and Northern Ireland. It is not merely a matter of reviving relatively little-used languages like Gaelic and Welsh but of actually shifting major authority including title to mineral wealth into regional hands."

In Canada, the separatists of Quebec—who wanted to withdraw from English-speaking Canada and to set up their own French-speaking state—used "devolution" as a less revolutionary-sounding word than "secession." The word seems closer to "evolution" than "revolution," and is useful to those who want to maintain a moderate-sounding position before demanding or declaring "independence."

DEWEY BLITZ   the second-ballot pressure by the Dewey forces that enabled them to wrest the nomination from Senator Robert Taft in the 1948 Republican convention.

Three Republican candidates led the field in 1948: Dewey, Taft, and

Harold Stassen. 548 convention votes meant nomination. On the first ballot, Dewey received 434, Taft 224, and Stassen 157. The favorite-son delegations of Senator Arthur Vandenberg (Michigan) and Governor Earl Warren (California) were considered least likely to change on the second ballot; the favorite-son delegations of Illinois and Tennessee were likely to switch to Taft. That meant Dewey had to pick up other favorite-son delegations, plus strength from Stassen, to hold his momentum.

Led by New York attorney Herbert Brownell, the Dewey organization "leaned on" (see FEET TO THE FIRE) the Stassen voters; important defections were achieved from the Iowa, Maryland, Nebraska, and South Dakota delegations. Though Stassen picked up scattered votes elsewhere, his second-ballot total dropped to 149; Dewey's increased to 515 and Taft's to 274. Thus, the Dewey second-ballot increase was 81 to Taft's 50—and the STAMPEDE was on.

If liberal columnist Max Lerner did not coin the phrase "Dewey blitz," he was at least an early user. Lerner wrote that Dewey won the nomination "not because he had principles or even appeal, but because he had a machine. The machine was ruthless and well oiled, run by a group of slick and modern operators. It combined the age-old methods of power politics with the newest strategies of blitz warfare and the precision tools of American industry and administration."

The word *Blitz* (German for "lightning") was still relatively new in its military context and referred to fast-moving mechanized warfare carried out by Nazi armored divisions in early World War II. In 1941 the Birmingham (U.K.) *Sunday Mercury* asked: "If the last war's *strafe* is this war's *blitz,* what will it become in the war after next?"

In its English form—lightning—the word enjoyed a brief political vogue in the 1880s. Alabama Democrats adopted a "lightning creed" in 1880, to turn out the Reconstruction Republicans and Negroes. "No man can be appointed (in Alabama)," Illinois Representative J. H. Rowell told the House in 1890, "to hold a precinct election unless he is known to be a 'lightning man,' a ballot-box stuffer, a false counter."

The Dewey blitz brought the word into U.S. politics; the phrase is still used by politicians to refer to excellent convention organization, and "blitz" has been adopted to describe saturation television campaigns.

A "TV blitz" in politics is a concentration of advertising in the last week of the campaign, aimed at the "undecided" and at turning out the vote of the committed. Since 1952, when admen Al Hollender and Rosser Reeves created the Eisenhower "spot" campaign, half-hour speeches have given way to spots of one minute, twenty-, or ten-second duration, selling hard to huge audiences. But like all MADISON AVENUE TECHNIQUES, they are troubling. "These new techniques," wrote James Perry in the *National Observer,* "are so overwhelming, so terribly effective. Some day, maybe they will elect a truly dangerous and sinister man to high office."

DIALOGUE   genuine two-way communication, or the pretense thereof.

The phrase "national dialogue" was popularized by Adlai Stevenson in his 1952 campaign as part of his theme, "let's talk sense to the American people." The word appealed to

John F. Kennedy, who used it often, as in a 1962 Yale speech: ". . . the dialogue between the parties—between business and government—is clogged by illusion and platitude . . ."

In current political usage, the word has an intellectual, slightly wistful connotation; a *dialogue* is more pointed than a *discussion,* less heated than an *argument,* less formal than a *debate.* It is used to describe the establishment of wary communication between divergent groups; when modified by "meaningful," the word becomes meaningless. See ISSUES, THE.

DIAPER IN THE RING, *see* **HAT IN THE RING.**

DIEHARDS dwindling handful committed to a losing cause, fighting long after hope of victory is gone.

In 1911 British Prime Minister Herbert Henry Asquith was determined to reduce the veto power of the House of Lords over the House of Commons. He extracted a trump card from the previous King, Edward VII, and held George V to it as well: if the House of Lords would not go along with a reduction of power, the King would appoint as many new peers to that House as necessary to get the deciding vote.

A substantial group in the House of Lords, led by Lord Halsbury, refused to go along; they said they would "die in the last ditch," and became known as the "Diehards." Wrote R. J. Minney in a history of 10 Downing Street: "Behind the scenes the 'Diehards' held angry meetings over dinner and exchanged letters in one at least of which violence was advocated if necessary." But other peers were not prepared to die hard; they accepted a two-year veto compromise and de-

serted the "Diehards." The King recorded in his diary: "The Halsburyites were, Thank God, beaten. It is indeed a great relief to me—I am spared any further humiliation by a creation of peers."

The British political use of diehard was taken from the nickname of the Middlesex Regiment, the 57th Foot; at the Battle of Albuera in 1811, Colonel William Inglis was badly wounded and refused to be taken to the rear, crying "Die hard, men, die hard!" The phrase was reinforced in America because George Washington's last words were reported to be "It is well. I die hard, but am not afraid to go."

DIME'S WORTH OF DIFFERENCE, NOT A a minor-party sneer at the similarity between the two major parties.

The phrase was central to the presidential campaigns of Alabama Governor George Corley Wallace, who stressed the need to SEND THEM A MESSAGE—"them," in Governor Wallace's eyes, being the "pointed-headed professors" in Washington who dominated the planning of both the Democratic and the Republican parties.

Governor Wallace informed the author in 1976: "I do not recall the exact date that we first used the phrases 'dime's worth of difference' and 'pointed-headed.' Both of these, I am sure, were used initially in 1967 as we were preparing for the third party campaign and gaining ballot positions. To the best of my knowledge, both of these expressions were original with me and something that I just thought of and put into an extemporaneous speech. The expressions were received well by the crowds and I continued to use them."

DINOSAUR WING an attack term against extreme conservatives.

A parenthetical remark by Adlai Stevenson in a speech at the Mormon Tabernacle, Salt Lake City, Utah, October 14, 1952, either coined or popularized the phrase: "Yet the same Republicans (the dinosaur-wing of that party) who object to service from our Government—who call everything 'creeping socialism' . . . who hint darkly of 'dictatorship'—these same men begin to hint that we are 'subversive,' or at best the tools of our country's enemies, when we boast of the great strides toward social justice and security we have already made . . ."

It is possible that Stevenson saw the word used in the *New York Times* the day before: "Anybody who gets indignant [over corruption] is a hypocritical old dinosaur." A similar metaphor was used in the mid-nineteenth century to describe former Whigs, "the fossil remains of an extinct party."

The predecessor phrase was "Neanderthal wing." The Truman Library has an unsigned memorandum dated June 29, 1948, probably written by Judge Samuel Rosenman, urging Truman to call back Congress after the Democratic convention because "it would keep a steady glare of publicity on the Neanderthal men of the Republican party . . ." Columnists Evans and Novak used "Stone Age Republican" in this sense.

In a story on Chicago Mayor Richard J. Daley, the *Saturday Evening Post* in 1964 gave the word a bipartisan connotation: "The last dinosaur wins again."

The dinosaur made another foray out of extinction in American business lingo when George Romney, then president of American Motors, launched a compact-car campaign attacking the "gas-guzzling dinosaurs" of the road. When he entered politics, it was just a question of time before he adapted his best-known phrase, and the time came in spring of 1967 when he told a political audience "the Great Society has become a tax-guzzling dinosaur."

The word "dinosaur" was coined by Sir Richard Owen in 1841 from the Greek *deinos* (fearful) and *sauros* (lizard) before it was discovered that the beast would have registered as a vegetarian.

See RADICAL RIGHT; BIRCHERS; LITTLE OLD LADIES IN TENNIS SHOES; KOOKS, NUTS AND. In the other direction, see PINKO; FELLOW TRAVELER; FLAMING LIBERAL.

DIRTY POLITICS unethical practices in campaigning: ballot-box stuffing, mudslinging, character assassination, and other chicanery.

Franklin D. Roosevelt Jr.'s characterization of Hubert Humphrey as a "draft-dodger" in the 1960 West Virginia primary (while Roosevelt was campaigning for John F. Kennedy) was described by the *Washington Star* as "a new low in dirty politics." Bruce Felknor, executive director of the Fair Campaign Practices Committee, in 1966 compiled a volume of low tricks, smears, and unethical attacks entitled *Dirty Politics*.

American slang includes *dirty pool, dirty wash, dirty linen, dirty work,* and *dirty word.* With a small addition of water, dirt becomes *mud,* leading to *political mudbaths,* MUDSLINGING, and *mudsills.*

Oddly, there is no antonym for dirty politics: clean politics is not a phrase in use. PRACTICAL POLITICS carries a connotation of cynicism, *power politics* and *smart politics* slightly more, and *dirty politics* the most.

Each phrase is purely subjective. Often a campaign manager will wire a protest about his opposition's radio or TV spots to the station manager just before an election, with a copy to the FCC, threatening a suit for libel. Unless the spots are in the candidate's own voice, the station will ordinarily take them off the air for at least several hours until a decision is made or the spots modified. The spots might have been accurate or innocuous, but the protest knocks them off for a while. To the party pulling the trick, it is smart politics; to the party on the receiving end, it is dirty politics.

DIRTY TRICKS   as "Department of Dirty Tricks," the nickname of the covert operations of the Central Intelligence Agency; since the Watergate scandals, a disapproving term for campaign smears and disruptive activities of a "black advance."

In the sixties, applied to the CIA, the phrase had a ring of derring-do, since it was felt that democracies had to fight cold-war fire with fire of their own: a *Time* cover story on Richard Helms (February 24, 1967) described a post he had held as "deputy chief of the plans division, the so-called 'dirty tricks' department . . ." Soon after criticism mounted of our support of South Vietnam, columnist Walter Lippmann began to wonder about those activities: "The question before us today is whether the activities of the CIA which are outside genuine intelligence, that is to say its black propaganda, its interventionist operations, its 'dirty tricks,' are truly in the national interest."

The phrase "dirty trick" can be traced back to 1674, but was rarely used politically, and if so, not in the way it was applied to the CIA: a lighthearted description of serious, sometimes murderous, acts. In 1972 it was used in a general sense by Margaret Truman in a biography of her father: "Along with the smears and lies Dad was continually rebutting, the Republicans threw in a few dirty tricks aimed specifically at our campaign train. A 'TRUTH SQUAD' followed us around the country, issuing statements that supposedly countered Dad's speeches. In Buffalo they hired a horde of school children who tried to drown out Dad with screams and catcalls, anticipating by twenty years the Students for a Democratic Society."

In March of 1973, however, the phrase in the CIA sense was applied to politics in the Watergate scandals. "Money from the safe, it is alleged," wrote the *National Observer* on March 10, "was used to finance Republican 'dirty tricks' during the campaign." The *New York Times* on April 29: "Last week, it was disclosed that a third private treasury of about $600,000 [was] used to finance a variety of dirty tricks." In the July 23 *New Yorker,* Common Cause president John Gardner told reporter Elizabeth Drew that the activity could not be minimized by using the ironic phrase: " 'Some of the highest officials of this nation carried on a sustained and systematic attempt to destroy our form of government. It wasn't "dirty tricks" within the system—it was an attempt to subvert the system . . .' "

Although Nixon speechwriter Patrick Buchanan sought to draw distinctions between time-honored pranks and illegal campaign practices (see HARDBALL), the phrase "dirty tricks" lost its smirk and became a serious term for criminal, or at least obviously unethical politicking. Right after the Watergate scandal, *New York Times* reporter Seymour Hersh broke the CIA scandal, and the new seriousness with which outside-the-law activities were perceived underscored the new meaning of "dirty tricks." As the bridge between the Watergate and CIA investigations, the phrase became embedded in the vocabulary of venality and is likely to be used as an attack phrase in the future—which, in itself, is a mild form of "dirty trick."

See SMEAR; ROORBACK; GUTTER FLYER.

DISADVANTAGED a euphemism for "poor," replacing "underprivileged" in social workers' jargon.

As a result of the civil rights movement of the fifties and sixties, it was felt that no citizen was "privileged," though many were "advantaged," thus the substitution. Since "underadvantaged" is cumbersome, "disadvantaged"—without the advantages of education and opportunity—was selected.

In the same way, what used to be called a "slum" is now delicately referred to as "a culturally deprived environment."

A cartoon by Jules Feiffer published in 1965 shows a man saying to himself: "I used to think I was poor. Then they told me I wasn't poor, I was needy. They told me it was self-defeating to think of myself as needy, I was deprived. Then they told me underprivileged was overused. I was disadvantaged. I still don't have a dime. But I have a great vocabulary."

DISASTER METAPHORS natural catastrophe is commonplace in political language. Beginning with a mild GROUNDSWELL (a heavy rolling sea due to a distant storm), a candidate's fortunes may move forward like a *prairie fire,* his headquarters *flooded* with telegrams of support, leading him to a WHIRLWIND CAM-PAIGN, but a *tidal wave* or FIRESTORM of criticism after a scandal has *erupted* may lead to an AVALANCHE of votes against him and an electoral LANDSLIDE for his opponent, leaving him *snowed under* and wondering how he could have been *blitzed* (German for "lightning," which candidates hope will strike) by a threat that seemed, at the beginning, *like a cloud no bigger than a man's hand.* (I Kings 18:44).

Typical of a political disaster comment was William Allen White's assessment of the defeat of Alfred Landon in 1936: "It was not an election the country has just undergone, but a political Johnstown flood."

DISGRACE TO THE HUMAN RACE, *see* **THREE-MARTINI LUNCH.**

DISH THE WHIGS to steal the opposition's clothes; to win by reversing long-held stands.

In nineteenth-century English slang, "to dish" was to defeat decisively, especially by trickery; the term probably came from the notion of cooking something and serving it well-done, though there is also speculation that it is derived from the Old English "disherit," now "disinherit": to take away one's inheritance.

When England's Conservative party surprised itself and the world by passing the radical Reform Bill of 1867—thereby enfranchising two million workingmen, a goal of its Whig opposition for many years—the Prime Minister, Lord Derby, said delightedly, "Don't you see we have dished the Whigs?" With the aid of Benjamin Disraeli, who was to succeed him as head of the Tories, Derby had indeed won support that had been taken for granted by the opposition.

The British phrase was a favorite of *Newsweek* columnist Stewart Alsop's, and is still used by history buffs to describe a flip-flop: "Seldom in Western politics since Disraeli's Reform Bill of 1867," declared a *New York Times* editorial about Nixon summiteering on February 10, 1972, "—when Lord Derby boasted, 'We've dished the Whigs'—has a national leader so completely turned his back on a lifetime of beliefs to adopt those of his political opponents."

The Derby reference was especially piquant, since his only other famous remark was: "When I first came into Parliament, Mr. Tierney, a great Whig authority, used always to say that the duty of an Opposition was very simple—it was, to oppose everything, and propose nothing." That statement has been shortened to "the duty of an Opposition is to oppose" and, ironically, is attributed to the politician who won by adopting the tenets of his opposition.

DISINFORMATION, *see* **PROPAGANDA.**

DISINTERMEDIATION, *see* **ECONOMIC JARGON.**

DISSENT, *see* **PRESIDENT OF ALL THE PEOPLE; ACTIVIST.**

DIVORCE ISSUE the question raised about the "morality" of a candidate who has been divorced.

The *youth issue* has died; the religious issue is weakening; but to some voters, the *divorce issue* is still strong. The marriage of Andrew Jackson to divorcee Rachel Donelson Robards caused a stir, particularly since her divorce was in question; and Wallis Simpson's divorced status made it necessary for King Edward VIII to abdicate in order to marry her.

The first divorced man to run for President was James Cox in 1920. According to some accounts, a deal was suspected: the GOP would not mention Cox's divorce, and the Democrats would not whisper about Harding's mistresses.

In modern times, divorce itself is not the issue; Adlai Stevenson had been divorced when he ran for President in 1952, and that fact was never very important. It is remarriage after a divorce that rankles a portion of the public, and "home-wrecking" is considered the worst sin of all.

Nelson Rockefeller was divorced in 1961; he was re-elected governor of New York in 1962 by a comfortable half-million votes. Before the election, social critic Cleveland Amory observed that "he's certain to get the divorce vote and remember that's one in four these days." But in May 1963 he married Margaretta Fitler ("Happy") Murphy, herself recently divorced, and without assured custody of her five children; there was a measurable reaction.

"People will forgive a politician they love almost any sin," wrote Theodore White, "—as witness James Michael Curley, Huey Long, Adam Clayton Powell, Jimmy Walker, and a score of others; in matters of romance, particularly, they will forgive him almost any peccadillo . . . so long as the peccadillo is not flaunted. But the frank and open acceptance of a new marriage was a breach with the general indulgence of the hypocrisy of politics . . ."

In the crucial California primary against Barry Goldwater in 1964, the divorce issue hurt Rockefeller—but until the final weekend, the polls showed him ahead. That weekend, "Happy" Rockefeller bore the candidate a son; the newspapers were filled with the story of Rockefeller's flying visit to the hospital, a fresh reminder of the divorce and remarriage. An insidious slogan, "Elect a leader, not a lover" was pressed home by word of mouth, and Rockefeller lost by a narrow margin. A Rockefeller campaign worker, later looking at a picture of robust Nelson, Jr., playing with his toys, sighed, "If only that little boy were three days younger, he'd be the son of the President of the United States."

DIXIECRAT Southern Democrats who bolted the national party in 1948 in opposition to President Truman's civil rights platform.

In a fiery speech to the 1948 Democratic convention, Hubert Humphrey posed the central issue to face his party in the decades ahead: "It is time for the Democratic party to step out of the shadow of STATE'S RIGHTS—and to walk forthrightly into the bright sunshine of HUMAN RIGHTS." Most Democrats followed his lead (although, twenty years later, many liberals—angered by the Vietnam policy of Lyndon Johnson, whom Humphrey served as Vice President —were reluctant to support him).

The States Rights Democrats from Alabama, Mississippi, Louisiana, and other Southern states held a convention of their own in 1948, nominating Senator J. Strom Thurmond as their candidate for President. The votes lost to the Democrats in the South were probably offset by votes Democrats gained in the North, no longer embarrassed by their party's civil rights divisions.

Coinage has been attributed to William Weismer, telegraph editor of the *Charlotte (N.C.) News,* who squeezed States Rights Democrats into a headline. *American Speech* magazine lists another headline on May 5, 1948, using the word in the *Birmingham News.* Alabama Governor Frank Dixon did not like the new nickname: "Dixiecrats leaves the wrong impression," he complained. "Our contention is that we are returning to the original concepts of the founding fathers of our nation and the Democratic party."

Harry Truman was having none of that. He wrote: "The States Rights Democrats claim that this was not a bolt from the Democratic party. They said they represented the true Democrats of the Southland. It was a bolt."

The technique of label-formation using one half of Democrat or GOP as an acronym lingers on. Derivations include "Dixiegop," for Southern Republican, and in 1966 Democratic supporters of Republican candidate for Florida governor Claude R. Kirk called themselves "Demokirks."

See BOLT; TAKE A WALK; OFF THE RESERVATION; OUTSIDE WORLD.

DR. FELL SYNDROME a voter's inexplicable distaste for a candidate whose positions would ordinarily command his support.

Stewart Alsop, writing in *Newsweek* in 1970, identified the "Dr. Fell Syndrome" as the cause of President Nixon's greatest political weakness— many of the people who liked what he stood for didn't like the way he stood.

The phrase is from the poem by Thomas (Tom) Brown written while he was a student at Christ Church, Oxford, during the 1600s. It is a loose translation of some lines in Martial's *Epigrammata,* written in the first century A.D.:

> I do not love thee, Dr. Fell.
> The reason why I cannot tell;

But this alone I know full well,
I do not love thee, Dr. Fell.

The real Dr. Fell, a seventeenth-century English divine, was able to maintain Church of England services despite Cromwell and was made dean of Christ Church after the Restoration. Though he was generally acknowledged to be a man of courage, rectitude, and vision, some people just couldn't warm up to him.

DOCTRINES   policies that have hardened with acceptance.

When the word is applied in retrospect, it usually sticks; when it is announced with a policy, it usually fades. President Monroe's decision to deny European influence in the Americas was not laid down as the *Monroe Doctrine;* it became known as that many years later. On the other hand, most Americans do not remember what was contained in the *Truman Doctrine* (aid to Greece and Turkey to fight Communism) or the *Eisenhower Doctrine* (same kind of containment in the Middle East).

Two of the most hotly debated doctrines in American history have faded from the language today: the *Freeport Doctrine* of Stephen Douglas, which held that the people of a territory could exclude slavery prior to the formation of a state constitution, and John Calhoun's *Doctrine of Non-Interference,* declaring that federal intervention on the slavery issue in a state was illegal.

In the Communist world, the *One Glass of Water Doctrine* is still remembered, but more in the breach than the observance. This held that good Communists should regard sexual desire as being no more important than a glass of water. Lenin revoked this doctrine after the Bolsheviks took power, but it remained for many years as gospel to Chinese Communists under the name *Pei-shui-chu-i.* It was the cause of some disaffection among the Viet Cong in South Vietnam.

The *Brezhnev Doctrine,* expounded by Leonid Brezhnev on November 12, 1968, after Soviet arms had crushed a turning toward freedom in Czechoslovakia earlier that year, holds that "the Socialist community as a whole"—that is, the Soviet Union—has the right to intervene in otherwise sovereign states when it detected a tendency toward capitalism subverting an already Communist state. This asserted Soviet military control of its satellites: "to protect Communist regimes even if it means the use of force."

"The Carter approach to foreign policy," said the State Department's Leslie Gelb in 1977, "rests in a belief that not only is the world far too complex to be reduced to a doctrine, but there is something inherently wrong in having a doctrine at all."

See NIXON DOCTRINE.

DO-GOODER   politician's derisive name for reformers and civic-action nonpartisans.

The phrase "do-goods" can be traced back to 1654 *(OED),* and the use of the compound word in a political context can be found in a 1923 issue of *The Nation:* "There is nothing wrong with the United States except . . . the parlor socialists, uplifters, and do-goods." Tracing the use of "good" back in political history, the pattern seems to be "Good Government Clubs," "goo-goos," "goody-goody"—with a separate branch for "holier than thou."

The City Club of New York came up with a district-level network of local action groups called "Good Government Clubs" in the 1890s.

Promptly dubbed the "goo-goos" by the *New York Sun,* the reformers raised the ire of Theodore Roosevelt: "The Republican machine men have been loudly demanding a straight ticket; and those prize idiots, the Goo-Goos, have just played into their hands by capering off and nominating an independent ticket of their own."

Like so many reform groups, the Good Government Clubs atrophied and died in a few years; the Democratic and Republican machines skillfully redistricted the city, and the reformers no longer knew which club they belonged to.

Just before the rise of the goo-goos, "holier-than-thou" was the name given the independent Republicans in 1884. This was derived from Isaiah 65:5: "Stand by thyself, come not near to me; for I am holier than thou."

DOLLAR DIPLOMACY   use of U.S. military and political power to further the interest of U.S. entrepreneurs in Latin America; or, enticement of foreign nations to follow U.S. political leadership with promises of economic aid.

Early in the twentieth century, under the Roosevelt Corollary to the Monroe Doctrine, U.S. Marines helped U.S. businessmen open up new markets in Latin America and protected those interests; protectorates were established over Cuba, Haiti, Nicaragua, and Santo Domingo. *Harper's Weekly* in 1910 referred to the phrase as it was then being applied to Secretary of State Philander C. Knox: "An attempt is made, necessarily sketchy, to outline simply and clearly what is meant by the term 'Dollar Diplomacy' as it has come to be commonly applied to certain of the activities of Secretary Knox as mani-

fested in Honduras, in Liberia, and in negotiations now in progress looking to the participation of American capital in railway construction in the Far East."

President William Howard Taft, in his annual message on December 3, 1912, defended the philosophy in what came to be known as the "Dollar Diplomacy" speech: "The diplomacy of the present administration has sought to respond to modern ideas of commercial intercourse. This policy has been characterized as substituting dollars for bullets. It is one that appeals alike to idealistic humanitarian sentiments, to the dictates of sound policy and strategy, and to legitimate commercial aims."

"Dollar diplomacy" became a term of criticism used by Latin American diplomats who resented economic arm-twisting. In its more general sense, the phrase has come to mean the dangling of economic plums in front of a hungry neutral or unfriendly nation. In 1965 President Lyndon Johnson offered a billion-dollar investment program in Southeast Asia if only the Communists would replace aggression with "peaceful cooperation." Wrote Arthur Krock in the *New York Times:* "Only from members of the small Republican minority . . . was any question raised . . . of the political psychology of a proposal reminiscent by its attendant circumstances of the crude era of American 'dollar diplomacy.' "

In late 1971, the phrase was used in derogation of hard-bargaining Treasury Secretary John Connally, but temporarily lost its pejorative connotation after a realignment of currency rates favorable to the U.S.

DOMINO THEORY   the concept that if one strategically placed nation in an area goes Communist, the others will quickly follow.

Dwight Eisenhower used the Joseph Alsop metaphor politically in 1954, in explaining his decision to offer economic aid to the South Vietnamese government of Ngo Dinh Diem. "You have a row of dominoes set up," said the President at a press conference, "you knock over the first one, and what will happen to the last one is that it will go over very quickly. So you have the beginning of a disintegration that would have the most profound influences." The theory derives from what historian Arthur Schlesinger, Jr., describes as "a popular construction, or misconstruction, of the Munich analogy." (See MUNICH, ANOTHER.) In any event, the idea was accepted widely. As Eisenhower told Churchill: "We failed to halt Hirohito, Mussolini and Hitler by not acting in unity and in time."

John F. Kennedy had reservations about the theory. Columnist Arthur Krock wrote after an interview with him: "I asked him what he thought of the 'falling domino' theory—that is, if Laos and Vietnam go Communist, the rest of Southeast Asia will fall to them in orderly succession. The President expressed doubts that this theory had much point any more because, he remarked, the Chinese Communists were bound to get nuclear weapons in time, and from that moment on the nations of Southeast Asia would seek to be on good terms with Peking."

Some of Kennedy's closest advisers, nevertheless, accepted the theory. His former Chairman of the Joint Chiefs of Staff, General Maxwell Taylor, told a House subcommittee shortly after Kennedy's death that if the U.S. withdrew from Vietnam, the country would quickly go Communist, and "the remainder of Southeast Asia would very shortly thereafter go

neutralist, possibly even Communist. Burma would be affected, India also. Indonesia would soon line up with the Communists. We would be pushed out of the Western Pacific back to Honolulu."

One of the most persistent critics of the theory, Senate Foreign Relations Committee Chairman J. William Fulbright, wrote in *The Arrogance of Power:* "The inference we have drawn from this is that we must fight in one country in order to avoid having to fight in another, although we could with equal logic have inferred that it is useless to fight in one country when the same conditions of conflict are present in another." A graphic metaphoric attack was made by novelist Norman Mailer during a 1965 anti-Vietnam demonstration at the University of California at Berkeley: "They are not dominoes but sand castles. Sand castles. And a tide of nationalism is on the way in."

U.S. News & World Report in 1968 termed the phrase "a cornerstone of U.S. reasoning about Vietnam since the Eisenhower years."

The phrase was parodied in 1968 by columnist Art Buchwald. He held that BRINKMANSHIP was named after a man named Brinkman, and the domino theory after one Sam Domino, who explained how he coined it: "Well, one evening we were having a buffet and there were about twenty people lined up with plates waiting for some chicken cacciatore when my uncle, who was first in line, slipped and fell backward. He knocked over my aunt standing in back of him and she, in turn, knocked over my cousin, who knocked over my son and so on until all twenty people were on the floor. It suddenly occurred to me that if this could happen to people, it could happen to countries."

DONKEY, DEMOCRATIC symbol of the Democratic party.

The donkey gained its acceptance as the Democratic symbol in 1874 as a result of Thomas Nast's cartoons (see ELEPHANT, REPUBLICAN), supported by Ignatius Donnelly's remark in the Minnesota Legislature: "The Democratic party is like a mule—without pride of ancestry or hope of posterity."

The donkey has provided cartoonists and speechwriters with an invaluable metaphor. For example, when the Democrats at their 1928 Houston convention nominated Al Smith (who favored repeal of Prohibition) and Senator Joseph T. Robinson of Arkansas (who favored Prohibition), the wisecrack was "the Democratic donkey with a wet head and wagging a dry tail left Houston."

Nast exercised good judgment in his selection of symbols. Clinton Rossiter writes that the difference between the two parties "is caught vividly in the choice of beastly emblems that was made for all of us long ago: the slightly ridiculous but tough and long-lived Donkey—the perfect symbol of the rowdy Democrats; the majestic but ponderous Elephant—the perfect symbol of respectable Republicans. Can anyone imagine the Donkey as a Republican and the Elephant as a Democrat?"

DO-NOTHING CONGRESS Harry Truman's epithet for the 1947–1948 Republican-controlled session that rejected much of his program.

"Do-nothing" is associated with Truman's criticism of the 80th Congress, since it was so instrumental in giving him an upset victory over Thomas E. Dewey in 1948. But the term was in use as early as the sixteenth century, and Franklin Roosevelt used it in referring to the "do-nothing policy of Hoover." In his memoirs, Truman quoted Will Rogers' addition to an old slogan: "Keep Cool with Coolidge and Do Nothing."

Truman picked it up when, crossing the U.S. in June 1948, he found audiences responding to his attacks on "the good-for-nothing, do nothing, Taft-Hartley 80th Congress" and the "worst Congress" ever. When he accepted the Democratic nomination, he declared: "On the 26th day of July, which out in Missouri we call 'Turnip Day,' I am going to call that Congress back in session, and I am going to ask them to pass some of these laws they say they are for in their platform. Now, my friends, if there is any reality behind that Republican platform, we ought to get some action out of the short session of the 80th Congress. They could do this job in 15 days if they wanted to. . . . What that worst 80th Congress does in its special session will be the test. The American people will decide on the record."

Dominated by Robert A. Taft and his disappointed followers, the special session accomplished nothing, and Truman was able to continue campaigning on what he considered its obstructionism and on the fact that he had to use the veto 62 times against it. It was a bold move for, as Democratic adviser Clark Clifford recalls: "We were on our own 20-yard line. We had to be bold. If we kept plugging away in moderate terms, the best we could have done would have been to reach midfield when the gun went off. So we had to throw long passes."

Instead of the traditional defense of the record of the Administration in power, the Truman strategy was to turn its own frustrations and defeats into an asset by furiously attacking those who had effectively hamstrung the Administration. The strategy worked.

DON'T CHANGE HORSES an expression urging voters to continue an Administration during a period of crisis.

The metaphor was Lincoln's, spoken at the Republican convention of 1864, to a delegation from the Union League Club which had hailed the action of the convention in nominating Lincoln. Reported Nicolai and Hay: "The President answered them more informally, saying that he did not allow himself to suppose that either the Convention or the League had concluded that he was either the greatest or the best man in America, but rather that they had decided it was not best to 'swap horses while crossing the river.' "

Sperber and Trittschuh traced the origin to an 1846 newspaper: "There is a story of an Irishman who was crossing a stream with mare and colt when finding it deeper than he expected, and falling off the old mare, he seized the colt's tail to aid him in reaching the shore. Some persons on the bank called to him, advising him to take hold of the mare's tail, as she was the ablest to bring him out. His reply was, that it was a very unseasonable time for swapping horses."

The expression was edited by usage into "Don't change horses in midstream," or "Don't swap horses while crossing the stream." In recent times, its best-known use was in the Roosevelt campaigns of 1940 and 1944.

Republican Chairman Joe Martin remained convinced that the unwillingness to shift leadership in a crisis was the root cause of the Willkie defeat in 1940: "The fall of France and the imminent danger to Britain filled the American people with a fear of switching administrations. 'Don't

change horses in the middle of the stream' was never a more potent argument in American history than it was then. Not even the third-term issue could prevail against it."

"The Democrats could not seem to fight their way out of the hard crust of inertia in Washington," wrote Irving Stone of the Roosevelt-Dewey campaign, "and the only effort they cared to make was the negative cry of 'Don't change horses in midstream.' " Dewey's slogan was "TIME FOR A CHANGE," and public opinion polls showed him closing the gap on the President. Dewey's 1944 campaign (in contrast to 1948) was slashing and vigorous; Roosevelt supporters, viewing the erosion of their margin of safety, urged FDR to drop his above-the-battle stance and hit hard. The FALA SPEECH soon followed, infuriating the Republicans and reminding independents that the Old Master had not lost his political touch.

The phrase is current. The *New York Times* editorialized in 1967: "President Johnson . . . clearly intends to run as the commander-in-chief appealing to patriotism and national unity in a time of war and crisis. This approach has numerous precedents, including Lincoln's 'don't swap horses in the middle of the stream' in 1864 and Franklin Roosevelt's 1940 and 1944 campaigns."

Heavy use of the phrase was made in the Hoover-Roosevelt campaign of 1932. The *New Republic* characterized the Republican campaign theme as "Don't change barrels while going over Niagara." Roosevelt supporters said, "Swap horses or drown!"

DON'T LET THEM TAKE IT AWAY an unofficial Democratic campaign slogan of 1948 and 1952.

The phrase appeared in the *New*

York Journal-American of December 28, 1946, as a kind of belated answer to the Republican "HAD ENOUGH?" that had been so successful in the 1946 off-year elections. It was used in the 1948 Truman campaign, though not nearly as much as "DO-NOTHING CONGRESS."

In 1952, Adlai Stevenson treated it lightly: "There have been times when I have wondered whether you, my friends here in Illinois, couldn't have found some easier way of getting rid of me. In fact, before the Convention I wrote a song about it, only the Democratic party took the song and changed the words. My song was called 'Don't Let Them Take Me Away.' "

This is a defensive slogan, similar to the British Conservative party's 1964 slogan: "It's your standard of living—keep it with the Conservatives." That did not catch on, either. For one that did, see YOU NEVER HAD IT SO GOOD.

DON'T WASTE YOUR VOTE slogan of a major party attempting to win back support lost to splinter parties; usually accompanied by the statement "A vote for [splinter party candidate name] is a vote for [major opposition party name]."

President Harry Truman, fighting his uphill battle in 1948, knew that Henry Wallace's Progressive party was drawing votes from people who would ordinarily be Democratic. As Truman ripped into the DO-NOTHING CONGRESS and its MOSSBACK committee chairmen, he said in Los Angeles: ". . . a vote for the third party plays into the hands of the Republican forces of reaction whose aims are directly opposed to the aim of American liberalism."

A classic example of a double don't-waste-your-vote effort was the four-way New York gubernatorial race in 1966. Republican Rockefeller was urging members of the splinter Conservative party not to waste their votes on Paul Adams, while Democrat Frank O'Connor was urging Liberal party members not to waste their votes on Liberal candidate Franklin D. Roosevelt, Jr. At the last minute, word was passed to Liberal district leaders that their party members should switch to the Democrat, though too few did so to influence the result.

Reformer William Evarts, who helped break up New York's Tweed ring, was running for U.S. Senator in 1884 and came up with a phrase to dissuade New Yorkers from paying attention to the man running on the Prohibition ticket. He called it "voting in the air."

The answer to the don't-waste-your-vote plea is, of course, a stand on principle. Said Hearst's *San Francisco Examiner* in support of a hopeless cause in 1908: "The vote for principle is never thrown away. It is the only vote that isn't thrown away." Felix Frankfurter, explaining his vote for Robert La Follette in 1924, agreed: "If clarification of American politics through the formation of a new party is required to make our politics more honest and more real, then all the talk of 'throwing one's vote away' is the cowardly philosophy of the BANDWAGON."

A question in the minds of many American voters is: "Is my vote really needed?" Third parties play on this nagging doubt by urging voters to "make your vote count" by registering a protest. Major parties appeal on these grounds as well. Recalling the importance of "a single vote in each election district" in the 1960 election, they point out that each vote is important and the front runner could lose if that particular voter did not turn out.

Worry about the wasted vote is particularly strong in Japan. "For some reason," wrote Nobutake Ike in 1958, "Japanese voters do not like to 'waste' their votes. They are therefore reluctant to vote for a candidate who clearly has no chance to win. By the same token, if they believe that a particular candidate will win by a wide margin, they might shift their vote to someone else. They feel that 'he is going to win anyway, so why shouldn't I make my vote count by giving it to another candidate.'"

For the opposite appeal, see SEND THEM A MESSAGE.

DOOLEY, MR.   a fictional creation of author Finley Peter Dunne, who made sage political observations in a thick Irish brogue.

Mr. Dooley first appeared in a Chicago newspaper in the 1890s and dispensed his wisdom up to World War I.

Dunne lifted his character out of his hometown Chicago sixth-ward commentary in the Spanish-American War, and gained national recognition in 1896 by commenting on the William Jennings Bryan campaign. Skepticism kept his epigrams astringent: "I see gr-reat changes takin' place ivry day, but no change at all ivry fifty years." His best-known line, now used after being rendered into proper English, was: "No matther whether th' Constitution follows th' flag or not, th' Supreme Coort follows th' iliction returns." See SUPREME COURT FOLLOWS THE ELECTION RETURNS.

A typical Dooley comment is this view of the vice presidency: "Ye can't be sint to jail f'r it, but it's a kind iv a disgrace. . . . It is princip'lly because iv th' vice-prisidint that most iv our prisidints have enjoyed such rugged

health. Th' vice-prisidint guards th' prisidint, an' th' prisidint, afther sizin' up th' vice-prisidint, con-cludes that it wud be betther f'r th' counthry if he shud live yet awhile."

The tradition of political humor in dialect is that of Petroleum V. Nasby and Artemus Ward. Mark Twain placed political observations in the mouths of Huck Finn, Tom Sawyer, and Pudd'nhead Wilson. Will Rogers carried the torch for a while, and in the seventies, without dialect, the field has been dominated by Art Buchwald and Russell Baker.

See BEANBAG.

DOOMSDAY MACHINE   a computer programmed to set off a nuclear war based on another nation's actions; carrying DETERRENT to the extreme.

The Doomsday Machine, properly constructed, should be capable of wiping out life on earth. It sits in the nation that built it, but its behavior is controlled by an enemy nation.

This means that the enemy nation knows that certain actions will trigger the machine, and that no fears or false hopes in the nation that built the machine can stop its use. The enemy is thus provided with a list of restraints which have been programmed into the computer and knows where the line is drawn. One such restraint could be "You may not build a Doomsday Machine."

"Although it is most unlikely that any nation would build such a device in the next ten to twenty years," admits Herman Kahn, author of *On Thermonuclear War,* "there clearly are some circumstances in which a nation might wish it had built one."

A related expression, the Doomsday Clock, has led to the use of the urgent phrase "two minutes to midnight." Since 1947, the Doomsday

Clock appears monthly on the cover of the *Bulletin of the Atomic Scientists.* Powered by mankind's activities regarding atomic energy, the clock ticks toward the world's midnight when, presumably, all bets are off. The clock was originally set at eight minutes to twelve; by September 1953, when both the Soviet Union and the U.S. had thermonuclear capability, the hands were moved ahead to two minutes to midnight. After the 1963 nuclear test-ban treaty, it was moved back to twelve minutes; by 1968 the hands were at seven minutes.

The *Domesday Dictionary* was published in England in 1964, defining the more frightening nuclear words in a deadpan manner; *domesday* is pronounced *doomsday,* and refers to the survey of England for taxing purposes made by William the Conqueror in 1085, which was recorded in the *Domesday Book.*

DOORBELL-RINGING house-to-house canvassing for votes; personal persuasion by party workers of individual voters, hallmark of a well-organized campaign.

A doorbell-ringing campaign is one in which the party's workers are mobilized to make a personal appeal to individuals in their residence. Some of the rules: (1) an index-card file must be prepared of all registered voters, with party preference checked, and need for babysitter or transportation on election day indicated; (2) no calls before 8 A.M. or after 9 P.M.; (3) teams of men and women to do the actual doorbell-ringing, to reassure the voter of his safety and to provide for the safety of canvassers.

A follow-up to, but not a substitute for, a doorbell-ringing campaign is a telephone blitz—calls made from a "boiler room" to remind favorably inclined voters to turn out on election day.

Theodore White, in *The Making of the President 1964,* held that it was the influence of strangers ringing the doorbells of lonely newcomers in California that tipped the scales from Rockefeller to Goldwater in the closing days of the 1964 primary campaign that decided the Republican nomination.

See CANVASS.

DOPE STORY information leaked to a reporter and published as his own analysis; useful method of launching TRIAL BALLOONS or conditioning public opinion.

A good example of this technique was the way President Harry Truman handled the special session of what he termed the "DO-NOTHING CONGRESS" in the campaign of 1948. A President's special message to Congress is ordinarily handled as top secret, but in this case presidential press secretary Charles Ross leaked its contents the week preceding its delivery. "Thus the Truman program got double exposure in the nation's press," wrote biographer Cabell Phillips, "first in the provocative form of 'dope stories,' and again when the message was made officially public. As a publicity gimmick, it was a small triumph."

Dope has a dual root in American slang. As a synonym for narcotics, it is extended to one who appears drugged or stupid, as "dopey." As slang for information, it spawned "inside dope," "dope out," "dope sheet," and "dope story." The narcotic meaning appears to come from the Dutch word *doop,* with a current meaning of "baptism" but an earlier one of "sauce"—and opium smokers deal with a gooey substance. ("On the sauce" is current slang for alcoholism.) But no plausible explanation has been given for the root of dope as "data," to the author's knowledge. It is not new; the *Dictionary of Americanisms* has an entry dating to 1901, from a book by George Hobart: "I've known Tommy for a long time, so he feels free to read his dope to me."

Richard Nixon was the first President to use the phrase publicly; on January 28, 1969, he told a large group of State Department employees: "I have been reading some dope stories lately about the rivalries that may develop between the various Departments in government . . ."

A conflict of meanings exists; in Washington, D.C., a man who knows no inside dope is considered fairly dopey.

See **BACKGROUNDER; NOT FOR ATTRIBUTION; LEAK; PLANT; THUMBSUCKER.**

DOUBLE DIGIT   inflation of 10 percent or over.

A digit, from the Latin *digitus,* is a finger. Children start counting on their fingers, which is how the word for "finger" became the word for "number." "Double digit" means two numbers, like 10 or more.

The phrase began as "double-figure inflation" in England in the sixties, taken from "double figures" in cricket scores. In the U.S. the coinage of the phrase "double digit" probably belongs to Leonard Silk, member of the editorial board of the *New York Times,* who wrote this lead editorial on March 22, 1974:

"For American consumers, it is slaughter at the checkout counters and the gasoline pumps. Food and fuel prices soared again in February, giving another big thrust to skyrocketing consumer prices. With last month's increase of 1.3 percent, the cost of living has climbed 10 percent

in the past twelve months—the first double-digit rate of inflation in consumer prices since the Korean War."

Mr. Silk recalls: "I remember coming up with the phrase and noticing how fast it was picked up afterward. Of course, we all know that coincidences happen, but I'd be surprised if there was prior publication, since my piece was right on the news, when the digits went double."

Though the phrase is usually confined to inflation, it can be used to describe any high, or inflationary, price. In an essay in the *Washington Post* about the casual names given expensive places, Frank Mankiewicz wrote in 1977: "Joe's Place, which used to guarantee . . . a friendly roadhouse with live music on Saturday nights, now could signal anything from an elegant boutique to a restaurant with double-digit entree prices."

See **HIGH COST OF LIVING; INFLATION; OVERHEATED ECONOMY.**

DOUBLE DIPPING   income, in the form of salary or pension, from two government sources.

A more complete definition was given to the author by CPA P. K. Seidman: "The practice of collecting a government salary or other money benefit on top of a pension from the same government, or using the same salary as the base of securing two pensions from related governments such as state and county."

Civilian employees who retire and then return to government service in a different capacity forfeit their pension during their working years. But this does not apply to members of the armed forces. A *New York Times* editorial on April 12, 1977, argued: "Double dippers are members of the military who retire young, then take civilian jobs with the Federal government and collect both a military pension and a civilian salary. There are already 150,000 of them . . . Double dipping is indefensible."

The defense put forward by some is that retired soldiers ought not to be penalized by losing their pension income for the "crime" of entering the civilian labor force of the government. On September 19, 1977, Harry W. Quillian wrote a letter to the *Washington Post* making this point: "As one who has no prospect of becoming a 'double dipper' I suggest that term be banished from reporting on and discussion of the dual compensation controversy. The implication it seems to carry—that it is reprehensible to earn a salary while receiving a pension—is absurd and doubtless painful to some honorably retired people supplementing their pensions by working at a second job."

The phrase comes from the ice cream parlor: a cone with two scoops of ice cream is a double dip. Additional pension benefits have not yet been termed "sprinkles."

DOVES believers in ACCOMMODATION as the route to peace, who reject the "appeasement leads to war" argument of the "hawks" (see WAR HAWKS).

The dove, perched on the arm of Aphrodite, Greek goddess of love and beauty, has been a symbol of peace and gentleness since ancient times. When modern painter Pablo Picasso lent his prestige and his palette to the Communist movement, the dove was seized upon as the symbol of peace used in Communist posters and at international conferences.

In the Soviet-American confrontation over the placement of missiles on Cuban soil in 1962, the "dove versus hawk" metaphor came to the fore. In the deliberations of the Kennedy cabinet, UN Ambassador Adlai Steven-

son was represented as a "dove" by reporters Stewart Alsop and Charles Bartlett; Robert Kennedy, Dean Rusk, and McGeorge Bundy were identified as the leading "hawks." Since a firm U.S. line resulted in a Russian backdown, subsequent identification as a dove in this crisis was in essence an attack at unwise softness, and friends of Stevenson objected strenuously to such leaks.

Concurrently, debate on the U.S. position in Vietnam was beginning. Those who wished to extricate the U.S. from what they felt was a hopeless quagmire were labeled *doves,* and those who felt it necessary to contain Communism and resist the new "wars of national liberation" at the South Vietnamese border were called *hawks.* With many exceptions, most liberals favored what came to be known as a "dovelike position," and most conservatives, with a history of attacking liberals as SOFT ON COMMUNISM, willingly identified themselves as hawks. (Senator George Aiken of Vermont preferred to describe himself as an owl.)

In the 1966 elections, many conservative candidates found it possible to adopt far more liberal domestic positions without losing their conservative support, as long as they held to a "hard line" in Vietnam; and vice versa.

Edmund Burke's address to Parliament on "conciliation with America" in 1775 made a basic point that applied to the position of the doves of the 1960s: "Terror is not always the effect of force: and an armament is not a victory. If you do not succeed, you are without recourse; for, conciliation failing, force remains; but, force failing, no further hope of reconciliation is left."

McGeorge Bundy, after he resigned as Johnson's chief adviser on national security matters to head the Ford Foundation, made a dovelike (or dove-ish, usually spelled dovish) differentiation for one so intimately identified with the hawks: "The real choice is not between 'doves' and 'hawks.' It is between those who would keep close and careful civilian control over a difficult and demanding contest, and those who would use whatever force is thought necessary by any military leader in any service." In this manner, he sought to label the center position as "dovelike," pushing "hawk" over to the extreme military-solution position. This would put the "moderate hawks" into dove's feathers, but it never caught on.

POLARIZED positions are traditional in U.S. politics: the *hards versus softs*, *lily-whites versus black and tans* and *doves versus hawks* are summed up in this analysis of the *tough-minded and tender-minded* by philosopher William James:

The tough think of the tender as sentimentalists and softheads. The tender feel the tough to be unrefined, callous, or brutal. Their mutual reaction is very much like that that takes place when Bostonian tourists mingle with a population like that of Cripple Creek. Each type believes the other to be inferior to itself; but disdain in the one is mingled with amusement, in the other it has a dash of fear.

Before its recent usage, "dove" was best known for the use New York Democratic Governor Al Smith made of a remark by his opponent in 1926 in which the luckless Republican said: "If I am elected Governor, I will get along with the Legislature like a cooing dove." Replied Smith: "Had I gotten along with the Legislature like a cooing dove, there would have been no automobile regulation . . . the people of New York want

clear-headed, strong-minded fighting men at the head of the government and not doves. Let the doves roost in the eaves of the Capitol—not in the Executive Chamber. So much for the doves . . ."

Appropriately, the goddess Aphrodite, referred to at the beginning of this entry, is associated with two symbols: the dove and the "apple of discord."

DO YOUR OWN THING, *see* COUNTERCULTURE.

DRAFT, PRESIDENTIAL   a demand by a party that a man not seeking the nomination accept it; upon rare occasion, applies to one who did not encourage his own candidacy.

The most recent authentic draft was at the Democratic convention of 1952. At that time a reluctant Adlai Stevenson, who was President Harry Truman's early choice, was drafted by the delegates who felt uncomfortable with Senator Estes Kefauver (who led on the first two ballots). Historian Richard Morris contends that "Stevenson, who did not seek the nomination, was the first Presidential nominee to be drafted since Garfield (1880)."

The Garfield draft (see PRESIDENTIAL FEVER) was a classic example of a man putting himself forward without appearing to do so. Supporters of former President U. S. Grant, led by party leader Roscoe Conkling, had the most strength; James Blaine of Maine and John Cooper of Ohio trailed close behind. Before the balloting began, a floor fight broke out over the seating of delegates who refused to take a party-loyalty pledge. Congressman James Garfield of Ohio, in a graceful speech, suggested a face-saving compromise. As he agreed to the compromise, Conkling sent Garfield a note on his potential nomination for the presidency.

The three-man deadlock lasted for 34 ballots when Wisconsin, whose votes had been scattered between Grant, Blaine, and Cooper, suddenly cast 16 votes for Garfield. Garfield jumped up to exclaim, "No man has a right, without the consent of the person voted for, to announce that person's name, and vote for him in this Convention." But Garfield had not objected when two Pennsylvania delegates voted for him on 30 previous ballots; his sudden protestation of unavailability triggered more support. On the 36th ballot, Garfield was drafted.

FDR felt he had to be drafted in 1940 by the Democratic convention, to prove he had no dictatorial ambitions and to blunt the third-term issue. For his technique in arranging the draft, see VOICE FROM THE SEWER. Though FDR used the word "muster" rather than draft when referring to military conscription, he embraced the word "draft" in his acceptance speech in 1940: "Only the people themselves can draft a president. If such a draft should be made upon me, I say to you, in the utmost simplicity, I will, with God's help, continue to serve . . ."

As a political word, *draft* remains best known for military conscription, and the "Draft Riots" in New York during the Civil War locked the word in the lexicon. In 1966, students chalked walls and wore buttons that played on another meaning of the word: "Draft beer not men."

DREAM TICKET politician's vision of a combination of candidates with an unbeatable appeal, simultaneously unifying the party's divergent wings; rarely comes true.

"GOP Dream Ticket" *Newsweek*

headlined in 1967, "Reagan and Brooke." Dreamily, the magazine continued: "Some professional Democrats now say privately that the strongest team the GOP can field in '68 is one headed by Ronald Reagan and Edward Brooke. The Negro Senator from Massachusetts might cost the ticket some Southern votes, they admit. But these would be more than offset by the votes he could capture for Reagan in the populous industrial states of the U.S. where elections are usually won or lost . . ."

A dream ticket not only balances geography, ideology, age, and religion but also puts together two personalities that are famous—neither of which is ever likely to accept the other at the top of the ticket. Republicans in 1960 talked of a dream ticket of Nixon and Rockefeller, and Nixon did urge the New York governor to be his running mate; Rockefeller, as most realists predicted, turned it down. See COMPACT OF FIFTH AVENUE.

The dream ticket means one that is especially strong; *a* dream ticket is one that is striking in its juxtaposition of personalities.

DROPBY, *see* **ADVANCE MAN.**

DUMP, *see* **JOE SMITH; KING-MAKER.**

DYED-IN-THE-WOOL descriptive of an all-out partisan, proud of his party label; most often used about Democrats.

The expression comes from the coloring of textiles while the material is in a raw, unfinished state; wool so dyed is likely to be more colorfast than that with color added later in the process.

The use can be traced to 1830, and likely originated earlier; in current use, alliteration has consigned *dyed-in-the-wool* to Democrats, and ROCK RIBBED to Republicans. *Whole hog* (Jacksonian origin) is applied mainly to Democrats, *staunch* to Republicans; HIDEBOUND belongs to extreme conservatives.

Senator Huey Long had some fun with the phrase. "I am a dyed-in-the-wool party man," he told the Senate in 1935. "I do not know just what party I am in right now, but I am for the party."

DYNAMIC CONSERVATISM
Eisenhower's attempt to define his approach to the economic and social needs of the nation.

The President and the more conservative Republican congressmen became more and more disillusioned with one another as his Administration drew on. He found that Democratic votes were often needed to save measures he thought necessary; the Republicans found a New Dealish tinge to many of those same measures. The result was a President who thought many of his party members were too Republican to be progressive, and a number of conservatives who found him too progressive to be a very good Republican.

The President, in 1955, was looking for a phrase which would have the right sound and sum up his basic philosophy. One he liked was "conservative dynamism." In his speech before the finance committee of the Republican National Committee on February 17, 1955, President Eisenhower turned it around before using it: "I have said we were 'progressive moderates.' Right at the moment I rather favor the term 'dynamic conservatism.' I believe we should conserve on everything that is basic to our system. We should be dynamic in applying it to the problems of the day so that all

our 165,000,000 Americans will profit from it."

But this term, too, failed to satisfy his desires and went the way of "progressive moderation" and "moderate progressivism."

To Adlai Stevenson, this fuzzy sloganeering was the subject of a 1955 Chicago press conference: "I have never been sure what progressive moderation means, or was it conservative progressivism? I have forgotten and I am not sure what dynamic moderation or moderate dynamism means. I am not even sure what it means when one says that he is a conservative in fiscal affairs and a liberal in human affairs. I assume what it means is that you will strongly recommend the building of a great many schools to accommodate the needs of our children, but not provide the money."

DYNASTY the recurrence of political power in generations of a single family; previously, the passing of power among a small group of the political elite.

In the U.S., the first "dynasty" to be denounced was the Virginia Dynasty—the succession of power from Jefferson to Madison to Monroe. The Jacksonian Democrats tagged a "dynasty" label on what was then an Establishment, and on their second try for national power, broke it up.

The dynasty charge, sometimes called "the nepotism issue," was an important part of the election of Benjamin Harrison, grandson of President William Henry Harrison. In 1888 the Democratic song was "Grandpa's pants won't fit Benny," and the Republican refrain went "Yes, Grandfather's hat fits Ben—fits Ben."

For his study of *American Political Dynasties,* Stephen Hess chose the following families: Adams, Lee, Livingston, Washburn, Muhlenberg, Roosevelt, Harrison, Breckenridge, Bayard, Taft, Frelinghuysen, Tucker, Stockton, Long, Lodge, and Kennedy.

Sociologist C. Wright Mills pointed out: "There are of course political dynasties in elite American politics—the Adams family being only the outstanding and best known. Yet, it can be safely said that throughout U.S. history well over half of the American political elite have come from families not previously connected with political affairs. They come more frequently from families highly placed in terms of money and position than political influence."

A startling cover of *Esquire* magazine in March 1967 capsuled the hopes and worries of many Americans about the Kennedy "dynasty." It showed four men in rocking chairs —John F. Kennedy, 35th President; Robert Kennedy, 37th President; Ted Kennedy, 38th President; and John-John Kennedy (John F.'s son) 39th President. This kind of frightening satire has long been associated with the Kennedy clan. John F. Kennedy was quoted as saying: "Joe [Junior] was supposed to be the politician. When he died, I took his place. If anything happened to me, Bobby would take my place. If something happened to Bobby, Teddy would take his place."

Despite two assassinations, because of their willingness and ability to have a great many children, the Kennedys have an especially strong chance at creating a dynasty. When Mrs. Robert F. (Ethel) Kennedy had her tenth child in 1967, her mother-in-law, Rose Kennedy, commented, "If I knew there was going to be a contest, I never would have stopped at nine."

EAGLE SYMBOL, *see* **BALD EAGLE.**

EASTERN ESTABLISHMENT a cluster of legal, financial, and communications talent centered in New York, generally liberal Republican in politics; not an organized group but influential all the same.

The late Senator Robert A. Taft spoke of the Eastern Establishment when, after losing the 1952 GOP nomination, he complained: "Every Republican candidate for president since 1936 has been nominated by the Chase National Bank." Barry Goldwater was another critic—as evidenced by his frequent, only half-jesting remark during the 1964 campaign that he would like to "saw off the Eastern seaboard" and set it adrift in the Atlantic.

Historian Arthur Schlesinger, Jr., offered an apt description of the Eastern Establishment—sometimes known as the "Eastern kingmakers" or simply as the "Establishment"—in *A Thousand Days:*

> He was little acquainted in the New York financial and legal community—that arsenal of talent which had so long furnished a steady supply of always orthodox and often able people to Democratic as well as Republican Administrations. This community was the heart of the American Establishment. Its household deities were Henry L. Stimson and Elihu Root; its present leaders,

Robert A. Lovett and John J. McCloy; its front organizations, the Rockefeller, Ford and Carnegie Foundations and the Council on Foreign Relations; its organs, *The New York Times* and *Foreign Affairs.* Its politics were predominantly Republican; but it possessed what its admirers saw as a commitment to public service and its critics as an appetite for power which impelled its members to serve Presidents of whatever political faith.

In *The Making of the President 1964,* Theodore White wrote:

> . . . how intertangled is the maze of the Eastern Establishment, even to a New Yorker—and how much more so to the primitives out beyond the mountains . . .
>
> From beyond the Alleghenies, the Eastern Establishment seems to inhabit a belt that runs from Boston through Connecticut to Philadelphia and Washington. Its capital is New York, a city shrouded in symbolic words like "Wall Street," "international finance," "Madison Avenue," "Harvard," *"The New York Times,"* "The Bankers Club," "Ivy League prep schools," all of which seem more sinister and suspect the farther one withdraws West or South.

"Eastern Establishment" is a specific political term; "establishment" alone is a general sociological term, originally coined in Great Britain by Henry Fairlie. See **ANGRY YOUNG MEN.** The *National Observer* objected to the overuse of the general term at the end of 1967: "If someone wishes to complain about something but hasn't a very clear idea of what, all he needs do is blame the problem on the 'establishment' and people will sagely wag their heads. . . . It is one of the great blessings of America that it has no 'establishment.' "

See COMMUNITY.

EAT CROW   to admit freely a bad mistake and to offer to accept the consequences.

The *San Francisco Picayune* of December 3, 1851, printed a story that had been making the rounds about a man who boasted he could eat anything: "The bet was made, the crow was caught and nicely roasted . . . he took a good bite, and began to chew away. . . . 'Yes, I can eat a crow! . . . but I'll be darned if I hanker after it.' " This joke's punch line became a part of American folklore.

The political use of the phrase appears to have taken hold in 1872, when a splinter group calling themselves Liberal Republicans bolted to the Democrats and persuaded them to nominate renegade Republican Horace Greeley to run against Republican President Ulysses Grant. "Mr. Greeley appears to be 'boiled crow' to more of his fellow-citizens," wrote *The Nation,* "than any other candidate for office in this or any other age . . . boiled crow he is to his former Republican associates; and now the Democrats are saying in a curious way that to them also he is boiled crow." By 1885, the *Magazine of American History* was saying: " 'To eat crow' means to recant, or to humiliate oneself. To 'eat dirt' is nearly equivalent."

While the expression has been adopted throughout the language, it appears to have a special place in poli-

tics. The *New York World* in 1881 reprinted the original story and gave it a political base: ". . . the delectable old story of the political sneak who, having been caught and convicted of slander and fed upon his own words, looked up piteously from the unsavory meal and murmured: 'I hev eat crow, and I kin eat crow, but I don't hanker arter crow.' " Its use in a cartoon without the complete punch line indicates its widespread use in 1900; Carl Schurz and his friends were shown eating a "silver" crow with the caption "We can eat it, but—"

In recent use, "boiled" has been dropped and the phrase used mostly about "experts" who have been wrong in political prognostications. The most poll-shaking example of this came in 1948, when Harry Truman amazed the pundits by defeating Thomas E. Dewey. As Truman and Vice President–elect Alben Barkley rode up Pennsylvania Avenue in their "home-coming" celebration, they saw a sign hung from the *Washington Post* building that read: "Mr. President, we are ready to eat crow whenever you are ready to serve it." Truman wrote in his memoirs: "I sent that great newspaper word that I did not want anyone to eat crow, that I was not elated or in a mood myself to crow over anyone."

That was a nice turn of phrase; "crow over" is another use of the image of the tough, raucous black crow. For another use, see JIM CROW.

ECOLOGY, *see* **ENVIRONMENTALIST.**

ECONOMIC JARGON   *Stagflation:* ". . . applause and acclaim awaits the creator of the newest star of economic slang: 'stagflation'," wrote *Washington Post* reporter Robert J. Samuelson on September 19,

1971. "The word is everywhere these days—in the London *Economist,* in speeches, in newspaper columns." But no claimant to the coinage came forward; Peter Jay, financial editor of the *Times* of London and late ambassador to the U.S., used the term in a 1969 article, but thought it came from the U.S.; economists here are inclined to attribute the word to a British use. The word describes a situation of unrelenting inflation combined with low (stagnant) economic growth and high unemployment—often called "the worst of both worlds."

Nixonomics: A pejorative term used to label the economic policy of the Nixon Administration, coined by Walter Heller in the summer of 1969, and popularized by columnists Rowland Evans and Robert Novak, with an assist from Larry O'Brien, chairman of the Democratic National Committee. O'Brien's definition: "Nixonomics means that all the things that should go up—the stock market, corporate profits, real spendable income, productivity—go down, and all the things that should go down—unemployment, prices, interest rates—go up." Ironically, the neologism had been independently suggested by this writer in early 1969 as a catch phrase to replace "gradualism", but was turned down as too contrived.

Liquidity crisis: Along with "credit crunch," this describes a lack of ready cash in banks for lending to companies. In the summer of 1970, with the Federal Reserve restraining the growth of the money supply to combat inflation, there were fears this would lead to a drying up of the funds needed for the conduct of business; at a White House dinner at that time, Federal Reserve Chairman Arthur Burns told a group of businessmen in plain terms, "There will be no liquid-

ity crisis," and there was not.

Disintermediation: This word was popularized in 1969, and again in 1971, by Federal Reserve Governor Andrew Brimmer and Assistant Budget Director Maurice Mann. When interest rates are rising, and the rates that may be paid by banks and savings and loan associations are restricted by legal ceilings, investors shift their funds from banks and S&Ls to bonds and other financial instruments that pay higher rates. "Intermediation" is the process by which lenders use an intermediary in passing funds to a borrower; an individual puts his money in a bank, and the bank lends it to a home buyer. Disintermediation cuts out the middleman, or bank, as the lender lends his money directly to the borrower by purchasing a bond.

See BAFFLEGAB; HOLD THE LINE; INFLATION; GAME PLAN; JAWBONING; NEW ECONOMICS; GUIDELINES; WE ARE ALL . . .; OVERHEATED ECONOMY; SNAKE IN THE TUNNEL; HIGH COST OF LIVING; DOUBLE DIGIT.

ECONOMIC ROYALISTS President Franklin D. Roosevelt's description of those people with great financial wealth who hoped to control the activities of government.

In his acceptance speech, following the 1936 Democratic convention in Philadelphia, Mr. Roosevelt said: "The economic royalists complain that we seek to overthrow the institution of America. What they really complain of is that we seek to take away their power."

The speech was written by Samuel I. Rosenman and Stanley High, although Judge Rosenman gives credit for the phrase—much repeated thereafter—to Mr. High. However, FDR fund-raiser Sidney Weinberg recalled that "economic royalist" was originally suggested by Robert Jackson, who later became a Supreme Court Justice.

The phrase awakened memories of "malefactors of great wealth," "robber barons," and VESTED INTERESTS. See RUNNING AGAINST HOOVER.

In 1977 President Carter lambasted oil-industry lobbyists for "the greatest rip-off in history" in opposing his energy proposals. His selection of an amorphous, faceless villain—rather than an opponent like Senator Russell Long—recalled the FDR tactic to many. "A President enters a slanging match," editorialized the *Washington Star,* "with the 'economic royalists' of the moment at his own risk, although most Democratic chief executives find the temptation to do so irresistible."

EDIFICE COMPLEX a monumental desire by a politician to leave behind great buildings.

When the Albany Mall was under construction in the sixties, New York Governor Nelson Rockefeller came under fire for spending too much taxpayer revenue on Ozymandian buildings. The governor, who in his youth helped manage Rockefeller Center in New York City, was accused of having an "edifice complex."

The pun is, of course, a play on "Oedipus complex," the yearning a child feels toward a parent of the opposite sex.

EFFETE SNOBS a more recent term for EGGHEAD; a derogation of the arrogance of pseudo-intellectuals.

"A spirit of national masochism prevails," Vice President Agnew told a dinner at New Orleans on October 19, 1969, "encouraged by an effete corps of impudent snobs who characterize themselves as intellectuals."

Headline writers dropped "corps of

impudent" to compress the epithet to "effete snobs," which is how it is generally remembered today. One reason the phrase caused such a fierce reaction was that many readers interpreted "effete" to mean "effeminate," which is not its meaning—"enervated," "wrung out," "intellectually barren" define the term properly and fit the context of his remarks.

The New Orleans speech was a lengthy, fairly dull exposition of the Nixon Administration's foreign and economic policies; however, the opening—including the controversial phrase—was prepared by the Vice President and gripped the audience. In it, he took care to blunt the charge of anti-intellectualism: "Persuasion through speeches and books is too often discarded for disruptive demonstrations aimed at bludgeoning the unconvinced into action. . . . Subtlety is lost, and fine distinctions based on acute reasoning are carelessly ignored in a headlong jump to a predetermined conclusion. Life is visceral rather than intellectual, and the most visceral practitioners of life are those who characterize themselves as intellectuals."

The term was used by Agnew critics as an example of POLARIZATION, "escalating the rhetoric," and—as expected—anti-intellectualism.

EGGHEAD an intellectual; a highbrow. When used derogatively, an effete, bookish person with intellectual pretensions; when used affirmatively, a man with brains.

Stewart Alsop, in his syndicated column, reported in September 1952:

After [Adlai] Stevenson's serious and rather difficult atomic energy speech in Hartford, Conn., this reporter remarked to a rising young Connecticut Republican that a good many intelligent people, who would be considered normally Republican, obviously admired Stevenson. "Sure," was the reply, "all the eggheads love Stevenson. But how many eggheads do you think there are?"

Alsop went on to define the word as "what the Europeans would call 'intellectuals' . . . [someone] interested in ideas and in the words used to express those ideas." Years later he revealed that the "rising young Connecticut Republican" was his brother, John (not Joe): "John says the word sprang unbidden into his mind, with the mental image of a thin outer shell with mushy white stuff underneath." *Newsweek* quoted the source, John Alsop, as recalling "Egghead . . . dredged up out of my unconscious . . . is a visual picture of speech, tending to depict a large, oval head, smooth, faceless, unemotional but a little haughty and condescending."

Stewart Alsop had not intended to attack Stevenson seriously, but there was a need for a new word to crystallize the prevailing anti-intellectualism. Novelist Louis Bromfield soon defined it as "a person of intellectual pretensions, often a professor or the protégé of a professor . . . superficial . . . feminine . . . supercilious . . . a self-conscious prig . . . a BLEEDING HEART." The *Baltimore Sun* observed: "Writers on the lower levels of the trade have sought in vain for a new way of saying 'highbrow.' 'Loftydome' was about the best they could do, until 'egghead' came along."

Stevenson tried to laugh it off. To a University of Wisconsin audience in October of 1952, he said: "For a few minutes I took this egg head talk personally in injured silence. But I couldn't stand it and summoned up the courage to ask them what an egg head was. The answer, I discovered, is that an egghead is anyone who has gone to college! So at least today I have a lot of company." Later he quoted Professor Madison Priest's Latin joke *"Dura est ovicipitum via,"* which translates freely into "The way of the eggheads is hard." He bravely kidded: "Eggheads of the world, unite; you have nothing to lose but your yolks."

But, as the MAN ON THE WEDDING CAKE hurt Dewey, and the BAREFOOT BOY FROM WALL STREET hurt Willkie, *egghead* hurt Stevenson. The familiar image had long gone unnamed, but was nonetheless etched in many minds. From the huge, bald head of the scientist in the comic strip "Buck Rogers" to the description of an intellectual by Mao Tse-tung ("swollen in head, weak in legs, sharp in tongue but empty in belly"), a stereotype existed of a balding, topheavy head bulging with brains and shaped like an egg.

For a while, subdivisions were made of eggheads that included "scrambled eggheads" for the confused variety to "hard-boiled eggheads" for the more tough-minded type. President Eisenhower, when asked about a Latin motto on his desk, *Suaviter in modo fortiter in re* (Gentle in manner, strong in deed) replied, "That proves I'm an egghead."

In the late sixties George Wallace sharpened the top of the egg to label his target "pointed-headed professors." See SEND THEM A MESSAGE.

EIGHT MILLIONAIRES AND A PLUMBER description of the original Eisenhower cabinet.

In selecting his original cabinet, President Eisenhower turned for administrative talent to the business community. Democrats naturally sniped at the business-weighted cabinet. When it came to choosing a Labor Secretary, Eisenhower later wrote: "I hoped to find a satisfactory man from the ranks of labor itself. Long before, the old Department of Commerce and Labor had been divided, and Commerce was now traditionally headed by a businessman; I thought as a counterbalance the Labor Department should be headed by one actually experienced in the labor movement."

Adviser Herbert Brownell suggested Martin Durkin, a Chicago Democrat, head of the Journeyman Plumbers and Steamfitters Union. The contrast of Durkin with the other cabinet members only served to accentuate the business orientation; Richard Strout, under the pseudonym "TRB" in the *New Republic*, wrote in the issue of December 15, 1952: "The next four years may see the biggest lobby drive since Grant's day to loot the public domain, reverse history and crown big business. Ike has picked a cabinet of eight millionaires and a plumber."

The phrase caught the public fancy; writing a follow-up on February 2, 1953, Mr. Strout observed: "We often ask ourselves how much influence a weekly column like ours has, and we still don't know the answer, though it is curious to note the following. In the December 15 issue of this magazine we commented casually, 'Ike has picked a cabinet of eight millionaires and one [*sic*] plumber.' The result was rather astonishing. We find the comment still traveling outward after being included by such excellent columnists as Alsop, Childs, Stokes, Fleeson and goodness knows how many others; it bounded the Atlantic into the London *Economist* and bounced back to America again in the *St. Louis Post-Dispatch*. Well, good luck, little quip—keep flying! Every-

body in Washington, of course, likes to see his ephemeral comment take into the air and buzz away; no question of paternity is ever asked."

Asked about its paternity in 1977, Mr. Strout recalled: "It came to me in the bar of the National Press Club and I carefully husbanded it, knowing that if I loosed it there it would be around before I had reached 14th Street."

Oddly, the phrase is now usually misquoted as "nine" millionaires and a plumber, perhaps because of the growth of the cabinet.

EISENHOWER DOCTRINE, *see* **DOCTRINES.**

EISENHOWER SYNTAX convoluted extemporaneous remarks; ad libs that appear confused.

Spoken English differs from written English. Good secretaries rephrase their bosses' dictation before presenting it for signature. John Steinbeck was one of the rare authors who occasionally dictate rather than write or type their prose. Journalists have often "covered" for extemporaneous speakers by adding punctuation and rearranging sentences.

Dwight Eisenhower had his good days and bad days with unprepared remarks. His off-the-cuff addition to a speech before the American Society of Newspaper Editors in 1956 was a model of clarity; in many press conferences, however, the written transcript was both fuzzy and contorted. (Earlier Presidents refused to permit direct quotation, and newsmen had to edit their sentences.)

Oliver Jensen, later an editor of *American Heritage*, rewrote the GETTYSBURG ADDRESS as Eisenhower would have ad-libbed it, satirizing both Eisenhower syntax and vocabulary:

I haven't checked these figures, but 87 years ago, I think it was, a number of individuals organized a governmental setup here in this country. . . . Well, now of course we are dealing with this big difference of opinion, civil disturbance you might say, although I don't like to appear to take sides or name any individuals. . . . But if you look at the overall picture of this, we can't pay any tribute—we can't sanctify this area—we can't hallow, according to whatever individual creeds or faiths or sort of religious outlooks are involved, like I said about this particular area. It was those individuals themselves, including the enlisted men—very brave individuals—who have given this religious character to the area. . . . We have to make up our minds right here and now, as I see it, they didn't put out all that blood, perspiration and—well, that they didn't just make a dry run here, that all of us, under God, that is, the God of our choice, shall beef up this idea about freedom and liberty and those kind of arrangements, and that government of all individuals, by all individuals and for the individuals shall not pass out of the world picture.

Columnist Arthur Krock observed that this kind of criticism dimmed the Eisenhower glory. "One reason is that glory withers in the controversial fires of politics. Others were supplied by the General himself: his frequent revelations at news conferences that he had not done his homework, his often blind and always labyrinthian syntax when extemporizing. These were gleefully seized on by the articulate 'liberals' who were his principal critics to lampoon him as an old fogey . . ."

It may be surprising to some that Eisenhower was a sharp and accurate editor of written copy; speech texts corrected by him show sensible tightening and clarifying. His first official words, following a brief prayer, spoken after taking his oath of office on January 20, 1953, were: "The world and we have passed the midway point of a century of continuing challenge." He had written on the margin of a draft: "I hate this sentence. *Who* challenges *whom? About what?*" He resisted the rhetoric, then agreed to use it. The author picked up a copy of an Eisenhower speech in 1952 after the General had edited it. Here is a typical sentence: "The Federal Government can make a~~tremen-~~ s including

dous contribution ~~through~~ the exam-

the   of

ple it sets in ~~how~~ ~~it~~ conducts its business."

Reporter Tom Wicker, reviewing William Manchester's *Death of a President,* showed that rambling ad libs were not confined to the Eisenhower era: "Kennedy gets only the best of verbs, adjectives and similes. Thus, a certain day was 'as clear and crisp as a Kennedy order'; this may be an allowable descriptive, but not to those who tried to decipher a large part of the Kennedy syntax as recorded at many news conferences."

ELDER STATESMAN   an older politician or adviser to Presidents, who is treated with much public respect and some veneration.

"You can always get the truth," said abolitionist Wendell Phillips in 1860, "from an American statesman after he has turned seventy, or given up all hope of the Presidency."

As a dead or retired reporter becomes a "journalist," many politicians who leave the arena become known as "statesmen"; and those who grow old in this often active limbo are sometimes dubbed "elder statesmen."

Like **PUNDIT**, the phrase was popularized in the U.S. by *Time.* An early use in that publication was September 16, 1929: "Last spring Elihu Root, gray Elder Statesman of U.S. diplomacy, good friend of Herbert Hoover, went to Geneva . . ."

Best known of the breed was financier Bernard Baruch, who in his Wall Street days gave new respectability to the word "speculator." A typical accolade was Arthur Krock's in 1943:

> Though others have titles, he has none. Yet he is the President's counselor, philosopher and guide. . . . He is an honored visitor at the Pentagon, the Navy Department, the Department of State. . . . His rooms at the Carleton and the Shoreham, and the bench in Lafayette Square where he likes to warm his old bones in the sunshine, are the gathering places for all those with problems growing out of the State's business. . . . He is the nation's elder statesman. He is Bernard Mannes Baruch.

President Harry Truman had a more acerbic view of B.M.B. "He had always seen to it that his suggestions and recommendations, not always requested by the President, would be given publicity. . . . Baruch is the only man to my knowledge who has built a reputation on a self-assumed unofficial status as 'adviser.' "

Elder statesmen are occasionally **PARTY ELDERS** as well; Harry Truman and Herbert Hoover, in their later years, qualified for both. But normally, an elder statesman is "above" partisan politics; he is turned to for advice and photographs by Presidents who wish to show the breadth and depth of their brainpicking, and he lends his prestige to projects like international arms control and efficiency in government.

Eleanor Roosevelt, writing about her husband's soul-searching before deciding to run for a third term, showed how the elder-statesman role has a powerful appeal: ". . . it became clearly evident to me, from little things he said at different times, that he would really like to be in Hyde Park, and that the role of elder statesman appealed to him. He thought he would enjoy being in a position to sit back and offer suggestions and criticisms." Unlike Theodore Roosevelt, who left the presidency and then changed his mind about being an elder statesman, Franklin Roosevelt decided that the edge of power was no substitute for the center of power.

ELECT A LEADER, NOT A LOVER, *see* DIVORCE ISSUE.

ELECTIONEER to campaign crassly; to appear to intrigue or try too hard to get votes.

The word was probably coined by English conservative Edmund Burke, used at the time of the Revolutionary War and later to connote a too narrowly partisan approach to the polls. "The whole judicial authority," wrote John Adams in 1798, "as well as the executive, will be employed, perverted and prostituted to the purpose of electioneering."

To this day, the word's negative connotation—similar to "profiteer" —is reinforced by signs posted some fifty yards from voting places by Boards of Elections that read: "No Electioneering between this point and the Polls."

Attacking Lyndon Johnson's diplomacy, reporters Edward Weintal and Charles Bartlett set forth their version of a meeting between the President and the British Prime Minister, Harold Wilson: "The President blasted the Prime Minister in no uncertain terms. 'I won't have you electioneering on my doorstep,' he stormed. 'Every time you get in trouble in Parliament you run over here with your shirttail hanging out . . .' "

ELECTRONIC EAVESDROPPING, see TAPS; BUGS.

ELEPHANT, REPUBLICAN

symbol of the GOP, born in the imagination of cartoonist Thomas Nast and first presented in *Harper's Weekly* on November 7, 1874.

An 1860 issue of *Railsplitter* and an 1872 cartoon in *Harper's Weekly* connected elephants with Republicans, but it was Nast who provided both parties with their symbols.

Oddly, two unconnected events led to the birth of the Republican elephant. James Gordon Bennett's *New York Herald* raised the cry of "Caesarism" in connection with the possibility of a third-term try for President Ulysses S. Grant. The issue was taken up by Democratic politicians in 1874, halfway through Grant's second term and just before the midterm elections, and helped disaffect Republican voters.

While the illustrated journals were depicting Grant wearing a crown, the *Herald* involved itself in another circulation-builder in an entirely different, nonpolitical area. This was the Central Park Menagerie Scare of 1874, a delightful hoax perpetrated by the *Herald.* They ran a story, totally untrue, that the animals in the zoo had broken loose and were roaming the wilds of New York's Central Park in search of prey.

Cartoonist Thomas Nast took the two examples of *Herald* enterprise and put them together in a cartoon for *Harper's Weekly.* He showed an ass (symbolizing the *Herald*) wearing a lion's skin (the scary prospect of Caesarism) frightening away the other animals in the forest (Central Park). The caption quoted a familiar

fable: "An ass, having put on a lion's skin, roamed about in the forest and amused himself by frightening all the foolish animals he met with in his wanderings."

One of the foolish animals in the cartoon was an elephant, representing the Republican vote—not the party, the vote—which was being frightened away from its normal ties by the phony scare of Caesarism. In a subsequent cartoon on November 21, 1874, after the election in which the Republicans did badly, Nast followed up the idea by showing the elephant in a trap, illustrating the way the Republican vote had been decoyed from its normal allegiance. Other cartoonists picked up the symbol, and the elephant soon ceased to be the vote and became the party itself; the jackass, now referred to as a donkey, made a natural transition from representing the *Herald* to representing the Democratic party that had frightened the elephant. See DONKEY, DEMOCRATIC.

Why the choice of an elephant? New York State Senator N. A. Elsberg in Francis Curtis' 1904 book, *The Republican Party,* explains: "Among the elephant's known characteristics are cleverness and unwieldiness. He is an animal easy to control until he is aroused; but when frightened or stirred up, he becomes absolutely unmanageable. Here we have all the characteristics of the Republican vote . . ."

A less sympathetic explanation came from Adlai Stevenson: "The elephant has a thick skin, a head full of ivory, and as everyone who has seen a circus parade knows, proceeds best by grasping the tail of its predecessor."

ELEVENTH COMMANDMENT
"Thou Shalt Not Speak Ill of Fellow Republicans."

When Dr. Gaylord E. Parkinson, a San Diego obstetrician, became California State Republican Chairman, he inherited a party that had been torn apart with internecine warfare every two years.

Just before the contest between actor Ronald Reagan and San Francisco Mayor George Christopher for the Republican gubernatorial nomination in 1966, Parkinson laid down the rule that he named the "Eleventh Commandment." Reagan, who had most to lose in a bitter battle and whose strategy was to "unify the party behind a candidate who can win," accepted the rule with alacrity; Christopher followed along and never really joined the "inexperience" issue.

Party chairmen traditionally try to heal breaches in primaries before they become so irreparable as to make a nomination valueless. Boss Frank Hague of Jersey City, plumping for Al Smith against FDR for the Democratic nomination in 1932, declared that Franklin Roosevelt would not carry a single state east of the Mississippi. FDR's manager, Jim Farley, made a mild reply, calculated to win the respect of the professionals: "Governor Roosevelt's friends have not come to Chicago to criticize, cry down or defame any Democrat from any part of the country."

Calling a truism a commandment, or endowing a fiat with commandment status, gives a jocose weight to any political advice. In July 1977 Vernon Jordan, head of the National Urban League, criticized President Carter for "not living up to the first commandment of politics—help those who help you."

ELITISM leadership by an aristocracy—whether of the intelligent, the wealthy, the tastemaking, the meritorious or the merely powerful.

In the Nixon attempt to identify and rally a cross-party "silent majority," a useful *bête noire* was "elitism." In 1968 Alabama Governor George Wallace had successfully exploited the resentment of lower-middle-class voters against unseen forces in faraway Washington that manipulated their lives; in the congressional campaign of 1970 President Nixon directed Vice President Spiro Agnew to "crack those elitists" who ran the power centers most critical of his Administration: the media, the academy, the foundations. This was an attempt at a turnabout: the liberal philosophy, which espoused the redistribution of income for the benefit of the greatest number of people, could be attacked as being guided by a small clique. The target was the leadership, not the recipient of liberalism's liberality.

The word, which had been popularized in sociology by C. Wright Mills (see POWER ELITE) gained its -ist and -ism forms in the early fifties in the writings of sociologist David Riesman. Freud, he wrote in 1950, "shared with . . . Nietzsche and Carlyle elements of an elitist position."

Although some conservatives preferred "illuminati," the term "elitist" became current as an attack word; defenders of the idea shied away from the word, which is definitely pejorative, and countered with "meritocracy."

In 1972 the editors of the *Public Interest,* a quarterly, surveyed the emergence of the new political-sociological favorite:

Elitist, of course, is closest to the surface. Perhaps it has already lost its esoteric quality. Who knows, any longer, that it derives from Mosca, Michels, and Pareto, and achieved a bastardized American birth through the midwifery of Harold Lasswell, James Burnham, and C. Wright

Mills. But in a populist society, elitist is a handy stick for all sides and for all seasons. In the *New York Times* Op-Ed page, that elitist sounding board for the vox populi, Jeffrey St. John denounces "public broadcasting" as appealing only to elitists, and concludes that therefore the U.S. Government should not provide a subsidy. In the *Village Voice,* where the radical shtick meet to read, and devour each other, Jimmy Breslin calls his fellow McGovern delegates who had voted for Sissy Farenthold instead of Tom Eagleton "elitist bastards." In the *New Human Services Newsletter,* Frank Riessman sounds the note for a new class war: "A major deterrent to improved, humanized service is professional elitism and this is a political, constituency-oriented problem. The professionals and their establishment will not easily give up their special status and power. This must be fought by the new professionals (the paraprofessionals), the consumers, the students, all of whom have strong interests opposed to traditional elitism." Not to be outdone, President Nixon, in responding to the report of the Environmental Council, according to the *New York Times,* "said at one point that the environment was in danger of becoming an 'elitist' issue and that the Council should 'reach down and include the fellow who never went to college.' " And, in the letters column of the *Village Voice,* that Miss Lonelyhearts of the counter-culture, a trans-sexual person denounces lesbian Jill Johnston for her "transvestite-hating . . . elitist and authoritarian stance."

By 1978 the word had become a standard blast at anyone with an undue regard for excellence as a criterion for the receipt of money or power. Next to "racism" and "sexism," the charge of "elitism" had to be vigorously resisted by those tagged. A good example was in this letter to the *Washington Star* from Michael Straight, deputy chairman of the National Endowment for the Arts:

Now that four-letter words have become respectable, we need new epithets, and "elitist," like "racist," has slid into frequent and careless employment. Like "racist," it confuses thought in an area that demands precision.

If "elitism" means anything in cultural terms, it means adherence to the position set forth by T. S. Eliot in his "Notes Towards a Definition of Culture." Eliot argued that "culture" could only be understood and transmitted by a small minority of well-educated citizens, and that the majority was and always would be incapable of appreciating the arts.

I happen to have spent eight years denouncing Eliot's position, which to me is wholly antithetical to the nature and purpose of the National Endowment for the Arts. I happen to believe that public funding for the arts is justifiable only on the assumption that they may and will be enjoyed by the majority of our citizens.

EMPTY CHAIR   a phrase dramatizing an opponent's refusal to debate.

When John Foster Dulles ran unsuccessfully against incumbent New York Senator Herbert Lehman, he was unable to draw Lehman into debate. To make his point, Dulles traveled with a "prop"—an empty chair he debated in lieu of Lehman.

The origin of this oratorical technique was provided the author by historian George Johnson. In 1924, while running for Vice President on Robert La Follette's Progressive ticket, Burton K. Wheeler attacked President Calvin Coolidge in a way Wheeler described in his *Yankee From the West:*

"In Des Moines, I hit on an original showmanship gimmick. The hall was jammed to the rafters . . . I said, 'You people have a right to know how a candidate for President stands on issues, and so far President Coolidge has not told you where he stands on anything . . . so I am going to call him before you tonight and ask him to take this chair and tell me where he stands.' People in the auditorium began to crane their necks to see if Coolidge really was somewhere on the premises. I pulled a vacant chair and addressed it as though it had an occupant. 'President Coolidge,' I began, 'tell us where you stand on Prohibition.' I went on with rhetorical questions in this vein, pausing after each for a short period. Then I wound up: 'There, my friends, is the usual silence that emanates from the White House.' The crowd roared in appreciation."

In the four-man gubernatorial race in New York in 1966 (Rockefeller, O'Connor, Roosevelt, Jr., and Adams), negotiations for a debate appeared interminable to Frank O'Connor's representative, Peter Straus. Straus threatened John Trubin, Rockefeller's representative and a law partner of Senator Jacob Javits, that O'Connor would go on alone and debate an empty chair. Trubin shook his head. "That's against FCC regulations," he said with a straight face. "This is a four-man race. You'd have to debate *three* empty chairs." See EQUAL TIME.

ENGAGE IN PERSONALITIES

phrase used to evade man-to-man political clash, always disappointing to newsmen.

The phrase is most closely associated with Dwight Eisenhower, and is consistent with his frequent ABOVE POLITICS stance. At one of the early press conferences of his 1952 campaign, he was reminded of his comment that the loss of China must not be repeated, and asked on whom he would pin responsibility for that loss. "I am not . . . going to engage in personalities in anything I have to say. I believe in certain principles, certain procedures and methods that I will discuss with anybody at any time. I am not going to talk personalities."

In office, Eisenhower held to his rule. Looking over a draft of a presidential message to Congress that implied criticism of some congressional leader's motives, he is reported to have said, "Look here, you and I can argue issues all day and it won't affect our friendship, but the minute I question your motives you will never forgive me."

A good many Democrats questioned Eisenhower's motives in refusing to tangle with Senator Joseph McCarthy in the tumult of MCCARTHYISM. In his memoirs, Eisenhower answered this criticism: "McCarthyism was a much larger issue than McCarthy. This was the truth that I constantly held before me as I listened to the many exhortations that I should 'demolish' the Senator himself. . . . Lashing back at one man, which is easy enough for a President, was not as important to me as the long-term value of restraint, the due process of law, and the basic rights of free men." See PHILIPPIC.

In *At Ease,* he wrote: "I make it a practice to avoid hating anyone. If someone's been guilty of despicable actions toward me, I used to write his name on a piece of scrap paper, drop it in the lowest drawer of my desk, and say to myself: 'That finishes the incident . . . and that fellow.' The drawer became over the years a sort of private wastebasket for crumbled-up spite and discarded personalities."

By steadfastly refusing to "engage

in personalities," Eisenhower did what many campaigners often promise but seldom observe. Wendell Willkie, who later engaged FDR forcibly, said: "We go into this campaign as a crusade. We shall fight the campaign on the basis of American liberty, not on the basis of hate, jealousy or personalities."

The phrase, as it stands, is confusing; it is a shortening of "engage in a discussion of personalities," and really means "You won't get me in the gutter with that guy."

ENEMIES LIST originally, Nixon counsel John Dean's roster of Administration opponents to be harassed; now used as a counterattack by any person considering himself targeted for criticism by those in power.

"This memorandum," Dean wrote on August 16, 1971, "addresses the matter of how we can maximize the fact of our incumbency in dealing with persons known to be active in their opposition to our Administration. Stated a bit more bluntly—how we can use the available federal machinery to screw our political enemies."

George Bell, an aide to presidential counsel Charles Colson, compiled a list in response to Dean's memo, which Colson forwarded to Dean under the heading "Opponents List." However, when Dean revealed his own memo and its answer in testimony before the Senate Watergate Committee, he called it an "enemies list"; the word "enemies," which he had used in his original memo, carried a far more savage connotation than "opponents." Curiously, the revulsion at this device exempted its author, Dean, and concentrated on Nixon, Colson and the rest of the "President's men." Among those on

the list were a fund-raiser (Arnold Picker of United Artists Corp.), a large contributor (Howard Stein of the Dreyfus Corporation), a labor leader (Leonard Woodcock of the United Auto Workers), a black congressman (John Conyers, D-Mich.) and "a real media enemy" (Daniel Schorr, CBS).

The "enemies list" became one of the phrases associated with the abuses of power charged during the Watergate investigation. Colson argued that it had been compiled "for the use of the social office" to exclude opponents from White House dinners, but it was apparent that the intent was to use the power of government to punish political adversaries.

William Sullivan, a former deputy to J. Edgar Hoover at the FBI, insisted that the idea "originated in the Bureau. In the Bureau it was called the 'No Contact List'. . . On the No Contact List went all individuals who had criticized the Bureau or Hoover personally."

The phrase has become generic, applying to any targets, similar to HIT LIST. In September 1977, when supporters in the Senate of President Carter's natural-gas program were filibustering against deregulation, and were unexpectedly abandoned by the White House, Senator James Abourezk (D-S.D.) cracked: "This Administration doesn't have an enemies list—it has a friends list."

As Watergate memories recede, the phrase has been used in gentle spoofs. On April 10, 1978, a *New York Times* editorial stated: "We have been compiling an enemies list: uppity words . . ." The ten on the list were *absent* ("when disguised as a synonym for 'without' "), **FEEDBACK**, *governance* ("except when accompanied by ELDER STATESMEN") *hold harmless, in place, massive* ("except in case of nuclear attack"), OPTION, *posture, thrust,* and *viable.*

ENTANGLING ALLIANCES a phrase of Jefferson's that is threaded through American history, most often used to justify a policy of ISOLATIONISM.

George Washington, who many people think first used "entangling alliances," only came close to using the phrase in his Farewell Address in 1796: "It is our true policy to steer clear of permanent alliance with any portion of the foreign world." In the same speech he also said: "Why, by interweaving our destiny with that of any part of Europe, entangle our peace and prosperity in the toils of European ambition, rivalship, interest, humor, or caprice?"

Two years later Thomas Jefferson wrote to T. Lomax: "Commerce with all nations, alliance with none, should be our motto." He reworked this sentence for his inaugural address in 1801: "Peace, commerce, and honest friendship, with all nations; entangling alliances with none."

Jefferson's crystallization of Washington's point became a rock of American foreign policy for over a century. When Woodrow Wilson tried to persuade Americans to accept the League of Nations, he addressed himself to the one phrase that most stood in his way, and tried to identify himself with it: "I am proposing that all nations henceforth avoid entangling alliances which would draw them into competitions of power. . . . There is no entangling alliance in a concert of power."

The phrase was handled just as gingerly by Franklin Roosevelt and his Secretary of State, Cordell Hull, in the mid-thirties. While denouncing *entanglements* (which everybody is automatically against) they had to lay the groundwork for *alliances* (which most people more or less favor). FDR said in 1935: "Our national determination to keep free of foreign wars and entanglements cannot prevent us from feeling deep concern when ideals and principles that we have cherished are challenged." Hull added in 1936: "While carefully avoiding any political entanglements, my Government strives at all times to cooperate with other nations to every practical extent in support of peace objectives . . ."

"Entanglement" has lost none of its effectiveness as an attack word. Walter Lippmann (see ATLANTIC COMMUNITY) wrote in 1965 that if Lyndon Johnson's conception of the Great Society were to fail, "it would not be because the conception is false. It would be because of some external cause—possibly because we had become diverted by some entanglement in another continent."

A serious threat of entanglement is now called a "quagmire."

ENVIRONMENTALIST an anti-pollutionary; one who puts the values of the preservation of the earth and its atmosphere ahead of economic development.

At the turn of the twentieth century, an environmentalist was a scientist who believed that a human being's behavior was determined more by his surroundings than by his genetic inheritance.

Until the sixties, the battle of heredity-vs.-environment colored the use of the word. However, another battle was beginning that gave the word new surroundings. Keith Mellanby, in *Pesticides and Pollution* in 1967, wrote of pesticides "which have recently been shown to constitute such an important contribution to environmental pollution." In 1970 a group of marine biologists wrote the *Times* of London that "we are actively involved in various facets of environmental science—a less emotive and more encompassing term than pollution studies."

By the seventies, "environmental impact" became a rallying phrase for a loose alliance of scientists and political activists who were worried about the encroachments of immediate comfort upon the long-term life of man; the word "ecology," which had meant a balance in nature of organisms and their environment, became a vogue term around 1970. "Ecologist," a term coined in 1873 by biologist Ernst Haeckel to describe the relationship of organisms to their environments, may replace "environmentalist" in time. However, "ecologist" has a more scientific connotation, and "environmentalist" still encompasses people who don't like chemicals in their drinking water or the smell of cigarette smoke in airplanes.

"Conservationist," the predecessor term, survives; perhaps it has been avoided by liberals interested in the restraint of technology because of its resemblance to "conservatism." George Reiger, conservation editor of *Field & Stream,* wrote the *New York Times* on January 10, 1978: ". . . you should permit the record to be set straight on conservation, a word popularized in America by Gifford Pinchot (a hunter) after it had been used in Great Britain for half a century to describe 'the wise use of renewable resources.'. . . People who believe that no creatures should be killed, that no forests should be cut, that, in fact, the goldfinch that comes to their feeder this winter is the very same bird that visited them a decade ago should be called ultra-preservationists, radical environmentalists,

unrealistic extremists, or residents of the twilight zone, but please, please, don't call them conservationists. They are not."

An old geneticist might say that political environmentalism inherited a natural schizophrenia: a stance that is outspokenly anti-development, pro-wilderness, and suspicious of technology's "advances" (which is seen as anti-business) also comes directly into conflict with the development of new jobs, and is thus attacked by organized labor as ELITIST.

"If there's ever a flat choice between smoke and jobs," said President Nixon to this speechwriter in 1970, "tilt toward jobs." The environmentalists, toward the end of the seventies, had succeeded in many of their goals of ensuring the consideration of the impact of polluting atmosphere and water on many business and governmental plans, but began to develop a backlash among those who felt their efforts limited the growth of the job market.

Demanding "a more vigorous approach to supply expansion," the NAACP issued a statement at the end of 1977 saying: "We cannot accept the notion that our people are best served by a policy based on the inevitability of energy shortage and the need for the government to allocate an ever-diminishing supply among competing interests." (See ZERO SUM GAME).

Republican Ronald Reagan seized on this statement as indicative of the "elitism" of environmentalists, whose best-known publication was *The Limits to Growth.* "The limits-to-growth people," said Reagan, "who are so influential in the Carter Administration are telling us, in effect, that the American economic pie is shrinking, that we all have to settle for a smaller slice . . . the best way . . . is for government to get out of the way while the rest of us make a bigger pie so that everybody can have a bigger slice."

E PLURIBUS UNUM, *see* **UNITED WE STAND.**

EPONYMY, *see* **QUISLING; MAVERICK; GERRYMANDER; SOLON; PHILIPPIC.**

EQUAL TIME a doctrine requiring radio- and television-station licensees to exercise fair play in making air time available to opposing candidates for public office or views differing from the station's editorial policies.

Curiously, the phrase "equal time" does not appear in any of the statutes or decisions of the Federal Communications Commission, the agency charged with regulating stations. In a 1968 letter to the author, FCC Secretary Ben F. Waple explained:

As you point out, in Section 315 of the Communications Act of 1934, as amended (47 U.S.C. 315), the phrase "equal opportunities" is used in reference to broadcasts by candidates for public office. The same phrase is used in the Commission's Rules regarding that subject (47 CFR 73.-120). The term "equal time" is used popularly in the broadcasting industry as an equivalent to "equal opportunities." "Equal time" has no official status and does not appear in the Commission statute, rules, or interpretive rulings; however, it may appear in press releases for the Commission's Office of Reports and Information.

(For an example of reluctant official adoption of a popular phrase, see MEDICARE.)

In essence, "equal time" requires stations to make provision for all candidates if they make their airwaves available to any, *unless* the coverage is part of a regularly scheduled news broadcast, interview, documentary, or on-the-spot coverage of a news event. To be on the safe side, most stations lean backward to provide equal time on interviews and regularly scheduled news broadcasts (over a period of time) as well.

Under its "historical notes," the FCC does use "equal time" to describe the special provision made in the 1960 presidential campaign to permit the Kennedy-Nixon debates without offering time to the splinter-party candidates.

The phrase, as used today, applies only to free, public service time proffered by stations and networks; on purchased time, candidates can and do obtain unequal time, depending on the financial capability and media choices of the parties. However, if one party "reserves the time" in a period shortly before election day, and the opposition decides to spend some money that night, stations must bend every effort to make equal "commercial" time available for sale, even though it might already be sold to others.

The equal time law, aimed at protecting minority rights to be heard, can be used as a shield for abuses. Jack Gould, television critic for the *New York Times,* showed how campaign strategists in 1964 used the law to their advantage:

In the last Presidential race, for example, established TV news programs sought appearances by President Johnson and Sen. Barry Goldwater. Virtually all the overtures were rejected by the White House, allegedly because the Democratic party saw no point in giving free exposure to the Republican aspirant. Unless both candidates agreed to appear, the networks were open to violation of the principle of equal time. In effect, therefore, if one candidate feels he is better known than his rival he can exert a veto power over his opponent's free appearance and force him to buy time. This strategic attitude also accounts for the invariable nonsense over challenges and counter-challenges on the subject of TV debates, which do not involve any campaign costs. One candidate, usually the one enjoying the publicity advantage of being an incumbent, sees no purpose in putting a rival on an equal stature in the public eye.

ERA OF GOOD FEELING the years 1817 to 1825, when James Monroe was President of the United States, and there was, in effect, no political opposition.

The term was probably first used by Benjamin Russell in the *Columbian Centinel* in 1817 while Monroe was making a northern tour. Russell, speaking for the defeated Federalists, expressed a wish that the Federalist faction, now practically defunct, should be treated as though past differences had never existed.

The "Good Feeling" was more apparent than real. Monroe's victory was largely the product of political organization, the Federalists' complete loss of credit because of their opposition to the War of 1812, and an attempt in New England to secede during that war. The result had been the sweeping Monroe victory in 1820 in which only one elector voted against him.

During the Era, factions were forming which eventually gave rise to political parties as we know them today. At that time there was the "Adamite" faction, Eastern-oriented, looking toward Europe and the sea. They were merchants and the new manufacturers, followers of John Quincy Adams, who would soon become the Whigs. Then there were the Jacksonites, farmers and frontiersmen, who were soon to become the leaders of the Democratic party.

The term has been continually revived. Victorious Northern Republicans used it after the Civil War, meaning by an "Era of Good Feeling," the hope that the Democrats and the South would accept their defeat gracefully.

Franklin D. Roosevelt used it in 1928 when, upon being elected New York governor, he described ". . . a period in our history known in all our school books as the 'era of good feeling.' It is my hope that we stand on the threshold of another such era in this State." As President, Roosevelt called in his second inaugural address for "a genuine period of good feeling." And Lyndon Johnson, after his overwhelming victory over Senator Barry Goldwater in 1964, expressed the hope that a new Era of Good Feeling would result.

It did not; and under conditions of political democracy, it never does for any appreciable length of time. Even in the days of Monroe there was continual conflict between individual supporters of John Quincy Adams and Andrew Jackson. President Johnson's hopes were based on the continued success of his policy of CONSENSUS and this, too, was frustrated. See PRESIDENT OF ALL THE PEOPLE; DEAL.

ERRING BRETHREN, *see* EUPHEMISMS, POLITICAL.

ESCALATE THE RHETORIC, *see* RHETORIC.

ESCALATION an increase in military activity, either in preparation for or during an armed conflict; by extension, acceleration of effort in any kind of campaign.

Escalation is one of the linguistic products of the cold war and the nuclear age. Scientists and strategists began writing what they called SCE-NARIOS of how nuclear war might occur and how it might be avoided. Herman Kahn, one of the most articulate of the thermonuclear thinkers, put it this way: "War by miscalculation might also result from the process . . . called 'escalation.' A limited move may appear safe, but set into motion a disastrous sequence of decisions and actions." Kahn even postulated a sixteen-step "escalation ladder" leading from "subcrisis disagreement" to the aftermath of "all-out war." Through the writings of Kahn and others in the 1950s, the term came into wide use as one of the relatively unusual cases in which both experts and laymen could share the same snippet of jargon. "But wars, large or small, are fought for victory," wrote *The Nation* early in 1961. "That means you pound the enemy with every available lethal assistance, with the inevitable result—to use the fancy new term—of escalation to all-out war."

Centuries ago, there had been another military term for an elevating device or act. *Escalade,* from the French, was used as a verb meaning to scale a wall or fortification. As a noun, *escalade* means the ladder used for this purpose. Sir Ernest Gowers in Fowler's *Modern English Usage* explains the preference for escalation over the older term by pointing out that escalation "has the advantage of novelty and a more native look, and a moving staircase provides a more up-to-date metaphor than a scaling ladder."

Escalation gained its widest currency not because of nuclear conflict but because of the war in Vietnam. Each time one side or the other introduced reinforcements or a type of weapon previously unused in the war, the act was branded as escalation. In the U.S., the word took on political overtones and a pejorative shading first because Washington was pledged to seeking peace rather than "widening" the war, and second because it gave opponents of the war a universally understood term with which to attack the Administration. Official spokesmen, said the *New York Times,* "have generally shied away from describing each new expansion of the air war as 'escalation' because of political sensitivity . . . [they] prefer to say that the air war is being widened, that pressure is being increased or that the war is being increased."

Time magazine lost all patience with the term in April 1967, calling it in a lead article "one of those windy words that are foisted on the public by military bureaucrats, interminably parroted by the press and kept in the vernacular long after losing any real meaning." Nonetheless, escalation seemed too deeply entrenched for exorcism. Dr. Martin Luther King, Jr., an opponent of the war, called on his followers for "an escalation of our opposition to the war in Vietnam."

Although real escalators run both up and down, the political term heads only upward. The antonym is *de-escalate,* which is awkward, or *descalate,* which the *New York Times* proposed on May 31, 1967, as a word for mutual reduction of military activity but which did not catch on.

When escalation of troop levels in Vietnam ceased to be an issue in the U.S., the word became part of a new cliché, "don't escalate the rhetoric," an admonition honored largely in the breach. See WINDING DOWN; VIET-NAMIZATION.

ESTABLISHMENT, *see* **EASTERN ESTABLISHMENT.**

ETHNIC PURITY   cultural or racial solidarity of a community; a phrase, conceded to be impolitic, used by Jimmy Carter in his presidential campaign.

"I have nothing against a community," said Jimmy Carter in April of 1976 as he approached the Democratic nomination, "that's made up of people who are Polish, Czechoslovakians, French Canadians or blacks who are trying to maintain the ethnic purity of their neighborhood. This is a natural inclination on the part of people."

The remark—intended to assuage Southern fears that the former Georgia governor was in favor of "forced busing" and other drastic remedies for segregation—instead ignited resentment among blacks and Northern liberals distrustful of the Carter candidacy. At first the candidate tried to explain what he meant, but the pressure soon caused him to withdraw the phrase and apologize for it. During this flap Congressman Andrew Young, a Carter supporter (later U.S. Ambassador to the UN) worked hard to allay black suspicions and earned the candidate's gratitude.

The phrase, like BENIGH NEGLECT, is occasionally used to remind voters of an old error. In August 1977 William Raspberry wrote in the *Washington Post:* "Despite his repeated, embarrassed, back-tracking attempts to explain, it never became clear just what Jimmy Carter meant by that 'ethnic purity' remark. I suspect the candidate himself didn't fully understand it. Some of us thought the phrase meant hardly anything at all, except possibly as veiled opposition to the establishment of public housing in white workingclass neighborhoods.

"He should have visited Chicago. Ethnic purity is alive and well in this city that has earned its reputation as the most segregated city in America."

ETHNICS   Americans who take pride in their national origin; now broadening to any group conscious of a cultural heritage that is not White Anglo-Saxon Protestant or black.

"Ethnic" began as an adjective, meaning "pagan" or "heathen"; a confusion with the Greek etymology gave rise to the mistake that it stems from "heathenic." At the start the meaning was limited to people neither Jewish nor Christian; later, in social science, the meaning was "racial," or ethnological; in 1941, sociologists W. Lloyd Warner and Paul S. Lunt, in *The Social Life of a Modern Community,* used the adjective for the first time as a noun, calling attention to their coinage by using quotation marks: "These groups . . . we have called 'ethnics.' "

By 1970, as the white BACKLASH took political form, a word was needed for lower-middle-class whites who felt threatened by the advancement of minorities. In a 1973 promotional piece for the *American Heritage Dictionary,* associate editor Alma Trinor wrote: "There is among many groups in the population a new sense of group identity and pride that has given rise to changes in nomenclature. Now we read not about hyphenated Americans, second-generation Americans, or religious minorities, but about *ethnics.*"

David Guralnik, editor of Webster's *New World Dictionary,* recalls: "Originally the term was created to refer specifically to Jews, Italians, and Irish in the large cities, but in Cleveland it is now pretty well restricted to people of central European extraction, but specifically excluding Jews."

As "ethnic groups" changed to a breezier "the ethnics," the term at first took on an anti–civil rights connotation (see HARDHATS) and then lost it. In 1972 *Newsweek* columnist Stewart Alsop wrote of the rules of television situation comedies: "The rules are: 'ethnics' are okay, Jews are okay, blacks are very okay, white Anglo-Saxon Protestants are a bunch of bigoted boobies."

By the presidential campaign of 1976, every campaign had ways of reaching the ethnics. In a televised debate on foreign policy, President Ford blundered by insisting that the East European nations were not under Soviet domination, the "captive nations" spokesmen denounced this as inaccurate. At the inauguration of President Carter, an inaugural official used two vogue words in his complaint: "There's no outreach to the ethnics."

In current use, "ethnics" is a slightly clinical, neutral, and inoffensive way of identifying national groups, though it carries a note of condescension to some ears. In a 1974 *Atlantic Monthly* article, Henry Fairlie, coiner of "Establishment," drew a useful distinction between the polemically loaded "ethnic" and the more clinical "ethnic group". "One *belongs* to an ethnic group, one *is* an ethnic, and there is a world of difference. To say that someone is a member of an ethnic group is implicitly to say that one is describing only one of his characteristics. To say that he is an ethnic is to imply that this is the most important characteristic about him, the determining characteristic . . ."

EUNUCH RULE provision in state constitutions forbidding governors from succeeding themselves, except after the lapse of another term.

In most states, particularly in the South, governors are rendered impotent—lame ducks from the moment they enter the Statehouse—by the "eunuch rule." This was designed to prevent four-year governors from building long-lasting machines. (In two-year term states, like Texas and Arkansas, succession is permitted.)

Wherever the eunuch rule applies, the governor starts thinking about (1) running for senator, (2) laying the groundwork for a career in private business, or (3) "modernizing" the state constitution to permit reelection.

Alabama Governor George Wallace, unable to achieve the necessary modernization that would have enabled him to succeed himself, beat the system by running his wife, Lurleen, in his place in 1966. She was elected, and the state received "two Governors for the price of one." Wallace himself was later re-elected.

EUPHEMISMS, POLITICAL avoidance of hard words; or, obvious avoidance to underscore a cliché with ironic humor.

The classic political euphemisms come out of the Civil War, which was delicately referred to as "the late unpleasantness" by humorist Petroleum V. Nasby. The Confederate states were sarcastically called "our erring brethren" by Northerners, or "our wayward sisters" (a phrase of General Winfield Scott's). After the war, the BLOODY SHIRT was called "the ensanguined undergarment." (A fine euphemistic difference is still drawn about this war. Northerners say "Civil War," but many Southerners say "The War Between the States," a phrase which carries less stigma of rebellion.)

Today, Pentagon officials estimate that World War III will cause 120 million deaths in the U.S., and more than 120 "megadeaths" (million deaths) in the Soviet Union; the euphemism for this cataclysm is an "All-Out Strategic Exchange," similar to a "future unpleasantness." Similarly, Hitler's genocidal campaign against the Jews was called the FINAL SOLUTION.

On the domestic scene, politicians dealing with the problem of the aged shy away from "old people," "the aged," or even "the elderly." An *Esquire* cartoon showed one of these people shouting at a television set: "Call me Gramps, call me an Old Fogy—call me anything except a Senior Citizen!"

The most derided euphemism of 1970 was "protective reaction," a military term for bombing raids against anti-aircraft installations, followed in a few years by "termination with extreme prejudice," a CIA term for assassination. In South Africa, "apartheid" was given the name of "plural relations."

In 1976 the influx of "illegal aliens" into the U.S. was recognized as a problem; since most of these were Mexicans, formerly derogated as "wetbacks" (from having to swim the Rio Grande River), many Americans felt they should be given legal status and changed their appelation to "noncitizens"; that still did not remove the stigma, and was further euphemized with "undocumented persons." (Spanish-speaking Americans usually eschew the euphemisms and call them *ilegales.*)

A U.S. Department of Labor dictionary of job definitions, published at the end of 1977, enshrined euphemism in a government document. To eliminate sex and age references, occupational analysts changed "busboy" to "dining-room attendant"; "batboy" to "bat handler"; "governess" to "children's tutor"; "repairman" to "repairer." Faced with deciding what to call people who wait on tables, the Labor Department came up with "waiter-waitress."

See DISADVANTAGED; POLICE ACTION.

EUROCOMMUNISM the form of un-international Communism espoused by leaders in West European nations who purport to be independent of the line set forth by the Communist party in the Soviet Union.

"The striking fact about Eurocommunism," said anti-Titoist Yugoslav Milovan Djilas in 1977, "is that for the first time opposition to Moscow flows from the democratic process."

Santiago Carrillo, General Secretary of the Spanish Communist party, wrote "Eurocommunism and the State" in 1977 and attacked the Soviet state as an obstacle to Communism. "The 'Eurocommunist' phenomenon is not a 'tactical maneuvre on the part of Moscow'. . . it is opposed both by those who think that Communism must be an instrument of Soviet policy and by those who see Europe as a simple extension of the American empire."

Carrillo's tract, when denounced by Moscow, drew this comment in the *New York Times:* "Eurocommunism, from Madrid to Moscow, is the greatest heresy in Soviet doctrine . . . it is the idea that threatens the Soviet regime . . ."

A contrary view was expressed by former Secretary of State Henry Kissinger: "We are entitled to certain skepticism about the sincerity of declarations of independence which coincide so precisely with electoral self-interest." Many others agreed that the professed independence of the Eurocommunists was a sham, and that "Communism with a human face" was a mask for international Communism with a local appeal.

Those suspicious of the motives of the Eurocommunists could point to a Lenin pamphlet of the 1920: "the specific peculiarities which this struggle inevitably assumes in each specific country according to the peculiarity of its politics, economics, culture, national composition, etc. . . ."

Eurocommunism received its biggest boost in Italy, where political pluralism was embraced by Italian Communist leader Enrico Berlinguer, who recommended a "historic compromise" whereby Communists could share power in the national government of Italy. In France, Communist party chief Georges Marchais set back the cause of Eurocommunism in September 1977 by dramatically breaking with the Socialists, driving a wedge in the "Union of the Left" with a demand for specifics in the nationalization of industry; as a result, the right was able to turn back the challenge from the left in 1978.

The phrase is a major post–Cold War coinage. Arrigo Levi, editor of *La Stampa,* informed *New York Times* correspondent Flora Lewis that the originator of the phrase was Franc Barbieri, a high-ranking Yugoslav Communist who settled in Italy in the early seventies. A follow-up query to Mr. Levi in Turin brought this reply:

The expression "Eurocommunism," to the best of my knowledge, was used for the first time in print by Franc Barbieri, a well-known Yugoslav journalist (former editor of *Nin* and *Politika*), an ex-Communist now writing for [Milan's] *Il Giornale,* whose editor is Indro Montanelli. Barbieri believes he used this expression, for the first time, in a leader article of *Il Giornale* whose title was "Brezhnev's Compromises," on June 26, 1975. He has explained that he coined this expression in opposition to that of "neo-

communismo," which I in particular had used occasionally in that same period of time (you may find an article of mine in *Newsweek* international ed., of July 14, 1975, which referred to "Berlinguer's neocommunism"); also a reference to it in J. F. Revel's book *La tentation totalitaire*): he wanted to stress the "European," rather than the "new" character of "eurocommunism," doubting of the seriousness of the novelties involved.

I believe that he was right: eurocommunism was soon accepted even by Berlinguer as an acceptable term, in interviews and articles; I doubt that he would have accepted "neocommunism." Only recently some communist leaders (Amendola) have expressed doubt as to the reality of "eurocommunism," preferring to speak of national communisms. Berlinguer and others still stick to it as a valid concept, not, of course, as indicating the existence of an alternative "communist central." Finally, I believe that I was one of the first to use the word "eurocommunism" in the international press, and was widely (though wrongly) quoted as the inventor of it."

See **HISTORIC COMPROMISE.**

EVERYMAN, *see* **JOHN Q. PUBLIC.**

EVERY MAN A KING   slogan of Louisiana Governor Huey P. Long.

This was the trigger phrase of Governor Long's Share-the-Wealth program, which he espoused from 1928 until his assassination in 1935. It was taken from William Jennings Bryan's "Cross of Gold Speech" to the 1896 Democratic National Convention.

Long held that 10 percent of the people in the U.S. owned 70 percent of the wealth, taking most of his populist ideas from Senator S. J. Harper. The full slogan used "Every Man" as

one word: "Everyman a King, but No
Man Wears a Crown."

EXCHANGE RATES, *see* SNAKE IN THE TUNNEL.

EXECUTIVE PRIVILEGE the
right claimed by a President to withhold information from Congress or
the judiciary.

"The doctrine of Executive privilege is well established," President
Nixon said publicly on March 12,
1973, as the Watergate case was about
to break. Citing its use since George
Washington, he said that both members and former members of his
White House staff "shall follow the
well-established precedent and decline a request for a formal appearance before a committee of the Congress."

Historian and former Kennedy
aide Arthur Schlesinger, Jr., took
sharp issue with this in the March 30,
1973, *Wall Street Journal:* ". . . the
very term 'Executive privilege' seems
itself to be of fairly recent American
usage . . . You will look in vain for it
as an entry in such standard reference
works as the Smith-Zurcher *Dictionary of American Politics,* or the *Oxford Companion to American History*
or Scribner's *Concise Dictionary of
American History.* It is not even to be
found, I was dismayed to discover, in
The New Language of Politics, compiled by William Safire of Mr.
Nixon's very own White House staff."

To correct that omission from the
earlier editions, here is the history of
the phrase taken from Schlesinger's
observations, a tracking of the term in
American Speech (Fall-Winter 1973),
and a contribution by an early user.

"In May 1954," Schlesinger recounted, "in the midst of the Army-
McCarthy hearings, President Eisenhower instructed employes of the

Department of Defense that, if asked
by the McCarthy Committee about
internal exchanges within the Department, they were 'not to testify to any
such conversations or communications or to produce any such documents or reproductions.' This was an
unprecedently sweeping denial to
Congress. But it had a certain moral
justification in the atrocious character
of the McCarthy inquisition, and it
was given legal color by an accompanying memorandum from Herbert
Brownell, the Attorney General . . ."

That was a point that was to trouble many scholars: if Mr. Eisenhower's evocation of "Executive privilege" (the idea, not the phrase) was
constitutionally right in the case of
withholding data from the "atrocious" Senator McCarthy, how could
Mr. Nixon's repetition of that maneuver be constitutionally wrong in withholding information from a Congress
operating with more public support?
Judge John Sirica supplied the answer. As *Time* reported in 1973,
Sirica "noted that the Supreme Court
in 1953 had recognized an Executive
privilege for military secrets . . . But
he made it clear that Executive privilege does not cover conversations relevant to a criminal investigation and
not involving performance of official
duties."

The practice of withholding information from Congress, without the
modern phrase, did begin with Washington. In the 1792 House inquiry
into the St. Clair expedition, President Washington gave the House the
documents it requested, and sent his
cabinet members to testify, but—according to Thomas Jefferson's diary
—agreed with his cabinet officers that
"the Executive ought to communicate such papers as the public good
would permit, and ought to refuse
those, the disclosure of which would

injure the public; consequently were to exercise a discretion."

The phrase grew out of the use of the word "privilege" in law, to mean "the royal prerogative," or privilege of clergy, or the privilege of Parliament. The 1953 citation by Judge Sirica was in the Supreme Court decision of *U.S.* v. *Reynolds,* when the Court referred to the government's "privilege against revealing military secrets." On May 17, 1954, Attorney General Herbert Brownell wrote: "Presidents have established, by precedent, that they and members of their Cabinets, and other heads of executive departments have an undoubted privilege and discretion to keep confidential, in the public interest, papers and information which require secrecy." Raoul Berger, in his 1974 *Executive Privilege: A Constitutional Myth,* traced the phrase to a 1958 article by Conrad D. Philos in the *Federal Bar Journal* (14:113) titled "Executive Privilege and the Release of Military Records," and a Federal Supplement (157:943/2), "The position taken rests on the claim of executive privilege."

The earliest use of the phrase by a high official of government that this lexicographer can find is in testimony by William P. Rogers (who, as Deputy Attorney General under Herbert Brownell, helped draft the 1954 memorandum) before the Senate Judiciary Subcommittee on Constitutional Rights on March 6, 1958, objecting to new disclosure requirements on administrative procedure legislation. The phrase was used three times in Mr. Rogers' summary:

"(1) the executive privilege applies to the executive functions of the independent agencies; (2) the executive privilege obviously does not apply to judicial functions; similarly (3) legislative inquiry into the legislative functions of the independent agencies is not limited by any executive privilege, but there are other restraining considerations . . ."

Coincidentally, Mr. Rogers was Richard Nixon's Secretary of State when the dispute arose in 1973 over the Nixon use of the separation-of-powers doctrine to keep Congress from digging into Administration actions about the Watergate affair. When Mr. Nixon turned to Mr. Rogers for legal support of his claim of executive privilege, Rogers advised that in having already directed aides to testify on related matters, the President had waived his claim to privilege.

Because its use was discredited in Watergate, the phrase (with the *e* not capitalized, as it should be if referring to the Office of the President) is rarely chosen by White House officials or cabinet officers as a cause for withholding information from the Congress now. When public opinion once again resists some congressional inquiry, as it did in the Joseph McCarthy era, the practice may reappear under a different name, such as "presidential privacy."

But not even the Watergate-tarnished phrase escaped commercialization: Bloomingdale's department store brought out a gift for Christmas, 1973, which it called "Executive Privilege": an electric paper shredder with a smoky Plexiglas shell to catch the shreds.

EXTREMISM a position at the end of an ideological spectrum; home of the politically far-out.

Senator Barry Goldwater, accepting the Republican nomination for President in 1964, drew a roar from his adherents and a gasp from his opponents in the party with this line in his acceptance speech: "I would remind you that extremism in the defense of liberty is no vice. And let me remind you also that moderation in the pursuit of justice is no virtue!"

In his text, Goldwater underlined the two sentences. (Authorship of these CONTRAPUNTAL PHRASES has been attributed to speechwriter Karl Hess.) In their campaign Democratic speakers underlined it as well, stunned—almost—at their luck in garnering from their chief opponent's own mouth a phrase unequaled in its service to the enemy since a Blaine supporter's condemnation of "Rum, Romanism and Rebellion."

Supporters of Goldwater, and the Senator himself, had been annoyed at the "extreme" label applied to them by the Republican MODERATES in the primary campaign. Some saw Goldwater's use of "extremism" as a way of "rubbing it in" to the defeated liberals; others felt it was an affirmation of his personal identity and point of view, as opposed to the usual unity approach after a difficult division. "My God," cried a reporter, "he's going to run as Goldwater!"

Republican Nelson Rockefeller, leader of the liberal wing, issued this statement the following day: "To extol extremism whether 'in defense of liberty' or 'in pursuit of justice' is dangerous, irresponsible and frightening. Any sanction of lawlessness, of the vigilante and of the unruly mob can only be deplored. . . . I shall continue to fight extremism within the Republican party. It has no place in the party. It has no place in America."

Richard Nixon, who sat on his hands during the enthusiastic demonstration after Goldwater's line, sought some unifying clarification from Goldwater three weeks later. Nixon and others pointed out to the candidate that his statement was being construed as a blanket endorsement of extremism. In a letter to Nixon, Goldwater backtracked to this extent: "If I were to paraphrase the two sentences in question in the context in which I uttered them I would do it by saying that wholehearted devotion to liberty is unassailable and that half-hearted devotion to justice is indefensible."

But the original statement could not be glossed over. Lyndon B. Johnson hammered it home at the conclusion of the campaign: "Extremism in the pursuit of the Presidency is an unpardonable vice. Moderation in the affairs of the nation is the highest virtue."

Extremism today remains as frowned upon by most people as in this 1639 English proverb: "Extremity of right is wrong." See RADICAL RIGHT; CODE WORDS.

EYEBALL TO EYEBALL   a direct international confrontation; a diplomatic crisis with war a distinct possibility.

In 1962 Senator Kenneth B. Keating (R.-N.Y.) charged that Russian missiles were being established in Cuba. Within weeks, the "Cuban missile crisis" had come to test the will of the Kennedy Administration which was still smarting from its earlier Cuban errors. See BAY OF PIGS FIASCO.

Reconstructing the events that led to the strong stand by the U.S. writers Charles Bartlett and Stewart Alsop, in the *Saturday Evening Post,* quoted Secretary of State Dean Rusk as saying: "We're eyeball to eyeball and the other fellow just blinked." Roger Hilsman of the State Department reported that the statement was made by Rusk to ABC newsman John Scali, who had helped in the negotiations, and the words used were: "Remember when you report this—that, eyeball to eyeball, they blinked first."

The metaphor, with its vivid picture of two men, foreheads pressed together, glaring into each other's eyes, soon became synonymous with "confrontation" and was as well known as BRINKMANSHIP in the Eisenhower years.

In current usage, an eyeball-to-eyeball situation is something that far-sighted diplomatic policy seeks to avoid. However, both the idea of confrontation and the phrase that so vividly describes it are not likely to disappear. In September of 1977, when U.S. Secretary of State Cyrus Vance became embroiled with eyepatch-wearing Israeli Foreign Minister Moshe Dayan in dispute over the make up of a Geneva conference,

columnist Joseph Kraft wrote: "They're eyeball to eye patch, and you can't tell who blinked."

The expression has a military origin, and is a contribution of black English. General Harold Johnson, U.S. Army Chief of Staff in the mid-sixties, tells the author he first heard the term used—and widely quoted—in November 1950, during the Korean conflict. Before President Truman desegregated the armed forces, the 24th Infantry Regiment was all-black; after a counterattack had caused a retreat of U.S. forces, MacArthur's headquarters sent an inquiry to the 24th Regiment, which was expected to bear the brunt of the fighting: "Do you have contact with the enemy?" The reply: "We is eyeball to eyeball."

FACT-FINDING TRIP   a serious effort to obtain firsthand information, or a ploy designed to impress the folks back home with a spurious interest in foreign affairs.

An overseas tour by a congressman or candidate is described by him as a *fact-finding trip,* and as a *junket* by his opponents, who usually add "at the taxpayer's expense."

A good test of whether a trip abroad is politically motivated is whether it covers "the three I's": Ireland, Italy, and Israel, points of origin or antecedence for many urban voters.

The appeal to voters of an "I want to see for myself" attitude was demonstrated by Eisenhower's "I shall go to Korea" pledge, which was heightened by the fact that he was a general going to study a war. But it works for civilians as well, and the year before a national convention, world leaders find their calendars filled with visits by aspiring U.S. politicians.

Another important use of a fact-finding trip is to keep a national political figure out of trouble for weeks at a time; when he returns for a ship- or plane-side interview, he is "fresh" news copy.

Massachusetts Attorney General Edward McCormack, campaigning (unsuccessfully) against Ted Kennedy for the Senate Democratic nomination in 1962, tried to dampen the effect of a Kennedy trip to Ireland by quoting—to Irish voters—a story in the *Dublin Sunday Independent:* "Arriving in Ireland today is Mr. Edward 'Ted' Kennedy, age thirty. . . . Why is he coming to Ireland? He's coming because later this year he is due to be involved in a political fight back home in Massachusetts. . . . You do not spend your time campaigning in your own little patch . . . you go out in the world far far afield, hit the headlines, hit the American voters in the right way. I think the trips are more political than fact-finding."

In labor negotiations, parties who do not wish to be bound by arbitration occasionally agree to a fact-finding panel, or one may be imposed by government.

On rare occasions the phrase is used in its past tense, as in this 1967 comment by Jacques Barzun, provost of Columbia University, on the subject of the spread of social research studies: "Judging from what is being studied, researched, and fact-found all over the world, it is clear that as a civilization we no longer know how to do anything . . . we repeatedly analyze the familiar and suspend action." See **NONPOLITICAL TRIP; JUNKETEERING GUMSHOES.**

FAIL-SAFE   a retaliatory strike that can be recalled if the original signal was a mistake; a system whereby bombers may be launched on an ambiguous warning.

Bombers operating on a "fail-safe" system can take off if an enemy attack appears to be under way, fly to a point of no return, and there get instructions from a central control whether or not to continue on to target. "In this way," wrote Herman Kahn, "the central authorities have additional time to confirm or deny the validity of the original warning."

UPI disclosed the existence of "fail-safe" in a story of the Strategic Air Command's operations in the Arctic, soon followed by a book and motion picture on the sensational subject. "It should have been possible," wrote Douglass Cater, later a White House aide, "to describe our military precautions without resorting to the phoney dramatics about bombers headed toward Moscow which alarmed our allies and provided propaganda material for the Soviets."

Fail-safe refers to a system with two signals: one to take off, the other to verify. If bombers headed for enemy territory "fail" to receive a confirmation signal, they return home, placing the communications failure on the "safe" side.

FAIR DEAL   the theme of President Truman's State of the Union message in 1949, updating the "New Deal" inherited from Roosevelt.

During his first eighteen months in office, President Truman worked under the shadow and confining legacy of Franklin Roosevelt's New Deal policies.

Truman needed a phrase and an image of his own. These he established in his first message to the 81st Congress: "Every segment of our population and every individual has a

right to expect from his government a fair deal."

The press picked up the phrase—a natural progression from the New Deal of FDR—and used it to label the domestic policies of the Truman Administration. Two generations before, Woodrow Wilson had used "Fair Deal" as a counterpart to Theodore Roosevelt's "Square Deal."

In 1967 Michigan's Republican Governor George Romney made a punning reference to the progression of "the Deals": "There was the New Deal of Franklin Roosevelt, the Fair Deal of Harry Truman and the ordeal of Lyndon Johnson."

See CARD METAPHORS.

FAITHFUL, *see* **PARTY FAITHFUL.**

FALA SPEECH   a Franklin D. Roosevelt campaign speech in 1944 that marked a return to partisan politicking from a previous "above the battle" posture.

In the summer of 1944 many Republican newspapers were printing a rumor that President Roosevelt's Scottie, Fala, had been left in Alaska after a presidential visit and that an American destroyer had to be turned around and sent back for him. More serious charges were being made, but FDR seized on this one to ridicule and cast doubt on all the others.

In a campaign speech to the Teamsters Union in Washington, President Roosevelt answered the Republican attacks this way:

> . . . Republican leaders have not been content with attacks on me, or my wife, or on my sons. No, not content with that, they now include my little dog, Fala. Well, of course, I don't resent attacks, and my family doesn't resent attacks, but Fala does resent them. You know, Fala is

Scotch, and being a Scottie, as soon as he learned that the Republican fiction writers in Congress and out had concocted a story that I had left him behind on the Aleutian Islands and had sent a destroyer back to find him—at a cost to the taxpayers of two or three or eight or twenty million dollars—his Scotch soul was furious. He has not been the same dog since.

I am accustomed to hearing malicious falsehoods about myself. . . . But I think I have a right to resent, to object to libelous statements about my dog.

The rest of the "Fala Speech" was a serious enumeration of the problems facing the U.S. and those points had considerable effect on the campaign of '44. However, the Fala reference made the speech come alive; speechwriter Samuel Rosenman, in retrospect, felt it was FDR's most effective single political speech.

The Democratic National Committee said after the speech: "The race is between Roosevelt's dog and Dewey's goat." See CHECKERS SPEECH; DEWEY BLITZ.

FALLBACK POSITION   an agreed-upon line of retreat.

"Fallback position" came into political use late in 1966, as Republican liberal leaders sought to avoid the divisions of 1964 that led to the nomination of a conservative. New York's Governor Rockefeller announced his support of Michigan's Governor George Romney, urging all Republican MODERATES to do the same. Romney pegged his campaign on his "winability," a dangerous route presupposing no slump in his popularity rating. When the slump came in early 1967, there was talk of a secret DEAL on a "fall-back position"; *New York Times* reporter Warren Weaver referred to Illinois freshman Senator

Charles Percy as "the backup candidate." This implied no active support for him unless Romney faltered, at which point the combined liberal forces would move—in impossibly disciplined fashion—to a second candidate.

A year before the 1968 convention, Senator Jacob K. Javits used the phrase in an interview with *Time*, reiterating his and Rockefeller's support of Romney. Obviously recognizing the weakening effect of the admission of any secret second choice, he insisted: "We have no fallback position. There are no alternatives." *Time* added: "None, that is, unless Romney happens to stumble." When he did, it became apparent that Rockefeller had occupied the fall-back position. See PENTAGONESE.

Jimmy Carter was the first President to use the phrase in diplomatic negotiation. In July 1978 he warned Israel that if direct negotiations between Egypt and Israel did not produce results, the matter could be placed in the anti-Israel UN: "The Geneva conference is . . . the basic framework for peace and that is always a fallback position if we fail as an intermediary or mediator."

FALLOUT   unfortunate side effects of a political policy or event; unanticipated negative reaction.

Senator William Fulbright wrote in 1966: ". . . the Vietnamese war thus far has had three major 'fallout' effects on East-West relations: first, it has generated a degree of mistrust and antagonism toward the United States . . . second, it has weakened the drive of the Eastern European countries toward greater independence of the Soviet Union; third, it has put a severe strain on the Soviet-American detente . . ."

The political use is an extension of

the scientific term coined after the explosion of the first atomic bombs in 1945. "Fallout" is defined in the April 1953 issue of the *Bulletin of the Atomic Scientists* as "the descent of the [radioactive] particles back to earth—[that] may occur in the immediate vicinity of the detonation or as far as several thousand miles away . . . although it is heaviest near the site."

Political usage should not be confused with "falling-out," or disagreement.

FAMILY JEWELS, *see* **CIA-ESE.**

FASCIST   originally, a believer in the corporate state; now a smear word intended to mean totalitarianism of the right.

Fascio is the Italian word for "bundle," or "group"; in 1895 a political organization called itself *fasci dei lavoratori,* and in 1915 the *fascio interventista* were called the *fascisti.* The movement grew in the early twenties as an especially brutal alternative to Communism, and under Benito Mussolini, controlled Italy from 1922 to 1943.

In current use, the word is an epithet directed often from the far left toward anyone on the right; in Communist terminology, it is the worst insult short of "revisionist." In the demonstrations of the sixties in the U.S., the phrase "fascist pig" was used so often that the word lost some of its sting.

See **TRAINS RAN ON TIME.**

FAT CAT   a man of wealth, particularly an important contributor to political campaigns. The phrase is both derogatory and respectful, since few politicians can go far without such supporters.

The phrase was popularized by Frank R. Kent of the *Baltimore Sun* in his 1928 book, *Political Behavior:* ". . . these capitalists have what the organization needs—money to finance the campaign. Such men are known in political circles as 'fat cats.' "

In politics, "fat" means "money." The word was used back in the last century: high-pressure fund-raising was called "fat-frying" in the campaign of 1888. Publisher Henry L. Stoddard wrote historian Mark Sullivan: "[Mark] Hanna was *a* fat-fryer. *The* fat-fryer was John P. Forster, President of the League of Young Republican Clubs. It was in 1888 that he wrote a letter suggesting 'to fry the fat out of the manufacturers.' "

The word is not always used in the campaign contributor sense. FDR in 1937 wrote to Ambassador Bowers in Spain: "All the fat-cat newspapers— 85% of the whole—have been utterly opposed to everything the Administration is seeking . . ."

By the forties, politicians had developed a taste for biting the hand that fed them. Republican Party Finance Chairman Ernest T. Weir tried to oust National Chairman Joe Martin after the Willkie defeat in 1940 by putting on a financial "freeze." At a private luncheon in the Capitol, in 1941, Wendell Willkie said, "The thing I like about Joe Martin is that he has the guts to tell those fat cats to go to hell."

Fund-raisers for John F. Kennedy organized "The President's Club" with a membership gained by a donation of $1,000. This was denounced by Republicans as evidence of "fat cats with axes to grind" getting contracts as special recognition for their contributions to Kennedy's campaign. Despite the negative publicity, "Governor's Clubs," "County Chairman's Clubs," etc., were formed by both parties to give the fat cats a warm hearth and a feeling that their purrings were heard by the man at the top.

See GREASE.

FAT CITY, *see* **FUN CITY.**

FAT-FRYING, *see* **SLUSH FUND; FAT CAT.**

FAVORITE SON a candidate who holds a state's votes together at a convention for brokerage purposes; not a serious candidate for the presidency, but one who seeks a trading position with a chance as a compromise candidate or Vice President.

The phrase was first applied to George Washington as "Freedom's Favorite Son" in the late 1780s. Probably its first use in a more partisan sense applied to Martin Van Buren, "New York's favorite son" in the 1830s, and Henry Clay, "Kentucky's favorite son" a decade later.

In current use, a state's political leader often announces his intention of going to a convention as a favorite son. In that way he appears not to be seeking the nomination seriously; he can be promoting the interests of his own state (Hiram Fong's demonstration at the 1964 Republican convention extolled the delights of Hawaii on national television), avoiding a divisive primary fight in his home state, or simply holding his delegates in line to act more influentially as a bloc.

The favorite-son candidacy gives an alibi to the potentially serious candidate for refusing to withdraw his name from preferential primaries in other states—such a disavowal would be "inconsistent" with being a favorite son. Because of its usefulness, the scornful implication of the phrase, prevalent in the later part of the nineteenth century, has disappeared.

Though "favorite son" is understood throughout the political U.S., "native son" is also used to mean the same, particularly in the Midwest. Harry Truman wrote in his memoirs: "I recalled the 1928 Democratic convention in Houston. There were two or three native-son nominations that year, including Jim Reed of Missouri . . ."

Jokingly, but prophetically, John F. Kennedy said in Arizona during his 1960 campaign that "if we keep working, we will just take Arizona out of Barry Goldwater's bag. In any case, we will make it easy for him to be a candidate in 1964. That is the least we can do for a favorite son."

FEAR ITSELF, *see* **NOTHING TO FEAR.**

FEDERALESE, *see* **PENTAGONESE; GOBBLEDYGOOK.**

FEDERALISM, *see* **CREATIVE FEDERALISM; NEW FEDERALISM.**

FEEDBACK response; voter reaction; information resulting from a TRIAL BALLOON.

A modern word, perhaps originating in the radio engineers' vocabulary, feedback describes the loud squeak that jars the nerves of an audience when loudspeakers are misplaced in such a way that they feed sound waves back into the microphone. In automation, feedback is the essence of automatic control, the return to input of part of the output of a machine, system, or process.

In politics, feedback is the information a candidate gets when he has probed in a given direction. It can be approving or critical, but it gives him the first test reaction before a major commitment. Example: "Put out a rumor that I'm supporting so-and-so and see what kind of feedback we get."

A second political meaning is negative reaction, similar to FALLOUT. The Suffolk (L.I.) *Sun* headlined its column of complaints and protests from readers "Feedback."

A *New York Times* editorial on April 10, 1978, included feedback as one of its ten least-liked words "except in analyses of computer or stereo performance."

See FLAK.

FEET TO THE FIRE pressure to fulfill a commitment.

The phrase is customarily used in regard to persuading delegates to conventions to honor their promises, and often implies economic coercion. "Who knows his banker? Who's his boss? Who does he do most of his business with? Put his feet to the fire."

Governor Ronald Reagan of California said in 1967 he would approve a withholding system of taxation only if "they held a hot iron to my feet." Senator Stephen Young told of a colleague who had switched his vote, and was congratulated by a friend for having "seen the light." The reply: "I didn't see the light, but I felt the heat."

The *New York Times* in 1968 used the phrase in this way: "Senator Robert F. Kennedy has been squirming rather uncomfortably at the edge of the national arena of late, and the man who has been putting his feet to the political fire has been his supposed comrade-in-arms, Senator Eugene F. McCarthy of Minnesota."

Admonitions of political pressure begin with a mild *talk to him,* rise to *twist his arm,* then *lean on him,* and finally *put his feet to the fire.*

See LEVERAGE.

FELLOW COUNTRYMEN, *see* **MY FRIENDS.**

FELLOW TRAVELER one who accepts most of the Communist doctrines, but is not a member of the Communist party; or one who agrees with a philosophy or group but does not publicly work for it.

Leon Trotsky was angered by some Russian authors of the twenties who were only interested in the Bolshevik Revolution, not dedicated to it. He made the distinction: "They are not the artists of the proletarian revolution, but only its artistic fellow travelers." The word in Russian is *poputchik.*

Max Lerner, in an article in *The Nation* in 1936 titled "Mr. Roosevelt and his Fellow Travelers," explained: "The term has a Russian background and means someone who does not accept all your aims but has enough in common with you to accompany you in a comradely fashion part of the way."

Since World War II, the term has been most often applied to those who are (or are accused of being) in general agreement with the Communist party.

In literal translation, Soviet Sputniks are fellow travelers: something (satellite) traveling with a traveler (the earth).

"Fellow traveler" is an attack phrase on Communists; the Communist attack phrase on the same subject, especially prevalent in China, has been "running dogs." See "ducks" under PROVERBS AND AXIOMS, POLITICAL.

FENCE, ON THE undecided; unwilling to take a position; straddling.

In its original use, "on the fence" meant refusing to take a firm stand for or against a candidate or issue and was an attack phrase. That sense continues, but a new use has arisen: to be "on the fence" is not all bad, because it shows that a political figure is considering all the alternatives.

The term blossomed in 1828 and was probably in use before then. The *Ohio Journal* in that year summed up the Senate split between supporters of President John Quincy Adams and Andrew Jackson:

Administration 22
Jackson 13
On the fence 1

The *Georgia Journal* in 1840 suggested a position that was later termed ALL THINGS TO ALL MEN to politicians of the time: "Our advice to all politicians who have a hankering after the praise of all . . . is to take a position near the fence, on the fence, or above the fence."

Carl Schurz, insisting on political independence, described his position (according to James Blaine) "as that of a man sitting on a fence, with clean boots, watching carefully which way he may leap to keep out of the mud."

This defense of fence-sitting remains a secondary meaning of the phrase: the best place to be before all the facts are in. Daniel P. Moynihan told the Americans for Democratic Action in 1967:

President Johnson is said to be fond of relating the experience of an out-of-work school teacher who applied for a position in a small town on the Texas plains at the very depths of the depression. After a series of questions one puckered rancher on the school board looked at him and asked, did he teach that the world was round or that the world was flat. Finding no clues in the faces of the other members of the board, the teacher swallowed hard and allowed he could teach it either way.

Johnson's Texas background led to

his being criticized as "tall in the straddle," a play on "saddle," when he took a position on the fence. "Straddle," its political use traced to 1843, carries a more negative connotation than being "on the fence."

FENCE MENDING   looking after interests in one's political POWER BASE; taking care of the folks back home.

When Senator John Sherman of Ohio made a trip home in 1879, ostensibly to look after his farm but actually to see to his political interests, he insisted to reporters that he was home "only to repair my fences."

The following interchange took place in the House of Representatives on August 16, 1888:

Mr. Dougherty:—I presume [the absent members] are at home seeking renomination or looking after their fences. . . .

Mr. Weaver:—I have "fences" as well as other gentlemen; but my friends will look after my "fences" while I am here. . . .

Mr. Springer:—I am very anxious that the public business would be dispatched as early as possible, and that we may return to our constituents; and then, if there are any "fences" to be mended, . . . we shall have our own time in which to attend to such matters.

A deeper sense of fence mending was given in Robert Frost's poem, "Mending Wall." In it the poet explains the comradeship and sense of mutual respect between two men who recognize each other's limitations:

Before I built a wall I'd ask to know
What I was walling in or walling
*   out . . .*
Something there is that doesn't love a wall,
That wants it down . . .
He ways again, "Good fences make good
*   neighbors."*

Fences have an important place in

politics. Fence mending—talking to local politicians, contributors, workers, and newsmen—is considered good and necessary, but *sitting on the fence* is often considered cowardly and *fence straddling* is opportunistic. See FENCE, ON THE. The underworld use of "fence"—as an intermediary for stolen goods—is not used in politics; however, a baseball metaphor, *hitting it over the fence* is occasionally used in politics to describe a successful speech, and politicians parry questions while *fencing* with reporters.

The British equivalent to fence mending is "nursing a constituency."

FETCHER BILL a legislative proposal designed to attract a bribe to bury it.

Like RIPPER BILL, this is statehouse lingo. Frank Trippet, in *The States: United They Fell* (1967), defined a fetcher bill as "a measure that, by threatening to curtail some commercial interest, provides incentive for a payoff to obtain the death of the bill."

Probably of English slang origin. The *OED* has a meaning for "fetch," beyond the usual verb "go get," as a noun to mean contrivance, stratagem or trick. A 1745 citation reads: "This might be another of their politick Fetches." A fetcher bill is one that fetches—or elicits, or goes and brings back—a bribe.

FIASCO, *see* BAY OF PIGS FIASCO.

FIELD EXPEDIENT an alteration in plans made on the stump without consulting campaign headquarters.

A field expedient is an army term for a makeshift substitute; an ingenious device, made from materials at hand, to take the place of a manufac-

tured item. A rifle barrel can be cleaned with a government-issue item consisting of a small lead weight, a chain, and a square of chamois cloth. When this is lost, soldiers come up with a "field expedient" of a small pebble, a string, and a piece of shirt-tail.

When General Eisenhower was campaigning through upstate New York in 1952, he was scheduled to broadcast to a New York City fund-raising dinner from Governor Thomas E. Dewey's mansion in Albany. A microphone and loudspeaker were set up in Dewey's office for the two-way broadcast of a conversation between dinner chairman Paul Hoffman in New York City and Eisenhower and Dewey in Albany.

A moment before the broadcast was to begin, the line went dead. Thinking quickly, the radio engineer made a telephone call to the Grand Ballroom of the Waldorf-Astoria, got Hoffman on that end of the line, and jammed earphones on the heads of Dewey and Eisenhower. The earphones were too small for Dewey and hurt his head; angrily, he muttered, "Save us from AMATEURS."

Eisenhower, who had been tense at the sudden change in technical setup and worried looks of the engineer and director, immediately relaxed when the engineer explained, "Field expedient, General." "Nothing to worry about," the nominee reassured Dewey. "This is a field expedient." Since the General seemed to expect him to understand the term, Dewey stopped glaring and coolly proceeded to introduce the broadcast.

FIFTH COLUMN any secret group of traitors or sympathizers with an enemy, prepared to rise up and strike on his behalf at the most propitious moment.

The term was coined by Emilio Mola, a rebel general in the Spanish Civil War. Javier Gaytan de Ayala, director of the Spanish Library of Information, says he believes the term was first used during an interview granted by General Mola while his troops were advancing on the then Loyalist-held capital of Madrid in October 1936. Mola described how four rebel columns were converging on the city; when asked by a reporter which column he believed would actually capture the city, he replied, "the fifth."

The phrase was used again and elaborated on in a radio broadcast on October 16, 1936. The exact words have been lost, but General Mola made it clear that by a fifth column he meant sympathizers of the Franco cause who would rise within the city at the appropriate time. General Mola died in an airplane crash on June 3, 1937, before the fifth column of which he boasted achieved the results he had predicted.

The world, wrote *Time* in 1947, "pounced on the phrase with the eagerness of a man who has been groping for an important word."

Ernest Hemingway titled his only play *The Fifth Column* and it was presented in a 1937 performance at Madrid's Florida Hotel, a center for foreigners sympathetic with the Loyalist cause.

The phrase was later used to describe the secret Hitler sympathizers in Western Europe, then to identify almost any hidden group of enemies. *Chicago Daily News* correspondent Leland Stowe, covering the fall of Norway to the Nazis in World War II, broadcast a description of that country's collapse in which he charged Norway had fallen "to its fifth column of Quislings and others." President Roosevelt used "sixth

column" to describe the "gossips and defeatists" during World War II.

In his 1946 IRON CURTAIN speech, Winston Churchill described Communist parties in Western countries as "Communist fifth columns [which] are established and work in complete unity and absolute obedience to the directive they receive from the Communist center."

FIFTY-FOUR FORTY OR FIGHT, *see* WAR HORSE.

FIGHTING THE PROBLEM
refusal to come to grips with a situation that requires action; pettifogging delay.

This is a military expression that is gaining some currency in political life. An army recruit who explains to the mess sergeant that unpeeled potatoes have more vitamins and better flavor than peeled potatoes is "fighting the problem": sooner or later, he will have to peel the potatoes.

"As Secretary of State," writes Harry Truman in his memoirs, "[General George C.] Marshall had to listen to more staff talk than when he was Chief of Staff. He would listen for a long time without comment, but when the debates between members of his staff seemed destined to go on interminably and he could stand it no longer, he would say, 'Gentlemen, don't fight the problem; decide it.'"

Defense Secretary Robert Lovett used another line in the same kind of situation: "Gentlemen, as one rat said to the other, 'To hell with the cheese, let's get out of the trap.'"

FIGHT THE GOOD FIGHT   to
stand up for one's convictions; a lifelong battle for principle.

The Bible is referred to as "the good book," and "the good fight" is an ethical fight. The outcome is less important to the definition than the idea of taking a stand on a question of principle. The phrase comes from the second epistle of Paul to Timothy (4:-7): "I have fought a good fight, I have finished my course, I have kept the faith."

Senator George Norris of Nebraska, a leader in battles to overthrow the arbitrary rule of House Speaker "Uncle Joe" Cannon, to introduce federal power in the Tennessee Valley, and to abolish the LAME DUCK Congress with the Twentieth Amendment, put it this way toward the end of his life: "I have fought the good fight with all that was in me. Now there is no strength left. Other hands must take up the burden. Remember, the battle against injustice is never won."

Adlai Stevenson titled his final television appeal of the 1952 campaign "The Good Fight." In political use, it has come to connote a worthwhile but losing battle.

FILIBUSTER a technique by which a minority of senators attempts to defeat or alter a measure favored by the majority through the device of continuous talking, or when a senator dramatically calls public attention to a bill he considers is being "railroaded through."

The entire process rests upon the Senate's pride in itself as the world's foremost chamber of enlightened debate. The vehicle is Rule 22, which provides for unlimited debate on any measure before it can be brought to a vote. Such debate is not possible in the House of Representatives where the rules limit the duration of any individual's right to speak, or in Great Britain's House of Commons, where Rule 20 permits the Speaker to direct a member "who persists in irrelevance" to "discontinue his speech."

The usual strategy is for the group of senators involved in a filibuster to follow one another in planned succession. As the vocal cords or imagination of one begins to tire, he yields to a successor. Subject matter need not be relevant—a common phrase is *reading the telephone book;* a synonym is *talkathon,* or marathon talk.

The word was first used to describe the sixteenth-century English and French privateers who began by raiding Spanish treasure ships in the waters of the Caribbean, then known as the Spanish Main, and who ended up, more often than not, as pirates.

The word is derived from the Dutch *vrijbuiter* (*vrij,* "free," and *buiter,* "booter") or "freebooter," a word commonly used to describe pirates. Freebooter was translated into French as *flibustier* and into Spanish as *filibustero,* and then back to English as "filibuster."

Whatever the origin, the term was already common in American politics in its present sense by the time of the Civil War. James Blaine claimed its first appearance occurred when a minority of senators succeeded in delaying the Kansas-Nebraska Act in 1854. In recent years it has most commonly been used in connection with civil rights legislation, the modern outgrowth of the slavery issue.

Until 1957, Southern senators were able to defeat proposed civil rights legislation by filibustering, and often merely by threatening to filibuster. The countermeasures employed by the majority were round-the-clock sessions, intended to wear the minority down, and cloture (more often used than "closure") a two-thirds vote to end debate. In this manner the 1957 Civil Rights Bill was finally passed; today, only a three-fifths vote is required to invoke cloture.

The all-time champion filibusterer is Republican—formerly Democratic

—Senator Strom Thurmond of South Carolina, who talked for more than twenty-four hours in the battle against the 1957 bill. The man considered to be his closest challenger was Democratic—formerly Republican— Senator Wayne Morse of Oregon. However, Senator Morse rejected the role, claiming his most strenuous long-talking efforts made in opposition to the Kennedy Administration's space satellite communication bill was not filibustering but merely "education."

In 1967 Senator Albert Gore (D-Tenn.), attempting to stop the tax checkoff measure for financing political campaigns, protested a delaying action taken by Louisiana Senator Russell Long. Long (whose father Huey set the then-record of sixteen hours in 1935) replied with an expression reminiscent of *Alice in Wonderland*'s "curiouser and curiouser." "When the Senator talks about delaying tactics," he said, "he is speaking as one filibusterer to another filibusterer."

A similar technique in the Japanese Diet is the "cow-waddle," used to delay a vote and express minority displeasure. As the vote is called, opposition members individually waddle— with infinite slowness, stopping to chat along the way—to the ballot box on the rostrum.

FINAL SOLUTION Hitler's planned extermination of the Jews; now used to mean any plan whose carrying-out would lead to a neat, if morally corrupt, conclusion.

This euphemism for mass murder was used by Reinhard ("The Hangman") Heydrich, then head of the Reich Security Police, in a letter of November 6, 1941, to the Nazi Quartermaster General. He had previously used the term (in German, *Endlö-sung*) in a secret report about Polish Jews to the German military officials in Poland in September of 1939.

"At the Nuremberg trials," Charles Whittier of the Library of Congress informs the author, "a memorandum from Hermann Göring to Heydrich, dated July 31, 1941, was cited: Göring claimed that *Endlösung* in that memo meant 'total' solution and not 'final' (*Gesamtlösung*, rather than *Endlösung*)."

Another user of the phrase was Franz Stuckart, who drafted the Nuremberg decrees in 1938, but in his use probably did not mean what has come to be called "genocide": Stuckart recommended the deportation of all Jews from Germany so as to make the Reich *"Judenrein,"* or free of Jewish taint.

The earliest use the author can find is in the March 10, 1920, *Völkischer Beobachter* ("Racial Observer"), using the term *Endziel*, or "final goal," and proposing concentration camps for Jews.

The phrase is now used ironically in the U.S., as an example of the furthest reach of euphemism. It was widely recalled when a phrase used by CIA bureaucrats surfaced: "termination with extreme prejudice," the polite term for murder.

See HOLOCAUST.

FINESSE as a verb, to use a stratagem of applying only as much power as is absolutely necessary to accomplish a political goal, yet not so much power as to induce a counterattack; as a noun, style (as viewed by an ally), trickiness, guile (as seen by an enemy).

In establishing the right of judicial review, Chief Justice John Marshall finessed President Thomas Jefferson. At the start of Jefferson's Administration, the Supreme Court was packed with Federalists appointed by John Adams. Jeffersonian Republicans let it be known that if the Court tried to invalidate important Republican measures, the President would defy the judges, thereby denying the Court the power to declare laws unconstitutional.

Marshall selected the case of *Marbury* vs. *Madison* to finesse the President. He invalidated a minor part of a bill that, ironically, would have given certain technical powers to the Supreme Court. Had he chosen an important Republican measure to declare unconstitutional, Jefferson would have joined the issue and disputed judicial review. But this was a minor, technical matter at hand, without even a specific court order for Jefferson to refuse to obey. The President was finessed, and the vital precedent was set.

On the point of applying "just enough" power, a common political expression is: "You don't use an elephant gun to shoot a rabbit."

The word entered political language through cardplaying (as did "new deal"). In bridge, a finesse is an attempt to take a trick with a lower card (while holding a higher card) in the hope that one's right-hand adversary holds an intermediate card of that suit. Also, in croquet, an opponent is finessed by placing the ball in a difficult position for him to make a shot, which is precisely what Marshall did to Jefferson. See CARD METAPHORS.

FINGER ON THE BUTTON

ready to launch an atomic war; a scare phrase used in attacking candidates who complain of a NO-WIN POLICY.

President Lyndon Johnson, campaigning on television in 1964, let the nation know that he considered Barry Goldwater TRIGGER-HAPPY: "You must have strength, and you must always keep your guard up, but you must always have your hand out and be willing to go anywhere, talk to anybody, listen to anything they have to say, do anything that is honorable, in order to avoid pulling that trigger, mashing that button that will blow up the world."

Former President Dwight Eisenhower, in a televised conversation with candidate Goldwater, did what he could to refute the implication: "This is actual tommyrot . . . you're not going to be doing those things that are going to be—what do they call it?—push button, you're not going to push a button here and start a war."

In a 1954 press conference, Eisenhower gave a more eloquent explanation of the restraints a President must keep on himself: "In many ways the easy course for a president, for the administration, is to adopt a truculent, publicly bold, almost insulting attitude. A president experiences exactly the same resentments, the same anger, the same kind of sense of frustration almost, when things like this occur to other Americans, and his impulse is to lash out."

Sorensen called the President "custodian of the nuclear trigger." "Trigger" and "button" are interchangeable in this sense, in both the U.S. and Britain. In the 1951 British election, the Labour party accused the Conservatives of being warmongers, an attack led by the *Daily Mirror*'s article, "Whose Finger on the Trigger?"

The derivation of trigger is from the Western "hair-trigger" as explained in the entry on "trigger-happy"; button, as in push-button war, is becoming preferred, and is probably derived from the "panic button" of World War II. Writing in

American Speech magazine, Lt. Col. James L. Jackson, USAF, suggests:

> The actual source seems probably to have been the bell system used in bombers (B-17, B-24) for emergency procedures such as bailout and ditching. In case of fighter or flak damage so extensive that the bomber had to be abandoned, the pilot rang a "prepare-to-abandon" ring and then a ring meaning "jump." The bell system was used since the intercom was apt to be out if there was extensive damage. The implications of the phrase seem to have come from those few times when pilots hit the panic button too soon and rang for emergency procedures over minor damage, causing their crews to bail out unnecessarily.

Soon after taking office in 1969, Richard Nixon removed an electric push-button window-opener from his White House bedroom, which had been installed by President Johnson. "I took that out," said President Nixon, "because I was afraid if I pushed the button, I'd blow up the world."

FIRESIDE CHAT   a warm, informal talk by a political leader to a few million of his intimate friends.

In 1938, President Roosevelt wasn't sure just how the term "fireside chat" began to be applied to his radio talks. "The name 'fireside chat,' " he said, "seems to be used by the press even when the radio talk is delivered on a very hot mid-summer evening."

Roosevelt's first fireside chat as President was made on March 12, 1933, dealing with the opening of banks the next day. However, he had used radio talks in the same way during his first term as governor of New York State, principally to woo upstate Republicans who received most of their information from Republican newspapers.

The title of the first speech made no mention of firesides; it was "An Intimate Talk With the People of the United States on Banking." In a letter dated October 30, 1933, FDR recalled the audience he had in mind: "I tried to picture a mason at work on a new building, a girl behind a counter, and a farmer in his field." As Joseph Abrell points out in an unpublished study of Roosevelt's radio usage, ". . . the term 'Fireside Chat' was not applied to his first such address but in promoting the second. Harry C. Butcher, who in 1933 was head of the CBS office in Washington, D.C., suggested the name, and from then on they were identified as such by everybody from the 'girl behind the counter' to Roosevelt himself."

Will Rogers thought the talk had so simply explained banking that "even bankers understood it." The *New York Times* editorialized: "His use of this new instrument of political discussion is a plain hint to Congress of a recourse which the President may employ if it proves necessary to rally support for legislation which he asks for and which the lawmakers might be reluctant to give him." Backhanded testimony came from defeated Republican candidate Alf Landon in 1938: "The Presidency is primarily an executive office, not a broadcasting station."

Roosevelt was so effective as a radio speaker that succeeding Presidents were urged by their advisers to give more radio and TV reports to the nation.

President Kennedy's journalist friends urged him so strongly to use the airwaves more often that he commented, "People seem to think Roosevelt gave a fireside chat once a week." Kennedy's staff found that

Roosevelt gave only thirty fireside chats during his twelve years as President; before World War II, he averaged only two a year. See OVEREXPOSURE.

The phrase was used as the basis for a gag in 1976 about Senator Henry Jackson's lacklustre speech delivery: "If he gave a fireside chat, the fire would go out."

When President Carter made a televised "fireside chat"—complete with crackling fire—in 1977, he included a wrinkle of his own: a cardigan sweater.

FIRESTORM   sudden, fierce controversy; a surge of public fury.

"Richard Nixon clung tenuously to office last week," wrote *Newsweek* in its issue of November 5, 1973, "in the face of the most devastating assault that any American President has endured in a century—a nationwide rebuke of such magnitude that one of Mr. Nixon's principal aides described it as 'a fire storm.'"

The anonymous aide who so described it was White House chief of staff Alexander Haig, a lifelong Army officer accustomed to the vocabulary of military catastrophe. The following April, *Newsweek* reprised the word to describe the scene: "It was a full five months since the Saturday-night massacre—the firing of Special Prosecutor Archibald Cox, the resignation of Attorney General Elliot Richardson and the ouster of his deputy, William Ruckelshaus—touched off the fire storm of public outrage that made the impeachment of a U.S. President a real possibility."

General Haig was familiar with the term since its use in the language of atomic warfare. After a heavy incendiary attack, or the dropping of an atomic bomb, rising hot air creates a vacuum that causes a "storm" of air

to rush in, causing further devastation. In 1959 the *New York Times* estimated casualties in an atomic attack in this way: "Nearly half of these could be expected to die instantly, killed by blast or incinerated in the fire-storms caused by the explosions." (The *OED* tracks the word back to 1581 in a curiously similar upward-sucking metaphor: "Helias . . . was taken up into Heaven in a fire storme.")

Although the word has occasionally been used in its political sense before Watergate (columnist James J. Kilpatrick wrote in 1970 that "the next revolutionary who strikes a match in Seattle may ignite a political firestorm"), its association with the most crucial moment in the Nixon decline annealed it to political crisis terminology. Hence, when President Gerald Ford issued his surprise pardon of Mr. Nixon, CBS correspondent Bruce Morton quoted a congressman as saying he predicted "a firestorm of criticism," a calibration more than criticism's usual storm. The *Wall Street Journal* used the same word for the same event the next month: "It may well be, as some of Mr. Ford's oldest and closest advisers say privately, that the President will soon recover from the fire storm that followed the Nixon pardon."

As in most catastrophic metaphor —from prairie fire to avalanche—the new word was soon trivialized. When Secretary of Agriculture Earl Butz made a racial slur in a joke told privately during the 1976 campaign, John Fialka wrote in the *Washington Star*: "What began as a casual conversation among three airline passengers—John Dean, Pat Boone and Earl Butz—has ended in a political firestorm that has cost Butz his job . . ."

In this way, firestorm (now usually

one word, sometimes hyphenated) has almost become synonymous with FLAP, which is unfortunate, since a word for a sudden public-opinion rage is useful.

FIRST IN WAR "To the memory of the man," read the resolution presented to the House of Representatives by Henry (Light Horse Harry) Lee on the death of George Washington in 1799, "first in war, first in peace, first in the hearts of his countrymen."

The line is as famous as any in American history primarily because of the circumstances in which it was spoken; at the death of a great president, the nation is attuned to a memorable phrase (Stanton on Lincoln: "Now he belongs to the ages").

The line also scans in three-syllable beats like the hoofbeats of a galloping horse: first-in-war/first-in-peace/ first-in-the / hearts-of-his / countrymen/. This rhythm has led to parroting, which overlooks the truth in the phrase: Washington was indeed the man who was most responsible for winning the Revolutionary War, for setting up a republic, and refusing a monarchy, and was the most popular American.

Like almost every familiar line, it has been parodied. When Tammany Hall scandals began to embarrass New York Governor Franklin Roosevelt in 1931, *Time* magazine wrote of Tammany: "First in war, first in peace, first in the pockets of its countrymen."

And in 1967, cartoonist Conrad in the *Los Angeles Times* pictured a colonial-looking Lyndon Johnson as "First in War, second in Peace, and 46% in the Polls of his countrymen."

FIRST LADY the wife of the President of the U.S.

British war correspondent William Howard Russell (who coined the phrase "thin red line" in his (London) *Times* coverage of the Crimean War) used "first lady" in *My Diary North and South,* published in 1863. "The gentleman who furnished fashionable paragraphs for the Washington paper has some charming little pieces of gossip about 'the first Lady in the Land.' " His use of the phrase in quotations indicates an earlier coinage, but no phrase detective has yet found an earlier reference than this one (in the *Dictionary of Americanisms*) to Mary Todd Lincoln.

American poet and novelist Mary Clemmer Ames used the phrase in describing the inauguration of President Rutherford B. Hayes on March 5, 1877. The phrase was a natural to describe Dolly Madison, the first presidential wife also to be a public figure. It became part of the language when playwright Charles Nirdlinger wrote a comedy about her in 1911, entitled *The First Lady in the Land,* which enjoyed a good run at New York's Gaiety Theatre.

When the President dies, the first lady ceases to be "first," but may remain a celebrity. Eleanor Roosevelt was consistently on the "most admired American" lists after 1945, and was often introduced as "First Lady of the World." Jacqueline Kennedy remained the center of some attention after Lady Bird Johnson became first lady in 1963.

Recently, the wives of governors and mayors have been referred to as first ladies; as this usage grows, the words describing the wife of the President are likely to be capitalized, to set her off from the pack. The wife of the Vice President is never called "the second lady."

FISCAL INTEGRITY the "motherhood" of money—everybody is for it.

Fiscal policy has to do with budgeting the government's taxes against its expenditures; *monetary* policy concerns itself with the interest rates that reflect and guide the flow of funds in a nation. A *balanced* budget and *deficit financing* are phrases in the fiscal area; *tight money* and *hard money* belong in the monetary area.

Fiscal integrity, then, has been used most often to describe a balanced budget. It is stressed more often by conservatives, who charge liberals with recklessness and "fiscal irresponsibility." With the advent of Lord Keynes (see NEW ECONOMICS), the rules appeared to change on fiscal integrity: if balanced budgets could lead to depressions, then perhaps fiscal integrity required deficit financing.

"I think the virtues of a 'balanced budget' can at times be exaggerated," wrote Harry Truman. "Andrew Jackson paid off the national debt entirely, and the budget was balanced when the unprecedented Panic of 1837 struck. Even the depression following the crash of 1929 overtook a government which was operating in the black."

Such a comment would have been considered heresy for a politician only a generation before. Its acceptance as a position without blinking now indicated that "fiscal integrity" was shifting away from balancing the budget and toward some amorphous "doing the right thing for the economy to ensure prosperity, full employment and no inflation." See PAY AS YOU GO.

FISHING EXPEDITION investigation without a specific goal; a probe undertaken usually by a committee dominated by one party into the affairs of another party, for the purposes of unearthing whatever "bait" might be useful in a campaign.

The phrase is used as a defensive smear of a legitimate investigation. Thomas L. Stokes wrote in 1940 about the Harding–Teapot Dome investigation of 1924: ". . . many voters, undoubtedly, were willing to accept the Republican explanation that it was just a 'political fishing expedition.'"

In a 1955 Eisenhower cabinet meeting, Philip Ray, general counsel to the Department of Commerce, explained why he refused to turn over department records to the House Judiciary Anti-Trust subcommittee, headed by Democrat Emmanuel Celler. Ray said that Celler seemed bent on a "fishing expedition," and Eisenhower agreed that the department should draw a line between what could and could not be released to a committee of Congress. According to reporter Robert Donovan's reading of the minutes of that meeting, Eisenhower said "he was never going to yield to the point where he would become known as a President who had practically crippled the Presidency."

Other fishing metaphors in politics include the familiar *fish or cut bait,* the graphic *floundering around,* and a fishing expression unique to politics, *going fishing,* which means *sitting out a campaign,* or not quite *bolting* (see BOLT) but refusing to help.

The July 2, 1876, the *Cincinnati Commercial* wrote: "There has been a great deal of inquiry as to whom Carl Schurz was going for in the presidential campaign. Perhaps he is not going for anybody, but is going a-fishing."

Writing on California Republican politics in the *New Republic* in 1967, Andrew Kopkind observed: "[Senator Thomas] Kuchel supported [Mayor George] Christopher against [candidate for Governor Ronald] Reagan, and 'went fishing' in the general election."

To *fish for votes* is a common construction, leading to this frequent admonition to candidates too willing to spend time on citizens too young to vote or too deeply committed to either side: "Fish where the fish are."

In the seventies, the expression's sharp edge of unwarranted intrusion was blunted by a frequent use meaning "feeler" (see PEACE FEELER) or TRIAL BALLOON. After Carter aides had sounded out television executives to find out if they would telecast a routine Fourth of July speech, Tom Shales wrote in the June 29, 1978, *Washington Post*: "This practice of testing the waters to gauge possible interest—'a fishing expedition,' one NBC executive calls it—has been common practice . . ." Defending the White House right to "think out loud," another executive—Sanford Socolow of CBS—used a locution that is the farthest-out form of fishing expedition: "Those guys are entitled to blue-sky once in a while."

FIVE PERCENTER one who claims to know government officials in high places and can be "helpful" for five percent of a contract.

Republicans, notably Senator Joseph McCarthy of Wisconsin, popularized the phrase in the friends-in-high-places scandals during the Truman Administration.

A New England furniture manufacturer, Paul Grindle, triggered a congressional investigation of influence peddlers in Washington. Grindle, a former reporter for the *New York Herald Tribune,* alleged that James V. Hunt, a management counselor in Washington, assured him that

he could introduce him to influential people for $1,000 down, $500 a month and five percent of any contract.

Grindle closed the deal and then put the *Tribune* on to the story. The newspaper story started a Senate investigating committee on Hunt's trail. Subsequent investigations uncovered other emoluments: the wife of an examiner of loans for the Reconstruction Finance Corporation received a $10,000 mink coat after the RFC had approved a loan for a Florida motel; Major General Harry Vaughan, President Truman's military aide, and other Washington notables received deep freezers as gifts. Remaining aloof from the controversy, Truman refused to get drawn into a detailed discussion of the five-percenter investigations. Vaughan said he was "bewildered and baffled" by the uproar about doing a few favors for friends.

As a result of the Senate investigations, the RFC was reorganized and there were some purges in both the Department of Justice and the Internal Revenue Service.

See INFLUENCE PEDDLER; MESS IN WASHINGTON.

FLAK opposition, especially noisy opposition to a new idea or program. To "run into flak" means to encounter some unexpected but not devastating criticism.

The word was coined in World War II to describe anti-aircraft gunfire, an acronym for the German *Flieger* (aircraft) *Abwehr* (defense) *Kanone* (gunfire). In politics, flak serves to bring down TRIAL BALLOONS.

The puffs of smoke of the exploding anti-aircraft shells also gave rise to another meaning of "flak": press agent, or government public information officer. The puffs refer derogatorily to "puffed-up" or inflated, exaggerated information; "puff pieces" are articles that flatter and swell the head of the subject.

The two meanings came together in a small footnote to history. While working on a speech in the White House one day in 1969, the author received a call from one David Young, who was an assistant to Henry Kissinger (and who later went on to some fame as the coiner of PLUMBERS). The young aide wanted to know what "flack" meant.

Since the first rule of bureaucratic survival is not to pass out any information without knowing its intended ultimate use, I deliberately misinterpreted the question and gave an answer that explained the German derivation of the acronym "flak."

Moments later the aide called back to say, "Dr. Kissinger doesn't need you to teach him German, but he says Joe Kraft just called him 'an Administration flack' and he wants to know whether he should take offense."

With the background understood, I passed along the current meaning of "flack" with a *c*—apologist, or paid proponent, with its pejorative but sometimes madcap connotation. To cheer up Dr. Kissinger, the thought was added that the role, if not the word, could be an honorable one, since a skilled advocate was needed to explicate foreign policy.

However, when next Dr. Kissinger passed by, he gloomed: "I decided to take offense." Perhaps he was wrong to worry about "flack"; in a few years he was to learn what it was to be the object of "flak" without a *c*, from this writer and others.

FLAMING LIBERAL attack word on a member of the political left;

more vivid than "radical."

Fire is often used to characterize radicalism. A *fiery* orator, or *firebrand*, *fires up* his audience; with *fire in his eyes*, he *inflames* their passions to *heated* argument about his *infernal* opinions. (Smoke, on the other hand, implies deviousness: see SMOKE-FILLED ROOM and SMOKE SCREEN.) The color of fire is red, and red is the name of everything radical. Some issues "burn"; others are merely "hot."

The phrase might have arisen parallel to the "flaming youth" of the twenties. All-encompassing labels like LIBERAL require adjectives to make a description more exact. During Prohibition, those who went along with repeal were called "Wets," and they opposed the "Drys"; but those who felt strongly about repeal were labeled "dripping Wets." Similarly, liberals are tagged KNEE-JERK liberals (who react without thinking), *professional* liberals (a favorite Harry Truman criticism of those who only talked liberalism), or *flaming* liberals.

A flyer put out by an extreme right-wing group in 1964 attacked "Hubert Humphrey The Flaming Liberal" as a member of "a semisecret, New York-based, Communist-appeasing group called the Council on Foreign Relations." The flyer did not add that other members of this group included Dwight Eisenhower, Lucius Clay, Edward Teller, and several of Barry Goldwater's foreign policy advisers.

FLAP, *see* **UNFLAPPABLE.**

FLAT-OUT a maximum effort applied from the beginning, with no consideration given to rest, overexposure, or saving a last burst of energy and money for the end.

The phrase is probably derived from auto racing, where it means maximum speed, accelerator flat on the floor.

Opposite of *flat-out* is PEAKING, planning a campaign so that all activity, expenditure, and voter interest reach a crescendo just before election day. In the campaign of 1960, Kennedy began as the underdog and ran a flat-out campaign, as an underdog must do; Nixon, who dropped back after the first debate on television, came on with a rush at the end, "peaking" just a few days too late to win. Wrote Arthur Schlesinger, Jr.: "Some close to Kennedy believed that, if the campaign had gone on three days more, he would have been beaten. The candidate himself knew the tide was shifting."

FDR believed in peaking, though the phrase was not current in his time. He began the 1936 campaign by going on a leisurely two-week cruise, allowing the Republicans to take center stage; his time would come nearer the decision date. "The Republican high command," he wrote his running mate, John Nance Garner, "is doing altogether too much talking at this stage of the game." See OVEREXPOSURE.

The flat-out campaigner runs the risk of being spent, physically and financially, on the crucial weekend before election; the campaigner concerned with peaking runs the risk of having energy and money left over when it is too late to use them.

The phrase, now current, is often misused for the shorter word *flat*. When Robert Kennedy and FBI Chief J. Edgar Hoover began trading charges in 1966 on who was responsible for electronic eavesdropping, one former Justice Department aide accused Hoover of "a flat-out lie." Lies and denials can be *flat* or *out-and-out;* campaigns and races are *flat-out*.

San Francisco Mayor George Christopher, Nelson Rockefeller's Northern California chairman in the 1964 Republican primary ultimately won by Barry Goldwater, gave this description of what it is like to be involved in an intense, flat-out campaign: "This morning I was sitting on the edge of the bed just holding a sock in my hand. My wife asked me what I was doing. I told her I was trying to figure out whether I was getting up or going to bed."

FLATTERIES OF HOPE, *see* **GLOOM AND DOOM, PROPHETS OF.**

FLOATER, *see* **SWING VOTER.**

FLOO-FLOO BIRD   a bird that flies backward, more interested in where it has been than where it is going; liberal's description of a conservative.

Frank Lloyd Wright referred to this curious creature in a 1938 speech to architects in Washington, D.C.:

> The cultural influences in our country are like the "floo floo" bird. I am referring to the peculiar and especial bird who always flew backward. To keep the wind out of its eyes? No. Just because it didn't give a darn where it was going, but just had to see where it had been. Now, in the "floo floo" bird you have the true symbol of our Government architecture . . . and in consequence, how discredited American culture stands in the present time. All the world knows it to be funny except America.

Frank Lloyd Wright did not hyphenate the floo-floo bird in his written remarks. Proper usage requires the hyphen, which looks both ways.

Just after Dwight Eisenhower's reelection in 1956, Senate Majority Leader Lyndon Johnson said the country supported the President because it felt that Eisenhower "was more interested in where he is going than where he has been." The lack of wisdom present in backward-looking was expressed by Negro baseball pitcher Satchel Paige, who counseled: "Never look back. Someone may be gaining on you."

Other birds in the mythical heavens include the "worry bird," a small desk ornament that does the worrying for executives; the "gooney bird," or weekend Air Force reservist flying around for practice; and the extinct dodo, subject of the expression, "dead as a dodo." The Johnson family's names (wife "Lady Bird" and daughter Lynda Bird) gave rise to some satire, as in the play *MacBird!* (produced in New York in 1966), parodying Shakespeare's *Macbeth*.

For the political menagerie's complete aviary, see this dictionary's Introduction to the first edition.

FLOOR FIGHT an argument, usually about platform demands or delegate credentials, that cannot be settled in committee and is taken to the floor of the convention for decision.

Floor fights are despised by most political professionals: compromise has failed, and sections of the party will consider themselves losers at the convention and may go home and sit on their hands.

Historian Stefan Lorant tells of the day in 1896 when a man burst into Republican boss Mark Hanna's St. Louis hotel room and announced: "Mr. Hanna, I insist on a positive declaration for a gold-standard plank in the platform."

Hanna looked up and said, "Who the hell are you?" The man replied, "Senator Henry Cabot Lodge of Massachusetts."

"Well, Senator Henry Cabot Lodge of Massachusetts, you can go plumb to hell. You have nothing to say about it."

"All right, sir," bristled Lodge. "I will make my fight on the convention floor." Replied Hanna: "I don't care a damn where you make your fight." But cooler heads prevailed, and a floor fight was averted. When it became known that the Democrats would declare for free silver, the platform committee placed the Republicans dead against it. ("Avert a floor fight," as used above, is a cliché. For a modern example of how to stop a floor fight before it starts, see COMPACT OF FIFTH AVENUE.)

A floor fight in the 1952 Republican convention over contested credentials swung the nomination away from Taft to Eisenhower (see THOU SHALT NOT STEAL); a floor fight on ideological grounds in the 1948 Democratic convention resulted in the bolt of the DIXIECRATS.

The meaning of "floor" as "forum," or "right to speak," predates American political history and comes from English parliamentary tradition. See HUSTINGS.

FLUGIE a rule that only benefits the maker of the rule, and can be changed to avoid having it benefit his opponent.

When Senator Russell Long (D-La.) wants to get special legislation passed for a constituent, and a fellow senator objects, Senator Long explains patiently that his proposal is "just like a flugie." When the objector wonders what that is, Senator Long eagerly tells the story:

Two men are playing poker; one gets a full house and starts to gather in the winnings, when another player —with not even two of a kind in his hand—stops him. "This is my pot," says the full-house man, "you don't have a thing." "Ah," says his opponent, "but nothing is a 'flugie.' Read the sign on the wall behind me." Sure enough, the sign says: "A Flugie Beats Everything." The man with nothing in his hand takes in the pot.

On the next hand, the man who just held the full house comes up with nothing, and starts to rake in his pot. "Wait," says the flugie expert, who this time has a pair. "Read the sign behind you." On the wall, the sign reads: "Just One Flugie Per Evening."

Washington Star reporter James Dickenson, recounting this in 1977, added: "The widespread notion of the U.S. Senate is that when it comes to tax legislation Long really wants, which very often benefits oil and gas producers, he consistently gets the only flugie of the evening."

The slang term "flugie"—or its variants "floogie," "floozie," "floosy" —usually describe a woman of loose morals. The World War II ditty "Flatfoot Floogie with a Floy-Floy" was said to mean, to the cognoscenti, a streetwalker with a venereal disease. This is evidently not the meaning Senator Long has in mind.

FLYER a small handbill or circular with a brief political message.

Political literature includes *handbills, handcards, doorknob-hangers, flyers, brochures, reprints,* and *mailers.*

In current use, *flyer* and *handbill* are used interchangeably to mean a cheap circular about an issue or one calling attention to an upcoming event or visit; a *handcard* is a picture of a candidate on heavier stock paper with a brief description of his background and occasionally a summary of his platform; a *brochure* is an expanded version of the handcard, often using pictures of the candidate in action and with improved graphic design, usually more elaborate than a flyer; a *doorknob-hanger* is a flyer saying that a volunteer called and giving some brief information about a candidate, with the top of the flyer slit or shaped so that it can be hung on a doorknob; a *reprint* is a photo-offset reproduction of a favorable article about the candidate, in flyer form to be handed out; a *mailer* (or *self-mailer*) is a brochure designed, with space left for address and stamp, to be mailed without an envelope.

Circular is no longer in current use in politics; HANDOUT is rarely used in this sense; its current meanings are a welfare payment or a press release.

Flyer (when not used to mean aviator or small venture in the stock market) is the most frequently used word in political literature. It can be traced to an 1888 speech in the House by Congressman T. E. Tarsney of Michigan: "[My opponent] placed upon every doorstep of every house in the city [of Saginaw] a flyer. 'Do not vote for Tim Tarsney: he is a free-trader.' "

For examples of how flyers can get far more vicious than the kind Tarsney complained about, see GUTTER FLYER; ROORBACK.

FOGGY BOTTOM the State Department.

Robert A. Lovett, who served as Secretary of Defense in the Truman Administration, had been dubbed "the Bald Eagle of Foggy Bottom" (see BALD EAGLE) from his earlier State Department days. State Department offices were built on land that had originally been called Foggy Bottom, and the name was reapplied because it recalled a fogginess of official language.

New York Times columnist James Reston tells the lexicographer that the reporter who first applied the phrase to the State Department was Edward Folliard of the *Washington Post*. "Eddie grew up down by the gasworks, between what is now the New State Department building and the K Street bridge," Reston recalls. "The coinage took place soon after State moved out of the building across the street from the White House, that's now the Old Executive Office Building."

The Library of Congress provided the author with a description of the derivation, from George R. Brown's 1930 book, *Washington.*

> Over in the old First Ward of an earlier day . . . where originally had been the little town of Hamburgh, which existed before Washington was even conceived, was—and still is—Foggy Bottom, lying west of Twenty-third Street and extending to Rock Creek and stretching from the river nearly to Pennsylvania Avenue. In its southern reaches it was formerly a section of swamps and flats, from which arose at night miasmatic vapors which gave to it its colorful cognomen.
>
> Indeed, that whole region which extends from the river to the White House, south of Pennsylvania Avenue, the western extremity of which is still known to the old families as "Foggy Bottom," became in time a fashionable neighborhood . . . which afterwards, however, declined, and is only just now experiencing a renaissance somewhat similar to that which Georgetown has enjoyed, as people of means and culture have flocked there . . .

As people in the foreign service flocked to the "western extremity," the State Department came to be known by the mildly mocking name. Wrote Arthur Schlesinger, Jr., in *A Thousand Days:* "The State Department sent over a document. . . . In addition to the usual defects of Foggy Bottom prose, the paper was filled with bad spelling and grammar."

FOLLOWING, *see* **BACKER.**

FOOTBALL, POLITICAL   an innocent civic or philanthropic project used to make a political issue.

Pity the low-flying, nonpolitical bird that finds itself the shuttlecock in a game of political badminton. This, to mix a **SPORTS METAPHOR,** is the political football, and it means "unfair use of a pure project for crass partisan gain." As can be seen, the phrase itself is an attack phrase, drawing sympathy to the nonpartisan ball that is getting kicked.

In 1800 Abraham Bishop wrote in *Connecticut Republicanism:* "Multitudes of rational men are for destroying that kind of religion which is made a football or stalking horse, and which operates only to dishonor God and ruin man."

Fiorello La Guardia, former New York mayor who headed the United Nations Relief and Rehabilitation Administration, got into a debate with Adlai Stevenson in 1946 over methods of providing emergency relief. Taking the offensive, the "Little Flower" accused Stevenson of "making a political football out of food." In the same way, Harry Truman said of Dwight Eisenhower's actions in the campaign of 1952: "Hard as it was for us to understand this side of Eisenhower now revealed to us, it was even more of a jolt to see our foreign policy used as a political football."

Mobster Charles "Lucky" Luciano, in a 1953 interview with the author, sat in a Naples bar and gloomily reviewed the causes of what he felt was his persecution: "I was sent to jail, I was sprung, and I was deported, all because I was a political football."

A new, more ominous use of "football" refers to the small, thirty-pound metal suitcase containing codes that can launch a nuclear attack. It is carried by a military aide to the President and follows the Chief Executive wherever he goes. See BAGMAN. For the use of football terminology in politics, See GAME PLAN.

FOOT-IN-MOUTH DISEASE

tendency to blunder when ad-libbing; error-prone.

The day after Eisenhower's Defense Secretary Charles E. Wilson made his famous BIRD DOG . . . KENNEL DOG comparison, he admitted his error and told reporters that some of his cabinet colleagues "seem to think I have foot-in-mouth disease."

This is a combined colloquialism of interesting parentage, now almost exclusively applied to political figures.

To put one's foot in it, presumably to step into a foul substance or tread heavily on thin ice, has long been a colloquial expression for a misstep or mistake. On matters verbal, the expression was narrowed to *put your foot in your mouth.* This was closely akin to the cattleman's problem, *foot-and-mouth disease* (or hoof-and-mouth disease), a contagious disease of livestock, especially of cloven-hoofed animals. "Foot and mouth" and "foot in mouth" sound identical when spoken quickly, thus spreading the political "disease."

The metaphor can be mixed. Newbold Morris, wealthy reform associate of Fiorello La Guardia and at one time president of New York's City Council, was derided as a man "born with a silver foot in his mouth."

Medical metaphors (see BODY POLITIC) offer political writers vast opportunities; in 1967, a *New York Post* editorial writer was able to pack five medical words into a single sentence: "After consultation with his political doctors, Governor Romney of Michigan has resolved to refrain from further comment in the near future on Vietnam; this self-imposed quarantine may help arrest his virulent attack of foot-in-mouth disease."

Foot-in-mouth disease should not be confused with *logorrhea,* which means speaking on and on past the point of no interest. To apologize in advance for a long speech and to avoid the appearance of verbal diarrhea, politicians often use the self-deprecating line: "This reminds me of the little girl who claimed she knew how to spell 'banana' but she didn't know when to stop."

See BLOOPER.

FOOTNOTE TO HISTORY a

seemingly insignificant detail, contributed long afterward to a great event or a historic person's life.

Samuel Rosenman felt that the story of Roosevelt's use of language was important, "not only as a footnote to history, but as an aid to the better understanding of the leadership exercised by Franklin D. Roosevelt." By designating his information as a footnote to history, the contributor strikes a modest pose; in addition, he calls attention to the detail—most people, like it or not, find their eyes dragged down to the bottom of a page by a footnote.

The phrase is from a book of that title by Robert Louis Stevenson.

Criteria for a footnote to history are that it be (1) hitherto unpublished, (2) from firsthand knowledge, (3) illustrative of character or mood, and (4) unpretentious. See the Kissinger story in FLAK as an example.

FOREIGN WARS, *see* AGAIN AND AGAIN AND AGAIN.

FORGOTTEN MAN single image for the millions left in economic desperation by the Depression.

Governor Franklin D. Roosevelt of New York, campaigning in 1932 for the Democratic presidential nomination, used this phrase in a short speech containing several ideas which would become basic during the first years of his presidency. The theme of this address was the need to come up with plans that "rest upon the forgotten, the unorganized but the indispensable units of economic power . . . that build from the bottom up and not from the top down, that put their faith once more in the forgotten man at the bottom of the economic pyramid."

The party's 1928 presidential candidate, former New York Governor Alfred E. Smith, saw it as a radical attack on business: "At a time like this, when millions of men, women and children are starving throughout the land, there is always a temptation to some men to stir up class prejudice . . ."

To the man out of work, already suffering or fearful of what lay ahead, the "forgotten man" was himself; the phrase played a part in Roosevelt's victory over Smith at the Democratic convention and then over Hoover.

The future President was not the man who coined the phrase, nor was Professor Raymond Moley, though he picked it up and inserted it in that initial speech. A sociologist at Yale University, William Graham Sumner, first used the phrase in an article written in 1883. Far from intending it to describe the destitute, Sumner had in mind the sturdy middle-class citizen who bears society's greatest loads: "Such is the Forgotten Man . . . he is not in any way a hero (like a popular orator); nor a problem (like tramps and outcasts); nor an object of sentiment (like the poor and weak); nor a burden (like paupers and loafers) . . . therefore, he is forgotten. All the burdens fall on him . . ."

Just how important FDR's use of the phrase was at the time is shown by a bitter verse printed in the *New York Sun,* a paper whose unyielding Republicanism was never in doubt, after Roosevelt's victory and just before his inauguration. The President had gone on a fishing cruise on Vincent Astor's yacht, the *Normahal.* The party included other well-to-do friends, which inspired the newspaper's poet to write:

They were just good friends with no selfish ends,
To serve as they paced the decks;
They were George and Fred and the son of Ted
And Vincent (he signed the checks);
On the splendid yacht in a climate hot
To tropical seas they ran;
Among those behind they dismissed from mind
Was the well-known Forgotten Man!

In 1972, on the 90th anniversary of Roosevelt's birth, the *New York Times* editorialized: ". . . to anyone under the age of 40, his name is likely to evoke nothing more than the shadow outline of a wartime statesman . . . Roosevelt is in danger of himself becoming America's greatest 'forgotten man.' "

FOR ROOSEVELT BEFORE CHICAGO, *see* **CUFFLINKS GANG.**

FOUNDING FATHERS a group of revolutionaries willing to take their chances on treason to pursue the course of independency—now viewed as sage, stately signers of the documents of U.S. freedom.

Although the phrase has the feel of an early Americanism, it is of twentieth-century origin.

At the instigation of Richard Hanser, television writer and phrase hunter, the Library of Congress researched the subject and came up with the unlikely originator: Warren Gamaliel Harding.

On George Washington's birthday in 1918, then-Senator Harding, told the Sons and Daughters of the American Revolution: "It is good to meet and drink at the fountains of wisdom inherited from the founding fathers of the republic." He repeated it in his campaign for the presidency in 1920 and used the phrase again in his inaugural address: "I must utter my belief in the divine inspiration of the founding fathers."

Without capitalization, the phrase now means the originator of any movement or organization; capitalized, the reference is primarily to the men who gathered at the Constitutional Convention in Philadelphia in 1787.

Richard Whelan used the phrase in a dynastic sense as the title of his biography of Joseph P. Kennedy.

Harding was fond of matching up words with the same beginning letter (see his "not nostrum but normalcy" line-up under ALLITERATION) and Founding Fathers functioned as the fulfillment of his forensic fancy.

FOUR FREEDOMS   objectives of U.S. policy as summarized by President Franklin D. Roosevelt in his message to Congress, January 6, 1941: freedom of speech, of religion, from want, and from fear.

In his State of the Union message, eleven months before the U.S. entered World War II, President Roosevelt suggested the Lend-Lease program to supply Great Britain with war equipment to fight the Axis Powers. He also outlined the "four freedoms":

In the future days, which we seek to make secure, we look forward to a world founded upon four essential human freedoms.

The first is freedom of speech and expression—everywhere in the world. The second is freedom of every person to worship God in his own way—everywhere in the world.

The third is freedom from want—which, translated into world terms, means economic understandings which will secure to every nation a healthy peaceful life for its inhabitants—everywhere in the world.

The fourth is freedom from fear—which, translated into world terms, means a worldwide reduction of armaments to such a point and in such a thorough fashion that no nation will be in a position to commit an act of physical aggression against any neighbor—anywhere in the world.

President Roosevelt, his speech writers, and his personal secretary, Dorothy Brady, were working over the fourth draft of his 1941 State of the Union message when FDR turned to his secretary and asked her to take down an addition. The addition was the passage he must have had in mind since the previous July, when he briefly mentioned the four freedoms in a news conference.

One of the speechwriters who was present at the meeting, Samuel Rosenman, later wrote that only a few words were changed from the way FDR dictated the four-freedoms passage to the final draft as it was delivered.

In his dictation, Mr. Roosevelt added "everywhere in the world" only to the first two freedoms.

Harry Hopkins suggested that "everywhere in the world" covered a lot of territory. He doubted that the American people were interested in "the people in Java."

President Roosevelt answered, "They'll have to be some day. The world is getting so small that even the people in Java are getting to be our neighbors now." In the final draft Mr. Roosevelt added "everywhere in the world" and "anywhere in the world" to the last two freedoms. The four freedoms were later incorporated into the Atlantic Charter.

FOURTH ESTATE the press; now outdated and used ironically. .

Books of quotations usually credit Edmund Burke with coinage, thanks to a citation by historian Thomas Carlyle in *Heroes and Hero-Worship*, written in 1839: "Burke said that there were three estates in Parliament; but, in the Reporters' Gallery yonder, there sat a Fourth Estate more important far than them all." When diligent research failed to turn up the phrase in anything Burke said or wrote, some quotation detectives assumed Carlyle was referring to Lord Macaulay, who said in 1828: "The gallery in which the reporters sit has become a fourth estate of the realm."

"Fourth estate" had been used much earlier in both England and France, usually in reference to "the mob" (the other estates being the king, the clergy and the commons, all powers whose agreement was necessary for legislation). The *OED* suggests that Lord Brougham used it in Commons in 1823 applied to the press, "and at that time it was treated as original."

The vote of this lexicographer for the coiner of the phrase as a definition of the press goes to English essayist William Hazlitt, who wrote on the character of William Cobbett in an 1821 *Table Talk*. Cobbett was a pamphleteer and editor, vituperative and often in trouble for libel both in England and America. Hazlitt wrote of him: "One has no notion of him as making use of a fine pen, but a great mutton-fist; his style stuns his readers . . . He is too much for any single newspaper antagonist; 'lays waste' a

city orator or Member of Parliament, and bears hard upon the government itself. He is a kind of *fourth estate* in the politics of the country."

The phrase was used to put the press on an equal footing with the greatest powers in a nation; in the twentieth century it was taken up by many editors in descriptions of the importance of journalism. The phrase lost its vividness as the other "estates" faded from memory, and now has a musty and stilted connotation. In current use "the press" usually carries with it the aura of "freedom of the press" enshrined in the U.S. Constitution, while press critics usually label it, with a sneer, "the MEDIA."

For a related etymology, see THIRD WORLD.

FOURTH OF JULY SPEECH an emotional speech appealing to the spirit of patriotism; a flag-waver.

A speech made on the Fourth of July is expected to be patriotic; when the term "Fourth of July speech" is used to describe a speech made on any other day, it is derogatory.

The expression dates far back in American history. Ohio Senator Stanley Matthews, on Feb. 13, 1879, asked his fellow senators: "Has the oratory that is peculiar to the Fourth of July come to be a hissing and a byword, a scorn and a reproach . . . is it enough to smother opposition and put down argument, to say that that is merely the sentimentality of a Fourth of July oratory?"

One example of how Fourth of July oratory came to have a bad name can be seen in this excerpt from a speech on July 4, 1827 by Edward Everett, Massachusetts governor, U.S. Secretary of State, and Harvard president (best known for his forgotten speech before Lincoln spoke at Gettysburg): "Let us then, as we assemble on the birthday of the nation, as we gather upon the green turf, once wet with precious blood, let us devote ourselves to the sacred cause of Constitutional Liberty! Let us abjure the interests and passions which divide the great family of American freemen! Let us resolve . . ." etc.

James Russell Lowell, a poet who served as ambassador to England, abjured that approach in his Independence Day speech in London in 1883: "Now the Fourth of July has several times been alluded to, and I believe it is generally thought on that anniversary the spirit of a certain bird known to heraldic ornithologists—and I believe to them alone—as the spread eagle, enters into every American's breast, and compels him, whether he will or no, to pour forth a flood of national self-laudation." Lest his English listeners think him unpatriotic, Lowell added: "I ask you, is there any other people who have confined their national self-laudation to one day in the year?"

Although Americans are traditionally self-conscious about excessive displays of patriotism (see SUPERPATRIOTS), and will deride such excess as "Fourth of July," there are limits to which derision is allowed. When Rufus Choate denounced the "glittering and sounding generalities that make up the Declaration of Independence" in 1856, Ralph Waldo Emerson snapped back with "Glittering generalities! They are blazing ubiquities."

FREEDOM FIGHTER, *see* **CIVIL DISOBEDIENCE; ACTIVIST; TERRORISM.**

FREEDOM NOW slogan of the civil rights movement, stressing impatience of delay in achieving equality in fact after achieving it in law.

"To the Negro demand for 'now,' " wrote Murray Friedman in the *Atlantic Monthly* in 1963, "to which the deep South has replied 'never,' many liberal whites are increasingly responding, 'later.' But the Negro will accept nothing short of first-class citizenship, now."

"Now" became one of the "in" words of the mid-sixties, probably stemming from its use in "Freedom Now," a militant civil rights slogan that preceded Stokely Carmichael's **BLACK POWER.** Its structural sloganeering predecessor was Clarence Streit's pre-World War II call for an international federation, "Union Now." In 1966, there were "now" dresses (miniskirts), "now" dances, and the "Now Generation" (from the "Lost Generation" via the "Beat Generation").

"Freedom," like democracy, justice, and peace, is a Humpty Dumpty word, meaning whatever the user chooses it to mean. In phrases, it was used in "freedom fighters" in Hungary in the early fifties, and **FREEDOM RIDERS** in the U.S. a decade later.

Theodore White wrote in 1965: "Perhaps the most necessary intellectual operation in American life is some redefinition of the word 'freedom.' I have attended as many civil-rights rallies as Goldwater rallies. The dominant word of these two groups, which loathe each other, is 'freedom.' Both demand either Freedom Now or Freedom for All. . . . It is quite possible that these two groups may kill each other in cold blood, both waving banners bearing the same word."

FREEDOM OF THE PRESS, *see* **RIGHT TO KNOW.**

FREEDOM RIDERS groups of Negroes and whites that rode buses through the South in the summer of 1961 testing the segregation of public facilities in interstate bus terminals.

In February 1960, four Negro students attempted to sit and eat at a lunch counter in Greensboro, North Carolina. They were evicted. For the next year, the director of the Congress of Racial Equality (CORE), James Farmer, raised money to hire buses and recruited Negro and white volunteers to ride them through the South to demand the right to sit and eat in a public place or to use facilities which the general public was permitted to use. CORE dubbed the buses "freedom buses," those who rode them "freedom riders." See FREEDOM NOW.

During the summer of 1961, the freedom riders did most of their riding and testing in Alabama. Riders were beaten in Birmingham; a bus was burned in Anniston. Attorney General Robert Kennedy sent more than 600 deputy federal marshals to Alabama. There were only a few minor incidents during the rest of the summer.

"The most nightmarish day of our freedom ride," wrote CORE's James Peck, who took 53 stitches after a beating, "was Sunday, May 14, Mother's Day. I identify the date with Mother's Day because when Police Chief Connor was asked why there was not a single policeman at the Birmingham Trailways terminal to avert mob violence, he explained that since it was Mother's Day, most of the police were off-duty visiting their mothers."

In September 1961, the Interstate Commerce Commission desegregated all facilities in terminals used in interstate bus travel and the Justice Department ordered the desegregation of public transportation. See SEGREGATION.

The phrase became secure enough to be parodied. When a New York State law threatened to invalidate "quickie" Mexican divorces, a stampede of unhappy spouses poured into Juarez, Mexico, before the law took effect. "Most of the New Yorkers flocking here are women," wrote the *Wall Street Journal* in 1967, "and many arrive on American Airlines flight 295 (which they call 'the Freedom Riders Special') . . ."

FREE ENTERPRISE   the practice of capitalism under representative government.

The Republican platform in 1936 charged President Roosevelt with having displaced "free enterprise with regulated monopoly." FDR fired back: "Private enterprise, indeed, became too private. It became privileged enterprise, not free enterprise."

A British economist, Alfred Marshall, wrote in 1890 of tracing "the growth of free enterprise in England." Woodrow Wilson used it in 1913 at the time the Federal Reserve System was being set up to help "resourceful businessmen . . . deal with the new circumstances of free enterprise . . ."

The term, used also as "freedom of enterprise" by Wilson in 1913, has been most popular with those who find the capitalistic system challenged by government regulation. For example, *Newsweek* wrote in 1938: "Management leaders representing the world's democratic countries agreed that free enterprise, not government control, is the key to better times."

Roosevelt felt the need to reaffirm his faith in 1944: "I believe in free enterprise—and always have. I believe in the profit system—and always have."

The term became more popular after 1936, primarily as a euphemism for *laissez-faire* which was no longer

considered politically acceptable. See
AMERICAN SYSTEM; AMERICAN WAY
OF LIFE; BLACK CAPITALISM.

FREE LUNCH   as to which there
is no such thing.

Nobel economics laureate Milton
Friedman has published articles, a
book and lectures using the title
"There Is No Such Thing as a Free
Lunch." His meaning is that everything, even what is seemingly "free,"
must be paid for by somebody in some
way and that there is no sense in hiding that fact.

Reached by letter, Dr. Friedman
replied that had no idea where his
much-quoted phrase comes from:
"I wish I did, but if wishes were
horses . . ." (An allusion to the saying
"If wishes were horses, beggars would
ride," to which novelist Vladimir
Nabokov once replied, "I'd wish for
Pegasus.")

Slanguist Stuart Berg Flexner offered the author this help: "*Free
lunch* dates from the 1840s and was
supposed to have moved from the
West to the East, getting fancier as it
approached eastern bars and hotels,
so sometime after the late 1840s I can
just see some bartender slapping the
hands of a customer and asking him
to buy that 5¢ beer before shoveling in
the victuals—though whether it was
ever used in that literal way or not by
bartenders, I don't know. It sure is a
great conservative line, though."

Thanks to the Friedman popularization, and to the seventies trend toward a fresh acceptance of conservative ideas, the phrase's use has
mushroomed. When a bill favoring
the maritime industry was defeated in
a surprise vote in Congress in 1977,
Common Cause president David
Cohen explained: "The maritime industry has had a free lunch on Capital
Hill before this, because there'd been

no publicity." In November 1977, reporter Fox Butterfield wrote in a *New
York Times Magazine* article about
an improbable welfare state in Mi-
cronesia, especially on the island of
Yap: "Yap is a living refutation that
there is no such thing as a free lunch,"
a U.S. official was quoted as saying.
"Here it's a smörgåsbord."

For a 1964 Goldwater use, see
SANTA CLAUS, NOBODY SHOOTS AT.

FREE RIDE   a campaign undertaken by an officeholder who runs for
a higher office without giving up his
own; if he loses, he continues to serve
in the first office.

Senators, serving six-year terms,
have the best opportunity for "free
rides" running for governor of their
states, or on a national ticket. In the
election of 1960, for example, Senator
John F. Kennedy, whose term did not
expire until 1964, had a free ride; in
1964 Senator Barry Goldwater,
whose term expired that year, did not.
Lyndon Johnson solved the problem
in 1960 by running simultaneously
for both Senator and Vice President.

In 1964 California Democratic
Senator Sheridan Downey was a possible gubernatorial nominee. "Downey would be getting a 'free ride,' "
wrote Leo Katcher, "in that, if he
lost, he would continue as Senator.
Nothing is dearer to a politician's
heart than such a free ride . . ."

In a more general sense, the phrase
means any effort that requires no sacrifice. Robert F. Kennedy, announcing his 1968 challenge to Lyndon
Johnson's renomination, said, "I
can't believe that anybody thinks that
this is a pleasant struggle from now
on, or that I'm asking for a free ride
. . . I'm going into primaries . . . I'm
not asking for a free ride . . ."

FREE SOIL, FREE MEN, FREMONT, *see* **REPUBLICAN.**

FREE WORLD   in the eyes of the Western democracies, any nation not under Communist domination.

The "free world" probably was in use as a phrase during both world wars, to describe the nations not under German or Axis control, but it gained currency in the late nineteen forties and early fifties as realization of the Communist expansion dawned. A 1955 Marcus cartoon was typical: an upstanding-looking gentleman labeled "free world," with his arm in a sling labeled "violation of Yalta agreements," is spurning the blandishments of a bear labeled "Russian honor," with the caption "Once bitten, twice shy."

Dwight Eisenhower used the phrase frequently: "I believe that the situation and actions best calculated to sustain the interests of ourselves and the free world . . ." (memo to John Foster Dulles, 1955).

Its constant use by Western orators made it uniquely an anti-Communist phrase that could not be turned around, as the Communists did with the phrase "people's democracy." This was revealed in Chairman Nikita Khrushchev's preface of the phrase with a SNEER WORD in an address to the 21st Congress of the Communist party, January 27, 1959: "The so-called free world constitutes the kingdom of the dollar . . ."

FRONTLASH, *see* **BACKLASH.**

FRONT-PORCH CAMPAIGN originally, a dignified campaign technique, eminently successful; now, a pompous approach to voters by a lazy candidate.

"McKinley stayed at home," wrote Harry Truman, "and spoke only to such delegations as came to his house from time to time. This was the first of the 'front porch' campaigns. I do not approve of 'front porch' campaigns. I never liked to see any man elected to office who did not go out and meet the people in person and work for their votes."

Although Harry Truman, in his 1948 campaign (see WHISTLESTOPPING) laid to rest for modern campaigners any thoughts of relaxed campaigning at home, his historical analysis is open to debate. There were three front-porch campaigns—Harrison in 1888, McKinley in 1896, and Harding in 1920—and the last two resulted in landslides for the front-porcher. McKinley, especially, had good reason to stay at home and entertain delegations to Canton, Ohio— he was not the stemwinding orator that his opponent, William Jennings Bryan was. It made more political sense to play to his strength, which was a homely, conservative, heartland-of-America stability.

Benjamin Harrison made speeches from his front porch in 1888, narrowly defeating Cleveland, and repeated the technique in 1892, losing to Cleveland. But it was McKinley's campaign that perfected the technique and coined the phrase. The delegations to Canton organized by Mark Hanna's Republican organization included railroad excursion fares, which made such a trip, in the *Cleveland Plain Dealer*'s disgusted opinion, "cheaper than staying at home." Though the candidate said he was "averse to anything like an effort being made to bring the crowds here," the delegations were met at the depot by a gaily uniformed escort of horsemen, conducted to the McKinley home in a noisy parade, and treated to a fine display of rustic Americana; they returned home with excellent word-of-mouth to pass on about the charming gentleman who shook each visitor's hand.

In his next campaign, in 1900, McKinley felt more confident about Bryan's opposition, and agreed to travel more. In 1920, the Harding managers thought it would be safer to keep their man mainly at home and out of the kind of trouble possible in a STUMP campaign.

What makes a front-porch campaign impossible today is that a candidate must never seem remote and inaccessible. But McKinley's accessibility—to those who would take the trouble to travel to see him—added to his appeal. English journalist George Steevens wrote: "If you want to see a Presidential candidate you ring the bell and walk in and see him. That is what he is there for. I rang and walked in; Mr. McKinley was sitting on a rocking-chair not ten feet from the door . . . he is gifted with a kindly courtesy that is plainly genuine and completely winning."

FRONT RUNNER the leading contender for a nomination.

Another racing term describes the front runner: "shows early foot." This means that the horse (or candidate) is capable of getting out of the starting gate well and sets the pace for the others in the field. Occasionally his lead becomes insurmountable, as Barry Goldwater's nomination race showed in 1964, and Jimmy Carter's capture of many convention states and early primaries showed in 1976, but the phrase as used today in politics carries ominous overtones of a likelihood of fading in the homestretch.

FDR, the front runner in 1932, received this letter from Robert W. Wooley about his leadership so early in the campaign: "Herein lies the dan-

ger . . . automatically you become the target of the other candidates, real and potential. There isn't a single favorite son whose delegation won't be held out of the Roosevelt column so long as there is a reasonable chance of getting something for that favorite son, even at your expense."

Ted Sorensen echoed this point about Kennedy a generation later: "There were disadvantages in being the 'front runner.' The Senator's critics became more open and vocal and his every word was politically interpreted."

The front runner must come thundering into the convention increasing his speed and with enough "kick" left for a final spurt. "When the balloting starts," wrote Thomas E. Dewey, "every candidate wants to show enough strength to be one of the leaders on the first ballot. He also wants to have enough strength in reserve so he can gain on the psychologically important second ballot. For example, in 1940, I led on the first three ballots out of six—the wrong three. I lost ground on the second ballot. That was the beginning of the end and everybody knew it." See DEWEY BLITZ.

Despite all the protestations of danger in being the front runner, candidates prefer that position to DARK HORSE because it has a greater chance of victory. However, the racing analogy is not complete. In 1953, a sports page of the *New York Times* pictured a victorious jockey completely splattered with mud. The caption explained that "it is evident McCreary's mount had to come from way back to win—front runners stay clean." Not so in politics.

FRYING THE FAT, *see* **FAT CAT.**

FUDGE FACTORY, *see* **WAFFLE.**

FULL-COURT PRESS an all-out effort.

"Something dramatic was in order," wrote *Time* in October 1977, describing Carter Administration plans for a counterattack on opponents of its energy legislation. "[Vice President Walter] Mondale spoke up and, using a basketball image, urged a 'full-court press' on energy. Carter liked the idea."

"Full-court press" became White House lingo in the late sixties; one of its most frequent users was counsel Charles Colson. In politics, the term has come to mean a strenuous effort to get legislation passed, probably because of its resemblance to "all-out pressure."

In basketball, however, the phrase is used only to describe a defense. When a professional team takes the ball into play from behind its own basket, it has ten seconds to cross mid-court; the defense sometimes employs a "full-court press" to harass and otherwise delay the offense from bringing the ball across. Other "presses" are half-court and (in college ball) zone; in each case, the meaning is to concentrate delaying pressure on the offense (in hockey, this is known as a forecheck).

However, in political usage the defensive image has dribbled away, and only the aggressiveness remains.

See SPORTS METAPHORS.

FULL DINNER PAIL symbol of prosperity, turn-of-the-century equivalent of a cornucopia, or horn of plenty; slogan of the 1900 McKinley campaign.

"Hurrah for a full ballot-box, a full dinner-pail, and continued prosperity!" The *Review of Reviews* in 1900 showed a picture of a large dinner pail featured in a Youngstown, Ohio, parade, with a caption: "Four more Years of the Full Dinner Pail."

William Jennings Bryan, in his second campaign against McKinley, stressed imperialism as the PARAMOUNT ISSUE: "Immediate Freedom for the Philippines" was the Democratic slogan. The Republicans emphasized prosperity, with vice-presidential candidate Theodore Roosevelt doing much of the campaigning, assuring the workingman that Republicanism and high tariffs would continue to keep the dinner pails full.

The dinner pail had long been a symbol in the growing labor movement. Thomas Nast used it in an 1880 *Harper's Weekly* cartoon, and Theodore Roosevelt wrote a friend in 1894: "I hear all around that the working men intend to vote 'for the policy of the full dinner pail' . . ."

In 1928 Herbert Hoover tried to update the phrase, holding the symbol for the "party of prosperity": "The slogan of progress is changing from the full dinner pail to the full garage." (See CHICKEN IN EVERY POT.) Writing about his defeat a year later, Democrat Al Smith described Republican strategy that had "brought down from the garret the old full dinner pail, polished it up and pressed it into service."

Since the Depression, Republicans have stayed away from symbols of prosperity in campaigning, though they have used the word prosperity itself; Democrats have hammered away at the "chicken in every pot"— which Hoover never said—denying Republicans the full dinner pail as a symbol. Since dinner pails are blue-collar rather than white-collar, the symbol may be expected to reappear in a more modern form.

FULL GENERATION OF PEACE the central theme and highest ideal of the Nixon presidency.

President Nixon attributed the phrase to Jawaharlal Nehru. As Vice President in 1953, on his first trip to India, he asked the Indian Prime Minister what was his nation's greatest single need. According to Nixon, Nehru replied, "The greatest need for India, and for any newly independent country is for twenty-five years of peace—a generation of peace."

Six months earlier (on May 11, 1953) soon after the death of Stalin, Winston Churchill had told the House of Commons that a "conference on the highest level" should be convened: "At the worst, the participants in the meeting could have established more intimate contacts, and at best we might have a generation of peace."

At a speech to the Air Force Academy in June 1969, Nixon began contrasting the record of the past generation with his hopes for the next: "In the past generation, since 1941, this Nation has paid for fourteen years of peace with fourteen years of war. In terms of human suffering, this has been the costliest generation in the two centuries of our history. Perhaps this is why my generation is so determined to pass on a different legacy. We want to redeem that sacrifice. We want to be remembered, not as the generation that suffered in war, but as the generation that was tempered in its fire for a great purpose: to make the kind of peace that the next generation will be able to keep."

On his arrival in India on July 31, 1969, Nixon referred to the Nehru observation, and made it his own theme: "It is essential, absolutely essential, that we have a generation of peace for Asia and the world."

By using the phrase again in his speech to the 25th anniversary of the United Nations, and repeating it in the 1971 State of the Union message, the President made it plain that he had found his central theme.

There was one thing odd about the concept, however; "only" one full generation of peace was a limited ideal, retaining the possibility of war in a later generation—considerably short of the idea of "permanent peace," or in Lincoln's phrase a JUST AND LASTING PEACE. This writer and others pointed out the need for an explanation of the limited nature of the goal, and the President addressed the subject in an appropriate forum, the dedication of the Woodrow Wilson International Center for Scholars in Washington, D.C., on February 18, 1971:

> Every war-time President since Woodrow Wilson has been tempted to describe the current war as "the WAR TO END WARS." But they have not done so because of the derision that the phrase evoked, a reminder of lost dreams, of lights that failed, of hopes that were raised and dashed.
>
> What I am striving for above all else, what this nation is striving for in all that we do is something America has never experienced in this century, a full generation of peace. . . . That is why I have set our sights on a span of time that men in positions of power today can cope with, just one generation, but one long step on the path away from perennial war.

FUN CITY   a sardonic reference to New York City.

Woody Klein, who was Mayor John Lindsay's first press secretary, wrote the author:

> As for the origin of "Fun City," I believe that the Mayor himself originated this term early in 1966, or possibly in late 1965 when he participated in an advertisement for an airline and he was asked about New

York. His reply contained the phrase "Fun City." It was Dick Schaap, columnist for the *World Journal Tribune*, who publicized the term with his regular columns entitled "What's new in Fun City."

Columnist Schaap turned the mayor's innocent remark into his regular lead for stories on pollution, traffic congestion, and everything wrong with a metropolis.

The adjectival use of the mass noun "fun" has been noted in Webster's *Third International* which cites "a fun hat" and "have a fun time." Linguists have been observing its use as an adjective like astronomers watching the sky, certain that a new star has to appear in a given spot.

Dwight Bolinger of Harvard explained in *American Speech* Magazine: "There was a hole in the semantic pattern. Other nouns of emotion have their corresponding adjectives meaning 'productive of': joy: joyful, joyous; fear: fearful; excitement: exciting. The noun fun had the disadvantage of seeing its adjective *funny* put to the irrelevant uses of 'laughable' and 'odd.' " Since *funny* did not mean "filled with fun," the noun *fun* had to double in brass as an adjective, the way the word "good" does.

University of Florida professor John Algeo explained: "Since the substantive fun is a mass noun, it often occurs in the predicate position without a determiner. In this position the word looks like an adjective, and thus analogy operates: 'That thing is good': 'That thing is fun': 'That is a good thing': 'That is a fun thing.' " Professor Algeo added solemnly: "The future development of adjectival *fun* needs watching . . . we may even anticipate being told that one car is funner than another, and that will be the funnest thing of all."

President Lyndon Johnson, in 1967, used a similar-sounding expression—"Fat City"—which was part of a hippie lexicon compiled by his daughter Lynda Bird. "I have kept my cool," said the President. "I haven't bugged out. I am still in Fat City." To bewildered reporters, the White House press office issued a definition: "Fat City: A state of mind characterized by mild to extreme euphoria, usually induced by a combination of salubrious climate and fortunate personal circumstances." Hip *Time* magazine commented: "The President might have cooled it with the phrase had he known that, to some hippies, Fat City is a synonym for Squaresville."

After the first edition of *The New Language of Politics* appeared, the author received this clarifying note from Ben J. Wattenberg, a Johnson speechwriter at the time of the episode:

Lynda indeed did compile a hippie lexicon for *McCall's*, but that is not where the President got the phrase. As I recall it, we were sitting in my office writing a humorous introduction for the President's speech to the White House Fellows or the Presidential Scholars and were toying around with the idea of the President using some hippie language. Ervin Duggan and I were working on the speech, but it was Carol Weida, my beautiful research assistant, who suggested the phrase "fat city," which she says she heard at Berkeley where her then-fiancé was studying. The day after the speech I was at the press briefing when a wild rumor circulated among the press that "fat city" was really an obscene phrase. At which point I lost my cool, I bugged out, and I felt that I could easily leave "fat city" in a state of disgrace. As it turned out, as you reported, the official definition came up tame, and we all survived.

FUSION coalition before election; a combination of minority parties to defeat the majority party.

Coalition is used to describe the alliance of different political groups who combine to form a government after an election, and therefore is mainly a word to describe non-American politics. *Fusion,* on the other hand, is a welding of interests before an election in the U.S. and particularly in big cities.

As a young novelist, Benjamin Disraeli described the usage in the 1840s in England: "Political conciliation became the slang of the day, and the fusion of the parties the babble of the clubs."

Edward Costikyan, the new-breed Tammany leader in 1964 who managed the 1977 Ed Koch campaign for mayor of New York, offered this definition: " 'Reformer' was a term of opprobrium within the machine, and reformers looked . . . to the occasional creation of an *ad hoc* political force which would sporadically 'throw the rascals out' and enjoy four years or so of steadily deteriorating governmental power, until the machine returned to power. In New York, this tradition became known as 'fusion.' "

New York fusion succeeded four times: in 1901, when Seth Low became a one-term mayor; in 1913, when John Purroy Mitchel became a one-term mayor; in 1933, Fiorello La Guardia for three terms; in 1965, John Lindsay. Lindsay was fond of quoting La Guardia's appeal to non-partisanship when speaking to voters registered Democratic: "There is no Republican way or Democratic way to clean the streets."

Bronx boss Ed Flynn expressed the feeling of the Democratic organization politician in New York for the two groups that caused him the most trouble: ". . . the 'other party,' which in New York is the Republican party; and the motley mob of political hacks that cluster periodically about benign old jurists and smart young boy gang-busters who raise the flag of 'Fusion.' "

FUTURE AND IT WORKS, *see* **WAVE OF THE FUTURE.**

FUZZINESS, *see* **ALL THINGS TO ALL MEN.**

GAFFE, *see* **BLOOPER.**

GAG RULE a parliamentary device or resolution to limit debate.

Both in England and America, sedition acts at the end of the eighteenth century were labeled "gags" by critics. The most famous American example of "gag rule" was a resolution passed by the House of Representatives in 1836 to cut off debate on the subject of abolishing or curtailing the institution of slavery.

In 1833 the American Anti-Slavery Society was founded. The House of Representatives was deluged by thousands of antislavery petitions and proposed measures, particularly bills demanding the abolition of slavery in the District of Columbia.

The answer of the slaveholding interests, operating within the Democratic party, was the "gag rule." The measure was actually proposed by a Northerner, Mr. C. G. Atherton of New Hampshire; and Northerners within the Democratic ranks supported it. It tabled any measures dealing with the subject.

Former President John Quincy Adams, who had entered the House as a representative after his term as Chief Executive, opposed it at the beginning of every session of Congress, writing later: ". . . then came Atherton of New Hampshire, the man of the mongrel gag."

In 1844 the "gag" was finally defeated, but not before it had become a national issue publicizing the antislavery forces. Adams was anathematized by some; however, John F. Kennedy in his *Profiles in Courage* refers to the Adams fight against the measure as "the brightest chapter of his history."

Action to limit debate by the device of cloture in Britain's House of Commons is usually referred to by the minority as "using the gag." The usual reaction of any parliamentary minority, faced with an attempt by the majority to limit debate, is to complain that they are being subjected to a "gag rule." See MUZZLE.

Rule is a word that harkens back to the American distaste of monarchy, and is almost invariably used pejoratively in politics. In addition to *gag rule,* there is *mob rule,* which usually means anarchy following a breakdown of law and order but occasionally is used in regard to organized racketeering; *boss rule,* the object of reformers' scorn; *rule-or-ruin,* from English poet John Dryden's "resolved to ruin or to rule the state," used in the U.S. in 1836 against the Whigs and now a condemnation of sore losers and bolters in primaries or conventions; *one-man rule,* first used against "King Andrew" Jackson, and *one-party rule,* the *bête noire* of the advocates of a TWO-PARTY SYSTEM. In Great Britain the sovereign *reigns but does not rule;* a positive use of the word is in *majority rule,* but even that came under attack with de Tocqueville's "tyranny of the majority"; about the only rules held sacred are the Golden Rule, the RULE OF LAW, and HOME RULE.

GAME PLAN   strategy; a plan with the ultimate goal permeating all tactics.

Paul McCracken, chairman of the Council of Economic Advisers, told the American Statistical Association on August 21, 1969: "There is one thing that perhaps the Council Chairman can do. That is to outline for you the Washington game plan for economic policy."

The game plan was to use both monetary and fiscal policy to restrain inflation; then, even before the results of that policy of tightening became fully apparent, to restimulate the economy and thereby avert a recession. The ultimate goal was a new steadiness of prosperity, not controlled by government, that would produce full employment and a stable dollar.

That was the plan; despite setbacks like more unemployment than the Administration expected and too slow a slowing of inflation, that remained the game plan. Halfway through the four-year term, the Nixon economists pointed out that inflation was indeed being curbed, that the mildest recession after a major inflation was already over, and a strong surge of the Gross National Product could be expected. Critics blamed the Administration for not using various forms of controls, for causing unemployment to rise to the average level of the Kennedy years, and for not slowing inflation soon enough; the central metaphor for their derision was the "game plan."

McCracken had used a phrase that was current in Administration circles because the President used it often in private conversation with his aides, usually as a verb: "We have to game-plan this." This was natural enough, as he was both an avid football fan and a believer in the GRAND DESIGN.

The expression proceeded to become hackneyed with overuse. Every suggestion had to be "game-planned" and those who suggested the term be banned were told sympathetically to submit a game plan on how this was to be done. When this writer used the phrase in a draft of an economic speech, the President struck it out— enough was enough.

Alan Otten wrote in the *Wall Street Journal* on December 23, 1970: "Government also tends to become infatuated with a phrase, and then abuse or misuse it. Thus officials in both foreign and economic policy areas have too eagerly embraced the 'game plan' image of the sports world. They now constantly project their 'economic game plan' or 'Vietnam game plan,' even though the phrase carries overtones of fun and frivolity that don't quite suit the serious business of ending the war in Southeast Asia or restoring economic vigor at home."

In professional football, a detailed game plan is drawn up by the head coach for both the offensive and defensive units to exploit the weaknesses of the opposition. The quarterback is told what to do under a variety of circumstances before the game begins: first down and ten yards to go deep in his own territory, third and short yardage at midfield, etc. "Part of the game plan deals with reactions to varying defenses," Edward Bennett Williams, one of the owners of the Washington Redskins, informs the author. "A game plan is quite detailed, even computerized. Of course, when you get behind, you sometimes have to scrub the game plan."

Thus, in football, the phrase has a more detailed, tactical connotation than in politics, where the meaning is more strategic. But in politics, too, when you get behind, you often scrub the game plan.

At a meeting in Camp David on Friday, August 13, 1971, the game plan was interred and the New Economic Policy—including wage and price controls—was born.

GANG OF FOUR, *see* **CHINA WATCHERS.**

GAP a phrasemaking word, much overused, to illustrate shortage, lack, insufficiency, a falling short, or a gulf between.

The original gap was the MISSILE GAP, a Democratic charge in 1959 and 1960; educators have used "reading gap," businessmen "experience gap," and many have used CREDIBILITY GAP against Lyndon Johnson, who talked of "bridging the gap between East and West" in his 1964 State of the Union message. See GENERATION GAP.

Russell Baker, the "Observer" of the *New York Times,* needled the gapsters in a 1967 column, calling attention to

the so-called gap gap, one of the most pressing problems confronting the Government today. Several of Washington's most important Cabinet officials illustrate the enormous range of gaps that have already been dealt with in intensive, two-year studies conducted by the nation's leading universities, and make a convincing argument that if the present rate of two-year studies is maintained the country will be out of gaps to keep its blue-ribbon committees employed by the end of 1969. The inescapable sociologist, Sean Moyni-

han, controversial as always, proposes solving the problem by lengthening all two-year gap studies to four years.

GARDEN-HOSE ANALOGY FDR's homely parable to explain Lend-Lease to the American people.

Late in 1940, Prime Minister Churchill wrote a 4,000-word letter to President Roosevelt reviewing Britain's military and financial position, and hoping that the U.S. would not "confine the help which they have so generously promised only to such munitions of war and accommodations as could be immediately paid for." At a press conference in Washington on December 17, 1940, Roosevelt pointed out that the more supplies Britain took—paid or not—the more quickly our own productive capacity would grow, and the war materials were more useful "if they were used in Great Britain, than if they were kept in storage here."

He went on extemporaneously telling a kind of parable:

Suppose my neighbor's home catches fire, and I have a length of garden hose four or five hundred feet away. If he can take my garden hose and connect it up with his hydrant, I may help him to put out his fire. Now, what do I do? I don't say to him before the operation, "Neighbor, my garden hose cost me $15; you have to pay me $15 for it." What is the transaction that goes on? I don't want $15—I want my garden hose back after the fire is over.

After the fire is put out, he puts the garden hose back, and if it is damaged beyond repair in putting out the fire, he (my neighbor) says, "All right, I will replace it."

Now, if I get a nice garden hose back, I am in pretty good shape.

The plain words about lending a garden hose to a neighbor to put out a fire—which, incidentally, might well spread to your own home—and later getting the garden hose back, or a duplicate, was Lend-Lease in its simplest terms. As complex a scheme as Lend-Lease turned out to be, it could not have been more simply or effectively placed before the American people.

Of course, the hose was never returned, nor did FDR ever expect it would be.

GARRISON STATE, *see* **WELFARE STATE.**

-GATE CONSTRUCTION a device to provide a sinister label to a possible scandal.

After WATERGATE, a scandal in France dealing with the adulteration of Bordeaux wines was promptly dubbed "Winegate." This led to the adoption of the -gate suffix as a scandalizer in other fields.

When it became known in 1976 that an investigation had been launched into corruption of members of Congress by the South Korean CIA, this writer started referring automatically to "Koreagate."

Similarly, when President Carter's Director of Management and Budget, Bert Lance, was charged with taking a SWEETHEART LOAN it was natural to label it "Lancegate"; and when mayoral candidate Mario Cuomo attacked New York Mayor Abe Beame for seeking to suppress an SEC report on the finances of the "Big Apple"— New York City—he called it "Applegate." More aptly, charges leveled at Congressman Daniel Flood in 1978 were called "Floodgate." The construction is too useful to fade quickly.

GENERATION GAP a frustrating lack of communication between young and old; or, a useful stretch of time that separates cultures within a society, allowing them to develop their own character.

Generation gap was not sired by *missile gap* out of *credibility gap,* though gapsmanship in general reinforced all three. The originator was Sir Winston Churchill, who wrote in *My Early Life* (1930):

"Come on now, all you young men, all over the world. You are needed more than ever now to fill the gap of a generation shorn by the war . . ." He went on to write:

"Don't take no for an answer, never submit to failure. Do not be fobbed off by mere personal success or acceptance. You will make all kinds of mistakes; but as long as you are generous and true, and also fierce, you cannot hurt the world or even seriously distress her. She was made to be wooed and won by youth."

GENOCIDE, *see* **HOLOCAUST; FINAL SOLUTION.**

GEOPOLITICS, *see* **HEARTLAND; LEBENSRAUM.**

GERRYMANDER drawing of political lines by the party in power so as to perpetuate its power; designing a district to fit a voting pattern.

This is one of the most triumphant political expressions, traceable to the early days of the Republic and still in current use.

Charles Ledyard Norton selected a picture of a gerrymander for the cover of his 1890 book, *Political Americanisms,* and detailed the derivation:

> The term is derived from the name of Governor [Elbridge] Gerry, of Massachusetts, who, in 1811, signed a bill readjusting the representative districts so as to favor the Democrats and weaken the Federalists, although the last named party

polled nearly two-thirds of the votes cast. A fancied resemblance of a map of the districts thus treated led [Gilbert] Stuart, the painter, to add a few lines with his pencil, and say to Mr. [Benjamin] Russell, editor of the Boston *Centinel,* "That will do for a salamander." Russell glanced at it: "Salamander?" said he, "Call it a Gerrymander!" The epithet took at once and became a Federalist war-cry, the map caricature being published as a campaign document.

Gerry's name was pronounced with a hard *g;* but because of the similarity of the word with "jerry-built" (meaning rickety, no connection with gerrymander) the letter *g* is pronounced as *j.*

Governor Gerry, a signer of the Declaration of Independence and later one of James Madison's Vice Presidents, has become—thanks to linguistics—one of the villains of American history. Actually, he never sponsored the redistricting bill and is said to have signed it reluctantly. But his name has been perpetuated in denunciations like this: "See where the hateful serpent of the gerrymander has wound his sinuous course," said an Indiana congressman in 1893. "See where in his glittering folds he has strangled the life out of the spirit of liberty."

The construction, with the governor's name up front, can be made more current. Critics of New York State's reapportionment in 1961 called it "Rockymandering" after Nelson Rockefeller.

Gerrymandering has created some odd-looking districts, such as the "Monkey-Wrench" district of Iowa, the "Dumb-bell" district of Pennsylvania, the "Horseshoe" district of New York, and the "Shoestring" district of Mississippi. For a modern use of the ancient technique, see ONE MAN, ONE VOTE. For other examples of eponymy, see MAVERICK; SOLON; PHILIPPIC; and QUISLING.

GETTYSBURG ADDRESS the Sermon on the Mount of politics, often quoted, seldom understood.

To most Americans, Lincoln's Gettysburg address is a string of revered catch phrases, beginning with "four-score and seven years ago" (a solemn way of saying eighty-seven) and ending with the familiar "of the people, by the people and for the people." See IDEAS. Some who memorized it in grammar school will also recall "the last full measure of devotion" and "that these dead shall not have died in vain." The back-of-the-envelope legend is recalled, along with a satisfying memory that the main speaker's address has been forgotten while the President's modest remarks are immortal.

The Gettysburg address is a poem based on the theme of national resurrection. Its opening sentence contains four images of birth—of a nation *"conceived* in liberty"—*"brought forth"* (born) by "our *fathers"* with all men *"created* equal." The speech then uses the forum of a national cemetery and the images of death ("final resting place," "brave men, living and dead") to symbolize purification and resurrection—that out of this scene of death, "this nation, under God, shall have a *new birth* of freedom."

Rather than addressing himself at length to the dead men in that cemetery, Lincoln used the occasion to recount the conception, birth, death, and rebirth of the nation. But the metaphor, central to Christianity, is never labored.

In his 266 words, Lincoln used the word "dedicate" five times. The first and second times refer to the nation's dedication to an ideal—"that all men are created equal." The third use refers to the specific purpose of the occasion, honoring the dead men buried at Gettysburg—"to dedicate a portion of that field as a final resting place." The fourth and fifth times refer to the ideals—"to the unfinished work" and "to the great tasks remaining before us."

The structure of this speech can be based on these uses of "dedicate"—a strong dedication to ideals first, then a passing dedication of ground for the dead, and finally a ringing rededication to the ideals.

The speech is so deceptively simple that it spawned the "jotted-on-the-back-of-an-envelope" legend. Most speechwriters feel that it was far too carefully constructed to have been written so casually.

For a parody, see EISENHOWER SYNTAX.

GHOSTWRITER one who writes another's speeches, articles, and planned "ad libs."

Seven categories of ghost (or "spook") haunt the political scene:

1. *Speechwriter,* a ghost who operates out in the open. Only a President, who the public has come to recognize is too busy to prepare all his own messages, can afford to permit it to become known who writes his speeches (see SPEECHWRITER).

2. *Ghostwriter,* or *ghost,* one who surreptitiously prepares written and oral messages for public figures below the highest levels.

3. *Phrasemaker,* one who improves upon speeches already drafted, who "punches up" or adds impact to remarks that contain no quotable passages.

4. *Wordsmith,* in current usage a hack ghostwriter, with the ability to transcribe thoughts into speakable English but with no ideas of his own.

5. *Sloganeer,* which can be a

pejorative word for phrasemaker, or an advertising copywriter whose assignment is to create slogans and define issues in a short headline.

6. *Research assistant,* who can be one ferreting out the facts on which to base a speech or with which a general speech can be made more specific; or a ghost or wordsmith on the public payroll whose euphemistic title conceals his public-relations or writing activities.

7. *Press aide,* or *press secretary,* (called *press agent* or *flack* by the press) also writes material for his employer, though the higher the public office becomes, the less likely the press aide is to handle the speechwriting function.

Campaigning in support of Republican congressional candidates in 1970, Vice President Spiro Agnew suggested that network news commentators be quizzed on the air by elected officials, to reveal their biases. Eric Sevareid of CBS fired back: "Unlike the Vice President, we don't possess a stable of ghost writers. Come to think of it, if there are mysteries around, unseen spirits motivating the public dialogue, maybe that's the place that could use the glare of public scrutiny—that stable of anonymity."

GIVEAWAY attack word against those who propose private development of natural resources, made by those who feel that public development would be more in the public interest.

If there is any counter to the conservative's charge of CREEPING SOCIALISM, it is the liberal's charge of "giveaway." The word became popular in the controversy in 1953–55 over who should provide power to the city of Memphis, Tenn.: the public Tennessee Valley Authority (proudest product of the New Deal), or a combine of private companies called "Dixon-Yates" after the names of the two company presidents.

Democrats charged that the Dixon-Yates proposal would "give away" some $5 million in profits annually to private enterprise, which could be "saved" if the TVA did the job. "Giveaway," "SELLOUT," and "steal" were the words most often used in the attack. Eisenhower in 1954 attempted to explain his position: "The issue is not . . . public power versus unregulated private power. The issue posed to us is federal monopoly of power, as against public or regulated power, freely chosen in each instance by the citizens of each area, with the federal government coming in as a cooperating partner where this seems necessary or desirable."

However, after a contract had been signed with Dixon-Yates, it was revealed that a consultant to the Bureau of the Budget was also an official of the banking firm that was to finance the deal, and the City of Memphis decided to build its own power plant.

Democrats felt they had a good campaign issue against the Eisenhower policy on power and conservation, but it became confused when the "natural gas lobby" overstepped the bounds of propriety in fighting for their bill in 1956. While agreeing with the purpose of the natural gas bill, Eisenhower vetoed it because of the nature of the lobbying, which left Majority Leader Lyndon Johnson, who supported the bill, holding the bag. After that, "giveaway" lost its bite, and Dixon-Yates gave way to new issues.

Some conservatives finally found use for the word in 1977: they charged that the Panama Canal treaty was a "giveaway" of U.S. sovereignty.

GIVE 'EM HELL, HARRY a Truman battle cry in 1948, now used to characterize a slugging campaign.

Enthusiasm for Harry Truman's candidacy was lacking among Democrats early in the 1948 campaign; signs at the convention read: "I'm just mild about Harry."

On September 17, as he began barnstorming the country (see WHISTLESTOPPING), Truman recalls he told his running mate, Alben Barkley: "I'm going to fight hard. I'm going to give them hell." As he ripped into the "gluttons of privilege" (see VESTED INTERESTS) and the DO-NOTHING CONGRESS, the crowds responded to the scrappiness of the underdog with welcome interruptions of "Give 'em hell, Harry!"

"I never give them hell," Truman smiled as he reviewed his technique in 1956. "I just tell the truth, and they think it is hell."

The phrase became closely identified with the former president in an affectionate way. When Oxford University presented him with an honorary degree in 1956 ("to Harricum Truman, Doctors in Iure Civili") the student cheer was "Harricum! Harricum! Give 'em hell, Harricum!"

The current generic use of the phrase is illustrated by this passage from Sherman Adams' memoirs: "[Len] Hall and I realized that it was futile to expect Eisenhower as the head of the party to make a 'give 'em hell' tour of the countryside . . ."

One slogan suggested to John V. Lindsay in 1972 to give him a fighting, Democratic image was "Give 'em hell with JVL." It did not help.

GLITCH a mechanical or electronic failure that afflicts campaigns and can rattle campaigners.

A monkey wrench that finds its way into a "well-oiled political machine"; the piercing sound of feedback when a speaker reaches a climactic moment in a speech; the loss of baggage on a campaign tour—all these come under the heading of "glitches," a term with electronic-error connotations.

A glitch, the mischief of a computerized gremlin, fills a linguistic need for an annoying and usually inexplicable failure of normal operations which results in a candidate's toe-stubbing or diplomatic gaffe. On Jimmy Carter's first trip abroad as President in December of 1977, he was unexpectedly troubled by a State Department interpreter's mistranslation of his "desire" to be in Poland as "lust" for Poles, and of his "leaving" the U.S. as "abandoning" the U.S. This was followed in India by the world wide coverage of Mr. Carter's whispered, private suggestion to Secretary of State Cyrus Vance that he send a "cold, very blunt" letter to the Indian Prime Minister upon their return to the U.S.; unknown to the President, a microphone was open nearby during a "photo opportunity," and the presidential whisper required fast backtracking by the press secretary, Joseph L. Powell.

"That private talk with Vance," wrote Vernon A. Guidry Jr. of the *Washington Star* on January 2, 1978, "is now likely to become a source of embarrassment to Carter. It became public through another one of the glitches that have plagued the President's foreign tour . . ." A *Star* copy editor, unfamiliar with "glitches," changed the word in the second edition to "snafus."

The word probably originated in the German and Yiddish *glitschen,* meaning "slip." According to the *Polyglot's Lexicon,* it entered the language in 1966, as a false signal, mishap or malfunction in spacecraft.

For a locomotive glitch, see the "idiot engineer" who undid candidate Thomas E. Dewey, under **BLOOPER.**

GLOBALONEY, *see* **BALONEY.**

GLOOM AND DOOM, PROPHETS OF the dismissal by the "Ins" of the viewing-with-alarm of the "Outs."

"My theory has always been," wrote Thomas Jefferson, "that if we are to dream, the flatteries of hope are as cheap, and pleasanter than the gloom of despair." Not so to a group of political pundits, or to almost any candidate running for another man's seat. The man seeking to oust the incumbent must convince voters that all is not rosy, that we are indeed in grave danger of a variety of catastrophies that could only be averted by a change of administration or representation.

Incumbent Democrats described Republicans in the campaign of 1936 as "disciples of despair" floundering in a "fountain of fear"; during the Eisenhower years, Republican Clare Boothe Luce denounced Democrats as "troubadors of trouble and crooners of catastrophe." Most common, however, is prophets of, or peddlers of, "gloom and doom."

One of the leading prophets, consistent through changes in Administrations, has been columnist Joseph Alsop. After World War II ended, Alsop predicted to Harvard's Signet Club that the cause of Western man was lost; he urged free men today to emulate the brave action of the Spartans at Thermopylae, to "comb their golden hair in the sunlight and prepare to die bravely."

The *Miami News* in 1967 wrote about the *Miami Herald:* "A gloom-and-doom piece in a Sunday newspaper here is rather typical of the nitpicking . . ." See NATTERING NABOBS OF NEGATIVISM.

GLUTTONS OF PRIVILEGE, *see* VESTED INTERESTS.

GNOMES OF ZURICH international bankers.

This phrase, coming into increasing usage in foreign economic policy coverage, was popularized by British Foreign Secretary George Brown in 1964. It paints a picture of busy elves in the Swiss financial capital, and was aimed at derogating the speculators who by questioning Great Britain's credit standing forced unpopular austerity measures on the government. Brown felt the "gnomes of Zurich" were out to make a killing at the expense of the pound sterling.

Reporter Paul Hoffman points out: "The term is a misnomer, since George Brown was actually referring to the Bank for International Settlements, which is in Basel."

The word "gnome" was coined by Philippus Aureolus Paracelsus, a sixteenth-century Swiss alchemist and physician, while investigating the mechanics of mining and the diseases of miners; the word is from the Greek *ge-nomos,* earth dweller, and originally meant a misshapen being who guarded the mines and quarries of the inner earth, able to move through earth as a fish moves through water.

The mining derivation of gnome made Brown's phrase especially apt: in Zurich, the gnomes deal in gold, a metal that was the quest of the alchemists.

Unlike MALEFACTORS OF GREAT WEALTH and ECONOMIC ROYALISTS, *gnomes of Zurich* has a manipulative rather than a predatory connotation. By 1968, the phrase had gained the top rank of bogeymen, as in this use in the *Wall Street Journal:* "Frankly, we had enough to worry about with the MILITARY-INDUSTRIAL COMPLEX, the Establishment, the gnomes of Zurich, the illuminati and the POWER ELITE. Now the arbiters of instant demonology have added the jet set."

George J. W. Goodman, using the pseudonym "Adam Smith" in *The Money Game* in 1968, called one character the Gnome of Zurich. His pessimistic credo: since men cannot long manage their affairs rationally, politicians make costly promises, trade surpluses evaporate, gold reserves trickle away, and a "dollar crisis" periodically results.

GO ALONG, *see* HOLD STILL . . . GO ALONG.

GOALS, *see* QUOTAS.

GOBBLEDYGOOK the stilted circumlocution of official directive, sometimes intended to be hard to comprehend but usually the result of a lazy lapse into legalese. Synonyms are OFFICIALESE, "federalese", PENTAGONESE, and BAFFLEGAB.

The coiner of this classic Americanism was Texas Congressman Maury Maverick, whose grandfather Samuel lent his name to the word for "rambuctious loner" (see MAVERICK).

"People ask me where I got gobbledygook." Representative Maverick wrote in the *New York Times Magazine* on May 21, 1944. "I do not know. It must have come in a vision. Perhaps I was thinking of the old bearded turkey gobbler back in Texas, who was always gobbledy gobbling and strutting with ludicrous pomposity. At the end of this gobble there was a sort of gook."

The congressman defined the term as "talk or writing which is long, pompous, vague, involved, usually with Latinized words. It is also talk or writing which is merely long, even though the words are fairly simple, with repetition over and over again [sic], all of which could have been said in a few words."

He gave an example, taken from a meeting he had recently attended. The congressman quoted the chairman: "We* * *" (long talk with no relation to the subject)* * * "face profound changes in our economic system." (He didn't explain the profundities, or what to do about them.) These, he said, "* * *inevitably spring from a broad frame of related and unrelated factors." Then: "Optimum production* * * maladjustments, coextensive with problem areas* * * alternative, but nevertheless meaningful minimae* * * must be correlation * * * conservation of human and natural resources* * * utilization of factors which in a dynamic democracy can be channelized into both quantitative and qualitative phases."

Maverick wrote: "My next-chair neighbor was squirming and getting red in the face. He had come a long way across America to attend this 'ad hoc'—whatever that is—meeting. 'That fellow,' he whispered angrily, 'must be a Communist.' "

In his seminal article, Maverick quoted Lewis Carroll's Alice in Wonderland: " 'Speak English,' said the Eaglet. 'I don't know the meaning of half these long words, and, what's more, I don't believe you do, either.' " And the Congressman found a text from the Bible: ". . . except ye utter by the tongue words easy to be understood, how shall it be known what is spoken? for ye shall speak into the air."

He discovered metaphoric arrogance in one cant phrase: "The Gobbledygookers are forever talking about 'levels' of government, as though the Federal Government, for which they work, is in the High Place." And he called for "a new language development in America which will rescue our present language from the curse of confusion. We must stop dragging in the corpses of dead languages. A man's language is a very important part of his conduct. He should be held morally responsible for his words just as he is accountable for his other acts."

Maverick must have been using the word in late 1943; it appeared in American Notes and Queries in April 1943 as "Maury Maverick's name for the long high-sounding words of Washington's red-tape language," and in Time on April 10, 1944: "Maury Maverick . . . railed against what he called Washington's 'gobbledygook' language."

Eric Partridge, in his introduction to the 1952 Chamber of Horrors, speculated on what might have been going through Mr. Maverick's mind: "When a term is so devastatingly apposite as gobbledegook, it walks unquestioned into the vocabulary, as quisling had done four years earlier in Britain. The allusion is to the gobbling noise made by a turkey cock; probably the word was an unconscious yet none the less inspired adaptation of 'gobble of the turkey cock,' the becoming de in imitation of stage foreigners' pronunciation, and cock becoming gook by assimilation to the g of gobble, and gock becoming gook perhaps under the influence of goon."

In 1975 the Washington Star began a series called "Gobbledygook" regularly exposing to ridicule some blatant examples of federal prose. With the word thus regularly featured, President Carter—like King Edward VIII making official the word "radio" (rather than "wireless") in his Churchill-written abdication—enshrined it in the language in 1978 as part of his first State of the Union address: "We have made a good start on turning the gobbledygook of federal regulations into plain English that people can understand, but we still have a long way to go."

GO-FER, *see* **GOPHER.**

GO FIGHT CITY HALL   an expression of helplessness in the face of bureaucracy; a shrugging acceptance of the insuperable difficulties of organized society.

The expression, which probably originated in New York City, is not to be taken literally and assumed to be a call to action. On the contrary, it means that you *cannot* fight City Hall. The speaker is really saying, "Don't bother me with your problem, take it up with the powers that be in government—and you won't get anywhere with them, either." The expression implies the same futility as "tilting at windmills," a reference to the foolish gallantry of Don Quixote.

In 1967, when Senator Albert Gore (D-Tenn.) was able to get enough votes to attach a rider calling for repeal of a campaign fund measure favored by Majority Whip Russell Long (D-La.), a Gore aide was quoted as saying happily, "You don't beat City Hall too often."

A *Wall Street Journal* headline illustrates the range of government "City Hall" refers to: "Fighting City Hall: Public Employees Turn Militant, Go On Strike to Back Wage Demands/New Jersey Teachers Force a Town to Curtail Classes; Firemen Stage a Slowdown."

When the phrase is used to mean the real city hall, it is a joke, as in this 1967 *Newsweek* usage about New York City's crackdown on diplomatic parking abuses: "For the smouldering diplomats, the encounter was a new lesson in international relations. Around the U.N., the word was being passed that you can say what you like about the United States, but you can't fight City Hall."

A frustrated characterization of organized society began with *City Hall,* and progressed to *Establishment, power structure,* and *System.*

GO FISHING, *see* **FISHING EXPEDITION.**

GO-IT-ALONE   to stand by oneself as a person or a nation.

American politicians have been either proud of themselves or critical of others for "going-it-alone" since about 1850, when card players began using the phrase to describe one who wanted to play the game of euchre single-handed. In the card game of four-handed euchre (not three-handed, or "cutthroat" euchre), a player's point total is doubled if he takes in his tricks by rejecting the help of a partner and "goes it alone."

In 1874 Senator G. F. Edmunds of Vermont said, "Our forefathers [did not act] upon the idea that a member of Congress was to take his carpet-bag and go it alone [in Washington]."

Early in 1953, Ohio Republican Senator Robert A. Taft suggested that "the U.S. might as well forget the United Nations as far as the Korean war is concerned. I believe we might as well abandon any idea of working with the United Nations in the East and reserve to ourselves a completely free hand." President Eisenhower didn't like Taft's idea and said so at a news conference on May 28, 1953: "If you are going to go it alone in one place, you have to go it alone everywhere." Taft later denied that he was advocating a policy of "go-it-alone."

Senator Charles Mathias (R-Md.) used the synonym for isolationism in 1978, with an ironic twist: "No matter how ready the rest of us are for a bipartisan foreign policy, we cannot go it alone. The President must provide the leadership."

See CARD METAPHORS; ISOLATIONISM.

GOOD FIGHT, see FIGHT THE GOOD FIGHT.

GOOD GUYS, see MR. NICE GUY; WHITE HATS.

GOOD OLE BOY, see REDNECK.

GOOD NEIGHBOR POLICY
Franklin Roosevelt's program for relations with Latin American nations.

FDR set forth the phrase "good neighbor" in his inaugural address drafted by brain truster Raymond Moley in March 1933: "In the field of world policy I would dedicate this nation to the policy of the good neighbor—the neighbor who resolutely respects himself and, because he does so, respects the rights of others." A month later he told the Pan-American Union: "Never before has the significance of the words 'good neighbor' been so manifest in international relations. Never have the need and benefit of neighborly cooperation in every form of human activity been so evident . . ."

The time was ripe for a fresh approach to Latin American relations. Phrases like "colossus of the north," "Yankee imperialists," and DOLLAR DIPLOMACY were in common use in Central and South America to show resentment toward the "big brother" in the north. At a conference in Montevideo, Uruguay, on December 26, 1933, Secretary of State Cordell Hull supported a pact declaring, "No state has the right to intervene in the internal or external affairs of another." FDR added two days later: "The definite policy of the U.S. from now on is one opposed to armed intervention."

There was some sniping from the opposition; the Republican candidate in 1936, Alfred Landon, commented, "We can be a good neighbor without giving away. the latch-key to our door." But the Latin American policy turned out to be the least controversial of all Roosevelt's foreign policies, supported by both isolationists and internationalists. The internationalists felt that a united hemisphere was useful in maintaining world peace; isolationists held that cross-hemispheric relations fell within a kind of "regional isolationism."

The policy was bolstered by the Act of Chapultepec in 1945, the Rio Treaty of 1947 (both pacts of mutual military assistance), and the creation of the Organization of American States. The policy was strained in U.S. dealings with dictators like Argentina's Juan Perón and, later, Cuba's Fidel Castro.

President Eisenhower felt it necessary to amend the phrase. "Our Good Partner Policy," he said in 1960, "is a permanent guide encompassing nonintervention, mutual respect and juridical equality of States." The phrase never took hold.

John F. Kennedy, reported Theodore Sorensen, "requested suggestions for a policy label as meaningful for the sixties as Roosevelt's 'Good Neighbor Policy' had been for the

thirties. I suggested 'alianza'. . . ."
See ALLIANCE FOR PROGRESS.

GOOD SOLDIER a politician willing to place the good of the party first; one who swallows personal pride and falls in line.

The phrase is often preceded by a gulp. In 1956, Ohio favorite son Michael Di Salle announced that he was throwing his support to Senator John Kennedy for vice-presidential nominee (he lost to Senator Estes Kefauver). William Coleman, Ohio state chairman, did not like Di Salle's decision but decided to go along. A *Columbus Dispatch* reporter asked him, "Mr. Coleman, is Senator Kennedy really your choice?" The grim-faced state chairman replied, "I am a good soldier."

He was echoing a phrase made famous by Missouri Senator James Reed at the 1932 Democratic convention. Reed, who had bitterly opposed Franklin Roosevelt, sat on the platform with what was described as "an expressionless face" while the final ballot showed 945 votes for Roosevelt, 190½ for Al Smith. The convention chairman asked him to address the convention in a display of unity, and he refused. FDR aide Arthur Mullen went to him and said, "We're all Democrats, Jim." Reed went to the microphone and calmed the disappointed Smith supporters: "At a time like this, every man who claims to be a Democrat should banish from his heart all feeling of disappointment, all sense of chagrin, and like a good soldier, fall in line, salute the colors and face the enemy."

Speaker of the House Sam Rayburn also used the phrase at a convention. In 1960, when John Kennedy urged him to convince his fellow Texan, Lyndon Johnson, to take second spot on the ticket, "Mr. Sam"

replied, "Well, there is always the thought in a fellow's mind that he might get to be President. Lyndon is a good soldier, and he will hear the call of duty."

Good soldier is a high accolade among politicians, a decoration for regularity. The ringing phrase must not be confused with *old soldier,* a funky cigar butt, or *dead soldier,* an empty whiskey bottle. See OLD SOLDIERS NEVER DIE; MILITARY METAPHORS.

GOO-GOO, *see* DO-GOODER; REFORM.

GOP Republican; initials for the Grand Old Party.

In the 1870s, "grand old party" and "gallant old party" were in use, mostly referring to Republicans. Meanwhile, in England, Prime Minister William Gladstone was being dubbed "the Grand Old Man," first used in 1882. Soon after, Gladstone was "the G.O.M." Soon after that, GOP made its bow. " 'The G.O.P. Doomed,' shouted the *Boston Post,*" wrote the *New York Tribune* on October 15, 1884; nobody has yet found the earlier *Boston Post* use.

In early motorcar days, the letters also stood for "get out and push"; in the sixties, the Republican National Committee launched a modernization program for the old acronym, referring to themselves as "the GO-Party," and in 1972 pointed to "Generation of Peace." Harry Truman said the initials meant "Grand Old Platitudes."

GOPHER one who will "go for" coffee and run errands in a political headquarters.

Political novices are sometimes startled by the calibre of people willing to act as "gophers" in the final stages of a campaign. Officeholders, district leaders and fat cats, anxious to be seen at headquarters by the candidate and his managers, will often willingly assume menial tasks. The word is often spelled "go-fer."

Just after John Lindsay took office as New York's mayor in 1966, a minor controversy arose when it was charged that policemen were being used as "gophers"—to bring coffee into the Lindsay offices.

The need for gophers, and the sustenance they bring harried workers, was recognized in 712 by Alexander Pope in *The Rape of the Lock* when the British poet wrote of "coffee, which makes the politicians wise."

In Philadelphia in the first part of the nineteenth century, tradesmen who lobbied were called "coffeehouse politicians." Coffee remains in the political lexicon (see COFFEE-KLATSCH CAMPAIGN).

The alternate spelling of "gopher," though with the identical meaning, was used in this doggerel by Fred Bruhn in the *Wall Street Journal* in 1974, commenting on a proposal for a permanent special prosecutor for top officials:

It's not the big black cars with chauffeurs,
It's not the maids, the aides, the go-fers,
It's not the top floor corner space
It's not the horsy country place
What stamps a man of power and wealth:
A prosecutor for himself.

In Texas the word used for a "gopher" is "Billy-do-boy." A similar-sounding word, coined on the same analogy as "gopher," is "two-fer," which originally meant two tickets for the price of one, and in politics is used to indicate that an appointee is both black and a woman, thereby pleasing two constituencies.

GOSPEL OF HATE, *see* **APOSTLE OF HATE.**

GO TO THE WELL followed by "too often," the phrase means the overuse of an asset; used as "a man to go to the well with," trustworthy.

Campaigning through the South in 1960 as John Kennedy's running mate, Lyndon Johnson overcame suspicions of Kennedy as a Catholic and a Yankee by assuring audiences that "Kennedy's a man to go to the well with." This was an effective regional idiom, referring to the danger of obtaining water when a frontier encampment was under siege by Indians.

In 1964 President Johnson stimulated some interest in his choice of a vice-presidential nominee by saying of the junior senator from Minnesota: "Gene McCarthy . . . is the kind of man—as we say in the ranch country in Texas—who will go to the well with you."

Newsweek wrote almost four years later: "But Hubert Humphrey was selected for that particular visit to the well, and McCarthy was piqued by a sense that he himself had been ill-used by the President. That resentment, some suspect, has carried over into his decision this year to try to dig a new Democratic well outside the Texas ranch country."

GOVERNANCE, *see* **PUNDIT.**

GOVERNMENT, *see* **ADMINISTRATION.**

GOVERNMENT BY CRONY an Administration in which advisers qualify not by experience or talent but by their longtime friendship with the Chief Executive.

Washington columnist Arthur Krock, in a February 9, 1946, piece titled "Government by Crony," wrote: "During the Truman administration, New Dealers and Conservatives found themselves together in opposition to what a press gallery wit has called a 'government by crony.' "

Krock suggested that many New Dealers held over from the Roosevelt Administration "opposed many of Truman's intimate White House circle because, they say, they are of courthouse caliber."

The columnist added: "Government by crony is not new in Washington. President Roosevelt appointed many persons of doubtful competence or eligibility because of personal relationships."

Soon after Krock's use of the phrase, Secretary of the Interior Harold Ickes (see CURMUDGEON) resigned with a blast at Truman: "I am against government by crony."

The author suspected that the anonymous "press gallery wit" quoted by Krock might be similar to "Western observer"—the reporter himself. Mr. Krock replied to a query: "As I recall, I was referring modestly to myself in that reference to 'a press gallery wit,' though I couldn't document that I am the originator. But I, too, have seen no previous use of the expression in the public prints."

There are a number of "government by" phrases used in the pejorative sense: "Government by organized money" (FDR in referring to the Republican Administration before 1932); "Government by epilepsy" (Brazilian President Janio Quadros describing Fidel Castro's Cuba in 1961); "Government by injunction" (John L. Lewis after the U.S. government found him guilty of abrogating the United Mine Workers contract with the government in 1946); "Government by golly" (anti-Eisenhower); "Government by Irish-Mafia" (anti-Kennedy); "Government by Texans" (anti-Johnson).

Most of the "government by" phrases of the last century were probably coined to compare unfavorably with the phrase Lincoln popularized, "government of the people, by the people, for the people." For the derivation of that phrase, see IDEAS.

GOVERNMENT-IN-EXILE a description of the Kennedy family, and their close associates, during the Administration of President Lyndon Johnson.

"On Capitol Hill," wrote William Manchester in 1967, "the two brothers [Robert and Ted Kennedy] inevitably came to be regarded as the nucleus of a government-in-exile."

Although President Johnson asked most of the Kennedy men (see IRISH MAFIA) to stay on after the assassination of John F. Kennedy ("I need you more than he ever did"), most left the White House to write books and form a coterie around other Kennedys. Ted Sorensen, Arthur Schlesinger, Jr., Richard Goodwin, Kenneth O'Donnell, Stephen Smith, and others of the "Clan" formed a circle around Robert, Ted, and Jacqueline Kennedy; Postmaster General Lawrence O'Brien, Poverty War head Sargent Shriver, and Defense Secretary Robert McNamara refrained from going into "exile."

The use of the phrase indicated an estrangement that grew within the Democratic party, which author Manchester was accused of exaggerating in *The Death of a President.*

In its traditional use, a "government-in-exile" has either been forced out by revolution or usurpation, or invaded and taken over by another nation, with the "legitimate" government taking refuge elsewhere. The use of the phrase in the Johnson-Kennedy context served to further polarize the situation.

A typical reflection of the tension between the two groups which led to a nomination fight in 1968, is the description of White House adviser John Roche (see INTELLECTUAL-IN-RESIDENCE) in a 1967 *New York Times* article: "He plainly enjoyed the recent row about the 'government in exile' at Harvard and candidly confesses that he has never had anything in common with 'that crowd of cold Kennedy cats operating exclusively on the star system.' "

After its nonce use in the Johnson Administration, the phrase was applied to the usually liberal Brookings Institution during the Nixon-Ford years, and then to the conservative American Enterprise Institute in the Carter years.

GOVERNMENT OF LAWS, NOT OF MEN   a maxim that suggests there is little human weakness in the administration of justice; or, that all stand equal before the bar.

The idea can be found in Baron Montesquieu's *Spirit of Laws,* a work written in 1748 that influenced many of the founders of the U.S. Constitution: "The rulers of republics establish institutions, and afterwards the institutions mould the rulers."

John Adams, in his preamble to the Massachusetts Constitution in 1778, used the phrase as his ultimate political goal: "In the government of the Commonwealth of Massachusetts the legislative, executive and judicial power shall be placed in separate departments, to the end that it might be a government of laws, not of men."

Chief Justice John Marshall picked up the Adams phrase in his decision in the landmark *Marbury* vs. *Madison:* "The government of the United States has been emphatically termed a government of laws, and not of men."

In England the phrase for the same idea is alliterative: MEASURES, NOT MEN. In the U.S. the phrase is often replaced by the august RULE OF LAW. During the year preceding Richard Nixon's resignation in 1974, the phrase was used both as an admonishment to the Nixon men (for putting themselves above the law) and as a spur to the forces favoring impeachment (holding the law above the elected officials.) Its most dramatic use came on the night of October 20, 1973, when Special Prosecutor Archibald Cox—just fired by the President in what came to be known as the SATURDAY NIGHT MASSACRE—issued a statement from his home: "Whether ours shall continue to be a government of laws and not of men is now for Congress and ultimately for the American people."

GRADUALISM, *see* TOKENISM; SALAMI TACTICS.

GRAFFITI   slogans and messages scrawled on walls.

"Cuba Sí—Yankee No," and "Ami Go Home," in paint or chalk on walls in the U.S. and abroad first brought this ancient art to the attention of U.S. politicians. The word originally applied to all scrawled messages, from "Kilroy Was Here" to the names of a boy and a girl with an arrow and heart, to outright smut, but its meaning has narrowed to messages with some social or political content.

A 1967 advertisement for "Books USA," a government-endorsed project to mail books abroad, showed a picture of a U.S. soldier standing next to graffiti that read "Go Home Yankee Dog," with this copy: "Read any good walls lately? Probably not. Few flattering things have ever been written on walls about anyone. And the unflattering truth is that there are walls like this in many countries, covered with words written in anger, mistrust and ignorance . . ."

A collection of *Graffiti: Selected Scrawls from Bathroom Walls* was made in 1967 by Robert Reisner, and included political graffiti like: "Yankee Go Home (via Pan Am)," "Peace is a cool scene," "Bomb Saigon," "Half the Way with LBJ," "Dulles Lives," "UNLEASH CHIANG KAI-SHEK." Often, graffiti are in the form of a dialogue, with answers or comments scrawled below, as: "What happened to all the high class graffiti?" "It got read." "Better read than dead."

The word is the plural of *graffito,* which refers to a method of ornamenting architectural plaster surfaces by scratching the top coat to reveal colored layers underneath, used in ancient cultures and refined in fifteenth-century Italian decorative art.

The spreading of slogans by graffiti is not unlike the dissemination of news via wall posters in China. "Posters written in big characters," said Mao Tse-tung, "are an extremely useful new type of weapon." See SNIPE. During the upheavals of the CULTURAL REVOLUTION, *tatzepao,* or big-character posters, served as the best way of getting news to the people and is still an approved form of communication in the People's Republic of China.

A combination of wall-poster news and commenting graffiti is to be expected. Reported KREMLINOLOGIST Harry Schwartz in 1967: "A traveler who recently returned from Hong Kong reports that among the graffiti he saw there was the assertion: 'Mao Tse-tung is a Hippie.' The suspicion must be strong that the author was a frustrated China-watcher expressing his conviction that only a user of LSD or marijuana could have been responsible for this past year's convulsions in China."

GRAFT money or property gained through political corruption.

A grafter is the one who receives the money, or seeks the payment. Standard English construction would ordinarily make him the *graftee,* and the one who makes the payment the *grafter;* this is not current usage, because the corrupter is considered less sinful than the official who "betrays a public trust."

The word is traceable as thieves' argot back to a *Police Gazette* of 1865: " 'Twas handy that we were so related, as, when about a 'graft,' or 'doing stur,' both sisters could keep each other company." Josiah Flynt in his *Tramping with Tramps* (1899) and *World of Graft* (1901) defined the word as "a generic slang term for all kinds of theft and illegal practices generally."

St. Louis circuit attorney Joseph W. Folk gave the word its political flavor soon after the turn of the century, and his war on what he called "grafters" took him to the governorship of Missouri in 1905. As politics took over the word, thieves' argot shifted to "grift."

Richard Leche, Louisiana governor who succeeded Huey Long, turned out to have an income in 1938 of $282,000 on a salary of $7,500. Shortly before he went to jail, Leche earned his place in political history with the comment: "When I took the oath as Governor, I didn't take any vows of poverty." However, outright bribery of major officials is now becoming rare.

Graft is specific, *corruption* general; graft is the currency of corruption. In 1914 Walter Lippmann overlooked the differentiation in explaining the emerging meaning of both words:

> We can see, I think, what people meant by the word graft. They did not mean robbery. It is rather confused rhetoric to call a grafter a thief. His crime is not that he filches money from the safe but that he betrays a trust. The grafter is a man whose loyalty is divided and whose motives are mixed. A lawyer who takes a fee from both sides in some case; a public official who serves a private interest; a railroad director who is also a director in the supply company; a policeman in league with outlawed vice; these are the relationships which the American people denounce as "corrupt." The attempt to serve at the same time two antagonistic interests is what constitutes "corruption."

See HONEST GRAFT; BOODLE; REACHED; WHIPSAW; GREASE.

GRAND DESIGN   a diplomatic master plan; a broad strategy to shape historical forces.

This phrase comes from the French, *Les Grands Desseins,* and "grand" is translated as "great" or "grand." The phrase, from the time of the French King Henry IV, was reintroduced by Franklin D. Roosevelt at the Teheran Conference in Iran, December 1943, where Stalin, Churchill, and Roosevelt planned an invasion of France and received a commitment from Stalin that Russia would enter the war against Japan. Roosevelt used "Great Design" and Churchill, in his war memoirs, "Grand Alliance" (after the English-Dutch-Hapsburg "Grand Alliance" of 1701).

At the 1944 Republican convention, former President Herbert Hoover traced the derivation: "During the past month Forrest Davis has published a circumstantial account of the Teheran Conference. It is said to have been authorized. It has not been denied. It relates to President Roosevelt's new peace method, called by him, the Great Design. A peace method under this same name, the Great Design, was proposed by Henry the Fourth, a French monarch, some 350 years ago. It has some similarities to Mr. Roosevelt's idea. . . . The American people deserve a much fuller exposition of this Great Design." This point was indicative of a Republican charge of "secret agreements" made after later Big Three conferences, especially Yalta.

FDR might have taken the phrase from its use by Theodore Roosevelt, who received a letter from some prominent Frenchman congratulating him on his efforts in international conciliation. TR later wrote: "They believe that the action of President Roosevelt, which has realized the most generous hopes to be found in history should be classed as a continuance of similar illustrious attempts of former times, notably the project for international concord known under the name of 'The Great Design of Henry IV' in the memoirs of his Prime Minister, the Duke de Sully."

Sully's memoirs refer to vague *Grands Desseins* based on the King's wish to avoid another European war. Until recently, a grand design kept that method-for-peace connotation; of late, it has taken on more of a means-of-defense meaning, not exactly the same.

Senator J. William Fulbright, in *Old Myths and New Realities,* outlined the cracks in the postwar plan:

> The "grand design" for Atlantic partnership envisioned the concurrent development of two sets of relationships: an evolving federation of Europe with institutions vested with specified supranational powers and a broader set of arrangements for link-

ing Europe and America to each other in a close military, political and economic partnership. . . . These expectations, it is now clear, were not well founded, nor are they likely to be fulfilled in the near future. General de Gaulle's policies have shown us that our hopes for an Atlantic partnership were premature and overly optimistic.

As the NATO alliance fell on difficult days (partially as a result of its own success in stemming communist expansion in Europe) economist Robert Lekachman surveyed the field in 1967 for the *New York Times:*

> Competing grand designs jostle each other—de Gaulle's Europe independent of American influence, the two-pillar notion of a unified Western Europe including Great Britain joined in friendship with the United States, in the broader concept of Atlantic Union as a confederation of nations happily led by the United States. At this writing, what appears most likely to succeed is none of these visions, but rather a continuation of the half-alliance, half-intramural quarrel which best describes our relations with Western Europe . . .

For another contribution to American political terminology by Henry IV, see CHICKEN IN EVERY POT.

GRANDPA'S PANTS WON'T FIT BENNY, *see* DYNASTY.

GRANTS-IN-AID, *see* TAX SHARING.

GRAPEVINE rumor factory; word-of-mouth communication of political secrets or background; inside gossip.

The grapevine is falling into disuse because reporters learn and print most rumors before politicians have a chance to pass them along. "I hear by the grapevine" between politicos has been almost altogether replaced by Mr. DOOLEY's "I see by the papers." The phrase persists mainly in the hints of jobs available and personnel shifts.

Hans Sperber thought the word may have had its origin in an episode told by Charles Howard Shinn, in a mining book about the Great Comstock lode in Nevada:

> That curious and vivid Western phrase, "grapevine telegraph," originated in 1859. Colonel Bee constructed a telegraph line between Placerville and Virginia City, attaching the wire to the trees; their swaying stretched it until it lay in loops on the ground, resembling the trailing California wild grapevines. Frequent breaks occurred from falling trees and avalanches, till the line became almost useless, being sometimes beaten into Sacramento by the Pony Express. California and Nevada papers took it up, and whenever a journalist wished to cast doubts on the freshness of his opponent's news he forthwith accused him of running a grapevine telegraph.

The phrase was used before 1859, however, in connection with the Underground Railroad, the abolitionists' method of aiding escaped slaves. The grapevine was their communications system, and was often used interchangeably with "the clothesline telegraph." Grapevines, it may be assumed, were used as a substitute for rope and the two phrases came into being together. Union captain John Truesdale, in an 1867 collection of Civil War anecdotes called *The Blue Coats,* showed how the clothesline could be used as an intelligence device: clotheslines were used as visual transmitters of espionage, with shirts of different colors hung out to dry used as a code to reveal the order of battle of the Confederate troops.

GRASSROOTS the ultimate source of power, usually patronized, occasionally feared; the rank and file of a party, or voters not normally politically active.

The phrase began with a rural flavor, implying simple virtues of the land as against city-slicker qualities. Recently the anti–big-city connotation has been disappearing, leaving only an anti–boss, up-from-the-people meaning. Accordingly, politicians seek support "from the grassroots and the sidewalks of the nation" to cover everybody.

The word has its own roots in mining terminology, used in 1876 to mean the soil just beneath the surface. An early metaphoric use was by Rudyard Kipling, in *Kim,* published in 1901: "Not till I came to Shamlegh could I meditate upon the Course of Things, or trace the running grass-roots of Evil." (Why "running"? Philip Howard of the *Times* of London wrote in 1977 that Kipling was probably referring to "*Agropyron repens,* the common couch or twitch grass, whose long creeping root-stalks or rhizomes run below the surface and make it a pestilential and ineradicable garden weed.")

An early political use was in 1912, when Senator Albert J. Beveridge told the Bull Moose convention in Chicago: "This party comes from the grass roots. It has grown from the soil of the people's hard necessities." The Farmer-Labor party used it as a slogan in 1920.

The phrase came into prominence with a Republican effort to organize a massive thrust to unseat FDR. In Springfield, Ill., on June 10, 1935, the Grass Roots Conference was held. "Issues are hard to find," reported *Common Sense,* "and the 'Grass Roots' Conference in Springfield, Illinois, found itself stumped." Three decades later, Republican Chairman Ray Bliss called a similar conference to mobilize grassroots (by now one word) support in the big cities, and claimed better results.

Most candidates now claim to run *grassroots campaigns,* where they get out to meet the people, just the opposite of a FRONT-PORCH CAMPAIGN. However, the best way to reach the grassroots is from a television studio, posing a semantic problem. Senator George McGovern used the word as the title of his memoirs in 1977.

Reporting on Attorney General Robert Kennedy's trip to the Far East in 1962, *Newsweek* came up with a good play on the phrase: "He sought to make U.S. policies understandable at the rice-roots level." See STREET SMART.

GRASS WILL GROW IN THE STREETS a threat of financial ruin if the opposition is elected, and specifically if a protective tariff is removed.

The phrase was made famous in recent times by Herbert Hoover in the campaign of 1932 as he was defending the Smoot-Hawley tariff against a suggested Democratic tariff proposal: "The grass will grow in the streets of a hundred cities, a thousand towns; the weeds will overrun the fields of millions of farms if that protection is taken away." This was fairly colorful language for Hoover, but it came with the election only a week away and did little good. Roosevelt used it in 1936, however, reminding responsive audiences: "I look for the grass which was to grow on city streets."

The grass-in-the-streets prophecy was a part of the most famous of all convention speeches: William Jennings Bryan's 1896 "Cross of Gold" address, which had a strong agrarian flavor. "Burn down your cities and leave our farms, and your cities will spring up again as if by magic," he orated, "but destroy our farms and the grass will grow in the streets of every city in the country."

Bryan, and later Hoover, only rephrased a metaphor used frequently before, especially in regard to tariffs. The October 13, 1892, issue of *The Nation* warns that an argument for a protective tariff "is the old 'howling wilderness' and 'grass-in-the-streets' argument for protection."

The earliest use found so far was in a speech by Jefferson Davis, shortly after his inauguration as President of the Confederate States of America. He predicted a short, victorious war, because soon "Grass will grow in the Northern cities."

The phrase is now obsolescent, partially because so many park-hungry urbanites would welcome grass wherever it grew within a city's limits.

See GLOOM AND DOOM, PROPHETS OF.

GRATITUDE, POLITICAL favors done now in anticipation of return favors to come.

Unlike normal gratitude, political gratitude looks forward and not backward. The phrase is used usually when a politician turns down a request from someone who helped him in the past. The rejected former helper, understandably cynical, murmurs "That's political gratitude," meaning the politician will be "grateful"—receptive—only to those who can help him in the future.

President Kennedy is reported to have said that "politicians do not have friends, they have allies." This was an adaptation of "the British Empire has no friends, only interests."

Newsweek columnist Raymond Moley wrote: "Sam Rayburn once told me that whenever he secured a job for a political applicant, he 'made nine enemies and one ingrate.' "

Rayburn was passing along a comment of Louis XIV, in Molière's *Siècle de Louis Quatorze:* "Every time I fill a vacant office I make ten malcontents and one ingrate." Thomas Jefferson in 1807 increased the enemies as he quoted obliquely: "Every office becoming vacant, every appointment made, *me donne un ingrat, et cent ennemis.*"

Essayist William Hazlitt ascribed to English man of letters Horace Walpole the following maxim, similar to one of La Rochefoucauld's: "The gratitude of place expectants is a lively sense of future favors."

GRAVEYARD top secret; an unbreakable confidence; or, a DEAD END.

Political secrets are often transmitted with the prefatory admonition: "This is graveyard." It appears to have gained currency in the 1950s and is common political usage today, although it rarely, if ever, is seen in print. Presumably the metaphor connotes a place of darkness, whispers, and trepidation, the proper atmosphere for a political confidence.

A second meaning of the word is "final political resting place," or "dead end." A reporter in 1967 asked New York Mayor John Lindsay, "Isn't the mayor's office a political graveyard?" Lindsay replied with a reference to two New York mayors who departed office under a cloud, James Walker and William O'Dwyer: "Some mayors have gone on to international fame. One went to Europe, one went to Mexico . . ."

GRAY EMINENCE from the French, *l'éminence grise;* a shadowy figure who exercises power through another; in current use, a manipulative adviser.

Armand Jean du Plessis, Duc de Richelieu, French statesman and cardinal, wore a red habit (unique at the time) that made him known as L'Éminence Rouge, "The Red Cardinal." As Prime Minister, he controlled Louis XIII, directing both foreign and domestic policy, successfully shifting the balance of power from the Hapsburgs to the Bourbons.

Cardinal Richelieu's private secretary, Père Joseph de Trembley, attired in a gray habit, became known as *L'Éminence Grise*—"the Gray Cardinal," who, while not a Cardinal at all, often exercised the power of a prince of the Church because of his influence on Richelieu.

The title's ghostly connotation made it eminently suitable for political use; a gray eminence is now used to describe any POWER BEHIND THE THRONE or KINGMAKER who has the ear of a political leader but does not often appear publicly.

The description was often applied to Louis Howe, a brilliant, gnomelike, lifelong adviser and confidant of Franklin Roosevelt. "Roosevelt's election," wrote Jonathan Daniels, "was, of course, Howe's final, unique triumph. He was to be remembered as the long-time friend, the Warwick, the alter ego, *l'éminence grise.*"

Japanese Liberal party leader Tsuji Karouki, a behind-the-scene power, was described as a "kuromaku," or "black curtain." See RUSTLING BEHIND THE JALOUSIES.

GREASE   as a verb, to smooth the way by bribery; as a noun, the money used in such corruption.

"Cash . . . is a necessary article in their business," wrote the *Columbian Centinel* in 1797, "and without daily application of this specific grease their

wheels must roll heavily on."

Grease can be used in a meaning limited to money ("We must have grease to run a campaign," Democratic leader John Thompson told the Ohio Central Committee in 1881) but the overtone that the money is corruptly obtained is more often present.

After a period in which the word was considered an archaism, it appears to be making a comeback: "U.S. Attorney Thomas P. Sullivan said yesterday," went a UPI report from Chicago in 1977, "a federal investigation is under way on charges that Mayor Michael A. Bilandic 'greased' an 11.7 percent city taxi fare increase last summer."

For the derivation of the monetary meaning of "fat," see FAT CAT: another, earlier use of "grease" is "to grease the fat pig," or to give to those who need it least, a proverb found in John Heywood's 1566 collection of sayings.

GREAT, POLITICAL USE OF   great, in the sense of GREAT SOCIETY, means *fine and magnanimous;* in the sense of GREAT UNWASHED, it means *a large body;* in the sense of GREAT DEBATES, it means *important;* as an adjective modifying "statesman" or "leader," it means *eminent.*

Historians who compare the greatness of Presidents use a wide variety of criteria, especially the ability to meet crises, make progress, and verbally exalt and inspire the nation. In this connection, they have created the comparative word "near–great."

In its political use, the word cannot be used as a synonym for "big": Big Government is not at all Great Government, and Great Business and Great Labor are never used, indicating that the political meaning of "Great" does not usually include the idea of size.

As an adjective in introductions, the word is intended to mean "noble" or "outstanding," but the meaning has been prostituted by its frequent application to nonentities and hacks.

Bitterness at its overuse in convention oratory was illustrated in this passage by novelist John Dos Passos about jobless men sleeping on the streets in 1932. "Try to tell one of them that the *gre–eat* Franklin D. Roosevelt, Governor of the *gre–eat* state of New York, has been nominated by the *gre–eat* Democratic party. . . . Hoover or Roosevelt, it'll be the same cops."

GREAT DEBATES in recent times, the series of televised debates between Kennedy and Nixon; earlier, the debates between Calhoun, Clay, and Webster.

Because "great" rhymes with "debate," there is a tendency to label important national discussions as "great debates." The first known widely by this title was the Senate debate of Henry Clay's package of compromises regarding slavery, including admission of California as a free state, and no restrictions on slavery in the territory acquired from Mexico.

In the debate that lasted through February and March 1850, Clay occupied the middle position, Daniel Webster spoke for the Union without slavery, John C. Calhoun (enfeebled by illness, his final speech read by another) advocated the halting of agitation on the slavery issue and opposed the compromise. During this debate Webster said, "I wish to speak today not as a Massachusetts man, not as a Northern man, but as an American. . . . I speak today for the preservation of the Union. 'Hear me for my cause.' "

Oddly, the debates between Lincoln and Douglas were not known as "great debates," simply as the Lincoln-Douglas debates. In recent times, a "great debate" was held at the United Nations in 1946 over the adoption of the Baruch plan for atomic control.

Senator Blair Moody, a Michigan newsman serving out the unexpired term of Senator Arthur Vandenberg in 1952, had the idea of a national confrontation of major presidential candidates. This failed to interest either Eisenhower or Stevenson in 1952; Stevenson was said to feel that a challenge to Eisenhower would be regarded as a gimmick. And Section 315 of the Federal Communications Act requiring EQUAL TIME for all candidates stood in the way. In August 1960, however, Congress temporarily suspended Section 315, and on the night of Richard Nixon's nomination, NBC board chairman Robert Sarnoff offered Democrats and Republicans eight hours of prime time for what he called "The Great Debate." Kennedy, lesser known, promptly accepted; four days later, Nixon did the same.

Nixon's gaunt appearance surprised many viewers on the first debate of four; "Was Nixon Sabotaged by TV Make-Up Artist?" asked the *Chicago Daily News.* When asked "Who won?" after the first debate, viewers tended to go along with the candidate they had previously supported, and radio listeners gave Nixon the edge. But the first debate gave the Kennedy campaign a powerful boost, and in retrospect, many viewers later said they thought Kennedy "won" the first debate.

"As they approached this brave new frontier of television," wrote Douglass Cater years later, "the two candidates were far more concerned about their images than their argu-

ments. Both proved remarkably
adaptable to the new art form. They
were marvels at extemporization,
wasting none of their precious time by
reflective pauses . . . the flowering of
television in politics had coincided
with the flowering of politicians particularly adapted to its special demands."

Pollster Samuel Lubell found "the
overwhelming majority responded in
terms of how the candidates looked
and handled themselves rather than
in terms of the issues that were argued
about."

According to Theodore White,
what the debates did best "was to give
the voters of a great democracy a living portrait of two men under stress
and let the voters decide, by instinct
and emotion, which style and pattern
of behavior under stress they preferred in their leader." White added:
"The salient fact of the great TV debates is not what the two candidates
said, nor how they behaved, but how
many of the candidates' fellow
Americans gave up their evening
hours to ponder the choice between
the two."

The televised debates between Gerald Ford and Jimmy Carter in 1976
were not billed as "great," but a
lengthy pause due to a GLITCH was
labeled "the Great Silence."

GREAT LEAP FORWARD a
Chinese Communist plan for dramatic economic advance, notable for
its failure; now, any dramatic diplomatic move in the Far East.

Mao Tse-tung's "Great Leap Forward" began to be mentioned in the
Chinese media in 1957, not as part of
any five-year plan, but as a special
effort to dramatically advance the
Chinese economy. It was officially
adopted at the second session of the
eighth Party Congress between May

and July of 1958, and is generally
considered to have ended in mid-
1960.

Westerners regarded the "leap" as
a colossal failure, and the expression
was used in derision throughout the
sixties. However, when President
Nixon announced his acceptance of
the invitation of the People's Republic of China to visit Peking, U.S.
media turned to the phrase and set
aside its previously pejorative connotation.

Max Frankel in the *New York
Times:* "President Nixon's success in
arranging a trip to China evoked the
widespread judgment here today that
American policy, in Mao Tse-tung's
phrase, was taking a great leap forward."

Columnist Mary McGrory: "Some
are saying the trip to China is merely
a step in the right direction. For Richard Nixon it could be the 'great leap
forward' that could not only bring a
long-deferred encounter with reality,
but also carry him back to the White
House."

Newsweek: "After years of fighting
each other, castigating each other,
fearing each other—and just plain
wondering about each other—the
most powerful nation in the world
and the most populous nation in the
world had decided to recognize each
other's existence. And that alone
represented a great leap forward."

In a related terminological development, President Nixon began substituting "mainland China" for "Red
China" or "Communist China" in
private meetings in 1970. In a toast to
Rumanian President Ceausescu in the
White House State Dining Room on
October 26, 1970, the President used
"People's Republic of China" for the
first time publicly, in a way that hindsight makes clear he was hinting at
his own future plans: "It happens that

in the world today because of the divisions, there are times when the leader of one nation does not have adequate communication with the leader of another. But as I was saying to the President earlier today, he is in a rather unique position. He heads a government which is one of the few in the world which has good relations with the United States, good relations with the Soviet Union, and good relations with the People's Republic of China."

In his report to the Congress on foreign policy of February 25, 1971, the President used the official name again, and this time it was noticed: "Each of the major powers of the Pacific region—Japan, the USSR, the People's Republic of China, and the United States—is faced with difficult decisions in adjusting its policies to the new realities of East Asia." In a spoken summary of this long document, he chose to use the official term again, which was taken as a gesture of respect by those who had been previously known in the U.S. as the Red Chinese.

GREAT SEAL OF U.S., *see* **UNITED WE STAND; BALD EAGLE.**

GREAT SOCIETY   slogan of the administration of President Lyndon B. Johnson.

President Johnson's first approach to the theme was made three months after he took office. When asked on a television program if he had a slogan as yet, he replied, "I haven't thought of any slogan, but I suppose all of us want a better deal, don't we?"

He tried "Better Deal" a few times in subsequent speeches, but it didn't catch on. The SQUARE DEAL–NEW DEAL–FAIR DEAL lemon had been squeezed dry.

Meanwhile Richard Goodwin, a Kennedy speechwriting holdover, suggested "Great Society." He prepared a draft of a speech presenting the first Eleanor Roosevelt Memorial Award to Judge Anna M. Cross on March 4, 1964. Jack Valenti, then the President's chief speechwriter, preferred another draft without the phrase, but held the thought for later trial.

When the "better deal" fizzled, the "Great Society" began popping up in Johnson speeches; the President was obviously anxious to drop the label "Kennedy-Johnson programs." At a White House ceremony on March 17, 1964, he tried: "We want to have the glorious kind of society." He asked a group of editors on April 21, to "accept with me the responsibility of developing a greater society." He told a Democratic fund-raising dinner on April 23: "We have been called upon —are you listening?—to build a great society of the highest order, a society not just for today or tomorrow, but for three or four generations to come."

Johnson liked the feel of the phrase and he used it at least sixteen times publicly thereafter. Goodwin, who was writing the May 22 speech at graduation exercises of the University of Michigan, then developed it in detail. The advance tests of the speech capitalized the phrase—"Great Society"—a clear signal to the press that the President had found his slogan.

> . . . in your time, we have the opportunity to move not only toward the rich society and the powerful society, but upward to the Great Society.
>
> The Great Society rests on abundance and liberty for all. It demands an end to poverty and racial injustice. . . . The Great Society is a place where every child can find knowledge to enrich his mind and to enlarge his talents. It is a place where

leisure is a welcome chance to build and reflect, not a feared cause of boredom and restlessness. It is a place where the city of man serves not only the needs of the body and the demands of commerce but the desire for beauty and the hunger for community. . . .

But most of all, the Great Society is not a safe harbor, a resting place, a final objective, a finished world. It is a challenge constantly renewed, beckoning us toward a destiny where the meaning of our lives matches the marvelous products of our labor.

Republican researchers promptly pounced on a previous use of the phrase by English Fabian socialist Graham Wallas, in a book titled *The Great Society*, published in 1914. Wallas told one of his Harvard students, Walter Lippmann, that the book was "an analysis of the general social organization of a large modern state . . ." Lippmann later amended the title for a more influential book of his own, *The Good Society*. Goodwin had never heard of Wallas' work.

Wallas, in turn, probably never read another use of the phrase in *Blackstone's Commentaries* of the 1760s, "Of the Nature of Laws in General":

Man was formed for society; and, as is demonstrated by the writers on the subject, is neither capable of living alone, nor indeed has the courage to do it. However, as it is impossible for the whole race of mankind to be united in one great society, they must necessarily divide into many, and form separate states, commonwealths, and nations, entirely independent of each other, and yet liable to a mutual intercourse.

In 1931 English socialist Harold Laski, in his *Introduction to Politics*, titled a chapter "The Place of the State in the Great Society."

Sir William Blackstone and Harold Laski used "great" as meaning "whole," or "total"; Wallas and later Johnson meant it as "noble" or "grand."

Adaptation is the sincerest form of recognition; Ronald Reagan used the phrase "creative society" in his campaign for California governor in 1966, Nelson Rockefeller used "a just society" after his reelection as governor of New York that year, and Senator J. William Fulbright said in 1967 that our preoccupation with Southeast Asia was making the U.S. a "sick society." Since then, the most successful use has been the title of a comic strip, "The Small Society."

GREAT UNWASHED   condescending view of the lower classes; now used ironically and not publicly by politicians.

Current use is typified in this passage from Negro novelist James Baldwin's *The Fire Next Time* (1963): ". . . as long as we in the West place on color the value that we do, we make it impossible for the great unwashed to consolidate themselves according to any other principle."

The phrase is now used to show how the WHITE POWER STRUCTURE is supposed to treat those beneath them with disdain, although it is rarely used by any member of any elite group, unless in an ironic sense.

The phrase was used in 1864 to describe the English lower classes of an earlier time by English novelist James Payn: "There were no such things as 'skilled workmen' or 'respectable artisans,' in those days. The 'people' were 'the Great Unwashed.' "

The phrase is said to have been used before that by Edmund Burke. In the U.S., political observer George Julian wrote in 1884 about the Polk-Clay race that the Whigs "insisted that . . . the larger element of ignorance and 'unwashed' humanity, including our foreign-born population, gave victory to Mr. Polk."

Throughout the nineteenth century the phrase was used to mean Democratic voters, and was often a self-description of some pride. A *Cleveland Leader* headline in 1884 read: "Thomas A. Hendricks Addresses The Great Unwashed at Cincinnati." William Allen White used the word in its Democratic sense as late as 1946: "When election time came around, this black abolition Republican, who was my mother, and this Stephen Douglas Copperhead Democrat, who was my father, still unwashed, still voting for Jackson, had their purple moments."

In current use, the phrase has dropped its specific party affiliation. Broadcasting executives and admen often refer to their audiences as "the great unwashed," in an effort to explain why they aim at a low common denominator. See VAST WASTELAND; SILENT MAJORITY; MIDDLE AMERICA.

GREAT WHITE FATHER   a term ridiculing the paternalism of the President of the United States.

Just after the 1936 Democratic convention, publicist Herbert Bayard Swope wrote to his friend Felix Frankfurter: "Probably you and I are the only ones left who have no hope of reward, or fear of punishment, from the Great White Father." (Frankfurter was rewarded with a Supreme Court Justiceship three years later; Swope—see COLD WAR—never found a government role.)

The phrase is used either in a spirit of mild affection, which was Swope's usage, or in a blast at all-powerful, centralized government. "It is devouring the substance of self-supporting people," wrote *Reader's Digest* in

1949, "to render them self-supporting no longer and to establish a condition of universal reliance upon the biased paternalism of a Great White Father."

In the early days of the Republic, the Great White Father was the name given the president by the Indians subjugated by the new nation, and the treatment was paternal indeed. President Thomas Jefferson, in 1808, nearing his retirement told a group of Indian chiefs gathered to bid him farewell:

Sensible that I am become too old to watch over the extensive concerns of the seventeen states and their territories, I requested my fellow citizens to permit me to live with my family, and to choose another President for themselves, and father for you. . . . Be assured, my children, that he will have the same friendly dispositions towards you which I have had, and that you will find in him a true and affectionate father. . . . Tell your people . . . that during my administration I have held their hand in mine; and that I will put it into the hand of their new father, who will hold it as I have done.

In political campaigns, donning an Indian headdress for photographers has become as encrusted a tradition as kissing babies. In his memoirs, General Eisenhower told this story about some unfortunate Indian campaigning by his rival for the 1952 nomination, Senator Taft: "The day before the Minnesota primary a Navajo medicine man conferred an Indian blessing on Senator Taft. Unhappily, however, he left his turkey-feather wand at home and at the site of the ceremony had to improvise one of chicken feathers. When reporters asked the medicine man afterward how he estimated Taft's chances, he replied glumly, 'Wand had chicken feathers instead of turkey feathers. Now Taft is finished.' "

An often-told political joke is that of the politician addressing a large crowd of Indians, who shouted "Oompa!" in response to his promises. Pleased with the enthusiastic reception, the politician began to move off the platform, only to be warned by an aged chief, who indicated a pile of manure, "Don't step in the oompa."

The phrase is probably associated with "Big Daddy" (the name of a character in Tennessee Williams' *Cat on a Hot Tin Roof*), which was used by critics of Lyndon Johnson. "Big Daddyism" means stiflingly paternalistic government.

The tag was a natural for President Johnson because he frequently used the word himself, as when he claimed FDR had been "like a daddy to me." In California, the term has most often been applied to the Democratic Speaker of the Assembly, Jesse M. Unruh. In 1968, after Unruh had reduced his weight from 285 to 200 pounds, Governor Ronald Reagan remarked, "It seems like it takes more than a tailor to change the image of Big Daddy," a comment that Unruh felt was "sort of poor taste on his part."

GROUNDSWELL popular support; enthusiasm for a policy or candidate from the lower levels of a party or from the general public.

To a sailor, a groundswell is a heavy undulation of the ocean, caused by a far-off gale or earthquake. The sense of depth and inexorability is kept in the political metaphor; when a genuine groundswell develops for one candidate, all the others are in choppy water.

"A ground swell, however," wrote President-to-be James Buchanan in

1856, ". . . among a noble people who had sustained me for more than thirty years forced me reluctantly into the field."

In March 1968, the *New York Times* observed: "By the politico-meteorological standards of New Hampshire, the sudden Rockefeller candidacy not only failed to qualify as a ground swell, but fell considerably short of a frost heave."

In current use, the two words are usually wedded, as with the similar GRASSROOTS; the word continues to refer to an unled, unmanipulated public opinion. For examples of other natural phenomena used in politics, see DISASTER METAPHORS.

GROUP OF 77, *see* **THIRD WORLD.**

GUARANTEED ANNUAL WAGE, *see* **LIVING WAGE.**

GUIDELINES (GUIDEPOSTS) a general standard of measuring wage and price increases to determine whether they are in what the federal government considers to be the national economic interest.

The national wage-price guidelines (suggesting a limit of 3.2 percent rise per year) were promulgated by President Kennedy in 1962; he resisted the charge that wages and prices were none of his business by pointing out "when things go badly . . . if we have another recession, the President of the United States is to blame. So I think it is our business."

Walter Heller called the guidelines (which he usually termed "guideposts") "the jawbone method" of holding wages and prices down, since they were founded on no statute and included no specific sanctions to violators. Kennedy never picked up the usage, probably suspecting that some critic would point out that Samson used "the jawbone of an ass."

Heller informs the author that he felt the word guidelines sounded "too interventionist—guideposts seemed to me less constricting." However, the press and public preferred the more activist "guidelines."

The rationale for the guidelines was that high wage demands, passed on as price increases, would inflate the economy and dissipate any real wage increase. Opponents argue that government intervention here was in effect wage-price control and a long step toward a "managed economy."

As guidelines began to erode in 1966, Heller took a more modest view of their intent: "First, the guideposts have been a useful moderating influence in 1961–1965. Second, since they are designed to function as a supplement rather than an alternative to overall fiscal monetary policy, they should not be expected to carry the burden of stabilization—nor should they be judged by the performance of wages and prices—in a period of excessive total demand."

"Guidelines" was not a new word in the use of presidential power; Eisenhower told a cabinet meeting in 1954 that he wanted guidelines laid out for departmental handling of congressional requests for information.

Franklin Roosevelt used another word for a more limited economic purpose than Kennedy's wage-price guidelines. Before he became President, he called for public competition with private power utilities, "at least as a yardstick." As President, he demanded that the Tennessee and Columbia rivers be the sites of federal power projects for use as "yardsticks" in measuring private utility services and costs.

The guideline phrase traveled. In the British general election of 1964,

the Conservatives were saddled with a "pay pause" phrase that one of their leaders had mistakenly used; Labour Minister John Hare announced that any pay pause would soon give way to a more flexible "guiding light."

GUILT BY ASSOCIATION a SMEAR technique, implying wrongdoing by a person because of the wrongdoing—or extremist connections—of those with whom he associates.

The phrase was used by civil libertarians against what they considered the WITCH HUNTS of the early fifties, when blacklists such as "Red Channels" cast doubts on the loyalty of many who belonged to Communist or Communist-front organizations, or were associated with or related to those who did.

The Supreme Court, however, in *Adler* v. *Board of Education,* 342 US 485 (1952), noted that people are indeed often judged by the company they keep, and a person's associations may be considered in determining loyalty. See SECURITY RISK.

The charge of using "guilt by association" was most often made against Senator Joseph McCarthy, when he headed the Senate Subcommittee on Permanent Investigations. J. B. Matthews, staff director, wrote an article for the *American Mercury* magazine in 1953 charging that "the largest single group supporting the Communist apparatus in the United States today is composed of Protestant clergymen." Though McCarthy was not aware of the article in preparation, he was obliged to stick by his appointee. There was protest from areas that had earlier kept silent about McCarthy; Eisenhower denounced the attack in a telegram to clergymen, and Matthews resigned.

"There was irony in this, too,"

wrote Robert Donovan, "because McCarthy, so far as anyone knows, had nothing whatsoever to do with Matthews' article. He was simply trapped in a case of guilt by association, which had been his own favorite snare for catching others."

Those who rely too heavily on character references are sometimes accused of seeking "innocence by association." See LOVED FOR THE ENEMIES HE MADE.

The phrase is secure enough to resist punning: during hearings to confirm Nelson Rockefeller as Vice President in 1974, it was revealed that he forgave large loans to his former government aides. This was dubbed "gilt by association."

GULAG acronym for the Soviet slave labor camps.

When Russian novelist Alexander Solzhenitsyn published *The Gulag Archipelago 1918–1956* in Paris in 1973, the word "gulag" entered the English language.

The word is an acronym for the main administration of correctional labor camps—in Russian, *Glavnoye Upravleniye Ispravitelno-trudovykh Lagerei.* When the U.S. State Department refers to this system, the acronym is spelled as an acronym ought to be—all in caps—but in most other use, the word is merely capitalized as "Gulag," as if it were a place. This has led to a widespread assumption that the Gulag is a large prison, or an island chain. But the metaphor Solzhenitsyn had in mind was a series of islands—or camps—in the sea of the USSR.

The term is now linked to almost any discussion of forced labor or the absense of human rights in the Soviet Union. See SAMIZDAT.

GUMSHOE CAMPAIGN, *see* **JUNKETEERING GUMSHOES.**

GUNBOAT DIPLOMACY the iron fist of threatened force inside the velvet glove of diplomatic relations.

The expression is always derogatory, and has always been used in the sense of those days being over. "It has been said that the days of 'gunboat diplomacy' in China are over," goes an *OED Supplement* citation from proceedings of the U.S. Naval Institute dated February 1927. In the United Nations in 1961, an Iraqi delegate termed a British action in Kuwait "gunboat diplomacy at its worst."

The phrase began in a description of Western domination of China in the early twentieth century, with U.S. and British interests maintained by gunboats on the main rivers and patrolling harbors. In 1937 the *"Panay* incident"* took place when a Japanese bomber sank a U.S. gunboat 27 miles north of Nanking on the Yangtse River, but that was an example of a gunboat being on the receiving end of force.

The gunboat has a long tradition in American naval history. The "gunboat system"—small armed craft manned by local seamen—was preferred by Thomas Jefferson to a more expensive regular navy for the defense of U.S. harbors, and in the war of 1812 defended New Orleans from the British until Andrew Jackson arrived. But the term gained an oppressive or imperialistic connotation from its Chinese experience.

Now the phrase is used exclusively to express dismay at what is considered JINGOISM. In 1976, when Republican Ronald Reagan charged that the Ford Administration's advocacy of black majority rule in Rhodesia "risks increased violence and bloodshed," Senator Joe Biden (D-Del.) commented: "There is a good deal of gunboat rhetoric that is misleading the American people."

For a rundown of the way "diplomacy" has been used to make phrases, see SHUTTLE DIPLOMACY.

GUNG HO enthusiasm undampened by experience, often shown by a political volunteer.

When a political operative is "gung ho," he is willing to undertake the impossible cheerfully, often overcoming obstacles that "old pros" consider too difficult to attack.

"Gung ho" was used by Allied armed forces in World War II to express a spirit of cooperation and enthusiasm, popularized by Colonel Evans F. Carlson's marine raiders. The word was drawn from the Chinese, roughly meaning "work together," the name of the industrial cooperatives set up by missionaries in China in the mid-thirties.

Nym Wales, an authority on Chinese affairs, wrote in 1938:

... the Gung Ho industrial cooperatives were to be neutral politically— to start co-ops for both Kuomintang and communists to help win the war —and to bring about the industrial revolution in the village, not in the treaty-port cities, as before.

Would Henry Luce sponsor the Gung Ho industrial cooperatives? This was a vital question. *Time* did give publicity to the infant Gung Ho cooperatives and Henry Luce agreed to be on the advisory board of the America Committee in Aid of Chinese Industrial Cooperatives along with Mrs. Franklin Roosevelt ...

In current use, the phrase may be used affirmatively (New York Mayor John Lindsay in 1967: "People are getting a bit gung ho for the City of New York, which is good") or derisively, as a modernization of Talley-rand's advice to diplomats: "Above all, not too much zeal."

GUNS BEFORE BUTTER the strain placed on consumer products and social-welfare projects by a nation that must place a higher priority on war supplies.

The phrase is generally attributed to Hermann Göring, who said in a radio broadcast in 1936: "Guns will make us powerful; butter will only make us fat." Earlier that year, Nazi Propaganda Minister Joseph Goebbels had said: "We can do without butter, but, despite all our love of peace, not without arms. One cannot shoot with butter but with guns."

The "guns before butter" slogan came to mean the domestic economic sacrifices any nation must face in preparing for war. In the U.S., however, the phrase has changed to "guns *and* butter," which is a charge that the President is refusing to face up to the sacrifices required. Senator Lyndon Johnson made this charge against President Harry Truman in the early stages of the Korean conflict; he was on the receiving end during his own presidency.

In his 1966 State of the Union message, Johnson told the joint session of Congress: "Time may require further sacrifices. If so, we will make them. But we will not heed those who will wring it from the hopes of the unfortunate in a land of plenty. I believe we can continue the Great Society while we fight in Viet Nam." No signal was needed; editorial writers and Johnson critics across the country called this "a guns and butter policy." A year later, following a House Appropriations committee's gentle handling of a public-works-project (**PORK BARREL**) bill, the *New York Times* asked: "If the nation can't afford guns and butter, can it afford guns and pork?"

GURU, *see* **RABBI.**

GUTFIGHTER a tough, no-holds-barred political operative always ready to go for the jugular vein of his opponent.

Wrote *Times* reporter Cabell Phillips: "The people voted for the homely, rumpled, irrational gutfighter, Harry Truman."

Curiously, *gutfighter* is generally used admiringly, unlike MUD-SLINGER or CHARACTER ASSASSIN, and is not to be confused with *gutter fighter,* which means one who drags a campaign down to the low level of the gutter.

Gutfighter is an inside political word, not yet fully taken up by the general public; politicians consider a gutfighter to be one who is totally committed, intensely loyal, and willing to do almost anything for his cause or candidate. Gutfighters are at their best dealing with GUT ISSUES.

Typical use in 1967 was by political writer John Hopkins, in the *Fort Lauderdale News:* "Florida's Democratic party is shadow-boxing when it should be gut-fighting . . . today they search for the knife-wielder who has not shown up yet." See INSTINCT FOR THE JUGULAR; HATCHETMAN; HARD-BALL.

GUT ISSUE a political-campaign theme that reaches beyond rational discussion and affects the emotions of the voter; a topic that engenders a visceral reaction.

Examples of gut issues are war-fever and war-weariness; depression or inflation; fear of crime or resentment of minority groups. A "switcher issue" is a gut issue to a limited group of voters, such as abortion and gun control, which can cause that group to abandon normal political alliances.

"Non-gut issues" include fiscal integrity, better highways, state constitution modernization. A "burning issue" is always discussed; a gut issue may be discussed or not.

A peripheral issue in one campaign can be a gut issue in another; urban renewal leaves the suburban voter cold while "slum clearance" can be a gut issue in a city. Restraint in foreign policy dealings was hardly a gut issue until the Johnson forces in 1964 tagged Goldwater as TRIGGER-HAPPY, and the fear of nuclear adventurism became a gut issue.

In modern campaigns, DEPTH POLLING is often used to determine what lies beneath the articulated problems worrying voters; this will often turn up the gut issue that can either be brought out into the open or alluded to subtly. In the 1966 Rockefeller campaign for governor, a gut issue that surprised politicians turned out to be a fear of crimes committed by narcotics addicts in poorer city neighborhoods. Rockefeller forces promptly gave major billboard space and television time to the governor's program to "get the addicts off the streets," a theme that had not even been considered early in the campaign.

Both "gut" and "guts" refer to the entrails, bowels, belly, intestines. While "gut" has come to mean emotionally or psychologically underlying, "guts" in current usage connotes courage and stamina. In World War II General George Patton was known as "Old Blood and Guts."

Fiorello La Guardia's radio signoff —"Patience and Fortitude"—recalled to many the "intestinal fortitude" of the scrappy mayor.

Author Louis Adamic offered the following definition in *A Study in Courage:* "There is a certain blend of courage, integrity, character and principle which has no satisfactory dictionary name but has been called different things at different times in different countries. Our American name for it is 'guts.' "

A gut issue should not be confused with the leading rational issue of a campaign. The *leading issue,* or *key issue,* of imperialism was called by William Jennings Bryan the *burning issue* and the PARAMOUNT ISSUE in 1900. But in 1970, it was hard to tell whether the *social issue* or the *economic issue* was the gut issue. See IS-SUES, THE.

GUTTER FLYER   the lowest variety of political literature, vicious and not traceable.

The "coffin handbill" of 1828 was the first important example of this genre. The one-page flyer recounting "some of the Bloody Deeds of General Jackson," was decorated with coffins, illustrating the murders of soldiers and others while he was commanding troops. Philadelphia publisher John Binns was credited later with the authorship of the handbill, which contained the text of the execution order for six men signed by Lieutenant Colonel (later Senator) Thomas Hart Benton and approved by Jackson. Most of the "victims" represented by coffins had been court-martialed for mutiny or desertion. One man Jackson had slain himself; the general had been tried, pleaded self-defense, and was acquitted. The handbill was effective, but Jackson won.

Another, more recent, gutter flyer was the "Nixon deed" used in the 1960 campaign. This was a blowup of the deed of the house in which Richard Nixon lived in Washington; like all other houses in that area, it contained a restrictive covenant. The flyer, clearly implying a racial bias by the candidate, was distributed widely in Negro neighborhoods in New York, Philadelphia, Detroit, and other urban areas. Democratic headquarters claimed no knowledge of the effort, but it appeared too well organized and financed to be the work of a single vicious entrepreneur. To force a halt, a young Republican volunteer thought of getting a similar deed on Kennedy-family homes in the Washington area, most of which contained a similar restrictive covenant. But wherever he looked in the town records, the sheet had been destroyed; the organizer of the "Nixon deed" plot had thought ahead.

In November 1963, John F. Kennedy was welcomed to Dallas with a gutter flyer in the form of a Bertillon police poster, with front and side views of Kennedy and the headline "Wanted for Treason."

In most cases, gutter flyers are unsigned. A federal law prohibits the use of unsigned literature in a campaign for federal office.

For an early example, see ROORBACK; for recent episodes, see DIRTY TRICKS.

HACK attack word on a long-time politician; a political drudge.

The word is derived from the hackney horse in England, a horse that was let out for hire, usually mistreated, and became dull, broken-down, and exhausted. See HOBSON'S CHOICE. The word was especially apt for politics because political hacks were disciplined by a party whip.

After the death of William Pitt in 1806, England was governed by a star-studded "Ministry of All the Talents," as the administration headed by Lord Grenville was dubbed. However, this was followed in 1807 by a less eminent—if more practical—group, soon derided as "All the Hacks."

The English word made the transition to American politics in the earliest days of the new nation; in 1828 the *New York Enquirer* said that other publications were calling those "friendly to Gen. Jackson 'political hacks.'"

A *hack,* in current usage, is one who works mechanically; he differs from a HENCHMAN, who works under clear direction, a HATCHET-MAN, who works ruthlessly, and a *hanger-on,* who does not work at all.

A hack writer, disdained in intellectual circles, is sometimes sought after in politics despite his hackneyed prose. "Find me a good hack writer," one local candidate told the author, "who will put down what I think, and you can keep all your Sorensens and Emmet Hugheses with their fancy ideas." For the PECKING ORDER of political writers, see SPEECHWRITER; GHOSTWRITER.

HACK IT to succeed; to come through after a struggle.

In a news conference on March 4, 1971, President Nixon used a phrase he attributed to General Creighton Abrams: "His evaluation after three weeks of fighting is that—to use his terms—the South Vietnamese can hack it . . ."

Several weeks later, commentator Howard K. Smith, in a televised conversation with the President, observed, "You also said that the Laos operation showed the South Vietnamese could hack it by themselves." The President again used the phrase in his reply: "When I use the term 'hack it' . . . we have now concluded, and this is General Abrams' assessment, that the South Vietnamese have now passed a milestone in their development."

The phrase appears to be an off-shoot of "cut it," a shortened form of "cut the mustard."

"HAD ENOUGH?" Republican campaign slogan in the off-year elections of 1946.

The phrase "had enough," with a modern variant "had it," is an old expression of mild disgust. When

Theodore Roosevelt decided not to run for a third term in 1908, he said, "I don't want it. I've had enough . . ."

In 1946 Harry Truman was in trouble. The cost-of-living index was climbing rapidly, more unions were striking than usual, shortages of meat, autos, and housing were continuing. The White House was the scapegoat. The creation of an advertising slogan that reflected the public mood—"Had Enough?"—is credited to the Harry M. Frost agency of Boston.

Wrote Eric Goldman: "A nation which had quite enough of inflation and the Russians, of strikes, shortages, and the atom bomb, of everlasting maybe's about peace and prosperity, rose up in a hiss of exasperation and elected the first Republican Congress since the far-distant days of Herbert Hoover."

See DON'T LET THEM TAKE IT AWAY.

HAIL OF DEAD CATS criticism accompanying the exit of an unpopular figure from public life.

The National Recovery Administration, a New Deal project, ran into severe criticism soon after Roosevelt's HUNDRED DAYS had ended, and was frequently labeled "the National Run-Around."

A series of strikes, especially in the textile industry, required National Guard action that resulted in a list of dead and wounded on the labor front. In the fall of 1934 General Hugh Johnson, controversial head of the NRA, resigned in what he called "a hail of dead cats."

Precipitation has an affinity for resignations. A "rain (or flood or deluge) of complaints" leads to a resignation "under a cloud"; a "storm of criticism" is followed by the most colorful expression of all, "a hail of dead cats."

The expression is probably not related to the "dead cats" of the circus (nonperforming lions and tigers) but may be akin to "catcall," a raucous noise expressing disapproval.

HALF-BREEDS, see STALWART.

HALF-TRUTH a statement accurate enough to require an explanation; and the longer the explanation, the more likely a public reaction of half-belief.

Senator Joseph McCarthy was often accused of using "half-truths, innuendos and smears." On the other hand, one defense of a charge that might be largely true was to label it a half-truth and denounce "McCarthy-type tactics" (except in areas where McCarthy had a strong following).

Alexander Gilchrist, in his *Life of William Blake,* quoted the English poet-artist-mystic as referring to "the great half-truth, Liberty." In Blake's *Auguries of Innocence,* this couplet appears:

> *A truth that's told with bad intent*
> *Beats all the lies you can invent.*

Philosopher Alfred North Whitehead wrote: "There are no whole truths. All truths are half-truths. It is trying to treat them as whole truths that plays the devil."

A political adage attributed to nobody is: "Half a truth is like half a brick—you can throw it twice as far." And the evasiveness of a half-truth is recognized in court oaths swearing in witnesses: "The truth, the whole truth, and nothing but the truth."

See BIG LIE.

HANDOUT a welfare payment; or, a press release; or, a handbill.

"Handout" is an attack word on

welfare payments. A political cliché is "People want a hand up, not a handout." The word has connotations of begging; the usage began in the late nineteenth century as hobo lingo, referring to the bundle of clothes or plate of food given at the back door. See HOTTENTOTS, MILK FOR.

A press handout is a story written by a political figure's press aide, or by himself, to be given to reporters at a press conference to save them the trouble of taking notes or asking questions. Good reporters profess to ignore "handouts" and dig for themselves; however, an informative handout can be helpful and timesaving. A *handout* is usually directly given by press agents to reporters; a *release* may either be handed out or mailed.

Handout is also an infrequently used word for political handbill. See FLYER.

HAND-PICKED   a candidate chosen or an appointment made by a powerful person; an allusion to boss rule.

Hand-picked is always an attack word; in the 1958 Democratic convention in New York State, the choice of District Attorney Frank Hogan for senatorial candidate was dictated by Tammany chief Carmine De Sapio. Hogan was promptly depicted by Republicans as "Boss De Sapio's hand-picked candidate" and was roundly defeated by Kenneth Keating.

In agriculture, hand-picked (vs. machine-picked) means carefully chosen, resulting in an unbruised fruit or berry or, more commonly, selected by hand from a larger group of the same product for quality. In politics, the opposite has come to be the meaning.

A "hand-picked successor" implies autocratic domination, subverting democratic processes, and is a charge hurled by whatever group refuses to hold still or go along. The vice-presidential candidate is usually handpicked by the presidential candidate, though Adlai Stevenson in 1956 made a point of permitting an "open convention" that chose Estes Kefauver over John F. Kennedy.

"In 1908," wrote Harry Truman, "William Howard Taft had been hand-picked by [Theodore] Roosevelt as his successor." He did not add that he himself had been hand-picked by another Roosevelt in 1944.

See HEIR APPARENT.

HANGER-ON, *see* HACK.

HANG TOUGH   strike a determined pose; or, remain resolute.

Eugene Landy's *Underground Dictionary* traces the phrase: "It is used to encourage individuals during a stressful situation, such as a period of withdrawal from a drug. Hang tough was commonly used at Synanon Foundation during the foundation's initial stages when addicts were allowed to withdraw after entering Synanon. Synanon's house in Santa Monica, California has a ship's white life preserver upon which is written 'S.S. Hang Tough' hanging on the wall."

The phrase, which has variant readings of "hang in there" and "tough it out," was used by Hugh Sidey in *Life* on June 19, 1970: "In sum, they agree that the emergence of Patton as a major figure in the Nixon Pantheon is a good sign, meaning that he will continue to hang tough in the crunches."

During the sixteen months of Watergate siege, President Nixon was urged by some to "hang tough," and the phrase has been used in reference to presidential resolution or irresolution ever since.

"Hang loose" is an older locution, from "hang it easy," a teen age phrase from the early fifties. Some slang authorities speculate that both "hang loose" and "hang tough" are sexual in origin, referring to the relaxed or tense condition of the genitals. Steven Weisman defined "hang loose" in the *New York Times* in 1976 as "the period when a legislator has not made up his mind."

New York Times columnist Tom Wicker speculated in a 1973 note to the author: "I believe 'hang in there' will be found to be a prize-fight term meaning that someone momentarily rocked by the other guy should 'hang in there,' maybe even literally hanging on to the ropes or hanging on to the other guy in a clinch."

"Tough it out" has a longer lineage in slang. R. L. Thornton has six citations in his *American Glossary,* beginning with an 1824 memoir: "We little fellows had to tuff it out as well as we could."

HAPPY DAYS ARE HERE AGAIN   campaign song of FDR in 1932.

Hit songs during the Depression ranged from "Brother, Can You Spare a Dime?" to "Happy Days are Here Again." Bronx Democratic boss Edward J. Flynn felt that the music to be played when FDR was nominated should be gay and optimistic.

Flynn and FDR-confidant Louis Howe were lying on the floor of Howe's hotel suite in Chicago listening to the nomination on the radio. Roosevelt, a former Navy man, had suggested that at the moment of nomination the convention band should play "Anchors Aweigh." When the musicians began to play the Navy song slowly, Flynn groaned to Howe:

"That sounds like a funeral march. Why don't we get them to play something peppy, like 'Happy Days are Here Again'?" Howe agreed, and Flynn telephoned the convention floor manager to suggest that the band switch to a lively rendition of "Happy Days." Flynn wrote later: "In a moment it began to come over the air. To me, it certainly sounded more cheerful and appropriate to the occasion."

The song soon came to mean for Roosevelt what "Sidewalks of New York" meant to Al Smith. Nobody bothered to point out that the song was written just before the crash of 1929 by Jack Yellen/Milton Agar for use in an MGM movie entitled *Chasing Rainbows.*

At the 1976 Democratic convention, the song was played to recall past Democratic glories for candidate Jimmy Carter.

The phrase "Happy Days," which is also a toast, was used as the title of a kids' television program in the mid-seventies, which was the disseminator of many nonce words.

HAPPY WARRIOR   Franklin Roosevelt's characterization of Al Smith.

Franklin Roosevelt, nominee for vice president on the losing Democratic ticket in 1920, crippled by poliomyelitis in 1921, made his political comeback in a nomination speech for Alfred E. Smith in 1924. Leaning on crutches, he walked to the podium and said of Smith toward the end of his speech: "He is the Happy Warrior of the political battlefield." The entire address, Walter Lippmann wrote Roosevelt later, "was a moving and distinguished thing. I am utterly hard-boiled about speeches, but yours seems to me perfect in temper and manner and most eloquent in its effect."

But Smith deadlocked with McAdoo, and John W. Davis received the nomination, only to lose to Coolidge. FDR repeated the "Happy Warrior" theme to the Democratic convention in Houston in 1928, this time to fifteen million Americans listening on radio. The bid for nomination was successful, thanks largely to Republican-turned-Democrat John Raskob, who ran the Smith campaign.

In 1932 Smith and Roosevelt competed for the Democratic nomination and bitterness developed between the two. Smith "took a walk" (see TAKE A WALK) during the first term of the New Deal, and attacked Roosevelt in the 1936 campaign. Roosevelt selected Senator Joseph Robinson, Smith's running mate in 1928, to answer the attack. Robinson hit where it hurt: for deserting his party, Smith was labeled "The Unhappy Warrior."

Roosevelt's reference was to English poet William Wordsworth's "Character of the Happy Warrior":

Who is the happy Warrior? Who is he
That every man in arms should wish to be?
. . . .
But who if he be called upon to face
Some awful moment to which Heaven has
*   joined*
Great issues, good or bad for human kind,
Is happy as a lover . . .

The story behind the 1924 speech was recounted in the *New York Times* obituary of Judge Joseph Proskauer, who died in 1971 at the age of ninety-four. As an aide to Governor Al Smith, Proskauer drafted the nominating speech for the man nominating him to give (a practice widely followed today). Roosevelt objected, "You can't give poetry to a political convention," and drafted a speech of his own.

Recalled Proskauer: "So I took Herbert Bayard Swope, the editor, with me to Roosevelt's place up the Hudson so that we could work it out.

"Swope made the mistake of the century. He picked up Roosevelt's speech, turned to me and said, 'Joe, this is awful. It's dull. It won't do.' And he flung it down on the floor.

"Then he picked up my 'happy warrior' speech. 'This is great, Frank,' he said to Roosevelt. 'You've done it just the way it ought to be.' Well, Roosevelt damn near went through the roof. We fought and fought. Finally I told him, 'Frank, I have this message from the Governor: Either you give this speech or you don't nominate him.' "

Roosevelt gave the Proskauer speech. "It's a good question whether it did Smith or Roosevelt the most good," grumbled the judge years later, "but I wrote the speech."

The sobriquet was later applied to Senator Hubert Humphrey, who espoused "the politics of joy."

HARDBALL rough political tactics; stronger than "practical politics" or "pranks," milder than DIRTY TRICKS.

In hearings on September 26, 1973, before the Senate Watergate Committee, Nixon speechwriter Patrick J. Buchanan gave a declension of roughness in politics: "My own view is that there are four gradations. There are things that are certainly utterly outragous and I would put that in with the kind of demonstrations against Vice President Humphrey in 1968 which denied him an opportunity to speak for almost a month. Then, there is 'dirty tricks.' Then, there is political hardball. Then there is pranks."

The author first heard the word used on December 20, 1972, by attorney (later Secretary of HEW) Joseph

Califano, complaining of Republican tactics during the campaign against Senator George McGovern: "Nobody ever played hardball like you guys." (He was unaware at the time that previous Presidents had used the FBI and CIA for campaign intelligence purposes.)

In trying to show that hardball, as practiced in the 1972 campaign by the Nixon forces, was not necessarily immoral or illegal, the author in his *New York Times* column used the expression "not every hardball is a beanball." *Times* sportswriter Walter "Red" Smith promptly corrected the mixed metaphor: "In sports terminology there is no such thing as 'a hardball.' When the word is used, which is seldom, 'hardball' means the game of baseball as distinct from softball. It does not mean a high, fast pitch. Probably Mr. Safire should be excused, for this was a column applauding Richard Nixon's forthright behavior in the Watergate case. It had an understandably agitated tone."

This word, popularized by Watergate, is likely to last longer than such specific usages as SATURDAY NIGHT MASSACRE, which refer to specific events. In May 1976 *Washington Star* columnist Edwin M. Yoder Jr. wrote: "This is a judicious way of accusing the Court of playing political hardball on the sly." In December 1976 Walter Pincus wrote in the *Washington Post* about "the hardball politics of a Cabinet appointment" which was headlined "Barbara Jordan Caught Up in Hardball Politics."

Though applied widely, the word still has a Nixonian connotation. *Time*'s Richard Schickel, reviewing the movie *King Kong,* wrote in December 77: "Grodin plays the honcho as a hard-baller of the sort that used to hang around the Nixon White House and creates a vicious, accurate parody of one of our more distressing contemporary types."

In political journalism a "softball" or "fat pitch" is a question designed to give an interviewee a rest.

For an earlier use of a game metaphor, see BEANBAG, FULL COURT PRESS, and GAME PLAN; also SPORTS METAPHORS.

HARD LINE a firm stand; recently, strong support of the CONTAINMENT of Communism; called "rigid" by soft-liners, who favor ACCOMMODATION.

The "line" appears to have come from PARTY LINE, a Communist phrase. Historian Samuel Eliot Morison wrote: "Thus the cold war began as soon as the hot war was over. Earl Browder, head of the Communist party in the United States, was the first victim of the 'hard line.' For his continuing to preach friendly collaboration between the United States and Russia, which he had been ordered to do in 1941, he was contemptuously deposed in May 1945, by orders from Moscow."

Western powers, led by the U.S., took note of the new Russian line and of Winston Churchill's IRON CURTAIN warning in 1946; NATO was formed, and the policy of containment followed. See CONTAINMENT; MR. X. The "hard line" was pursued in the Korean War, and was subsequently identified with Secretary of State John Foster Dulles throughout the Eisenhower years. At the onset of the war in Vietnam, however, the wisdom of the "hard line" came under increasing attack in the U.S. and abroad.

The *Wall Street Journal* wrote in 1967:

Such hard-liners as Sens. Bourke Hickenlooper (R.-Iowa) and Frank Lausche (D.-Ohio) can't shake the fear that the various national Communist parties around the world still want to seize political and social control everywhere, that they still have the common goal of toppling capitals. Former Ambassador Kennan, a hard-liner himself during Stalin's day, contends this economic goal is becoming increasingly theoretical. Eastern Europe policy-shapers may continue to make mischief for the West, but for reasons that are uniquely Russian, or Polish, or Rumanian, and not because they're "Communist."

The "Hards" and the "Softs" date back more than a century in U.S. history. New York State sent two warring factions to the 1848 Democratic convention in Baltimore: the *Hunkers,* known as the *Hard Shells* or *Hards,* and the *Barnburners,* known as the *Soft Shells* or *Softs.* The Hards supported the Polk Administration's policy opposing the Wilmot Proviso prohibiting slavery in California and the rest of the Mexican cession; the Softs were against the Democratic Administration's opposition, and fought to limit the extension of slavery. Efforts at a compromise failed, and neither faction took part in the convention.

Digging back, Charles Ledyard Norton in 1890 traced the hard and soft "shells" to sects of the Baptist denomination, so called by their critics because of their supposed similarity to crabs in different stages of development.

Hard-liners are often described as "hard-nosed"; for some reason, soft-liners are never described as "soft-nosed." According to lexicographer Kenneth Hudson, "hard-nosed" was originally applied to bulls: "A hard-nosed bull is one who does not respond when the ring through the cartilage of his nose is twitched by the person leading him on a pole or rope."

HARD MONEY   historically, metallic versus paper currency; recently, applied symbolically to anti-inflationists.

One of the great debates of early U.S. history pitted the "hard-money" against the "soft-money" men. In an 1816 debate Daniel Webster formulated the classical defense of gold and silver currencies: "The framers of the Constitution, and those who enacted the early statutes on this subject, were hard-money men; they had felt and therefore duly appreciated the evils of a paper medium."

Andrew Jackson tied the Democratic party to a hard-money policy during his battle with the banks, and they became known as "Perish Credit, Perish Commerce" men. But in 1840 the party split into hard and soft money factions.

Nowadays, paper currency is universally accepted, but the hard and soft terms are still applied symbolically. The hard-money men favor a slow, measured expansion of the money supply, generally no more than 2 or 3 percent a year. The soft-money men—often Democrats, Keynesians, or both—approve pumping greater quantities of currency into circulation as a stimulus to employment and consumption.

HATCHED   removed from political activity by virtue of the Hatch Act.

The Hatch Act, bearing the name of Senator Carl Hatch, a Democrat from New Mexico, whose bill was passed in 1939, says: "It shall be unlawful for any administrative person employed in any administrative position by the United States, or by any department, independent agency, or other agency of the United States . . . to use his official authority for the purpose of interfering with, or affecting the election or the nomination of any candidate . . ." Its purpose was to prevent political appointees from unduly influencing government workers.

The phrase "subject to the restrictions of the Hatch Act" was soon shortened to the verb "hatched" which present usage no longer capitalizes.

In 1970 George Shultz, who had been promoted from Secretary of Labor in the Nixon cabinet to Director of the Office of Management and Budget, was routinely asked to make a speech supporting a candidate in his home state. Shultz looked up from his desk as if he had just pecked his way out of an eggshell and replied, "I can't. I've been hatched."

Presidential advisers use this rule of thumb: if you are on the White House payroll, or you are in a job that has called for Senate confirmation—you've not hatched.

In the late seventies, there was agitation to repeal the Hatch Act because it limited some people's rights to political expression; in this way, reformers were calling for reform of reform.

HATCHETMAN the associate of a politician or officeholder who takes on the unpleasant assignment of forcing supporters into line; also a public figure who engages in strong partisan attacks.

Louis Howe was FDR's private hatchetman, Harold Ickes his public hatchetman in political wars (see MAN ON THE WEDDING CAKE; BAREFOOT BOY FROM WALL STREET). Sherman Adams was occasionally Eisenhower's private hatchetman; Richard Nixon was often accused of being Eisenhower's public hatchet-

man because of the Vice President's willingness to play a partisan role in contrast to Eisenhower's above-politics position.

Robert Kennedy was the one most often accused of being John Kennedy's hatchetman, though Kenneth O'Donnell often had to perform that function. Lyndon Johnson occasionally used Hubert Humphrey as a public hatchetman (in the partisan public-figure sense); privately, White House aide Marvin Watson was accused of doing the necessary hatcheting, although President Johnson—with his Senate Majority experience—occasionally did the job himself. In 1971 the *Wall Street Journal* sunk the appellation in the head of Nixon counsel Charles Colson.

The derivation indicates both the public and private senses of the expression. In the public sense—one who engages in partisan attacks clearing a path for the above-politics leader—derivation is from American colonial military vocabulary. A hatchetman, or ax-man, was used to chop foliage in advance of a military group operating in woods or jungle. General George Washington wrote to one of his subordinates: "I think it will be advisable to detain both mulattoes and negroes in your company, and employ them as Pioneers or Hatchetmen."

In the private, arm-twisting sense, the derivation is from the Chinese tong wars of the 1880s, where "hatchet-armed killers" were the "enforcers" of their era, murdering enemies of the tongs for pay.

In current political usage, then, a politician differentiates between the public, or openly partisan, hatchetman and the insider who does the dirty work for a public figure. A HENCHMAN is one cut above a *hanger-on* but one cut below a *hatchet-*

man, though he may be used for hatcheting chores from time to time.

The work performed is called a "hatchet job" as well as "hatcheting." Harry Truman's assessment of the Republican party in the 1948 campaign: "Gluttons of privilege . . . all set to do a hatchet job on the New Deal."

When peace is made the hatchet is buried.

See GUTFIGHTER.

HAT IN THE RING announcement of active candidacy.

Former President Theodore Roosevelt was actively working to get the Republican presidential nomination in 1912, but had not yet announced that he really wanted to run against his protégé, William Howard Taft.

A number of governors signed a petition asking Roosevelt to take hold of the progressive forces in the GOP and make a run for the nomination. With the petition in his pocket Roosevelt couldn't help answering a reporter's question about his possible candidacy one cold night in Cleveland. "My hat's in the ring. The fight is on, and I'm stripped to the buff."

Roosevelt popularized a boxing phrase used on the American frontier. When a Westerner decided he was willing to fight all comers, he threw his hat in the prize ring, similar to "throwing down the gauntlet" in the days of chivalry.

After newspapers had picked up Roosevelt's "hat in the ring" quote, *Harper's Weekly* said of the bitter feud between Roosevelt and Taft: "Hate, not hat, is in the ring." The construction is flexible and current. Harold Ickes derided young Thomas E. Dewey for "throwing his diaper in the ring," and the *New York Times* in 1967 said that congressional candidate Shirley Temple Black "threw her curls in the ring."

HAVE AND HAVE-NOT NATIONS   phrase used to dramatize the gulf between the nations rich in resources and industry, and those yet undeveloped and dependent.

Miguel de Cervantes coined the phrase. In the second book of *Don Quixote,* chapter XX, Sancho Panza observes that his grandmother always used to say, "There are only two families in the world, the Haves and the Have-Nots." The Spanish *el tener* and *el no tener* is sometimes translated "have-much and have-little." A parallel aphorism is Rabelais' "one half of the world knows not how the other half lives."

The phrase has always filled a need. Lord Bryce used it in *The American Commonwealth:* "In the hostility of rich and poor, or of capital and labour, in the fears of the Haves and the desire of the Have-nots . . ." Theodore Roosevelt wrote in 1918: ". . . to oscillate between the sheer brutal greed of the haves and sheer brutal greed of the have-nots means to plumb the depths of degradation."

The phrase is used in its general sense defining the chasm between economic classes, and in a more specific sense pointing to the difference between rich and poor nations. H. L. Mencken used the general sense in his blast at Democratic candidate John Davis in the 1924 campaign: "Dr. Coolidge is for the Haves and Dr. La Follette is for the Have Nots. But whom is Dr. Davis for? . . . himself."

Talking about foreign affairs in 1948, Harry Truman used the more specific: "The world was undergoing a major readjustment, with revolution stalking most of the 'have-not' nations. Communism was making the most of this opportunity, thriving on misery as it always does."

America's responsibility toward the "have-not" nations has been a running controversy (see HOTTEN-TOTS, MILK FOR) in domestic politics. Frequently, when the "have-nots" bite the hand of the "haves" that are trying to feed them, there is a reluctance to continue the largesse (or fulfill the social responsibility, depending on the point of view).

The tension between the two "families" Sancho Panza spoke of is not likely to lessen. Journalist and former U.S. Ambassador to Guinea William Attwood wrote in 1967: "The number one problem of our planet in the years ahead will no longer be the cold war but the war on poverty; our world could live in peace half-slave and half-free, but it cannot live in peace, not in this age of mass communications, one-third rich and two-thirds poor."

Walter Lippmann struck a hopeful note:

> We have seen a breakthrough— that we are escaping from the immemorial human predicament of the haves and the have-nots. This predicament has been based on the assumption that the size of the pie to be divided is fixed and that therefore if some have more others must take less . . . the result of this change is a benign revolution which makes it possible that the costs of improving schools and colleges, of reducing poverty, of rebuilding slums can be covered by calculated increases in the national output of wealth.

See THIRD WORLD.

HAVE THE TICKETS, *see* TICKET.

HAWKS, *see* WAR HAWKS.

HEARTBEAT AWAY FROM THE PRESIDENCY   a reminder to voters to examine the shortcomings of a vice-presidential candidate.

"The Republican Vice Presidential candidate," Adlai Stevenson said in the Cleveland Arena in 1952, "—who asks you to place him a heartbeat from the Presidency—has attacked me for saying in a court deposition that the character of Alger Hiss was good." Stevenson then launched into a blast at Richard Nixon.

Nixon supporters in the 1960 campaign took a leaf from Stevenson's text. They compiled a list of every one of vice-presidential candidate Lyndon Johnson's votes against civil rights legislation as a representative and senator and circulated a flyer entitled "Only a Heartbeat from the Presidency."

McKinley manager Mark Hanna, seeking to block Theodore Roosevelt from the vice-presidential nomination, used the thought but not the phrase in 1900. "It must always be remembered," one report quoted him —"that there is only one life between the Vice President and the Chief Magistracy of the nation." Another report of the same statement: "Don't any of you realize that there's only one life between this madman and the White House?"

U.S. history to date has shown that there are better than two chances in ten that the President's heartbeat will stop during his term in office. Tyler took over for Harrison; Fillmore for Taylor; Johnson for Lincoln; Arthur for Garfield; Roosevelt for McKinley; Coolidge for Harding; Truman for Roosevelt; Johnson for Kennedy.

The scary phrase was used by reporter Jules Witcover as the title of a book about the forced resignation of Spiro Agnew: *A Heartbeat Away.*

Former presidential aide John Ehrlichman, noting the frequent references President Carter made to Vice President Walter Mondale as his "full partner," confided in a 1977 book review:

"For decades presidential candidates have promised to make the vice president a 'full partner,' 'deputy president,' 'total participant' in the Presidency. Up to and through the Nixon years those promises have been broken by each succeeding President and Vice President. Kennedy's Johnson was as frustrated and unused as Johnson's Humphrey. Hundreds of hours of the Nixon staff's time were spent on the Agnew relationship. Nixon himself was continually trying Mr. Agnew's square peg in one round governmental orifice and then another. At the nadir of his tolerance for Agnew, Mr. Nixon spoke to me more than once of his desire to induce the Vice President to resign so that John Connally might take his place. Nixon even considered offering Agnew a seat on the Supreme Court to get him to move. The specter of Senatorial confirmation chilled that idea."

HEARTLAND the strategic central area of a nation or a land mass; in American political usage, those non-coastal sections where spiritual and moral values are said to be most revered.

The geopolitical theory expounded by Sir Halford Mackinder in 1904 held that Eastern Europe's "heartland" could dominate the continent of Eurasia. From the Elbe to the Amur, the idea went, a self-sufficient area existed that could not be challenged by British mastery of the seas, and held the key to world domination. Naturally, this theory was vigorously disputed by exponents of British seapower.

The modern political use of the word stemmed from Dwight Eisenhower's 1945 Guildhall speech in London, where he referred to his boyhood in Abilene, Kan.: "I come from

the very heart of America." There was a double meaning to this, geographic and spiritual, which was picked up by Richard Nixon in the Landon Lecture he delivered at Kansas State University, September 16, 1970: "Now, twenty-five years later, as I speak in the heart of America, I can truly say to you here today you are the heart of America—and the heart of America is strong. The heart of America is good. The heart of America is sound. It will give—you will give us—the sound and responsible leadership that the great promise of America calls for . . ."

Political analyst Kevin Phillips applied the old geopolitical word to modern U.S. politics in his 1969 book, *The Emerging Republican Majority:* "Twenty-one of the twenty-five Heartland states supported Richard Nixon in 1968. . . . Over the remainder of the century, the Heartland should dominate American politics in tandem with suburbia, the South, and Sun Belt–swayed California." See SUNBELT.

Although the word continues to have this geopolitical meaning, it is more commonly used in a less specific context. "I am always pleased to be here in this great heartland of America," President Nixon told a group of Indiana's elderly citizens in 1971. Garnett Horner, writing in the *Washington Star* on June 25, 1971, used the word in its current spiritual-geographic sense: " 'It gives me a lift,' President Nixon remarked during an unscheduled sixty-eight-mile sentimental auto journey through a corn growing section of the heartland of America." *New York Times* correspondent Seymour Topping wrote on July 16, 1971: "The willingness of the President to travel to Peking, to the heartland of the Asian Communist world, cannot fail to impress the Chinese . . ."

HEARTS AND MINDS, see **SLO-GANS.**

HECKLE to harass a person, usually a speaker, with comments or questions in the hope of embarrassing or silencing him.

Nikita Khrushchev was heckled at a dinner of the Economics Club of New York in 1959, and won the respect of his audience by skillfully handling the heckler: "I am an old sparrow, so to say, and you cannot muddle me by your cries."

The Middle English word "hekele" meant to comb flax, to tease or ruffle hemp. As early as 1808, a Scottish dictionary began carrying a second definition for "heckle"—"to tease with questions."

Few hecklers today stop at teasing. Most try to make the heckled angry. If the heckled loses his temper, the heckler has won his point.

In 1906 the *New York Times* considered the word fit enough to use in that way and ran a headline: "Hearst is Heckled Into Talking Taxes."

Campaigning politicians are continually heckled. Their retorts, often carefully written ad libs, if clever enough, can quiet the hecklers quickly. During the 1960 campaign John F. Kennedy was often met by determined and loud young Republican hecklers. Whenever he was faced with a "We want Nixon!" chant, he replied with a good-humored, "I don't think you're going to get him." This was not brilliant repartee, but it pleased crowds and eased the tension and embarrassment of a crowd toward the hecklers within it.

In the same campaign Richard Nixon found that all heckling need not be audible, nor even in English. In Chinatown, Los Angeles, courtesy of Democratic prankster Dick Tuck, there was a huge billboard with a smiling picture of Nixon with the words "Welcome Nixon." However, in Chinese characters the sign asked, "What about the Hughes loan?," a Democratic allegation that Nixon had abused the trust of his office to obtain financial aid for his family.

Sometimes a hard answer can turn away a wrathful heckler. 1964 Republican presidential candidate Barry Goldwater was giving a relatively quiet speech at Rutgers University when a young man leapt to his feet and shouted, "You goddam Fascist bastard!" Goldwater won cheers from a generally hostile audience when he replied, "If you call me a bastard again, I'll meet you outside." Some observers found it fascinating to note at which word he took offense.

Most American politicians, accustomed to what they consider the art of heckling, are amazed at the violence of the heckling in England. On the stump, British candidates often have great difficulty in making themselves heard over the shouts and catcalls of groups of men who come equipped with loudspeakers. However, charming heckling is also a British trait. Sir Alec Douglas-Home, when he was a British Foreign Secretary, said he received the following telegram from an irate citizen: "To hell with you. Offensive letter follows."

HEFT, POLITICAL weight or substance as a candidate, based on experience or intellectual capacity, or the seriousness with which the public treats his candidacy.

This is a word used frequently in discussions of a candidate's potential, but the author is unable to find a written reference. "He's got heft," the opposite of "He's a **LIGHTWEIGHT,**" is usually accompanied by a rising and falling motion of the hand, as if the pleasurable weight of a roll of dimes was being hefted.

An ancient meaning of the word is to raise aloft ("Inflamed with wrath his raging blade he heft"—Spenser), a past tense of "heave"; a colloquial meaning has long been "influence," which is figurative weight, and its usage increased among politicians in the sixties.

HEGEMONY domination by one state over others.

Hegemony (preferred accent on the "gem") is the dirty word for leadership. In Greek, a *hegemon* is a leader; among the warring Greek city-states, Athens sought hegemony. Among individuals, this sort of leadership is often seen as laudable, but among states it has always been perceived as predatory. In 1860 the *Times* of London wrote: "No doubt it is a glorious ambition which drives Prussia to assert her claim to the leadership, or as that land of professors phrases it, the 'hegemony' of the German Confederation." In the U.S., *Forum* wrote in 1904: "The hegemon of the Western Hemisphere is the United States."

The word was popularized more recently by Mao Tse-tung. "Dig tunnels deep," he counseled, "store grain, and never seek hegemony." As the split developed in the Communist world, the crucial epithet became "hegemony"—secondarily the domination of imperialism, but primarily Mao's denunciation of the attempt by the Soviet Union to dominate China. When Communist parties in Western Europe sought to show their independence from Moscow so as to improve their appeal locally, "hegemony" was their attack word as well. One Italian Communist suggested that the Marxist "dictatorship of the proletariat" be changed to "the hegemony of the

working class." See EUROCOMMUNISM.

In his 1977 book, *A Civil Tongue*, Edwin Newman had some fun with the word:

The Soviet and Chinese governments have a way of insulting each other that is peculiarly their own. You seek hegemony, the Chinese will tell the Russians. You seek hegemony, the Russians will tell the Chinese. In the 1950's, some of us on the outside thought that the two governments might be seeking hegemony together, but their paths parted. Ever since, according to the Chinese, the Russians have been looking for hegemony high and low and in every nook and cranny, while according to the Russians the Chinese are obsessed with hegemony and think of nothing else except, in lighter moments, inciting a third world war. An unnamed Pakistani has told the *New York Times,* "The Indians have been bitten by the bug of wanting hegemony of the subcontinent." The *Times* found an Indian to deny it. The hegemoniacal debate goes on.

HEIR APPARENT the chosen successor, who does not always succeed in a democratic society.

If the man at the top feels secure enough, he will designate an heir apparent to carry on his policies after his term or life is over. From the boss's viewpoint, the advantage is a cessation of bickering below; the disadvantage is boredom below, or an unexpected bid for power by the second in command. See HAND-PICKED.

Martin Van Buren was Andrew Jackson's heir apparent, and William Howard Taft had been publicly tapped by Theodore Roosevelt. But "Little Van" could not carry the Jacksonian tradition past a single term. Roosevelt turned on Taft and ran as an independent against him, splitting the Republican vote enough to elect Woodrow Wilson.

Splitting heirs, the *heir expectant* is one who is simply in line for some inheritance; the *heir presumptive* is one who will succeed if the top man dies or quits immediately, but who can be replaced by the birth of a closer relative; and the *heir apparent* is the man to stop when the top man lets his power slip.

HELL BEFORE BREAKFAST, *see* **RIGHT TO KNOW.**

HELLBENT FOR ELECTION determined to the point of recklessness; evoking an image of a spirited, horn-blowing, flag-flying campaign.

The phrase appears to have its political origin in Maine in 1840, year of the "Tippecanoe and Tyler Too" election. Edward Kent won the gubernatorial election handily, and a ditty ran: "Maine went Hellbent For Governor Kent."

See **FLAT-OUT**.

HENCHMAN in fact, a member of the staff of a candidate or party; in an attack, a stooge, hatchetman, hanger-on.

This word has deep roots, starting with the Anglo-Saxon *hengest,* or horse; a hengest-man was a groom, squire, or page. In the Scottish Highlands, the henchman became a gillie, or right-hand man, to the clan leader, where the word picked up its political meaning of a loyal supporter and active worker.

The word is only used pejoratively; nobody ever claims to be anybody else's henchman. Typical use was by Alfred Landon in 1936: "Idealists may have been at the front door preaching social justice, but party henchmen have been at the back door handing out jobs."

A rare but colorful synonym is *janissary,* taken from the sultan's guard in Turkey. For differentiation in current usage, see **HACK; HATCHETMAN**.

HIDEBOUND narrow-minded, reactionary, stubborn; an attack word on conservatives.

In a cliché fight, *a hidebound conservative* could square off with a *bleeding-heart liberal.* The *OED* tracks the word back to Cooper's *Thesaurus* of 1559, talking about a "sickenesse of cattall . . . when their skynnes dooe cleve fast to their bodies, hyde bounde."

See **DYED-IN-THE-WOOL; ROCK-RIBBED; MOSSBACK**.

HIGHBINDERR, *see* **SPELL-BINDER.**

HIGH COST OF LIVING perennial political complaint about inflation; standard charge by the party out of power.

The 1972 *OED Supplement* credits American author William Dean Howells with the earliest use of "cost of living" in 1896: "The pay is not only increased in proportion to the cost of living, but it is really greater."

The earliest political use that this lexicographer has spotted is in the 1912 *Republican Campaign Textbook,* where the subject is addressed as "The Advance in the Cost of Living." The Taft Administration was under attack by Democrats on the tariff issue, and the Republican National Committee defended itself in this way:

"The increasing cost in recent years of the common necessaries and comforts of life has presented a serious problem to the masses of the people, not alone from the practical side of adjusting expenses to earnings, but also as to the political and economic side, as to whether the advance is to conditions peculiar to the system being applied in our government. It has been charged and is being constantly charged that it is due, in some mysterious way, to the protective tariff and to other conditions assumed to be related to the protective system.

"The most striking feature of the situation, however, is that the advance is not confined to this country or to the countries having protective tariffs, but is world wide, and that in every country the same kind of an agitation is going on, with more or less effort to lay the blame upon 'the party in power'. . ."

The Republicans, split by Teddy Roosevelt's "Bull Moose" party, lost in 1912 to Woodrow Wilson. By 1920, after eight Democratic years, the Republican texbook added an adjective and made the issue its own, using "The High Cost of Living" as its chapter heading:

"To the plain citizen of the United States the term 'High Cost of Living' has a clear and definite meaning. It sums up the hardship and suffering that the American people have borne during the past five years, because of the great rise in the prices of the goods and of the services upon which their income is ordinarily spent." The Republicans had the reason: "The prime cause of the 'High Cost of Living' has been, first and foremost, a fifty percent depreciation of the purchasing power of the dollar, due to a gross expansion of our currency and credit." The party also blamed "reduced production, burdensome taxation, wage advances and the increased demand for goods."

Two generations later the charge and phrase are in current use. The word INFLATION is used when the consumer price index is approaching DOUBLE DIGIT proportions, and the plainer "high cost of living" (no longer capitalized)—with its vague suggestion that the cost can be brought down—is used to express general dissatisfaction when inflation is not so high.

HIGHER LAW an appeal to moral or spiritual authority to excuse refusal to obey the laws of man.

This was an abolitionist phrase, probably used first by William Ellery Channing in 1842: "On this point the Constitution, and a still higher law, that of nature and God, speak the same language; and we must insist that these high authorities shall be revered." Senator Daniel Webster agreed. The phrase was taken up by William Seward, of New York, in an antislavery speech in the Senate in 1850: "I know there are laws of various kinds, which regulate the conduct of men . . . But there is a higher law than the Constitution, which regulates our authority over the domain."

Democrats and Whigs (including Abraham Lincoln) thought Seward had gone too far; later this phrase, along with Seward's 1858 characterization of the slavery issue as "an irrepressible conflict," led to Seward's defeat and Lincoln's victory at the Republican convention of 1860.

The idea of a "higher law" has usually conflicted with the RULE OF LAW and a GOVERNMENT OF LAWS, NOT OF MEN. It has been used by dissenters from established laws as justification for civil disobedience. In 1968 the *National Observer* wrote: "America must renounce the popular and poisonous philosophies that glorify anarchy as a heroic response to a 'higher law.'"

The phrase, however, has an idealistic or moralistic ring, and is not usually considered anarchic, or—as used against Seward—anticonstitutional.

See CIVIL DISOBEDIENCE.

HIGHEST AUTHORITY, *see* **AUTHORITATIVE SOURCES; BACKGROUNDER.**

HIGHEST NOTE IN THE SCALE THEORY, *see* **OVEREXPOSURE.**

HIGH MUCKEY-MUCKS, *see* **MUCKEY-MUCKS.**

HIGH ROAD . . . LOW ROAD rational approach versus emotional appeal; sticking to the issues versus going for the jugular; Marquis of Queensberry rules versus no-holds-barred.

The phrase became popular in the presidential campaign of 1948, when Republican Thomas E. Dewey selected "the high road" and let voters draw their own conclusions as to what road President Harry Truman was trudging. When Truman compared Dewey's mustache to Adolf Hitler's, Dewey wired Republican state chairmen to see if they thought he should take off the gloves and reply in kind (in earlier campaigns, Dewey had gained a reputation as a slashing speaker). "They all agreed," said GOP speechwriter John Franklin Carter, "that the proper thing for Dewey to do was to ignore Truman's personal attack and continue along the high road to the White House."

Politicians do not consider a "low road" charge the worst kind of insult. In 1958's off-year elections, Eisenhower aide Sherman Adams rehashed charges of Democratic catastrophes like losing our atomic secrets, losing China to the Communists, and described the Korean War as the one "they couldn't end." In Adams' memoirs, he admits: "I was loudly (and

not quite inaccurately) accused of 'taking the low road' while the President was keeping his campaign oratory on a high and dignified level."

But the low road is not always an effective course. In the Democratic primary contest for Massachusetts senator in 1962 between Attorney General Edward McCormack and Ted Kennedy, McCormack, trailing, decided to attack Kennedy in a televised debate. The political editor of the *Boston Herald* wrote: "[McCormack's] attack on Kennedy, and the latter's refusal to be drawn into an Army base brawl, apparently created unfavorable reaction to the Attorney General among many viewers, especially women. . . . Kennedy took the high road, and, although he was battered and mauled by McCormack, probably won a strategic victory with the huge TV audience."

Ted Kennedy was following John F. Kennedy's strategy at the 1960 Democratic convention, when Lyndon Johnson baited him in a debate before a joint caucus of the Texas and Massachusetts delegations. *Washington Post* publisher Philip Graham urged Johnson to present himself as a man of wide experience in defense and foreign affairs and avoid the kind of comments about Kennedy's health and his father's alleged pro-Nazi record that Johnson supporters were spreading. Pro-Kennedy historian Arthur Schlesinger, Jr., wrote later: "During the debate Johnson opened with Graham's 'high road' but went on to attempt the personal thrusts which Kennedy parried with such ease and mastery."

Derivation: a "high road," or highway, is the easy way in English usage. In London today the "high streets" are the main traffic arteries. However, the takers of low roads can sometimes make better time, as the balladeer in

"*Loch Lomond*" indicates: "O ye'll take the high road and I'll take the low road and I'll be in Scotland afore ye . . ."

HILL, THE   Capitol Hill; term for the legislative branch of U.S. government, as White House is for the executive branch.

"On the Hill" is frequently used in roundups of news from Washington, D.C.; White House aides for legislative liaison take messages "up to the Hill." (The judiciary has a similar metaphor, with indictments being handed "up"—to the bench—and decisions handed "down"—from the bench.)

The Hill is real as well as figurative. The base of the Capitol sits 88 feet above sea level, as compared with the White House's 55 feet, with lower areas in between. Before November 21, 1800, when Congress moved from Philadelphia and held its first session in the new Capitol, the eminence was known as "Jenkins Hill," presumably from one Thomas Jenkins, who rented the land from one Daniel Carroll, who owned it. Both George Washington and Pierre L'Enfant, who laid out the city of Washington, referred to "Jenkins Hill" in letters.

It is by no means the tallest hill in Washington—the hill on which the National Cathedral stands is over 300 feet—but it is the one that dominates the scene.

Although *the Hill* implies power, an unrelated metaphor, *over the hill*, implies the diminution of power, as even legislators become as *old as the hills.*

HIPPIE LANGUAGE, *see* **COUNTERCULTURE.**

HISTORIC COMPROMISE   the bid by Italian Communists to accept a share of national power as part of a multiparty coalition.

In the early seventies, as the Italian Communist party grew in voting strength in local elections, the idea was broached that a coalition might be possible with the long-ruling rightist party, the Christian Democrats.

Arrigo Levi, editor of Italy's *La Stampa,* replied to the author's query with this derivation of the phrase:

"As to 'historic compromise': this was coined by [Enrico] Berlinguer himself, in the famous articles which appeared in the pci's [Italian Communist Party] weekly *Rinascita,* also republished in *l'Unità,* after the end of [Chilean President Salvatore] Allende, as a comment on the reasons that had led to his fall. Fundamentally, Berlinguer criticized Allende's policy of trying to split Chilean Christian Democracy, stated that the pci's policy in Italy was to try and achieve a 'historical compromise' with the whole of Democrazia Cristiana, in order to prevent the kind of reaction which happened in Chile. Though later somewhat criticized by the former leader Luigi Longo, who didn't like the word 'compromise' because of its negative connotations, it has remained as the official 'line' of the party. The *Rinascita* articles appeared on September 28, October 5 and 10, 1973."

See **EUROCOMMUNISM.**

HIT LIST   persons or projects targeted for removal.

In underworld lingo, a "hit" is a murder; a "hit man" is a hired assassin. On the analogy of an older phrase, "shit list," it followed that a "hit list" was a group of individuals to be exterminated.

In politics, the phrase is usually used at a time of transition between Administrations, when the new "Ins" are examining rosters to see what plums are available for replacement with the faithful. If those who are selected for removal can claim any civil service protection, they charge that they have been placed on an Administration "hit list," giving a sinister connotation to old-fashioned PATRONAGE.

The term's use is growing. *New York Daily News* correspondent Paul Healy wrote from Plains, Georgia, in August 1977: "President Carter reluctantly signed yesterday a $10 billion public works appropriation bill that includes money for 10 water projects on his 'hit list.' "

When conservative fund-raiser Richard Viguerie said in 1977 that he "couldn't care less about party labels," Senator Charles Mathias (R-Md.) took this as a threat to oppose less conservative Republicans in primaries. Ken Bode wrote in the *New Republic* on December 10: "Verbal skirmishing about ideology versus party broke into open hostility last month when moderates discovered that at least three of their number [Senators Ed Brooke and Clifford Case, and Representative John Anderson] were on what they termed 'hit lists'—targeted by conservative groups for primary contests in 1978." (See IDEOLOGY.)

The opposite of a hit list for projects is a "must list," a term for top-priority legislation. *New York Times* Albany reporter Steven Weisman wrote in 1976: "In the Capitol, where one man's 'must' is another man's 'maybe,' all the leaders circulate their 'must lists' among themselves to make sure that the bills that 'must' be passed are, in fact, passed. Lists are so popular in Albany that some aides keep lists of their lists." (See ENEMIES LIST.)

The nonmurderous, but besmear-

ing, use of "hit" appears to be growing. Carter Administration Attorney General Griffin Bell denounced a newspaper story about him as "nothing less than a 'hit job,' " thus being the first to marry "hit" to "hatchet job," and the *New York Times* on November 17, 1977, reported that the writer so accused "resented [the story] being characterized, even without naming her, as a 'hit job.' "

HIZZONER   a sobriquet bestowed on all mayors by writers with an instinct for the jocular.

"Hizzoner the Mayor," for "His Honor the Mayor," was a frequent sound in New York during the incumbency of Fiorello H. La Guardia. Since "the Little Flower" was not stuffy, the playful derogation of the honorific title seemed in place, and has become a part of big-city mayoralties, much as "Veep" has loosely attached itself to the vice presidency. A refinement was introduced when Richard Daley of Chicago was known as "Hizzoner duh Mare."

In December 1977, *Time* reported that the West Virginia town of Coalton was having trouble finding a citizen to serve as mayor, for a salary of only $100 a year. The headline: "It's No Honor to Be Hizzoner."

HOBSON'S CHOICE   a take-it-or-leave it proposition; in politics a situation in which you vote for one candidate or do not vote at all.

English poet Thomas Ward wrote in 1630: "Where to elect there is but one/'Tis Hobson's choice,—take that or none."

Sir Richard Steele, in *The Spectator,* No. 509, explained the derivation:

> Mr. Tobias Hobson [Thomas Hobson, 1544–1631] from whom we have the expression . . . was a carrier

... the first in the Island who let out hackney-horses. He lived in Cambridge, and observing that the scholars rid hard, his manner was to keep a large stable of horses, with boots, bridles, and whips.... When a man came for a horse, he was led into the stable, where there was great choice, but he obliged him to take the horse which stood next to the stable-door; so that every customer was alike well served according to his chance, and every horse ridden with the same justice. From whence it became a proverb, when what ought to be your election was forced upon you, to say Hobson's Choice.

Theodore Bernstein, author of *The Careful Writer,* points out that it is incorrect to use the phrase as if it meant the kind of choice involved in a dilemma, as in this sentence: "But how long, in Berlin, must we rely on this cruel Hobson's choice between honoring pledges and eviscerating the world?"

The correct use was in this 1910 New Jersey campaign address by Woodrow Wilson, which marked an early use of "new deal" as well: "If it is reorganization, a new deal and a change you are seeking, it is Hobson's choice. I am sorry for you, but it is really vote for me or not vote at all."

HOLD STILL . . . GO ALONG
the grudging willingness of a politician to accept publicly, or not to fight privately, a proposed project.

Hold still indicates a greater degree of personal objection and an unwillingness to support publicly; *go along* in current political usage means the political leader will remain passive and indicate his support when asked. For example, "We can't get him to go along, but he'll hold still—he'll have to bite the bullet, but he won't bolt."

When Alice Roosevelt Longworth expressed doubts to George Harvey

about the selection of Warren Harding as a candidate, Harvey explained that Harding was best because he would "go along."

Wrote John F. Kennedy in *Profiles in Courage:* "The question is how we will compromise and with whom. For it is easy to seize upon unnecessary concessions, not as means of legitimately resolving conflicts but as methods of 'going along.' "

An old saying in the U.S. Senate is: "The way to get along is to go along." In 1958 Arthur Krock wrote a bit of doggerel called "Wisdom of a House Freshman" that sums up the point:

> *I love Speaker Rayburn,*
> *His heart is so warm,*
> *And if I obey him*
> *He'll do me no harm.*
> *So I shan't sass the Speaker*
> *One least little bitty*
> *And then I'll wind up*
> *On a major committee.*

Degrees of "going along" range from "willingly" to "grudgingly" to "kicking and screaming." The last cannot be used with "hold still."

HOLD THE LINE   government
efforts to restrain the economy; anti-inflation moves.

Four months after he became President, Harry Truman issued an Executive Order gradually relaxing controls over prices, wages, and production as the wartime economy made its transition to peace. This became known as the "hold-the-line order."

"Holding the line against inflation" remains a cliché, taken from a football metaphor ("Hold-that-line!") which in turn comes from a military expression (a line of soldiers trying to prevent an enemy breakthrough).

Other inflation bromides include *inflationary spiral* and *runaway infla-*

tion which *erodes the purchasing power of your dollars* and hurts most those on *fixed incomes.* See INFLATION; DOUBLE DIGIT; OVERHEATED ECONOMY.

Columnist Art Buchwald quoted a mythical professor of the Grim Economic Institute as predicting for 1968: "An inflationary spiral followed by a wage and price merry-go-round which will eventually lead to a roller coaster ride ending on a ferris wheel cycle of high interest rates."

HOLIER THAN THOU, *see* **DO-GOODER; RELIGIOUS META-PHORS.**

HOLOCAUST, THE the systematic murder of six million Jews during the Nazi regime in Germany.

After World War II the murder of the Jews spawned a new word, "genocide," the coinage of U.S. scholar Raphael Lamkin, and the United Nations in 1948 passed a Convention on the Punishment of the Crime of Genocide.

Somehow, "genocide" was too clinical a description of what had happened; the similar "homicide" is a bureaucratic word for "murder." In 1965 A. Donat published a book titled *The Holocaust Kingdom,* and two years later N. Cohn, in *Warrant for Genocide,* wrote that "by the end of 1944 the holocaust was nearing its conclusion." In 1968 the *Manchester Guardian* reported: "There is now within modern history a compartment of 'holocaust studies'—dealing with the wholesale destruction by the Nazis of European Jewry."

"Holo" is rooted in "whole" and "caust" in "burn"—a holocaust is a burnt offering, extended to mean an all-consuming conflagation. In 1977, when Egyptian President Anwar el-Sadat became the first Arab chief of state to visit Israel, Prime Minister Menachem Begin conducted him to the mausoleum of Yad Vashem, the shrine to the six million Jews who died in what—since only the mid-sixties—has come to be known as the Holocaust.

In the mid-sixties a group of militant U.S. Jews formed the Jewish Defense League to demonstrate against those they considered anti-Semites. Though most established Jewish organizations disavowed its sometimes violent activity, and considered its leader, Rabbi Maier Kahane, harmful to the interests of Jews in the U.S., they could not dispute its slogan, based on the Holocaust: "Never Again."

See FINAL SOLUTION.

HOMELAND word used by a group seeking an independent state to assert a moral or historic claim to the territory.

This incendiary, evocative term was first used in a political context by Theodor Herzl, at the First Zionist Congress in Basel, Switzerland, in 1897. The "Basel Declaration" called for a Jewish homeland: the German word used was *Heimstätte,* which translates more as "homestead" than the more common *Heimatland,* or "homeland." In 1917, in an effort to marshal Jewish support for the Allies in World War I, British Prime Minister Arthur Balfour embraced the idea in a communication to the second Baron Rothschild.

The Balfour Declaration came close to using the word: "His Majesty's Government view with favor the establishment in Palestine of a national home for the Jewish people . . . nothing shall be done which may prejudice the civil and religious rights of existing non-Jewish communities in Palestine . . ." Formally approved at Versailles in 1919, Balfour's pledge of a "national home" became the basis of the League of Nations Mandate for Palestine. After World War II, a combination of guilt felt by the Allied powers at their inability to stop the murder of six million Jews in Europe (see HOLOCAUST), gratitude for Jewish efforts in North Africa in the face of some Arab support of the Axis powers, and a fierce determination by Jews for "eretz Israel" led to the UN resolution creating a state out of the Jewish "homeland."

When Arabs on Israel's borders failed, after four wars, to conquer the new nation, they made demands for the "rights" mentioned in the Balfour Declaration; although the Palestine Liberation Organization interpreted those rights as a return of Israel to Arab rule, other Arabs—and their UN supporters—saw "the legitimate rights of the Palestinian people" as meaning a separate state in the West Bank of the Jordan river and in the Gaza Strip. This "moderate" demand took the form, in the mid-seventies, of a call by third parties for a "homeland" for the Palestinian refugees. Israelis pointed out that the Jewish state had absorbed all Jewish refugees from Arab states, while Arab states had refused to absorb the Palestinians, using the festering camps as a weapon against Israel. Jewish leaders took umbrage at the use of "homeland"—their word—against them.

Israel's supporters were dismayed when, on March 21, 1977, President Carter told a Clinton, Mass., audience: "There has to be a homeland provided for the Palestinian refugees who have suffered for many, many years." Later he denied that "homeland" meant a separate state, as most people construed it; the President said he preferred an "entity," of ambiguous nature, tied to Jordan.

Another example of the power of the word (which stirs feelings akin to, though not as aggressive as, LEBENS-RAUM) was in its appropriation in the early seventies by the white leadership of the Union of South Africa. Some tribal Bantustans, occupied by blacks, were made politically independent, though they remained economically dependent upon South Africa. Columnist James J. Kilpatrick wrote in 1978 that "this widely scorned program of creating 'homelands' " rested upon "the fundamental fact of South African life: the political, cultural and social identity of the blacks is not national; it is tribal." Columnist William Raspberry countered: "They will play at 'reform'—removing racial barriers at only the country's most expensive hotels, for instance—because they value world opinion. For the same reason, they will put new names on old policies—'homelands' instead of 'bantustans' or 'native reserves.' "

HOME RULE the demand that a state government grant more autonomy and local self-government to cities and counties.

"In campaign season," wrote the *New York Sun* in 1905, "politicians of all stripes and kinds howl for 'Home Rule!' Then they flood to Albany and ask the Legislature to tinker up what they consider imperfect in the city government."

Injection of the phrase into big-city politics was probably begun by Tom Loftin Johnson in his campaigns for mayor of Cleveland, Ohio, in the early 1900s. The full slogan of the Democratic ticket was: "Home Rule; Three Cent Fare; and Just Taxation."

Opponents of Frank "I AM THE LAW" Hague, mayor of Jersey City, in 1939 elected five anti-Hague commissioners in Bayonne, N.J., on the slogan "Home Rule—Not Hague Rule."

The argument for home rule has always been, "the best government is that government which is closest to the people." The argument against it is that many localities are hesitant to take unpopular but necessary steps in taxation, school construction, etc. The argument reaches its highest pitch when a major city in a state is controlled by one party and the state government by another.

Origin of the phrase is English, about 1860, in connection with agitation for self-government in Ireland. Benjamin Disraeli, speaking in Manchester in 1872, suggested that with international troubles brewing, England might be wise to have a loyal Ireland to call upon: "Our connection with Ireland will then be brought painfully to our consciousness, and I should not be at all surprised if the visor of Home Rule should fall off some day, and you beheld a very different countenance." The Home Rule movement, led by the Sinn Fein, ultimately founded the Irish Free State; Northern Ireland remained a part of Great Britain, operating under a Home Rule Act. Modern descendants of the Home Rule movement continue to agitate for an end to partition.

See SHORTCHANGE; DEVOLUTION.

HONCHO   as a noun, the one in charge; as a verb, to follow through.

This Japanese word was brought to the White House in the late sixties by staffers from California; it began as a noun—"who's the honcho on this project?"—and soon acquired a verb usage: "Honcho this and don't let it get lost in the bureaucracy."

HONEST GRAFT   money made as a result of political power, without doing anything illegal—no longer considered permissible.

New York newspaperman William Riordon took down and reshaped the thoughts of Tammany leader George Washington Plunkitt as he held court on his favorite rostrum, the New York County Court house bootblack stand in 1905:

Everybody is talkin' these days about Tammany men growin' rich on graft, but nobody thinks of drawin' the distinction between honest graft and dishonest graft. There's all the difference in the world between the two. Yes, many of our men have grown rich in politics. I have myself. I've made a big fortune out of the game, and I'm gettin' richer every day, but I've not gone in for dishonest graft—blackmailin' gamblers, saloonkeepers, disorderly people, etc.—and neither has any of the men who have made big fortunes in politics.

There's an honest graft, and I'm an example of how it works. I might sum up the whole thing by sayin': "I seen my opportunities and took 'em." . . .

I'll tell you of one case. They were goin' to fix up a big park, no matter where. I got on to it, and went lookin' about for land in that neighborhood.

I could get nothin' at a bargain but a big piece of swamp, but I took it fast enough and held on to it. What turned out was just what I counted on. They couldn't make the park complete without Plunkitt's swamp, and they had to pay a good price for it. Anything dishonest in that?

Times have changed, and such graft is no longer considered "honest." Such gains by a politician or any member of his family are now considered ill-gotten; bribery is permissible only to the extent of "something that can be eaten or smoked in a single day."

Today's "honest graft" is more ephemeral: government officials, when they retire, take jobs with private industry. Admirals who have steered government cargo to certain steamship lines, planning commissioners who have pressed certain zoning matters, find themselves paid off in a way that arouses little or no criticism. It is considered "honest." But it is graft. In the late seventies, this practice became known as the "revolving door," and President Carter proposed legislation that would curb the modern version of Plunkitt's technique.

See BOODLE; GRAFT.

HONEYMOON PERIOD the short time after first taking office during which a public official is not set upon by the press.

"Kingdoms have their honeymoon," wrote Thomas Fuller in 1655, "when new Princes are married unto them." The political use is among the first *OED* citations of the word.

"The honeymoon is over." This phrase is used as the interval between election and disenchantment is about to end. In this period, the news generated by an administration on any level of government is primarily appointments, announcements of plans, often a quick vacation that the public considers well-deserved. The opposition cannot carp without appearing to be sore losers; the press has little to criticize and many reporters are even willing to give the new man the benefit of the doubt. In historian Charles Beard's phrase, a "golden glow" emanates from the press.

"Every newly elected Governor," wrote Adlai Stevenson's biographer, Kenneth S. Davis, "has his 'honeymoon' period with the press of the State. Stevenson's [in Illinois] was unusually ecstatic and unusually prolonged."

On the other hand, California Governor Ronald Reagan took some controversial steps regarding the University of California soon after assuming office in 1967 and was promptly blasted by many newspapers. After four months in office, he said: "If this has been a honeymoon, then I've been sleeping alone."

The shortest honeymoon on record for any President was recounted by columnist Murray Kempton in the *New York Post* in December 1977. Colonel Robert McCormick, late publisher of the *Chicago Tribune,* was watching the news tickers in his office in March of 1929, as President Herbert Hoover's inaugural address was being dispatched. After the fourth paragraph he fired his response to his Washington bureau: "This man Hoover wont do. McCormick."

The word refers, of course, to the vacation after a marriage and before settling down, and is derived from the thought that the honeymoon, or full moon, begins to wane from the moment it is full.

HONKIE, *see* **CHARLIE.**

HOOPLA devices and techniques to stimulate enthusiasm.

"Hoo" is the sound of excitement and gaiety. "Hooray" and "Hoohah!" along with "Whoopee" and "Whoop-de-do" all probably derive from the excited squeals of children.

In politics, hoopla is a necessary ingredient to campaigns to give them bounce, youthfulness, and a sense of fun. At the opening of Rockefeller headquarters at the New York Hilton in the 1966 campaign for governor, the man in charge of hoopla was discussing budget with the office manager. He pointed out that an opening rally required balloons, buttons, a sound truck with bunting, and hats and sashes for the "Rockyettes." Multicolored confetti, he explained, cost 10 cents a package, but it was cheaper if you bought it by the pound, at 50 cents per pound.

"I can't give you a budget," the rally man explained, "until I know how big a rally you want."

"Figure a thousand people," the office manager said.

"You want a lot of hoopla?"

The man in charge of the budget took out a requisition slip and calculated rapidly. "Give me fifty pounds of hoopla."

See BALLYHOO; BANDWAGON.

HOOVERIZE originally, to behave in a humanitarian way; since the Depression, to pauperize.

The word reflects the extremes of attitudes toward the late President Herbert Hoover. The verb was first used in 1917, after the first regulations of Hoover's Food Administration were published. It was widely and favorably applied after Hoover's postwar feats—providing food for the Belgians and sending aid to Russia and other devastated lands.

During the Depression, the Democrats made the word synonymous with poverty and despair. A whole class of related words came into being: Hoovervilles—the shabby shantytowns occupied by the jobless, also known as Hoover villages; Hoover soup; and Hoover prosperity. The Democrats ridiculed Hoover's originally optimistic attitude toward the Depression. "Prosperity," they said, "is just Hoovering around the corner." Today, rhetoric warning of economic doom is called RUNNING AGAINST HOOVER.

See RUGGED INDIVIDUALISM; CHICKEN IN EVERY POT.

HORSE-AND-BUGGY hopelessly old-fashioned; out-of-date.

The phrase became political parlance when Franklin Roosevelt denounced the Supreme Court decision in 1935 striking down the National Recovery Act (see NINE OLD MEN). FDR called the decision "horse-and-buggy law."

A generation later, Rev. Martin Luther King, Jr., used the metaphor in his letter from a Birmingham, Alabama, jail: "The nations of Asia and Africa are moving with jetlike speed toward the goal of political independence, and we still creep at horse-and-buggy pace toward the gaining of a cup of coffee at a lunch counter."

HORSE-TRADING hard political bargaining to a conclusion of a deal.

Horse-trading implies a more naked display of power than *bargaining* or *negotiating* and has a no-nonsense connotation.

A good example of the technique was outlined by William V. Reichel, Republican national committeeman from California, to the California delegation committed to Earl Warren in 1944: "We have fifty convention delegates and we're going to get something. At the convention, our votes will get us a Western cabinet member, a Western Supreme Court Justice, and a Western man on every high policy-making body in the government. That's what Warren will be bargaining for. We'll get them or they won't get our votes." As it happened, Warren wound up the vice-presidential nominee on the Dewey ticket, but its loss to Truman and Barkley meant that the horse-trading was all for naught.

HOT LINE direct teletype link between world leaders, designed to prevent "accidental war."

The idea for a direct communications link between the heads of government in Washington and Moscow was proposed by newsman Jess Gorkin, editor of the Sunday supplement *Parade,* in 1960. He tells the author he got the idea from the Strategic Air Command's "red telephone" system; in the October 30, 1960, issue of *Parade,* Gorkin referred to a "hot line" that provided the SAC controller with "instant contact with 70 bases in ten countries on four continents."

President John F. Kennedy wrote Gorkin on April 23, 1963: "It is heartening to me that the Soviet Government has agreed in principle to the United States suggestion for a 'hot line' between our two countries. I remember when you first brought this new and imaginative idea to my attention back in 1960 . . . your advocacy of faster communications between the United States and the Soviet Union was sharply underlined during the Cuban crisis . . ."

Jack Raymond, in *Power at the Pentagon,* wrote: "The proposal was made by the United States in the light of the Cuba experience, during which, at times, the President and his aides were uncertain whether the Soviet leaders fully understood the import of steps that could lead to nuclear war." After negotiations in Geneva, the "hot line" was set up in September 1963.

White House press secretary Pierre Salinger recalls that he had discussed the matter with one of his counterparts, Mikhail Kharlamov, in January 1962. "It is a chilling, but historic, fact," Salinger wrote later, "that the Russians did not agree to 'hot line' negotiations until after the Cuban missile crisis of October 1962. The delay could have been fatal."

The first non-test use of the first hot line (other lines between different capitals have followed the White House–to–Kremlin line) was in the Arab-Israeli war in 1967. The story was in this *New York Daily News* dispatch:

Washington, June 8. . . . President Johnson told Soviet Premier Kosygin on the Washington-Moscow hot line today that an American ship had been attacked in the Mediterranean and planes from the U.S. 6th Fleet were flying to its aid.

The White House said Johnson told the Kremlin about the incident so that it wouldn't misinterpret the scrambling of the American planes.

Press Secretary George Christian announced that Johnson and Kosygin had used the hot line teletype link "a number of times" since Monday, when the Arab-Israeli war erupted.

The first message was from Kosygin to Johnson Monday. Johnson responded the same day. The series of messages was the first time the hot line has been used in an actual crisis situation since it was installed August 30, 1963.

The hot line is a leased teletype circuit from the White House in Washington to the Kremlin in Moscow. Transmissions are in English from Washington and Russian from Moscow, with instantaneous translations at the other end.

HOT PROPERTY   an attractive candidate, as seen through the eyes of his political sponsors; a comer.

Columnist Max Lerner wrote in the sixties about Governor Ronald Reagan: "He is the hottest upcoming property on the horizon, as the politicians put it."

The term probably comes from show business, where agents often refer to clients in terms of inanimate chattels, and "properties" are people whose talents are salable. A play, scenario, book, or script may also be termed a hot property if it shows commercial promise.

In 1967 the *New York Times* combined the show-business and political meanings in an editorial objecting to the sponsorship of a television series begun by Mayor John Lindsay: "If the Mayor's program were unsponsored, it would be quite another matter. But lending his name and office to a sponsored program is commercialism. The Mayor of New York should be nobody's hot property."

"Hot" is not used in the sense of "hot potato," an issue to be avoided because of its sensitivity, but rather in the sense of Wall Street's "hot issue," an underwriting that is oversubscribed and highly sought-after. See **POLITICAL CAPITAL, TO MAKE.** Another corporate phrase turned political is **LAME DUCK**; another show-business phrase used in politics is "waiting in the wings."

The word "upcoming," as used by Lerner (above) is journalese, its meaning fluctuating between "forthcoming" and "up-and-coming." Bernard Kilgore, chairman of the board of Dow Jones, sent this note to a *Wall Street Journal* editor: "If I see 'upcoming' in the paper again, I'll be downcoming and someone will be outgoing." (This formulation was used in 1977 by novelist Peter De Vries to denigrate the word "downplay": "If I heard a speaker use it I would upget and outwalk.")

HOTTENTOTS, MILK FOR attack on foreign aid to underdeveloped nations.

On May 8, 1942, Vice President Henry Wallace made his "century of the common man" speech (see **COMMON MAN, CENTURY OF THE**), disputing the point of view of the Luce publications that the coming hundred years would be "the American Century." Wallace had been raising the hackles of conservatives with his demand for full employment ("sixty

million jobs") and pressing forward on New Deal legislation that had been eclipsed by the war effort. During his speech, he said that he had told the wife of the Soviet ambassador—half in fun and half seriously: "The object of this war is to make sure that everybody in the world has the privilege of drinking a quart of milk a day."

The statement was used as a weapon against Wallace. The Hottentots, a nomadic southwest African tribe with a catchy name, had been used as a symbol of an undeveloped—and undevelopable—people even before Lord Salisbury's "Hottentot Speech" in Parliament in 1886 opposing Irish Home Rule. Dutch explorers named the African tribe Hottentot, according to a 1670 Dutch lexicographer, because of the "clucking speech" of the aborigines. Edgar Allen Poe, in 1840, had used the tribal name as typical of preposterous-sounding words: "The Hottentots and Kickapoos are very well in their way. The Yankees alone are preposterous." Wallace's statement was stretched by conservatives into a policy of "milk for the Hottentots."

"Many of Wallace's progressive and well-meaning speeches," wrote Samuel Rosenman, "about improving the standards of living in backward areas of the world had been so unfortunately phrased that they were distorted by the isolationist press into a statement of readiness to embark on crackbrained and unrealistic projects of worldwide charity handouts."

The phrase remains a symbol of selfless aid, with a connotation of hopelessly impractical idealism. Herman Kahn, listing typical U.S. foreign policy aims in 1962, chose four for discussion: **RULE OF LAW, JUST AND LASTING PEACE, FOUR FREEDOMS,** Milk for the Hottentots."

See HAVE AND HAVE-NOT NA-
TIONS; THIRD WORLD.

HOUSE an ideological, business,
or political entity or movement.

House, like "covenant," is a Biblical word borrowed for political use.
"All the house of Israel," "dwell in
the House of the Lord," and reference
to a church as a House of Prayer or
House of God laid the groundwork
for the metaphor.

Lincoln in 1858 took a quotation
from Mark 3:25, "If a house be divided against itself, that house cannot
stand," shortened it to "A house divided against itself cannot stand,"
and added, "I believe this government
cannot endure permanently half slave
and half free."

The Houses of Parliament and
houses of Congress refer more to the
political bodies than to the buildings
containing them. European business
empires such as Rothschild and
Krupp referred to themselves as
"houses," and a young American
banker or broker still seeks a position
in a "fine old Wall Street house."

In May 1937, a strike at the Republic Steel plant in Chicago erupted into
violence, where thirty strikers were
shot, ten of whom died. This "Memorial Day Massacre," low point of
labor relations in the "sit-down
strike" era of the thirties, brought a
surprising remark from FDR: "A
plague on both your houses." Later
the President tried to explain away
his quotation from Shakespeare as applying only to extremists of both
sides, but CIO president John L.
Lewis turned Roosevelt's use of
"house" into the familiar "House of
Labor" and intoned over nationwide
radio: "It ill behooves one who has
supped at labor's table and who has
been sheltered in labor's house to
curse with equal fervor and fine im-

partiality both labor and its adversaries when they become locked in
deadly embrace."

Woodrow Wilson used a variation
on the theme when he referred to
Warren G. Harding as a man with "a
bungalow mind." Lyndon Johnson
told a group of reporters during a
1964 stroll: "The Democratic party
has been the House of Protest since it
was born."

When Barry Goldwater in 1960
urged his followers to work within the
Republican party, despite their dissatisfaction with the Rockefeller-
Nixon COMPACT OF FIFTH AVENUE
that ensured a liberal platform, he
told the convention: "This great Republican party is our historic house.
This is our home." The shelter metaphor (price "ceilings," tariff "walls,"
"floor" fights, "fireside" chats) is used
as often as the anatomical metaphor.
See BODY POLITIC.

HOUSEHOLD WORD a satiric
reference to a political figure's low
"recognition factor."

Like RED HERRING, this was a
phrase used by a reporter in a question that gained fame when accepted
and repeated by the man being interviewed.

Richard Nixon's choice of Spiro T.
Agnew to be his running mate came
as a shock to newsmen covering the
Republican convention in 1968. On
August 8, just after his choice had
been announced, the VP-to-be held a
news conference at the Hilton Hotel
in Miami Beach. Mike Wallace of
CBS observed, "The name of Spiro
Agnew is hardly a household political
word across the nation." Agnew replied, "I would certainly agree with
that, yes." Wallace then went on to
ask, ". . . what political strength do
you actually bring to the ticket?" The
candidate answered, "I can't analyze

any strength I bring, and I agree with you that the name of Spiro Agnew is not a household name. I certainly hope that it will become one within the next couple of months."

It did. Two years later, columnist James J. Kilpatrick used the now-famous phrase as a synonym for the Vice President: "The Household Word said some things about higher education, and especially about the folly of 'black quotas' that needed badly to be said."

In use, "household name" became transmuted to the more familiar "household word". With Agnew's forced resignation in 1973, use of the phrase diminished and is recalled now with irony or distaste; on his leaving office, he popularized the Latin phrase *nolo contendere*, a plea of guilty without an admission of guilt.

HOUSEKEEPING BILL seemingly innocuous legislation.

"A tricky term with two meanings that are the opposite of each other," wrote *New York Times* Albany reporter Steven R. Weisman of "housekeeping bill" in 1976. "One meaning refers to a measure that embodies a minor technical or procedural alteration in a law. But when a Democrat (or a Republican) gets up in one of the chambers to say 'this is just a little housekeeping bill,' it's a signal to Republicans (or Democrats) to scrutinize the measure to make sure something of consequence isn't being slipped through by subterfuge."

HUMAN ELEMENT personal quirks or characteristics that must be taken into consideration in a political plan; the one element over which detailed planning has no control.

Railroad-accident reports occasionally give as a reason for a disaster "human error," often a euphemism for "the engineer dozed off." In political planning, on a tight schedule, time must be allotted for the human element: a trip to the men's room, or a short belt of gin, or a quick phone call to an old girl friend in the city visited. Allowances must be made for the distressing fact that not all politicians act logically; a known grafter can upset his enemies' plans with an inexplicable burst of altruism or social responsibility, or the man counted on for an introduction can get laryngitis.

When Arthur Schlesinger, Jr., at the 1960 Democratic convention, urged Robert Kennedy to move quickly to conciliate the disappointed Stevenson supporters, Kennedy replied, "Arthur, human nature requires that you allow us forty-eight hours. Adlai has given us a rough time over the last three days. In forty-eight hours, I will do anything you want, but right now I don't want to hear anything about the Stevensonians. You must allow for human nature."

At the same convention, a classic example of the human element was Robert Kennedy's comment regarding the confusion around the selection of Lyndon Johnson as the vice-presidential nominee: "My God, this wouldn't have happened except that we were all too tired last night."

The human element enters into far less consequential political matters. Ambassador Richard C. Patterson, New York City's official greeter during the Robert Wagner administration, called his speechwriter late one night with a problem. He was to introduce South Korean President Syngman Rhee at a Waldorf-Astoria luncheon the next day; part of the introduction was to be a telegram from General Douglas MacArthur praising Rhee's "courage and his indomitable will."

"So you'll read the telegram," the speechwriter said, "and everybody will clap. What's the problem?"

"You're forgetting the human element," said Patterson. "Nine people out of ten will flub on the word 'indomitable'—including me. I can just hear myself saying 'indominitabubble' and everybody laughing and embarrassing the guest of honor. Go ahead—you try it."

"Easy," said the speechwriter, "Indominitabubble."

"You see? Let's substitute another word. We can release the accurate text in written form."

The speechwriter thought a moment. "I got it. You got a pencil? 'Indefatigable.' " There was a long silence as Patterson considered hiring a new speechwriter. Then they settled on "steadfast," and the human element triumphed again.

HUMAN RIGHTS   the idea that each person is born with the moral claim on some political freedom which ought not to be denied by any government.

"Ignorance, neglect or contempt of human rights," reads a declaration of the first National Assembly of France, "are the sole causes of public misfortunes and corruptions of government."

The phrase in French was *droits de l'homme* ("the rights of man") taken from the concept of "natural rights" espoused by English political philosopher John Locke in the seventeenth century. Locke held that man, in a theoretical state of nature, was born free; after he mixed his labor with the common property of nature's abundance, he had property of his own. Man then traded part of his absolute freedom to government, for protection of his person and his property "rights."

Locke's "natural rights" were also called "inherent" and "imprescriptible"; when Thomas Jefferson referred to them in the Declaration of Independence, they were "inalienable." When people were denied these rights by kings, Locke argued with some discretion, they could "appeal to Heaven"—a euphemism for revolution, since the cautiously couched theory struck at the root of the divine right of kings.

For nearly two centuries after the American and French revolutions, human rights were called "the rights of man." That was the title of Thomas Paine's book on the subject, and in Herman Melville's *Billy Budd,* the name of the ship on which his moral tale took place was *The Rights of Man.*

In his book *Political Theory and the Rights of Man* (1967), Professor D. D. Raphael, of the University of Glasgow, explained why the name was changed:

The concept of Human Rights, as they are called in the English text of the [UN] Universal Declaration of 1948, is of course a revival of the eighteenth-century concept of the Rights of Man. According to Mrs. Eleanor Roosevelt, who was Chairman of the United Nations Commission on Human Rights, the old phrase was changed because of an interpretation given to it, at an early stage of international discussion, by a delegate from some benighted country. "I assume," he blandly remarked, "that when we speak of the rights of man, we mean what we say. My government, of course, could not agree to extend these rights to women." The French text of the Universal Declaration retains the traditional *droits de l'homme,* perhaps because the French . . . are familiar with the dictum that, in the language of the law, "the male is presumed to embrace the female."

Throughout the fifties and sixties, however, the movement for "rights" was directed at the *civil* rights of American Negroes; having achieved their fundamental "human" right to freedom, blacks demanded the equality in voting, education and housing that belonged to them in civil law. The phrase "human rights" was, in those decades—as it was when Woodrow Wilson used it—a ho-hum expression of idealism.

Although President Harry Truman had told the UN conference at San Francisco in 1945 that "the Charter is dedicated to the achievement and observance of human rights and freedoms," the Charter's article 2, section seven, limits that dedication in this way: "Nothing contained in the present Charter shall authorize the UN to intervene in matters which are essentially within the domestic jurisdiction of any state . . ."

In the early seventies an international organization named Amnesty International, based in London, raised the money to expand its research and did much to publicize the extent of limitations on political freedom in many countries. In 1974 the House of Representatives International Relations Subcommittee on International Organizations and Movements, chaired by Donald Fraser (D-Minn.), held hearings and published a report that thrust the subject into American political debate.

Daniel Patrick Moynihan, the most outspoken of the American UN ambassadors, became most closely identified with the articulation of human rights in a world grown more statist. He challenged many other diplomats who had hitherto criticized the U.S. with impunity, while their own countries routinely denied citizens basic human rights.

At that time the policies of Secretary of State Henry Kissinger, promoting DETENTE. with its QUIET DIPLOMACY and pragmatic acceptance of the differences between societies, were coming under widening attack. By the beginning of the election primaries of 1976, "the human rights issue" began to flower, offering hardline conservatives and moralistic liberals common ground: the assertion of American values in a world made up of so many totalitarian states.

Among conservatives, Ronald Reagan picked up the issue in his nearly successful attempt to wrest the Republican nomination from President Gerald Ford; during that primary season, Democratic candidate Jimmy Carter also embraced the subject and the phrase in his desire to incorporate a different approach into his foreign policy statements.

In his inaugural, Mr. Carter put forward the idea in ringing terms: "Our commitment to human rights must be absolute." When he corresponded with Soviet dissenter Andrei Sakharov, this displeased the Soviet Union, which responded angrily in its propaganda, identifying the American human rights campaign as a part of the hawkish "anti-détente faction of Senator Henry Jackson." At the urging of many foreign policy professionals, and to the dismay of some of his early supporters, President Carter moderated the tone of his speaking out about human rights by the end of his first year in office.

In current political usage, *human rights* means more liberty for dissenters in totalitarian lands; *civil rights* is associated with equality for blacks; and *civil liberties* connotes grim approval for the free speech of people espousing unpopular causes.

For Hubert Humphrey's dramatic use of the terms at the 1948 Democratic Convention, see DIXIECRAT.

HUMOR, SELF-DEPRECATING

a politician's attempt to take the sting out of a charge by kidding about it; acknowledging a disadvantage in such a charming way as to turn it to an advantage.

Abraham Lincoln joked about his height and plain looks. "Here am I and here is Mrs. Lincoln. That's the long and short of it." And "The Lord prefers common-looking people. That's the reason he makes so many of them."

Humor has been used often in politics, especially in ridiculing an opponent (Churchill re MacDonald: "sheep in sheep's clothing," see IN-VECTIVE, POLITICAL) but not until the 1950s did the Lincolnesque technique of poking fun at oneself come into such universal political vogue.

Adlai Stevenson led the way in defeat, quoting Lincoln's story about the little boy who stubbed his toe and was too big to cry and hurt too much to laugh. A few months later he added, "A funny thing happened to me on the way to the White House," and when his auto was delayed by a military funeral he observed, "Military heroes always seem to be getting in my way."

John F. Kennedy carried self-deprecating humor forward. Criticized for appointing his younger brother Attorney General, he innocently observed, "I see nothing wrong with giving Robert some legal experience before he goes out to practice law." Robert Kennedy did not think this was very funny, according to historian William Manchester, and objected; his brother told him he had better get used to kidding himself, because people liked it. "Yes, but you weren't kidding yourself," Robert replied, "you were kidding *me*."

Later, Robert Kennedy did apply the technique, introducing candidate Adlai Stevenson III in Illinois with the remark, "If there's one thing I can't stand, it's a fellow running on his family's name." Senator Ted Kennedy, who bore the brunt of a "nepotism" and "dynasty" charge in Massachusetts, said that he wanted to be judged on his own so much that he thought of changing his name—from Teddy Kennedy to Teddy Roosevelt. Defusing the "born with a silver spoon" bomb, Ted Kennedy quoted a factory worker who said to him, "Senator, I hear you never worked a day in your life, and this is what a lot of people have against you. I want to tell you, you haven't missed a thing."

Alan L. Otten, *Wall Street Journal* political analyst, wrote in 1966: "This type of humor has obvious advantages. It's usually a quick throwaway line, less likely to bore an audience than the old-fashioned long anecdote. It disarms critics by making their target appear unafraid of the criticism. It makes the listener feel this can't be such a bad fellow after all."

HUMPTY DUMPTY   sure loser; a sacrificial lamb.

This nursery rhyme character who "sat on a wall" and "had a great fall" was popularized by Lewis Carroll as an early example of anything-goes linguistics: a word, to Humpty Dumpty, meant anything he chose it to mean.

In politics, a Humpty Dumpty is selected to take a great fall in a hopeless race against an unbeatable opponent. The appellation is always contemptuous.

The name was subtly revived after Nixon's fall by reporters Bob Woodward and Carl Bernstein, in their title *All the President's Men*; the allusion was to the inability of Nixon's aides to put together the Nixon presidency after the cracks of Watergate appeared.

A related term, opposite in meaning, is *Mickey Mouse,* used when any candidate chosen to run could beat the unpopular opponent (see LAUNDRY TICKET). This phrase is also used to mean "inadequate" in more general terms; Roy Innes, director of the Congress of Racial Equality, told a CBS interviewer on June 30, 1968: "I am disgusted with the Mickey Mouse welfare programs . . ."

For the political use of related characters, see TWEEDLEDUM AND TWEEDLEDEE.

HUNDRED DAYS most often applied to the productive special session of Congress summoned by Franklin D. Roosevelt in 1933 to cope with the Depression.

The historical parallel to FDR's Hundred Days was Napoleon's escape from Elba and his triumphant march across Europe that finally culminated in disaster at Waterloo. The time span between Napoleon's escape and abdication, however, was 116 days; the hundred days was applied to Louis XVIII's absence from Paris beginning March 20, 1815, as Napoleon arrived, to June 28, when the King returned in state after Napoleon's defeat. The Count de Chambord, prefect of Paris, coined the phrase: "A hundred days, sire, have elapsed since the fatal moment when your Majesty was forced to quit your capital in the midst of tears." When used in reference to that period, the phrase has now come to mean the time of Napoleon's return rather than the King's exile.

Roosevelt's Hundred Days were equally eventful. During the period from March 9 to June 16—exactly one hundred days—the 73rd Congress enacted such milestone legislation as vast public works and relief measures, guarantees of bank deposits, and tighter federal regulation of the banks, agricultural subsidies, the Tennessee Valley Authority, and others.

"The legislative record it set," wrote Raymond Moley, one of FDR's brain trusters, "the impression it created on the public, its impact upon the economy of the nation, and the incredible speed with which important legislation was planned, considered, proposed and enacted has no parallel in the earlier history of the Republic. Nor has there been any parallel since, except under the exigencies of the war that began eight years later." Not even Lyndon Johnson's 89th Congress was comparable, said Moley, because much of its program "had been inherited from the Kennedy years" or were traceable to the Roosevelt era.

While John F. Kennedy was working on his inaugural address, Theodore Sorensen wrote in *Kennedy,* the late President at one point said impatiently, "I'm sick of reading how we're planning another 'Hundred Days' of miracles. Let's put in that this won't all be finished in a hundred days or a thousand." His finished speech thus read: "All this will not be finished in the first hundred days. Nor will it be finished in the first thousand days, nor in the life of this Administration, nor even perhaps in our lifetime on this planet. But let us begin." Historian Arthur Schlesinger, Jr., chose *A Thousand Days*—the approximate length of the Kennedy Administration—as the title of his history of the period. See **"LET US CONTINUE."**

Britain's Harold Wilson was less reluctant to exploit what had become a cliché. "What we are going to need," he said during his successful 1964 campaign to lead Labour to power and himself to the prime ministership, "is something like what President Kennedy had after years of stagnation—a program of a hundred days of dynamic action."

HUNDRED FLOWERS a governing doctrine that permits open disagreement within an Administration.

In 1957 Mao Tse-tung made a speech that appeared to embrace sweet reason: "Ideological struggle is not like other forms of struggle. Crude, coercive methods should not be used in this struggle, but only the method of painstaking reasoning." He went on to use a vivid metaphor: "Let a hundred flowers blossom and a hundred schools of thought contend."

However, when the flowers blossomed, they were ruthlessly cut down. Historian Sidney Hook wrote: "The Communist Party loosed another fierce campaign of purge and suppression, branding these flowers of doctrine as poisonous weeds which must be chopped down." Peking's *People's Daily,* four months after Mao's speech, completed the metaphor: "Only by letting poisonous weeds show themselves above ground can they be uprooted." Two decades later, after Mao's death and the fall of the radical "gang of four," a limited amount of debate was permitted, especially in the form of wall posters. This recalled the "hundred flowers" phrase, but Chinese leaders disagreed with great circumspection: they had learned their lesson.

In American political usage, the phrase is employed—usually sardonically—in descriptions of public disagreements by Administration leaders. This is often referred to in the press as a "let-a-hundred-flowers-bloom technique," and is more frequently condemned for its seeming confusion than praised for its acceptance of open debate.

HUNKER, *see* **BARNBURNERS; HARD LINE.**

HURTING, *see* **CRUNCH.**

HUSTINGS specifically, any place from which a campaign speech is made; generally, the campaign trail.

The original meaning was an assembly, any deliberative body; before written ballots became the law in England in 1872, the husting was the place from which candidates for Parliament addressed the electorate. The best-known husting was the upper end or platform of the Guildhall, where the mayor held court.

The etymology is interesting. In Scandinavian countries the word *thing* is currently the name of legislative assemblies and courts of law, taken from the Old Norse *husthing,* literally "house meeting." Old English dropped an *h* to form *hūsting,* which is now used only in the plural, construed as singular, as "The hustings is a place . . ."

In a classic English translation of Demosthenes' *Oration on the Crown,* the Greek orator says: "In what spirit was I to mount the hustings? In the spirit of one having unworthy counsel to offer?—I should have deserved to perish!"

In current use, *on the hustings, on the stump,* and *on the campaign trail* are synonymous, though the archaic *hustings* is more often used semihumorously.

HYMIE'S FERRYBOAT an analogy about the COATTAIL effect of a strong candidate.

Hymie Schorenstein, Brooklyn's Democratic district leader in the twenties, received a complaint from one of his candidates for a local elective office.

"Why is it, Hymie, that your whole budget for posters and literature is for Governor Roosevelt, and nothing for the candidates on the local level? I need to become better known, Roosevelt doesn't. How about a few signs for me?"

Hymie did not answer directly. "You ever watch the ferries come in from Staten Island?" The candidate allowed as how he had, and waited for Hymie's point.

"When that big ferry from Staten Island sails into the ferry slip, it never comes in strictly alone. It drags in all the crap from the harbor behind it." Hymie let the message sink in before adding, "FDR is our Staten Island Ferry."

That is the way the story is most frequently recounted as it worked its way into political legend. When political reporter Richard Reeves used the anecdote (with an early edition of this dictionary as a source), he received a letter in 1976 from John Rae of New York City, an eyewitness to its telling: "I was at a party with Jimmy Walker and Hymie Schorenstein. The ferry story concerned Hymie's nonentity nephew running for the Assembly at the time Walker was running for Mayor. Walker assuaged Hymie by saying he would pull Hymie's nephew in—he coined the ferryslip story which Hymie loved to repeat as did Beau James."

Schorenstein, who despite an inability to read operated most effectively as a county clerk, was preceded in the use of this metaphor by the president of Columbia University, Nicholas Murray Butler, who heard it from Boise Penrose, a leader of the Pennsylvania delegation in the Republican convention of 1912. In the midst of a fistfight between supporters of former President Theodore Roosevelt and President William Howard Taft, Butler wondered how men of that type ever were selected for the responsibility of choosing a presidential nominee. Penrose replied, "Oh, those are the corks, bottles and banana peels washed up by the Roosevelt tide."

HYPE, *see* **MEDIA EVENT.**

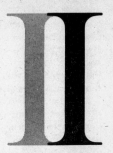

I AM THE LAW   example of the height of political imperiousness.

Mayor Frank Hague of Jersey City, big-city boss and full-time autocrat, received a bum rap from history on this quotation. The episode involved two youths who wanted to change from day school to night school so that they could go to work, but who were denied working papers by the Board of Education's Special Services Director because the law required them to stay in day school. Mayor Hague cut through the red tape and ordered the official to give the boys working papers. As he proudly recounted the matter before the Men's Club of Emory Church in Jersey City on November 10, 1937: when the school official told him, "That's the law," he replied, "Listen, here is the law. I am the law! Those boys go to work!"

Today such an action would be lauded as the action of a public official pushing aside an unresponsive bureaucracy to "meet human needs"; but Hague had a well-deserved reputation for high-handedness, and the phrase soon lost its context and was used against him.

During World War II Charles de Gaulle irritated Churchill and Roosevelt with his insistent remark, "*Je suis la France.*" This phrase reminded them, and others, of Louis XIV's supposed remark to the 1665 Parliament of Paris, "*L'état, c'est moi*" ("I am

the state"). In his 1825 Bunker Hill Monument oration, Daniel Webster gave this interpretation, which could also apply to Hague's remark: "When Louis XIV said I am the state, he expressed the essence of the doctrine of unlimited power. These ideas, founded in the love of power, and long supported by the excess and abuse of it, are yielding in our age to other opinions . . ."

The phrase is current. On April 1, 1978, after L. Patrick Gray and other former FBI officials were indicted for violating the civil rights of members of a terrorist group, cartoonist Herblock pictured two agents in raincoats carrying a black bag labeled "illegal operations" and asking: "We broke the law? We *are* the law!"

IDEAS   a catchword for a number of political movements that enjoyed some fame in the U.S.

"One-idea parties" was a nineteenth-century label placed first on anti-Masons and then all minority or splinter parties by members of larger parties. However, some of the ideas were worth looking into:

1. *The idea of freedom:* Associated with the abolitionist cause, the phrase was introduced by Theodore Parker at a New England antislavery convention held in Boston on May 29, 1850. Parker's idea was of "a democracy, that is, a government of all the people, by all the people, for all the people; of

course, a government after the principles of eternal justice, the unchanging law of god; for shortness' sake, I will call it the idea of freedom." (Part of this statement was later adopted by Lincoln at Gettysburg.)

2. *The Ohio idea:* The Democratic platform of 1868 stressed the redemption of national debts in specie. Senator George H. Pendleton summed up this "Ohio Idea" in 1881:

> The Ohio idea is the absolute equality of all men before the law; absolute and equal justice to all men by the law; and, in the administration of our State affairs, the administration of the few powers committed to our State affairs, the administration of the few powers committed to our State legislature by the Constitution in such wise that every man may pursue his own avocations and his own scheme of domestic life according to his tastes . . . as is consistent with the order of society and the peace of the community. And in national affairs, the Ohio idea is the absolute performance of every act to which the plighted faith of the nation is given.

3. *The Plattsburg idea:* With World War I under way, those who advocated preparedness for the U.S. introduced the Plattsburg idea in April, 1915—two years before America's entry into the war. Named for the northern New York State site of a training camp, it called for military training for civilians at similar spots.

4. *The Wisconsin idea:* Graduates of the enlightened University of Wisconsin, which encouraged its students to seek wealth, power, and influence for the betterment of society, fostered the idea. They envisioned a progressive, agrarian-democratic commonwealth—and from 1900 to 1914 they went a long way toward making the idea a reality. With Robert La Follette, Sr., as governor, advocates of the Wisconsin idea enacted a direct primary, tax reform, laws controlling the railroads, initiative and referendum provisions, a corrupt-practices act, child- and female-labor laws, workmen's compensation, regulatory agencies for utilities and transportation, and laws covering campaign expenditures, civil service, lobbying, safety, public health, conservation, and the schools.

In current campaign oratory, there is a tendency to discard the word "idea," on the grounds that it appears too sudden a notion, substituting the less exciting "plan" or "program," or the more pretentious "concept."

IDEOLOGY   originally, a system of ideas for political or social action; in current political use, a mental straitjacket, or rigid rules for the philosophically narrow-minded.

French philosopher Destutt de Tracy coined the word in 1796, to mean a rationalist "science of ideas" opposed to ancient metaphysics, and made it the title of his 1801 book, *Idéologie*. Napoleon Bonaparte was the first to give the word a bad name: "It is to the doctrine of the ideologues . . . one must attribute all the misfortunes which have befallen our beautiful France." British historian Thomas Carlyle tried to rescue the word in 1839: "Does the British reader . . . call this unpleasant doctrine of ours ideology?" But when Marx and Engels joined Napoleon in condemning the word in their 1845 attack on German radicals, titling their book *The German Ideology*, the term could never shake its connotation of foolish rigidity. When the Marx book was finally printed in English in 1927, the word gained currency in the U.S.

"I think 'ideology' is a scare word to most Americans," observed former

California Governor Ronald Reagan to columnists Evans and Novak in 1978. "But a basic political philosophy is the reason for a party existing."

The observation, with the counterpoint use of "philosophy," was semantically accurate. In current use, "ideology" carries the connotation of alien theory, and "ideologues" are seen as demagogues hawking extreme points of view. Such TRUE BELIEVERS practice "cannibalism" within a party by seeking to PURGE its minority elements, refusing to accept the formulation attributed to Senator William Borah: "A Republican is anybody who calls himself a Republican." In this attack, the BIG TENT advocates deprecate the divisiveness of "narrow ideology."

In response, principled partisans who believe a party should "stand for something" insist it must offer a CHOICE, NOT AN ECHO to avoid "metooism" (see ME TOO) and TWEEDLEDUM AND TWEEDLEDEE comparisons that show "not a DIME'S WORTH OF DIFFERENCE." The riposte can be typified in this statement by conservative Howard Phillips, who challenged liberal Republican Senator Edward Brooke of Massachusetts in 1978: "When liberals challenge conservative Republicans, they call it 'base-broadening.' But when conservatives oppose liberal GOPers, it is called 'cannibalism.'"

In this big-tent vs. stand-for-something argument, which bothers Republicans more than Democrats, the meeting ground is "philosophy," or "basic philosophy." The safest phraseology for both sides is an assertion that "certain principles" and "values" cannot be compromised, provided they are not defined.

IDIOT ENGINEER, *see* **BLOOPER.**

I'D RATHER BE RIGHT   Henry Clay's statement that began as an example of his idealism but now has a flavor of sour grapes.

"I would rather be right than be President." Kentucky Senator Clay made this statement several times to his friends, in a letter in 1839, and in a Senate speech in 1850.

"The Great Compromiser" and "The Great Pacificator" achieved major-party presidential nominations twice and was defeated. See CAN'T-WIN TECHNIQUE. Like Senator Robert A. Taft, a century later, he was too strictly a congressional leader to build nationwide coalitions beyond Congress. After losing the presidency, he tired of hearing his immortal words quoted and said dryly that this particular sentiment "had been applauded beyond its merit."

Clay's use of the statement in a Senate speech was in reply to those that said his Missouri Compromise would hurt his chances for the presidency. For years, congressmen quoted the remark until it became a political bromide; House Speaker Thomas B. Reed answered a Clay-quoter with "the gentleman need not be disturbed, he will never be either."

George M. Cohan wrote a Broadway musical entitled *I'd Rather Be Right* in the thirties, kidding the Administration of Franklin Roosevelt. In it, the President would turn to his secretary and say, "Mac, take a law." FDR enjoyed this and often turned to his secretary, Grace Tully, and said, "Grace, take a law."

Variations on Clay's remark can be found before and after he first sounded it. William McKinley, before his 1896 election, told a friend, "If I cannot be President without promising to make Tom Platt Secretary of the Treasury, I will never be President." Marcus Tullius Cicero

(106–43 B.C.) said of the Pythagoreans, "I would rather be wrong with Plato than right with such men as these."

IFFY QUESTION a hypothetical question; phrase used by Franklin Roosevelt to avoid giving iffy answers.

"If you run next year, who will your Vice President be?" This type of question is designed to elicit not one answer, but two (Who will be the Vice President? Will you run next year?). Many press conference traps of this kind were neatly avoided by FDR, who merely smiled and said, "That's an iffy question."

New York Governor Averell Harriman, campaigning against Nelson Rockefeller in 1958, was asked if he planned to retain Tammany leader Carmine De Sapio as Secretary of State, and replied, "I think that's an iffy question that doesn't—that I needn't deal with today." Since "bossism" was an important thrust of Rockefeller's campaign, and since the "if" in the question was hardly hypothetical but pertinent to post-election plans, the Harriman use of "iffy question" was an ill-advised evasion. The phrase appears to work only when the question is indeed hypothetical, or "iffy."

For example, Robert Kennedy was asked by reporters in 1964 if he would accept a vice-presidential nomination. He answered such obvious speculation with: "The question reminds me of my brother. When he was posed with such a question, he used to say that is like asking a girl if she would marry that man if he proposed."

Other types of questions include: loaded, slanted, planted, tricky, and innocent.

IF YOU CAN'T LICK 'EM . . . join 'em. A frequent bit of advice, origin obscure, given in areas dominated by one party.

The phrase, akin to the Scottish proverb "Better bend than break," carries no connotation of surrender; it is used to indicate that the way to take over the opposition's strength is to adopt their positions and platform. See ME TOO; CO-OPT.

President Harry Truman in his 1948 campaign warned farmers about a variation of this technique supposedly practiced by Republicans: "It's an old political trick: 'If you can't convince 'em, confuse 'em.' But this time it won't work."

IF YOU CAN'T STAND THE HEAT . . . get out of the kitchen. A motto often attributed to President Harry S. Truman.

President Truman stressed two facets of the presidency with colorful phrases: "The BUCK STOPS HERE" on the need for decisiveness, and "If you can't stand the heat, get out of the kitchen" on the cheerful expectancy of pressure.

As a senator, Lyndon Baines Johnson phrased the same philosophy in this way: "My daddy told me that if I didn't want to get shot at, I should stay off the firing lines. This is politics."

This phrase is as closely associated with Truman as "GIVE 'EM HELL," "DO-NOTHING CONGRESS" and "RED HERRING," and needs no specific attribution to him for identification. Daniel P. Moynihan, then of the Joint Center for Urban Studies, wrote complaining of an attack on him in *Transaction* in 1967: "A better political scientist than I said the final word on government executives either standing the heat or getting out of the kitchen, but there are levels of personal abuse that make one wonder whether it is worth it." (It was; Moynihan went on to become senator from New York.)

When Sir Walter Raleigh, nibbling his nails, wrote "Fain would I climb, yet fear to fall," the more direct Queen Elizabeth I is said to have written in reply: "If thy heart fails thee, climb not at all."

"I HAVE A DREAM"   a memorable speech construction by Rev. Martin Luther King, Jr., at the Lincoln Memorial during the March on Washington, August 28, 1963.

> I say to you today, my friends, that in spite of the difficulties and frustrations of the moment I still have a dream. It is a dream deeply rooted in the American dream . . .
> I have a dream that one day on the red hills of Georgia the sons of former slaves and the sons of former slaveowners will be able to sit down together at the table of brotherhood . . .
> I have a dream that my four little children will one day live in a nation where they will not be judged by the color of their skin but by the content of their character . . .
> I have a dream today . . .

For other examples of vision and inspiration in speeches, see **"I SEE" CONSTRUCTION; AMERICAN DREAM; VISION OF AMERICA.**

ILLEGITIMI NON CARBORUNDUM   a pseudo-Latin phrase meaning "Don't let the bastards grind you down."

Small signs and plaques carrying this message have appeared in U.S. business offices and army posts for at least a generation, since General "Vinegar Joe" Stilwell used it as his motto in World War II. *Carborundum* is a trademark for silicon carbide, a leading commercial grinding

substance, probably a blend of the words "carbon" or "carbide" and "corundum" (the hardest mineral except for the diamond), also used as an abrasive.

In politics, the motto was popularized by 1964 Republican nominee Senator Barry Goldwater, who hung the sign in his office. It expressed a suitable be-yourself, don't-compromise attitude that fit "Mr. Conservative."

The *New Republic* in 1967 used a ridiculously bowdlerized translation in reporting on its use by a group of senators who had been characterized as doves: "The Administration brought General Westmoreland all the way from Vietnam to overawe its critics, but the Senate's Democratic and Republican dissenters appropriated Barry Goldwater's old dog-Latin motto, 'Illegitimi non Carborundum,' which roughly means, 'Don't let the so-and-so's shut you up.' "

ILLUMINATI, see POWER ELITE.

IMAGE   the impression of himself that a public figure attempts to convey; the merchandising of reputation.

Political images and image-makers are post–World War II offspring of television and big-league advertising and public relations. All politicians in all times, of course, seek public affection and respect. But turning this search into a constant and major effort is a recent innovation. John Brooks observed that the preoccupation with "image" sprang from an "unholy . . . liaison between promotion and psychology" that "invaded American politics about the time Eisenhower came to the White House." Almost as one, political writers picked up the term and have yet to put it down. Sir Ernest Gowers in Fowler's *Modern English Usage* calls it an overused "vogue word" but still a valid one in an era when "politicians and advertisers and other advocates of themselves or other causes can . . . project their images into our very homes" via TV.

The personal use of the word, to mean more than a reflection in a glass, was begun by psychologists; "father image" is a familiar psychiatric term. The word was picked up by advertising men as "brand image," meaning the conception on the part of the consumer of a manufacturer's trade name or product; this led to "corporate image," a conception that a public (stockholder, financial community, local community, the trade, etc.) has of a corporation. "A brand image is what you say you are," public relations men like to say, "but a corporate image is what you really are."

As image became a sales tool for opinion molders, it became a handy and modern-sounding word to describe the total public posture and impression of a public figure. Many politicians misuse the word to mean something that belongs to them, much as Peter Pan's shadow, and feel lost without it; the fact is that an image belongs to the public.

The activating verb used with *image* goes back to the use of the word as a reflection, or picture. Images are "projected," as one would project a movie on a screen.

The use of the word may be new, but the idea isn't. The seventeenth-century English writer Thomas Fuller lamented that "Fame sometimes has created something of nothing." It has also created political myths. Charles Evans Hughes, the Republican candidate for President in 1916, was the victim of the so-called ice myth that portrayed him as so with-

drawn from the common man that he "communed in the Alps with Kant, solid geometry and Lycurgus." Hughes replied, "I'll plead guilty to knowing Kant, but not guilty as to the solid geometry charge. As to Lycurgus . . . do you think it is anything intoxicating?" Hughes lost the election.

News media play their part in image-making, of course. Calvin Coolidge gave reporters so little good copy that embroidery became necessary to keep editors and readers awake. Henry Suydam, recalling his days as a Washington correspondent, wrote: "Mr. Coolidge would observe, with respect to a certain bill, 'I'm not in favor of this legislation.' The next morning Washington dispatches began as follows: 'President Coolidge, in a fighting mood, today served notice on Congress that he intended to combat, with all the resources at his command . . .'"

Perhaps the ideal example of a politician's attitude toward his image was expressed by Oliver Cromwell in the instructions to the man painting his portrait: "I desire you will use all your skill to paint my picture truly like me, and not to flatter me at all; but remark all those roughnesses, pimples, warts, and everything as you see me: otherwise I will never pay one farthing for it."

See MADISON AVENUE TECHNIQUES; SELLING CANDIDATES LIKE SOAP.

IMPACT, POLITICAL effect on public opinion; jargon that has replaced *repercussions* and *ramifications* and even *results* in current usage.

"Impact" is a word that first became a cliché in the advertising business in the fifties, to describe the effect of an ad on a reader. In a classic "house" ad, the Young and Rubicam agency showed a picture of a boxing glove shattering a boxer's jaw—with the word "impact" printed below—to describe the effectiveness of their brand of advertising.

Some pretentious political public relations practitioners use the phrase often, as "We have to assess the political impact of such an unpopular stand"; the pros dismiss it as jargon.

In the seventies, the noun regressed to a verb, as "How does this impact on the grassroots?" It impacts awkwardly.

IMPERIAL PRESIDENCY a charge that the Executive Branch has gained more power than the Constitution warrants.

At the end of 1973 Arthur Schlesinger, Jr.—historian of the Jackson era and the New Deal who served as a White House aide during the Presidency of John Kennedy—published *The Imperial Presidency,* which was taken to be an attack on the growth of presidential power. Since the book came out in the midst of the fall of Richard Nixon, it provided an intellectual underpinning to those liberals who otherwise were having problems of consistency with their previous enthusiasm for the growth of power under FDR and their fierce disapproval of its growth under Nixon.

"In recent years the imperial Presidency," read the book's inside-cover blurb, "having established itself in foreign affairs, has made bold bid for supremacy at home. Through a diversity of means—through the mystique of the mandate, through the secrecy system, through executive privilege and impoundment, through political and electronic surveillance in the name of national security, through the use of the White House itself as a base for espionage and sabotage against the political opposition—the imperial Presidency has threatened to become the revolutionary Presidency."

Schlesinger, who was then unaware of many of the abuses of civil liberty that a Senate committee in 1975 showed to have taken place in the sixties, was careful in his introduction to disclaim any desire to cripple the powers of the President: "The answer to the runaway Presidency is not the messenger-boy Presidency. The American democracy must discover a middle ground between making the President a czar and making him a puppet." His timely book confronted the dilemma of all those who had long urged an "activist" presidency and who had been dismayed when too much activisim had led to Vietnam and Watergate.

As in the POLITICS OF, a Schlesinger book title became the construction for many variations in phrasemaking. Laurence Silberman, at the American Enterprise Institute, published a critique of expanding judicial power which he called "the imperial judiciary"; after the War Powers Act and the forced resignation of Nixon, Congress gained much power and was frequently criticized as "the imperial congress"; and in May 1978 Robert Manning wrote in the *Atlantic* (which had printed some of Schlesinger's original material in its pages): "Americans wanted no part of an Imperial Presidency. Neither will they tolerate an Imperial Press."

IMPUDENT SNOBS, *see* **EFFETE SNOBS.**

INCOMES POLICY government influence upon or regulation of wages, prices, and profits, ranging from mild JAWBONING to direct controls.

In the late fifties, U.S. economists,

who had been using "wage-price policy" to describe this general area, switched to the British usage, "incomes policy." This was because labor economists felt that wages and prices did not cover the subject of dividends and profits.

The new phrase came to public attention in the late sixties, when inflation persisted longer than most economists had expected. Because of its vagueness, it was especially popular as a solution to inflation by those who wanted to go beyond the customary methods of fiscal and monetary policy, without advocating wage and price controls.

The phrase was given a more specific definition, and the policy a strong boost, by Dr. Arthur Burns, who in 1970 became chairman of the Board of the Federal Reserve System. He called for an incomes policy, centering his proposal on a wage-price stabilization board—relying on voluntary compliance, short of mandatory controls.

Burns's espousal of a stabilization board, at a time when the Administration was using a milder form of incomes policy, moved the definition of the phrase in popular usage toward a more activist meaning. When the author pointed out to the Federal Reserve Chairman that the policy he was proposing was directly in conflict with all he had written in the past, Burns replied, "I am not afflicted with the notion that what I write is chiseled in granite."

Incomes policy is often confused with, but has a totally different meaning from, *incomes strategy*. The latter has to do with providing money, rather than services or food, to those dependent on public support. Proponents of an incomes strategy hold that the least demeaning way to help the needy is to give them the cash to buy their own essentials; opponents point to ignorance about nutrition standards and the danger of misuse of the welfare money by the recipients.

INCUMBENT   in office; running against a challenger.

An incumbent, in its original sense, is one who lies down on the job; the word has the same root as "recumbent" and "succumb." The idea of resting is illustrated in the phrase "It is incumbent upon us," which means "It rests with us," and is as stilted as "It behooves us" (better usage is "We should" or "We must").

Based on past performance, the odds are two to one that an incumbent President will be re-elected. Fourteen have succeeded (FDR three times) out of twenty-one attempts. Those who failed were John Adams in 1800, John Quincy Adams in 1828, Martin Van Buren in 1840, Grover Cleveland in 1888, Benjamin Harrison in 1892, William Howard Taft in 1912, Herbert Hoover in 1932, and Gerald Ford in 1976. See SITTING PRESIDENT. Those who failed of later nomination by their own party were John Tyler in 1844, Millard Fillmore in 1852, Franklin Pierce in 1856, Andrew Johnson in 1868, and Chester Arthur in 1884; of these, only Pierce had already been elected President "in his own right."

In almost every political race, the incumbent has an edge. Incumbent congressmen have a franking privilege that enables them to regularly report to or survey their constituents, showing themselves busily at work without incurring direct-mail advertising costs. Officeholders can also use their title as part of their name in campaign posters. The extreme example of this was the advertising approach of Jack Tinker and Partners in the 1966 New York campaign for governor: "Governor Rockefeller for Governor." Campaign aide Harry O'-Donnell, explaining the choice of the slogan to reporters, said, "It was either that or 'Nelson Rockefeller for Nelson.' "

With the same thought in mind, Republicans in 1971 called their citizens' committee "Committee for the Re-election of the President," which Republican National Chairman Bob Dole dubbed CREEP.

INDEPENDENTS, *see* **SWING VOTER; SWITCHER.**

INDISPENSABLE MAN a term that indicates that the U.S. government can get along without anybody, including the sitting President.

FDR repeated this statement of Woodrow Wilson's, who was running against both a sitting President, William Howard Taft, and former President Theodore Roosevelt seeking a comeback as a third-party candidate: "There is no indispensable man. The government will not collapse and go to pieces if any one of the gentlemen seeking to be entrusted with its guidance should be left at home."

Just before President Eisenhower's heart attack in 1955, as Republicans were urging him to announce his intentions of running again in 1956, he told a gathering of Republican state chairmen at the Brown Palace hotel in Denver, "We don't believe for a minute that the Republican party is so lacking in inspiration, high-quality personnel and leadership that we are dependent on one man . . . humans are frail and they are mortal. Finally you never pin your flag so tightly to one mast that if a ship sinks, you cannot rip it off and nail it to another. It is sometimes good to remember." Within two weeks the President suffered a heart attack, and his words

sounded suddenly prophetic.

On the other hand, when Eisenhower wrote about General Alfred M. Gruenther, who succeeded him as Allied Commander in Europe, he referred to him as "practically an indispensable individual."

The origin of the phrase is in the French proverb: *"Il n'y a point d'homme nécessaire."*

I NEED HIM statement made by President Eisenhower after his assistant, Sherman Adams, admitted to a congressional subcommittee that he had exchanged gifts with a New England textile manufacturer on whose behalf Adams had made phone calls to government agencies.

President Eisenhower's words were: "I personally like Governor Adams. I admire his abilities. I respect him because of his personal and official integrity. I need him . . ."

On September 22, 1958, under substantial pressure from Republicans worried about the midterm elections, Adams resigned.

President Eisenhower's statement was played up by his critics as an admission of dependency by a weak Chief Executive. See ABOMINABLE NO-MAN.

INFLATION loss of the purchasing power of money; in politics, an issue of greatest concern to those on fixed incomes.

Basically, there are two forms of inflation: *demand-pull,* when there are too many dollars chasing too few goods, and *cost-push,* when wage increases sharply exceed productivity increases, pushing prices ever higher.

The first great quarrel in the U.S. over inflation was tied in with the long-running debate between hard- and soft-money men. The hards warned in 1837 that "a bubble will be inflated more disastrous in its explosion than the present one."

In 1933, after the burst of a particularly great bubble and the onset of the Depression, the government began talking of "reflationary" measures, such as massive deficit spending. As Raymond Moley wrote: "One zealot said to me at the time that the $3.3 billion"—the amount appropriated for the National Industrial Recovery Act's "reflationary" public works program—"would be better used if it were scattered by aircraft over the country in $1 bills. I suggested that $2 bills would be more appropriate because in the resulting inflation a dollar would mean so little."

During his 1952 campaign, Dwight Eisenhower hit hard at Democratic inflation and promised to correct it. In *Mandate for Change,* he wrote:

To illustrate inflation I had used a length of board (sawed to the breaking point in two places) to represent the buying power of a 1949 dollar. To demonstrate the decline in the dollar between 1945 and 1952, I would break off the first third of the board. To illustrate the decline that was probable with eight more years of Fair Deal policies, I would break off another chunk of the board, ending up with a wooden equivalent of a 33¢ dollar in terms of 1945 values. We expended a large pile of lumber in this lesson, but the point got across.

With John F. Kennedy's Administration the Keynes-oriented "new economists" (see NEW ECONOMICS) made deficit spending and a moderate dose of controlled, continuing inflation official policy.

After inflation gained momentum in the late sixties under pressure of heavy defense spending, the federal government moved to a "full-employment budget" concept—the limit on spending set at the amount that the tax system would produce at full (4%) employment.

The word most closely associated with inflation is "spiral"; an "inflationary spiral," like a Vandyke beard, is a phrase that is most often defined by a gesture of the fingers. The pace of inflation ranges from "creeping" to "galloping," and orators denounce the way it "eats away" at the purchasing power of the dollar. Campaigns using the theme often print tiny replicas of dollar bills and call them "Johnson (or whoever the opponent is) dollars."

In the early seventies, "stagflation" came into use, which *Fortune* magazine defined as "continuing inflation under conditions of stagnant output and rising unemployment." This situation was also described, in a paraphrase of Voltaire's Dr. Pangloss, as "the worst of both worlds."

See HOLD THE LINE; HIGH COST OF LIVING; DOUBLE DIGIT.

INFLUENCE PEDDLER one who has, or claims to have, the contacts and "pull" supposedly necessary to get government contracts and favors from public officials, for a fee.

Testifying before a special Senate subcommittee in 1949, one of many of the FIVE PERCENTERS being investigated said, "I have nothing to sell but influence."

The phrase became common during the concluding years of the Truman Administration as Republicans sought to discredit the Democrats (see MESS IN WASHINGTON; GOVERNMENT BY CRONY).

President Truman was never accused of profiting personally by corruption. But testimony showed that his military aide and close friend, Major General Harry Vaughan, had been active on behalf of people interested in getting to France to bring in

perfume base at a time when transportation for such activities was not
available. General Vaughan had in-
terceded successfully for others wanting structural steel, then in short supply, in order to put up a race track in
California and, in fact, had helped
others get military contracts.

Vaughan denied having kept anything for himself, and President Truman staunchly sustained him, as he
did special assistant and fellow Mis-
sourian Donald Dawson, who was
charged by another committee
(headed by Senator J. William Fulbright) with being the man to see if a
loan was wanted from the Reconstruction Finance Corporation.

Synonymous with "influence peddler" was "five percenter," a man
who claimed to be able to get government contracts for which he wanted,
in return, 5 percent of the value. During that period, sixty-six employees of
the Bureau of Internal Revenue were
purged and nine went to prison.

Nothing, however, had quite the
impact as gifts of deep-freeze units
made by a former Army officer, Colonel James V. Hunt, at the suggestion
of General Vaughan. They were sent
to Mr. Truman's Independence, Missouri, home, to Chief Justice Fred
Vinson, and to Secretary of the Treasury John Snyder. Their value was
much less than other examples of giving or getting things to which one was
not entitled but the "deep freeze"
gifts gripped the public mind, as did
vicuña coats years later.

President Truman's insistence on
standing up for old friends, despite his
private fury over having been "sold
down the river," hurt his party in
1952.

The predecessor of "influence" was
"pull," which Charles Ledyard Norton described in 1890 as "what influence, honorable or dishonorable, can

he bring to bear to secure his election,
or further party interests." The word
is a shortening of "wirepulling," and
can be found in "The Boss," a poem
by James Russell Lowell:

*Skilled to pull wires, he baffles Nature's
    hope
Who sure intended him to stretch a rope.*

INFRASTRUCTURE   skeleton; a
political entity's internal administrative apparatus.

This word proves that nobody—
not even a great world leader and
master of language—can kill a really
tenacious bit of jargon.

Winston Churchill tried. Emanuel
Shinwell, Labour Minister of Defence, reviewed for the House of
Commons in 1950 the results of a
meeting of the Consultative Council
of the Brussels Treaty Western
Union, a predecessor of the Common
Market. Shinwell explained that the
installation of signal communications, preparation of the headquarters, and division of the airfields were
activities now known collectively as
working on the "infrastructure."

Churchill rose and gave the use of
the word fair warning: "As to this
new word with which he has dignified
our language, but which perhaps was
imposed upon him internationally, I
can only say that we must have full
opportunity to consider it and to consult the dictionary."

Two months later, in a debate on
the Schuman plan to pool European
coal and steel, the word appeared
again and Sir Winston was ready for
it: "In this debate we have had the
usual jargon about 'the infrastructure
of a supranational authority.' The
original authorship is obscure; but it
may well be that these words 'infra'
and 'supra' have been introduced into
our current political parlance by the

band of intellectual highbrows who are naturally anxious to impress British labour with the fact that they learned Latin at Winchester."

Considering the prestigious source of the ridicule, infrastructure lay dormant. In the American diplomatic community in Vietnam in the sixties, the word reared its head cautiously. In discussing the need for pursuing the OTHER WAR, diplomats and generals briefed correspondents on the need for a "viable indigenous governmental apparat," i.e., a local Vietnamese government that would be accepted by the people, able to continue after U.S. forces left. This became known as the "infrastructure."

The adjective most often used to modify infrastructure is "viable." "That 'viable' phrase drives me mad," Defense Secretary Robert McNamara once said. "I keep trying to comb it out, but it keeps coming back."

With Churchill gone, linguistic defense collapsed and infrastructure triumphed to describe the organization of both the "friendlies" and the Viet Cong. Typical home-front use was in this 1967 *New Republic* article by Andrew Kopkind: "If [Ronald] Reagan had appeased the people, he had also alienated the major economic interests. California's corporatism, perhaps more than any other state's, relies heavily on the production of technicians and intellectuals to support its 'infrastructure.' Huge technological parks go up around every new campus, the better to feed off the state-subsidized resources."

This indicates that the word has also absorbed the pejorative meaning of "superstructure," or excess organization. John Kenneth Galbraith, in *The New Industrial State,* labeled the "organized intelligence" directing modern industrial production as the "technostructure."

"Structure" has recently become a vogue verb, its meaning drifting from "build," "create," "plan," to "organize."

For another word that could not be stopped, see MEDICARE.

INITIALESE, *see* ACRONYMS, POLITICAL; ALPHABET AGENCIES.

INITIALS, PRESIDENTIAL a contribution made by newspaper-headline writers to American history.

Prior to 1932, the President was referred to in headlines as the President, or by his last name, occasionally by his nickname ("Teddy," "Cal"), once by his initials (T.R. for Theodore Roosevelt). Presidents, in signing brief memos, would often use the initial of their first name (A. Lincoln). Franklin D. Roosevelt initialed memos "FDR" and his staff referred to him that way.

This proved a boon to headline writers, saving six spaces on both "Roosevelt" and "President." Use of initials was terse but not disrespectful, as "Frank" might have been. English newspapers had long followed the practice—Gladstone was headlined as "GOM" (Grand Old Man). Following FDR, HST was immediately adopted as short for Harry S. Truman (which may reappear in the eighties meaning hypersonic transport). Though Eisenhower initialed short notes "DE," his nickname was short and famous enough to take the place of initials, though "Ike" was considered too familiar for the *New York Times.*

Irreverent headline writers referred to John F. Kennedy as "Jack" before his election, quickly changing to "JFK" afterward. Sorensen wrote:

"JFK—as he persuaded the headline writers to call him, not to imitate FDR but to avoid the youthful 'Jack.' "

Dating even before his association with FDR, LBJ was preoccupied with initials: Lady Bird Johnson, Lynda Bird, Luci Baines all carried the same initials, as did his ranch. "All the Way With LBJ" was used as a pre-convention slogan in 1960, but achieved no national recognition. Johnson became LBJ outside his own circle only when he became President. In 1964 he used his initials in campaign advertising: "USA for LBJ" and "All the Way With LBJ."

Jimmy Carter avoided using his initials because "J.C." is usually associated with Jesus Christ.

Nixon's last name was short, which meant headline writers did not need "RN"; miffed, the former President used the initials as the title of his 1978 memoirs. Ford's name was even shorter, doing away with the need for a gruff "GRF."

INNER CLUB a small, informal group which is reported to hold leadership power in both the House of Representatives and the Senate, especially the Senate.

The phrase is attributed to columnist William S. White, who wrote of the "Inner Club where emphasis is still put on seniority and skill in negotiation." It is apparently a relative of the much older description of the U. S. Senate as "the most exclusive gentlemen's club in the world."

Its members, whatever their political affiliation, have certain things in common: some degree of seniority and a secure seat; a working belief in compromise; the quality and force of their personality; and a willingness to do solid, difficult work in the committees where legislation is forged.

The members of the Inner Club are by no means always the best-known or eventually the best-rewarded. During his senatorial years John F. Kennedy was never considered a member of the Senate's Inner Club, nor did he aspire to be. Neither was his younger brother, Senator Robert Kennedy.

An example of the group's cohesive power occurred in Hubert Humphrey's first term in the Senate. He came to the upper house as an outspoken liberal, proceeded to launch an attack on Virginia's conservative but highly respected Senator Harry Byrd, and was firmly squelched for his presumption. Senator Humphrey's attitude to the Club organization underwent so strong a change that a few years later he was Assistant Majority Leader under the most ardent exponent of Clubmanship of all, Senate Democratic Majority Leader Lyndon B. Johnson.

The phrase goes beyond the Senate. Kennedy-appointed State Department official Roger Hilsman wrote of the time he and two other aides waited until a large group left the President's office. "The three of us trooped into his oval office through the curved side door from the room his private secretary, Mrs. Lincoln, occupied and found the President rocking away in his chair before the fireplace, reading and signing the last of a pile of letters. He looked up and grinned. 'And now,' he said, 'we have the "inner club." ' "

More often, the group closest to the President or a candidate is called the "inner circle."

INOPERATIVE the epitome of arrogant ground-giving; a correction without an apology.

On April 17, 1973, press secretary Ronald Ziegler came before the

White House press corps just after President Nixon had announced "new developments" were forthcoming in the Watergate case. When asked about his own previous statements on the case, as well as the President's earlier speeches denying that anyone on the White House staff was involved, the press secretary said—six separate times—that the "operative" statement was the most recent one issued by the President.

Then, in a situation similar to that which ensnared Harry Truman on RED HERRING, a reporter used the word that later became famous and asked the spokesman if he would adopt it. R. W. "Johnny" Apple of the *New York Times* asked, "Ron, could I follow up on your comment on the 'operative' statement? Would it be fair for us to infer, since what the President said today is now considered the operative statement, to quote you, that the other statement is no longer operative, that it is now inoperative?"

Ziegler, as columnist Nick Thimmesch later put it, "dropped his guard and took the sucker punch." After a minute's fencing, the press secretary replied using the word the reporter knew would provide a devastating lead: "The President refers to the fact that there is new material; therefore, this is the operative statement. The others are inoperative."

The bit of jargon, with its mechanistic metaphor, stirred great derision. The *New York Daily News* White House correspondent, Paul Healy, said, "I think he should resign. His credibility has been ruined." The National Press Club professional relations committee denounced the way Ziegler "has misled the public and affronted the professional standards of the Washington Press Corps." Seven weeks later, the battered Ziegler turned over the briefing function to his deputy, Jerry Warren.

"Inoperative," with its Watergate cover-up connotation, continues to carry a burden of coldly brushing off the past; in 1975, in a *New York* magazine competition, "inoperative statement" was defined as "a lie that no longer works." Ziegler, who was never accused of knowingly telling a lie by the Special Prosecution force, was saddled in history by the word he allowed a reporter to lead him into saying.

The word can be found four times in amendments to the U.S. Constitution, and until the Ziegler usage, was best remembered from Abraham Lincoln's statement on September 13, 1862, explaining why he had not issued an Emancipation Proclamation: "What good would a proclamation of emancipation from me do, especially as we are now situated? I do not want to issue a document that the whole world will see must necessarily be inoperative, like the Pope's bull against the comet." (The Proclamation was announced nine days later; Lincoln had deliberately misled his callers. He misled himself about the papal bull: though Pope Calixtus III decreed "several days of prayer for averting the wrath of God" when Halley's Comet appeared in 1456, the story that he excommunicated the comet by papal bull has been disproven and is inoperative.)

IN PLACE   an informer situated in a position of trust in the enemy camp.

The word is taken from espionage, where to have an "agent in place" is the most productive form of covert operation. Spy novels and movies gave the phrase currency, and the occasional political use of the idea has kept it current. See the sub-entry on "mole" under CIA-ESE.

In most large campaigns, a covert operation existed to put a secretary, office boy, or messenger into the opposition headquarters. This "agent in place" often does nothing more than bring copies of press releases to opposition headquarters as they are delivered to the press, giving the opposing camp time to prepare a counterrelease. Post-Watergate, this practice was usually seen to be more trouble than it was worth, since it ran the risk of a DIRTY TRICKS charge.

The phrase had an antecedent political use before it shifted in meaning to become part of the undercover intelligence lexicon. Abolitionist Wendell Phillips, welcoming the crisis caused by Lincoln's election in 1860, told his followers: "Not an abolitionist, hardly an anti-slavery man, Mr. Lincoln consents to represent an anti-slavery idea. . . . He seems to govern; he only reigns. . . . Lincoln is in *place*, Garrison in power."

INPUT, *see* **DECISION-MAKING PROCESS.**

INS AND OUTS   the party in power and the party out of power; used to show basic similarity in political ideology.

Democrats in 1892 sang this song for the return of Grover Cleveland:

Grover, Grover, four more years
    of Grover—
In we'll go, Out they'll go,
Then we'll be in clover!

When asked "What is the difference between the Republicans and the Democrats?" a host of political figures have been credited with the remark: "The only difference is—they're in and we're out."

Herbert Hoover, campaigning against Franklin Roosevelt, in 1932, tried to draw a wider distinction: "This election is not a mere shift from the ins to the outs. It means deciding the directions our nation will take over a century to come." Adlai Stevenson in 1952 derided Republicans for "being out of patience, out of sorts, and . . . out of office."

Attorney General Griffin Bell, criticized for replacing Republican U.S. Attorneys with Democrats despite campaign pledges by Jimmy Carter as candidate to keep politics out of such appointments, surprised reporters with his candor in January 1978: "We have two parties in this country. The 'in' party right now happens to be the Democrats."

There are other meanings to the phrase. An experienced politician is one who *knows the ins and outs* of politics. An *in-and-outer,* however, is a "trimmer," one who cannot be trusted. But in the sense of "in power," and usually capitalized, the Ins of today are the Outs of tomorrow.

INSTANT ANALYSIS   the reaction of television commentators following a presidential speech.

The phrase was coined by Vice President Spiro Agnew in his first speech castigating much of the media, in Des Moines, Iowa, on November 13, 1969: ". . . a week ago, President Nixon delivered the most important address of his Administration, one of the most important in our decade. His subject was Vietnam. His hope was to rally the American people to see the conflict through to a lasting and just peace in the Pacific. . . . When the President completed his address—an address that he spent weeks in preparing—his words and policies were subjected to instant analysis and querulous criticism. The audience of seventy million Americans—gathered to hear the President of the United States—was inherited by a small band of network commentators and self-appointed analysts . . ."

This speech, which was written by Nixon aide Patrick Buchanan, was telecast in its entirety on prime time and did much to make the Vice President both a rallying point and a lightning rod.

The phrase grew out of "instant history," a pejorative term for articles and books about current events on recent Administrations, which in turn percolated from "instant coffee." The use of "instant"—similar to the description of a graduate of Officers Candidate School as a "90-day wonder"—plays on the suspicion of any quick assumption of expertise.

Although Agnew's remarks were roundly denounced by most television newsmen as an infringement of freedom of the press, the subsequent character of analyses following presidential addresses changed markedly from rebuttal to wrap-up.

INSTINCT FOR THE JUGULAR
ability to ferret out and attack the hidden weakness of the opponent; willingness to launch an attack that will do lasting damage.

To the tough-minded, the phrase is a compliment; to the tender-minded, it is a reference to the cruelty of wolves who slash at the jugular vein of their quarry to guarantee a kill. Most politicians admire an "instinct for the jugular" in other politicians, but do not like it to show publicly in their candidates.

The vivid phrase, still current, is one of the oldest in U.S. politics. It was coined by Massachusetts Senator Rufus Choate (coiner of "glittering generalities"), directed at another Massachusetts man, John Quincy

Adams, sixth President of the U.S. "He has peculiar powers as an assailant, and almost always, even when attacked, gets himself into that attitude by making war upon his accuser; and he has, withal, an instinct for the jugular and the carotid artery, as unerring as that of any carnivorous animal."

The metaphor used as the opposite of this was reported by Eliot Marshall in the *New Republic* (January 29, 1977): "One former [Henry] Kissinger aide told Les Gelb of the *New York Times,* 'Neither Henry nor I in the first years thought [James] Schlesinger was a man to be taken seriously. Given Jim's turn of mind, his interest in the technical rather than policy issues, we thought he had an instinct for the capillaries.'"

And it can be punned upon: humorist Russell Baker was referred to by a colleague as a man with "an instinct for the jocular."

See GUTFIGHTER; HATCHETMAN.

INSURGENT, *see* REFORM.

INTEGRATION, *see* WITH ALL DELIBERATE SPEED; SEGREGATION; BUSING.

INTELLECTUAL-IN-RESIDENCE
a presidential adviser set up in the Johnson Administration to bridge the gap between the White House and the "intellectual community."

First to hold the job was Princeton professor Eric Goldman, who resigned after a year with a blast at the President's unwillingness to accept new ideas. He was succeeded by John P. Roche, former chairman of Americans for Democratic Action. "I am not a governess to the intelligentsia," Roche said in describing his duties. "I am not the President's ambassador to the *Partisan Review* or the Metropolitan Opera." His assignment was primarily as a bridge-builder to such outspoken intellectual critics of the Administration as University of Chicago professor Hans Morgenthau, who promptly said: "He conceives his official task to be the HATCHET MAN who will try to ruin the reputation of those intellectuals who dare openly to disagree with his master."

On NBC's *Meet the Press,* December 25, 1966, former Kennedy and Johnson national security aide McGeorge Bundy (now president of the Ford Foundation, once a Harvard Dean and an administration spokesman in the "teach-ins") was asked to compare the two Presidents on their relations with the academic community. "I think we exaggerated the optimism in 1961 and 1962," he replied, "and we exaggerated the disharmony that exists in the last year or two."

President Johnson said in a 1966 Princeton University speech: "Each time my Cabinet meets I can call the roll of former professors—Humphrey and Rusk, McNamara and Wirtz, Katzenbach . . . Gardner and Weaver. The 371 appointments that I have made as President . . . collectively hold 758 advanced degrees."

Despite these statements, the academicians remained unconvinced. "When President Johnson named an intellectual-in-residence in 1964," wrote University of Toronto professor Lewis S. Feuer, "he assigned him the job of seeking the ideas and cooperation of the intellectuals. If the philosophers were not kings, they were to be honored advisers to a Democratic President. Yet no President in American history has evoked the animosity of intellectuals as much as Lyndon Johnson has."

The phrase originated with *poet-in-residence* and *writer-in-residence,* a method used by some colleges to provide the upkeep for a well-known poet or author while enhancing the school's reputation. The whatever-in-residence is rarely expected to teach, but is expected to inspire students with his creative presence.

A misunderstood word contributed to intellectual estrangement soon after Roche took office. To an interviewer, he referred to "the West Side [of New York] Jacobins"; most intellectuals would have taken this allusion to the radicals of the French Revolution in stride, but the word was reported in the *Partisan Review* (quoting a "nationally syndicated column") as "jackal bins," which started a mild furor in the intellectual community reminiscent of Charles E. Wilson's BIRD DOGS . . . KENNEL DOGS.

INTELLECTUALS, *see* **EGG-HEAD; ALIENATION.**

INTERESTS, *see* **VESTED INTERESTS.**

INTRANSIGENT unwilling to compromise; obstructionist, especially regarding peace negotiations.

During the Mideast SHUTTLE DIPLOMACY of 1974, a "senior official aboard the Secretary's plane" (the phrase denoting Secretary of State Henry Kissinger speaking on background) complained that the Israelis were being "intransigent" in his attempt to negotiate an agreement with Arab states. Since this was the first overt criticism of Israel by a high U.S. official, and was soon accompanied by a threat of a "reassessment" of U.S. support, the word received much attention.

"Intransigence," although hard to pronounce, is a word deeply rooted in diplomacy. *Transigere* is Latin for "drive through," and its participle is *transactus,* the basis for "transact": thus, "intransigent" means "unwilling to do business." In diplomacy, this has been interpreted as "uncompromising," and has long been used as a criticism of one party in peace negotiations.

INVECTIVE, POLITICAL personal abuse, vituperation, and ridicule of another; usually wistfully referred to as "a dying art," but never quite dead.

John Randolph of Virginia, who coined "doughface" to describe the supporters of the Missouri Compromise, served as a power in the House and Senate from 1799 to 1829, U.S. minister to Russia in 1830, and died insane in 1833. Recognized as the master of American political invective, Randolph said of Edward Livingstone, then a House member and later Secretary of State: "He is a man of splendid abilities, but utterly corrupt. Like rotten mackerel by moonlight, he shines and stinks."

Throughout his life it was rumored that Randolph was impotent. Congressman Tristram Burges of Rhode Island said in the House about Randolph, "I rejoice that the Father of Lies can never become the Father of Liars," to which he replied, "You pride yourself upon an animal faculty, in respect to which the slave is your equal and the jackass infinitely your superior."

Public blows as low as this, unheard-of today, were commonplace in England and America in the eighteenth and nineteenth centuries. John Montagu, fourth Earl of Sandwich, predicted that his former friend John Wilkes "would either die on the gallows or of a loathsome disease." Wilkes, in a reply usually credited to Disraeli, lashed back: "That depends, my lord, on whether I embrace your principles or your mistress."

Modern American invective has often been reduced to simple name-calling, as with John L. Lewis' description of John Nance Garner: "a poker-playing, whisky-drinking, evil old man." In the thirties, name-calling and invective flourished with General Hugh Johnson, Westbrook Pegler, and Harold Ickes (for Ickes' contributions, see CURMUDGEON). Johnson, a New Dealer turned against Roosevelt, called New Dealers "economic pansies," "a cockeyed crew of wand-waving wizards," and selected Senator Sherman Minton to be "the messenger-boy in chief for the White House janissariat." See HAIL OF DEAD CATS.

Hugh Johnson should not be confused with Hiram Johnson, first two-term (of four years) governor of California, who held this opinion of *Los Angeles Times* publisher Harrison Grey Otis: "He sits there in senile dementia with a gangrene heart and rotting brain, grimacing at every reform, chattering impotently at all things that are decent, frothing, fuming, violently gibbering, going down to his grave in snarling infamy . . . disgraceful, depraved . . . and putrescent."

Westbrook Pegler, whose most frequent target was Eleanor Roosevelt, did much to popularize the phrase "bleeding-heart liberal" (see BLEEDING HEART), hit gossip columnists as "gents-room journalists," hit intellectuals as "double domes," and infuriated the FBI by widely disseminating left-wing Congressman Vito Marcantonio's description of J. Edgar Hoover as "a Stork Club detective."

Winston Churchill is commonly thought to have directed his famous dig "sheep in sheep's clothing" at Clement Attlee. In a review of the first edition of this book, British historian D. W. Brogan set the record straight: "Sir Winston Churchill never said of Clement Attlee that he was a 'sheep in sheep's clothing.' I have this on the excellent authority of Sir Winston himself. The phrase was totally inapplicable to Mr. Attlee. It was applicable, and applied, to J. Ramsay MacDonald, a very different kind of Labour leader." MacDonald was a favorite target of Churchill's, as illustrated in the following classic of invective without rancor, on a low key: "I remember, when I was a child, being taken to the celebrated Barnum's Circus, which contained an exhibition of freaks and monstrosities, but the exhibit on the programme which I most desired to see was the one described as 'The Boneless Wonder.' My parents judged that that spectacle would be too revolting and demoralising for my youthful eyes, and I have waited fifty years to see the Boneless Wonder sitting on the Treasury Bench."

In current use, political invective has become more decorous; personal attacks are whispered rather than spoken publicly, for fear they will boomerang. Perhaps Francis Bacon's words are being considered: "Anger makes dull men witty, but it keeps them poor."

INVESTIGATIVE REPORTER, see **MUCKRAKER.**

INVISIBLE GOVERNMENT any group accused of creating public policy immune from public criticism or electoral recall.

"The Invisible Government," wrote David Wise and Thomas B. Ross in their 1964 book of that title, "is not a formal body. It is a loose, amorphous grouping of individuals and agencies drawn from many parts of the visible government. It is not limited to the Central Intelligence Agency, although the CIA is at its heart. . . . This shadow government is shaping the lives of 190,000,000 Americans. Major decisions involving peace or war are taking place out of public view."

In 1967 the editors of *Ramparts* magazine disclosed that foundations acting as conduits for CIA funds had secretly subsidized trips abroad of U.S. student groups. The public reacted severely to this disclosure of a covert operation, and President Johnson ordered it ended. A political cartoon showed a scruffy-looking, bearded beatnik trudging along on a campus, observed by a pair of coeds, one of whom says, "Oh, is he CIA? I thought he was FBI."

After *New York Times* reporter Seymour Hersh broke the story of the CIA's illegal activities in 1975, the "agency"—or as it was also known, "the company"—lost much of its clout. With repeated disclosures (see "family jewels" under CIA-ESE), the intelligence organization ceased to be known as an "invisible government," and adopted the benign term "intelligence community."

"Invisible" is a word with deep and mistrusted roots in American history. Albert Beveridge, senator, orator, and Lincoln biographer, used the phrase at the 1912 Progressive Party convention that nominated Theodore Roosevelt: "These special interests, which suck the people's substance, are bipartisan. They use both parties. They are the invisible government behind the visible government . . . it is this invisible government which is the real danger to American institutions." The phrase was used heavily in the three-man Taft-Roosevelt-Wilson campaign; Wilson joined in denouncing the "special interests" and added: " . . . an invisible empire had been set up above the forms of democracy."

In 1923 the *Review of Reviews* reported that "Governor Parker of Louisiana appeared in Washington to consult with President Harding and the Department of Justice regarding an 'invisible government' that was alleged to be interfering with the administration of justice in his own state and in other parts of the South." The reference was to the Ku Klux Klan, known since the Civil War as "the invisible empire of the South."

The Klan became an issue at the 1924 Democratic convention. Liberal, urban forces behind New York Governor Al Smith wanted to denounce the Klan by name in the party platform; agrarian Democrats behind Wilson's son-in-law, W. G. McAdoo, took a more ambivalent attitude toward the extremists, not wishing to alienate the rural vote where the Klan was strongest. As Barry Goldwater did forty years later with EXTREMISM, McAdoo took the key phrase of his opposition, gave it a twist, and flung it back; playing on the "invisible empire" description of the Klan, he spoke of "the sinister, unscrupulous invisible government which has its seat in the citadel of privilege and finance in New York City."

With William Jennings Bryan's support, McAdoo won the battle against naming the Klan in the platform by a single convention vote. But the bitterness of this issue, as well as the League of Nations, brought forth a moderate dark horse, and John W. Davis was selected as the nominee.

"Invisible government," as a phrase, touches a responsive chord in the minds of people already suspicious of faraway federal government. In the early sixties, ardently anti-Communist Dallas newsletter writer Dan Smoot published a book about the Council on Foreign Relations, titled *The Invisible Government*, which preceded the better-selling Wise-Ross book of the same title.

See DIRTY TRICKS.

IN YOUR HANDS a Lincoln construction used by John Kennedy; an oratorical device of involvement.

From Lincoln's first inaugural: "In your hands, my dissatisfied fellow countrymen, and not in mine, is the momentous issue of civil war."

From Kennedy's inaugural: "In your hands, my fellow citizens, more than mine, will rest the final success or failure of our course."

IRISH MAFIA the Bostonians of Irish descent who were John Kennedy's earliest and closest political aides.

According to Theodore Sorensen, a Nebraskan with no known Irish blood, Irish Mafia was a "newspaper designation bitterly resented by its designees when first published." Stewart Alsop probably printed it first, but by the time the Kennedy Administration took office in January 1961, Irish Mafia was a smart "in" phrase. Among the group's prominent members were Kenneth O'Donnell, who became Kennedy's appointments secretary; Lawrence O'Brien, chief of congressional liaison and later Democratic National Chairman; and David Powers, a general White House factotum.

Another group, drawn primarily from the academic world typified by McGeorge Bundy, Kennedy's assistant for national security affairs, was often contrasted with the practical politicians of the O'Donnell-O'Brien group. Pierre Salinger, who by background belonged to neither camp, said stories of power struggles between the eggheads and the Mafia "would arouse JFK to profane anger."

The inference that the Kennedy clan leaned heavily on power plotters who rarely saw the sun from their SMOKE-FILLED room hardly blended with the idealistic NEW FRONTIER image. Even worse was the connotation of gangsterism. The original Mafia—named after the Sicilian slang word for boldness or swagger—consisted of primitive racketeers. When an Italian-American group objected in the seventies to what they felt was an ethnic slur, the word was avoided by many law officers.

Although the first use in politics of the word was to compare the most useful qualities of a mob hierarchy to those of men surrounding a President, and to salute the loyalty, dedication, common background and toughness common to both, the jocular tone of the phrase was jolted by revelations in 1975 that the "real" Mafia may have been used by the "Irish Mafia"—or at least the CIA, with Kennedy knowledge—to carry out an assassination attempt against Fidel Castro.

In 1964 political writers showed their nonpartisanship by dubbing Barry Goldwater's Republican coterie from home the "Arizona Mafia." A subsequent article in the *New York Herald Tribune* about English governesses in the U.S. was entitled "The Nanny Mafia." By 1978 the "real" Mafia cloud had passed, and the men in the Carter Administration—Georgians Joseph L. "Jody" Powell, Hamilton Jordan, Griffin Bell, Robert Lipshutz, and others—were often called "the Georgia Mafia," or "Magnolia Mafia."

IRON CURTAIN a barrier to communication between peoples, lowered to permit a regime to operate in a society isolated from outside criticism.

This was one of the two great figures of speech in the generation following World War II (for the other, see COLD WAR). It was popularized by Winston Churchill, who had used it several times before deciding to use it strongly in a speech at Fulton, Missouri, on March 5, 1946: "From Stettin in the Baltic to Trieste in the Adriatic, an iron curtain has descended across the continent. Behind that line lie all the capitals of the ancient states of central and eastern Europe. . . . The safety of the world, ladies and gentlemen, requires a new unity in Europe from which no nation should be permanently outcast."

The forum Churchill chose was an odd one. The president of tiny Westminster College at Fulton wrote to alumnus General Harry Vaughan, President Truman's military aide, inviting Churchill to speak at the college during a forthcoming trip to the United States. Truman endorsed the idea, passed it on to Churchill, who replied that he had something he would like to say.

The "iron curtain speech" of Churchill marked the end of a peaceful honeymoon with Soviet Russia that had existed in the minds of many Americans after World War II. It became the symbol of Soviet oppression, and the rallying cry for the Western European military organization that came to be NATO.

Phrase detectives—principally Ignace Feuerlicht, writing in *American Speech* magazine—tracked down a variety of previous uses. It began as a theatrical phrase. A theater in Lyons, France, introduced a curtain in the eighteenth century to prevent the spread of fire, and in 1794 the Drury Lane Theatre in London did the same. Throughout Europe, "iron curtain" was the name for the fireproof curtain in theaters, and the Earl of Munster, writing of travels in India, used it as a metaphor in 1819: "As if an iron curtain had dropped between us and the Avenging Angel, the deaths diminished."

H. G. Wells used it in 1904 in *The Food of the Gods* as a metaphor for enforced privacy; American author George W. Creel in *A Mechanistic View of War and Peace* in 1915 described France as "a nation of 40 millions with a deeprooted grievance and an iron curtain at its frontier."

The London *Times Literary Supplement* recalled a 1920 use by Viscountess Snowden in her account of a visit to Russia after the war, entitled *Through Bolshevik Russia.*

German militarists liked the phrase. Writing in 1923, Walther Nicolai, who served as intelligence chief of the German General Staff during World War I, used the metaphor about a news blockade the wartime allies had planned to impose upon Germany: "It became clear that in case of war, the enemy would shut off Germany from the outside world as with an iron curtain."

The Moscow *Literary Gazette* carried an editorial headlined "Iron Curtain" in January 1930. The writer, Lev Nikulin, suggested that the bourgeoisie was trying to lower an iron curtain between Russia and the West. The theatrical simile was clear here, because Nikulin was showing how the bourgeoisie was attempting to prevent the spread of the fire of communism.

Hitler's minister of finance, Ludwig Schwerin von Krosigk, was credited with the phrase as well; Nazi propaganda minister Joseph Goebbels used it often, as in this Reuters dispatch appearing in the *Manchester Guardian* of February 23, 1945:

"If the German people lay down their arms, the whole of Eastern and Southern Europe, together with the Reich, will come under Russian occupation. Behind an iron curtain mass butcheries of people would begin."

Later that year, on November 15, Senator Arthur Vandenberg used the phrase in a Senate speech. Meanwhile, on May 12, 1945, Churchill had wired Truman: "An iron curtain is drawn down upon their frontier. We do not know what is going on behind." In his memoirs, Churchill called this "the iron curtain telegram." Ten months later, he popularized the term at Fulton, Missouri.

Predecessors to the iron curtain were the *cordon sanitaire,* which was drawn around western Russia at the end of World War I in an early attempt at "containment" of Communism; the "Wall of China" has often been used as a figure of speech saying "Keep out" in international language, later echoed by the Berlin Wall (see WALL, POLITICAL USE OF); and the French military establishment was denounced during World War II for its "Maginot Line thinking."

Derivatives of the iron curtain are fascinating. Probably the longest-lived was "bamboo curtain," describing the outlook of Communist China. Others included: "Jim Crow curtain," coined by Adam Clayton Powell; the "sand curtain" (between the Arabs and Israel); the "marble curtain" (between newsmen and the government), a coinage of Senator Hubert Humphrey; "cobweb curtain" (separating the English press from the royal court); and a "lace curtain" (the closing of New England to Russian tourists) coined by *Pravda,* its unconscious humor noted by some Irish-Americans.

"I SEE" CONSTRUCTION   a favorite device of speechwriters, outlining a vision of the future punctuated with "I see."

Orator Robert G. Ingersoll, who coined the "Plumed Knight" title for candidate James Blaine, offered an example of this highly effective technique in 1876:

I see our country filled with happy homes. . . .

I see a world where thrones have crumbled. . . .

I see a world without a slave.

. . .

I see a world at peace . . . a world where labor reaps its full reward.

. . .

I see a world without the beggar's outstretched palm . . . the piteous wail of want. . . .

. . . and, as I look, life lengthens, joy deepens, love canopies the earth; and over all, in the great dome, shines the eternal star of human hope.

When Samuel Rosenman prepared a speech for FDR's inaugural in 1937, he used the "I see" repetition in a reportorial, rather than visionary, sense: "I see tens of millions of its citizens" denied the "necessities of life"; "I see millions denied education . . ." Rosenman wrote later: "I had written on the original of the second draft a summation of all the 'I sees' with a final 'I see' . . . the President rubbed out all I had written in pencil after that final 'I see' and after a moment's reflection substituted in his own hand his own summation: 'I see one third of a nation ill-housed, ill-clad, ill-nourished.'"

Rosenman and Robert E. Sherwood collaborated on an FDR speech in 1940 that used the "I see" construction in its visionary sense:

I see an America where factory workers are not discarded after they reach their prime. . . .

I see an America whose rivers and valleys and lakes . . . are protected as the rightful heritage of all the people.

I see an America where small business really has a chance to flourish and grow.

I see an America of great cultural and educational opportunity for all its people.

I see an America where the income from the land shall be implemented and protected. . . .

I see an America devoted to our freedom . . . a people confident in strength because their body and their spirit are secure and unafraid.

Toward the close of his 1952 campaign, Adlai Stevenson outlined his own vision and dream:

I see an America where no man fears to think as he pleases, or say what he thinks.

I see an America where slums and tenements have vanished and children are raised in decency and self-respect.

I see an America where men and women have leisure from toil—leisure to cultivate the resources of the spirit.

I see an America where no man is another's master—where no man's mind is dark with fear.

I see an America at peace with the world.

I see an America as the horizon of human hopes.

This is our design for the American cathedral . . .

Variations of this construction include "I look forward to" and "I HAVE A DREAM." Stevenson used the "I look forward" structure in a Los Angeles speech on the American future on September 11, 1952; John Kennedy used it in 1963, a month before his assassination:

I look forward to a great future for America, a future in which our country will match its military strength with our moral restraint, its wealth with our wisdom, its power with our purpose.

I look forward to an America which will not be afraid of grace and beauty. . . .

I look forward to an America which commands respect throughout the world not only for its strength but for its civilization as well. And I look forward to a world which will be safe not only for democracy and diversity but also for personal distinction.

Preparing his acceptance speech at the 1968 Republican convention, Richard Nixon reviewed all the foregoing, and offered his own vision of America in the year 2000:

I see a day when Americans are once again proud of their flag. . . . I see a day when the President of the United States is respected and his office is honored because it is worthy of respect and worthy of honor. . . . I see a day when we will again have freedom from fear in America and freedom from fear in the world. I see a day when our nation is at peace and the world is at peace and everyone on earth—those who hope, those who aspire, those who crave liberty—will look to America as the shining example of hopes realized and dreams achieved.

In what press secretary Joseph L. Powell described as an "ambitious new text," candidate Jimmy Carter incorporated a passage by speechwriter Patrick Anderson in May 1976: "I see an America that has turned its back on scandals and shame . . . I see an America that does not spy on its own citizens . . ." (See VISION OF AMERICA.)

ISM   a political, social, or economic belief or system; in its proper form as a suffix, a way of converting names or ordinary descriptive words into broad labels.

In pragmatic America, dogma (whether right or wrong) has always been slightly suspect. Oswald Garrison Villard, summarizing Calvin Coolidge's appeal to businessmen during the 1924 campaign, said, "He is just what the country needs, a quiet, simple, unobtrusive man, with no isms and no desire for reform."

Derived from the Greek -ismos, ism can be attached to almost anything for the sake of a catchword either to defend or attack. During William McKinley's Administration, Secretary of War Russell Alger became a controversial figure because of the conduct of his department during the Spanish-American War. "Algerism" became a short-lived but lively topic of conversation—and target for political shafts. Senator Joseph McCarthy died in 1957, but MCCARTHYISM remains a forensic point of departure.

Capitalism, militarism, pacifism, nationalism, AMERICANISM, and scores of other isms are part of common political discourse, although the meaning of any one term varies widely, depending on the ideology of the user and the context of the use. Charles de Gaulle's concept of nationalism, for instance, differs widely from that of a leader of a former French colony in Africa. The British diplomat Sir Andrew Cohen observed in 1958: "To campaign against colonialism is like barking up a tree that has already been cut down."

Quincy Wright noted that social scientists have "long deplored" such terms because they are "highly sentimentalized, ambiguous, controversial and changeable." But, conceded Wright, it is impossible to "give precise definition to these words or to substitute other words with no connotation in the popular vocabulary."

Two of the angriest political epithets today are RACISM and SEXISM.

ISOLATIONISM the theory that American interests are best served by a minimum of involvement in foreign affairs and alliances.

Isolationism became a major issue in American politics and a fixture in the American political vocabulary in the post–World War I fight over whether the United States should join the League of Nations. Woodrow Wilson, the great pro-League advocate, castigated those who would have the U.S. retreat into "sullen and selfish isolation." Warren Harding responded: "We seek no part in directing the destinies of the world." Harding prevailed and the country entered its last period of separation from international power politics although even during the 1920s it participated in arms-control conferences.

The rise of Nazism in Germany and the Spanish Civil War once again made isolationism versus internationalism a major domestic issue here. Throughout most of the thirties the country's traditional preference for separation from Europe—what Thomas Jefferson called "the exterminating havoc of one-quarter of the globe"—continued at least nominally in force.

Even Franklin Roosevelt, whose name was to become irrevocably linked with internationalism, said in 1936: "We are not isolationists except insofar as we seek to isolate ourselves completely from war. . . . If we face the choice of profits [from munitions exports] or peace, the nation will answer—must answer—'we choose peace.'" But by 1941 the United States had become the ARSENAL OF DEMOCRACY, and Pearl Harbor ended the isolationists' dream forever. Senator Arthur Vandenberg, one of the many Republican leaders who abandoned isolation, watched German V-rockets assaulting London

in 1944 and mused, "How can there be any immunity or isolation when men can devise weapons like that?" Said the *New Republic:* "Hank Jones, American, is sick of isolation."

After World War II, with relatively little dissent at home, successive Administrations kept the U.S. very much in the mainstream of world affairs. But a variation of the old dispute arose when American involvement in Vietnam became bloody and costly. Lyndon Johnson's Administration was accused, in effect, of extending internationalism beyond the bounds of reason and prudence. Many of the critics were liberals who had favored earlier foreign intervention. Defenders of the Vietnam commitment charged the dissenters with "neo-isolationism." To this Henry Steele Commager, the historian, responded that too much U.S. military activity abroad was leading the country into "intellectual and moral isolationism." See ENTANGLING ALLIANCES; GO-IT-ALONE.

Objectively, the antonym is *internationalism;* isolationists prefer to denounce *interventionism* and *adventurism.*

ISRAEL LOBBY, *see* **CHINA LOBBY.**

ISSUES, THE important but dull subjects, treated rationally, which most candidates solemnly promise to campaign upon; a promise usually honored in the breach.

"I intend to campaign on the issues," a candidate frequently announces, and that pledge is dutifully reported as "So-and-so pledged an issue-oriented campaign." The candidate who proclaims his fealty to "the issues" usually refuses to ENGAGE IN PERSONALITIES, which is what interests most voters.

Real issues run the gamut from GUT ISSUE to "burning issue" to the more recent "social issue" and the recurring BREAD-AND-BUTTER ISSUE; but spoken in the plural, construed as singular, "the issues" is gaining a do-good, bogus-intellectual connotation.

The phrase was probably popularized by Senator William E. Borah in the campaign of 1928. On March 10 of that year he charged that the Republican National Committee had accepted over a quarter-million dollars from oil magnate Harry Sinclair, adding that "the people are baffled and discouraged because they cannot get the issues squarely and fairly presented." He then delivered a quotable line: "Give the people issues, and you will not have to sell your souls for campaign funds."

In 1972, after presidential candidate George McGovern dropped Senator Thomas Eagleton from the ticket, a New York *Times* editorial adjured the Democratic team to address "itself vigorously to the real issues," which caused *Times* columnist Russell Baker to comment: "The odd thing about Senator McGovern's Vice Presidential entr'acte was the amount of noise from the press urging that the Vice Presidential crisis be disposed of quickly so that the campaign could proceed to deal with the issues—sometimes called 'the real issues.' Reviewing Presidential campaigns back into the nineteen-fifties, we are led to suspect that the press people who wanted to move on to these 'real issues' were trying to cheat us of what will probably be our one opportunity to perceive Mr. McGovern as he might actually behave in the White House."

In 1977, after a campaign in which he had been accused of being "fuzzy on the issues," President Jimmy Carter told reporter John Sherwood of the *Washington Star* that he felt a kinship with successful congressional campaigners: "We're all fuzzy on the issues. That's proven by the fact that we did get elected. The advantage of being a presidential candidate is that you have a much broader range of issues on which to be fuzzy."

"The issues" is becoming an issue in itself. Richard Reeves, speculating about a possible 1980 Democratic primary race between Jimmy Carter and California Governor Jerry Brown, wrote in the *Washington Monthly:* "Since both can afford pollsters, Carter and Brown will not be that far apart on what the *New Republic* calls 'issues.' " Tom Bethell seized on this line in *Harper's* (January 1978): "There at last were the issues—the Issues—being referred to within ironical quotation marks. As indeed they should be, if it is true that candidates' (or incumbents') positions are now determined by the findings of pollsters rather than by the principles of officeholders or -seekers. If this is so, then 'the issues' have in an important sense disappeared and fully deserve their quotation marks, because they are no longer the object of decision on the part of 'decision-makers' in Washington . . . thus the Issues have become mere ornaments, the wearing of which would inevitably attract such a careful student of style as *Women's Wear Daily.* "

ITCH TO RUN a yearning for elective office, used most often as a "presidential itch"; a symptom of POTOMAC FEVER and PRESIDENTIAL FEVER.

Rutherford B. Hayes in 1871 wrote in his diary: "If I thought there was the slightest danger of so obscure a personage as I being attacked with that wretched mania, an itching for the White House, I would beg for the prayers of your church for my deliverance." Five years later he was off and running, and won.

The expression is common in English politics as well. Alfred Austin,

poet laureate of England at the turn of the century, wrote:

You want a seat! Then boldly sate your itch;
Be very radical, and very rich.

ITEM VETO, *see* **RIDER.**

JACOBINS, *see* **INTELLECTUAL-IN-RESIDENCE.**

JANISSARY, *see* **HENCHMAN.**

JAWBONING the use of presidential admonition as a tool of IN-COMES POLICY.

"The jawbone method" was the phrase used by Walter Heller, chairman of the Council of Economic Advisers in 1962, to describe GUIDE-LINES set down to restrain prices and wages. The most vivid example of this technique was the confrontation between President Kennedy and the steel industry (see S.O.B.).

When the guidelines began to break down in 1965, the word "jawboning" gained a connotation of ineffective protest. President Nixon flatly told the Cabinet Committee on Economic Policy in early 1969: "I'm against jawboning." In economic speeches, he said the economy needed more backbone, not more jawbone. Even after his announcement of a new economic policy on August 15, 1971, the President retained his distaste for the ineffective connotation of the word; in September, describing the phase of policy that would follow the wage-price freeze, he told a press conference, "you cannot have jawboning that is effective without teeth," which was an appropriate extension of the metaphor.

Jimmy Carter, as President, preferred the phrase "moral suasion," and assigned Robert Strauss, a former Democratic National Chairman, to the job of jawboning business and labor in 1978.

JIM CROW laws and customs that discriminate against, segregate, or humiliate Negroes.

"I was offered the Ambassadorship of Liberia once," said Ralph Bunche, after becoming Undersecretary of the United Nations in 1960, "when that post was earmarked for a Negro. I told them I wouldn't take a Jim Crow job."

At the Republican convention in San Francisco in 1964, a band of Negro demonstrators marched in front of the Cow Palace shouting and clapping "Jim Crow [*clap, clap*]— must go!"

A crow is black. A Kentucky plantation song, sung early in the eighteenth century, coined the name for a dance, or jig:

> *First on the heel tap, den on de toe,*
> *Ebery time I wheel about*
> *I jump Jim Crow.*

In 1829, entertainer Thomas Dartmouth Rice blacked his face and "jumped Jim Crow" in a Louisville theater. Soon after, the name became synonymous with Negro, and around 1840 the segregated Negro car on the Boston Railroad became known as the "Jim Crow." In 1841 the abolitionist *Liberator* told of the indignity to Negro editor and later diplomat Frederick Douglass: "The conductor . . . ordered Douglass to leave, and to take his seat in the forward car; meaning the 'Jim Crow,' though he felt ashamed to call it by that name."

President Truman took a major step in ending Jim Crow by desegregating the armed services. "Experience on the front has proved," he wrote, "that the morale of troops is strengthened where Jim Crow practices are not imposed." With great pride Truman recounted the reaction of Southern Democrats to his insistence on a strong civil rights plank in the 1948 Democratic platform. As South Carolina Governor J. Strom Thurmond walked out of the convention with his followers, a reporter pointed out, "Truman is only following the platform that Roosevelt advocated." "I agree," Thurmond replied, "but Truman really *means* it."

The legality of Jim Crow was crushed by the Supreme Court desegregation decision of 1954 (see WITH ALL DELIBERATE SPEED). The most dramatic challenge to Jim Crow customs as well as laws came with the "freedom rides" of young Negroes in the South in 1961 (see FREEDOM RIDERS). With education and transportation desegregated, Negroes made their next target housing. Although Lester Maddox won a narrow victory in Georgia in the 1966 race for governor on a slogan of "Your Home Is Your Castle—Protect It," his ardor cooled somewhat after election day. For subsequent developments in the lexicon of civil rights, see SEGREGATION; BUSING; RACISM.

JINGOISM   shrill, aggressive superpatriotism   (see   SUPERPATRIOTS); chauvinism.

In a Venezuelan boundary dispute between Great Britain and the U. S. in 1895, New York Police Board chief Theodore Roosevelt warned: "We will settle the Venezuelan question in Canada. Canada would surely be conquered, and once wrested from England it would never be restored."

To Senator Henry Cabot Lodge, Roosevelt said, "This country needs a war," but added that "the bankers, brokers and Anglomaniacs generally" seemed to favor "PEACE AT ANY PRICE."

Horrified, President Charles William Eliot of Harvard asked whether anything could be more offensive "than this doctrine of Jingoism, this chip-on-the-shoulder attitude of a ruffian and a bully," and added that both Roosevelt and Lodge were "degenerated sons of Harvard." (Roosevelt became calmer in later years, his best-known remark beginning with "Speak softly.")

The doctrine of jingoism Eliot referred to, along with Roosevelt's PEACE AT ANY PRICE remark, came from the English parliamentary battle in 1876, with Gladstone on one side facing Queen Victoria and Disraeli on the other. The issue was intervention in Turkey over alleged persecution of Christians there. Gladstone held that Britain should support the Christian minorities against the Turks, threatening to bundle the Turks out of Europe "bag and baggage." Disraeli and the Queen felt it was all a plot by the Russians to expand at the expense of Turkey. When Disraeli threatened the Russians with war if they did not halt the flow of "volunteers" into Turkey, this refrain was heard in the music halls of London:

We don't want to fight, but by Jingo, if we do,

We've got the ships, we've got the men,
We've got the money, too!

"Jingoism" quickly became a synonym for bellicose remarks and national cockiness. Disraeli was initially forced into neutrality, but when Russia invaded Turkey in 1878, he sent in the British fleet and helped arrange what he called a PEACE WITH HONOR.

In recent times, "jingoism" has been a charge leveled at U.S. participation in the war in Vietnam. In answer, McGeorge Bundy wrote that the American people "have refused to give support to easy wrong answers at either extreme. Open opposition has flourished. There has been less jingoism than in any previous war in our history." In 1978, opponents of the Panama Canal treaties, who charged GIVEAWAY, were denounced as "jingoes."

The synonym is SUPERPATRIOTS or chauvinists, from the French *chauvin,* the name of a real Napoleonic veteran in Scribe's play *Le Soldat Laboureur.*

Winston Churchill wrote in *My Early Life:* "I have always been against the pacifists during the quarrel, and against the Jingoes at its close."

JOB SEEKS THE MAN a philosophy of office believed in by the fatalistic, the idealistic, or the lazy.

A paradox exists in the mind of the American voter. He expects a candidate for high office to be mildly reluctant at first, as "the office seeks the man"; then, with the possibility implanted, he expects the candidate to hungrily seek the office. The man must not try too hard at first; he must not fail to try his hardest toward the end. Many a man has played "hard to get" a little too long, the possibility of his candidacy does not take root, and he is dismissed with his acquiescence unspoken.

President Harry Truman, in a passage about "luck" in his memoirs, observed:

If a man starts out to make himself President, he hardly ever arrives. Henry Clay is an outstanding example. He was so sure he would be President that he twice refused the vice-presidency, and in both cases he would have succeeded to the highest office because of the death of the President. James G. Blaine was another such man. And I was convinced . . . that Thomas E. Dewey was another whose determined efforts to make himself President would never materialize.

Richard Nixon took the same fatalistic view: "I have a theory," he said in 1958, "that in the United States those who seek the Presidency never win it. Circumstances rather than a man's ambition determine the result. If he is the right man for the right time, he will be chosen."

Adlai Stevenson, subject of a rare genuine draft in 1952, appeared to many to have overplayed reluctance and humility. In his acceptance speech, he reminded the delegates, "I would not seek your nomination for the presidency because the burdens of that office stagger the imagination . . . its potential . . . smothers exultation and converts vanity to prayer." Many politicians felt he made the right speech at the wrong moment.

The concept of "the job seeks the man" applies less to lesser offices than to president. In the case of Supreme Court Justice, however, it applies most of all. When Governor Abraham Ribicoff of Connecticut, a strong and early Kennedy supporter, was asked if he had hopes for the high court, he replied, "He who does not seek is often found. The one thing you should never seek is the Supreme Court."

Columnist Clayton Fritchey wrote in 1967 about the way California Governor Ronald Reagan ducked the question of national candidacy: "When asked about White House aspirations, he declined to be drawn out because, as he reminded the reporters, in this country 'The Office seeks the man,' not the other way around." He added: "Like Lola, what The Office wants, The Office gets. Ask Eisenhower. The General fled to Paris in 1952 and tried to hide out in NATO, but it didn't work. . . . It's time somebody seeks The Office instead of vice versa."

In this expression, *job* and *office* are used interchangeably; job is more recent usage, and seems to be ascendant.

JOE SMITH   surprise star of the 1956 Republican convention; a fictitious nominee for Vice President, the name put in by a delegate who wanted to "dump Nixon."

After Harold Stassen's effort to replace Richard Nixon as the Republican nominee for Vice President proved abortive (see **KINGMAKER**), the nomination was a foregone conclusion. Speaker Joseph Martin, convention chairman, had been tipped off by Interior Secretary Fred Seaton of Nebraska that "a misguided and recalcitrant Nebraska delegate" was going to put Seaton's name in nomination, using that as a wedge to make a nominating speech. In that proposed speech, National Chairman Len Hall suspected some alarming things were to be said about President Eisenhower's health; Hall urged Martin to avoid giving the Nebraska delegate, Terry Carpenter, a chance to speak.

When Nebraska was reached on the roll call, the head of the delegation said that Carpenter wanted the floor. "Who does he desire to nominate?" asked Martin, probably out of order. The Nebraska chairman did not know. Martin explained that the reason he was asking was that he had a note from "a distinguished son of Nebraska" (Seaton) stating he wanted no part of being nominated. This robbed Carpenter of his candidate, but he thought fast.

"Mr. Chairman," he called out, "we are going to nominate Joe Smith."

"Joe who?"

"Joe Smith!" Amid a roar of laughter in an otherwise cut-and-dried convention, newsmen clustered around the Nebraska delegation. Martin thundered the classic order of the day: "Take your Joe Smith and get outa here!"

See **CHARLIE REGAN**.

JOHN BULL, *see* **UNCLE SAM**.

JOHN Q. PUBLIC   the mythical average man, or **MAN IN THE STREET**; often cartooned as bespectacled, long-suffering, clad in a barrel, but eternally optimistic.

In the fifteenth century his name was *Everyman,* hero of English and Dutch morality plays; when Death called him, he asked his friends Beauty, Kindred, and Worldly Goods to go along. They turned him down, and only one—Good Deeds—accompanied Everyman to heaven. See **EVERY MAN A KING**.

In the Progressive movement of the nineteenth century, he was *The Man of Good Will;* William Graham Sumner called him *the forgotten man* (not be be confused with FDR's **FORGOTTEN MAN** who lived "on the bottom of the economic pyramid"); and Woodrow Wilson idealized him as *the* man on the make from "out of the unknown homes" who was the hope of America. Wilson's aim was to set up a government "where the average man, the plain man, the common man, the ignorant man, the unaccomplished man, the poor man had a voice equal to the voice of anybody else in the settlement of the common affairs, an ideal never before realized in the history of the world." See COMMON MAN, CENTURY OF THE.

William Allen White, editor of the *Emporia Gazette,* took the side of the consumer in a 1937 speech: "We are all the children of John Q. Public, and our interests as members of the consuming public are after all our chief end and objective as citizens of our democracy. . . . If labor insists," he warned, "upon maintaining its class lines of bitter intransigent hostility to all capital, the American middle class —old John Q. Public and his heirs and assigns—will not support labor."

He signs specimen checks under the name of *John Doe* and *Richard Roe;* his wife, *Jane Doe,* signs specimen subscription orders for women's magazines. To a younger set, he has a glazed expression that asks, "What— me worry?" and answers to *Alfred E. Newman.* In other incarnations, he appears as *Joe Zilch* and *Joe Blow.* In China he is known as *Old Hundred Names.* Theatergoers know him as *Littlechap,* who cries, "Stop the world—I want to get off!" Only the Devil himself (Satan, Mephisto, Scratch, Old Nick, Lucifer, etc.) has more aliases.

John is the most common first name, with the "Q" added to give a distinctive, humorously dignified fillip; the last name has genuine built-in dignity, its Latin root *pubes,* "adult."

Not every writer pays him respect. Robert Bendiner wrote in 1960 about the political diminutives—*"little man, common man, small businessman, small farmer,* and the like. In an election year, we seem to have an enormous population of midgets. The candidate's immediate audience, however, is never made up of these wee folk; it is made up of *the great people of this great state.* That's you. The little people are your relatives and neighbors."

JOHNSON TREATMENT in the broad sense, the "LBJ brand," or style of presidency; in a narrow sense, the technique of badgering, dickering, and overpowering that President Johnson was reputed to use in person-to-person persuasion.

The broad sense is less often used. Jack Bell, AP White House correspondent, called his book about the President *The Johnson Treatment,* subtitled "How Lyndon B. Johnson Took Over the Presidency and Made It His Own."

The Treatment, as it was more specifically known, was described by a recipient, Texas Lieutenant Governor Ben Ramsey, in explaining to Governor Allan Shivers in 1956 why he suddenly switched his support on a matter from Shivers to Johnson: "Lyndon got me by the lapels and put his face on top of mine and talked and talked and talked. I figured it was either get drowned or joining."

The Johnson treatment was generally described as an all-stops-out display of pressure, cajolery, threats, promises of *quid pro quo,* and refusal to take no for an answer. Rowland Evans and Robert Novak described this scene of the persuasion of Senator Richard Russell to become a member of the Warren Commission on the assassination of President Kennedy: "In a conversation lasting most of an hour, Johnson unleashed The Treatment, dormant now for three years. Emotionally, he recalled their long, intimate association. He appealed to Russell as his friend, and he appealed as the President of the United States. 'If you say no,' Johnson said, 'I'll have you drafted.' Russell accepted, and the Commission was complete."

Used in its general sense, the Johnson treatment is synonymous with his presidential style. The word *style* is almost always used admiringly in regard to Kennedy, derisively regarding Johnson; those who like his style use the Western metaphor, *brand*. Harvard professor Theodore Levitt made the case in favor of The Treatment in the *Harvard Business Review:*

> At best Johnson gets pejorative praise, summarized in tasteless references to the "Johnson Treatment" —the endless telephone calls, implied threats, stubborn push, pleading entreaties, back-room quid pro quos . . .
>
> But . . . Johnson's great achievement is that he has changed people's perceptions. They see new, different, and more congenial things than they ever did before when they look at today's Presidency, today's federal government, and the needs of modern society. That is the essence of the Treatment. It works not because it is ruthless, persistent and threatening, which is the lapidary logic of most observers, but because it is perceived by its "victims" as the opposite— as being conversational, sensible, congenial, just plain common sense . . .
>
> The Johnson Treatment is nothing more or less than his practice of taking business and other opponents, or potential opponents, into his private and genuine confidence, to talk comfortably about the problems of our people, not intellectually about the issues of our times.

JOURNALESE At the BACK-GROUNDERS held by AUTHORITATIVE SOURCES, which can be MEDIA EVENTS in themselves, members of the FOURTH ESTATE—evoking the public's RIGHT TO KNOW—refuse to settle for NO COMMENT or OFF THE RECORD. Instead, reporters protected by a LID and on a NOT FOR ATTRIBUTION basis probe the SOURCES for material for their TICK-TOCKS and KEEPERS, sometimes seeking to enliven MEGOS with the technique of RULE OUT.

Meanwhile, some PUNDITS—anxious for LEAKS but suspicious of PLANTS and scornful of HANDOUTS —reportedly write such infuriating DOPE STORIES, THINK PIECES, and THUMBSUCKERS that they wind up on the ZOO PLANE.

All of the above have separate entries herein, explicating the hype of the highest authority.

JUICE   political power.

Among the many slang meanings of "juice" (liquor, gasoline, hot money) is "electrical current," which is the metaphoric base of this 1970s political term. To be able to apply "juice" is to be able to flip the switch that generates great political power.

Reporter Nicholas Horrock wrote in the *New York Times* of August 7, 1977, of a plan proposed by the Director of Central Intelligence, Admiral Stansfield Turner, to take over "line authority" of intelligence agencies currently under the Defense Department: "But reportedly, Vice President Mondale . . . opposed the plan on the ground that it would have placed too much of what in Washington is called 'juice' at the admiral's fingertips."

When a surprise roll-call vote overturned an expected voice-vote approval of cargo-preference legislation on October 19, 1977, the *Washington Post* reported the bitter comment of an aide to House Merchant Marine Chairman John Murphy: "We got ju-iced."

The word appears to be squeezing out CLOUT.

JUNKET, *see* **NONPOLITICAL TRIP; FACT-FINDING TRIP.**

JUNKETEERING GUMSHOES derisive description of a European fact-finding tour taken by two members of Senator Joseph McCarthy's subcommittee staff.

Roy M. Cohn and G. David Schine visited U.S. Information Service libraries in Europe during 1954, and recommended certain books be removed from the shelves. Mr. Cohn informs the author it was Theodore Kaghan, at the U.S. High Commissioner's office in Germany, who coined the phrase.

"It turned out to be one of the most publicized journeys of the decade," wrote Cohn in 1968, characterizing the trip as a "colossal mistake."

"What we failed to foresee was the propaganda uses to which our critics would put the journey. David Schine and I unwittingly handed Joe McCarthy's enemies a perfect opportunity to spread the tale that a couple of young, inexperienced clowns were bustling about Europe, ordering State Department officials around, burning books, creating chaos wherever they went, and disrupting foreign relations."

"Junket" and "junketeer" carry connotations of joyride, a vacation at public (or anyone else's) expense. Congressmen called these NON-POLITICAL TRIPS, inspection tours, or FACT-FINDING TRIPS; critics call them junkets. When a business firm

or tourist board invites newsmen on a junket, it is so labeled; some newspapers insist on paying the equivalent air fare to the destination.

"Gumshoe" has a long history. Present word for the item it originally identified is "sneaker"—a canvas shoe with rubber sole and heel used most often in sports. Because the wearer can move most quietly, the gumshoe became synonymous with stealth. See PUSSYFOOTING. Martin Van Buren, who had acquired a certain reputation for wiliness, was accused of "rowing to his object with muffled oars," and "making his way to the White House in gumshoes," A "gumshoe campaign" was used at the turn of the century, especially in the Midwest, to describe a quiet campaign; currently the word is slang for "detective," used often as a verb.

Kaghan's skillful combination of the two words made it an effective derogation of McCarthy's investigators, and led to the BOOKBURNER speech by Eisenhower.

JUST AND LASTING PEACE a Lincoln coinage about the Civil War, used in regard to the settlement of every war since then.

The phrase comes from Lincoln's second inaugural address, along with "bind up the nation's wounds" and "with malice toward none": ". . . to do all which may achieve and cherish a just and lasting peace among ourselves, and with all nations."

President Eisenhower, in his statement at Geneva in 1955, departed slightly from the text to refer to "a just and durable peace," but returned to report to the American people that "we will make constantly brighter the lamp that will one day guide us to our goal—a just and lasting peace."

"Bad" peaces are usually described

as *uneasy* or *shaky;* "good" peaces are referred to as *peace with justice* or PEACE WITH HONOR. The overriding ideal, however, appears to be permanence; the Chartist petition of 1828 in England called for the universal suffrage that would bring "true and lasting peace."

JUST WAR, *see* **WAR OF NATIONAL LIBERATION.**

K

K₁C₂ a 1952 Republican campaign symbol, combining the three key charges: Korea (and the Democrats' inability to end the war), Communism (SOFT ON) and Corruption (the MESS IN WASHINGTON).

Combinations of numbers and letters resembling chemical symbols are sometimes appropriate political devices. For use in the 1964 Goldwater campaign, see **AuH₂O = 1964**. In Great Britain, "C three C 3" referred to a population classification of the mentally and physically deficient, and came to be a colloquialism for "unfit," similar to the U.S. "4-F."

KANGAROO TICKET one in which the vice-presidential candidate has greater political appeal than the presidential candidate.

Unnamed friends of Treasury Secretary John F. Connally were described by R. W. Apple in the *New York Times* of October 23, 1971, as saying he would run for Vice President in 1972 if asked by President Nixon, but one condition was "he would insist that the Nixon-Connally partnership be advertised as a 'kangaroo ticket.'"

The phrase may have originated in 1932, when some thought that John Nance Garner, the Democratic vice-presidential nominee (the hindquarters in this analogy), had more spring than Franklin D. Roosevelt (the forequarters).

The kangaroo, an herbivorous, leaping marsupial mammal native to Australia, has made other contributions to American slang. It has been used as a variant of "rump convention," because it has a muscular rear end; in an issue of the *Sonora Democrat,* published in Santa Rosa, California, in 1868, *kangaroo convention* was used in a way that indicates previous coinage: "Among those who are reflecting infamy on Virginia in the Kangaroo Convention at Richmond is a nigger named Lewis Lindley."

A *kangaroo court* is an irregular tribunal, such as a trial by prisoners in a jail, or a minor court in a frontier jurisdiction. *Kangaroo closure* occurs when a chairman or speaker selects only those amendments of a bill he is interested in as subject to debate. In underworld lingo, a kangaroo is a shoplifter with capacious pockets.

KEEPER a news story held for use at a more newsworthy time.

This journalistic term can be used to describe an innocent delay of a story until a more propitious moment, or a manipulative delay of a story until it can do the most damage.

"It is largely in the executive offices of the printed press and the networks that slanting the news and its editorial evaluation is to be found," wrote Arthur Krock, former Washington correspondent of the *New York Times,* in a 1975 book. "Important in the process are: the placement of the news by which it can be minimized or magnified; and holding back news stories called 'keepers' for publication on a date when they will have the stronger impact in forming public opinion aligned with the editorial policy of the newspaper concerned."

KENNEDY ROUND a series of negotiations begun in 1964 and concluded in 1967 between the U.S. and European nations that succeeded in reducing tariff barriers.

Economists in the Kennedy Administration felt that the General Agreement on Tariffs and Trade—GATT—could be supplemented by U.S. entry into the complex discussions on the reduction of tariffs, with the aim of "freer trade." The Kennedy Administration's Trade Expansion Act of 1962 enabled the U.S. to begin the discussions; though the President was assassinated before the negotiations began, they continued to bear his name.

"Once the Kennedy Round is over," wrote the *New York Times* in 1967, "there will be need for a Johnson Round. . . . If the negotiations produce a package containing reduction in both industrial and agricultural tariffs, the President would have little difficulty convincing Congress and the nation that executive authority for concluding new bargains is essential."

The "Kennedy Round" is a seldom understood phrase. Soon after Lyndon Johnson became President, he turned to Bromley Smith, a member of the National Security Agency staff, and asked plaintively, "Can you tell me in one clear sentence what the Kennedy Round is?"

Tariff is a word rooted in the Arabic *arifa*, to "explain" or "define."

See **WALL, POLITICAL USE OF; SNAKE IN THE TUNNEL.**

KEY AIDE, *see* **STAFFER.**

KEYNOTER one who delivers the keynote, or theme-setting, address at a convention.

In recent years the advent of television has changed the keynote speech, the last refuge of full-blown oratory, into a showcase for young political talent. Each party, anxious to put its best foot forward to the home viewers as well as to the delegates in the hall, has been choosing young, good-looking, articulate keynoters (examples: Mark Hatfield for the Republicans, Frank "Where, Oh Where" Clement for the Democrats).

Writing of the old-style keynoter, Walter Lippmann said: "A keynoter must never say that two and two make four. It is also the rule that the orator must never use one adjective if he can think of three adjectives, or make one statement except in superlative terms."

Senator Alben Barkley, keynoting the 1932 convention that nominated Franklin Roosevelt, roused the troops in this manner: "Two weeks ago in this place, the Republican party promulgated what it called a plank on the Eighteenth Amendment. It is not a plank. It is a promiscuous agglomeration of scrap-lumber!" See **PLATFORM.**

After Barkley's **STEMWINDER,** Will Rogers wrote: "This was no note . . . this was in three volumes . . . but it had to be a long speech for when you start enumerating the things the Republicans have got away with in the last twelve years you have cut yourself out a job."

KINGFISH self-proclaimed nickname of Huey Long, governor and later senator from Louisiana, assassinated in 1935.

The nickname was drawn from "Kingfish of the Lodge," a Negro character on the popular *Amos 'n Andy* radio program. Long's choice of the name showed a good instinct for self-deprecating humor that was to become fashionable a generation later. His son, Russell Long, managed to live down the nickname "Princefish," and became one of the powers of the Senate.

"Share the Wealth" and "EVERY MAN A KING" were two of Long's short slogans.

KINGMAKER one who places another in a position of power when, for reasons of personality, circumstance, or preference, he cannot or will not place himself there.

"In elective governments," wrote English royalist Roger L'Estrange in the time of Cromwell, "there is a tacit covenant that the king of their own making shall make his makers princes." In 1595 an English writer described a manipulative earl as "that great Kingmaker Warwick."

Rarely do kingmakers serve their sovereigns without expectation of reward. Theodore Roosevelt passed the mantle of the presidency to his personal choice, William Howard Taft, and was convinced he acted with the purest altruism. But when Taft wrote Roosevelt immediately after the election that "you and my brother Charlie" made him President, the estrangement began. Roosevelt wondered to a friend what "brother Charlie" had to do with it, and soon was taking umbrage at what he felt were slights by the new President.

Most famous American kingmakers were Henry Clay, who delivered the swing vote necessary to elect John Quincy Adams and received the post of Secretary of State in return, enraging the Jackson men ("Bargain and Corruption" was their slogan); Mark Hanna, Cleveland industrialist who masterminded William McKinley's election; and Harry Daugherty, who spotted Warren Harding, a handsome, small-town newspaper editor in Ohio, and helped him up the ladder through the SMOKE-FILLED ROOM (in which Daugherty was not present) to the White House. Years later Daugherty said of Harding: "I found him sunning himself like a turtle on a log, and I pushed him into the water."

However he exaggerates his own importance, the manipulative politician knows that he is dispensable after power is achieved by his candidate. Since kings tend to resent Pygmalions, the wise counselor admits only to having "helped."

Most recently, television advisers have been given Warwick's sobriquet. In a *New York Times Magazine* article on advisers Jerry Rafshoon and David Garth, opposed in the 1977 New York mayoral campaign, reporter Joseph Lelyveld described Rafshoon's national reputation as the man who helped "create" Jimmy Carter: "When the votes were in, [Carter] sent his media man a lightly ironic note that hangs now above the fancy new desk in Rafshoon's fancy new office, a block from the White House. 'I'll always be grateful,' the note says, 'that I was able to contribute in a small way to the victory of [the] Rafshoon agency.' "

Mr. Garth, who was Mayor John Lindsay's media adviser, has this quotation on his wall, from Niccolò Machiavelli: "Whoever causes another to become powerful is ruined, because he creates such power either with skill or with force; both these factors are viewed with suspicion by the one who has become powerful."

See GRAY EMINENCE; POWER BE-
HIND THE THRONE.

KISS OF DEATH unwelcome
support from an unpopular source,
occasionally engineered by the opposition.

Occasionally, unpopular organizations move in Machiavellian ways,
publicly supporting the candidate
they most want to defeat. More often,
they will quietly "pass the word" to
their members to support a candidate
they would like to see elected and
then scrupulously avoid making any
public statements in his support that
might embarrass him.

Governor Al Smith of New York
popularized the phrase in its political
context in 1926, when he called William Randolph Hearst's support of
his opponent, Ogden Mills, "the kiss
of death."

Walter Lippmann discussed the
technique in 1936: "Thus it has recently been said that Senator Borah
received 'the kiss of death' when Dr.
Townsend gave him his blessing.
Governor Landon has received the
kiss of death because Mr. Hearst is for
him. Senator Vandenberg has received the kiss of death because someone took it into his head to say that
Mr. Hoover is for him. . . . Colonel
Knox has been repeatedly kissed to
death because certain not too savory
Illinois machine politicians are for
him . . ."

The phrase is derived from the kiss
of Judas and the betrayal of Christ. It
is also described as coming from a
gangland custom called *omerta,* said
to have begun in Sicily. "In the
mobs," wrote Russell Baker, "a kiss
from the boss is tantamount to arriving at the office one morning and
finding your rug gone. When [Joseph]
Valachi got the kiss and noted that
Johnny Dio was oddly anxious to

have him step into the privacy of the
showers, Valachi concluded that he
was a 'dead duck' and defected."

KITCHEN CABINET informal
advisers to the President who, while
holding only minor offices themselves
—or none at all—exert more influence on policy than the real cabinet
because of their close personal relations with the Chief Executive.

Early in his first Administration,
Andrew Jackson for a time suspended
formal cabinet deliberations. His enemies accused him of substituting the
judgment of five of his friends—two
editors and three minor Treasury Department officials—for that of the
regular department heads, especially
in directing the attack against the
United States Bank. Despite their
presumed influence, it was no compliment to be called a member of the
kitchen cabinet. Said Davy Crockett
in 1834: "I might easily have been
mistaken for one of the Kitchen Cabinet, I looked so much like a ghost."

Presidents before and after Jackson
were similarly charged. Thomas Jefferson was accused of forming "an invisible, inscrutable, unconstitutional
cabinet" that dealt in "back-stairs influence." Jackson's frontier coterie
was the first designated as the
"kitchen" cabinet, presumably because of his and their reputation for
unpolished manners. But the kitchen-
ites had their defenders. The *Washington Globe* described them as "men
fresh from the ranks of the people,
acquainted with their wants and understanding the current of their opinions."

The term began to lose its sting
after Jackson's time and today is
rarely used. But because most Presidents do have circles of personal
friends, the idea remains. Theodore
Roosevelt had his "tennis cabinet."

Jonathan Daniels refers to Warren Harding's "poker cabinet." Herbert Hoover had an exercise-loving "medicine ball cabinet." Even governors can play the game. In writing of New York's Alfred Smith, Ed Flynn mentions the "golfing cabinet."

Harry Truman facetiously organized what he termed his "kitchen cabinet," consisting of a Secretary for Inflation, Secretary of Reaction, Secretary for Columnists and Secretary of Semantics ("to furnish me with 40- to 50-dollar words").

More than most modern Presidents, Truman was accused of relying too much on the advice of buddies (see GOVERNMENT BY CRONY). John F. Kennedy later observed: "Congressmen are always advising Presidents to get rid of presidential advisers. That's one of the most constant threads that run through American history, and Presidents ordinarily do not pay attention."

The expression is current. When it became known in 1977 that President Carter's Special Trade Representative, Robert Strauss, was becoming the most listened-to adviser in the President's cabinet, the Texan was asked when he expected to move his office into the White House. "You don't have to be inside the kitchen," he replied, "to be a member of the kitchen cabinet."

KITCHEN DEBATE   the conference between Vice President Nixon and Soviet Chairman Nikita Khrushchev in the "typical American home" at the U.S. exhibition in Moscow in 1959.

There were two debates that day. At the color television exhibit, Khrushchev unexpectedly attacked U.S. policy before the cameras, with the Vice President parrying the remarks, trying to be the good American-exhibition host. By the time the Russian leader strolled out of the studio, however, it was clear that this was only the opening round; the main bout would be elsewhere.

American press agents publicizing the "typical American home" exhibit arranged for a mixup in the flow of the crowd, trapping the leaders in their exhibit. Nixon felt that an American kitchen was a suitable forum for a discussion of standards of living and the variety of choice available to American working people. In *Six Crises*, Nixon wrote:

> The conversation began innocently enough. We discussed the relative merits of washing machines. Then I decided that this was as good a place as any to answer the charges that had been made in the Soviet press, that only "the rich" in the United States could afford such a house as this.
>
> I made the point that this was a typical house in the United States, costing $14,000, which could be paid over twenty-five or thirty years. Most U.S. veterans of World War II have bought houses like this, in the $10,000 to $15,000 range, I told him, adding that most any steelworker could buy one.

Khrushchev retorted, "We too can find steelworkers and peasants who can pay $14,000 for a flat." He accused American builders of planning obsolescence—building a house to last twenty years, while Soviets build for generations. "If an American citizen does not have dollars," he pointed out, "he has the right to buy this house or sleep on the pavement at night."

The debate was sharp, accompanied by jabbing fingers and lapel-grabbings. Nixon tried to end it with a light touch: "Isn't it better to be talking about the relative merits of our washing machines than the relative strength of our rockets?" But Khrushchev stayed angry: "Yes, that's the kind of competition we want, but your generals say we must compete in rockets. . . . We are strong, we can beat you." Nixon came back hard behind a pointed finger: "You are strong and we are strong. . . . For us to argue who is the stronger misses the point. If war comes, we both lose." ·

To the observers in the kitchen, the two leaders appeared to be using, rather than losing, their tempers. After a discussion about threats and ultimatums, Nixon broke off the debate with a light remark and Khrushchev picked up the cue, thanking the refrigerator demonstrator "for letting us use her kitchen for our argument."

The event was initially dubbed the "Sokolniki Summit" (after Sokolniki Park, in which the exhibition was held) by Harrison Salisbury of the *New York Times.* However, Salisbury was accompanied in the kitchen by an American press agent (the author) who assured the Russian guards the reporter was a "refrigerator demonstrator." The press agent, anxious to publicize the house and kitchen rather than the Russian park, told other reporters about the "kitchen conference." Salisbury adopted the phrase in briefing other reporters, and it is still recalled as the "kitchen debate" or "kitchen conference."

KLONG a reaction of dismay at a crisis caused by one's own thoughtlessness.

Senator George McGovern's 1972 campaign manager, Frank Mankiewicz, who coined the term, defined it simply as "a sudden rush of shit to the heart."

Klongs are divided into the *petit klong,* which can be the horrified realization that you have invited a dozen people to dinner for one hour ago and you are still in the office, and the *grand klong,* which comes to a prosecutor who carefully prepares a case and brings it to fruition one day after the statute of limitations has run out.

KNEE-JERK LIBERAL an unthinking intellectual; an attack phrase on automatic support of causes favored by the political left.

In current usage, a PROFESSIONAL liberal is the most uncommitted, a FLAMING LIBERAL is the most militant, and a *knee-jerk* liberal the most dull-witted. For answering charges, see HIDEBOUND; ROCK-RIBBED; MOSSBACK.

Knee-jerk is among the most descriptive and least pedantic medical words coined in the past century. Sir Ernest Gowers, a giant of linguistics who edited the second edition of Fowler's *Modern English Usage,* told of its origin in *Plain Words* (1948): "Some seventy years ago a promising young neurologist made a discovery that necessitated the addition of a new word to the English vocabulary. He insisted that this should be *knee-jerk,* and *knee-jerk* it has remained, in spite of the efforts of *patellar reflex* to dislodge it. He was my father; so perhaps I have inherited a prejudice in favor of home-made words."

KNOCK ON THE DOOR, *see* **RAP IN THE NIGHT.**

KNOW-NOTHING a derisive term for a member of a political faction, active during the 1850s, which opposed immigration and sought anti-Catholic measures; hence, a bigot or reactionary.

The Know-Nothings sprang from a

number of splinter groups that today would be called part of the radical right. They had several names, such as the Order of the Star-Spangled Banner, the American Party, and the Native American Party (leading to a nickname, "Sams," after Uncle Sam). They were widely described as Know-Nothings because they refused to tell outsiders of their activities. Explained the *Cleveland Plain Dealer* in 1854: "When one Know Nothing wishes to recognize another, he closes one eye, makes an O with his thumb and fore-finger and places his nose through it, which, interpreted, reads eye-nose-O —I know nothing."

Although the party had some successes in the 1854 elections, it soon broke up because of internal disputes. Its members joined other parties, but to be accused of having been associated with the Know-Nothings was a political liability. This led Abraham Lincoln to say in 1855: "I am not a Know-Nothing. How could I be? How can anyone who abhors the oppression of negroes, be in favor of degrading classes of white people?" (Note: "Negro" was not at that time capitalized; current usage requires it.)

Although the Know-Nothings disintegrated, their spirit lived on in such organizations as the American Protective Association and the Ku Klux Klan. The phrase is still used occasionally to describe reactionaries, SUPERPATRIOTS, and other residents of the far right, as when *Time* magazine described George Wallace as seeking to run for President in 1968 "under a neo–Know Nothing banner."

In 1969 historian Eric Goldman, who as a Johnson aide tried and failed to bring together the White House and the intellectual community, passed this judgment on the conduct of both camps at an ill-fated arts festival, in *The Tragedy of Lyndon Johnson:* "I had seen a President reacting with arrogant know-nothingism, and influential figures in the cultural world reacting with an equally arrogant know-it-allness."

See THIRD-PARTY MOVEMENT; UN-AMERICAN; YAHOO.

KOOKS, NUTS AND extremists; far-right- or left-wingers; distinguished by hate campaigns, occasional scruffiness, and unconventional political behavior.

Gook was a word used by American soldiers to describe any Asiatic, friend or foe; *kook* made its appearance in the late fifties as teen-age slang to replace *drip* or *jerk. Kooky* described far-out behavior, changing to *kicky* in 1966 regarding mini-skirted clothes with op-art and pop-art patterns, and to *kinky* in the seventies as a description of taboo sex habits.

Politically, the "nuts and kooks" came into popularity to describe some of the more extreme supporters of Senator Barry Goldwater before his nomination in 1964. Goldwater himself used the word, according to publisher John S. Knight in a post-convention interview: "He [Goldwater] remarked with a wry smile that some of the 'kooks' supporting him are convinced that the concept of metropolitan government is the handiwork of the Communist Party."

The Goldwater managers did what they could to discourage demonstrations of the "kooks," since they were a source of embarrassment easily exploited by the Democrats. Reported Theodore White at the 1964 convention:

> The floor itself was comparatively quiet, Goldwater discipline holding firm; and here one had the full contrast that plagued all reporters

throughout the year—the contrast between the Goldwater movement and the Goldwater organization. There is not, and was not, anywhere in the entire high command, in the brains trust or in the organizational structure of the Goldwater campaign, anyone who remotely qualified for the title "kook." Nor was there evident any "kook" on the floor. But the "kooks" dominated the galleries, hating and screaming and reveling in their own frenzy.

Governor Nelson Rockefeller, subjected to the fury of the "kooks" in the galleries, had his finest political moment as he exchanged barbed comments with them.

In 1965 the word "kook" was applied less to right-wingers and more to members of the New Left, especially those who burned draft cards and participated in antiwar demonstrations. "The Movement attracts some of the best young people in the country," wrote Jacobs and Landau in *The New Radicals,* "contrary to the vulgar popular notion that those who are involved are only 'beats,' 'kooks,' and 'potheads.' "

According to William Manchester (who presumably heard it from either Jacqueline Kennedy or Kenneth O'-Donnell), President Kennedy, on his way to Dallas in 1963, looked at a violently anti-Kennedy advertisement in the *Dallas News,* and commented, "We're heading into nut country today."

A different meaning of "nut" is found in campaign financing: "the nut" is the basic amount needed to get a campaign started. In New York it specifically denotes the two years' salary which candidates for judgeships are expected to contribute before getting the nomination.

One cannot use the word "nut" with impunity. In 1977, when the author described some of the threatening mail that had been in the private files of J. Edgar Hoover as having come from "nuts and kooks," a man who called himself a member of the "Mental Patients Liberation Front" wrote the *New York Times* in protest: "This is offensive . . . he is lumping together all people who act differently, in ignorance of the issues . . . as one of those kooks, who knows a great number of other kooks, I have been in an organization struggling for our liberty, a liberty which has been denied by 300 years of psychiatric abuse."

As can be seen, even admitted nuts and kooks defend themselves from linguistic slurs. Thus, to be quite fair, in current usage a "nut" or "kook" is considered by the speaker to be crazy—hence the synonym "crazies"—but this ought not to be taken for a lack of intelligence. A punch line of an old joke, wherein an asylum inmate helps a confused visitor, is illustrative: "I may be crazy, but I'm not stupid."

KOREAGATE, *see* **GATE CONSTRUCTION.**

KREMLINOLOGIST   a Western observer who interprets the intricate workings of Soviet government.

Former Syracuse University professor Harry Schwartz, now a *New York Times* expert on Soviet affairs, wrote in 1967: "The recent shift in the leadership of the Soviet secret police, perhaps the most sensitive single post in the Moscow bureaucracy, has given Kremlinologists around the world a shot in the arm. From Washington to Peking the effort to analyze the meaning of the change and its impact on the future of Soviet leadership is now in high gear."

Specialists in Russian affairs study the play of news in *Pravda* and *Izvestia,* examine photographs of Red

Leaders on Lenin's Tomb reviewing troops on May Day to see who stands closest to the top man, and sift reports of travelers to the Soviet Union. According to *Time* magazine, "in an office of the U.S. embassy in Bonn, a rotund Sovietologist digests a stack of reports that may originate from any one of a thousand sources—a barber in East Berlin, a whorehouse madam in Vienna . . ."

An -ologist is a "student of"; Kremlinologists are expected to keep up with the latest papers issued on their specialty. A variant of the expression is Sovietologist, and the counterpart term for Chinese Communists is "Pekingologist." See CHINA WATCHERS. In a kind of back-formation, Soviet analyst of U.S. affairs Georgi Arbatov was described in 1978 as an "Americanologist."

Soviet leaders treat the interpretations of foreign pundits with much the same disdain as U.S. officials look askance at predictions by specialists on Washington matters. Said Khrushchev in 1955 of the press interpretation of Soviet attitudes: "They pay little attention to what we say and prefer to read tea leaves."

KU KLUX KLAN, *see* **INVISIBLE GOVERNMENT.**

LABELS oversimplified identification of ideological position; widely used and universally deplored by politicians unwilling to be pigeonholed.

FDR positioned himself "a little left of center" (see LEFT WING, RIGHT WING; LIBERAL) but once told a press conference about appointees: "If we have the right kind of people, the party label does not mean so much."

Party labels are readily accepted by political figures in those areas where that party's registration dominates, but it has become popular in recent years to denounce ideological labels. In his 1960 State of the Union message, Dwight Eisenhower said: "We live, moreover, in a storm of semantic disorder in which old labels no longer faithfully describe. Police states are called 'people's democracies.' Armed conquest of free people is called 'liberation.' Such slippery slogans make difficult the problem of communicating true faiths, facts and beliefs . . ."

Six years earlier, however, President Eisenhower had tried to come to grips with ideological labels in a well-known statement: "When it comes down to dealing with the relationships between the human in this country and his government, the people in this administration believe in being what I think we would normally call liberal, and when we deal with the economic affairs of this country, we believe in being conserva-

tive." (See Adlai Stevenson's riposte in DYNAMIC CONSERVATISM.)

Judging by his popularity, Eisenhower was able to solve a dilemma that had long been plaguing Republicans. More Americans considered themselves "liberal" than "conservative," and the Republicans are more closely identified with conservatism, often placing them in an electoral bind. Thomas E. Dewey was frank to admit it: "One of the standard weapons of party conflict both between conventions and during campaigns is the effort to pin labels on individuals or movements, attractive or sinister, depending upon the point of view. On the whole, the Democratic party in recent years has been the more successful in this use of semantics."

Lyndon Johnson adopted a few labels and rejected labeling in a 1958 statement of his political philosophy:

I am a free man, an American, a United States Senator, and a Democrat, in that order.

I am also a liberal, a conservative, a Texan, a taxpayer, a rancher, a businessman, a consumer, a parent, a voter, and not as young as I used to be nor as old as I expect to be—and I am all these things in no fixed order.

I am unaware of any descriptive word in the second paragraph which qualifies, modifies, amends, or is related by hyphenation to the terms listed in the first paragraph. In consequence, I am not able—nor even the least interested in trying—to define my political philosophy by the choice of a one-word or two-word label.

The reasons for political squirming when it comes to ideological labeling are these: (1) A label excludes more voters than it includes, and no politician wants to say "I am not one of you" to a large portion of the electorate. (2) Although in one area one label may predominate, politicians are ambitious; acceptance of a label may preclude advancement. See PRESIDENT OF ALL THE PEOPLE. (3) A label is simplistic, and thoughtful people reject its rigidity.

LADIES IN TENNIS SHOES, *see* **LITTLE OLD LADIES IN TENNIS SHOES.**

LAME DUCK an officeholder whose power is diminished because he is soon to leave office, as a result of defeat or statutory limitation. See EUNUCH RULE.

During the 1920s this venerable phrase was modernized and widely publicized by the campaign for the "lame-duck amendment" which in 1933 was finally ratified as the Twentieth Amendment to the Constitution. Previously the incoming President was forced to wait until March to assume office while the old Congress—some of whose members had been retired at the last election—met in December and held nominal legislative powers until March.

The new system brings November's winners into office in January, thus halving the difficult lame-duck period for the outgoing Administration and, in the absence of an emergency, eliminating the lame-duck session of Congress. Franklin D. Roosevelt's New Deal was the first beneficiary of the change, but not until after the historic HUNDRED DAYS had to be deferred by the last application of the old schedule. Said Rexford Tugwell: "The old stretch of four months, devised for a country without rapid transportation, was a dangerous hiatus in the [Depression] circumstances of 1932–33."

"Lame duck" was originally an eighteenth-century import from Britain meaning a bankrupt businessman; by the 1830s the phrase was used to label politically bankrupt politicians. In 1910 *The Nation* described Election Day casualties hoping for better days as "lame ducks in the sense that they have been winged, but hope to preen their plumage again." Today it is often used snidely, as when a mayor, governor, or President makes "lame-duck appointments" by rewarding friends with judicial posts during his last days in office.

This particular fowl has an honored position in American slang. In addition to lame duck, there is a "sitting duck" (vulnerable), "queer duck" (odd), "dead duck" (finished), and "ducky" (great, unless used scornfully). See Walter Reuther's use of "If it quacks like a duck" in PROVERBS, POLITICAL.

LANDSLIDE a resounding victory; one in which the opposition is "buried." ("Snowed under" is better suited for an AVALANCHE.)

In its natural-disaster sense, the word made its appearance about 1838, and headline writers began applying it politically a few years later. (For usage differentiation from "tidal wave," "prairie fire," etc., see DISASTER METAPHORS.)

Alfred M. Landon, "the Coolidge of the West," sported an optimistic slogan in 1936: "Land Landon with a Landslide!" A landslide it was— Roosevelt carried 46 states with 523 electoral votes, Landon 2 states with 8.

The electoral college system makes landslides look more severe than they are. Landon managed to get 16 million votes to Roosevelt's 27 million—37 percent of the popular vote looks a little better than 1.5 percent of the electoral vote.

When Lyndon Johnson squeaked through a senatorial election in Texas —a post–Election Day correction gave him a majority of 87 votes out of almost a million cast—he was dubbed "Landslide Lyndon." The phrase was used again, minus the sarcasm, in 1964—Johnson carried 61 percent of the popular vote. This was not quite as high as Roosevelt's 63 percent in 1936 or Harding's 64 percent in 1920, but it was enough to qualify as a genuine landslide. Before those, the great landslides were Andrew Jackson in 1828 and 1832; U. S. Grant in 1872; Theodore Roosevelt in 1904.

Senator Henry Jackson made a unique use of the word after his New York State Democratic primary victory in April 1976. Against a sizable field, including Jimmy Carter, Senator Jackson won a plurality but fell short of his hoped-for 50 percent of the total vote. Reminded that he had predicted a landslide, he replied, "We got a landslide, but we missed a majority."

After the resounding election defeat of George McGovern in 1972, Senator Thomas Eagleton—who was forced to quit the Democratic ticket when it was revealed he had a history of mental illness—dismissed the episode involving him as merely "one rock in a landslide." Five years later Senator McGovern wrote: "Perhaps that is true, but landslides begin with a single rock."

LAND WAR IN ASIA, *see* **WRONG WAR; LET ASIANS FIGHT ASIANS.**

LAST HURRAH   exit of a politician, especially one who has had a boisterous career; more generally, the final, losing campaign.

The phrase was coined by Edwin O'Connor, who used it as the title for his 1956 novel, *The Last Hurrah,* loosely based on the life of Boston Mayor James Curley, showing the calculations and compromises—as well as the rapport with the people—of an Irish politician in Massachusetts in the first third of the twentieth century.

The title was based on the "hurrah boys," name of the Andrew Jackson enthusiasts in 1828 and 1832, which then became the phrase for any noisy supporter in a campaign filled with HOOPLA. "When General Jackson was first brought before the public," wrote the *Ohio State Journal* in 1828, "his admirers . . . earned for the pains, the appropriate name of 'hurra boys.' " George William Curtis, editor of *Harper's Magazine,* told this story in a collection of speeches published in 1894:

> An anti-Jackson partisan fell into the water, and, when nearly drowned, was seized by the hand and drawn to the surface, while his excited rescuer, delighted to save him, expressed his joy in the familiar phrase, "Hurrah for Jackson!" "What d'you say?" asked the drowning man thickly, but not so far gone that he could not hear the obnoxious name . . . "Hurrah for Jackson!" replied the other. "No, I'll be darned if I'll be saved by a hurrah-for-Jackson man" said the first, shaking off his hand and sinking back into the water.

The word "hurrah" is a seventeenth-century derivation from "huzza," an imitative sound expressing joy and enthusiasm.

In current use the phrase—while usually connoting farewell—can refer to a final win as well. The *National Observer*, after the 1966 New York gubernatorial election, titled an article "The Almost Perfect Political Campaign," with the subtitle "Nelson Rockefeller's Last Hurrah." It was not. And columnists Evans and Novak wrote in the spring of 1977: "Although even staunch Reaganites believe he is too old for anything other than a KINGMAKER's role in 1980, he has by no means ruled out a last hurrah."

LATE UNPLEASANTNESS, *see* **EUPHEMISMS, POLITICAL.**

LAUNDERED MONEY funds passed through a foreign account to conceal illegitimate origins.

The corrupt connotation to "launder" was popularized in the 1973 Watergate hearings, as $200,000 in contributions was sent to Mexico and later used to finance illegal Nixon campaign operations of dubious merit.

The word had previously been used in this sense to describe the way "hot money"—that is, gambling profits or undeclared funds from foreign sources—was legitimized before re-entering the country. Metaphorically, the money laundry was used to "cool" rather than "clean" the money, as in this citation supplied the author by lexicographer Peter Tamony in the *San Francisco Call-Bulletin* of June 3, 1935: "There is not a hot money passer in America who will 'wash' this money exchanging it for 'cool' currency—unless it is offered him at such a tremendous discount that he can afford to hold it for years, if necessary, before attempting to pass it."

Mr. Tamony speculates: "As the mob/syndicate took over in Cuba in the decades preceding Fidel Castro, circa 1959, it is probable the *washing/ laundering* was done there until Mexico became handy again fifteen years ago."

The locution was used in 1977 to describe the contributions of Korean lobbyist Tongsun Park, who was said to use various cultural foundations as means of "laundering" funds for passage to U.S. congressmen.

LAUNDRY TICKET jocular symbol of the popularity of an individual candidate who does not need organization support to win.

Franklin Roosevelt, running for President in 1932, wanted the strongest possible Democratic candidate to succeed him as governor of New York, helping him to carry the state. Former Governor and presidential nominee Al Smith, although by now a bitter enemy of FDR, united with him in supporting Herbert Lehman, then Lieutenant Governor, but Tammany leader John Curry opposed Lehman.

At the state convention, just an hour before the balloting, both Smith and Roosevelt threatened to denounce Curry on the floor if Lehman was not nominated. What's more, added Smith, he personally would run for mayor and "take the town away" from Curry and Tammany.

"On what ticket?" Curry sneered, with some logic.

"Hell," replied Smith, supremely confident of his power with New York voters, "on a Chinese-laundry ticket."

A related phrase, "laundry list," has a different meaning: a long, soporific list of items in a speech, or a series of patronage requests by a political supporter after a successful campaign.

LAW AND ORDER   stress on repression of violence; regarded by strong civil rights supporters since 1964 as the "code words" for repression of Negro rights.

Some candidates, while not going so far as to oppose integration and civil rights legislation, sought to appeal to the anti-Negro BACKLASH by stressing law and order and urging control of "crime in the streets." Civil rights advocates, who could not argue against law and order, instead concentrated their fire on the CODE WORD concept, charging this was part of Senator Goldwater's 1964 SOUTHERN STRATEGY aimed at winning anti-integration votes in the South without blatantly appealing to racist feelings.

An editorial in *The Insurgent,* a publication of the W. E. B. DuBois Clubs (a far-left group) said: ". . . the law is built to defend the white power structure. 'Order' means keeping people 'in their place.' "

On the other hand, many "moderates," who in no way intended to attack what they considered legitimate Negro aspirations, did feel strongly about violence in the streets, which reached a peak during riots in Detroit and Newark in the LONG HOT SUMMER of 1967. But they found it difficult to stress "law and order" without being attacked in turn for using the same phraseology as the subtle racists.

With the mood of the nation turning against violent demonstrations and riots in the mid-sixties, the "code word" counterattack generally failed, and those espousing "law and order" —for whatever motives, sincere or not—found the issue effective.

The ability to cope with a breakdown in "law and order" was the quality that projected Calvin Coolidge on the scene of U.S. politics. Massachusetts Governor Calvin Coolidge met the crisis of the Boston police strike of 1919 with the statement "There is no right to strike against the public safety by anybody, anywhere, anytime." He was nominated in 1920 for Vice President on the Harding ticket after a convention demonstration with "Law and Order" banners waving.

Wrote Donald R. McCoy, his biographer, in 1966:

Thus Coolidge, who was no rabble-rouser, had become the uncrowned king of the rabble-rousers and the Saint George of the innocently frightened. He who had given little thought to Marxism had become the champion of the anti-Marxists. He who had often been labor's friend had become a hero of antilabor forces. He who had not wanted to become involved had become deeply involved. He who had been the last in acting had become the first in receiving credit.

The phrase reaches far back into American political history. In the first half of the nineteenth century, Rhode Island was governed under a Colonial charter with a property qualification so high that less than one third of its citizens could vote. A Suffrage Party was formed by Thomas Dorr, which led to "Dorr's Rebellion" in 1842. The political group opposing suffrage called itself the "Law and Order Party."

See CRIME IN THE STREETS.

LEADER, *see* **BOSS, BOSSISM; SACHEM; SATRAP; BIGWIG; MUCKEY-MUCKS; MOVERS AND SHAKERS.**

LEAK disclosure of information, usually concerning government or political activity, through unofficial channels or what some consider improper means.

Lexicographers in the U.S. have had their eye on this term for a long time. In 1832 Noah Webster defined "to leak out" as "to escape privately from confinement or secrecy; as a fact or report," and G. W. Matsell in his 1859 *Vocabulum* defined "to leak" as "to impart a secret."

One of the earliest sensational leaks on record occurred in 1844, when Senator Benjamin Tappan of Ohio gave a copy of the still-secret treaty of annexation with Texas to the *New York Evening Post.* The *Post* printed it, an uproar ensued, Tappan admitted his part in it and was censured.

The commonest leaks are those sprung by middle-echelon officials in order to get publicity for themselves or their agencies: an official tips off one reporter or a small group in advance of a general announcement in the hope that the exclusivity will get the story better coverage than it would otherwise enjoy.

Franklin Roosevelt complained bitterly about a number of leaks, including one about Henry Morgenthau's controversial plan (later shelved) to strip Germany of all industry after World War II. In 1955 Dwight Eisenhower said: "I have been plagued by inexplicable, undiscovered leaks in this government." President Johnson was accused of corking leaks by changing his plans once information had come out prematurely.

The *courtesy leak* is used when an official owes a reporter a favor—or would like the reporter to owe him a favor—and uses information as currency. A favorite type of story for use in this transaction is advance word about presidential appointments. Thus a handful of reporters got a scoop on Earl Warren's appointment as Chief Justice. However, while a courtesy leak makes the scoopers happy, the scooped segment of the press thinks morosely of revenge.

There are also *authorized leaks*—disclosures given with euphemistic attribution such as "informed sources" and "government officials." In this case the government wishes to see something in print but would rather not be on the record as formally committed to a particular policy or view. See TRIAL BALLOON; NOT FOR ATTRIBUTION. Some argue that the press should not allow itself to be used in this way. Others justify the practice by pointing out that news BACKGROUNDERS—the sessions at which such information is conveyed —are better than news blackouts.

Authorized leaks have been known to backfire. In one of his first informal meetings with the press, Defense Secretary Robert McNamara disclosed that there really was no MISSILE GAP. This flatly contradicted an important point made during the Kennedy campaign, much to the embarrassment of the new Kennedy Administration.

The most massive leak in U.S. history was "the Pentagon Papers," given by former national security consultant Daniel Ellsberg to the *New York Times*, which caused the Nixon Administration to go to court seeking to enjoin publication. The suppression effort failed.

Director of Central Intelligence Stansfield Turner wrote in the *Washington Post* in 1977 that no nation should countenance the free-wheeling disclosure of its military secrets, and that our society should "trust the judgment of its public servants regarding what should and should not be withheld from the public."

Daniel Schorr, a journalist who had handled more than his share of leaks, wrote in reply: "The awareness that 'secrets' may leak tends to have a healthful, ombudsman effect in government, making covert operators ask themselves how their plans would look if they were exposed. In balance, this nation has probably been harmed much less by undue exposure than by undue secrecy."

Richard Neustadt, professor of government at Harvard, agreed: "The class of confidential communication commonly called 'leaks' play, in my opinion, a vital role in the functioning of our democracy. A leak is, in essence, an appeal to public opinion. Leaks generally do not occur in dictatorships."

An overreaction to leaks led to Richard Nixon's downfall. In May of 1969 Nixon, Attorney General John Mitchell and National Security Adviser Henry Kissinger determined to crack down on "national security leaks," using a series of wiretaps by the FBI; when J. Edgar Hoover was reluctant to pursue this technique, a Kissinger aide—David Young—was assigned to a leak-plugging unit that he later dubbed the PLUMBERS.

See PLANT; BACKGROUNDER; WHISTLEBLOWER.

LEBENSRAUM literally, "living space"; an excuse for territorial expansion.

The word was coined by Swedish scientist Rudolf Kjellén and appropriated by a German geographer, Dr. Karl Haushofer, to describe what he considered to be Germany's needs and, therefore, rights.

An English phrase, "land-hunger," had been used earlier to describe the state of a nation whose population is expanded too rapidly for its territory to support.

The Nazis used *Lebensraum* to mean that Germany was crowded, that the fertile portions of Russia were occupied by inferior beings, thus Germany, as the home of the "master race," had the right to take the geographical areas she wanted by war.

Haushofer's views on geography as related to politics, which he called *Weltpolitik* and "geopolitics," were considered gospel by the Nazis, whom he supported enthusiastically.

In 1942, during a visit to Washington by Winston Churchill, Franklin Roosevelt made a speech that greatly impressed the British Prime Minister, especially the line "The world is too small to provide adequate 'living room' for both Hitler and God." "Whoever wrote that sentence," Churchill told FDR, "I'd like to take with me to England." The President did not reply; dramatist Robert E. Sherwood was too valuable to him.

After World War II a German novelist told reporter John Gunther what impressed him most about the U.S.: "Space. *Lebensraum.* The impression that no crisis can be really severe or permanent in this country because people are free to move around so much."

The word has been used by ENVIRONMENTALISTS to project some of the troubles of the world of the future. In the June 1955 *Fortune* magazine, John von Neumann wrote:

In the first half of this century the accelerating industrial revolution encountered an absolute limitation —not on technological progress as such, but on an essential safety factor. This safety factor . . . was essentially a matter of geographical and political *Lebensraum:* an ever broader geographical scope for technological activities, combined with an ever broader political integration of the world. Within this expanding framework it was possible to accommodate the major tensions created by technological progress.

Now this safety mechanism is being sharply inhibited; literally and figuratively, we are running out of room. At long last, we begin to feel the effects of the finite, actual size of the earth in a critical way.

See PLACE IN THE SUN.

LEFT WING, RIGHT WING the ideological spectrum; reading from left to right, radical, liberal, centrist or moderate, conservative, reactionary.

The presiding officers of the French National Assembly seated the radicals at the *côté gauche* (left side), the moderates in the center directly in front, and the conservative nobles on the right. Like so many political terms, the "wings" derived from military use, with the use of "left wing" of an army traceable to 1707.

The left-wing–right-wing spectrum is not a straight bar; the relationships are better explained by considering it as a kind of horseshoe. An extreme leftist, or radical, or Communist, has more in common with an extreme reactionary, or fascist, than either has with the moderate.

Franklin Roosevelt established his position in a 1944 press conference when reporter May Craig asked him if he was going "left or right politically." He replied, "I am going down the whole line a little left of center." See LABELS. Another reporter asked about recent appointments of conservatives. He said, "I have got a lot of people in the Administration—oh, I know some of them are extreme right and extreme left, and everything else. . . . Just think, the crowd here in this room—my gracious, you will find every opinion between left and extreme right."

Sociologist C. Wright Mills, who coined NEW LEFT, defined the "right" as "celebrating society as it is: a going concern," and "to be left" as meaning to "connect up with cultural and political criticism."

One on the left is called: RED, pink, PINKO (PARLOR PINK is radical in theory only), commie, bomb-thrower, COMSYMP, FELLOW TRAVELER, ultraleft.

One on the right is called RADICAL RIGHT, DIEHARD, MOSSBACK, Bourbon, bitterender, ultrarightist, OLD FOGY, standpatter (see STAND PAT), and LITTLE OLD LADIES IN TENNIS SHOES.

CENTRISTS and MODERATES are: ON THE FENCE, STRADDLERS, MIDDLE OF THE ROADERS, OPPORTUNISTS, and ALL THINGS TO ALL MEN, though they claim to be the MAINSTREAM.

Winging nuance: those on the left resent being called "left-wingers" more than those on the right resent being called "right-wingers."

LEGISLATIVE VETO, *see* ONE-HOUSE VETO.

LET ASIANS FIGHT ASIANS a recurrent proposal to replace American troops with allied Asian troops in warfare in the Far East.

In the 1952 presidential campaign, Dwight Eisenhower held that the U.S. commitment of ground troops might be curtailed, the men replaced by South Korean troops. "If there must be a war there," he is reported to have said, "let it be Asians against Asians."

A few days before the election, as Stevenson realized the power of Eisenhower's "I shall go to Korea" promise, the Democratic candidate attacked the General's Asian suggestion:

" 'Let Asians fight Asians' is the

authentic voice of a resurgent isolationist. In 1939 the Republican Old Guard, faced with the menace of the Nazi world, was content to say 'Let Europeans fight Europeans', ignoring completely the fact that the menace of Nazism was a menace to Americans . . ."

The thought has a genuine appeal, similar to the fervent desire to avoid a "land war in Asia." In 1964, President Lyndon Johnson said: "We are not about to send American boys nine or ten thousand miles away from home to do what Asian boys should be doing for themselves."

See VIETNAMIZATION.

L'ÉTAT, C'EST MOI, see I AM THE LAW.

LET 'EM EAT CAKE   the height of political patronization; an attack phrase against economic suggestions that do not directly benefit "the little man."

This is supposed to be one of the examples of hauteur by Marie Antoinette that helped bring about the French Revolution. She never said it.

The reference appears in the sixth book of Jean-Jacques Rousseau's *Confessions,* written about 1767, two or three years before Marie Antoinette's arrival in France: "At length I recollected the thoughtless saying of a great princess, who, on being informed that the country people had no bread, replied, 'Let them eat cake.' "

The remark (in French, *"qu'ils mangent de la brioche"*) is still used to signify unconcern with the needs of the people. When Vice President Agnew delivered a keynote address at a National Governors' Conference in 1971 that included a defense of the profit motive, it was denounced by an anonymous Democratic spokesman as "Marie Antoinette economics."

LET ME MAKE ONE THING PERFECTLY CLEAR, see POINTER PHRASES.

LET SLEEPING DOGMAS LIE, see UNLEASH CHIANG.

LET'S LOOK AT THE RECORD a rousing appeal to reason by presidential candidate Alfred E. Smith.

The New York governor began using "Let's look at the record" in his campaign against Herbert Hoover. See WHISPERING CAMPAIGN.

The phrase was used both as a defense and an attack phrase in its early days, though in recent years it has become a bromide mainly used in attacks on the opposition record. "As Al Smith used to say, 'Let's look at the record,' " has been used so often that it elicits yawns. For more aggressive attacks on past performance, see TWENTY YEARS OF TREASON.

For other Smith coinages, see BALONEY; DOVES; LAUNDRY TICKET; KISS OF DEATH; LULU; and SANTA CLAUS, NOBODY SHOOTS AT.

LET'S TALK SENSE, see DIALOGUE.

LET THE DUST SETTLE, see WATCHFUL WAITING.

"LET US CONTINUE"   Lyndon Johnson's exhortation as he stepped into the presidency after the death of John F. Kennedy.

Five days after the Kennedy assassination, President Johnson told a joint session of Congress:

On the twentieth day of January in 1961, John F. Kennedy told his countrymen that our national work would not be finished "in the first thousand days, nor in the life of this Administration, nor even perhaps in our lifetime on this planet. But," he said, "let us begin."

Today, in this moment of new resolve, I would say to all my fellow Americans, let us continue.

This is our challenge—not to hesitate, not to pause, not to turn about and linger over this evil moment, but to continue on our course . . .

The words were crafted by Kennedy speechwriter Ted Sorensen, but the President's Texas accent grated on the nerves of some of the former President's greatest admirerers—the pronunciation of "continya" was later mocked. (Kennedy and Johnson were the only two Presidents up to that point in the twentieth century to have strongly regional accents.)

But the choice of the phrase was apt, recalling the early phrase of Kennedy's and updating it, thereby gracefully acknowledging another's leadership while asserting a leadership of one's own.

Author John Dos Passos has written of the need for this kind of reaching back and establishing the sense of continuity: "In times of change and danger when there is a quicksand of fear under man's reasoning, a sense of continuity with generations gone before can stretch like a lifeline across the scary president."

By 1967 the context of solemnity in which Johnson had used the phrase was long forgotten, and columnist Russell Baker wrote:

It is curious that we let beloved old phrases expire and trundle off the Old Phrases' Burying Ground without even noticing that they have left us . . . what about "Let Us Continue!"? Gone, simply gone, and all unnoticed. Can it mean that somewhere back there, without noticing it, we stopped continuing? If so,

when? If we could pinpoint the moment when we stopped hearing "Let us continue!" we could probably tell to the second when the Vietnam war really started.

LEVELS, *see* **GOBBLEDYGOOK.**

LEVERAGE indirect pressure that can be brought to bear on politicians, particularly delegates at conventions.

The "delegate book" that each serious presidential candidate brings to an open convention includes data on each man's social and business background, as well as his political leanings. This book is for the purpose of "getting to him"—finding some Achilles heel that makes him receptive to the candidate.

Typical question before the convention, while the delegate book is leafed through, is "What kind of leverage do we have there?" In other words, is the delegate's best friend, wife, employer, most important customer, school chum, banker, country club president—anyone in a position to exert pressure—a crowbar to pry that delegate's support away from another candidate?

The process is as old as balloting. Daniel Manning, Grover Cleveland's manager in the 1884 MUGWUMP campaign, gave these instructions to William C. Hudson, who was to open the Cleveland headquarters at Chicago for the convention: "Now, I want you to devote yourself to these doubtful men. Find out the conditions surrounding them, the influences political, commercial and moral. . . . We must subject them to pressure, but first we must learn the sort of pressure that should be applied."

See **FEET TO THE FIRE.**

LIBERAL currently one who believes in more government action to meet individual needs; originally one who resisted government encroachment on individual liberties.

In the original sense the word described those of the emerging middle classes in France and Great Britain who wanted to throw off the rules the dominant aristocracy had made to cement its own control.

During the 1920s the meaning changed to describe those who believed a certain amount of governmental action was necessary to protect the people's "real" freedoms as opposed to their purely legal—and not necessarily existent—freedoms.

This philosophical about-face led former New York Governor Thomas Dewey to say, after using the original definition, "Two hundred years later, the transmutation of the word, as the alchemist would say, has become one of the wonders of our time."

In U.S. politics the word was used by George Washington to indicate a person of generosity or broad-mindedness, as he expressed distaste for those who would deprive Catholics and Jews of their rights.

The word became part of the American vocabulary in its earlier meaning during a rump convention of Republicans dissatisfied with the presidency of Ulysses S. Grant, at Cincinnati in 1872. German-born Carl Schurz, who chaired the convention, used the word often. So did the leading journalist-thinker of the rebellion, Edwin L. Godkin of *The Nation,* who began his career in England. The short-lived party born of the convention was called "The Liberal Republican" party.

In its present usage, the word acquired significance during the presidency of Franklin D. Roosevelt, who defined it this way during the campaign for his first term: ". . . say that civilization is a tree which, as it grows, continually produces rot and dead wood. The radical says: 'Cut it down.' The conservative says: 'Don't touch it.' The liberal compromises: 'Let's prune, so that we lose neither the old trunk nor the new branches.' "

Liberalism takes criticism from both right and left, leading to various terms of opprobrium. See LEFT WING, RIGHT WING; BLEEDING HEARTS. Herbert Hoover in a magazine article referred to ". . . fuzzy-minded totalitarian liberals who believe that their creeping collectivism can be adopted without destroying personal liberty and representative government."

To its opponents, liberalism and liberals seem to call out for qualifying adjectives expressing contempt. Barry Goldwater, trying to combat the popularity of President Johnson with businessmen, told a U.S. Chamber of Commerce conference, "If you think President Johnson is going to give you any better attention than you have got, you're very, very mistaken. If he's a conservative," said the senator, "I'm a screaming liberal."

Sometimes even liberals cannot avoid the temptation to assault the term. Adlai Stevenson, quoting an uncertain source, once described a liberal as "one who has both feet firmly planted in the air." And columnist Heywood Broun, who came to consider himself a radical, wrote: "A liberal is a man who leaves a room when a fight begins," a definition adopted by militant Saul Alinsky.

The word has fallen on hard times. In the 1976 presidential primaries, Representative Morris Udall told columnist David Broder: "When a word takes on connotations you don't like, it's time to change the label."

Henceforth, Udall said—though he would think of himself as a liberal—he would use the word "progressive" instead because the word "liberal" was "associated with abortion, drugs, busing and big-spending wasteful government."

Liberals are variously described as LIMOUSINE, double-domed, screaming, KNEE JERK, professional, BLEEDING HEART; also see PINKO; PARLOR PINK; NEW LEFT; COMMITTED; EGGHEAD.

LIBERATION OF CAPTIVE PEOPLES the promise of the Republican platform of 1952 and subsequently of the Eisenhower Administration that the U.S. would help the people of the countries under Communist rule gain their freedom.

The 1952 platform was meant to cast aspersions on any "secret agreements" made at Yalta by Roosevelt, Stalin, and Churchill. Russian power, combined with the vague wording of the Yalta agreement, had led to the seizure of most of Eastern and Central Europe by Communist factions, dominated by the Soviet Union.

In the Republican platform, Yalta was condemned as aiding "Communist enslavements." The plank went on: "It will be made clear, on the highest authority of the President and the Congress, that United States policy, as one of its peaceful purposes, looks happily forward to the genuine independence of those captive peoples."

General Eisenhower amplified this in an address during the campaign to the American Legion in which, after reciting the litany of Communist-dominated nations, he said: "We can never rest—and we must so inform all the world, including the Kremlin—that until the enslaved nations of the world have in the fullness of freedom

the right to choose their own path, that then, and then only, can we say that there is a possible way of living peacefully and permanently with Communism in the world."

In reply, Democratic candidate Adlai Stevenson warned of the dangers such words created. He said to a predominantly Polish audience on Labor Day of 1952: ". . . the cruel grip of Soviet tyranny upon your friends and relatives cannot be loosened by loose talk or idle threats. It cannot be loosened by awakening false hopes which might stimulate intemperate action that would only lead your brothers to the execution squads . . ."

President Eisenhower's biographer, Robert J. Donovan, and the long-time State Department troubleshooter, Robert Murphy, both insisted that the liberation referred to was to come only by peaceful means; John Foster Dulles told a Senate committee that "liberation does not mean a war of liberation."

This was not quite clear to restive elements in Communist-dominated ("enslaved") countries, many of whom were convinced that American troops would come to the aid of the Hungarian people when they staged their uprising in 1956. In the U.S., the abortive Hungarian revolt marked the beginning of the end of the "liberation of captive peoples" as a political phrase, and it soon went the way of UNLEASH CHIANG.

In a 1976 televised debate with Jimmy Carter, President Ford refused to recognize the dominance of East European nations by the Soviet Union, which was widely interpreted as a foreign-policy political gaffe.

Liberation, a noble World War II word that came to mean the acquisition of booty (as in "liberating" a wine cellar), is also frequently used in

Communist terminology. See WAR OF NATIONAL LIBERATION. In recent years it has been adopted by small terrorist groups in the U.S. (the "Symbionese Liberation Army," which kidnapped Patricia Hearst) and large groups abroad (the Palestine Liberation Organization).

LID an assurance of inactivity.

Political reporters need to know not only when news is breaking, but when news is not breaking—so they can plan their lives accordingly. This need to know when there is nothing to know has led to the invention of the pressroom "lid," the assurance to reporters that no news is scheduled for distribution, or press conference planned, until an announced time when the "lid" ends. Reporters can use this promise of suspended animation to protect themselves while they cover other stories, or sun themselves in nearby spas, secure that they will not be caught napping—unless an emergency arises, at which point all lids are off.

The word is taken from "The lid's off," a turn-of-the-century expression for no-holds-barred activity. "Commissioner of Police McAdoo," wrote the *Philadelphia Public Ledger* in 1904, ". . . has taken frequent occasions to deny that the 'lid' was off, to use the slang definition of a lax police administration."

In modern political-press parlance, a lid may be "soft" ("Probably nothing happening, but stick around") to "hard" ("I'm going to the beach, too").

For examples of other forms of "masterly inactivity", see WATCHFUL WAITING.

LIFE IS UNFAIR the apology for economic or social inequity; a gentle shrugging off of egalitarian demands.

In a press conference on March 21, 1962, President John F. Kennedy was asked about demonstrations by army reservists who—having "done their time" in the armed forces—resented being mobilized to fight in the Vietnam war. After observing that the calling up of the reservists had "strengthened the foreign policy of the United States," he extemporized in a more philosophical vein:

"There is always inequity in life. Some men are killed in a war and some men are wounded, and some men never leave the country, and some men are stationed in the Antarctic and some are stationed in San Francisco. It's very hard in military or in personal life to assure complete equality. Life is unfair . . ."

The phrase did not at first appear to fit in the ringing, high-minded Kennedy rhetoric; as years went by, it was remembered more than the more carefully crafted utterances in his speeches, and gained an added overtone of fatalism after his assassination.

President Carter, in a press conference on July 12, 1977, used the same argument (with a rough approximation of the phrase) in handling a question about the Supreme Court decision that the federal government was not obligated to provide money for abortions for women who cannot afford them. "There are many things in life that are not fair," the President replied, "that wealthy people can afford and poor people can't. But I don't believe that the federal government should take action to try to make these opportunities exactly equal, particularly when there is a moral factor involved."

The unintended evocation of John Kennedy's remark was widely noted, and reinforced journalistic usage of the phrase. *Washington Post* columnist George F. Will, writing about the Panama Canal treaty negotiated by Ambassador Sol Linowitz, observed: "Carter inherited the negotiations, and the general shape of the outcome. The fight for ratification will diminish his popularity, and defeat—a real possibility—would diminish his stature. It isn't fair, but as has been said, life is unfair."

LIFT OF A DRIVING DREAM Nixon's description of idealism.

At the Highway Hotel in Concord, New Hampshire, on February 3, 1968, Richard Nixon made the first speech of his second presidential campaign, beginning with "The finest hours in our nation's history have been triumphs of the American spirit. We now are engaged in a great test of that spirit."

The use of a Churchill phrase— "finest hours"—and the use of the Lincolnian construction "We are now engaged"—reflected the candidate's dual purposes: to rally and to heal. The centerpiece of the speech, written with the help of Ray Price, was this line: "What America needs most today is what it once had, but has lost: the lift of a driving dream."

As President, he returned to the theme and the phrase in an impromptu talk to the members of the American Revolution Bicentennial Commission, responsible for planning the observance of the nation's 200th birthday: "I would charge this Commission . . . to move forward, move forward, yes, in reaching the great material goals of which we know we are capable—that is the easiest part of the job—but recognizing that the best fed, best clothed, best housed people in the world, that the strongest nation in the world, and the richest nation in the world still will not deserve to be the hope of the world unless it has

that splendid spirit, the lift of a driving dream which meant so much to the world in 1776 and for 200 years since that time."

Correspondent Nancy Dickerson, interviewing the President with other network commentators on January 4, 1971, brought up the earliest use of the phrase and observed "many people have failed to perceive the lift of a driving dream." The President replied in part: "Before we can really get the lift of a driving dream, we have to get rid of some of the nightmares we inherited . . ."

After the Watergate revelations had driven Nixon to resignation, his successor, Gerald Ford, evoked the same image in his first speech and most memorable line: "Our long national nightmare is over."

One would think that this phrase would disappear from the political language as the Nixon presidency recedes in memory, but Ray Price's phrase may have staying power independent of memories of its speaker. "It is unclear whether Carter, the problem-solver," wrote Hedrick Smith in the *New York Times Magazine* on January 8, 1978, "understands that his greatest shortcoming so far has been his failure to rouse the nation with the lift of a driving dream . . . he has not used the White House effectively as a BULLY PULPIT."

LIGHTNING MAY STRIKE the wish of the dark-horse or long-shot candidate; the possibility of a sudden shift in fortune that may nominate a man for major office.

In the California primary before the 1964 Republican nomination, Rockefeller supporters looked in vain for help from other liberals and middle-of-the-roaders in the campaign against Barry Goldwater. "It's understandable," said Nelson Rockefeller, tongue in cheek, four days before Goldwater's narrow victory. "All of them are available for the nomination and hoping that lightning will strike. What other position could they take?" Obviously, if Rockefeller had stopped Goldwater in California, the other Republican leaders who helped him would not be the compromise choice—lightning could only strike someone acceptable to both camps.

The phrase has been in use, in its precise meaning today, for at least a century. R.W. Thornton's *American Glossary* has this definition: "The lightning is said to strike, when a person or a place gains sudden and unexpected fame, notoriety, or good fortune. Not in the dictionaries." He offers this example from the *Congressional Record* of 1879:

"Mr. Sparks: I wish to suggest to the gentleman from Iowa that in districts near his own the lightning has been striking . . .

"Mr. Price: Oh, no . . . no danger of that kind of lightning in my district."

A vivid use of the phrase was made by magazine publisher and parachutist Bernarr Macfadden in 1936. Alva Johnson reported that Macfadden was bilked of a quarter of a million dollars by a group that convinced him he had a chance for the presidency against FDR. "If lightning strikes," the eccentric publisher announced, "it will find me a willing victim."

LIGHTWEIGHT   a shallow public figure behind an impressive façade; a politician lacking either intellect, grasp of administrative detail, or guts.

"Lightweight" is an attack word, often as cruel and hard to shake as "loser," usually accompanied with "he just doesn't have it." See STRAW MAN.

A political aide useful for minor roles, but not one to be delegated major responsibility, is also tagged as a lightweight. The opposite—"heavyweight"—is rarely used in the first sense applied to public figures; more often, it refers to political aides who carry prestige and authority. "We need a heavyweight to operate on the top level."

Classic definition of a lightweight, attributed in 1960 to Brooklyn Republican leader John Crews about New York Mayor Robert Wagner: "He's light enough to do a tap dance on a charlotte russe." (Another pastry metaphor was used by newswoman Louise Lamprey in 1897, in a remark later attributed to Theodore Roosevelt: "President McKinley has no more backbone than a chocolate eclair.")

The word, revived recently and now in frequent political use, can be traced back to 1809 and an allusion to "lightweight princes." In 1882 New York Congressman S. S. Cox said on the House floor, "I never took my friend from New Jersey [George Robeson] to be a lightweight in any regard."

In boxing, a lightweight can be an excellent fighter, even a champion; not so in politics. In the political arena, weight categories do not exist to protect the light from the heavy, and the fastest lightweight is easily taken by the slowest heavyweight.

Other boxing terms used in politics include ARENA; HAT IN THE RING; "throw in the towel," "take off the gloves," "hit below the belt," "on the ropes." Wrestling terms include "eye-gouging" and "no holds barred." See HEFT, POLITICAL.

LIMITED WAR   a military conflict in which the goal is defined as something short of total victory and in which one or both combatants may use less than full military resources.

"Limited war" a variant of TOTAL WAR, became a common phrase—and a politically contentious one—during the Korean conflict. The Truman Administration called its intervention to save South Korea a POLICE ACTION rather than actual war and described its strategy as "limited warfare." The diplomatic rationale for circumlocution was clear: Washington wanted to keep Peking and Moscow out of the fighting and did not want to intensify the battle either rhetorically or militarily. General Douglas MacArthur could not live with the restrictions and Truman finally dismissed him as commander. See NO SUBSTITUTE FOR VICTORY; NO-WIN POLICY.

The Truman-MacArthur showdown and the frustrations of fighting an indecisive war under unusual conditions in a remote land set the issue. The goal of total victory and unconditional surrender in World War II was so fresh in the national consciousness that many forgot, as historian Samuel Eliot Morison pointed out, that "limited war is also in the American tradition." We had fought such wars with Great Britain, Spain, and Mexico. Nonetheless, when the Eisenhower Administration took office, Defense Secretary Charles Wilson said: "We can't afford to fight limited wars. We can only afford to fight a big war, and if there is one, that is the kind it will be."

As a result of this policy decision, the American military establishment during the 1950s emphasized strategic nuclear weapons at what critics said was the expense of conventional forces. But the change was temporary. Secretary of State John Foster Dulles acknowledged that the country had to be flexible enough in its arsenal to inflict less than MASSIVE RETALIATION.

While still a senator, John Kennedy insisted that "limited brushfire war," rather than all-out nuclear conflict, was the more likely threat. As President, Kennedy favored "balanced forces" and "flexible response" and had the military reorganized along these lines.

See PEACE WITHOUT VICTORY; MEASURED RESPONSE.

LIMITS TO GROWTH, *see* ENVIRONMENTALIST.

LIMOUSINE LIBERAL one who takes up hunger as a cause but never felt a pang; who will talk at length about the public school system but sends his children to private schools.

Mario Procaccino used this scornful phrase in New York City's mayoral campaign of 1969, casting aspersions of hypocrisy at John Lindsay's followers on the Upper East Side of Manhattan. "Proc" was disdained by opponents who passed along bloopers like "I want every kid in New York to have the same chance I did—to come up the hard way."

But "limousine liberal" was a phrase that stung, alliteratively caricaturing people of relative wealth who felt that the downtrodden should have more at the expense of the lower middle class. Race was of course a factor here—some aristocratic liberals who spoke out for open housing had no fear of blacks moving into the expensive apartment next to them.

Of course, there has never been a need for a man to be poor to be liberal, and some aristocrats—FDR, for example—did more for the indigent "one-third of a nation" than did any member of that third. Thus, in its broadest sense, the application was unfair. In a narrower sense, however, it had substance as brought out by Tom Wolfe in *New York* magazine, who dissected "radical chic"—the sponsorship of groups like the Black Panthers by some of New York's cultural elite.

Both terms had a sobering effect on many old-line liberals who had to take into consideration the needs and votes of HARDHATS, homeowners and people not poor enough for welfare.

Scorn at hypocrisy is offered in international affairs as well. Egyptian President Anwar el-Sadat, rejecting radical Arab criticism after his 1977 visit to Israel, said, "Those militants in nightclubs are going about while the real militants are there in jail in Israel." The "nightclub militant" is a metaphoric cousin of the "limousine liberal."

See PARLOR PINK.

LINKAGE a global negotiating strategy holding that progress on one front is necessary to, or helpful to, progress on other fronts.

The word was used by Dr. Henry Kissinger, President Nixon's national security adviser, in a background briefing on February 6, 1969, explaining what the President had said in a press conference about not wanting to dissociate arms control from political issues. "To take the question of linkage between the political and the strategic environment," said Kissinger, " . . . the President would like to deal with the problem of peace on the entire front in which peace is challenged and not only on the military one."

Linkage was intended to describe a tie between nuclear-arms talks and discussions of political tensions; in the public mind, however, it has come to mean a "package deal" in geographic terms—that is, the U.S.

would agree to reduce tensions in an area where the Soviets wanted such reduction, in return for détente in another part of the world where superpower interests were in conflict.

Ironically, the word was used by U.S. diplomats in the mid-sixties to object to the Soviets' connection of U.S. bombing of North Vietnam to détente elsewhere. The popularizer of the term—originally, in the sense of tying foreign affairs to domestic concerns—was James Rosenau, then professor of international relations at Rutgers, who titled a 1968 collection of essays *Linkage Politics*.

The word surfaced again in the Carter Administration, as National Security Adviser Zbigniew Brzezinski sought to establish a linkage between Soviet desire for arms control with Soviet support of Cuban troops in Africa.

LION AND THE FOX combination of strength and craftiness.

Niccolò Machiavelli wrote in *The Prince:*

> A prince must imitate the fox and the lion, for the lion cannot protect himself from traps, and the fox cannot defend himself from wolves. . . . a prudent ruler ought not to keep faith when by so doing it would be against his interest.

This view of morality is the essence of "Machiavellianism." James MacGregor Burns, in *Roosevelt: The Lion and the Fox,* wrote: "To the idealists who cautioned him he responded again and again that gaining power—winning elections—was the first, indispensable task. He would use the tricks of the fox to serve the purposes of the lion."

The phrase crops up fairly frequently in political columns. On the death of former German Chancellor Konrad Adenauer in 1967, columnist

Max Lerner wrote: "Konrad Adenauer had considerable of the lion in him, and even more of the fox —a combination, as Machiavelli was one of the first to see, that gives a man a galloping advantage in politics."

LIQUIDITY CRISIS, *see* ECO-NOMIC JARGON.

LITTLE GROUP OF WILFUL MEN a small, powerful clique disposed (in its opponent's view) to put its own interests above the public's.

During the post–World War I fight over U.S. entry into the League of Nations, Woodrow Wilson characterized the opposition—centered in the Republican Senate leadership—as stubborn obstructionists. Later writers attributed "little group of wilful men" to Wilson as his theme during the League dispute. In fact, Wilson coined it just before rather than after the war in a speech attacking roughly the same group of Senate isolationists after their successful filibuster killing his bill to allow the arming of merchant vessels. "A little group of wilful men," Wilson said on March 4, 1917, "representing no opinion but their own, has rendered the great government of the United States helpless and contemptible." Perhaps because the same issues and personalities dominated the 1919–20 League campaign, the phrase has been applied indiscriminately.

Wilson's "little group" is often misquoted as a "little band," as that phrase has often been applied to valiant fighters against superior forces. It dates from a group of three hundred Thebans who fought in the fourth century B.C., were annihilated at Chaeronea, and became known to history as "the Sacred Band."

Despite the rather specialized Wilsonian use of "little group," later Presidents borrowed the idea in fights of their own. It became a favorite political gambit to portray oneself as the public's defender against predatory oligarchs and power brokers. Franklin D. Roosevelt answered conservative critics of his economic policy in 1941 by saying: "Beware of that small group of selfish men who would clip the wings of the American eagle in order to feather their own nests."

Harry Truman, faced with labor crises early in his Administration, summed up: "This is no contest between labor and management. This is a contest between a small group of men and their government." And John F. Kennedy, in his 1962 confrontation with the steel industry over prices, attacked "a tiny handful of steel executives whose pursuit of private power and profit exceeds their sense of public responsibility."

Vice President Spiro Agnew, in his campaign supporting Republican congressional candidates in 1970, chose "band" over "group," but deliberately used the rhythm of the Wilson sentence to recall Senatorial obstructionism: "Will a little band of radical-liberals, with no constituency but each other, succeed in frustrating the will of the new majority of the American people?"

LITTLE OLD LADIES IN TENNIS SHOES characterization of feminine right-wing extremists.

Columnist Robert Novak informs the author that the phrase was coined in 1961 by Stanley Mosk, then Attorney General of California, in a report on right-wing activity.

The expression was one of many attacking Senator Barry Goldwater's campaign for the Republican nomination in 1963 and 1964. Republican liberals, members of what Goldwater supporters called the Eastern Establishment (Goldwater: "We ought to saw off the Eastern seaboard and float it out to sea") denounced the conservative champion as the captive of the John Birch Society and other extremist groups, which included "nuts and kooks" (see KOOKS, NUTS AND). Among these were a resolute, intensely dedicated women's group—Western (or at least not Eastern urban), unsophisticated, white-haired, and wearing rimless eyeglasses. They were called "the little old ladies in tennis shoes" with considerable disdain. However, their doorbell-ringing helped upset the Rockefeller forces in the crucial California primary.

The tennis-shoes metaphor can be contrasted with the SILK STOCKING metaphor; other political uses of foot coverings include "the heel of a dictator" and Adlai Stevenson's "hole in the shoe" symbol, as well as "gumshoe campaign."

Ronald Reagan, campaigning for governor of California in 1966, joked about the charge of ultraconservative support by addressing audiences occasionally as "Gentlemen—and little ladies in tennis shoes . . ."

As used on the attack, however, the phrase currently can flash on edge of viciousness: "It is not little old ladies in tennis shoes who are the hate merchants of the '70s," said AFL-CIO leader George Meany in 1977. "It is slick Madison Avenue types . . ."

Editors of *The New Yorker* magazine have frequently pointed out that they were not editing their publication for "the old ladies in Dubuque." In *Here at The New Yorker,* Brendan Gill wrote that the founder-editor, Harold Ross, launched the publication "with the stipulation that it was *not* to be edited for the old lady in Dubuque." The phrase came to mean a low common denominator of taste,

and is almost always used patronizingly. There may be a relationship between the ladies in Dubuque (Iowa) and those in tennis shoes (anywhere).

LITTLE MAN, *see* **JOHN Q. PUBLIC.**

LITTLE TIN BOX   symbol of graft; a hiding place for money.

Thomas M. Farley (no relation to James A.) was sheriff of New York County in the early thirties, and a Tammany SACHEM. In his investigation of corruption that led to the resignation of Mayor James Walker, Judge Samuel Seabury discovered that Farley had deposited $396,000 in his bank account over a six-year period. In that time, his total salary had been $90,000. Seabury's interrogation of Farley led to the coinage of the phrase.

> "Where did you keep these moneys that you had saved?"
> "In a safe deposit box at home in the house."
> "Whereabouts at home in the house?"
> "In a big safe."
> "In a little box in a big safe?"
> "In a big box in a big safe."
> "And, Sheriff, was this big box that was safely kept in the big safe a tin box or a wooden box?"
> "A tin box." [It turned out that Farley's bank deposits, year after year, came from this tin box, which seemed to generate cash all by itself.]
> "Kind of a magic box, wasn't it, Sheriff?"
> "It was a wonderful box."

In 1959 a musical based on Mayor La Guardia's life called *Fiorello!* was produced by Harold Prince. One of the hit songs was "A Little Tin Box" by Jerry Bock and Sheldon Harnick:

Mister X, May we ask you a question?
It's amazing, is it not?
That the City pays you slightly less
    than fifty bucks a week
Yet you've purchased a private yacht.
I am positive Your Honor must be
    joking
Any working man could do what I
    have done.
For a month or two I simply gave up
    smoking.
And I put my extra pennies one by
    one
Into a little tin box, a little tin box
There's a cushion for life's rude
    shocks.
There is faith, hope and charity,
Hard won prosperity,
In a little tin box. *

The word's meaning was inverted by Abraham Beame, controller of the City of New York, who used it to refer to the container for sealed bids by banks for city financing. The *New York Times* reported on July 8, 1971: "The ritual of unlocking the city's 'little tin box' and then unsealing the bids got under way at 11:03 A.M. yesterday . . ." In this sense, the box is a symbol of financial fairness and rectitude.

There is no connection between the "little tin box" and the "loose box" of British usage, which refers to the seats set aside for Edward VII's mistresses at his coronation, in turn taken from an enclosure for horses that permits them to move about without tethering.

LITMUS-TEST ISSUE   a subject used as an indicator of a candidate's ideological purity.

This phrase made its appearance in the mid-seventies to fill the need for a description of topics that separated

---

the **COMMITTED** from the **CENTRISTS**, or the **TRUE BELIEVERS** from the **OPPORTUNISTS**.

The most frequently discussed "litmus test" was a Republican's position on the Panama Canal treaties of 1977, which supporters of Ronald Reagan said would determine whether any candidate could get the 1980 presidential nomination. A Democratic litmus test was the Humphrey-Hawkins bill to reduce unemployment, and a Republican litmus test was the campaign for an Equal Rights Amendment for women.

In discussing the sale of war planes to Saudi Arabia in 1978, Mr. Reagan told this writer: "It isn't a litmus-test issue"—that is, conservatives could differ without having it considered a test of ideological virtue.

Professional politicians, to whom winning is the paramount issue, like to avoid the litmus. "Whatever Republican disunity may develop," wrote *New York Times* reporter Adam Clymer on June 25, 1978, "the party is doing one thing right, and that is not squabbling much in 1978. The party's right and middle (it has no real left) distrust each other, but they are working hard at electing Republicans without resorting to litmus-test issues . . ."

The phrase comes from the organic dye that turns blue in alkaline solutions, red in acid.

See **SWITCHER**.

LIVING WAGE   enough earnings to pay for necessities and a little more; a frequent promise of politicians seeking labor votes.

This has its roots in a "living price," or the price at which a businessman can make a profit and thereby earn his living. Congressman John Lind of Minnesota said in the House in 1890: "Things are at a

---

standstill. We have plenty to sell but no buyers at 'living' prices."

Father Coughlin, "the radio priest," who later became a bitter isolationist and anti-Semite, was an ardent supporter of Roosevelt in the early New Deal days, calling for currency inflation, nationalization of the banks, and "a living annual wage."

"Living" wages were contrasted with "starvation wages"; both terms are falling into disuse with the accent on "fringe benefits" and a "guaranteed annual wage." For a related usage, see HIGH COST OF LIVING.

LOBBY   as a verb, to attempt, as a private citizen or group, to influence governmental decisions and particularly legislative votes; as a noun, a group organized for this purpose.

The practice of lobbying is doubtless as old as the practice of legislating, but the term did not come into vogue until the mid-seventeenth century, when the large anteroom near the English House of Commons floor became known as the lobby. The word is akin to the Old High German *lauba,* meaning a shelter of foliage; when adopted into English, it came to mean a covered walk or passageway. The lobby was a public room, and thus one in which Members of Parliament could be approached by special pleaders, with or without protective foliage.

In the early nineteenth century those who lobbied were called "lobbiers" in the U.S., later "lobbyists." In England a "lobbyist" came to mean a reporter covering Commons, while a "lobby-agent" meant one who urged particular measures.

But in the U.S. during the politically venal 1800s, lobbying and lobbyists earned a bad name from which their professional descendants today, no matter how pure in motive and

deed, have yet to clear themselves completely. To Walt Whitman, "lobbiers" were among the "lousy combings and born freedom sellers of the earth." Dennis Tilden Lynch, writing of New York State politics circa 1820, said that "corruption has erected her court. . . . Her throne is the lobby."

In such low repute were lobbyists —universally considered buyers-up of votes and sellers-out of the public welfare—that to be branded one was an almost automatic disqualification for public office. Mark Hanna was William McKinley's political strong man and an intimate as well. But it is said that when Hanna pressed a particular appointment on McKinley, the President replied, "Mark, I would do anything in the world for you, but I cannot put a man in my cabinet who is known as a lobbyist." By this time lobbyists were considered so numerous and powerful that they were sometimes referred to collectively as the Third House of Congress.

Lobbying has grown more diverse. The federal government and some of the states have imposed legislative restrictions in an attempt to end the more blatant abuses. Most lobbyists now operate openly as registered advocates for their employers and clients, appearing before legislative committees and regulatory agency proceedings, where they are often useful in supplying information on complex issues.

At the same time, government has grown so large and complicated that executive agencies sometimes are cast in the role of lobbyists before Congress in competing with other departments for appropriations. Jack Raymond wrote in 1964: "The military services' own public relations and lobbying apparatus has disturbed some observers. The question has been posed whether the total effect of the military pleadings is contrary to the national interest."

When a reporter asked President Harry Truman in 1948, "Would you be against lobbyists who are working for your program?," the President replied, "We probably wouldn't call those people lobbyists. We would call them citizens appearing in the public interest."

For a derogation of pressure groups in international affairs, see CHINA LOBBY; for a melancholy view of lobbyists, see POCATELLO, YOU CAN'T GO BACK TO.

LOBBY TERMS, *see* **NOT FOR ATTRIBUTION.**

LOG CABIN humble origins which, when part of a candidate's personal history, are presumed to be worth many votes (now used mostly in a humorous vein).

When the Whigs nominated William Henry Harrison for President in 1840, one of his detractors observed that if someone gave Harrison a supply of hard cider, a small pension, and his choice of how to spend his time, the old hero of Indian fighting would sit contentedly by his log cabin the rest of his days. At that point Harrison owned some 2,000 acres of farmland and a mansion built around the old cabin, but his friends seized on the cider-cabin remark after it was printed in the *Baltimore Republic* as a way of emphasizing their man's plebian past. Harrison himself campaigned from a log cabin built on a wagon bed that had a seemingly bottomless cider barrel attached. The crowds loved it.

Complained a Democrat: "We defend the policy of the administration; the Whigs answer 'log cabin.' We urge the honesty, sagacity, statemanship of Van Buren; the Whigs answer

that Harrison is a poor man." Harrison won in what became known as the "Log Cabin and Hard Cider" campaign. See BANNER DISTRICT.

As a specific prop, the log cabin remained a Harrison monopoly, but rare is the candidate or incumbent who fails to point out his close relations with the common man, to the public's apparent approval. From Lincoln's log cabin to Harry Truman's haberdashery store, the lean yesterdays of Presidents are milestones of political folklore—all the more so, it appears, in this era when personal wealth and political success are hardly unrelated. John Nance Garner, a two-term Vice President under Franklin D. Roosevelt, said in 1959, "That log house [in which he was born] did me more good in politics than anything I ever said."

LOGORRHEA, *see* **FOOT-IN-MOUTH DISEASE.**

LOGROLLING mutual aid among politicians, especially legislators who must vote on many items of economic importance in individual states and districts.

H. L. Mencken traces the use of logrolling back to 1820. Hans Sperber and Travis Trittschuh have tracked down derisive newspaper comments of "great log rolling captains" in politics to 1809.

In the *Apocolocyntosis,* written early in the first century A.D. and attributed to Seneca, Hercules urges the gods to deify the Emperor Claudius. The Latin *(Deinde tu si quid volueris, in vicem faciam)* translates: "And then if you may desire something, I would reciprocate."

Among settlers in the wilderness, cooperation in handling logs for land clearing and construction was a force overriding any differences among neighbors. So too in politics. "If you will vote for my interest," said Congressman B. F. Butler in 1870, "I will vote for yours. That is how these tariffs are log-rolled through."

Reformers have inveighed against the practice as assiduously as the practitioners have pursued it. In 1871 the *New York Times* complained of Republicans who established "corrupt alliances with the enemy in the way of log rolling legislation." And in 1967 *Time,* cataloging the problems of the Post Office—then an institution as afflicted by bad politics as any in the country—noted "construction programs pressured on the one side by budget vagaries and on the other by congressional log rolling." *Time* still prefers the two-word usage; most current writers join the two words.

The classic description of the theory of logrolling is attributed to Simon Cameron, Pennsylvania politician who served as Lincoln's first Secretary of War: "You scratch my back and I'll scratch yours."

LONELIEST JOB IN THE WORLD description of the presidency, emphasizing its "awesome burdens."

It is a wonder that there are any applicants.

Thomas Jefferson, who served first as Vice President, said: "The second office of this government is honorable and easy, the first is a splendid misery." Andrew Jackson called the presidency "a situation of dignified slavery." The term of office has been likened to a term in jail by George Washington, who felt like "a culprit, going to the place of his execution." Warren Harding said, "This White House is a prison. I can't get away from the men who dog my footsteps. I am in jail." Harry Truman agreed; returning from a pre-breakfast stroll,

he sighed and told a reporter, "There is the big white jail." He wrote in his memoirs: "To be President of the United States is to be lonely, very lonely at times of great decisions."

"My God," said James Garfield two months after taking office, "what is there in this place that a man should ever want to get into it?" James Buchanan called it "a crown of thorns."

Several Presidents thought it a ruiner of friendships. Grover Cleveland wrote: "Henceforth, I can have no friends . . . I must face the difficulties of a new official life almost alone." John F. Kennedy, who enjoyed the presidency, agreed that it "is not a very good place to make new friends."

Old friendships are often strained. General Omar Bradley had called Dwight Eisenhower "Ike" for forty years; when he properly addressed him as "Mr. President," Eisenhower felt a twinge of isolation. He wrote: "His salutation put me on notice: from then onward, for as long as I held the office, I would . . . be separated from all others, including my oldest and best friends. I would be far more alone now than when commanding the Allied Forces . . ."

Wendell Willkie asked FDR why he kept Harry Hopkins so close to him. FDR replied, "Someday you may well be sitting here where I am now as President of the United States. And when you are, you'll be looking at that door over there and knowing that practically everybody who walks through it wants something out of you. You'll learn what a lonely job this is, and you'll discover the need for somebody like Harry Hopkins who asks for nothing except to serve you."

Of all the burdens of the presidency, loneliness is the one complaint that threads through the writings of the occupants, or inmates, of the White House. William Howard Taft summed it up to Woodrow Wilson on the latter's inauguration day: "I'm glad to be going—this is the loneliest place in the world."

LONER   politician who "goes his own way," "keeps his own counsel"; used pejoratively, as one who will not mix or take good advice.

Probably derived from "lone wolf" or "Lone Ranger," the word is applied to those who reject the camaraderie of political life, and on the policy level, who know enough (or think they do) to arrive at conclusions on issues independent of advisers. A loner is not necessarily a maverick; he may not oppose the organization but he does not give the organization a sense of participation in his decisions and his future.

Chicago Democratic Boss Jake Arvey assessed Senator Paul Douglas' beginnings in politics this way: "Paul was a 'loner' in Chicago politics. He was an alderman and somewhat of a stormy petrel. . . . I knew Paul Douglas was thinking about maybe running for Mayor. The indications were that if he did run, he would make the race as an independent Democrat. This was in line with Douglas' history of being a 'loner.'" Arvey talked Douglas out of running for mayor and into running for senator, with Adlai Stevenson running on the same ticket for governor. "In neither case," Arvey continued, "were these men 'developed' in the sense that they came out of the organization. Stevenson was a political unknown about to break on the public consciousness; Douglas had made himself in politics by bucking the organization on many important issues."

Though each man was, in a different way, a "loner," the organization used and was used by them.

Although Henry Kissinger once described himself to Italian interviewer Oriana Fallaci as a kind of lonely cowboy on the international scene—evoking the "Lone Ranger" image, which was followed by some derisive hooting from critics—a "loner" is not a reputation political figures usually seek. Joan Mondale, wife of the Vice President, used the word and its current antonym, "team player"—which, during the Watergate hearings, temporarily gained a negative connotation—in a comment about her husband to reporter Brock Brower in 1977: "He is very much a team player, not a loner."

See MAVERICK.

LONG HOT SUMMER   a threat of violence in Negro ghettos, when summer heat shortens tempers and crowds gather out of doors.

The phrase began as the title of a 1958 movie based on a number of works by William Faulkner; a television series based on the characters, also called *The Long Hot Summer,* ran on the ABC-TV network in 1965.

"It's going to be a long, hot summer" was a frequent prediction by Negro leaders in the spring of 1966; the author has not been able to trace the first political use of it, though it probably was used in this sense in 1964. The reference was to the likelihood of violence, from crime in the streets to full-scale rioting.

In June 1967, before the riots of Newark and Detroit, Martin Luther King, Jr., said, "Everyone is worrying about the long hot summer with its threat of riots. We had a long cold winter when little was done about the conditions that create riots." The phrase used to try to calm troubled neighborhoods was usually "Cool it."

Michigan Governor George Romney, who was to face a riot in Detroit that required federal troops to quell, said in April 1967 that the U.S. faced not only long hot summers at home but "the equally forbidding prospect of a long, hot century" throughout the world.

Faulkner's phrase was an apt turnaround of an earlier image that connected unrest with winter. *The Winter of Our Discontent* was a 1961 book by John Steinbeck, its title taken from Shakespeare's *King Richard III:* "Now is the winter of our discontent/ Made glorious summer by this sun of York."

John F. Kennedy used that earlier season image in a remark at the conclusion of the frigid 1961 Vienna meeting with Khrushchev: "It's going to be a cold winter."

LOOSE BOX, *see* **LITTLE TIN BOX.**

LOSER, *see* **CAN'T-WIN TECHNIQUE.**

LOVED FOR THE ENEMIES HE MADE a campaign cry of Grover Cleveland supporters in 1884; innocence by dissociation.

Grover Cleveland, mayor of Buffalo and later governor of New York, did not work well with the SA-CHEMS of Tammany Hall. While this caused him some difficulty in his home state, the opposition of Tammany leaders was an asset in the campaign for the Democratic nomination. With Samuel Tilden ill and declaring himself out of the running, Cleveland was the leading candidate. In a seconding speech Governor Edward S. Bragg of Wisconsin electrified the delegates with: "They love him most for the enemies he has

made." (Senator Joseph McCarthy used the same slogan in a full-page ad in the *Milwaukee Journal* in 1952, as he ran for a second term; New York Mayor Robert F. Wagner was to make substantially the same turning-on-Tammany appeal running for his third term in 1961.)

Franklin D. Roosevelt knew how to exploit the appeal of enmity from an unpopular source. In a Madison Square Garden speech bringing his 1936 campaign to a climax, he zeroed in on the enemy: ". . . financial monopoly, speculation, reckless banking, class antagonism, sectionalism, war profiteering." In a hard voice he said: "Never before in all our history have these forces been so united against one candidate as they stand today. They are unanimous in their *hate* for me—*and I welcome their hatred.*"

Presidents have taken private reassurance from the source of attacks as well. When Harry Truman fired Secretary of Commerce Henry Wallace, he incurred the wrath of the far-left wing. Writing to his mother, the President observed: "Well, now he's out, and the crackpots are having conniption fits. I'm glad they are. It convinces me I'm right."

IBM president Thomas J. Watson, Jr., observed: "Make no little enemies —people with whom you differ for some petty, insignificant reason . . . cultivate 'mighty opposites'—people with whom you disagree on big issues, with whom you will fight to the end over fundamental convictions."

LOVE FEAST humorous exaggeration of a friendly meeting, especially one that could have revealed tensions and bitterness but ends amicably.

The phrase was originally religious, to describe the "agape," or love feast, among early Christians—an informal dinner, with songs and prayers, prevalent in the first two centuries of Christianity. Suspicions of bacchanalian zeal were voiced early, as the Book of Jude warned of "blemishes on your love feasts"; Pope Paul in 1967 disapproved of changes in the celebration of the Eucharist, following reports of experiments in the liturgy that included mass at home accompanied by modern music, with non-Catholics participating. "Such masses," reported the *New York Times* "are frequently thought of as imitations of the 'agape,' or love feast, common in the early church, and the emphasis is on the close fellowship of small numbers of believers."

Colonel Edward House set up a luncheon for Franklin Roosevelt and Massachusetts Democratic leaders in 1932 to discourage Al Smith. Ralph Martin wrote in *Ballots and Bandwagons:* "Uninvited to this 'love feast', promoted by Colonel House, [former Boston Mayor James] Curley not only showed up with Roosevelt, but invited his own press and newsreel people . . ."

The religious phrase was probably introduced into politics by Mark Twain and Charles Dudley Warner in 1873, in the novel *The Gilded Age,* a story about the politics of Reconstruction. The newspaper in their fictional Washington, D.C., is so much the supporter of the corrupt status quo that it is called the *Daily Love-Feast.*

In 1901 William Jennings Bryan wrote a Republican friend about the revolt of the Western progressives: "Your party is entering upon a struggle by the side of which our contest will seem a love-feast." A more restrained form is "mutual admiration society."

LOW PROFILE   self-denigration to reduce vulnerability; abhorrence of the vivid or dramatic in public posture.

A low profile is one step short of a PASSION FOR ANONYMITY; one who maintains a low profile gets some public exposure, but does not invite attack. It is normally used to describe the low-keyed approach of an individual, but can also be used to characterize an Administration.

This figure of political speech probably has a military origin; in tank warfare, a vehicle with a low profile is less readily identified through binoculars and presents less of a target for artillery.

The phrase is in active current use. Presidential assistant Leonard Garment told an associate in early 1970, "I've kept my profile so low for so long, I've got a permanent backache." The meaning of the expression was best captured in John F. Kennedy's advice to his speechwriter, Ted Sorensen: "Stay out of sight and you stay out of trouble."

And it has achieved a certain linguistic universality. "In last year's election campaign," wrote the *Wall Street Journal* on November 15, 1977, in a story about Canadian separatists, "unlike previous contests, the Parti Québécois kept what its strategists called 'le low profile' on the independence issue."

LOW ROAD, *see* **HIGH ROAD . . . LOW ROAD.**

LOYAL OPPOSITION   the role of the political opposition in a republican form of government, implying the responsibility to oppose with patriotic motives.

In eighteenth-century Britain when political parties were first being formed, the term was meant to indicate that the party in opposition, like the party in power, was true to the Crown—in fact, loyal—but felt that the best interests of the nation would be served by different policies. It is officially used to describe the party out of power in Great Britain, as "His (Her) Majesty's Loyal Opposition."

In the U.S. it was popularized by Wendell Willkie in a radio speech delivered several days after he and the Republican party had been defeated by President Roosevelt in November 1940.

Willkie spoke of the war already under way in Europe, and of the calls by some for a coalition cabinet of Democrats and Republicans. He rejected such a cabinet (though FDR had already enlisted Republicans Frank Knox and Henry Stimson) and described what he considered to be the role of the Republican party: "A vital element in the balanced operation of democracy is a strong, alert and watchful opposition . . . I say: 'Your function during the next four years is that of the loyal opposition.' . . . Let us not, therefore, fall into the partisan error of opposing things just for the sake of opposition. Ours must not be an opposition against—it must be an opposition for—an opposition for a strong America . . ."

Commented Republican leader Joe Martin: "Willkie got off on the right foot with the whole country, Republicans included, with his Loyal Opposition speech." It was not easy, for the "duty" of the opposition was still felt by many to oppose, and not to cooperate.

That principle had long been articulated. Winston Churchill told of his father, Lord Randolph Churchill, quoting an early-nineteenth-century politician as saying bluntly: "The duty of an Opposition is to oppose."

This might have been a simplifica-tion of a statement attributed to a Whig leader named Tierney by Edward Stanley, Earl of Derby. Tierney is quoted as having said: ". . . the duty of an opposition was very simple—it was, to oppose everything, and propose nothing."

In his years as Senate Majority Leader, Lyndon Johnson established himself as a Democratic leader who was frequently prepared to support legislation desired by the Republican Administration of Dwight D. Eisenhower. He expressed his philosophy to fellow Democrats at a Senate conference early in 1953: "I have never agreed with the statement that it is 'the business of the opposition to oppose.' I do not believe that the American people have sent us here merely to obstruct."

But there are those who still subscribe to the Tierney theory. Fred Vinson, Supreme Court Chief Justice from 1946 to 1953, told the story of a Kentucky politician who was asked whom he was going to support in a primary election. The politician's answer: "I don't know yet. I'm waiting to see what the opposition does, so I can take the other side."

"Loyal opposition" is an oxymoron (a phrase made memorable by the jarring juxtaposition of contradictory words); more recent oxymorons are *profitless prosperity*, UNTHINKABLE THOUGHTS, and WAGING PEACE.

As a member of the loyal opposition, Churchill in 1936 flung a handful of oxymorons at the government of Stanley Baldwin: "So they go on in strange paradox, decided only to be undecided, resolved to be irresolute, adamant for drift, solid for fluidity, all-powerful to be impotent."

A not-so-loyal member of the Canadian opposition, René Levesque of the secession-minded Parti Québecois, in 1978 called a plan by Prime Minister Trudeau "profoundly insignificant."

LOYALTY OATH a pledge of fealty to a government; more specifically in recent years, a promise of abstinence from subversive activities and causes.

The latest concern with loyalty oaths started soon after World War II. Charges of Communist infiltration of the American government became the biggest domestic issue of the late forties and early fifties. Although President Harry Truman sometimes scoffed at it (see RED HERRING), he also issued an Executive Order in 1947—called the "loyalty order"—which prescribed security procedures for the executive branch.

The issue seems to be one that arises periodically after great wars and upheavals. The "red menace" after World War I also made the country security-conscious, and loyalty oaths had a brief vogue.

Another form of loyalty oath is often required by a political party of its convention delegates; it is a pledge to abide by the decision of the convention and not to bolt if dissatisfied. Columnist Arthur Krock wrote: "Without the discipline which was enforced by the 'loyalty' requirement at the Democratic Convention of 1964, a political party as such loses its identity as a responsible group accountable to the people."

During the Civil War, Congress enacted legislation that required Confederate sympathizers to take the *ironclad oath* if they wished to regain their civil rights. No former rebel could hold important public office, for instance, without swearing his opposition to the Confederate cause. Sometimes called the *amnesty oath* in the North, it was more often termed the *damn nasty oath* in the South.

In *Andrew Johnson and Reconstruction*, Eric McKitrick wrote of the Southern girl who was brought before a Union captain and told she had to swear an oath of loyalty to the Union. "The girl refused on the grounds that it was wrong to swear an oath—her church forbade it, her mother told her that no lady ever swore. The captain insisted that she swear the oath and the girl finally agreed, saying: 'I will swear an oath, but it will be forever on your conscience. Damn all you Yankees to hell! There, Captain, I swore my oath!' "

LULU payment made to legislators "in lieu of" expenses.

Instead of requiring a detailed accounting of expenditures from its legislators, New York State sets a fixed fee to be paid them in lieu of expenses; if the legislators can skimp on the outlay, they can keep the extra money. Governor Al Smith named them "lulus," a play on the word "lieu" and the meaning of the girl's name in current slang as a whopping mistake, or a "beaut." (Fiorello La Guardia: "When I make a mistake, it's a beaut.")

"Lulu" is in current, if regional, use; attacks on the expense system are made periodically.

See POLITICAL MILEAGE, TO MAKE; PERKS.

LUMPENPROLETARIAT, *see* **PROLETARIAT.**

LUNATIC FRINGE persons or groups with extreme political views.

The emergence of militant right-wingers and professional anti-Communists since the 1940s revived "lunatic fringe." Since then it has usually been used to denote the farout right.

In one of his last campaign speeches, Franklin Roosevelt in 1944 attacked "labor baiters, bigots and some politicians who use the term Communism loosely." This "fear propaganda," he said, had been used by fascist blackshirts, Nazi brownshirts, and "in this country by the silver shirts and those on the lunatic fringe." Since then the term has been most frequently applied to "extremism" or the RADICAL RIGHT.

It was not always so. Theodore Roosevelt is generally credited with first using the phrase, or at least giving it currency, in 1913, when he wrote: "Every reform movement has a lunatic fringe." Although himself a progressive and a reformer, Roosevelt said he was talking about "the votaries of any forward movement." The left connotation was clear as TR wrote: "I am always having to fight the silly reactionaries and the inert, fatuous creatures who will not think seriously; and on the other hand to try to exercise some control over the lunatic fringe among the reformers."

Thus, left-leaning radicals were targets of the lunatic label before their rightist cousins. The Republicans in the 1948 election accused the Democrats of being hospitable to a "lunatic fringe" and the Republicans were so charged in 1964.

In current usage, labeling from near right to far right goes "rightist," "far rightist," "reactionary," "ultrarightist," MOSSBACK, "dinosaur wing," "troglodyte," and "lunatic fringe."

See LITTLE OLD LADIES IN TENNIS SHOES; KOOKS, NUTS AND.

LUNCHING HIM OUT, *see* **ADVANCE MAN.**

M

MACHINE POLITICS the election of officials and the passage of legislation through the power of an organization created for political action.

The phrase is derogatory because it suggests that the interests of the organization are placed before those of the general public.

Machine politics in the United States is closely linked with New York's Tammany Hall and with urban politics. The Vare organization in Philadelphia (Republican), the Kelly-Nash machine in Chicago (Democratic), and the recent Democratic organization of Richard Daley, are all examples of machine politics in the classic sense.

The beginnings of big-city organization politics can be tracked back to Tammany (see TAMMANY TIGER). Theodore Roosevelt, himself a politician of substantial skill, wrote that "Van Buren was the first product of what are now called 'machine politics' put into the Presidential chair. The people at large would never have thought of him for President of their own accord; but he had become Jackson's political legatee."

The creation of the first political machine in the U.S. at the end of the eighteenth century in New York has often been credited to Aaron Burr, though recent scholarship downgrades his importance. His political acumen was praised by those who won the right to vote through his political manipulations, and damned by those, led by Alexander Hamilton, whose possession of property had previously held control of the franchise.

The word "machine" is believed by Mencken to have been Burr's invention, though it did not come into general use until after the Civil War. It generally means strict organization, with rewards of one kind or another going to those who work for the organization and observe its disciplines. Discipline is important. As Edward Flynn, the Bronx County Democratic leader who was a national figure in the Roosevelt era, wrote: ". . . the so-called 'independent' voter is foolish to assume that a political machine is run solely on good will, or patronage. For it is not only a machine; it is an army. And in any organization as in any army, there must be discipline."

The charge against machines is that they are undemocratic and invariably encourage corruption. One answer is the primary elections whereby candidates for office may be selected directly by the voters who register for one political party or the other. But the primary system often means selection of the best-known candidate, or the one supported by the organization leadership who can use "troops" to turn out the vote.

To the reformer, the machine is dominated by a BOSS and consists of his HENCHMEN and "dupes"; to a regular, the organization is headed by a "leader" and consists of ACTIVISTS and "public-spirited citizens."

In Japan, the word for political machine is *jiban,* literal translation "base" or "foundation," which is one view of the function of the machine in the party system.

MACHINERY OF GOVERNMENT metaphor to show complexity of interrelationships within public administration.

"I think we have more machinery of government than is necessary," wrote Thomas Jefferson in 1824. He might have seen the phrase in Edward Gibbon's *Decline and Fall of the Roman Empire,* written between 1776 and 1788: "The nice and artificial machinery of government was out of joint."

Geared to press the *panic button* at the first *feedback* from *machine* politicos, government planners *mesh* their thinking to get *traction* for their programs to *spark* action, *engineering* their budgets so as to ignore *start-up* costs, and *mechanically* warn those *automatons* and *cogs* whose *machinations* might throw *monkey wrenches* into the *works* that *counterproductive* people usually get the *shaft.* See INOPERATIVE; WHEELS WITHIN WHEELS.

President William Howard Taft listened in wonderment to an adviser who spoke of "the machinery of government" and said later to a friend, "You know . . . he really thinks it *is* machinery."

In 1969 a White House aide told President Nixon he would relay a request "to the appropriate mechanism." The President proceeded to reminisce to the author about a visit he had made to Poland in 1959: "There was a steel mill on the itiner-ary. The Polish diplomat who was my escort officer—a brilliant fellow—turned me over to the plant manager for the usual guided tour. The manager was especially proud of the new machinery in the plant, and he told me all about what it cost and how it speeded up the process. He got a little impatient when I stopped to shake hands with the workers around whatever machine he was showing off. In the car on the way back from the mill, the diplomat said something I've always remembered. 'It's not hard to find men who understand machinery,' he said. 'Our trouble is we don't have enough men who understand men.' "

In 1978 the metaphor was cranking along as merrily as ever. "Carter's an engineering officer, a protégé of Admiral [Hyman] Rickover," said the President's Energy Secretary, James Schlesinger, to Hedrick Smith of the *New York Times.* "Rickover has to know how every single engine or pump works. Carter is that way. He looks upon government as machinery to be improved, to be lubricated."

MACHISMO condescension of the swaggering male; the trappings of manliness used to dominate women and keep them "in their place."

Pronounced ma-*chees*-mo, the word is a favorite of WOMEN'S LIB. In the first issue of the magazine *Ms.* in December 1971, the political "machismo factor" (or anti-machismo stand) was defined as "personal rejection of the traditional 'masculine' role . . . and opposition to militarism and violence." A Mexican term, machismo is based on the Spanish *macho,* "manly." In March 1967, sociologist David Riesman wrote: "In Spanish-America the term machismo designates efforts of a man to appear manly in the approved way, often caricaturing himself in the process."

Politically the word (sometimes as *macho,* or as "manhood") is most often used as a criticism of intervention. When President Ford in 1975 reacted sharply to the attack on the merchant ship *Mayagüez,* Secretary of State Henry Kissinger explained, "We are not going around looking for opportunities to prove our manhood." Lucy Komisar responded in a *New York Times* Op-Ed article: "It was a curious comment for the question had never been asked, and it made it clear that at a level very close to his consciousness, Secretary Kissinger knew that this was precisely what America's reaction had been all about."

MADISON AVENUE TECH-NIQUES   the other side's gimmicky, slick use of the communications media to play on emotions, contrasted with your own forthright use of modern advertising methods to "get the message to the people."

The phrase "Madison Avenue," in its present sense descriptive of the advertising community, was born in 1944, when an article in the *New Republic* describing advertising's contribution to the war effort was signed "Madison Avenue." "The avenue," as columnists soon called it, covered agencies on Park, Third, and Fifth avenues as well.

"Madison Avenue techniques" is a phrase used to derogate "the Hidden Persuaders" (author Vance Packard's term) who are **"SELLING CANDIDATES LIKE SOAP"**—neatly packaged, making popular appeals in catchy phrases, always new, ever-improved.

Madison Avenue techniques can be startlingly successful in politics. In Picoaza, a town of 4,000 in Ecuador, the producer of "Pulvapies," a foot powder, tied in to the local campaign for mayor in 1967 with the following slogan: "Vote for any candidate, but if you want well-being and hygiene, vote for Pulvapies." Well-being and hygiene turned out to be GUT ISSUES in Picoaza, and the human candidates were chagrined when the voters chose Pulvapies, the foot powder, over the human candidates for mayor. "Cynics may feel," editorialized the *Wall Street Journal,* "the ensuing result reflects on the literacy of Ecuadorans, but we're not so sure. There are times in this enlightened land when the citizenry would welcome a chance to vote for a ticket that promised, not PIE IN THE SKY, but something down to earth and believable."

See MEDIA EVENT.

MAGNOLIA MAFIA, *see* **IRISH MAFIA; SMELL OF MAGNOLIAS.**

MAIDEN SPEECH   a first speech, usually in a legislative body.

Probably the best-known example was a fiasco. Benjamin Disraeli, destined to be Prime Minister of Great Britain twice and to enter the House of Lords as the Earl of Beaconsfield, was at the time he first secured a seat in the House of Commons merely an ambitious young man of thirty-two. His maiden speech to that body was badly received; in fact, so raucous was the laughter of the members that Disraeli was forced to take his seat, his speech unfinished. His parting words were: "The time will come when you shall hear me."

The Senate of the United States, which likes to think of itself as the world's greatest deliberative body, long had a tradition that new senators did not deliver their virgin speech-making efforts until they had sat through a congressional session in silence. This rule has been discarded in recent years with the election of men already nationally prominent to that body; for example, the maiden speeches of men like Robert Kennedy of New York and Edward Brooke of Massachusetts, delivered shortly after having taken their places in the Senate, were given careful attention all over the nation. In Great Britain, however, the tradition is current; Winston Churchill called Sir Alan Herbert's maiden effort "a brazen hussy of a speech."

MAINSTREAM   the central current, as in philosophy or political doctrine.

"Mainstream" — or variations thereof—has long appealed to writers and statesmen as a symbol of the broad MIDDLE OF THE ROAD. A Japanese proverb notes that "one man can stand still in a flowing stream, but not in a world of men." In 1792 Mary Wollstonecraft wrote in *A Vindication of the Rights of Women:* "In every age there has been a stream of popular opinion that has carried all before it, and given a family character, as it were, to the century."

John F. Kennedy often used the mainstream image, or byplays on it. He told James MacGregor Burns: "Some people have their liberalism 'made' by the time they reach their late 20's. I didn't. I was caught in cross-currents and eddies. It was only later that I got into the stream of things." Addressing the Irish Parliament in Dublin on June 28, 1963, he returned to the image: "Ireland is moving in the mainstream of current world events. Your destiny lies not as a peaceful island in a sea of trouble but as a maker and shaper of world peace."

No modern politician has used the word more often, however, than New York's Governor Nelson Rockefeller. "The mainstream of American political thought and action" was one of his favorite phrases. Speechwriter Hugh Morrow recalls that Rockefeller's first use of the term was in a statement released July 14, 1963:

> . . . it has now become crystal clear that the vociferous and well-drilled extremist elements boring within the Party utterly reject these fundamental principles of our heritage. They are, in fact, embarked on a determined and ruthless effort to take over the Party, its platform and its candidates on their own terms— terms that are wholly alien to the sound and honest conservatism that has firmly based the Republican Party in the best of a century's traditions, wholly alien to the sound and honest Republican liberalism that has kept the Party abreast of human needs in a changing world, wholly alien to the broad middle course that accommodates *the mainstream of Republican principle.* This cannot be allowed to happen.

During the 1964 Republican presidential convention, Rockefeller supporters, in a futile effort to halt Barry Goldwater's drive for the nomination, unfurled a 30-foot canvas banner urging Republicans: "Stay in the Mainstream." But the votes were not there; as the old English proverb states, "the stream cannot rise above its source."

In politics, there are streams within streams. While the banner at the 1964 convention referred to the mainstream of political thought, eschewing EXTREMISM, the mainstream of thinking within the Republican party shifted to the right in the seventies; the *Washington Star* editorialized in 1977 that a liberal nominee to the Federal Elections Commission "is not what could be considered a 'mainstream' Republican."

An antonym for the term may be "out of touch," a description that critics began applying to such congressional leaders as Democratic Speaker of the House John McCormack and Senate Minority Leader Everett M. Dirksen in the mid-1960s.

A related meaning is in the use of the word as a verb. In *Time* (January 2, 1978), Stefan Kanfer wrote: " 'Mainstreaming' is the short form of a long process: the education of disabled children alongside the normal.'"

See DON'T CHANGE HORSES; EXTREMISM.

MAJORITY RULE, *see* **ONE MAN, ONE VOTE.**

MAKE THE WORLD SAFE FOR DEMOCRACY   a rallying phrase as America entered World War I which acquired a hollow sound after the war and is currently used as an example of foolishly idealistic intervention.

President Woodrow Wilson's phrase was: "The world must be made safe for democracy." His speech, delivered before Congress on April 2, 1917, went on to disclaim any "selfish ends" on the part of the U.S.

Had it not been for one man, however, Wilson's phrase might never have caught on. Senator John Sharp Williams of Mississippi, a good orator himself, but at this time aged and almost deaf, was leaning forward, concentrating intently on the speech. When Wilson said, "The world must be made safe for democracy," he began slowly—and alone—to clap, continuing until others joined him. This underlined for the reporters in the press gallery that a phrase had been turned.

In the fall of 1941 Adlai Stevenson, at that time representing the Committee to Defend America by Aiding the Allies, said in debate that the U.S. must provide aid for Great Britain because "I do not think that with tyranny in four-fifths of the world, freedom can endure in one-fifth." Caly Judson of the America First committee replied, "The question we must answer before it is too late is: 'Is this our war?' If it is our war, then we should be in it without delay, even though it will not be the comparatively simple job it was the first time we saved the world for democracy."

The construction has been used in recent years in that sarcastic manner, as in this official statement by Kenya's ruling party, the African National Union: "America's presence [in Vietnam] is not in the interests of the people. It is there to make the Far East safe for Coca-Cola."

President Nixon in 1971 varied the phrase: "By his example, Woodrow Wilson helped make the world safe for idealism."

See WAR TO END WARS.

MALEFACTORS OF GREAT WEALTH   the irresponsible rich; an early attack phrase on Big Business.

Annoyed by continued attacks on him as the destroyer of business and the author of the Panic of 1907, Theodore Roosevelt declared in a speech at Provincetown, Mass., on August 20, 1907, that the trouble had been caused, at least in part, by "ruthless and determined men" hiding "behind the breastworks of corporate organization." He added: "It may well be that the determination of the government to punish certain malefactors of great wealth has been responsible for something of the trouble, at least to the extent of having caused these men to bring about as much financial stress as they can in order to discredit the policy of the government."

For Franklin D. Roosevelt, "ECO-NOMIC ROYALISTS" and "pluto-crats" were latter-day equivalents of his cousin's famous "malefactors."

Words like "malefactor" and "infamy," rarely used but immediately understood, give solemnity and significance to a phrase. "Malefactor" (directly from the Latin *evil-doer*) is used less frequently than its opposite, "benefactor" *(good-doer)* and made TR's phrase successful.

MA, MA, WHERE'S PA? *see* SMEAR.

MANAGED NEWS information generated and distributed by the government in such a way as to give government interest priority over candor.

News management surfaced in October and November 1962 along with the Russian offensive missiles in Cuba to give a name to one of the oldest truisms in the relations of government officials and journalists. Long before he was President, John F. Kennedy warned an aide about the press: "Always remember that their interests and ours ultimately conflict." To the reporter, news is the publication of information that will interest and enlighten his reader. To the official, it is what may affect his own political future.

Newspapers, magazines, and broadcasters harped on news management as soon as the worst of the missile crisis was over, with much justification. There had been some fibbing in high places. Assistant Defense Secretary Arthur Sylvester later talked about the "government's right, if necessary, to lie" and of news as "weaponry." Reporters were barred from ships on blockade duty around Cuba. The White House made requests about self-censorship but refused to impose official censorship. Sylvester in the Pentagon and his counterpart Robert Manning in the State Department imposed requirements irksome to reporters that all interviews be either monitored or reported to an official's superior.

Some critics of these policies recalled Nazi propaganda minister Joseph Goebbels' statement: "During a war, news should be given out for instruction rather than for information." However, the policies were not new. Pierre Salinger, who as Kennedy's press secretary had to take much criticism for news management, pointed out that the very phrase was invented to describe not his activities but those of his predecessor under Dwight Eisenhower, James Hagerty. The author was James Reston of the *New York Times,* who discussed Hagerty's "management of the news." Charles Hurd recalls that Franklin D. Roosevelt was frequently accused of "using the press." Lyndon Johnson was chided for holding too few formal press conferences, too many informal press conferences, for talking too much and saying too little and for having created a CREDIBILITY GAP.

It was ironic that the issue of "news management" should have reached such a peak in the Kennedy Administration. Kennedy himself had usually seemed adept at his press relations and had enjoyed generally favorable coverage. Yet he had his share of scrapes, as when he banned the *New York Herald Tribune* from the White House for its too-vigorous coverage of the Billy Sol Estes case. Robert Kennedy, then Attorney General, was accused of pressuring hostile reporters. The President quipped in the spring of 1962, when asked how he liked the press: "Well, I'm reading it more and enjoying it less."

But the missile crisis was unique in the grayness of its status between war and peace. The government was groping for solution by trying to keep all factors—including information—in fine balance. Douglass Cater later wrote: "Certainly news is bound to be regarded as a weapon by officials who are involved in struggles of statecraft. But they are foolish if they expect to say so out loud and get away with it."

See MEDIA EVENT; PROPAGANDA.

MANDATE the authority to carry out a program conferred on an elected official; especially strong after a LANDSLIDE victory.

Before the midterm elections in 1918, Woodrow Wilson appealed to the nation for a "mandate" to carry out his policies in the form of a Democratic Congress. He did not get one, and later he hit on the idea of a "Senatorial mandate." Wilson's unusual idea was to have those senators who opposed him on such issues as the League of Nations resign, then run in a special election. If they won a clear mandate, Wilson said, he would appoint one of the opposition leaders—perhaps Henry Cabot Lodge—as Secretary of State. Then he and his Vice President would resign, automatically making the Republican Secretary of State the new President—under the Succession Act as it then worked.

In the U.S., the TWO-PARTY SYSTEM has helped ensure the transfer of mandates at frequent intervals. Thus, in 1936, Franklin Roosevelt noted that "it will never be possible for any length of time for any group of the American people, either by reason of wealth or learning or inheritance or economic power, to retain any mandate, any permanent authority to arrogate to itself the political control of American public life."

Significantly, Dwight Eisenhower, who was elected after twenty years of Democratic control of the White House, titled the first volume of his memoirs *Mandate for Change*.

How many votes constitute a mandate for the winner? He must receive at least one vote more than the loser. In his first inaugural address, FDR interpreted his sizable victory as "a mandate [for] direct, vigorous action." John F. Kennedy, on the other hand, won narrowly, yet did not shrink from acting for that reason. "The fact remains that he won," wrote Theodore Sorensen in *Kennedy*, "and on the day after election, and every day thereafter, he rejected the argument that the country had given him no mandate. Every election has a winner and a loser, he said in effect. The margin is narrow, but the responsibility is clear. There may be difficulties with the Congress, but a margin of only one vote would still be a mandate."

Nonetheless, the closeness of his victory often acted as a brake. "Kennedy had very little leverage," wrote Arthur Schlesinger, Jr. He had been elected "by the slimmest of margins; no one could possibly claim his victory as a mandate for radical change."

In 1955 Walter Lippmann described how a mandate may be achieved by means other than electoral. "Political ideas acquire operative force in human affairs when . . . they acquire legitimacy, when they have the title of being right which binds men's consciences. Then they possess, as the Confucian doctrine has it, 'the mandate of heaven.' "

An interesting use of the word occurred during the British general election in the midst of the worldwide depression of the 1930s. A coalition government was then in power, and it asked voters for a "doctor's mandate"—one that would prescribe the proper treatment for the country's ills.

MANIFEST DESTINY   the doctrine that it was the duty and fate of the U.S. to expand to the Pacific coast —and beyond.

One of the earliest uses of the phrase is attributed to Andrew Jackson. In 1824, according to biographer John Ward, Jackson described the U.S. as "a country manifestly called by the Almighty to a destiny which Greece and Rome, in the days of their pride, might have envied."

An enthusiastic promoter of the concept was John O'Sullivan, an American diplomat and journalist. In 1839 O'Sullivan wrote: "In its magnificent domain of space and time, the nation of many nations is destined to manifest to mankind the excellence of divine principles." Six years later an unsigned editorial in the expansionist journal *The United States Magazine and Democratic Review* noted that certain foreign governments were trying to prevent the U.S. annexation of Texas and spoke of "our manifest destiny to overspread the continent allotted by Providence for the free development of our yearly multiplying millions." O'Sullivan, it was later learned, was the author of the editorial.

His views were echoed elsewhere. In a congressional debate on the U.S. treaty with Great Britain settling the borders of Oregon in January 1846, Massachusetts' Representative Robert C. Winthrop declared that it was "the right of our manifest destiny to spread over this whole continent." Through the century the phrase echoed and reechoed. James Gordon Bennett wrote in a *New York Herald* editorial on April 3, 1865: "It is our

manifest destiny to lead and rule all other nations." The doctrine, to be sure, disturbed many Americans. In his *Journals,* Emerson wrote in 1865: "That word, 'manifest destiny,' which is profanely used, signifies the sense all men have of the prodigious energy and opportunity lying idle here."

It did not lie idle for long. In 1898 President William McKinley told George Cortelyou, an aide, "We need Hawaii just as much and a good deal more than we did California. It is manifest destiny." McKinley's critics saw in this attitude an imperialistic "greed of conquest," but Hawaii was annexed in July 1898. Former President Grover Cleveland, who never cared much for the idea, wrote to a friend at the time: "Hawaii is ours. As I look back upon the first steps in this miserable business and as I contemplate the means used to complete the outrage, I am ashamed of the whole affair."

MAN IN THE STREET   the average man; JOHN Q. PUBLIC; the voter of ordinary intelligence.

The phrase was popularized by Ralph Waldo Emerson, in his 1841 essay "On Self-Reliance," regarding the spiritually debilitating effect of civilization on man: "A Greenwich nautical almanac he has, and so being sure of the information when he wants it, the man in the street does not know a star in the sky."

The phrase had been traced by the *OED* to 1831, and Theodore Roosevelt used it in a 1900 letter: "But the man in the street naturally does not look as far ahead as this." Lord Bryce, in *The American Commonwealth,* used "man in the cars" in 1888 in a sense that holds up well today as a condemnation of how too many men in the street form their opinions:

> . . . one need only try the experiment of talking to that representative of public opinion whom the Americans call "the man in the cars" to realize how uniform opinion is among all classes of people, how little there is of that individuality in the ideas of each individual which they would have if he had formed them for himself, how little solidity and substance there is in the political or social ideas of nineteen persons out of every twenty. These ideas, when examined, mostly resolve themselves into two or three prejudices and aversions, two or three prepossessions for a particular leader or section of a party, two or three phrases or catchwords suggesting or embodying arguments which the man who repeats them has not analyzed.

MAN OF THE PEOPLE public figure identified with humble origins and usually a POPULIST philosophy.

"The President will not be a man of the people," warned Founding Father James Wilson in 1787, "but the minion of the Senate." Wilson held that the senatorial veto of presidential appointments would cripple the office of Chief Executive, but the Constitutional Convention disagreed. See ADVICE AND CONSENT.

The meaning of the phrase was narrowed to nonaristocrats with the emergence of Andrew Jackson, whose background and manner were far more plebeian than Washington, the Adamses, Jefferson, Madison, or Monroe. As Harry Truman assessed him: "Jackson was recognized as the 'man of the people'—an advocate of the liberal interpretation of democracy as practised by Jefferson."

In current use, the phrase has dropped most of the "humble origin" connotation and is concerned more with a man who identifies himself with the needs and aspirations of the common man. Thus, a man of wealth —Franklin Roosevelt, for example— could be classed "a man of the people" even to the extent of being a TRAITOR TO HIS CLASS.

Wealthy candidates still seem to feel a need, however, to prove that even if they are rich, they are still "regular guys"—witness Nelson Rockefeller munching a hot dog, Averell Harriman a knish, and supporters of Adlai Stevenson making much of a hole in his shoe. When Wendell Willkie pointed out his Hoosier origins, Harold Ickes nailed him with BAREFOOT BOY FROM WALL STREET.

MAN ON HORSEBACK a military figure with political potential; or a would-be dictator; or any strong, authoritarian leader.

The idea, though not the phrase, appeared in a scaffold statement by English rebel Richard Rumbold, hanged in 1685: "I never would believe that Providence had sent a few men into the world, ready booted and spurred to ride, and millions ready saddled and bridled to be ridden."

The phrase was introduced to American politics by General Caleb Cushing, who described to a group of Maine Democrats assembled in Bangor on January 11, 1860, what the impending civil strife would mean to the nation: ". . . cruel war, war at home; and in the perspective distance, a man on horseback with a drawn sword in his hand, some Atlantic Caesar, or Cromwell, or Napoleon."

The predecessor phrase, with the same metaphor, is "on a high horse." Shakespeare had Marc Antony say of Julius Caesar that he "sits high on all people's hearts," and the Reverend John Brown, in a letter to David Garrick dated October 27, 1765, complained of Dr. Samuel Johnson's criticism of Shakespeare: "Altogether upon the high horse, and blustering about Imperial Tragedy!"

Hans Sperber concluded that the phrase was drawn from the "solitary horseman" appearing in six books by a popular novelist of the period, G. P. R. James.

Lincoln professed not to be concerned about the chances of a military dictatorship. In a letter to General Joseph Hooker, who had said the nation needed a dictator, Lincoln wrote: "Only those Generals who gain successes can set up dictators. What I now ask of you is military success, and I will risk the dictatorship."

General George B. McClellan, true to Cushing's prophecy, did turn out to be the Democratic nominee of 1864, losing to Lincoln by 400,000 votes out of 4,000,000. But the "man on horseback" phrase was first applied to a presidential candidate in Ulysses S. Grant's 1868 campaign, and "Vote as You Shot" was a slogan of veteran's groups for many years after the Civil War.

Military men who made it to the top in U.S. history include George Washington, Andrew Jackson, William Henry Harrison, Zachary Taylor, U.S. Grant, Theodore Roosevelt (as a "Rough Rider," he is on the edge of this category), and Dwight D. Eisenhower. Generals who lost presidential bids were Lewis Cass in 1848, Winfield Scott in 1852, McClellan in 1864, and Winfield Scott Hancock in 1880. In addition, Admiral George Dewey and General Douglas MacArthur awaited lightning that never struck. Of the thirty-eight Americans who have served as President, twenty —more than half—had some armed-service background.

Eisenhower, for one, was disturbed

by the "man on horseback" image. Sought by both parties for the 1948 nomination, he declared: "The necessary and wise subordination of the military to civil power will be best sustained . . . when lifelong professional soldiers, in the absence of some obvious and overriding reasons, abstain from seeking high political office."

In 1961 E. M. Dealey, chairman of the board of the *Dallas Morning News,* said in an angry letter to President John Kennedy that "we need a man on horseback to lead this nation, and many people in Texas and the Southwest think that you are riding Caroline's bicycle."

Kennedy replied indirectly in a Los Angeles speech, referring to those "voices of extremism" who "look suspiciously at their neighbors and their leaders. They call for a 'man on horseback' because they do not trust the people . . . they object quite rightly to politics intruding on the military— but they are very anxious for the military to engage in their kind of politics . . ."

MAN ON THE WEDDING CAKE characterization of Republican presidential candidate Thomas E. Dewey in 1944.

Coinage is in vociferous dispute. In the first edition of this book, the author tentatively wrote: "Though columnist Walter Winchell was often credited with the coinage . . . Harold Ickes, FDR's Secretary of the Interior, was possibly the author."

Winchell promptly took issue: "From page 250 of a new book about the new language of politics: ' "Man on the wedding cake" (a characterization of Republican candidate Thomas E. Dewey in 1944) was often credited to Walter Winchell, but Harold Ickes, FDR's Secretary of the Interior, was possibly the author.' But Mr. Ickes wasn't. Alice Longworth and many others were credited with its coinage. 'Dewey, the Little Man On The Wedding Cake' was auth'd by 'Paul Revere, II' in *P.M.*, a New York pro-Democrat newspaper. . . . Mr. Paul Revere, II was not the name-de-ploom of Harold Ickes, but of WW, then under contract to the *New York Mirror*, which was pro-Dewey. (Catch on?)"

Columnist Leonard Lyons took a different position: "The fact is Ethel Barrymore created the line. I printed the story November 3, 1944, quoting Mrs. Longworth: 'Ethel Barrymore said that, and she's mad as hell because I've been getting credit for it.' "

Since Mrs. Alice Roosevelt Longworth, daughter of Theodore Roosevelt and grande dame of Washington society, is obviously a central figure in the case, the author sent her a query, and received this reply:

"Thanks for your letter. I did *not* coin the phrase 'little man on the wedding cake'. The first time I heard it Mrs. Flandrau remarked 'Dewey looks like the bridegroom on the wedding cake.' I thought it frightfully funny and quoted it to everyone. Then it began to be attributed to me. To everyone who asked if I originated it, I said no and told just what I have written here, though I did admit that 'I gave it currency.' "

Thus, it can be stated with some assurance that the phrase was coined in 1944 by either Walter Winchell, Ethel Barrymore or author Grace Hodgson Flandrau, probably not Harold Ickes, and was given currency by Mrs. Longworth. Additional claims will be met with suspicion.

Four years later Mrs. Longworth peppered candidate Dewey with "You can't make a soufflé rise twice," and "You have to know Dewey really well to dislike him thoroughly." (She is also credited with the "weaned on a pickle" characterization of President Coolidge, which she attributed to her doctor in her 1933 autobiography. None of her victims fire back, because she is a distinguished lady, very old and frail, and she can kill you.)

Dewey was short, mustachioed, formal-looking; calling him "the little man on top of the wedding cake" was as inspired as it was cruel. Walter Winchell added insult to this injury with "He's the only man able to walk under a bed without hitting his head."

Dewey was also young for a presidential candidate, which was not implied in the wedding-cake reference; Ickes completed the description when the New York governor formally announced his candidacy by commenting, "Dewey has thrown his diaper in the ring."

MAOISM the militant philosophy of Mao Tse-tung, especially as redefined by the split in the Chinese Communist hierarchy in the mid-sixties.

Probably the best-selling book in the world in 1966 was "the little red book," containing quotations from the speeches and writings of Mao, read as scripture by his followers and brandished at demonstrations.

Traditionally, after the revolutionaries come the pragmatists—men with a zeal to administer rather than overthrow. In China this evolution was interrupted by the desire of the architect of the Communist revolution to recapture its revolutionary, doctrinaire spirit. Mao tried to rekindle the spirit of the generation of the Long March in his Red Guards, young men who formed the cadres that launched the CULTURAL REVOLUTION.

Maoism's book of quotations, like

most scripture, is written to permit widely varying interpretations. "The Maoists," writes Columbia professor Doak Barnett, "can appeal to certain writings which emphasize the need for revolutionary radicalism and self-sacrifice; while the anti-Maoists can stress others, which prescribe pragmatic realism and the need to adapt policy to reality."

Essentially, Maoism teaches "uninterrupted revolution" and the overriding role of the human will in history: "Nothing in the world is difficult for one who sets his mind to it." The indoctrinated revolutionary character of the people is essential. "An army without culture [revolutionary zeal] is a dull-witted army, and a dull-witted army cannot defeat the enemy."

Philosophies or techniques named after statesmen rarely last. Reference is still made to Socratic reasoning and Aristotelian ethics, Jeffersonian democracy and Churchillian prose, but Stalinism, Gaullism, Titoism, and Maoism are likely to fade not long after the deaths of their authors. Marxism-Leninism, however, seems assured of a place in the philosophic lexicon.

MARCH ON WASHINGTON a civil rights rally held in Washington, D.C., in August 1963; the largest demonstration to that date in the city's history.

Its purpose, in the words of its initial proposer, Negro labor leader A. Philip Randolph, was to give voice to "a great moral protest against racial bias."

Mr. Randolph had proposed such a march twenty years earlier to President Franklin D. Roosevelt as a protest against discrimination against Negroes in war industries. The President had used a series of protest meetings in several of the larger American cities as an excuse to issue his Executive Order No. 8802, designed to end such discrimination. That 1943 march never was held.

The Democratic President in the White House in 1963, John F. Kennedy, did not look forward at first to the realization of Mr. Randolph's proposal. One reason for Kennedy's early lack of enthusiasm was his fear that a march, ending at the Capitol as originally intended, would make it appear the Congress was being besieged and thus would have a negative effect on the civil rights bill then being considered.

When the plan was changed to a demonstration around the Lincoln Memorial, the President gave it his public support. In a mid-July news conference he said he understood it would be "a peaceful assembly calling for a redress of grievances" and added, "I think that's in the great tradition." He had no other choice.

There were two basic problems. The march had received so much nationwide publicity that it would seriously jeopardize the civil rights legislation (1) if the number of those attending did not exceed the promised one hundred thousand and (2) if there was any violence.

Both these dangers were overcome. The march, as organized by civil rights leader Bayard Rustin, brought almost a quarter of a million people to the rallying point at the Washington Monument.

When the area around the monument was almost completely filled with people, the demonstrators quietly walked down to the Lincoln Memorial, where several civil rights leaders addressed them. See "I HAVE A DREAM."

At nightfall the demonstrators departed for their home cities. It had been a powerfully moving and peaceful event. President Kennedy said the next day, "This nation can properly be proud."

This nonviolent event was a contrast to the Bonus March of 1932, when the participants rioted and terrified the capital. The *March of Time* film documentaries, and the "March of Dimes" campaign against polio, further popularized the metaphor.

In current use, although a *march* implies military organization and discipline, it has become less "militant" than a *demonstration*. A curious but revealing linguistic attitude toward *demonstration* was shown in a statement made by an FBI agent in a crowd of several hundred lawmen at the arraignment of former FBI officials in April 1978: "This is not a demonstration. This is a show of support."

MARTIN, BARTON AND FISH a campaign catch phrase used with devastating effectiveness by Franklin D. Roosevelt in his campaign for a third term.

Working on a speech for FDR in 1940, Judge Samuel I. Rosenman and dramatist Robert E. Sherwood wanted to mention the Republican party's opposition to moves for preparedness. In the first draft they cited GOP Congressmen Bruce Barton and Hamilton Fish of New York and Joseph Martin of Massachusetts, in that order. Rosenman recalled in *Working With Roosevelt:*

> We sat around—I remember we were writing in my apartment in New York City—working on that paragraph. Then as we read those names, we almost simultaneously hit on the more euphonious and rhythmic sequence of Martin, Barton and Fish. We said nothing about it when we handed the draft to the President,

wondering whether he would catch it as he read the sentence aloud. He did. The very first time he read it, his eyes twinkled; and he grinned from ear to ear. . . . He repeated it several times and indicated by swinging his finger in cadence how effective it would be with audiences.

In his own memoirs, *My First 50 Years in Politics,* Martin notes that the line followed the meter of "Wynken, Blynken and Nod." Though he wrote that "I felt no particular resentment over it," Martin did tell FDR that it was "a bit unfair" to blame the GOP alone for the sad state of U.S. military preparedness. As for the famous phrase, Martin declares that the three men cited had always been good friends. "Roosevelt's attack lent a new bond to our friendship," says Martin. "Afterward, whenever we three would meet one another here and there we used to refer to ourselves as 'members of the firm.' "

MASSIVE RESISTANCE, *see* **TOKENISM.**

MASSIVE RETALIATION national strategy that threatens to meet foreign military challenge with nuclear attack.

Secretary of State John Foster Dulles said in a speech on January 12, 1954, to the Council on Foreign Relations: "Local defense must be reinforced by the further deterrent of massive retaliatory power." Immediately and universally, via microphone and printing press, "massive retaliatory power" changed to "massive retaliation," and American policy had a label.

Actually, there was little new in Dulles' statement. The Eisenhower Administration had been in office for a year when Dulles made the speech and had already begun to de-emphasize "conventional" or nonnuclear strength while stressing the nuclear. Defense Secretary Charles Wilson had already foreclosed post-Korea LIMITED WAR and put the label of "BIGGER BANG FOR A BUCK" on his goal. And five days before Dulles' speech, Eisenhower himself in his State of the Union address had stressed the need for "massive capability to strike back" against any aggression.

Out of the massive retaliation strategy came generations of nuclear bombers and missiles—and seemingly never-ending controversy as well. General Maxwell Taylor, Army Chief of Staff under President Eisenhower, left the service furious that the Army was being reduced and wrote an angry book called *The Uncertain Trumpet,* in which he called massive retaliation a "great fallacy." Other officers, and writers too, chose sides and debated the issue for years.

As soon as the Kennedy Administration took office, General Taylor was recalled from retirement and eventually installed as Chairman of the Joint Chiefs of Staff. Robert McNamara became Defense Secretary. After one week in office McNamara reported: "A strategy of massive nuclear retaliation . . . [is] believed by few of our friends and none of our enemies." Conventional forces were emphasized, and the bywords became "flexible response" and "MEASURED RESPONSE."

The adjective "massive"—as used in "massive aid to the cities"—became a vogue word in the liberal lexicon during the sixties, along with "decent," "obscene," "unacceptable," "root cause," and "human needs."

MAVERICK   one who is unorthodox in his political views and disdain-

ful of party loyalty, who bears no man's brand.

Maverick drifted into the political vocabulary around the turn of the century; *McClure's* magazine mentioned the occasional appearance of a "maverick legislator." The simplicity and aptness of the metaphor made it both durable and universally understood.

This is an eponymous word, taken —like "boycott" and "bloomer," "cardigan" and "sandwich"—from a person's name. Samuel Maverick, son of an Anglican minister in England, settled in Massachusetts about 1624. Contrary to some reports, he does not seem to have been an "eccentric innkeeper," but a man noted for his hospitality; later an inn, Maverick House in Boston, was named after him and became a well-known political hangout.

His direct descendant, Samuel Augustus Maverick, established himself as a Texas rancher in the mid-1800s (see F. C. Chabot, *With the Makers of San Antonio,* San Antonio, 1937). This Maverick became known for his unbranded calves.

J. David Stern, author of *Maverick Publisher,* advises the author of one theory behind this practice: "Old man Maverick, Texas cattleman of the 1840s, refused to brand his cattle because it was cruelty to animals. His neighbors said he was a hypocrite, liar, and thief, because Maverick's policy allowed him to claim all unbranded cattle on the range. Lawsuits were followed by bloody battles, and brought a new word to our language."

Theodore Roosevelt wrote in 1887 for the edification of Eastern tenderfeet: "Unbranded animals are called mavericks, and when found on the round-up are either branded by the owner of the range . . . or else are sold for the benefit of the association."

Ten years later TR was back in New York himself, winning his reputation as a maverick on the political range. When Cousin Franklin ran for Vice President in 1920 on the Democratic ticket, TR's son, Theodore Jr., was tapped by the Republicans to dispel the idea that FDR was son or political heir to the recently deceased former President. "He's a maverick," said young Theodore about FDR. "He doesn't have the brand of our family."

Despite this pejorative use, independence—and hence maverick's status—has traditionally been considered something of a virtue, especially at election time. Many of the nation's most successful politicians, going back to Andrew Jackson, were mavericks at some stage. Russell Baker wrote Estes Kefauver's epitaph: "From Harry Truman in the White House down through the bull-roasting-and-clambake crowd, the party professionals despised him. He was a maverick." In American politics, one who wins many enemies among the pros often wins many friends among the more numerous laymen; thus it is often more difficult for a maverick to get nominated than elected.

See LONER; MUGWUMP.

MAYORALTY, *see* HIZZONER; DEAD END.

MCCARTHYISM
the approach with which the late Senator Joseph R. McCarthy won fame as a Communist-hunter, now applied to any investigation that flouts the rights of individuals in pursuit of its ends.

McCarthy burst into prominence after a speech in Wheeling, W.V., on February 9, 1950. "While I cannot take the time to name all of the men in the State Department who have been named as members of the Communist Party and members of a spy ring," he said then, "I have here in my hand a list of 205 that were known to the Secretary of State as being members of the Communist Party and who nevertheless are still working and shaping the policy of the State Department."

Over the next four years the free-swinging charges, the well-timed announcements and press releases that caught newspapers right on deadline, the McCarthy manner during hearings (see POINT OF ORDER) became familiar. His many supporters felt that he succeeded in alerting the nation to the danger of internal subversion.

Probably the first to use the term "McCarthyism" was *Washington Post* cartoonist Herblock (Herbert Block), who, in 1950, showed the word crudely lettered on a barrel of mud that rested precariously on a tower made up of buckets of mud. Said Harry Truman: "A powerful group of men in the Republican Party is now determined to rise to power through a method of conduct as hostile to American ideals as anything we have ever seen. This method has come to be known as McCarthyism."

In *The Fourth Branch of Government,* Douglass Cater noted that "McCarthyism's greatest threat was not to individual liberty or even to the orderly conduct of government. It corrupted the power to communicate, which is indispensable to men living in a civilized society."

McCarthy, a Republican, was a particularly painful problem for the first Republican Administration in twenty years. When a White House aide drafted a strong anti-McCarthy statement, President Eisenhower rejected it, saying, "I will not get in the gutter with *that* guy." The President made it clear, nonetheless, how he felt about the senator's tactics. "McCarthyism," he wrote in his memoirs, "took its toll on many individuals and on the nation. No one was safe from charges recklessly made from inside the walls of Congressional immunity. Teachers, government employees, and even ministers became vulnerable . . . The cost was often tragic."

When McCarthy attacked the Protestant clergy and the U.S. Army early in 1954, Eisenhower abandoned some of his restraint. He denounced him as one who tried "to set himself above the laws of our land" and "to override orders of the President." On December 2, 1954, the Senate condemned McCarthy. The word "censure," for some reason, was avoided. His power faded quickly thereafter; he died in 1957.

The issue of McCarthyism plagued John F. Kennedy during his 1960 campaign for the presidency. As a senatorial candidate in 1952, Kennedy had gone out of his way to avoid antagonizing McCarthy. "Hell," he later explained to historian Arthur Schlesinger, Jr., "half my voters in Massachusetts look on McCarthy as a hero." McCarthy did not enter Massachusetts to campaign against Kennedy, and as columnist Emmet John Hughes wrote, if JFK's "view of Joe McCarthy had been publicly and candidly more critical, at a time when such courage counted, he almost certainly would not have reached the White House in 1960."

In the 1968 primary campaign, liberal Democratic Senator Eugene McCarthy of Minnesota labeled the attacks on his patriotism by President Johnson's supporters as "McCarthyism."

The original meaning of the word —of misuse of information by a congressional committee—was echoed in 1976, when a suppressed report by the House Select Intelligence Committee chaired by Otis Pike (D-N.Y.) was printed in the *Village Voice,* including this line: "On September 24, 1975 . . . the Deputy Secretary of State raised for the first time an innuendo that the Committee's action [demanding Executive documents] resembled McCarthyism."

See PHILIPPIC; JUNKETEERING GUMSHOES; CHARACTER ASSASSIN; PROFILES IN COURAGE.

MEANWHILE, BACK AT THE RANCH a Western movie and radio cliché *(The Lone Ranger)* used to refer to Temporary White House activities at the LBJ Ranch near Johnson City, Texas.

An economic report by Goldman, Sachs & Co. analyzed a tax-increase decision and concluded with a paragraph titled "Meanwhile, Down at the Ranch" to show what was under consideration by the President.

Western metaphors were common with Johnson: the "LBJ Brand" of leadership "lassos votes" and "corrals support" for key measures before the Congress. An alternate to "the ranch" is "the Pedernales," pronounced "Purd'nalis," a Texas river flowing through the LBJ Ranch. Columnist Russell Baker observed that anyone who knew and used the word Pedernales had "an inner grasp of the Great Society." See COONSKIN ON THE WALL.

MEASURED RESPONSE the exercise of restraint in response to provocation or even attack, especially in the military sense.

The phrase was frequently used by President Lyndon Johnson, along with the wish for "no wider war," to describe a stepping up of military activity, carrying the implication that the new action was the result of provocation and was carefully controlled.

These were measures short of total war, a step beyond—but similar in tone—to Franklin Roosevelt's 1939 phrase to help allies of the U.S.: "There are many *methods short of war,* but stronger and more effective than mere words, of bringing home to aggressor governments the aggregate sentiments of our own people." The phrase was promptly misquoted as "measures short of war," and is so remembered.

A generation later the measures short of war became measures of war short of annihilation, spawning *measured* response and its cousins, *controlled, flexible,* and *selective* response. See PENTAGONESE.

These were devised as a military philosophy of the nuclear age, describing a response to an act of aggression against this country which will demonstrate the nation's preparedness to react to such an act with a positive counterstroke but will also signal clearly that peace is desired rather than "all-out" war.

"The rhetoric of restraint," as former presidential aide McGeorge Bundy called it, has not always been the prevailing tone of American politics. Still, whether domestic or international matters are involved, it has always had its advocates. Daniel Webster put it this way: "Liberty exists in proportion to wholesome restraint." See LIMITED WAR.

MEASURES, NOT MEN an alternative phrase for GOVERNMENT OF LAWS, NOT OF MEN and RULE OF LAW.

The inbuilt distrust of rulers and the desire to see rights guaranteed in writing underlies the concept of "measures, not men," a phrase coined by Philip Stanhope, Earl of Chesterfield, in a March 6, 1742, letter. Picked up by Oliver Goldsmith ("Measures, not men, has always been my mark") and later by Edmund Burke, it was attacked by George Canning (later a Prime Minister) in the House of Commons in 1801: "Away with the cant of 'Measures, not men!'—the idle supposition that it is the harness and not the horses that draw the chariot along. If the comparison must be made, if the distinction must be taken, men are everything, measures comparatively nothing."

Canning, who had the courage to blast the fine-sounding phrase, was associated with it not as its denouncer, but as its author; the *New York World* of September 18, 1874, warned: "There is danger in the blind following of Canning's maxim, 'Measures, not men.' " Obviously, there is danger in a politician's head-on attack of a favorite phrase.

In modern times the idea is best remembered in the form given it by John Adams in his preamble to the Massachusetts Constitution in 1778: "In the government of the Commonwealth of Massachusetts the legislature, executive, and judicial power shall be placed in separate departments, to the end that it might be a GOVERNMENT OF LAWS, NOT OF MEN."

MEDIA a slightly sinister or clinical word for "the press," often intended to carry a manipulative or mechanical connotation.

As Dwight Eisenhower discovered in the roar of approval that followed his 1964 comment about "sensation-seeking columnists and commentators," considerable public sentiment is directed against the press. That latent hostility was dramatized by the reaction to a speech objecting to "instant analysis" and other presumed press sins by Vice President Spiro Agnew in Des Moines in 1970.

In the nineteenth century, "mediae" was a term in phonetics to describe an intermediate sound between the tenues and the aspirates, and in biology for a middle membrane of an artery. Of course, it is the plural of "medium," and the first famous use of that word in the sense of communications was by Lord Francis Bacon in 1605: "But yet is not of necessitie that Cognitions bee expressed by the Medium of Wordes." Another sense, that of an intervening substance, was used by Burton in his *Anatomy of Melancholy* (1621): "To the Sight three things are required, the Object, the Organ and the Medium."

"Mass medium" came into the language, according to the latest *OED Supplement,* in a 1923 article by S. M. Fechheimer in N. T. Praigg's *Advertising & Selling,* where he also used the plural: "Class appeal in mass media." In 1927 *American Speech* "finally decided to allot a definite media to each member," and in 1929 E. O. Hughes wrote in an advertising magazine: "The advertising media to which reference will be made . . . are newspapers, journals, magazines and such-like printed publications."

J. S. Huxley took a benign view of the emerging word and industry in 1946: "The media of mass communication—the somewhat cumbrous title (commonly abbreviated to 'Mass Media') proposed for agencies, such as the radio, the cinema and the popular press, which are capable of the mass dissemination of word or image. . . . The use of the mass media to foster education, science and culture . . . Regarded from this angle, the mass media fall into the same general category as the libraries and museums —that of servicing agencies for man's higher activities."

Political advertising had much to do with the change in attitude toward the word from a neutral conveyor of information to a manipulator of minds. As television and its use rose in importance in politics, so did the "media adviser" (see SELLING CANDIDATES LIKE SOAP). In the sixties, concern for the changing of opinion by television spot increased with its effectiveness, and "media manipulation" became worrisome.

Around 1970 the phrase "news media" began to gain in frequency of use, which married the fear of advertising with some doubts about the credibility of the purveyors of information. This was exploited by those who believed that too much power was concentrated in "an unelected elite" from too few news organizations.

The press itself extended the use of the word, dividing into "electronic media" and "print media," discussing "media campaigns," "media event" (for PSEUDO-EVENT), and "media hype" (for too much promotion and attention). In May 1973 the *New York Times* "Winners and Sinners" sheet sent to editorial employees complained: "Media . . . there is no need to overwork the word, which we and everybody else have been doing. Twice in one sentence is a little too much: 'It would appear counterproductive for the Administration to continue to attack the media at a time when it has, in effect, accepted media accounts of the Watergate case' (April 24). Try words like 'journalism,' 'the press,' 'broadcasting,' 'news accounts,' 'newspapers.' "

The word is plural, like data, and takes a plural verb. "Media" is a word, but the media are thousands of newspapers, television stations, underground printing presses and the mimeograph machine, eagerly covering the words of political leaders blasting "the media."

MEDIA ADVISER, *see* **KING-MAKER.**

MEDIA EVENT an occasion so stage-managed for wide coverage that the coverage becomes more important than the occasion.

For the background to this phrase, see PSEUDO-EVENT. "Pseudo" has been replaced by "media," but the word "media" has acquired the phoniness of "pseudo." People who are concerned about the manipulation of public opinion, including many in the press (a more likable term for news media), tend to derogate any occasion that appears to be arranged for maximum publicity.

A second meaning of "media event" is an occasion that is important not in itself, but in how the media interprets it. On January 30, 1976, the night Jimmy Carter's victory in the Iowa presidential caucus, CBS News correspondent Roger Mudd told anchorman Walter Cronkite: "The English [meaning "twist"] that is applied to these results is going to be applied by the media and the politicians themselves. It's not exactly the precise figures that will be important, it's whether the media and the politicians agree that this man won and this man lost."

Joseph Lelyveld of the *New York Times,* who was covering the coverage, wrote: "That was a working definition of a 'media event': an occasion on which the discussion overwhelms and finally obscures the fragile reality that gives rise to it."

That is the sophisticated definition; most references are rooted in "pseudo-event," or touting of an unimpor-

tant story. When Carter Attorney General Griffin Bell held a much-heralded briefing of congressmen about the Justice Department's investigation into payoffs by South Korean businessman Tongsun Park, Representative Patricia Schroeder (D-Colo.) said, "This was a big P.R. media event. I feel gypped. I feel like a co-conspirator in a cover-up."

Investing a minor occurrence with false importance is called "hype," or "media hype," from the euphoric kick one gets from an injection of a narcotic with a hypodermic needle.

MEDICARE a government program of health insurance for the elderly.

The creation of this word shows how bureaucracy crumbles before a mighty coinage. It is worth a detailed examination.

In his "economic bill of rights," FDR had called for "the right to adequate medical care and the opportunity to achieve and enjoy good health." In 1945 the Wagner-Murray-Dingell bill providing compulsory health insurance was proposed; this, along with some other Truman health proposals, was attacked as "socialized medicine" and defeated.

The word "medicare" cropped up in early 1956. It was the name applied to the Dependents Medical Care Program of the Department of Defense, probably used first by Jerry Gross, editor of the *Washington Report on Medical Sciences.* The original program called for medical care of dependents of armed services personnel.

But the word outgrew this narrow use in the mid-fifties. Defense Department officials were troubled by the term, which newspapers began to apply both to plans for general medical care and for assistance to the elderly, then being discussed as part of the Social Security program. Dr. Frank Berry, senior medical adviser to the Assistant Secretary of Defense for Manpower, wrote to Abraham Ribicoff, President Kennedy's first Secretary of Health, Education and Welfare, about the confusing overlap in the use of the term. On April 27, 1961, Secretary Ribicoff made one of the most short-lived semantic stands of the decade: "This will acknowledge your letter of April 7 concerning the use of the term 'Medicare.' I am sure that we have no intention of using this term in connection with any present or planned programs to be administered by this Department." (Compare this with Churchill's resistance to IN-FRASTRUCTURE.)

The scene shifts from Defense to HEW. Wallace Kendall, an information officer, unforms the author:

In 1964 and early 1965, we in social security were trying as hard as we could to discourage use of the term "medicare" in connection with the limited program of hospital insurance for older people which was under consideration in Congress. HR-1 and earlier Administration bills would have provided only hospital insurance, not medical insurance, and for this reason we thought "medicare" would be a misleading term.

After the medical insurance part was added in Congress and Public Law 89–97 was passed, the law had been called "the medicare law" in so many newspaper articles and radio-TV broadcasts that it was impossible for us to avoid using it. We were still reluctant; we used it in an appositive way for some weeks: 'the program of health insurance for the aged, often called "medicare." ' Then we were urged by many people to go ahead and use the term in a more forthright way. At this point, I called Colonel McKenzie to find out

whether or not the Department of Defense would object . . .

Kendall, with a good sense of history, kept a record of his August 12, 1965, conversation with Lieutenant Colonel Vernon McKenzie, assistant for special projects and new programs (health and medical) in the office of the Assistant Secretary of Defense, which McKenzie has seen and corroborates:

Col. McKenzie said that he personally stopped using the term "Medicare" in connection with the programs of the Dept. of Defense about two years ago. He said that the term had never been entirely satisfactory in the Dept. of Defense because of the confusion about what it meant.

When the term was first introduced the Dept. of Defense intended to use it as a specific and meaningful term and they went so far as to register use of the term with the copyright office in the Library of Congress. Col. McKenzie told me that this gave them no legal rights to use of the term; it simply established the fact that they were using it in a certain sense at a certain time. Several private insurance companies later tried using the term, and in at least one case the Dept. of Defense wrote to the company and pointed out that the term was a registered one with a specific meaning within the Dept. of Defense. I gather that the companies stopped selling "Medicare" policies after receiving these letters from the Dept.

After a while, however, Col. McKenzie and other officers in the Dept. of Defense began to realize that the term was causing confusion instead of clearing it up. Some people used it to mean the entire program of medical care within the Dept. of Defense both for active duty military personnel and their dependents and retired people. Others used it to refer to all kinds of medical care for the dependents of people on active duty. A third group used it to mean only the care of dependents in civilian hospitals.

These confusing factors, plus the increasing use of the term "Medicare" not only by reporters and radio and television news people, but also by Members of Congress and by Presidents—these factors all combined to cause Col. McKenzie to stop using the term "Medicare" in his own work about two years ago.

In passing he observed that it seemed to him that the term "Eldercare" would have been a much more accurate term for the social security bill as it finally passed the House. He had also thought about the term "Fedicare" but he said that there was a certain logic of events that seems to be requiring the Social Security Administration to use the term "Medicare" for the bill now under consideration.

Col. McKenzie said that he has never done anything official about halting the use of the term "Medicare" in the Dept. of Defense but he will now give some thought to the idea of recommending that the military bow out and not use the term any further in order to clear the way for its use by the Social Security Administration.

A question arises: Who in the Department of Defense had the foresight to register the use of the word with the copyright office?

Paul I. Robinson, M.D., was the major general in charge of the Dependents Medical Care Program from 1956 to 1958 and was later chief medical director of the Metropolitan Life Insurance Company. He credits the late Jerry Gross with the word's coinage, and points out that Gross's further sponsorship of "eldercare" was more descriptive. As to the decision to protect the use of the word legally, he recalls: "Soon after the word began being used early in 1956, I received a call from a man who was making a patent medicine for acne, which he called 'Medicare.' He told me to tell the Defense department to cut it out. I called the Judge Advocate General to tell him of this, and he said not to worry about it." Immediately afterward, the government copyrighted its use of the name.

State governments adopted such versions as *medicaid* and *medi-Cal,* and a tax-credit plan is *medicredit.* In the sixties, *medi-* was almost as popular a prefix as *mini-,* but in the seventies, the less colorful "health insurance" signified the declining political appeal of the subject.

MEGO rhetorical soporific; the acronym for "My Eyes Glaze Over."

This useful term is newsmagazine lingo. Like "violin piece" and TICK-TOCK, it was introduced to the author in 1969 by Mel Elfin, Washington bureau chief of *Newsweek.* "A MEGO is something that is both undeniably important and paralyzingly dull," Elfin reports. "Latin American policy is a MEGO. Petrodollars is a MEGO. I'm falling asleep explaining this to you."

MELTING POT the process by which immigrants become Americanized; a nation that assimilates all nationalities and cultures.

The phrase originated in *The Melting Pot,* a turn-of-the-century play by Israel Zangwill, and was quickly accepted as expressing a sense of pride in America's tradition of immigration, alongside Emma Lazarus' poem beginning "Give me your tired, your poor . . ." A predecessor phrase was "Asylum of the Oppressed of Every Nation," from the 1856 Democratic platform.

However, the big-city politician who takes the phrase seriously is soon disabused. Nathan Glazer and Daniel

P. Moynihan pointed out in their study of ethnic patterns in New York City, *Beyond the Melting Pot,* that the Italian, Irish, Jewish, Negro, and Puerto Rican communities of New York are more separate than similar. Ticket-balancing and ethnic appeals are still important to the big-city vote-getter. "New York City is not a melting pot," Thomas E. Dewey told reporter John Gunther in 1947, "it's a boiling pot."

Least assimilated, of course, is the nonwhite American. Political leaders in recent years have exhorted all Americans to apply the melting-pot principle to blacks; John F. Kennedy, in a 1963 civil rights message, called the denial of equal access to public accommodations "a daily insult which has no place in a country proud of its heritage—the heritage of the melting pot, of equal rights, of one nation and one people."

According to the melting-pot theory, immigrants would become Americanized and assimilated. The existence of persistent patterns of social, cultural, and educational life within large cities shows that this theory did not materialize. A more realistic approach, called "cultural pluralism," is now current, treating the American system more as a salad bowl than a melting pot. "If the 'melting pot' had completed its work," wrote Henry Fairlie in 1974, "there would be no 'ethnics.'"

See ETHNICS.

MENDING FENCES, *see* **FENCE-MENDING.**

MEN OF THOUGHT   livers of the life of the mind; frequently contrasted with "men of action."

The phrase "men of thought and men of action" was popularized by Woodrow Wilson, but the concept of the tension between the two types has a long history. British essayist William Hazlitt, in an essay "On Thought and Action," observed: "Thought depends on the habitual exercise of the speculative facilities; action, on the determination of the will. The one assigns reasons for things, the other puts causes to act." Personally, he disclaimed the ability to act: "I . . . had rather write one of these Essays than have to seal a letter."

Historian Thomas Babington Macaulay, noting the criticism of men of action, explained: "A politician must often talk and act before he has thought and read. He may be very ill-informed respecting a question . . . but speak he must; and if he is a man of talents, tact, and intrepidity, he soon finds that, even under such circumstances, it is possible to speak successfully." Thomas Carlyle was another man of thought who admired action: "The end of man is an action, and not a thought, though it were the noblest."

Although John Galsworthy held that "a man of action, forced into a state of thought, is unhappy until he can get out of it," Theodore Roosevelt, a man with credentials in both areas, disagreed: "Power undirected by high purpose spells calamity; and high purpose by itself is utterly useless if the power to put it into effect is lacking." Men of action also describe men of thought with the same respect. Argentine dictator Juan Perón said in 1950: "The Peronist movement needs men of action, but it also requires preachers of the doctrine."

John F. Kennedy, early in 1960, hoped "to reopen the channels of communication between the world of thought and the seat of power," and did much to activate thinkers. Richard Nixon, in a 1966 speech on academic freedom, pointed out that

"Woodrow Wilson's distinction between men of thought and men of action can no longer be made. The man of thought who will not act is ineffective; the man of action who will not think is dangerous."

For praise of dreamers, see MOVERS AND SHAKERS; for derogation of intellectuals, see EGGHEAD.

MEN'S ROOM OF THE KREMLIN, *see* SALT (LEXICON).

MENTOR, *see* RABBI.

MERCHANTS OF DEATH armament manufacturers; more recently, sellers of firearms by mail or over the counter to minors or incompetents.

The phrase comes from the title of a 1934 book by H. C. Engelbrecht and F. C. Hanighan, one of many exposés in the twenties and thirties attempting to prove that the causes of war were economic.

Businessmen have often been suspected of being "profiteers," a word based on the "privateers," free-lance pirates in the service of a nation but not officially part of its navy. Thomas Jefferson observed in a letter in 1814 that "merchants have no country." The German House of Krupp was most commonly identified as the "merchants of death." The "captains of industry" celebrated by Thomas Carlyle became the MALEFACTORS OF GREAT WEALTH of Theodore Roosevelt and the ECONOMIC ROYALISTS denounced by Franklin Roosevelt.

Interventionists have often been accused of economic motives. Vermont ("the Granite State") Senator Redfield Proctor, after the sinking of the battleship *Maine,* made a speech supporting President McKinley's policy of disputing Cuba with Spain.

Speaker Thomas B. Reed dismissed the marble king's remarks with: "A war will make a large market for gravestones."

One Swedish explosives manufacturer was particularly sensitive to characterizations that later became phrased as "merchant of death." Alfred B. Nobel, who invented dynamite by combining nitroglycerine with more stable elements, established a will that made his name synonymous with peace rather than death.

After the Kennedy assassination in 1963, attempts were made to limit the sale of firearms through the mail, which was Lee Harvey Oswald's method of purchase of a gun. The efforts were resisted by the National Rifle Association, quoting the Constitution: ". . . the right to bear arms shall not be abridged." A new use of "merchants of death" sprang up to describe sellers of guns to incompetents, minors, and those likely to participate in race riots. Editorialized the *New York Times* in July 1967: "In community after community, more and more Negroes and whites alike take advantage of the nation's insanely lax laws on firearms and buy rifles, pistols and other weapons. Imaginative merchants of death help the process along by advertising 'long hot summer specials' as a means of boosting their sales."

MESS IN WASHINGTON specifically the 1952 Republican campaign characterization of the state of affairs; generally, the way the "Outs," of whatever party, always see conditions in the capital under the "Ins."

"It was the 'mess in Washington,' that, more than any other single factor, caused President Truman's image to fade as his term drew to a close," wrote Cabell Phillips in *The Truman*

Presidency. There was, he added, a "climate in which a handful of cheats, frauds and simple fourflushers in the government managed to spray the tint of corruption across his second Administration," and by 1952 Truman's popularity was down to 26 percent in public opinion polls.

General Harry H. Vaughan, the President's friend and military aide, became the focus of the charges. A Senate investigating subcommittee reported that FIVE PERCENTERS who hung around the Defense Department, the War Assets Administration, and the Reconstruction Finance Corporation relied on Vaughan's friendship to steer contracts and projects their way. Though the subcommittee found no evidence of direct payoffs, it noted that Vaughan became the channel for some generous contributions to the Democratic party and himself received a deep-freeze from the grateful client of a friend. The deep-freeze (see INFLU-ENCE PEDDLER) came to symbolize the "mess."

Talk of a "mess" irked Truman. In his memoirs he noted that Adlai Stevenson, campaigning in Oregon in 1952 under the Democratic banner, said he would clean up "the mess in Washington." Wrote Truman: "I wondered if he had been taken in by the Republican fraudulent build-up of flyspecks on our Washington windows into a big blot or 'mess.' For several years the Republican opposition had tried to make a case against the Administration, only to find that the Administration was always alert in rooting out corruption or bad practices wherever they existed."

Though Dwight Eisenhower's speechwriter, Emmet John Hughes, said that he wanted to shun the mess phrase as "petty, self-righteous and extravagant," other advisers urged

him to use it. He did. As Eisenhower wrote in his memoirs, the furor over Richard Nixon's campaign fund in 1952 was especially welcome to the Democrats "because of the emphasis we had been putting on the 'mess in Washington' . . . so much evidence of woeful negligence and apparent crookedness had turned up . . . that I had again and again talked about the need for an Administration that would renew Americans' faith in the government."

As a phrase, "the mess" is no newcomer to Washington: when Theodore Roosevelt was being urged to seek the presidency again in 1912, he resisted at first, saying, "I'm not in the running and I'm not going to be dragged into it. Taft created the mess and let Taft take his spanking for it."

ME TOO a general lack of originality; specifically applied by conservatives to Republicans who stand on liberal platforms.

The phrase first became current when Thomas C. Platt of New York resigned as senator in 1881, following the lead set by his colleague, Senator Roscoe Conkling, after a dispute with President Garfield over patronage appointments in the Empire State. A cartoon of the day showed Platt as a small boy sticking out of Conkling's pocket, with a card labeled "Me, too!" tied to one of his hands.

With the New Deal well launched by 1936, Franklin Roosevelt began ridiculing Republicans for "me too" speeches in which they endorsed his goals but attacked his methods. During his campaign for a second term, he said:

> Let me warn you and let me warn the nation against the smooth evasion which says—of course we believe all these things; we believe in social security; we believe in work

for the unemployed; we believe in saving homes. Cross our hearts and hope to die, we believe in all these things; but we do not like the way the present Administration is doing them. Just turn them over to us. We will do all of them—we will do more of them—we will do them better; and, most important of all, the doing of them will not cost anybody any-thing.

In 1940 the *New York Daily News* sneeringly referred to the GOP candidate for President as "Me Too" Willkie, complaining: "Instead of a knockdown and drag-out political fight, this is getting to be a LOVE FEAST." As Socialist Norman Thomas said of Wendell Willkie: "He agreed with Roosevelt's entire program of social reform—and said it was leading to disaster."

The "me too" label has been pinned on liberal Republicans ever since. In 1948, after New York's Governor Thomas E. Dewey won the presidential nomination, the *Chicago Tribune* protested: "For the third time, a Republican convention fell under vicious influences and nominated a 'me-too' candidate who conducted a 'me-too' campaign." Harry Truman had some fun with the theme. Referring to Dewey's promises, during a Pittsburgh speech on October 23, 1948, he noted: "The candidate says, 'Me, too.' But the Republican record still says, 'We're against it.' These two phrases, 'me, too' and 'we're against it,' sum up the whole Republican campaign."

Adlai Stevenson, campaigning in Denver in September 1952, echoed Truman's earlier speech: "The Republican candidates seem to have clasped all of the social gains of the past 20 years to their bosoms with a 'me-too' fervor that is touching to a Democrat, for imitation still remains the sincerest form of flattery."

Defending liberal Republicans pinned with the "me too" label, Dewey noted during a 1950 series of lectures at Princeton: "There are some loud voices in the Republican Party denouncing all the platforms and nominees with the epithet 'me too.' The complaint and the epithet largely originated with those who hold isolationist or extremely conservative views, or both. As for myself, and I believe most of the members of the Republican Party, we refuse to be against the Ten Commandments just because the Democrats say they are for them."

Significantly, Barry Goldwater, the least "me-tooish" GOP candidate in a generation, campaigned in 1964 on the slogan "A CHOICE—NOT AN ECHO," and suffered one of the worst drubbings in the party's history.

See ROAD TO DEFEAT; BIG TENT.

METROAMERICAN, *see* **MIDDLE AMERICA.**

MICKEY MOUSE, *see* **HUMPTY DUMPTY.**

MIDDLE AMERICA   the payers of most of the taxes, the holders of most of the values, the electors of most of the candidates.

Columnist Joseph Kraft coined the term in a piece on June 23, 1968: "For two years before that," he informs the author, "I had been beating around the term, talking about ordinary Americans, middle-class Americans, Americans who were not young or poor or black and that kind of thing. My focus on that group was stimulated in 1967 by a Labor Department study of living costs for people in the $7,000 to $10,000 income bracket in the major cities. It showed that their requirements were outrunning their earnings and I was struck by the fact and have been writing about it ever since."

Time magazine named Mr. and Mrs. Middle America the Man and Woman of the Year at the end of 1969: "Above all, Middle America is a state of mind, a morality, a construction of values and prejudices and a complex of fears. The Man and Woman of the Year represent a vast, unorganized fraternity bound together by a roughly similar way of seeing things."

With this news peg, Kraft returned to the subject: ". . . the Middle Americans are the chief beneficiaries of the past decade of unbroken prosperity—the great mass of some 40 million persons who have recently moved from just above the poverty line to just below the level of affluence. . . . Middle Americans have switched from renting to owning their homes, from public to private transportation, from beer to whisky. No longer is the emphasis on economic security. Middle Americans now want ease of life. . . . Upper America, in countless ways, is always sticking its finger in the eye of Middle America. The universities revered by Upper Americans have been the source of a cultural revolution combining an assault on the Army and police, which Middle Americans regard as essential to discipline, with a mockery of the kept hair, tidy clothes, and harmonious music which Middle Americans identify with decency. . . . But this is not to say that Middle America is right. On the contrary, on almost all the major issues—on attitudes towards blacks and browns, on school decentralization, on humanizing the police, on keeping federal tax as high, to say nothing of foreign and defense and economic policies—Upper America is right. The present requirement, accordingly, is not to abandon enlight-

ened conviction. It is to gear for survival in difficult times . . ."

A variety of phrases have been coined in recent years to replace JOHN Q. PUBLIC and are used interchangeably. However, there are some nuances of difference:

"Un-young, un-poor, and un-black" is a *statistical* concept, according to Richard Scammon, who used it in response to a question in early 1968. Someone who is none of the three is not necessarily conservative; as Scammon puts it, a left-winger who commands high legal fees and is fifty or so is neither poor, young, nor black.

Middle America is primarily an *economic* concept, as Kraft uses it, showing the conflict between the middle class and the classes above and below, though the phrase is sometimes used to mean a state of mind.

The SILENT MAJORITY is a *social* concept, referring to those who uphold traditional morality, and who resent the attention given by the media to the demonstrators and noisemakers.

The Real Majority, title of a book by Scammon and Ben Wattenberg, and *The Emerging Republican Majority,* title of a book by Kevin Phillips, are *political* concepts—the former a brief for political centrism, the latter a brief for conservatism.

The FORGOTTEN MAN is the predecessor phrase for Silent Majority, and is interchangeable with it; an antonym for both, coined by historian Eric Goldman in 1969, is Metroamerican, who is youthful, wealthy, educated, public-spirited, ambivalent, and, as the coiner puts it, "liberal but without ideology . . . flexible, pragmatic, and a devotee of the ironic edge."

The GREAT UNWASHED has fallen into disuse, despite the fact that television sets outnumber bathtubs in America.

MIDDLE OF THE ROAD the place where most U.S. national political candidates, Democratic and Republican, take their stand; the land equivalent of the MAINSTREAM.

"The objective of a nominating convention," Henry L. Stoddard wrote in his 1938 book, *It Costs to Be President,* "is not a candidate who is strongest in states certain to be carried by his party, but one who is likely to be the strongest in those states in which party prospects are weakest— in other words, a middle-of-the-road man."

At the turn of the century the term characterized Populists who opposed joining the Democratic party. An 1892 Populist campaign song went:

Side tracks are rough, and they're hard to walk,
Keep in the middle of the road:
Though we haven't got time to stop and talk,
We keep in the middle of the road.

To some, though, it seemed a barren place. "I am a middle-of-the-road man," said Populist James Baird Weaver in 1894, "but I don't propose to lie down across it so no one can get over me. Nothing grows in the middle of the road."

German politician August Bebel, speaking to a congress of the German Social-Democratic party in Dresden in 1903, echoed the theme: "The field of politics always presents the same struggle. There are the Right and the Left, and in the middle is the Swamp. The Swamp is made up of the know-nothings, of them who are without ideas, of them who are always with the majority."

Robert Frost, the poet, took note of Dwight Eisenhower's characteriza-tion of his government as middle-of-the-road and snorted: "The middle of the road is where the white line is— and that's the worst place to drive."

Nonetheless, a U.S. President who departs from the middle will find himself in dangerous territory. "Missouri friends represented Mr. Truman as a 'middle-of-the-road' man on all current political and economic issues," complained *New York Times* columnist Arthur Krock in September 1945, "but the 'middle of the road' was way off to one side."

Eisenhower firmly planted his feet in the middle in a 1949 Labor Day speech in St. Louis. "The path to America's future," he said, "lies down the middle of the road between the unfettered power of concentrated wealth . . . and the unbridled power of statism or partisan interests." After his inauguration in 1953, he was advised to stay right there by former President Herbert Hoover. "All you can do is to try to turn away gradually from the path leading to paternalism until it takes a central course, and then stick with it. And both sides will dislike you." Ike took his advice, and declared in his first State of the Union message: "There is, in our affairs at home, a middle way between untrammeled freedom of the individual and the demands for the welfare of the whole nation. This way must avoid government by bureaucracy as carefully as it avoids neglect of the helpless."

He never lost that conviction. In October 1963, three years out of office and irritated at LABELS, he wrote: "I despise all adjectives that try to describe people as liberal or conservative, rightist or leftist, as long as they stay in the useful part of the road." Even more, he added, he despised those who "go to the gutter on either the right or the left, and hurl rocks at those in the center." The next month he noted: "People talk about the middle of the road as though it were unacceptable. Actually, all human problems, excepting morals, come into the gray areas. Things are not all black and white. There have to be compromises. The middle of the road is all of the usable surface. The extremes, right and left, are in the gutters."

See CENTRIST; OPPORTUNIST.

MIDTERM ELECTION, see OFF YEAR.

MILITARY-INDUSTRIAL COMPLEX a combination of forces that, left unchecked, would soon control the U.S. economy and foreign policy.

Dwight Eisenhower, a military man whose best friends were industrialists, startled the nation with his farewell address on January 17, 1961, warning of the danger of military-industrial power. Speechwriters Malcolm Moos and Ralph Williams had drafted the speech for Eisenhower and are credited with having submitted the famous passage: Until World War II, Eisenhower said, the U.S. had no permanent armaments industry.

But . . . we can no longer risk emergency improvisation of national defense. We have been compelled to create a permanent armaments industry of vast proportions. Added to this, three and a half million men and women are directly engaged in the defense establishment. . . . Now this conjunction of an immense military establishment and a large arms industry is new in the American experience. The total influence—economic, political, even spiritual—is felt in every city, every State House, every office of the Federal Government. . . . Our toil, resources and livelihood are all involved; so is the very structure of our society.

In the councils of Government, we must guard against the acquisition of unwarranted influence, whether sought or unsought, by the military-industrial complex. The potential for the disastrous rise of misplaced power exists and will persist.

Asked about this statement at a farewell press conference a few days afterward, he added that he was thinking not so much of a willful abuse of power, but of "an almost insidious penetration of our own minds that the only thing this country is engaged in is weaponry and missiles—and I'll tell you we can't afford that."

Walter Lippmann, who had grown increasingly critical of Eisenhower, called his farewell address "in the great tradition. Washington made the theme of his farewell address a warning against allowing the influence of foreign governments to invade our political life. That was then the menace to the civilian power. Now Eisenhower, speaking from his experience and looking ahead, is concerned with a contemporary threat to the supremacy of the civilian power."

Political scientist Harold Lasswell had coined a term in 1941 on this subject. In *The Garrison State* he warned: "The military men who dominate a modern technical society will be very different from the officers of history and tradition. It is probable that the specialists on violence will include in their training a large degree of expertness in many of the skills that we have traditionally accepted as part of modern civilian management." See WHIZ KIDS.

The concept of restraining the military is at least as old as Cicero, who said in 60 B.C.: "Let the soldier yield to the civilian." Woodrow Wilson, preparing for war, insisted "one thing that this country never will endure is a system that can be called militarism.

. . . Men who are in charge of edged tools and bidden to prepare them for exact and scientific use grow very impatient if they are not permitted to use them . . ."

But the danger pointed out by Eisenhower was more subtle than militarism, or civilian control of the military. He recognized that there was no line of demarcation between "civilian" and "military" in the modern defense establishment, where huge companies depended on defense contracts. These companies, through their economic impact on an area, had political power of their own that contributed to military appropriation decisions, building a vicious circle or "complex."

MILITARY METAPHORS Soon after the opening gun of the CAMPAIGN, the STANDARD-BEARER was denounced as a HATCHETMAN, an OLD FOGY, and a *flash in the pan* by the LEFT WING, and it appeared to DIEHARDS that the old WAR-HORSE'S BOOM was a *lost cause;* but the MAN ON HORSEBACK turned out to be a GOOD SOLDIER, and the TROOPS— from PALACE GUARD to OLD GUARD to the FIFTH COLUMN in the enemy *camp*—closed ranks, ignored the SMOKESCREEN, and did not hesitate to *wave* the BLOODY SHIRT; the CALCULATED RISK of the BANNER DISTRICTS was *saluted* at a victory RALLY, with the SPOILS divided by a TASK-FORCE at campaign headquarters before the new Administration's first HUNDRED DAYS.

Of the military phrases above so often used in politics, the not-so-obvious are "hatchetman" (who cleared the woods for General Washington's troops), "flash in the pan" (a cannon charge that misfires), "spoils" (originally of war), "left wing" (of a military front) "hundred days" (Napoleon's final campaign), and OLD FOGY (from "phogy," seniority pay for officers). The others appear elsewhere under individual entries. Also see FIELD EXPEDIENT; FIGHTING THE PROBLEM; HOLD THE LINE; LOW PROFILE; ON THE POINT.

Military images appear in international diplomacy (arsenal of democracy), and words born in hot and cold wars are used in politics (FIFTH COLUMN, EYEBALL TO EYEBALL); in return, politicians create phrases for warriors (bigger bang for the buck, overkill).

The chaos and waste of a political campaign make metaphors of military campaigns particularly applicable; in a more profound sense, poets like Matthew Arnold apply the metaphor to life in general, as in "Dover Beach":

And here we are as on a darkling plain
Swept with confused alarms of struggle
*   and flight,*
Where ignorant armies clash by night.

In the application of metaphor to politics, only sports (particularly racing) compares to the military. See SPORTS METAPHORS. WAR-GAMING WORDS will direct the reader to those new words created for military-political use, and PENTAGONESE to more current military jargon.

Even SLOGAN comes from a Scottish war cry.

MILK FOR HOTTENTOTS, *see* **HOTTENTOTS, MILK FOR.**

MINISTRY OF ALL THE TALENTS, *see* **HACKS.**

MINK COATS, *see* **INFLUENCE PEDDLER.**

MINORITY euphemism for "nonwhite," which is usually a euphemism for black.

When a sociologist refers to a minority, it can be any segment of a public which is not a majority. In political usage, however, the term is usually employed to mean black or Hispanic: a promise to include minorities in appointments is taken to mean that blacks, Puerto Ricans and Mexicans will get a share of the patronage.

In national life, Jews are a minority, just as White Anglo-Saxon Protestants are a minority (11 percent) in New York City, but the word's literal meaning must not be confused with its political meaning: "minority" connotes nonwhite, and usually poor.

In a 1974 *Atlantic Monthly* piece on the language of politics, Henry Fairlie pointed out the change in meaning this word had undergone in two generations: "Fifty years ago, when Ortega y Gasset wrote *The Revolt of the Masses,* 'minorities' meant the privileged few at the top: '. . . the masses are today exercising functions which coincide with those hitherto seemed reserved to minorities . . .' The 'minority' was the elite opposed to 'the masses' . . ."

Curiously, the word "minority" is also applied to women crusading for equal rights, although in 1976 women were 51.2 percent of the U.S. population, outnumbering males by over 5 million. The word has such an oppressed-underdog connotation that it is preferred by a group even when that "minority" is a majority.

Ethnic groups, though certainly demographic minorities, are not meant when a politician speaks of "minority employment"; for a discussion of this related subject, see ETHNICS.

MIRV, *see* **SALT (LEXICON).**

MISCALCULATION the danger of war through a mistaken assessment of another power's intentions or capabilities.

"A favorite Kennedy word," wrote Ted Sorensen, "from my earliest association with him was 'miscalculation.' Long before he read Barbara Tuchman's *The Guns of August*—which he recommended to his staff—he had as a student at Harvard taken a course on the origins of World War I . . . he would cite the 1914 conversation between two German leaders on the origins and expansion of that war, a former chancellor asking 'How did it all happen?' and his successor saying, 'Ah, if only one knew.' "

Recalling the Soviet miscalculation of the U.S. reaction to placing missiles in Cuba, Kennedy told an aide that the sequel to *The Guns of August* could be "the missiles of October." Kennedy had used the word "miscalculation" in his meeting with Khrushchev in 1961, according to Arthur Schlesinger, Jr., and it irritated the Russian leader. "It was a vague term," he said, and it suggested to him "that America wanted the Soviet Union to sit like a schoolboy with hands on the top of the desk . . . the West should put the word 'miscalculation' into cold storage, for its use did not impress the Soviet Union." Kennedy tried to explain that he meant any nation could be prone to misjudgments, as was the U.S. in failing to foresee Chinese intervention in the Korean War.

In that instance, the Indian ambassador in Peking had already relayed to the U.S. a warning that the Chinese Communists would send in "volunteers" if General MacArthur's troops crossed the 38th parallel in his 1951 counterattack. Dean Rusk, then several steps removed from Secretary of State, contributed to the decision to overlook the warning; later he said frankly, "I was wrong."

That was the second miscalculation in Korea. The first was the mistaken belief by the Communists that if

North Korea invaded the south, neither the U.S. nor the UN would respond militarily. Fifteen years later, in Vietnam, the same danger existed in trying to outguess "the other side's" motives, capability, and potential backing. "Miscalculation," wrote the *New York Times* in the spring of 1967, "remains an obvious danger—one that President Johnson himself has often recognized. Last week, in fact, he was disclosed to have told his daughter Luci one night last summer, as the first raids on Hanoi and Haiphong were on the wing, that if a Soviet ship were accidentally bombed it could well lead to World War III."

This was a misuse of the word. Inadvertent or accidental war differs from miscalculation, which is part of the risk taken in consciously playing power politics on the international scene. War by miscalculation could come about by overconfidence in weaponry, by underestimation of the other side's willingness to "take a stand," or by steady escalation with no settlement along the way.

See **ESCALATION; PREVENTIVE WAR; DOOMSDAY MACHINE; FAIL-SAFE; MEASURED RESPONSE; CALCULATED RISK; SALT (LEXICON).**

MISHMASH confusion; meaningless material.

"Mishmash" is an English word in use for five centuries, particularly applicable in politics to describe the intellectual content of a speech.

Mishmash suggests a picture of lumpy, gray porridge, tasteless and not especially nourishing. A perfect use can be shown in the following communication from an attaché of the Soviet embassy in Washington, D.C.

Haydon Burns, a governor of Florida, misaddressed an invitation to Soviet Foreign Minister Andrei Gromyko as "Ambassador to the United Nations," asking him to speak at a lecture series in Florida. By the time an answer was forthcoming, a new governor had replaced Burns; this is the text of the letter sent Governor Claude R. Kirk:

Dear Sir:

Sometime ago, we received a letter signed by the Honorable Haydon Burns with the kind invitation to visit the place and speak before Daytona Beach Open Forum. We apologize for an unfortunate delay in answering the letter since there was some mishmash in it.

Andrei Gromyko whom the letter was applied to as "Ambassador to the United Nations" is the USSR Foreign Minister in the course of the last ten years. . . .

Besides that, any speaker of our Embassy is not able to participate in "the Open Forum program—1967" as this particular place is restricted to travel by Soviet citizens.

Yours sincerely,
Alexander A. Kokorev
Attaché
USSR Embassy

A second communication, published in *The Groucho Letters,* illustrates a common belief that the word mishmash has a Yiddish derivation:

To the Hon. William R. Scranton, Governor of Pennsylvania
                    February 24, 1964

Dear Sir:

If you contemplate campaigning in any more Jewish neighborhoods, I suggest you learn how to pronounce "mishmash." It is not pronounced "mash" as you said on "Meet the Press," but rather as though it were spelled MOSH.

Sincerely
yours,
Groucho Marx

The author wrote the first draft of this entry under the impression that the word did indeed have a Yiddish derivation; one of his editors sent it back with proof from the *OED* that the word was English, and the entry was accordingly revised. However, when the copy editor saw the revision, she penciled a note in the margin paraphrasing the punch line of an old Jewish joke: "Funny, it doesn't *look* English." She backed up her doubts with a copy of the Groucho letter.

Under this usage pressure, the first editor returned the manuscript to the author with the following note: "Here we go again on mishmash. The word is *not* Yiddish. However, the pronunciation of the word, as if *mishmosh,* is probably due to Yiddish influence in certain regions in the U.S. Perhaps it would be a good idea to add a short sentence of explanation: it's not Yiddish but maybe the pronunciation *-mosh* is due to Yiddish influence— though this pronunciation is not that of the majority of Americans."

Note to publisher: *print as is.* This entry is enough of a mishmash (pronounced mishmosh) already.

MISSILE GAP   a Kennedy charge that U.S. missile production lagged behind Soviet production; a hot issue in the 1960 presidential campaign, it was soon afterward coolly dismissed as nonexistent by the new Administration.

The Eisenhower Administration decided in the late 1950s not to invest heavily in intercontinental ballistic missiles, on the grounds that they were technologically inadequate; Defense Secretary Neil McElroy was charged by Democrats in Congress with planning a "missile gap." General James Gavin resigned from the Army in 1958 with a blast at the "missile lag." The charge became a

key point in the 1960 Kennedy campaign (along with "the prestige gap") but was dismissed by the new Defense Secretary, Robert McNamara, soon after his appointment by Kennedy.

Arthur Schlesinger, Jr., later frankly labeled it a "fake issue"; Ted Sorensen, taking the most charitable view, wrote: "Kennedy's error in 1960 on the 'missile gap' had been the result of the public's being informed too little and too late—even after the facts were certain—about a danger which he had in good faith overstated."

When Pentagon leaks in 1966 indicated an authentic missile gap was developing, the *St. Louis Post-Dispatch* remembered that the first gap turned out to be a myth, adding: "Somebody ought to ask whether the intelligence on which these proposals are based is any better than that of the first missile gap. . . . Once bitten, twice shy; that ought to be the motto in Congress."

For other phrases spawned by this phrase, see GAP; CREDIBILITY GAP.

MISSILES OF OCTOBER, *see* **MISCALCULATION; EYEBALL TO EYEBALL.**

MODERATE   positioned slightly to the left of center; a word more acceptable to conservatives than *liberal,* more dynamic than *middle-of-the-roader.*

President Eisenhower began using the word "moderation" in cabinet meetings in late 1954, just after the mid-term elections. Robert Donovan, who had access to cabinet-meeting minutes, reported that the President said on November 4, 1954, that the next two years would be extremely critical ones for the Administration's policy of moderation.

A year later Adlai Stevenson told a

fund-raising dinner in Chicago: "I agree that moderation is the spirit of the times. But we best take care lest we confuse moderation for mediocrity, or settle for half answers to hard problems. . . . Moderation, yes! Stagnation, no!" At the same dinner New York Governor Averell Harriman, a potential foe of Stevenson's for the 1956 Democratic nomination, disagreed: "There is no such word as 'moderation' in the Democratic vocabulary."

Senator Lyndon Johnson, however, on December 12, 1955, declared, "I have always thought of myself as one who has been a moderate in approaching problems." He had used "moderation" often, as had Eisenhower; Joseph Rauh, chairman of Americans for Democratic Action, suggested, "It would make sense to try to figure out what Eisenhower moderation is versus Johnson moderation, if indeed there is a difference."

By the late fifties, "moderate" had established a centrist meaning, weighted slightly liberal. The word was relatively quiescent during the Kennedy years, but reappeared strongly in the Rockefeller-Goldwater fight for the Republican nomination of 1964. Rockefeller National Campaign Director John A. Wells, an attorney who had managed Jacob Javits' landslide victory for the Senate in 1962, urged that Rockefeller use "moderate" rather than "liberal" in describing his philosophy in the New Hampshire primary, in the hope of capturing mildly conservative voters who might not identify with "Mr. Conservative," Barry Goldwater. "Moderate" and "MAINSTREAM" became the bywords of the stop-Goldwater movement, and moderate appears to have become a permanent label. Conservatives see through it. In describing Illinois Senator Charles

Percy as "a sort of inbetween Republican," columnist William F. Buckley Jr. added: "I resist the word 'moderate' because it is a base-stealing word for the benefit of GOP liberals."

Its predecessor word, "moderation," has had a long history in politics. Robert Clive, in a hot parliamentary debate in 1773, exclaimed, "By God, Mr. Chairman, at this moment I stand astonished at my own moderation!" In 1875 Leon Gambetta, who was to become Premier of France, told the Assembly, "Moderation is the reason of politics."

In his essay "Of Faction," written in 1597, Francis Bacon set forth the epitaph for Republican liberals before the 1964 nomination: ". . . it is often seen, that a few that are stiff, do tire out a great number that are more moderate."

MODERN REPUBLICANISM

a philosophy of government "liberal in human affairs, conservative in fiscal affairs"; an attempt to give a more progressive label to the GOP.

In 1955 Arthur Larson, then Under Secretary of Labor and a former dean of the University of Pittsburgh Law School, wrote *A Republican Looks at His Party.* Sherman Adams and the President's brother, Dr. Milton Eisenhower, had been anxious to focus on some articulation of the Eisenhower philosophy. Adams brought the book to the President in Walter Reed Hospital, where he was recovering from his ileitis operation, and the President subsequently said the book "expressed my philosophy of government as well as I have seen it in a book of that size."

Though Larson wrote mainly of a "new" Republicanism, his liberal approach was dubbed "modern," and he was attacked by conservatives—Republicans and Democrats alike—

when he was appointed to head the U.S. Information Agency. Conservative journalist George Sokolsky complained that the Republican party under Eisenhower "has gone so modern that it is indistinguishable from the New Deal." Illinois Representative Noah Mason said, "Essentially Ike's New Republicanism is a form of bribery, a program to buy votes with the voter's own money."

As the 1956 Eisenhower landslide rolled in on election night, the President told Richard Nixon what he planned to discuss on the air after Stevenson's concession. "I think I'll talk about Modern Republicanism." He formally used the phrase for the first time that night:

"Modern Republicanism, as I have said time and again, is to follow the Lincoln dictum of what government is for, and then to do it within the concept of competitive economy, sound fiscal arrangement and a sound dollar." The President was referring to this comment of Lincoln's: "The legitimate object of government is to do for a community of people whatever they need to have done, but cannot do at all, or cannot so well do, for themselves—in their separate, and individual capacities. In all that the people can individually do as well for themselves, government ought not to interfere."

"As the publicizer of Modern Republicanism," Sherman Adams wrote, "Larson became a marked man." When he was named to head USIA, Democrats and conservative Republicans joined to slash its budget from $144 million to $105 million. "Eisenhower did not need to be told," said Adams, "that Modern Republicanism as well as economy was behind the attack on Larson's budget."

Though Eisenhower's Administration was marked by its breadth of support, the "modern Republican" phrase was curiously divisive. It implicitly labeled the Old Guard as "OLD FOGY". In the sixties it was used only occasionally, with the "moderns" adopting the more conciliatory "moderate Republican," and in the seventies, NEOCONSERVATIVE.

See MAINSTREAM; MODERATE; ME TOO.

MOLLYCODDLE as a verb, to pamper—a charge made by opponents of many social welfare benefits that recipients are being treated with undue solicitude, to the detriment of working taxpayers; as a noun, a weakling.

Said John Jay Chapman, an American writer and critic, in *Practical Agitation* in 1900: "In a martial age the reformer is called a mollycoddle; in a commercial age, an incompetent, a disturber of values; in a fanatical age, a heretic. If an agitator is not reviled, he is a quack."

In politics, the word is most closely associated with Theodore Roosevelt, who espoused "the strenuous life." In his autobiography he referred to those who opposed the building of battleships and the fortification of the Panama Canal as "the large mollycoddle vote, people who are soft physically and morally."

Like MOSSBACK and SNOLLYGOSTER, it was one of President Harry Truman's favorite Americanisms. "I wasn't going to go down in history," he promised toward the end of his term, "like Pierce or Buchanan or Chester Arthur or Benjamin Harrison—he was one of the most mediocre Presidents we ever had. I wasn't going to be one of your arm-rolling cheek-kissing mollycoddles!"

-MONGER a suffix meaning "peddler of," used to create derogatory phrases.

Ever since the sixteenth century, "monger"—an Anglo-Saxon word for trade—has had a connotation of petty, disreputable trafficking. Ironmongers and fishmongers carry on respectable enough businesses, as once did warmongers—the word for a mercenary soldier. Boroughmongers were wealthy landowners in England who sold representation of the ROTTEN BOROUGHS.

The suffix has been particularly used to describe people who pass along information: gossipmongers, scandalmongers, rumormongers. In politics, one who warns of imminent danger is sometimes attacked as a panicmonger, or more seriously as a warmonger.

As with other phrases using the idea of war (see WAGING PEACE), a turnaround has taken place and those who speak against containment or intervention have been labeled "peacemongers."

MONROE DOCTRINE, see DOCTRINES; DOLLAR DIPLOMACY.

MOONLIGHTING working for a second source of income; in politics, doing private work for pay at night while on the public payroll during the day.

The word originally applied to the nighttime raids of poverty-stricken Irishmen in the 1880s, to punish unpopular tenants or prevent payments of rents. The concept of working for a second employer after putting in a full day elsewhere was called "smooting" in England at that time, and was prohibited by the trade unions, which wanted to spread the work to as many different members as possible.

A political issue is occasionally raised as to whether policemen and firemen should be allowed to supplement their income by taking a second job during their off-hours. Opponents argue that moonlighting drains the worker's stamina for his civic job; and they claim it leads to conflict of interest in the case of white-collar public workers or officials.

See DOUBLE DIPPING.

MORAL EQUIVALENT OF WAR fervor without destructiveness; an acknowledgment of man's psychological need for the martial arts, with a recommendation that the need be satisfied through peaceful challenges.

William James, in an essay entitled "The Moral Equivalent of War," published in the *International Concilium* in February 1910, wrote: "So long as anti-militarists propose no substitute for war's disciplinary function, no *moral equivalent* of war, analogous, as one might say, to the mechanical equivalent of heat, so long they fail to realize the full inwardness of the situation."

Four U.S. wars later President Jimmy Carter used the James phrase in his address to the nation on the energy problem on April 19, 1977. He pictured the situation as "the greatest challenge that our country will face in our lifetimes," adding: "Our decision about energy will test the character of the American people and the ability of the President and the Congress to govern this nation. This difficult effort will be the 'moral equivalent of war' —except that we will be uniting our efforts to build and not to destroy." His writers felt that the last phrase, although redundant, was necessary to stress that the President was not advocating any kind of "shooting" war.

After the Senate had refused to pass legislation that would have raised fuel taxes and continued the control of all natural-gas prices, as the President had requested, Mr. Carter took the occasion of a press conference on October 13, 1977, to castigate the oil and gas industry in Trumanesque terms: "Back in April when our national energy policy was presented to the Congress and to the people, I said that because of the importance of it that this was 'the moral equivalent of war' . . . as in the case in time of war, there is potential war profiteering in the impending energy crisis. This could develop with the passing months as the biggest ripoff in history."

Columnist Anthony Lewis of the *New York Times* wrote a few days later: "Even by oil company standards there is something staggering in the pretense that 'freeing' the oil companies to produce more will meet a challenge as critical to this country as import dependence over the next decade. That was even more deserving of President Carter's angry rhetoric than the greed that provoked his talk of war profiteering. (Could he please drop the war image, incidentally? Recent examples of its use, starting with the WAR ON POVERTY, are not very happy.)"

As usual, the targets of the attack used the attacking phrase in their counterattack. A committee of economists supporting the oil industry blazed back in a full-page ad: "Congress has been told that it must rush to pass Mr. Carter's current energy plan. 'This is the moral equivalent of war.' And what is that? William James, from whom President Carter borrowed the phrase, defined 'the moral equivalent of war' as nonmartial suffering, something which involves 'discomfort and annoyance, hunger and wet, pain and cold, squalor and filth.' We do not believe that the American people deserve to have 'discomfort, pain, squalor, etc.' imposed upon them by their government."

The lofty James phrase received its cruelest blow from *New York Times* columnist Russell Baker, who took to using its feline acronym: MEOW.

MORATORIUM   an officially declared stoppage or delay; applied to politics, a truce.

This sonorous word, invariably attached to the verb "declare," stems from the Latin for "delay" but has a more majestic connotation. In 1931 Herbert Hoover called for a one-year moratorium on war-debt payments, and this "debt holiday" was called "the Hoover moratorium." When Lyndon Johnson traveled to a conference of Asian leaders just before the off-year elections of 1966, Republican leaders were compelled to declare a moratorium on foreign-policy criticism while he was gone, for fear of appearing to undercut the president abroad on the business of all the people.

When political figures want to tell their friends to shut up while they try to settle a sticky situation, they find it more polite to "request a moratorium." Ted Sorensen wrote that civil rights leaders in 1963 "were angry at the Kennedys for requesting a moratorium on demonstrations while an agreement was worked out . . ."

NBC correspondent Herbert Kaplow, chafing at candidate Richard Nixon's moratorium on Vietnam discussions during the 1968 campaign, suggested to this writer: "You ought to hold your next rally in a huge moratorium."

MORKRUMBO   journalese, especially "bogus titling."

Said Wallace Carroll, editor of the

Winston-Salem Journal and Sentinel,
in 1969:

The Morkrum printer that brings
wire reports into the newspaper
offices chugs along at sixty-six words
a minute. . . . The machine is might-
ier than the mind, and news writing
must sacrifice all grace and clarity to
accommodate these physical limitations. . . . Identification must be
crammed together in front of a
man's name so that everyone gets an
awkward bogus title. All the flexibility and lilt must be squeezed out of
the writing so it reads as if the machine itself had composed whatever
is written.

And we get leads like this:
"Teamsters union president
James R. Hoffa's jury-tampering
conviction apparently won't topple
him from office under a federal law
barring union posts to any one convicted of bribery."

Clickety-clickety-click. It's not
English—it's *Morkrumbo,* the language of the Morkrum printer. . . .

"Former North Carolina State
University's head basketball coach
Everett Case today declared . . .
Clickety-clickety-click."

No real liberty is taken with the
language in changing "Patricia Harris, the Secretary of Housing and
Urban Development," to "Housing
Secretary Patricia Harris"; in such
cases the Morkrumbo is anti-bureau-
cratese. But the abhorrence of com-
mas has led to an outbreak of what
Carroll called "bogus titling," and
sometimes the titles appear to gain
the force of law. That is what happened to "Consumer Advocate Ralph
Nader."

MOSSBACK a reactionary; one
who furiously resists progress of any
kind.

The word is derived from a sea
creature so ancient that it has moss or
seaweed growing on its back. During
the Civil War it was used to describe
those who fled to the swamps and forests to evade the draft; in the 1870s
the word was given a political meaning as a Northern counterpart to a
Southern Bourbon.

Emporia Gazette editor William
Allen White, in his famed "What's
the Matter with Kansas?" editorial in
1896, thundered: "We have an old
moss-back Jacksonian who snorts
and howls because there is a bath tub
in the State House; we are running
that old jay for Governor . . ."

Pennsylvania Congressman J. C.
Sibley drew a typical word picture in
1900: "Primitive man lived in caverns, clothed himself with skins, and
ate his meat raw, sitting on his haunches; and there has never occurred a
change for the higher and better
forms of life without arousing the
hostility of some old mossback, conservative hunker[s], who will prate of
those fairer and better days of old,
when their grandfathers swung by
their tails from the limbs of the trees."

Will Rogers told defeated Democratic candidate Al Smith in 1929:
". . . taken out from under the influence of a lot of these old Mossbacks,
you are a pretty progressive fellow,
Al, and with you and this fellow
Roosevelt as a kind of nucleus, I think
we can, with the help of some Progressive young Democratic governors
and senators and congressmen, make
this thing into a Party, instead of a
Memory."

The word was relatively dormant
during the thirties and early forties,
but President Harry Truman gave it
new life in the 1948 campaign. In the
Far West he charged that the Republican party's domination by "eastern
mossbacks" would stifle the economy
of the West. Throughout the country,
he denounced the Republican chairmen of Senate and House committees

as "a bunch of mossbacks."

One of the lines that best describes a mossback was leveled at House Speaker "Uncle Joe" Cannon: "If he had been present at Creation, he would have voted for Chaos."

See DO-NOTHING CONGRESS.

MOST FAVORED NATION not, as the phrase implies, special treatment in trade, but an assurance that relations will be "equal to that of the most favored nation."

The essense of "MFN" is that "nobody else gets a better deal." The idea, if not the phrase, appears in the commercial treaty Oliver Cromwell of England negotiated with Sweden in 1654 that won recognition of his commonwealth: people of either confederate "shall have and possess in the countries, lands, dominions and kingdoms of the other as full and ample privileges, and as many exemptions, immunities and liberties, as any foreigner doth or shall possess in the dominions and kingdoms of the said confederate." Cromwell got this idea from the Turkish "capitulations": extraterritorial privileges granted in the twelfth century by Byzantium's successors to the Italian city-states. The *OED* does not have the first use (probably in the late seventeenth century) but a typical phrasing can be found in a 1905 British-Rumanian pact: ". . . the commerce, navigation and industry of each country shall be placed, in all respects, on the footing of the most favoured nation."

The underlying idea behind MFN, as it came to be called in the sixties, is a fair field with no favor: any special privileges demanded by one nation, and agreed to by another, then becomes available to all. That is the "unconditional" MFN, guaranteeing equal treatment without any reciprocal strings attached.

The founders of the U.S., however, recognizing that their new nation was a newcomer to world commerce, and faced with English, French, and Spanish attempts to exclude the newcomer from their overseas possessions, came up with a new wrinkle on the hoary clause: the "conditional" MFN. Only if other nations permitted access to their markets would the U.S. permit access to its own.

That conditional principle can be found in the first U.S. trade treaty, concluded with France, in July of 1778. The idea was to make trade reciprocal and dependent upon receipt of equal treatment. Secretary of State John Quincy Adams wrote in 1818 that such reciprocity could not confer special treatment on any one nation: "If any such advantage is granted for an equivalent, other nations can have no right to claim its enjoyment, even though entitled to be treated as the most favored nation, unless by the reciprocal grant of the same equivalent." (Curiously, Adams' sobriquet was "Old Man Eloquent.")

After World War I, however, the U.S.—which originated the conditional most-favored-nation clause—found it no longer useful, since the condition allowed other countries to discriminate against U.S. exports. "By offering complete and nondiscriminatory treatment," reads a 1974 staff study by the Senate Finance Committee, "the United States sought to obtain the same treatment from other countries . . . Authority for the U.S. to offer unconditional MFN was included in the Tariff Act of 1922 . . . The Trade Agreements Act of 1934 included an unconditional MFN provision and made it a requirement of United States domestic law." From this open policy flowed the U.S. participation in the international General Agreement on

Tariffs and Trade (GATT), which puts MFN in its first provision of Article 1.

The Cold War turned U.S. policy around again. In 1951, Congress directed President Truman to withdraw MFN status from Communist countries. He did so, excepting only Tito's Yugoslavia. When, in 1972, détente became the order of the day, another switch in MFN was sought: Nixon Administration trade experts, led by Peter Flanigan, lobbied to remove this barrier. The verbal approach Flanigan used was not to seek to make the Soviet Union "a most favored nation" (implying special favors to Russia, in the untutored mind) but "to end trade discrimination" ("discrimination" was a word most people were accustomed to being against).

However, when the USSR began to levy exit fees on emigrants, Senator Henry Jackson led Congress into forbidding the extension of most-favored-nation status to "non-market economy" nations which denies its citizens the right to emigrate; the Jackson-Vanik amendment to the Trade Act of 1974 enshrined the principle in law. (See QUIET DIPLOMACY.)

Proof that the 200-year-old phrase had permanently entered the language could be found in a *Newsweek* cover story (February 13, 1978) on the entertainment industry, which defined a Hollywood "Most Favored Nation Clause" as "a contractual promise to a star who signs early that no latecomer will get a better deal."

MOUNTAINTOP, TAKE HIM TO THE a private promise, made prior to a convention, of high appointive office or a place on the ticket, in return for delegate support.

This phrase rarely appears in print but is current usage in spoken negotiations. "Take him to the mountaintop" implies, first, complete privacy in dealing—unbugged, unwitnessed conversation, promises made that would be denied if repeated. Second, the "mountaintop" offers a pulse-quickening view of the vista below, glimpses of far horizons that persuade the man with the delegates to come across and stay across. A typical use:

"How's Jones in Kansas?"

"Committed the wrong way. I think the other side promised him Secretary of Agriculture."

"They took him to the mountaintop this early in the campaign?"

"It's a busy mountaintop. I know two other guys who think they have that job sewed up."

In December 1967, Drew Pearson and Jack Anderson wrote that Senator Eugene McCarthy entered Democratic primaries opposing Lyndon Johnson because "McCarthy is bitter at the man who, he thinks, took him up on the mountain to the Vice Presidency, then pushed him off into the Atlantic City breakers."

The phrase appears as "take him up the mountain," "take him on the mountaintop," as well as "take him to the mountaintop."

Mountaintop also appears in labor relations, as "now we have to get them down off the mountaintop." In early stages of negotiations, a labor leader often makes unrealistic demands, fully expecting to scale them down for a settlement. However, his rank and file becomes enamored of items like a four-day week and other "asking prices," and the union leader at settlement time has to bring his own men "down off the mountaintop."

The phrase originates in the temptation of Christ (Matthew 4:8–9):

". . . the devil taketh him up into an exceeding high mountain, and sheweth him all the kingdoms of the world and the glory of them; and saith unto him, All these things will I give thee, if thou wilt fall down and worship me." The stern, get-thee-behind-me response of Jesus led later political tempters to be both more specific and more successful.

MOVEMENT, THE   in the nineteenth century, the progressive tradition; in the early twentieth century, organized labor; in the fifties, civil rights; in the sixties, an amalgam of civil rights and the NEW LEFT; in the seventies, WOMEN'S LIB.

Paul Jacobs and Saul Landau, in *The New Radicals* (1966), defined the phrase this way:

> The Movement is a melange of people, mostly young; organizations, mostly new; and ideals, mostly American. . . . Those in The Movement feel that modern American liberals have substituted empty rhetoric for significant content, obscured the principles of justice by administrative bureaucracy, sacrificed human values for efficiency, and hypocritically justified a brutal attempt to establish American hegemony over the world with sterile anti-Communism. . . .

> The new movement is also a revolt against the postwar "over-developed society," with its large bureaucracies in government, corporations, trade unions, and universities. To those in The Movement the new technologies of automation and cybernation, with their computers and memory-bank machines, are instruments of alienation, depersonalizing human relations to a frightening degree.

The labor movement and the civil rights movement had more clear-cut goals, and were readier to communicate their needs to the general public. The amorphous Movement of the six-ties appeared to many Americans to have adopted the techniques of previous movements (sit-ins, protests, demonstrations, strikes) without their direction or national leadership.

Some leaders of the sixties Movement were anti-leadership. Tom Hayden warned of "maintaining a dependency on fixed leaders, who inevitably develop interests in maintaining the organization (or themselves) and lose touch with the immediate aspirations of the rank and file." Stokely Carmichael of SNCC, trying to avoid the taint of leadership, assumed the title of "field hand." Vocabulary of the Movement leans heavily on "participate," "initiate," "hang-ups," "community," and "people" (never "masses").

Did the Movement of the sixties lose its battle? Not so, *Commentary* magazine editor Norman Podhoretz told television interviewer Ben Wattenberg in June 1978: "The movement with a capital M, as it used to be called, was made up of a kind of a political arm and a cultural arm. The political arm was called The NEW LEFT, the cultural arm was called the COUNTERCULTURE . . . I think it disappeared because it won. Its critique of American society and institutions came to be widely accepted by people who were not themselves members of that movement . . . You see an ominous growth of neo-isolationist sentiment . . . the idea that the United States is not a benevolent force in world affairs but a malevolent force."

The Movement moved in the seventies to the efforts of women to gain equality in U.S. society, centered often on the campaign to ratify the Equal Rights Amendment. See SEX-ISM.

MOVERS AND SHAKERS   opinion leaders; influentials, especially those who are political or economic activists.

Mass-communications theorists like Columbia professor Paul I. Lazarsfeld hold that there is a "two-step flow" of most communication: from source, to opinion leader in that idea's category, to the great number of people.

"Movers and shakers" is applied to both the source group and the transmitting opinion leaders; a strict definition would narrow it down to those who decide policy, develop new ideas, and—most important—make it happen.

Clinton Rossiter explained the self-image of Democratic voters: "They delight in the whole sweep of American history, certain that they have been the 'movers and shakers' and their opponents, whether Federalists or Whigs or Republicans, the 'stick-in-the-muds.' "

Walter Heller used the phrase to describe how Lyndon Johnson sought to achieve consensus, using both private meetings and public pronouncements: ". . . this method combines Presidential persuasion and education of hundreds of the country's 'movers and shakers' *in person* in small White House meetings . . . with public persuasion of millions of citizens by performance under the resulting policies and legislation."

The phrase was coined by nineteenth-century English poet Arthur O'Shaughnessy:

We are the music-makers,
And we are the dreamers of dreams . . .
Yet we are the movers and shakers of the
world forever, it seems.

The phrase is often used with a faint note of derision at those who believe themselves to be powerful. See MUCKEY-MUCKS.

MR. CLEAN, *see* BOY SCOUT.

MR. DOOLEY, *see* DOOLEY, MR.; SUPREME COURT FOLLOWS THE ELECTION RETURNS; BEANBAG.

MR. NICE GUY   everybody's friend; a practitioner of the politics of pacification.

"Nice guys finish last" was the dictum of Brooklyn Dodger baseball manager Leo Durocher in the 1940s, and to a degree this has application to modern politics. Writing about Senator Edmund Muskie in October 1971, David Broder of the *Washington Post* pointed out: "Tagged as a cautious, cool Mr. Nice Guy by most observers, the Maine Senator has turned into a deliberately hard-nosed, independent character, often seeming to go out of his way to demonstrate he is his own man."

As used in politics, the appellation connotes scorn; when a man tries too hard not to make enemies, he appears to lack leadership potential. A skillful politician is one who takes positions that seem uncompromising and forthright—and still does not make enemies.

The phrase was popularized by a joke current in the mid-fifties. Hiding out in South America, the story went, Hitler deputy Martin Bormann sought to convince his former chief to return to Germany and take over a neo-Fascist movement. Reluctantly Adolf Hitler agreed to make a comeback, warning, "But this time—no more Mr. Nice Guy."

A variation appeared in the seventies: "good guys," usually plural, was used to mean WHITE HATS or heroes, and intended to be ironically simplistic, as in the good-guy–bad-guy Western movies. Jimmy Breslin's 1975 book about Congressman Thomas P. "Tip" O'Neill was titled *How the Good Guys Finally Won* over the "bad guys" of the Nixon Administration.

"Nice guy," as in "Mr. Nice Guy," connotes weakness, while "good guy" has an aura of moral strength (see GOOD FIGHT). On February 7, 1978, the *Washington Post* ran an article by Lynn Darling on local government officials who found the demands of the political life too demanding—the headline was "Good Guys Bow Out"; and the "good guys" were defined as "These are the types who spend a vacation writing a rent control bill and read much of the night on Wednesday to prepare for a hearing on Friday because all of Thursday will be taken up by a work session . . . In high school, these men and those like them might have been the class grinds, the kind who got straight A's, were captain of the debate team, worked two paper routes and won the science fair to boot."

See BOY SCOUT.

MR. REPUBLICAN   a sobriquet for the recognized embodiment of party leader; not always helpful in the general election.

Putting "Mr." before a generic word and applying the name to an individual locks up that area—but may also lock a man inside that area. Senator Robert A. Taft of Ohio was "Mr. Republican" in 1952, but it only served to emphasize the "can't win" charge, since Democratic votes are needed for a Republican nominee to win.

Similarly, Barry Goldwater was styled "Mr. Conservative," which focused and dramatized his specific strength, but limited his appeal.

Richard Nixon, in his introduction of Goldwater at the 1964 Republican convention, sought to overcome the problem in a progression of phrases:

He is the man who earned and proudly carries the title of Mr. Conservative.

He is the man who, by the action of this Convention, is now Mr. Republican.

And he is the man who, after the greatest campaign in history, will be Mr. President—Barry Goldwater.

MR. X   a sinister figure who cannot be named; or, the nom de plume of George Kennan.

Mr. X—sometimes called Mr. Big —occasionally appears as a character in the last few days of an election campaign. In the New York City mayoralty race of 1953, Manhattan Borough President Robert F. Wagner, Jr., choice of the regular Democrats, was being overshadowed in the press by independent Democrat Rudolph Halley, former chief counsel of the Kefauver crime-investigating committee. A Wagner backer was given some anti-racketeering information damaging to local Republicans, but with not enough proof to substantiate a charge against a specific individual. He passed the information to the candidate, who alluded to it in a "Who is Mr. X?" broadcast —capturing the headlines and the curiosity of the voters during the final weekend of the campaign. Wagner was elected.

The danger of any "Mr. X" charge is in mistiming; it must come toward the very end of a campaign, or else voters begin demanding that the speaker answer his own question or shut up. Mishandled, it can also appear to be a desperate last-minute ruse, which it sometimes is.

This is an extension of a technique New York Mayor James J. Walker used to infuriate Fiorello La Guardia, whom he defeated decisively in 1929 despite a variety of scandal charges against the Walker administration. "The question I would like to ask Mr. La Guardia," Walker would say solemnly in many of his speeches, "is: What was he doing in Providence on a certain day in 1926?" Of course, Walker had no evidence La Guardia had ever been in Providence, or if he had been, what he was doing there. It succeeded in needling his opponent.

In foreign affairs, "Mr. X" is now a well-known figure. George F. Kennan, a U.S. State Department policy planner in 1947, wrote a long memorandum to his superiors urging a new, tougher policy toward Communist expansionary aims. Part of the memo was printed in *Foreign Affairs* under the title "Sources of Soviet Conduct," signed by "X." (See CONTAINMENT.) Kennan later surfaced as one of the United States' chief planners on Soviet affairs.

MUCKEY-MUCKS (MUCK-A-MUCKS)

big shots; term of derision for party leaders by party workers.

The expression is still often heard as "high muck-a-muck" because of its probable derivation from Chinook jargon, *hiu* (plenty) *muckamuck* (food); hence, one who has plenty to eat, or a man of power, a big wheel.

The *Democratic State Journal* of California in 1856 wrote: "The professors—the high 'Muck-a-Mucks'—tried fusion, and produced confusion." A comic-strip character in the *Chicago Tribune* in 1947 said, "They's a high-mucky-muck in th' radio business vacationin' here, so we gotta be good."

Synonyms are PARTY ELDERS, the INNER CIRCLE, POWER BROKERS, BOSSES. For other American Indian expressions in politics, see SACHEM; TAMMANY; GREAT WHITE FATHER; MUGWUMP; RAINMAKER.

MUCKRAKER

a journalist who searches through the activities of public organizations seeking to expose conduct contrary to the public interest.

The term, while still used to describe columnists like Jack Anderson, reached its greatest popularity in the days of the crusading magazines between 1903 and 1909.

Theodore Roosevelt first used it in its present meaning at a time when he was suspected of being antibusiness by the businessmen who formed an important part of his own Republican party. Articles exposing certain activities in business had already shocked the public when President Roosevelt, first in an off-the-record Gridiron Club speech and later in a speech at the laying of the cornerstone for the new House of Representatives Office Building on April 14, 1906, warned that this kind of antibusiness journalism could go too far. Roosevelt said "the men with the muckrakes are often indispensable to the well being of society; but only if they know when to stop raking the muck, and to look upward to the celestial crown above them, to the crown of worthy endeavor. There are beautiful things above and round about them; and if they gradually grow to feel that the whole world is nothing but muck, their power of usefulness is gone."

Roosevelt's reference was to the Man with the Muck Rake in Bunyan's *Pilgrim's Progress,* the man who could never look any way but down; when offered a celestial crown, he refused to gaze upward and continued to rake the filth on the floor.

The President was repeating a phrase he had found successful at the

Gridiron Club dinner of March 17, 1906. Then he had used it more strenuously to describe men who attacked those who had acquired means merely because of wealth "but [who] were prepared to condone crimes of great brutality, including murder, if those committing them can obtain the support of powerful labor organizations."

It was not completely new to politics; as early as 1871 it was used to describe the ambitious politician who rakes in muck, hoping to come up with valuable ammunition.

Mr. Roosevelt's version caught on immediately. One of the most famous —though least virulent—of the school, Ray Stannard Baker, was hailed by a friend on the street almost immediately after the speech with the cheery salutation "Hello, Muckraker." Baker said he didn't know what was meant at the moment but was quickly educated.

Lincoln Steffens, whose articles in *McClure's* magazine made him the leader of the school, wrote in his autobiography: "I did not intend to be a muckraker. I did not know that I was one till President Roosevelt picked the name out of Bunyan's *Pilgrim's Progress* and pinned it on us and even then he said that he did not mean me."

He and others such as Baker and Ida Tarbell, did not long resent the word. According to historian Mark Sullivan, "all the writers of exposure accepted the epithet that was meant for some of them, and in the eyes of most of the public, 'muckraker' became a term of approval."

For a short time the pages of *McClure's, Collier's,* the *American Magazine, Cosmopolitan,* and others were rife with stories of misconduct, previously sheltered from public exposure. In its day, when the exposés

in the popular magazines came weekly, a favorite muckraker story was of the wealthy Alaskan miner who walked into a magazine office demanding a crusade. Said the editor, "You certainly are a progressive, aren't you?"

"Progressive!" the miner roared. "I'm a full-fledged insurgent. Why, man, I subscribe to thirteen magazines."

Today's muckrakers prefer the term "investigative reporter." The breed was criticized by Bert Lance, President Carter's first Director of the Office of Management and Budget, who had been driven from office by press criticism of his financial affairs. Lance warned the American Society of Newspaper Editors in April 1978 that censorship could follow press irresponsibility:

The press has always had its share of professional cynics, as quite properly it should. But that once healthy dash of cynicism appears to have become a pervasive and destructive cynicism, another sad legacy of Vietnam and Watergate.

Along with this unhealthy climate of suspicion is a change in the standards governing publication of allegation, rumor and gossip, and an intense post-Watergate competition among investigative reporters. There are more muck*rakers* around these days than muck*makers*.

MUDSLINGING wild, unsubstantiated charges; a word, like **"SMEAR,"** used to turn an attack back on the attacker.

"Calumniate! Calumniate! Some of it will always stick," advised Beaumarchais in *The Barber of Seville* in 1775. This was based on ancient Latin advice, *Fortiter calumniari, aliquia adhaerebit,* or "Throw plenty of dirt and some of it will be sure to stick."

Sometime after the Civil War, *dirt-*

throwing picked up some water to become *mud-throwing, mud-gunning* and the word that gained pre-eminence, *mudslinging.* The *New York Tribune* of April 13, 1876, disagreed with the Latin dictum: "Mud doesn't stick to Mr. Blaine any better than it does to Mr. Bristow. The slander peddlers are having a bad season." The word was so well entrenched by 1878 that the *Tribune* could refer to it obliquely, as "the dredging machine was set at work again yesterday, and brought up a small load of sediment from the dirty stream of Louisiana politics."

Bruce Felknor, of the Fair Campaign Practices Committee, in the sixties classified six presidential campaigns as "spectacularly dirty": Jackson's first election, Lincoln's second, the Hayes-Tilden debacle, Cleveland's first election, Theodore Roosevelt's third campaign and the Hoover-Smith clash of 1928. Harry Truman agreed on the last, recalling: "Al Smith was given the nomination, and that set off the most vicious anti-Catholic, anti-Jewish, anti-Negro movement that we have ever had in any political campaign . . . there was more slander and mudslinging going on than at any time I can remember."

"Mudslinging" (from dirt-throwing) and "dirty politics" are obviously from the same source. "I was told repeatedly not to enter politics," said then-Governor Nelson Rockefeller, "that politics is a 'dirty' business. . . . Politics is the lifeblood of democracy. To call politics 'dirty' is to call democracy 'dirty.' "

Adlai Stevenson in 1954 combined a couple of earthy metaphors to put together a Confucianist epigram: "He who slings mud generally loses ground."

MUGWUMP   bolter; MAVERICK.

Anyone who bolted his political party was a mugwump, especially those Republicans who refused to support the presidential candidacy of James Blaine in 1884. The true mugwump went a step further and gave his support to the Democratic nominee, Grover Cleveland of New York.

The first known use of the word was by John Eliot in his *Indian Bible,* published in 1663, from the Algonquin language, in which the word *mugquomp* is used to define a chief or another individual of high rank. See SACHEM.

In June 1884 it was popularized politically by the *New York Sun* and quickly became common parlance. The Republicans had met in convention and picked Blaine as their candidate. Many figures of stature (though not much influence) in the party decided they could not accept a man they felt was so corrupt. They met June 7, 1884, in Boston and decided to support Cleveland. The *Sun* jeeringly referred to them as "Little Mugwumps," meaning little men attempting to be big chiefs. Little they were not: their ranks sparkled with such names as President Eliot of Harvard, Carl Schurz, Charles Francis Adams, and George William Curtis.

The "little," in fact, was soon dropped; the term "mugwump" persisted and, indeed, those so labeled soon accepted and even affected the description after Admiral Horace Porter defined a mugwump as "a person educated beyond his intellect."

"Mugwumpery" or "mugwumpism" has persisted both here and in Great Britain to describe bolters, though most usually the term has been applied to independent Republicans.

Political lexicographers have always felt obligated to report that a mugwump was described by the *Blue Earth* (Minn.) *Post* in the early 1930s as "a sort of bird that sits on a fence with his mug on one side and his wump on the other."

Theodore Roosevelt, who was persuaded to party orthodoxy in 1884 by Henry Cabot Lodge of Massachusetts, called mugwumps "dudes"— they had also been called "pharisees." Roosevelt professed contempt for mugwumps through the years, right up to the time he bolted the Republican party and ran for the presidency as an independent in 1912.

MUNICH, ANOTHER   symbol of a place of appeasement leading to war.

Cities that are the scene of a great event, when they are not major capitals that are the scene of too many other great occasions, are often identified with the meaning of that event.

Yalta was the scene of the last meeting of Roosevelt, Churchill, and Stalin toward the end of World War II. "Another Yalta" has come to be used as a warning against gullibility in dealings with Communist leaders.

Guernica, a small city in Spain, was bombed by German aircraft in support of the Franco forces in April 1937; its obliteration came to mean ruthless attacks against defenseless cities, until it was superseded by "another Rotterdam."

Sarajevo, a town in what is now southern Yugoslavia, was the scene on June 28, 1914, of the assassination of the Archduke Ferdinand, which history texts dubbed "one of the immediate (but not underlying) causes of the World War." "Another Sarajevo" means a spark that ignites a major conflict.

Munich was the scene of an agreement between British Prime Minister Neville Chamberlain, French Pre-

mier Édouard Daladier, Hitler, and Mussolini on September 30, 1938, granting Germany the Czech territory of the Sudetenland as well as its defense border. The Czechs were not present at their "sellout." Today, "another Munich" means an agreement that appeases an aggressor at the expense of a weak nation and only leads to greater war later.

Writer Bernard Fall, killed in Vietnam in 1967, wrote a year earlier: "If Munich is not a good example of how to settle the Vietnamese conflict, neither is Guernica, or Sarajevo."

See PEACE IN OUR TIME.

MUSICAL METAPHORS   "For if the trumpet give an uncertain sound, who shall prepare himself to the battle?" (I Corinthians 14:8) This Biblical musical metaphor has occasionally been applied to political leadership, most recently by former Army Chief of Staff General Maxwell Taylor as the title of a book, *The Uncertain Trumpet,* attacking the downgrading of conventional army units in the fifties.

The Defense Secretary who later worked closely with Taylor, Robert McNamara (see WHIZ KIDS), became the subject of a musical metaphor. "McNamara's Band," the nickname for his organization, was taken from a turn-of-the-century song beginning "My name is McNamara, I'm the leader of the band . . ."

New York Mayor Fiorello La Guardia orchestrated his administration with sirens chasing fire engines and explosions of temper against "tinhorn gamblers and two-bit politicians." One night at Radio City Music Hall, listening to the organist at intermission, "the Little Flower" explained his theory of administration to his City Council president and protégé, Newbold Morris: "Newbold, that's how our city must be run. Like that organist, you must keep both hands on the keyboard and both feet on the pedals—and never let go!"

A celestial harp was used subtly and skillfully by Abraham Lincoln as a metaphor in his first inaugural address, perhaps the best metaphor of any kind used by any U.S. President: "The mystic chords of memory, stretching from every battlefield and every land, will yet swell the chorus of the Union when again touched, as surely they will be, by the better angels of our nature." The composing of this passage, originally suggested by Secretary of State William Seward, is described in the Introduction to the third edition of this dictionary.

MUTUAL AND BALANCED, *see* **CODE WORDS.**

MUZZLE to censor; to stifle criticism; an attack word on an attempt to present a united front.

Controversy-seeking journalists have applied the word to the requirement by Eisenhower, Kennedy, and Carter Administrations that all policy speeches by military men be approved by the government and changed or suppressed if they differ materially with official policy.

The best-known example occurred during the first week in office of President Kennedy. The Russians, at the time, were holding several American fliers whose reconnaissance plane had been shot down near Russian waters. Negotiations for their return were in progress. The Chief of Naval Operations, Admiral Arleigh Burke, voluntarily submitted a speech which had a strong anti-Soviet tone. When the speech was toned down and the fact became known, the President was accused of "muzzling" the military.

Kennedy replied: "If a well-known,

high-ranking military figure makes a speech which affects foreign policy or possibly military policy, I think that the people and the countries abroad have a right to expect that that speech represents the opinion of the national government. . . . The purpose of the review . . . is to make sure that . . . government speaks with one voice."

An investigation by a senatorial committee headed by Senator Strom Thurmond sought to equate the policy with censorship and being SOFT ON COMMUNISM. The committee received encouragement from a statement made by former President Eisenhower, who somewhat deplored a similar policy of speech review required during his two terms, saying that "after mature consideration" he now felt the policy should be dropped.

Columnist Walter Lippmann felt otherwise, writing, "the talkativeness of American military men, most of them reading speeches written by professional speech writers who are paid by the government, is an international scandal."

The word has been used in a purely political context, since at least 1880, when *Harper's Weekly* described a "unit rule" (see GAG RULE) as "a muzzle and gag unworthy of honorable men." In the 1952 campaign, Adlai Stevenson, speaking of the original, liberal Republican supporters of General Eisenhower's candidacy, said their voices seemed to have been absent since the convention. "Someone seems to have muzzled them. It may be they sounded too much like Democrats."

Reporters insist the public has a RIGHT TO KNOW the differences of opinion within the military establishment; Administration officials feel that a general's lobbying encroaches on civilian control of the military.

Despite "the word" from the White House, generals and admirals find a way to leak their points of view to friendly correspondents. A muzzle prevents a dog from biting and barking, but not from growling.

MY (USE OF POSSESSIVE PRONOUN) used as "my ambassador," either a slip of the tongue leading to an attack for royalist tendencies, or a deliberate presidential effort to undercut the State Department.

In the campaign of 1940, Franklin Roosevelt referred to Joseph P. Kennedy, Ambassador to the Court of St. James's, as "my ambassador," a phrase which the Republicans promptly pounced on as proof of his dictatorial ambitions in their "no-third term" drive. Similarly, in 1966, Lyndon Johnson played into Republican hands with a reference to "my Congress," giving Richard Nixon an opportunity to flay the "do-anything Congress," a play on Harry Truman's DO-NOTHING CONGRESS.

Abraham Lincoln was attacked in 1858 for his use of "I" in speeches— the *Burlington Gazette* said; ". . . he is known all over Suckerdom by the name of 'the Perpendicular pronoun.' " But President Andrew Johnson drew the most fire on the subject —the *Cleveland Press* made a count of personal and possessive pronouns in an 1866 Johnson speech: "This humble individual, one; myself, two; me, nine; my, 28; I, 69. That's not much, only 109 allusions to himself in a 15 minute speech . . . President Johnson is a my-ty man."

Although John F. Kennedy did not refer to "my" ambassadors in any speech, Arthur Schlesinger, Jr., made this point: "He felt this [the State Department] in some particular sense 'his' department . . . in the relationship between the President and the ambassadors, there had been, it is true, a slippage since Roosevelt's day. Roosevelt regarded them correctly as 'my' ambassadors and encouraged them to supplement their reports to the State Department by personal communication with him." Ambassadors like Kenneth Galbraith in India and George Kennan in Yugoslavia often communicated directly with President Kennedy.

Dwight Eisenhower, a team player, consciously avoided the possessive pronoun. "I don't believe," wrote reporter Robert Donovan, "that Eisenhower has ever used the expression 'my administration' or 'my cabinet.' He speaks of *the* Cabinet or *the* administration."

A speech General Eisenhower made in 1945 in New York City at a dinner in his honor as a war hero suggests that his selection or rejection of the personal pronoun had always been deliberate: "You have great hospitals in your city that are filled with wounded men. I call them 'my wounded men'; they came back from my theatre. I don't want to see any more of them there, ever."

MY FRIENDS FDR's use of a salutation to establish a warm, personal bond between himself and his audience.

Running for the New York State Senate in 1910, Franklin Roosevelt admired the way his fellow campaigner, Richard Connell, running for U.S. congressman in that area, established quick rapport with his listeners. FDR copied Connell's "My friends" for that and subsequent campaigns, but the phrase became identified with him because of the lilt of his pronunciation and the special requirement for warmth in radio addresses. No longer was the audience "vast" and "out there"; most listeners were in small groups in their own living rooms, and FDR pressed the intimacy with frequent use of "you and I know . . ."

Roosevelt probably did not know of the trouble the phrase caused for one of his predecessors as governor of New York, Horatio Seymour. When, trying to calm a group of draft rioters at City Hall in 1863, he opened his remarks with "My friends," Republicans attacked him for being unduly friendly to those "copperheads" who opposed the Civil War.

Salutations are overlooked as formalities by most speakers, which (as Seymour discovered) is a mistake. Abraham Lincoln chose his salutations with great care: to the citizens of Springfield, Illinois, upon his departure, he used "My friends," because many of them were his lifelong friends; at Gettysburg he used no salutation at all, appropriate in that atmosphere of solemnity; in his inaugural addresses he said "Fellow countrymen," which, along with "My countrymen," is traditional for inaugurals.

In 1781 John Witherspoon, president of Princeton and coiner of AMERICANISM in the sense of a word peculiarly American, unsuccessfully made the case against "fellow countrymen" as a salutation:

Fellow countrymen. This is a word of very frequent use in America. It has been heard in public orations from men of the first character, and may be daily seen in newspaper publications. It is an evident tautology, for the last word expresses fully the meaning of both. If you open any dictionary you will find the word countryman signifies one born in the same country. You may say fellow citizens, fellow soldiers, fellow subjects, fellow Christians, but not fellow countrymen.

Napoleon gave a martial ring to his addresses and messages to his troops: a simple, forceful "Soldiers." By contrast, the Selective Service system bureaucratically addressed its soldiers-to-be with a ludicrous "Greeting," and a draftee became known as one who "got his greetings."

Nicolai Lenin made "Comrades" famous to the point where all communists were called, often derisively, comrades.

Chief Tecumseh addressed General "Tippecanoe" Harrison with a translation of a dignified Indian greeting: "Friend and Brother." Members of the American labor movement address letters to each other as "Dear Sir and Brother," harking back to more fraternal times.

Jefferson chose "Friends and fellow citizens," and both William Howard Taft and John F. Kennedy preferred "Fellow citizens," with Harry Truman and Dwight Eisenhower leaning toward "My fellow Americans." During the 1940 campaign, Republican nominee Wendell Willkie made "fellow Americans" his own, rasping out his hoarse "Feller Amurr-ricans . . ."

The most effective "example" of the use of a salutation as a weapon is supposed to be the opening of Franklin Roosevelt's speech to the Daughters of the American Revolution following a dispute about the DAR's emphasis on white Anglo-Saxon lineage. FDR did *not* begin his speech, as legend has it, with "Fellow immigrants." The closest he came to this was a line in his speech to the DAR of April 21, 1938: "Remember, remember always, that all of us, and you and I especially, are descended from immigrants and revolutionists."

It is a shame that "Fellow immigrants" is apocryphal—it would have been the most pointed salutation in history.

MYTH frozen point of view attacked by John Kennedy; later, ironically, used to describe the aura of legend around Kennedy.

"Myths Respecting American Government" was the title of a speech given by President John F. Kennedy at Yale University, June 11, 1962. "Mythology distracts us everywhere —in government as in business, in politics as in economics, in foreign affairs as in domestic policy." In considering the "myth and reality in our national economy," he said that the dialogue between business and government was "clogged by illusion and platitude," adding, "For the great enemy of the truth is very often not the lie—deliberate, contrived and dishonest—but the myth, persistent, persuasive and unrealistic. Too often we hold fast to the clichés of our forebears. We subject all facts to a prefabricated set of interpretations. We enjoy the comfort of opinion without the discomfort of thought."

The Yale speech was a left-handed holding out of an olive branch to business leaders convinced that the Kennedy Administration was souring on them. (See **S.O.B.**) Historian Richard Hofstadter had used "The Agrarian Myth and Commercial Realities" as a chapter title in a 1955 book.

Senator J. William Fulbright picked up the "myth and reality" theme in a foreign-affairs context two years later: "We are clinging to old myths in the face of new realities, and we are seeking to escape the contradictions by narrowing the permissible bounds of public discussion, by relegating an increasing number of ideas and viewpoints to a growing category of 'UNTHINKABLE THOUGHTS.' " In-

cluded among the "old myths" in this speech (which became expanded into a book entitled *Old Myths and New Realities*) were U.S. policy regarding Cuba, Panama, and Vietnam.

Negro author James Baldwin also picked up the myth motif. He wrote in *The Fire Next Time:*

> The American Negro has the great advantage of having never believed that collection of myths to which white Americans cling: that their ancestors were all freedom-loving heroes, that they were born in the greatest country the world has ever seen, or that Americans are invincible in battle and wise in peace, that Americans have always dealt honorably with Mexicans and Indians and all other neighbors or inferiors, that American men are the world's most direct and virile, that American women are pure. Negroes know far more about white Americans than that . . .

Critics of Kennedy also liked the myth phraseology. Author Victor Lasky published a scathing attack on Kennedy in 1963 titled *JFK: The Man and the Myth.* The book was climbing on the best-seller lists until November, when it was withdrawn after the assassination, not to be marketed again for nearly fifteen years. With the martyrdom of a youthful President, the Kennedy mystique or image did soon achieve the proportions of an ancient myth, a high point being the publication of William Manchester's *The Death of a President,* with the controversy surrounding the Kennedy family's revisions in the manuscript. Reviewing the book in the *Times,* Tom Wicker referred to the myth:

> For my part, I reject the myth . . . I refuse to believe that any but a particular light went out . . . Above all, in Kennedy's case or any other, I refuse to deny the harsh reality of

death—that life goes on anyway, not unchanged, for the death of any man must diminish the sum of humanity, but undaunted, unabated in all its glory and misery. That is the meaning of the "ghastly futility" at Dallas. That is what the Kennedy myth distorts. And that is what, in the end, William Manchester's monument obscures.

The use of the myth as a rhetorical strawman is current and active. At Wake Forest College, in March 1978, President Jimmy Carter made the keynote of a hard-line defense speech his attack on "the myth" that the U.S. was unwilling or unable to help defend its allies around the world.

NABOB, *see* **NATTERING NABOBS OF NEGATIVISM.**

NAME OF THE GAME the goal; the quintessence; the heart of the matter.

Talking about U.S. foreign policy goals in Europe, presidential National Security Adviser (later Ford Foundation head) McGeorge Bundy said in 1966: "Settlement is the name of the game." Senator Frank Church added: "If we are going to play the game, we must remember that the ball is labeled 'relations with the Soviet Union.' If we are not going to play, we will discover that the game will go on without us, and we will soon become spectators in Europe rather than participants."

Campaign literature for Governor George Romney, put out by the Romney for President organization in 1967, carried a banner headline: "Winning is the Name of the Game." This slogan emphasized Romney's early strength in public opinion polls against President Johnson, subtly pressing the "Nixon can't win" theme.

Brooding about the decline of the Broadway column after the collapse of a New York newspaper in May 1967, columnist Robert Sylvester told the *New York Times:* "Now Lee Mortimer is dead, Dorothy Kilgallen is dead, Danton Walker is dead, Louis Sobol is retired. Some of these people

were the powerhouses. Some of these people were the name of the game."

In the seventies, the locution was usually replaced by "what it's all about," as "Settlement is what it's all about"; or "where it's at," as "Winning is where it's at."

See **SPORTS METAPHORS.**

NATION OF SHOPKEEPERS derisive description of England; meant to imply small-minded, business-dominated, greedy people.

Earliest known use was not in a pejorative sense. Josiah Tucker, Dean of Gloucester Cathedral (1712–68), wrote in 1763: "What is true of a Shop-keeper is true of a Shop-keeping nation."

The phrase was given currency in 1776 by Adam Smith in *Wealth of Nations:* "To found a great empire for the sole purpose of raising up a people of customers may at first sight appear a project fit only for a nation of shopkeepers. It is, however, a project altogether unfit for a nation of shopkeepers; but extremely fit for a nation whose Government is influenced by shopkeepers."

The phrase was probably already in current usage when Smith used it; on August 1, 1776, American revolutionary Samuel Adams reportedly said in Philadelphia: "Men who content themselves with the semblance of truth and a display of words talk much of our obligations to Great

Britain for protection. Had she a single eye to our advantage? A nation of shopkeepers are very seldom so disinterested. Let us not be so amused with words; the extension of commerce was her object."

The phrase became secure in the political lexicon when Napoleon Bonaparte applied it in scorn: *"L'Angleterre est une nation des boutiquiers."*

NATIVE RESERVES, *see* **HOMELAND.**

NATTERING NABOBS OF NEGATIVISM a new version of a denunciation of pessimists as PROPHETS OF GLOOM AND DOOM.

In the congressional campaigns of 1970, alliteration was one device Vice President Spiro T. Agnew used to call attention to his speeches. "Pusillanimous pussyfooters" and "vicars of vacillation" were his targets, and the phrases had a ring that reporters could not ignore. After the first few speeches, the looked-for alliteration was delivered tongue-in-cheek, culminating in a display of oratorical pyrotechnics in San Diego on September 11, 1970. Working with the Vice President on that speech, this writer offered a choice of alliterations to parallel the Stevenson "gloom and doom" phrase, but the VP chose to go with both: "In the United States today, we have more than our share of the nattering nabobs of negativism. They have formed their own 4-H Club—the 'hopeless, hysterical hypochondriacs of history.'"

As intended, the line got a laugh from the audience; it was taken seriously by James Reston of the *New York Times,* who called it "the worst example of alliteration in American history." (See Harding's "not nostrums but normalcy, not revolution but restoration, not agitation but adjustment . . . not experiment but equipoise . . ." under ALLITERATION.) Columnist William F. Buckley Jr. picked it up to apply to the British Prime Minister's problems over the sale of arms to South Africa: "Heath's point was that he has not been elected Her Majesty's first minister in order to take orders on matters affecting English security from nattering nabobs of negativism."

In the construction of the phrase, negativism was the basic word. A practitioner, beginning with *n,* was added next; nabob is a Hindi word for governor, and the word in English has come to mean a self-important potentate, carrying a jocular connotation. (See John Adams' 1776 use under SACHEM.) Nattering, the offbeat adjective that made the phrase memorable, was the last to be found, and its meaning of "complaining" was disputed by columnist Stewart Alsop, who insisted that the word was of British origin and meant "chattering."

The reason this entry is written with such dreary authority is that this lexicographer was the coiner, while serving as a speechwriter-on-loan to Mr. Agnew in the fall of 1970. The unwritten Speechwriters' Code, which proscribes writers from claiming their clients' prose as their own, is suspended in this case because the disgraced former Vice President has publicly ascribed the phrase to this scribe, requiring him to deny repeatedly authorship of other Agnewisms such as "effete corps of impudent snobs," "When you've seen one slum, you've seen 'em all," and INSTANT ANALYSIS.

The phrase is current, not directed against its original target, but used derisively against politicians who complain about the press. From the

Washington Star of December 20, 1977: "Ray Blanton, the Tennessee governor who's constantly being castigated by political rivals as well as those nattering nabobs of negativism, the media . . . says he's not going to answer reporters' questions any longer 'unless you report the positive side.' "

The phrase helped repopularize "nabob," and the word—one cut below a "nizam" in Hindi—is now synonymous with SATRAP, PANJANDRUM, POOH-BAH, high MUCKEY MUCKS, and other members of the POWER ELITE. But some writers have to be different: in the *New York Times Magazine,* (January 15, 1978) humorist S. J. Perelman used an alternate Hindi spelling—nawab—in a description of the patrons of Manhattan's "21" Club: "Here congregated tycoon and political nawab, screen idol and press overlord, rock star and capo of capos, secure in the knowledge that no losers were present. Here the illuminati rubbed elbows with the cognoscenti, publishers rubbed knees with nascent lady novelists, male dress designers rubbed thighs and spat at each other like cats. The drumfire of epigrams and the bray of egotism were rising to sawmill pitch . . ."

NEANDERTHAL WING, *see* **DINOSAUR WING.**

NEOCONSERVATIVE a political philosophy that rejects the utopianism and egalitarianism espoused by liberals, but departs from conservatism by embracing collective insurance and cash payments to the needy; a temperate philosophy, not sharply ideological, that takes modern democratic capitalism to be the best course in most cases.

Neoconservatism (the word has tri-

umphed over "the new conservatism") was spawned in the pages of a quarterly, the *Public Interest,* edited by Irving Kristol and Daniel Bell, published by Warren Manshel, and frequently contributed to by Daniel Patrick Moynihan and Seymour Martin Lipset. These former liberals were troubled by the failures of Lyndon Johnson's "Great Society" and dismayed at the way political orders throughout the world—especially the social democracies—were becoming statist and simultaneously less stable. When Keynesian economics began to fail to contain inflation, neoconservatives felt the economic basis for social democracy as it has been practiced began to erode. The last straw for many of the lifelong Democrats was the strident discontent of the youthful counterculture of the sixties, which made liberal elders uncomfortable with the culture that produced it. As it became fashionable all along the political spectrum to be alientated by "big government," that cultural chasm between "new" left and "old" left that widened: many of the former liberals could not stomach the permissive attitudes toward pornography, homosexuality, and rejection of group responsibility so often espoused by the inheritors of liberalism.

What distinguished neoconservatism from the "old" conservatism? The novel feature of the new conservatism is a relaxed attitude toward collective responsibility: "A welfare state, properly conceived," wrote Irving Kristol in the *American Spectator* in 1977, "can be an integral part of a conservative society." Such a statement is conservative heresy; conservatism teaches that statism leads to a repression of individuality. But Kristol plunged ahead: "It is antisocialist, of course . . . but it is not upset by the fact that in a populous, complex, and affluent society, people may prefer to purchase certain goods and services collectively rather than individually . . . People will always want security as much as they want liberty, and the 19th-century liberal-individualist notion that life for all of us should be an enterprise at continual risk is doctrinaire fantasy."

Kristol and "the *Public Interest* crowd," as the neoconservatives are frequently called, see liberal institutions such as Social Security to be bulwarks against further socialization. They hope the effect of their movement will be to remove utopian dreams from practical government. To the socialists (who want to center more power in the state), as well as to the "old" conservatives (who want to place more reliance on the individual), the neoconservatives say that the system the U.S. has now evolved "is certainly not the best of all possible worlds—but the evidence of the twentieth century is quite conclusive that it is the best of all available worlds. That makes it very much worth defending."

An early use of the phrase was by James Schall in *Time* (August 23, 1971): "Judaism and Christianity have always placed primacy in man. Now this primacy is attacked by what I call the neoconservative ecological approach to life." Senator Moynihan recalls that it was Michael Harrington, writer on poverty, who popularized the term at about that time in its present context.

The trend toward intellectual acceptance of neoconservatism has drawn fire. British journalist Henry Fairlie wrote in the *New York Times* on January 1, 1978: "The neo-conservatives have settled for popularity, instead of success—the slow, subterranean movement that genuinely alters the landscape. There is not a conserv-ative chortle or rumble or guffaw or belch among them. They have made conservativism dull and respectable again, when it is dullness and respectability that have killed every other American conservative movement in the past." Fairlie's observation caused some head-shaking amid the neoconservative faithful, who had just assembled at a dinner honoring the *American Spectator* at which the neoconservative honoree delivered a hilariously drunken harangue.

NEPOTISM, *see* DYNASTY.

NERVOUS NELLIES the easily upset; President Johnson's characterization of some critics of his Vietnam policy.

On May 17, 1966, the President spoke of "some Nervous Nellies and some who will become frustrated and bothered and break ranks under the strain. And some will turn on their own leaders and their own country, and on our own fighting men."

In slang, the word "nervous" has acquired the connotation of cowardly; "nervous in the service," Army slang, means a psychological disorder leading to a medical discharge, as well as a milder impatience or "itchiness." "Nice Nellie" is slang for prude.

Johnson's exact words show that he differentiated between "Nervous Nellies" and other dissenters, but the catch phrase was so strong that many critics of the policy soon used it as though Johnson had labeled all anti-involvement or anti-escalation forces "Nervous Nellies." A year later, the President added fuel to the fire with a remark about "cussers and doubters."

A useful political technique is to seize on a colorful phrase used by the opposition leader about some segment of your own group, and interpret it as though he referred to everyone opposed to him. For example, a Long Island, New York, candidate in 1962 called a bearded heckler a "greasy pig." The opposition promptly distributed banners and stickers with a drawing of a pig and urged voters to join the "greasy pig campaign." The candidate who made the remark, running in a "safe" district, was defeated; many voters had been convinced that he referred to all his opposition as "greasy pigs."

By 1975 the term had been parodied so often that it became part of the Johnson Administration lore, and was included in a satiric song in a Gridiron Club revue. To the tune of "A Wand'ring Minstrel, I," a reporter portraying Henry Kissinger sang:

> A wandering merchant, I
> Who deals in confrontation,
> Détente and consternation
> And schemes that mystify.
> Bismarck and Metternich
> And me and Machiavelli
> I'm not a Nervous Nelly!
> I've slippery rhetoric—
> Yes, slippery rhetoric.

NEUTRALIST a nation that refuses alignment with either Communist bloc or Western bloc, acting as mediator between, or beneficiary of, both.

Laotian Premier Souvanna Phouma defined the art of being a neutralist in 1961: "I am a good friend to Communists abroad but I do not like them at home." *Neutral*—as for example, applied to Sweden and Switzerland during World War II—differs from *neutralist,* uncommitted, or *nonaligned* nation. In the U.S. a neutral is considered merely a nonbelligerent, but a neutralist (a term having a pejorative connotation from most Americans' point of view) is a nation

that does not understand the threat of world Communism, or that cooperates with the U.S. only when it suits its interests and is not a good "ally" in a pinch.

This is a far cry from Woodrow Wilson's explanation of U.S. neutrality in 1915: "The basis of neutrality is not indifference; it is not self-interest. The basis of neutrality is sympathy for mankind. It is fairness, it is good will, at bottom. It is impartiality of spirit and of judgment."

About the same time, Benito Mussolini was saying: "Neutrals never dominate events. They always sink. Blood alone moves the wheels of history."

Secretary of State Dean Rusk tried to take the edge off the antineutralist feeling in the U.S.: "I do not believe that we ourselves should be unduly concerned about what might be called genuine neutralism because if a new nation is internally vigorous, viable, strong, progressive, its orientation in foreign policy is not so important as its health and strength. . . . I do not believe we ought to ask commitments of a sort that would make it difficult for them to lead their own peoples in development." See SCRAP OF PAPER.

Neutralism was frequently called "the Third Way" in 1957, preparing the ground for the adoption of THIRD WORLD as its replacement.

NEUTRALITY, *see* SCRAP OF PAPER.

NEVER AGAIN, *see* HOLOCAUST.

NEVER LOST A WAR OR WON A PEACE Will Rogers' assessment of U.S. diplomacy: "The United States has never lost a war or won a peace." A frequent criticism of peace negotiations by the "out" party.

See WINNING THE PEACE.

The point of view simultaneously carries a banner of patriotism and a partisan lance leveled at the bungling peacemakers who "sold out" our national interests. Some Republicans bitterly attacked Woodrow Wilson for advocating U.S. entry into the League of Nations. After World War II, Republicans were suspicious of "secret agreements" purportedly made at Yalta by President Roosevelt.

Thomas E. Dewey made the debatable point in 1950:

> During the First World War we said we wanted nothing for ourselves and nothing is what we got. In the Second World War again we said we wanted nothing and again nothing is what we got. At other times in our history we have known what we wanted and got it. Consider the War of 1812. The actual hostilities were indecisive and often humiliating for us. But at the peace conference which produced the Treaty of Ghent, the United States won a very advantageous frontier with Canada and all the other national objects for which we had fought. That was a war we did not win but we won the peace.

There is substance to the observation that the U.S. has been more successful in warmaking than peacemaking. Canadian Prime Minister Lester Pearson, in receiving the Nobel Peace Prize in 1957, gave one reason: "The grim fact is that we prepare for war like precocious giants and for peace like retarded pygmies."

NEW, POLITICAL USE OF   in the past century, no word stands out like "new" in the framing of themes for political movements.

Clement Laird Vallandigham, Ohio Democrat, in 1871 stirred his party with his *new departure:* "It is

not a New Departure but a Return: the restoration of the Democratic party once more to the ancient platform of Progress and Reform." Despite the disclaimer, the phrase caught on and helped rejuvenate the staggered Democrats.

Theodore Roosevelt, known for the "Square Deal," also pressed his *New Nationalism* in 1912: "This New Nationalism regards the executive power as the steward of the public welfare."

Woodrow Wilson titled the collection of his campaign speeches *The New Freedom,* taken from this line: "And the day is at hand when it shall be realized on this consecrated soil— a New Freedom—a Liberty widened and deepened to match the broadened life of man in America . . ." Theodore Roosevelt knew a good slogan when he heard one, and quickly tried to put it down: " 'The New Freedom' is nothing whatever but the right of the strong to prey on the weak."

But the Wilson phrase clicked, and spawned a wide range of others: the New Poetry, the New History, the New Art, the New Democracy, the New Woman—"the new anything," wrote historian Eric Goldman, "so long as it was new and gave an intoxicating sense of freedom."

As Adolf Hitler was talking of a *New Order,* Franklin Roosevelt was expounding the *New Deal;* in the campaign of 1960, John F. Kennedy talked of a *New Frontier* and Edmund Muskie in 1972 called for a *New Beginning.*

Adlai Stevenson captured this theme in a 1956 address: "There is a *New America* every morning when we wake up. . . . The New America is the sum of many small changes—a new subdivision here, a new school there, a new industry where there had been swampland—changes that add up to a broad transformation of our lives . . ."

In President Jimmy Carter's inaugural address, he invoked a *"new spirit"* several times, but the time was evidently not ripe for the phrase. See GREAT, POLITICAL USE OF.

NEW AMERICAN REVOLUTION, *see* **REVOLUTION OF RISING EXPECTATIONS.**

NEW BROOM, *see* **SPOILS SYSTEM; CLEAN SWEEP.**

NEW CLASS   the technical and managerial elite.

Communist doctrine teaches that with the destruction of capitalism, a classless society will emerge. That has not happened in the Soviet Union; what has emerged instead is a bureaucracy of party and government which substitutes power and perquisites for money, and enables an elite to enjoy luxuries that capitalists use money to buy.

The phrase was coined by Yugoslav Communist Milovan Djilas, in his book *The New Class: An Analysis of the Communist System* (1957). Djilas, later harassed and jailed by Marshal Tito, held that "the new class, the bureaucracy, or more accurately the political bureaucracy, has all the characteristics of earlier ones . . . the Party makes the class, but the class grows as a result and uses the Party as a basis. The class grows stronger, while the Party grows weaker; this is the inescapable fate of every Communist party in power."

In the early seventies Professor Irving Kristol and other NEOCONSERVATIVES used the phrase to describe the academic-technical-governmental-foundation elite that sought to represent and to help, but not be a part of, the working class in the U.S.

A related term is TECHNOCRAT, a back-formation from "technocracy," an intellectual movement in the early thirties that argued for the replacement of consumer-dominated capitalism with an economic system that gave its priority to production at capacity. Because of its similarity to "bureaucrat," with the lowering of public regard for that occupation, the word "technocrat" gained a mechanical and bloodless connotation. In the early seventies Zbigniew Brzezinski, who later became Jimmy Carter's National Security Adviser, coined "the technitronic age" to herald the new society ahead, but that phrase never caught on. Well-educated managers and students of the "new class," whether technocrats, social workers or members of "the CHARLES RIVER GANG," are sometimes distrusted by people who are vaguely worried about machines and computers having too much to do with their lives.

NEW DEAL   Franklin D. Roosevelt's program, enunciated in his acceptance speech at the 1932 Democratic convention; since divided into First New Deal (1933–35) and Second (1935–37).

"I pledge you," Roosevelt told the convention, "I pledge myself, to a new deal for the American people. Let us all here assembled constitute ourselves prophets of a new order of competence and of courage. This is more than a political campaign; it is a call to arms. Give me your help, not to win votes alone, but to win in this crusade to restore America to its own people."

This brief peroration, perhaps by Samuel Rosenman, offered commentators four possibilities for a slogan: "new order," which became known as Adolf Hitler's program; "crusade," which became Dwight Eisenhower's theme; "call to arms," which was never picked up by anybody; and "new deal."

On the day of the speech, cartoonist Rollin Kirby drew a sketch of a man leaning on a hoe, looking bewildered but hopeful, watching an airplane flying overhead labeled "New Deal." This was an indication to the Roosevelt forces and the Democratic National Committee that they had an exciting catch phrase. (Cartoonists can do much to propagate a phrase; see MCCARTHYISM.)

"I had not the slightest idea that it would take hold the way it did," wrote Rosenman later, "nor did the Governor [Roosevelt] when he read and revised what I had written. In fact, he attached no importance to the two monosyllables. . . . Some have said that it was intended to be a combination of the Square Deal of President Theodore Roosevelt and the New Freedom of President Woodrow Wilson. There was no such intention when it was written or when it was delivered . . . when I handed him the scrap of paper on which the few paragraphs had been written he said that he thought they were all right as a peroration. . . . It was simply one of those phrases that catch public fancy and survive—short, concise, and yet comprehensive enough to cover a great many different concepts."

Other versions of the origin exist. Both Judge Rosenman and Professor Raymond Moley reviewed some of the Roosevelt entries in this book, and in this case, these were Professor Moley's comments:

> You will find an account of the preparation of the acceptance speech on pages 23–27 inclusive in my "After Seven Years." When Rosenman says that he wrote it he is in error. The expression "new deal" was in the draft which I left at Albany with Roosevelt. What happened at Albany was not the rewriting of the speech but a rearrangement of it in a somewhat shortened version. If you will look at the exhibit opposite page 14 in my book you will see where the expression appeared first. I merely put this in to carry out the rhythm of the sentences at that point.
>
> Of course, I have in my possession the original drafts before Rosenman and Roosevelt worked on them in Albany and some of the original drafts have Roosevelt's notations on them.
>
> I was not aware that this would be the slogan of the campaign. It was a phrase that would have occured to almost anyone, and it certainly did not come from the book written by Stuart Chase, for I had not seen the book at that time.

The first person who spotted the importance of the phrase was Herbert Bayard Swope, who wrote a letter to me immediately after the speech was delivered, saying that it should be pulled out and made the keynote of the campaign. I don't know about Rollin Kirby's cartoon.

Later Roosevelt allowed the New Deal legend to be embellished by pointing to Mark Twain's Connecticut Yankee, who said that "when six men out of a thousand crack the whip over their fellows' backs, then what the other nine hundred ninety four dupes need is a new deal" [see CARD METAPHORS].

English reporters pointed out that "A New Deal for Everyone" was David Lloyd George's campaign slogan in 1919, one year before FDR ran unsuccessfully for vice president. Other phrase hunters came up with a few lines from a Woodrow Wilson speech on October 24, 1910: "If it is reorganization, a new deal and a change you are seeking, it is Hobson's Choice. I am sorry for you, but it is really vote for me or not vote at all."

Robert La Follette had written in his 1912 autobiography that his Committee of 100 "believe that the time has come for a new deal," and Carl Schurz had used it several times in the previous century, as in 1871: "There were the spoils ahead, with the prospect of a 'new deal.' " Petroleum V. Nasby wrote a year after Lincoln's assassination: "Wilkes Booth's ghost came in, and wanted to know what he wuz to hev in the new deal, 'for,' sed he, 'ef't hadn't been for me, where'd yoo all hev bin?' " And Nicholas Biddle, head of the Bank of the U.S., received a letter in Jackson's day calling for "a new bank and a New Deal." Further search seems unrewarding.

Around the time the speech was delivered, Stuart Chase had written an article in the *New Republic* titled "A New Deal for America," which Rosenman does not recall ever having seen. Suffice it to say the phrase was in the air and meant little until it was given the context of the man, the time and place. Indeed, "time and place" without the man meant nothing; on that same day and from that same rostrum, speaking several hours before Roosevelt, John McDuffie of Alabama nominated John Nance Garner for Vice President with the words: "There is a demand for a new deal in the management of the affairs of the American people."

The phrase was promptly parodied as "New Dole," "Raw Deal," and even "Jew Deal"; a generation later, Adlai Stevenson characterized Dwight Eisenhower's cabinet, made up mostly of businessmen, as "The Big Deal," and George Romney called Lyndon Johnson's administration "The Fast Deal." See DEAL.

NEW DEPARTURE a recurrent phrase urging a fresh approach, based on a nautical metaphor. See SHIP OF STATE.

Senator John C. Calhoun of South Carolina used "new departure" frequently in the 1830s: "My aim is fixed, to take a fresh start, a new departure on the States Rights Republican tack." "Tack," of course, is a sailing term; Massachusetts Senator Henry Wilson, one of the founders of the Republican party, picked it up in 1871 in an *Atlantic Monthly* article titled "New Departure of the Republican Party," and sailed on further: ". . . the new under-currents in the popular mind . . . have driven and drifted the ship of state from its former course, and rendered necessary new observations, new calculations and a new departure." Clement Laird Vallandigham, a COPPERHEAD briefly banished by Lincoln to the Confederacy during the Civil War, popularized the phrase in seeking a reorientation of the Democratic party in Ohio in 1871.

At the same time, Republican Henry Wilson was selected by Ulysses S. Grant to run as his Vice President in his second term, opposing the Liberal Republican–Democratic coalition headed by Horace Greeley.

Thus both sides in the campaign of 1872 were hammering away at their own "new departure," successfully preventing a fine theme from gaining any real identity.

NEW ECONOMICS political economic thought stemming from the school of John Maynard Keynes, holding that government fiscal and monetary policy can help end depressions and stimulate orderly economic growth.

"We are all Keynesians now," admitted Milton Friedman, leading conservative economist and defender of what was left of the laissez-faire philosophy, to *Time* magazine in 1965. See WE ARE ALL.

Lord Keynes's publication in 1936 of the *General Theory of Employment, Interest and Money,* followed by Alvin Hansen's "translation" into understandable English and application to the U.S. economy, in turn followed by Paul Samuelson's "neoclassical synthesis" combining the Keynes position with some classical economic theory, resulted in a startling approach to managing a nation's business.

Keynes and his followers, dubbed "new economists" in the late fifties, sought new ways to provide full employment and a high annual growth rate at a minimum cost to the stability of prices and the balance of trade. The concept of "pump-priming," used in the thirties, was vastly expanded, and the idea of reducing deficits by reducing, rather than increasing, taxes at certain stages was introduced. In what was probably the last stand of the old-line economists, Treasury Secretary George Humphrey said in 1957 about government spending during business declines, "I don't think you can spend yourself rich."

The increase in revenues after the 1964 tax cut (which stimulated business and thereby increased the amount of tax revenues received) probably provided the breakthrough for "new economics" in the councils of government. A large question remained: If the new thinking could stimulate the economy out of recessions, could it restrain the economy from inflation?

A key word in the new economist's new vocabulary is TRADE-OFF. Former chairman of the Council of Economic Advisers Walter Heller explains:

The political economist typically thinks in terms of *trade-offs*—for example, the trade-off between jobs and inflation, the problem at which we pitch our Phillips Curves (relating the behavior of prices to the behavior of unemployment); the trade-off between international payments equilibrium and internal expansion, for which monetary policy did the twist (pushing short-term interest rates up to discourage the outflow of volatile funds, while holding long-term rates down to encourage capital spending); the trade-off between price-wage stability and unfettered markets, for which we erected the wage-price guideposts (providing guides to noninflationary wage and price behavior).

The new economics marked the entry of "the Respectable Professors of the Dismal Science," in Carlyle's phrase, into the top level of government planning. John R. Commons, whose "progressive individualism" was a controversial economic approach at the turn of the twentieth century, believed that "the place of the economist is that of adviser to the leaders, if they want him, and not that of propagandist to the masses." But which economist to trust was a dilemma agonizingly expressed by Warren G. Harding: "I know somewhere there is an economist who knows the truth, but I don't know where to find him and haven't the sense to know and trust him when I find him. God, what a job!"

John F. Kennedy tried to take some of the controversial sting out of the new economics by making it appear to be simple, good business management: "What is at stake in our economic decisions today is, not some grand warfare of rival ideologies which will sweep the country with passion, but the practical management of a modern economy."

NEW FACE a candidate unscarred by previous major contests, unencumbered by known positions, offering politicians and voters a fresh choice.

A striking example of "new faces" on the national scene was the choice offered Republicans at their 1940 convention: Robert A. Taft, elected senator from Ohio just two years before; Thomas E. Dewey, who had recently been defeated in his first race to be governor of New York; and Wendell L. Willkie, a businessman who had never run for public office. That year the newest face (Willkie's) won; in 1944 Dewey's face was no longer new, but won; in 1948 Dewey's face was the "oldest" by virtue of his previous election defeat, and won again. Both lost to the smiling old face of FDR.

The desire for a new face—"untarred by the brush of defeat"—is perennial at national conventions, but is usually at its peak long before the convention meets. The balance sheet of every well-known candidate includes liabilities: enemies made in previous contests, a possible lost election and a CAN'T-WIN aura, perhaps a haunting record on what has become an embarrassing issue, and often a contempt-breeding familiarity with his voice and his personality. Because the presence of some new and mysterious candidate like a William Jennings Bryan or a Dwight Eisenhower is a thrilling uncertainty, the appeal of a new face in an "out" party is understandable.

As the Brookings Institution pointed out in 1960, "the limitations of well-known candidates are likely to be about as well understood as their potentialities. But both limitations and potentialities of less-known men can only be guessed at—unless the testing process before the convention is sufficient to bring out evidence."

Suspicion about a new face's "trustworthiness"—i.e., willingness to work with a party—increases as convention time approaches, and public demand for specific stands rises. These combined forces lessen the appeal of a new face, reminding delegates of the security of an "old face"—one less likely to blunder on the campaign trail, one who understands their local political problems, and above all, one whose victory will mean victory for themselves.

The phrase itself was popularized in the Broadway theater by Leonard Sillman, who began producing a series of *New Faces* revues in 1934.

See TIME FOR A CHANGE.

NEW FEDERALISM a political philosophy that seeks to wed the need for national action with the desire for much greater local participation.

The phrase was coined, and the idea expounded, in a speech to the nation by President Nixon on August 8, 1969. "After a third of a century of power flowing from the people and the States to Washington it is time for a New Federalism in which power, funds and responsibility will flow from Washington to the States and to the people." (See CREATIVE FEDERALISM; POWER TO THE PEOPLE.) That morning, at a ceremony in the Rose Garden of the White House, Republican National Chairman Rogers Morton—who had read the speech draft—jumped the gun with this comment: "These are bold new steps toward a new Federalism, a new participation of the people of this great country in the pluralism that is essential to our democracy."

Revenue sharing (see TAX SHARING) was a step in the direction of decentralization, which the President developed with a much more heavily funded proposal the next year; on the other hand, welfare reform (see **WORKFARE**) was a step toward centralization. To explain this seeming anomaly, the President encouraged his aides to do some thinking and writing on the subject.

That brought forth memoranda from "Publius" (this writer) and "Cato" (Tom Charles Huston, an outspoken conservative who later gained notoriety as author of a scheme of admittedly illegal counterespionage known as the Huston Plan.)

Wrote Publius in January of 1970, in "New Federalist Paper #1":

> We like the blessings of strong central government: a clear direction toward social goals, a willingness to counteract economic freezings and overheatings, a single voice in world affairs. But we are repelled by centralization's side effects: ineffective administration that breeds resentment, inflexible bureaucracy that breeds alienation.
>
> We also like the blessings of decentralization or "home rule," with its respect for diversity, its ready response to local demands, its personality tailored to its constituents. But we are repelled by frequent local unwillingness or inability to meet human needs.
>
> Do we have to choose one way or the other—centralization or decentralization—taking the bitter with whatever we consider the sweet? Many think not, and have spent the past year working out a synthesis of the most desirable in both central government and home rule. It has been called "The New Federalism."
>
> ... The purpose of the New Federalism is not to wrap liberal principles in conservative clothing, or vice versa; the purpose is to come to grips with a paradox: a need for *both* national unity and local diversity; a need to protect *both* individual equality at the national level and individual uniqueness at the local

level; and a need to *both* establish national goals and decentralize government services.

Replied Cato the following month:

> ... what New Publius is really advocating is not a New Federalism but a **NEW NATIONALISM** (a phrase which Theodore Roosevelt unfortunately preempted nearly sixty years ago). At the heart of New Publius' contrived synthesis is this simple proposition: while decision-making must be nationalized, administration should be decentralized ... he simply brushes aside States rights as a constitutional guarantee; he, New Publius, declares (the Constitution of the United States notwithstanding) that States rights have now become rights of first refusal. Perhaps one should give him the benefit of the doubt and assume that in his eagerness to replace the melting pot with the salad bowl he has inadvertently mixed apples with oranges. If, for example, New Publius is simply saying that within the scope of legitimate federal authority Congress may choose to give the States first option on the administration of a federal program, such a statement is unobjectionable. If, however, New Publius is saying that once the Federal Government determines that a problem—any problem—exists and decides that something should be done about it, the States have the first option to take action and if they refuse, the Federal Government may rightly act on its own—if this be his argument, then not only is it objectionable, it is revolutionary.

George Shultz, then Secretary of Labor, set forth what he considered to be the credo of the New Federalist in a speech on March 19, 1970:

> We must act as one nation in determining national goals: We must act as a federation of States and localities in meeting those goals, providing leeway for local option and individual diversity; The Federal government and the courts must

provide checks against any unfairness inflicted by local government, and local government must be able to provide checks against unfairness caused by national standards; Power must be permitted to seek its own level of efficient response, flowing to that level of government closest to the people and willing and able to exercise it; Local innovation and voluntary action must be aggressively encouraged, which limits the liability of the failure of worthwhile experiments and raises the chances of finding practical solutions; We must reinstill a new respect for individual responsibility and personal freedom, recognizing that the dignity of work is the counterpart of human dignity. The individual citizen must think and act on two levels: He must contribute to the determination of our national goals and then must involve himself locally in making those goals a reality where he lives. This may not seem like a revolutionary credo, but if it is followed in our time, it could have the same revolutionary impact that followed the acceptance of the ideas of the original Federalists.

These two schools of thought contended, on varying levels and in many ways, throughout the next year; in the 1971 State of the Union message, President Nixon espoused much of the philosophy described in the Publius memorandum and the Shultz speech.

A wide range of choices were provided to the President for a phrase to describe his philosophy in August 1969, with aide Patrick Buchanan's suggestion finally chosen. "The New Federalism" was an intellectual slogan, which was what the President had in mind, and not a promissory one. He did not expect it to be the "New Deal" of his Administration, and it was not; pre-Watergate, it did serve the purpose of providing

thoughtful supporters and critics a focus for discussion.

NEW FREEDOM the slogan used by Woodrow Wilson in the presidential campaign of 1912.

Wilson believed with Louis Brandeis, who had won fame as a trust buster and whom he would later appoint to the Supreme Court, that the greatest enemies of the American people were the growing trusts and bigness in industry and commerce in general. He felt that the only instrument which could, and should, do something about this was the federal government.

His New Freedom called for government intervention to safeguard the democratic rights of small business against the industrial behemoths. Wilson described it thus: ". . . a revival of the power of the people, the beginning of an age of thoughtful reconstruction, that makes our thought hark back to the great age in which democracy was set up in America." See CURSE OF BIGNESS.

Wilson's belief that bigness was evil brought him into direct conflict with Theodore Roosevelt, also a candidate. Former President Roosevelt, an early believer in defining an Administration's political philosophy with a slogan—"SQUARE DEAL"—had a new slogan of his own, "THE NEW NATIONALISM." Bigness, with a certain necessary minimum of regulation, was perfectly natural from Roosevelt's point of view, and late in life he found nothing reprehensible in trusts.

On this subject Wilson drew the issue: "I take my stand absolutely, where every progressive ought to take his stand, on the proposition that private monopoly is indefensible and intolerable."

His writings and speeches of the

campaign were gathered in a 1913 book called *The New Freedom.*

NEW FRONTIER style adopted by the Kennedy Administration.

"A new frontier had been discovered," a hard-driving presidential candidate told a crowd in West Middlesex, Pennsylvania, ". . . the frontier of invention and new wants. Under our American way of life, men with courage and imagination were free to occupy this new frontier and develop it. They built a greater America."

The candidate was Alf Landon, the date August 22, 1936. Landon used the phrase several times in his campaign against Roosevelt, but he could not make too much of it, since *New Frontiers* was the title of a book published two years before by Henry A. Wallace.

Senator Arthur Vandenberg of Michigan strung a few clichés together in a speech in South Dakota, October 11, 1938:

Man cannot live by bread alone. What profiteth it a man if he gain the whole world and lose his own soul? Those who try to trade liberty for security usually wind up by losing both. Eternal vigilance is the price of liberty. Every journey to the forbidden land begins with the first step. These new frontiers that are offered to us are anticonstitutional, antidemocratic, antiliberal Frontiers. They are the potential boundaries of the collectivist state.

In 1951 Walter Prescott Webb wrote a pessimistic piece in the *Atlantic Monthly* decrying the boosterism of those who "speak of new frontiers," adding: "The businessman sees a business frontier in the customers he has not yet reached . . . The social worker sees a human frontier among the suffering people whose woes he has not alleviated . . . If you watch these peddlers of substitute frontiers, you will find that nearly everyone

wants you to buy something, give something, or believe in something . . . They are all fallacies, these new frontiers, and they are pernicious in proportion to their plausibility and respectability."

Of course, "previous usages" can be found of almost any famous phrase in the English language (see NEW DEAL; GREAT SOCIETY); the important usage was by John F. Kennedy, accepting the Democratic nomination in the Los Angeles Coliseum in 1960: " . . . we stand today on the edge of a new frontier—the frontier of the 1960s, a frontier of unknown opportunities and paths, a frontier of unfulfilled hopes and threats. . . . The new frontier of which I speak is not a set of promises—it is a set of challenges. It sums up not what I intend to offer the American people, but what I intend to ask of them."

Who suggested it to Kennedy? Arthur Schlesinger, Jr., points out in *A Thousand Days* that he had given a speech himself a few months before titled "New Frontiers of American Liberalism"; reporter David Wise credited Walt Whitman Rostow, then an MIT economic historian, with suggesting the phrase to Kennedy at a Boston cocktail party a month before the nomination; later both Rostow and Max Freedman, Washington correspondent for the *Manchester Guardian,* are supposed to have submitted separate drafts of the acceptance speech, each containing the "New Frontier" theme. But a Kennedy intimate informs the lexicographer that neither Freedman nor Rostow submitted any material for this particular speech. He adds that rough draft material was solicited from many sources, including Professor Allan Nevins of Columbia, but that the term itself was in none of them.

The origin here was probably similar to "NOTHING TO FEAR BUT FEAR ITSELF," when Louis Howe—probably—picked it up from a newspaper advertisement and suggested it to FDR. The phrase "new frontier" was in the air in early 1960. For example, the U.S. Chamber of Commerce appointed a Committee on New Frontiers in Technology in April of that year, with the name chosen months before that. "The Chamber would not have adopted this name if it had been already used by and identified with Mr. Kennedy," the secretary of that committee writes the author. After Kennedy made the phrase his own, the Chamber ruefully changed the name of its "new frontiers" committee to the more pedestrian "Committee on Science and Technology."

In *Kennedy*, Ted Sorenson, who prepared the acceptance speech for the candidate, takes a defensive stance: ". . . the basic concept of the New Frontier—and the term itself—were new to this speech. I know of no outsider who suggested that expression, although the theme of the Frontier was contained in more than one draft. Kennedy generally shrank from slogans, and would use this one sparingly, but he liked the idea of a successor to the New Deal and Fair Deal."

Thus Kennedy popularized, probably at Sorensen's suggestion, a phrase that was "around."

NEW LEFT a movement, deliberately leaderless, begun in England in 1957 by young radicals who rejected the "old" liberal philosophy; joined in the next decade by pacifists and civil rights militants, who oppose the "power structure" that robs them of their freedom and individuality.

Sociologist C. Wright Mills is credited with the coinage of the phrase in the late fifties. In England, two university periodicals merged in 1959 to form the *New Left Review*, staffed largely by disenchanted young Marxists. At that time in the U.S., a group calling itself SLATE was formed at the University of California's Berkeley campus, and a similar student political party was formed in Chicago. The young intellectuals adopted new vocabularies and new forms to contrast with the "liberal establishment" they felt no longer met their needs. See MOVEMENT, THE.

Mills wrote in 1960: "If there is to be a politics of a New Left, what needs to be analyzed is the structure of institutions, the foundation of policies. In this sense, both in its criticisms and in its proposals, our work is necessarily structural—and so, for us, just now—utopian." His followers seized upon this rationale for their emphasis on questions over answers, their apparent negativism and lack of a program.

In recent use, it encompassed the antibureaucracy, alienated groups who dissociated themselves from the liberals of the "old" left.

From the point of view of Democrats and "regular" liberals, the new left represented a splintering of support or an embarrassment; many Republicans considered it a collection of Vietniks and far-out radicals, with whom no communication was possible, overlooking the common ground possible in a mutual distaste for strong centralized government. See COUNTERCULTURE.

NEW LOOK a change in defense strategy in 1953, as the Korean War ended, de-emphasizing "conventional" forces and relying more on nuclear deterrents. See BIGGER BANG FOR A BUCK.

The phrase came from the fashion world, where it was used in 1947 to describe the Paris-inspired change to radically lower hemlines and softer details after the austere fashions of wartime. The phrase fitted a reassessment of the nation's defense attire.

Defense's new look appealed to those who wanted a reduction in total defense spending, and who felt that our preparation for nontotal "brushfire" wars diminished our threat of nuclear retaliation. It was opposed by many Army generals who agreed with retiring Chief of Staff Matthew Ridgway in assailing the "overemphasis" on air power and MASSIVE RETALIATION.

In his memoirs General Eisenhower traced both the coinage and what he felt was an OVERREACTION:

> At about the time of the changeover in the Joint Chiefs of Staff, active fighting in Korea ended. This fact, along with the epochal developments which were transpiring in nuclear armaments, occasioned what Admiral [Arthur] Radford described in a talk late in the year as a "New Look" [at the Press Club, Washington, December 14, 1953]. It happened that this term had a definite place in the parlance of the day; it had been coined to describe noticeable changes in the style of women's dresses (not entirely an improvement, some men felt). Thus the tag "New Look" probably suggested to many minds a picture of a far more radical change in the composition of our armed forces than was truly the case.

NEW NATIONALISM Theodore Roosevelt's progressive program of 1910, designed to lead the Republican party toward more liberal paths.

The former President was stamping about Africa in 1910, bored and regretting not having sought a third term. His friend Judge Learned Hand sent him a book by Herbert Croly, *The Promise of America,* which differed from the Jeffersonian ideal of the least government being the best

government, and restated and extended much of Roosevelt's own thought. On his return, TR invited Croly to tea in Oyster Bay and promptly took over the program; biographer Henry Pringle thinks the phrase "new nationalism" came from Croly as well.

In a speech at Osawotomie, Kansas, the former President said: "The New Nationalism puts the national need before sectional or personal advantage. . . . This New Nationalism regards the executive power as the steward of the public welfare. It demands of the judiciary that it shall be interested primarily in human welfare rather than in property, just as it demands that the representative body shall represent all the people rather than any one class or section of the people."

Elihu Root shrugged it off with "The only real objection I see to it is calling it 'new,' " but many other Republicans considered it heresy. Two years later, in the Wilson-Taft-Roosevelt "Bull Moose" campaign of 1912, Woodrow Wilson adopted most of the principles expressed by the "New Nationalism" with the exception of an attitude toward trusts, which TR felt were good if properly supervised and Wilson felt were the embodiment of evil. Wilson called his own program "the NEW FREEDOM"; President William Howard Taft was the only candidate running with nothing "new."

Ironically, ten years after Roosevelt introduced the term, Warren G. Harding—apostle of "normalcy"—declared Roosevelt's Osawotomie speech the basis of his platform, but he did not later become known as a proponent of a strong central government.

NEW ORDER   program of Hitler's regime in Germany.

The phrase, in English, is from British poet Alfred Lord Tennyson: "The old order changeth, yielding place to new,/And God fulfils himself in many ways,/Lest one good custom should corrupt the world."

Hitler's use of the phrase was adapted by Prince Konoye, Premier of Japan, in 1938, as he called for "a new order in East Asia." Before both Hitler and Konoye, Woodrow Wilson had used the phrase. See NEW DEAL; UNITED WE STAND.

In the seventies, the phrase was picked up by leaders of have-not nations demanding a redistribution of wealth under a "new economic order." See THIRD WORLD.

NEW POLITICS   the self-description of a grouping on the left that was occasionally successful in attracting new politicians.

Syndicated columnist Milton Viorst described it as of June 30, 1970:

Basically, the New Politics is a movement on the left and insofar as it can be defined at all, is ideological and anti-organizational. It invented Eugene McCarthy and almost made him president, but it neither began nor ended with the 1968 campaign . . .

On the same day, columnist David Broder observed:

. . . the parties have been weakened plenty in recent years, particularly the 'new politics' reformers expected. Instead of elevating us to a new plane of issue-oriented direct democracy, it may sweep us backwards toward the primitive brutalities of tribal warfare. When voters lose the habit of identifying themselves as Republicans or Democrats, they may not, as the reformers hoped, begin to think of themselves

as conservatives or liberals, or even hawks or doves. They may instead view electoral politics as a power struggle between Italians and Irish, Catholics and Yankees, or blacks and whites. And that we could do without.

Another point of view was expressed by the *Wall Street Journal:*

A GRASS-ROOTS upsurge for Eugene McCarthy in the Democratic Party gets labeled "the new politics," something better than old ways. Yet, as we recall, a grass-roots upsurge for Barry Goldwater in the Republican Party got labeled political atavism, or something like that. . . . It will be horrible, most of the pontificators tell us, if all those who support Mr. McCarthy are left feeling their efforts did not influence either major party. But somehow no one weeps over the far more fundamental alienation felt by the supporters of George Wallace. How healthy our political system is, it seems, depends a good deal on whose political ox is gored. All of which suggests to us there are no old politics and no new politics. Only politics.

The phrase triggers excitement because it appears to sever ties with the entrenched political leadership, and triggers resentment because it appears to fly a false banner—the techniques are not new at all.

"Hypocrisy" and "expediency" were the twin villains of participants of the new politics, but as reformers come to power, terms like "practical politics" and "necessary compromise" come to the fore. Many people who objected to the new politics focused on the fact that the techniques were far from new, which was hardly in dispute—the trouble was that the new participants expected immediate gratification in their quest for the "old" political power.

NEW WORLD ECONOMIC ORDER, *see* **NEW ORDER; THIRD WORLD.**

NICKEL-AND-DIMING, *see* **BUTTONHOLING.**

NICKNAMES derisive or laudatory sobriquets that familiarize or stigmatize a politician.

Since the earliest days the chief statesmen of this country have been given nicknames, some of them familiar to every schoolboy: "Father of his Country" for Washington; "Honest Abe" for Lincoln; "Old Hickory" for Jackson; "The Little Giant" for Stephen A. Douglas.

Not every schoolboy is informed that Washington, in his lifetime, was often referred to as "The Stepfather of his Country" and "The Old Fox." Lincoln was derided by Confederates and Northern Democrats alike as "The Baboon" and his wife as "The She-Wolf." U. S. Grant, observed Mencken, "because he was always the soldier more than the politician, escaped with nothing worse than 'The Butcher,' but his successors got it hot and heavy."

Hayes was "The Fraud" as well as "The Hero of '77"; Arthur was "The Dude" and "America's First Gentleman"; Cleveland, "The Stuffed Prophet" and "Perpetual Candidate"; Theodore Roosevelt was "Bull Moose," **"MAN ON HORSEBACK"** and "Teddy the Meddler." Wilson was "The Phrasemaker" and "The Schoolmaster." Coolidge was "Silent Cal."

The two Roosevelts and Wilson probably provoked more invective than any other Presidents. Franklin Roosevelt was known variously as "Boss," FDR, "Houdini in the White House," "Sphinx," "Squire of Hyde Park," and **"THAT MAN IN THE WHITE HOUSE."**

Nicknames are often borrowed and transferred: "Great Commoner" (Pitt the elder) to Henry Clay and, later, to William Jennings Bryan; "Bald Eagle of Foggy Bottom" (Robert Lovett, Secretary of Defense) from "The Bald Eagle of Rhode Island," Tristram Burges (1770–1853), a member of Congress.

New York's Mayor John Lindsay was known as "Mr. Clean" and "Batman." President Truman enjoyed "Give 'Em Hell Harry" but not "High Tax Harry." President Eisenhower was simply "Ike." Nixon was "Tricky Dick." With Franklin Roosevelt, John Kennedy, and Lyndon Johnson, presidential initials became popular. President Johnson was both LBJ and "Big Daddy." James Earl Carter, Jr., was the first to formally adopt the informal style with "Jimmy."

MR. DOOLEY, referring to "Tiddy" (Teddy Roosevelt), was told not to be disrespectful; he retorted that he was not being disrespectful, he was being affectionate.

The "nick" in nickname comes not from the variety of characterizations given the Devil (Old Nick) but from the Middle English *eke,* meaning something added, an extension, or (as a verb) to increase or lengthen (still used as "eke out a living") and an *ekename* became a nickname, or an extra surname applied in jest or familiarity.

See **INITIALS, PRESIDENTIAL; SOBRIQUETS.**

NIGHTMARE, *see* **LIFT OF A DRIVING DREAM.**

NIGHT MAYOR a city official of whatever rank assigned to remain at City Hall or tour the city on official business during the night hours.

Begun by the administration of John Lindsay of New York in 1966, the program was intended to publicize the wide-awake, round-the-clock officials and give them an opportunity to make surprise inspections that often resulted in newspaper photos.

The practice derived from the military CQ (charge of quarters) and OD (officer of the day, or on duty) who is responsible for any decisions requiring immediate attention when ordinary authority is off duty.

The phrase itself was coined by James J. Walker, who served as a sparkling, beloved mayor of New York and who resigned in 1932 as a result of Samuel Seabury's investigation of municipal corruption: "Some folks call me the 'night mayor' of New York."

NIGHT OF THE LONG KNIVES

a time of purge; a savage, surprise attack by one's supposed friends.

"It was no secret that this time the revolution would have to be bloody," Adolf Hitler told the Reichstag meeting at the Kroll Opera House on July 13, 1934, explaining the events of the weekend of June 29 to July 2; "when we spoke of it, we called it 'The Night of the Long Knives' [*die Nacht der langen Messer*]. . . .

"In every time and place," Hitler continued, "rebels have been killed . . . I ordered the leaders of the guilty shot. I also ordered the abscesses caused by our internal and external poisons cauterized until the living flesh was burned."

In the summer of 1934 Hitler was Chancellor, his rise to power helped by the Brown Shirts headed by Ernst Röhm. But the leaders of Germany's regular army were worried about Röhm and the private Nazi militia, who were calling for a "second revolution" to overthrow the military and industrial elite in Germany. Hitler made a deal to enhance his power in government while wiping out his undisciplined former comrades, and personally directed Heinrich Himmler and Reinhard Heydrich of the Gestapo, and their boss, Hermann Göring, to arrest and execute eighty-three of the leaders of the storm troopers. After that weekend, Hitler's power was unchallenged.

The "night," then, was originally supposed to be a time of revolution conceived by Hitler, Röhm and the early Nazis; to its planners the phrase denoted an entire weekend of purge and the elimination of an obstacle to complete power. Ironically, the "night" that took place eliminated one of the men who had planned it, and turned the "second revolution" into an internal purge.

Today, the phrase is an example of the use of catastrophic terms to describe far less bloody developments, like "massacre" for extensive firings. In *Time*'s obituary of Charles Chaplin on January 2, 1978, Stefan Kanfer wrote: "Let a man rise in show business, even to so stratospheric a level as The Tramp's, and there comes an evening of the Long Knives. . . . he became embroiled in a series of affairs . . . after the war, he could no longer be saved from his enemies."

See PURGE and PUTSCH; for other Nazi-era terms, see FINAL SOLUTION; HOLOCAUST; and MUNICH, ANOTHER.

-NIK SUFFIX

as in the derisive terms *beatnik, peacenik, Vietnik,* and others. Suggests youth, scruffiness, beardedness, and irresponsibility.

A 1963 *New York Times* headline read: " 'BEATNIK' TROUBLES LEXICOGRAPHER." The lead: "Dr. Charles Talbot Onions . . . celebrated his 90th birthday here recently worrying about the word 'beatnik.' "

Those who "knew their Onions" worried as well; was it a neologism that would last, deserving a place in a dictionary—or a "nonce word" that struts and frets and then is heard no more?

The popularization of the suffix -nik probably started with Al Capp, creator of the "Li'l Abner" comic strip, who developed a subseries in the country of "Lower Slobbovia," a land of ice, wolves, and miserable people who spoke a combination of English, Russian, and Yiddish. "Leettle Noodnik" (from the Yiddish nudnik, "tedious fellow," or "dope") was one of the characters. The suffix is of Russian origin; -nik when added to stems of Russian words means "one who."

-nik crashed like a meteorite into the English language with the launching of the Soviet Sputnik (from iskust-vennyi sputnik zemli, "artificial satellite [literally: fellow traveler] around the earth") on October 4, 1957. When a second satellite, containing a dog, was launched on November 4, several newspapers tagged it a "muttnik," and the fad of the -nik construction was launched as well.

There were no-goodniks and far-outniks, beatniks, and sickniks. Even the typical suburban home shown at the U.S. exhibition in Moscow—not split-level, but with a walkway splitting it—was called the "Splitnik," coined with inordinate pride by the author.

After some flirtation with "folk-nik" and "peacenik," public fancy in 1958 appeared to settle on "beatnik," probably an outgrowth of the "beat generation," novelist Jack Kerouac's switch on Gertrude Stein's "lost generation." Columnist Herb Caen coined the term in the San Francisco Chronicle of April 2, 1958: "Look Magazine, preparing a picture spread on S.F.'s Beat Generation (oh, no, not AGAIN!) hosted a party in a No. beach house for 50 Beatniks . . ." The term was active as a derogation of young people who let their hair grow and refused to work, to be replaced in the late sixties by "hippie," a somewhat different subculture.

Time and Newsweek turned "beatnik" to "Vietnik" in October 1959, and the pejorative connotation of beatnik—lazy, irresponsible—was transferred to the word for war protesters.

In the mid-seventies the suffix was returned to its country of origin, by way of giving an English word a Russian flavor. A headline in the New York Times letters section in June 1977 read: "Robert Toth Explains Refuseniks' Role." A "refusenik" is a Soviet citizen, often Jewish, who has been refused permission to emigrate.

NINE OLD MEN a description of the nine Justices of the Supreme Court, a majority of whom blocked Franklin Roosevelt's programs in the mid-1930s.

The average age of the Supreme Court members in 1936 was seventy-one (in 1968 it was sixty-five). Throughout his first term, Roosevelt had no opportunity to make a single appointment. "Chance and the disinclination of the individuals to leave the Supreme Bench," said Roosevelt, "have now given us a Court in which five Justices will be over 75 years of age before next June and one over 70."

FDR came up with a plan to bring the Court out of what he called "the horse and buggy age." He proposed that for every Supreme Court Justice who failed to quit the bench within six months after reaching his seventieth birthday Congress empower the President to appoint a new Justice up to a total of six.

Roosevelt had overreached himself; his plan was denounced as court-packing, and he found himself on the defensive. "If by that phrase 'packing the Court' it is charged," he said, "that I wish to place on the bench spineless puppets who would disregard the law and would decide specific cases as I wished them to be decided, I make this answer: that no President fit for his office would appoint, and no Senate of honorable men fit for their office would confirm, that kind of appointee to the Supreme Court."

Roosevelt's plan died in committee on July 22, 1937; however, the President's purpose was served when the Court began to show its shifting position. Justice Owen Roberts threw the balance of power to the liberals, and the Court soon upheld a minimum-wage law for women, a National Labor Relations Act, and the Social Security Act.

"By the time the Court recessed for the summer," wrote Samuel Rosenman, "it was obvious that the liberal dissenting views of the minority in 1935 and 1936 had in large measure become the majority views of the Court. As a contemporary wag put it: 'A switch in time saved nine.' "

The phrase "nine old men" was coined by Drew Pearson and Robert S. Allen in a 1936 book dealing with the Court, and was further made famous by a characterization of them as a kind of chorus line in the 1937 Rodgers-Hart musical, *I'd Rather Be Right.*

Since that time, attacks on the age of Supreme Court Justices or senators have been rare. The word "senator" is Latin for "old man" and is based on the same root as "senile."

NITTY-GRITTY   detail work; difficult minutiae to be handled by staffers after strategy has been decided higher up.

"SNCC's resources for nitty-gritty organizing—" wrote the *New Republic* in 1967, "and perhaps its will to work in a low key over a long period of time—are thin."

This expression of Southern Negro origin is in common current use, and one can speculate on its derivation: "nit" means the egg of a louse, something tiny and distasteful; "nit-picking," or fault-finding, uses "nit" in a sense of something small or detailed. (Shakespeare's *Taming of the Shrew:* "Thou flea! thou nit, thou Winter-cricket, thou!")

"Grit" is rooted in sand, or dust, and later in coarse meal (as "hominy grits"); as a verb, it means to grind in sand, and to "grit one's teeth." Thus, the rhyming words mean to take tiny details (nitty) and grind them carefully (gritty). Speculation aside, somebody probably thought of it in a flash of inspiration, as with other rhyming compounds like "willy-nilly" (willing or not) and "helter-skelter" (from the German *holter-polter*). These are reduplicated or ricochet words; a political "flip-flop" is called a gradational compound.

NIXON DOCTRINE   a foreign policy that sought to maintain U.S. involvement in the affairs of the world, in a way that required allies to bear the manpower burden of their own defense.

In his November 3, 1969, SILENT MAJORITY speech, President Nixon first used the phrase publicly: "Let me briefly explain what has been described as the Nixon Doctrine." (Somewhat self-conscious about using the phrase with his name in it, he toned it down with "what has been described as." Needless to say, he wanted it described exactly that way.) These were the three principles of the doctrine as set forth in that speech:

First, the United States will keep all of its treaty commitments. *Second,* we shall provide a shield if a nuclear power threatens the freedom of a nation allied with us or of a nation whose survival we consider vital to our security. *Third,* in cases involving other types of aggression, we shall furnish military and economic assistance when requested in accordance with our treaty commitments. But we shall look to the nation directly threatened to assume the primary responsibility of providing the manpower for its defense.

The doctrine first presented at Guam was in a **BACKGROUNDER** not for direct quotation, and Nixon could not correctly say it was "announced" there. The operative verb, appropriate for **DOCTRINES** generally, is "enunciated."

NOBLE EXPERIMENT   sarcastic characterization of Prohibition, based on a phrase of Herbert Hoover's.

Hoover wrote Senator William E. Borah on February 28, 1928, of "a great social and economic experiment, noble in motive and far-reaching in purpose." But there were 327 murders in Chicago alone in one Prohibition year, and not a single conviction for murder that year; the "wets" quoted Isaiah (24:11): "There is a crying for wine in the streets; all joy is darkened, the mirth of the land is gone."

Hoover is best remembered for phrases he nearly said, or claimed he did not originate, or denied having said at all. He did not say **"CHICKEN IN EVERY POT"**; he said he did not originate **"RUGGED INDIVIDUALISM,"** and as seen here, he did not quite say

"NOBLE EXPERIMENT." And he certainly did not name the collection of Depression shacks "Hoovervilles."

"Noble experiment" is applied now to hopelessly lost causes. Its predecessor phrase was "Holy Experiment," English Quaker William Penn's term for his 1682 colony of Pennsylvania. That experiment worked.

See **RUNNING AGAINST HOOVER**.

NOBODY DROWNED AT WATERGATE   a slogan used by Nixon partisans to express resentment at what they believed was a double standard of political morality.

In the early stages of the Watergate scandal, many of the President's supporters believed that the break-in at Democratic headquarters was little more than had been described by press secretary Ron Ziegler: a "third-rate burglary." To them, the **COVER-UP** which aroused such widespread indignation was similar to the attempts made by Senator Edward F. Kennedy in 1969 to seal information at an inquest in Edgartown, Mass., following "the Chappaquiddick incident."

At Chappaquiddick, a young woman named Mary Jo Kopechne had died when a car Senator Kennedy was driving plunged into a river. Nixon supporters, claiming that Senator Kennedy was not subjected to the same rigorous examination that a non-Kennedy would have been under similar circumstances, suggested that the loss of life in the Chappaquiddick incident made it far more important and worthy of investigation than the Watergate break-in. Hence the phrase "nobody drowned at Watergate," which was in the air some months before the *Wall Street Journal* quoted Secretary of Agriculture Earl Butz saying it in 1974.

A curious twist on the construction

came in 1978 when Georgia supporters of banker Bert Lance believed he
was being hounded out of his job
as Jimmy Carter's Director of the Office of Management and Budget for
minor irregularities committed when
he ran a bank in Calhoun, Georgia.
The resentment took the form of a
bumper sticker reported to be on a
car in southern Georgia: "Nobody
Drowned at the Calhoun Bank."

NO COMMENT an outdated,
pretentious phrase to ward off a reporter's query, now used by political
novices with no skill at fencing.

When the expression was fairly
fresh, Winston Churchill used it with
zest. After a White House meeting
with President Truman in 1946, he
evaded questions with: "I think 'No
comment' is a splendid expression. I
got it from Sumner Welles."

Before making that discovery,
Churchill—early in his career—used
a form of excruciating euphemism to
avoid a position. When asked, in
1906, if the British government was
condoning slavery of Chinese labor-
ers in South Africa, he replied, "It
could not, in the opinion of His Majesty's Government, be classified as
slavery in the extreme acceptance of
the word without some risk of terminological inexactitude."

Before he was a candidate for President, Franklin Roosevelt said he
knew the value of "sitting tight, saw-
ing wood and keeping my mouth
shut"; his cousin Theodore had once
written: ". . . what is needed for me is
to follow the advice given by the New
Bedford whaling captain to his mate
when he told that all he wanted from
him was silence and damn little of
that."

At press conferences FDR's favorite evasive action was "That's an IFFY
QUESTION." Grover Cleveland was

much more blunt; once when asked
something he preferred not to answer,
he glared at the reporter and said,
"Young man, that is an issue too big
to be brought up in a brief interview
that is drawing rapidly to a close."

Best known for his taciturnity was
"Silent Cal" Coolidge, who answered
critics with a mild "I have noticed
that nothing I never said ever did me
any harm." President Lyndon Johnson, when pressed, avoided the words
"No comment," substituting something like "I don't have anything to
say about that at this time." He
passed along advice given him by former House Speaker Sam Rayburn:
"You don't have to explain what you
don't say."

Another riposte is to challenge the
basis or the phraseology of the question or to play tricks with language: at
his first press conference as head of
the Council of Economic Advisers,
Walter Heller listened to a reporter
object to a lack of cost estimates of the
Administration's anti-recession program. "The inference will be drawn,"
said the reporter, "that you don't care
very much about how much they'll
cost." Heller snapped back with a
smile: "That may be the inference,
but not the implication."

Diplomats must say nothing nice to
reporters; Harold Macmillan said of
the post of Foreign Secretary, "He is
forever poised between a cliché and
an indiscretion." UN Secretary General Dag Hammarskjöld phrased his
"No comment" as "I never discuss
discussions."

Political managers often advise
their candidates to say nothing. Tammany chieftain Charles Murphy advised young Mayor-to-be James
Walker: "Most of the troubles of the
world could be avoided if men opened
their minds instead of their mouths."
A century earlier, banker Nicholas

Biddle told party managers to pass the word to "Tippecanoe" Harrison: "Let him say not one single word about his principles, or his creed—let him say nothing—promise nothing. Let no committee, no convention—no town meeting ever extract from him a single word about what he thinks or what he will do hereafter. Let the use of pen and ink be wholly forbidden."

The reason for Biddle's advice was explained by Alexis de Toqueville in *Democracy in America:* "The general interest of a party frequently demands that members belonging to it should not speak on great questions which they understand imperfectly; that they should speak but little on those minor questions which impede the great ones; lastly, and for the most part, that they should not speak at all. To keep silence is the most useful service that an indifferent spokesman can render to the Commonwealth."

John Selden, who served in Parliament in the seventeenth century, observed: "Wise men say nothing in dangerous times." Three centuries later, physicist Albert Einstein reduced this advice—and that of Tammany boss Murphy—to the following formula: "If A equals success, then the formula is A equals X plus Y plus Z. X is work. Y is play. Z is keep your mouth shut."

Charles de Gaulle put it this way in *The Edge of the Sword:* "There can be no power without mystery. There must always be a 'something' which others cannot altogether fathom, which puzzles them, stirs them, and rivets their attention. . . . Nothing more enhances authority than silence. It is the crowning virtue of the strong, the refuge of the weak, the modesty of the proud, the pride of the humble, the prudence of the wise, and the sense of fools . . ."

But there is such a thing as carrying a zipped lip too far. In an unauthenticated speech made to party and army cadres in Peking in July 30, 1977, Foreign Minister Huang Hua recalled his use of the phrase when he was China's UN ambassador: "While I was in New York, a Swedish reporter once asked me if he could be of service to me. I said: 'No comment.' That reporter then asked me if we Chinese really had nothing to say except 'No comment.' I repeated: 'No comment.' As a socialist country, however, it does not seem right if our responsible comrades have learned only to say 'No comment.' Sometimes we should give out some news."

NO-DEAL, *see* **DEAL.**

NONPARTISAN without thought of party politics.

In current usage, *bipartisan* means the cooperative efforts of both parties in an area usually the scene of party disagreement; *nonpartisan* (or, as Senator Arthur Vandenberg preferred, *unpartisan*) means areas of civic or patriotic interest where party or ideological difference never arises. The meaning corresponds to the prefixes: two-party, no-party.

The phrase most closely associated with nonpartisan is ABOVE POLITICS; with bipartisan, WATER'S EDGE.

Pleas for nonpartisanship stem from Washington's farewell address deploring the "baneful effects of the spirit of party," Madison shaking his head at "faction," and Jefferson stating flatly, "If I could not go to Heaven but with a party, I would not go there at all."

When FDR in 1939 called for "cooperation . . . without trace of partisanship," speechwriter Samuel Rosenman properly called it "a plea for nonpartisanship in the form of bipartisanship."

Denunciations of partisanship and of party connection have been prevalent throughout U.S. history, particularly by weaker candidates who felt the need to prove their independence. Zachary Taylor, for example, whose long military COATTAILS helped popularize that expression, took no controversial positions as a Whig in 1848: "If elected, I would not be the mere president of a party. I would endeavor to act independent of party domination. I should feel bound to administer the government untrammeled by party schemes." Taylor won, but the Whigs lost Congress.

Nonpartisanship is also called for by leaders of a party under attack, with some reason, for corruption. Charles Evans Hughes, a tower of integrity in the Harding Administration, said as scandals like Teapot Dome began to be exposed: "Neither political party has a monopoly of virtue or of rascality. Let wrong be exposed and punished, but let no partisan Pecksniffs affect a 'holier-than-thou' attitude. Guilt is personal and knows no party." Adlai Stevenson, fighting off the "mess in Washington" charge in 1952, used Hughes's statement to no avail.

Rarely if ever do public figures stand foursquare in favor of partisanship, though all will speak up for the TWO-PARTY SYSTEM, another way of saying the same thing. Bronx Democratic boss Ed Flynn got to the heart of the matter: "There is no such thing as nonpartisanship. If there were, there would be no need for elections. The phrase 'nonpartisanship' has a high moral tone. It is used by men running for public office to attract votes, but deep down in their hearts these men know that it is only a word without real meaning. There is, and

always must be, honest disagreement. All of us have our likes and dislikes. And that is the genesis of partisanship."

See PARTISAN; PRESIDENT OF ALL THE PEOPLE.

NONPOLITICAL TRIP tongue-in-cheek term for a political tour, or "swing around the circle," made to appear "nonpolitical" for strategic or fund-raising reasons.

When an officeholder travels on official business, the public pays his way; on an admittedly politically motivated journey, he must get his party or his supporters to finance him. In the case of Presidents, the very appearance of acting as President is more potent than any purely or frankly "political" act; therefore, presidential press secretaries straight-facedly announce "nonpolitical" trips that must, whether intended or not, have strong political overtones. (For a similar construction, see FACT-FINDING TRIP.)

Washington attorney Clark Clifford, appointed Defense Secretary in 1968 and an adviser to Democratic candidates and Presidents for a generation, wrote a campaign memo to Harry Truman in 1948 that charted one portion of what was to be a stunning upset:

Since he is President, he cannot be conspicuously active politically until well after the convention. So a President who is also a candidate must resort to subterfuge. He cannot sit silent; he must be in the limelight. . . . He must resort to the kind of trip Roosevelt made famous in the 1940 campaign—the inspection tour. . . . No matter how much the opposition and the press pointed out the political overtones of those trips, the people paid little attention, for what they saw was the Head of State performing his duties.

Manchester Guardian correspondent Alistair Cooke wrote of a 1964 campaign tour of Lyndon Johnson's: ". . . on this 'non-political,' two-day 9000-mile trip, somebody saw to it that 10,000 people turned up in Great Falls, Montana, 25,000 in Blaine, Washington, that he paid a swift courtesy call on the Mormon Church in Salt Lake City, and that he touched down at Seattle, Portland, and Sacramento, the political power stations of the West Coast."

It is hard to get passionate about this practice, especially since Thomas Jefferson and James Madison visited New York in 1791 for political reasons, blandly letting it be known they were looking for wild flowers and a rare species of butterfly in the Hudson Valley. John F. Kennedy, early in the 1960 primaries, referred to this excuse and added, "But I'm not looking for butterflies. I'm looking for votes."

NONSTUDENT   a participant in campus political activity at an institution of higher learning who is not an enrolled student.

The word entered the language in the mid-sixties in connection with demonstrations and other political activity at the Berkeley campus of the University of California. When the university officials sought to curb on-campus activities of "nonstudents," these young people, along with many students and faculty members, strenuously objected. The issue of "academic freedom" vs. "faculty control" was raised, and became a part of the gubernatorial campaign between Democratic Governor Edmund "Pat" Brown and Republican candidate Ronald Reagan in 1966, with Reagan advocating a "crackdown" to restore discipline.

The use of *non-* as a prefix in coining new words is growing. NONVIO-

LENCE is in the civil rights lexicon; *Time* magazine coined "non-book" to describe the many "quickie" books being compiled and published with a minimum of writing or thought; a presidential trip during a campaign is often derisively described as NON-POLITICAL. And novelist Herbert Gold told in 1967 of a poet who believed in the value of silence: "Marshalling his McLuhan, the dropped-out, anti-word poet declared non-speech to be a bigger gas than speech."

It is now possible to use *non-* five times in a short sentence: "A nonstudent with a non-book under his arm made a nonpolitical speech to a group of nonviolent nonentities."

NONVIOLENCE   a technique of bringing about social change through peaceful though dramatic demonstrations.

The word is most closely associated with Mohandas K. Gandhi as "the first article of my faith." But the Mahatma's method of "passive resistance" was improved upon by leaders of the civil rights movement in the U.S. in the early 1960s.

The Reverend Martin Luther King, Jr., called 1961 "a year of the victory of the nonviolent method; although blood flowed, not one drop was drawn by a Negro from his adversary."

In Birmingham, Alabama, in 1963, King and his followers were criticized by clergymen of that city for provoking violence. In "Letter from a Birmingham Jail" King answered that criticism: "Is not this like condemning the robbed man because his possession of money precipitated the evil act of robbery?" He added: "I have tried to stand between these two forces saying that we need not follow the 'do-nothingism' of the complacent or the hatred and despair of the black nationalist. There is the more excellent way of love and nonviolent protest. I'm grateful to God that, through the Negro church, the dimension of nonviolence entered our struggle. If this philosophy had not emerged I am convinced that by now many streets of the South would be flowing with floods of blood."

By the mid-sixties, however, the word was used to mock Negro leaders unable to moderate their own extremists. Though the Student Nonviolent Coordinating Committee had nonviolence in its title, it became an anachronism to SNCC leaders like H. "Rap" Brown, who called in 1967 "for less rooting and more shooting."

NORMALCY period of retrenchment, of stability; the promise of Warren G. Harding.

"Not heroism but healing, not nostrums but normalcy" was the campaign theme of Ohio publisher Warren Harding in 1920, running with Coolidge against Cox and Roosevelt. For the rest of the quotation, see AL-LITERATION; for variations, see CATCHWORD.

"After a diet of strong occasions," wrote political scientist Harold Laski, "a nation, like an individual, turns naturally to the chance of a quiet time. 'Normalcy' is always certain to be popular after crises." Wrote Eisenhower in his memoirs: "Twice in this century the United States, at the end of a war, had celebrated the victory, brought the troops back home, and with relief and hope tried to return to 'normalcy.' " Harding's use of the word might have been a mistake; some say the word was written "normality" and fluffed, but if true, the mistake was fortunate: the word caught on to symbolize not only a campaign but an era.

The much-abused Harding (whose talent for alliteration led to his coinage of FOUNDING FATHERS) was defended on the charge of error by no less an authority than H. B. Woolf, editorial director of G. & C. Merriam Company, who wrote *New York Times* reporter Israel Shenker in 1972: "It is true that Harding's use of *normalcy* subjected him to considerable criticism, but he defended himself by pointing out he found it in the dictionary. (See the *Times* for July 21, 1920.) The word dates from at least 1857, and it is an entry in the 1864, 1890, and 1909 editions of the Merriam-Webster Unabridged."

In a less sloganeering way, Harding returned to the theme that elected him in his inaugural address: "Our supreme task is the resumption of our onward, normal way . . . the normal balances have been impaired, the channels of distribution have been clogged, the relations of labor and management have been strained . . . we must strive to normalcy to reach stability."

NORMALIZATION, *see* **VIETNAMIZATION.**

NO SUBSTITUTE FOR VICTORY the rallying cry of General of the Army Douglas MacArthur, in his address to Congress of April 19, 1951, following his removal from command in the Far East by President Truman. Said MacArthur:

> I know war as few other men now living know it, and nothing to me is more revolting. I have long advocated its complete abolition, as its very destructiveness on both friend and foe has rendered it useless as a means of settling international disputes. . . .
>
> But once [war] was forced upon

us, there is no other alternative than to apply every available means to bring it to a swift end. War's very object is victory, not prolonged indecision.

In war there can be no substitute for victory.

This statement put him into conflict with another theory of war that had been gradually evolving: that it is possible to wage deliberately controlled, LIMITED WAR for limited objectives.

The statement should be considered in the context of the times. General MacArthur had ruled Japan since World War II as something of a proconsul, neither brooking nor being offered much interference. He had conducted the Korean conflict in much the same spirit. But he had been refused permission to turn the 600,-000 Chinese Nationalist troops on Formosa loose against the mainland with American logistical support. He had been denied the large numbers of reinforcements he had demanded and refused permission to send bombers against enemy bases north of the Yalu River, the border between North Korea and China.

The General's pressure led President Truman and his advisers to consider MacArthur's removal. When the General wrote a letter to Republican House Minority Leader Joseph Martin, which he read in the House of Representatives, Truman determined to replace his Far East Commander. The recall came hastily when it became known that the *Chicago Tribune,* a paper friendly to the General's views, was about to break the story.

The immediate result was a furor in which personalities, strategies, and constitutional positions were thoroughly intermixed. A senatorial investigation was begun by those friendly to the General's views, but the course of the investigation ran eventually in the Administration's favor.

The conflicting theses were stated in May 1951 when Senator Leverett Saltonstall quoted from a speech by Dean Rusk, then Assistant Secretary of State, who formulated the core of the limited-war concept: "What we are trying to do is to maintain peace and security without a general war. We are saying to the aggressors, 'You will not be allowed to get away with your crime. You must stop it.' At the same time we are trying to prevent a general conflagration which would consume the very things we are now trying to defend."

General MacArthur totally rejected the new theory. "I think," he said, "that introduces into the military sphere a political control such as I have not known in my life or have ever studied."

See NO-WIN POLICY; OLD SOLDIERS NEVER DIE.

NOT FOR ATTRIBUTION   an agreement between journalist and news source to use information without revealing where it came from.

Not for attribution should not be confused with OFF THE RECORD, when the information is given with the understanding that it will not be used, or with *background,* where a source may be indicated but not named.

Until late 1971 (when the *Washington Post* began to object to "collusion" between government and press) the Washington press corps had generally accepted the Lindley Rule, named after journalist Ernest K. Lindley, enabling the President to discuss affairs of the day with reporters without either being quoted or referred to at all. In an article in the *Columbia Journalism Review* entitled

"The President Nonspeaks," Ben Bagdikian wrote: "Under the Lindley Rules . . . no meeting took place so far as the public is concerned. If reporters want to use something the nonspeaker has said at the nonmeeting, they must paraphrase the nonspeaker and attribute his ideas to their own intuition or some nameless source." See BACKGROUNDER; TRIAL BALLOON; PLANT.

Mr. Lindley, in 1968 a Special Assistant to Secretary of State Dean Rusk, informed the author (for attribution):

> The Lindley Rule was laid down early in the Truman Administration to enable high ranking officials to discuss important matters—especially those involving international and military affairs—without being quoted or referred to in any way. It was, and is, a rule of no attribution —thus differing from the usual "background rule" permitting attribution to "official sources" or "U.S. officials," etc. Thus the paragraph you quote from Bagdikian is not quite correct—attribution to a "nameless source" is not permitted under the Lindley Rule.

The point is a fine one, but there can be no arguing with Hoyle himself: "not for attribution" means the newsman must take responsibility for the statement without hinting where it came from. This is also called "deep background."

The British use "on lobby terms" for the same technique, from "lobby journalist" who picks up his news outside legislative halls. "Under this system," wrote M.P. Anthony Wedgewood Benn in 1964 in the *Manchester Guardian,* "Ministers and M.P.'s can talk 'on lobby terms' to journalists, confident that nothing they say will be attributed to them; and journalists can always find out what is really happening without bothering to dig on their own. . . . One day some political correspondent is going to tumble to the fact that he would do far better to abandon the cosy comfort of 'lobby terms' and set up the sort of private political intelligence unit that every newspaper should have."

NOTHING TO FEAR BUT FEAR ITSELF a classic phrase of Franklin Roosevelt's, from the opening of his first inaugural address, March 4, 1933.

"This is no occasion of soft speaking or for the raising of false hopes." FDR crossed out that line in an early draft, and substituted the more positive statement:

> This is preeminently the time to speak the truth, the whole truth, frankly and boldly. Nor need we shrink from honestly facing conditions in our country today. This great nation will endure as it has endured, will revive and will prosper.
>
> So, first of all, let me assert my firm belief that the only thing we have to fear is fear itself—nameless, unreasoning, unjustified terror which paralyzes needed efforts to convert retreat into advance.

Who wrote it? This has been the subject of some heated controversy among Roosevelt intimates. The copy of the first draft of the speech, in Roosevelt's handwriting, and with a cover note from FDR attesting to its composition at Hyde Park, February 27, 1933, from 9 P.M. to 1:30 A.M., does not contain the famous opening. "The final draft," wrote Samuel I. Rosenman, who edited the Roosevelt public papers, "was typed on March 3. . . . In that last draft the . . . 'fear' sentence had been inserted. The way it was changed was typical of what the President could do with a speech —even in the great rush . . ."

Rosenman never asked Roosevelt

where the "fear" sentence came from, and did not notice until after FDR's death that it was not in the first draft. He speculated: "It bears a striking resemblance to a statement about fear written by Henry David Thoreau: 'Nothing is so much to be feared as fear.' Eleanor Roosevelt has told me that one of her friends had given the President a copy of some of Thoreau's writings shortly before the day of inauguration, and that it was in his suite at the hotel while this speech was being polished."

In *FDR: The Lion and the Fox,* historian James MacGregor Burns puts that speculation in such a way that the reader can only draw one conclusion: "In his hotel room Roosevelt worked over the speech. Nearby was a copy of Thoreau, with the words, 'Nothing is so much to be feared as fear.' "

Brain truster Raymond Moley dismisses all this. He stated positively in 1966 that Louis Howe wrote the "fear" line, and that Howe got the idea from a newspaper ad that featured the quote a few weeks before. "I was in Roosevelt's Mayflower suite," Moley wrote this lexicographer, ". . . I saw no books there. Nor was I familiar with Thoreau. I had been with Roosevelt more than a year and never heard him mention Thoreau. . . . And Howe, whose reading—which his asthma-provoked insomnia required—was confined exclusively to detective stories and newspapers, may never have heard of Thoreau."

Moley's history marches to the beat of a different drummer: he was with FDR at Hyde Park on the night of February 27, and submitted a draft of the inaugural to him. "He read over my draft carefully and then said that he had better write out the text himself because if Louis Howe (who was expected the next morning) failed to see a draft in his (Roosevelt's) handwriting, he would 'have a fit.' " Presumably FDR wanted to conceal from Howe the fact that he had a ghostwriter. After Roosevelt copied out the speech, Moley says he tossed his own first draft into the fire. "Then, in the morning, as had been anticipated, Howe got his hand into the composition. He proceeded to redictate the draft, adding . . . a first paragraph. . . . I do clearly remember that the phrase appeared in a department store's newspaper advertisement some time earlier in February. I assume that Howe, an inveterate newspaper reader, saw it too. . . . To Howe's everlasting credit, he realized that the expression fully fitted the occasion."

The who-wrote-it controversy is dwelt on in some length here because it illustrates (1) the difficulty of pinning down the originator of a phrase, and (2) the relative unimportance of the writer as compared to the speaker and the forum. The message was in the ad, assuming Moley's recollection is correct, but who cared? Who even noticed, besides a gnomelike man who had the ear of the President-elect? The phrase did not belong to Howe, nor to the advertising copywriter, nor to all those who had used it previously (including Sir Francis Bacon: "Nothing is to be feared but fear . . ." Epictetus, Cicero, Burke, William James, and others). It was Roosevelt's phrase, and it might have rated only a modest mention in a news story had it not been spoken in a momentous inaugural address.

In current use, "nothing" takes precedence over "the only thing," as in a 1968 cartoon by Mahood in the *Times* of London showing Dean Rusk reading a newspaper to a worried Lyndon Johnson: "Apart from

Kennedy, McCarthy, Nixon, the Viet Nam war, the Senate Foreign Relations Committee and the price of gold, you have nothing to fear but fear itself."

NOT TOO MUCH ZEAL, *see* GUNG HO.

NOVEMBER REPUBLICANS
voters who register in one party to participate in its primary but who intend to vote for the other party in the general election.

This is a Texas expression. Since the Democratic party dominates Texas politics on the local level, many voters who wish to have a voice in the selection of a candidate for sheriff will register Democratic. But their voting habits in the general election, especially on the national scene, run to the opposite party—hence, "November Republicans."

See CROSSOVER VOTERS.

NOVUS ORDO SECLORUM, *see* UNITED WE STAND.

NOW, POLITICAL USE OF
crucial word in the mid-sixties to indicate (1) Negro impatience and (2) youthful rejection of "old-fashioned" ideas.

Clarence Streit's pre–World War II plea for world government, *Union Now*, was the precursor of the civil rights movement's slogan, FREEDOM NOW. The use of "now"—a small but powerful word—occurred frequently at rallies and on petitions and statements by civil rights leaders, frustrated by promises of evolutionary change and future equality. In *The White Liberal's Retreat*, the American Jewish Committee's Murray Friedman wrote: ". . . to the Negro demand for 'now,' to which the deep South has replied 'never,' many lib-

eral whites are increasingly responding 'later.' But the Negro will accept nothing short of first-class citizenship, now."

Teen-agers in 1966 ("teeny-boppers") picked up the word to apply to fashions ("now" dresses and "now" hairdos) and students sought "now" philosophies.

NO-WIN POLICY   attack phrase
on what is considered an overly cautious military effort, leading not to victory but to stalemate.

The phrase illustrates the exasperation felt by many people at LIMITED WARFARE. General Douglas MacArthur (see NO SUBSTITUTE FOR VICTORY) told the Republican convention in 1952: "It is fatal to enter any war without the will to win it." When General Mark Clark returned home in 1953 after the truce in the Korean conflict, he reflected the unsatisfied attitude of many Americans: "I return with feelings of misgiving from my third war—I was the first American commander to put his signature to a paper ending a war when we did not win it."

The fact that Eisenhower was a Republican, conservative at least in fiscal affairs, and a former general with an overwhelming reputation for military judgment, muted the ultraconservative attacks on the lack of a "victory plan" against Communism. But when the Democrats returned to power in 1961, and especially after the Bay of Pigs, a typical comment was made by Rear Admiral Chester Ward (Ret.), of the right-wing American Security Council: "Americans are tired of surrenders covered up as 'negotiated settlements.' . . . For the first time in sixteen years of the cold war, a demand for victory is beginning to roll into Washington."

Barry Goldwater's biography was titled *Victory Is His Flight Plan.* Moderates and liberals had difficulty finding phrases that counseled patience and firmness without provocation. "In the face of right-wing attacks," wrote sociologist David Riesman, "the administration denies that it is pursuing a 'no-win' policy; it argues instead that it is just as combative, only more clever or roundabout."

Bayard Rustin, organizer of the March on Washington, made the phrase part of the civil rights lexicon: he charged Negro radicals who rejected the help of white liberals with having a "no-win" attitude, seeking shock with no legislative or social goal. "My quarrel with the no-win tendency," Rustin wrote in the February 1965 *Commentary,* ". . . parallels my quarrel with the moderates outside the movement. As the latter lack the vision or the will for fundamental change, the former lack a realistic strategy for achieving it. For such a strategy they substitute militancy. But militancy is a matter of posture and volume and not of effect."

The turnaround of the phrase, proving its permanence, took a long time to come. It was not until November 30, 1977, that the *Washington Star* carried a headline: "On the Middle East, Carter Lucks into a 'No-Lose' Position."

NOW IS THE TIME . . . for all good men to come to the aid of the party. A typewriter exercise and not a political slogan.

Charles E. Weller, a court reporter in Milwaukee in 1867, devised the sentence to cover most of the keys on the typewriter, a new invention by his friend Christopher Latham Sholes. It has about as much political signifi-cance as "the quick brown fox jumps over the lazy dog," which is much more useful, since it covers all 26 letters in the alphabet, compared to Weller's 18.

NUCLEAR PROLIFERATION the growth in the number of nations who possess atomic or hydrogen bombs.

The phrase is a mouthful, and a constant challenge to speakers. Atomic jargoneers say that when the possession of atomic weapons *diffuses* among many nations, the result of scientific information's *dissemination,* what takes place is nuclear *proliferation.*

"Proliferation" comes from a Latin root meaning "offspring," and was mainly used in biology to denote division of cells or budding of plants.

Adlai Stevenson used it politically, possibly for the first time, in his 1949 inaugural address as governor of Illinois, describing the process by which state departments mushroomed into large bureaucracies. One newsman told the new governor he had looked up the word and as far as he could tell, it had something to do with the way coral spreads. "That's good," laughed Stevenson, "better than I thought."

As the U.S. Ambassador to the UN, Stevenson used the word often, as in a 1964 broadcast about Soviet attitudes: "They, too, want to insure the world against the proliferation of nuclear weapons."

President Kennedy had said much the same thing, using a smaller word: "The struggle against nuclear spread is as much in the Soviet interest as our own." The word "spread" means the same in this case, is far easier to handle and understand, and was often used later by Senator Robert Kennedy. However, the subject is momentous, and the word "proliferate" is properly ominous.

See SALT (LEXICON).

NUCLEAR TRIGGER, *see* **FINGER ON THE BUTTON; TRIGGER-HAPPY; TRIPWIRE.**

NUMBERS GAME the misleading use of statistics in political argument.

"Figures don't lie, but liars do figure" is an expression often applied to those who play the numbers game. An effective attack phrase against those who marshal sound or unsound statistical arguments, "numbers game" connotes gambling ("the numbers racket").

When the White House in 1954 announced that 2,427 SECURITY RISKS had been removed from their jobs since the Eisenhower administration took office, Adlai Stevenson dubbed it a "numbers game," pointing out that this figure included many who had resigned their posts unaware that they had ever been considered "risks."

"Through two political campaigns," wrote Cabell Phillips in *The Truman Administration,* referring to 1954 and 1956, "Republican party spokesmen played an avid 'numbers game' with the monthly statistics of the Loyalty Review Board to demonstrate the GOP's prowess in cleaning out the Communists left behind by the Democrats. The totals were made to look impressive by lumping voluntary resignations with dismissals. When this bit of chicanery was exposed by the press, the 'numbers game' fell into disuse."

A similar expression is "crowdsmanship," the technique of inducing a police official to overestimate to reporters the number of people in a rally crowd. A cooperative cop can turn a meager airport turnout (adding the pilot and crew, innocent bystanders and the reporters and police themselves) into "a few hundred enthusiastic supporters, despite the threatening weather." Some policemen try to be scientific, estimating crowds by figuring two square feet per person; others have been known to straight-facedly explain, "I get down on my haunches, count the feet, and divide by two."

NUT-CUTTING dirty work; a slang allusion to castration, its political meaning is the denial of favors and the removal of power.

To "get down to the nut-cutting" means to abandon broad policy discussion and deal with hard specifics of patronage and pecking order. The phrase was inadvertently used by Richard Nixon publicly at the end of the 1968 campaign in its second meaning of detail work or "brass tacks" (see NITTY-GRITTY). Other taboo expressions with the same metaphoric source used in and out of politics include "ballbuster" (a slave-driving boss, or a particularly difficult problem) and "by the short hairs" (to have another in circumstances where control is an easy matter).

See SHORT HAIRS; HANG TOUGH.

NUTS AND KOOKS, *see* **KOOKS, NUTS AND.**

OBSOLETE POLITICAL TERMS

amen corner (automatic support)

anxious seat (potential candidate, probable loser)

backstairs influence (manipulation by hidden supporters)

barnacle (hanger-on)

bashaw (high-ranking politician, from Turkish *pasha*)

big bug (replaced by big shot, big wheel)

black-and-tans (pro-Negro Southern Republicans)

bogus baby (bad legislation)

bottle holder (adviser, from boxing)

buffalo hunt (cover for territorial acquisitions)

bullwhacker (tough political boss)

candle-box returns (phony votes)

come-outer (bolter)

crawfish (back out of a firm position)

cuttlefish (obscure an issue, confuse)

dirt eater (Southerner favoring Union)

doughface (Northerner favoring slavery)

fat-frying (fund solicitation)

fire eaters (Southern secessionists)

floater (swing voter)

forty thieves (politicians in control of finances)

fugelman (henchman)

half-breed (splinter group, antiregular)

heroite (Jackson supporter)

hewgag (clarion call for action)

hunker (conservative Democrat)

leg treasurer (official who absconds with money)

loaves and fishes (spoils, plums)

Loco Foco (anti-Tammany, hard-money Democrats)

mucker (reformer)

off horse (disgruntled politician)

organ grinder (partisan newspaper-man)

pap (government handouts)

persimmon (plum)

rag baby (greenback Democrat)

regulators (vigilantes)

ring (derogatory, political organization)

rooster (Democratic symbol)

Salt River (place of political defeat)

scratcher (split ticket voter)

shreaker (a bolter)

soap (graft)

still hunt (undercover investigation)

straight-outs (Democrats who tend to bolt)

subsoil (secretly laying the groundwork)

Sunday School (civil service reformers)

Swartout (to run away with the public money)

swing around the circle (tour the country)

taffy (phony promises)

tin pan (a caucus)

trimmer (opportunist)

wide-awakes (independent Republican clubs)

wire worker (small-time political manager)

young scratcher (antimachine Republican)

OBSTRUCTION OF JUSTICE, *see* SMOKING GUN; STONEWALL; COVER-UP.

OFFICE SEEKS THE MAN, *see* JOB SEEKS THE MAN.

OFFICIALESE government jargon, intended to impress, conceal, or confuse; often the result of writing with scissors and pastepot.

Probably the first word along these lines was *legalese,* coined by an exasperated layman who could not make sense out of a legal opinion. However, legalese has the virtue of eliminating ambiguity, and should be read more as a mathematical equation than as prose, anything herein to the contrary notwithstanding.

Commercialese is a clean-prose movement aimed at killing ult., inst., per, and enclosed please find.

Gamalielese was H. L. Mencken's word for BLOVIATION by Harding.

Charles Dickens wrote humorously of "circumlocution"—which he treated as a combination of circumnavigate and elocution—to describe the lofty pretension of *officialese.* Congressman Maury Maverick coined GOBBLEDYGOOK, and Milton Smith coined BAFFLEGAB.

For examples, see PENTAGONESE; COMMUNIST TERMINOLOGY; CIAESE.

OFFICIAL FAMILY the appointees of a Chief Executive of nation, state, or city, especially those of great importance or who work closely with him.

In listing the Secret Service code names in use November 1963, author William Manchester grouped the *first family* (Lancer, Lace, Lyric, and Lark—the President, wife, daughter, and son), the *vice-presidential group* (Volunteer, Victoria, Velvet, Venus, Vigilant—the Vice President, wife, two daughters, and aide) and the *official family*: the President's personal secretary, press secretary, military aide, Air Force aide, naval aide, and a White House assistant—all with code names beginning with W—the President's physician, and the Secretary of State.

Current usage of official family is loose. It does cover all cabinet officials, the secretary of the cabinet, if there is one, assistants to the President, his legal counsel, speechwriters and ranking White House aides. It often applies to appointees down to Assistant Secretaries, but at that point the line blurs. A regional director of HUD whom the President is never likely to meet and does not know is equivalent to a second cousin once removed: a member of the family in a formal sense, but whose passing is not mourned unless an inheritance is involved.

Walter Lippmann in 1942 considered men in the official family to be those "participating in the action," as in this passage denouncing publicity men and ghostwriters, whose role the columnist considered cosmetic:

> The address of a President should be an event and not a lecture or a public reading, and the decision about when he should speak and what needs saying can be wisely made, not by supposed experts on public opinion, but only by men participating in the action he is going to talk about. There is all the difference in the world between being assisted by his official family and being assisted by GHOST WRITERS.

President Grover Cleveland, preparing to bolt the Democratic party in 1896 over the issue of "free silver" being drawn by candidate William

Jennings Bryan, used the phrase in a letter to his Secretary of the Interior, Hoke Smith: "You know how free my association with my official family has been . . ." Smith had said: "While I shall not accept the platform, I must support the nominees of the Chicago Convention." Cleveland told him: "It seems to me like straining at a gnat and swallowing a camel."

OFF THE RECORD not for publication; for a reporter's private knowledge only, and not to be used in any way.

Although H. L. Mencken attributed the coinage of this heavily used phrase to Al Smith, he probably meant "LET'S LOOK AT THE RECORD"; Mathews in the *Dictionary of Americanisms* traces "on the record" to 1900, but none of the dictionaries pinpoint the origin of "off the record."

It probably stemmed from FDR's press conferences in the thirties, which had these categories of answers: *direct quotation* when specifically permitted; *indirect quotation,* but directly attributable to the President, as "The President said that he . . ."; *background information* (see NOT FOR ATTRIBUTION; BACKGROUNDER) that could not reveal the President as a source; and *off-the-record* information that could not be used at all. Wrote Douglass Cater: "Roosevelt played the various categories with tremendous skill, keeping the correspondents informed even when it did not suit his purpose to inform the public."

Charles Hurd, a White House correspondent in the early thirties, wrote: ". . . the press conference reached, prior to 1941, a pre-eminent place in our system of government. It did bring into the language, unfortunately, the phrase 'off the record.'

Soon everyone, from the divorcee being interviewed by the society columnist in the Blue Angel to the ward heeler talking to a police reporter, was preceding answers to inquiries with the phrase 'off the record,' thinking thereby to make their words sound more important—and more likely to be printed."

The new weapon occasionally backfired; Ambassador to Great Britain Joseph P. Kennedy gave what he claimed was an off-the-record interview to a *Boston Globe* reporter, who promptly printed Kennedy's thoughts about the King's speech impediment, the Queen's housewifely appearance, Churchill's fondness for brandy, and the notes he kept getting from Eleanor Roosevelt asking him "to have some little Susie Glotz to tea at the Embassy." At that point Kennedy's political future in his own right was finished.

"Off the record" can be abused by reporters who break the confidence to the embarrassment of the source; sources who are embarrassed by an on-the-record comment, and while not willing to lie about not having said it, are willing to claim they said it off the record; and the compromising of reporters by giving them information "off the record" that they would soon be able to find out elsewhere, thereby temporarily blocking them from publishing their story.

OFF THE RESERVATION remaining nominally within a party, but refusing to support the party's candidate.

Off the reservation, in current use, is one step short of TAKING A WALK —supporting the other party's candidate—and two steps short of an outright BOLT—switching to the other party permanently.

Former President Harry Truman

explained in his memoirs: "The South's opposition to [Democrat] Al Smith gave Hoover many southern states, and he won by a comfortable margin. In the general election two years later, however, almost all the people who were running for office in the south and had supported [Republican] Hoover were defeated. That was the price they had to pay for going 'off the reservation' in 1928."

In Truman's usage, the phrase included those who actively supported the opposition candidate; most politicians consider outright support of the opposition a shade stronger than "off the reservation."

The phrase refers to Indian reservations in the days when unscrupulous whites would trade "firewater" for goods, and "off the reservation" was a lonely and dangerous place for a red man to be.

OFF YEAR elections that take place in the middle of a presidential term, where the turnout is always lower than those years that feature a presidential election; or, an odd-numbered year in which local elections are held.

The expression, in use since the 1870s, indicates the fall-off of enthusiasm from its antonym, "the presidential year." Since candidates for President run every four years, and congressional elections are every two years, every other congressional race is in an "off year"; further, candidates for local offices, as well as some governors, run in years between congressional elections, but there is no special expression for these way-off years.

President Eisenhower told a press conference in 1954 that he did not think a President should intervene "too intensively and directly in off-year Congressional elections," but rather create an "umbrella of accomplishment" under which candidates for his party could run. A reluctance to campaign in off years is a characteristic of Presidents; traditionally, the party in control of the White House loses seats in Congress in off years.

The "average" fall-off in House seats ranges from twenty to forty, depending on how far back one wishes to start and whether one chooses all midterms or comparable first or second terms. The Republicans did badly at Eisenhower's midterms, well at Nixon's; the Democrats did well under Kennedy, badly under Johnson.

The expression is in a state of flux. Since "midterm" is a more accurate term for the nonpresidential congressional years, it is gaining in current usage, while "off year" is being applied more to odd-numbered years in which elections for local offices take place.

OHIO GANG, *see* **SMOKE-FILLED ROOM.**

OLD CHINA HANDS Western journalists or diplomats, often the children of missionaries, who spent years in China.

Author Pearl Buck and Time, Inc. founder Henry Luce, both children of missionaries to China, were the best-known "Old China Hands." Authors Edgar Snow and Alice Tinsdale Hobart were included in this category, along with diplomats John Davies and John Service, who were attacked as Communist sympathizers in the fifties.

"The prime time of Old China Hands," writes Nym Wales (herself one), "was in the thirties. . . . There are still a few Old Hands living in China, notably Anna Louise Strong, now in her eighties, whose first book described the 1927 revolution and who still sends out a newsletter favoring Mao and the Red Guards. . . . Living in China is always a searing experience; the letter 'C' remains branded on every China Hand."

China Hand differs from CHINA WATCHER: "hand" connotes previous residence, "watcher" (or *Pekingologist*) connotes observation from outside.

OLD FOGY reactionary; burdened with the barnacles of backwardness.

The word may have a military origin. A fogy is an old military officer, or anyone who receives a "phogey"— seniority pay to one who has served three years in wartime or five years in peacetime. The *Dictionary of American English* traces this use back to 1879, and indicates the likelihood of previous use.

Earlier, author William Makepeace Thackeray used it in *The Book of Snobs,* published in *Punch* in 1846–47: ". . . the honest, rosy old fogies, the mouldy old dandies, the waistbelts and glossy wigs and tight cravats of these most raucous and respectable men." *John Donkey,* an imitator of *Punch,* gave it a political twist a year later in an article titled "The Political Old Fogy."

Congressman John C. Breckenridge, later a Vice President and a candidate against Lincoln in 1860, said in 1852: ". . . their principles are denounced in the cant language of the day as 'old fogyism,' and themselves as 'old fogies' . . . wholly incompetent to fathom the ideas or control the policy of this generation."

Current use has not changed at all. In 1967 the *New Republic*'s "T.R.B." wrote: "When the House repeatedly backed an amendment for direct election of senators and the Senate

refused to act, the threat of a constitutional convention finally brought the old fogeys around."

As can be seen, there are any number of ways to spell the phrase; currently, fogy and fogys are preferred over phogy, fogey, fogies, or fogeys.

Youthful conservatives are occasionally referred to as "Young Fogys," but elderly insurgents are not called "Old Turks."

OLD GUARD hard-core loyalist; strongly conservative Republican.

Nobody represents himself as being a member of the Old Guard, since it now has the connotation of hidebound and stodgy. It is most often an epithet used by Democrats against conservative Republicans, or by insurgents against regulars. Among Republicans, the party's wings in the 1880s were the Stalwarts vs. the Half-Breeds; in the 1900s the Regulars vs. the Progressives; in recent years, the Old Guard vs. the Modern Republicans, or (as characterized by liberal Republicans) extremists vs. moderates, or (as characterized by conservatives) me-tooers vs. real Republicans.

When the Old Guard is used in its broadest sense—an entrenched conservative faction in either party—its opposing faction is often called the YOUNG TURKS, or ANGRY YOUNG MEN.

Most Old Fogies and Guardsmen are derided as "implacable." Humorist Vic Gold, in his 1969 book *So You Want to Be a Liberal,* defined "implacable" as *"hard-line, old guard, last ditch.* Pertaining to Non-Liberal zealotry, as distinguished from *principled,* the approved description of Liberal implacability."

When the Republican platform in 1944 "accepted the purposes" of the National Labor Relations Act, the Social Security Act, and other New

Deal legislation, Franklin Roosevelt solemnly read the Republican plank to a Democratic audience and commented: "The whole purpose of Republican oratory these days seems to be to switch labels. . . . Can the Old Guard pass itself off as the New Deal? I think not."

Adlai Stevenson, just before his first defeat in 1952, said, "It is a tragedy that the Old Guard has succeeded in doing what Hitler's best general could never do: they have captured Eisenhower."

The expression was used politically in the U.S. as early as 1844. "The Old Guard knows how to die," quoted the *Ohio State Journal*, "but the Old Guard does not know how to surrender. So said Napoleon on a celebrated occasion. So will all the Whigs say . . . we have gallant Whig champions and a glorious cause: 'The Old Guard will never surrender!' " (The Whigs' Clay lost to the Democrats' Polk; after one more victory, Zachary Taylor's, the Whigs surrendered.)

The Old Guard became identified with the Republican party in 1880, by advocates of a third term for Ulysses Grant. Author Don Chidsey writes: "Three hundred and six of them stood on the burning deck when all but them had fled. One, Chauncey I. Filley, went so far as to have 306 Grant medals struck, and he distributed these: they bore not only the much publicized number, but also the words 'The Old Guard,' and thereby gave Republican reactionaries . . . a new title."

Source of the term was Napoleon's Old Guard, his most loyal troops. Count Pierre-Jacques-Étienne Cambronne, who was captured at the Battle of Waterloo, supposedly said about them: "The Guard dies, but never surrenders." According to French writer Edouard Fournier in 1859, the remark was invented by a reporter named Rougemont; Count Cambronne went to his grave denying he ever said it. The count is remembered today by a monument erected to him in Nantes, upon which is inscribed: "The Guard dies, but never surrenders." This story may be counter-apocryphal, but the count's response to a surrender demand was really supposed to have been *"Merde!,"* which is known in France as *le mot de Cambronne.*

The Young Americans for Freedom, a conservative group, gave the diehard phrase a fresh fillip in the seventies by naming their magazine *The New Guard.*

OLD PRO one richly experienced in politics, regardless of age; the highest accolade among professionals.

"Old pros," not to be confused with PARTY ELDERS, may be found among: (1) officeholders who "know the ropes" and "where the bodies are buried"; (2) self-proclaimed "amateurs," who can be depended upon to run citizen's movements in a sound professional manner every few years; (3) party professionals, who "can count" and can be distinguished from "hangers-on," "hacks," and "henchmen."

Curiously, old pros on different sides of the political fence know of one another, but seldom know one another well. This contrasts with opposition-party elected officials, who come to know and often like one another because of their daily contact. To them, Shakespeare's words about lawyers apply: "Adversaries . . . in law strive mightily, but eat and drink as friends."

But professional campaign managers often make it a point to honor their respected foes by not socializing with them. Julius C. C. Edelstein,

New York Mayor Robert F. Wagner's executive assistant and campaign planner, once explained why he never met John A. Wells, an eminent attorney who often manages major Republican campaigns in New York. Edelstein told a story about a college student in Chicago in the 1920s. "The student had made contact with a gang of mobsters, and asked if he could observe some of their activities for his course in criminology. The mobsters were strangely delighted by the prospect of a 'perfesser' studying their habits, and they took him under their wing," according to Edelstein's recollection. "One day the student inquired why the gang had to import out-of-state torpedoes to kill off rival hoodlums. Didn't the gang have its own able trigger men? The gangsters explained that the local hoodlums, in all the rival gangs, had grown up together in the same neighborhood. When one was assigned to rub out another, he just couldn't pull the trigger—friendship and sentiment stood in the way. So they had to hire guns from out of town to do the job that only a stranger could do.

"Now, I wouldn't say that campaign managers are quite like torpedoes," Edelstein went on. "But a man who manages a political campaign is in the hottest end of politics, and he is often called on to strike hard for his candidate with no thought of personal consideration."

Edelstein added: "That's why Jack Wells and I are not likely to meet."

OLD SOLDIERS NEVER DIE sentimental touch introduced by General Douglas MacArthur at the conclusion of his speech in 1951, after having been relieved by President Truman.

MacArthur, who favored "hot pursuit" of Communist aircraft into China, was relieved by President Truman, who felt he was insubordinate and trying to dictate rather than carry out policy decided by civilians. Upon his return, MacArthur spoke to a joint meeting of Congress (not a joint session; only Presidents address joint sessions):

"I still remember the refrain of one of the most popular barracks ballads of that day which proclaimed most proudly that old soldiers never die; they just fade away. And like the old soldier in that ballad, I now close my military career and just fade away, an old soldier who tried to do his duty as God gave him the sight to see that duty."

The last few words, overlooked in the rush to look up and issue a recording of "Old Soldiers Never Die," were reminiscent of a phrase in Lincoln's second inaugural: ". . . with firmness in the right, as God gives us to see the right . . ." See NO SUBSTITUTE FOR VICTORY.

OLD-TIME RELIGION conservative economics.

Herbert Stein, chairman of the Council of Economic Advisers in 1973, frequently referred to "that old-time religion" in discussing economic politics to eliminate or restrain inflation. Dr. Stein liked the phrase because conservative economics, like fundamentalist religious worship, has been honored more with lip service than with church attendance.

The phrase is in current use, usually with a derisive cast, but not always. "Discipline and patience are required," wrote Tilford Gaines in a Manufacturers Hanover Bank newsletter (September 1974), "if the 'old-time religion' is to work, and there is every reason to hope that it will."

The expression was popularized in the forties by bandleader Phil Harris' rendition of "Gimme Dat Old-time Religion."

OLD WINE IN NEW BOTTLES a derogatory characterization of peace proposals presented in a fresh form but holding to the previous position.

At the Paris peace talks on September 17, 1970, the North Vietnamese and Viet Cong delegations presented an eight-point plan for ending the war that U.S. Ambassador David E. K. Bruce promptly labeled "old wine in new bottles."

This vivid figure of speech made the U.S. delegation's point more dramatically than any ordinary diplomatic rejection as "nothing new." The phrase became part of the language of diplomacy, and when Henry Kissinger, President Nixon's national security adviser, was going over the language of an October 7, 1970, U.S. proposal for a standstill cease-fire and immediate prisoner exchange, he remarked to this writer: "It's new wine."

When the Communists presented another proposal on June 30, 1971, Marilyn Berger of the *Washington Post* wrote: "There appeared to be a determined U.S. effort, however, not to dismiss the Communists' seven point plan in the way the chief U.S. negotiator at the Paris peace talks turned aside the last Communist proposal as 'old wine in new bottles.'"

In 1968 the National Advisory Commission on Civil Disorders—the Kerner Commission, its staff headed by Washington attorney David Ginsburg—reported that "What is new about Black Power is phraseology rather than substance . . . the rhetoric is different, but the ideas are remarkably similar." The heading for that section of its report was "Old Wine in New Bottles."

A much earlier use was remarked by Herman Melville, who noted in a diary during a European tour in 1849 that he had been given a book by Dr. Augustus Gardner entitled *Old Wine in New Bottles, or Spare Hours of a Student in Paris.*

The phrase is a switch on a line in the Gospel according to St. Matthew (9:17), in which Jesus says: "Neither do men put new wine into old bottles; else the bottles break, and the wine runneth out, and the bottles perish: but they put new wine into new bottles, and both are preserved." In that time, bottles were made of leather, and used bottles could not bear the fermentation strain of new wine; the parable means that the old Law of the Hebrew religion could not encompass the new spirit of Christ's gospel.

In the original use, new wine in old bottles was destructive; in current use, old wine in new bottles is deceptive.

No wine is so old that a pun cannot be uncorked: on May 19, 1976, strategist Stanley Hoffmann scoffed at Secretary of State Henry Kissinger's attempt to put a good face on Franco-American relations with a *New York Times* Op-Ed piece titled "Old Whine, New Bottles."

OLEAGINOUS LINGO, *see* **BUNK; WEASEL WORDS**.

OMBUDSMAN an official intermediary between citizen and government to counteract the delay, injustice, and impersonality of bureaucracy.

The word comes from the Old Swedish *umbud,* meaning proxy, or power to act for another. In modern Swedish, an ombudsman can be any kind of agent, from commercial representative to member of Parliament (Riksdag), but the world-wide meaning of the term is taken from what the Swedes call the "JO": *Riksdagens Justitieombudsman,* Parliamentary Commissioner for Justice.

The office was started in Sweden in 1809, has been adopted in varying forms by other Scandinavian countries, New Zealand, and the Philippines, and has aroused world-wide interest as the complexity of government administration grows. In 1967 the State of Hawaii adopted an Ombudsman Act: ". . . the Ombudsman may establish procedures for receiving and processing complaints, conducting investigations, and reporting his findings" without regard to "the finality of any administrative act." The crucial point in his powers is the right to look into "unreasonable, unfair, oppressive, or unnecessarily discriminatory" acts by government officials *"even though* in accordance with law" (italics in the act).

"A key characteristic of the Ombudsman," writes Professor Stanley Anderson of the University of California, "is his accessibility to the public. Anyone may file a complaint simply by writing a letter. This is especially important to those deprived of their freedom in jails, hospitals, sanitoria, etc."

A similar function is provided by the military in the U.S. in its office of Inspector General, which overlooks "channels" in its investigations. The argument against ombudsmen is that they take over functions that properly should be handled by mayors, district attorneys, and other elected officials. If these officials are not responsive to legitimate citizen complaints, they should be replaced, not circumvented.

To counter Republican Mayor John V. Lindsay's plan for "little City Halls" throughout New York, Democratic City Council President Frank O'Connor put forth an idea in 1967 that had been proposed often by Democrat Paul O'Dwyer—the ombudsman. Wrote the *New York Times* in support:

An ombudsman for New York City would be the supergrievance committee chairman, a bridge between the people and their complex and scattered government. If New York were a tiny crossroads, it wouldn't need an ombudsman. But the very bigness of modern government and its inevitable remoteness can hurt both the citizen and the officials supposed to serve him. The ombudsman, "a person of distinguished accomplishments in the field of law or administration," would be available to help ameliorate the frictions of urban life.

OMNIBUS BILL, *see* **PACKAGE DEAL.**

ON ALL FOURS, *see* **UP TO SPEED.**

ONE GLASS OF WATER DOCTRINE, *see* **DOCTRINES.**

ONE-HOUSE BILL legislation intended for grandstanding only, not for passage into law.

Lobbyists in state capitals often work on one-house bills: getting passage in the state senate or assembly with the tacit assurance that the bill will be killed in the other house. The lobbyist can then show his client proof of some success without disturbing the status quo. (See FETCHER BILL.)

Another meaning has to do with divided legislatures, when one house is Democratic and the other Republican, and the passage of the bill is not venal but equally hopeless, unless it can be tied to another "one-house bill" and a deal struck.

ONE-HOUSE VETO a provision in laws that enables either the House or the Senate to cancel Executive actions.

When President Carter vetoed the Department of Energy Authorization Act in November 1977, he said: "It limits the constitutional authority of the President through three one-house veto provisions."

Presidents do not like one-house vetoes; they argue that it erodes the separation of powers. Congressmen like the device, since it gives their institution more control over federal expenditures.

On January 9, 1978, the Supreme Court let stand a decision by the U.S. Court of Claims, which—as Morton Mintz wrote in the *Washington Post* the next day—refrained from striking down "the one-house veto, which enables either the House or the Senate to decide unilaterally whether any of a wide range of governmental actions will survive."

The formal phrase is "legislative veto." In a message to the Congress on June 21, 1978, President Carter said he understood why Congress has been asserting itself in the seventies, but asked that such mistrust not be directed at him: "The desire for the legislative veto stems in part from Congress' mistrust of the Executive, due to the abuses of years past. Congress responded to those abuses by enacting constructive safeguards in such areas as war powers and the budget process. The legislative veto, however, is an overreaction which increases conflict between the branches of government." Attorney General Griffin Bell added his definition: "Legislative veto is a device whereunder . . . the power is transferred to the Congress to do things that ordinarily the executive department would do."

Mr. Carter pointed out that the legislative veto was first used in 1932, in a bill which authorized President Hoover to reorganize the Executive Branch. (Congress had tried earlier, but Woodrow Wilson was having none of that encroachment.)

An early use, and possible coinage, of the term was by John Millett and Lindsay Rogers in the Winter 1941 *Public Administration Review*: "The Legislative Veto and the Reorganization Act of 1939." In the article they wrote that "a new device has been invented: a mandate to the executive to act, and, if the result is not liked, a *legislative veto.*" To help FDR reorganize the Executive Branch in 1938, Congress gave him a concurrent resolution, which was a two-house veto. When he demanded a joint resolution instead (which he could veto), Republicans accused him of being a dictator, to which the President responded, "I have none of the qualifications which would make me a successful dictator."

ONE-IDEA PARTIES, *see* **IDEAS.**

ONE MAN, ONE VOTE a slogan urging reapportionment of legislatures so that each legislator represents approximately the same number of people.

Peter Straus, owner of New York radio station WMCA, brought the lawsuit that resulted in the Supreme Court decision setting forth the principle of one man, one vote. He told the author in 1968:

We wanted to do a radio spot campaign to back up our editorials about reapportionment. But how do you get anybody excited about anything sounding as dull as "reapportionment?" Some people thought we were talking about "proportional representation," and most people don't even know what that is. We needed a phrase, a handle, that would make this issue come to life. Digging through the literature on the subject, and the booklets by the League of Women Voters, one of our writers came across "one man, one vote." We used it, and we hit it hard.

The Supreme Court in 1963 picked up the phrase in its decision in *Gray* v. *Sanders* to forbid a state from electing governors or senators by the county unit system, but modified the slogan to include women voters: "The conception of political equality from the Declaration of Independence, to Lincoln's Gettysburg Address, to the Fifteenth, Seventeenth and Nineteenth Amendments can mean only one thing—one-person, one-vote."

In a subsequent decision, the Court held: "While it may not be possible to draw Congressional districts with mathematical precision, that is no excuse for ignoring our Constitution's plain objective of making equal representation for equal numbers of people the fundamental goal for the House of Representatives." On June 15, 1964, the Court capped the series of decisions with an order to apportion both houses of all state legislatures on the basis of population only.

Since the Senate of the United States is not elected on the basis of population, opposition to the Court's decisions could naturally be expected to be articulated there. Senator Everett Dirksen (R-Ill.), then Minority Leader, called attention to some of the points made in dissent by Justice Harlan: "Legislators can represent their electors only by speaking for their interests—economic, social, political—many of which do reflect the place where electors live," and thus geographic area, as well as population, should be represented. ". . . by focusing exclusively on numbers . . .

the Court deals in abstractions which will be recognized even by the politically unsophisticated to have little relevance to the realities of political life." Dirksen proposed a constitutional convention—only the second in U.S. history—to set the matter straight.

Politically, the issue was the transfer of power from rural areas to urban areas, and the slogan did much to crystallize the issue that had been hidden in abstract words. Wrote Arthur Krock: "The one-man, one-vote principle on which the Supreme Court ruling is based has the quality of those political slogans which appeal to the strong streak of idealism in the American people."

The phrase was coined in England early in the nineteenth century in a different context: Major John Cartwright (1740–1824), a radical Member of the House of Commons, called "the Father of Reform," led the fight against "plural voting" with the slogan "one man, one vote." At that time it was possible for a man to cast two ballots, one on the basis of his residence and the other a "business" or "university" qualification. The House of Lords rejected bills passed by the House of Commons on this subject for more than a century; in 1948 the Representation of the People Act finally abolished the right to exercise more than one vote in a parliamentary election.

Both slogan and issue resurfaced in the mid-seventies, as international pressure was applied to the white leadership of Rhodesia and South Africa to allow "majority rule," which many blacks saw as the end of intolerable repression by whites, and which many whites took to be revolution by the blacks. A dispatch to the *London Daily Telegraph* from Salisbury, Rhodesia, dated September 26,

1977 read: "The Rhodesian Government will accept the principle of "one man, one vote" only if there are adequate safeguards written into a new constitution . . ." That newspaper's conservative columnist, Peregrine Worsthorne, held that "this theory can mean nothing less than a whole great continent's return to primitive savagery" and asked: " 'One man, one vote.' When Dr. [Foreign Secretary David] Owen continues to talk about this liberal idea (in relation to Africa) is he not really being as shockingly dishonest as those Marxists who insist on pretending that what is happening behind the Iron Curtain has anything to do with 'the withering away of the State' or 'the dictatorship of the proletariat'?"

When Vice President Walter Mondale visited South Africa in 1977, he raised the issue of majority rule using the phrase "one man, one vote"—readily understandable in the U.S. but causing consternation among his hosts.

ONE-PARTY PRESS   an accusation that the news media favors one political party, and as a result denies the opposition equal or fair coverage. Andrew Jackson's supporters called any newspaper who opposed their man "the kennel press." In that tradition, Harry Truman wrote: "As far as I was concerned, they had sold out to the SPECIAL INTERESTS, and that is why I referred to them in my campaign speeches as the 'kept press and paid radio.' " Truman reminded his staff that in the elections since 1800, the press had played an important role in thirty-six; eighteen times behind the winner, eighteen times behind the loser. "That was the clearest proof I needed that I had nothing to fear regarding the influence of the newspapers . . ."

Although abolitionist Wendell Phillips had been certain "we live under a government of men and morning newspapers," Democratic candidates in more recent times found press opposition did not ensure defeat. In 1936 FDR told Samuel Rosenman: "Wait till October comes around when we really get a chance to tell the people the facts—which they're not getting now from their newspapers." Harold Ickes confided to his diary that "the outstanding thing about the campaign was the lack of influence of the newspapers . . . the very bitterness of the assault upon the President by the newspapers reacted in his favor."

At that same time, in England, Prime Minister Stanley Baldwin was making much the same discovery. The combined attack of Lord Beaverbrook and Lord Rothermere, the press peers, together with the denunciations of Winston Churchill, did not succeed in destroying Baldwin's leadership of the Conservative party. "It disclosed," wrote historian R. J. Minney, "that the influence of the popular press was by no means as wide and effective as had been imagined." Baldwin suffered in silence, then finally lashed back: "What the proprietorship of these papers is aiming at is power, and power without responsibility: The prerogative of the harlot throughout the ages."

Adlai Stevenson popularized the phrase "one-party press" in 1952 in a speech to newspapermen of Portland, Oregon:
> . . . the overwhelming majority of the press is just against Democrats. And it is against Democrats, so far as I can see, not after a sober and considered review of the alternatives, but automatically, as dogs are against cats. As soon as a newspaper—I speak of the great majority, not of

the enlightened ten per cent—sees a Democratic candidate it is filled with an unconquerable yen to chase him up an alley. . . . I am in favor of a two-party system in politics. And I think we have a pretty healthy two-party system at this moment. But I am in favor of a two-party system in our press too. And I am, frankly, considerably concerned when I see the extent to which we are developing a one-party press in a two-party country.

Democrats are not the only ones to suffer from what they feel is slanted treatment from the press. Richard M. Nixon, in what he promised would be his "last press conference" after his unsuccessful race for the governorship of California in 1962, bitterly reminded the reporters covering his campaign of the press's responsibility to "put one lonely reporter on the campaign who will report what the candidate says now and then."

ONE-PARTY RULE

charge made by candidates of a minority party in areas where the majority is entrenched; a system that often leads to corruption and inefficiency.

Republicans in the South and in big cities, and Democrats in suburbs and rural areas in the North, join in denouncing "one-party rule." Its opposite is the TWO-PARTY SYSTEM, and its predecessor phrase was probably "one-man power," used to attack Andrew Jackson and his followers, who favored a strong executive branch.

Congressman (later Speaker of the House) Thomas B. Reed said in 1880: "The best system is to have one party govern and the other party watch." This was an excellent argument against coalition and in favor of the two-party system—provided the parties changed places from time to time.

See SOLID SOUTH.

ONE-TERM PRESIDENT

if said about an incumbent, a charge of weakness and vulnerability; if said about a past occupant of an office, a cool and cruelly accurate account.

The first noted use of the phrase was by Jacob Brinkerhoff, a two-term congressman from Ohio, on the House floor January 13, 1845: "The North had been taunted with the fact that it never had any but one-term presidents, democratic or federal."

Dwight Eisenhower used the phrase in 1968 about Richard Nixon, in a way that imputed courage to the one-termer: "I think Dick's going to be elected President but I think he's going to be a one-term President. I think he's really going to fight inflation, and that will kill him politically." Nixon must have remembered the phrase: in a line he added to the speech he made on April 30, 1970, announcing an incursion into Cambodia, he said: "I would rather be a one-term President and do what I believe is right than to be a two-term President at the cost of seeing America become a second-rate power . . ."

In the twentieth century, the only one-term Presidents—assuming the phrase to cover one full term of four years, not shortened by death—were William Howard Taft and Herbert Hoover. However, since the nearly five terms beginning with Kennedy's election in 1960 have seen five Presidents (Kennedy, Johnson, Nixon, Ford, Carter), the U.S. has been averaging one term per President in recent years.

Perhaps that new low average prompted the use of "one-term President" in regard to President Jimmy Carter in the fall of 1977. *New York Times* columnist Tom Wicker caught and extended the phrase in a column headed "One Term for Carter" on October 18: "People who think and talk about politics are beginning to ask each other openly: 'Is Jimmy Carter a one-term President?' The question may seem strange and premature, when the man has been in office less than a year; yet it has a certain validity."

The power of the incumbency used to make any President an odds-on favorite to succeed himself, but as Wicker pointed out: "When television makes everything visible and immediate, defeats and failures are not exceptions; those who are elected by the tube can be defeated by the tube."

Six months later a lead editorial in the *Times* began: "The story is told in Washington of two Senators. Senator A says, 'Carter is beginning to look like a one-term President.' Senator B replies, 'Yes, but when does it begin?' "

ONE THIRD OF A NATION FDR's memorable phrase calling attention to poverty in America.

There was probably more revising and rewriting of President Roosevelt's second inaugural address of January 20, 1937, than any other major Roosevelt speech. Thomas Corcoran, Stanley High, Donald Richberg, and Samuel Rosenman submitted drafts and made changes. FDR insisted on a human treatment of the statistics. "I see tens of millions of its citizens" denied the "necessities of life"; "I see millions denied education, recreation, and the opportunity to better their lot and the lot of their children"; and there followed several other examples of what "I see."

Rosenman had written in an early draft a summation of the "I see's" with a final "I see." He recalls: "I do not remember nor is there a record of what that summation of mine was, for the President rubbed out all I had written in pencil after that final I see

and after a moment's reflection substituted in his own hand his summation: 'I see one-third of a nation ill-housed, ill-clad, ill-nourished.' " See **"I SEE" CONSTRUCTION.**

The fraction as a phrasemaking device, particularly in regard to the poor segment of society, had been successful before. Said Winston Churchill in 1950:

I remember in Victorian days anxious talks about "the submerged tenth" (that part of our people who had not shared in the progress of the age) and then later on in the old Liberal period (the grand old Liberal period) we spoke of going back to bring the rearguard in. The main army we said had reached the camping-ground in all its strength and victory, and we should now, in duty and compassion, go back to pick up the stragglers and those who had fallen by the way and bring them in.

In 1957 President Dwight Eisenhower gave the FDR "one third" turn of phrase a more global view: "From the deserts of North Africa to the islands of the South Pacific, one third of all mankind has entered upon an historic struggle for a new freedom: freedom from grinding poverty." At about the same time, Senate Majority Leader Lyndon Johnson upped the ante: "We live in a world where over two-thirds of the people are 'ill-housed, ill-clad, ill-nourished.' When the madness of the nuclear arms race is halted, mankind's creative efforts can be turned to their relief." See **WAR ON POVERTY.**

ONE WORLD internationalist, liberal Republican philosophy of Wendell Willkie, expressed after his defeat by FDR in 1940.

After his campaign, Willkie made a 31,000-mile trip to the Soviet Union, the Middle East, Africa, and China. In Chungking, he called on the Allies to recognize that World War II was not "a simple tactical problem for task forces. It is also a war for men's minds."

On his return he reported to Americans that the U.S. had a vast "reservoir of good will" that was being drained because our war aims were not being articulated. "The United States has lost moral force," he said after U.S. dealings with Admiral Darlan upset liberals, "and by it, we may lose the peace . . . I hate this false finagling with expediency . . ."

Willkie put these thoughts and others in a 1941 book titled *One World*. In one chapter Willkie held "the attitude of the white citizens of this country toward the Negroes has undeniably had some of the unlovely characteristics of an alien imperialism —a smug, racial superiority, a willingness to exploit an unprotected people." To Willkie, "one world" meant a peace founded without regard to a nation's size, wealth, power, or the color of its citizens. "Our western world and our presumed supremacy are now on trial. Our boasting and our big talk leave Asia cold. Men and women in Russia and China and in the Middle East are . . . coming to know that many of the decisions about the future of the world lie in their hands."

One World sold two million copies within two years. "Bookleggers" in China overlooked the copyright and published it under a title that translates: *Within Four Seas, All Are Brothers.*

After the explosion in 1945 of the first atomic bomb, a group of scientists put forth a statement headed "One World or None." Radio commentator Elmer Davis asked: "Has it occurred to them that if their one world turned out to be totalitarian and obscurantist, we might better

have no world at all?" See BETTER RED THAN DEAD.

ONLY THING WE HAVE TO FEAR, *see* NOTHING TO FEAR BUT FEAR ITSELF.

ON THE POINT   the vulnerable position of being in the lead of a group of candidates; the position of the FRONT RUNNER.

The phrase has only recently entered the political lexicon. The derivation is from military terminology: the member of a squad of soldiers who "takes the point" (often a volunteer, or a more experienced member of the squad) moves out ahead of his comrades and is the man in the greatest danger. He is more frequently called the "scout" than the "point man," but the terms are synonymous. In an ambush, the experienced ambushing force will allow the scout to penetrate, in order to entrap the entire squad; for this reason, the squad is instructed to be spread wide enough so that the last two men of the wedge are far enough back to avert capture or killing, and can warn the main force. The men at the ends of the inverted "V" (farthest from the "point man" in the middle front) are called the "getaway men," a phrase not yet adopted by politics.

The man "on the point" is the object of "Stop (Whoever)" movements by coalitions of other candidates, and the man whose every misstep is given greatest play by the press.

Colorado Governor John A. Love was asked by a reporter what he thought of the attacks being made in 1967 on then Republican front runner George Romney. He replied: "It's a hard place to live, out there on the point."

In 1977 President Carter's Ambassador to the United Nations, Andrew

Young, who had stirred controversy when he hinted at a forthcoming improvement of relations with Cuba, and who created a furor when he said Cuban forces in Angola were "a force for stability" in Africa, agreed on a television panel interview to a description of himself as "a point man" —that is, one who goes out in front of events and takes the heat.

A *Washington Post* editorial disagreed: "To toss off personal opinions —or (in Young's words) to play 'point man'—and then be repudiated is to lose a certain part of one's claim on another government's or the public's attention: to lose effectiveness."

The mixing of horse racing and military metaphors is common in politics. A *front runner* (racing) is *on the point* (military); a *campaign* (origin military) can be a *horse race* (turf); there can be a *boom* (military cannon origin) for a *dark horse* (racing); a *TV blitz* (World War II) in the *home stretch* (last two weeks, racing), as the two *camps* (military) come *down to the wire* (racing) with the *standard-bearers* (military) in a *dead heat* (racing), and the *right wing* (military) threatening to *bolt* (racing). See MILITARY METAPHORS.

"Point man," rather than "on the point," is a Carter Administration contribution, and has been used to describe other advance agents of controversy besides Ambassador Young. The *National Journal* of October 1, 1977, titled a piece about California Congressman James Corman "The House Point Man on Welfare."

A synonym is "cutting edge," as in this *New York Times* editorial (1977): "Secretary Califano has become the cutting edge of the Government's affirmative action drive . . ." The phrase was popularized by Spiro T. Agnew as a self-description of his role in 1970.

OPEN CONVENTION a political convention which begins with no single candidate having a near majority.

"I don't think any one candidate has enough votes to win," said California Governor Earl Warren on the eve of the 1948 Republican convention. "As long as that prevails it's a wide-open convention."

In 1956, former President Harry Truman let it be known that he favored an open Democratic convention, thereby helping block Adlai Stevenson from "locking everything up" before the convention began. New York Governor Averell Harriman announced he was "for Stevenson" but not necessarily "for him for president." ("What does he think I'm running for," asked Stevenson, "county coroner?") Truman supported Harriman, but Stevenson was able to overcome that challenge as well as Senator Estes Kefauver's.

At that point, Stevenson in turn announced that he favored an "open convention" in the choice of a vice-presidential nominee. The delegates, who couldn't remember a previous opportunity to choose a Vice President freely, almost went for Senator John F. Kennedy, but finally chose Kefauver.

At the 1960 convention Harry Truman didn't feel that John Kennedy "was ready" and again called for an "open convention." Kennedy told an aide: "Mr. Truman regards an open convention as one which studies all the candidates, reviews their records and then takes his advice."

Origin of the phrase is probably from gambling terminology: a "wide-open" town is one in which gambling, as well as prostitution, is permitted.

For the usage of open convention compared with "rigged" or "locked up" convention, see **BROKERED CONVENTION**.

OPEN COVENANTS Woodrow Wilson's call for "open diplomacy" without secret agreements.

The Fourteen Points included: "Open covenants of peace, openly arrived at, after which there shall be no private international understandings of any kind, but diplomacy shall proceed always frankly and in the public view."

Clemenceau, Lloyd George, and others were dismayed at Wilson's apparent naïveté, because "in the public view" seemed to mean "no confidential discussions" without which diplomacy could not operate. To correct this, Wilson sent his closest adviser, Colonel Edward House, to explain to world leaders what he meant before armistice negotiations began. House used a memorandum, approved by Wilson, on this point:

> The purpose is clearly to prohibit treaties, sections of treaties or understandings that are secret. The phrase "openly arrived at" need not cause difficulty. In fact, the President explained to the Senate last winter that his intention was not to exclude confidential diplomatic negotiations involving delicate matters, but to insist that nothing which occurs in the course of such confidential negotiations shall be binding unless it appears in the final covenant made public to the world.

In effect, Wilson's high-sounding words—which had an appeal to millions who were curious about what went on behind the scenes at international conferences—had a meaning to Wilson that required confidential explanation. As Walter Lippmann wrote in 1932: ". . . great masses of people cannot negotiate. They can no more negotiate than they can make love or write books or invent. They

can approve or disapprove the results, but if they participate in the negotiation itself they merely shout themselves hoarse and fall into a hopeless deadlock."

At the end of World War II, Republicans were able to use "open covenants" against the party of Wilson. In his "Equal Justice Under Law" speech attacking the war-crimes trials, Senator Robert A. Taft clearly set up the line about secret agreements: "The Atlantic Charter professed a belief in liberty and justice for all nations, but at Teheran, at Yalta, at Moscow, we forgot law and justice. Nothing could be further from a RULE OF LAW than the making of secret agreements distributing the territory of the earth in accordance with power and expediency."

"Open covenants" as used today still requires explanation with every use. It means "no secret agreements," but it also means "sensible private discussions" and as much as says "forget that part about 'openly arrived at.'" Lippmann in 1961 made the point: "By open diplomacy, which only too often means loud-mouthed diplomacy, we can do little to assuage, indeed much to exacerbate these crises. For then one side or the other has to back down if there is to be any accommodation. But in quiet diplomacy, there is no loss of face if a country backs away from an extreme position which has proved to be untenable. For this reason, quiet diplomacy is for the time being the hope of the world."

The word "covenant" rather than treaty or agreement appealed to Wilson. The Covenant of the League of Nations was his phrasing, chosen because he liked the Biblical solemnity of the word. It is possible he took the idea from "The Solemn League and Covenant" of 1643, unifying religious practice in England, Scotland, and Ireland.

Abolitionist leader William Lloyd Garrison liked the word too, in 1831 calling a U.S. Constitution that permitted slavery a "Covenant with Death and an Agreement with Hell," which became a slogan for the Massachusetts Anti-Slavery Society.

See PITILESS PUBLICITY; QUIET DIPLOMACY.

OPEN DOOR POLICY   the policy at the turn of the twentieth century, that all important trading nations should have equal trading rights with the Chinese government, with all respecting that country's territorial integrity.

McKinley's Secretary of State, John Hay, goaded by the British government, acted at a time when it looked as though every powerful nation was about to fall on the hapless Chinese government and tear away both concessions and territory. This supported neither British nor American interests. Britain already had rich concessions in the Yangtze Valley; the U.S., though it wanted to share the Chinese market, was not prepared to fight for it.

China in these last days of the Manchu Empire had been badly defeated in a short but decisive war waged against her by Japan. Only the combined disapproval of all the Western nations currently involved in China at the time (1895) had prevented the Japanese from slicing off chunks of the prostrate Celestial Empire.

At British insistence, Hay sent a series of notes to the concerned powers, which included Italy, Japan, and France, as well as Britain and the U.S., asking for assurances that existing treaties would be observed with China.

Secretary Hay did not reveal the contents of the replies but announced in September 1899 that all had concurred. A new series of notes followed, asking all to agree to China's territorial and administrative integrity. Again, this time on January 2, 1900, Mr. Hay pronounced common accord, though keeping the notes from the public eye.

However, the Boxer Rebellion and the Russo-Japanese War of 1904–05 resulted in further encroachments on China, largely by the Japanese government.

The U.S. continued to talk of the Open Door and used the $25 million forced from China as reparations after the Boxer Rebellion to educate young Chinese in America. For some time, successive Chinese governments felt friendly to the U.S. as the least voracious of all the nations which were busily involved in taking away the country's wealth.

In current usage, diplomats refuse to "close the door" on negotiations.

OPEN SHOP,   see CLOSED SHOP; RIGHT TO WORK.

OPEN-SKIES PROPOSAL   President Eisenhower's suggestion at the 1954 Geneva Convention to permit unlimited aerial photography of the U.S. and the Soviet Union.

President Eisenhower laid the proposal before Premier Bulganin and Communist party chief Khrushchev:

I propose . . . to give each other a complete blueprint of our military establishments, from beginning to end, from one end of our countries to the other; lay out the establishments and provide the blueprints to each other. Next, to provide within our countries facilities for aerial photography to the other country— we to provide the facilities within our country, ample facilities for aerial reconnaissance, where you can make all the pictures you choose and take them to your own country to study; you to provide exactly the same facilities for us and we to make these examinations, and by this step to convince the world that we are providing as between ourselves against the possibility of great surprise attack, thus lessening danger and relaxing tension.

When the Soviets showed no inclination to accept this proposal, the U.S. proceeded to open up the Russian skies unilaterally and secretly with U-2 flights. When the "U-2 Incident" broke up a summit conference, the U.S. State Department took pains to point out that the flights had begun immediately after the rejection of our "open skies" proposal. Senator Lyndon Johnson, who frequently built phrases on top of other phrases, added in 1957: "We must create a new world policy. Not just of 'open skies'—but of open eyes, ears, and minds, for all peoples of the world. I call for the 'open curtain.' Let truth flow through it freely. Let ideas cleanse evil just as fresh air cleanses the poisoned, stagnant mass of a long-closed cavern."

OPEN SOCIETY   a social order in which the people are granted a **RIGHT TO KNOW** as opposed to a "closed society" of a totalitarian state, in which secrecy is predominant.

The phrase achieved common political usage in the fifties, especially after the "open skies" proposal by President Eisenhower in 1954; there was another flurry of usage after the U-2 incident in 1959 when it was explained that the U.S. was an "open society" and needed to find ways to explain the goings-on in "closed societies."

Dwight Eisenhower coined one of his best metaphors around the subject of an open society in a draft for a speech that was never delivered. Had the President been permitted to visit the Soviet Union, he would have delivered a speech in Leningrad on May 12, 1960, about Soviet-American relations that used these words:

When I was a boy, we put blinders on horses so they would not shy in fright of a scarecrow, a shadow, a rabbit. But today we human beings deliberately put blinders on ourselves, not to avoid the sight of frightful things, but to ignore a central fact of human existence.

I mean that mankind too often blinds itself to the common lot, to the common purposes, to the common aspirations of humanity everywhere. I mean that all of us too much live in ignorance of our neighbors; or, when we take off our blinders, view them through the contortionist spectacles of propaganda.

And we will continue that way— forever fearful, forever suspicious— until we convince ourselves that the only way to peace is through the mutually open society. Then, at long last, seeing our human neighbors as they really are, we shall come to realize that we need no more fear them than the horse the rabbit.

The phrase is often used in discussions seeking to explain the necessity of (or deploring the actions of) the Central Intelligence Agency. Walter Lippmann wrote in 1967 about covert CIA support of student groups: ". . . black propaganda, secret interventions, intrigue and subornation are incompatible with our open society. They are the methods of a totalitarian state and without a totalitarian environment of secrecy and terror, they are unworkable. This most unpleasant and embarrassing affair is the proof than an open society cannot act successfully like a totalitarian society."

Said President Johnson soon after, about the bad press he was getting: "There is something about our open society that gives the play to what went wrong instead of what went right." Defense Secretary Robert A. Lovett looked at the problem another way: "I cannot escape the feeling that, as a government, we tend to talk too much. To be sure, we are an open society, but we give the impression of being unbuttoned."

After the phrase was in common use, a new meaning was introduced as part of the language of the civil rights movement. "Open" instead of meaning "nonsecret" was defined as "available to all"—as in "open occupancy" or "open housing." *Ebony* magazine quoted Dr. Leo K. Bishop in this context: "In two decades the Jews and the Roman Catholics have moved into the open society of the United States, and the Negroes will make it too."

OPIATE OF THE PEOPLE   a metaphor by Karl Marx about religion, used against Marxism and Communism by its critics for more than a century.

"Religion is the sigh of the oppressed creature," wrote Marx in 1844, in his *Critique of the Hegelian Philosophy of Right,* "the feeling of a heartless world, just as it is the spirit of unspiritual conditions. It is the Opium of the People." The German phrase *Opium des Volkes* can be translated "opium of the people," or "opiate of the people"; the latter is now more commonly used.

Although Marx went on to stress the point—"the first requisite for the people's happiness is the abolition of religion"—Communist leaders in countries with strong religious traditions have tried to water down the metaphor. "Marx's position is widely misunderstood," wrote the Socialist Labor party's official organ in 1959. ". . . When the essay was written, opium was used in Europe almost exclusively for relieving pain. . . . Marx was using the word 'opium' in this sense and not in the sense that religion is a stupefier deliberately administered to the people by agents of the ruling class."

As president of Columbia University in 1950, Dwight Eisenhower made a typical attack on the "Godlessness" of Communism, using Marx's vivid phrase against him: "Hundreds of millions behind the Iron Curtain are daily drilled in the slogan: 'There is no God, and religion is an opiate.' But not all the people within the Soviet accept this fallacy; and some day they will educate their rulers, or change them."

Clare Boothe Luce played with the phrase in 1955, calling Communism "the opiate of the intellectuals . . . but no cure, except as a guillotine might be called a cure for a case of dandruff."

But the best turnaround was in a 1967 editorial in the Suffolk (L.I.) *Sun,* about the LSD prophet, Dr. Timothy Leary, "who hopes to make opiates the religion of the people."

OPINION LEADER   a person or organization able because of position, expertise, or facilities to influence the convictions of others.

An obvious influence might be a newspaper. In 1859 John Stuart Mill wrote in obvious regret: "The mass do not now take their opinions from dignitaries in church or state, from ostensible leaders, or from books. Their thinking is done for them by men much like themselves, addressing them or speaking in their name, on the spur of the moment, through the newspapers."

Congressman Robert La Follette, seeking a second term against the opposition of the regular leaders of the Republican party in Wisconsin, devised a technique for reaching those he considered opinion leaders. Before the 1886 elections, he had the voter list broken down into townships. He then sent such a list to a supporter in that particular area, requesting the names of any of the local men considered to be people whose names had local leadership significance. To these people, he regularly sent accounts of his congressional actions and copies of his speeches. The system worked; despite continued party opposition he was renominated and reelected.

Columbia University behavioral scientist Paul Lazarsfeld led the way to the formulation of the "opinion leader" idea. His theory of the "two-step flow of communication" held that the general public did not take its opinions directly from the mass or class media; instead, these messages were filtered through a layer of respected activists. These opinion leaders, however, do not lead in all categories. For example, a sophisticated high-society type may be an opinion leader in matters of fashion, but she may be a follower of a gregarious housewife in marketing matters, and both these leaders may be followers of a League of Women Voters president in political affairs.

The power of television has eroded the opinion-leader concept in recent years, as persuasive candidates have been able to affect mass opinion "over the heads" of the opinion leaders.

Many politicians accumulate a "Kefauver Christmas list," named after Estes Kefauver's extensive list of contacts, contributors, casual acquaintances, and correspondents who received a Christmas card from the Tennessee senator. Presumably, a good portion of these people are opinion leaders.

OPINION OF MANKIND, *see* **WORLD OPINION.**

OPPORTUNIST one who sacrifices principle to expediency; a frequent attack word used against ambitious or fast-rising political figures.

The word grew popular in the political lexicon in the fifties, although Arthur Krock accused Senator Robert Taft of playing "obvious or even opportunist politics" in 1946.

One who is attacked as an opportunist is (1) on the way up, (2) in the public eye, and (3) controversial. As an attack word, "ambitious" was losing its sting because ambition pervades politics and in the proper degree is an excellent trait. The predecessor word, now obsolete, was "trimmer," from one who trims his sails to capture the prevailing breeze.

An opportunist, in current usage, is one who changes his position to comply with what is presently popular (see ALL THINGS TO ALL MEN). "Theodore Roosevelt," said Robert La Follette, "is the ablest living interpreter of what I would call the superficial public sentiment of a given time, and he is spontaneous in his reactions to it." Britain's Harold Wilson attacked Harold Macmillan: "Cynical opportunism in place of leadership, an appeal to cupidity rather than to the moral purpose of the nation."

On the other hand, one who sticks to a single position can be attacked as "inflexible," "mossbacked," "unwilling to meet new situations with new solutions." The most common defense of one who has radically switched his position (Arthur Vandenberg on isolationism, Lyndon Johnson on civil rights) is that the individual has "matured," or "been man enough to admit a mistake," or has become "pragmatic."

In 404 B.C., a member of the Athenian oligarchy named Theramenes was nicknamed *cothurnus,* which was a sandal that could be worn on either foot, because he was considered an opportunist. From this came the expression "He wears the sandals of Theramenes," i.e., he is not to be trusted. Brewer in his *Dictionary of Phrase and Fable* said: "He blew hot and cold with the same breath."

In 1597 Francis Bacon pointed to an example of opportunism still practiced today: "It is commonly seen, that men once placed, take in with the contrary faction to that by which they enter; thinking, belike, that they have the first sure, and now are ready for a new purchase."

Republicans in 1967 were surprised when Michigan Governor George Romney called fellow Republican, Illinois Senator Charles Percy, an opportunist; he later explained that he meant that Percy understood timing, that he knew how to seize an opportunity. This is a positive sense the word may one day gain, but neither was nor is current usage.

The word is rooted is the Latin *ob,* "before," and *portus,* "the harbor," and bears a relation to the man who keeps hoping his ship will come in. According to former Nixon speechwriter Benjamin Stein, writing in *Esquire* in 1977, Henry Kissinger's assessment of Mr. Carter's national security adviser, Zbigniew Brzezinski, carried the wistful tone of one whose ship had come and gone: "He's a bit of an opportunist."

No publication ever gave the idea more of a metaphoric blast than the *Liberation Army Daily,* published in Peking. After the overthrow of the radical "Gang of Four," the army paper attacked a group of unnamed opportunists who had not been swept from power by Chairman Mao's successor, Hua Kuo-feng: "The main features of those who follow the wind are steering the boat according to which way the wind blows and the advocacy of opportunism. Their color changes when they hear the wind, and they sell their soul at a discount. Speculation has become their habit, and they treat any woman who gives them milk as their mother . . . They are like grass growing atop a wall, bending with the wind. They are as changeable as clouds and rain. Their necks function like ball bearings and their waists like spring bands, and wind gauges are planted on their heads." This dazzling display of anti-opportunistic rhetoric was reprinted in the *People's Daily* on January 6, 1978, in the same space where—only two years before—a similar attack on opportunists had been launched by those later labeled the Gang of Four.

See CENTRIST.

OPTIONS   choices; alternatives.

In a sophisticated political sense, the existence of a number of options offers freedom to maneuver; as options are narrowed, the decision-maker loses leverage on his adversaries because his chances for TRADE-OFFS are decreased, and the element of surprise is lessened. See NEW ECONOMICS.

President Lyndon Johnson was often quoted as insistent on "keeping my options open." The word "open," in this sense, is used to mean "not narrowed by elimination." Whenever Franklin Roosevelt asked Congress for discretionary authority in legislation, he called it "room to turn around."

The word became popular in Washington in the sixties, probably from the **WAR-GAMING** vocabulary. The doctrine of flexible response (see **MEASURED RESPONSE**) and a decision about which weapons systems to develop depends largely on what—and how many—options are available.

This is a far cry from George Washington's use of the word: "There is an option left to the United States of America, whether they will be respectable and prosperous, or contemptible and miserable, as a nation." More often today, the option is between the lesser of two evils; as entertainer Maurice Chevalier said on reaching seventy-two: "Old age isn't so bad when you consider the alternative."

In the early seventies, as a result of National Security Adviser Henry Kissinger's use of the term in backgrounders, "Option Three" became synonymous with compromise. In a choice of five options, option three is nicely situated between extremes, and is the easiest to choose; an option three philosophy is not conducive to bold leadership.

As a verb, *opt* is gaining in popularity, connoting a more impulsive selection than the thoughtful *choose*. Bergen Evans used it precisely in *Comfortable Words:* "Confronted with a choice between *choose* and *opt,* my impulse is to opt for *choose.*"

See **TRADE-OFF**.

OPT OUT, *see* **-OUT CONSTRUCTION.**

OTHER BODY an arch reference by a member of the Senate to the House, and vice versa.

Both houses in a bicameral legislature are jealous of their prerogatives; in the U.S., the "other body" is a way for a legislator to refer to the Senate or the House of Representatives without appearing to pay it too much respect; in current use, the pronunciation attempts to reproduce the "sound" of quotation marks.

The phrase originated in a rule of the British Houses of Parliament which states that a member of one house may make no reference to the proceedings of the other, a vestige of the days when rivalry between the House of Commons and the House of Lords could have led to a constitutional crisis. To get around the old custom, English politicians call their other body "another place."

-OUT CONSTRUCTION a rhetorical device to express alienation.

The removal of an individual from reality, as in "pass out" for a drunk becoming unconscious, was popularized in the sixties as "to drop out," or to leave school. This progressed to "opt out," a deliberate decision to separate one's self from most of society. By 1977, to "flick out" meant to go to the movies (flicks) in such a determined manner as to immerse one's self in an escapist world.

The -out construction is often used by political campaigners who wish to appear "in," but sometimes results in a false camaraderie that leads to charges of **SELLOUT**.

OUT OF CONTEXT, *see* **QUOTED OUT OF CONTEXT; DEFOLIATE.**

OUT OF POCKET, *see* **UP TO SPEED.**

OUT PARTY, *see* **INS AND OUTS.**

OUTSIDE WORLD a **SPLINTER PARTY**.

A measure of the xenophobia of

politicians is shown in this expression. A party is a world of its own and
threats to TAKE A WALK or BOLT lead
to an outside world—cold, barren
unexplored, with wild voters roaming
the tundra.

Don Oberdorfer of the *Washington
Post* on July 23, 1971, wrote about
plans being made by supporters of
former Senator Eugene McCarthy for
a fourth party (assuming Governor
George Wallace would be a third-
party candidate in 1972). An unnamed McCarthy aide said the independent route might be taken if their
candidate should lose the Democratic
nomination "unfairly": "If we get
beat up in the streets and screwed in
the caucuses . . . then the 'outside
world' is always fair." Oberdorfer
correctly defined "outside world" as
"the euphemism for a fourth party."

OUT TO LUNCH, *see* **UP TO
SPEED.**

OVAL OFFICE   the formal office
of the President of the United States;
by extension, the center of Executive
power.

A headline on page 16 in the *Washington Post* of July 6, 1934, read:
"President's New Oval Office/Care-
fully Planned for Beauty—FDR"
The story predicted that the West
Wing of the White House would have
"a main floor unchanged except for
filling in the clothes yard . . ."

According to the January 1935
issue of *Building Modernization,* the
expansion of space from 15,000 to
40,000 feet "was accomplished by
filling in the old 'drying yard'—a lat-
tice-inclosed square adjacent to the
old laundry once used for drying presidential wash. In its place along the
side portico, opening on a rose garden, is the office of the President and
his personal staff." The office was de-

scribed as "oval in shape and besides
the fact that it is almost always
flooded with southern sun, its chief
feature is its large bay made up of a
series of steel sash windows of immense proportion."

Although White House curator
Clem Conger can find citations of the
"oval office" in the thirties, the President's office—one of several oval
rooms in the White House, including
the Diplomatic Reception Room and
the "Yellow Room" on the second
floor of the residence—did not become known as such through several
Administrations. When Harry Truman gave his farewell address from
his office on January 15, 1953, he said:
"This is the President's Office in the
West Wing of the White House."
Dwight Eisenhower used "West
Wing" to mean center of action during his Presidency and in his book
Mandate for Change.

Although "The President's oval
office" was heard by White House
aides in the Johnson Presidency, the
phrase did not come into the general
language until Mr. Nixon's term. The
author recalls that among White
House aides who were his colleagues,
"Oval Office"—capitalized, and without "the President's" in front of it—
was a phrase used to hint at decision
making by the President without
using his name.

The phrase was speeded into wide
public use as a result of Watergate:
the earliest Merriam-Webster citation
is an October 19, 1972, story by Robert Semple Jr. in the *New York Times:*
"At the moment, the White House
feels, the alleged conspiracy is perceived by most of the public as a distant and even amateurish intrigue far
removed from the Oval Office . . ." J.
Anthony Lukas reported in the *New
York Times Magazine* on July 22,
1973, that "John Dean says [Egil]

Krogh told him that orders for the burglary came 'directly from the Oval Office.' " That notion—of the Presidency being more of a place than a man, and thus less personally accountable—was behind the early internal use of "Oval Office," and later led to its popularization.

Lexicographers report a rush of citations late in 1974 and 1975; the White House Historical Association, which in previous editions of its guide referred to "the President's Office", switched in 1973.

"Oval Office," in initial caps, seems to be the only Watergate-era word that carries no unpleasant connotation into the present. Soon after the election of Jimmy Carter, Leslie Gelb —a *New York Times* reporter destined to serve in the Carter State Department—wrote: "A crisis like another Middle East war, saber-rattling by Moscow, the embrace of the foreign policy bureaucracy and the enormous complexity of issues and pressures when viewed from the Oval Office could consign the most ardently believed campaign rhetoric to oblivion."

The phrase has become a neutral reference to the Presidency; similarly, "the West Wing" refers to the President's Senior staff, the "East Wing" to the First Lady's offices.

OVEREXPOSURE   the fear held by public figures that continuous publicity leads to public boredom.

Kennedy biographers are fond of quoting a passage from this letter by Franklin Roosevelt to Ray Stannard Baker, dated March 20, 1935, that had earlier been quoted by Richard Neustadt in *Presidential Power:*

> I know . . . you will be sympathetic to the point of view that the public psychology and, for that matter, individual psychology, cannot,

because of human weakness, be attuned for long periods of time to a constant repetition of the highest note in the scale. . . . Whereas in this country there is a free and sensational press, people tire of seeing the same name, day after day, in the important headlines of the papers, and the same voice, night after night, over the radio . . . if I had tried [in 1935] to keep up the pace of 1933 and 1934, the inevitable histrionics of the new actors, Long and Coughlin and Johnson, would have turned the eyes of the audience away from the main drama itself . . .

Because it is quoted frequently, the "highest-note-in-the-scale" theory has become a kind of credo of political mass communications. "I do not believe it is possible," wrote Ted Sorensen loyally, "to 'overexpose' a President like Kennedy." Then he became pragmatic, to use a word popular in the Kennedy era: "Nevertheless he could not, with any effectiveness, go on the air to denounce Big Steel, or announce a Cuban quarantine, or deliver some momentous message, every month of the year. . . . As a commander saves his biggest guns for the biggest battles, so Kennedy limited his direct national appeals to situations of sufficient importance to demand it and sufficiently fluid to be helped by it."

Eisenhower press secretary James Hagerty felt sufficiently confident of the magnetism of Eisenhower's presence to permit—for the first time— the filming of presidential press conferences, despite the danger of "overexposure." Kennedy extended this to "live" coverage and more frequent conferences; Lyndon Johnson, early in his Administration, made a great many television appearances to "put his stamp" on the presidency. As Arthur Krock wrote: "He does not share the fear of some friends that he is taking too heavy a toll of his incredible energy, and has already incurred whatever political peril there may be in 'overexposure.' " By 1967, however, Johnson made it a point to say less and appear less.

Krock's successor as the Washington correspondent of the *New York Times,* James Reston, applied the exposure yardstick with a photography metaphor to Senator Robert Kennedy in 1967, after a Kennedy dispute with J. Edgar Hoover over wiretapping, and Kennedy's handling of Manchester's book on the assassination: ". . . publicity is not the same thing as power, and while it is often useful to a rising politician, it can sometimes be the opposite. . . . He is better known now, but he looks a little underdeveloped and overexposed."

OVERHEATED ECONOMY   an economy headed toward uncontrollable inflation, with price and wage rises far outpacing productivity.

A classic example of the unconscious use of jargon is this passage from Walter Heller's *New Dimensions of Political Economy (1967):* "Let us assume that a nation which has accepted the idea of tax cuts to overcome slack, to close a 'deflationary gap,' should undertake tax increases to cool off an overheating economy, to close an 'inflationary gap.' "

In pointing to the metaphoric use of "gaps," Heller overlooked his own use of "overheating economy," a piece of economic jargon. Like FLAT-OUT, it is an automobile metaphor; overheated refers to an engine raced too long or loaded too heavily.

See HOLD THE LINE; INFLATION; BAFFLEGAB; NEW ECONOMICS.

OVERKILL   a surfeit of power; more nuclear destruction capable of being inflicted than is needed to kill an enemy's entire population.

"In describing the aftermath of a war," Hudson Institute operations analyst Herman Kahn wrote coolly in 1960, "it is not particularly illuminating to use such words as 'intolerable,' 'catastrophic,' 'total destruction,' 'annihilating retaliation,' and so on. Such words would be useful only if it were really true that in a modern war all possible targets would be overkilled by factors of five or ten, as many people have assumed." After coining the word, he advocated a shelter program that would, he thought, cut U.S. casualties from eighty million down to forty million. See UNTHINKABLE THOUGHTS.

U.S. strategic planners picked up the word in explaining their policy of "limited deterrence," which held that if the U.S. had enough atomic weapons to inflict "unacceptable" damage to an enemy, any further expenditure on weapons would only be for "overkill" and a waste of money.

One of the charms of political language is its ability to absorb colorful words, no matter how shocking or bloody the concept. Writing about the ovation given Robert Kennedy at the 1964 Democratic convention, political columnists Rowland Evans and Robert Novak observed: "It brought second thoughts to the politicians who had accused Johnson of overkill in deploying the powers of the Presidency on The Bobby Problem."

In a 1969 speech, William McChesney Martin, then chairman of the Federal Reserve Board, showed how the word could be used in an economic context as well. He described a conversation he had with President Johnson in 1965, in which he pointed out that increased expenditures required higher taxes to avert inflation. "I remember him saying to me, 'Well, yes, I think so too, but we can't do it now. We'd risk overkill.' That was the first time I'd heard that expression used, but I've heard it plenty over the years since, when all the while the economy—and inflationary pressures as well—were burgeoning."

OVERREACT to respond more strongly than necessary, revealing a tendency to panic; in politics, the mark of an amateur.

When President Harry Truman received reports on June 24, 1950, that North Korean troops had invaded South Korea, he was careful not to overreact. "Don't make it ALARM-IST," he told reporters. "It could be dangerous, but I hope it isn't. There has been no formal declaration of war that I know of. I can't answer any more questions until I get all the facts." This illustrates one sense of the word: the comment, or "reaction," from a public figure immediately following an event.

The second sense is to take more action than is necessary to counter an opponent's thrust. When steel companies raised their prices in 1962 (See **S.O.B.**) President Kennedy marshaled all the strength of the presidency to force them to roll back their increase. Wrote Sorensen: "When it was all over, several Republicans . . . would term these various administration efforts an example of 'over-reacting,' 'tyranny' and 'executive usurpation.' "

The use of "overreact" as an attack word is evident in this 1967 *Wall Street Journal* editorial: "When the United States has used overwhelming force, as in Eisenhower's intervention in Lebanon or Johnson's dash into the Dominican Republic, the results have been relatively happy despite initial charges of overreaction."

The use of the word has traveled. *The Economist* of London urged in

1967 an end to the "baiting" of Foreign Secretary George Brown: ". . . one of Mr. Brown's faults is that he is inclined to over-react. The more he is hounded by the gossip writers (as he is) the more likely he is to over-react and provide them with additional copy. The more he is made to look politically vulnerable by being forced (unnecessarily) to restate major speeches, as he has had to do twice this week, the more likely he is to over-react with a real resignation."

OVERSIGHT presumed vigilance of a government operation by a congressional committee.

In a working paper for the House Select Committee on Committees, Walter Oleszek wrote in June 1973: "A result of this expansion [of administrative agencies since the New Deal] has been an enlargement of Congress' oversight function, a traditional legislative function that philosopher John Stuart Mill considered as the most important responsibility of a legislature."

This "oversight function" of the U.S. Congress is relatively new, first formally authorized by Section 136 of the Legislative Reorganization Act of 1946: "To assist the Congress in appraising the administration of the laws and developing such amendments or related legislation as it may deem necessary, each standing committee of the Senate and the House shall exercise continuous watchfulness of the execution by the administrative agencies concerned of any laws, the subject matter of which is within the jurisdiction of such committee . . .

"Continuous watchfulness," Congressmen felt, was too vague, or too time-consuming; in 1970 this was changed to "legislative review." In practice, the investigative part of "oversight" was largely neglected by the Congress, which was more interested during the fifties and sixties in legislative reach—adding to the laws regulating commerce or creating new agencies.

However, with the CIA revelations of the Senate Select Committee on Intelligence in 1975, it became apparent that Congress had been remiss in its obligation to act as a check on actions of the executive branch, especially in the intelligence area. The word "oversight" became voguish in the mid-seventies, not only as an accusation of lack of previous vigilance but as a means of extending congressional power. A related term, "accountability," has a positive connotation, while "monitoring" often carries an intrusive, pejorative tone.

Ted Sorensen, the Kennedy speechwriter who was rejected by the Senate in 1977 as nominee to be Director of Central Intelligence, once wrote wryly: "The word 'oversight' has two meanings, and they chose the wrong one."

"The oversight function," as the word is sometimes attenuated, is occasionally confused with "overview," a favorite term of social scientists. "Oversight" implies supervision or at least some modicum of control, while "overview" implies either a perspective or a survey conducted with Olympian detachment. "Overview" has good lineage: "Too bitter is thy jest," says the King in *Love's Labour's Lost,* written by Shakespeare in 1588. "Are we betrayed thus to thy overview?"

OXYMORON, *see* **LOYAL OPPOSITION; UNTHINKABLE THOUGHTS; WAGING PEACE.**

PACIFICATION euphemism for crushing guerrilla resistance in an area, either by extermination or, preferably, by constructing a stable socio-economic system that will persuade them to change sides.

In the minds of military men, pacification has both of the above meanings. The choice of the word—"to make peaceful"—enables political leaders to concentrate on the positive sense and overlook the "or else" implicit in the program.

In the war in Vietnam, the U.S. government wished to make clear that it was assisting in repelling invaders from the North who were using local Vietcong troops as aides to their invasion, rather than accept the Communist view that it was a civil war between South Vietnamese, with "outsiders" meddling. Accordingly, the "war" was against the North Vietnamese, and "pacification" aimed at Vietcong activities.

"Unlike the direct campaign against major Communist military units," wrote McGeorge Bundy in 1967, "the political effort, in all its forms, can take effect only as it engages the energies and convictions of the Vietnamese people themselves. So we must not be surprised that real pacification is hard to get in the Vietnamese countryside.

Lyndon Johnson, in a Nashville, Tennessee, speech on March 16, 1967, used pacification in its constructive sense, again separating it from military success against troops from the North: ". . . our military success has permitted the ground work to be laid for a pacification program which is the long-run key to an independent South Vietnam."

In American history, the word had been relatively dormant since its use as the nickname for Senator Henry Clay of Kentucky, "The Great Pacificator." See INFRASTRUCTURE; OTHER WAR.

PACKAGE DEAL an omnibus bill, often containing something for everybody; a compromise that enables an executive to get legislation he wants in return for agreeing to sign legislation he has opposed.

Running for re-election as governor of California in 1950, Earl Warren stressed his nonpartisan stance, resisting efforts to get him to support any other Republican on the ticket, including Richard Nixon for senator: "I have no present intention of endorsing candidates for other offices in the November 7 election. We are all running independent campaigns. I've never believed in package deals. I believe the public is entitled to make its own selection and I'm just interested in one campaign—my own."

This was and is a merchandising expression, referring to the two-for-the-price-of-one sales appeals, or the inclusion of a tube of toothpaste in the same package with a toothbrush.

In an early Eisenhower cabinet meeting, it was pointed out that conservatives resisted a negotiated peace in Korea because they felt it might lead to recognition of Red China. Defense Secretary Charles E. Wilson, a businessman all his life, popped up with: "Is there any possibility for a package deal? Maybe we could recognize Red China and get the Far East issues settled." As Sherman Adams recalled later, "Eisenhower managed to control himself." Emmett Hughes commented, "Quite a few cabinet meetings were jerked to quivering attention by such remarks." (In retrospect, "Engine Charlie" seems more prescient than his more sophisticated colleagues.)

The President explained that such a quid pro quo was not feasible; the phrase "package deal" was not used again in cabinet meetings. However, in his 1957 message to Congress on mutual security, Eisenhower put together a series of foreign operations recommendations into "one vital parcel which we must not neglect."

In 1978, when Jimmy Carter linked the promised sale of jet fighters to Israel with a similar sale to Egypt and Saudi Arabia, his Secretary of State, Cyrus Vance, presented the plan publicly as "a package," and Congress approved the three items in series.

See CHRISTMAS TREE BILL; LINKAGE.

PACKING THE GALLERIES
placing the supporters of one candidate at a national convention in the galleries to the exclusion of others, in the hope of stampeding the delegates.

"We want Willkie! We want Willkie!" The thunderous demand from the galleries at the 1940 Republican convention heartened many a Willkie supporter among the delega-

tions on the floor, and convinced many waverers that a bandwagon was rolling.

The floor manager for Senator Robert A. Taft, R. B. Creager, stormed up to the platform with a complaint to Chairman Joe Martin: when Taft supporters showed up for their gallery seats, they found them already occupied by Willkie fans who were using counterfeit tickets. (For counterfeiting instructions, see SPONTANEOUS DEMONSTRATION.) "It was an open scandal," Martin admitted later, "that several hundred counterfeit tickets had been printed and given to a Willkie claque who filled the best seats in the gallery to the exclusion of holders of bona fide tickets." Creager wanted to be recognized in order to denounce the tactics, but Martin talked him out of it. "We had no evidence in hand . . . we weren't even sure that we could distinguish the counterfeit tickets from the real ones, so skillfully were the former printed."

As the hollering continued, Martin banged his gavel: "I regret to have to admonish those in the galleries to be quiet, and to remind them that they are the guests of this convention . . ."

"Guests, hell," a voice was heard to shout, "we *are* the convention!"

After Willkie was nominated, Taft men insisted that the packing of the galleries had "put over" Willkie. Roscoe Drummond, then a *Christian Science Monitor* correspondent, disagreed: "Willkie was no more 'put over' on the Republican convention than Babe Ruth was 'put over' on the New York Yankees."

Wilkie's gallery-packing was in the grand tradition of the first candidate of the Republican party. According to historian Carl Sandburg, Lincoln supporter Ward Lamon had been to the printers of tickets for seats to the Republican convention held in Chicago's Wigwam in 1860: "Young men worked nearly a whole night signing the names of convention officers to counterfeit seat tickets so that the next day Lincoln men could jam the hall and leave no seats for the Seward shouters."

PAID HIS DUES, *see* **CARD-CARRYING.**

PAIRING an agreement between two legislators, in disagreement about an upcoming vote, that neither will be present at the voting; thus, each is on record without the necessity of appearance.

When supporters of John F. Kennedy explained that their candidate was seriously ill at the time of the McCarthy censure, liberal Democrats refused to accept the excuse because, they argued, "the Senator could have been paired against McCarthy."

The system is a useful device when absence is caused by illness or other important official business; similarly, it is an alibi-ruiner. However, Ralph Waldo Emerson made a case against the idea:

> What a vicious practice is this of our politicians at Washington pairing off! as if one man who votes wrong, going away, could excuse you, who mean to vote right, for going away; or as if your presence did not tell in more ways than in your vote. Suppose the three hundred heroes at Thermopylae had paired off with three hundred Persians: would it have been all the same to Greece, and to history?

PALACE GUARD attack word on the leader's inner circle from one who has been excluded; those who protect or "insulate" a President, taking an undue share of power.

"Either make up your minds," Eisenhower chief of staff Sherman Adams said to two department heads in some dispute, "or else tell me and I will do it. We must not bother the President with this. He is trying to keep the world from war." Adams (see **ABOMINABLE NO-MAN**) was denounced by Senator Joseph McCarthy for heading a "palace guard," usurping power by "insulating" the Chief Executive from decisions properly only his.

From the point of view of one unable to reach the leader's ear, the sin of the palace guard is insulation. F. Clifton White, who organized the Draft Goldwater movement only to find himself frozen out when Goldwater was nominated, said nothing against the candidate but was bitter about what he termed "the tight little coterie that insulated him from all other Republicans."

According to Lyndon Johnson, House Speaker Sam Rayburn told Harry Truman soon after Truman became President: "Harry, they'll try to put you behind a wall down here. There will be people who will surround you and cut you off from any ideas but theirs. They'll try to make you think that the President is the smartest man in the world. And, Harry, you know he ain't and I know he ain't."

James Farley broke with FDR in 1940, when he thought there was a possibility of a presidential nomination for himself. Of those days, he wrote: "Housing Administrator Nathan Straus brought me word that the White House 'palace guard' realized the anti-Catholic campaign against me had failed . . ." Earlier, when Farley was a member of that guard, he explained the political subtlety behind the willingness of Louis Howe, FDR's closest adviser, to permit Farley to be close to Roosevelt: "The reason Louis had faith in me and trusted me was that he knew I didn't want to get between him and Roosevelt. In other words, Louis didn't have anything I wanted, see?"

A good political campaign appears to "stay loose," to avoid the strict lines of authority that discourage influential supporters from reaching the candidate or his manager. If the circle of men around a candidate freezes into a few familiar faces, there is a tendency for those men to identify too closely with the candidate and an understandable reluctance of others to try to "break in."

The idea of the palace guard probably comes from the Praetorian Guard, an imperial bodyguard established by the Emperor Augustus which, under later Roman emperors, assumed considerable power of its own. In 1791 James Madison warned that the "stockjobbers will become the praetorian band of the Government, at once its tool and its tyrant." Around "King Andrew" Jackson's time, the White House was referred to as "the palace," a usage William Leggett objected to in 1837: "The word 'palace' . . . as applied to the President's house is entirely out of place . . ."

The phrase was applied to the Nixon senior staff by Dan Rather and Gary Paul Gates in a 1971 book of that title; because of the Germanic origin of some of the key aides' names (Haldeman, Ehrlichman, Kissinger, Ziegler) the Nixon palace guard was also known as the "Berlin wall."

In the Carter Administration, the number of Georgians on the staff (Joseph Powell, Hamilton Jordan, Robert Lipshutz, Stuart Eizenstadt) led to the occasional use of the "Magnolia Mafia." Carter cabinet secretary Jack Watson insisted: "The White House

staff will not be a palace guard giving commands to the rest of government." Asked why he had placed a stern call to a cabinet member, Watson replied, "He will constantly need a presidential perspective on issues, and the White House staff has to give him that perspective." See IRISH MAFIA.

As used today, *palace guard* is a mild term of reproof to the circle of advisers that must be near a President or governor; *inner circle* (see INNER CLUB) is a term of respect or awe; KITCHEN CABINET is a group of trusted, unofficial advisers on policy; *coterie* implies congeniality, or circle of cronies; *retinue* is critical of the number of people who travel with the executive; *clique* is definitely pejorative, connoting snobbism; *mafia* imputes fierce loyalty, often used in admiration mixed with a dash of fear; OFFICIAL FAMILY is wide-ranging and imputes no criticism; *set,* as in the "Cliveden Set" in wartime England, or "Georgetown cocktail party set," is snobbish with a sinister overlay; *privy council,* used by Roosevelt, never caught on in the U.S.; BRAIN TRUST connotes professors: "the back door to the White House can only be opened with a Phi Beta Kappa key."

PAPER THE FILE, *see* **COVER YOUR ASS.**

PAPER TIGER   exaggerated danger; false ferociousness; in diplomacy, a blustering nation with no real strength.

"All reactionaries," Mao Tse-tung told correspondent Anna Louise Strong in 1946, "are paper tigers. In appearance, the reactionaries are terrifying, but in reality they are not so powerful."

On other occasions Mao said of imperialists and feudalists: "Look! were these not living, iron tigers, real tigers? But in the end they changed into paper tigers, dead tigers, bean-curd tigers." And of the threat of nuclear destruction: "The atom bomb is a paper tiger which the U.S. reactionaries use to scare people. It looks terrible, but in fact it isn't."

Paper is a word used to symbolize the name of a thing rather than the thing itself; a picture of a cow drawn on paper cannot be milked, nor can a picture of a tiger on paper harm the viewer. Hence, "paper blockade," declared but not enforced; "paper profits," real but unrealized; and "to paper the house," to distribute free tickets to give the illusion of a sellout crowd.

Tiger metaphors have long stalked politics. "Riding the tiger" is an ancient image, used in 1936 by Winston Churchill: "Dictators ride to and from upon tigers from which they dare not dismount. And the tigers are getting hungry." A Tammany chieftain is said to have mounted a tiger's head on an old fire engine to rally his voters, and Thomas Nast locked in the image of a hungry TAMMANY TIGER in a cartoon.

PANJANDRUM   mock title for a self-appointed big shot; a more intellectual form of POOH-BAH.

In a 1977 book review by *New York Times* cultural writer John Leonard, the mouth-filling word was used in its intended meaning: "As we might expect from Mr. [Ben] Wattenberg—co-author of *The Real Majority,* adviser to Senator Henry Jackson, panjandrum of the 'centrist' Coalition for a Democratic Majority and public-television personality—*Against All Enemies* has more on its mind than mere entertainment."

Panjandrum was a word concocted by playwright Samuel Foote in 1755 to test the memory of a character who claimed to be able to repeat anything after having once heard it: "And there were present the Picninnies, and the Joblillies, and the Garyulies, and the Grand Panjandrum himself, with the little round button at top."

PARAMOUNT ISSUE   the overriding concern on the minds of voters in a campaign.

The phrase was popularized by William Jennings Bryan, in regard to free silver, and has had a steady use since. Michigan Governor George Romney called Vietnam the "paramount issue" of 1967 (see UNTHINKABLE THOUGHTS).

Paramount issue implies importance, for rational discussion; BURNING QUESTION is irrational discussion from entrenched positions, as on the question of slavery; GUT ISSUE is one which is not so much discussed as it is felt, as resentment about Negro gains or fear of social change; POCKETBOOK ISSUE is economic. In recent years, TOPIC A has been in use to define the subject at the tip of many tongues.

Before an issue can become paramount, it must (1) be drawn so as to show a difference between parties, (2) show voters that the issue-drawing party's side is close to their own, and (3) hit home—be important to the voter.

PARITY   the price at which a farmer maintains his purchasing power.

Parity and "price supports" are used interchangeably, further confusing a farm program that most Americans do not understand.

Parity, like "par" and "peer," is from a Latin root meaning "equal." In agricultural policy, it is the price established by government statisticians that will bring the farmer a return equal to a previously favorable base period. The "parity price" gives the farmer a fair return on his investment in comparison with his costs.

To make sure the farmer was adequately paid for his goods, government price supports were begun, meaning that the federal government promised a farmer to purchase his crop at 90 percent of the parity price —provided the farmer planted only on those acres fixed by the government. As Dwight Eisenhower explained it: "At harvest time, if the market price had fallen below the support price . . . a farmer could get a loan from the government, with his crops as collateral, for the full support price. If the market price then rose above the support price, the farmer paid the government back; if not, he kept the loan, and the government took his crop."

The program had been denounced in the New Deal's early days as "a program of scarcity in a hungry land" and mock tears were shed for "little pigs not born" because of the element of the plan that restrained production. Republicans in the sixties pressed a program of "flexible price supports," with farmers compensated at between 75 percent and 90 percent of the parity price, depending on scarcity and timing.

Politically, the issue has always been hot, with both parties attacking the other's position as the one that stimulates overproduction, causes huge surpluses, helps the big farmer but not the small, and does not give the farmer his share of national prosperity. Secretaries of Agriculture from Henry Wallace to Ezra Taft Benson to Earl Butz have been centers of political controversy, with "parity" the incendiary word.

In a different sense, the word is in active use in strategic arms control. As the Soviet Union approached (and in some respects outstripped) the United States in the ability to conduct nuclear war, a word was needed to change the desired American posture from continued "superiority." In 1969, "sufficiency" was discussed, but "parity" persevered. ("Equality" would have been misleading, since each superpower led in certain categories and trailed in others.) Nixon speechwriters, distressed that the President could no longer say "America must remain number one" in strategic arms, found their answer in a ringing but accurate "America must be second to none," a positive way of presenting parity.

New Yorker writer Elizabeth Drew wrote in 1978 that Carter Secretary of State Cyrus Vance "suggested that language about parity in weapons be changed to 'essential equivalence.' In the President's [Wake Forest College] speech, this became 'functional equivalence.' [Zbigniew] Brzezinski says that 'functional equivalence' is a new phrase, and a new concept. He says, 'I thought "essential equivalence" didn't convey the point. The term "functional equivalence" means that our weapons need not be identical or similar.' " See SALT (LEXICON).

PARK-BENCH ORATOR   a private citizen outspoken about public affairs, especially in places of public assembly.

The picture of a man seated, spouting opinions with no responsibility for their consequences if undertaken, is also expressed by ARMCHAIR STRATEGIST. However, "park-bench orator" has a less pejorative connotation, and is less noisy than "soapbox orator," especially since Bernard Baruch made a park bench his headquarters.

When in Washington, Baruch's favorite bench was located in Lafayette Park near the White House, where he would sit bundled in a heavy overcoat in his later years holding conferences with important government officials and newsmen. "His bench," wrote biographer Margaret Coit, "to which mail was duly addressed and delivered, was just off dead center of the park, near the end of the equestrian statue of Andrew Jackson. It was four feet six inches long, just enough to accommodate Baruch and one average-sized Cabinet officer."

The studious lack of ostentation was ostentatious in itself, but the ELDER STATESMAN's stature was such that he could carry it off. Two generations earlier, Baruch had taken the edge off what had been a dirty word by telling the Pujo Committee that his occupation was "speculator" and then defining the need for speculators in the making of markets; in his old age, Baruch did much the same for "park-bench orator."

Current use is illustrated in this 1967 *Wall Street Journal* item: "[defining Communism] . . . A pastime for park-bench orators and intense collegians has rather suddenly blown into an important Congressional debate . . ."

PARLOR PINK socialite socialist; attack word on a leftist or FELLOW TRAVELER who limits his political radicalism to cocktail-party discussions.

Theodore Roosevelt was the coiner of the "parlor" end in a Minneapolis speech, September 28, 1917: "The *parlor pacifist*, the white-handed or sissy type of pacifist, represents decadence, represents the rotting out of the virile virtues among people who typify the unlovely, senile side of civilization. The rough-neck pacifist, on the contrary, is a mere belated savage who has not been educated to the virtues of national patriotism."

A year later, in a magazine article, Roosevelt applied the noun-become-adjective to the left as "parlor bolshevism." See PROFESSIONAL.

Since Bolsheviks were "reds," their sympathisers were called pinks, or pinkos, especially from the thirties through the fifties; the alliteration of the Roosevelt adjective and the noun locked up the phrase as "parlor pink."

The phrase outlived the use of the word "parlor" in American speech; with changes in housing, the parlor—a small formal sitting room for guests—became merged into a general living room or den. As the room was designed out of houses and apartments, the word parlor—from the French verb *parler*, "to speak"—atrophied, except for its political use in this phrase, and in invitations from spiders to flies. In current use, the phrase has been replaced by "radical chic," a coinage of journalist Thomas Wolfe. In France, the current term is *la gauche de salon*.

See PINKO; RED; FELLOW TRAVELER; LEFT WING, RIGHT WING; LIMOUSINE LIBERAL.

PARTICIPATORY DEMOCRACY, *see* TELL IT LIKE IT IS; COMMITTED.

PARTISAN praised as basic to the TWO-PARTY SYSTEM, the adversary system of arriving at truth in government; attacked as introducing unnecessary strife, placing party advantage above the public interest. (For differentiation between partisans, see BIPARTISAN; NONPARTISAN.)

The dispute about the pros and cons of partisan political activity can be illustrated by the following quotations, only some of which are familiar.

George Washington: "The alternate domination of one faction over another, sharpened by the spirit of revenge natural to party dissension, which in different ages and countries has perpetrated the most horrid enormities, is itself a frightful despotism."

Joseph Addison in *The Spectator:* "There is nothing so bad for the face as party zeal. It gives an ill-natured cast to the eye, and a disagreeable sourness to the look. . . . I never knew a party-woman that kept her beauty for a twelve-month."

On the other hand—

John Stuart Mill: "A party of order or stability, and a party of progress or reform, are both necessary elements of a healthy state of political life."

Graham Wallas (see GREAT SOCIETY): "Something is required simpler and more permanent, something which can be loved and trusted, and which can be recognized at successive elections as being the same thing that was loved and trusted before; and a party is such a thing."

In this century, statesmen like Woodrow Wilson felt free to say, "The trouble with the Republican Party is that it has not had a new idea in thirty years," and Dwight Eisenhower, who was ABOVE POLITICS, was not above referring to Democrats in high office as "too big for their britches and too small for their jobs."

The object of that last crack, Harry Truman, enjoyed the heat of the kitchen: "There never was a non-partisan in politics. A man cannot be a non-partisan and be effective in a political party. When he's in any party he's partisan—he's got to be. The only way a man can act as a non-partisan is when he is in office, either as President or head of a state or

country or city." See IF YOU CAN'T STAND THE HEAT . . .

Truman is regarded by many as the example of HAPPY WARRIOR partisanship in the twentieth century, just as Andrew Jackson came to be the focus of partisan attack and support in the formative years of the American party system. (It is true that Jackson wrote President Monroe in 1818, "Now is the time to exterminate the monster called party spirit," but that can be dismissed as a burst of youthful exuberance and is never quoted at Democratic Jackson Day dinners.)

In his preliminary notes for *Profiles in Courage,* John F. Kennedy wrote of Senator Robert A. Taft: "He was partisan in the sense that Harry Truman was—they both had the happy gift of seeing things in bright shades. It is the politicians who see things in similar shades that have a depressing and worrisome time of it."

In 1971, at the dedication of the Johnson Library, President Nixon applied a phrase of Albert Beveridge's to Lyndon Johnson: "a partisan of principle."

See NONPARTISAN; BIPARTISAN; FUSION.

PARTY, *see* TWO-PARTY SYSTEM.

PARTY ELDERS   the "Grand Old Men" of a party, venerated for their age, presumed sagacity, party service, and present or past political power.

Party elders are occasionally turned to for mediation because they have no political ambitions of their own. In the deadlock of the 1920 Republican convention, a group of what historian Mark Sullivan called the "party elders" gathered to resolve the impasse between General Leonard Wood and Governor Frank Lowden.

See SMOKE-FILLED ROOM. Seven senior senators were in the group, and one of them, Henry Cabot Lodge, put forth the name of Warren G. Harding, a man without enemies, who was chosen. Harry Daugherty, Harding's prime mover who was not present at the meeting, referred to the elders as "the Sanhedrin of the Solemn Senators" (a reference to the supreme council of Jews in ancient Jerusalem).

Party elder is probably derived from "church elder," and from the Council of Elders who "appealed" to Napoleon to take over France after the Revolution. The phrase is more partisan than "ELDER STATESMAN," though in the case of former Presidents Harry Truman and Herbert Hoover, each was both a party elder and elder statesman simultaneously. General Eisenhower, who had remained ABOVE POLITICS, was considered only an elder statesman and not a party elder.

A party elder is not to be confused with an OLD PRO, which refers to political experience and not to age. A man can be referred to as an "old pro" in his forties. White hair has been a requirement for party elders, with the exception of Speaker Sam Rayburn, who was bald.

PARTY EMBLEMS identifying symbols at the top of a ballot, originally as a signal to illiterate voters, now used as a kind of trademark.

At the time of the Jackson Administration, the Democratic party emblem was a hickory pole and broom ("a new broom sweeps clean" [see CLEAN SWEEP]) which was replaced in the 1840s by a rooster. The story of how the change came about is probably apocryphal, but legend has it that a Democratic leader named Chapman had a reputation for crowing like a gamecock. When the Democrats won, an expression arose: "Tell Chapman to Crow." In 1842 and 1844, after Democratic victories over the Whigs, the rooster became the usual party emblem.

Republicans in the 1850s and 1860s needed a counterpart. While Democrats were being urged to "vote for the big chick," Republicans were told to "vote for the bird on the dollar," an eagle.

In the 1950s, however, with the "white rooster" closely identified with segregation in the South, Democrats there dropped the emblem and replaced it with a variety of others, most often a star.

Minor parties have used the torch and the scale of justice (mainly Socialist), the Liberty Bell (Liberal party), the arm and hammer (labor parties); the Prohibitionists always featured the fountain.

Party emblems differ from party symbols. See ELEPHANT, REPUBLICAN; DONKEY, DEMOCRATIC. National emblems differ from national symbols (John Bull of England, Marianne of France, UNCLE SAM of the U.S.).

For America's national emblem, see BALD EAGLE. Other national emblems include the lion of England (see TWISTING THE LION'S TAIL); the cock, as well as the fleur de lis, of France; the double-headed eagle of Austria, and the black eagle of Prussia.

PARTY FAITHFUL the rank-and-file regulars; the hard-core voters and soft-touch contributors.

The originally militant implication of "faithful," taken from its religious usage, appears now to be used of the long-suffering, often overlooked regulars taken for granted by politicians who spend their time wooing the "swing vote."

There is a wistfulness in today's use of the phrase, as if the faithful's hope for ultimate reward is far in the future. The phrase is a cliché in the reportage of fund-raising functions, where "eight hundred of the party faithful turned out to munch rubber chicken and listen to . . ."

REGULAR, with its military origin, implies militant fidelity; *faithful,* with its religious origin, implies mystic, spiritual fidelity; RANK-AND-FILE, from military via labor, implies fidelity to orders from above; TROOPS, military, are more disciplined than rank-and-file, and will go out and ring doorbells.

See RELIGIOUS METAPHORS.

PARTY LINE   the official position of a political organization.

There are several political meanings of this phrase: (1) the principles or position set down by an authoritarian political organization, to be adhered to at lower levels without deviation; (2) the line or column on a ballot or voting machine displaying the party's nominees (when the display is horizontal, the word *row* is gaining preference over *line*); and (3) in the plural, the lines of demarcation between parties, which regulars do not cross but issues often do.

"Each Communist is entitled to his opinion," said Nikita Khrushchev in 1963 to the party's central committee, "but when the Party adopts a decision, maps out a general line, then all Party members toe the line and do what has been worked out by the collective thinking and will of the party."

Most Americans think of party line as originating with Communist terminology, and use it sweepingly, as communists use "general line"; thus, the "general line of the transition period" in China was a broad directive to Communist cadres to place themselves in strategic positions "in a state of readiness." Later, more specific lines set more immediate targets for takeover and national indoctrination. In the U.S., specific Communist party lines zigzagged before World War II as the Soviet Union first reached an accommodation with, and later fought, Nazi Germany.

The phrase was then adopted in the U.S. as an ironic description of Democratic and Republican positions on specific issues. When Defense Secretary Robert McNamara insisted on military officers clearing all speeches with his office, there were objections to the establishment of "a military party line." See MUZZLE; HUNDRED FLOWERS.

In the second sense of a position on the ballot, a party with a poor comparative registration in an area likes to play down its Democratic or Republican designation, and urges voters to "Vote Row A All the Way"; individual candidates in that position advertise "the next to the last name on Line C."

The third sense was illustrated by Wendell Willkie's call in his 1940 acceptance speech: "Party lines are down; nothing could make that clearer than the nomination by the Republicans of a liberal Democrat who changed his party affiliation because he found democracy in the Republican party and not in the New Deal."

In discussing the Republican choice of Eisenhower over Taft in 1952, Harry Truman used the phrase in that context: "The Republicans, being a minority party, knew they had to borrow strength from the Democratic and independent vote. Their only hope of gaining such strength was to find a candidate whose appeal to the voters would cut across party lines."

Going back in American history, the lines converge. Thomas Hart Benton, writing in the 1830s, used the phrase in a meaning that covered both "the official position" and "demarcation between parties": "Look at the vote in the Senate : . . as clearly defined by a party line as any party question can ever be expected to be." The phrase "Old Line Whigs" referred to the party principles as well as the party periphery, and was probably drawn from the military skirmish line.

PARTY LOYALTY   the ability to support a candidate of an IDEOLOGY not one's own against another party's candidate who does espouse one's own ideology, in the belief that only by "closing ranks" now can your faction come to party power in the future.

"Sometimes party loyalty asks too much," said John F. Kennedy to a Democratic friend, excusing him for supporting Republican Leverett Saltonstall for senator of Massachusetts.

The argument against party loyalty is usually founded on "principle": a liberal Democrat finds it sticks in his craw to support a conservative Democrat against a liberal Republican, and vice versa for both parties. Yet this overlooks the nature of the TWO-PARTY SYSTEM in America; the two parties are not ideologically divided, as in England where Labour faces the Conservatives. The BIG TENT of each American party includes factions of the left and right, struggling for control. When one faction wins, it naturally expects its opposing faction to support the majority choice against the other party. If discipline breaks and the minority faction bolts, it surrenders its right to the loyalty of the

opposite faction in the next election. Thus, the bolters see their "principle" temporarily upheld as the other party wins, but they are not likely to ever gain control of a united party that can win.

"Party loyalty among too many Liberal Republicans is not even skin deep," wrote Goldwater organizer Clif White after the 1964 debacle. "You either play it their way, or they play for the other side." Asked Goldwater of George Romney: "Where were you, George, when the going was rough?"

Liberal Republicans answered that in 1964 the conservatives were first to break the rules of party loyalty: Goldwater supporters, after so long out of control of the Republican party, offered no olive branch to the losing liberals at the convention, which is traditional in healing party wounds. See EXTREMISM.

Party loyalty can be attacked as blind and unprincipled, but to those who view politics as a practical route to the position of power that can make principles operative, party loyalty is essential.

That is what Benjamin Disraeli was getting at when he said: "Damn principles! Stick to your party."

PARTY OF PRIVILEGE   frequent Democratic characterization of the Republican party.

The Democratic platform of 1908 dispensed with subtleties and the gray areas of party overlapping: "The Democratic party is the champion of equal rights and opportunities to all; the Republican party is the party of privilege and private monopoly." As if this were not a wide enough gulf, the platform went on: "The Democratic party listens to the voice of the whole people and gauges progress by the prosperity and advancement of the average man; the Republican party is subservient to the comparatively few who are the beneficiaries of governmental favoritism."

The Republican nominee in 1908, William Howard Taft, won handily, but the emerging phrase was to plague Republicans for years to come. Calvin Coolidge did his best to knock it down. "The governments of the past," he said in 1924, "could fairly be characterized as devices for maintaining in perpetuity the place and position of certain privileged classes . . . The Government of the United States is a device for maintaining in perpetuity the rights of the people, with the ultimate extinction of all privileged classes."

But not even Coolidge sounding like Lenin could alter the stereotype that was forming in the mind of most of the American electorate. Political scientist Clinton Rossiter put it bluntly: "Most men recognize the Republicans as the party of the upper and upper-middle classes and the Democrats as the party of the lower and lower-middle classes. The short title for the former classes is 'the rich,' for the latter 'the poor.' "

In phraseology applied to parties, the Democrats have been fairly successful in tagging Republicans as the "party of privilege" and styling themselves as the PARTY OF THE PEOPLE. For a partial offset, see WAR PARTY. Also see VESTED INTERESTS.

PARTY OF THE PEOPLE
Democratic party's characterization of itself.

"Our party is the party of the people," wrote Democrat Grover Cleveland in 1896, "because in its care for the welfare of all our countrymen it resists dangerous schemes born of discontent . . . reinforced by the insidious aid of private selfishness . . . ."

In that year William Jennings Bryan, whose "dangerous scheme" of free silver caused Cleveland to bolt, asked in his "Cross of Gold" speech: "Upon which side will the Democratic party fight: upon the side of 'the idle holders of idle capital' or upon the side of 'the struggling masses?' . . . The sympathies of the Democratic party . . . are on the side of the struggling masses who have ever been the foundation of the Democratic party." See TRICKLE-DOWN THEORY.

Renegade and embittered Republicans helped the Democrats seal their slogan throughout the twentieth century. In the Bull Moose campaign of 1912, the Theodore Roosevelt campaign against President Taft included this challenge: "Let us find out whether the Republican party is the party of the plain people; or whether it is the party of the bosses and the sinister interests of special privilege." Democrat Woodrow Wilson, echoing these sentiments, was able to defeat the divided Republicans. After the Dewey defeat by Truman in 1948, liberal Republican Russell Davenport, a top Willkie campaign aide in 1940, complained: "The theme of the last sixteen years (which must now become twenty years) has been—the Republican party versus the people. And the people have won . . ."

Truman in 1948, and Adlai Stevenson in both of his campaigns, did not neglect the populist theme which had been absorbed by the Democrats. Said Stevenson: ". . . the Democratic Party is the people's party, not the labor party, not the farmer's party, not the employer's party—it is the party of no one because it is the party of everyone."

Lyndon Johnson, using orthography which would have appealed to Noah Webster and George Bernard

Shaw, spelled it out in 1966: "The people . . . P-E-E-P-U-L . . ."

PARTY UNITY the vital ingredient to winning an election, when dissident factions accept the majority decision and unite behind the nominee, grumbling only in private.

American parties have no monopoly on the desire for party unity. "This democratic method of resolving contradictions among the people," wrote Mao Tse-tung in 1957, "was epitomized in 1942 in the formula 'unity, criticism, unity.' . . . It means starting from the desire for unity, resolving contradictions through criticism or struggle and arriving at a new unity on a new basis."

The argument for national unity can be applied to parties. When Lincoln asked, "The Union, is it a marriage bond or a free-love arrangement?" or when Jefferson ameliorated dissension with "every difference of opinion is not a difference of principle," the point was made that splitting was losing.

The Democratic party prides itself on its ability to split wide apart in primaries and come together in time for elections. "No, sir, th' dimycratic party aint on speakin' terms with itsilf," said Mr. DOOLEY to Mr. Hennessey. "Whin ye see two men with white neckties go into a sthreet car an' set in opposite corners while wan mutthers 'Thraiter' an' th' other hisses 'Miscreent' ye can bet they're two dimmycratic leaders thryin' to reunite th' gran' ol' party."

"Party harmony" is used almost interchangeably with "party unity": James Garfield nominated John Sherman "in the interests of party harmony," and Henry Clay, after a nomination defeat was certain, said, "If my name creates any obstacle to Union and Harmony, away with it,

and concentrate upon some individual more acceptable to all branches of the opposition."

However, *party harmony* is milder than *party unity*, which is militant; *party loyalty* is the spirit that results in *party regularity*, which in turn is the key to *party unity*.

PASSION FOR ANONYMITY

a willingness to submerge one's identity for the benefit of a public figure; a passion that sometimes passes as the price of memoirs rises.

Franklin Roosevelt took the phrase from Louis Brownlow, who was chairman of his Committee on Administrative Management in 1936–37. Brownlow was thinking of men like Harry Hopkins and Felix Frankfurter; the Reorganization Act of 1939 permitted the President to add six assistants to his staff, each with what Brownlow had described as a "passion for anonymity."

Historian Eric Goldman directed the author to the source of the phrase. Brownlow, who entitled his 1958 autobiography *A Passion for Anonymity*, credits it to Welsh politician Tom Jones, who served as private secretary to three British Prime Ministers: David Lloyd George, Ramsay MacDonald, and Stanley Baldwin. Brownlow related Jones's comments in 1939 about the need for one key aide.

> Being both a Welshman and a veteran of many parliamentary and ministerial battles, he was inclined to put the emphasis on the man rather than on the institution and, therefore, talked more about Sir Maurice Hankey than he did about the Cabinet secretariat. Then he asked me if I would take a message to President Roosevelt for him, a mission which I gladly undertook. The message was this: "Tell the President that the way to solve his

problem is to find that one man who would turn out to be another Maurice Hankey, a man possessed of high competence, great physical vigor, and a passion for anonymity." Later, when we rejected the one-man idea and proposed, among other new aids recommended for the President, six administrative assistants, we used Tom Jones's language to describe their qualifications . . .

During his second term FDR chose assistants less colorful than in his first. "The later careers of Moley, Tugwell and Hugh Johnson," wrote Samuel Rosenman, ". . . indicate that there is something about administrative power along the Potomac that excludes the concept of anonymous helpfulness which was the basis of the success of the original BRAIN TRUST."

President John F. Kennedy, in speaking of assistant Kenneth O'-Donnell, sketched the qualities he wanted in a White House aide: "He has good nerves and a good memory. He has a passion for anonymity. He is always optimistic." Ted Sorensen wrote that "while few of us had a 'passion for anonymity,' most of us had a preference in that direction." President Kennedy told him to turn down requests for speeches and magazine profiles: "Every man that's ever held a job like yours—Sherman Adams, Harry Hopkins, House, all the rest—has ended up in the [Sorensen substituted a blank for the next word]. Congress was down on them or the President was hurt by them or somebody was mad at them. The best way to stay out of trouble is to stay out of sight."

The ability to stay out of sight is invaluable, of course, to members of what came to be called the INVISIBLE GOVERNMENT, the Central Intelligence Agency. As might be expected, CIA chief Allen Dulles told Congress of the kind of men he was trying to recruit: "The agency should be directed by a relatively small but elite corps of men with a passion for anonymity . . ." Twenty years later, as angry CIA operatives published books, they were denounced by old hands as having a "passion for notoriety."

PATERNALISM, *see* **GREAT WHITE FATHER.**

PATRONAGE governmental appointments made so as to increase political strength.

> Dear Tit:
>   The bearer understands addition, division and silence. Appoint him!
>   Your friend,
>   Bill

According to Charles Ledyard Norton, writing his *Political Americanisms* in 1890, these "qualifications of a successful lobbyist or unscrupulous political worker" first appeared in the *New York Sun* of March 15, 1872, in a letter alleged to have been written by W. H. Kemble, then State Treasurer of Pennsylvania, to T. J. Coffey of Washington, introducing G. O. Evans. This may be legend; the source has of "addition, division and silence" also been given as New York Boss William Marcy Tweed and Pennsylvania Boss Matthew Quay.

Patronage, a necessary ingredient in political life, has always been described by Presidents as an odious task. Thomas Jefferson said: "No duty the President had to perform was so trying as to put the right man in the right place." Andrew Johnson tried to defend himself: "Congress, factious, domineering, tyrannical Congress has undertaken to poison the minds of the American people, and create a feeling against me in consequence of the manner in which I have distributed the public patronage."

Dwight Eisenhower came out of a cabinet meeting on October 9, 1953 in a bad temper. "Everything seems to have been patronage this morning," he said as he left.

The power of appointment carries with it the stigma of favoritism, nepotism, and dishonesty. "Our present mayor," said a clergyman about John ("Honey Fitz") Fitzgerald in 1906, "has the distinction of appointing more saloon keepers and bartenders to public office than any previous mayor."

Some political figures, like Woodrow Wilson in 1913, took a high-minded view and refused to allow political considerations to dictate appointments. Wilson told Albert S. Burleson, his Postmaster General and dispenser of patronage, "On appointments I am not going to advise with reactionary or standpat Senators or Representatives." Burleson quietly pointed out that this meant: ". . . the defeat of the measures of reform that you have next to your heart. The little offices don't amount to anything. They are inconsequential. It doesn't amount to a damn who is postmaster at Paducah, Kentucky. But these little offices mean a great deal to the Senators and Representatives in Congress. . . . If they are turned down, they will hate you and will not vote for anything you want. It is human nature . . ." Wilson gave in.

Rarely do politicians articulate a defense of patronage. Tammany leader Edward Costykian, who was forced by his reform associates to rename his "Patronage Committee" the "Government Appointments Committee" wrote: "How does one secure good government with good people, and strengthen a political party through the use of the power to appoint people to government office? This is the basic problem in dealing with 'patronage,' and it is one which our mythology prevents us from dealing with effectively. . . . The basic lesson I quickly learned was that a political leader cannot afford to insult his supporters by rewarding his opponents."

The opprobrium connected with patronage, and its association with phrases like **"SPOILS SYSTEM"** and the "power of public plunder" did not originate with politics. Originally, patronage meant the protection of the rights of the Church. The *OED* traces the word back to 1412: "He . . . sal noth iniure na disese the place throuch na titil of patronage bot as it is granttit . . . in this indenture." Following its defense-of-religion use, the word became associated with the patronage of authors and artists by the Church and the nobility. "Patron of the arts" stems from this.

In Great Britain, patronage in politics has remained "support received" and has not made the change—as in the U.S.—to "jobs to be given out." Wrote the *Times Literary Supplement* in 1958: "The ideal back-bencher would be one who is wholly unfettered by any obligation to particular bodies, and who is sufficiently well off financially not to depend on the patronage of any kind of pressure group."

The effect of the patronage of either kind on the morale of the receiver, was observed by Cardinal Wolsey in Shakespeare's *Henry VIII:* "O, how wretched is that poor man that hangs on princes' favours."

In 1976 the U.S. Supreme Court, in *Elrod, Sheriff et al.* v. *Burns et al.,* held that the practice of patronage dismissals in a sheriff's office violated the First and Fourteenth Amendments. In the majority opinion, Justice William Brennan wrote: "More recent times have witnessed a strong decline in [patronage's] use, particularly with respect to public employment. Indeed, only decades after Andrew Jackson's administration, strong discontent with the corruption and inefficiency of the patronage system of public employment eventuated in the Pendleton Act (1883), the foundation of modern civil service. And on the state and local levels, merit systems have increasingly displaced the practice."

In a footnote the Court cited *To the Victor* (1971), a book by Martin Tolchin and Susan Tolchin, as expert in modern patronage, and its authors in 1978 supplied this lexicographer with their most current definition: "The traditional view had been that patronage referred only to jobs. We defined patronage—after consultation with scores of politicians who said that they were not pressed for jobs but for many other governmental favors—as the disbursement of the discretionary favors of government in exchange for political support."

The purpose of such disbursement was best described by Chicago boss Jacob Arvey: "Politics is the art of putting people under obligation to you."

PAY AS YOU GO   the technique of the withholding tax, in which taxes are deducted as income is received; previously, a balanced budget.

"It is incumbent on every generation," Thomas Jefferson wrote a friend in 1820, "to pay its own debts as it goes—a principle which, if acted on, would save one-half the wars of the world." Jefferson took the phrase from an old proverb, often attributed to Benjamin Franklin—"pay as you go" used along with "never live beyond your means."

The phrase has had a long political application. Thurlow Weed, who later became a power in the Republican party, wrote in 1839 in reference to the Erie Canal: "The Democracy proclaimed itself in favor of the 'pay as you go' policy." John Randolph of Roanoke cried in Congress, "Mr. President! I have found the Philosopher's Stone! It is contained in four words: Pay-as-you-go!" Until the adoption of the withholding tax, espoused by Beardsley Ruml, the phrase continued to mean a policy of balanced budgets. With the adoption of the "estimated tax," tax policy extended "pay as you go" to all income, not just wages.

PEACE, *see* **FULL GENERATION OF PEACE; JUST AND LASTING PEACE.**

PEACE AT ANY PRICE   a slogan formerly used in earnest, now an attack phrase on those considered appeasers.

The idea of a "price" to be paid for peace probably stemmed from the price for liberty. "Eternal vigilance is the price of liberty" is the "quotation" developed out of Irish Judge John Philpot Curran's ."The condition upon which God hath given liberty to man is eternal vigilance . . ."

English poet Arthur H. Clough attributed the first use of "peace at any price" to French poet and Minister of Foreign Affairs in 1848, Alphonse de Lamartine. Lord Avebury, in *The Use of Life*, wrote in 1849: "Though not a 'peace-at-any-price' man, I am not ashamed to say I am a peace-at-almost-any-price man."

In 1856 in the U.S., the phrase was used without sarcasm as the rallying cry of the KNOW-NOTHINGS behind former President Millard Fillmore, who ran behind James Buchanan and John Frémont. "Peace at any price— peace and union" was the slogan of those willing to pay the price of slavery to avoid civil war.

A strangely familiar "quotation of the day" appeared in the *New York Times* on January 31, 1959, attributed to Admiral Arthur W. Radford: "The things that will destroy America are prosperity at any price, peace at any price, safety first instead of duty first, the love of soft living and the get-rich-quick feeling of living." The quotation, with the substitution of "life" for "living" at the end, is from Theodore Roosevelt, who liked to inveigh against the "professional pacifists, the peace-at-any-price, nonresistance, universal arbitration people" who he felt were "seeking to Chinafy this country."

On February 1, 1916, Woodrow Wilson told an Iowa audience: "There is a price which is too great to pay for peace, and that price can be put in one word. One cannot pay the price of self-respect."

Senator William Borah, in 1919, attacked Woodrow Wilson's peace treaty and League of Nations with "Would you purchase peace at the cost of any part of our independence?" In 1937 Harold Macmillan urged England to "settle with Germany now, or coerce her now. But don't let us purchase an uncertain peace at a terrible price to be paid later."

The idea of peace having a high price, worth paying, but not going so far as "any" price remains a current political metaphor. At the height of the Cuban missile crisis, President Kennedy said on television: "The cost of freedom is always high, but Americans have always paid it." Bernard Baruch, urging the United Nations to adopt a plan for atomic weapons control in 1946, gave the phrase an added dimension: "The solution will require apparent sacrifice in pride and in position, but better pain as the price of peace than death as the price of war."

PEACE BLOC, *see* **BLOC.**

PEACE CORPS a 1960 Kennedy campaign phrase and idea appealing to youthful idealism, which was translated into an effective program after the campaign.

Senator Hubert Humphrey, along with Senator Richard Neuberger and Congressman Henry Reuss, had proposed several ideas in the late fifties for sending voluntary technical assistance workers overseas. Senator Humphrey provided the author with this background:

Congressman Henry S. Reuss of Wisconsin played a very important role in a government-sponsored youth service corps. After a visit to Cambodia in 1957, he created the Point Four Youth Corps which he submitted to the House of Representatives early in 1960, calling for a study on his proposal. The study was eventually assigned to the University of Colorado Research Foundation and put under the general direction of Dr. Maurice Albertson. The Albertson report was completed in May 1961. Much of the concrete planning of the present Peace Corps was based on it.

On June 15, 1960, while I was a Senator, I introduced the "Works for Peace" bill. This bill differed from that of Congressman Reuss' in that instead of asking for a study of the Peace Corps, it asked for the Peace Corps itself. President Kennedy took the Peace Corps idea and continued to call it by that name.

After pointing out its origin in

Humphrey's work, Arthur Schlesinger, Jr., adds:

> General James Gavin urged a similar plan on Kennedy. Kennedy himself advanced the idea a little tentatively during the campaign—it was mid-October and two in the morning—to an audience of students at the University of Michigan. The response was unexpectedly warm. . . . Later, in California, Kennedy called for the establishment of a peace corps, broadening it from Humphrey's original conception to include women as well as men and older people as well as young.

Ted Sorensen, however, played down Humphrey's contribution in his recollection of the origin: "The Peace Corps proposal, for example, was based on the Mormon and other voluntary religious service efforts, on an editorial Kennedy had read years earlier, on a speech by General Gavin, on a luncheon I had with a Philadelphia businessman, on the suggestions of his academic advisors, on legislation previously introduced and on the written response to a spontaneous latenight challenge he issued to Michigan students."

General Gavin, in response to the author's query, reports that his idea germinated at an October 18, 1960, meeting of a committee of the U.S. Chamber of Commerce.

> The more I thought about it, the more I became convinced that the country should organize something like a Peace Corps.
>
> I returned to Arthur D. Little, Inc., and discussed it with some of my colleagues. One of them wrote a memo to me recommending the title, "Peace Corps." I personally was a bit reluctant to use the "Corps" because of its military connotation. Several days later I addressed a group of educators in Miami, Florida, on Thursday, October 27,

and advanced the idea of a Peace Corps to them. A bit to my surprise they greeted my idea with great enthusiasm and applause. I was sitting between the Governor of South Carolina and the Governor-Elect of Florida at the time and we were all very worried about the outcome of the presidential election. The Governor-Elect of Florida suggested that I should call John F. Kennedy and urge him to adopt the idea.

> I returned to Wellesley on Friday, October 28, and got in touch with Mr. Kennedy by phone. He asked me to send him a brief memo on the subject to San Francisco. I wrote the paper over the weekend and referred to the undertaking as the "Peace Corps." Mr. Kennedy spoke on it in San Francisco the following Wednesday, urging the adoption of such a program.

Who, then, "coined" Peace Corps? Humphrey probably coined the phrase, if you define coinage as "first use." General Gavin and his aide at Arthur D. Little "coined" it, if you define coinage as setting up the concept and suggesting the label. John F. Kennedy "coined" it, if you define coinage as making a phrase famous.

Ideas generated in the heat of a campaign rarely see the light of election day (heat and light metaphors may be mixed). To the surprise of many politicians, this suggestion of Gavin's did.

PEACE FEELER a diplomatic probe, real or imagined, to end hostilities.

A feeler has long been defined as a remark or proposal put forth to ascertain the attitudes of others. Colloquially, "to feel out" means to subtly find out another's opinion or disposition.

"Peace feeler" came strongly into the political terminology during the war in Vietnam, as the U.S. sought some receptivity to negotiations by the North Vietnamese government. In 1966, the Johnson administration was criticized for ignoring peace feelers supposedly extended through the United Nations. When Robert Kennedy traveled abroad in 1967, a controversy arose as to whether a peace feeler was extended to him. A Mauldin cartoon showed Senator Kennedy arriving home with a snakelike vine twitching behind him, which he asked: "Can I help it if a peace feeler followed me home?"

Lyndon Johnson gave the phrase the presidential seal on March 15, 1967, in a speech to the Tennessee legislature. "We have just lived through another flurry of 'peace feelers.' " In the context in which the President used it, the phrase carried a connotation of vain hopes, of illusory approaches.

PEACE FOR OUR TIME   British Prime Minister Neville Chamberlain's optimistic prediction before World War II; now used derisively.

Chamberlain returned from the Munich Conference September 30, 1938, convinced that his concessions to Hitler dismembering Czechoslovakia had paved the way to peace. For a fuller discussion, see MUNICH, ANOTHER; SELLOUT.

Paraphrasing a remark of Disraeli's (see PEACE WITH HONOR), Chamberlain said, "My good friends: This is the second time in our history that there has come back from Germany to Downing Street peace with honor. I believe it is peace for our time."

The phrase is often misquoted as "Peace *in* our time," perhaps because it appears in that form in Morning Prayer: "Give peace in our time, O Lord."

PEACEFUL COEXISTENCE   as seen in the U.S., a proposal for fair competition of ideologies ("live and let live"); as often expressed in the USSR, a program for evolutionary triumph over capitalism.

On June 30, 1954, President Dwight Eisenhower was asked at a news conference: "Mr. President, what are the possibilities for peaceful coexistence between Soviet Russia and Communist China, on the one hand, and the non-Communist nations on the other?" He replied in part:

> For a long, long time, everybody in the United States had urged that we attempt to reach a proper basis for peaceful coexistence. We had found, though, an aggressive attitude on the part of the other side that had made such an accomplishment or consummation not easy to reach. In other words, there had to be good faith on both sides. Moreover, we had to make certain that peaceful coexistence did not mean APPEASEMENT. . . . We have got to find ways of living together.

The phrase can be traced back to Lenin in 1920, who spoke of "peaceful cohabitation with the peoples, with the workers and peasants of all nations." The Ninth All-Russian Congress of Soviets used the term in January 1922: "peaceful and friendly coexistence."

The phrase had its greatest impact when Nikita Khrushchev made it the subject of a speech on January 6, 1961, just before a new American President—John F. Kennedy —was to be inaugurated. Khrushchev's definition: ". . . the policy of peaceful coexistence, as regards its social content, is a form of intense economic, political, and ideological struggle of the proletariat against the aggressive forces of imperialism in the international arena."

This was in line with Russian policy enunciated by Lenin: "International imperialism disposing of the might of capital cannot coexist with the Soviet Republic. Conflict is unavoidable."

However, in October of 1961 the Communist line appeared to change. In the "Programme of the Communist Party of the Soviet Union" a softer line was evident:

Peaceful coexistence of the socialist and capitalist countries is an objective necessity for the development of human society. War cannot and must not serve as a means of settling international disputes. Peaceful coexistence or disastrous war—such is the alternative offered by history. . . . Peaceful coexistence implies renunciation of war as a means of settling international disputes, and their solution by negotiation. . . . Peaceful coexistence serves as a basis for the peaceful competition between socialism and capitalism. . . . The policy of peaceful coexistence is in accord with the vital interests of all mankind, except the big monopolymagnates and the militarists.

The zigzags in the PARTY LINE confused many Americans who were under the impression that "peaceful coexistence" meant "live and let live." Barry Goldwater warned in 1961, "Nor is there such a thing as peaceful coexistence." In 1963 John F. Kennedy urged "peaceful cooperation" at the UN, and a year later UN Ambassador Adlai Stevenson defended coexistence as the alternative to "coextinction."

Thus, the phrase means—in the words of Humpty Dumpty—"whatever I choose it to mean."

PEACENIK, see **-NIK SUFFIX.**

PEACE SCARE, see **WAGING PEACE.**

PEACE WITH HONOR   a wartime leader's excuse for not concluding a peace; or, an explanation to a leader's people that the peace concluded was a good one; or, an assertion that an end to war would not or does not mean surrender.

The earliest use was negative: in 49 B.C. Cicero wrote *turpi pace*, or "peace with dishonor." Burton Stevenson, in his book of proverbs, maxims and phrases, traced the early uses of "peace with honor": Theobald, Count of Champagne, in a letter to Louis the Great in 1125; Shakespeare's *Coriolanus*, twice ("We have made peace/with no less honour to the Antiates/than shame to the Romans"); Sir Kenelm Digby's letter to Lord Bristol in 1625; and Edmund Burke's *Conciliation with America* in 1775.

"Honor" became closely associated with "peace" over the years, always increasing the difficulty of negotiations. In 1864, "peace with dishonor" was thrown by Republicans against the Democratic platform that claimed the Civil War had been a failure and called for peace talks.

The phrase is best remembered and occasionally quoted today because of its use by Benjamin Disraeli, Lord Beaconsfield, Queen Victoria's Prime Minister in 1878. When the Russians forced the Turks to a "dishonorable" peace in the Treaty of San Stefano, Great Britain intervened and demanded a European Congress; fearing war with England, the Russians agreed, and Disraeli traveled to Berlin to negotiate. He forced Russia to give back Macedonia to the Turks, and came away with Cyprus for England in the bargain. He said on his return: "Lord Salisbury and myself have brought you back peace—but a peace I hope with honor, which may satisfy our sovereign and tend to the welfare of the country."

Disraeli was a hero; but England was soon involved in a war in Afghanistan, another against the Zulus in South Africa, a crop failure led to a recession, and Disraeli was turned out of office eighteen months after his "peace with honor."

Today, the phrase is often used along with "peace without surrender," and "no reward for aggression."

PEACE WITHOUT VICTORY

a Wilsonian phrase urging a limitation to the objectives of World War I and a peace settlement not so harsh to any side as to bring about a future war.

Coming as it did from a neutral U.S. early in 1917, Woodrow Wilson's proposal did not set well with leaders of France and England who were fighting a war against Germany: ". . . it must be a peace without victory. . . . The world must be made safe for democracy." See MAKE THE WORLD SAFE FOR DEMOCRACY.

Like "TOO PROUD TO FIGHT," Wilson's "peace without victory" was greeted with disdain in America as well. He had just won a close election over Charles Evans Hughes, and Wilson's slogan had been "He Kept Us Out of War," but the nation was closely divided and memories of Theodore Roosevelt's "Big Stick" were still green.

When unrestricted submarine warfare brought the U.S. into the conflict later in 1917, "peace without victory" was forgotten in the enthusiasm and fury of war. The traditional American demand for "unconditional surrender" was recalled (the War of 1812 was always forgotten) and Wilson's Fourteen Points as a basis for a peace

treaty were taken with a grain of salt by other Allied leaders.

In World War II, unconditional surrender was again the goal, and Churchill's "V" sign assured the allies that peace would indeed come with victory. Not until the Korean War did the idea of LIMITED WAR appear, and that was met by a statement that there was "NO SUBSTITUTE FOR VICTORY" and denunciations of a "NO-WIN POLICY."

However, most Americans in the sixties were ready to accept "peace without victory," as they did in Korea, provided an "honorable solution" could be found. Senator J. William Fulbright touched a sensitive nerve in *The Arrogance of Power:*

> When we talk about the freedom of South Vietnam, we may be thinking about how disagreeable it would be to accept a solution short of victory; we may be thinking about how our pride would be injured if we settled for less than we set out to achieve; we may be thinking about our reputation as a great power, fearing that a compromise settlement would shame us before the world, marking us as a second-rate people with flagging courage and determination.

Wilson's phrase, "peace without victory," was not used by DOVES in their argument, perhaps because the compromise they were willing to accept was more of a peace without defeat.

PEAKING

a campaigning technique that seeks to build to a crescendo in the forty-eight hours before Election Day.

Franklin Roosevelt pointed out the difficulty of maintaining the "highest note on the scale" (see OVEREXPOSURE); a candidate who "peaks" too early rarely regains the momentum of his campaigning. For a discussion of the opposite type of strategy, see FLAT-OUT.

The word was probably first used by pollsters, or those studying the popularity charts submitted by pollsters. Graphically, a line showing a rise and fall in voters' attitudes toward a candidate forms a peak. The term was popularized during the Nixon-Kennedy campaign of 1960, with Nixon strategy calling for a steady rise in activity and intensity "peaking" once about three weeks before Election Day, and then peaking again just before the final decision. Kennedy strategy called for a "flat-out campaign," sometimes called an "all-out scramble," starting from the beginning. The closeness of the contest leaves the question of which strategy is "best" unresolved. Many politicians feel the wisest strategy is the one that best fits the nature and stamina of the individual candidate.

"Peaking" today is still closely identified with Nixon. Democratic Congressman Michael J. Kirwan writes that the Nixon-Brown race for Governor of California in 1962 "contrasted the so-called 'peaking' campaign techniques followed by Nixon to the 'all-out scramble' technique of Brown." D. E. Butler and Anthony King, in *The British General Election of 1964,* wrote:

> Like Mr. Richard Nixon in America, Mr. Wilson believed in the need to "phase" his campaign carefully in order to avoid "wearying" the electorate. He was haunted by the belief that Mr. Gaitskell had lost in 1959 partly because his campaign had "peaked" too early; Labour had drawn ahead mid-way through the campaign only to fall behind in the closing stages. As the period of intensive electioneering drew near, Mr. Wilson was determined to make a great initial impact on the Wembley rally planned for September

12th, then to ease up for a week or two, and then to hit hard in the final fortnight.

Peaking is regarded as a more sophisticated technique than flat-out campaigning, or scrambling, and is usually given more thought by those who start out slightly ahead. Underdogs are best advised to run HELL-BENT FOR ELECTION. When Republican Norbert Tiemann ran against Val Peterson in a 1966 primary for governor of Nebraska, he put in 600 appearances over 65,000 miles and edged out the favored Peterson by 15,000 votes. "We paced him just right," said Tiemann's campaign manager, David Pierson. "When election day came, we figured he was just about 14 hours away from total collapse."

When President Nixon announced in 1971 that Henry Kissinger had arranged for his visit to China, an Administration punster, worried about the reaction of U.S. conservatives, asked, "Peking too soon?"

PEANUT POLITICIAN attack word on a politician, deriding him as mean and insignificant.

"I know them—a set of peanut agitators," said Representative Mike Walsh of New York on May 19, 1854. An editorialist in the *New York Mail* on May 27, 1887, inveighed: "If the Governor would consent not to play peanut politics . . ."

The word "peanut," perhaps because of its sound, has had a long history as a synonym for "insignificant." But politicians are careful not to offend anyone. Another congressman told the House: "It would be gross disrespect to a great commercial product of several States in this Union for me to denounce the course pursued by this Administration . . . as 'peanut politics.'"

The phrase has been traced to the *New York Mail* of 1887—"If the government would consent not to play peanut politics"—and at one time had a lowdown, dirty connotation, as writers pointed out that a peanut (which is a vegetable and not a nut) grows and ripens underground.

Big spenders habitually refer to small sums as "peanuts"; this is probably the meaning from which the phrase is derived. However, another derivation is suggested in an 1880 book by Al G. Field: "Those from the West Side chewed tobacco. All ate peanuts. Special appropriations were requested by John Ward, city hall janitor, to remove the peanut hulls after each talk fest. And thus it was that peanut politics and peanut politicians came to be known in Columbus [Ohio]. Peanut politics like all infections spread until the whole political system became affected."

In World War II, to show his contempt for Generalissimo Chiang Kaishek, General Joseph Stilwell gave him the code name "Peanut."

Since President Jimmy Carter was a peanut warehouseman, it was natural to assume the phrase would be thrown at him, although he countered with the use of peanuts in campaign parties and a small package of peanuts in lieu of a button. The most frequent use of the metaphor was by those leaving his Administration, who would say, "I'm tired of working for peanuts."

PECKERWOOD, *see* **REDNECK.**

PECKING ORDER unofficial hierarchy; status of aides to a chief executive of city, state, or nation, or within a government department. Emerges when no "table of organization" is provided.

Like a linguistic Inspector Javert,

Professor Porter G. Perrin of the University of Washington followed the origin and development of this phrase from its technical inception to its modern political use. His evidence, along with other contributions to *American Speech* magazine, is summarized here.

During and following World War I, a Norwegian zoologist-psychologist named Thorleif Schjelderup-Ebbe made some remarkable studies of the social organization of birds, particularly hens. Due to the nature of his subject, he had to develop a group of compound nouns beginning with *hacka*—to peck—such as *hackkombination,* and *hackordning,* or "peck order." University of Chicago zoologist W. C. Allee explained Schjelderup-Ebbe's findings in the U.S.:

> He recognized a so-called peck-order in which the animal highest in the order pecks and is not pecked in return while that at the extreme bottom of the order is pecked without pecking in return. The social order is indicated by the giving and receiving of pecks, or by reaction to threats of pecking; and hence the social hierarchy among birds is frequently referred to as the peck-order.

A minor government official would do well to study this followup comment by Mark A. May in a 1929 psychology text: "It seems that the bird which is despot over only a few shows its annoyance at the pecks to which it itself is exposed by especially furious pecking, while the birds that rank high in the pecking order, and so are seldom pecked, are more reasonable."

Professor Allee saw the political possibilities: "I pass over the possibilities of studying the peck-order in women's clubs, faculty groups, families or churches . . . we may be able to work out an adequate control even for the prestige problems of the international peck-order."

Novelist Aldous Huxley, who liked to turn scientific theory to use in fiction dealing with social experiments, picked up the idea in *Point Counter Point:* "Observing the habitual and almost sacred 'pecking order' which prevails among the hens in his poultry yard . . . the politician will meditate on the Catholic hierarchy and Fascism."

Anthropologist Margaret Mead used the phrase in a 1942 book, *And Keep Your Powder Dry.* That year, poet W. H. Auden used the phrase in its original sense in *Nones:* ". . . the smug hens,/Passing close by in their pecking order . . ."

Then the Alsop brothers got hold of it in 1954, using it four times that year, in their syndicated column and magazine articles, from a straightforward "in the Washington officialdom, a secretaryless official is at the very bottom of the pecking order," to a less intelligible "Prediction was the by-word, with a number of variables used in multiple regression equations determining the pecking order in the status hierarchy." (Explain that to Schjelderup-Ebbe!)

Professor Perrin concluded:

This brief case history of pecking order illustrates the typical progress of words from specialized to general usage, and in addition suggest: (1) that this particular word is definitely established in English and now runs the full range of usage from gobbledygook to poetry; (2) that, when it is used of human beings, its connotation is generally dyslogistic [unfavorable]; and (3) that once acquired, pecking order tends to be habit forming.

PEERLESS LEADER   ironic description of a precinct captain or local boss.

The "Peerless Leader" in American history was William Jennings Bryan, three times nominated by the Democrats. Along with "The Great Commoner," a sobriquet that had been applied to William Pitt the elder and later to Henry Clay and Thaddeus Stevens, Bryan was given the sobriquet of "peerless leader," which later was the title of a 1929 biography by Paxton Hibben. (Opponents termed the ticket of Bryan and Arthur Sewall "Brine and Swill.")

Because of the rhyme, the phrase is often rendered "fearless leader" (a Helen Gray Cone poem called Pickett's men at Gettysburg "peerless, fearless, an army's flower"). The pomposity of the phrase has led to its sarcastic use today.

PEKINGOLOGIST, *see* **CHINA WATCHERS; KREMLINOLOGIST.**

PENTAGON PAPERS, *see* **RIGHT TO KNOW; LEAKS.**

PENTAGONESE   military-industrial jargon designed to provide its users with a convenient linguistic shorthand which often serves only to obfuscate the obvious, or to lend a sense of importance to routine communications.

In common with other jargon, Pentagonese—a word that entered the language in 1952—provides an "in group" with the sort of security that children achieve when they share a secret handshake and wear rings with hidden compartments. Pentagonese is used not only within the Pentagon but also throughout the U.S. military establishment. A sample: Within the *parameters* of a problem (the range of possibilities, not a perimeter), there exist several *options* (alternatives) for *tradeoffs* (trades) that will *maximize* (strengthen) the *software* (thinking) to *escalate* (raise) the *state of the art* (what can be done now).

Had experts at Pentagonese gotten their hands on the Gettysburg Address, *New York Times* columnist Arthur Krock wrote in 1962, they might have changed "We are now engaged in a great civil war" to read: "We have entered upon a period of civil uncertainty involving fairly high mobilization." After the 1962 Cuban missile crisis, he constructed this imaginary statement for Defense Secretary Robert McNamara: "Let's be sure we have plenty of options and be certain there will be no overkill. And then, I think, after these options are mirror clear, and to pursue this further would be counter-productive, we can melt this ball of wax and move the hardware from the shelf."

Similarly, *Time* magazine in 1967 parodied Pentagonese by bringing Mr. Flap and General Redstone on stage, while a goggle-eyed student and the dean of the school he wants to enter look on:

> *Flap:* Order of magnitude, expedite, implement, reorient, inter-occupational mobility, mission-oriented—
> *Redstone:* Component forces, readiness levels, destruct—
> *Student:* Excuse me—
> *Redstone* (ignoring him):—credibility, paramilitary, departmentwide contingency plans, preemptive war, scenario, remote area conflict . . .
> *Dean:* It's no good, son. Once the civilian and the military start arguing, it can go on for years.

A kissing cousin of Pentagonese is State Departmentese. As Arthur Schlesinger, Jr., wrote in *A Thousand Days:*

> The intellectual exhaustion of the Foreign Service expressed itself in the poverty of the official rhetoric. In meetings the men from State would talk in a bureaucratic patois bor-

rowed in large part from the Department of Defense. We would be exhorted to "zero in" on "the purpose of the drill" (or of the "exercise" or "operation"), to "crank in" this and "phase out" that, to "pinpoint" a "viable" policy and, behind it, a "fallback position," to ignore the "flak" from competing government bureaus or from the Communists, to refrain from "nit-picking" and never to be "counterproductive." Once we were "seized of the problem," preferably in as "hard-nosed" a manner as possible, we would review "options," discuss "overall" objectives, seek "breakthroughs," consider "crash programs," "staff out" policies—doing all these things preferably "meaningfully" and "in depth" until we were ready to "finalize" our deliberations, "sign on to" or "sign off on" a conclusion (I could never discover the distinction, if any, between these two locutions), and "implement" a decision.

As *Newsweek* noted in 1967, nuclear weapons "unleashed a fallout of acronyms, neologisms, euphemisms and technical jargon," and the development of antiballistic missiles "has produced a second generation of Strangelovisms." Among the additions to Pentagonese: *megadeaths,* for millions of deaths; *credible deterrent,* a defense that needn't be effective as long as the enemy thinks it is; *preferential defense,* protecting some areas but not others; *rippled attack,* sending missiles in salvos to trick an enemy into using defensive missiles on the first few waves, leaving no defense for later waves.

The Pentagon has popularized, or in some cases invented, scores of other words, from *cost-efficiency* to *quantification* (a reference to McNamara's reliance on facts and figures) and *spasm* (meaning a reflexive response to an enemy attack, real or imagined).

Malcolm McLean, in the *Foreign Service Journal* in 1968, wrote of a survey made at the National War College by Marine Colonel Ralph Spanjer. Lecturers were clocked in the 1966–67 year as to the number of times they used Pentagonese. These were the most frequently used bits of jargon:

quid pro quo	pragmatic
vis-à-vis	caveat
per se	viable
dialogue	ambivalence
xenophobia	scenario
charisma	academician
thrust	escalate
exacerbate	expertise
dichotomy	low silhouette
hegemony	quantum jump
cost effective	flexible response
proliferation	rapprochement
counterproductive	détente

Less frequently used, but mentioned in the survey, were: boggle, simplistic, in-house, time frame, pluralistic, poly-centrisms, infrastructure, real world, bipolar, confrontation.

Not mentioned in the survey, but important expressions of the Vietnam war, were "body count," "protective reaction," "sanctuaries," "captured documents," and "enemy situation deteriorating." See VIETNAMIZATION.

Herman Melville wrote: "A man of true science uses but few hard words, and those only when none other will answer his purpose; whereas the smatterer in science thinks that by mouthing hard words he proves that he understands hard things."

See OPTIONS; ESCALATION; UNFLAPPABLE; SCENARIO; FALLBACK POSITION; VIETNAM LINGO; WHIZ KIDS; PACIFICATION; FALLOUT; INFRASTRUCTURE; WAR-GAMING WORDS; SALT.

PEOPLE'S DEMOCRACY a phrase with a redundant root adopted by Communists to differentiate between "their" democracy and "capitalists' " democracy.

Though the political glorification of the word "people" is best known in the close of the Gettysburg Address, "people's party" and "people's ticket" were familiar phrases throughout the nineteenth century. In China, the Manchu dynasty was overthrown in 1911 by forces whose ideological leader was Dr. Sun Yatsen; among his "Three Principles of the People" was a "Principle of People's Democracy," a long-range plan to be started by the revolutionary leaders.

Later in the twentieth century, Communist governments adopted the style of "people's republics" and Communist terminology used "people's democracies" as a generic phrase for Communist or Communist-dominated nations.

In a good twist on the phrase, the New York Stock Exchange in the early fifties began publicizing "people's capitalism" to dramatize the degree of stock ownership in the U.S. (over 30 million individuals owned shares in 1978). The Exchange recognized the Communist capture of the word "people," and by combining it with the word most often attacked by Communists put forth a useful counterphrase to "Wall Street warmongers."

PEOPLE'S REPUBLIC OF CHINA, *see* GREAT LEAP FORWARD; MAOISM; LET A HUNDRED FLOWERS BLOSSOM; CULTURAL REVOLUTION.

PERENNIAL CANDIDATE attack phrase on one who has tried and failed before.

Republican Harold Stassen is the man most often identified as a "perennial candidate" in recent times; in the previous century, the honor belonged first to Grover Cleveland (the "perpetual candidate") and then to thrice-defeated William Jennings Bryan.

Said Stassen in 1967: "I suppose there is a lot of misunderstanding about me. People try to understand me as seeking office. Actually it's not the office itself. Not at all. It's the office in relation to what I'm trying to do, what I'm seeking. I want a progressive Republican Party."

A similar attack was launched by President Lyndon Johnson in 1966 on Richard Nixon, labeling him a CHRONIC CAMPAIGNER. The effect was to focus attention on Nixon in the closing weeks of the midterm elections, helping him help Republican candidates win back 47 House seats.

PERKS   clipped form of perquisites; the delicious trappings of power; the cherry on the cake of public service.

"Perks!" wrote Michael Satchell in the *Washington Star* in January 1977. ". . . hundreds of public servants enjoy the perquisites of power, the freebies, privileges, emoluments and prestige that go along with the job, that make life at the office a little nicer, that stamp the individual as a favored employe. Perks! For politicians, Cabinet officers and ranking career bureaucrats, they mean limousines, government jets and even boats to get you from A to B with a corps of chauffeurs, military aides, escort officers, staff assistants, coat holders and Filipino Navy stewards to make sure the steaks are rare, the martinis cold, the trip smooth and trouble-free."

The word was originally a Briticism, according to Merriam-Webster, but appears to be taking hold firmly in coverage of American officialdom. In the sixties, "with perks" was most frequently a description of "fringe benefits" available to corporate officers. "When the day's work is done," wrote the *Wall Street Journal* on July 15, 1971, "Alexander Farkas and his wife whisk out to balmy Westhampton, Long Island, in the company helicopter. That's called a perquisite, or perk, and it's an increasingly popular kind of reward for the executive who has everything but a favorable tax bracket."

Politicians' perks—especially limousine service—came under attack in the mid-seventies, led by Senator William Proxmire's harassment of Pentagon officials whose salaries were supplemented by extra, untaxed services. President Carter, sensitive to the anti-Washington, anti–big shot feeling of most taxpayers, did away with many of the frills enjoyed previously by the White House staff; White House press secretary Jody Powell grumbled good-naturedly about being denied a White House car to take him to work, a perk granted all his predecessors. The well-publicized cutback of perks did much to reduce resentment over substantial White House salary increases.

Perks are not inexpensive trappings; a car and driver supplements a government official's salary by a value of at least $20,000. The new word, and the new interest in the subject, saves the taxpayer sizable amounts, although it is not so much the money as the principle: if the voter has to pay for his haircut, then why, he wonders, should his congressman get one free? The system that used to permit the local cop on the beat to swipe an apple from the vendor, as a right of his job, now frowns on—and even threatens to tax—some of the extra income that is taken in the form of service.

Perks cover a range of presumed rights, including *freebies,* which are small gifts or costless tickets; *annie oaklies,* which are always tickets or passes; and *junkets,* which are ostensible official trips (see JUNKETEERING GUMSHOES). Perquisite is not related to "perky," which comes from the verb "to perch," but is rooted in the Latin *quaerere,* "to seek"—thus, a "query" about a "perk" digs for its own root.

PERORATION   the stirring conclusion of an address, exhorting or uplifting the audience; in political slang, the ZINGER or *snapper.*

"Perorations usually add nothing to the context of the speech," wrote Samuel Rosenman, who wrote many for FDR, "they are more inspirational than informative. Every oration needs one, however, and a well-written peroration can clinch an argument or inspire confidence or lift morale."

In the peroration of his 1932 acceptance address FDR introduced "New Deal": "I pledge you, I pledge myself, to a new deal for the American people." (For the dispute over who wrote it, see NEW DEAL.) Perhaps the most famous peroration was at the conclusion of Lincoln's second inaugural, beginning "With malice toward none . . ."

A well-prepared, well-delivered speech, without peroration, dribbles off and leaves an audience unsatisfied. Simple, clear English prose, the stuff of good speeches, is difficult to make soar; there cannot be many thrilling moments or high notes in any speech, and if there is to be one, the place the audience will remember it most is at the end. Reminder: a reference to God's help is expected, especially on solemn occasions.

"His enthusiasm kindles as he advances," wrote Edmund Burke of a good orator, "and when he arrives at his peroration it is in full blaze." Here is a peroration (closing of Woodrow Wilson's first inaugural) that includes a disclaimer of pride, an element of suspense, a question, a challenge, a summons to the audience to help, a reference to the Deity, and a promise of success:

> This is not a day of triumph; it is a day of dedication. Here muster, not the forces of party, but the forces of humanity. Men's hearts wait upon us; men's lives hang in the balance; men's hopes call upon us to say what we will do. Who shall live up to the great trust? Who dares fail to try? I summon all honest men, all patriotic, all forward-looking men, to my side. God helping me, I will not fail them, if they will but counsel and sustain me!

The word, in Shakespeare's time, meant an overblown, flowery speech ("What means this passionate discourse? This peroration with such circumstance"); since that time, it has come to mean the conclusion or wrap-up of a speech, where some passion is permitted to flower.

PERSON   in its political meaning, a woman; or, an ostentatious inclusion of women.

In the early seventies, during the "consciousness-raising" of women (see WOMEN'S LIB), the word "man" was held to be offensive in its assumption that only men held certain jobs. To avoid offending feminists, some congressmen began calling themselves "congressperson" (eschewing the choice between congressman and congresswoman), and some chairmen chose "chairperson."

This lent itself to derision ("Go down to the personbox and see if the personperson left any person"), and by the late seventies some of the more extreme male-avoidance was depersonalized. With the increase of working women, however, the formerly archaic word "spouse" was brought back into more frequent use, along with its jocular plural, "spice"; also, the term "worker" became preferred to "workingman."

See EUPHEMISMS.

PERSONALLY OBNOXIOUS verbal signal that calls down the wrath of "senatorial courtesy"; the Senate then refuses to confirm an appointment opposed by a senator from the state affected.

Senatorial courtesy, or *courtesy of the Senate,* is the gun; *personally obnoxious,* or *personally objectionable,* is the trigger. The system was explained by *Harper's Weekly* in 1870: "Senator Fowler of Tennessee claimed the right which the courtesy of the Senate affords every member of vetoing the appointment of any postmaster in the place of his residence who is not agreeable to him." Ten years later the magazine defined the phrase in more political terms: "The courtesy of the Senate is an exceedingly smooth phrase. It means control of patronage."

Woodrow Wilson first attempted to fight this system, then gave way. See PATRONAGE. His closest adviser, Colonel Edward House, and Treasury Secretary William McAdoo, both Democrats from New York, sought to break Tammany's power by dispensing patronage to reformers. Senator James O'Gorman of New York, while not closely allied with Tammany, saw this as an effort to build a New York machine that might be a danger to him. He warned the President that such appointments would be "personally obnoxious" to him, and they were not made.

Dwight Eisenhower ran into the same problem when he started making appointments in 1953. He planned to name Val Peterson, a former Nebraska governor, as ambassador to India, but Nebraska Senators Hugh Butler, and Dwight Griswold, old political enemies of Peterson's said no. "They informed me," wrote Eisenhower, "that if I should send his name to the Senate they would find it necessary to state on the Senate floor that he was 'personally objectionable'; the Senate has normally honored such an announcement . . ." The President appointed Peterson to several other jobs not requiring Senate approval, and ultimately—after the two senators were gone—as ambassador to Denmark. But it bothered him. "I believe that the custom of allowing one disgruntled senator to block an appointment by the phrase 'personally objectionable' is unjustified and should be disavowed by the Senate."

There has in recent years been a tendency to replace "obnoxious" with "objectionable," a milder word. This is a shame, as "obnoxious" so well describes the true feeling of the dissenting senator.

See BLUE SLIP.

PHANTOM COINAGE, *see* BACKLASH; MEDICARE; ESCALATION.

PHILIPPIC diatribe; tirade; vitriolic attack.

"Forensic Philippics" was FDR's description of some of the Supreme Court decisions striking down New Deal measures. See NINE OLD MEN. The word comes from the three orations of Demosthenes, rousing his fellow Athenians to resist Philip of Macedon; subsequently, the orations of Cicero against Mark Antony were also called Philippics.

Dwight Eisenhower was urged by many friends to ENGAGE IN PERSONALITIES with Senator Joseph McCarthy, using the prestige of the presidency to condemn his methods. In this unpublished letter to broadcaster John R. ("Tex") McCrary, President Eisenhower wrote on December 4, 1954:

. . . I would not, under any circumstances, glorify—or at least publicize—such an individual by attempting a Presidential Philippic, with him as the target. When any individual or any idea goes completely outside the realm of logic and of reason, I doubt that elimination can be achieved through argument! In fact, it is only the persistent and senseless publicity he has achieved that has made the matter of any concern to our people.

My own reaction to this whole messy business has been to uphold Americanism and preach fairness, justice and decency. Moreover, where I had any knowledge of facts in a case, I've made a point of praising Marshall, Zwicker, etc. If young or old want a President who will indulge in billingsgate—and bemean the office as it has been bemeaned before—they'll have to find another.

PHILOSOPHY, see **IDEOLOGY.**

PHONY WAR   the quiet period after the fall of Poland in 1939 and the German attack on Norway and Denmark in the spring of 1940; also called a "sitzkrieg."

"Sitzkrieg" of course was a play on "blitzkrieg." To some Americans, the desultory warfare in this period showed that Britain and France did not really want to fight, but simply entered the war grudgingly, committed as they were to the defense of Poland; these critics also held that Hitler wanted no war with France and Great Britain.

The *London News-Chronicle* on January 19, 1940, headlined: "This is Not a Phoney War: Paris Envoy." The story explained that "phoney" was "American slang, anglicized about 1920."

French Premier Paul Reynaud used the phrase in a radio speech on April 3, 1940: " *'Il faut en finir'; tel fut, dès le debut, le refrain qu'on entendit. Et cela signifie qu'il aura pas de* 'phony peace' *après une guerre qui n'est nullement une* 'phony war.' " (" 'It must be finished'; that is the constant theme heard since the beginning. And that means that there will not be any *'phony peace'* after a war which is by no means a *'phony war.' "*)

During this time Neville Chamberlain continued as prime minister of England. When the British fleet was repulsed trying to land troops in Norway, he came under heavy criticism in Parliament. On May 9, 1940, he asked Winston Churchill to join his government; Churchill refused. After the German invasion of Holland and Belgium on May 10, Chamberlain agreed to turn over the reins completely to Churchill. There was no more talk of "phony war" nor of weak leadership in Great Britain.

According to Eric Partridge, the word can be traced back to 1781 when "the ring-dropping game, one of the old everlastings for fooling the credulous, was known as the fawney rig, the fawney trick, fawney being an English attempt at the Irish *fáinne*, a finger ring." In Great Britain, the word is spelled *phoney;* in the U.S., *phony.*

PHRASEMAKER   one who captures the essence of an issue in a few highly quotable words.

Sloganeer, which now has acquired a pejorative connotation, is the closest synonym. *Ghostwriters, speechwriters,* and *research assistants* who prepare speeches may be *phrasemakers* or they may not. For a discussion of usage, see GHOSTWRITER. A phrasemaker is similar to a "play doctor" who is called in to add lines and sharpen the scenes of another playwright.

A phrasemaker should be capable of taking an ordinary speech and adding a news lead in the form of inflammable words or a stunning new thought in quotable form. He should also be anonymous; the public has come to accept the idea of a public figure employing a speechwriter, but a phrase must "belong" to the public man and not be attributable to a man behind the scenes, at least not for the life of an Administration.

President Eisenhower called an early assistant of his, Emmet Hughes, "a writer with a talent for phrasemaking."

Some presidents, notably Abraham Lincoln and Theodore Roosevelt, had a genius for phrasemaking. In politics, however, every talent is attackable; among Woodrow Wilson's nicknames were "schoolmaster in politics," "coiner of weasel-words," "professor"—and equally damning, "phrasemaker."

How is a phrase made? If original inspiration is lacking, a play on a previous phrase is customary: "Johnson's War on Poverty has now become a War on Prosperity." This word-substitution in a familiar phrase is a frequent technique; in the congressional campaign of 1966, the Republican decision was to attack President Johnson on the subject of inflation. Possibilities: "Johnson Inflation," "Johnson Dollars Buy Less." Neither very catchy, and the word "inflation" is rather abstract. The High Cost of Living was a well-known and well-understood phrase,

and it needed a tight identification with the President. Hence, "the High Cost of Johnson" was used and served its purpose, although it never became a part of the language.

Seminal phrases are rare: for coinages, see MEDICARE; COLD WAR; for emphasis using contrast, see CONTRAPUNTAL PHRASES; for adaptation, see TURNAROUNDS; for the most useful phrasemaking word, see NEW, POLITICAL USE OF.

PIE IN THE SKY scornful characterization of liberal or populist promises.

In the vocabulary of rhetorical counterattack—"empty promises," "cruel demogogery", "callous vote-buying"—none has been more durable than "pie in the sky." In the face of this withering return fire, even the word "promise" has disappeared from campaign oratory, supplanted by the more solemn "pledge."

The origin of "pie in the sky" was supplied the author by laborlore specialist Archie Green, a professor of English at Ohio State University. The phrase was coined around 1910 in "the Preacher and the Slave," a composition by legendary labor hero Joe Hill, which became part of the widely distributed "little red songbooks" of the Industrial Workers of the World (the I.W.W., or Wobblies").

You will eat, bye and bye,
In that glorious land above the sky;
Work and pray, live on hay
You'll get pie in the sky when you die.

Professor Green rightly calls this phrase "the most significant Wobbly contribution to the American vocabulary." Conservative speakers have been seizing on it for denunciation for three generations.

An example of its currency is in a cartoon by Auth for the *Philadelphia*

Inquirer in November 1977: people in line for unemployment benefits are shown looking skyward at a vision of a pie labeled "Humphrey-Hawkins," a bill designed to bring down the rate of unemployment in the U.S. And after Larry Flynt, publisher of the raunchy *Hustler* magazine, announced his spiritual rebirth in 1978 thanks to an airborne conversion by Ruth Carter Stapleton, the *Washington Post's Potomac Magazine* headlined: "Piety in the Sky."

See CAMPAIGN ORATORY; for a don't-you-believe-it lexicon, from BALONEY to FREE LUNCH (food is often associated with the metaphors for disbelief), see SANTA CLAUS, NOBODY SHOOTS AT.

PINKO   epithet for anyone in a spectrum ranging from liberal to Communist, but most often applied to FELLOW TRAVELERS, a smear word.

Pinko, pink, and the more effete PARLOR PINK were often used against Democratic candidates. Just as Republicans after the Civil War said "Not all Democrats were rebels, but all rebels were Democrats," some conservatives in this century have used "Not all Democrats are pinkos, but all pinkos are Democrats."

Those who found Communism "a god that failed" and those who changed their minds about fellow-traveling were the foremost users of the word. When the CIO purged its membership in 1949 of the United Electrical Workers Union because of their Communist links, former pinko Michael J. Quill, colorful boss of the Transport Workers Union, lashed out at the "pinks, punks and parasites."

In 1926, when *Time* was popularizing the Homeric adjective ("Berkshire-cradled," "Beethoven-locked," "Yankee-shrewd"), its editors were fond of "pinko-liberal" and "pinko-

political." See PUNDIT for other *Time* coinages.

PIPELINE, IN THE   in the process of being developed, but not ready for public disclosure; on its way.

Government officials answer complaints of inaction with the assurance that work is "in the pipeline." The phrase was popular in the White House in the early seventies, sometimes carrying a connotation of inexorability: once some proposal got in the pipeline, it could not be stopped, and any attempts to sidetrack it was met with "That train has left the station."

A subtlety of this phrase is in the understanding that not everything in political affairs is cause-and-effect, and that often an event comes about not by virtue of its apparent cause, but because it had already been "in the pipeline." When a project is cut off, it may continue for years because funds to support it were "in the pipeline."

Another meaning of "pipeline" is "channel of information," as "we have a pipeline into the Joint Chiefs."

PISS ANT   one who is a stickler for detail; a derogation of a too-technical minor functionary.

In a 1977 *New Republic* piece on former Defense Secretary James Schlesinger, who had been named by President Carter to be his energy chief, Eliot Marshall wrote: "He began his career in the Nixon administration in 1969 as a second-rung functionary in what was then the gritty Bureau of the Budget. As one departing cabinet aide put it, he began as a mere 'pissant' . . . His worldly skills are sometimes referred to as his 'practical sense,' or his appreciation of detail. It explains why he once was considered a pissant."

The word can be used as an adjective ("every piss-ant line in the Budget") and is usually written as two words. Origin unknown.

PISSING POST, *see* **POWER BASE.**

PITILESS PUBLICITY as Wilson used it, the purifying power of the public gaze on the operations of government, where secrecy can breed corruption; now also the encroachment on privacy by reporters seeking sensation.

Woodrow Wilson used the phrase often in his New Jersey gubernatorial campaign of 1910, and in the presidential campaign of 1912 against Taft and Roosevelt, taking it from Ralph Waldo Emerson's use in "The Conduct of Life": "As gaslight is found to be the best nocturnal police, so the universe protects itself by pitiless publicity."

In the 1912 campaign, Wilson explained: "Publicity is one of the purifying elements of politics. Nothing checks all the bad practices of politics like public exposure. An Irishman, seen digging around the wall of a house, was asked what he was doing. He answered, 'Faith, I am letting the dark out of the cellar.' Now, that's exactly what we want to do."

True to his pledge of welcoming "pitiless publicity," Wilson inaugurated the regular presidential press conference after he took office. At the first, he told reporters: "A large part of the success of public affairs depends on the newspapermen—not so much the editorial writers, because we can live down what they say, as upon the news writers, because news is the atmosphere of public affairs."

The same concern for shining a beam of publicity in the dark corners of diplomacy led to his expression "OPEN COVENANTS, openly arrived at"; but just as he modified that position to include confidential discussions, in his later years in office he withdrew from the regular press conference routine.

A related phrase, "the white light of publicity"—the same metaphor as "letting the dark out"—was coined a few years later by writer Theodore F. MacManus in a 1915 *Saturday Evening Post* article: "In every field of human endeavor, he that is first must perpetually live in the white light of publicity."

The word *publicity* has a double image today. In the Wilsonian sense, it is regarded as a good thing, calling politicians immediately to account for almost every action. Joseph Pulitzer told his editors at the *New York World* in 1895: "Publicity, PUBLICITY, PUBLICITY, is the greatest moral factor and force on our public life."

On the other hand, the press agent or publicity man is often scorned as he inveigles "free publicity" for his "publicity hound" client, either through "cheap stunts" or the manipulative devices of "hidden persuasion."

As a result of this bad publicity, people in the field often shy away from the phrase "publicity man" or even the word "publicist," which once meant a man dedicated to the affairs of the public, and adopted "public relations counsel." To them, publicity—getting space in the press and time on the air for the client's product or principle—is a single arrow in the large quiver of public relations techniques.

As a result of this double image, "pitiless publicity" in current usage is something the public not only gets the benefit of, but which it is constantly subjected to.

The phrase is also used to express concern with too-zealous reporters and photographers who invade privacy, particularly in the coverage of tragedies.

PLACE IN THE SUN justification for expansion and conquest.

Kaiser Wilhelm II, speaking at Hamburg on August 27, 1911, laid the basis for Germany's claim to territorial growth: "No one can dispute with us the place in the sun that is our due."

"Place in the sun" became a German rallying cry during World War I and during the rise of Hitler; the Nazis, however, preferred LEBENS-RAUM, "living room."

The phrase can be found in the *Pensées* of Blaise Pascal (Kennet's translation, 1727): "This Dog's mine, sayd the poor Child: this is my place, in the Sun. From so petty a beginning, we can trace the Tyranny and Usurpation of the whole Earth."

PLANT as a verb, to induce a reporter to ask a question at a press conference; as a noun, a news story released to a single reporter which benefits the person leaking the story; or, an individual placed in an opposition camp.

Anthony Leviero, a Washington correspondent of the *New York Times,* broke an exclusive story in 1951 about the details of the Truman-MacArthur conference on Wake Island. Following MacArthur's dismissal (see OLD SOLDIERS NEVER DIE) it occurred to the reporter that the assumption about total agreement between Truman and MacArthur at Wake might be false, and that the Administration might be ready to release the document to refute MacArthur's charges.

Leviero pointed out how he went after the story in a memo, and added:

This disposes of the stories about a "plant," although I or any other Washington correspondent would gladly accept a planted authentic document. . . . A final word on the claims of discomfited rivals that this was an Administration "plant." Without conceding the story came from the White House, I can say that never in more than three years of covering the place did a member of the President's staff offer me a story. But I often scored by asking at the right time.

In current political usage, a LEAK is usually deliberate, sometimes inadvertent; a *plant* is always deliberate, and connotes "control" of the reporter's story; an *exclusive* has a more legitimate ring, although reporters left out are envious; a *scoop* or *beat* carries the least stigma of deliberate origination by the source, and usually means the reporter dug out the information by his own enterprise.

Question-planting in the U.S. is always surreptitious, and most press secretaries disclaim any use of the practice. On the other hand, French President Charles de Gaulle practiced it openly, according to former Kennedy press secretary Pierre Salinger: "His aides plant every question in advance with pro-Administration reporters, and *Le Président* carefully rehearses the answers."

PLATFORM ideally, the standards to which the wise and honest voters can repair; in practice, a list of principles and positions designed to attract most and offend least, important mainly in the work it gives a convention to do other than select a candidate.

Francis Bacon, in 1623: "The wisdom of a lawmaker consisteth not only in a platform of justice, but in the application thereof." In most early use in the U.S., the word related to the principles of a church, taken from the French word for ground plan of a building. Since the word also came to mean a raised area from which a person could speak, its metaphoric use in politics married both senses. Like STUMP and HUSTING, a place to stand soon was allied to a place to take a stand.

As early as 1803, the *Massachusetts Spy* was writing about "The Platform of Federalism," but it was William Lloyd Garrison in his antislavery *Liberator* who would help popularize the term; in 1844, the first national party platforms were adopted and by 1848 the word was a political standby.

The word "plank" was a natural derivative: in the 1848 "Bigelow Papers," one line of doggerel read: "They kin' o' slipt the planks frum out th' old platform one by one/An' made it gradooally noo, 'fore folks know'd wut wuz done . . ."

In current use, a party platform is taken with great seriousness at a convention, since it enables many compromises to be made and gives appointment plums to many factional leaders, but is soon forgotten in the campaign. A frequent saying, of obscure origin, is that "A platform is not something to stand on, but something to run on" and is soon followed by "A platform is what you start by running on and end by running from."

PLAYING POLITICS placing partisan gain above the public interest; more mildly, to adeptly embarrass a political opponent.

While it is proper to *participate in* politics, and stimulating to *talk* politics, it is considered reprehensible to *play* politics.

Notwithstanding Frank R. Kent's book title, *The Great Game of Politics,* when politics is played rather than engaged in, the gambling verb (*to play*) casts suspicion on the otherwise innocent noun (*politics*). Walter Lippmann wrote in 1955 that "a political figure must never in so many words admit that in order to gain votes he sacrificed the public good, that he played 'politics.' "

Warnings about playing politics have been popular with Presidents; Herbert Hoover in 1930 in connection with unemployment relief said, "They are playing politics at the expense of human misery"—a charge that was to be repeated a generation later as "playing politics with poverty." Franklin Roosevelt, in his MARTIN, BARTON AND FISH speech before the election of 1940, cautioned Republicans about "playing politics with national defense," and Dwight Eisenhower in 1954 applied it to White House-Capitol Hill relations: "History shows that when the Executive and Legislative Branches are politically in conflict, politics in Washington runs riot. . . . The public good goes begging while politics is played for politics' sake."

A middle ground between the laudatory "participate in politics" and the accusatory "playing politics" appears to be the turning of the noun "politics" into verb or participle: "to politic," or "politicking" has the neutral connotation of campaigning.

For allusions to political activity as gambling, see CARD METAPHORS; as a sport, see SPORTS METAPHORS.

PLAY IN PEORIA to elitists, the criterion of the crass; to antiestablishmentarians, the measurement of acceptability in the heartland.

Some White House aides excuse cornball gestures by a politically savvy President with a shrug and "It'll go over well in the boonies," or —in the Nixon Administration— "It'll play in Peoria."

New York Times columnist Russell Baker disparaged the language of the Nixon men in a June 9, 1973, essay: "If the Administration's critics (Eastern liberal intellectuals, 'establishmentarians,' 'elitists') complained that they could not understand the language, much less the name of the game, the Nixon men had a standard rebuttal. 'It will play in Peoria,' they said." ˉ

The phrase has a hucksteresque quality (see SELLING CANDIDATES LIKE SOAP) derived from its metaphor of politics as a performance; it probably originated in vaudeville, as entertainers discussed how an act would be received in the hinterland. Its coiner, White House aide John Ehrlichman, informs the author: " 'Play in Peoria' appeared in a *Wall Street Journal* story after I'd run the school for advance men in NYC in 1968. I used the expression there. Onomatopoeia was the only reason for Peoria, I suppose. And it personified—exemplified—a place, removed from the media centers on the coasts, where the national verdict is cast, according to Nixon doctrine."

Everett Dirksen (R-Ill.), the Senate Minority Leader, did not like the faint put-down implicit in the phrase, as if Peoria were not cosmopolitan. In 1969, reminiscing about his youth to the author, he gave the connotation attributed to Peoria a different note: "I was born in Pekin, Illinois. A lovely town, kind of on the quiet side. But for those young rakes who wanted excitement—not too far away were the bright lights of Peoria."

PLOY an artful device aimed at deception; a maneuver of indirection to achieve an objective without revealing the ultimate goal.

This ancient Scottish derivative of "employ"—meaning "escapade" or "merry mischief" to Highland clans —gained in political usage in the 1960s, stimulated by the popularity of Stephen Potter's frequent use in his "one-upmanship" series.

Another possible derivation of ploy comes from the military "deploy"; in infantry terminology, a "ploy" is a means used to diminish the front exposed to the enemy, or to form a column from a line.

Ted Sorensen referred to a diplomatic ploy in discussing the many "inside" accounts of the Kennedy Administration's handling of the Cuban missile crisis in 1962: "Much information has been written about this series of meetings, about who said what, and about such terms as 'hawks and doves,' 'think tank,' 'Ex Comm' and 'Trollope ploy' which I never heard used at the time."

The "Trollope ploy" derives from the nineteenth-century romantic novels of Anthony Trollope, in which the heroine interprets—or deliberately misinterprets—the squeeze of her hand as a proposal of marriage. In the Cuban missile crisis, it was suggested that the most recent communication from Khruschev be ignored, and the U.S. make its reply to an earlier communication as if the most recent message had not been received. "It was Robert Kennedy," wrote Roger Hilsman in 1967's *To Move a Nation,* "who conceived a brilliant diplomatic maneuver—later dubbed 'The Trollope Ploy' . . ."

The word has political promise, because of its alliteration with politics (a "political ploy"), the degeneration of "gimmick" into so wide a variety of meanings as to make it useless, and the lack of color in "device" or "maneuver." The word it will have to compete with is "gambit," which comes from an opening chess move sacrificing a pawn to improve position and which became a diplomatic word for a concession to begin discussions. In politics, *gambit* is currently synonymous with *ploy* and *trick*.

PLUM, POLITICAL an appointive job, especially a sinecure; PA-TRONAGE.

"Shaking the plum tree" is attributed to Matthew Stanley Quay, political boss of Pennsylvania in 1885 and later U.S. senator.

The idea of political plums falling from a tree is evident in this reply by presidential candidate William Howard Taft in 1908, to a query by editor William Allen White about how Taft got started so young: "I always had my plate the right side up when offices were falling."

The meaning has remained unchanged. Raymond Moley, writing in *Newsweek* in 1967 about Postmaster General Lawrence O'Brien's plans to remove the "political plum tree" from the U.S. postal system by turning it into a nonprofit corporation, reminisced: "Starry-eyed idealists have long since deplored the use of government jobs, contracts and favors as rewards for political service. But they fail to realize that keeping the plum tree is not a happy lot."

The predecessor word, no longer used in politics, was *persimmon*.

PLUMBER one who investigates and seeks to plug up leaks of information; specifically, the inept crew of lawbreakers who undertook that task in the Nixon Administration.

Room 16, in the basement of the Old Executive Office Building across West Executive Avenue from the White House, was assigned to G.

Gordon Liddy and David Young in 1970. One of their overt jobs was to track terrorist groups, at home and abroad, and to inform White House staffers of means to avoid letter-bombs and other dangers. Another, less spoken about, part of their job was to find out who was leaking what information to the press, an activity that fascinated the President and Henry Kissinger.

Liddy later went on to fame and prison as one of the leaders of the Watergate break-in; Young did not get involved in those illegal matters. His contribution to history, however, was the sign he drew and placed on the door of Room 16: "The Plumbers." After the Watergate break-ins were exposed, all eavesdropping operations—from the seventeen FBI wiretaps of newsmen and White House aides to the bungled attempts by agents hired by the Plumbers—were widely publicized, culminating with disclosure of clandestine break-ins and other abridgments of Fourth Amendment protections committed by the FBI and CIA in previous Administrations.

When people spoke of the Plumbers in the late seventies, it was usually applied to the Special Investigation Unit, headed by Howard E. Hunt and G. Gordon Liddy, that was pressed into action in 1971, after the publication of the Pentagon Papers. The most famous bungled target of the Plumbers was the office of Daniel Ellsberg's psychiatrist, in a search for material that could be used to discredit the leaker of the secret history of the Vietnam war.

See "black bag jobs" under CIA-ESE; and the word from which "plumbers" sprung, LEAK.

PLUMED KNIGHT, *see* **THE MAN WHO; STALWART.**

PLUMP   to give active support; to strive for the election of another without reservation.

An obscure meaning of the word "plump" is "cluster," or group; voting as a bloc, or using a group's votes in a cumulative manner, was known as "to vote plump."

John Adams used it in that way in 1776: "New Jersey has dethroned Franklin, and in a letter, which is just come to my hand from indisputable authority, I am told that the delegates from that county 'will vote plump.' "

The word "plumping" came to have opposite meanings on the same subject in England and the U.S.: "One of the English election phrases for which there is no equivalent in the United States," wrote the *New York Tribune* in 1880, "is 'plumping.' Whenever [an English] constituency returns two members, each voter can give one vote each to any two candidates but he cannot give his two votes to any one candidate. If he chooses he can give one vote to only one candidate, and this is termed 'plumping.' "

In 1904, in the U.S., *Weber's Weekly* showed how the word came to mean the opposite of the English word: "The practice of casting three votes for one candidate has come to be known as 'plumping.' By 'plumping' the minority may concentrate its votes."

This is the same as cumulative voting, practiced in many publicly owned corporations in the U.S., where a number of votes for a slate of directors can be lumped together to be cast for a single director, encouraging minority representation on the Board.

In current use, *plump* has lost its cluster connotation, and has come to mean to solicit support for a candidate, preferably in large clusters. In its verb form, it is sometimes confused with **STUMP**.

POCATELLO, YOU CAN'T GO BACK TO   A melancholy expression about the loss of hometown roots by those who flower in Washington, D.C.

"This is one case in which you can cite your source with confidence," the popularizer writes the author. "It was invented by Dick [Oregon Senator Richard L.] Neuberger and myself in 1943 or 1944."

Present at the creation was Jonathan Daniels, in 1978 editor emeritus of the *Raleigh News and Observer,* and from 1943 through 1945 administrative assistant and later press secretary to President Roosevelt. He recounted the origin of the phrase in his book *Frontier on the Potomac,* published in 1946:

> Neuberger had just come back from Alaska and was telling me about the cold up there and the state of his kidneys.
>
> "There's Worth Clark," he said suddenly.
>
> Neuberger regards the State of Idaho as a part of his personal province as a writer.
>
> The ex-Senator joined a party at a table.
>
> "Is he living here now since he was defeated?" I asked. "He probably doesn't know it, but he's a distant cousin of mine."
>
> "Yes," said Dick. "I think he is practicing with Tommy Corcoran."
>
> He drank from a glass of milk.
>
> "You know," he said suddenly, "somebody ought to write an article, 'You Can't Go Back to Pocatello.' "
>
> "Pocatello?"
>
> "That's his home town. It's a big town for Idaho. Oh, I guess twenty thousand people."
>
> "Why can't he go back?"
>
> "It isn't Clark. They just can't. They come down here to the Senate

or something. Then they get beat. It isn't easy to go back and practice local law and live local lives."

"It is not only the little towns it's hard to go back to," I said.

And while we watched, big Jim Watson, of Indiana, walked across the room. Nobody noticed him. He had been Republican majority leader of the Senate under Hoover. He was an old man, eighty, I guessed. He had been defeated, too, but he was in Washington still.

"You can't go back to Pocatello," I said.

It would be a good story. You couldn't tell in the big dining room who hadn't gone back but had stayed as bureaucrats on the other side of the street. The lobby and the government were laughing together. The only difference would be which picked up the check. And suddenly the big, wicked lobbyists seemed, above the noise of people eating and talking on expense accounts that auditors far away would approve and the Bureau of Internal Revenue might pass, less wicked than sad.

In current use, the phrase is an insider's alternative to POTOMAC FEVER and is usually changed to "They never go back to Pocatello." In a 1975 editorial the *Washington Star* referred to the bittersweet line as evidence that the much-condemned Washington atmosphere was not all bad: "Whatever its drawbacks—and we acknowledge some—the number of politicians who come here and 'never go back to Pocatello' would indicate that the Nation's Capital is a pretty good place after all."

POCKETBOOK ISSUE   a voter's concern with what is happening to his income and its buying power.

"The great mass of the people," Boston politician Martin Lomasney discovered, "are interested in only three things—food, clothing and shelter."

In the midst of depression or inflation, pocketbook issues take precedence over more esoteric, philosophical appeals, and can exert a greater influence than personalities.

Republicans in 1966 decided to make pocketbook issues their theme; a piece of literature distributed in several areas of the nation was a long paper in the shape of a supermarket cashier's tape, with comparative food prices on it and a denunciation of "Johnson INFLATION." This could be considered fair play, as "Hoover depression" had been a Democratic approach to pocketbook issues for a generation.

A *pocketbook issue* is synonymous with BREAD-AND-BUTTER ISSUE. AFL-CIO President George Meany said of the 1970 congressional race: "The gut issue is going to be the pocketbook issue." See PARAMOUNT ISSUE; GUT ISSUE; ISSUES, THE.

POCKET VETO   on bills passed within ten days of congressional adjournment, the ability of the president to effectively veto by withholding his signature.

The President may retain a bill for ten days before either signing or vetoing it. If, during that time, the Congress adjourns, the President will have vetoed it merely by "putting it in his pocket."

In practical terms, this means that the President need not give reasons for vetoing the bill, which is why the term originally applied was "silent veto"; such a veto may not be overridden by a two-thirds vote of the Congress, which is no longer in session.

Andrew Jackson brought the practice into full flower. "The silent veto," wrote Daniel Webster, "is, I believe, the exclusive adoption of the present administration. . . . In an internal improvement bill of a former session,

and in the State interest bill, we have
had the silent veto, or refusal without
reasons." The *Ohio Statesman* headlined "Pocket Vetoes" in 1842.

Abraham Lincoln, at odds with
Thaddeus Stevens about the severity
to be shown to the South after the Civil
War, gave the pocket veto a new
twist. He let it be known that he was
not going to sign the harsh Wade-
Davis bill, and that a "pocket veto"
would take effect; however, instead of
refusing to give his reasons, he issued
a proclamation to show which parts
of the legislation he would accept. But
the Radicals were in no mood for conciliation. Thaddeus Stevens exploded:
"What an infamous proclamation!
The idea of pocketing a bill and then
issuing a proclamation as to how far
he will conform to it . . ."

In effect, the ten-day rule gives the
President the power to accept or reject legislation passed in the last ten
days of any session; congressional
leaders try to get important bills
through before the President gets this
uncheckable power.

The word "veto" comes from the
Latin, meaning "I forbid." Louis XVI
and Marie Antoinette were called
Monsieur and Madame Veto by the
Jacobins, because of abuse of the veto
power given him in 1791 by the Constituent Assembly.

The origin of "pocket" as a synonym for "suppress" was given the author by Senator Edward Kennedy,
who referred to the word in a *Virginia
Law Review* article (April 1977). In
Shakespeare's *The Tempest,* Antonio
asks: "If but one of his pockets could
speak, would it not say he lies?"
Sebastian replies: "Ay, or very falsely
pocket up his report." .

For a look at the way the Congress
evens the score with the President, see
ONE-HOUSE VETO.

POINT FOUR PROGRAM, *see*
CONTAINMENT.

POINT MAN, *see* **ON THE POINT.**

POINT OF ORDER   cry of interruption made famous by Senator Joseph McCarthy in 1954.

"Our counsel, Mr. [Ray] Jenkins,"
said temporary chairman Karl
Mundt of the Senate Subcommittee
on Investigations, "will now call the
first witness—"

"A point of order, Mr. Chairman,"
said Senator McCarthy at the televised Army-McCarthy hearings.
"May I raise a point of order?"

The senator's insistent use of parliamentary device had schoolchildren
repeating a phrase that had been limited to formal debates and congressional hearings.

The hearings marked the high
point—and the beginning of the decline—of the senator's "era." See
MCCARTHYISM. Eric Goldman
wrote: "The children stopped saying
'Point of order, point of order.' The
housewives went back to 'I Love
Lucy.' A different subject was filling
conversations."

The phrase became the title of a
film documentary and articles on the
senator, who was censured by the
Senate in 1954 and who died in 1957.
Though he did not always use the device for determining a breach of the
rules, here is why he was able to get
the floor from the chairman whenever
he chose, from *Robert's Rules of
Order:*

> While it is the duty of the presid-
> ing officer to enforce the rules, mem-
> bers might differ from the Chair as
> to whether the rules are being vi-
> olated or the Chair might have no-
> ticed a violation of the rules. In ei-
> ther case, the member who thinks
> there is breach of the rules has the

right to raise the question as to whether they are being violated, and this is called raising a question of order or making a point of order. The point of order must be made at the time the breach of order occurs.

In the House of Commons in 1978, visitors protesting the presence of British troops in Northern Ireland threw three bags of manure at the legislators. One Member responded, "Politics is a dirty business," and another called for "a point of ordure."

POINT WITH PRIDE ... VIEW WITH ALARM clichés associated with national party platforms.

A classic party platform has been said to include these elements:

1. "Pointing with pride" at past accomplishments;
2. "Viewing with alarm" the blundering record of the opposition;
3. Clearcut positions on issues long since resolved;
4. Cautious, ambivalent positions on current issues;
5. One nervously-taken stand on a controversial matter.

In 1878, *The Nation* used the phrase in connection with one Republican platform: "Besides 'pointing with pride,' the remainder of the platform approves of 'temperance among the people' and the navigation laws, and exposes the evil designs of the Democrats . . ." In 1892, the same magazine reported: "The Republican Convention in the Portland (Me.) district . . . adopted a platform which 'points with pride' to the McKinley Law . . ."

The phrases are often used today in the full knowledge that they are clichés, most often with the same irony and quotation marks as used a century ago. Anyone using them seriously is considered a blowhard.

POINTER PHRASES speechwriters' term for verbal signals that underscore essential points in a speech.

"Let me make one thing perfectly clear," Richard Nixon used to like to say. He stopped using the phrase, just as John Kennedy stopped using the word "vigor" when it became the target of parody. "Quite clear," "crystal clear," and even plain, unadorned "clear" became taboo words in the lexicon of those working with Nixon on speeches.

A speaker who uses a pointer phrase is consciously trying to help his audience understand his message. A reader of written prose can skip back to catch an important point; the listener cannot. The technique appears an oversimplification when transcribed to text for reading, but is a helpful device for the listener whose attention tends to wander. When this writer included a pointer phrase—"make no mistake about it"—in an early draft for a Nixon speech, the President crossed it out with the comment, "Leave this out of the text—if it comes naturally for me to say it, I will."

Here are some other pointer phrases in frequent use today:

My point is this:
Let me be quite blunt:
It all comes down to this:
In plain words:
In a nutshell:
Let's face it:
The most important thing to remember is this:

In the use of pointer phrases, the most important thing to remember is this: when any particular phrase is used to excess, it becomes an object of ridicule. A cartoon by Gardner in the *Washington Star* in 1971, soon after the announcement of President Nixon's plan to travel to China, showed Secretary William Rogers bursting into the State Department's translation division to ask: "How do you say 'Let me make one thing perfectly clear' in Chinese?"

POL short for politician.

Use of this shortened form indicates a spurious familiarity with politics. It is an inexperienced reformer's kind of word, resented by those who do not resent "politician"; the user tries to insinuate himself into the political world by using a word that he does not know is disliked by insiders.

Fletcher Knebel, reporter and novelist, put his finger on it in 1964: " 'Pol' is to politician what 'cop' is to policeman."

POLARIZE to accentuate the differences within a party; to drive men ordinarily in agreement on many positions to extremes of disagreement.

In California in 1946, moderate Democrat Will Rogers, Jr., campaigned against strongly liberal former Congressman Ellis Patterson for the Democratic nomination to the Senate. "The battle between Rogers and Patterson," Democratic candidate for Governor Robert Kenny said, "polarized the party. It was the one highly emotional issue and it became a touchstone. Nothing else mattered to the partisans of the two men. . . . They just didn't give a damn."

Polarization in a primary often results in the defection of the losers in the general election, and because of that is resisted by both party leadership and the leaders of the "wings." Such polarization is of course encouraged by the opposite party.

"There are many more areas in which we agree than where we disagree," is the cliché often used to try to smooth over differences. See ELEV-ENTH COMMANDMENT; SURRENDER ON MORNINGSIDE HEIGHTS. In 1948 the Democratic party polarized to the point of dropping off both ends: Dixiecrats followed Strom Thurmond, ultraliberals followed Henry Wallace, leaving Harry Truman with just enough of a center to win. In 1964 the ideological split between Goldwater and Rockefeller polarized the Republican party, leaving very little middle at all, and this kind of polarization— the kind CENTRISTS dread—resulted in a Lyndon Johnson landslide.

In optics, to "polarize" means to affect light waves so that they vibrate in a definite pattern. The general sense of the word used to be "to set a trend." But politics changed the general sense of the verb, and "polarity" has come to mean the concentration of forces in diametrical opposition.

In foreign policy tracts of the early seventies, and especially in the writings and interviews of Carter National Security Adviser Zbigniew Brzezinski, the term "bi-polar" was used to signify a world dominated by the opposition of two superpowers, and in contrast to "multi-polar," where power centers included China, the THIRD WORLD, the West European bloc, etc.

See LITMUS-TEST ISSUE.

POLICE ACTION diplomatic euphemism for a war conducted under United Nations auspices; specifically, the Korean War.

When the North Koreans invaded South Korea in 1950, the Soviet delegate was in the midst of a boycott of UN Security Council sessions, and the U.S. was able to get through a resolution providing a UN umbrella for our decision to intervene. Thus, U.S. troops could serve with some others as "United Nations forces" in Korea.

The phrase, like RED HERRING, was placed in President Harry Truman's mouth by a reporter. At his first press conference after the North Korean attack, a reporter asked: ". . . are we or are we not at war?"

"We are not at war," Truman replied positively, and gave newsmen the unusual (at the time) permission to quote him directly, adding that the U.S. was only trying to suppress a "bandit raid" on the Republic of Korea.

"Would it be correct," asked another reporter, "to call this a police action under the United Nations?" Truman said yes, that was what the action amounted to. Headline writers took this as "Truman Calls Intervention 'Police Action,' " which associated the President closely with the phrase.

Since the President was so definite in his statement that this was not a war, and since no declaration of war was ever made, legislative attorneys drawing up bills to make veterans of the not-a-war eligible for benefits called it "the Korean Conflict." Similarly, a later war's legislative euphemism became "the Vietnam Era."

POLICE BRUTALITY, see **CIVILIAN REVIEW.**

POLICEMAN OF THE WORLD attack phrase on America's assumption of responsibility as guardian of non-Communist borders.

"We Americans," said Benjamin Harrison in 1888, "have no commission from God to police the world."

Theodore Roosevelt disagreed. In his message to Congress on December 6, 1904, he claimed the duty of the U.S. was to exercise an "internal police power" in the Western hemisphere because "chronic wrongdoing, or an impotence which results in a general loosening of the ties of civilized society, may . . . ultimately require intervention by some civilized nation."

With the adoption of a policy of CONTAINMENT of Communist expansion early in the fifties, Roosevelt's corollary to the Monroe Doctrine was extended throughout the world. Critics of this policy took the position that the United Nations, not the U.S., was properly charged with the responsibility for keeping world peace; moreover, they held, this policy was escalating wars rather than keeping the peace. Supporters of the "world policeman" idea, while rejecting the phrase as slanted to their opponents' arguments, believed the Soviet veto made the UN ineffective in halting aggression; in the vacuum, the U.S. had to step in on the basis of its own long-range self-interest, as well as the ideal of preserving the self-determination of nations.

Senator J. William Fulbright, after quoting Abraham Lincoln's use of the Biblical phrase "judge not that ye be not judged," said: "The United States must decide which of the two sides of its national character is to predominate—the humanism of Lincoln or the arrogance of those who would make America the world's policeman." In the latter half of his sentence, the Foreign Relations Committee chairman was referring to Theodore Roosevelt, but his sense of new reality kept him from attacking a well-loved old myth.

Speaking in Montreal in May 1966, Defense Secretary Robert McNamara surprised and delighted DOVES with "neither conscience nor sanity, itself, suggests that the United States is, should, or could be the Global Gendarme." Without credit to President Harrison, he added, "The United States has no mandate from on high to police the world, and no inclination to do so . . .''

Secretary of State Dean Rusk felt obliged to say a year later that our efforts to pursue peace "does not mean that we are the world's policeman. It does not mean that we aspire to a *pax Americana*." This was a play on "pax Britannica," meaning the peace imposed upon the world by the power of the British Empire.

George Ball, former Undersecretary of State who served Lyndon Johnson as the leading dissenter on the escalation of the Vietnam war, objected to the use of this cliché in *Foreign Affairs* (July 1969): ". . . man is still so bedeviled by greed and passion that force and authority must be ever at hand if he is not to blow the world up. So, unhappy as may be the policeman's lot, if we do not walk his thankless beat, who will?"

POLICE STATE, *see* **TOTALITARIAN.**

POLITICAL ANIMAL what man is supposed to be; usually employed with open—or grudging—admiration.

Aristotle said it in his *Politics:* "Man is by nature a political animal." Some have since complained that man is too much the political animal, but George Bernard Shaw, for one, was not among them. "It is very doubtful whether man is enough of a political animal," GBS noted in a speech in New York on April 11, 1933, "to produce a good, sensible, serious and efficient constitution. All the evidence is against it."

In *The Kennedy Circle,* Lester Tanzer noted of John Kennedy's Secretary of Defense: "As a political animal, McNamara defies classification. In 1960 he made four campaign contributions. Three of the candidates he

supported were liberal Republicans— Senator Clifford Case of New Jersey and John Sherman Cooper of Kentucky, and Paul Bagwell, the unsuccessful Republican candidate for governor of Michigan. The fourth was a Democrat, John F. Kennedy."

The term was often applied to Lyndon Johnson. Writing on May 24, 1964, *New York Times* columnist Arthur Krock noted: "The most political animal to occupy the White House since Andrew Jackson, if not since the creation of the Federal Government, has just completed the first six months of his presidency."

Winston Churchill in 1942 classified animals as to air, sea, and land, and assigned allies their proper roles: "We were sea animals, and the United States are to a large extent ocean animals. The Russians are land animals. Happily, we are all three air animals."

If the accent is placed on the second word—as "political *animal*"— the phrase can become an epithet. Reported *Newsweek* in 1967: "Mrs. Lenore Romney became so upset when the governor [George Romney] angrily denounced the President as a 'political animal' that her eyes filled with tears." In 1978 House Speaker Thomas P. "Tip" O'Neill denounced a Republican prosecutor, David Marston, as "He's nothing but a Republican political animal." The Republican leader, John Rhodes, correctly took offense.

See STIR UP THE ANIMALS; for canine metaphors, see BIRD DOG . . . KENNEL DOG.

POLITICAL CAPITAL, TO MAKE to take unfair partisan advantage; capital is used in the sense of considering political prestige, notoriety, and influence as "property."

"I tell you," said Senate Majority

Leader Lyndon Johnson in the debate on the 1957 civil rights bill, "out of whatever experience I have, that there is no political capital in this issue. Nothing lasting, nothing enduring has ever been born from hatred and prejudice—except more hatred and prejudice." In voting for civil rights legislation for the first time in his life, Senator Johnson was determined to make the civil rights bill his own, and it served to add to his political capital as a national, rather than sectional, leader.

The phrase has been traced as far back as an 1842 issue of the *Ohio Statesman:* ". . . the attempt of the whigs . . . to make 'political capital,' as was avowed by whig members, fizzles out . . ." The use of quotation marks indicates the phrase was used earlier than that, and its frequent current use makes this phrase an important political Americanism.

Adlai Stevenson in 1952 tried to blunt the SOFT ON COMMUNISM issue this way: "It is never necessary to call a man a Communist to make political capital. Those of us who have undertaken to practice the ancient but imperfect art of government will always make enough mistakes to keep our critics well supplied with standard ammunition. There is no need for poison gas."

A year after that election, Eisenhower Attorney General Herbert Brownell charged that Harry Dexter White, a Truman Assistant Secretary of the Treasury, was "a Russian spy." Eisenhower recalled later: "The central point in this case was this shocking FBI evidence, but a host of partisan critics chose to ignore this and to attack the Attorney General for 'trying to make capital' out of incontrovertible evidence."

Business has not contributed nearly as many metaphors to politics as religion, sports, or the military. "Stock" is occasionally used, as in this 1836 *Scioto Gazette* comment: "The rapid advance of Jackson stock in the political market presented too splendid a speculation to be eluded by such jobbers as the house of Van Buren & Company . . ." and the 1876 *Cleveland Leader's* headline, "Hayes Stock Is Strong."

LAME DUCK is the best-known borrowing from finance, with "gravy train," "angel," "blue sky laws," and BOOM AND BUST used often. For an up-and-coming borrowing, see HOT PROPERTY.

POLITICAL MILEAGE, TO MAKE   to seize an opportunity to take political advantage; to make use of the voter appeal inherent in an issue or position.

The word "mileage" was first used to describe a legislator's allowance for traveling costs. Benjamin Franklin in 1754 wrote of "Member's Pay . . . milage for traveling expenses." The word, with an *e* added, gained political significance when the Whigs in 1850 called for "mileage reform." At the time, "constructive mileage" was paid when an extra session of Congress was called; if legislators happened to have remained in Washington, they were paid the cost of a trip to the capital even though they never took the trip. See LULU.

The new meaning is evidently built on this, but the current use is not in any dictionary. Senator Joseph McCarthy discovered plenty of mileage in the SOFT ON COMMUNISM charge; there was mileage in the frustration of Americans about a stalemate in Korea in 1952. John F. Kennedy made political mileage of an ephemeral missile gap, Lyndon Johnson discovered the mileage in poverty, and George Wallace (and later,

Jimmy Carter) made mileage out of a general resentment directed at the federal bureaucracy.

Making political mileage implies less unfairness than making political capital (see previous entry).

POLITICAL MIRACLE cliché indicating an upset or unexpected development.

"Barring a political miracle," wrote *Time* magazine in 1948 about the Dewey-Warren combination favored to swamp Truman, "it was the kind of ticket that could not fail to sweep the Republican party back into power."

Four years later, a WRITE-IN campaign was begun in Eisenhower's behalf by a citizen's group in Minnesota, just after his New Hampshire primary victory over Robert Taft. Professionals warned Eisenhower against it, feeling its likely failure would slow down the bandwagon. Bradshaw Mintener, state chairman of "Minnesotans for Eisenhower," appealed to the voters for "a political miracle." As the General commented later: "It appeared to have happened: more than one hundred thousand people wrote in varying versions of my name."

The word "political" seems to have a particular affinity for the words *miracle, suicide,* and of late, *cool.* Taking any unpopular stand, or one that used to be unpopular and still gives the illusion of courage in opposing it, is called POLITICAL SUICIDE by tut-tutters; and keeping one's "political cool" means refusing to OVERREACT in adversity or triumph.

POLITICAL SUICIDE an obviously unpopular action, which may result in defeat at the polls.

These suicides, like the report of Mark Twain's death, are usually ex-

aggerations. Actions that are unpopular on their face often redound to a candidate's credit as evidence of courage; it may appear to some commentators as "political suicide" to question or oppose automatic increases in funds for education, but some governors who take this controversial step find they may stay alive by proving they have made a white elephant more efficient, or held the line on taxes, or whatever the other side of the coin enables them to say.

The phrase, sometimes expressed as "political hara-kiri" (mispronounced Harry Carey), does not mean taking one's own political life deliberately; it means, rather, taking an action that some other people feel will lead to political oblivion.

In that second sense, the word was used by Woodrow Wilson in a letter to Bernard Baruch in 1916 early in the presidential campaign, and could have been applied to Lyndon Johnson's strategy in the 1964 campaign: "I am inclined to follow the course suggested by a friend, who says that he has always followed the rule never to murder a man who is committing suicide."

POLITICIAN one who engages in a career either in government or in a political party on a full-time, usually professional, basis.

In most countries the practice of politics is considered a respectable profession, worthy of this 1770 definition by English parliamentarian Thomas Burke: "It is the business of the speculative philosopher to mark the proper ends of government. It is the business of the politician, who is the philosopher in action, to find out proper means towards those ends, and to employ them with effect."

That was a far cry from the derogation in Shakespeare's *Richard III:*

"meerly a politician, and studied only his owne ends." In 1879 Sir George Campbell reported to his countrymen that "the word 'politician' is used in a bad sense in America as applied to people who . . . are skilled in the area of 'wirepulling.' " In the U.S. the politician has been looked upon with suspicion from the first, because the Colonists felt themselves misunderstood and mistreated by a government in London (in which they were not represented) that inflicted on them such distasteful regulations as the various Acts of Trade and the Stamp Act.

Thomas Jefferson summed up his feeling as "that government is best which governs least." George Washington expressed the feeling of most of his countrymen when in his Farewell Address he referred to "the mere politicians." Later, Artemus Ward said: "I am not a politician, and my other habits are good."

In more recent times, the practice of politics in this country has become more acceptable, and a growing number of men are prepared even to accept the appellation without wincing. One who bore the badge proudly was former President Harry Truman, who told the Reciprocity Club in 1958: "A politician is a man who understands government, and it takes a politician to run a government. A statesman is a politician who's been dead ten or fifteen years."

A professional politician's image is similar to that of the professional soldier: patronized in peacetime, lionized in wartime. Between campaigns, the politician is an embarrassment and a pest to many government officials; at campaign time, he is leader, guide, and confidant.

In current usage, a *public figure* is a celebrity; a *political figure* is an officeholder or likely candidate; a *professional politician* is usually a technician without ideology; a POL is one of *the boys in the backroom;* a GOPHER is the lowest political functionary; a *political expert* or *political observer* is often a reporter's fiction for quoting himself without appearing to do so, and an OLD PRO knows enough ropes to hang himself.

POLITICS OF   a framework for titles, to suit all purposes.

In the 1949 English edition of his book *The Vital Center,* the title used by Arthur Schlesinger, Jr., was *The Politics of Freedom.* He informs the author that titles like *The Strategy of Terror* by Edmund Taylor might have inspired his frequent use of this construction.

Schlesinger followed this with *The Politics of Upheaval* in 1957, and *The Politics of Hope* in 1962. In the 1968 presidential campaign, Hubert Humphrey tried out "the politics of joy," and in 1970 Senator Edward Kennedy denounced Vice President Agnew's "politics of fear."

On the politics of anything: the word "politics" is construed as singular, as in "Politics is fun," but when it is used to denote a set of beliefs, the plural takes over, as "My politics are nobody's business."

POLLSTER   one who measures public opinion, especially with an eye to predicting election results.

"A pinch of probably is worth a pound of perhaps," wrote James Thurber. The politician's desperation for reassurance combined with a journalist's curiosity led to the rise of public opinion polling, a technique in use in the U.S. since the Adams-Jackson-Clay-Crawford presidential race of 1824.

The word "poll" comes from the Middle English *polle,* meaning "top of the head," the part that showed when heads were being counted. Today, a *poll tax* is a head tax; *the polls* are where the heads are counted; and *a poll* is a counting of a sampling of heads, selected at random or by prearrangement, to reflect the opinion of a given populace. Dr. Elmo Roper and Dr. George Gallup were the leaders in the field for many years, establishing their profession in the thirties, blossoming after the debacle of the *Literary Digest* poll of 1936. See STRAW POLL.

"Pollster" is a relatively new word, popularized in—and especially after—the Truman upset of Dewey in 1948. Wrote *Time,* wrong as any, afterward: "The press . . . had failed to do its own doorbell-ringing and bush-beating, it had delegated its journalist's job to the pollsters." The "-ster" suffix is slightly jazzy (jokester, trickster, hipster) and not at all scientific; the people in the business do not like it.

> To the best of my memory, the first time the word "pollster" was ever applied to me [Dr. Roper informs the author] was in the summer of 1944, but again according to my memory it didn't achieve anything like its present currency until the campaign of 1948. Since we have always tried to do something above and beyond a mere nose counting job—seeking always for the reasons *why* people were going to do whatever it was they were about to do— I have always preferred to be called a "public opinion analyst." But the press—in its normal omniscience— apparently needs a shorter phrase and I haven't ever developed what might be called an active resentment against the word "pollster." . . . Our organization has never used the word "poll." When we started the first published "poll," we insisted on calling it "The Fortune Survey."

Dr. Gallup recalls an early use of the word in a book by Lindsay Rogers, *The Pollsters.*

See DEPTH POLLING; TRIAL HEAT.

POLLUTION, *see* **ENVIRONMENTALIST.**

POOH-BAH big shot; pompous functionary.

The word has a huffing and puffing sound, imitative of the "high MUCKEY-MUCKS" it describes. A favorite of Justus Lawrence, aide to General Dwight Eisenhower at Supreme Headquarters Allied Powers, Europe, the term has been given frequent political usage.

When the "McGovern Victory Special" rolled in June of 1972, Haynes Johnson wrote in the *Washington Post:* "They all climbed aboard that train today; movie stars, jocks, beautiful people, old politicians, new politicians, erstwhile Kennedy and McCarthy followers, big pooh-bahs of the press and other assorted people on the make."

In January 1977, columnist Joseph Kraft supported the doomed nomination of Theodore Sorensen as Director of Central Intelligence: "He is an avowedly political man, not the kind of antiseptic pooh-bah usually picked to build public confidence."

The word is sometimes thought to be derived from A. A. Milne's *Winnie-the-Pooh,* but Pooh-bear is not the source.

The complete derivation is given in this answer to the author's query by Stuart Berg Flexner, co-author of the *Dictionary of American Slang:*

> *Pooh-Bah* was first heard the night of March 14, 1885, when Gilbert & Sullivan's *The Mikado* opened (in London's Savoy Theatre, the one Richard D'Oyly Carte built for their operas). Pooh-Bah was the name of the pompous bureaucrat

holding many offices and titles, though his real title was "The Lord High Everything Else."

Pooh-Bah really starts the action of the opera because he's the one who informs the Lord High Executioner Ko-Ko that he must execute someone within a month or lose his office, Ko-Ko eventually reporting that he has executed Nanki-Poo (the son of the Mikado traveling in disguise) who has fallen in love with Yum-Yum.

W. S. Gilbert loved these cute/humorous names, Pooh-Bah, Ko-Ko, Nanki-Poo, Yum-Yum, etc. Since he wrote the book and lyrics, everyone assumes he chose the names, and Pooh-Bah merely comes from his combining the two negative exclamations *pooh!* plus *bah!*, typical put-downs from a typical bureaucrat.

By the 1890s the English were using the name Pooh-Bah in a general way, to mean any pompous person with a lot of bureaucratic offices and titles (the English almost always retain the capital P and B though we don't). I don't find any info on when the term was first used in the U.S., but it obviously came from the other side of the Atlantic. Incidentally, the first A. A. Milne *Winnie-the-Pooh* book didn't appear until 1926, but since that toy bear is somewhat pompous and Milne was also a playwrite, liked Gilbert and Sullivan, and had Winnie say "pooh" a lot, he may have had Pooh-Bah in the back of his mind.

In 1968 King Taufa'ahau Tupou IV, the 300-pound monarch of Tonga (an island group between New Zealand and Samoa) presided over the Independence Day of his nation happily, and confided: "I'm a bit of a Pooh-Bah, you know, except that I don't cut off any heads."

POPULIST attuned to the needs of "the people"; now used with a con-

notation of old-fashioned radicalism; a liberalism rooted deeply in U.S. history.

Lyndon Johnson was called by friendly writers a political leader "in the old populist tradition." When Jimmy Carter inveighed against favoritism (and the Nixon pardon) in his 1976 acceptance speech with "I see no reason why big-shot crooks should go free, while the poor ones go to jail"—that, too, was described as "populist."

The word is used today with a small *p* as a reminder of the theories rather than the structure of the Populist or "People's party" (see PARTY OF THE PEOPLE), which was a political party of a radical nature that won substantial backing in the U.S.

Periodic depressions and a conviction that the government was dominated by large money interests inimical to both the farmer and the mechanic led to some informal alliances between these groups and socialists. In 1890 a state party calling itself the People's party was founded in Kansas. In that same year, various Farmer's Alliance groups, founded largely to fight the railroads, scored heavily in the South and the West; there, candidates advocating new economic legislation favored by the Alliances were elected in five senatorial contests, six gubernatorial, and forty-six congressional races.

This led to the organization of a national "Populist" party in 1891. At its convention in Omaha it demanded, among other things, public ownership of the railroads, the telegraph and telephone systems; direct election of U.S. senators; a graduated income tax; and cheaper money. The delegates, coming predominantly from the farmers' organizations and the Knights of Labor, wrote a radical platform calling for "a permanent and perpetual . . . union of the labor forces of the United States. . . . The interests of rural and civic [urban] labor are the same, their enemies are identical. . . . We believe that the time has come when the railroad corporations will either own the people, or the people must own the railroads."

Other planks were no more friendly to capitalists. When the Populist candidate, General James B. Weaver, won 22 electoral-college and 1,029,846 popular votes in the 1892 election, many people, including some considered liberals, were fearful of impending revolution.

Watching Populist congressmen in action, novelist Hamlin Garland foresaw "a great periodic upheaval similar to that of '61. Everywhere as I went through the aisles of the House, I saw and heard it . . . the House is a smouldering volcano." A woman announced she was going to Europe "to spend my money before those crazy people take it."

The party lingered on until 1908, but most of its members had returned to the Democratic fold by then and the word is used now by politicians who want to identify with "the little man," who can be found under JOHN Q. PUBLIC.

PORK BARREL the state or national treasury, into which politicians and government officials dip for "pork," or funds for local projects.

The classic example of the pork barrel is the Rivers and Harbors bill, a piece of legislation that provides morsels for scores of congressmen in the form of appropriations for dams and piers, highways and bridges.

The phrase probably is derived from the pre–Civil War practice of periodically distributing salt pork to the slaves from huge barrels. C. C.

Maxey wrote in the *National Municipal Review* in 1919:

Oftentimes the eagerness of the slaves would result in a rush upon the pork barrel, in which each would strive to grab as much as possible for himself. Members of Congress in the stampede to get their local appropriation items into the omnibus river and harbor bills behaved so much like Negro slaves rushing the pork barrel, that these bills were facetiously styled ."pork barrel" bills, and the system which originated them has thus become known as the pork-barrel system.

A story by E. E. Hale called "The Children of the Public," which appeared in an 1863 issue of *Frank Leslie's Illustrated Newspaper,* probably also helped popularize the term. In Chapter I, entitled "The Pork Barrel," Hale wrote: "We find that, when an extraordinary contingency arises in life, as just now in ours, we have only to go to our pork barrel, and the fish rises to our hook or spear."

By the 1870s, congressmen were regularly referring to "pork," and the word became part of the U.S. political lexicon. *Time* magazine noted in 1948 that one Peter J. McGuinness "fished in Tammany's pork barrel for 28 years to bring improvement to 'me people.' " In a Baltimore speech on inflation in 1952, Adlai Stevenson pledged "no pork-barreling while our economy is in its present condition."

Getting rid of the practice is next to impossible, as former Senator Paul H. Douglas, (Dem-Ill.) wrote: "As groups win their battle for special expenditures," he said, "they lose the more important war for general economy. . . . They are like drunkards who shout for temperance in the intervals between cocktails." See DELIVER.

POSITION PAPER a statement of policy on an issue in a campaign, for guidance of speechwriters and supporting speakers; in diplomacy, an *aide-mémoire* at an international conference.

Before any major campaign begins, bright young lawyers are brought in to work on position papers. They check past speeches by the candidate on the subject to be careful of inconsistency, draft the latest "new ideas" on the subject, farm out extra research to academicians specializing in the area. Papers are then drawn on subjects like urban renewal, agricultural policy, air and water pollution, transportation, crime, and housing; in more local campaigns, on "home rule" and traffic congestion, and in national campaigns, on foreign affairs and broad themes of social welfare.

The position papers are useful in briefing a candidate on areas he knows little about and getting a briefing from the candidate on areas he has definite ideas about. They are usually packaged in a looseleaf folder and made available to the writers and headquarters staff; in abridged form they may be sent to canvassers (see CANVASS) to equip them with answers to questions likely to be asked when they ring their doorbells.

A position paper is detailed, including a background statement of position; it should not be confused with a brief. When Adlai Stevenson said in 1952, "each day their statement of position moves in like a new fog bank," he was deriding sweeping Republican policy pronouncements, not detailed papers.

In diplomacy, a WHITE PAPER is a formal report issued by a government to define its policy; a *position paper* is a private guide to its diplomats. "A full-scale international conference involves difficult and intricate preparation," wrote Dwight Eisenhower; " 'position papers'—documents on all

conceivable issues, setting forth the position the government intends to present at the meeting—have to be carefully written and approved." He added sharply: "Position papers can be written only after a chief executive has decided precisely what his position is to be."

One-page position papers, prepared as answers to anticipated press-conference questions, make up a President's "black briefing book."

POSITIONS OF STRENGTH power from which to negotiate; diplomatic muscle.

Secretary of State Dean Acheson started the phrase, in slightly different form, on February 16, 1950: "The only way to deal with the Soviet Union, we have found from hard experience, is to create situations of strength."

By the process of double translation, into and from the Russian, the phrase has become "positions of strength" in current usage.

POSTER, *see* **SNIPE.**

POTOMAC FEVER the proximity to power that turns a PASSION FOR ANONYMITY into a notion for notoriety.

An ordinary human being whose statements have been ignored all his life will, upon taking a job in Washington, D.C., find his statements quoted and his picture appearing in newspapers across the country. The sensation that follows, often linked with the drinking of "heady wine," is euphoric; men who have always decried "personal publicity" find it necessary, after their appointment, to utilize the avenues of mass communication to get across their agency's message.

"The rivalry for the attention and

support of Congress," wrote Harry Truman in his memoirs, "was, in part, responsible for many news leaks. 'Potomac fever,' too, creates a great desire on the part of people to see their names in print."

Speaking to the National Newspaper Association in 1966 about his role as Lyndon Johnson's press secretary, Bill Moyers, pointed out: " 'Potomac Fever' can produce a bloated sensation—particularly in the area of the ego—that causes Press Secretaries to take themselves much too seriously. There are many symptoms of this, including hypervexation over the annoyances any reporter—especially the pathological troublemakers—can generate; myopia, which blurs their vision of things afar; and the tiger-in-the-tank syndrome manifested by supercharged reaction to criticism, justified and unjustified."

A similar disease, contracted before arrival in Washington, or a particularly virulent strain contracted while in Washington on a senatorial level, is PRESIDENTIAL FEVER transmitted by the PRESIDENTIAL BUG.

See POCATELLO, YOU CAN'T GO BACK TO.

POWER BASE   a politician's foundation of support, usually his home district or state.

A favorite axiom of Democrat Jim Farley was this: "The most important lesson for a politician to learn is that he must always be sure he can carry his own precinct."

De Tocqueville took note of this phenomenon in his *Democracy in America.* In aristocracies, he said, a member of the legislature "is rarely in strict dependence on his constituents." But in the United States,

a representative is never sure of his supporters, and, if they forsake him, he is left without a resource. . . . The seeds of his fortune, therefore, are sown in his own neighborhood; from that nook of earth he must start, to raise himself to command the people and to influence the destinies of the world. Thus it is natural that in democratic countries the members of political assemblies should think more of their constituents than of their party, while in aristocracies they think more of their party than of their constituents.

The importance of preserving this base of power has other effects. "There is nothing quite like a Curley or Hague or Crump or even a De Sapio in other countries that have well-developed party systems," writes Clinton Rossiter in *Parties and Politics in America.* "To be a real boss, and not just a flunky, a politician must have his own base of power and immunity from external discipline, if not from internal revolt."

Not even Presidents are immune from this requirement. Charles Hurd, in *When the New Deal Was Young and Gay,* notes that "all Presidents have had permanent residences that they maintained during their periods in office, partly out of sentiment and partly in order to maintain political 'roots.' "

The term "pissing post" is occasionally used to refer to one's power base, or home district, or political *pied-à-terre.* The author's attention was drawn to this phrase by Professor Edward Banfield of Harvard, who reported its use in Cook County, Illinois, as a "trivial base."

A surprise loss in his home district in Greenwich Village to Ed Koch (later Mayor of New York) toppled Tammany leader Carmine De Sapio from his position as the most powerful Democrat in New York State. For a method of maintaining communications in one's power base, see FENCE MENDING; BACKER.

POWER BEHIND THE THRONE
unofficial adviser of great influence; used to attack an Administration when the President himself is popular.

William Pitt the Elder coined it in 1770: ". . . there is something behind the throne greater than the King himself." Negro leader Frederick Douglass echoed it toward the end of the Civil War, but in a benevolent sense: ". . . we are not to be saved by the captain, at this time, but by the crew. We are not to be saved by Abraham Lincoln, but by the power behind the throne, greater than the throne itself."

Woodrow Wilson had his Colonel Edward House, FDR his Louis Howe and later Harry Hopkins, Eisenhower his Sherman Adams. In modern usage, a GOVERNMENT BY CRONY and KITCHEN CABINET are mildest in terms of extralegal influence; a power behind the throne is more severe, PALACE GUARD and a GRAY EMINENCE more sinister, a RUSTLING BEHIND THE JALOUSIES more feminine, and a *Svengali* or a *Rasputin* imply complete control from behind the scenes.

POWER BROKERS
those who control a bloc and can DELIVER its support; or, a middlemen trusted by disparate forces who can help bring about a coalition.

Though the President of the U.S. may exercise great power, he "is endowed with far greater responsibility than authority," says Douglass Cater in *Power in Washington.* "To make his office operable, the President often finds himself serving as broker among the power groups rather than as banker drawing on his own limited reserves of power."

Wilfred Funk traces "broker" to the French *brokiere,* or broacher, one who taps wine casks. The broker eventually turned into a middleman, handling anything from marriages to mutual funds.

Bismarck was known as the "honest broker" at the Berlin Conference of 1878 after the Russo-Turk War because all the powers involved won new territories except Germany. But the German Chancellor had achieved an important objective for Germany —the continued isolation of France. At the turn of the century Senator Nelson Aldrich, the Rhode Island Republican, was known as "Morgan's floor broker in the Senate."

During his mayoral campaign and often after he was elected, former Republican John Lindsay spoke scornfully, and often despairingly, of the "power brokers" (a phrase coined by Theodore White) who ran New York behind the scenes. A less detrimental reference appeared in *Newsweek* magazine in 1967. Discussing how critics of the Vietnam war boycotted a 1965 art festival sponsored by the White House, the magazine quoted a Johnson Administration official as saying: "Presidents deal with power. Power is real. Power is not pretty. And I guess these people don't understand power brokers like they do art brokers."

Novelist Peter De Vries told the "usage panel" of the *American Heritage Dictionary* in 1977 that he thought "power broker" was "an adroit coinage, but will probably turn out to be one of those tendentious words that proliferate the reality they presume to denote, so that soon we shall have powerbrokers under every bed just as now we have the establishment lurking in every corner." Former Senator Eugene McCarthy agreed: ". . . it doesn't describe either the political reality or the function of a broker." Nevertheless, the word (as two words) is in current, if declining, political use.

Such brokerage as does go on takes place in "the corridors of power," evoking images of transactions made while walking to and from the "center of power." British novelist C. P. Snow coined the "corridors" in a novel of that title, while Stewart Alsop popularized "the center" in the title of his nonfiction work.

POWER CORRUPTS a charge usually made by Outs against Ins to persuade voters that it's time for a change.

In a speech in the House of Lords on January 9, 1770, William Pitt the Elder declared: "Unlimited power is apt to corrupt the minds of those who possess it." Sir John Acton later amended this to: "Power tends to corrupt; absolute power corrupts absolutely."

Lord Acton's famous maxim was quoted frequently when Franklin Roosevelt was being chided for trying to pack the Supreme Court. John F. Kennedy also touched on the idea. In a speech at Amherst College in October 1963, honoring Robert Frost, Kennedy said: "When power leads man toward arrogance, poetry reminds him of his limitations. When power narrows the area of man's concern, poetry reminds him of the richness and diversity of existence. When power corrupts, poetry cleanses."

Some see politics as an inevitable sullier of souls. In a 1945 essay on "The Evils of Politics and the Ethics of Evil," Hans Morgenthau wrote:

Only the greatest dissenters of the age have been clearly aware of this necessary evilness of the political act. A great non-liberal thinker writing in the liberal age, such as Lord Acton, will find that "power corrupts . . . absolute power corrupts

absolutely," or he will, like Jacob Burckhardt, see in politics the "absolute evil"; or, like Emerson, in force "a practical lie" and corruption in every state.

Others have been less gloomy. "Power does not corrupt men," George Bernard Shaw wrote. "Fools, however, if they get in a position of power, corrupt power." In *The Short Reign of Pippin IV,* novelist John Steinbeck wrote: "The King said: 'Power does not corrupt. Fear corrupts, perhaps the fear of a loss of power.' "

See **ARROGANCE OF POWER.**

POWER ELITE a charge that there exists an interlocking directorate of moneymen, politicians, and military men who shape national policy no matter who is elected.

The phrase was the title of a book (1956) by sociologist C. Wright Mills, who held that "neither professional party politicians, nor professional bureaucrats are now at the centers of decision. These centers are occupied by the political directorate of the power elite." Mills said this elite was composed of "the political directorate," the "corporate rich," and the "ascendent military." Together, they formed "over-lapping cliques [which] share decisions having at least national consequences. Insofar as national events are decided, the power elite are those who decide them."

Journalist, later presidential aide Douglass Cater disagreed, calling Mills's theory "too pat to be convincing." He argued that "it would be difficult to document the thesis that an elite really rules on matters of national consequence . . . the growth of giant organizations has not brought cumulatively greater power to the individuals who head them. . . . The swaggering tycoons of business and labor unions no longer exist to dictate their demands to the subservient politicians. . . . Mills' concept of a sinister and cynical power elite hardly seems applicable to decision-making in Washington today."

As Mills argued in the fifties that a power elite kept intellectuals and liberals out of the decision-making process, conservative journalist William F. Buckley Jr. was arguing that an "establishment" of intellectuals and liberal politicians was freezing out the prudent, businesslike conservative who understood the American system best.

Mills's theory received an unexpected boost from Dwight Eisenhower in his farewell address. See **MILITARY-INDUSTRIAL COMPLEX.**

"Elite," a word used earlier to describe specially trained Swiss troops, came to mean the socially select; in this sense, it was widely popularized by a radio program of the thirties and forties, "Duffy's Tavern," "where de elite meet t'eat." In current political use, "intellectual elite" is a derisive term that appears to be as common now as "power elite." In the sixties, **WHITE POWER STRUCTURE** was the black leaders' phrase for "power elite," and "power structure" lingered into the seventies as "structure" became a vogue word.

Jet set and the *Beautiful People* are not usually members of the power elite, though the old elite and the new sometimes meet on press junkets. Columnist John Roche likes *mandarinate; media biggies* is a phrase that waggishly describes the potentates of the press; and *illuminati* is used to give an intellectual cast to the banal "celebrity." "Illuminati" has been in political use since 1800: "We have thrown some useful light upon the Illuminati of Connecticut and Massachusetts," wrote the *Philadel-*

phia Aurora, "and lately upon a similar propaganda in Delaware State." It originally described the holders of candles at baptisms.

POWER GRAB attempt to take over leadership; attack word on insurgents.

This is a curious phrase, since those who denounce a power grab do not call themselves "powerholders." Consequently, it is most often used by supporters once removed from the seat of power, with the implication that the reason the insurgents want power is not for the opportunity to render public service, but to have it for power's sake or to use it for their own selfish ends.

The phrase, along with **CARPETBAGGER,** was used often against Robert Kennedy in his successful campaign against Senator Kenneth B. Keating in 1964. Since both candidates were liberals, there was little ideological argument; Keating, to overcome Kennedy's fame and name, played on his opponent's reputation for ruthlessness.

This particular thrust reached its high, or low, point when a small boy appeared at a Kennedy rally carrying a sign: "Don't use *me* in your cynical power grab."

"Grab" is a classic political Americanism. The opponents of the Embargo Act of 1807 spelled the word backwards and called it the "O Grab Me" Act, because they felt it favored the agricultural interests of the South over the shipping and commercial interests of New England.

Railroad tycoons were attacked as "land grabbers" for the way they bought valuable land from the government at low prices, often by laying original track in serpentine patterns to pick up added acreage.

The "salary grab" is the best-known use of the word before "power grab." Congress in 1873 raised the President's salary from $25,000 to $50,000, gave raises to many other federal officials and judges, and increased a congressman's own draw from $5,000 to $7,500. This might have gone through with mild public criticism had not the raises been made retroactive to the start of the Congress then sitting. The "salary grab" became an issue, and the next Congress cut back all salaries except the President and Supreme Court.

POWERHOUSE   place of action.

In New York City, "The Powerhouse" is a nickname of the Catholic Archdiocese of New York, in recognition of the political and economic power inherent in the Church. (Similarly, the thirteen subcommittee chairmen of the House Appropriations Committee are called "the College of Cardinals.")

In an article on the Archdiocese in the *World Journal Tribune* in 1967, just before that newspaper's demise, the Church leadership was described as operating

> out of the south wing of the old Whitelaw Reid mansion on the east side of Madison Avenue between 50th and 51st Streets. (The north wing is occupied by Random House, a piddling operation—by Church standards—even after its recent merger with Radio Corporation of America.)

The press and some laymen refer knowingly to the Archdiocesan Chancery offices as *The Powerhouse*. The clergy, and others who have business there, call it simply "Madison Avenue." Interestingly, it is in the heart of the area advertising people also call "Madison Avenue." The same turf, but an entirely different world.

In a more general sense, the word is used to describe a place of action and turbulence. "Originally installed in the predominantly feminine East Wing," wrote the *New York Times Magazine* of the shifting position of the INTELLECTUAL-IN-RESIDENCE at the White House, "[John P.] Roche took just two months to become the first academic in recent White House history to be allowed into the powerhouse setting of the West Wing."

POWER POLITICS   political or diplomatic action guided by the principle that "might makes right."

Professor Hans J. Morgenthau, who became well known in the sixties for his attacks on U.S. policy in Vietnam, wrote in 1950: "The illusion that a nation can escape, if only it wants to, from power politics into a realm where action is guided by moral principles rather than by considerations of power . . . is deeply rooted in the American mind." He made the point that world politics as practiced in 1950 and power politics were synonymous: "The choice is not between moral principles and the national interest, devoid of moral dignity, but between one set of moral principles, divorced from reality, and another set of moral principles, derived from political reality."

"Reality" is the operative word in power politics. "Uncle Joe is a realist," FDR was reported to have said about Joseph Stalin. And REAL-POLITIK is now used interchangeably with *power politics,* though the former has a scientifically impersonal connotation, and the latter calls up a picture of a big nation pushing little nations around. PRACTICAL POLITICS has some pejorative connotation, but is usually considered the ART OF THE POSSIBLE. *Power play* is the art of running roughshod over the opposition.

POWER STRUCTURE, *see* WHITE POWER STRUCTURE.

POWER TO TAX ... the power to destroy.

"An unlimited power to tax involves, necessarily, the power to destroy," argued Daniel Webster before the U.S. Supreme Court in 1819. The case was the landmark *McCullough* v. *Maryland,* when the state of Maryland sought to tax a branch of the new Bank of the United States. The issue was federal supremacy of the young nation's monetary system, which sought to curtail the issuance of currency by state banks.

Chief Justice John Marshall, writing the Court's decision, agreed "that the power to tax involves the power to destroy; that the power to destroy may defeat and render useless the power to create . . . [the states] have no power, by taxation or otherwise, to retard, impede, burden or in any manner control the operations of the constitutional laws enacted by Congress."

In another decision in 1930, Justice Oliver Wendell Holmes wrote: "The power to tax is not the power to destroy while this court sits."

The phrase has current usage in attacks on the very institution it originally defended—the federal government and its tax policies. Arguing against a federal tax increase for 1967, economist Pierre Rinfret said: "The power to tax is the power to destroy, and a tax increase at this time would destroy our economic growth."

POWER TO THE PEOPLE slogan of dissident groups, especially the Black Panthers.

"Power to the Soviets!" was a battle cry of the Bolsheviks during the Russian Revolution.

In the 1960s, advocates of "participatory democracy" like Tom Hayden of Students for a Democratic Society were calling for a transfer of power to the "people," whom they were able to identify as themselves. Power became a vogue word of the civil rights movement (see BLACK POWER) later parodied as Irish Power and ultimately, for elderly people, Geezer Power.

"Power to the People," shouted with clenched fist raised in a mock fascist salute, was publicized as a Black Panther slogan at a meeting under the leadership of Bobby Seale in Oakland, California, on July 19, 1969. Earl Caldwell of the *New York Times* reported: "They came with long hair and in faded old Army field jackets, in bulky sweaters and in worn and ragged levis. Most of them were white; some were youthful hippies. The majority were students, and they came off the campuses fired with what they called revolutionary fervor. 'Power to the people,' they shouted. 'Power to the people.' They made it a chant and they used it again and again. When they did, their arms shot into the air with their fists clenched."

PRACTICAL POLITICS to some, a euphemism for cynical or dishonest dealing; to others, a coming to grips with the reality of people's prejudices and foibles.

"Practical politics," wrote historian Henry Adams in 1906, "consists in ignoring facts." The phrase was in current use at the time, having been popularized by British Prime Minister Gladstone in his "bag and baggage" speech of 1877, dismissing the Turks as "out of the range of practical politics."

A century before Gladstone, Edmund Burke's letter to the Sheriffs of Bristol made a case for practicality in politics: "I was persuaded that government was a practical thing, made for the happiness of mankind, and not to furnish out a spectacle of uniformity to gratify the schemes of visionary politicians. Our business was to rule, not to wrangle; and it would have been a poor compensation that we had triumphed in a dispute, whilst we lost an empire."

Thomas Jefferson, a student of Burke, surprised his friends with his willingness to occasionally set idealism firmly aside. "What is practicable must often control what is pure theory, and the habits of the governed determine in a great degree what is practicable." He considered his own Louisiana Purchase unconstitutional, but he told Congress the agreement with Napoleon must be ratified, "casting behind them Metaphysical subtleties."

The dual meaning of the phrase was evident in 1890, when Charles Ledyard Norton defined "practical politics" in *Political Americanisms:* "The minor details of party management, including practises that are corrupt and criminal, as well as those that are legitimate and honorable. The phrase in the sense was in common colloquial use in 1875."

Theodore Roosevelt, fighting President William Howard Taft for the Republican nomination in 1912, was offered a deal on delegates that might have won him the nomination, but he turned it down unless all "stolen" delegates were purged. See THOU SHALT NOT STEAL. After Taft had won, *New York Times* Washington correspondent O.K. Davis asked the former President why he had been so rigid. The reply defined a practical politician as applying to one who might cut a few corners but who

would not do anything basically dishonest: "Yes, I am a practical politician," said Roosevelt, "and I have played the game. But that was something different. . . . It had gone far beyond the mere question of expediency or political shrewdness. It was a fundamental question of morality."

Teddy's cousin Franklin Roosevelt was often accused of compromising his ideals and gave this Lincoln example to a group of young people questioning him about it: "Lincoln was one of those unfortunate people called a 'politician' but he was a politician who was practical enough to get a great many things for this country. He was a sad man because he couldn't get it all at once. And nobody can." FDR was also fond of quoting Grover Cleveland's practical remark: "We are faced with a condition and not a theory."

In the Eisenhower years, the word *practical* was used for *cynical,* though it fell short of *dishonest.* In his memoirs, Eisenhower told of the amazement of party leaders when he told them he was determined to redeem every one of the 1952 Republican platform's provisions. "More than once I was to hear this view derided by 'practical politicians' who laughed off platforms as traps to catch voters. But whenever they expressed these cynical conclusions to me, they invariably encountered a rebuff that left them a bit embarrassed."

Correspondent Arthur Krock, after the election of the Kennedy-Johnson ticket in 1960, used the word in the same sense as Eisenhower had used it: "Rarely had there been an instance of more cynical 'practical' politics than the choice of Johnson to run on a platform pledging him to major policies and legislation he has steadfastly opposed."

In the Kennedy years, and again in

the seventies, *pragmatic* gained popularity for political leaders who thought of themselves as "problem-solvers." Although "pragmatic" is rooted in "affairs of state," its meaning became close to "practical" with a modern flavor, and is now lodged between *dogmatic* and *principled*.

See REALPOLITIK.

PRAIRIE FIRE, *see* **WHIRLWIND CAMPAIGN; DISASTER META-PHORS.**

PRANKS, *see* **HARDBALL; DIRTY TRICKS; RATFUCKING.**

PRECINCT CAPTAIN a local commander of political TROOPS, equivalent to a sergeant in an infantry platoon; one who is called on to DE-LIVER the vote.

"In the old Tammany days," writes former Tammany leader Ed Costikyan, "a political captaincy was a much-prized honor. . . . Such a captain . . . would build up a following among his voters loyal to both his party, his leader, and to him. Ultimately several hundred people would follow his direction on election day, and vote for whichever candidates he told them to."

While the position still carries some local respect, the function has changed. The captain's job now calls for education and persuasion of voters by precinct leaders and their canvassers (see CANVASS) who might not be well acquainted with their target voters. With the welfare function of the local political organization taken over by the government, the captain's service function has been reduced to steering constituents through the maze of government machinery to get "what you might not realize you're entitled to."

With voters increasingly concerned with the campaigns for major office that they see, hear, and read about in mass media, the precinct captain's job is to point out the importance of local campaigns for minor offices, using the "top of the ticket" to help the rest of the party's slate.

Many political leaders at the top level recognize the importance of providing COATTAILS for local precinct workers to cling to, in return for turning out the vote for the major candidate on Election Day. That was why Mayor Edward Kelly of Chicago said in 1940: "Roosevelt is the greatest precinct captain I've ever known. He's made the job of our workers easy."

PRE-EMPTIVE STRIKE, *see* **PRE-VENTIVE WAR.**

PREFERENCE POLL, *see* **TRIAL HEAT.**

PRESENCE diplomatic word for "showing the flag"; particularly, a United Nations force on the scene to avert or end hostilities.

Traditionally, a great power would send a naval squadron to a trouble spot within its SPHERE OF INFLU-ENCE to remind the locals of the power the squadron symbolized. This is now considered heavy-handed. Modern diplomacy requires the dispatch of military advisers or an economic mission to establish a "presence" underscoring the power's commitment in the area. A specific "military presence" differs from the old-fashioned "showing the flag" by the continuity of the assignment—an extended stay rather than a brief display.

The word has a United Nations origin. In November of 1958, British troops left Jordan; despite inter-Arab "good neighbor" pledges, King Hussein's country was not expected to remain independent. UN Secretary-General Dag Hammarskjöld sent a thirty-man mission to Jordan headed by Pier Spinelli, Italian chief of the UN European office in Geneva. Spinelli's mission established what came to be called "UN presence" in Amman, Jordan, providing a steadying effect in the area by virtue of evidence of continuing UN interest.

Wrote Andrew Boyd of *The Economist:* "Hammarskjöld also proposed to appoint a 'high-level' representative at UN headquarters who could visit the various Arab countries as required for 'diplomatic actions.' But this official (at once nicknamed 'the absent presence') was never appointed; the Secretary-General found things going smoothly enough to dispense with the idea."

The UN presence was applied to all UN peacekeeping efforts "in the field" as in the Congo and the Gaza Strip. The idea was to keep the great powers out of small wars that could, with Soviet or U.S. intervention, become world wars. When Secretary-General U Thant quickly acceded to Egyptian demand for the withdrawal of the UN force in 1967, he was sharply criticized in the aftermath of the Arab-Israeli conflict.

By that time the usage had spread to non-UN bodies. The U.S. Sixth Fleet in the Mediterranean was "the U.S. presence" and the British Colony at Hong Kong was called "the threatened Western presence on China's border." But a part of the word's effectiveness is its vagueness—a presence can be a visiting diplomat, an aircraft carrier, a permanent military base, or a force of troops. Hammarskjöld, author of the idea, liked the flexibility of the term and insisted on what he called "a completely pragmatic" view: "There is a UN presence wherever the UN is present."

In 1978, Israelis striking into southern Lebanon to punish Palestinian terrorists announced that they would accept a UN presence in their stead; the presence called itself a "peacekeeping force."

PRESIDENTIAL BUG   a mythical insect whose bite results in PRESIDENTIAL FEVER; breeds best where the opposition has been swamped, or in an atmosphere charged with power.

The phrase possibly originated with Abraham Lincoln's "chin fly" story, told to Henry Raymond, editor of the *New York Times.* Lincoln's Treasury Secretary, Salmon P. Chase, was often critical of the President, perhaps because he wanted the top job himself. Raymond quoted Lincoln:

". . . you were brought up on a farm, were you not? Then you know what a chin fly is. My brother and I . . . were once plowing corn on a Kentucky farm, I was driving the horse, and he holding the plough. The horse was lazy but on one occasion rushed across the field so that I, with my long legs, could scarcely keep pace with him. On reaching the end of the furrow, I found an enormous chin fly fastened upon him, and knocked him off. My brother asked me what I did that for. I told him I didn't want the old horse bitten in that way. 'Why,' said my brother, 'that's all that made him go!' Now if Mr. C[hase] has a presidential chin fly biting him. I'm not going to knock him off, if it will only make his department go."

The only trouble with this story is that Lincoln's brother died before he was old enough to plow. Maybe Lincoln was exaggerating.

See POTOMAC FEVER; ITCH TO RUN.

PRESIDENTIAL FEVER a raging desire for the top job, accompanied by the "sweating out" of delegates' decisions.

New York Governor Al Smith said in 1924: "A plague on all individuals who would like to be president!" This particular plague is called "presidential fever," and was so termed at least as far back as 1858, when abolitionist clergyman Theodore Parker wrote: "The Land Fever is more contagious than the Presidential Fever, and equally fatal to the moral powers."

Leading up to his final SHERMAN STATEMENT, General William Tecumseh Sherman said in 1879: "I am not now, and do not intend to get, infected with the presidential fever." Five years later he phrased it slightly differently, as "infested with the poison of presidential aspiration."

In 1879, in tandem with Sherman, Republican James Garfield of Ohio was making feverish notes in his diary. On February 8: "I have so long and so often seen the evil effect of the Presidential fever upon my associates and friends that I am determined it shall not seize me. In almost every case it impairs if it does not destroy the usefulness of its victim." On April 20, 1880, two months before the convention: "I long ago made the resolution that I would never permit the Presidential fever to get lodgment in my brain. I think it is the one office a man should not set his heart upon." When Grant and Blaine were deadlocked, Garfield's name came up, the fever rose, and he became the twentieth President.

PRESIDENTIAL INITIALS, see INITIALS, PRESIDENTIAL.

PRESIDENTIAL SEAL, see BALD EAGLE.

PRESIDENTIAL TIMBER, see TIMBER, PRESIDENTIAL.

PRESIDENT OF ALL THE PEOPLE the desire of every President to represent a unified nation, not limited to any blocs, groups, or partisans that elected him.

Of course the President of the United States, as chief of state, *is* "President of all the people" not just those who voted for him. Yet there is a nagging doubt in the minds of most Presidents that they do indeed lead everybody; this doubt has led each President to urge the concept and many to use the phrase.

The first President to phrase the thought in the way that is now familiar was James K. Polk, in his 1845 inaugural address: "Although in our country the Chief Magistrate must almost of necessity be chosen by a party and stand pledged to its principles and measures, yet in his official action he should not be the President of a part only, but of the whole people of the United States." Since the idea was not to extend authority over those who did not vote for him, but to recognize and show respect for the right to dissent, Polk added eloquently: ". . . he should not be unmindful that our fellow-citizens who have differed with him in opinion are entitled to the full and free exercise of their opinions and judgments, and that the rights of all are entitled to respect and regard."

Herbert Bayard Swope wrote Franklin Roosevelt in 1936 that his strategy should be: ". . . to be firm without being ferocious; to be kindly rather than cold; to be hopeful instead of pessimistic; to be human rather than to be economic; to be insistent upon every man having a chance, and above all, to make yourself appear to be the President of *all* the people . . ."

Writing in 1963 about the early days of the Roosevelt Administration, historian James MacGregor Burns used the phrase: "Like Jefferson and Wilson before him, Roosevelt was starting his administration off on a high, non-partisan note. He would be President of all the people . . ."

President Harry Truman used "whole people" rather than "all the people": "As the President came to be elected by the whole people, he became responsible to the whole people. I used to say the only lobbyist the whole people had in Washington was the President of the United States." Truman biographer Cabell Phillips adds: " 'The representative of all the people,' which he conceived the President to be, was no simple slogan but a deeply felt obligation laid upon him by Providence."

Dwight Eisenhower used the phrase in his memoirs: "The man in the White House, I believe, should think of himself as President of all the people."

Eisenhower succeeded more than most in achieving a recognition of leadership by almost all Americans. Wrote Arthur Schlesinger, Jr., about Eisenhower's successor, John Fitzgerald Kennedy: ". . . it seemed that Kennedy suffered from the illusion so common to new Presidents (even Roosevelt had it till 1935) that he, unlike any of his predecessors, could really be President of all the people and achieve his purpose without pain or trauma . . ."

The President most closely identifies with the phrase, because of his often-expressed yearning for CONSENSUS, was Lyndon Baines Johnson. Speaking in Minneapolis on June 27, 1964, he used the phrase publicly for the first time and used it again often: "As long as I am President, this Government will not set one group against another—but will build a creative partnership between business and labor, farm areas and urban centers, consumer and producer. This is what I mean when I choose to be a President of all the people."

As can be seen, the phrase is favored by public figures and by historians. A joke during the 1964 campaign was: "If Johnson loses more than eight states, he will refuse to serve because he wants to be 'President of all the people.' "

In the sixties, as Lyndon Johnson's popularity fell, a related phrase came to the fore: the "only President we've got," taken from a frequent remark along those lines by Mr. Johnson. (In the seventies, when former Director of Central Intelligence Richard Helms said, "I only work for one President at a time," the single-President theme was accentuated.) Evidence that the "only President" phrase is part of the political language came in a July 9, 1978, column by Tom Wicker of the *New York Times*, satirically reviewing the Carter Administration as if it were a baseball team managed by Charles Kirbo, Carter's long-time confidant: " 'Remember,' drawls Country Kirbo, who has too many smarts to be a playing manager, particularly in this club, 'Peanuts is the only centerfielder we've got.' "

President John F. Kennedy took the idea a step forward: "For each President, we must remember, is the President not only of all who live, but, in a very real sense, of all who have yet to live. His responsibility is not only to those who elected him but also to those who will elect his successors for decades to come."

PRESSING THE FLESH   handshaking; any form of physical contact between candidate and voter.

The phrase, possibly originating as part of the rhyming jive talk of the 1940s, was politically popularized by Lyndon Johnson in 1960. "I just want to tell you how happy I am that you would come here and howdy and shake hands with us this morning," the vice-presidential candidate told small crowds at whistlestops. "You make us feel so wonderful to come out here and look us in the eye and give us a chance to press the flesh with you."

In the 1960 presidential campaign, a pickpocket in a Los Angeles crowd was reported to have groped inexpertly for someone's wallet and found himself, instead, shaking the hand of the Democratic candidate. Kennedy's grandfather, "Honey Fitz" Fitzgerald, was supposed to have perfected the art of the "Irish Switch": a technique of shaking one voter's hand while talking to a second voter, simultaneously smiling and winking at a third.

G. Mennen "Soapy" Williams, running for governor of Michigan, felt it was necessary to grasp the hands of at least two thousand voters a day. A *Detroit Free Press* reporter chronicled his method of working an auto plant in Flint at the time of a shift change, with hundreds of men streaming in and out:

> Williams was standing in a familiar position, straddling the two stairways the men must take for entering the plant. Perhaps one man in 75 would try to slip by the Governor without shaking his hand. He couldn't get away with it. Williams would quickly spot him veering away and give chase. Two or three quick steps and his long legs would be planted firmly in the man's path. He would reach out, grab the man's hand, pump it once and say: "Nice to see you." Then he would smile proudly and step back in front of the

two staircases, one foot blocking each.

Senator William Proxmire of Wisconsin estimates that he shakes approximately 300,000 hands a year and has a formula for avoiding politician's grip: always avoid the possibility of knuckle-crunching by shoving your hand into the voter's hand right up against the thumb.

Harry Truman's receiving-line technique was to use the handshake to pull the greeter along and deposit him with the next person on the line.

Politicians agree that "pressing the flesh" requires concentration on the crowd, even when "Irish Switching." Wendell Willkie broke this rule while campaigning in Rushville, Indiana, in 1940, and absent-mindedly shook hands with his own wife. When she protested, he apologized: "Gosh, Billie. Excuse me, I was thinking."

Senator Robert Kennedy often leaned across a platform and reached out with both hands to touch the outstretched hands, thereby covering more people than individual handshakes; Governor Nelson Rockefeller liked to backslap and squeeze arms with his familiar "Hiya, fella."

In an era of television campaigning, the necessity of physical contact is still with us; white candidates in black areas are especially told by their managers of the need to "press the flesh" and "lay on the hands" so as not to appear unwilling to be in close touch.

PRESS SECRETARY, *see* **GHOST WRITER.**

PRESSURE GROUP attack phrase on a lobbying organization or bloc advancing its own cause.

Political parties gain broad power over short periods; pressure groups seek narrow power over long periods. As organized labor "punishes its enemies and rewards its friends," pressure groups work inside the political system to promote their causes on a continuing basis no matter who is in power.

James Madison, in the *Federalist* Number 10, defined "faction" as we now use "pressure group": "a number of citizens, whether amounting to a majority or minority of the whole, who are united and actuated by some common impulse of passion, or of interest, adverse to the rights of other citizens, or to the permanent and aggregate interests of the community."

Although in Madison's view factions could operate for good or evil, the phrase "pressure group" has a bad connotation. Dwight Eisenhower, describing Henry Cabot Lodge's plea to him to campaign for President in 1952, said the former senator painted the possibility of "at least a partial reversal of the trend toward centralization in government, irresponsible spending, and catering to pressure groups . . ."

The common denominator in any definition of pressure groups is *interest;* if the interest is *special* or *vested,* the pressure is venal, but if the interest is *public,* the pressure is benevolent. "We call them 'interest groups' when we are feeling clinical," wrote historian Clinton Rossiter, " 'pressure groups' when we are feeling critical, and 'lobbies' when we are watching them at work in our fifty-one capitals."

See VESTED INTERESTS; LOBBY; BLOC.

PREVENTIVE WAR an attack aimed at destroying a prospective enemy before he can launch an attack of his own.

On November 20, 1948, Pacifist Bertrand Russell approached the subject in this way: "Either we must have a war against Russia before she has the atom bomb," he told an audience at the Westminster School, "or we will have to lie down and let them govern us."

Once Moscow acquired nuclear weapons, Lord Russell became more disposed to lying down. See BETTER RED THAN DEAD. But others have argued that preventive war might be preferable to a devastating sneak attack—presumably from Russia or China—in the future. There was some talk of it when mainland China threatened the offshore islands of Quemoy and Matsu in 1955 and again in 1958. During the Berlin crisis in 1961, John F. Kennedy told an interviewer that "a clear attack on Western Europe" might require the U.S. to use nuclear weapons first. As Theodore Sorensen wrote in *Kennedy,* "others read 'preventive war' or 'preemptive strike' overtones into this, but it was in fact longstanding policy and depended on an initial attack by the Soviets."

In Mario Pei's *Language of the Specialists,* Robert E. Hunter says that a first strike must be directed against enemy nuclear systems or else it will leave the attacker open to terrible retaliation.

A first-strike strategy might be adopted where an attacker has a vulnerable force, and must strike first (i.e. before being struck) if at all; where an attacker wishes to achieve "victory" through surprise attack, particularly against a strategically inferior nation (preventive war); where an attacker wishes to preempt a threatened enemy attack; or where a strategically inferior nation wishes to bring about catalytic war involving other powers.

Herman Kahn, in *Thinking About the Unthinkable,* notes:

Almost all authorities agree that at present the advantages of striking first are so great that, should there seem to be a high probability that the other side is actually attacking, it might be better to risk the certainty of a relatively small retaliatory strike, rather than the high probability of a much more destructive first blow.

Preventive war is still a phrase looked on with revulsion by most Americans; *pre-emptive strike,* however, lost much of its pejorative connotation when it was used to describe the Israeli thrust against the Arabs following Gamal Abdul Nasser's closing of the Gulf of Aqaba in 1967. See SALT (LEXICON).

PRIMARY   an intraparty election to select candidates for a forthcoming general election.

The *closed primary* is restricted to registered members of a particular party. In an *open primary,* voters may cross lines, regardless of their party affiliation, to vote for candidates of another party. See CROSSOVER VOTE.

Designed to give a party's rank-and-file a greater voice in the choice of candidates (and of convention delegates as well), the primary began appearing in the early nineteenth century. Mencken traces one to New York City in 1827. In the early twentieth century, the presidential-preference primary was launched by the progressive Republicans of the Middle West who wanted to reduce the influence of state party machines in the nomination of candidates. As governor of Wisconsin in 1901, Robert La Follette promoted a direct-primary bill. By 1916 both Republicans and Democrats chose a majority of their national convention delegates by this method. It lost ground for a time,

but in the early seventies more states saw political and publicity advantages in holding them.

Their importance is hotly disputed. In 1952 Senator Estes Kefauver of Tennessee won most of the preferential primaries he entered, but Adlai Stevenson won the Democratic nomination nonetheless. Stevenson considered the presidential primary "almost a useless institution." In 1958 he described it as confusing and time-consuming, and added, "Finally, it is terribly expensive; it's exhausting physically; you burn up yourself, you burn up your ammunition, you burn up your means. I think that it's a very, very questionable method of selecting Presidential candidates and actually it never does. All it does is destroy some candidates."

But it did get John F. Kennedy on the road to nomination in 1960, it provides a "shakedown cruise" for a campaign staff, and it settles arguments about vote-getting ability with some finality. By 1976 Jimmy Carter proved that the winner of most of the early primaries could gain an unstoppable momentum for nomination.

PRIORITIES, *see* **REORDERING PRIORITIES.**

PRIVILEGED   SANCTUARY base from which attacks can be made without reprisal to that base.

General Douglas MacArthur transferred the phrase from the religious or bird-refuge sense to the military-political in a communiqué on November 6, 1950, after the Chinese Communist "volunteers" entered the Korean War:

In the face of this victory of United Nations arms the Communists committed one of the most offensive acts of international lawlessness of historic record by moving without any notice of belligerency elements of alien Communist forces across the Yalu River into North Korea and massing a great concentration of possible reinforcing divisions with adequate supply behind the privileged sanctuary of the adjacent Manchurian border.

Nine days later President Harry Truman stated: "United Nations forces are now being attacked from the safety of a privileged sanctuary."

Since that time, the phrase has appeared in hawkish statements whenever a nonbelligerent provided airfields or supplies for belligerents, where a nation at war could not permit "hot pursuit" by planes or troops without enlarging the war.

The adjective and noun have been married at least since 1788, when Edward Gibbon wrote *The Decline and Fall of the Roman Empire:* "The ancient privilege of sanctuary was transferred to the Christian temples."

"Right of asylum," almost synonymous in one sense, is considerably different in political usage, meaning the protection granted by one state to an individual citizen of another. Oddly, the "right" of asylum is more of a privilege, and the "privilege" of sanctuary is more of a right.

In 1970 President Nixon ordered U.S. troops into Cambodia to counter a North Vietnamese invasion after a pro-Western government overthrew a neutralist regime. Explaining this move to the American people on television, he said: "For the past five years . . . North Vietnam has occupied military sanctuaries all along the Cambodian frontier with South Vietnam . . . neither the United States nor South Vietnam has moved against those enemy sanctuaries because we did not wish to violate the territory of a neutral nation . . ."

The successful operation, which Nixon carefully labeled an "incursion" rather than an "invasion," caused a sharp protest in the U.S. Anthony Lewis suggested this definition in the *New York Times:* "Privileged sanctuary: Area where the enemy can rest and regroup in safety. See Laos, Cambodia. Do not see Thailand, Hawaii, or other base and recreation areas for American forces."

PRIVY COUNCIL, *see* **BRAIN TRUST.**

PROBE, *see* **WITCH HUNT; WHITEWASH.**

PROCEDURAL SAFEGUARD, *see* **RED TAPE.**

PROCESS, THE the majesty of the machinery; the inexorable procedures of government; more broadly, the American way of self-government.

"I realize that, in our democratic process," said Office of Management and Budget Director Bert Lance in July 1977, "government officials at times come under public and political scrutiny. That is part of the process."

"Process" came into vogue in the mid-seventies, a clipped form of both "the democratic process" and the DECISION-MAKING PROCESS, and as a partial replacement for "the SYSTEM" in its positive sense. A favorite word of the Carter White House, it reflected President Carter's interest in the management of the workings of government. Vice President Walter Mondale, assessing President Carter's first year in office to a group of reporters at the end of 1977, said of the President: "Now he has had a year's experience. He has seen this process work first hand. He is anxious that in succeeding years that what he has learned about that process permits him to better schedule and pace his proposals."

Meanwhile, in the office of the Governor of California, an aide described Democrat Edmund "Jerry" Brown's approach to *Washington Post* columnist David Broder, who had been asking about "a core of policy" in Governor Brown's philosophy: "No, I see a particular kind of process reflected in the way the place operates and in the people who are here. He really does want a lot of dialogue. But no consistent philosophy. It drives a lot of people nuts when he quotes Gandhi: 'the means are the ends in process.' Sometimes it drives me nuts, too."

See MACHINERY OF GOVERNMENT.

PROFESSIONAL an experienced, cool political operative; or one who protests too much his allegiance to a cause.

For the definition of the first sense, see OLD PRO. For the second, See LIMOUSINE LIBERAL. In the second sense, the adjective turns completely around: a "professional liberal" or "professional intellectual" is one who poses as a liberal or intellectual but does not accept responsibility for the work of promoting a cause. In the same way, a "professional Irishman" is a politician who cultivates his brogue and acts in such a way as to appear to be the very model of what he thinks other Irish-Americans expect an Irishman to be, in an effort to identify with what may no longer be a voting bloc.

In 1918 Theodore Roosevelt used the word as it is used today: "Prominent, although not always powerful, among the latter are the professional intellectuals, who vary from the soft-handed, noisily self-assertive fre-quenters of frowsy restaurants to the sissy socialists, the pink tea and parlor Bolshevists . . ."

One prevalent use of the term today is not political: "professional virgin" is a frustrated suitor's epithet.

In the first sense, the antonym is "amateur"; in the second sense, the antonym is "authentic."

PROFILES IN COURAGE any courageous political act, in a phrase popularized by a 1955 book of that title by Senator John F. Kennedy.

"Richard Nixon etched his profile in political courage," wrote columnist Murray Kempton in 1966, "by mentioning the word 'Rockefeller' in Syracuse." This was a sardonic comment about Nixon's strong support of Rockefeller's gubernatorial candidacy in a conservative Republican area of New York. But the "profiles in courage" phrase is frequently used without irony (evoking memories of the assassinated President) whenever any act that will offend voters is undertaken by a political figure.

That was the point of Kennedy's analysis of the crucial moment in the lives of eight American politicians, mostly senators. "It may take courage to battle one's President, one's party or the overwhelming sentiment of one's nation; but these do not compare, it seems to me, to the courage required of the Senator defying the angry power of the very constituents who control his future."

This particular point was flung back at Kennedy, who had remained silent on MCCARTHYISM, by Mrs. Eleanor Roosevelt: "I feel that I would hesitate to place the difficult decisions that the next president will have to make with someone who understands what courage is and admires it, but has not quite the independence to have it." After blasts like these, a friend suggested to Kennedy that he had paid a price for giving his book that title. "Yes," he replied dryly, "but I didn't have a chapter in it on myself."

See POLITICAL SUICIDE.

PROGRESSIVE   a movement of social protest and economic reforms; a word now offering an alternative to those who do not wish to be labeled LIBERAL.

The late nineteenth century brought the first great progressive surge to the U.S. Russell B. Nye wrote in *Midwestern Progressive Politics:*

> Spreading outward after 1870, diminishing in force as it encountered increased resistance from adjacent and politically different areas, the so-called Midwestern spirit of "progressivism" (or "insurgency" or "radicalism") became a real force in American political life. The Grangers, the Populists, the "progressives," the "insurgents," the Non-Partisan Leaguers, even the Socialists represented phases of this movement.

Progressivism reached high tide in the first decade of the twentieth century. The "Wisconsin idea," a progressive experiment, bore fruit in Robert La Follette's governorship at the beginning of the century. In 1912 the GOP split into progressive and conservative factions, with Theodore Roosevelt leading the progressives. The split is still reflected in divergent wings of the party.

The word retains its attraction. For a time during and after World War II, it was pre-empted by the far-left followers of Henry Wallace, but its frequent use by Republicans—especially in the Theodore Roosevelt context—has restored its luster. In 1948, in an essay titled "What Is Liberalism?," Earl Warren, then governor of Cali-

fornia and later Chief Justice of the Supreme Court, wrote:

> I would divide people into three groups—reactionary, progressive and radical. I particularly like the term "progressive," not necessarily as a party label, but as a conception. To me it represents true liberalism and the best attitude that we could possibly have in American life. It is distinguishable from both reaction and radicalism, because neither of these philosophies makes for real progress. The reactionary, concerned only with his own position, and indifferent to the welfare of others, would resist progress regardless of changed conditions or human need. The radical does not want to see progress because he hopes that our democratic institutions will fail and that he will be able to take over with some form of alien tyranny.

Similarly, President Lyndon Johnson, in a March 16, 1964, interview, said, "I want to be progressive without getting both feet off the ground at the same time. . . . If I had to place a label on myself, I would want to be a progressive who is prudent." Housing and Urban Development Secretary George Romney had said on several occasions: "I'm as conservative as the Constitution, as liberal as Lincoln and as progressive as Theodore Roosevelt."

PROLETARIAT   the lowest class in society; or, the industrial working class.

From the Latin *proletarius,* a member of the lowest class in Roman society, the word entered the English language in the mid-seventeenth century.

Karl Marx defined "proletariat" in a critique of Hegel's *Philosophy of Right:*

> It is not the naturally arising poor but the artificially impoverished, not the human masses mechanically op-

pressed by the gravity of society but the masses resulting from the drastic dissolution of society, mainly of the middle estate, that form the proletariat, although, as is easily understood, the naturally arising poor and the Germanic serfs gradually join its ranks.

Marx's solution to proletarian poverty was never more forthrightly stated than as the conclusion of his *Communist Manifesto:* "The proletarians have nothing to lose but their chains. They have a world to win. Workingmen of all countries unite!" (The last line is often more excitingly translated: "Workers of the world unite!") More specifically, Friedrich Engels, in a letter to a friend in 1875, spelled out the steps by which the proletariat could gain power: "The organization of the working class as a class by means of the trade unions . . . is the very essential point, for this is the real class organization of the proletariat, in which it carries on its daily struggle with capital, in which it trains itself."

Communist dogma, of course, holds that "the dictatorship of the proletariat" lies just beyond bourgeois rule. Returning to Russia in 1917 to prepare for the Bolshevik takeover, Lenin wrote:

> The peculiarity of the present moment in Russia consists in the transition from the first stage of the Revolution, which gave power to the bourgeoisie because of the insufficient class-consciousness and organization of the proletariat, to the second stage, which must give power to the proletariat, and the poorer peasantry.

Joseph Stalin described proletarian rule in hard terms: "The dictatorship of the proletariat is the domination of the proletariat over the bourgeoisie, untrammeled by law and based on violence and enjoying the sympathy and support of the toiling and exploited masses."

Walter Lippmann, in a column called "How Liberty is Lost," urged the West in 1938 to avoid creating the conditions for a revolution in the name of the proletariat.

> The greatest evil of the modern world is the reduction of the people to a proletarian level by destroying their savings, by depriving them of private property, by making them the helpless employees of a private monopoly or of government monopoly. Unless the means of independence are widely distributed among the people themselves, no real resistance is possible to the advance of tyranny. The experience of Europe shows clearly that when a nation becomes proletarian, the result is not, as the Communists taught, a dictatorship by the proletariat but a dictatorship over the proletariat.

Lumpenproletariat, a German word dressing the lowest class in rags, is occasionally used for emphasis or out of affectation.

PROMISES, *see* **CAMPAIGN ORATORY; PIE IN THE SKY.**

PROPAGANDA   attack word on an adversary's ideas and publicity techniques.

Your side *disseminates information, deals with the issues, communicates the facts, publicizes the truth, gets the message to the people;* the other side engages in **PSEUDO-EVENTS,** *puffery, deliberate distortion, the* **BIG LIE, SMOKE SCREENS,** *media hype* and *propaganda.*

In two centuries, the word has traveled from religion to war to politics. The ninth edition of the *Encyclopaedia Britannica* (1875) has an archbishop covering the subject, pointing out its derivation in Pope Gregory XIII's commission of cardinals *de propaganda fide* in the sixteenth century, and Pope Urban VIII's *collegium de propaganda* set up in 1627 to train missionaries. In *Britannica*'s fourteenth edition (1929), the article is concerned with war propaganda; in the current edition, the essay is contributed by political scientist Harold Lasswell.

Senator Daniel Webster, speaking about a revolution in Greece in 1824, helped the word enter the political vocabulary in its adjectival form, as the "emanation of a crusading or propagandist spirit." President Millard Fillmore said in 1852 that the founding fathers knew that "it was not possible for this nation to become a 'propagandist' of free principles without arraying against it the combined powers of Europe."

The religious usage became limited in the nineteenth century, replaced by the political. An English magazine in 1844 wrote that "we did not fight to propagandize monarchical principles," and an 1843 dictionary of science, literature, and art by W. T. Brande gave a definition that is quite current: "Derived from this celebrated society [for the propagation of the faith] the name *propaganda* is applied in modern political language as a term of reproach to secret associations for the spread of opinions and principles which are viewed by most governments with horror and aversion." The transmutation of the word from evangelism to sinister political persuasion is not surprising: the word continues to carry its meaning of persuasion by faith rather than by fact. The sinister connotation was emphasized by books on war propaganda after World War I, with titles like *Falsehood in War-Time, Atrocity Propaganda 1914–1918,* and *Spreading Germs of Hate.*

Nazi Minister of Propaganda Paul Joseph Goebbels, however, raised the word and the art to an instrument of national policy and blackened its name forever. In 1923, he said, "It is the absolute right of the State to supervise the formation of public opinion," and in 1943 wrote in his diary: "Not every item of news should be published: rather must those who control news policies endeavor to make every item of news serve a certain purpose." See MANAGED NEWS.

In the U.S., "white propaganda" meant the selection of favorable items for persuasion, and "black propaganda" (jokingly called "impropaganda") the spreading of lies and false rumors. To dissociate our techniques from those of the Nazis, "psychological warfare" was a useful term. Publicist Leo J. Margolin added "paper bullets" in a book title, a phrase from Shakespeare's *Much Ado About Nothing.* A tried-and untrue technique of black propaganda is *disinformation*, or misinformation which is deliberately spread. CIA operatives were especially proud of the way disinformation—untrue statements inserted into the text of Nikita Khrushchev's "secret speech" and leaked by U.S. agents—embarrassed Soviet propagandists.

Despite occasional efforts to insist the word is neutral, that there is "good" propaganda, current usage is definitely pejorative. Charges of "Communist propaganda" and "imperialist propaganda" are traded, making this word (because of its Latin root and bad connotation) one of the few that mean the same to both Communists and anti-Communists. Sociologist Erwin W. Fellows wrote in 1959 that some of the wartime sting has come out of the word. "The recent shift to a less unfavorable attitude probably reflects . . . increased public recognition and acceptance of the use of powerful channels of communication by special interest groups . . . an increasing awareness of the techniques used to influence opinion and an indifference toward the content communicated."

While all this has been going on, the Society for the Propagation of the Faith continues its work, and visitors to St. Peter's in Rome continue to stroll up the *via Propaganda.*

PROPHETS OF GLOOM AND DOOM, *see* GLOOM.

PROTEST VOTE a ballot cast for a candidate who stands no chance of winning, registering dissatisfaction with the other candidates.

Eugene Debs, who served a term in jail for his opposition to World War I, polled 920,000 votes on the Socialist ticket in 1920. At least half of these were non-Socialists who "threw their vote away" on Debs; they were disillusioned with Wilson but were unwilling to vote Republican. See DON'T WASTE YOUR VOTE.

"Vote 'No' for President" was a button worn during the 1964 and 1972 campaigns. A voter unhappy with the choice in the TWO-PARTY SYSTEM has three choices: to pick the lesser of the two evils, to stay home, or to cast a protest vote. Whenever there is a third candidate in the field, he is likely to rate higher in public-opinion polls than his final vote reflects. This is because most voters talk protest during a campaign, but when it comes to the final moment in the voting booth, revert to party or choose the man with a chance whom they dislike least.

PROVERBS AND AXIOMS, POLITICAL GO FIGHT CITY HALL (resigned version); *You can't fight*

City Hall (helpless version).
YOU CAN'T BEAT SOMEBODY WITH NOBODY.

You scratch my back, I'll scratch yours. Attributed to Pennsylvania politician Simon Cameron, Lincoln's first War Secretary.

When the water reaches the upper deck, follow the rats. Attributed to FDR's Secretary of the Navy Claude Swanson.

To the victor belong the spoils of the enemy. William Marcy. See SPOILS SYSTEM.

Few die and none resign. Thomas Jefferson.

ROOT, HOG, OR DIE.
THE OFFICE SEEKS THE MAN.

In politics a man must learn to rise above principle. No attribution found for this, or its more recent version: *We'll doublecross that bridge when we come to it.*

IF YOU CAN'T STAND THE HEAT, *get out of the kitchen.* A favorite of Harry Truman's.

Never murder a man who is committing suicide. Woodrow Wilson. See POLITICAL SUICIDE.

Nobody shoots at Santa Claus. Al Smith. See SANTA CLAUS, NOBODY SHOOTS AT.

I don't care what the papers say about me as long as they spell my name right. Attributed to Tammany leader "Big Tim" Sullivan.

If you don't go to other people's funerals, they won't go to yours. (Put positively, this delightful proverb suggests that if you do go to other people's funerals, they will attend yours —as ghosts, presumably. No known attribution—probably some anonymous ghostwriter.)

If you have an elephant on a string, and the elephant starts to run—better let him run.

Forgive but never forget. Attributed to John F. Kennedy by Ted Sorensen in a 1968 television interview.

If it walks like a duck, and quacks like a duck, then it just may be a duck. (On how to tell a Communist, attributed to labor leader Walter Reuther.)

A rising tide lifts all the boats. John Kennedy, on how a general economic upturn affects specific depressed areas.

Any party which takes credit for the rain must not be surprised if its opponents blame it for the drought. Dwight Morrow.

Ticker tape isn't spaghetti. Fiorello La Guardia.

Never hold discussions with the monkey when the organ grinder is in the room. Attributed to Winston Churchill, replying to a query from the British ambassador in Rome as to whether he should raise a question with Mussolini or Count Ciano, his Foreign Minister.

Don't roll up your pants legs before you get to the stream. Congressman Emanuel Celler (D-N.Y.).

You can't make a soufflé rise twice. Alice Roosevelt Longworth, on Thomas E. Dewey's second presidential campaign.

No man ever went broke underestimating the intelligence of the American voter. H. L. Mencken.

How you stand depends on where you sit. Attributed to former Bureau of the Budget employee Rufus E. Miles, by University of Chicago professor Arnold Weber.

When the going gets tough, the tough get going. Attributed to John Mitchell by Jeb McGruder during the Watergate hearings; earlier attribution to Joseph P. Kennedy.

You can get a lot more done with a kind word and a gun, than with a kind word alone. Gangster Al Capone, quoted jocularly by economist Walter Heller, in connection with wage and price controls.

If it ain't broke, don't fix it. Bert Lance, President Carter's Director of the Office of Management and Budget, on government reorganization.

Every man has his price. From a comment made in the House of Commons in 1734 by Sir Robert Walpole: "I know the price of every man in this House . . ."

Don't just do something, stand there! An objection to government meddling; used in a speech in 1970 by Labor Secretary George Shultz.

Speak softly and always carry a big stick. The saying is always identified with Theodore Roosevelt, but he attributed it in this manner: "I have always been fond of the West African proverb . . ."

Watch what we do, not what we say. Attorney General John Mitchell.

Whenever you have to start explaining—you're in trouble. Barber Conable (R-N.Y.).

The duty of an Opposition is to oppose. Attributed by Lord Derby to a Whig named Tierney. See DISH THE WHIGS.

PROXY WAR great-power hostility expressed through client states.

"The first case of a proxy war between China and the Soviet Union," was the way National Security Adviser Zbigniew Brzezinski described the fighting between Vietnam and Cambodia that resulted in a break of relations on New Year's Eve of 1978. He cautioned that the two nations had a tradition of enmity, "but the larger international dimension of the conflict speaks for itself."

Cambodian Communists had the support of the People's Republic of China, while the Soviet Union supported Vietnam. Tass, the official Soviet news agency, wanted no part of a "proxy war" and charged Mr. Carter's aide with trying to "palm off the desired as reality" and attempting to "whip up animosity between the peoples of China and the Soviet Union."

The phrase is probably rooted in "proxy fight": attempt to get control of a corporate management through a contest for stockholders' proxy votes. Its first citations are in 1955, taken to mean "localized conflict", then synonymous with "brush-fire war"—meaning a war that was likely to spread quickly unless put out.

PSEPHOLOGY the study of elections and voting behavior.

In their 1970 book, *The Real Majority: An Extraordinary Examination of the American Electorate,* Richard M. Scammon and Ben J. Wattenberg popularized the word and provided the derivation: "from the Greek *psephos,* or pebble. The derivation comes from the ancient Greek custom of voting by dropping colored pebbles into the equivalent of our ballot box."

The authors had a significant impact on the 1970 congressional elections with their argument that "the social issue" was becoming decisive—that voters were most concerned with unrest, alienation, drugs, crime, and changing morality rather than the traditional bread-and-butter issue. Candidates of both parties made much of the social issue, and not until late in the campaign did Democrats take advantage of the economic issue, which Republicans had feared most all along.

The Greek pebble-dropping provides the root for a more familiar political word. The Greek *ballein* means "to throw" and is the origin of both "bullet" and "ballot."

Time editor Ronald Kriss credits the coinage of psephology to writer Michael Demarest in the 1964 election issue of *Time.*

PSEUDO-EVENT contrived news; a happening that is made to take place for the purpose of the coverage it will get, or centered on people famous for being well known.

The phrase is Dr. Daniel Boorstin's, coined in *The Image; or, What Happened to the American Dream?* Boorstin, now Librarian of Congress, held that American life has become unreal, based on illusion and images, with heroes replaced by celebrities. The manufactured "event"—a headquarters opening, a press conference for the dissemination of nothing much, a staged picture of a ribbon-cutting or "topping out" ceremony—have taken the place of much real news, designed to manipulate and promote rather than inform. As Boorstin puts it, a pseudo-event "is not a train wreck or an earthquake, but an interview."

The predecessor phrase was "pseudo-statement" used by I. A. Richards in his 1926 *Science and Poetry*: "A pseudo-statement is a form of words which is justified entirely by its effect in releasing or organizing our impulses and attitudes . . . a statement, on the other hand, is justified by its truth."

Reporter Richard Rovere described Senator Joseph McCarthy's skillful use of the press:

He knew how to get into the news even on those rare occasions when invention failed him and he had no un-facts to give out. For example, he invented the morning press conference called for the purpose of announcing an afternoon press conference. . . . This would gain him a headline in the afternoon papers:

"New McCarthy Revelations Awaited in Capital." Afternoon would come, and if McCarthy had something, he would give it out, but often enough he had nothing, he wasn't quite ready, that he was having difficulty in getting some of the "documents" he needed or that a "witness" was proving elusive. Morning headlines: "Delay Seen in McCarthy Case—Mystery Witness Being Sought."

Why are Americans prone to a diet of pseudo-events? Because, wrote Boorstin, "Pseudo-events are more sociable. . . . Their occurrence is planned for our convenience."

Boston University political scientist Murray B. Levin, in an analysis of the Edward Kennedy–Edward McCormack Massachusetts Democratic senatorial primary in 1962, suggested that "Edward Kennedy's rise to power and subsequent political stardom, and that of many other candidates, was based partly on . . . Kennedy's ability to pay for the services of men expert in the business of creating and selling pseudo-events."

The concept of the pseudo-event overdramatizes the degree of successful manipulation in American commercial and political affairs; a surprising and newsworthy position taken in an interview is not rendered counterfeit by the fact that it was arranged for maximum coverage. But the idea and the phrase are helpful in both planning for and watching out for "pseudo-events."

In the 1972 campaign for the Democratic presidential nomination, several candidates announced their intention to formally announce their candidacy at a later time. That ploy qualified as a pseudo pseudo-event.

The phrase seems to be in the process of being replaced by MEDIA EVENT.

PUBLIC INTEREST, CONVENIENCE AND NECESSITY

phrase binding the broadcasting industry to a degree of public-service programming, as they act as licensees of the public airwaves.

The phrase has traveled a long legal road. The Federal Communications Commission informs the author that "Picon's" predecessor can be found in the Interstate Commerce Act of 1887, as "public convenience and necessity." Before that, in 1876, in *Munn v. Illinois,* 94 U.S. 113, the Supreme Court permitted regulation of prices in a "business affected with a public interest." A new word was slipped into the phrase in the Radio Act of 1927, Public Law 632: "Public convenience, interest or necessity." In 1934, when the Communications Act was passed, an unknown legislator apparently felt that "public convenience" sounded too much like a toilet, and switched the words around to their present "public interest, convenience and necessity."

Speaking to a group of broadcasters while he was still a senator, John F. Kennedy said:

Will the politician's desire for reelection—and the broadcaster's desire for rating—cause both to flatter every public whim and prejudice—to seek the lowest common denominator of appeal—to put public opinion at all times ahead of the public interest? For myself, I reject that view of politics, and I urge you to reject that view of broadcasting.

In current usage, "public interest" has become a useful antonym to VESTED INTEREST and "special, selfish interest." Franklin Roosevelt used it in his 1936 annual message to Congress, appealing from "the clamor of many private and selfish interests, yes, an appeal from the clamor of partisan interest, to the ideal of the public interest."

The phrase can be traced back at least two centuries to England's Lord Chief Justice Hale's treatise on private property: when "affected with a public interest, it ceases to be *juris privati* only."

Who determines the public interest? Often the "public" member of a board or commission, who serves with an industry member and perhaps a labor member. But the public, writes sociologist C. Wright Mills, "consists of the unidentified and the nonpartisan in a world of defined and partisan interests. . . . What the 'public' stands for, accordingly, is often a vagueness of policy (called 'open-mindedness'), a lack of involvement in public affairs (known as 'reasonableness') and a professional disinterest (known as 'tolerance')."

PUBLIC OFFICE IS A PUBLIC TRUST phrase popularized by Grover Cleveland, used today in charges of graft or calls for codes of ethics for public officials.

"When a man assumes a public trust," Thomas Jefferson remarked to Baron von Humboldt in 1807, "he should consider himself as public property."

A variety of public men and writers began to mold this into a useful phrase. Henry Clay in 1829: "Government is a trust, and the officers of the government are trustees; and both the trust and the trustees are created for the benefit of the people."

Senator John C. Calhoun, in 1835, began a paragraph: "So long as offices were considered as public trusts, to be conferred on the honest, the faithful, and capable, for the common good, and not for the benefit or gain of the incumbent or his party . . ." By 1872 Senator Charles Sumner was observing, "The phrase, 'public office is a

public trust' has of late become common property."

The Democratic national platform in 1876 muddied up the phrase as follows: "Presidents, vice-presidents, judges, senators, representatives, cabinet officers—these and all others in authority are the people's servants. Their offices are not a private prequisite; they are a public trust."

W. C. Hudson, a newsman working for Grover Cleveland in the campaign of 1884, was looking for a phrase to embody integrity in government. He recalled the 1876 platform statement, and found in previous Cleveland speeches statements like "Public officials are the trustees of the people" and "We are the trustees and agents of our fellow citizens, holding their funds in sacred trust." Hudson felt all this provided the basis for a slogan and wrote later:

I went at the making of one. . . . Public Office is a Public Trust was the result. . . . It was the dogmatic form of what he had expressed with greater elucidation. . . . I took it to the Governor for his inspection. His eye at once went to the top line and pointing to it, he asked:

"Where the deuce did I say that?"

"You've said it a dozen times publicly, but not in those few words," I replied.

"That's so," he said. "That's what I believe. That's what I've said a little better because more fully."

"But this has the merit of brevity," I persisted, "and that is what is required here. The question is, Will you stand for this form?"

"Oh, yes," replied the Governor. "That's what I believe. I'll stand for it and make it my own."

Hudson later learned that the slogan had predated his coinage but insisted he had never been aware of an earlier use when he showed it to Cleveland. The phrase was accepted and used by everyone except Cleveland; as his biographer, Robert McElroy, pointed out: " . . . throughout the campaign, and throughout the remainder of his life, Grover Cleveland continued to express this, his most cherished conviction, not in the words of Hudson's brilliant slogan, but in ponderous phrases of his own which he persisted in considering better because longer."

Campaigning against Herbert Hoover in 1932, Franklin D. Roosevelt gave the phrase a twist: "Private economic power . . . is a public trust." Adlai Stevenson, in 1952, extended the idea of public office to those (like his opponent, General Eisenhower) who hold public confidence: "A man who has the confidence of the public has a public trust not to abuse that confidence for any ends, let alone his own."

PUBLIC TROUGH, FEEDING AT THE the practice of politicians and their hangers-on of fattening themselves on public funds; in current jocular use.

The phrase has Biblical roots, recalling how the Prodigal Son, at his nadir, ate from a trough with the swine. *Emporia Gazette* editor William Allen White referred to the story when, in the 1920s he rejected a friend's suggestion that he write a biography of Warren G. Harding. "It isn't Harding's story," said White of the late President and the scandal that followed his death, "it is the story of his times, the story of the Prodigal Son, our democracy that turned away from the things of the spirit, got its share of the patrimony ruthlessly, and went out and lived riotously and ended it by feeding among the swine."

An article in the *New York Tribune*, in 1881, noted that "the Republican Party is tired of bossism, quarrels about patronage, slavery to the machine, and the statesmanship of the feed trough." The word "troughman" was also used to describe a politician who spoons funds from government treasuries—that is, from the public trough. *The Nation*, in 1904, said grafters included "a number of lesser persons spoken of as 'troughsmen.' These used to be called 'henchmen,' then 'heelers,' but the newer word may be accepted without cavil."

A variation of the trough is the "public crib." In his *Thirty Years' View*, Senator Thomas Hart Benton wrote: "They have no other view than to get one elected who will enable them to eat out of the public crib." Still another variation, though one less redolent of corruption and the spoils system, is "public teat." Here the image is warmer, connoting a more paternalistic—or maternalistic —government.

Today the phrase is used less by critics than by politicians in a spirit of camaraderie. Perhaps this is because the image of a hog hungrily munching his garbage or a piglet rooting at its mother is too strong for criticism, crossing over into an area of mild irony. A politician often greets a friend who has just been elected or reappointed with "Still on the public teat?"

PUMP-PRIMING using federal funds to stimulate the economy, usually during a recession or depression.

In the *OED*, to prime a pump is defined as "to pour water down the tube with the view of saturating the sucker, so causing it to swell, and act effectually in bringing up water." The phrase became popular during Franklin Roosevelt's presidency, when vast expenditures for the Public Works and Works Progress Administrations were characterized as pump-priming.

"Most revolutionary of all," wrote Charles Hurd in *When the New Deal Was Young and Gay,* "was the theory that when business slackens, the government should spend money—even if it has to go into debt—to 'prime the pump' of the economy." During the 1937–38 recession, FDR said: "The things we had done, which at that time were largely a monetary and pump-priming policy for two years and a half, had brought the expected result, perfectly definitely." He blamed the recession on a drop in pump-priming caused by congressional economizers and the Supreme Court's nullification of several of his agencies.

Pump-priming, its critics point out, can be overdone. As a May, 1722, edition of the New England *Courant* pointed out: "No covetous person will use more Water to fetch the Pump than he designs to pump out again."

The phrase is current enough to be punnable. In June 1978 a *New York Times* editorial commenting on the plan of President Carter's media adviser, Gerald Rafshoon, to restore some of the imperial trappings to the presidency, was headlined: "Priming the Pomp."

See TRICKLE-DOWN THEORY.

PUNDIT a political analyst, usually associated with a newspaper or a sizable broadcasting outlet.

A *New York Times* editorial of 1921 admired the writing style of President Warren G. Harding: "[He] is not writing for the superfine weighers of verbs and adjectives, but for the men and women who see in his expressions their own ideas, and are truly happy to meet them . . . [it] is a good style, let the pundits rage about it as they will."

In his column about the press in the *Village Voice,* Alexander Cockburn wrote in June 1976: "The use of the word 'governance,' incidentally, is the sure mark of a pundit; the other favored word is 'polity.' "

The word lends itself to spoofing, since its first syllable is about word play. *Time* in the fall of 1977 headed an article about a conservative, pun-loving columnist: "Punder on the Right."

The word comes from the Hindu phrase for "learned man." A group of Yale undergraduates founded a club called the Pundits, sponsored by William Lyon Phelps. When Yaleman Henry R. Luce started *Time,* he recalled the term and began applying it, as a courtesy title, to playwright Thornton Wilder and columnist Walter Lippmann.

Today the term is widely applied to almost any member of the newspaper and radio-television fraternity encompassed in Eisenhower's "sensation seeking columnists and commentators." Historian Arthur Schlesinger, Jr., calls them the "PANJANDRUMS of the opinion Mafia."

Also to the American discourse contributed *Time: tycoon, moppet, socialite, cinemactor,* and *adman,* as well as the weird, backward construction of this sentence.

PUNT AND PRAY, *see* SPORTS METAPHORS.

PUPPET (GOVERNMENT) a nation or individual controlled by another; a SATELLITE.

Just before the off-year elections of 1966, Defense Secretary Robert McNamara went to the LBJ Ranch in Texas to appear at a press conference with President Johnson. After he made an optimistic report on the progress of the war in Vietnam, Richard Nixon said he had demeaned his office and called him a "Charlie

McCarthy," referring to the dummy created by ventriloquist Edgar Bergen which was popular in the heyday of radio (the late thirties, early forties). When General William Westmoreland visited the U.S. in 1967 to enlist support for a long, hard war, Senator George McGovern (D-S.D.) —in a speech calling for an end to escalation—said the general "is obviously doing both in Vietnam or in New York exactly what he is told to do by his commander in chief, the President." Senator Spessard Holland (D-Fla.) rose to say he did not think that "General Westmoreland is a Charlie McCarthy to come over here and tell the people of this country what someone else wants them to hear."

Puppetry is a deep-rooted political metaphor. Political satire was part of the *Punch and Judy* shows of the seventeenth century in England; *Punch,* a satiric British magazine first published in 1841, got its name from the lead character; and "pleased as Punch" comes from the self-satisfaction Punch received from his mischief.

In 1670 Baruch Spinoza used the metaphor in his *Writings on Political Philosophy:* ". . . the object of government is not to change men from rational beings into beasts or puppets, but to enable them to develop their minds and bodies in security, and to employ their reason unshackled . . ." John Adams, in 1775, warned of American subjugation in which "we should be little better than puppets, danced on the wires of the cabinets of Europe."

"Puppet government" achieved its popularity in World War II, when conquering Nazi forces set up local civilian regimes (see QUISLING); however, when Communist-dominated regimes were set up in Eastern Europe after the war, they were mainly referred to as "satellites" and only rarely as puppets.

"Puppet" is frequently used by Communist speakers to refer to small nations supporting the Western position. However, domination of small states is not so easy as it seems. According to McGeorge Bundy, former Kennedy and Johnson national security aide, "Anyone who thinks that the lines of influence from Washington are like so many strings to so many puppets has never sat at the pulling end."

PURGE   to forcibly eliminate opposition within a party; to retaliate for party irregularity.

The word entered the political vocabulary early: "Pride's Purge" in 1648 was the ejection of ninety-six Presbyterian Members of Parliament by Colonel Thomas Pride in the Cromwell era. In modern history, the term is most often associated with the bloody crackdowns of the Communists. As Thomas Dewey said in his 1950 lectures at Princeton: "In the Soviet Union and its satellites today the purge is both the instrument of change and the means of securing the leadership in undisputed control."

When leaders get the urge to purge, the NIGHT OF THE LONG KNIVES is recalled: on the weekend of June 29 to July 2, 1934, Adolf Hitler and Heinrich Himmler's Black Shirts pounced on eighty-three followers of Ernst Röhm's Brown Shirts and killed them all, establishing Hitler's complete control of the Nazi movement.

The bloodless purge, however, has also been used as an instrument of party politics in the U.S. In 1870, after the Senate defeated President Grant's attempted annexation of Santo Domingo, a party-wide purge followed. "Grant showed vindictive traits," wrote Matthew Josephson in

The Politicos, and there was much "cutting off of political heads." One victim was Carl Schurz, the transplanted German liberal who had fled to the U.S. after the abortive 1848 Revolution and later became a U.S. senator from Missouri. After refusing to back Grant on the annexation, Schurz found the White House door closed to him and complained to a friend: "Grant has read me out of the Republican Party." See READ OUT OF THE PARTY.

In the 1938 midterm election, Franklin Roosevelt tried to purge those congressmen who consistently torpedoed his programs—particularly three Democratic senators. All three won re-election.

Dwight Eisenhower on several occasions resisted the temptation to attempt a purge. When Senator Ralph Flanders of Vermont launched his censure effort against Senator Joseph McCarthy, for example, Republican Majority Leader William Knowland resisted and indirectly warned Ike against trying to punish him for it. As Ike wrote in Mandate for Change: "Sensing my sympathy with Senator Flanders' action, he [Knowland] cited President Franklin Roosevelt's efforts to 'purge' Senators he did not like. I told him that I would not be trapped into any purging action . . ."

John F. Kennedy was similarly mindful that a purge can backfire. But he also hinted that if he was re-elected in 1964, he would not be too kindly disposed to those in the Democratic party who had thwarted his programs or had opposed him personally. "We can make loyalty to the ticket the test in 1964," he said in 1962, "and then we can deal with those who failed to support the ticket."

In 1970 Vice President Agnew denounced Republican Senator Charles Goodell of New York, who was trailing his Democratic and Conservative opponents, as a RADIC-LIB. As expected, many anti-Agnew Democrats switched to Goodell, enabling Conservative James Buckley to win. In 1978, Republican National Chairman Bill Brock denounced right-wing challenges to liberal Republican officeholders as "cannibalism." See IDEOLOGY.

PUSSYFOOTING   sidestepping an issue; being mealy-mouthed; not treading where angels fear to tread.

This was a sobriquet of W. E. "Pussyfoot" Johnson, an ardent advocate of Prohibition, who was so named because of his stealthy, unrelenting, catlike approach to revenue-evaders in the Indian Territory. "Special Agent Johnson," wrote the Muskogee (Georgia) Democrat in 1907, "he of the 'Panther' tread, has resented the action of the peddlers of bogus beer and had them all indicted by the Grand Jury. It is evidently lèse majesté to sue a velvet-shod emissary of Uncle Sam's Booze Department."

The word probably began with a note of sneakiness: earliest noted reference was in Scribner's magazine of 1893, about men who "were beginning to walk pussy-footed and shy at shadows"; the Atlanta Constitution later spotted Theodore Roosevelt's Vice President, Charles Warren Fairbanks, "pussyfooting it around Washington."

Pussyfooting has lost its stealthy connotation and has acquired a meaning of evasion of hard issues. James Farley wrote in 1932: "We Democrats must meet the issue fairly, without any pussyfooting." Wendell Willkie in 1944: "I'm getting pretty sick of the pussyfooters who try to catch the WPA and the National Association of Manufacturers with the same kind of talk."

Pussyfoot today has a more cautious, fearful connotation than *straddle* or *on the fence,* works harder at evasion than *sidestep,* is less blatant than *to carry water on both shoulders,* is less investigative than GUMSHOE, and is not as Machiavellian as being ALL THINGS TO ALL MEN. See CREEP.

PUTSCH   a minor revolt that fails; an unsuccessful attempt at takeover of the party or government machinery.

A *rebellion* is a *revolution* that failed; a *putsch* is a rebellion that was not considered a serious threat. History teacher George Johnson defined the word as "a *coup d'état* that went *kaput.*"

Adolf Hitler's Beer Hall Putsch took place on November 8, 1923, as the National Socialists, with General Ludendorff as a front, attempted to force the leaders of Bavaria to form a new government under Hitler. "The putsch," wrote William L. Shirer, "even though it was a fiasco, made Hitler a national figure and, in the eyes of many, a patriot and a hero. Nazi propaganda soon transformed it into one of the great legends of the movement." Hitler, tried for treason, was sentenced to five years, serving nine months during which he dictated *Mein Kampf* to Rudolf Hess.

Because of its Nazi association, *putsch* is used now as an attack word on insurgents in any political situation.

QUADRIAD   A grouping of four of the President's leading economic advisers: the Chairman of the Council of Economic Advisers, the Secretary of the Treasury, the Director of the Office of Management and Budget, and the Chairman of the Federal Reserve Board.

"We originally called this assemblage 'the Fiscal and Financial Advisory Group'," Walter Heller, former Chairman of the Council of Economic Advisers, informs the author, "but that was a cumbersome designation. I went to the unabridged Webster's in my office and turned to 'quar.' The word 'quartet' seemed prosaic, but then I came across 'quadriad' and was intrigued by the definition: 'a group of four—*rare.*' I suggested this in a note to President Kennedy, and the next time he saw me he said, 'You're a rare group, all right—we'll call it the Quadriad.'"

When the group meets without the Federal Reserve Chairman, it is called the **TROIKA**.

The designation is handy. On August 13, 1971, when President Nixon was discussing plans for a new economic policy at Camp David with a dozen advisers, he was able to cut the group down to decision-making size without offending anyone—including the speechwriter—by saying, "Now I want to meet with the Quadriad."

QUALITY OF LIFE   the pursuit of happiness unsullied by the drawbacks of modern life; excellence of environment, idealistically reaching beyond an improved standard of living.

Democratic candidate Adlai Stevenson used the phrases "quality of life" and "quality of living" frequently in the campaign of 1956. The phrase was probably coined by TV commentator Eric Sevareid, who answered this writer's query: "Long ago, I think in '56, I wrote a radio broadcast for a Sunday series we called 'Newsmakers' about the nature of Adlai Stevenson. I put in the phrase 'the quality of life' to try to describe his approach to the national condition as it differed from the stock New Deal approach which, it seemed to me, was pretty directly concerned with more quantities for every group. He read the script later, on an airplane trip; twice, in notes to me, he expressed gratitude for the phrase. He used it often in his speeches."

Stevenson, however, did not elevate the phrase to slogan status. Arthur Schlesinger, Jr. recognized its potential and did more than anyone to popularize it in the intellectual community. In 1955 he wrote a memorandum comparing the "quantitative liberalism of the thirties" to the necessary "qualitative liberalism" of the future, as the needs of people in a depression change in a time of affluence. This memo was published in the *Reporter* magazine in the spring of 1956.

When conservation and pollution, in the mid-sixties, suddenly became transfigured into "the environment" and a new political cause, the "quality of life" phrase was born again—this time to stress the other-than-material needs of the AFFLUENT SOCIETY.

The phrase is now an unassailable political cliché, indispensable to environmentalists, useful as shorthand for orators appealing to youthful voters turned off by promises of a higher standard of living.

A related cliché is "life style," sociologese for "way of life." (Vice President Agnew castigated the drug culture as "a lifestyle that has neither life nor style.") That word was coined by psychologist Alfred Adler in 1929.

"Quality of life," so well established as a generalized national goal, is overdue for a turnaround, but proponents of zero population growth have yet to denounce "the quantity of life."

See ENVIRONMENTALIST.

QUARANTINE euphemism for blockade, or one-sided embargo.

The health of the BODY POLITIC has long been a rich vein of metaphor for politicians. Jefferson talked of "the disease of liberty" and Lincoln of "the scourge of war."

In the fall of 1937 Franklin Roosevelt wanted to speak out against Hitler and Mussolini. Norman Davis of the State Department drafted a speech that included the phrase "war is contagion." Harold Ickes told Roosevelt that a neighborhood had a right to "quarantine" itself against threatened infection; according to the Interior Secretary, FDR jotted down

the word and said he would use it sometime.

"When an epidemic of physical disease starts to spread," FDR said in Chicago, "the community approves and joins in a quarantine of the patients in order to protect the health of the community against the spread of the disease." How to stop this "epidemic of world lawlessness"? He ended on an ambivalent note: "We are adopting such measures as will minimize our risk of involvement, but we cannot have complete protection in a world of disorder . . ."

The next day, reporters led by Ernest K. Lindley (see "Lindley Rule," under NOT FOR ATTRIBUTION) tried to pin him down. How did a quarantine fit in with a policy of neutrality laid down by act of Congress? "I can't give you any clue to it," the President parried, "you will just have to invent one . . ." How about sanctions? "Sanctions is a terrible word. They are right out the window." Is a quarantine a sanction? "No. I said don't talk about sanctions." A reporter said, "This is no longer neutrality." Roosevelt replied, "On the contrary, it might be a stronger neutrality."

By the time John F. Kennedy was faced with the threat of Russian missiles installed in Cuba, the word "quarantine" was installed in the American political lexicon as a kind of stern but peaceful act risking dangerous involvement in a good cause.

Kennedy, according to Roger Hilsman, "again repeated his preference for a blockade and at this time supplied the word quarantine to describe it. This was a phrase with obvious political advantages both at home, where it was reminiscent of President Roosevelt's 'quarantining the aggressors' speech, and abroad, where it struck a less belligerent note than the word blockade."

QUICK AND THE DEAD, THE

the living contrasted with the dead; phrase used by ELDER STATESMAN Bernard Baruch to dramatically pose the choice of mankind in the atomic age.

"My fellow citizens of the world," said Bernard Baruch on June 14, 1946, to a UN meeting in New York's Hunter College gymnasium, "we are here to make a choice between the quick and the dead. . . . That is our business. Behind the black portent of the new atomic age lies a hope which, seized upon with faith, can work our salvation. . . . We must elect World Peace or World Destruction."

The Baruch Plan for an international authority of atomic inspection "with teeth in it" was bravely proposed, supported strongly by President Truman, but was met coldly by the Soviets and took some criticism from the U.S. Senate. It might, however, have begun some foundation-laying for a nuclear test-ban treaty that took place almost twenty years later.

The Baruch phrase might have been the work of his publicist and friend, Herbert Bayard Swope, who said it was; however, while Baruch freely admitted his "COLD WAR" phrase was Swope's, he would never credit the former *World* editor with "the quick and the dead."

The phrase occurs twice in the Bible (Acts 10:42, 1 Peter 4:5) in the context of Judgment Day. In Shakespeare's *Hamlet,* Laertes leaped into Ophelia's grave saying, "Now pile your dust upon the quick and dead . . ."

The phrase is recalled from time to time by columnists writing about disarmament. In 1963 Arthur Krock wrote in the *New York Times:*

> It has been a long time since Bernard M. Baruch, representing the

United States, offered the U.S.S.R. the "choice between the quick and the dead" that he said was presented by our proposal of a nuclear weapons test-ban, effectively supervised. The total absence of this proviso from the Moscow compact demonstrates, not only that time has passed, but also the whole concept that our national security can never be risked on the good faith of the U.S.S.R.

QUIET DIPLOMACY

behind-the-scenes efforts, held to be more effective in achieving desired ends than attempts to publicly embarrass another nation into acceding to the first nation's wishes.

"Through quiet diplomacy," Secretary of State Henry Kissinger told the Synagogue Council of America on October 19, 1976, "this Administration has brought about the release or parole of hundreds of thousands of prisoners throughout the world and mitigated repressive conditions in numerous countries. But we have seldom publicized our specific successes.

"The most striking example has been the case of Jewish emigration from the Soviet Union," Kissinger went on. "The number of Soviet Jews who were permitted to emigrate in 1968 was four hundred; by 1973 that number had risen to 35,000. The reason for this quantum leap lies largely in persistent but private approaches . . . quiet personal discussions . . . no public announcement or confrontation ever took place . . . When even greater advances were sought by confrontation and legislation, the result was tragic. Today Jewish emigration from the Soviet Union has dropped to 10,000 a year . . . moral ends are often not enough in themselves. The means used also have a moral quality and moral consequences."

Kissinger was attacking the "Jackson-Vanik amendment" to trade legislation that publicly and specifically tied MOST FAVORED NATION treatment to emigration policies.

The argument against "quiet diplomacy" was that without public pressure, neither the U.S. government nor the Soviets, with whom it was seeking détente, would enter into any talks at all to protect human rights; also, the dissidents within Iron Curtain countries wanted not so much specific loosening of their personal repression, but were willing suffer personal deprivation in order to induce basic changes in the Communist system.

Candidate Jimmy Carter, in 1976, firmly allied himself with the forces in favor of human rights publicly sought; after his election, he tempered his rhetoric. But observers noticed. "The shift in President Carter's human-rights campaign from shrill publicity to quiet diplomacy," wrote columnists Evans and Novak in October 1977, ". . . has cost him a powerful cutting edge for domestic politics, but quiet diplomacy . . . may be having a more productive impact on Moscow than the headlines of early 1977."

The counter to that was expressed by Senator Daniel P. Moynihan (D-N.Y.), one of the earliest spokesmen for the human rights campaign, in a *Commentary* article: "It is entirely correct to say that quiet diplomacy is effective in obtaining concessions from totalitarian regimes with respect to particular individuals who need our help. But the result of proceeding in this fashion is that the democracies accommodate the dictators. The dictators let the occasional prisoner out of jail in return for our silence about those jails."

See HUMAN RIGHTS; SAMIZDAT; MOST FAVORED NATION; OPEN CONVENANTS; LINKAGE. For a 1967 usage, see SUMMITRY.

QUISLING a collaborator with the enemy; a traitor; one who cooperates with a foreign country in the overthrow of his own, and especially one who then serves in a PUPPET GOVERNMENT.

Major Vidkun Quisling, head of the Nazi party in Norway and of that country's puppet government during World War II, spawned the word. He was executed for treason in 1945.

On May 11, 1940, the *London Daily Express* turned the name into a word: "Two thousand Quislings had been rounded up by Thursday night." On May 22 the *Manchester Evening News* wrote: "Major Quisling, the betrayer of Norway, has given us one of the first new words of the war." In the U.S., *Time* magazine's issue of May 24 dropped the capitalization: "South America becomes very quisling conscious." The *London Star,* on July 10, explained why the word caught on: "The Norwegian traitor was cursed with a name which by its very sound conveyed all the odious, greasy wickedness of the man." The *Manchester Guardian* wondered on October 19: "So far the most significant and valuable addition in this war has been Quisling. Will there be a verb, to quisle?" There was not.

Quisling is an eponymous word, taken from the name of an individual. Other people whose names have become words include Captain Charles Cunningham Boycott, a land agent in County Mayo, Ireland; Miss Amelia Bloomer, American feminist; British General Henry S. Shrapnel; and a seventeenth-century English hangman named Derrick.

Eponymy in politics includes GERRYMANDER, SOLON, SHERMAN STATEMENT, ROORBACK, and the verb HOOVERIZE, meaning to conserve food, stemming from Herbert Hoover's relief activities in World

War I. Best known is MAVERICK. Once removed from eponymy are phrases like "to pull a Wallace" (to start a third party, to bolt) and "another Stassen" (a PERENNIAL CANDIDATE).

QUOTA the number permitted or required; in civil rights terminology, government-set numerical standards to require admission or employment of blacks, on the grounds that this helps to compensate for two centuries of discrimination.

The Latin *quotus* asks the question "How many?" In the first half of this century, the political use of this word was concerned with immigration policy (how many should be let into the U.S. from which other nations) or with discrimination against Jews and Catholics (how many should be allowed into medical schools, country clubs, corporations).

In the civil rights backlash of the 1970s, the word "quota"—like BUSING—became politically sensitive, as many who had been proponents of civil rights for blacks in theory did not like the practice; they believed it abridged civil rights for whites. When black activists sought a form of reparations for past prejudice, on the grounds that special preference was due to enable them to enter the "mainstream" of American life, this was attacked as "reverse discrimination"; the argument was made that the Constitution must remain "color-blind" or the courts would be filled with pleas for preference by every minority and ethnic group, undermining the tradition of the MELTING POT.

The critical words in the issue were "affirmative action," "goals," "quotas," and "reverse discrimination."

Affirmative action, as a phrase, was conceived during the Eisenhower Ad-

ministration; former Nixon Treasury Secretary George Shultz tells the author he recalls that it was being used in the 1955 White House Conference on Equal Job Opportunity. Evidence that this phrase was bubbling up through the bureaucracy was its first official use, six weeks into the Kennedy Administration, in Executive Order 10925 (March, 1961): "The contractor will take affirmative action to ensure that applicants are employed, and that employees are treated, during employment, without regard to their race, creed, color or national origin." These actions came to mean providing remedial education or compensatory training, making certain that testing did not incorporate forms of discrimination, and aggressive recruiting—in other words, sincerely trying to find, and hire or admit qualified blacks.

Goals are numerical targets, set to put a specific criterion before a school or employer or union, which can be achieved through "affirmative action" on agreed "timetables." If good-faith efforts are made to provide equal opportunity, failure to reach the goal would not trigger a government penalty such as cancellation of contracts.

Quotas do not permit of explanations: if the number set by population percentages is not met, penalties ensue; this rigidity results in the hiring or admission of minority applicants less qualified than other applicants, primarily on the basis of race, and the charge of *reverse discrimination.*

In *Regents of the University of California* v. *Allan Bakke,* decided on June 28, 1978, Justice Lewis Powell, writing for the Supreme Court, swept aside the differences between "goals" and "quotas"—at least as applied in that case—as "semantic distinction beside the point." The point was that nobody could be denied admission to a college specifically by virtue of his race; Bakke, who was white and had claimed "reverse discrimination," won entry. At the same time, the Court held that "race or ethnic background may be deemed a 'plus' in a particular applicant's file"—in other words, that race could be taken into consideration provided it was not the only element in the admissions decision.

This overrode the contention that the Constitution was "color-blind" made by opponents of affirmative action. Ironically, they took this word from the 1896 opinion of John Marshall Harlan in *Plessy* v. *Ferguson*, dissenting from "the wrong this day done" by a Court that upheld SEPARATE BUT EQUAL facilities: "Our constitution is color-blind and neither knows nor tolerates classes among citizens. In respect of civil rights, all citizens are equal before the law. The humblest is a peer of the most powerful."

When this was used by whites in the seventies to protest "reverse discrimination"—the affirmative action taken to redress past discrimination —four justices in the Bakke case held: "We cannot . . . let color blindness become myopia which masks the reality that many 'created equal' have been treated as inferior."

QUOTED OUT OF CONTEXT a defensive charge that one's words have been quoted in such a way as to twist the original meaning of the statement.

During the French Revolution, Jean Paul Marat was arrested and tried by the Convention for alleged outrages against that assembly in 1793. In his successful defense, he said: "I demand a consecutive reading . . . for it is not by garbling and mutilating passages that the ideas of an author are to be learnt, it is by reading the context that their meaning may be judged of."

In the 1944 presidential campaign, Franklin Roosevelt was irritated at Thomas E. Dewey's jabs at FDR's "promise" not to campaign "in the usual sense" when he accepted the Democratic nomination. He planned to use the following passage in a speech:

In accepting the nomination in this campaign I said: "I will not campaign, in the usual sense, for the office."

Apparently the Republican campaign orators came to the conclusion that meant that they were free to say anything they wanted without contradiction. . . . But in their habit of tearing sentences from their context, which they seem to do in their campaign speeches with great facility, they decided to overlook what I said in the same paragraph. It was this: "I shall, however, feel free to report to the people the facts about matters of concern to them and especially to correct any misrepresentations."

So last week, I exposed their misrepresentations . . .

Speechwriter Samuel Rosenman felt this was intemperate and out of character, and FDR agreed not to use it. Instead, he made the point obliquely: "I am quoting history to you. I am going by the record. And I am giving you the whole story and not merely a phrase here and a half a phrase there . . ." There was an outburst of laughter at that point and the master orator promptly scrapped the rest of the line: ". . . picked out of context in such a way that they distort the facts." Instead, he said: "In my reading copy there's another half-sentence. You've got the point and I'm not going to use it."

On November 15, 1954, during the

debate on Senate resolution 301 to censure Wisconsin Senator Joseph McCarthy, Senator Samuel J. Ervin, Jr. (D-N.C.) told the Senate:

I now know that the lifting of statements out of context is a typical McCarthy technique . . . practiced by a preacher in North Carolina about 75 years ago. At that time, the women had a habit of wearing their hair in top knots. This preacher deplored that habit. As a consequence, he preached a ripsnorting sermon one morning on the text "Top Knot Come Down."

At the conclusion of his sermon an irate woman, wearing a very pronounced top knot, told the preacher that no such text could be found in the Bible. The preacher thereupon opened the Scriptures to the 17th verse of the 24th chapter of Matthew and pointed to the words: "Let him which is on the housetop not come down to take anything out of his house." Any practitioner of the McCarthy technique of lifting things out of context can readily find the text "top knot come down" in this verse.

RR

RABBI   political patron.

In political usage, as Paul Hoffman pointed out in the January 21, 1969 *New York Post,* this word has no religious or spiritual significance. A rabbi in politics is primarily a sponsor or protector, although there is a second meaning of mentor or teacher. "Who's his rabbi?" is a question often asked by wary hatchetmen before cutting loose at a target.

When a speechwriter escaping the White House in 1973 asked *Newsweek* pundit Stewart Alsop to "be my rabbi" in giving advice about which newspaper offer to accept, Alsop—a self-described "confirmed WASP"— delightedly signed all future correspondence with his colleague "Your rabbi, Stew."

The more frequently used term for mentor is *guru,* from the Indian "holy man" or "teacher," which began to lose its religious connotation in 1949 when Arthur Koestler used it in *The God That Failed* as "My self-confidence as a *Guru* had gone." In political usage, *guru* is for outsiders, *rabbi* for insiders.

RACIAL BALANCE, *see* **BUSING.**

RACISM   originally, an assumption that an individual's abilities and potential were determined by his biological race, and that some races were inherently superior to others; now, a political-diplomatic accusation of harboring or practicing such theories.

"This word [racism]," wrote Harvard Professor J. Anton De Haas in November 1938, "has come into use the last six months, both in Europe and this country . . . Since so much has been said about conflicting isms, it is only natural that a form was chosen which suggested some kind of undesirable character."

Racism was at first directed against Jews. In the nineteenth century, anti-Semites who foresaw a secular age in which religion would not be such a rallying force against Jews put forward the idea of Jewishness being less a religion than a race. Adolf Hitler, with his "master race" ideology, turned theory into savage practice.

Anne Soukhanov, associate editor of Merriam-Webster, informs the author: "Our citations for *racism* ran very heavy from the late 1930s through the late 1940s; most of them referred to fascism. Then they thinned out until the late 1950s, when references to U.S. (and, in particular, to Southern) racism began to build up. The citations seemed to peak for that sense in the Sixties."

Meg Greenfield, writing in *Newsweek* on November 24, 1975, agreed: "US Ambassador [to the UN] Daniel P. Moynihan observes that the term 'racism' only became a fixture of official General Assembly prose sometime in the mid- to late 1960s. The same is true of official prose in this

591

country. I remember being astonished in 1968 by the abandon with which the Kerner commission, appointed by President Johnson to study the causes of civil disorder in our cities, stigmatized vast segments of the American population with the charge of 'white racism.' "

Curiously, the term which had originally characterized (and derogated) attacks on Jews then became associated with the black civil rights movement, returned as an attack on Jews when the UN General Assembly, dominated by a Soviet-Arab-African coalition, passed a resolution condemning Zionism as a form of racism.

Ambassador Moynihan, on November 10, 1975, observed in the UN: "The term derives from relatively new doctrines—all of them discredited—concerning the human population of the world, to the effect that there are significant biological differences among clearly identifiable groups, and that these differences establish, in effect, different levels of humanity." Opposing the resolution, he declared that "today we have drained the word 'racism' of its meaning . . . The United States of America declares that it does not acknowledge, it will not abide by, it will never acquiesce in this infamous act."

"Racism" became a favored term of Mr. Moynihan's successor, Andrew Young, who returned to the sixties usage regarding blacks, and in Great Britain told his hosts that England "invented racism." When he observed that even Abraham Lincoln, as well as more recent Presidents, had been racist, defining the word to mean "insensitive to racial aspirations," he took some of the passion out of the word.

Both word and problem are likely to remain in the political discourse.

Seymour Martin Lipset, writing in the October 1977 *American Spectator,* was pessimistic: "The racism and ethnic tension that have been potent aspects of human experience from ancient days down to the present continue as strong or stronger than ever . . . the story of people's hatred of each other for reasons of ancestry, culture, religion, race or language is far from over."

In the landmark *Bakke* decision, the Supreme Court held in 1978 that race could be considered as a factor determining admission to a college, provided it was not the only factor. "To get beyond racism," wrote Justice Harry Blackmun, "we must first take account of race. And in order to treat some persons equally, we must first treat them differently."

RADICAL CHIC, *see* **LIMOUSINE LIBERAL; PARLOR PINK.**

RADICAL RIGHT   attack phrase on right-wing EXTREMISTS, especially on an angry segment that believes treason motivates many of the government's leaders.

Prince Klemens von Metternich, who put the stamp of reaction on the Congress of Vienna in 1814, coined a predecessor phrase—"white radicals" —to define the activists of the far right, counterbalancing the "red radicals" of the left. And attorney Clarence Darrow, who defended a teacher's right to discuss evolution at the Scopes "monkey trial," liked to refer to the Catholic hierarchy as "the right wing of the right wing."

Telford Taylor, a prosecutor at the Nuremberg war-crimes trials, is credited with the coinage of "radical right" in the foreword to his 1954 book, *Grand Inquest.*

Sociologist Daniel Bell picked up

the phrase in a 1955 book, *The New American Right,* which he updated and retitled *The Radical Right* in 1963. Bell defined the group as a melange of

> soured patricians . . . whose emotional stake lay in a vanishing image of muscular America defying a decadent Europe . . . the "new rich"—the automobile dealers, real-estate manipulators, oil wildcatters—who needed the psychological assurance that they, like their forebears, had earned their own wealth, rather than accumulated it through government aid, and who feared that "taxes" would rob them of that wealth; the rising middle-class strata of the ethnic groups, the Irish and the Germans, who sought to prove their Americanism, the Germans particularly because of the implied taint of disloyalty during World War II; and finally, unique in American cultural history, a small group of intellectuals, many of them cankered ex-Communists, who, pivoting on McCarthy, opened up an attack on liberalism in general.

Writers who use this attack phrase are unanimous in their denunciation of the far right. Alan Barth, writing in 1961:

> They are commonly called "Rightist"—a term which connotes conservatism. But in sober truth there is nothing conservative about them. They are much more in a rage to destroy than a fervor to conserve. . . . Sometimes they are referred to as the "radical Right." But the fact is that there is nothing radical about them. They offer no novel solutions to the problems that plague them; indeed, they offer no solutions at all. . . . They are fundamentally and temperamentally "aginners." And perhaps the commonest characteristic among them is anger.

See BIRCHER; LITTLE OLD LADIES IN TENNIS SHOES; EXTREMISM; KOOKS, NUTS AND.

RADIC-LIB shortened form of radical liberal; a linkage of the unpopular far left with the left, which at election time must move for support to the center.

"What's a good word to describe radical liberals?" Vice President Spiro Agnew wondered aloud to a group of his writers at the start of the 1970 congressional campaign. "Radillectual" sounded anti-intellectual, which wouldn't do; nobody had a good word to describe radical liberals, so the two words remained as a kind of working title until a better one could be found. However, the use of the two words caused great consternation in the liberal community, whose candidates were then climbing in and out of sheriffs' cars to show their concern for law and order, and the search for an alternative phrase was quickly abandoned. (It is similar to the movie producer who asked, "Who can we get for the Henry Fonda role?" and somebody responding, "How about Henry Fonda?") One night, on his own, the Vice President tried out the short form—radiclibs—which caught the fancy of headline writers and incensed liberal opponents, who equated it with **"COMSYMP"** a short form of Communist sympathizer popularized by the Birch Society.

On November 2, 1970, Max Ways wrote in *Fortune* magazine:

> "As he employs the phrase . . . radical liberal seems to be an elastic blanket covering a huge bed, strangely cohabited by "the northeastern Establishment," the more inflamed students and the militant blacks. The term radical liberal is bitterly resented by many as an effort to smear liberalism with the unpopular tar of radicalism. . . . To be fair, Agnew did not invent the guilt-by-verbal-association form of terminological confusion. Some

years ago, the phrase "radical conservative" was used in both liberal and radical circles. This horrid hybrid, radical conservative, every bit as monstrous as radical liberal, was supposed to describe activist conservatives, such as members of the John Birch Society, who were inclined to ideologize their principles and who exhibited some stylistic similarities to leftist radicals . . .

In the 1840s a British Whig faction described itself as radical liberal; in 1968 the phrase was the title of a book by UCLA professor Arnold S. Kaufman.

RAINMAKER a lawyer or public relations man capable of making political manna fall on his client.

This apt term, of obscure origin, burst back into the political lexicon in 1968 when new trans-Pacific airline routes were to be awarded, and a half-dozen of President Johnson's former political associates wereretained by individual airlines to lobby for their interests. On May 28, 1968, the *Atlanta Journal* printed this dispatch from David Hoffman of the *Washington Post:* "Among airline men, corporate officials and consultants with high political contacts are referred to as 'rainmakers'. Half in jest and half in jealousy, airline men say the so-called rainmakers can precipitate new route awards for companies that employ them."

The next year, columnists Rowland Evans and Robert Novak wrote: "No sooner had President Johnson announced his decision on December 19 [1968] in the malevolently contested trans-Pacific air case, than two major airlines—American and Eastern—began a quick search for Republican rainmakers."

Former Attorney General John Mitchell gave a sophisticated definition of the term during his first trial in April 1974 after which he was acquitted. Sometimes a lobbyist will claim to have done something for a client but the effort leads nowhere; still, he claims to have made it rain. Mr. Mitchell said that a New Jersey Republican leader approached him on behalf of financier Robert Vesco, and asked him to set up a meeting with SEC chairman William J. Casey. But Casey was on vacation and the meeting was never arranged. According to Mitchell: "Rainmaking is a situation where an individual who is trying to obtain a favor for a client does things for the record that never happened."

The word, in its original sense, is associated with the American Indian. The earliest use of the word in print found so far is in Adair's Indians, in 1775: "When the ground is parched, their rain-makers (as they are commonly termed) are to mediate for the beloved red people, with the bountiful holy Spirit of fire." Two centuries later, cloud-seeding operations proved somewhat more reliable, but in both literal and political senses, the rainmaker often takes the credit for rain that was already on the way.

See FIVE PERCENTER; INFLUENCE PEDDLER; LOBBY.

RALLY as a noun, an event to stimulate and channel enthusiasm; as a verb, to enlist support.

"Rally round the flag" may or may not have been said by General Andrew Jackson at the Battle of New Orleans, but it illustrates the military use of the word, from the French *rallier,* to re-ally or join again, to reassemble scattered troops to fight again. Poet Robert Burns warned of repercussions, "ere we permit a foreign foe,/On British ground to rally."

As might be expected, the military phrase was given a political interpretation in the campaign for a military hero, William Henry ("Tippecanoe") Harrison. "If Pennsylvania should adopt him as her candidate," wrote the *Scioto Gazette* in 1835, "the west will rally around the Old Pioneer." Abolitionist Wendell Phillips followed an extension of the word in the *Liberator* in 1844: ". . . until slavery be abolished, the watchword, the rallying-cry, the motto on the banner of the American Anti-Slavery Society shall by 'No Union With Slave Holders!' "

The political rally, as practiced today, can be a *streetcorner rally,* one of many brief appearances by the candidate on a city-wide tour, providing an event for local supporters to organize in a neighborhood; a *headquarters rally* or *kick-off rally* to "open" a headquarters largely for the benefit of cameramen; a *coffee klatsch,* a gathering of supporters in a home but nevertheless a rally of sorts (see COFFEE-KLATSCH CAMPAIGN); and the all-stops-out, ring-a-ding, HOOPLA-filled *"Garden" rally* (after Madison Square Garden in New York) or *major rally,* which is also called the *wind-up rally,* at the end of a national campaign, bringing in celebrities, raising funds by charging admission to a section of the best seats, generating publicity and enthusiasm.

A good rally can be potent. Reluctant candidate Dwight Eisenhower wrote General Lucius Clay from Paris in early 1952: "My attitude has undergone a quite significant change since viewing the movie of the Madison Square Garden show . . ."

A checklist prepared by public relations man Gilbert A. Robinson for a Rockefeller for Governor rally in 1966 provides an indication of preparations for one rally:

    I. *Invitations:* (a) telegrams to county chairmen; (b) mail cards to volunteers; (c) bulk invitations to organizations.

    II. *Program:* (a) music—rock 'n' roll combo; (b) celebrities; (c) emcee; (d) introductions and speeches; (e) balloon and streamer drop from ledge overhead; (f) decorate upstairs headquarters with bunting and posters.

    III. *Equipment:* (a) flatbed truck with mounting steps; (b) police parking permit; (c) platform for TV cameras; (d) sign for front of hotel, U.S. and state flags; (e) sound equipment, two speakers on flat bed, two on station wagons roaming area to bring crows; (f) 150 hand signs on sticks, 160 hats, 50 sashes, 5000 buttons, 500 balloons, 50 pre-rally signs saying "at noon today" to be posted in AM; (g) "Days to Go" sign with removable numbers placed next to elevator in headquarters; (h) walkie-talkie communications.

    IV. *Crowd:* (a) telephone team calling volunteers three days before rally; (b) Young Republicans to guarantee 150; (c) tables in crowd with 3 girls manning each to sign up volunteers; (d) police notified and present.

    V. *Press arrangements:* (a) invitations; (b) TV arrangements and power; (c) phone follow-up to invitations.

This was a small, successful headquarters opening rally, which attracted about a thousand people and good press coverage. For a major rally, multiply complexities by fifteen. Good managers always distribute ten times as many tickets as there are seats in the hall. See BALLYHOO; BANDWAGON; SPONTANEOUS DEMONSTRATION.

RANK AND FILE the broad range of party members; the TROOPS, more active than the average voter registered with a party.

Al Smith, making a late effort to get the Democratic nomination in

1932, stated that "it would be wiser . . . not to instruct delegates to the convention in favor of any candidate . . ." This ploy was aimed at eroding delegate strength already pledged to Franklin Roosevelt. FDR immediately objected to "the kind of national convention which became merely a trading post for a handful of powerful leaders, and where the nomination itself had nothing to do with the popular choice of the rank and file of the party itself. . . . The rank and file of the party should be heard." See **POWER BROKERS.**

The phrase, often used in the labor movement, is from the military, where it means the whole body of enlisted men, including corporals but sometimes excepting sergeants. See **MILITARY METAPHORS.**

RAP IN THE NIGHT symbol for police state that rules by fear; a frightening sound, preliminary to arrest or search.

The crash of gun butts on the door in the dead of night is a device to strike terror into a populace. Nighttime is chosen because the resident is startled out of sleep, and a fear of the dark is added to the fear of authority. The Gestapo made it a kind of trademark. In some cases, night is chosen to avoid publicity.

"The clearest way to show what the rule of law means to us in everyday life," said Dwight Eisenhower in 1958, "is to recall what has happened when there is no rule of law. The dread knock on the door in the middle of the night . . ."

This became a political issue in the U.S. in 1962 following an increase in the price of steel. President John F. Kennedy put pressure on the steel companies to roll back their increase, because he felt it was unjustified and inflationary. As part of this pressure, Attorney General Robert Kennedy asked the Federal Bureau of Investigation to check into newspaper reports of remarks made by Bethlehem Steel executives at a stockholders meeting. "Unhappily," writes Arthur Schlesinger, Jr., "though the instruction went to the FBI in the afternoon, it was apparently passed on to Philadelphia by Pony Express, for the reporter involved was not called till three the next morning. The FBI's postmidnight rap on the door caused a furor."

The "rap in the night" was used against Robert Kennedy in his 1964 senatorial campaign as an indication of his ruthlessness; it was also phrased as "rap on the door" and "knock in the night." In a way, this explains why political canvassers are told by their leaders not to ring doorbells or knock on doors after 9 P.M.

RATFUCKING secretly, sometimes illegally, disrupting a opponent's campaign.

This odious word has its origin in Southern California campus politics, where fierce struggles to determine class presidencies sometimes featured underhanded tactics to confuse or irritate the opposition. In undergraduate politicking, it was considered harmless pranksterism, similar to the mock fury of much intermural sport, but transmitted to the national scene it was seen to be **HARDBALL** or **DIRTY TRICKS.**

Donald Segretti was identified by *Time* and by reporters Robert Woodward and Carl Bernstein of the *Washington Post* in October 1972 as having been hired by the Nixon White House to sabotage the Democratic campaign. "Those who did know of the disruption campaign," reported the *New York Times* on October 16, "referred to it as 'rat———,' an obscene phrase alluding to the Democratic candidate victimized by the program. The phrase is understood to be one commonly used on California campuses when some men linked to the case, including Mr. [Dwight] Chapin and Mr. Segretti, were in college there."

The use of the word "rat" to mean "a politician who deserts his party" (as distinguished from "ratfucking," in which a politician dishonors his party) was traced by glossarian Richard H. Thornton to use by Earl Malmesbury in 1792. In the U.S. it made its first appearance in the saying "like a rat deserting a sinking ship" about 1800, and this metaphor was alluded to by Thomas Jefferson in a letter to James Maury dated April 25, 1812: "I think the old hulk [England] in which you are is near her wreck, and that, like a prudent rat, you should escape in time."

Jefferson's element of prudence remains in the use of the metaphor today. A political proverb attributed to FDR Navy Secretary Claude Swanson is "When the water reaches the upper level, follow the rats."

See "black advance," under AD-VANCE MAN.

RATHER BE RIGHT, *see* **I'D RATHER BE RIGHT.**

RATTLE THE CAGE   attempt by a political figure to break out of the restraints imposed on him by his staff.

This phrase is an arrogation of importance by political staffers who jokingly speak of themselves as zookeepers of gorillas that must be protected from their own rampages.

When Nixon special counsel Charles Colson arranged a night out at the Kennedy Center for Richard Nixon to conform to a sudden presidential whim, he was dressed down by chief of staff H. R. Haldeman in these terms: "You could have put the President's life in jeopardy. The Secret Service wasn't prepared." Asked what to do when the President expressed a desire for an unscheduled public appearance, Colson writes he was told: "Just tell him he can't go, that's all. He rattles his cage all the time. You can't let him out."

A second meaning, when the keeper rather than the gorilla is doing the rattling, is "to warn," as in this *Wall Street Journal* use on July 5, 1977: "A congressional staffer recalls that a lobbyist for the American Israel Public Affairs Committee, after noting that a friendly congressman wasn't on hand for a key vote, ordered the congressman's aide to 'get up there and rattle his cage and get him down here.' "

The metaphor of center of power as prison is not new: Harry Truman referred to the place he worked as "a big white jail."

RAW MEAT, *see* **STIR UP THE ANIMALS.**

REACHED   bought off; corrupted.

A public official may be *approached* with no implication of wrongdoing on his part; when he has been *spoken to,* the implication is that he is neutralized or partially persuaded pending a final decision; when he is *reached,* however, he has been bought and sold.

California Attorney General Earl Warren, launching a gambling investigation in 1939, used the word in its current meaning:

It is impossible to open a big, notorious gambling operation without buying off public officials. Every time you see such a place, you can be sure they are paying off someone for the privilege to operate. This does not necessarily mean a sheriff or a District Attorney or a chief of police is being reached. Most often, it is someone higher up . . .

The question "Can he be reached?" or "Is he reachable?" is occasionally answered with another word, taken from Chicago gangland investigations and in turn from the Hindu caste system: "untouchable."

See GRAFT; BOODLE; BAGMAN.

REACTIONARY one who believes in returning to governmental and economic conditions of an earlier time; often an attack word on a conservative.

The origin seems to have been French, applied to the conservative groups who opposed the Revolution's extremists.

H. L. Mencken says it was first used in J. A. Froude's *History of England* in 1858, "in the current sense of a political conservative reactionary. . . . It is now used to designate any opponent of a new device to save humanity." The word was used earlier as a religious term.

Populists and Democratic supporters of William Jennings Bryan popularized it in this country, but as early as 1868, *Harper's Weekly* used "reaction" to describe the Democrats who met in their party's national convention in Ohio: ". . . the resuscitation of every notorious copperhead to control the government is the beautiful plum which 'the great reaction' offers the country."

In more recent times, President Roosevelt said in a 1939 radio speech: "A reactionary is a somnambulist walking backward." Six years later Herbert Hoover, accustomed to the label, wrote: "If it be 'reactionary' to be for free men then I shall be proud of that title for my remaining days." Communist China's Chairman Mao

Tse-tung wrote in *Political Science:* "Reactionaries must be deprived of the right to voice their opinions. Only the people have that right."

Like LIBERAL, MIDDLE OF THE ROADER, CENTRIST, and CONSERVATIVE, reactionary—and its counterpart on the left, radical—is a subjective label shifting in meaning with each labeler. However, left-wingers are more likely to be proud of the title "radical" than extreme right-wingers of the label "reactionary." In the late seventies, some ultraconservatives—picking up in the growing use of NEO-CONSERVATIVE—called themselves "neoreactionaries."

Forces of reaction is often used as an alternate to the adjective, and *fossilized thinking* and DINOSAUR WING shore up the antediluvian picture of the word. See MOSSBACK; EXTREMIST; HIDEBOUND; OLD FOGY; OLD GUARD.

READ OUT OF THE PARTY declared *persona non grata* by party leaders, usually after a BOLT.

The situation is similar to a dismissed employee grumbling, "You can't fire me, I quit." When a party leader or public figure within the party commits some unpardonable sin (like supporting the opposition), he has in effect deserted; any metaphoric expunging of his name from the party rolls simply vents the spleen of the party leadership deserted. It makes no difference, except to make it more difficult for the bolter to return.

Nobody actually "reads" anybody out of a party; if a man says he is a Democrat, he's a Democrat, no matter what Democratic leaders say or how many Republicans he votes for. The phrase is merely a way of showing party disapproval.

Like PARTY ELDERS, the origin is in the Church. As the *Guidebook* in the Administration of the Discipline of the Methodist Episcopal Church states: "It is made the duty of the 'official minister or preacher' at every quarterly meeting to read the names of those who have been excluded from the Church during the preceding quarter. . . . When persons are thus read out of the society by the official minister," etc. "Reading out the banns" in church was the thrice-repeated notice of intended marriage; it was also a sovereign's summons to his vassals for military service.

Political use was evident in 1840, when the *Logansport* (Indiana) *Herald* wrote: "If their candidates in expectancy are guilty of the unpardonable sin of telling the truth . . . they're immediately read out of the party."

When Republican Frank Knox, Alfred Landon's running mate in 1936, accepted a post in the Roosevelt Administration, Republican National Chairman John Hamilton "read him out" of the party. When Earl Warren, who had turned down the offer to be Thomas E. Dewey's running mate in 1944, was asked to run with Dewey in 1948, he felt he had to accept. "If he did turn Dewey down," wrote Warren biographer Leo Katcher, "he would be reading himself out of politics."

See PURGE.

REALPOLITIK POWER POLITICS with a scientific sound; international diplomacy based on strength rather than appeals to morality and world opinion.

The coiner was German writer Ludwig von Rochau, in his 1853 *Grundsätze der Realpolitik* (Fundamentals of Realpolitik), attacking what he felt were the unrealistic policies of the German Liberals. "The term was particularly applied to Bismarck's policy during and after the years of German unification," writes Professor Donald Cameron Watt in the *Fontana Dictionary of Modern Thought*, "and is to be distinguished from a policy of selfish self-interest or from a ruthless reliance on naked power."

"Historians may argue for years," wrote *Time* magazine about the brief Israeli-Arab war in 1967 (dubbed the "blintzkrieg"), "over who actually fired the first shot. . . . But the *Realpolitik* of Israel's overwhelming triumph has rendered the question largely academic." The *New York Times* editorially noted on June 8, 1967, that "The Kremlin now is trying to cut its losses without too much damage to its posture as 'friend of the Arabs,' " and described the effort as "Russia's Unrealpolitik."

On a different subject—the need to withdraw U.S. forces from Europe to help stem a gold drain—*Time* had written a month earlier: "For an America caught up in a war in Asia, and a vigorous Europe with no foreign entanglements, the first major withdrawal of 'cold war' troops from the Continent also signaled a belated adjustment to *Realpolitik* in the '60s."

In 1939, after the Soviets had signed a nonaggression pact with the Nazis, American Communists were forced to do a sharp zigzag in their party line, causing *The Nation* magazine to scoff at their dialectics. A clergyman wrote a letter to *The Nation*'s editor patiently explaining that Stalin was only fighting for the life of his regime, adding: "I would suggest that you leave the morals of the situation to us parsons and concentrate yourselves upon the realities in terms of *Realpolitik.* "

The German word is pronounced re-*al*-pol-i-*tik;* in Europe, it continues to mean "power politics," but in the

U.S. the word is used to mean "the realities of politics," which puts it closer to PRACTICAL POLITICS.

See QUIET DIPLOMACY; WORLD OPINION.

REAPPORTIONMENT, *see* **ONE MAN, ONE VOTE.**

RECESSION, *see* **BAFFLEGAB.**

RED   color originally symbolizing radicalism and anarchy, now identified with Communism.

Les républicains rouges, so called for their red caps and occasional willingness to dip their hands in the blood of their victims and then wave them in demonstrations, gave the anarchistic tinge to the color associated till then with magic and the Church.

This did not occur, as popularly assumed, during the Revolution of 1789 and the Reign of Terror that followed; the "red Republicans" earned their nickname in the insurrection of June 1848, which led to the establishment of the short-lived Second Republic. The red flag, however, had been used in the 1789 Revolution and was adopted by the Communists in the twentieth century, it had been used in the Roman Empire as a call to arms.

German revolutionaries in the midnineteenth century called themselves *rote Republikaner,* and the *Cleveland Plain Dealer* in 1856 made an interesting comparison: "They call themselves 'Red Republicans,' indicating by that name their bloody and revolutionary purposes. They have found congenial spirits in a party in this country called 'BLACK REPUBLICANS.'"

A character in *Uncle Tom's Cabin,* by Harriet Beecher Stowe, warned that "the masses are to rise, and the under class become the upper one."

The answer was, "That's one of your red republican humbugs, Augustine!" At the same time, the specter of Communism was haunting Europe, in the Marx-Engels word picture, and the timing was perfect for the color and the cause to come together.

PINKO and PARLOR PINK are obvious derivatives; BLEEDING HEART might have an association. See COLOR METAPHORS.

RED HERRING   a side issue that draws attention away from the main issue.

From the expression "neither fish nor flesh nor good red herring" in Dryden's *Duke of Guise;* a herring, cured with saltpeter and slowly smoked, turns red. Dragged across a trail, the strong smell irritates the nostrils of tracking dogs.

An early political use was by Alfred E. Smith, Governor of New York, campaigning for president in 1928. To an audience in Oklahoma City, he said:

The cry of Tammany Hall is nothing more nor less than a red herring that is pulled across the trail in order to throw us off the scent.

Now this has happened to me before in my State campaigns but I did not consider it of enough importance to talk about. But it has grown to a proportion that compels me to let the country know that at least I know what's behind it; it's nothing more nor less than my religion.[See WHISPERING CAMPAIGN.]

For a phrase to explode into an issue, it needs both forum and context. President Harry Truman's first use of it had the forum of his acceptance speech to the Democratic convention in July 1948, but the room was not gas-filled when the match was struck:

"I am going to call Congress back and ask them to pass laws to halt rising prices, to meet the housing crisis —which they say they are for in their platform. . . . They are going to try to dodge their responsibility. They are going to drag all the red herrings they can across this campaign . . ."

The phrase made no big impression at the time because there was no double meaning to "red." But during the special session of Congress, the House Un-American Activities Committee found two witnesses who unfolded a spectacular tale of Communist intrigue at high government levels. Elizabeth Bently and Whittaker Chambers started labeling "spy" and "collaborator" such officials as Lauchlin Currie, ex–White House aide; William T. Remington of the Department of Commerce; and the State Department's Alger Hiss.

On Thursday, August 5, 1948, in this new context, a reporter took Truman's convention-speech red-herring phrase and asked, "Mr. President, do you think that the Capitol Hill spy scare is a 'red herring' to divert public attention from inflation?" Truman replied, "Yes, I do," read a prepared statement saying the hearings "are serving no useful purpose," and ad-libbed at its conclusion: "And they are simply a 'red herring' to keep from doing what they ought to do." The reporter asked for permission to quote him directly on the ad lib, and Truman agreed.

Now the phrase had its context and its second meaning—red Communism. Republicans attacked Truman on it, but the issue had not yet ripened —Hiss had not yet been convicted— and the tone of the Dewey campaign did not permit a slashing attack. But by the time the 1952 campaign was under way, "SOFT ON COMMUNISM" was an issue and "red herring" was its shibboleth. Eisenhower, stung by Stevenson's wit, asked, "Is it funny when

evidence was discovered that there are Communists in government and we get the cold comfort of the reply, 'red herring'?"

Thus, Truman's first use of the phrase, which passed unnoticed, gave him confidence to accept a reporter's use of it a few weeks later; in the meantime, however, the context and meaning had changed enough to make the use of the phrase a major blunder that haunted Democratic candidates for years. As Senator Robert Taft's wife Martha summed up: "To err is Truman."

REDLINING   delineating an area as a slum in which mortgage financing is not available, thereby speeding its decline.

"Redlining," wrote U.S. District Court Judge David Porter in 1976, "contributes to the decay of our cities." A *Washington Post* editorialist added: "It is a self-fulfilling prophecy. When the first signs of blight or impending racial or economic change appear, some lending institutions, anticipating a drop in market value, draw an imaginary red line around the endangered neighborhood and make not further investments within it. This usually makes it impossible for responsible and credit-worthy people to buy homes and for landlord to make improvements in the 'red-lined' neighborhood."

Since many urban slums are inhabited largely by blacks, the practice has been attacked as RACIST. At the behest of liberal legislators, the Connecticut House of Representatives passed a bill prohibiting banks from refusing mortgages on geographic-decline grounds. The California Association of Realtors defined "redlining" in October 1976 as "the practice of denying the availability of home financing without regard to the credit worthiness of the individual or the soundness of the structure," a definition that implies disapproval.

A conservative writer, Robert Bleiberg in *Barron's* magazine, held that government intervention rather than racism was the cause of much urban blight: "Owing to rent control, which, in an age of inflation inexorably forces property owners to the wall, real estate, water and sewer levies go uncollected and the tax base steadily erodes. Physical deterioration spreads from the bombed-out sectors of Bedford-Stuyvesant and the South Bronx to the increasingly beleaguered borough of Manhattan. Much of the city is redlined—who in his right mind will sink his own or other people's money into a vast slum—and building grinds to a near-halt."

The word crossed into diplomatic usage when Israelis told Syrian leaders in 1976 not to cross a "red line" in Lebanon, close to the Lebanese-Israeli border. This was a corruption of "deadline," which originated in Civil War prison camps as a limit beyond which a prisoner could not walk.

RED MEAT, *see* STIR UP THE ANIMALS.

REDNECK   a bigoted rural white, especially Southern; used as an attack word on all Southern conservatives or segregationists.

The *Dictionary of American English* offers no definition, but traces the use back to 1830, when Mrs. Anne Royall in her *Southern Tour* wrote of "the Red Necks, a name bestowed upon the Presbyterians in Fayetteville [North Carolina]." The word came to mean *poor white* or *white trash* in some usages, the *backwoods vote* in others; throughout, however, there runs the strain of racial prejudice.

The word belongs in the political lexicon: Albert Kirwan's book on Mississippi politics from 1876 to 1925 was titled *Revolt of the Rednecks*. In his novel *All the King's Men* (1946), about Southern politics, Robert Penn Warren included a line: "Mason county is red-neck country and they don't like niggers . . ."

Huey Long's appeal to the Louisiana rednecks was a source of his power, though he was not what would be called today a racist. Civil rights workers and liberal writers in recent years have popularized the regional term nationally, using it to identify members of White Citizens Councils. The noun "redneck" can also be used as an adjective, though copy editors prefer to dress it up as "rednecked."

"Look," Florida Governor Claude R. Kirk told a *Saturday Evening Post* writer in 1967, "I'm not one of these red-necked governors like Lester Maddox . . ."

Red-necked, hyphenated, means angry, contrary to the *Post* transcription of the word Kirk used; it probably derives from the flush of blood to the neck and face in a moment of fury, and is not related to "redneck," though a connection could be made in the anger of a bigot.

In current usage, *prejudiced* is genteel, more concerned with religion than race; *discriminatory* legalistic; *bigoted* blunt; *biased* mild; *anti-Negro* intellectual and literary; *nigger-baiting* colloquial and rarely used (since the person using it would not be likely to use "nigger"); *hate-peddling* reminiscent of the thirties and now outdated; and *redneck* descriptive of what the speaker thinks is ignorant, rustic, anti-Negro, and anti-Northerner.

George Wallace, campaigning in 1968, described some of his followers as "peapickers," "peckerwoods," and "woolhats." Semanticist Mario Pei suggested that "these are evidently to be taken as complimentary replacements for less flattering terms, such as 'redneck' and 'cracker.'"

In *Redneck Power: the Wit and Wisdom of Billy Carter* (1977), the President's brother was quoted as drawing the distinction between the complimentary "good ole boy" and the derogatory "redneck": "Well, a good ole boy . . . is somebody that rides around in a pick-up truck— which I do—and drinks beer and puts 'em in a litter bag. A redneck's one that rides around in a truck and drinks beer and throws 'em out the window."

RED TAPE bureaucratic sluggishness; unnecessary paperwork; administrative delay.

"Steel Pipes and Red Tape Don't Mix," advertised the British steel industry in 1964, warning voters that a vote for Labour was a vote for nationalization of their industry, with all the bureaucracy it was expected to entail. This was not a borrowed political Americanism, but a coinage attributed to Charles Dickens and popularized by Thomas Carlyle. The author cannot find Dickens' use of the phrase, but a passage from *Little Dorrit*, written in 1857, illustrates the point: "Whatever was required to be done, the Circumlocution Office was beforehand with all the departments in the art of perceiving how not to do it."

In the 1850s, Carlyle in *Latter Day Pamphlets* described a politician as "little other than a redtape Talking-machine, an unhappy Bag of Parliamentary Eloquence." Official documents in England were tied with a string or tape of a reddish color, and many lawyers followed the practice in packaging their briefs. At the turn of the nineteenth century, Washington Irving used the phrase in the U.S., as "His brain was little better than red tape and parchment."

The phrase, along with BUREAUCRACY, is a convenient weapon for citizens frustrated by what might be the delay of sensible administrative review, or what may be, in Shakespeare's phrase, "the insolence of office and the law's delay." *Washington red tape* and the need to *go through channels* called for the creation of *expediters* in World War II, whose job was to *cut through the red tape* and open up *bottlenecks* in war production.

The result of their paperpushing depresses the most industrious; the late rocket scientist Werhner von Braun said in 1958: "We can lick gravity, but sometimes the paperwork is overwhelming."

The only known defense of red tape was made in 1977 by Herbert Kaufman of the Brookings Institution: "One person's red tape may be another's treasured procedural safeguard . . . We are ambivalent about the appropriate trade-offs between discretion and constraint, each of us demanding the former for ourselves and the latter for our neighbors . . . Accepting red tape as an ineradicable foe is not to give up the fight, but to join battle on the only terms that offer any hope of success."

Mr. Kaufman livened up the pages of his iconoclastic tract with a cartoon by Lichty: "Gentlemen, the bad news is the company is in a state of bankruptcy . . . the good news is we have complied with federal rules and regulations."

REFORM the creation of a temporarily organized opposition to an Administration or party hierarchy based upon its corruption, assumption of privilege, or, in some cases, its refusal to share power.

Reformers, often capable of defeating those in power, are less successful in maintaining themselves on top. This fact was bemoaned by Lincoln Steffens, who wrote: "It is an emotional gratification to go out with the crowd and 'smash something.' This is nothing but revolt, and even monarchies have uprisings to the credit of their subjects. But revolt is not reform and one revolutionary administration is not good government."

Steffens was writing about an attempt by a reform mayor, Seth Low, to win re-election in 1903; the Tammany motto was: "To Hell with reform." Tammany won.

Professional politicians have always had disdain for reform movements and reformers. Tammany Mayor John F. Hyland told the Civil Service Reform Association in 1918: "We have had all the reform that we want in this city for some time to come." Another New York mayor, Jimmy Walker, quipped: "A reformer is a guy who rides through a sewer in a glass-bottomed boat."

Reformers have taken abuse from more distinguished sources. Senator Frank Lausche, when governor of Ohio, fought through a compromise increase in unemployment compensation when liberal and reform elements were demanding a much larger increase. Of them, he said, "There can be such a thing as too much reform, if it takes the wheels off the wagon." Earlier, Speaker of the House Thomas Reed wrote his own sardonic definition of reform: "An indefinable something is to be done, in a way nobody knows how, at a time nobody knows when, that will accomplish nobody knows what . . ."

George Washington Plunkitt, of Tammany Hall, expressed his own conviction that reform will always fail: "The fact is that a reformer can't last in politics. He can make a show for awhile, but he always comes down like a rocket. Politics is as much a regular business as the grocery or the dry-goods or the drug business. You've got to be trained up to it or you're sure to fail."

Enthusiasm, moral fervor, and a conviction that reform will save the city, state, nation, and world is a hallmark of the genuine reformer, but to the philosopher George Santayana, it was all spurious. In *The Life of Reason* he wrote: "A thousand reforms have left the world as corrupt as ever, for each successful reform has founded a new institution, and this institution has bred its new and congenial abuses."

It is easy enough to find disdainful references to reform, but the intermittent movement is a vital part of the political system. Those associated with reform movements need not be stereotyped as "goo-goos," the nickname of New York's Good Government Clubs of the 1890s. Mrs. Eleanor Roosevelt, retired Senator Herbert Lehman, and former Air Force Secretary Thomas K. Finletter were the tough, politically savvy leaders of the reform movement in New York in the late fifties and early sixties.

Columnist Murray Kempton gave an insight into the steel behind Mrs. Roosevelt's charm in quoting a remark she made to congressional candidate Gore Vidal, who had introduced former Tammany leader Carmine de Sapio at a dinner. "The dear old lady," wrote Kempton, "gazed across those hills ennobled by our history and said sweetly, 'I told Carmine that I would get him after what he did to Franklin [Jr.] at the 1954 state convention.' "

Those who try to upset party leadership always call themselves *reformers;* the entrenched leadership prefers to call them *insurgents.*

The word became a euphemism for any planned revision in law in the sixties and seventies. When the Hatch Act (protecting government employees from political influence from their superiors at election time) was attacked as unfairly limiting the political activity of appointees, the suggested return to the old ways was called "reform reform."

"Mr. Carter wants 'legal and judicial reform,' " wrote columnist James J. Kilpatrick in February 1978. "He wants 'criminal code reform.' He wants 'wiretap reform.' He wants 'mining law reform.' He wants 'a series of reforms'. . .'long-needed reforms'. . .'to reform the sewage treatment construction grant program' . . . In times past, Presidents have regularly asked that various programs be enlarged, expanded, strengthened, enhanced, improved or even reorganized, but this is not Mr. Carter's approach. Politically, he is the inheritor of Luther, Calvin and Knox. Reform!

"My own thought," concluded Kilpatrick, "is that reform is like garlic in the dressing: a little bit, as every cook knows, goes a very long way."

REGIME, *see* **ADMINISTRATION.**

REGULAR the party-designated candidate in a primary, as opposed to the insurgent; or a loyal party voter, usually a member of a local organization.

In a primary fight within a party for a specific nomination or for local party leadership, the "ins" proudly display "Regular Democratic [or Republican] Candidate" on their posters and literature; the "outs," who cannot very well call themselves "irregulars," usually choose "Independent Republican Candidate" or "Reform Democratic Candidate." See INS AND OUTS.

Most politicians today use a yardstick of willingness to vote in a primary as a test of "regularity": if a voter registers with a party at a general election, he is a *registered Democrat* (or *Republican*), but if he takes the trouble to turn out at a primary— and about three out of ten do in a contest—he may be considered a *regular,* if he votes for the "ins."

A *regular* is more active than a *registered voter,* less active than a *party worker.* Though a regular is a PARTISAN, a partisan is not necessarily a regular. The *regular vote* is the hardcore strength of any party on Election Day, which usually needs to be supplemented by the independent or SWING VOTE for victory.

See MILITARY METAPHORS.

REIGN OF TERROR, *see* **TERRORIST.**

RELEASE, *see* **HANDOUT.**

RELIGIOUS ISSUE, *see* **WHISPERING CAMPAIGN; UNPACK; REVERSE BIGOTRY; BAILEY MEMORANDUM; RED HERRING.**

RELIGIOUS METAPHORS all the following political expressions have religious derivations, some not so obvious, which are covered under their separate entries:

ALL THINGS TO ALL MEN
BLEEDING HEARTS
BORN AGAIN
BULLY PULPIT
CRUSADE
CULT OF PERSONALITY

GRAY EMINENCE
HELLBENT FOR ELECTION
LOVE FEAST
OPEN CONVENANTS
PARTY ELDERS
PATRONAGE
PUBLIC TROUGH
QUICK AND THE DEAD, THE
READ OUT OF THE PARTY
SANTA CLAUS, NOBODY
 SHOOTS AT
WITCH HUNT

Used in politics, but not primarily political phrases, are *Bible belt* (a coinage of H. L. Mencken); *holier than thou* (a coinage of Ezekiel); *side of the angels* (Disraeli opposing the apes on evolution); *sacred cow* (from the Hindus).

RENDEZVOUS WITH DESTINY
fated to be great.

FDR told the 1936 Democratic convention: "There is a mysterious cycle in human events. To some generations much is given. Of other generations much is expected. This generation of Americans has a rendezvous with destiny."

Historian Frank Freidel credits the phrase to Roosevelt's speechwriter Raymond Moley; others say Roosevelt's aide Thomas Corcoran suggested it to the President. Poetic and effective, it stimulated strong reaction. H. L. Mencken warned soon after the speech that "The Rooseveltian 'rendezvous with destiny' will turn out, in November, to be a rendezvous with a bouncer."

Thomas E. Dewey, seeking the Republican nomination in 1940 that ultimately went to Wendell Willkie, tried a substitution: "The President has said we have a 'rendezvous with destiny.' We seem to be on our way toward a rendezvous with despair."

Why was the word "rendezvous" chosen rather than "date with destiny" or "appointment with destiny"?

Perhaps because the previous generation of Americans had a "rendezvous with death," in the phrase of U.S. poet Alan Seeger, killed while fighting with the French army in 1916:

But I've a rendezvous with Death
At midnight in some flaming town,
When spring trips north again this year,
And I to my pledged word am true,
I shall not fail that rendezvous.

This poem had an effect on a later President. Arthur Schlesinger, Jr., wrote of John F. Kennedy: "On Cape Cod, in October, 1953, when he returned from his wedding trip, he had read his young wife what he said was his favorite poem. She learned it for him by heart, and he used to love to have her say it. It was Alan Seeger's *I Have a Rendezvous with Death.*"

President Lyndon B. Johnson was intrigued by "this generation of Americans," the beginning of the rendezvous with destiny phrase. In his 1964 campaign he said that Barry Goldwater offered a "doctrine that plays loosely with human destiny, and this generation of Americans will have no part of it." The allusion to FDR's "rendezvous with destiny" was subtle; however in a Nashville, Tennessee, speech on March 16, 1967, Johnson edited FDR's construction into mediocrity: "This generation of Americans is making its imprint on history."

REORDERING PRIORITIES
putting first things first, though what is first to the reorderer is not always first to the reorderee.

This phrase achieved the status of a thundering cliché in the late sixties, when debate began about limiting the size of U.S. defense and space expenditures and directing those resources to "meet human needs." While not the coiner, John Gardner, first at the

National Urban Coalition and later at Common Cause, is identified with the phrase.

"Top priority" was heavily used in World War II, and "high priority" became bureaucratese subsequently. In calling for change, the participle used is never *changing* or *reorganizing;* it is occasionally *resetting* or *reassessing* but most frequently *reordering.* A measure of that frequency is the dropping of the hyphen. The word usually appears near another vogue term, "agenda."

In a calculated fashion, and with the relish experienced by soldiers who capture enemy guns and turn them around, the conservative writer of the 1972 budget message of the President led the huge document with this brief review: *"To the Congress of the United States:* In the 1971 budget, America's priorities were quietly but dramatically reordered: for the first time in twenty years, we spent more to meet human needs than we spent on defense."

REPORTEDLY a leading WEASEL WORD in journalism; a modifier that uses the fact of repetition to impute truth.

"Alleged," a word whose roots are linked with "litigate," has long been used to avoid libel litigation; the word has since become such a transparent, albeit ineffective, libel-ducker that newsmen now prefer "charge with" or "accused of."

Less precise than "alleged" is "reported" or "reportedly," which is a form of the gossipy "they say"; it implies "nobody has been sued using this before, so here goes." In Communist terminology, the preferred construction is "as is well known."

When *New Yorker* profilist Geoffrey Hellman died, Alden Whitman of the *New York Times* wrote in an obituary that Hellman "feuded fiercely" with his colleagues on the magazine. "One such feud was with Brendan Gill . . . the two were reportedly not on speaking terms." Mr. Gill blazed back in a letter to the editor: "Certainly he and I never had a feud. Moreover, having adjacent offices at the magazine, we spoke almost daily up to the time he fell ill, and we often lunched together. It is a fact that as an old friend of Geoffrey's I was one of the last of his colleagues to be granted the privilege of visiting him as he lay dying. So much for 'reportedly'—a word that has little to recommend its use in write-ups of the distressed living and the defenseless dying."

President Carter's Attorney General, Griffin Bell, put it this way in 1977, justifying his practice of correcting journalistic errors: "Once information is published, it is likely to be reprinted by journalists yet unborn unless a denial has been posted in neon at Times Square."

For a list of other terms which will be used by journalists yet unborn, see JOURNALESE.

REPUBLICAN advocates of a democratic form of government, as their Democratic opponents are advocates of a republican form of government.

John Adams worried about the word in 1790: ". . . all good government is and must be republican. But, at the same time, you can or will agree with me, that there is not in lexicography a more fraudulent word. . . . Are we not, my friend, in danger of rendering the word republican unpopular in this country by an indiscreet, indeterminate, and equivocal use of it?"

Thomas Jefferson, who used the word as an antonym for "monarchic" all his life, disagreed in 1816: ". . . of the import of the term republic, instead of saying, as has been said, 'that it may mean anything or nothing,' we may say with truth and meaning, that governments are more or less republican as they have more or less of the element of popular election and control in their composition . . ."

Jefferson's party became known as the Republicans; he preferred it to "anti-Federalists" and referred to his opposition as "the anti-republicans."

Hans Sperber and Travis Trittschuh pointed out in the *Dictionary of American Political Terms,* "since the Constitution guarantees to every state a republican form of government, it would seem that republican from the beginning had every chance of becoming a unifying not a partisan word." The party became known as the Democratic-Republicans, and their opposition as the National Republicans, because of this unifying sense of the word in its form-of-government meaning.

In the Jacksonian era, the word's previous bipartisan use led both parties, beginning to take adversary positions after the Era of Good Feeling, to drop it completely. Democratic-Republicans became "Democrats," National Republicans became "Whigs."

As the Whig party fell apart, the term "Republican" began to be bandied about, probably around 1852. In 1854 A. E. Bovay wrote to *New York Tribune* editor Horace Greeley: "Urge them to forget previous political names and organization, and to band together under the name I suggested to you at Lovejoy's Hotel in 1852, while Scott was being nominated. I mean the name Republican." About the same time, Greeley wrote a friend regarding the formation of an antislavery party: "Call it Republican —no prefix, no suffix, but plain Republican." At Jackson, Michigan, in

1854, the party was organized and chose that name, picking John C. Frémont as its first presidential candidate in 1856 with the slogan "Free Soil, Free Men, Frémont."

Strictly speaking, a *republic* is a form of government in which the people exercise their power through elected representatives, while a *democracy* is a government where the people exercise their powers directly *or* through elected representatives. In current usage, the two terms are interchangeable, which is why the definition at the beginning of this entry is not as flippant as it seems.

See DEMOCRAT, a back formation from "democracy."

REVENUE SHARING, *see* TAX SHARING.

REVERSE BIGOTRY the technique of crying "foul" to solidify a racial or religious group behind the candidate supposedly being fouled.

In the 1960 campaign, Republicans who carefully did not raise the "religious issue" felt that John F. Kennedy was raising it at every opportunity in cities with large Catholic populations. His speech to the Houston ministers, pleading for no prejudice in the campaign, was telecast often in major cities where—Republicans said—many regular Republicans who were Catholics were persuaded to switch to one of "their own" who was being unfairly attacked because of his religion. This, they charged, was "reverse bigotry." See BAILEY MEMORANDUM.

Congressman Abraham Ribicoff, running for governor of Connecticut in 1954 against John Davis Lodge, said, "Nowhere except in the Democratic party could a boy named Abe Ribicoff be nominated for governor of this state." In *America's Political*

Dynasties, Stephen Hess wrote: "The Republicans charged that this was a form of reverse bigotry: Ribicoff, in reply, justified his statement by citing some stories from New York newspapers as evidence that his opponents were conducting an undercover smear campaign against him."

Obviously, "reverse bigotry" is a charge as hotly denied as "bigotry." It applies to racial as well as religious appeals. When the House of Representatives in 1967 denied a seat to Congressman Adam Clayton Powell of New York because of his contempt of court citations and improprieties with committee funds, he claimed that his skin color was the only reason for the censure. The *Miami Herald* disagreed: "By crying again and again that his misfortunes are owed to his race, Powell has persuaded the Harlem constituency that Congress excluded him only because he is a Negro. This ignores a congressional record of almost incredible tolerance." Black activist James Meredith decided to challenge Powell in an election, then changed his mind under pressure from civil rights leaders. ". . . there won't be any election in the contested sense," observed the *Herald.* "Adam Clayton Powell's appeal to reverse bigotry has seen to that."

REVERSE DISCRIMINATION, *see* **QUOTAS.**

REVISIONISM a Communist charge that the accused seeks to alter basic tenets of Marxism-Leninism.

In **COMMUNIST TERMINOLOGY,** *deviationism* is internal criticism or refusal to recognize the official party line at any given moment; *revisionism* is a far more serious charge, as explained in the *Political Dictionary,* published in Moscow in 1958:

A tendency in the workers' movement which, to please the bourgeoisie, seeks to debase, emasculate, destroy Marxism by means of revision, that is, reconsideration, distortion, and denial of its fundamental tenets. . . . Contemporary revisionism seeks to defame the teaching of Marxism-Leninism, declares it antiquated, allegedly to have lost, at present, significance for social development. Revisionists seek to undermine the faith of the working class and toiling people in socialism.

Communists recognize revisionism as carrying the seeds of self-destruction (and the source of that cliché can be found in **BODY POLITIC**). Nikita Khrushchev said on January 6, 1961: "We must always keep our powder dry and wage implacable war on revisionism which tries to wipe out the revolutionary essence of Marxism-Leninism, whitewash modern capitalism, undermine the solidarity of the Communist movement, and encourage Communist Parties to go their separate national ways."

Those who are charged with deviationism and revisionism reply that their accusers are afflicted with *dogmatism*—a sin that, according to the 1961 party program, hinders "a correct appraisal of the changing situation and the use of new opportunities for the benefit of the working class and all democratic forces." Another defense is a countercharge of *sectarianism* defined by the Moscow *Political Dictionary* as "striving to quit the masses and to enclose oneself in a narrow circle, and throttles down the initiative of the toiling masses."

Thus, *revisionists* and the milder *deviationists* stand on one side, with *dogmatists* and the milder *sectarians* on the other. In 1964, Communist China began issuing polemics saying that the Soviet Union was led by revisionists: "The revisionists are producing their own opposites and will be buried by them."

The Chinese charge could not be more serious in terms of Communist philosophy. Chairman Mao Tse-tung had said in 1957: "The revisionists deny the differences between socialism and capitalism, between the dictatorship of the proletariat and the dictatorship of the bourgeoisie. What they advocate is in fact not the socialist line but the capitalist line. In present circumstances, revisionism is more pernicious than dogmatism." In the -ISM crossfire, the Chinese in the sixties and seventies added HEGEMONISM to their charge of Soviet revisionism, which meant that the Soviets were not only corrupting the Marx-Engels ideal, but seeking to impose their corruption on China.

The split in the Communist camp, magnified first by Chinese and later by Soviet leaders, calls to mind an observation by anthropologist Ruth Benedict in her classic *Patterns of Culture:* "Even given the freest scope by their institutions, men are never inventive enough to make more than minute changes. From the point of view of an outsider the most radical innovations in any culture amount to no more than a minor revision."

REVOLUTION OF RISING EXPECTATIONS unrest caused by extravagant promises; or, the constructive desire for change based on an optimistic view of society's future; or, the increased demand for a high standard of living that comes when the communications media bring evidence of affluence into poor people's homes.

"Reflections on the Revolution of Rising Expectations" was the title of a 1949 speech by U.S. diplomat Harlan Cleveland. Fifteen years later, in a speech to the UN, Cleveland said:

"The phrase has since been attributed to nearly every literate American of our time, but I think this was the first time that phrase saw the light of day." He titled his UN speech "The Evolution of Rising Responsibilities." For a coinage Cleveland resisted, see SALT (LEXICON).

When Theodore Sorensen was asked to list the qualifications of a USIA director to President-elect John F. Kennedy, one of the key points was: . . . "should comprehend the 'revolution of rising expectations' throughout the world, and its impact on U.S. foreign policy."

In 1968 London's *Economist* titled a review of Gunnar Myrdal's *Asian Drama: An Inquiry into the Poverty of Nations* "The Revolution of Falling Expectation?"

"Revolution," a slashing political word, was somewhat defanged by this phrase, and the process has continued in recent years. When violent protesters preached revolution in the late sixties and early seventies, their word was pre-empted, and thereby softened, by Establishment figures. "The American Revolution is a continuing one," said industrialist David Mahoney, upon taking the chairmanship of the American Revolution Bicentennial Commission in 1970, "a peaceful revolution in a system capable of managing change." In his 1971 State of the Union address, President Nixon labeled his revenue sharing, welfare reform, and government reorganization plans "a New American Revolution."

Semantically, *revolution* is violent change, and *evolution* peaceful change, but the assumption of the word "revolution" by those opposed to violence has taken out a lot of the sting; it is a good example of how a democratic system can counter a threat by absorbing its terminology.

In a similar way, President Johnson's use of WE SHALL OVERCOME and President Nixon's use of POWER TO THE PEOPLE (in connection with REVENUE SHARING) deafened the original users of the phrases with the System's echoes.

REVOLVING DOOR, see HONEST GRAFT.

RHETORIC originally, the study of persuasive presentation of argument, as in speeches; now, bombast, high-flying oratory.

Several forces combined to give a pejorative cast to a word once honored by Aristotle. "DEEDS, NOT WORDS" was a favorite saying of Eisenhower's; "lower our voices" was urged by Nixon in his inaugural; and with the escalation of ESCALATION, the phrase "de-escalate the rhetoric" was aimed at political speakers like Vice President Agnew. Rhetoric was associated with the expansive promises of the Kennedy and Johnson Administrations, and when delivery fell short of promise, emptiness insinuated itself into the definition of rhetoric.

In a 1968 column, Art Buchwald conducted an imaginary interview with a man "manufacturing" political rhetoric as if it were bunting and buttons:

"What item has been moving the best?"

" 'Law and Order' has been the biggest seller this year. We can't even keep the law and order rhetoric in stock. The minute it's put out on the counter, it's grabbed up."

"What else is selling?"

" 'Peace at Home and Abroad' is a very big item. I don't think there's a politician running for office this year who hasn't brought at least one. 'The Crisis of the Cities' is also moving very well, but the one that really

surprised us was 'A Piece of the Action.' We made a few samples, and before we knew it, everybody was using it to describe what the minorities wanted. . . ."

"Another big surprise is our 'Erosion' kit. It comes in a set: 'Erosion of the Cities,' 'Erosion of the Dollar,' 'Erosion of Moral Values,' and 'Erosion of America's Prestige Abroad.' We've also been doing well with 'Rebuilding the Urban and Slum Areas' and 'Facing up to the Challenges and Responsibilities of the Disenfranchised.' "

Rhetoric, as a word, is now most often demeaned by those who admired the effective and inspiring use of language by FDR, Adlai Stevenson, and John F. Kennedy. In denouncing its use, Hubert Humphrey in 1968 used a little himself: "It is time to have done with the language of promise; to have done with the language of excess, of exaggeration. It is time not to carry more sail by way of rhetoric than the ship of state in fact can carry."

See BLOVIATE; TROT OUT THE GHOSTS; VISION OF AMERICA; PERORATION.

RHYME, POLITICAL USE OF
the device of rhyme can make phrases memorable, as in the American GLOOM AND DOOM and the British description of a price-and-wage-control policy, "squeeze and freeze."

It may also be used subtly, appearing to be more rhythm than rhyme, as an oratorical device, as in this speech by John F. Kennedy to the UN in 1961: "We prefer world law, in an age of self-determination, to world war in the age of mass extermination." The cadence of Jimmy Carter's "a dis-*grace* to the human *race,*" about the tax system, was rhetorically effective. See THREE-MARTINI LUNCH.

Or rhyme can be used with a kind

of light-hearted determination, as in Churchill's "Better jaw-jaw than war-war," or his message to FDR prior to the Yalta Conference in 1945: "No more let us falter. From Malta to Yalta. Let nobody alter."

For political use of poetic construction, see MARTIN, BARTON AND FISH; for poems that spawned political phrases, see MOVERS AND SHAKERS; STROKE OF THE PEN; CRADLE AND THE GRAVE; and TWEEDLEDUM AND TWEEDLEDEE.

RICH MAN'S WAR, POOR MAN'S FIGHT protest against inequities in military conscription; of special concern in recent years to civil rights leaders and advocates of student deferments.

The slogan appears to have originated in the Confederacy in 1861, as a protest against laws favoring wealthy plantation owners; it was then picked up in the North and used in the New York draft riots of 1863. At the time, it was possible for a wealthy man to put up cash to have a "substitute" serve in his stead.

Resentment about who does the financing and who does the fighting exists between allies as well; some Britons in 1940 said, "America will fight to the last drop of English blood," and isolationist Americans turned the phrase around to use against the British.

Regarding student deferments during the Vietnam war, University of Chicago sociologist Morris Janowitz pointed out in *Trans-action* magazine that "a young man's chances of serving in the armed forces are decreased to the extent that he applies his energies to extending his education beyond four years of college." Obviously, this slanted student deferments toward wealthier students who could afford postgraduate education.

During the Korean conflict, the casualty rate of the lowest income groups was four times higher than that of the highest income groups, and black casualties—considering their proportion to the population—was twice as high as white. The Rev. Martin Luther King, Jr., an opponent of U.S. involvement in Vietnam, spoke out often in 1967 about what some Negro leaders were calling a "white man's war, a black man's fight." "There are twice as many Negroes in combat in Vietnam," said Dr. King, ". . . and twice as many died in action in proportion to their number in the population as whites." Others answered that black re-enlistments ran three times higher than white, accounting for a higher proportion in military service. This was countered with the point that black re-enlistments were high because career opportunities outside the service were almost nonexistent for blacks.

Negro leader Floyd McKissick said in 1966 that the war in Vietnam was "a way of drafting black men to go fight yellow men in order to protect this land that the white men stole from the red men."

RIDER a provision added to a bill not necessarily germane to the bill's purpose.

A bill passed by a legislative body must be signed by a Chief Executive to become a law; in most cases, an "item veto" is not permitted, and the President, governor or mayor must accept it all or reject it all. Riders are tacked on to unrelated legislation for two reasons: (1) an objectionable rider, sure to be vetoed, is added so as to force a veto of the portion of the bill the rider-sponsoring legislator is trying to "bring down"; (2) a bill that would likely be vetoed by itself is added to important appropriations legislation so as to "slip past" the Chief Executive.

Said President Roosevelt in 1938: "I want you to know that I completely agree with your criticism of legislative 'riders' on tax and appropriation bills. Regardless of the merits or demerits of any such 'riders'—and I do not enter that phase of the discussion at the moment—the manifest fact remains that this practice robs the Executive of legitimate and essential freedom of action in dealing with legislation."

Charles Ledyard Norton offered a fanciful derivation in 1890: "In common speech, a rider is the top rail of a zig-zag fence. Such a fence is 'staked and ridered' when stakes are driven in the angles and a rider laid across them. A rider is not an essential part of a fence, nor of a bill, but it adds considerably to the effectiveness of both."

In fact, the *OED* traces the expression back in English jurisprudence to 1669: "That which is certified shall be annexed to the Record, and is called a Rider-roll."

Riders, carried to an extreme, result in "Christmas Tree Bills." The *New York Times* in 1967 deplored the attempts by protectionists "to tack a series of riders sought by domestic industry onto the Administration's proposals for higher old-age benefits. Their hope is that Congress will give its approval to the entire 'Christmas tree' package. . . . The only sure way to stop the Christmas-tree bill is to chop it down before it is planted."

Elliot Richardson, then Secretary of Health, Education and Welfare, said in 1970: "Until I became Secretary, I had never heard 'Christmas tree' used as a transitive verb." Explained Alan Otten in the *Wall Street Journal* (December 23, 1970): "On Capitol Hill, the practice of tagging a host of special-interest amendments to a popular bill is known as 'Christmas-treeing' the bill."

RIF to discharge from a government job; or, to eliminate a job category or slot in such a way as to make it difficult for the employee to stay.

To rif—from the initials of Reduction in Force—is a sixties Washington acronym that has spread to state capitals. The term is usually heard during the transition between Administrations, and is a euphemism intended to make cooly impersonal what is usually a personal or political decision.

"I thought you'd be interested in a word that has entered the Albany argot as a result of Governor [Hugh] Carey's budget cutbacks," reporter Paul Hoffman wrote the author in 1977, "—the verb *to rif,* usually used in past tense, as 'I've been riffed,' or 'He was riffed.' Meaning to lose one's job as the result of a Reduction in Force."

Spelled both RIF and "riff," the verb is in Merriam-Webster's *New International Dictionary* (3rd edition); its first citations were from 1953. After a generation, it is fair to assume the transition from acronym has been made, though its specific origin inclines this lexicographer to prefer one *f.*

See HIT LIST; ACRONYMS, POLITICAL.

RIGGED CONVENTION, *see* **BROKERED CONVENTION; OPEN CONVENTION.**

RIGHT TO KNOW a new "right" that journalists say exists, justifying their inquiries; often conflicts with right to privacy and right to a fair trial.

Arthur Hays Sulzberger, president of the *New York Times,* stated the case for the "right to know" in 1956: "The crux is not the publisher's 'freedom to print'; it is rather, the citizens' 'right to know.' "

Ten years later, columnist Max Lerner took a different view, in connection with Jacqueline Kennedy's successful effort to edit material she had given in confidence to author William Manchester:

Clearly there are limits on such a right. We have no right to know about top-secret documents which have not yet been declassified. . . . Nor have we a right to know private things, even about public officials or their families against their wishes.

Thus the right to know is circumscribed by public policy, by taste, by codes of fairness, by the right of privacy.

More important than the right to know is the right to publish.

This too, is a limited right—limited by the obscenity statutes, by libel laws, by judicial interpretations of both. But the right to publish becomes a precious right when there are unwarranted censorship efforts to prevent publication.

The right to know is a philosophical extension, rather than justification, of freedom of the press. In the nineteen sixties, the controversy grew over the issue called "free press vs. fair trial." The Supreme Court held in 1966 that Dr. Samuel Sheppard had been denied his right to a fair trial—i.e., by a jury unprejudiced by information obtained outside the courtroom—because of the press campaign against him conducted primarily by the *Cleveland Press.*

The new "right" shoulders its way among other established rights and resists enthusiastic support. There is an upright ring to "the right to know." But when a newsman accepts a court citation for contempt in refusing to reveal a source, he is in effect denying the public's right to know his source, on the grounds that it will—in the long run—make it impossible for him to keep the public informed, which he maintains is the public's "right."

In 1971 the *New York Times* published selections from a secret 47-volume study of the origins of the Vietnamese war, which they labeled "Vietnam Archive" but which promptly became known as the "Pentagon Papers." After the series began, the government moved to enjoin publication; the Supreme Court ultimately upheld the right of the *Times* and other newspapers to publish the documents. Chief Justice Burger, in a dissenting opinion, used the phrase in this way: "The newspapers make a derivative claim under the First Amendment; they denominate this right as the public right-to-know; by implication, the *Times* asserts a sole trusteeship of that right by virtue of its journalist 'scoop.' The right is asserted as an absolute. Of course, the First Amendment right itself is not an absolute, as Justice Holmes so long ago pointed out in his aphorism concerning the right to shout of fire in a crowded theater."

This decision made clear that under circumstances presenting a clear danger to lives or an overriding national interest, the courts would uphold the public's right *not* to know. Soviet dissident and author Alexander Solzhenitsyn (see GULAG) used that phrase in a cultural rather than legal context at a Harvard commencement address in June of 1978: "People also have a right not to know, and it is a much more valuable one. The right not to have their divine souls stuffed with gossip, nonsense, vain talk. A person who works, who leads a meaningful life, does not need this excessive flow of information." Cartoonist Edward Sorel mocked this view in *Esquire* magazine with a drawing of the well-to-do and the flag wavers marching under the banner of "Americans for a Closed Society."

The controversy recalled to some writers George Washington's complaint in 1777: "It is much to be wished that our Printers were more discreet in many of their Publications. We see almost in every Paper, Proclamations or accounts transmitted by the Enemy, of an injurious nature. If some hint or caution could be given them on the subject, it might be of material Service."

General William Tecumseh Sherman went further. He arrested one of Horace Greeley's correspondents covering the Civil War for the *New York Herald*, charged him with spying and would have shot him were it not for President Lincoln's intervention. Upon hearing that three other correspondents were killed by artillery, General Sherman observed, "Good, now we shall have news from Hell before breakfast."

RIGHT TO WORK   a movement to stop making union membership a requirement for employment.

Management has clearly won the battle of semantics with labor while labor has won the more substantive victories. *Right to work* is a management slogan that has been adopted as the generic term for anticompulsory-union legislation, which labor refers to as *union-busting laws*. Management's term for a factory that will employ only a union member is CLOSED SHOP, connoting the sinister shutting out of men who refuse to join a union, while the labor term is *union shop*, connoting a smiling band of collectively organized workers; "closed"

is the word accepted by the public.

The Taft-Hartley Act permits the union, or closed, shop, but its Section 14b also permits states to pass laws prohibiting them—"right-to-work legislation." In 1958, this turned out to be a SLEEPER issue that upset two well-known Republicans.

Senate Minority Leader William Knowland, a powerful vote-getter in California, was running for governor in 1958 against Attorney General "Pat" Brown. Sam Brightman, publicity head of the Democratic State Committee, asked Brown where he stood on right-to-work. "Oh, I'm against Right-to-Work," Brown said, "but I don't think it's a big issue in California." Brightman disagreed: "The national platform opposes so-called [see SNEER WORDS] 'Right-to-Work.' Speaking out on the issue will help identify you with the national party and it'll help you with labor." Brown spoke out at a press conference, Knowland took issue and made it the focal point of the campaign, and Brown upset the better-known candidate.

Meanwhile, in Ohio, the issue upset Republican Senator John Bricker, heir to Robert A. Taft as a symbol of conservatism, with labor-supported Stephen M. Young winning by 150,-000 votes. The Ohio Republican State Chairman, Ray Bliss, had urged the party to evade the issue, was overruled, and emerged from the debacle a political sage.

By 1968, nineteen states had right-to-work laws, but not a single major industrial state had one on its books after Indiana repealed its eight-year-old law in 1965. The laws exist in states anxious to attract industry and with no appreciable labor influence. Though organized labor has not been able to repeal Section 14 b of Taft-Hartley on the national level, it has successfully defeated right-to-work in every major state contest since the issue broke.

"So the right-to-work movement is pretty much dead, right? Wrong," wrote the *Wall Street Journal* in 1967. "The [National Right To Work] Committee is ambitiously building its field staff in selected states and planning bigger public campaigns. And labor is vowing to spend all that's necessary to beat back the attack."

Popularization of the phrase in a different meaning belongs to Socialist leader Eugene V. Debs: "Every man has the inalienable right to work." Ralph Waldo Emerson, in his essay on politics, said, "every man has a right to be employed," and in the first half of the nineteenth century, the phrase was The Right to Labor. A German writer in 1808 wrote of *das Recht zu Arbeit,* and French social scientist François Fourier published, in the same year, a theory of four movements that included *le droit du travail.* In Franklin Roosevelt's 1944 campaign, the most vital part of his "economic bill of rights" was, "the right of a useful and remunerative job," though he hastened to add, "I believe that private enterprise can give full employment to our people."

In all those cases, the "right to work" meant, "the opportunity to make a living must be given to all."

Early use of the phrase in its present meaning was in a Bernard Partridge cartoon—"the Right to Work" —in *Punch,* April 3, 1912. John Bull is saying to a striker: "I can't make you work if you won't; but if this man wants to, I can make you let him. And I will." The capture of the phrase by management was a master stroke, with its built-in implication that unions prevented some men from making a living.

The same turnaround—taking a negative or defensive position and fashioning it into a positive slogan— was used by opponents of abortion in the seventies, who changed their appellation from "anti-abortion" to "right to life."

For another example of slanted generics, see **"TRUTH-IN" CONSTRUCTION.**

RIPPER BILL   action of a legislature to emasculate, or "rip out," power held by a lower body or administrative agency dominated by the opposite party.

"Some of the warmest arguments in the legislature," wrote Al Smith, ex-governor of New York, in 1929, ". . . occurred over what were called 'ripper' bills. The party in power would legislate their opponents out of office."

By "Special Acts," state legislatures would set up municipal characters, grant franchises, transfer powers between state agencies, and restrict or expand the powers of governors. A state legislature controlled by one party can "rip" the charter of a city controlled by the other party, and thus elicit demands for **HOME RULE;** by this means, party leaders can also punish reform elements in their own party.

ROAD TO DEFEAT   conservative Republican charge that liberal **ME TOO** tactics have failed.

Senator Everett Dirksen stood at the rostrum in the Chicago Stockyards at the 1952 Republican convention and waved a finger at twice-defeated New York Governor Thomas E. Dewey, now supporting Dwight Eisenhower against Senator Robert A. Taft.

"We followed you before," Dirksen intoned, "and you took us down the road to defeat." Taft men rose and booed Dewey, who sat stonily; the New York delegation returned the jeers, and hecklers shouted at the speaker and each other. Dirksen, who had brought the latent resentment to a head with his "road to defeat" remark, promptly reversed his field: "This is no place for Republicans to be booing any other Republican."

Dirksen was able to live down the divisive statement and become Senate Minority Leader, but Goldwater supporters frequently recalled the remark in the 1964 primary fight against Nelson Rockefeller.

The political-road metaphor is well traveled. The MIDDLE OF THE ROAD is favored on the *campaign trail;* and HIGH ROAD ... LOW ROAD is referred to by men with sights set on *Pennsylvania Avenue* who decry GUTTER FLYERS and MADISON AVENUE TECHNIQUES as efforts to confuse the MAN IN THE STREET.

ROCK AND A HARD PLACE, BETWEEN A   to be in difficulty; in recent usage, to be faced with either a moral dilemma or a HOBSON'S CHOICE.

John Ehrlichman used this phrase in testifying before the Senate Watergate committee; it was common parlance in the White House in the early seventies and became a vogue phrase in politics in the mid-seventies.

With the emphasis on "hard," the phrase seems to suggest that the choice faced is between a rock and a substance even harder than a rock. The meaning is similar to "between the devil and the deep blue sea."

In the *American Thesaurus of Slang,* Lester Berrey and Melvin Van Der Bark place the phrase under the entry for "Bewildered; perplexed; baffled" and include it with "against

the wall," "flummuxed," "hot and bothered."

In 1921 B. H. Lehman, writing in *Dialect Notes* about words used in California, gave a different interpretation. "To be between a rock and a hard place" is defined as "to be bankrupt." Professor Lehman reported the verb-phrase was "common in Arizona in recent panics, sporadic in California."

The expression has a Western flavor, and many of the aides in the Nixon White House were Westerners; it is likely that they popularized it in a media center like Washington, much as the Japanese word HONCHO was picked up in California and blossomed in the District of Columbia.

In current use the meaning of "confusion" seems to have atrophied; the phrase is generally used now along with another vogue phrase, "to be in big trouble," and carries a special meaning of being torn or tortured by a moral choice.

Washington Post editorial writers Philip Geyelin and Meg Greenfield toyed with, but decided against, the notion of titling an editorial about Afghanistan "Between Iraq and a Hard Place."

ROCK-RIBBED   inflexible, used by a critic; steadfast, or staunch, used by a friend.

"Rock-ribbed" is an adjective that has become associated with conservative Republicans, much as DYED-IN-THE-WOOL is a Democratic term. Poet William Cullen Bryant, in *Thanatopsis,* wrote of "The hills/ Rock-ribbed and ancient as the sun . . ." which Senator Andrew Johnson quoted in a political context in 1861: ". . . we stand immovable upon our basis, as on our own native mountains—presenting their craggy brows, their unexplored caverns, their summits, 'rock-ribbed and ancient as the sun'—we stand speaking peace, association and concert to a distracted Republic."

This hyphenated adjective often has a shifting pronunciation. If the noun does not follow, the emphasis is on the second word, as "He is rock-*ribbed*," but if the noun follows, the emphasis is on the first word, as "He is a *rock*-ribbed Republican."

ROORBACK a fictitious slander, an outrageous lie told to smear a political figure during a campaign.

"A roorback!" declared *New York Times* columnist James Reston to a colleague, denouncing a false story about presidential candidate Jimmy Carter during the 1976 campaign. He was not able to find the word in any of the standard dictionaries.

As election day drew near in 1844, the *Ithaca* (N.Y.) *Chronicle* printed what it claimed was a portion of "A Tour Through the Western and Southern States" by a "Baron Roorback," stating that Democratic candidate James K. Polk had bought forty-three slaves and branded his initials on their shoulders. Other newspapers picked up the story, which later turned out to be a forgery by an Ithaca abolitionist. The name is now applied to any last-minute smear, and is why many newspapers are leery of publishing damaging stories on the day before election.

See SMEAR; GUTTER FLYER.

ROOT, HOG, OR DIE a political proverb meaning "work for your office, or leave it."

In lean years, a hungry hog must learn to root in the ground for his food or starve. This proverb probably had nonpolitical origins, but it was popularized early in the Andrew Jackson era.

The *Calumet and War Club* publication in 1836 spelled out the SPOILS SYSTEM agreement of the Jacksonians: "Root, hog, or die—work for your office, or leave it—support the party, right or wrong—are the terms of the agreement."

The original spoils system connotation has worn off and the current occasional use is now a rough exhortation to get out and campaign.

See PROVERBS AND AXIOMS, POLITICAL.

ROSE GARDEN RUBBISH supposedly ad-lib remarks made by the President on minor occasions, usually prepared in note form by the most junior of White House speechwriters.

Political leaders are expected to make "appropriate remarks" at informal ceremonies, and often wish to have ideas submitted in advance, around which they can extemporize. Since many of these ceremonies take place in places like the White House Rose Garden, the phrase "Rose Garden rubbish" was coined in the Lyndon Johnson speechwriting staff to derogate the job of preparing the seemingly off-the-cuff appropriatenesses. Peter Benchley, a junior speechwriter who later gained fame as the author of the novel *Jaws,* popularized the term in a *Life* article.

The phrase is too self-critical to be used officially around the White House; in the Nixon era, the unloved task was referred to by the President with a musical metaphor: "Grace notes."

John B. McDonald, one of the second-string Nixon speechwriters in 1972, wrote an open letter to the Jimmy Carter speechwriters in the *Washington Post* in 1977, cautioning them that not all presidential prose was earth-shaking or even important:

"You're not yet acutely familiar with Rose Garden Rubbish—but you soon will be. Why is the President delighted that Miss Teenage America is calling on him? What does he say to the head of the American Dental Association? What does he tell someone who is off to deliver two musk oxen to the People's Republic of China? . . . these are all real items and the President can't wing them—somebody has to develop some background suggestions for lines of credible commentary. Don't look around—you're it."

The outdoor area near the Oval Office—a small lawn surrounded by flower beds, with magnolia trees in the corners—is called the Rose Garden, though it contains few rose bushes. White House gardeners rarely put red rose plants in, because they consider dark colors "heavy" for a garden, which is the sort of fact a speechwriter would provide a President who was welcoming a delegation of horticulturists.

ROTTEN BOROUGHS districts with unusually large representation for a small population.

In England from the sixteenth through eighteenth centuries, "rotten" or "pocket" boroughs existed with as few as a hundred voters sending a representative to Parliament. These seats were controlled by landowners who either bribed or coerced the voters in their area to vote their way; the seats were often sold by "borough-mongers" (see -MONGER). Reform bills in 1832 and 1867 eliminated the practice.

The phrase is traceable to 1771 in England and to Civil War days in the U.S.; the *Cincinnati Enquirer* in 1874 wrote: "The Republican South is Grant's 'rotten borough.' " States like Nevada and Delaware, with two senators despite their small population,

were attacked as rotten boroughs, though the Constitution provided two senators for the express reason of protecting the rights of the smaller states.

In recent years the phrase has been used in the campaign to reapportion voting districts in accordance with the principle of ONE MAN, ONE VOTE. The connotation of seats bought and sold is now gone, the meaning of unfair representation remaining. "Three cases protesting apportionment," wrote the *New Republic* in April 1967, "plus a fourth in Virginia, are now before the Supreme Court testing how far one-man, one-vote shall dissolve rotten boroughs. There are about 90,000 local political bodies in the U.S., of which perhaps 20,000 would be affected by a court ruling."

See GERRYMANDER.

RUBBER-CHICKEN CIRCUIT the interminable series of public luncheons and dinners which are an inescapable part of campaigning and officeholding.

"Rubber" chicken is tough. So is campaigning. Robert Phelps of the *New York Times* described in 1964 the stamina needed by a presidential candidate: "The candidate must be capable of covering up to 200,000 miles by air, ingesting 600 chicken dinners, delivering 2500 speeches, clasping hands with a million persons and smiling gaily while being smacked with 10 tons of confetti." Another *Times* reporter in 1967 wrote of George Wallace's presidential campaign: ". . . his political advance men soon discovered that the baked chicken and green pea circuit was not only willing, but often eager, to have him as a speaker."

FAT CATS at $100-a-plate affairs get steak or roast beef and rissolé potatoes (why always rissolé potatoes?) but at non-fund-raising affairs, where the purpose is to meet the candidate and $10 covers the cost of the function, chicken is *de rigueur.* Candidates are expected to make appearances sitting on the dais of several functions per evening, many philanthropic or civic, at which they make nonpolitical remarks and make a pass at their plates.

The result is often a combination of mental and physical malnutrition, brought on by a revulsion toward hotel food in general, and chicken in particular. Senator Jacob Javits of New York eats at home before going to a dinner and spends his time at the dinner visiting every table, starting with the rear balcony. Robert Price, former campaign manager for Mayor John Lindsay, insisted that his candidate "must eat one meal of red meat a day—no matter what."

"When the dinners run out," said candidate John F. Kennedy in 1960, "the luncheons begin, and when the luncheons run out, the breakfasts begin. We may all meet next week to get the campaign out of the red with a midnight brunch at eighty-five dollars a person—and I will be there."

According to restaurateur George Lang, the rubberization of chicken requires (1) a miscalculation of timing by the organizing committee, allowing the juices of the chicken to congeal while the dais is being introduced; (2) a chef whose oven is too hot; and (3) a food buyer with a sharp eye for stringy birds. A practiced rubberizer cooks the chicken hours before the function and reheats it for serving; when this is not possible, a tender roast chicken can be made quite rubbery by exposure to a steam table for a few minutes.

In recent years, testimonial dinners have come under fire, especially after employees of Connecticut Senator Thomas Dodd leaked the senator's files to columnist Drew Pearson, raising the question of the diversion of campaign funds to the personal use of the senator. This caused the *Washington Post* to editorialize in April 1967: "By and large, the 'testimonial dinner' is a political fraud, a gastronomical affront, an ethical outrage, a colossal bore, an insufferable social disaster and financial shakedown."

A counterpart in England is "function fish." In the U.S., the key to the phrase is "circuit": *baked (or roast) chicken circuit, roast beef circuit, chicken-and-mashed-potatoes circuit* are among the many variations. The phrase derives from vaudeville use, when performers were booked into a string of theaters; the word bore a treadmill connotation which has carried over into politics.

See WAXWORKS.

RUBBER STAMP a legislature or political figure taking orders from a political leader, or dominated by the executive branch.

"They centered all their powers in the Executive," Herbert Hoover reported Al Smith as saying in 1936 about the last two Congresses, "and that is the reason why you read in the newspapers reference to Congress as the rubber-stamp Congress."

In 1967, former FDR brain truster Raymond Moley disagreed. "The seventy-third Congress was no 'rubber stamp.' Its leadership was rich in talent and experience. The concept of an assembly line from the White House to the Congress cannot be sustained by the facts."

Theodore Roosevelt's biographer, William Thayer, used the phrase in 1919, as an exhortation William Howard Taft (long dominated by Roosevelt) might have heard: "Be your own President; don't be anybody's man or rubber stamp." Edward Conrad Smith, in his 1924 *Dictionary of American Politics,* wrote: "... the term was first used to characterize several members of President Wilson's cabinet who seemed to have practically no influence on the conduct of affairs."

On a television program in 1962, Harvard Law Professor Mark DeWolfe Howe objected to Ted Kennedy's candidacy for senator from Massachusetts: "Seeking an office in the United States Senate, while his brother is in the White House, seems to me to represent a total misunderstanding of the responsibilities of a United States Senator. To have a rubber stamp Senator is to me an offense against the whole tradition that there should be a separation of powers in our government."

In Huey Long's heyday, the Louisiana state legislature was known as "Huey's trained seals." As senator, Long ran the state through the supremely acquiescent Governor O. K. Allen, about whom Huey's brother Earl once said, "A leaf blew in the window of Allen's office one day and fell on his desk. He signed it."

RUGGED INDIVIDUALISM
Herbert Hoover's philosophy of economic freedom, equal opportunity, and personal initiative, as opposed to what he considered paternalistic government.

Toward the close of the 1928 campaign against Democrat Al Smith, Herbert Hoover spoke in New York on October 22, determined, as he recalled years later, to "draw the issue of the American system, as opposed to all forms of collectivism." He sketched the background of the necessary government involvement in the economy in World War I, then posed the peacetime dilemma:

We are challenged with a peacetime choice between the American system of rugged individualism and a European philosophy of diametrically opposed doctrines—doctrines of paternalism and state socialism. The acceptance of these ideas would have meant the destruction of self-government through centralization of government. It would have meant the undermining of the individual initiative and enterprise through which our people have grown to unparalleled greatness.

The Republican Party from the beginning resolutely turned its face away from these ideas ...

Six years after the phrase became a part of the American political lexicon, Hoover disclaimed coinage: "While I can make no claim for having introduced the term 'rugged individualism,' I should be proud to have invented it. It has been used by American leaders for over a half-century in eulogy of those God-fearing men and women of honesty whose stamina and character and fearless assertion of rights led them to make their own way in life."

At the time and for many years afterward, opponents of Hoover used the phrase with a sneer. Socialist Norman Thomas, two weeks after the speech was delivered, used the phrase as his text: "Mr. Hoover calls his capitalism 'rugged individualism' and professes to find some peculiar virtue in the wasteful and chaotic mismanagement of coal, in our frantic real-estate speculation ..."

In 1936, Franklin Roosevelt was too cagey to tackle individualism head-on at the Democratic convention; his reference was oblique: "I believe in individualism ... up to the point where the individualist starts to operate at the expense of society." But the association of Hoover with the phrase itself enabled FDR to make it a target in a campaign speech:

> . . . I know how the knees of all of our *rugged individualists* were trembling four years ago and how their hearts fluttered. They came to Washington in great numbers. Washington did not look like a dangerous bureaucracy to them then. Oh, no! It looked like an emergency hospital. . . . And now most of the patients seem to be doing very nicely. Some of them are even well enough to throw their crutches at the doctor.

As hatred of Hoover cooled, the use of "rugged individualism" lost some of its built-in sarcasm, and came to be regarded by most as a quaint hearkening-back to the simple virtues of America's early days. But President Harry S. Truman chose to RUN AGAINST HOOVER as well as Dewey in 1948:

> Many of you remember 1932. . . . Out here on Eighth Avenue veterans were selling apples. Ragged individualism, I suppose that's what you would call it.

RULE OF LAW   the rubric used to attack the assumption of extralegal authority or "inherent power" by the Executive; the assertion that a nation's leaders must abide by a written constitution or unwritten common law.

Though Tom Paine had said a century before that we stood as a nation "where the law is king," the phrase was popularized by A. V. Dicey, in his 1885 *Introduction to the Law of the Constitution.* In his definition, the "rule of law" in England meant that ordinary courts determined every man's legal rights and liabilities; that executive officers had less arbitrary power and more limited discretion than in other European countries; and that government officials could be brought to court for wrongs done even under the cloak of official authority.

In the U.S., this idea is more frequently expressed as GOVERNMENT OF LAWS, NOT OF MEN. Although the maxim "Necessity knows no law" is sometimes used as a justification for emergency actions, most politicians concede that—when the emergency is over—the extralegal acts are not to be condoned. ("Extralegal" is a forgiving euphemism for "illegal," which in turn is less severe than "unlawful.")

Historian J. G. Randall, in his 1926 classic *Constitutional Problems under Lincoln,* wrote of Civil War repression: "Instead of the 'rule of law' prevailing, as Dicey defined it, men were imprisoned outside the law and independent of the courts; and governmental officers were given a privileged place above the law and made immune from penalties for wrongs committed . . . Legally, the Civil War stands out as an eccentric period, a time when constitutional restraints did not fully operate and when the 'rule of law' largely broke down."

See MEASURES, NOT MEN; HIGHER LAW.

RULE OR RUIN, *see* GAG RULE.

RULE OUT   to deny the existence of even a remote possibility.

The use of a question that begins "Are you ruling out . . ." is a sign of journalistic desperation. On dull news days, reporters are forced to ask a question that gives them a weak lead either way it is answered.

The only story more tenuous than "The President today ruled out any chance of [whatever]" is "The President today refused to rule out consideration of [whatever]."

The rule-out question gained popularity in the late sixties, especially at press conferences of White House press secretary Ronald Ziegler. An attempt is made occasionally to blunt the surefire either-way story with an odd use of language: "I'm not ruling it out, but that doesn't mean I'm ruling it in."

RUMP SESSION a gathering of dissidents; or, a legislative body that refuses to disband according to law.

"It is not fit that you should sit here any longer!" shouted Oliver Cromwell to the "Rump Parliament." ". . . You shall now give place to better men." After England's Second Civil War of 1648, Cromwell's Colonel Pride ejected ninety-six Presbyterian members from Parliament who were suspected of dealings with the defeated King Charles ("Pride's Purge"), and the remaining sixty were known as the Rump.

The word "rump" is from the Scandinavian word for the hindquarters of an animal, its meaning crossing over to "remnant" or "tail end."

The word was popularized in the U.S. around the time of our own Civil War. In 1860 Stephen Douglas was called the candidate of a "rump convention," and Congress in Reconstruction days was called a "rump Congress" by Democrats who felt it did not represent all the states and was therefore in unlawful session. The most famous rump convention was Theodore Roosevelt's "Bull Moose" split-off from the Republicans in 1912.

In current use, "rump" is used with *caucus, convention, session,* and *meeting,* usually connoting a sorehead minority that cannot lose gracefully.

RUNNING AGAINST HOOVER making a theme, rather than an individual, the target or villain in a campaign.

"Every campaign needs a villain," Thomas E. Dewey told the author in 1969. He recommended that President Nixon make inflation his villain, just as FDR did with ECONOMIC ROYALISTS and Truman with SPECIAL INTERESTS. "Roosevelt never ran against me," said the man who had twice lost to FDR. "He just kept running against Hoover."

"Running against Hoover," in political parlance, has little to do with Herbert Hoover as an individual. Instead, the phrase denotes campaigning against the memory of hard times, the fear of joblessness and depression.

As personal recollections of depression days have faded in the minds of most of the population, another fear —frustration, really—has made itself felt, at first articulated by George Wallace in his SEND THEM A MESSAGE campaign against big government, the Establishment, the "pointed-headed professors." Nixon, too, in 1968 would "run against Washington," but in a more muted way, decrying "more of the same" from Hubert Humphrey, but unable—after his own years as Vice President and in Congress—to credibly adopt an outright anti-Washington stance.

"Running against Washington" was frequently imputed to be candidate Jimmy Carter's basic strategy; as an "outsider," he could credibly evoke the widespread resentment against faceless and distant government felt by so many people who were most often described as "alienated" or afflicted with feelings of "powerlessness."

Perhaps alone among the other Democratic candidates, Hubert Humphrey in 1976 took on those who were "running against Washington." In March, as Jimmy Carter began winning his first primaries, the warhorse from Minnesota said: "Candidates who make an attack on Washington are making an attack on government programs, on the poor, on blacks, on minorities, on the cities. It's a disguised new form of racism, a disguised new form of conservatism."

An earlier use of "running against" a theme was for a politician to be "against sin." That comes from a legend in the twenties that Mrs. Calvin Coolidge asked her taciturn husband the subject of a sermon he attended. He replied, "Sin." She asked, "What did the preacher have to say?" The President is said to have answered, "He was against it."

RUNNING DOGS, *see* **FELLOW TRAVELER.**

RUNNING FOR THE EXERCISE going through the motions of campaigning in a hopeless cause.

Asked on February 10, 1976, who he thought his most likely Democratic opponent would be, President Ford told reporters he thought all along it would be Senator Hubert Humphrey "—and I think all the rest of them are running for the exercise."

When a candidate enlists in a seemingly impossible campaign, he enters a self-hypnotic experience that soon magnifies a *remote possibility* into an *outside chance* into a probability of *making a good showing* into a *good bet for an upset.* He points out that he is not "running for the exercise"; his friends still think he is.

An American *runs* for election; an Englishman *stands* for election; the French verb is *se battre,* to *"struggle,"* or *se présenter,* to *"present oneself,"* for election. The English metaphor is based on a trial: the candidate stands for election as he would "stand trial." The American metaphor is that of a race.

"Run" has a place in a variety of political expressions, its usage traceable to Alexander Hamilton in 1792. See **RUN SCARED; RUNNING MATE; FRONT RUNNER.** The *Ohio State Journal* in 1840 pointed out that "General Harrison constantly *runs ahead of his ticket."* A campaign is most frequently compared to a *race,* and an easy victory is *winning in a walk.* Former Interior Secretary Harold Ickes, referring to a poor speech at the Gridiron Club by Senator John Bricker in 1946, said, "Before his speech . . . Bricker thought he was running for the Republican nomination for President. Now he is not only walking, he is limping . . ."

The antonym is **SHOO-IN,** also a racing expression.

RUNNING LIKE A DRY CREEK describing a campaigner who is not hitting as hard as some of his supporters would like.

Nineteen newspapers of the Scripps-Howard chain ran a front-page editorial in 1952, six weeks after Eisenhower was nominated, declaring "Ike is running like a dry creek." This was just after he half-heartedly defended General George C. Marshall against criticism by Senator William Jenner of Indiana, concluding, "Maybe he made some mistakes. I don't know about that." The editorial said that the General sounded like "just another **ME-TOO** candidate" and criticized him for not "coming out swinging." "If Ike doesn't know [about Marshall], he had better find out. For that's one of the big issues of this campaign. Ask any mother, father, or wife of a soldier now in Korea. . . . We still cling to the hope that . . . he will hit hard. If he doesn't, he may as well concede defeat."

The phrase appears to be Western

in origin, has been in politics for some time, and is in frequent current use. Campaigns also *never get off the ground* or *never catch fire.*

In Eisenhower's case, of course, the *dry creek* wound up in a *flood* of votes, a *tidal wave* of support, as he received *thunderous* ovations and a *shower* of contributions, *snowing under* his opponent and establishing his *don't-rock-the-boat* position in the *mainstream.* For other watery metaphors, see TRICKLE-DOWN THEORY; PUMP-PRIMING.

RUNNING MATE a candidate running on the same ticket, for a lower office; most often used in connection with the vice-presidential nominee.

"Governor Marshall bears the highest reputation," said Woodrow Wilson on July 4, 1912, ". . . and I feel honored by having him as a running mate." This was the first recorded use of the phrase by a presidential nominee, though the racing term had been in use in 1900. "Men of all parties," wrote the *Review of Reviews,* "will admit that Mr. Root's name would add positive strength, and that a better man could hardly be selected as Mr. McKinley's 'running mate.' "

In horse racing, a single stable will often enter two horses in a race, the lesser horse used as a pacesetter and called a running mate. This second horse usually vanishes into obscurity. Vice President Hubert Humphrey, reminiscing in 1966 about the 1964 campaign against the Goldwater-Miller ticket: "To this day I have a great deal of respect for Barry Goldwater and his running mate, what's-his-name." This was soon followed by a satiric song by Tom Lehrer, "I Wonder What Happened to Hubert."

When the running mate is stronger or better-known than the candidate for the top job, the result is called a KANGAROO TICKET.

RUN SCARED an admonition to avoid complacency; to run as if a good chance to lose existed, despite indications of likely victory.

"I expect to win running like a singed cat," said Adlai Stevenson in 1952. Dwight Eisenhower in 1956, who had less reason to campaign aggressively, said, "I believe when you are in any contest you should work like there is—to the very last minute —a chance to lose it. This is battle, this is politics, this is anything."

The candidate whose polls show him behind needs no advice to run scared; he does so automatically. The phrase is directed in particular to the candidate who is in the position of Thomas E. Dewey in 1948, considered a SHOO-IN. Hindsighted politicians now say Dewey should have "run scared"—conducted a more aggressive, fighting campaign—but the fact was that the Dewey managers did run scared, at the behest of party leaders—scared of saying anything that would "rock the boat," afraid of making a mistake that would give Truman an opening. See STIR UP THE ANIMALS.)

RUSTLING BEHIND THE JALOUSIES intervention in political affairs by the candidate's wife.

John A. Wells, a New York attorney who has managed campaigns for such Republicans as Nelson Rockefeller, Jacob Javits, Louis Lefkowitz, and others, once agreed to manage a political campaign provided, as he put it to the candidate, "there is no rustling behind the jalousies." His condition was met: the candidate's wife, noted for her outspoken opinions about the scheduling of the candidate's time, was effectively silenced for the duration.

The phrase is not as strong as **POWER BEHIND THE THRONE** or **GRAY EMINENCE**; its reference is exclusively feminine. A jalousie is a slatted screen, providing concealment without stopping whispered henpecking or the sound of a swishing skirt.

SACHEM   a party leader.

"Take me to your leader," a bromide used in dealing with savages, is reflected in the first recorded use of "sachem": "They brought us to their Sachim," the 1622 *Journal of the Plantation at Plymouth* records, ". . . very personable, gentle, courteous, and fayre conditioned." The word is from the Narraganset, an Algonquian language, meaning "sagamore" or "party chief," and was used by Tammany leaders as early as 1876. A political joke based on this construction is the grafter's request: "Lead me to your taker."

John Adams, in 1776, wrote of "The patricians, the sachems, the nabobs . . . [who] sigh, moan and fret." The braves and warriors of Tammany named their leader the Grand Sachem, who presided over meetings held at the "wigwam"; today, political leadership meetings are frequently termed "powwows."

The word is not used currently by politicians, but is frequently used—along with SATRAP—by political columnists and reporters. For other Indian words in politics, see MUCK-EY-MUCKS; MUGWUMP; CAUCUS; RAINMAKER.

SAFE   applied to a politician, reliable; applied to a district or constituency, taken for granted.

In James Russell Lowell's *Bigelow Papers* of 1862, a character says, "Long 'z ye sift out 'safe' canderdates thet no one aint afeared on." Lincoln Steffens wrote in a 1905 issue of *McClure's:* "The gubernatorial chair [in Rhode Island] never had amounted to much more than an empty honor for 'safe men.' "

In its political use, "safe" means regular and not likely to bolt. Mencken defined it as "not radical," but a radical can be safe to other radicals if he is not likely to turn conservative. When presidential candidates total up likely delegate support, the categories are "safe," "shaky," and "leaning away."

"They don't concede [Harold] Stassen one chance in a million," wrote John Gunther in 1947, ". . . they know that the better the prospects of Republican victory in 1948, the less are Stassen's own chances for the nomination—since, if victory is certain, there is no temptation to choose any but the 'safest' candidate." In 1952 Eisenhower was not nearly as safe to delegates as Senator Robert A. Taft, but after twenty years out of office they preferred a safe bet for election to a safe candidate.

SALAMI TACTICS   little by little; gradualism.

This figure of speech was a favorite of the Alsop brothers. Wrote Stewart Alsop in *Newsweek,* April 28, 1969: "It remains to be seen just how far the Russians and their Czech and Slovak stooges will have to go in order to complete the process of rescaring the people. One theory is that press censorship, secret-police pressure, and salami tactics will do the trick. Alexander Dubcek will certainly not be the last of the liberals to fall victim to the salami knife."

Two years later, in his syndicated column, Joseph Alsop denounced "the orgy of public hypocrisy touched off by the *Times'* collection of stolen Pentagon documents," pointing out that the two men whose advice was taken by President Johnson were Dean Rusk and Ambassador Llewellyn Thompson: "Both of them pressed strongly for the salami-slicing approach—for 'gradualism' as they called it."

In *The Harper Dictionary of Modern Thought,* Alan Bullock and Oliver Stallybrass credit the coinage to Matyas Rakosi of the Hungarian Communist party, who in 1945 described how he came to power by getting his opposition to slice off its right wing, then its centrists, until only those collaborating with Communists remained in power.

SALT Strategic Arms Limitation Talks, begun in November 1969, between the Soviet Union and the U.S. Most often used redundantly, as "SALT talks."

According to John Newhouse, in his *Cold Dawn: the Story of SALT* (1973), the man who invented the acronym SALT is Robert Martin, who was a low-level staffer in the State Department's Bureau of Political-Military Affairs.

"In the Spring of 1968," wrote Newhouse, "when the prospect of talks suddenly brightened, bureaucrats began having to write cables about limiting strategic arms. Any combination of words labeling the

process was inevitably cumbersome. Martin, who was then a member of the political section of the U.S. Nato mission in Brussels, finally gave up and concocted SALT. His ambassador, Harlan Cleveland, resisted the term for a while; so did a number of Washington officials, finding it too cute. ACDA [the Arms Control and Disarmament Agency] disliked it. The issue arose at a meeting of senior officials; the CIA finally insisted on formal adoption of SALT because its filing system was already being organized around the term."

Robert Martin confirms this. Reached in 1978 at the U.S. embassy in Teheran, where he is counselor for Political-Military Affairs, he responded: "The acronym SALT is one that I developed in order to save . . . some of that precious commodity —time . . . The initial reaction, both in Brussels and Washington, was negative. Harlan Cleveland, my Ambassador at USNATO, kept scratching it out, insisting that the four words be spelled out . . . he did not view the acronym as being sufficiently formal and serious for the exercise that the U.S. proposed to begin."

As often happens, the man who resisted the term got credit for it. A German newspaper reported Cleveland (see REVOLUTION OF RISING EXPECTATIONS) to be the author of the acronym. "He sent me a marvelous letter," writes Martin, "expressing delight at the credit being heaped upon him for something he had so belittled originally; yet further proof, he pointed out, that the Chiefs get all of the credit while the poor blighters in the trenches do all the work."

Sometimes "limitations" is used, but Martin shoots the plural down: "As created, it was singular, and for the purist it remains so." How does the acronym translate during negotiations? "Even the Soviets who work on SALT use the term when speaking Russian."

The vocabulary of nuclear warfare causes some shudders (see THINKING THE UNTHINKABLE), and in some cases, deliberately mocks itself: the acronym for "Mutual Assured Destruction" is MAD. Despite these trepidations, things must have names, and in 1975 the Arms Control and Disarmament Agency issued its revised "SALT lexicon," selections from which follow:

Arms Stability: A strategic force relationship in which neither side perceives the necessity for under taking major new arms programs in order to avoid being placed at a disadvantage.

Assured Destruction: The ability to inflict an "unacceptable" degree of damage upon an aggressor after absorbing any first strike. [Mutual assured destruction is a condition in which an assured destruction capability is possessed by opposing sides. See also "Unacceptable Damage."]

Ballistic Missile: Any missile which does not rely upon aerodynamic surfaces to produce lift and consequently follows a ballistic trajectory (i.e., that resulting when the body is acted upon only by gravity and aerodynamic drag) when thrust is terminated.

Intercontinental Ballistic Missile (ICBM): A land based, rocket-propelled vehicle capable of delivering a warhead to intercontinental ranges (ranges in excess of about 3,000 nautical miles).

Circular Error Probable (CEP): A measure of the delivery accuracy of a weapon system used as a factor in determining probable damage to targets. It is the radius of a circle around the target at which a missile is aimed within which the warhead has a .5 probability of falling.

Cold Launch: The technique of ejecting a missile from a silo before full ignition of the main engine, sometimes called "Pop-up."

Collateral Damage: The damage to surrounding human and non-human resources, either military or non-military, as the result of action or strikes directed specifically against enemy forces or military facilities.

Counterforce Strike: An attack aimed at an adversary's military capability, especially his strategic military capability. [This means the enemy's missiles.]

Countervalue Strike: An attack aimed at an opponent's cities or industries.

Coupling (strategic): The linking of a lower-level conflict, e.g., Soviet/Warsaw Pact military aggression in Europe, to the use of U.S. strategic deterrent forces such as ICBMs, heavy bombers, and SLBMs.

Cruise Missile: A guided missile which uses aerodynamic lift to offset gravity and propulsion to counteract drag. The major portion of a cruise missile's flight path remains within the earth's atmosphere.

Endoatmosphere: From sea level to about 40 nautical miles altitude.

Exoatmosphere: Higher than about 40 nautical miles above sea level.

First Strike (nuclear): The launching of an initial strategic nuclear attack before the opponent has used any strategic weapons himself.

Forward-Based Systems (FBS): A term introduced by the USSR to refer to those U.S. nuclear systems based in third countries or on aircraft carriers and capable of delivering a nuclear strike against the territory of the USSR.

Fractional Orbital Bombardment System (FOBS): A missile that achieves an orbital trajectory, but fires a set of retrorockets before the completion of one revolution in order to slow down, reenter the atmosphere and release the warhead it carries into a normal ballistic trajectory toward its target.

Hardening of Silos: Protection of a missile site with concrete and earth and other measures so as to withstand blast, heat, or radiation from a nuclear attack.

National Technical Means of Verification: Techniques which are under national control for monitoring compliance with the provisions of an agreement. [Such as spy satellites; this overcomes Soviet objections to on-site inspections.]

Payload: The reentry vehicle(s) placed on ballistic trajectories by the main propulsion stages and bus.

There are several general types of payload configurations, such as: (a) single reentry vehicles, (b) multiple reentry vehicles (MRV) and (c) multiple independently targeted reentry vehicles (MIRV). (See Reentry Vehicle).

Preemptive Strike: A nuclear attack initiated in anticipation of an opponent's decision to resort to nuclear war. [This is also used in non-nuclear warfare; the Israelis called their attack on the massing Arab armies in 1967 a "pre-emptive strike."]

Reentry Vehicle (RV): That portion of a ballistic missile designed to carry a nuclear warhead and to reenter the earth's atmosphere in the terminal portion of the missile trajectory. *Multiple Independently Targetable Reentry Vehicle (MIRV):* Two or more reentry vehicles carried by a single missile and capable of being independently targeted. [Writer Peter Ognibene called MIRV "separate but equal warheads integrated into a single missile but bused to different targets."]

Second Strike: A term usually used to refer to a retaliatory attack in response to a first strike.

Strategic Arms Limitation Talks (SALT): A series of negotiations between the U.S. and the USSR which began in Helsinki in November 1969. The negotiations seek to limit and eventually reduce both offensive and defensive strategic arms.

Throw-Weight: Ballistic missile throw-weight is the maximum useful weight which has been flight-tested on the boost stages of the missile. The useful weight includes weight of the reentry vehicles, penetration aids, dispensing and release mechanisms, reentry shrouds, covers, buses and propulsion devices with their propellants (but not the final boost stages) which are present at the end of the boost phase.

TRIAD: The term used in referring to the basic structure of the U.S. strategic deterrent force. It is comprised of land-based ICBMs, the strategic bomber force, and the Polaris/Poseidon submarine fleet.

Unacceptable Damage: Degrees of destruction anticipated from an enemy second strike, which is sufficient to deter a nuclear power from launching a first strike.

Verification: The process of determining the degree to which parties to an agreement are complying with provisions of the agreement.

Warhead: That part of a missile, projectile, or torpedo that contains the explosive intended to inflict damage.

Yield: The force of a nuclear explosion expressed in terms of the number of tons of TNT that would have to be exploded to produce the same energy.

The Arms Control agency cautions readers and negotiators that "the Lexicon is intended for quick reference only, not as a basis for adjudicating definitional problems that might arise in negotiation or in final treaty or agreement language."

One term not in the lexicon is *fratricide,* the first capital crime in the Bible, which Vice President Walter Mondale used in 1978 first in its strategic and later its political sense: "There is a concept in missilry, where you fire too many missiles too close together and they kill each other off—fratricide." Referring to the possibility that President Carter had overloaded the Congress with legislative initiatives in 1977, he added, "I think it can be fratricide—too many issues landing at the same time."

Saltniks seldom intersperse their jargon with shortened words or pet names, but *nuke* occasionally surfaces: as a verb, to make a "nuclear strike," or as a noun, to mean a "nuclear device," which is a euphemism for a bomb. Writing about the MX intercontinental missile in the *New York Times* on January 4, 1978, former systems analyst Earl Ravenal livened up his copy with a reference to a remark made by (and used against) Senator Barry Goldwater in 1964: "Mobile or with multiple bases, it [MX] would carry up to fourteen 200-kiloton MIRV warheads to within 100 yards of their targets. That kind of accuracy could finally realize Senator Barry Goldwater's vision of lobbing a nuke right into the men's room of the Kremlin." The writer immediately slipped back into the normal SALT idiom: "But, combined with silo-busting yields, it would also make the MX a highly unnerving first-strike counterforce weapon."

SALUTATIONS, *see* **MY FRIENDS.**

SAMIZDAT the underground press in the Soviet Union.

"By *samizdat,*" wrote *Time* on September 7, 1970, "Russians endlessly retype and clandestinely circulate the work of such banned writers as Alexander Solzhenitsyn."

John L. Hess, writing in the *New York Times* on June 12, 1971, reported that the latest Solzhenitsyn novel, *August 1914,* had an epilogue to its foreign edition noting that the book could not be published in the USSR "except in samizdat" because of censorship: "Samizdat is the hand-to-hand distribution of manuscripts, typed or photographed, of works rejected by Soviet printing houses."

The word comes from the Russian *sam* (self) *izdat* (the first part of the word for publishing), meaning to publish by one's self, probably coined as a pun on Gosizdat, the State Publishing House in Moscow.

The mid-sixties birth of the word coincided with the beginning of recognition outside the USSR that an organized opposition was operating within the Soviet regime. The word was first used in an official Soviet publication, the weekly magazine *Ogonyok,* in September 1971, in a story about dissident physicist Dmitri Mikheyev, defining the word as "in effect, anti-Soviet."

New York Times Soviet expert Harry Schwartz noted soon afterward that the spread of unofficial publications like *Chronicle of Current Events* raised the question of whether a "zone of tolerance" had been created in the USSR for illegal publication of dissent, providing a safety valve for political malcontents.

Through the seventies, that tolerance waxed and waned; after Solzhenitsyn's departure for the West, Soviet physicist Andrei Sakharov became the best-known dissenter, his positions made known by *samizdat.* In time a similar word—*tamizdat,* "published over there"—came to cover publication abroad, with copies smuggled back into the USSR.

By the late seventies, *samizdat* came to mean the material of dissent as well as its system of distribution.

See HUMAN RIGHTS; MOST FAVORED NATION; QUIET DIPLOMACY.

SANCTIONS, see QUARANTINE.

SANITIZE of a document, to delete damaging statements; of a person, to make innocent by association.

"The President has moved in seven months," wrote John Osborne about Jimmy Carter in the *New Republic* in 1977, "from thought of opening Cabinet meetings to the press, to maybe releasing edited transcripts of Cabinet discussions, to having a White House press officer attend meetings and afterward give reporters a sanitized account."

In that sense, "to sanitize" is to make palatable, or less embarrassing. The cleanliness metaphor—removing political dirt—is obvious, as in the instruction given to H. R. Haldeman to "clean up the tapes," i.e., to remove the material that might raise doubts or eyebrows.

A less obvious meaning of the term is to remain in place after a scandal affecting one's colleagues, thereby proving one's absence of taint. Many Nixon appointees asked to be kept on in the first year of the Ford Administration in order to be thus "sanitized."

Sometimes the word carries a political sting. Members of the House committee investigating the CIA (the "Pike Committee") objected in 1975 to the lack of cooperation they received from the intelligence agency. In the report, which was published in the *Village Voice* by CBS correspondent Daniel Schorr after the House decided to suppress it, the committee

stated: "We were given heavily 'sanitized' pieces of paper. 'Sanitized' was merely a euphemism for blank sheets of paper . . ."

Ordinarily the word is only mildly pejorative, as sanitization is taken to be the customary manner of protecting insiders from publication of their indiscreet or unduly frank observations. The extreme of sanitizing is "shredding," the product of the electric paper shredder; a more venal or deceptive form of avoiding detection is LAUNDERING.

SANTA CLAUS, NOBODY SHOOTS AT political proverb about folly of attacking government benefit programs.

Former Governor Alfred E. Smith, in a press conference in New York late in 1933, said, "No sane local official who has hung up an empty stocking over the municipal fireplace is going to shoot Santa Claus just before a hard Christmas."

In 1936, when Smith, the embittered 1928 Democratic presidential candidate, was campaigning against Roosevelt, he shortened the point to a simple "nobody shoots at Santa Claus."

Barry Goldwater, campaigning for the Republican presidential nomination in 1964, told the Economic Club of New York: "It is my chore to ask you to consider the toughest proposition ever faced by believers in the free-enterprise system: the need for a frontal attack against Santa Claus—not the Santa Claus of the holiday season, of course, but the Santa Claus of the FREE LUNCH, the government handout, the Santa Claus of something-for-nothing and something-for-everyone."

Another man to shoot at Santa Claus was Orville Freeman, campaigning for a fourth term as governor of Minnesota. According to economist Walter Heller, Freeman went around the state telling people frankly that the services they wanted could only be paid for with higher taxes—that, in his phrase, "There ain't no Santa Claus." He also lost.

A synonym for Santa Claus is "tooth fairy," after the practice of telling a child that if a recently extracted tooth is placed under the pillow at night, a fairy will come and replace the lost tooth with a coin. "Tooth fairy," to mean "a story told to believing children," is in growing use; it carries the same connotation of suspended-reality as Santa Claus, though Santa retains an exclusive franchise for government largesse. USC economics professor Arthur B. Laffer, who provided the intellectual underpinning for the TAX REVOLT in California in 1978, wrote in the July 1978 American Enterprise Institute *Economist*: "In the absense of the 'tooth fairy' the resources spent by the government are the total tax burden on the economy's productive sector."

In the don't-you-believe-it lexicon, BALONEY is the harshest denunciation; PIE IN THE SKY severe but fondly archaic; FREE LUNCH is usually limited to economic affairs; *tooth fairy* requires the most childlike belief; *Santa Claus* and *Uncle Sugar* are most associated with government handouts.

SATELLITE   a state formally independent but in fact subordinate to a large imperialist power; occasionally, an official under the domination of another.

The first part of the above definition, used in the Communist *Political Dictionary* (Moscow, 1958), can be agreed to by those members of the FREE WORLD who consider the Soviet Union "a large imperialist power."

This is a politically subjective word; to most Russians, the word refers to nations like some of those in Latin America, and even the British Commonwealth; these "lackeys" are within—to continue the metaphor—the U.S. "orbit." To Americans, satellites include the states of Eastern Europe as well as Cuba, whose economy depends on Soviet largesse. Senator Thruston Morton of Kentucky, urging the adoption of a consular treaty with these countries in 1967, hoped that it would lead to changes in "the so-called satellite countries." However, many Americans with ethnic roots in East-European nations preferred the phrase "captive nations."

"Satellite" is of Middle French origin, meaning "attendant" or follower, later applied to those sycophants who fawned on French princes; it is a word popularized by politics, not astronomy. In the original sense, Charles de Gaulle characterized the removal of Western Europe from what he considered American domination as "desatellization." See PUPPET.

SATRAP   minor party official.

This imperial word has had a rough time in politics. Originally from the Old Persian *xshathrapavan,* protector of the imperium, used by Persian provincial governors, the word "satrap" became associated with the unpopular military governors of the South during Reconstruction.

President Andrew Johnson popularized the word in 1866: "I could have remained at the capital with fifty or sixty millions of appropriations . . . with my satraps and dependents in every township." In the off-year election that followed in 1866, this was used against him in a campaign flyer: "Mr. Johnson said that, with forty or fifty millions of dollars placed at his disposal, under the Freedmen's Bureau bill, with his satraps scattered throughout the land, he could make himself a dictator. . . . Satraps, you know, are Turkish officers who are liable to lose their heads by the scimitar if they do anything to displease the Sultan." In 1876 the *New York World* linked "the miserable scallawag and oppressive black satrap."

The word has continued its use as a minor official inclined to officiousness, although John Gunther called the older brother of Missouri boss Thomas Pendergast "a satrap of considerable eminence."

In current use, BOSS, SACHEM, *leader* are on the top level, with *satrap*, HENCHMAN, HATCHETMAN, and *functionary* below, and TROOPS, *braves*, FAITHFUL *workers*, RANK AND FILE at the bottom. POOH BAH, high MUCKEY-MUCK, and PANJAN-DRUM are spoofs of big shots.

Another word associated with the Turkish sultans occasionally used in politics is *janissary*, Turkish slave-soldiers dating back to the fourteenth century, whose 1826 uprising ended in their massacre. An FDR clique in the forties was called the Janissariat.

SATURDAY NIGHT MASSACRE

the events of the evening of October 20, 1973, when the two top officials of the Department of Justice refused to fire the Watergate Special Prosecutor, and were swept out along with him, leading to a public-opinion FIRE-STORM.

Nixon chief of staff Alexander Haig told Attorney General Elliot Richardson to dismiss Special Prosecutor Archibald Cox, who had been pressing hard for subpoenaed White House tapes. Richardson, with tears in his eyes (as Haig later told the author), demurred; he had promised the Sen-

ate, as part of his confirmation, he would not fire the Special Prosecutor for any reason other than malfeasance. Haig then called Deputy AG William Ruckelshaus, replacing Richardson as the nation's top law enforcement officer; when Ruckelshaus declined, he reported Haig to have said: "Your commander-in-chief has given you an order. You have no alternative." Ruckelshaus said he did, and resigned. Haig then reached the Solicitor General, Robert Bork, who believed that there was a constitutional requirement that somebody in charge of the Justice Department carry out a legal order from the nation's elected leader. Bork intended to fire Cox and then resign, but he was persuaded to stay on.

At 8:25 P.M., press secretary Ron Ziegler told reporters in the White House briefing room that the three officials had been removed and the Special Prosecutor's office "abolished." At 9:05, FBI agents took positions inside the Special Prosecution Force offices at 1425 K Street on orders from Haig, who had heard that members of Cox's staff had been removing files for several days (which Cox aide Richard Ben-Veniste later confirmed as true in his Watergate memoirs).

"There was blood all over the floor," said White House aide Leonard Garment to this writer and others during that weekend, and the blood image—as a "massacre"—quickly took hold. By Monday the "Saturday Night Massacre" had become a phrase locked into Watergate terminology.

"Massacre" has long been a sloganizing word: the "Boston Massacre," on the night of March 5, 1770, led to the celebration of "Massacre Day" in Boston until 1783, when the celebration was switched to the Fourth of

July. Fans of gangland movies recall the "St. Valentine's Day Massacre." As with many terms of catastrophe or bloodshed, the word "massacre" has been absorbed into politics to denote bloodless coups, and is used ironically: when Admiral Stansfield Turner began dismissing 800 members of the CIA's clandestine branch in late October 1977, the laid-off agents and operatives called it the "Halloween Massacre."

Saturday night, before nearly everybody's day off, has a festive, sometimes violent connotation. In his book *With Nixon* (1978), speechwriter Ray Price compared the angry television commentaries of that crucial weekend in 1973 to "Saturday-Night Specials, the television equivalent of those cheap but lethal handguns that have given Saturday night a bad name."

SCALAWAG   rascal; an archaic political epithet.

Harper's Monthly in 1868 said that "Southern men who side with the Republican Party are called 'Scalliwags.' " The spelling varies, but the term, by the end of the Civil War, was used by Southerners to describe other whites from their own region who helped the Northern officials get established throughout the former Confederate states and who were answerable primarily to the radical Republican faction then dominant in Congress.

In 1865 the *Washington Morning Chronicle's* correspondent wrote that "Whenever a white man appears to vote [in Alabama] every one of these infuriated devils . . . set up a yell calling him 'white negro,' 'low trash,' 'Scalwag.' " The distinction between "scalawag" and CARPETBAGGER was that the latter was of Northern origin.

The word possibly derives from an old Scandinavian word, "scurryvaig"; another theory is that its origin can be traced to the Scallaway district of Scotland famed for dwarf cattle. Its first known usage in the U.S. was in 1848 when the word "scalaway" was common in western New York State to describe a mean person, a scapegrace, but all etymologies on this word are speculative.

Early in the Civil War, the *Kelso Stars and Bars* indicated that it was used as a term of general, not necessarily political, contempt. In 1863 this Southern paper wrote that "companies of armed men, gangs of ruffians, gentlemen and scallwags . . . white trash and black trash, were pouring into town from every quarter."

The Reconstruction word has returned to its earlier meaning. Scalawag now means a rascal, one who is never up to any good, rather than a Southerner intent on grinding down his own kind. ·

See COPPERHEAD.

SCENARIO   military-diplomatic jargon for a detailed plan or likely course of action.

"He believed in giving good men their head," wrote Arthur Schlesinger, Jr., of Ambassador Averell Harriman. "When long, detailed instructions would come across his desk intended for ambassadors in the field —'scenarios,' in the jargon, designed to deprive envoys abroad of all discretion—Harriman, before clearing the message, liked to add a liberating introductory sentence: 'For your guidance, you may wish to consider the following.' "

"Scenario," a theatrical word derived from the Latin *scēna,* is used in war-gaming to mean the manner in which military action is expected to develop. Author Herman Kahn, in a

1967 book review, wrote: "Let me now write a scenario for what might have happened if the United States had not reinforced South Viet Nam." Using a conditional construction, Kahn outlined a sequence of what he considered probabilities—North Vietnam's victory and the unification of the country, the fall of Laos, and the likely Communist domination of Thailand, the reinforcement of guerrillas in Malaysia—and "It is now possible to write, if with difficulty, a scenario in which this turned the balance in Indonesia . . . either turning communist or at least joining China as a firm ally." Kahn added, "While the above scenario is not wildly plausible, it is not wildly implausible."

White House correspondent Max Frankel also wrote in 1967 of the extrapolation of likelihoods in "peace games" that go on within warring governments: "Both are regularly confronted, it seems, by 'scenarios' to step up the war, to step down the war or, in various ways, to interrupt the war—all presented as the quickest way to conclude the war."

See PENTAGONESE; WAR-GAMING WORDS.

SCRAP OF PAPER   attack phrase on a treaty; cavalier treatment of a written diplomatic agreement.

On August 14, 1914, Germany's Theobald von Bethmann-Hollweg wrote to Great Britain's Sir Edward Goschen: "Just for a word—neutrality, a word which in war-time has so often been disregarded—just for a scrap of paper Great Britain is going to make war." The "scrap of paper" was Britain's treaty with Belgium guaranteeing that nation's neutrality. When Belgium was attacked, the British were true to their written guarantee.

"In and ever since 1914," wrote

Eric Partridge in *Usage and Abusage,* "one totalitarian state has sneered at the validity of a *scrap of paper.* Bethmann-Hollweg's famous phrase . . . caused Lord Samuel, in 1937, to say that, 'under stress, treaties may become mere scraps of paper.' "

The phrase has currency in writing about international affairs, especially in connection with the phrase "honoring our commitments." A similar phrase on another subject is "STROKE OF A PEN."

SEAL OF THE PRESIDENT, *see* BALD EAGLE.

SECOND-CLASS CITIZEN   one deprived of his rights, especially voting rights, and particularly the Negro.

"The Constitution does not provide for first and second class citizens," wrote Wendell Willkie in *An American Program.* A generation later Dwight Eisenhower used the phrase several times, but historian Samuel Elliot Morison commented: "It was all very well for President Eisenhower to declare, 'There must be no second-class citizens in this country'—there were, and still are."

Oddly, before the Civil War there was no definition of the term "citizen of the United States." Each state determined federal citizenship, until the Fourteenth Amendment stated that "all persons born or naturalized in the United States, and subject to the jurisdiction thereof, are citizens of the United States and of the States wherein they reside." The "subject to the jurisdiction thereof" clause was inserted to deny citizenship to children of foreign ambassadors and to Indians.

In the post-bellum reaction against Reconstruction, blacks were denied the right to vote by impossible "literacy tests," poll taxes, and direct intimidation. Congress in 1957 passed a civil rights law, the first since 1875, to protect the Negro's right to vote, adding other legislation in later years to strengthen it.

In the sixties, "second-class citizen" lost some of its voting-rights meaning and came to mean those to whom education and economic benefits were denied. To new black voters, Republicans pointed to the enactment of the first civil rights legislation under the Eisenhower Administration, and to the Lincoln Republican tradition. Democrats in the North dissociated themselves from "segregation forever" Southern Democrats, and pointed to social welfare legislation inspired by their party.

"Second-class" became a phrase to be avoided generally; transportation companies with "first-class" accommodations offered "coach," "tourist," "economy" (even "royal coach" and "deluxe economy") in an effort to get away from "second-class." The only area where the phrase has a happy sound is in the postal service, as publishers seek "second-class mailing privileges," which are in effect a subsidy of distribution costs.

SECRET AGREEMENTS, *see* **OPEN COVENANTS; GRAND DESIGN.**

SECURITY RISK a person considered likely to commit anything from an indiscretion to an act of espionage harming the safety of the U.S.

The expression was popularized during what is loosely termed "the McCarthy era" (see MCCARTHYISM) when the Wisconsin senator charged that the State Department was harboring hundreds of security risks. The phrase broadly covered those who could easily be blackmailed (alcoholics and homosexuals), those who have had or currently have Communist associations or belonged to groups considered subversive by the Justice Department, and those whose close relatives' associations may compromise them.

Attorney General Herbert Brownell charged in 1954 that the Truman Administration harbored a Treasury Department official, Harry Dexter White, who was "a known traitor." Some 2,427 "security risks" were removed from government service in two years, the White House announced, drawing a charge from Adlai Stevenson that it was participating in a NUMBERS GAME.

America's best-known security risk was atomic scientist J. Robert Oppenheimer. He contested the suspension of his secret "Q" clearance before a board set up by the Atomic Energy Commission, which decided he had "fundamental defects of character" because of his "associations" and his nonconforming attitude toward his sworn official obligations. The criteria were set up in the McMahon Act, the commission's regulations, and a White House directive of April 1953.

Testifying on Oppenheimer's behalf before the board, former High Commissioner for Germany John J. McCloy pointed out that scientists like Oppenheimer were needed, and that if anything was done "to dampen their fervor . . . to that extent the security of the United States is impaired . . . a security risk in reverse." See REVERSE BIGOTRY.

When a lady reporter labeled two State Department employees as "well-known security risks" in a press-conference question, President Kennedy flared in anger, saying he believed the men could carry out their assignments "without detriment to the interests of the United States, and

I hope without detriment to their characters by your question."

See LOYALTY OATH.

SEGREGATION attack word on the doctrine of SEPARATE BUT EQUAL facilities; the enforced separation of races in fields such as education, housing, and social and economic affairs.

Proponents of what is now accepted as segregation preferred the word "separation," as used in the Supreme Court decision in *Plessy* v. *Ferguson* in 1896: "Laws permitting, and even requiring, their separation in places where they are liable to be brought into contact do not necessarily imply the inferiority of one race to the other . . ." Some proponents accepted the word and defended the practice, as did Judge Thomas P. Brady before the Commonwealth Club of California in 1957: "Segregation in the South is a way of life. It is a precious and sacred custom. It is one of our dearest and most treasured possessions. It is the means whereby we live in social peace, order and security."

Opponents of separation adopted the words "segregation" and "integration," making them a part of the vocabulary as abrasive confrontation terms, joining the issue that was resolved in their favor by the Supreme Court in 1954.

A new word for extreme segregation, popularized by South African Prime Minister Daniel F. Malan, appeared in 1949: *apartheid.* It was derived from the Dutch *apart* (same meaning as English) and *heid* (-hood), or "apartness," the state of being totally segregated. It was not adopted in the U.S.

Wrote South African author Alan Paton in 1960: " 'Segregation' is such an active word that it suggests some-

one is trying to segregate somebody else. So the word 'apartheid' was introduced. Now it has such a stench in the nostrils of the world, they are referring to 'autogenuous development.' "

In its slang form, the word is "segged"—with a hard *g*—for segregated, "de-segged" for desegregated, which became preferred over "integrated." In an Alabama primary early in his career, George Wallace said he had been "out-segged" by a more extreme opponent.

The sale of houses to blacks in formerly all-white neighborhoods is attacked as "blockbusting," taken from the World War II bombing term.

See BUSING TO ACHIEVE RACIAL BALANCE; CIVIL RIGHTS; JIM CROW; FREEDOM RIDERS; RACISM; SEPARATE BUT EQUAL; SIT-IN; WITH ALL DELIBERATE SPEED; QUOTAS.

SELF-APPOINTED, *see* SNEER WORDS.

SELF-DETERMINATION the right of a people to choose its own form of government.

The phrase "national self-determination" is associated with President Woodrow Wilson, and is generally considered to be one of the most important of his Fourteen Points, although it was not one of them at all. Wilson called later for a fairly traditional nationalism based largely on language and common cultural heritage, with boundaries drawn on that basis and the people within them free to choose their own leadership.

The idea had wide appeal for propaganda purposes at the close of World War I; the Versailles settlement, to the surprise of cynics, largely succeeded in achieving Wilson's self-determination aim. Winston Churchill, in 1929, wrote: "Probably less than 3 per cent of the European population are now living under Governments whose nationality they repudiate . . ."

Churchill and Franklin Roosevelt included "self-determination" in the 1941 Atlantic Charter. Three years before, in a speech at the Sportpalast in Berlin, Adolf Hitler made Czechoslovakia his "last territorial demand" and said: "In 1918 Central Europe was torn up and reshaped by some foolish or crazy so-called statesmen under the slogan 'self-determination and the right of nations.' . . . To this, Czechoslovakia owed its existence." Hitler spoke of the oppression of the German-speaking people of that state and sharply reversed his field: ". . . at last, nearly twenty years after, Mr. Wilson's right of self-determination for the 3,500,000 [Germans] must be enforced and we shall not just look on any longer."

SELLING CANDIDATES LIKE SOAP a charge that MADISON AVENUE TECHNIQUES are being used in a campaign, appealing to emotion rather than reason.

The company that advertises most is Procter & Gamble, manufacturer, among many other things, of Ivory Soap. Successful soap-selling is thus a hallmark of excellence in the advertising fraternity.

Admen have long been active in politics. Bruce Barton, of Batten, Barton, Durstine & Osborn, was the congressman immortalized by FDR's MARTIN, BARTON AND FISH; Chester Bowles, of Benton & Bowles, served as a Kennedy State Department official; his partner, William Benton, was senator from Connecticut. But it is the adman behind the scenes in every political campaign that is most often criticized, with the gibes sometimes

written by the admen on the other side. See KINGMAKER.

Since an attack on the Eisenhower spot television campaign was part of Adlai Stevenson's message in 1952, the phrase was used often in that campaign. A typical Stevenson use:

Man does not live by words alone, despite the fact that sometimes he has to eat them. Alas, in this world he sometimes, or perhaps too often, lives by CATCHWORDS. SLOGANS are normally designed to get action without reflection. This one, "TIME FOR A CHANGE", fits these specifications admirably. This may not be too serious when all that is at stake is whether to buy one cake of soap or another, but I don't think it furnishes a sound basis for deciding a national election.

"Soap" has many uses in politics. In the 1880 Republican campaign it was used as a code word for money in dispatches, was deciphered, and for many years meant funny money, or graft; it is now obsolete. "Soft soap" is a soothing, ingratiating string of platitudes, and a "soapbox" has an origin similar to STUMP: a makeshift platform used by street-corner speakers, with a connotation of use by blowhards or extremists.

SELLOUT betrayal; attack word on a political compromise.

A weak political party that supports an opposition party's candidate in return for patronage is said to sell out; in its simplest sense, a politician who takes graft sells out his constituents.

The phrase has been traced to 1857, when the *Lawrence* (Kansas) *Republican* wrote: "If the *Times* has not been 'sold out' to the Border Ruffian party, it looks very much as if it had been 'chartered.' " In O. Henry's *Trimmed Lamp* (1906), a cynical character said, "When I sell out it's not going to be on any bargain day."

Soon after he became President, Harry Truman demanded that the Russians invite anti-Communist Poles into the Polish government as his price for admission of Poland into the United Nations. The Russians made a small gesture in this direction in 1945 and agreed to drop their objection to the admission of Argentina. When the U.S. agreed to the deal, anti-Communist Poles charged this was "the great sellout."

Previously the best-known diplomatic use of the phrase occurred after the Munich conference of 1938, when British Prime Minister Neville Chamberlain was charged with "selling Czechoslovakia down the river," a phrase with its origins in slavery.

The word is the most popular attack of TRUE BELIEVERS.

SENATORIAL COURTESY, *see* **PERSONALLY OBNOXIOUS.**

SEND THEM A MESSAGE a plea to vote symbolically for a candidate who is given little chance to win but whose votes will be seen as endorsement for a different point of view; a way for voters to object to policies of the party in power.

"The average voter," wrote *Washington Post* analyst David Broder in 1972, "sees a great gulf between himself—struggling with the family budget, problems in his kids' schools, the uncertainties of his job and the threats to his neighborhood—and the politicians in power, who act as if they have it made, which they probably do.

"It is that sense of distance—and of indifference from the top—that George Wallace exploited with his brilliant slogan, 'Send Them a Message.'

"That slogan came closer to capturing the mood of the American voters this year than anything else—a mood of distrust for the self-satisfied power possessors . . ."

That was the mood presidential candidate Jimmy Carter sought to catch in his long campaign for the Democratic nomination, which began in earnest in 1974. Like Wallace, he talked the "little man's" language, even spoke in the same accent, but was able to dissociate himself from the Wallace "segregation forever" stigma. Carter avoided the RACIST "message," but ran against Washington—exploiting the resentment at unfeeling bureaucrats, or musclebound government.

The phrase is current, though the Wallace origin is becoming obscured. Deploring the "instant sociology" that analyzed the thievery during a New York City power blackout in 1977, a *Washington Star* editorialist wrote: "In the book of instant sociology, human behavior is invariably conditioned behavior. People never do anything for the hell of it, or because they're bored, let alone for lack of the disciplines of civility. No, the looters must be trying to send us a Message."

In that usage, "message" was capitalized and given an added meaning, of social significance, as in the propagandistic "message movies." Looking toward the elections of 1978, however, House Minority Leader John Rhodes used the phrase in its traditional form: "I think the watchword should be, 'Send Jimmy Carter a message. Give him a Republican Congress.' "

See DIME'S WORTH OF DIFFERENCE.

SENIOR CITIZEN, *see* **EUPHEMISMS, POLITICAL.**

SEPARATE BUT EQUAL the phrase at the heart of the civil rights dispute, posing the question: Can separate facilities ever be equal?

Justice Henry B. Brown, speaking for the majority of the Supreme Court in the 1896 case of *Plessy* v. *Ferguson,* found that "separate but equal accommodations" satisfied the demands of the Fourteenth Amendment, adding: "We consider the underlying fallacy of the plaintiff's argument to consist in the assumption that the enforced separation of the two races stamps the colored race with a badge of inferiority. If this be so, it is not by reason of anything found in the act, but solely because the colored race chooses to put that construction upon it."

John Marshall Harlan, in dissent, wrote: "If evils will result from the commingling of the two races upon public highways established for the benefit of all, they will be infinitely less than those that will surely come from state legislation regulating the enjoyment of civil rights upon the basis of race. The thin disguise of 'equal' accommodations for passengers in railroad coaches will not mislead any one, nor atone for the wrong this day done . . ."

The doctrine was reversed in a series of decisions of the "Warren Court" in 1954, the most famous of which was handed down on May 11: "We conclude that in the field of public education the doctrine of 'separate but equal' has no place. Separate educational facilities are inherently unequal." And on May 17: "Does segregation of children in public schools solely on the basis of race, even though the physical facilities and other 'tangible' factors may be equal, deprive the children of the minority group of equal education opportunities? We believe that it does. . . . We

conclude that in the field of public education the doctrine of 'separate but equal' has no place."

The phrase has its American political origin in the Declaration of Independence, where this nation dissolved its bonds with Great Britain "to assume among the powers of the earth, the separate and equal station to which the Laws of Nature and of Nature's God entitle them." For cross references to other civil rights phrases, see SEGREGATION.

SEPARATISM, *see* **DEVOLUTION.**

SET, *see* **COMMUNITY.**

SEXISM gender-engendered bias; a condemnation, usually made by women, of discrimination on account of sex.

The above definition gingerly avoids sexism. Alma Trinor, a feminist and lexicographer with the *American Heritage Dictionary* in 1973, noted the difference in a Merriam-Webster definition ("prejudice or discrimination against women") and the *American Heritage* definition of the same term: "Discrimination by members of one sex against the other, especially by males against females, based on the assumption that one sex is superior." Another example of sex in lex, she charged, was the definition of "spokeswoman," which a rival lexicographer called "a female spokesman" and she defined as "a woman who speaks on behalf of another or others."

"Sexism" was popularized on the analogy of RACISM, as sex followed race in the fight against discrimination. The campaign to pass the Equal Rights Amendment beginning in the late sixties focused attention on the charge of "sexism," which covered everything from unintentional slights to serious bias in employment or pay scales.

In a good-humored letter to this lexicographer, Ms. Trinor wrote: *"The New Language of Politics* includes: the average man; the common man; the man in the street; the man of the people; the man who; one man, one vote. At this rate, how will women ever get into politics?" Her point: "I find that the word 'man' in its extended senses is the most overworked noun in the language, and it is a word that most definitely excludes women, no matter what dictionaries say to the contrary."

As job discrimination because of age is attacked, a continuation of the racism-sexism pattern can be expected; in mid-1977, Representative Claude Pepper (D-Fla.) sponsored legislation to end "age-ism," which President Carter signed in 1978.

See CONSCIOUSNESS-RAISING; WOMEN'S LIB.

SHADOW CABINET (GOVERNMENT) a formal organization of leaders of the party out of power, to take issue with their counterparts in government.

The system is British, and is drawn from the rarely used meaning of shadow as image or reflection. Whenever a party loses power and becomes the LOYAL OPPOSITION, the specialists in the various departments—who have often served as ministers in the previous government—form a cabinet-out-of-power and sit on the "front bench" of their party in Parliament. "The 'front bench' is more closely in touch with the members on the back benches when the party is in Opposition," writes Sir Ivor Jennings, "than when it is in office."

See BACKBENCHER.

Each member of the shadow cabinet contributes his expert knowledge to the prompt criticism of the government ministry he observes; the public understands that he is the man chosen in advance by the opposition as likely to head that ministry if the party wins the forthcoming election.

Advantages of the shadow cabinet system are that it provides quick, expert rebuttals to government decisions; a certain order to the party position; a coherence to the overall party program, often with a series of specific alternatives. Disadvantages are that too much party discipline leads to rigidity and that young men find it difficult to advance through party hierarchy.

Why hasn't it been adopted in the U.S.? Probably because the TWO-PARTY SYSTEM in America differs sharply from the mainly two-party system in England. There, the parties differ on ideology; here, the parties are much closer in ideology, with a conservative-liberal split within each party. It is difficult to reach a party consensus in the U.S., as convention platform fights indicate, and the TITULAR LEADER of the party out of power in the U.S. has no real authority to speak for the party or to appoint "shadow" ministers.

The closest Americans came to having a "shadow cabinet" was in 1948, when Thomas E. Dewey, considered the likely winner over Truman, chose several advisers who were widely understood to be his cabinet appointees after his victory; John Foster Dulles, when he spoke on foreign affairs, was referred to as "Dewey's likely Secretary of State." Since that time, candidates running against SITTING PRESIDENTS have avoided picking cabinets in advance, lest it look presumptuous.

During the Vietnam war the phrase was given a new meaning, playing on the sinister connotation of "shadow." The Viet-Cong controlled a large portion of South Vietnam by night, slipping into villages to collect "taxes" from people ostensibly under the authority of the anti-Communist regime. After an 83 percent turnout of voters in the 1967 elections, columnist Max Lerner wrote: ". . . with the Cong 'shadow government' which operates at night in the unpacified villages, it took some courage to make this affirmation."

SHEEP IN SHEEP'S CLOTHING
Churchillian characterization of Ramsay MacDonald (not, as is usually suggested, Clement Attlee).

Churchill's play on "wolf in sheep's clothing" is sometimes quoted as "sheep in wolf's clothing," but this can slip by unnoticed; "sheep in sheep's clothing" cannot be missed as a jab at mediocrity.

It is the best insult of its kind, aimed at showing a smallness of spirit. Theodore Roosevelt called William Howard Taft a man who "means well but means feebly," and Horace Greeley said of agitator Wendell Phillips that "he cannot conceive of a tempest outside of a teapot." See INVECTIVE, POLITICAL.

SHERMAN STATEMENT final
and irrevocable declaration of noncandidacy; frequently used term, rarely taken action.

Conservative Republican leader Charles Halleck was disconsolate after a talk with Senator Barry Goldwater in early 1963 about the possibility of a Goldwater candidacy. "He was throwing cold water on the whole idea," Halleck told F. Clifton White, who was to organize the draft-Goldwater movement, "and he was throwing it by the bucketful—with ice cubes in it."

"At least," replied White, "he didn't pull a Sherman on us."

Issuing a Sherman statement— "pulling a Sherman"—is the extreme of nonavailability. General William Tecumseh Sherman, Civil War hero second only to U. S. Grant, wired John B. Henderson, chairman of the Republican National Convention in Chicago on June 5, 1884: "I will not accept if nominated, and will not serve if elected." The directness of this statement has been corrupted by history books into a more pretentious "If nominated I will not accept; if elected I will not serve."

This early twisting of Sherman's statement was prophetic; hopeful supporters of genuinely reluctant public figures always seek to find loopholes in declarations of no interest.

The general's reluctance was no surprise. Twenty years earlier, he had written a friend: "If forced to choose between the penitentiary and the White House for four years, I would say the penitentiary, thank you." In 1868 Governor Horatio Seymour of New York told the Democratic convention: "I must not be nominated by this convention. I could not accept the nomination if tendered, which"— he hurriedly closed a loophole—"I do not expect."

When President Harry Truman was considered a sure loser in 1948, some Democrats turned to Justice William O. Douglas, who affected a horsewrangler's drawl in reply, "I never was a-running'. I ain't a-runnin', and I ain't goin' tuh."

In that year, Dwight Eisenhower issued a whole series of Sherman statements. To Democratic Senator Claude Pepper: "No matter under what terms, conditions, or premises a proposal might be couched, I would refuse to accept the nomination." To Republican publisher Leonard W.

Finder: "I am not available for and could not accept nomination for high public office. My decision is definite and positive. The necessary and wise subordination of the military to civilian power will be best sustained when lifelong professional soldiers abstain from seeking high political office." And to a young reporter at a Pentagon press conference: "Look, son, I cannot conceive of any circumstance that could draw out of me permission to consider me for any political post from dogcatcher to Grand High Supreme King of the Universe."

Can a Sherman statement be taken literally—would any man turn down a firm nomination? There is vicepresidential precedent: one man did say no after formal nomination. Silas Wright, senator and later governor of New York, was nominated as James W. Polk's running mate in 1844 by the Democrats. Angry at Martin Van Buren's defeat, he telegraphed the convention: "I am not and cannot under any circumstances be a candidate before your convention for that office," and he was hastily replaced.

While politicians will take a Sherman statement as evidence of a genuine "no," nobody takes it literally; the man might not campaign, but he would serve. Consider the dialogue between James Farley and FDR in 1940, when Farley—who wanted the nomination himself—tried to persuade the President not to run for a third term.

"What would you do in my place?" the President asked.

"Exactly what General Sherman did many years ago," Farley replied; "issue a statement saying I would refuse to run if nominated and would not serve if elected."

"Jim, if nominated and elected, I could not in these times refuse to take the inaugural oath, even if I knew I would be dead within thirty days."

The cadence of the Sherman phrase is so familiar that it can be used as the basis for parody. When it was important in 1969 for Henry Kissinger to gain a reputation as a "secret swinger" to create a DR. STRANGE-LOVE reputation and to provide cover for secret trips, he would appeal to White House wags and their friends (Richard Moore, this writer, and television producer Paul Keyes) for lines making that point. An opportunity arose when a picture appeared in many newspapers of Dr. Kissinger at a cocktail party with feminist leader Gloria Steinem, who scotched gossip rumors with an icy mock statement: "I am not now, and have never been, a friend of Henry Kissinger's." The writers huddled, and Kissinger went before a Washington Press Club dinner to recall that rejection, and to add: "But she did not say that if nominated, she would not run"— long pause—"or if elected, she would not serve."

SHIP OF STATE a nation, particularly in regard to its diplomacy.

Sailors always refer to ships as "she"; this expression might be the cause of the use of the feminine reference to nations, as "America will defend her national interests." The description of a nation as a vessel on a course can be traced in English to 1675 and can be found in ancient Greek poetry.

Lincoln liked the metaphor. "If we do not make common cause," he said in 1861, "to save the good old ship of the Union on this voyage, nobody will have the chance to pilot her on another voyage." Grover Cleveland in 1894 wrote much the same thing: "The Ship of Democracy, which has weathered all storms, may sink through the mutiny of those on board." In more recent times, when candidate Thomas E. Dewey in 1948 said, "We need a rudder to our ship of state and a firm hand on the tiller," Republican Joe Martin shrugged, "Sounds good and brings the applause. But promises nothing."

The metaphor offers a tool for criticism; an 1883 reference in the *Congressional Record* says "Twenty percent of the employees in all Departments in the City of Washington . . . are really barnacles upon the ship of state."

Most dramatic use of the phrase was in a message from President Franklin Roosevelt, given to defeated Republican candidate Wendell Willkie in 1941 to take to Winston Churchill, quoting an 1893 poem by Henry Wadsworth Longfellow:

Thou, too, sail on, O Ship of State!
Sail on, O Union, strong and great!
Humanity with all its fears,
With all the hopes of future years,
Is hanging breathless on thy fate!

Other nautical metaphors in politics include Sir Walter Scott's "sea of upturned faces" and Lord Acton's maxim, "The ship exists for the sake of the passengers." *Groundswells* lead to *tides of support*.

George Shultz, Director of the Office of Management and Budget, concluded a 1971 economic speech with the nautical reference: "Those of you familiar with sailing know what a telltale is—a strip of cloth tied to a mast to show which way the wind is blowing. A captain has the choice of steering his ship by the telltale, following the prevailing winds, or to steer by the compass. In a democracy, you must keep your eye on the telltale, but you must set your course by the compass. That is exactly what the President of the United States is

doing. The voice from the bridge says, 'Steady as you go.' "

On March 20, 1969, Senator Everett Dirksen delivered a speech drafted by this writer, who vaguely recalled the Dewey usage, and included the line: "Around the world there is the feeling that there is a firm hand on the rudder of our ship of state." One reader of the *Washington Post,* Karl G. Sorg, wrote a letter to the editor observing: "When I am on the high seas, I would like my skipper to keep a firm hand on the tiller, and to leave that rudder alone. Any skipper with a firm hand on the rudder is likely to be in water way over his head." This convinced one speechwriter that ship metaphors are best left to sailors.

See NEW DEPARTURE.

SHIRTSLEEVE   DIPLOMACY informal, plain-speaking international relatiions, contrasted with the diplomatic niceties of "striped-pants" diplomacy.

The phrase has a pleasantly hardworking connotation to Americans in current usage, from the expression "roll up one's sleeves" (to get to work). Earlier use of the phrase suggested that American ambassadors were chosen as a result of political contributions; and their demeanor was boorish compared to the conservative mannerisms of diplomats of nations steeped in international affairs.

London's *Pall Mall Gazette,* reporting in 1908 on American customs, wrote: "The Congressmen have a preference for what they picturesquely describe as 'Shirt-sleeve Ambassadors'—men who they think will labor for their country's interests and scorn social fascinations."

John Hay, Theodore Roosevelt's Secretary of State, was probably the first diplomat associated with the phrase. Wrote the *Cyclopaedia of*

American Government in 1914: "Shirt Sleeve Diplomacy. A title which has been given to some of the diplomacy of recent years which has disregarded much of the circumlocution and indirectness of earlier practice and has stated clearly the purpose of the negotiation and the methods by which a state proposed to attain the purpose. This term has been particularly applied to the diplomacy of the United States from the late years of the nineteenth century."

Wealth and social standing are supposed to inhibit the willingness to work in shirtsleeves (to deal informally, directly, often harshly). Columbia University president Nicholas Murray Butler referred to "a society like ours of which it is truly said to be often but three generations 'from shirtsleeves to shirtsleeves.' "

For a different type of diplomat, see COOKIE PUSHER.

SHOO-IN a certain winner; a candidate who can only be defeated by a POLITICAL MIRACLE.

Like FRONT RUNNER, BOLT, DARK HORSE, and many others, the metaphor is taken from racing, but this one has a fraudulent background. When jockeys form a "ring" and bet on a single horse, they hold back their own mounts and "chase in" or "shoo in" the horse selected to be the winner. *Racing Maxims and Methods of 'Pittsburgh Phil,'* published in 1908, points out: "There were many times presumably that 'Tod' would win through such manipulations, being 'shooed in,' as it were." In *The Underworld Speaks* (1935), A. J. Pollack defines shoo-in as "a horse race in which the winner is the only horse trying."

"To shoo" is a colloquialism meaning to urge gently a person or animal to go in a desired direction. It made its first recorded appearance around the turn of the twentieth century. "Shoo-in"—minus its crooked connotation, now only meaning "sure thing"—began to be used politically in the forties. "Taft Appears to Be Shoo-In for Top Senate G.O.P. Job" headlined the *San Francisco News* in 1948, and *Life* predicted, "Dewey looks like a shoo-in for the presidency."

The word was sufficiently secured in the political lexicon in 1967 to rate a turnaround. The *Wall Street Journal* called the candidate hopelessly running against popular Congressman Adam Clayton Powell in New York's Harlem "a shoo-out."

SHOOT FROM THE HIP, *see* TRIGGER-HAPPY.

SHOOTING WAR, *see* COLD WAR.

SHORTCHANGE to deny to a city those state services which it considers its due because of taxes paid to the state by residents of the city.

The shortchange charge is made when the different levels of government are controlled by opposing parties. For example, Mayor Robert F. Wagner of New York City, a Democrat, charged that New York State had been shortchanging the city when Thomas E. Dewey, a Republican, was governor. When Averell Harriman, a Democrat, became governor in 1954, the charge was muted, until Republican Nelson Rockefeller became governor in 1958; at that point Mayor Wagner returned to the familiar shortchange theme. When Republican John V. Lindsay became mayor in 1965, he could not make shortchanging an important charge against Rockefeller, whom he supported; instead, he charged Democratic President Lyndon Johnson with short-changing cities in federal aid.

The shortchange charge is usually made something like this: "The taxpayers of this city pay ten million dollars in taxes to the state, and receive back in services only six million dollars. Yet the farmers in the rural areas pay four million in taxes and get back four million in services." The defense by the higher body is usually: "When this Administration took office, services to localities totaled only four million. Now it is six." A more sophisticated argument, citing the need for state hospitals that can be used by city residents, is seldom made. The shortchange charge is usually not stressed between candidates for the same office, since one group of voters usually benefits from the apparently higher rate paid by other voters, and neither candidate wants to offend an entire bloc; however, the more local candidate has no such restriction on attacking the higher body, provided it is of the opposite party.

Another use of shortchange is made in PORK BARREL legislation, when congressmen feel their district is being overlooked in the dispensing of federal projects. Typical comment was made in 1961 by Representative Ken Hechler of West Virginia: "I am firmly against the kind of LOGROLLING which would subject our defense program to narrowly sectional or selfish pulling and hauling. But I am getting pretty hot under the collar about the way my state of West Virginia is shortchanged in Army, Navy, and Air Force installations. . . . I am going to stand up on my hind legs and roar until West Virginia gets the fair treatment she deserves."

SHORT HAIRS sensitive point by which a person or faction can be controlled.

In current slang, "to have someone by the short hairs" means to have the other in a totally controllable position; its pubic-hair connotation inhibits its use in polite society. It is not known when "short hairs" acquired this connotation, since the "Short-Hairs"—crew cut workingmen and pugilists—were members of John Kelly's administration of Tammany Hall in the 1870s. Opposing the Short-Hairs were the wealthy supporters of Samuel Tilden, the "Swallow-Tails" (after their formal clothes), who attempted to seize control of the Democratic party in the state. Tammany continued to fight New York Governor Tilden on the national scene, and the *Cincinnati Democratic Gazette* reported in 1876: "The anti-Tilden New Yorkers began to realize the fact last night that the rowdy or *short hair* element of their forces was disgusting the country delegates and reacting in Tilden's favor."

According to Charles Ledyard Norton in 1890, the Short-Hairs gained their nickname "in deference either to their 'fighting cut' or the supposed recent release from prison." Tammany leader John Morrissey, a retired prizefighter, spoofed the "Swallow-Tail" faction one morning by dressing up in full evening dress and carrying a French dictionary under one arm. He explained that "this sort of thing was necessary in order to retain one's influence."

Throughout the sixties, the wearing of long hair by men was a sign of rebellion; those young men who wore their hair short were considered "jocks," insensitive to political affairs. Some idea of how fast and far the pendulum swings was felt in 1978 when a military honor guard suspended two of its members for "too-short hair."

See NUT-CUTTING.

SHOWING THE FLAG, *see* **PRESENCE.**

SHREDDING, *see* **SANITIZE.**

SHRIMPS WHISTLE a Russian figure of speech indicating a day never to come.

When Russian Premier Nikita Khrushchev heard a Western suggestion in 1955 that the Soviet Union's fidelity to Communism might fade with the years, he replied, "Those who' wait for that must wait until a shrimp learns to whistle."

The image became a favorite of editorial writers doing pieces on PEACEFUL COEXISTENCE. The *New York Times,* suggesting in 1967 that Rhodesian Prime Minister Ian Smith surprise the world by making progress toward majority rule, wrote: "A move so contrary to Mr. Smith's every act since entering public life would confound African experts around the world. Shrimps, in Mr. Khrushchev's colorful expression, would surely whistle."

The nearest American expressions are "until the cows come home" or "until hell freezes over."

SHUTTLE DIPLOMACY negotiations assisted by a middleman hurrying between capitals by jet plane; in particular, the Kissinger peace attempts after the 1973 Arab-Israeli war.

"At week's end," wrote *Time* on March 4, 1974, "Kissinger was to return . . . to the Middle East for another round of 'shuttle diplomacy'— this time to Damascus, Jerusalem and Cairo : . ." By June 24 the magazine had dropped quotation marks and extended the metaphor: "The only possible accomplishment left for Henry Hercules is for him to become an astronaut, and then maybe he could be the first space-shuttle diplomat."

The word "shuttle" might have been introduced to diplomacy by talk of NASA's "space shuttle," which in turn came into the language from the Eastern Airlines Boston–New York–Washington "shuttle," which probably had its origin in New York's Pennsylvania Station–Times Square subway shuttle. All these transportation metaphors are extensions of the weaving shuttle that shoots the thread of the woof between the threads of the warp.

"Diplomacy" has long been a convenient word with which to conclude a new phrase. From DOLLAR DIPLOMACY to GUNBOAT DIPLOMACY, the phrasemaking progressed to the more recent "ping-pong diplomacy" regarding the Chinese, QUIET DIPLOMACY and "media diplomacy," which, for a time, replaced "shuttle diplomacy."

See STEP BY STEP.

SICK MAN OF EUROPE originally Turkey; applied in modern times to whatever European nation is in political or economic trouble.

"To make an aliiance with Turkey," writer François Chateaubriand quoted a diplomat in 1807, "is the same as putting your arms around a corpse to make it stand up." This echoed the judgment of Sir Thomas Roe, British ambassador in Constantinople two centuries earlier, who said the Ottoman Empire had "the body of a sick old man who tried to appear healthy, although his end was near." In 1853 Russian Czar Nicholas I told British Ambassador Sir George Seymore, "We have on our hands a sick man—a very sick man," and Turkey was tagged throughout the remainder of the nineteenth century "the sick man of Europe."

The patient changes, but the phrase lingers on. Australian editor Colin Bingham wrote in 1967: "For years after the Second World War, France was frequently described as 'the sick man of Europe,' but by 1966 the United Kingdom's economic difficulties prompted a transient application of the epithet to Britain."

SIGN OFF ON   approve; specifically, to initial one's endorsement.

"If you want to make sure the President will sign off on something," Carter White House aide Stuart Eizenstadt told *New Times* writer Robert Shrum in July, 1977, "the best way is to get Bert [Lance] to agree."

This off-again, on-again locution became popular in government in the sixties. (See the Arthur Schlesinger, Jr., puzzlement in **PENTAGONESE**.) Seeking approval is "running it past" an official, but getting that approval is inducing him to "sign off on" it. In radio parlance, "to sign off" is to go off the air; the noun "signoff" is the conclusion of a broadcast day with an announcement including the call letters, or sign, of the station.

From this, one can extrapolate to the meaning of "sign off" as termination, or final approval—in the sense that the **BUCK STOPS HERE**, at the top executive's desk. But why the "on"? One may speculate that if "to sign off" is taken to mean "to approve," then the "on" refers to the placement of initials on a document.

The awkward phrase is in rampant Washington use. At the end of 1977 President Carter proudly announced: "I've signed off on the budget." Similar to the military "endorse," the phrase has replaced "clear with" as a verb that helps a bureaucrat share responsibility. See **COVER YOUR ASS; CLEAR IT WITH SIDNEY**.

An element of "accountability," a favored Washington term in the mid-seventies, is connected with the phrase. Elizabeth Drew, writing in *The New Yorker* (May 1, 1978) about National Security Adviser Zbigniew Brzezinski, pointed to a debate within the Carter Administration about accountability in the President's executive order on intelligence oversight: "The executive order requires that the President must 'sign off' on any activity of any importance. Brzezinski is known to believe that the President should have broad flexibility, including 'deniability'—that is, it should be possible to carry out operations in a way that would enable the President to deny he knew about them."

The vogue use of "on"—as in "add on," or even the Americanization of the British "early on"—is ongoing.

SILENT MAJORITY   the remarkable legion of the unremarked, whose individual opinions are not colorful or different enough to make news, but whose collective opinion, when crystallized, can make history.

The voices of the Vietnam dissenters were relatively muted during the first nine months of the Nixon presidency; in October, 1969 a moratorium was organized, featuring a march on Washington, D.C., with more strident demonstrations planned the following month.

In the midst of this rebirth of demonstrations, President Nixon made a televised address, in prime time, that effectively countered the mounting dissent. The November 3 "silent majority" speech might well have had more of an effect on public opinion than any since the FDR acceptance in 1932, buying time for the Vietnamization program. The antiwar demonstrations did not make important news again until the Cambodian incursion six months later.

"If a vocal minority," the President warned, "however fervent its cause, prevails over reason and the will of the majority, this Nation has no future as a free society. Let historians not record that when America was the most powerful nation in the world we passed on the other side of the road and allowed the last hopes for peace and freedom of millions of people to be suffocated by the forces of totalitarianism. And so tonight—to you, the great silent majority of my fellow Americans—I ask for your support."

Nixon, who wrote this speech with no help from his speechwriters, was not consciously "making a phrase." The words in the phrase were not capitalized, nor was the phrase repeated, but it did fill a need for a description of all the people who were not demonstrating, and was promptly taken up by the media.

Though the phrase officially came into the political language on November 3, 1969, it had of course been used previously, and Nixon had used the thought many times.

In a radio speech during the primary campaign, on May 16, 1968, he referred to "the silent center, the millions of people in the middle of the American political spectrum who do not demonstrate, who do not picket or protest loudly. . . . We must remember that all the center is not silent, and all who are silent are not center. But a great many 'quiet Americans' have become committed to answers to social problems that preserve personal freedom."

Throughout the campaign he came back to those "quiet Americans" and "forgotten Americans," and occasionally used "quiet majority."

John F. Kennedy wrote in *Profiles in Courage* (1956): "They were not all right or all conservatives or all liberals. Some of them may have been representing the actual sentiments of the silent majority of their constituents in opposition to the screams of a vocal minority, but most of them were not."

The phrase "silent center" had been used by Senator Paul Douglas in a speech in 1967. Much earlier, Alexis de Tocqueville warned of "the excessive love of the whole community for quiet" leading Americans to ignore military problems until they became acute, and Bulwer-Lytton in 1848 described "the universal noiseless impression through all England" that Harold, last of the Saxon kings, "was now the sole man on whom rested the state—which, whenever it so favors one individual, is irresistible."

Previous usage of any famous phrase can be found. The September 1874 issue of *Harper's New Monthly Magazine* had an article entitled "The Silent Majority"; it was about burial customs around the world, the phrase taken from ancient Greek references to the dead. In Plautus' *Trinummus, ad plures penetrare*—"to join the great majority"—is used as a euphemism for dying.

Vice President Agnew used the phrase in its non-lugubrious sense on May 9, 1969: "It is time for America's silent majority to stand up for its rights, and let us remember the American majority includes every minority. America's silent majority is bewildered by irrational protest . . ."

During that spring of 1969, David Broder of the *Washington Post* asked historian Theodore White to reflect on the paradoxes that marked the previous election year. Said White: "Never have America's leading cultural media, its university thinkers, its influence makers been more intrigued by experiment and change; but in no election have the mute masses more completely separated themselves from such leadership and thinking. Mr. Nixon's problem is to interpret what the silent people think, and govern the country against the grain of what its more important thinkers think."

Six months later, as White predicted, Nixon rallied "the silent majority." In the late seventies the phrase carried the opprobrium generally accorded Nixon-Agnew utterances, but its users were careful to deride the phrasemakers rather than the group described. See MIDDLE AMERICA; GREAT UNWASHED.

SILENT VOTE the unmeasurables, who may or may not turn out.

Different meanings: (1) a sector of the public unhappy with the sameness of both parties, which can be turned out only by offering a CHOICE, NOT AN ECHO; (2) a sector that remains "undecided" to pollsters, for such reasons as religious preference, bigotry, or BACKLASH, and remains an unknown quantity until Election Day; (3) the wistfully hoped-for vote that was simply never cast. See STAY-AT-HOMES; TURNOUT.

"In the next election," the *Cincinnati Campaigner* predicted in 1848, "the silent vote for Van Buren will be immense." The former President, running on a third party ticket, picked up one tenth of the vote cast. "The silent vote, as it is called," wrote the *New York Times* in 1880, "is what will tell in November." This is usually a fairly safe prediction. In that case, James Garfield squeaked past Democrat Winfield Scott Hancock with 10,000 votes out of 10 million cast, with a "silent vote"—possibly costing Hancock the election—going to the Greenback splinter party.

The phrase is most often used today by apologists for candidates who are far behind in the public opinion polls; workers for Goldwater in 1964 cheered themselves up with the assurance that an enormous "silent vote" would appear on Election Day.

Of those people old enough to vote for President, about 40 percent do not. Conservatives have long claimed this vote is essentially conservative; others say these potential voters are simply apathetic, illiterate, ill or infirm, or have moved too recently to qualify, and are of all political persuasions.

SILK STOCKING wealthy; originally used to derogate the upper class, now only as descriptive of a high-income area.

The phrase can be found in the writings of Jefferson ("the Gores and the Pickerings will find their levees crowded with silk stocking gentry, but no yeomanry; an army of officers without soldiers") and Lincoln ("They came not like 'the silk stocking gentry' as they are called by their opponents; but as farmers, mechanics, etc.").

In the era of knee britches and silk hose, only the wealthy could afford silk stockings. The term was used by Jeffersonian Republicans against the well-to-do Federalists. The meaning changed only slightly later, as described by the *Cyclopaedia of American Government* in 1914: "a derisive appellation bestowed by the 'PRACTICAL POLITICIANS' upon those citizens of wealth and high social position who occasionally interfere in politics in support of some reform measure or candidate."

Over the years, *kid glove politics, swallow-tail politician,* and *ruffled shirt* appeared as synonyms, but silk stocking outlived them all, and is similar to "lace curtain" (as opposed to "shanty") used to describe the social classes of Irish-Americans. Louis Howe said he had originally sized up Franklin Roosevelt as a "spoiled, silk-pants sort of guy."

The best-known use of the phrase in its current sense was popularized by Theodore Roosevelt: "I was a Republican from the 'silk stocking' district, the wealthiest district in New York." The *New York Post* wrote in 1903 of "the 'silk stocking' quarter—the middle reaches of Manhattan, between 14th and 96th Street." But it is used generically as well. "In as chairman," wrote *Time* magazine in 1948, "went 47-year-old Hugh Scott, Jr., a three-term congressman from a suburban Philadelphia 'silk stocking' district."

SIT-IN a technique of demonstration launched by civil rights activitists in 1960 to dramatize segregation in the South.

Four black youths from North Carolina Agricultural and Technical College entered the F. W. Woolworth store in Greensboro, North Carolina, on February 1, 1960, and sat down at the "white" lunch counter. "It is regrettable," said Mayor William G. Enloe of Raleigh as the sit-ins spread throughout the state, "that some of our young Negro students would risk endangering Raleigh's friendly and cooperative race relations by seeking to change a long-standing custom in a manner that is all but destined to fail."

The sit-ins, at first dismissed as a college fad, were destined to bring into prominence the Congress of Racial Equality (CORE) and to change the pattern of segregation throughout the South.

The "-in" construction quickly caught on, leading to *kneel-ins* and *pray-ins* in the early sixties, *teach-ins*

in 1965 (first organized in Michigan by Students for a Democratic Society), and subsequently *love-ins, be-ins, eat-ins,* etc.

John Kennedy, campaigning for President in September 1960, caught the significance of the sit-ins and turned a phrase about them: "He [the President] must exert the great moral and educational force of his office to bring about equal access to public facilities, from churches to lunch-counters, and support the rights of every American to stand up for his rights, even if he must sit down for them."

As the "-in's" proliferated in the sixties, and the original civil rights connotation was diluted by the "hippies," Clark Kerr, ousted president of the University of California, predicted in 1967: "The sit-in will gradually join the coonskin coat as an interesting symbol of a student age retreating into history."

The former meaning of the phrase "to sit in" was "to have a place as a player of a game," especially of cards, and although it remains a colloquialism, it has been traced by the *OED* to 1599.

See FREEDOM RIDERS.

SITTING ON THE FENCE, see FENCE, ON THE.

SITTING PRESIDENT a President in office; the power of incumbency in achieving renomination or reelection.

The phrase derives from a sitting monarch, whose throne is a seat of power, and from a sitting hen, whose inactivity conceals a procreative purpose. A judge is sitting when court is in session, and sitting judges (those holding judicial office, whether court is in or out of session) are rarely considered as candidates (Alton B. Parker was the only one to run for President).

Harry Truman put it this way: "When the President is sitting in the White House, the National Convention of his party has never gone against his recommendations in the choice of a candidate or in the formation of a platform on which that convention is to operate." In his memoirs, the former President pointed out how sitting President Theodore Roosevelt in 1908 could dictate the choice of his successor, William Howard Taft; but in 1912, with all his popularity, Roosevelt could not take the nomination away from the incumbent Taft. He did not add that he, Truman, as a sitting President, found it simple to designate Adlai Stevenson as his choice in 1952, but in 1956 he was unable to deliver for Averell Harriman.

For a time in the mid-sixties, there was talk of Senator Robert Kennedy challenging President Lyndon B. Johnson for the 1968 presidential nomination, which was dismissed by Kennedy associates as "impossible against a sitting President." After a strong showing by Senator Eugene McCarthy in the New Hampshire primary, Kennedy changed his mind and made his move. Similarly, Ronald Reagan's 1976 challenge to President Gerald Ford made the presidential seat more insecure; in 1978, as Jimmy Carter slipped in polls, pundits fanned talk of a challenge to him in the 1980 primaries by California Governor Edmund "Jerry" Brown.

Florida Governor Claude Kirk, warning Republicans against overconfidence early in 1968, told a press conference: "A sitting president is never a sitting duck."

See INCUMBENT.

SITZKRIEG, *see* **PHONY WAR.**

SIXTY MILLION JOBS, *see* **HOTTENTOTS, MILK FOR.**

SLATE   a list of candidates, presented as a "package"; hopefully, take-one-take-all.

TAMMANY boss Charles Murphy re-elected his candidate for mayor, George B. McClellan, Jr., in 1906 and promptly submitted a list of names for patronage. McClellan, backed up by New York Governor Charles Evans Hughes, proceeded to fire some Tammany men who already had jobs and turned down most of Murphy's suggestions. When asked by McClellan to supply some more acceptable alternatives, Murphy snapped: "That's my slate. Take it or leave it. I got no other candidates." Ultimately, the Tammany boss won.

The name is taken from the material used in school blackboards; a slate on which students write offers the convenience of easy erasure, something often needed in assembling political teams. Its use can be found as early as 1842.

The word acquired a special meaning for the New Left in the late fifties, when a group of students at the University of California at Berkeley submitted a "Slate of Candidates" to run the student government. As they became involved in a wider field, organizing demonstrations against the House Un-American Activities Committee, the group continued to be known as SLATE.

See TICKET.

SLEEPER   an amendment slipped into a bill to nullify or alter its intent; or, a piece of legislation whose significance is not realized until after it has been passed.

The political derivation is from

both horse racing and cards. In racing, a sleeper is a horse that had been held back in previous races to build up its odds, and then allowed to go full speed in a race on which its owner had bet heavily. (For another fraudulent racing scheme turned into a political expression, see SHOO-IN.) In cards, the 1866 *American Hoyle* states: "A bet (in faro) is said to be a sleeper, when the owner has forgotten it, when it becomes public property, any one having a right to take it." See CARD METAPHORS.

The denunciation of "sleeper amendments" is difficult and embarrassing, since it usually includes an admission that the denouncer was not awake enough to catch the legislation when originally offered. Sleeper has generally replaced the previous slang word—"joker." For a "sleeper issue," one which assumes surprising importance in a campaign, see RIGHT TO WORK.

SLOGAN rallying cry; catch phrase (see CATCHWORD); a brief message that crystallizes an idea, defines an issue, the best of which thrill, exhort, and inspire.

Good slogans have rhyme, rhythm, or alliteration to make them memorable; great slogans may have none of these, but touch a chord of memory, release pent-up hatreds, or stir men's better natures.

It is in the nature of slogans to appeal to emotions, slipping past rational argument. "Men suppose that reason has command over their words," wrote Lord Bacon in the sixteenth century, "still it happens that words in return exercise authority on reason."

Themes recur in sloganeering. Many of the following have separate entries in this book, but this is an attempt to show some common denominator.

There are slogans that are essentially *promissory*: Reconstruction's Forty Acres and a Mule (which dwindled to Three Acres and A Cow, taken from British radical agrarian Jesse Collings by American populists); The Full Dinner Pail; Every Man a King; $2 a Day and Roast Beef; I Shall Go to Korea; He Can Do More for Massachusetts; Peace and Prosperity.

Other slogans are primarily *warnings*: Don't Let Them Take It Away; Coolidge or Chaos; Hoover and Happiness, or Smith and Soup Houses; You Never Had It So Good; Save the American Way of Life; No Third Term; Let's Keep What We've Got; Your Home Is Your Castle—Protect It.

A call for *change* has been quite effective: Had enough?; Turn the Rascals Out; Time for a Change; Let's Get America Moving Again.

Overtly *rational* slogans have failed: Let's Look at the Record; Let's Talk Sense to the American People; Experience Counts; as has one overtly *anti-rational*: In Your Heart You Know He's Right.

Challenging is a good slogan technique: Fifty-Four Forty or Fight; Freedom Now.

Appeals to *gratitude* seem weak, but have worked: One Good Term Deserves Another; Keep Him on the Job; He Kept Us Out of War.

There has been a time for *evocative* slogans: A Country Fit for Heroes; General Taylor Never Surrenders; Vote as You Shot.

Alliterative slogans abound: Ban the Bomb; Beat the Bosses; Love That Lyndon; Rum, Romanism, and Rebellion; Tippecanoe and Tyler Too; Wilson's Wisdom Wins Without War; Win with Willkie.

So do *rhyming* slogans: I Like Ike;
Jim Crow Must Go; All the Way with
LBJ; In Hoover We Trusted, Now
We Are Busted; the Grin Will Win.

There are occasional *symbolic* slogans: Log Cabin and Hard Cider; I
Am As Strong As a Bull Moose.

And *punning* slogans: Keep Cool
with Coolidge; Land a Job with Landon; (and Franklin Pierce won despite) We Polked You in 1844, We
Shall Pierce You in 1852.

Slogans have been *frantic* (Anything to Beat Grant); *sardonic* (Make
Love, Not War; Draft Beer, Not Students); *vicious* (Elect a Leader Not a
Lover; Twenty Years of Treason);
meaningless (Nixon's the One) and
questioning (Why Not the Best?).

In his 1960 campaign John F.
Kennedy gave a general review of slogans, including the names of programs as slogans: "The Democratic
party's candidates in this century
never ran on slogans like 'Stand Pat
with McKinley,' 'Return to Normalcy with Harding,' 'Keep Cool
with Coolidge,' and 'Two Chickens in
Every Pot with Hoover.' I don't know
what Dewey's slogan was because he
never worked it out. . . . Our slogans
have meaning. Woodrow Wilson's
New Freedom, Franklin Roosevelt's
New Deal, Harry Truman's Fair
Deal, and today, we stand on the
threshold of a New Frontier."

The knack of turning a phrase was
explained by Theodore Roosevelt to
his young aide, Lieutenant Douglas
MacArthur, in 1906. MacArthur had
asked the President to what he attributed his popularity, and Roosevelt replied, "To put into words what
is in their hearts and minds but not in
their mouths." ("Hearts and minds"
later became a slogan of sorts, as what
had to be won in Vietnam.)

There are those who think sloganeering is a danger. "Slogans are both

exciting and comforting," said educator James Bryant Conant in 1934,
"but they are also powerful opiates
for the conscience: some of mankind's
most terrible misdeeds have been
committed under the spell of certain
magic words or phrases." Examples
of this category include: Workers of
the World, Unite; Mare Nostrum;
Tomorrow the World.

Fowler's *Modern English Usage*
defines slogans as "those catchwords
with which in the modern world
politicians, ideologists, and advertisers try to excite our emotions and at-
rophy our minds." The word itself
comes from the Gaelic *slaugh-gairm,*
from *slaugh* (army) and *gairm* (yell),
the army-shout or war cry of the Scottish Highlanders, and has been in use,
according to the *OED,* since 1513. An
early American political use occurs in
Harper's Weekly in 1854: "As party
bitterness has died away . . . let us
take up the old slogan: Hurrah for
Jackson!"

Good sloganeering advice was provided by University of Wisconsin professor Robert T. Oliver in the February 1937 issue of *American Speech*:
"The party out of power would do
well to mass its attack behind one or
two key phrases. Thus it will gain the
same concentration that advertisers
seek with their reiteration of They
satisfy! Not a cough in a carload! Ask
the man who owns one! In the use of
slogans, it would appear, the chief
poverty is riches. The force of vivid
impression through which slogans
operate is vitiated when there are too
many."

In the seventies there was a trend
toward facetious slogans. "Support
Mental Health or I'll Kill You" appeared on buttons, but a candidate for
local office in Washington won on
"Dog Litter—An Issue You Can't
Sidestep."

SLOGANEER, *see* **GHOST-WRITER.**

SLUMLORD a landlord who realizes unconscionable profits on crowded slum dwellings, packing in tenants and withholding money for maintenance.

In cities, crusades against slumlords are frequent in local political campaigns, since there are relatively few voters who own real estate and a great many in ghetto areas who resent absentee landlords.

The word appeared in the midfifties; an early citation is from a 1957 *New York Times Magazine* article: "The landlord had bitterly protested to the Buildings Commissioner that he was not a 'slumlord' and avowed that he was ready to put the building in condition if he could get a guarantee that it would stay that way; otherwise he had no alternative but to demolish it." Added *Barron's* magazine in 1960: "To prevent the enrichment of slumlords, for example, the General Accounting Office, in fixing property values, would rule out all income earned in defiance of local ordinances."

Slumlords defend themselves by claiming that tenants overcrowd their facilities without their permission, and that vandalism is the cause of most of the complaints. This cuts no ice with campaigning candidates; a typical picture in this genre was Mayor Robert F. Wagner of New York touring a slum dwelling and coming face to face with a large rat.

There is a long tradition against landlords, particularly absentee. Dean Jonathan Swift inveighed against the English landlords of Ireland in the early eighteenth century, and this comment by Richard Hildreth in *Memoirs of a Fugitive* was typical of complaints against Southern plantation owners before the Civil War: "The absentee aristocracy congregates in Charleston, or dapples and astonishes the cities and watering places of the North by its profuse extravagance and reckless dissipation. The plantations are left to the sole management of overseers."

"Slumlord" is a word born with its time out of joint. The word was created by the substitution of the "land" in "landlord" with "slum," which was slang for "room" (possibly from "slumber") in the early nineteenth century, later coming to mean "poverty-stricken neighborhood." But as *slumlord* was being coined, so were euphemisms for *slum;* linguistic urban renewal replaced it with *culturally deprived environment* or *urban ghetto* or *inner city,* making *slumlord* a word in dire need of relocation.

SLUSH FUND a collection of money for payoffs or for personal use without proper accounting; an attack word on any collection of political contributions.

"Is Dodd Dead?" went the political question early in 1967, a play on the theological argument "Is God Dead?" As a result of an exposé by columnists Drew Pearson and Jack Anderson, Connecticut Senator Thomas Dodd was censured by the Senate for personal use of funds collected ostensibly for campaigning purposes.

Though "slush fund" was used often in Dodd's hearings, the meaning of the phrase is usually narrowed to a specific fund. Richard Nixon was accused by Democrats of having a slush fund in 1952, which he defended in the CHECKERS SPEECH concurrently releasing contributors, amounts, and purposes. Soon afterward Adlai Stevenson was discovered by Republicans to have a fund as Illinois governor for supplementing the salaries of state employees. Since neither fund had a nefarious purpose, the furor soon died down.

The word is probably derived from the Swedish *slask,* meaning wet, or filth. Naval vessels would sell the slush and other refuse on board; the proceeds went into a fund to purchase sundries for the crew. Later this practice was extended to war-damaged equipment as well, and to military as well as naval refuse and equipment. "The polite Commissary informed us," wrote the *Rio Abajo Press* in 1864, "that they received twelve dollars a barrel for the [coffee] grounds, and thus added materially to the 'slush fund.' "

The first political use found was in 1874. Connecticut Congressman S. W. Kellogg, referring to a $5 million appropriation administered by the Treasury Secretary, said:

> It was a matter of economy and good judgment . . . to consolidate all these offices into one bill, and dispense with what has been received out of . . . the "slush fund." . . . We have had this "slush fund" since 1866. It is the fund which my friend from Indiana (Mr. Holman) and my friend from Kentucky (Mr. Beck) talk so much about, although during Andrew Johnson's administration that "slush fund" was five or six times larger than it ever has been since.

Congressman Champ Clark used the term in 1894 in the sense of a campaign fund gathered for propaganda purposes, as he defended President Grover Cleveland, who "was not elected in 1888 because you had got the 'fat fried' out of your manufacturers; because of pious John Wanamaker and $400,000 of campaign slush funds. . . ." See FAT CAT.

What gives a slush fund its sinister current meaning is its inherent lack of accountability—the money goes into a pot and is ladled out without public scrutiny. From the original "fringe benefit" connotation in naval vessels, the phrase has gained a thieving image, as in this 1924 comparison of chicanery by Will Rogers: "If I was running for office I would rather have two friends in the counting room than a Republican slush fund behind me."

SMART POLITICS, *see* PRACTICAL POLITICS.

SMEAR   as a verb, to slander, or to bribe, or to devastate; as a noun, a malicious lie, or a payment.

"I know this will not be the last of the smears," said vice-presidential candidate Richard Nixon in 1952, at the conclusion of his television defense of the "Nixon fund." See CHECKERS SPEECH. "In spite of my explanation tonight, other smears will be made. . . . And the purpose of the smears, I know, is this: to silence me, to make me let up."

Both the word and the political device are ancient. The word appears in a variety of languages: the Greek *smyris,* unguent; the Old Norse *smör,* fat or butter; the Old English *smeoru,* grease; Middle English *smere;* modern English *smear.* As a verb, one of its meanings is to besmirch, or pollute, and that sense—of tainting a reputation—is its most common political meaning.

A second political meaning—to bribe—comes from the political use of GREASE as graft money; a related idea is to "know which side your bread is buttered on." This is usually pronounced *schmear,* or *schmier,* from the German verb "to spread."

"Be thou as pure as snow," Hamlet told Ophelia, "as chaste as ice, thou shalt not escape calumny." An attack on a reputation can be labeled pretentiously as *"impugning integrity."* A more legalistic mind uses *slander* (spoken) or *libel* (written). A recent label, implying systematic smearing, is CHARACTER ASSASSINATION.

Peggy Eaton, wife of Andrew Jackson's Secretary of War, was ostracized by Washington society for supposedly living with her husband-to-be before her first husband committed suicide, and the President accurately diagnosed the attack on the young woman as "a plot by Clay and Calhoun to separate Eaton and me." The lady herself put it quaintly: "It was the designs of politics that led to the slander of my fair frame . . ." Fathering a bastard, one of the dirtiest of smears, was used unsuccessfully against Grover Cleveland, who admitted he supported an illegitimate child; a campaign song was "Ma, Ma, where's Pa?"

A third, and less frequent, meaning of smear is to devastate, or "to cream," from the football use of the word for a crunching tackle, or the baseball use as an overwhelming victory. There is an overlap here, as a person who has been effectively slandered can be pictured as left lying on the ground.

Smear was popularized during the latter part of the Hoover Administration, when Democrats blamed Herbert Hoover for breadlines; the President said that Charlie Michelson, a former *New York World* reporter acting as head of the Democratic National Committee's publicity department, "came out of the smear department of yellow journalism."

John J. Raskob, Chairman of the Democratic National Committee in 1932, taunted the Republicans on their "smear" charge. "Upon consulting the dictionary," he told the national convention, "we found a definition of the word 'smear' to mean, 'to prepare a dead body with sacred oils before burial.'"

The Republicans in 1936 continued to complain about the "Smear Department of the New Deal," but in the next decade the use of the word became bipartisan. In political terminology, it was a useful antonym to "whitewash": Harry Truman wrote that his senatorial investigating committee "was not going to be used for either a whitewash or a smear in any matter before it but was to be used to obtain facts . . ." Senator Margaret Chase Smith, in her 1950 "Declaration of Conscience" aimed at Senator Joseph McCarthy, said: "The American people are sick and tired of being afraid to speak their minds lest they be politically smeared as 'Communist' or 'Fascist.' The American people are sick and tired of seeing innocent people smeared and guilty people WHITEWASHED . . ."

The spring and summer of 1960 was a high point of smearing. John F. Kennedy's West Virginia primary campaign featured a smear by Kennedy supporter Franklin D. Roosevelt, Jr., to the effect that Senator Hubert Humphrey had been a draft dodger; the Lyndon Johnson forces, led by Texas Governor John Connally (injured when Kennedy was assassinated, three years later), accused Kennedy's father of harboring anti-Semitic sentiments during World War II.

A question arises: Can the truth be a smear? The Johnson supporters claimed that John Kennedy was a victim of Addison's disease, requiring regular cortisone treatment. The Kennedy forces admitted only "a mild adrenal deficiency," but an article in the *Journal of the American Medical Association* in 1967 substantiated the original charge. Nevertheless, most politicians consider the original attack a smear; while truth may be a legal defense against libel, the spreading of a damaging story about a candidate—even if true—can be considered a smear. Journalists do not agree.

The predecessor word was ROOR-BACK; also see GUTTER FLYER and DIRTY TRICKS.

SMELL OF MAGNOLIAS the difficulty of being a Southerner in a national campaign; or, Southern charm exercised with great political finesse in the South.

"Johnson the candidate," wrote *Life* magazine in 1956 about the candidacy of Senator Lyndon Johnson of Texas, "has grave and probably decisive drawbacks as he, despite the hopes of his supporters, well knows. He has little support in organized labor. He 'smells of magnolias,' *i.e.,* is a Southerner."

Though the phrase seldom appears in print, it has a lively political usage as "magnolia talk"—an intimate, richly accented, we-have-the-same-roots seduction—and as "smell of magnolias," the odor that causes Southern conservatives to sigh and Northern liberals to sniff.

When Richard Nixon impressed the Republican platform committee in 1960 with the need to adopt a strong civil rights plank, a Southern lady from Louisiana told reporter Theodore White, "I know what you Northerners think. But we've lost Louisiana, I tell you, we've lost Louisiana. Lyndon Johnson's going to come across the border now and talk 'magnolia' to them and they'll vote Democratic and we could have had Louisiana, we could have had it." See CORN PONE.

In the presidential campaign of 1976, the presence of a Southerner, Jimmy Carter, at the top of the Dem-ocratic ticket led to a new use of the magnolia metaphor: unfriendly writers referred to his wife, Rosalynn Carter, as "the steel magnolia." In April 1978, *Time* magazine referred to the group of Georgians working in the White House as the "magnolia mafia."

SMOKE-FILLED ROOM a place of political intrigue and chicanery, where candidates are selected by party bosses in cigar-chewing session.

This sinister phrase is usually attributed to Harry Daugherty, an Ohio Republican who supported Senator Warren Harding for the party's presidential candidacy. Daugherty sensed that the two best-known candidates, General Leonard Wood and Governor Frank Lowden of Illinois, would start off with almost equal support. "The convention will be deadlocked," Daugherty is quoted as having said, "and after the other candidates have gone their limit, some twelve or fifteen men, worn out and bleary-eyed for lack of sleep, will sit down about two o'clock in the morning, around a table in a smoke-filled room in some hotel and decide the nomination. When that time comes, Harding will be selected."

Daugherty later denied having said any such thing, calling "The Fable of the Senatorial Clique" an "amazing yarn." But William Allen White, editor of the *Emporia Gazette* and a respected Republican figure, corroborated the Daugherty prediction. A story filed at 5 A.M. on June 12, 1920, by Associated Press reporter Kirke Simpson, led off with the words "Harding of Ohio was chosen by a group of men in a smoke-filled room early today as Republican candidate for President." Newsmen call this "putting the story in the lead."

Present in Colonel George Harvey's room at the Blackstone Hotel that night were some of the most respected political figures in the U.S.: Senators Wadsworth, Calder, Smoot, Watson, McCormick, and Lodge, along with Joe Grundy, a political boss who later became a senator. Not present were most of those later to become known as "the Ohio gang."

Historian Mark Sullivan, curious about the birth of a famous saying, elicited a letter from New Yorker Charles E. Hilles, who (Sullivan wrote) "was present at, so to speak, the obstetrical bedside of this verbal birth." The first-hand Hilles account: "Daugherty was hastily packing his bag in a Waldorf Astoria Hotel room when two reporters called. He expressed regret that he had not time for an interview. One of the reporters persisted . . . he said that he presumed that as Daugherty could not support by an authetic table of delegates his boast that Harding would be the nominee, it followed that Daugherty must expect to win by manipulation —probably in some back room of a hotel with a small group of political managers reduced to pulp by the inevitable vigil and travail.

"The reporter went on to say to Daugherty," Hilles recounted, "that he presumed the conferees would be expected to surrender at 2 A.M. in a smoke-filled room. Daugherty, unaffected by the taunt, retorted carelessly, 'Make it 2:11.'"

(For similar tales of phrases planted by reporters, see RED HERRING and INOPERATIVE.)

As Harry Truman pointed out, "the 'smoke-filled room' was nothing new but Harding's nomination dramatized the tag and made it stick." That kind of session was bound to happen, wrote Thomas E. Dewey, "where there are enough strong candidates to prevent anyone from getting a majority and there is a stalemate."

The era of air-conditioned hotel rooms has blown away most of the literal meaning, but the symbolism makes the phrase current and useful.

Carmine de Sapio, Tammany leader in the fifties, had an eye ailment that made it impossible for him to endure cigarette smoke. In tagging him with a "bossism" charge, his opponents continued to charge him with "operating in a smoke-filled room."

SMOKE SCREEN disguising intentions or evading issues by creating a diversion or giving a deliberately false impression.

British Prime Minister Harold Wilson attacked a London newspaper, the *Daily Express,* for revealing government secrets in 1967, despite a special commission's findings that the paper was innocent of the charges. Speaking in the House of Commons, a Conservative leader, Reginald Maudling, said of Mr. Wilson, "It is one of his most unlovable characteristics that he is never prepared to admit he is wrong. On the frequent occasions when he is, he tries to escape by throwing up a smokescreen."

The term is in active use in American politics as well. A 1940 cartoon in the *Rochester* (N.Y.) *Times-Union* shows a Democratic donkey flying an airplane which is putting down a smoke screen around various articles labeled "Taxes," "Extravagance," "Third term," "Public debt." At that time Republicans were charging the Roosevelt Administration with trying to hide its domestic errors behind the dangers of this country becoming involved in World War II. The cartoon is captioned "War Issue."

A linguistic spin-off is the word "spoofing," nuclear jargon for creating false alarms or making diversions.

This is designed to swamp or confuse an enemy's thermonuclear defense so that it is unable to identify a genuine attack when launched.

The derivation of "smoke screen" is naval, from the days when destroyers would dash at high speeds between an enemy fleet and their own, laying down large quantities of black smoke to conceal the movements and intentions of their own vessels. Later, airplanes were sometimes used to accomplish the same aims on the battlefield.

In Japanese politics, a more poetic phrase is used to describe the effort to evade an issue by creating a diversion. Translated literally, it is "throwing up cherry blossoms."

SMOKING GUN incontrovertible evidence: the proof of guilt that precipitates resignations.

"The chaplain stood with a smoking pistol in his hand," wrote A. Conan Doyle in a Sherlock Holmes story (1894). Such a stance is generally considered suggestive of obvious (sometimes too obvious) guilt.

During the Watergate investigation, Nixon defenders insisted that while much impropriety could be observed, no proof of presidential obstruction of justice—no "smoking gun"—had been found. Then, on the release of the June 23, 1972, tape, H. R. Haldeman was shown to have said to the President that "the FBI is not under control" and that the CIA could be used to block the FBI investigation. When Haldeman said, "And you seem to think the thing to do is to get them the FBI to stop?," the President replied, "Right, fine."

Representative Barber Conable, a conservative Republican, said that the evidence on the June 23 tape "looked like a smoking gun." The term, which had been "in the air" for months, was widely quoted. Within days the President resigned, and the simile's incontrovertible-evidence meaning was reinforced.

The term did not die with Watergate. Covering the Marvin Mandel corruption trial in Maryland, reporter Jerry Oppenheimer wrote in the *Washington Star* in 1977: "While no 'smoking gun' of new damaging evidence is expected to be introduced by the government, knowledgeable observers of the case believe that the 'morality of Maryland politics' in general will stand trial."

See **WATERGATE WORDS.**

SNAKE IN THE TUNNEL an agreement that one nation's exchange rates will fluctuate within a narrower band than other nations' rates; an attempt to give some limited flexibility to fixed exchange rates, opposed by free-marketers who want an unrestricted "float."

This is as good a metaphor as the invisible hand of the "dismal science" of economics has ever crafted, and is remembered more for the vividness of its image than the longevity of its practice. The word-picture combines the evil lurking in "snake in the grass" with the hope implicit in "light at the end of the tunnel." When this lexicographer went to Professor Herbert Stein, who served as a member, and later Chairman, of the Council of Economic Advisers during the early seventies when the snake was in the tunnel, the answer received went more to the way all catch phrases are born than to the serious business of politico-economic etymology.

"It seems that one day in 1972," recounts the droll Dr. Stein, "at a reception following a meeting of the Group of 10 in Paris, Dr. Karl Schiller, German Minister of Economics and Finance, found that the cream cheese had been spread on the lox, instead of vice versa. *'Diese snack ist im eine tummul!'* he exclaimed, meaning, of course, that the snack was mixed up.

"The information director of the Group of 10, who was British, thought Schiller had said that the snack is in the *tunnel,* the underground passage connecting the Château de la Muette with the OECD office building. At a press briefing later, when asked what Dr. Schiller's opinion was, he quoted Schiller as saying that the snack is in the tunnel.

"A stringer for the *Wall Street Journal,*" Dr. Stein continued, "misunderstood and cabled to New York that Schiller had said, 'The *snake* is in the tunnel.' And so it all began.

"This story," concludes the eminent economist, "while uninteresting, is also unauthenticated." Coming finally to the object of the author's query, he added: "However, I do have it on good authority that the expression was coined by Dr. Schiller."

Reached in West Germany, and responding in all seriousness, Dr. Schiller recalled the birth of the expression in Brussels at the end of 1970. "The meaning was quite simple," he wrote in March 1978. "At the time, we still had a fixed par value system and it was decided to agree on a narrower margin in the actual exchange rates between EEC countries as a preparatory step towards an economic and monetary union in Europe (Werner Plan) . . . this situation created the so-called 'Tunnel' within which the European exchange rates, i.e., the 'snake,' moved.

"Now that we have a joint floating of the currencies of some European countries against the dollar," Dr. Schiller explains, "we speak of the Snake only as a group consisting of some EEC member and some non-

member counties. The Tunnel has, so to speak, disappeared."

Thus, for the reader who wants a straight-faced explanation of the expression, what economists needed was a metaphor for a long, narrow band in which Common Market countries' currencies could go up or down by 1⅛ percent (the snake) while they could vary twice that much up or down against the U.S. dollar (the tunnel). Like a nervous arm in a sleeve, or a wriggling snake in a tunnel.

More important, however, is an understanding of Dr. Stein's points: that folk etymology is easily born, even in economics, and that in multilingual international conferences, much flavor is gained, rather than lost, in translation and transmission.

SNEER WORDS adjectives that cast aspersions on high-sounding nouns, or are used as a defense against entrapment by loaded phrases.

"Self-appointed" is probably the most frequently used sneer word, used to modify "guardian," "protector," and "watchdog" of the public interest. Also in this category is "self-proclaimed," "self-styled," and "self-annointed."

"So-called" is often used as a defensive adjective, when a shining phrase has been adopted generically by the opposition. Western diplomats use "so-called 'People's republic' " to show they don't really believe that the people run the republic; enclosing the sneer word and the noun it modifies within quotation marks completes the dissociation. Union leaders opposing "right-to-work" laws acknowledge that the slanted phrase has become generic, and refers to "so-called 'right-to-work' laws, which are really union busting laws . . ."

"Called" or "said to be" is not limited to English in its aspersion-casting sense; Charles de Gaulle scornfully referred to the United Nations as *"Les nations dites unies."*

A curled lip can be used in spoken English to show derision, but the use of quotation marks creates the same effect in written prose, as "My opponent 'forgot' to say" or "This entry 'neglects' to mention . . ."

SNIPE as a noun, a candidate's poster slapped up on "free space" such as fences, walls, telephone poles; as a verb, to post such advertising clandestinely.

This is a splendid little word long overlooked in political etymology. A "snipe" is a small bird with a long bill, akin to a woodcock; a "snipe hunt" is an elaborate practical joke in which the victim is left in a lonely field at night holding a sack and a tennis racket, one origin of the phrase "left holding the bag"; a snipe is also a fool, or a contemptible person, as in Churchill's "bloodthirsty guttersnipe" reference to Hitler; and it has been used to mean cigarette or cigar butt, as well as a member of a railroad section gang. Somewhere there must be a link that brings all these meanings together.

In its current political use, a snipe is a poster. An explanation is given in *The Relations Explosion,* a 1963 book by this writer:

> Perhaps you have been surprised one morning to see a candidate's "snipes" posted on fences and walls all over town, despite "Post No Bills" warnings. In almost every city, there is an organization well acquainted with building superintendents and construction crews, which will put up a candidate's snipes for a fee. The plastering-up is done in the dead of night, with no questions asked, but never covers up the snipes of the opposing candidate, for whom

the same snipers also work. Amateur snipers soon see their posters covered or disfigured with beards and mustaches.

> An effective political poster should be in glaring color, and should have the candidate's name filling at least a quarter of the poster, visible across streets, with few words of copy.

> We have been speaking here of the "free" poster space, not the normal outdoor billboard advertising. A larger portion of the campaign budget should go to billboards and snipes if the candidate is well-known. Billboards and posters are "reminder" media—they cannot carry much of a message.

In New York City, the sniping business, or racket, or profession, was for many years headed by the night manager of the Waldorf-Astoria.

In China, *tatzepao,* or big-character posters, are an effective propaganda tool; sometimes posted by angry students or supporters of disgraced officials. This form of communication occasionally reflects the genuine feelings of a minority.

In Japan, the word for reputation or prestige is *kamban;* its literal translation is poster, signboard, or "snipe."

SNOLLYGOSTER an unprincipled politician; according to Harry Truman, "a man born out of wedlock."

President Truman revived this obsolete Americanism in a 1952 Labor Day speech at Parkersburg, W. Va., twitting politicians who pray in public to win votes.

The replating of a fanciful term coined during or prior to the Civil War sent reporters to the *Dictionary of American English,* where an entry from the *Columbus Dispatch* in 1895 quoted a Georgia editor's definition:

"A snollygoster is a fellow who wants office, regardless of party, platform or principles, and who, whenever he wins, gets there by the sheer force of monumental talknophical assumnancy [sic]."

On September 3, 1952, the *Baltimore Sun* ran an editorial headed "Snolly and Snally" suggesting that the word came from the German *schnelle Geister,* or "Wild Host," which it defined as "birds of prey that terrorize man" and compared such a bird to an "ostentatious, vociferous politico."

Senator Charles Mathias (R-Md.) has supplied the author with "information about the Maryland Snallygaster which is apparently a different species from the Missouri Snollygoster mentioned in your *Language of Politics* . . . as you will see, the Maryland Snallygaster was a crude and cruel beast employed against black voters." Senator Mathias enclosed a copy of an article that appeared in the *Valley Register* on March 5, 1909, intended to frighten black voters who intended to go to the polls. The headline was: "Emmitsburg Saw the Great Snallygaster/It Ate a Coal Bin Empty and Then Spit Fire/Looked Like a 'Coonscooper.' "

Webster's *New International Dictionary* (3rd edition) uses the Maryland "a" spelling and defines: "[perhaps a modification of . . . *schnelle geeschte,* literally quick spirits] a mythical nocturnal creature that is reported chiefly from rural Maryland, is reputed to be part reptile and part bird, and is said to prey on poultry and children."

Presidential use of an obscure political term gives it currency and enriches the vocabulary; for other once-obsolete terms that made it back, see CARPETBAGGER and MERCHANTS OF DEATH; for ones that did not, see OBSOLETE POLITICAL TERMS.

S.O.B. abbreviation for "son of a bitch," an appellation which creates a furor whenever the public learns that a President of the United States has used it.

President Harry Truman's military aide, Major General Harry Vaughan, was criticized by columnist Drew Pearson for accepting a medal from Argentine dictator Juan Perón. On February 22, 1949, in Arlington, Va., where Vaughan was being given another award by the Reserve Officers Association, President Truman expressed his feelings:

"I am just as fond of and just as loyal to my military aide as I am to the high brass, and want you to distinctly understand that any s.o.b. who thinks he can cause any one of these people to be discharged by me by some smart aleck statement over the air or in the paper has got another think coming."

White House stenographer Jack Romagna changed s.o.b. to "anyone" in the official transcript, but most newspapers quoted Truman verbatim. The *Christian Science Monitor* simply said "He used a vulgar abbreviation" but the *Chicago Tribune* felt it necessary to explain that "s.o.b. is an abbreviation for a vulgar expression casting reflection on a person's parentage." The *Indianapolis Star* added, "The phrase, freely translated, means male offspring of a female canine." Although Michigan Republican Clare Hoffman declared that "a man who feels impelled to use that sort of language" is not "the kind of man who should hold the office honored by Washington and Lincoln," a few editorial writers applauded the President. Wrote the *St. Louis Post-Dispatch*: "We can well understand the President's use of the term s.o.b. as applied to a certain showman and think that, considering all the circumstances, it was very well applied." Drew Pearson himself capitalized on the attack by urging his listeners and readers to become "Sons of Brotherhood."

Senator William Jenner of Indiana harkened back to the "tall-talk" construction of the mid-nineteenth century in describing columnist Pearson in 1950. "This Drew Pearson," he fulminated carefully, "is a self-appointed, self-made, cross *t*'d, dotted *i*'d, double-documented, super-superlative, revolving s.o.b."

In 1951 Senator Joseph McCarthy denounced Truman as "an s.o.b. who decided to remove MacArthur when drunk."

During the Eisenhower years the use of the epithet and its abbreviation appeared to subside in politics. The Truman-Pearson outburst took a mildly disapproved phrase and made a public issue out of it. In 1946, gentlemanly Senator Leverett Saltonstall of Massachusetts had made light of the fact that like all residents of the Senate Office Building, he received mail addressed "Leverett Saltonstall, S.O.B., Washington, D.C." No eyebrows were raised. The phrase had even had a heroic connotation, when Marine Sergeant Daniel Daly coined a World War I battle cry at Belleau Wood: "Come on, you sons of bitches! Do you want to live forever?" Frederick the Great made a similar statement at Koslin, June 18, 1757.

The phrase made a political comeback in connection with the steel-price rise and rollback in 1962. After U.S. Steel chairman Roger Blough had left the President's office, John F. Kennedy was widely reported to have said: "My father always told me that all businessmen were sons of bitches."

This time, however, the furor was not over the President's choice of language (it was in private conversation) but on whether he actually said "all businessmen." Asked about his "rather harsh statement" at a press conference, Kennedy replied, ". . . the statement which I have seen repeated is inaccurate. It quotes my father as having expressed himself strongly to me, and . . . I quoted what he said and indicated that he had not been . . . wholly wrong . . . as it appeared in a daily paper . . . I think the phrase was 'all businessmen.' That's obviously in error, because he was a businessman himself. He was critical of the steel men. But he confined it, and I would confine it. . . . I felt at that time that we had not been treated altogether with frankness, and therefore I felt his view had merit. But that's past."

In May 1961 Kennedy had inadvertently left behind a staff paper at a meeting held with Canadian Prime Minister John Diefenbaker that supposedly referred to the Canadian as an s.o.b. This Kennedy denied. "I couldn't have called him an s.o.b.," Kennedy told Sorensen later. "I didn't know he was one—at that time."

Thus, current use indicates that the phrase is politically acceptable when used by anyone in private conversation; it is considered tasteless when used by public officials in public; and it shocks and horrifies when used publicly by a President.

SOBRIQUETS   terms of affection or derision used interchangeably with the names of famous men. More grandiose than a nickname.

Tracing the line of American Presidents: *The Father of His Country,* or the *American Fabius,* was succeeded by the *Colossus of Independence,* sometimes called the *Machiavelli of*

Massachusetts, and followed by the *Sage of Monticello,* or *Long Tom.* The *Father of the Constitution* was next, and then the *Last of the Cocked Hats,* author of the famous Doctrine; *Old Man Eloquent* (son of *Colossus*) gave way to *Old Hickory* (*King Andrew* to his enemies), and then his protégé, *The Little Magician,* or *Wizard of Kinderhook. Tippecanoe* died in office, making way for the *Accidental President,* then *Young Hickory* (we're up to Polk now) and *Old Rough and Ready.* The *American Louis Philippe* succeeded him, followed by *Purse*—just a play on the name Pierce—and then the *Old Public Functionary,* or *Bachelor President. Father Abraham* came next (called by some the *Illinois Baboon*), with *Sir Veto, Unconditional Surrender, President de Facto* (Tilden supporters wouldn't concede that Hayes was *de jure*), the *Dark Horse,* and the *First Gentleman of this Land,* taking us up to Cleveland, the *Man of Destiny* or *Stuffed Prophet. Grandpa's Grandson* (Tippecanoe was the Grandfather) ushered in *Prosperity's Advance Agent,* succeded by his Vice President, the *Rough Rider,* and then by William Howard Taft, who was not blessed with an outstanding sobriquet. *The Phrasemaker,* or *Professor,* was followed by Harding (no sobriquet), then *Silent Cal, The Chief, That Man in the White House,* and *Give 'Em Hell Harry.* Sobriquets have paled in recent years—Ike, JFK, LBJ —and a great tradition has come to an end.

Tom Braden, in a 1971 column, bemoaned the disappearance of the sobriquet:

> . . . our people have gradually and unconsciously deprived themselves of the romance which once accompanied the nation's business. Suppose today that instead of discussing

the relative showing in the polls of Richard Nixon and Edmund Muskie we could speak of the rivalry between Silver Dick and the Boy Orator of the Platte. How much more fun, how much more romantic. . . . Imagine a candidate for President whom people referred to as 'The Plumed Knight,'—which was the way the followers of James C. Blaine talked about their leader. And after Bryan, Czar Reed was speaker of the House, Blackjack Pershing was leader of American forces in World War I, Fighting Bob La Follette was to run for President on the Progressive ticket and silent Cal Coolidge was to win. . . . But why has the sobriquet gone? Was Eugene McCarthy getting close to the national mood when he wrote a poem about the disappearance of "Kilroy," that sobriquet for the American soldier who—in every battleground and staging area of World War II—"was here." McCarthy hinted that the disappearance of Kilroy meant the disappearance of pride, and maybe we are lacking in that pride in being American which caused us to sprinkle our politics with characters like Old Rough and Ready, Tippecanoe, Fuss and Feathers, and the Little Giant. Or for that matter, Honest Abe? The new standard is cool and polite, and correct, and not much fun.

SO-CALLED, *see* SNEER WORDS.

SOCIAL ISSUE, *see* PSEPHOLOGY.

SOFT ON COMMUNISM attack phrase used by those convinced that the United States is in danger from internal Communist subversion, or at those who refuse to accept a HARD LINE posture abroad.

The charge was most often heard during the peak of Senator Joseph

McCarthy's influence. The Soviet Union had acquired nuclear weapons and increasingly efficient rockets, a legitimate cause for American concern. In a series of trials and hearings, seemingly respectable and in several cases comparatively highranking government officials were accused of having been involved in espionage on behalf of Russia. Truman's peremptory defense of RED HERRING made the charge more potent.

The case which gave most ammunition to those making the "soft on communism" charge was that of Alger Hiss, who had held a series of high governmental posts, including working with the U.S. delegation to the Yalta conference. Hiss was later convicted for perjury.

Democratic presidential candidate Adlai Stevenson was attacked by Republicans for having made a deposition saying that Alger Hiss's reputation was good. Stevenson said that in the deposition he had testified as a lawyer should, saying what he knew —no more, no less. He went on, "My testimony in the Hiss case no more shows softness towards Communism than the testimony of these Republican leaders (Taft, Bricker, and Joe Martin) shows softness towards corruption."

In the same campaign, retiring President Harry Truman, belatedly recognizing the public appeal of the attack, said, "The most brazen lie of the century has been fabricated by reckless demagogues among the Republicans to the effect that Democrats were soft on Communism."

Mr. Truman, in whose Administration those attacked had held office, also said that the Stevenson forces had made a serious tactical error in allowing themselves to be put on the defensive in the campaign by the "soft on Communism" charges.

Current use of the phrase is more often directed against those who minimize the threat of external Communist aggression, rather than at internal subversion. In its original internal sense, such charges are still leveled by what has come to be labeled the RADICAL RIGHT but the technique is not confined to those of any single political persuasion.

See MESS IN WASHINGTON; K₁C₂.

SOFT-PEDAL a political decision to de-emphasize an issue or topic, without ignoring it completely.

In the 1964 presidential campaign, on the subject of President Johnson's choice of close personal aides, Republicans proceeded to "bear down on" Bobby Baker, but to "soft-pedal" Walter Jenkins because of the personal tragedy involved in his arrest on a morals charge. Because of the distasteful nature of the charges, a sharp attack on Jenkins might have backfired; hence the decision to "soft-pedal" by oblique references to the need for high moral standards in high places, to the great pressures put on aides by an overly demanding President, etc.

Editor Henry Stoddard wrote in 1938: "The weakness of the Hoover Administration was . . . in handling Prohibition. . . . When the campaign [of 1932] opened, [Hoover] handed over to Walter Brown, his Postmaster-General, the task of soft-pedaling Prohibition through the contest. Brought up in Ohio politics Brown knew how to gumshoe so that you have to listen intently to hear the fall of his foot, or to know whether he was coming or going. He handled the issue that way for Hoover, until both realized its futility. It was then too late to change."

While cautious politicians shy from hot issues, GUTFIGHTERS revel in them. "Since political campaigns are played for keeps," wrote reporter Robert Donovan in 1956 about Democratic charges that Stevenson had been hit below the belt, "a campaigner does not soft-pedal a good issue just because it offends the opposition."

The phrase is used in auto racing (to tread lightly on the accelerator pedal) and probably originated in piano playing (the soft pedal cuts down the reverberations of the strings).

SOLID SOUTH the supposedly monolithic vote of the Southern states for the Democratic party, used now more in the breach than in the observance.

Southerners knew after the Civil War that (1) Lincoln and his BLACK REPUBLICANS freed the slaves, and (2) the CARPETBAGGERS and SCALAWAGS descended on them during Reconstruction under a Republican regime. Not surprisingly, the Democratic party had an appeal for white Southerners.

The phrase "solid South" was popularized by General John Singleton Mosby, a cavalry leader (Mosby's Rangers) on the staff of Confederate General J. E. B. Stuart. Mosby, with his impeccable Southern credentials, startled his Southern friends by coming out in 1876 for Republican Rutherford B. Hayes against Democrat Samuel Tilden. In a letter that was widely publicized at the time, he wrote: "Suppose Hayes is elected with a solid South against him—what are you going to do then?"

Though this phrase has been used by House Speaker Schuyler Colfax in 1858, Mosby's use—in the context of a Southerner fighting against the solidity of the South—gave it political excitement. "The Solid South," re-

ported *Harper's Weekly* immediately afterward, "is the Southern Democracy seeking domination of the United States through the machinery of the Democratic party."

The phrase delighted Republicans; coined by a renegade Democrat, it helped Republicans slightly in the South and strongly in the North. The *New York Tribune* got the origin wrong, but the end result right: "The claim of a 'solid South' is likely to do the Democrats fully as much harm as good. They originated the expression, and the Republicans are using it with great force against them . . ."

In an article titled "The Solid South" in *Century* magazine, Edward Clark wrote:

The Solid South . . . came into vogue during the Hayes-Tilden canvass of 1876. The Democratic tidal wave in the elections of 1874 had shown a powerful, if not irresistible, drift toward Democracy in all the then lately reconstructed States, as well as in their sisters on the old borderline which had also maintained slavery, but which had not gone into the rebellion. The alliterative term commended itself to the Republican stump speakers and newspaper organs as a happy catch-word, and the idea which underlay it was impressive enough to arrest the attention of the whole country.

Thomas E. Dewey made the same point in 1950: "The only danger nationally has been that one party might become too strong, or able to use the enormous new powers of government to perpetuate itself in office, as is the case in politically lop-sided, machine-dominated cities or in the 'Solid South.' "

Through the years, the South remained solid for the Democratic party; in 1928, when Democrat Al Smith was the candidate, his Catholicism and support of Prohibition repeal defeated him in Texas, Florida, Tennessee, and Virginia; all four of those states went for Republican Dwight Eisenhower in 1952 and 1956, and all but Texas for Nixon in 1960. In 1964 the South was almost solid again, but this time for Republican Barry Goldwater in a vote attributed to the BACKLASH over black civil rights gains.

The tension between Northern Democratic liberals and Southern Democratic conservatives led to an open break in 1948. Governor Strom Thurmond of South Carolina led a delegation of six Democratic governors to a tense meeting at Democratic National Headquarters in Washington, demanding "the highly controversial civil rights legislation" be "withdrawn." Turned down, they issued a joint statement: "The present leadership of the Democratic party will soon realize that the South is no longer 'in the bag.' " Thurmond ran as a third-party candidate to punish Truman (see DIXIECRAT) and later became a Republican.

The South today is still Democratic in local elections, though not nearly as much as before; in national politics, the bloc was busted by Republicans, notably in 1964 by Goldwater, but solidified again for the candidacy of Southerner Jimmy Carter in 1976. But the political tradition of the "new South" is a far cry from the situation described in an anecdote used by Harry Dent in his book *The Prodigal South Returns to Power* (1978):

"In 1924 Senator Coleman L. Blease, Democrat of South Carolina, was alarmed to learn that Republican Calvin Coolidge had won 1123 of 50,-131 votes cast in South Carolina in the presidential race.

" 'I do not know where he got them,' Blease supposedly said. 'I was astonished to know they were cast and shocked to know they were counted.' "

Today the phrase is used mainly by commentators showing that the "solid" South has turned fluid. See SOUTHERN STRATEGY; SUNBELT.

SOLON headlinese for legislator; originally meant "wise statesman," now used ironically.

A headline writer who uses "Solons Probe" rather than "Legislators Investigate" saves eleven letters, providing space for two more clichés. Neither solon nor probe is used in the spoken political language.

Solon, an aristocratic Athenian born about 640 B.C., was referred to by Plato in the *Symposium* as "the revered father of Athenian laws," and was also an economist and the first Attic poet.

For other eponymous words in politics, see QUISLING; MAVERICK; PHILIPPIC; GERRYMANDER.

SONS OF THE WILD JACKASS political irregulars inclined to vote against the party line, especially liberal Republicans; also, reformers in general.

John Hay, later Secretary of State, used "wild ass" in the sense of "unreasonable reformer" in an 1890 letter to Theodore Roosevelt: "You have already shown that a man may be absolutely honest and yet practical; a reformer by instinct and a wise politician; brave, bold, and uncompromising, and yet not a wild ass of the desert."

William Jennings Bryan suggested in 1896 that reforming asses occasionally kicked each other's heads in:

> I remember that a few years ago a Populist in Congress stated that the small burros that run wild upon the prairies of South America form a group, when attacked by a ferocious

animal, and, putting their heads together and their feet on the outside of the circle, protect themselves from the enemy. But he added that the advocates of reforms sometimes showed less discretion, and turning their heads toward the enemy, kicked each other.

(The reference, Hans Sperber and Travis Trittschuh suggest, comes from the "wild asses in the desert" in the Book of Job, 24:5.) The wild asses of reform or independence were popularized a generation later. In 1929 Republicans included a number of Westerners who were indifferent to party discipline. Since they were politically akin to the Populists of an earlier generation, the liberal Westerners tended to look upon the more conservative Eastern portion of the party with suspicion as "lackeys of Wall Street." Senator George H. Moses of New Hampshire, lamenting the alliance between these Republicans and liberal Democrats, which blocked the higher tariffs the GOP leadership wanted, said on the Senate floor in 1924: "Mournfully, I prophesy that the program of these sons of the wild jackass who now control the Senate will probably go forward to complete consummation."

Senator Moses later said his inspiration came from the Old Testament, Jeremiah 14:6: "And the wild asses did stand in the high places, they snuffed up the wind like dragons."

The Western liberal Republicans of whom Senator Moses complained were men like Senators Johnson of California, Norris of Nebraska, La Follette of Wisconsin, and Shipstead of Minnesota. In recent times, Eastern and Western Republicans are—or have been—again divided, but lately it has been the conservative Republicans of the West looking with suspicion upon the more liberal Republicans of the East.

SOREHEADS, see **TAKE A WALK.**

SOUL deep understanding and sympathy for a cause; a civil rights word of the mid-sixties.

"Soul food" is a term for chitterlings (chit'lins) and other food items popular in black communities; indigenous music is called "soul music." In 1965, "soul brother" began to become popular to describe one sympathetic to black militancy.

During the Newark riots of 1967, black shopowners scrawled "Soul Brother" in soap across their windows, in hopes of deterring looters.

In current usage, "to have soul" politically is to identify with black unrest and dissatisfaction.

SOURCES a word used by reporters who want to show they are not originating some information to identify people who are passing on the information but do not want their identity known.

During "impeachment summer" of 1974, New York Times Washington bureau chief Clifton Daniel, concerned about the overuse of anonymous tips in the news columns, posted a memo to his staff:

"Sources" has become a discredited word in our business. Let's stop using it.

Sources are people (or pieces of paper). We should identify them whenever possible. When we cannot identify them, we should describe them as fully and accurately as circumstances permit. We should never misrepresent them—as, for example, by pluralizing a single source.

If we cannot identify or describe a source but have absolute confidence in it, we can use information from that source without attribution. A phrase such as "reliably reported" is better than "sources said." If we don't have confidence in a source, we should not use the information, whether attributable or not.

Sources are usually described as "reliable," sometimes as "usually reliable," never as "an unreliable source." Since the Daniel memo, the phrase "who asked that his name not be used" has been used more frequently. Reporters at the *Times* were also urged to locate sources, as in "an FBI source" or "an Administration source," which sometimes indicates the possible bias at the point of origin. "Sources close to the investigation" usually mean police or prosecution.

The noun has been turned into a verb as well: a story that is not "sourced" is considered "unsourced."

See AUTHORITATIVE SOURCES.

SOUTHERN STRATEGY an attack phrase attributing RACIST or at least political motives toward any position taken on desegregation or BUSING that would be well received by most Southern whites.

In the summer of 1963, the conservative weekly *National Review* published a map showing how Senator Barry Goldwater could win the 1964 election, which included a sweep of the Deep South. In answer to the author's query in 1971, *National Review* publisher William Rusher disclaimed coinage of the phrase itself and added: "I would guess that it goes back to some point in the early 1960's at which the liberals finally became aware of the strategy by which the Goldwater forces proposed to win the nomination and the election of 1964. It seems to me much more likely that the term 'Southern strategy' was invented by the liberals and fastened by them upon the strategy, since the pejorative implication was that the Goldwater forces were preparing to turn their backs upon the blacks and sell out to southern bigotry. (From our standpoint, of course, the correct term would have been 'Southern-Midwestern-Western strategy', since that was what we really had in mind —a coalition of these three against the dominant Northeast; but obviously such a term would have been too cumbersome.)" See SUNBELT.

Somewhat testily, Senator Goldwater nailed down the coinage in a letter to *Business Week* October 1971:

The first writer to use the term "southern strategy" was Joe Alsop, after his visit to my office back in the 1950s. At that time I was chairman of the Senate Campaign Committee and had conducted a very in-depth survey of voting trends in the U.S. for President Eisenhower. This survey showed that the only areas in the whole United States where the Republican Party had been making gains were in the Southwest. For that reason we decided to put more emphasis on that part of the nation, where Republicans historically had not done well.

That is the so-called "Southern strategy." It has nothing to do with busing, integration, or any other of the so-called closely held concepts of the Southerner. The South began to move into Republican ranks because of the influx of new and younger businessmen from the North who were basically Republican. And they were aided by young Southern Democrats who were sick and tired of the Democratic stranglehold on the South and switched over to the Republican Party. Nowhere in any platform adopted by the Republican Party since I can remember can there be found any thing aimed directly at the South which could be indicative of some strategy employed by the Republican party that the Republican Party does not employ elsewhere."

Goldwater did carry the Deep South in the Johnson landslide, giving the phrase a "losing" connotation, as not only a racist strategy, but a politically mistaken one. In the 1968 presidential campaign, when Nixon's Southern manager, Howard "Bo" Callaway, called for support from voters leaning toward George Wallace, Ward Just wrote in the *Washington Post* that some Republicans "are worried lest Nixon pursue a 'Southern strategy' in his election campaign that would compromise potential support among minority groups and moderates in the North."

Nixon managers let it be known that the 1968 strategy centered around the "battleground" states: California, New Jersey, Pennsylvania, Ohio, Illinois, Michigan, and Texas, only one of which—Texas— was below the Mason-Dixon line. Wrote Don Irwin in the *Los Angeles Times* on July 14, 1968: "Richard M. Nixon's avowed determination to concentrate on voters in large industrial states if he wins the Republican presidential nomination tells much about the election campaign he has in mind. It appears to bar revival of the all-out 'Southern strategy' that proved so disastrous for the GOP in 1964."

At the Gridiron Dinner spoofing the Nixon Administration in 1970, the hit song of the evening was sung to the tune of "A Dixie Melody":

Rock-a-bye the voters with a Southern strategy;
Don't you fuss; we won't bus children in ol' Dixie!
We'll put George Wallace in decline
Below the Mason-Dixon line
We'll help you save the nation
From things like civil rights and inte-gra-tion!

Weep no more, John Stennis!
We'll pack that court for sure.
We will fight for voting rights—
To keep them white and pure!
A zillion Southern votes we will deliver;
Move Washington down on the Swanee River!
Rockabye with Ol' Massa Nixon and his Dixie strategy!

To practical politicians, any strategy that wins one region at the expense of all others is nonsense; however, any national election strategy that seeks to include Southern support is attacked as a "Southern strategy" because it helps the attacker disaffect the opposition's support elsewhere.

Although Georgian Jimmy Carter swept the South in 1976 (excepting Virginia), his strategy was never considered to be "Southern"; he won that region because that was where he came from.

The phrase is firmly fixed in the political lexicon not as a strategy, but as a charge of deviousness and discrimination. See SOLID SOUTH.

SPECIAL   INTERESTS,   *see*
VESTED INTERESTS.

SPEECHWRITER one who writes speeches on assignment; for differentiation between *ghost, wordsmith, research assistant,* and *press secretary,* see GHOSTWRITER.

Robert Smith, who had done a creditable job as Secretary of the Navy under Thomas Jefferson, faced a problem when he was promoted to Secretary of State by the new President, James Madison. Smith was no writer. Wisely, he accepted the ghostwriting services of the best writer in the federal employ at the time: President Madison.

The President did not consider it menial work; Jefferson and Hamilton and he had helped Washington in the preparation of his Farewell Address, which stands out over most of the first President's turgid prose. Washington had asked them to look over his version, which he asked be "curtailed, if too verbose; and relieve of all tautology, not necessary to enforce the ideas in the original or quoted part. My wish is that the whole may appear in a plain stile; and be handed to the public in an honest; unaffected; simple garb."

Judge Samuel Rosenman, who worked on speeches with FDR, justified a presidential speechwriter's existence on the basis that "there just is not enough time in a President's day" to handle the chore. Some point out that Abraham Lincoln served in a busy era, wrote his own speeches, and turned out some of the best in the English language. But Lincoln, it is argued, had a knack for it; the presidency has grown in complexity; Chief Executives—even senators and congressmen—should not take time from their busy schedules to labor over a speech, certainly not its first draft. And since presidential words carry such import, why not get a great writer to put them down in the clearest, most inspirational way?

Walter Lippmann in 1942 was having none of this. In a column entitled "Something Off My Chest," he wrote:

A public man can and needs to be supplied with material and advice and criticism in preparing an important address. But no one can write an authentic speech for another man; it is as impossible as writing his love letters for him or saying his prayers for him. When he speaks to the people, he and not someone else must speak. For it is much more important that he could be genuine, and it is infinitely more persuasive, than that he be bright, clever, ingenious, entertaining, eloquent, or

even grammatical. It is, moreover, a delusion, fostered into an inferiority complex among executives by professional writers, that in an age of specialists some are called to act and some are called to find the right words for men of action to use. The truth is that anyone who knows what he is doing can say what he is doing, and anyone who knows what he thinks can say what he thinks. Those who cannot speak for themselves are, with very rare exceptions, not very sure of what they are doing and of what they mean. The sooner they are found out the better.

Lippmann's view did not prevail; the public does not frown on a President having speechwriters, indeed has come to expect a President to work from others' drafts. The idea of a speechwriter's assignment, in most people's minds, is one gently sold by every top-level speechwriter: to discuss the speech ideas with the public figure, reflect his point of view clearly and in organized fashion, to submit extra phrases and slogans for the top man's consideration, and to rewrite according to the speaker's wishes. This is sometimes exactly what happens.

Who were the modern speechwriters for Presidents? FDR's became well-known: Professor Raymond Moley, Judge Samuel Rosenman, editor Stanley High, dramatist Robert E. Sherwood, lawyer Donald Richberg were among them. Truman's writers were almost totally anonymous: Clark Clifford, Charles J. Murphy, and William Hillman would occasionally surface, and Rosenman contributed from time to time. Dwight Eisenhower used Malcolm Moos, Bryce Harlow, college president Kevin McCann, banker Gabriel Hauge, and journalist Emmet Hughes, among others. With Kennedy, writers became famous again: Ted Sorensen, Arthur Schlesinger, Jr., John Galbraith, and Richard Goodwin led the pack. Lyndon Johnson began with Kennedy holdovers, soon found journalist Douglass Cater, Horace Busby, Joseph Califano, and Harry McPherson, with Jack Valenti both writing and editing.

The Nixon writing and research operation was headed by James Keogh for two years, with Raymond K. Price replacing him. The senior writers, along with Price, were Patrick Buchanan and the author. Other writers included Lee Huebner, Noel Koch, John Andrews, John McLaughlin, and Tex Lezar, with researchers Ceil Bellinger and Anne Morgan.

Gerald Ford's speechwriters were Robert Hartman, Aram Bakshian, Milton Friedman and gagwriter Bob Orben. Jimmy Carter employed the services of James Fallows, Jerome Doolittle, Hendrik Hertzberg, Achsah Nesmith, and Griffin Smith.

One question nags public figures employing speechwriters: writers are dangerous, because they publish—will this or that speechwriter kiss and tell? Emmet Hughes, who enjoyed Eisenhower's confidence and did some of his best campaign speechwriting, infuriated Republicans later with what they considered a too-revealing book, *The Ordeal of Power;* Ted Sorensen, John Kennedy's alter ego of the written word, respected many confidences in his memoirs and was criticized for writing a memoir too discreet and defensive. At the first meeting of the Nixon campaign team for the 1968 race, the author was introduced, only half in jest, with ". . . and watch what you say—he's a writer."

SPELLBINDER   an orator capable of fascinating and persuading an audience, at least temporarily; also, a speech of that type.

This is based on *spellbound,* which means fascinated in the way a cobra is spellbound by a fakir's flute. Its political debut occurred in the 1888 presidential campaign. The *New York Tribune* wrote: "A big and successful dinner was given at Delmonico's by the Republican Orators—'Spellbinders'—who worked during the recent campaign." The Republican stump speakers were widely publicized during that race between Cleveland and Harrison (which Republican Harrison narrowly won); William Cassius Goodloe was quoted in 1888 as pointing to one and remarking, "Here comes another of the spellbinders!"

The word is current; historian Eric Goldman termed General Omar Bradley as "the last man anyone would pick for a spellbinder" in Bradley's surprisingly effective attack on General MacArthur's Korean strategy in 1951. See WRONG WAR.

A fascinating speech is a *spellbinder;* a rousing speech is a STEM-WINDER; a low blow, or a bodyguard, is a *sidewinder;* an influential but crude or dishonest politician is a *highbinder,* as in this 1920 use by *Emporia Gazette* editor William A. White: ". . . a lot of old high-binder standpatters who haven't had an idea since the fall of Babylon . . ."

SPEND AND SPEND . . .   a New Deal philosophy, attributed to Harry Hopkins, emphasizing the vote-getting potential of federal projects.

Harry Hopkins, who had replaced the late Louis Howe as FDR's closest aide, is supposed to have said to theatrical producer Max Gordon at the Empire Race Track in New York in August 1938: "We will spend and spend, and tax and tax, and elect and elect."

Others in Gordon's box that day denied having heard any such thing; Hopkins denied it; that left Gordon, who had passed the remark to a columnist, out on a limb. He had not realized how the phrase could be used against his friend Hopkins, but he could not call it back. The theatrical producer has been in this dilemma for forty years, and it bothers him. When reached on the telephone by the author, he said—as if reading from a small card in his desk blotter—"I have absolutely nothing whatsoever to say about the incident, thank you and goodbye."

Whether or not Hopkins said it, the phrase has been used to attack BIG GOVERNMENT as having raised the PORK BARREL to national policy.

Jonathan Daniels wrote in 1966 of the Tennessee Valley Authority: "As the most damned New Dealer, Harry Hopkins had little to do with its building, yet . . . it loomed as the embodiment of his supposed philosophy 'spend and spend, tax and tax, elect and elect.' "

The phrase is often remembered in this form: tax, tax, tax—spend, spend, spend—elect, elect, elect. A 1967 cartoon by Hesse of the *St. Louis Globe-Democrat* showed President Johnson groping in an empty bag for dollars saying, "Like I say—tax, tax—spend, spe . . ."

SPHERE OF INFLUENCE an economically undeveloped or militarily weak area under the domination of a great power, usually with the agreement or tacit acceptance of other great powers.

Winston Churchill could remember the Anglo-Russian agreement of 1907 dividing Persia into separate spheres of influence—the North for Russia, the South for England; the phrase came naturally to him in 1946, in his IRON CURTAIN speech at Fulton, Mo.: "Warsaw, Berlin, Prague, Vienna, Budapest, Belgrade, Bucharest and Sofia, all these famous cities and the populations around them lie in what I might call the Soviet sphere, and all are subject, in one form or another, not only to Soviet influence but to a very high and in some cases increasing measure of control from Moscow."

The diplomatic phrase, described by Webster's *New International Dictionary* (2nd edition) as "regions more or less under the control of a nation, but not constituting a formally recognized protectorate or suzerainty," has been used along with *sphere of interest, sphere of action, field of operations,* and *zone of influence* for more than a century.

SPIRIT OF   the aura of hope surrounding summit meetings, born of the chance that reasonable men can lessen the threat of war.

"The Spirit of '76" was a favorite name for newspapers just after the American Revolution. On September 13, 1808, a Richmond, Virginia, journal was issued under that name; in Goshen, New York, the *Orange County Patriot;* or, *The Spirit of Seventy-Six* started five months later. The phrase was frequently used as a colorful masthead for political campaign newspapers, but made its greatest impact as the title of a painting of a boy, an old man, and a Continental Army soldier by Archibald Willard in 1876 shown at the Philadelphia Centennial Exhibition. (The painting now hangs in the Marblehead, Mass., town hall.)

In its international relations sense, "spirit of" was originated by President Eisenhower at the Geneva Conference of 1955. On July 15, before he left for Geneva, Eisenhower warned "as long as this spirit that has prevailed up to now continues to prevail in the world, we cannot expose our rights, our privileges, our homes, our wives, our children to the risk which would come to an unarmed country." Three days later, at the conference, he said, "We are here in response to the peaceful aspirations of mankind to start the kind of discussions which will inject a new spirit into our diplomacy . . ." On his return, he continued to summon that spirit in a July 25 speech: ". . . if we can change the spirit in which these conferences are conducted we will have taken the greatest step toward peace . . ."

By August 25 the word had caught on enough for him to title a speech to the American Bar Association "The Spirit of Geneva," making this point:

Whether or not such a spirit as this will thrive through the combined intelligence and understanding of men, or will shrivel in the greed and ruthlessness of some, is for the future to tell. But one thing is certain. This spirit and the goals we seek could never have been achieved by violence or when men and nations confronted each other with hearts filled with fear and hatred. At Geneva we strove to help establish this spirit.

British Prime Minister Anthony Eden returned home with what he called "this simple message to the world: it has reduced the danger of war." Foreign Minister Harold Macmillan, who had gleefully said, "there ain't gonna be any war," discovered at a Foreign Ministers conference three months later that the Soviet attitude had hardened; "once more we are back in the strange nightmare where men use the same words to mean different things." But Macmillan remained optimistic: "The Ge-

neva spirit if it is anything is an inward spirit. Its light is not bright today. It burns low. But it burns."

What Eisenhower had heralded as "evidence of a new friendliness in the world" proved illusory. Soviet activity in the Middle East late in 1955 added to the disenchantment.

The next spirit to be conjured was "The Spirit of Camp David," scene of another Khrushchev-Eisenhower meeting in 1959. Camp David is a presidential mountain retreat, called "Shangri-La" by FDR. (That name was taken from FDR's evasive reply when asked where U.S. aircraft that attacked Tokyo early in World War II were based. FDR took the mythical name from a James Hilton novel; Eisenhower renamed the camp after his grandson.) Pictures of the two world leaders strolling through the rustic setting raised hopes once more, quickly dashed by the abortive Paris summit conference and the incident of the downed U-2 reconnaissance plane.

Sherman Adams asked Eisenhower if he noticed at Camp David any hint of the hostility later shown in Paris. "None at all," Eisenhower replied. "At Camp David, they never showed the slightest intimation of any unfriendly intentions. As a matter of fact, when Khrushchev and I were alone together at Camp David he was very convivial with me, especially eager to be friendly. He kept belittling most of our differences and gave every indication of wanting to find ways to straighten them out through peaceful compromise."

A spirit-haunted President Kennedy met Khrushchev in Vienna in 1961. The new President, wrote Ted Sorensen, "wanted no one to think that the surface cordiality in Vienna justified any notion of a new 'Spirit of Geneva, 1955,' or 'Spirit of Camp

David, 1959.' But he may have 'over-managed' the news. His private briefings of the press were so grim, while Khrushchev in public appeared so cheerful, that a legend soon arose that Vienna had been a traumatic, shattering experience, that Khrushchev had bullied and browbeaten the President and that Kennedy was depressed and disheartened."

Meeting in a place called Hollybush, in Glassboro, New Jersey, in the aftermath of the Arab-Israeli war of 1967, President Johnson and Soviet Premier Alexei Kosygin met in a world atmosphere that no longer took its spirits straight. Wrote the *Times* of London: "Atmospherics, of course, tend to be transient. The spirit of Geneva and the spirit of Camp David were short-lived."

Thus the use of "spirit of" changed from hope to derision, or at least suspicion and more recently back toward hope. The Soviet Union, in the late seventies, often complained that the Carter campaign for HUMAN RIGHTS endangered the "spirit of DÉTENTE."

The skeptical attitude is that of Hotspur's, in Shakespeare's *Henry IV,* Part I, who replied to Glendower's boast that he could "call spirits from the vasty deep" with "Why, so can I, or so can any man; But will they come when you do call for them?"

See SUMMITRY.

SPLENDID MISERY, *see* LONELIEST JOB IN THE WORLD.

SPLINTER GROUP   a dissident faction that splits away from a larger group; if it forms a party, it becomes a splinter party.

"When you get too big a majority," House Speaker Sam Rayburn used to say, "you're immediately in trouble." This became known as "Rayburn's Law," growing out of the Speaker's difficulty in keeping his party in line during FDR's second Administration. "Mr. Sam" felt that lopsided majorities had a way of producing splinter parties and factions along regional, ethnic, or economic lines.

Wooden metaphors abound in politics: PRESIDENTIAL TIMBER, PLATFORM, *plank,* and *splinter,* the least significant of them all.

A great many splinter groups or parties—called the multiparty system, as against the TWO-PARTY SYSTEM—often produce a weak government; the expression "always falling, never fallen" referred to the tendency of French governments to fall as factions bickered, though the French Republic went on. In postwar France, the political return of Charles de Gaulle fused many of the parties of the center and the right; the General himself called one of the smaller splinter groups "that party with six members and seven tendencies!"

In the 1972 presidential campaign, McGovern manager Frank Mankiewicz went to a Reform Democratic club on the West Side of Manhattan to instill enthusiasm for his candidate. After several hours with the articulate, highly splintered group, he came out and said, "Every little meaning has a movement all its own."

See BOLT; THIRD-PARTY MOVEMENT.

SPLIT TICKET   a ballot cast by a voter without regard for party slates.

A party regular will vote a *straight ticket;* an independent is more likely to vote a *split ticket,* choosing a candidate for governor from one party, a senator from another, an assemblyman possibly from a third.

The man at the top of the ticket is expected to discourage ticket splitting (see COATTAILS); a candidate's strength is sometimes measured in terms of how many of the opposing party regulars he can get to split their tickets and vote for him. However, it is considered disloyal to appeal to voters to vote a split ticket—in effect, this urges voters to cast their ballots against a candidate's running mates. For this reason, separate committees are formed, called "Democrats for [some Republican]" and vice versa, or "Independents for—."

The expression is found in an 1846 biography of Martin Van Buren: "I was reproached by you for having voted a 'split ticket.'" In 1904 the *New York Post* patiently explained to voters: "To vote a split ticket, which is one for candidates of different parties, the voter should make a cross mark before the name of every candidate for whom he wishes to vote."

Political scientist Clinton Rossiter pointed out in 1960 that the American electorate was tending toward greater reliance on issues and personalities, less on party affiliation.

Thanks to the looseness of legal definitions of party affiliation, to the fact that most of us are called upon to vote several times a year, and to the multiplicity of choices to be made in any one election, we enjoy unusual opportunities to be inconstant and even wayward; and every study made of this subject in recent years confirms the suspicion, with which our politicians must live bravely, that we seize these opportunities gaily. If ticket splitting is our privilege, ticket splitting is our delight.

For other types of tickets, see LAUNDRY TICKET and BALANCED TICKET; for a look at those most likely to split, see SWING VOTER; for the most selective of all, see BULLET VOTE.

SPOILER a candidate with no hope of winning himself, but who is capable of splitting another's vote, thereby spoiling his chances.

Rarely is a candidate defeated for a nomination so vindictive as to run in the general election solely to spoil the chances of the nominee who defeated him. It is not smart politics, as it throws away the chance of toppling the chosen nominee another day. More often, a third party motive is (1) to provide a place for a PROTEST VOTE on a matter of principle, (2) to build a third party into a balance-of-power situation, (3) a long-shot chance of winning.

National Review editor William Buckley ran for mayor of New York in 1965 on the Conservative ticket against Republican-Liberal John Lindsay and Democrat Abraham Beame. His purpose was not to win (when asked what he would do in that eventuality, Buckley replied, "Demand a recount") but to build the Conservative party in New York State and build in a threat to Republicans not to nominate too-liberal candidates. Lindsay supporters dubbed him a "spoiler."

In *Tigers of Tammany*, Alfred Connable and Edward Silverfarb wrote in 1967 of the fight between the "Barnburners" and the "Hunkers" in 1848; when the conservative Hunkers won, nominating Michigan Democrat Senator Lewis Cass, the antislavery Barnburners bolted and joined the Free Soilers to nominate Martin Van Buren. "Martin Van Buren's last political act was to run on principle and thereby doom to defeat the party which he had once unified . . . Tammany's allegiance was split . . . Van Buren was the 'spoiler' in a three-way race."

Conservative Republicans after Goldwater's defeat in 1964 placed a portion of the blame on Governor Nelson Rockefeller, whose primary battles had placed the TRIGGER-HAPPY tag on Goldwater. Conservative Congressman John M. Ashbrook of Ohio said of Rockefeller in *Fortune* magazine in 1967: ". . . he's a great administrator and has a fine personality. But the heart of the problem is his party posture—he's a spoiler." Ashbrook went on to challenge President Nixon in the 1972 primaries.

SPOILS SYSTEM   the fruits of party victory to loyal partisans; opposite of "merit system."

Senator William Marcy of New York, defending President Andrew Jackson's appointment of Martin Van Buren as ambassador to Great Britain from an attack by Senator Henry Clay, said in 1832:

> It may be, sir, that the politicians of New York are not as fastidious as some gentlemen are as to disclosing the principles on which they act. They boldly preach what they practice. When they are not contending for victory, they avow their intention of enjoying the fruits of it. . . . If they are successful, they claim, as a matter of right, the advantages of success. They see nothing wrong in the rule, that to the victor belong the spoils of the enemy.

Clay turned the phrase into a weapon against the Democrats in his 1840 statement: "If we acted on the avowed and acknowledged principle of our opponents, 'that the spoils belong to the victors,' we should indeed be unworthy of the support of the people."

William Marcy, who served later as governor of New York, Secretary of War and Secretary of State, is remembered mainly with scorn because of the coinage of the phrase; his reputation was further besmirched when a Tammany politician named Richard Tweed was said to have named his son after the distinguished American statesman, and William Marcy Tweed—and his "ring"—became the essence of bossism. But the naming was probably a canard: in his 1977 book, *Tweed's New York*, Leo Hershkowitz held that William Marcy was not well known when Tweed was born—that his middle name was "Magear," which was his mother's maiden name, and the "Marcy" was inserted by newsmen who wanted to associate the New York boss with the father of the "spoils system."

The word "spoils," in its sense of Roman plunder, was used in the Bible as the Israelites were told, "Ye shall spoil the Egyptians," an instruction carried out in 1967, and in Shakespeare: "Are all thy conquests, glories, triumphs, spoils, shrunk to this small measure?" The first political use found so far in the U.S. was in 1812, in the Massachusetts House of Representatives: "The weaker members of the party would be overlooked . . . whilst the more powerful would disagree in the division of the spoils." Two years before Marcy made it famous, Congressman J. S. Johnson said: "The country is treated as a conquered province, and the offices distributed among the victors, as the spoils of the war."

Jackson's Administration increased the use of patronage started by Jefferson, and historians like to quote an 1818 letter from Jackson to President Monroe: "By selecting characters most conspicuous for their probity, virtue, capacity and firmness without regard to party . . . you will acquire for yourself a name as imperishable as monumental marble."

When Jackson was queried later about this letter by one of his private secretaries, he replied, "We are never too old to learn."

Actually, Jackson was not the spoilsman he was made out to be; despite the "new broom" and the CLEAN SWEEP, only about 9 percent of federal officeholders were removed in his first year of office, and less than 20 percent of all previously appointed officeholders were removed on political grounds during his entire two terms. (On the other hand, Benjamin Harrison changed 31,000 out of 55,000 local postmasters within one year.)

The spoils system became the target of civil service reformers, aided by statements like this made by Tammany boss Richard Croker after the election of Thomas Gilroy as mayor of New York in 1893: "You may say for me that offices will be held by politicians." Carl Schurz ripped into the system in 1894: "The spoils system, that practice which turns public offices, high and low, from public trusts into objects of prey and booty for the victorious party, may without extravagance of language be called one of the greatest criminals in our history, if not the greatest."

In modern usage, spoils as a word is used mainly for historical purposes, the slightly less pejorative PATRONAGE having replaced it in regard to appointments. The nature of spoils has changed as well; today, favoritism toward certain aerospace companies, franchises granted large contributors, discretion shown in the prosecution of possible antitrust cases, the placement of bond issues and insurance policies through FAT CAT supporters, and post-government employment to friendly officials add up to a much more lucrative version of spoils than the primitive fruits of an earlier day. See HONEST GRAFT.

Political leaders now meet to *slice the pie* rather than *divide the spoils;* RIPPER BILLS are a help in placing power in party hands, and DESERVING DEMOCRATS is a phrase now only used by Republicans.

In *The Beautiful and Damned,* novelist F. Scott Fitzgerald coined an unusually apt turnaround: "The victor belongs to the spoils."

SPOKESMAN, *see* **BACK-GROUNDER.**

SPONTANEOUS DEMONSTRATION a carefully planned, organized, and routed march around a convention hall by delegates in support of a candidacy.

At the Bull Moose convention in 1912, historian George E. Mowry reports:

> Fifteen thousand people roared their welcome [to Theodore Roosevelt]. For 52 minutes, wildly waving red bandanas, they cheered him as they had never cheered anyone else. Here were no claques, no artificial demonstration sustained by artificial devices. None were needed. Men and women simply stood on their feet for an hour because they liked him and believed in him. When Roosevelt himself finally sought to stop the demonstration, the crowd once more broke into song.

In the 1940 Republican convention, the balconies were "packed" with Willkie supporters; their overpowering "We Want Willkie" chant, cued by the candidate's campaign managers, helped sway the convention delegates away from Taft. Ever since, tickets have been carefully allocated to prevent a recurrence. See PACKING THE GALLERIES.

In the 1964 Republican convention at San Francisco's Cow Palace, these were the ground rules laid down by the Republican National Committee for spontaneous demonstrations:

1. Goldwater and Scranton demonstrations to last 22 minutes

before gaveling; Rockefeller 11 minutes; all others as long as they like up to 11 minutes.

2. No more than 200 outside demonstrators permitted inside the hall, inclusive of candidate's band, and they must exit at end of demonstration. Twelve-piece National Committee band available for all demonstrations.

3. Only those signs and banners carried by 200 demonstrators permitted; no "stashing" inside hall beforehand; delegates could also carry in signs.

4. Parade route carefully delineated, not to obscure television cameras inside hall.

5. No "drops" of balloons from ceiling.

In practice, each of these rules was deliberately broken by each candidate. Tickets were counterfeited by Goldwater and Scranton forces; Rockefeller had lent most of his convention staff to Scranton, and his skeleton crew had to purchase the counterfeit tickets for an extra hundred demonstrators from the other two camps, (from the Goldwater group at $3 each, from Scranton managers at $5 each). Ticket takers at the gate would collect tickets from incoming demonstrators, sell them to floor managers, who would toss them over the fence to more demonstrators.

Each group had a secret cache of signs, banners, and noisemakers inside the hall; the Goldwater managers infuriated the Scranton men by springing a "drop" of gold confetti instead of balloons, staying within the letter of the rules.

The only truly "spontaneous" demonstration was for Senator Hiram Fong of Hawaii, whose small demonstration was joined by many delegates who felt like a walk around the hall and could hardly be criticized for paying tribute to the first non-Caucasian placed in nomination.

After one losing candidate's demonstration, the floor manager (this writer) was given the supreme accolade by the campaign manager: "I watched it on television, and you couldn't tell it from the real thing."

"A convention feels about demonstrations somewhat like the big man who had a small wife who was in the habit of beating him," wrote William Jennings Bryan. "When asked why he permitted it, he replied that it seemed to please her and did not hurt him."

See VOICE FROM THE SEWER.

SPOOK   a ghostwriter; or, a professional spy.

Speechwriters occasionally refer to themselves as "spooks"; derivation from a synonym for ghost. Also used as a verb, "to spook a book."

From the phantomlike operations of its covert agents, "spook" is a friendly, bantering name for spy. In a 1967 story on the Director of the Central Intelligence Agency, *Time* magazine wrote: "Dick Helms has been, in Washington parlance, a 'spook' for nearly 25 years."

After *New York Times* reporter Seymour Hersh in 1975 revealed massive spying on American citizens by the CIA, and a Senate select committee chaired by Frank Church reported on its investigation, the term lost its madcap, likable, breezy quality and absorbed much of the disapproval directed at the intelligence agency. A controversy arose in 1977 over the use of journalists as "cover" by the CIA, which the *Times* denounced: "American readers have a right to assurance that the journalists they trust for information are not in any sense accountable to unseen paymasters." However, in an editorial entitled "The Spooks and the Press," the *Washington Star* approvingly quoted former columnist Joseph Alsop: "I've done things for [the CIA] when I thought they were the right thing to do. I call it doing my duty as a citizen."

See CIA-ESE.

SPORTS METAPHORS   Shakespeare recognized the value of a sports metaphor in politics; King Henry V exhorted his troops before Harfleur: "I see you stand like greyhounds in the slips, straining upon the start. The game's afoot . . ."

It has been afoot ever since, given an impetus by the Duke of Wellington's "The battle of Waterloo was won on the playing fields of Eton." Football is especially well represented: "Politics is like football," John F. Kennedy told Pierre Salinger. "If you see daylight, go through the hole." Woodrow Wilson put it more formally: "I have always in my own thought summed up individual liberty, and business liberty, and every other kind of liberty, in the phrase that is common in the sporting world, 'A free field and no favor.' " Soon after taking office in 1933, FDR claimed his Administration had made some "ten-yard gains," adding, "but it is a long field." Truman-campaign strategist Clark Clifford said after the 1948 victory, "We were on our own 20-yard line. We had to be bold. If we kept plugging away in moderate terms, the best we could have done would have been to reach midfield when the gun went off. So we had to throw long passes . . ."

Truman, during the campaign, used a horse to rally his dispirited troops. Citation, one of the great racing thoroughbreds, would lay back at the start of a race and come on with a rush at the end. "I am trying to do in politics what Citation has done in the horse races. I propose at the finish-line on November 2 to come out ahead . . ."

FDR brushed off occasional failures with "I have no expectation of making a hit every time I come to bat," and Sherman Adams dismissed the first Russian Sputnik with a refusal to become engaged in "an outerspace basketball game."

Winston Churchill, defending the Speaker of the House of Commons in 1951, observed: "In these hard party fights under democratic conditions, as in football matches and the like, there are moments when the umpire gets a very rough time."

Political commentators use sports metaphors as well, occasionally mixing them: Theodore White, in *The Making of the President 1964* wrote: "Like aging prize-fighters, short of wind and stiffening of muscle, the Southerners were left with no resource but cunning; and cunning told them to delay, day by day, hour by hour, until somewhere, somehow, there might be a turning of national sentiment. It was the strategy, said someone, of 'punt and pray.' "

For boxing metaphors, see HAT IN THE RING and ARENA; for racing metaphors, see DARK HORSE. For football, see FOOTBALL, POLITICAL and GAME PLAN; for baseball, see HARDBALL; for basketball, FULL-COURT PRESS.

Sports metaphors relate closely to many people, which is why politicians spend the time to create them; at other times, they are tossed off without thinking because they are already a part of the language. After a Kennedy aide appeared on Lawrence Spivak's television panel show *Meet the Press,* the President called to say, "They never laid a glove on you." It is the classic remark of a trainer to a prizefighter who has been belted all over the ring.

Ron Nessen, President Ford's press secretary, wrote in 1978 that a favorite White House expression in the Ford years was "Welcome to the NFL"—a term used by announcers for the National Football League when a rookie received his first savage tackle.

SPUTNIK, *see* -NIK SUFFIX.

SQUARE DEAL   Theodore Roosevelt's campaign slogan, originally directed against the trusts; also, honest dealing (see CARD META-PHORS).

"We demand that big business give people a square deal," said President Roosevelt in 1901, urging government curbs on the new U.S. Steel Corporation. He took the issue to the people in a tour, urging his "square deal" —a phrase Lincoln Steffens claimed to have suggested—adding, "We do not wish to destroy corporations, but we do wish to make them subserve the public good." Campaigning for election he hammered home, "If elected, I shall see to it that every man has a square deal, no more and no less."

He continued to use the phrase, but the emphasis changed with the years. In 1910 he told a conservative Kansas audience:

I stand for the square deal. But when I say that I am for the square deal, I mean not merely that I stand for fair play under the present rules of the game, but that I stand for having those rules changed so as to work for a more substantial equality of opportunity and of reward for equally good service. One word of warning, which, I think, is hardly necessary in Kansas. When I say I want a square deal for the poor man, I do not mean that I want a square deal for the man who remains poor because he has not got the energy to work for himself. If a man who has

had a chance will not make good, then he has got to quit.

When he wrote his autobiography in 1913, he came back to his original use of the phrase in modified form: "We demand that big business give the people a square deal; in return we must insist that when any one engaged in big business honestly endeavors to do right he shall himself be given a square deal."

Every man's phrase is used against him. William Howard Taft, under strenuous attack from his former sponsor, said in 1912: "Mr. Roosevelt prides himself in being a true sportsman. . . . The maxim which he has exalted above all others is that every man is entitled to a square deal. . . . Is he giving me a square deal?"

The Square Deal was followed up by the NEW DEAL of Franklin Roosevelt and the FAIR DEAL of Harry Truman; in its square form, it was used by Wendell Willkie against FDR in 1940. When Lindon O. Pindling, first black Prime Minister of the Bahama Islands, wanted to show his closeness to the U.S., he took broadcaster Tex McCrary's advice and called his 1966 program "The Square Deal."

In current use, the phrase has lost most of its Roosevelt association and reverted to mean simply "honest dealing," as it had when Mark Twain used it in *Life on the Mississippi* in 1883: "Thought I had better give him a square deal." In this general form it was used in 1893 by Missouri Congressman Champ Clark ("What I want is a square deal and a 'divy' all around"), and by Huey Long in 1932 thanking columnist Claude Bowers for a friendly piece: "As a rule, I don't care a damn what any crooked newspaperman says about me, because they're mostly goddam liars; but you gave me a square deal and I want to thank you for it."

STAB IN THE BACK treachery.

"On this 10th day of June, 1940," said Franklin Roosevelt, "the hand that held the dagger has struck it into the back of its neighbor." When Italy attacked France, French Premier Paul Reynaud had cabled FDR asking for help, using the phrase "stab in the back." When a draft of the President's speech was submitted by the State Department, FDR inserted his version of the phrase but was dissuaded from using it by Sumner Welles. Other Democratic political leaders suggested this phrase might alienate the Italian-American vote in the coming election. However, on his way to the University of Virginia at Charlottesville, FDR wrote it in again and used it.

His successor, Harry Truman, used the same word-picture in a more partisan sense. Addressing 75,000 farmers and their families in Dexter, Iowa, in the 1948 campaign, Truman attacked: "The Republican Congress has already stuck a pitchfork in the farmer's back. They have already done their best to keep price supports from working . . . when you have to sell your grain below the support price because you have no place to store it, you can thank this same Republican Congress." Truman's use of the phrase annoyed Earl Warren, campaigning as Dewey's running mate: "Restraint is not easy when the President accuses Republicans of sticking a pitchfork into the backs of our farmers."

A familiar reflex to military disaster is the *Dolchstoss in den Rücken,* or *Dolchstosslegende,* which Prussian officers used to explain their 1918 defeat; Hitler revived the charge in the thirties, blaming the defeat on Jews. Historian Seymour Martin Lipset held in 1955 that the radical right was using this same kind of alibi for the loss of Eastern Europe, China, and Indochina: "The theory that these events occurred because we were 'stabbed in the back' by a 'hidden force' is much more palatable than admitting that the Communists have stronger political assets than we do."

FDR probably did not realize how apt the phrase was, or how sensitive the Germans would be to that figure of speech. In the medieval legend of the *Nibelungenlied* the hero, Siegfried—tired from being pursued, stopping to drink from a spring—was murdered by a man thrusting a spear into his back, spawning the *Dolchstosslegende,* and making Germans culturally aware of the duplicity of a stab in the back. To Americans, a similar episode is the shooting of Jesse James.

STAFFER a full-time member of a public figure's headquarters group.

In military terminology, there is a distinction between "line" and "staff" —between combat command and headquarters command. In government, "line" came to mean executive departments and "staff" the White House staff; though the staff started to grow in the Roosevelt years, the term "staffer" became prevalent in the Eisenhower years.

The **PECKING ORDER**: *adviser* or *counselor* carries the most prestige, an *assistant* comes next, a *staffer* follows (with a connotation of permanence), and an *aide* usually brings up the rear, though "aide" can be used to refer to all of the above, and journalists often try to unlock secrets by calling staffers "key aides."

As a verb, "to staff out" means to solicit a variety of views on a recommendation before submission to the decision maker.

STAGFLATION, *see* **INFLATION; ECONOMIC JARGON.**

STALKING HORSE a decoy; a candidate put forward to split a vote or deadlock a convention, concealing another candidate's plan.

In hunting, a stalking horse is used to conceal a sportsman stalking game, allowing the hunter to get close to his quarry; from this the expression has come to mean a person put forward to mislead. "He uses his folly like a stalking horse," wrote Shakespeare in *As You Like It*, "and under the presentation of that he shoots his wit."

Political writers and politicians have used it freely for over a century. *Niles' Register*, in 1846, said: "The 54–40 Doctrine is a mere stalking horse." In 1866 *Harper's Weekly* wrote of President Andrew Johnson: "He must know that they would willingly use him as a wedge to split the Union party, as a stalking horse to their own purposes, as a springboard to leap into power." In 1872 Hamilton Fish called Horace Greeley "the stalking horse of the secessionists."

In 1971 columnist Marianne Means wrote: "Senator George McGovern is plagued by this problem more than the other candidates. He has been accused of being a Kennedy stalking horse, sent out merely to soften up Muskie and divide the field until an eventual Kennedy blitz occurs." See STRAW MAN, SPOILER.

STALWART an unwavering party regular; a staunch supporter.

James G. Blaine ("The Plumed Knight") of Maine, wrote the *Boston Herald* in 1877: ". . . the Boston Press no more represents the stalwart Republican feeling of New England on the pending issues than the same press did when it demanded the enforcement of the Fugitive Slave law in 1851."

Commented *The Nation* four years later: "The epithet 'Stalwart' as applied to a class of politicians was first used by Mr. Blaine in 1877 to designate those Republicans who were unwilling to give up hostility and distrust of the South as a political motive."

Blaine used the adjective as an accolade; more often, it was an epithet. This was because Republicans had divided into two factions: "Stalwarts," regulars who opposed Blaine, and "Half Breeds," independents who supported him. Blaine was in the position of having his own word appropriated by the opposition. The "Stalwarts," led by N.Y. Senator Roscoe Conkling, organized the "Home Guard" behind General Grant at the Democratic convention; the "Half Breeds" pressed for Blaine. In the deadlock, dark horse James Garfield won the nomination and election.

Blaine was an avid reader of Sir Walter Scott, who frequently used "stalwart." The word is of Anglo-Saxon origin, meaning "foundation-worthy," the Old English meaning "serviceable," which stalwarts are to a party.

Current use has dropped the anti-Southern connotation, retaining the loyal-party-worker meaning. Dwight Eisenhower, in his memoirs, wrote of Senator Robert A. Taft: "In some things I found him unexpectedly 'liberal,' specifically in his attitudes on old-age pensions, school aid, and public housing—attitudes, incidentally, which were miles away from those of some self-described 'Taft stalwarts.' "

Stalwart Democrats are DYED-IN-THE-WOOL, BRASS COLLAR, and YELLOW DOG; and stalwart Republicans are ROCK-RIBBED.

STAMPEDE as a noun, panic-stricken decision on the part of delegates to jump on a bandwagon as it gathers speed; as a verb, to stimulate such a movement.

President William McKinley, looking over the field of candidates for his second-term running mate, told Senator Joseph B. Foraker, "I hope you will not allow the convention to be stampeded to Roosevelt for Vice-President." That was Foraker's recollection; true or not, the use of the word is unchanged from its early use and present use.

The Mexican-Spanish word is *estampida,* or *stampedo,* meaning a sudden rush of frightened cattle. The *New York Times* used a political application in 1876: "It is well known that many nominations, both in State and national Conventions, have been made by what is known as stampedes. A candidate runs ahead of all competitors, but while yet far short of the required number of votes, some County or State which has not kept tally supposes the Plurality man to be nominated, and wishing to be on the winning side changes to him."

Though the noun is most closely identified with convention action, the verb has frequent use in relation to movements rather than people. Thomas E. Dewey in 1948 sounded like an incumbent: "Ours is a magnificent land. Every part of it. Don't let anybody frighten you or try to stampede you into believing America is finished." And Dwight Eisenhower wrote: "Stories written with the purpose of damaging the reputation of a candidate have been a sleazy feature of many political campaigns. I resolved not to let such a story stampede me." See BANDWAGON.

STANDARD-BEARER the candidate, who carries the nomination of his party as his "standard."

From the French word meaning "banner," a standard is carried by a leader, as on a flagship. George Washington gave it an early use in America by calling on the delegates to the Constitutional Convention in Philadelphia to "raise a standard to which the wise and honest can repair."

The *New York Herald* in 1848 wrote: "It is on the old platform of principles, and for the good old cause, that the new standard-bearer is to be chosen." For a time, the phrase applied to the vice-presidential candidate as well. "The national convention," recorded the *Congressional Record,* ". . . summoned Garret A. Hobart to be standard-bearer with William McKinley." The President–vice president team is still referred to as "standard-bearers" but the Vice President individually is *a,* and never *the,* standard-bearer.

At the Democratic convention of 1884, Daniel Lockwood rose to nominate Grover Cleveland, asking the delegates "to go to the independent and Democratic voters of the country, to go to the young men of the country, the new blood of the country, and present the name of Grover Cleveland as your standard bearer."

The word, despite its archaic tone, is in current use. Theodore White on the 1964 campaign: "So many major Republican candidates avoided their standard-bearer whenever he entered their states that it was an act of grace when Charles Percy appeared in the late afternoon of Goldwater's second day in Illinois for three joint whistle-stop appearances."

In a 1975 *New York Times* column, a political hypocrite was denounced as a "double standard bearer." See BANNER DISTRICT; MILITARY META-PHORS.

STAND IN THE DOORWAY to resist symbolically; to make a dramatic show of opposition.

Governor George C. Wallace promised to "stand in the doorway" to block the admission of two black students into the University of Alabama on June 13, 1963. This phrase became a symbol of Southern resistance to school integration, much as "he should have taken her by the hand" was a much-used criticism of Eisenhower's refusal to make a dramatic personal gesture at Little Rock, Arkansas.

Wallace, making good his pledge, stood in the doorway of the university administration building at Tuscaloosa and blocked the entry of the two students and federal marshals. President Kennedy promptly federalized part of the Alabama National Guard, which soon arrived on campus. His symbolic show of resistance recorded by cameramen, Wallace retreated and the students were registered.

Both the "take her by the hand" and "stand in the doorway" expressions were used by Ted Sorensen: "There were recurring suggestions that the President should personally appear in Birmingham and take a Negro child by the hand into a school or lunch counter. But that suggestion badly confused the physical presence of the President with the official presence of his powers. It would have demeaned the dignity of the office by relying on the same kind of dramatic stunt and physical contest that was staged by those Southern governors who 'stood in the doorway.' "

Andrew Kopkind reported in The New Republic in 1967 that California Governor Ronald Reagan sought early in his administration to cut funds spent on education and then funds allocated for mental hospitals. "First Reagan stood in the schoolhouse door," he quoted an economist

as saying, "then he stood in the nuthouse door." As pressures built up, Reagan restored the cuts and retreated from the doorways.

STAND PAT   to adhere to a position; to accept the status quo; has assumed a reactionary connotation.

"We will stand pat!" Senator Mark Hanna, the foremost McKinley supporter, was supposed to have said in 1900; this has led to the assumption that "Stand Pat with McKinley" was a slogan in that election. This appears to be wrong.

Mark Hanna did give a new political meaning to the poker expression but not until 1902. Hans Sperber and Travis Trittschuh dug out the September 28, 1902, *Cleveland Plain Dealer* that reported on a Hanna speech the preceding day at Akron. Said Hanna: "About a year ago it was my privilege to attend the opening meeting of the Republican party, and after thinking and looking over the situation, I came to the conclusion—'Let well enough alone.' That was the whole chapter: that is all there was in the campaign of interest to you. Now I say stand pat." The *Plain Dealer* went on to explain what Hanna meant:

> The player "stands pat" when he declines to discard from his hand, and draw other cards, and the supposed earning quality of such a hand is superior to that of three aces. According to the rules of the game it is perfectly honest, however, for a player to hold a pat hand when it has little or no value, and if successful in scaring his opponents into laying down their hands he wins the bank or "pot." This is, we are informed, called a "bluff." Thus it will be seen that Dr. Hanna in his Akron speech invented a singularly appropriate figure of political speech.

Obviously the senator was needled after using this expression; politicians were considered too distinguished to be familiar with poker terminology. "When I told the people 'stand pat,' " Hanna told the *Cincinnati Enquirer* on October 3, 1902, "it was merely to use a familiar saying to express the situation. I have been told that this is a phrase used in the game of poker; but everybody understands it just the same . . ."

The *Enquirer* commented: "Senator Hanna probably got the suggestion of his 'stand pat' speech from some fellow who played poker; but the Senator didn't know that, of course."

Although Hanna popularized the expression (apparently in 1902, casting doubt on its use in the 1900 campaign), he was not the first to use it politically. Speaker Joseph G. ("Uncle Joe") Cannon used the expression in the House in 1896 regarding adherence to high tariffs. The *Congressional Record* of February 28, 1896, reported the following exchange:

Mr. J. G. Cannon:—That proposition was fought bitterly in the House; but the Senate *stood,* if the gentlemen will allow me the expression, *pat;*. . . and they had their own way, because no bill can pass without an agreement between the two houses.

Mr. G. L. Johnson of Calif.:—I understand the explanation made by the gentleman from Illinois, with the single exception of some technical, abstruse term which he used, but which I suppose is well understood in Illinois, though unfamiliar in California. I will ask the gentlemen however why should not the House "stand pat" as the Senate did?

Mr. Cannon:—Oh no: It was invented in California and put into the dictionary there.

After being popularized by Hanna, "stand pat" and "standpatter" came to mean REACTIONARY. Progressive Robert La Follette equated the two words in a comment on Calvin Coolidge's first message to Congress: "It was an able, concise and frank presentation of the stand pat reactionary theory of government." This criticism could not have come as a surprise to Coolidge who had given the following advice to political leaders of Massachusetts when he became Governor there ten years before:

Expect to be called a standpatter, but don't be a standpatter. Expect to be called a demagogue, but don't be a demagogue. Don't hesitate to be as revolutionary as science. Don't hesitate to be as reactionary as the multiplication table. Don't expect to build up the weak by pulling down the strong. Don't hurry to legislate. Give administration a chance to catch up with legislation."

In his 1960 campaign John F. Kennedy scorned "Stand Pat with McKinley" as an example of Republican reaction. Richard Nixon learned in that campaign that a political phrase could have an embarrassing double meaning. He countered Kennedy's "Let's get America moving again" with his own "America cannot stand pat." When it was pointed out that his wife, Pat Nixon, might take offense, he hurriedly changed that line in subsequent appearances to "America cannot stand still."

On January 17, 1978, Arthur Schlesinger, Jr., turned it into a one-word -ISM with a *Wall Street Journal* piece entitled "Carter's Retreats into Standpattism."

STATE OF THE UNION   annual report to the Congress required of the President.

Like the few extra vertebrae on the end of the human backbone that used to be the start of a tail, this phrase preserves a word that was once of great political import. The word "union," capitalized when it refers to the United States, was first used in an American context in Massachusetts in 1754: "A motion was made that the Commissioners deliver their opinion whether a Union of all the Colonies is not at present absolutely necessary for their security and defense." Jefferson in 1775 wrote: "A Committee of Congress is gone to improve our circumstances, so as to bring the Canadians into our Union."

It is used casually in Article II, Section 3 of the Constitution, directing that the President "shall from time to time give to the Congress information of the state of the union, and recommend to their consideration such measures as he shall judge necessary and expedient . . ."

At the time of the Civil War, "Union" became a dramatic word, meaning something worth fighting to preserve and, as an adjective, describing Northern forces. A word for Northern soldiers was "Unions," as in this use by Mark Twain in 1874: "When de Unions took dat town . . . dey all run away and lef' me all by myse'f."

By the late nineteenth century, "Unionist" and "Union man" ceased to mean a supporter of a federal union against nullification or secession; gradually, it changed to mean a member of a labor union.

State of the Union *messages* (preferred over *speeches, addresses,* or *reports* just as inaugural speeches are always formally called addresses) have inclined to be lengthy statements of legislative intent; they are a method by which a President takes the initiative in shaping a legislative program for his Administration. An exception was FDR's 1941 message, which became known as "the FOUR FREE-DOMS speech." In that speech, as in most State of the Union messages, the phrase itself was used: "Therefore, as your President, performing my constitutional duty to 'give to the Congress information of the state of the Union,' I find it unhappily necessary to report that the future and the safety of our country and of our democracy are overwhelmingly involved in events far beyond our borders."

John F. Kennedy gave the traditional usage a twist in 1963: "I can report to you that the State of this old but youthful Union, in the 175th year of its life, is good." Gerald Ford was the first to say "The State of the Union is not good"; Jimmy Carter called the state in 1978 "sound."

STATES RIGHTS DEMOCRATS, *see* DIXIECRAT.

STAY-AT-HOMES those eligible to vote who do not.

"They are not radical," wrote sociologist C. Wright Mills, "not liberal, not reactionary. They are inactionary. They are out of it. If we accept the Greek's definition of the idiot as an altogether private man, then we must conclude that many American citizens are now idiots."

Political pollsters call them the "politically inert." Politicians call them the SILENT VOTE.

When a person who usually votes stays away from the polls because he is dissatisfied with both candidates, he "goes fishing" (see FISHING EXPEDITION). The great majority of stay-at-homes, however, are apathetic. Political scientist Clinton Rossiter made a breakdown of the stay-at-homes in the 1956 presidential election: 62 million people voted out of 100 million eligible. Of the 38 million who did not, 6 million were "trapped in the political morass of the South"—kept from voting by intimidation and unfair local voting laws. Five million were transient—unable to meet local residence requirements. Another 5 million were ill on Election Day. Two and a half million were away from home and did not cast absentee ballots; another 2.5 million were illiterate. Six hundred thousand were in prisons, homes for the aged, and other institutions, and a like number were residents of the nonvoting District of Columbia.

"This leaves a total of 15.5 million Americans," wrote Rossiter, "who simply found it inconvenient. . . . a staggering number of Americans who thought it quite unimportant to act the parts of responsible citizens of a great democracy."

In 1948 President Harry Truman castigated those Democrats he considered responsible for the DO-NOTH-ING CONGRESS who, "because they stayed at home and did not vote last year, got just the kind of Congress they deserve."

Political scientist Sam Lubell, analyzing the 1948 Truman-Dewey election, came up with a surprising observation: "Far from costing Dewey the election, the [Democratic] stay-at-homes may have saved him almost as crushing a defeat as Landon suffered in 1936."

An elaborate campaign plan was drawn up by the GOP in the 1952 Eisenhower campaign; it claimed that the greatest potential GOP strength was among 45 million "stay-at-homes" and recommended a style of campaign "which could inspire a crusading zeal that is impossible to engender by the 'ME TOO' approach, or anything which promises only to better what the present Administration is doing . . . the recommended strategy is: 'Attack! Attack! Attack!' "

Overcoming the ennui of stay-at-homes is likely to remain an unreached goal of campaigners. A more subtle approach, playing on their guilt, was made by poet Ogden Nash:

They have such refined and delicate palates
That they can discover no one worthy of their ballots,
And then when someone terrible gets elected
They say, There, that's just what I expected!

The problem of stay-at-homes plagues both parties and is not limited to this country or this time. British political philosopher Edmund Burke wrote: "The only thing necessary for the triumph of evil is for good men to do nothing." And the French have a saying: *"Qui s'excuse, s'accuse."*

See TURNOUT.

STAYING BOUGHT constancy in corruption.

Simon Cameron, Lincoln's first Secretary of War, who was later censured by Congress for remarkably lax administration, defined "an honest politician" as "a man who, when he's bought, stays bought."

The phrase reappeared and was made part of the political language after the campaign of 1904. Although the Democrats put up Judge Alton B. Parker, a gilt-edged conservative, Republican Theodore Roosevelt was able to attract financial support from Morgan, Rockefeller, Depew, Frick, Harriman, and other industrial and financial titans. Judge Parker accused Roosevelt of having blackmailed the financial giants, promising them immunity from trustbusting if they contributed heavily. At least one, Henry Clay Frick—Andrew Carnegie's man for many years—felt he had been given commitments in return for his donation to Roosevelt.

"He got down on his knees before us," Frick angrily claimed. "We bought the son of a bitch and then he did not stay bought!"

STEAMROLLER rough tactics used by those in control of a political party to overpower those who disagree with them.

The steamroller began to roll at the Republican convention in June 1908. The word was probably first used in this country by a newsman in Chicago, Oswald F. Schuette of the *Inter-Ocean,* about the Roosevelt-Taft supporters within the Republican National Committee is disposing of those who protested against the seating at the convention of slates of Taft delegates from Alabama and Arkansas.

Turnabout was called unfair play in 1912 when the Roosevelt supporters at the Republican convention complained that their Southern slates were being steamrollered by a Taft-dominated Republican National Committee.

The word had already been used in international politics some years earlier. In 1902 *Munsey's Magazine* said of Russia: "She sought to achieve her end by means of the 'steam roller' of the concert of Europe."

In 1932 Roosevelt forces surrendered their plan to get the Democratic convention to give up the hoary two-thirds rule on the selection of candidates; it had become obvious they could not win the fight. Candidate Roosevelt wrote the convention acknowledging that asking for revision at that time might be considered unfair by some and saying: ". . . I decline to permit either myself or my friends to be open to the accusation of poor sportsmanship, or to use the methods which could be called, even falsely, those of a steamroller . . ."

In 1956, knowing his nomination was a certainty, President Eisenhower, wired his aide, Sherman Adams, that he must "guard against steamrollering, no matter what the proposition is." He remembered 1952, and the charge made by Ike's supporters against Robert Taft.

Steamrollering is often defined as using overwhelming strength unfairly, or even illegally, mainly by those who have been defeated. As Senator Robert La Follette said in his autobiography: "Whether one is on top of or under the steamroller influences somewhat one's point of view."

STEMWINDER an orator, or a speech, capable of rousing a crowd.

A stemwinding speech, like a good stump speech, is intended for delivery at large rallies, where roars of approval add to its effectiveness; the whirling image of the word pictures the orator "winding up" and flinging stimulating words and phrases. In current political usage, the word is used to describe a loud, partisan speech, either approvingly or mockingly. Its opposite is a low-key, reasonable-sounding, "sincere" speech, best used on television to reach people at home.

The word is derived from the stemwinding watch or clock, which was a major advance in timepieces patented in 1866. It soon became the word for modernity and excellence—"Ain't he a stem-winder" can be traced to 1892, and short-story writer O. Henry used it in 1902 in that sense: "There's a new bank examiner over at the First, and he's a stem-winder." Dictionaries of slang at the turn of the century included the word as "the best of its kind; a keyless watch, at the time a new and exquisite improvement."

Though its usage as "excellent" is archaic (battery-powered watches have no stems at all), the word is actively used in politics. Often one quality of a vice-presidential candidate is his ability to deliver stemwinders, while the presidential candidate delivers less partisan speeches. For comparative usage, see SPELLBINDER.

STEP BY STEP diplomacy that proceeds cautiously, seeking bilateral agreements rather than a comprehensive solution.

Garry Wills, in the *New York Review of Books* (July 12, 1975), covered much of the vocabulary of Mideast diplomacy in a sentence: "For a country with scholar-rulers, Israel's debates live to an extraordinary degree on slogans: one side's 'step by step' is the other's 'SALAMI TACTICS,' just as a friend's 'piece of peace' is a foe's 'intangible for tangibles.'"

The phrase was associated in 1974 with Secretary of State Henry Kissinger's SHUTTLE DIPLOMACY; coinage was claimed by writer Edward Sheehan in an article in *Foreign Policy* magazine, but reporter David Zuckerman found a quotation dated June 1, 1953, by Secretary of State John Foster Dulles, pledging that the U.S. would help bring about "a step-by-step reduction of tensions in the area and the conclusion of an ultimate peace."

On September 20, 1977, Moshe Dayan, Israeli Foreign Minister in Menachem Begin's government, told a group of Washington reporters that "step by step is dead," and defined the phrase as "a piece of land for a piece of peace." However, Israel soon became uncomfortable with President Carter's plans for a comprehensive settlement at a Geneva conference, fearing a veto over Arab moderation by Arab radicals and the Soviet Union. When Egyptian President Anwar el-Sadat made his dramatic visit to Jerusalem in 1977, talk of direct dealings between Israel and Egypt dominated the Mideast, and "step-by-step"—though never generating the same enthusiasm as when it was first expressed—did not seem such a bad approach to a solution.

Step-by-step (usually hyphenated when used without the "diplomacy") was at first totally identified with Kissinger, although it was originally an Israeli idea, adopted—as Kissinger said on September 16, 1975—after "every attempt to discuss a comprehensive solution failed." The phrase was the subject of a George Ball critique in 1975 in *Newsweek,* and was part of the title of a book about Kissinger by Israeli Matti Golan: *The Secret Conversations of Henry Kissinger: Step by Step in the Middle East.* To dissociate himself from the author of the previous policy, Carter's National Security Adviser Zbigniew Brzezinski referred to an approach of "concentric circles."

STEPPINGSTONE springboard to higher office; used to show ambition, demeaning the office held at the time or currently aspired to.

Harry Truman offered the vice-presidential nomination in 1948 to Supreme Court Justice William O. Douglas. He considered the offer for a weekend, and then called the President: "I am very sorry, but I have decided not to get into politics. I do not think I should use the Court as a steppingstone."

The only judges to run for President were Alton B. Parker in 1904 and Charles Evans Hughes in 1916; John F. Kennedy once jotted in a notebook: "No congressional leader of the very first rank save James Madison has been elected Pres.,—and apart from Polk, Garfield, McKinley and Truman no parliamentarians of the 2nd rank."

Certainly, House Speakers had tried. Henry Clay in 1824, James Blaine in 1876, Champ Clark in 1912, John Garner in 1932, all tried and failed; only James Polk succeeded. Thirteen men who had served as senators made it, but only one—Harding —made it directly from the Senate in the twentieth century, before the election of 1960, when for the first time two senators (Kennedy and Johnson) ran on the same ticket, against two former senators (Nixon and Lodge).

This was not what Thomas Jefferson had foreseen. "Congress is the great commanding theatre of this nation," he wrote William Wirt in 1808, "and the threshold to whatever department of office a man is qualified to enter." But the best steppingstone to the presidency has been the governor's chair—thirteen governors became President—and the vice presidency, where eleven became President, eight by succession at the President's death. Senator Henry Cabot Lodge at the turn of the century said that the vice presidency should not be looked on with disdain by great men, but should be desired by "our most ambitious men . . . as a stepping stone to higher office." Theodore Roosevelt, on the other hand, called it "a steppingstone . . . to oblivion."

The cabinet, especially in our early history, was an excellent steppingstone (nine made it), and the man to be was Secretary of State; in the twentieth century, Taft of the War Department and Hoover of the Commerce Department became Chief Executive.

In current usage the word is often employed to attack a candidate for having his sights set on greater things than the office he is currently running

for. This attack was potent in California, as William Knowland discovered, but New Yorkers were delighted to vote for a governor who could be presidential material.

Critics of Michigan Governor George Romney, and later of candidate Jimmy Carter, seizing on what they considered an overly devout, evangelical nature, spread a joke that their target was "only seeking the White House as a steppingstone."

STIR UP THE ANIMALS   start an unwanted controversy; take a position that could needlessly incur criticism.

Reviewing the 1948 campaign strategy, Dewey's (later Eisenhower's) press secretary James Hagerty said: "The main campaign worry was not to rock the boat. While Governor Dewey set the strategy, he was greatly influenced by the state chairmen and local leaders. They kept saying, telegraphing, and writing that the campaign had to be kept on a low [quiet] level, that there was no need to stir up the animals."

Obviously, this is a zoo or circus metaphor, referring to the commotion caused by sleeping denizens when wakened. For an early use of a similar metaphor, see POLITICAL ANIMAL.

"The animals" is a half-jocular, half-derisive reference to a lower order of life; news reporters frequently call broadcasting technicians by that name, which is never appreciated. (See ZOO PLANE.) "Animals" alone is also a derogation of criminals, with overtones of up-from-the-jungle racism. When an outbreak of looting followed a power outage in New York City in July 1977, the blacks and Hispanic citizens who were pictured carting away looting stores were castigated as "animals" by black businessmen. The accusation by blacks of other blacks made possible the television use of a word that would ordinarily be taboo because of its African-jungle connotation.

A closely related expression is "raw meat," or "red meat," which means material in a speech designed to elicit a strong reaction from the audience. This has to do with controversial subject matter more than style; in current usage, "Let's give 'em some raw meat" is defined as an instruction to deal with matters that will make an audience, like a lion, roar its approval. See RATTLE THE CAGE.

STONEWALLING saying "NO COMMENT"; HANGING TOUGH; a policy based on those actions.

The word was popularized during the Watergate investigation. As transcribed from the Nixon tapes, White House counsel John Dean assured the President on February 28, 1973: "We are stonewalling totally." Mr. Nixon picked up the word, which was in widening use, and on March 22 directed: "I want you to stonewall it, let them plead the Fifth Amendment, cover up or anything else . . ."

Several witnesses before the Senate Watergate Committee attributed the word to John Mitchell. During an interrogation in which the former Attorney General volunteered nothing, Senator Lowell Weicker (R-Conn.) asked if his testimony was "an exercise in stonewalling." Mitchell replied, "I don't know that term. Is that a Yankee term from Connecticut?"

In his 1976 campaign, candidate Jimmy Carter castigated President Ford's "inaccessibility" by charging: "In this Administration a stonewall seems to mean not letting American people have a right to know what's our own business."

The word's roots had heroic, if de-

fensive, connotations. On July 21, 1861, at the First Battle of Bull Run, Confederate General Thomas Jonathan Jackson held his position and earned his sobriquet when a soldier was said to have cried, "There stands Jackson like a stone wall—rally behind the Virginians!"

As a verb, it comes from Australian cricket slang, meaning to block balls persistently, playing only on the defensive. In the sense of obstruction as a strategy, the word was transferred to the business and political worlds in that region; the *Victorian Hansard* in 1876 asked "whether the six members constituted 'the stone wall' which was to oppose all progress?"

A related second meaning is to delay, filibuster, or stall. James Reston wrote in the *New York Times* in 1961 that the Kennedy Administration was "stonewalling for time in order to close the missile gap . . ."

"To stonewall" is to impede an inquiry, usually through silence, sometimes through delay, and is not as pejorative as COVER UP, which is a more sinister form of obstruction of justice. The word now appears to be firmly fixed in the political lexicon; in a letter to the author from federal prison dated July 23, 1977, former Attorney General John Mitchell wrote: "Please keep after the establishment and make them account. You should continue to have a field day with Koreagate. Sooner or later they will have to quit stonewalling and get on with the fireworks."

STRADDLE, *see* **ON THE FENCE.**

STRAIGHT TICKET, *see* **TICKET; SPLIT TICKET.**

STRANGE BEDFELLOWS enemies forced by circumstances to work together; members of an unlikely alliance, often attacked as an UNHOLY ALLIANCE.

"True it is," wrote Charles Dudley Warner in 1850, "that politics makes strange bedfellows." Warner, editor of the *Hartford* (Conn.) *Courant,* was co-author with Mark Twain of *The Gilded Age;* he might have taken the expression from Edward George Bulwer-Lytton's novel *The Caxtons,* published in 1849, which contained the phrase "Poverty has strange bedfellows."

More likely, the source for both was Act II, scene 2 of Shakespeare's *The Tempest,* when a storm drives Trinculo to seek shelter under a gabardine sheet with Caliban, whom he regards as a monster: "There is no other shelter hereabout: misery acquaints a man with strange bedfellows. I will here shroud until the dregs of the storm be past."

In current usage, both misery and poverty have given way to politics as the excuse for strange bedfellows. Historian Mark Sullivan titled a chapter "Strange Bedfellows" when he wrote in *Our Times* (1930) about the cooperation between Senator "Pitchfork Ben" Tillman and his arch-enemy, Theodore Roosevelt, on a bill to end rate preferences on railroads.

The most dramatic strange bedfellow in modern times was Joseph Stalin. When the Soviet Union signed a nonaggression pact with anti-Communist Germany in 1939, later following Hitler's invasion of Poland with an invasion of their own from the east, British cartoonist David Low presented the paradox in all its absurdity: the two leaders bowing to each other over the smoking ruins of Poland, Hitler saying to Stalin, "The scum of the earth, I believe?" and Stalin courteously replying, "The bloody assassin of the workers, I presume?"

After Russia was attacked by Ger-

many, Stalin became Churchill's strange bedfellow. When the British Prime Minister was asked how he could say anything good about the Communist dictator, he replied, "If Hitler invaded Hell, I would make at least a favourable reference to the Devil in the House of Commons."

In recent years the phrase has been heard more frequently, perhaps because odd alliances for expediency's sake are growing more common. Editorialized the short-lived *New York World Journal Tribune* in February 1967: "Everybody knows that politics makes strange bedfellows. It doubtless would surprise Robert Kennedy to wake up any morning now in the same bed with Arkansas' Sen. J. William Fulbright. At least they would have conversational rapport over crumpets and coffee as dissenters in foreign policy."

When columnists decided to speculate about a Rockefeller-Reagan Republican ticket for 1968, the phrase came naturally. James Reston in the *New York Times:* "No candidate has ever lost New York and California and won the Presidency. This is the beginning of the strange bedfellows story." Max Lerner in the *New York Post:* ". . . a good Presidential ticket, like a good marriage, does not have to be logically consistent, nor one of sweet harmony. Sometimes it is the neurotic interactions in marriage that make it hold together—which may be true of political bedfellows as well. In fact, the very daring of matching this particular pair of partners might enable them to get away with the absurdity of it."

The latent double meaning of the phrase surfaced in the House of Representatives in the thirties. Former House Speaker Joe Martin recalled a member shouting, "I say to you, Mr. Speaker, that politics makes strange bedfellows. Especially since women got into 'em.''

STRAW MAN (MAN OF STRAW)
a weakling; one who is all façade, no substance; also, a false issue or phony candidate set up to distract and draw attack.

"Condemn me if you will," said President William Howard Taft in 1912, under savage attack from the man who made him President and who now wanted the job back, "but condemn me by other witnesses than Theodore Roosevelt. I was a man of straw; but I have been a man of straw long enough. Every man who has blood in his body, and who has been misrepresented as I have . . . is forced to fight."

A man of straw—one who looks like a man but is stuffed with straw—comes from the farmer's scarecrow, and from its military use as a false target set up to draw enemy fire. The phrase was used by Taft in the sense of LIGHTWEIGHT; in the following use, the synonym would be STALKING HORSE.

Columnist Clayton Fritchey wrote with some sarcasm in 1967 that "The Fearless Ninetieth [Congress] . . . has shown once more that it wears no strawman's collar" by enacting a bill against race riots "which is aimed at the strawman of the mythical 'outside agitator.' "

A more profound term, very similar, is *hollow man*. The quality of bloodlessness equates *straw* and *hollow*, as in this use by Jersey City Democratic leader Frank Hague about Governor Franklin Roosevelt: ". . . a weather vane, beautiful against the sky, shining and resplendent, built of hollow brass." *The Hollow Men* is a poem by T. S. Eliot, the title of which is said by some analysts to characterize the postwar politicians of the Western world. The poem concludes: "This is the way the world ends/Not with a bang but a whimper." Historian Samuel Eliot Morison wrote: "Congress, too, was full of hollow men. William E. Borah, perpetual senator from Idaho, was the most pretentious and the emptiest, although he looked more like a statesman than any senator since Daniel Webster. Borah would support any liberal bill with great rumbling oratory, yet in the end vote with the regular Republicans. Senator Norris said of him, 'He fights until he sees the whites of their eyes.' " See TURNAROUNDS.

The danger of the emptiness of the straw or hollow man, stressing the nonhuman quality, was shown by Barbara Garson in 1965 in *MacBird*, a play in Shakespearean verse suggesting that Lyndon Johnson was responsible for the death of John Kennedy. A character most readily identified as Robert Kennedy, called Robert Ken O'Dunc, says at the end in the accents of Macduff:

To free his sons from paralyzing scruples
And temper us for roles of world authority
Our pulpy human hearts were cut away.
And in their place, precision apparatus
Of steel and plastic tubing was inserted.
The sticky, humid blood was drained and
   then
A tepid antiseptic brine injected.

Not all writers attack the emptiness of politicians; many members of the NEW LEFT identify with the feeling, and "hollow" is often used to articulate ALIENATION: "The sense of the body growing empty within," as novelist Norman Mailer explained it to a Berkeley crowd, "of the psyche pierced by a wound whose dimensions keep opening, that unendurable conviction that one is hollow, displaced, without a single identity at one's center."

The phrase itself can be tracked to English proverbs popular in the early seventeenth century: "A man of straw is worth a woman of gold" and "A man of straw eats a servant of steel."

An African affairs scholar, Sue Cott Wunderman, informs the author that the phrase has an independent West African root. Tribes were reluctant to have their real chiefs deal with French colonial officials. William Foltz points out in *From French West Africa to the Mali Federation:* "Usually a younger man or an elder of infeior caste or status was put up by the people themselves as a 'straw chief' to deal with the conqueror, but beneath the dignity of the tribesman really in charge."

See CHARLIE REGAN.

STRAW POLL (STRAW VOTE)

originally an informal survey of a small group to determine opinion; now becoming a term for a scientific, large-scale poll based on the theory of a random sample.

"Ballads, bon mots, anecdotes, give us better insight into the depths of past centuries than grave and voluminous chronicles," wrote Ralph Waldo Emerson in his *Journals.* " 'A Straw,' says Selden, 'thrown up into the air will show how the wind sits, which cannot be learned by casting up a stone.' "

Emerson was right in the point he was making, though he took some liberties with the quotation from John Selden (1584–1654), who wrote, "Take a straw and throw it up into the Air—you may see by that which way the Wind is," adding, "More solid things do not show the Complexion of the times so well, as Ballads and Libels." However, an earlier use of a similar phrase can be found

in Shakespeare's *Merchant of Venice,* Act I, scene 1: "I should be still/ Plucking the grass to know where sits the wind."

A straw is metaphorically *powerful* (the *last straw* can break a camel's back), *necessary* (you can't *make bricks* without it), empty (STRAW MAN), and *not so powerful* (a *straw boss* is a foreman who can give orders but carries no executive responsibility).

A *straw in the wind,* probably derived from Selden's usage, is a rough indication or portent, similar to a *cloud no bigger than a man's hand* on the horizon. The term *straw vote* is traced to the *Cleveland Leader* in 1866, with indications that it had been used long before: "A straw vote taken on a Toledo train yesterday resulted as follows: [Andrew] Johnson 12, Congress, 47." Surveys had often been taken on river steamboats, and *steamboat vote* was a predecessor phrase that was considered "a straw," as in this item in *Old Zack,* an 1848 publication about Zachary Taylor: "Straws.—For a while the Locofoco papers ventured to publish steamboat votes . . . A vote was taken on the Steamer Fairmount on her trip to Pittsburgh.—This is the vote: Taylor 75, Cass 37, Van Buren 4."

Most modern public-opinion surveys create a panel of voters, based on age, previous voting record, location, socioeconomic background, ethnic group, and so on, hoping to build a cross-section of the actual population make-up. However, straw polls—if they gather enough straws, or votes— can reflect the attitudes of the population of an area if they adhere rigidly to a "random sample" of, say, every hundredth person in a telephone book, and not just those easiest to reach or passing by a certain corner.

Best-known of these wide-scale

straw polls is the one conducted at election time in New York City by the *Daily News,* which has called elections correctly on all but two occasions in almost forty years. The first error was when the poll was just getting started, and the second in 1965, when it predicted Abraham Beame over John Lindsay for mayor. When the *News* poll technicians select a name out of phone books or voter registration lists, an interviewer is sent to that apartment; if the resident is not home, he keeps returning, because going next door for a substitute would throw the random sample out of kilter. If he is unable to get his target straw, the interviewer gets another name from the statistician.

Strength of a big straw poll is in the size of its sample, and the fact that most people do *not* change their vote in the final two weeks; weakness of such polling is that some people *do* change their minds, which can be decisive in a "squeaker," and the pollsters are stuck with straws carefully gathered in a final go-around that begins several weeks before Election Day.

When the poll shows a candidate behind, his supporters say with O. Henry in a 1913 story: "A straw vote only shows which way the hot air blows."

See POLLSTER; DEPTH POLLING; TRIAL HEAT.

STREET MONEY, *see* **WALKING-AROUND MONEY.**

STREET SMARTS savvy; cunning; intuitive understanding of the way the urban voter will react.

"To have the smarts" is to be mentally sharp; the specific "street smarts" is a political insider's term, rarely in print, meaning sensitivity to opinions at the grassroots, gained by experience, without benefit of polls.

In 1972, reporter Paul Hoffman wrote: "Street smarts—in New York City, Wagner, Lefkowitz and Javits have it, Rockefeller and Lindsay do not."

Beyond politics, the phrase is used to mean an understanding of the ways of the real world. In a 1972 article on the rock group the Rolling Stones, *Time* reported: ". . . the Stones from the start based their appeal partly on their reputation as delinquents. They were always too shaggy, too street smart . . ."

In the Southern U.S., new-products marketer Phyllis Y. Bishop reported in 1977 that a variant phrase with the same meaning is "street sense."

STRICT CONSTRUCTIONIST in law, one who tends to interpret the Constitution literally, as meaning exactly what it says and no more, much as a fundamentalist interprets the Bible; in politics, one who feels that judges in their broad interpretation of the law have been encroaching on the lawmaking function of the legislative branch.

The *Congressional Globe,* in 1841, defined a "strict constructionist" as "a Pharisee's Pharisee." In 1850 a Pennsylvania congressman named Chandler explained the breed to his House colleagues in this way: "You remember the anecdote of the youngster who received an admonition from his father that it was time to be steady, make some money and take a wife. 'Why, sir,' said he, 'I like the money-making, but whose wife shall I take?' He was a strict constructionist."

"We need more strict constructionists on the highest court of the United States," said Richard Nixon in a law-and-order speech on October 22,

1968, reprising a theme he had made frequently during the campaign. The emphasis was on the "strict."

The phrase connoted hard-line judges, who would not hamstring law enforcement officials with pettifogging procedural complaints. It connoted something else as well—judges who would not let their own social beliefs carry them into the lawmaking region reserved to Congress.

That is the general understanding of the term today, which distresses many lawyers who believe that such usage confusingly encompasses two different doctrines—one of *strict construction,* and the other of *judicial restraint.*

In law, according to Bouvier's *Law Dictionary,* "A *strict* construction is one which limits the application of the provisions of the instrument or agreement to cases clearly described by the words used. It is called, also, literal.

"A *liberal* construction is one by which the letter is enlarged or restrained so as more effectually to accomplish the end in view. It is called, also, equitable."

Judicial restraint, or self-limitation, deals with a related but different matter: the extent to which judicial decisions on cases "make" law. Justice Frankfurter in 1937 put the case for judicial restraint in these words: "Such self-limitation is not abnegation; it is the expression of an energizing philosophy of the distribution of governmental powers. For a court to hold that decision does not belong to it, is merely to recognize that a problem calls for the exercise of initiative and experimentation possessed only by political processes, and should not be subjected to the confined procedure of a lawsuit and the uncreative resources of judicial review."

President Nixon did not put a strict construction on his use of the term "strict construction"; he interpreted it broadly, to include judicial restraint. Explaining his appointment of Warren Burger to be Chief Justice, he said: "I happen to believe that the Constitution should be strictly interpreted, and I believe, as did Mr. Justice Frankfurter . . . [who] felt it was his responsibility to interpret the Constitution, and it was the right of the Congress to write the laws and have great leeway to write those laws, and he should be very conservative in overthrowing a law passed by the elected representatives at the state or Federal level . . ."

While most strict constructionists are also believers in judicial restraint, it would be possible to abandon judicial restraint in pursuit of strict construction.

Historically, the "construction," or interpretation, of the Constitution is our longest-lived controversy. Soon after the document was written, public opinion was divided between the "strict constructionists" (the Democrat-Republicans behind Thomas Jefferson) and the "loose constructionists" (the Federalists, favoring a strong central government, behind Hamilton).

Chief Justice John Marshall made a case for loose construction in *Maryland* v. *McCulloch:* "Let the end be legitimate, let it be within the scope of the Constitution, and all means which are appropriate, which are plainly adapted to that end, which are not prohibited, but consist with the letter and spirit of the Constitution, are constitutional." In modern times, Justice Hugo Black, whose liberal opinions often made him the target of many who considered themselves strict constructionists, used this language in dissenting from a decision that extended the Due Process clause to include the need to prove guilt "beyond a reasonable doubt": "In two places the Constitution provides for trial by jury, but nowhere in that document is there any statement that conviction of crime requires proof of guilt beyond a reasonable doubt. The Constitution thus goes into some detail to spell out what kind of trial a defendant charged with crime should have, and I believe the Court has no power to add to or subtract from the procedures set forth by the Founders." Justice Black was also fond of pointing to the words in the First Amendment that read "Congress shall make no law . . ." and commenting, " 'No law' means *no law.* "

STRIKE A BLOW FOR FREEDOM a pleasant drink in a politician's office, accompanied by informal political discussion; a legislative code phrase.

"On a hot afternoon in 1958," wrote Rowland Evans and Robert Novak in 1966, "Speaker Sam Rayburn's 'BOARD OF EDUCATION' met in his offices, as it did almost every day after work to 'strike a blow for freedom'—good political talk accompanied by good whiskey." The phrase is especially used among Texans and effectively confuses outsiders; when Texas Congressman Olin E. Teague invited the author to "strike a blow for freedom" one evening in 1963, about the last thing expected was a glass of Early Times bourbon along with a general discussion of the political scene.

New York Daily News columnist Ted Lewis, who covered Washington for United Press in the early thirties, attributes coinage to Vice President John Garner. He informs the author: "Garner called it striking a blow for liberty. He was a stingy man with the liquor, though—he could strike a blow with a thimbleful."

A similar phrase has long existed in England. To a tavernkeeper, an "Act of Parliament" is a small (which means weak) beer, stemming from an ancient requirement that landlords billeting soldiers had to provide five pints of small beer free to each—"by Act of Parliament."

The "strike a blow for freedom" phrase is sufficiently pretentious to make it useful for an ironic twist, even to the extent of giving it a meaning of enjoying a straight shot of whiskey. However, some political leaders still use the phrase in the original context. Said Rhodesian Prime Minister Ian Smith in 1965 as he broke from Great Britain: "We have struck a blow for the preservation of justice, civilization, and Christianity; and in the spirit of this belief we have this day assumed our sovereign independence." Thirteen years later he acquiesced in majority rule by blacks, which many felt was more of a "blow for freedom."

STRIKE FORCE, *see* **TASK FORCE.**

STRIPED-PANTS DIPLOMACY, *see* **SHIRTSLEEVE DIPLOMACY.**

STROKE as a verb, to persuade soothingly, or to hold in line with murmured reassurances; as a noun, influence.

When the White House is concerned with a legislator's possible defection on a vote, instructions are passed to the congressman's colleagues or to lobbyists to "stroke" him (from the image of the raised hackles of an angry or frightened animal.)

The noun form is less frequently used, and has a different meaning: a person with "stroke" is one with

CLOUT; the metaphor is possibly from golf or tennis.

When the author used this definition in a *New York Times* article in 1975, Meridyth Senes of Wynnewood, Pa., wrote: "If anything, 'stroke' . . . would have derived more from the street phrase 'different strokes for different folks,' with its obvious sexual connotation." The suggestion that "stroke" as a verb has to do with the rhythm of intercourse is not far-fetched: in Navy slang, "to stroke around" is to wander about, looking for company, similar to the Air Force term "strafing the *Strasse.*" Significantly, "to stroke" in auto-racing argot means to mill the crankshaft for a longer plunge.

Russell Baker of the *New York Times,* on April 4, 1978, compared stroking to another form of presidential persuasion, JAWBONING: "President Nixon, revolted by such direct methods, preferred what he called 'stroking,' a process of jawboning so sweet to the strokee's earbones that the victim fell into a hypnotic state in which he could be deboned without realizing it."

STROKE OF A PEN   by executive order; action that can be taken by a Chief Executive without legislative action.

Candidate John F. Kennedy said in 1960 that the President could end discrimination in federally financed housing with a "stroke of the pen," a phrase that was then current with civil rights leaders impatient with Eisenhower. When Kennedy, as President, delayed taking such action himself, Martin Luther King, Jr., called on him to "give segregation its death blow through a stroke of the pen," and disenchanted civil rights advocates began sending pens to the White House as a not-so-subtle reminder.

Typical prose use was in this passage from a 1966 book by Raymond Moley: "The closing of the banks was the anesthetic before the major operation. A proclamation that had been considered for weeks, assured of authority under the law, required merely the stroke of a White House pen. The hard part lay ahead."

In 1971 Leonard Woodcock, president of the United Automobile Workers, objected to a wage-price freeze in these words: "If this Administration thinks that just by issuing an edict, by the stroke of a pen, they can tear up contracts, they are saying to us they want war. If they want war, they can have war."

The political coinage was by stockbroker-poet Edmund Clarence Stedman (1833–1908) in a poem titled "Wanted—A Man":

Give us a man of God's own mould,
Born to marshal his fellow-men;
One whose fame is not bought and sold
At the stroke of a politician's pen.

STUMP   as a noun, the campaign trail; as a verb, to exhort informally, usually outdoors, in a campaign.

To achieve a dominating posture, a frontier speechmaker would use a convenient tree stump as a platform. The earliest reference clearly shows the origin; Ann Maury, in her 1716 *Memoirs of a Huguenot Family,* wrote, "I went down to the Saponey Indian town. There is in the center of the circle a great stump of a tree. I asked the reason they left it standing, and they informed me that it was for one of their head men to stand upon when he had anything of consequence to relate to them, so that being raised, he might the better be heard."

By 1838 it was part of the American political vocabulary. The *New York Herald* tells of the Speaker of the House, James K. Polk, "Stumping it about the State of Tennessee." And the *Hamilton* (Ohio) *Intelligencer* was editorializing sniffily about this innovation which it was quite certain would not last: " 'Stumping it' is a new game for candidates for Governor in Ohio, and we very much doubt whether the 'Experiment' will be sanctioned by a dignified people."

Congressman Isaac N. Arnold of Illinois, reminiscing in an address before the House of Representatives about the career of Abraham Lincoln, recounted how, a few years earlier, "The friends of Lincoln were not without anxiety when the challenge was given, and accepted, for a campaign on the stump" (with Stephen A. Douglas as the opposition).

As with other apt phrases, this one was picked up across the ocean, sometimes in exalted circles. Prime Minister Gladstone displeased Queen Victoria by campaigning for a broadening of the eligible electorate in a tour through Scotland while she was staying at her Balmoral residence in the same area. Her Majesty's secretary, General Ponsonby, noted "his constant speeches at every station. . . . The Queen is utterly disgusted with his stump oratory—so unworthy of his position—almost under her very nose."

Others have defined stump oratory in the same vein, as bombastic, even inflammatory; generally the word is accepted today in its original sense, and no candidate can afford to let a campaign go by without taking to the stump. See HUSTINGS; STEMWINDER.

Another meaning of stump, as a verb, is to pose a question that the person asked cannot answer. It is possible that this is connected with embarrassed stump speakers.

After listening to a speech by President Harding in 1921, H. L. Mencken wrote: "The stump speech, put into cold type, maketh the judicious to grieve. But roared from an actual stump, with arms flying and eyes flashing and the old flag overhead, it is certainly and brilliantly effective." See THE SPEECH.

SUAVITER IN MODO, *see* **EGGHEAD.**

SUFFICIENCY, *see* **PARITY.**

SUMMITRY   the art of dealing at the top level; the notion that diplomacy can best be practiced by face-to-face meeting of world leaders.

Winston Churchill, unhappy with the international impasse in 1950 that his friend Bernard Baruch had described as the COLD WAR, recalled the wartime meetings with Stalin and Roosevelt and issued a call for a "parley at the summit."

Immediately, diplomats around the world pointed out that such a meeting would bring about little of substance, that the hopes of the world would be raised and dashed, and that many months of intricate preplanning on lower levels would be necessary before any decisions could be made as to what would be discussed.

Churchill dismissed all this. "This conference should not be overhung by a ponderous or rigid agenda or led into mazes of technical details, zealously contested by hordes of experts and officials drawn up in a vast cumbrous array."

As a rule, foreign ministers resist summit conferences, on the theory that world problems are too complex to be left to world leaders and the world is led to expect too much;

what's more, the second echelon is left to fight over what was said, meant, and not meant. "Conferences at the top level are always courteous," career diplomat Averell Harriman said in 1955. "Name-calling is left to the foreign ministers."

After his first conference with Nikita Khrushchev (see SPIRIT OF), Dwight Eisenhower found that conferences at the top level can be disastrous. The 1959 summit conference in Paris was aborted by Khrushchev over the U-2 incident. On his way home, the disappointed President spoke to the staff of the U.S. embassy in Lisbon: "Did you see that cartoon not long ago where it says, 'The next speaker needs all the introduction he can get'? Well, I rather feel that way, after coming from this last meeting in Paris."

Turning a careful phrase in 1959, Senator John Kennedy said, "It is far better that we meet at the summit than at the brink." As President, he had a rough session at the summit with Khrushchev in 1961. But, wrote Sorensen, "The Soviet leader also made clear his belief in summitry. If the heads of state cannot resolve problems, how can officials at a lower level? He liked as much personal contact as possible, he said, no matter how able one's ambassadors might be —just as natural love is better than love through interpreters."

An unexpected defense of summitry came from Indian diplomat Arthur Lall in *Modern International Negotiation* in 1967: "The public exhortations, the invitations to Washington and Moscow, the wooing by important powers, praise for the acumen and wisdom of its statesmen, appeals in the interest of world harmony, and the spotlight and the publicity of international conferences, go to make up a much more accept-able political context for action by most governments than a courtroom or than wholly QUIET DIPLOMACY."

A question that always arises in debating the use of summitry is: How much freedom of action does a world leader have? How bound is he by past policy, and how much leeway does his Politburo or Congress or public opinion at home give him? The quiet style of Alexei Kosygin led this question to be asked in 1967 before the summit conference with Lyndon Johnson at Glassboro, New Jersey. This meeting was arranged hurriedly, during a trip to the UN to debate the Arab-Israeli war, proving that the need for extended advance preparation was not as overwhelming as it seemed. Though the conference was fringed with warnings not to expect much, and indeed did not produce much, President Johnson expressed this attitude afterward: "It does help a lot to sit down and look at a man right in the eye and try to reason with him, particularly if he is trying to reason with you." See COME NOW, AND LET US REASON TOGETHER.

In late 1971, on the eve of several international conferences, Peter Lisagor of the *Chicago Daily News* wrote: "On the face of things, the President would seem to have another spectacular in the works, designed to reduce the terror on earth even as it enhances his own fortunes. The mixture is hard to deplore. Yet summit diplomacy is risky business, consuming presidential prestige and power in enterprises that may produce a small return. It often is an act of self-exaltation, an ego trip."

In *Present at the Creation*, Dean Acheson wrote in 1970 that summitry traced back to the early sixteenth century, and that in only two cases was it clearly successful: the meetings at Münster and Osnabrück in 1648 that ended the Thirty Years' War with the Peace of Westphalia, and the Congress of Vienna in 1814.

Summits have "all too often been a gamble, the experience nerve-wracking and the results unsatisfactory," wrote the former Secretary of State, quoting advice given to Woodrow Wilson's aide, Colonel Edward House, on the eve of Wilson's journey to Europe. "The moment President Wilson sits at the council table with these prime ministers and foreign secretaries," the adviser said, "he has lost all the power that comes from distance and detachment . . . he becomes merely a negotiator dealing with other negotiators."

Acheson added: "When a chief of state or head of government makes a fumble, the goal line is open behind him."

In a nondiplomatic context, the best-known uses of the word *summit* were Napoleon's ("Soldiers, from the summits of the pyramids, forty centuries look down upon you") and Edmund Burke's eulogy of Charles James Fox, quoted by John Kennedy as the keynote in *Profiles in Courage,* and recalled after the Cuban missile crisis of 1962: "He may live long, he may do much. But here is the summit. He never can exceed what he does this day."

SUNBELT that string of states across the South, Southwest, and Western U.S. which—by virtue of attractive climate and economic opportunity—have seen their populations grow dramatically, thereby becoming important (and often conservative) political forces.

Kevin Phillips, dubbed by *Newsweek* columnist Meg Greenfield "the prophet-geographer of the New Right," coined the phrase while writing his book *The Emerging Republi-* *can Majority* in 1967. That work, however, was not published until 1969; in the meantime, writer Garry Wills used it in a magazine article, quoting Phillips as the source, just before the Nixon Administration took office. In his book, Phillips held that a new political cycle was coming, its trend conservative and anti-Establishment. He rested a portion of his argument "on the post-1945 migration of many white Americans (including many of the traditionally Democratic white ethnic groups) to suburbia and the Sun Belt states of Florida, Texas, Arizona and California."

After its coinage in that political context, and its subsequent denunciation as part of a SOUTHERN STRATEGY, writers of demographic and economic stories found "sunbelt" useful. In the first half of the seventies, while the population of the twenty-one Northeastern and North Central states remained static, the population of the "sunbelt" states (using the phrase to include all the South and West) increased by about 2 percent per year. Advertising executive Mary Wells Lawrence called the growth area "the golden horseshoe": its U-shape stretched from Washington, D.C., around to Southern California and up the West Coast to Washington State. She pointed to the social impact of the new dominance of these areas: increased mobility, indoor-outdoor living, and a divorce rate double that of the Northeast.

In most current use, Phillips' two-word phrase is compressed to one word: A *New York Times* headline of January 25, 1978, read: "Census Data Show Growth Slowing in Part of Sunbelt." The absence of quotation marks illustrated the wide acceptance of the phrase.

The parent of the phrase was

"Bible belt," a coinage of H. L. Mencken.

SUNSET LAW a provision in a bill shutting off a program on a specific date, requiring re-examination and a fresh authorization in the future; a device to worry bureaucrats.

The technique, and the phrase, began in Colorado. Answering the author's query, Rosalie Schiff of Colorado Common Cause states: "The phrase 'sunset law' was coined by Mr. Craig Barnes, a member of our Board of Directors, at an Issues committee meeting in May 1975 . . . To our knowledge the term had not been used or suggested elsewhere. Mr. Barnes coined the term to describe a process whereby agencies would terminate periodically unless they could justify their continued existence. Since affirmative legislative action would be required for continued life, should an agency fail to prove a public need for its existence, the 'sun would set' on said agency.

"The two-fold purpose of Sunset is to require more public accountability from these agencies and to reduce the proliferation and growth of bureaucracy."

The idea behind the mechanism was expressed in *Go East, Young Man* by Supreme Court Justice William O. Douglas: "The great creative work of a federal agency must be done in the first decade of its existence if it is to be done at all. After that it is likely to become a prison of bureaucracy and of the inertia demanded by the Establishment of any respected agency. That is why I told FDR over and over again that every agency he created should be abolished in ten years. And since he might not be around to dissolve it, he should insert in the basic charter of the agency a provision for its termination. Roosevelt would al-

ways roar with delight at that suggestion, and of course never did do anything about it."

Because administrative agencies tend, after a while, to identify with the interests they are supposed to administer or regulate, the idea of incorporating a termination date appealed to many Colorado liberals; conservatives could be expected to be for any antibureaucratic measure. As a result of this broad appeal, sunset provisions passed handily in that state, later in Florida (perhaps due to an interest in SUNSHINE LAWS) and—with the sponsorship of Senator Edmund Muskie—nationally. Said Senator Muskie in proposing a "spending reform" act in 1976, the sunset plan was "a sensible plan for making certain that the programs we approve are working, and for ending those programs which are no longer needed."

The cut-off idea was embraced by candidate Jimmy Carter in his 1976 campaign, as the legislative counterpart of his administrative ZERO-BASE BUDGETING. "Sunset is the congressional complement to zero base budgeting in the Executive Branch," wrote Senator Muskie. "Sunset, too, is considerably more than program evaluation." However, the sun sometimes sets on a good coinage: the bill he put forward to require new budget authority every five years was titled "The Program Evaluation Act of 1977."

Colorado's new law caused some of its proponents to glow with pride. "We kayoed the athletic commission, flushed the sanitary engineers, and clipped the barbers," claimed Senate president Fred Anderson in 1977. The triple metaphor attracted the attention of *Rocky Mountain News* reporter Peter Blake, writing in *Inquiry* magazine: "The athletic commission never did much anyway, since there is virtually no professional boxing in Colorado. The main function of the board for professional sanitarians was to bestow honorary appendages on certain government employees, like 'Esq' for a lawyer. And as for the barber board, it was not clipped at all; it was merely combined with the cosmetology board (which controls hairdressers) and it is stronger than ever. In short, all the Colorado legislature has done so far is put a few dying animals out of their misery. Most regulatory agencies continue to bask in the noonday sun."

SUNSHINE LAWS measures to force the conduct of public business in public.

"Publicity is justly commended," wrote Supreme Court Justice Louis D. Brandeis, "as a remedy for social and industrial disease. Sunlight is said to be the best disinfectant and electric light the most efficient policeman."

The Florida Sunshine Act was first proposed in 1961; while it was being debated for six years, five other states —Arkansas, Indiana, Nebraska, New Jersey, and New Mexico—enacted open-meeting laws. The Florida act directed "All meetings . . . at which official acts are to be taken are declared to be public meetings open to the public at all times, and no resolution, rule, regulation or formal action shall be considered binding except as taken or made at such meeting."

In proposing similar legislation on the national level, Florida Senator Lawton Chiles wrote in 1974: "Experience under the sunshine law has shown that the open meeting principle does not hamper public business operations, but rather increases public confidence in government . . . Closed doors are not necessary to sound resolution of conflicting views and interests."

Many legislators who do not like to derogate open meetings publicly disagree privately: in the horse trading that goes on in closed committee sessions, they hold, sensible compromises are reached that could not be struck in the harsh light of PITILESS PUBLICITY. Although the Freedom of Information Act has made much material in the executive branch available to citizens, Congress has been unwilling to provide such access to its own files and deliberations. In states with sunshine laws, it is charged, much of the public business is done in advance of open meetings—in secret, making the "open" meeting a charade.

Despite the criticism of impracticality, and the derision leveled at OPEN COVENANTS, OPENLY ARRIVED AT, the pressure toward "government in the sunshine" has helped the trend toward more public disclosure of the governmental activities. For example, the author received a notice from the U.S. Commission on Civil Rights: "In accordance with the Government in the Sunshine Act, we are providing you notice of a change in the Dec. 8, 1977 activities of the Commission." The notice listed a new time and place of meeting, adding: "Agenda: a discussion of the Sunshine Act."

SUPERPATRIOTS flag-waving extremists; attack phrase on those who protest too much their love of country.

"I don't think the United States needs super-patriots," wrote President Eisenhower in 1962. "We need patriotism, honestly practiced by all of us, and we don't need these people that are more patriotic than you or anybody else."

Carl Schurz defined "mock patriotism" as "the kind of sentiment which leads a man to say with Decatur 'Our country, right or wrong.' " During the Spanish-American War, William McKinley warned the hotheads: "Impatience is not patriotism."

Time wrote in 1939 of a type called the "patrioteer," harshly defined as "the professional patriot, the kind of refuge-seeking scoundrel who waves a red-white-and-blue handkerchief when he should be wiping his own nose."

Dr. Samuel Johnson found plain—not even super—patriotism "the last refuge of a scoundrel." Some are more charitable. Adlai Stevenson, writing of the McCarthy era: "We have survived it. We shall survive John Birchism and all the rest of the super patriots—but only at the price of perpetual and truly patriotic vigilance."

The fashion in "super" words—from supercolossal to superduper and superpower—was set by George Bernard Shaw. Nietzsche's *Übermensch* had been translated as "Overman" or "Beyondman"; Shaw coined "Superman," who later left politics to become a comic strip "man of steel." "Superstar" became a familiar word of the sixties in both show business and sports, and "superpower" and appellation in world politics. "We will never become a superpower," Chinese Premier Chou En-lai told the Canadian Broadcasting Company in July of 1971; "we are opposed to the POWER POLITICS of the big powers." Though Chou used the term pejoratively, as leaders of nonsuperpowers occasionally do, the word is more generally used neutrally in reference to the U.S. and the Soviet Union.

A synonymous prefix, "ultra," is also used politically. There are ultraconservatives and ultraliberals; though there are superpatriots, there are no supertraitors.

Conservative satirist Vic Gold spoofed the fashion of denigrating patriotic fervor as "superpatriotism" by titling a fictitious work "Paul Revere and the Superpatriotic Tradition in American History."

See **KOOKS, NUTS AND; LITTLE OLD LADIES IN TENNIS SHOES; TURN-AROUNDS.**

SUPREME COURT FOLLOWS THE ELECTION RETURNS a cynical view that the supposedly dispassionate and disinterested Supreme Court bench usually reflects the current political scene.

This bit of irreverence was the work of Finley Peter Dunne's "Mr. Dooley."

America's war against Spain had just been concluded. The majority of Congress, swept up by a new feeling of America's **MANIFEST DESTINY** had approved the taking of the Philippines and of Puerto Rico from Spain. Puerto Rico was not part of the U.S.; yet our government claimed the right to collect taxes and to levy tariffs among its people. The Democratic party, in convention in 1900, had contended that wherever U.S. sovereignty extended, the people of that area gained the rights and protection of the U.S. Constitution; in the phrase of the day, "We hold that the Constitution follows the flag." The Democrats lost.

The Court labored until it came up with a fuzzy doctrine: territories like Puerto Rico weren't exactly foreign, since the U.S. had acquired them; on the other hand, they weren't really domestic, either, so the U.S. government did have the right to levy taxes on these unrepresented people. This, more or less, agreed with the position of the winning Republicans.

All of which drew from Mr. Dooley the caustic comment, "No matter whether th' Constitution follows th' flag or not, the Supreme Coort follows the iliction returns."

Chief Justice Hughes once said, "We are under a Constitution, but the Constitution is what the judges say it is." By and large, the members of the Court reflect their time and the judgments of the populace, giving support to Dunne's gibe.

See NINE OLD MEN; DOOLEY, MR.

SURFACE   to allow to become known; to bring a secret supporter into public view.

In many campaigns, there are those who are willing to provide ideas, solicitation efforts, and money on an "off-the-record" basis. In addition, there are those whom the candidate may not wish to have publicly support him.

When these supporters decide to switch from covert to overt, they are said to "surface"; often they are forced to surface by inquisitive newsmen.

Politics adopted the word from espionage, where the word is used in the same way. "CIA Director Richard Helms's public record for the next five years is a total blank," wrote *Time* magazine. "When he surfaced in 1952, it was as deputy to the chief of the plans division, the so-called 'dirty tricks' department . . ."

Apparently the word, as a verb and in its present sense, comes from the action of a submerged submarine coming to the surface of the water.

SURRENDER ON MORNING-SIDE HEIGHTS   a party-unity conference between Eisenhower and Taft after the bruising fight for the 1952 nomination, which Democrats tried to exploit.

Like the Nixon-Rockefeller COMPACT OF FIFTH AVENUE in 1960, the meeting between Dwight Eisenhower and Robert A. Taft in 1952 was an attempt at unifying a party that was immediately characterized as a SELL-OUT by the opposition party, as well as by some disgruntled Republican liberals.

The meeting took place on September 12, 1952, at 60 Morningside Drive in New York City, Eisenhower's residence as president of Columbia University. Earlier, Taft had let it be known from his post-convention vacation retreat in Murray Bay, Canada, that his price for active support of the ticket would be some written assurances on policy. This Democrats called "the ultimatum of Murray Bay," but it did not catch on; Adlai Stevenson's characterization of the meeting as "the surrender on Morningside Heights" had greater appeal.

A statement issued after the meeting had a strong Taft flavor. They had agreed that an issue at home was "liberty against creeping socialization" and Taft added, "General Eisenhower emphatically agrees with me in the proposal to reduce drastically over-all expenses. . . . General Eisenhower has also told me that he believes strongly in our system of Constitutional limitations on Government power and that he abhors the left-wing theory that the Executive had unlimited powers. . . . General Eisenhower has also told me that he believes in the basic principles of the Taft-Hartley Law, its protection of the people and the freedom of the union members themselves against the arbitrary use of power by big business or big labor, and is opposed to its repeal . . ." He concluded, "It is fair to say that our differences are differences of degree."

Stevenson slammed away at the

meeting throughout the campaign: "I wonder what happened to all those declarations of undying principle we heard from both sides while they were calling each other nasty names in Chicago. . . . It looks as if Taft lost the nomination but won the nominee . . . when he walked out of the General's house in New York with the surrender in writing I have never seen such a contented smile since the cat swallowed the canary . . . part of the price of the embrace on Morningside Heights has been to lay no affirmative program before this nation for its approval."

Eisenhower recalled:

Some journalists and the Democratic nominee, however, seemed to think that here was raw drama. The opposition saw in this meeting a great "surrender on Morningside Heights." The fact was that Senator Taft and I had agreed emphatically on the need for fiscal sanity in the government, as on most other issues, long before the breakfast talk. In the succeeding weeks he evidenced his enthusiasm for our common cause by a rugged round of campaigning which included more than thirty speeches in nineteen states.

This is one of the classic minuets of politics. A savage primary is followed by a sullen requirement for assurances; these are then given at a sweetness-and-light unity meeting or LOVE FEAST; this is then attacked and derided by the opposition which tries to keep the primary split from healing; that attack is then pooh-poohed by the unifying candidates. The French analysis of this type of activity was given by Alphonse Karr in 1849: *"Plus ça change, plus c'est la même chose"*—the more things change, the more they stay the same.

SURROGATE CANDIDATE, *see* **ADVANCE MAN.**

SWAP HORSES, *see* **DON'T CHANGE HORSES.**

SWEETHEART   shorter than arm's length; collusive.

In labor terminolgy, a "sweetheart contract" is one in which a union leader makes an unfavorable settlement for his fellow employees and then takes an emolument from management on the side.

The adjective has crossed into political parlance without the specifically illegal meaning, but with a connotation of favoritism. In 1977 President Carter's Director of the Office of Management and Budget, Bert Lance, was accused by this author of arranging for a "sweetheart loan"; that is, one on abnormally favorable terms. *New York Times* columnist Tom Wicker used the word in July 1977 in its most modestly pejorative sense: "The Administration's broader anti-inflation policy is based on a vague, soft, sweetheart reliance on business voluntarism . . ."

In business, a "sweetener" is an acceptable extra incentive to close a deal; in politics, such sweetness strikes a sour note.

SWING AROUND THE CIRCLE, *see* **NON-POLITICAL TRIP.**

SWING VOTER   one who votes for the man, not the party; the independent vote that often "swings" elections one way or the other.

Several political scientists have estimated that not more than 60 percent of the American electorate is partisan and regular in its voting habits. As personalities and issues have become more significant than party affiliation, the size of the swing vote has grown. Pollster Samuel Lubell noted in 1959 that the electorate "seems to have undergone a curious quickening of its voting reflexes" in elections since 1948, making it "easier to shift the party allegiance of the American voter."

"Swing vote" and "swing voter" are not used to any extent in England; instead, an obsolete American expression, "floater," defines the independent group. In the U.S., floater enjoyed its greatest popularity in 1888, when the Treasurer of the Republican National Committee, W. W. Dudley, was charged with recommending to the Indiana state committee that they secure "floaters in blocks of five." This was construed to mean the purchase of votes wholesale; politicians in ancient Greece dealt out bribes to voters in "blocks of ten."

The slang term for public is rooted in fickleness; the word "mob," considered slang but in use in the English language since the sixteenth century, is traced to Claudius, a Latin poet of the third century B.C., who wrote of *mobile . . . vulgus* (the fickle crowd). Johann Wolfgang von Goethe came up with a simile that explains one reason for the growth of the swing vote: "In politics, as on the sickbed, people toss from one side to the other, thinking they will be more comfortable."

SWITCHER registered voter in one party likely to "split his ticket" (see SPLIT TICKET) on the basis of having done so before.

Pollster Oliver Quayle includes a "switcher analysis" in most of his surveys of the voting complexion of an area. These are voters who have crossed party lines in previous elections, indicating a lack of deep party commitment and a likely source of votes for an attractive opposition candidate.

Independents and SWING VOTERS have no party alliances; *switchers* do, if only nominal.

Adlai Stevenson told a story in 1952 about "the little boy who asked his father what a convert was, and the father—evidently a politically minded father—said, 'Well, son, if a Republican becomes a Democrat, he is a convert.' And what, asked the boy, is a Democrat who becomes a Republican? With a scowl his father said, 'Why, he's a traitor, of course.' "

A "switcher issue" is one that causes a fiercely committed voter to abandon all other patterns and preferences: in the seventies, abortion and gun control were switcher issues.

SYNTAX, PRESIDENTIAL, *see* **EISENHOWER SYNTAX.**

SYSTEM, THE the political structure, not to be despised when it works for you.

Originally "the System" was a phrase accompanied by a sneer, synonymous with "City Hall" or "the Establishment" or "the bureaucracy." In 1974, however, as the forces of government joined the anti-Nixon protestors, the phrase "The System Works" came into wide use, and the System took on a rosy glow as a protector of individual rights.

The nonpejorative use of the System was, in turn, parodied. In the *American Spectator* (January 1977), editor R. Emmet Tyrrell disparaged the Carter election victory as having been the result of a bored electorate: "The voice was faint: 27.5 percent of the people said Jimmy, 26 percent said Jerry, and a whopping 46.5 percent said yecch. The system works!"

Although the phrase was used in a positive sense, it had not lost its overtone of entrenched-authority-to-be-opposed. In 1978, when Philadelphia U.S. Attorney David Marston, a Republican, was fired with an explanation from Democratic Attorney General Griffin Bell that "we have a system" (see INS AND OUTS), Marston retorted, "I don't agree with that. They had a system too in Philadelphia before I got there and I didn't accept that system." In the sense used by Marston, "the system" was a matrix of official corruption and mob influence.

As "the System" has replaced "the Establishment," it has been overtaken in some ways by the "PROCESS," which is not capitalized; see that entry for differences, and AMERICAN SYSTEM for origins.

TAKE A WALK   leave the party after a dispute.

The phrase entered the political language with Al Smith's comment after the renomination of FDR in 1936: "I guess I'll have to take a walk." Democrats lashed back at him with his own symbol: "The brown derby has gone high hat."

Those who BOLT—a racing term— are called MUGWUMPS—an Indian term—and *soreheads,* from the expression, "mad as a bear with a sore head." An *Albany* (N.Y.) *Weekly Argus* correspondent wrote in 1848: "I have just returned from a ringed, striped, and speckled 'sore-head' demonstration at Sharon Springs," in regard to the formation of the Free Soil party.

Bolters have been denounced by party regulars as "shreakers" (now obsolete) determined to "rule or ruin" (still in use). To *bolt* and to *take a walk* and to *change stripes* is to make an (almost) irrevocable decision to *cross the street* to the other party; to *sit it out* or to *go fishing* means to remain within the party without supporting—but not publicly rejecting— its candidate in a particular election. To go OFF THE RESERVATION is to take a short, temporary walk, opposing a candidate of one's own party with the intention of returning to the fold after the election.

TAKE HER BY THE HAND, *see* **STAND IN THE DOORWAY.**

TAMMANY TIGER   symbol of big-city machines.

The Society of Tammany was a fraternal organization which controlled the New York Democratic party from the middle of the nineteenth century to the middle of the twentieth: often corrupt, sometimes effective, it was the prototype of all urban political machines in the U.S. and remains the best known today.

At its height, the motto of its leadership might well have been the remark made by Tammany leader George Washington Plunkitt: "I seen my opportunities and I took 'em."

The organization was founded in 1789 by New Yorkers who thought they saw a dangerous drift toward aristocracy in the popularity among the wealthier and wellborn of such societies as St. Andrew's. The Society, named after a Delaware chief famed for his sagacity—Chief Tamany, or more likely, Tamanend—dedicated itself to the defense of democracy. At the beginning of the nineteenth century, with Aaron Burr's help, it became the most efficient political organization of the day.

Legend has it that the tiger symbol came from a stuffed tiger's head on the front of a fire engine used by Tammany in parades; cartoonist Thomas

Nast popularized the tiger symbol in his attacks on the Tweed Ring, which is believed to have stolen anywhere from $200 to $300 million in its heyday.

Those who thought Nast's attacks and the subsequent exposures meant the end of Tammany were mistaken. "Honest John" Kelly took over, creating the classic structure of absolute, unquestioning autocracy which was inherited by Richard Croker and later by Charles Murphy.

Reformers were in continual battle with Tammany; nearby boroughs were determined to keep their minions out. In 1876 R. G. Ingersoll said, "Tammany Hall bears the same relation to a penitentiary as a Sunday-school to the church." And in Brooklyn, the motto was: "The Tiger shall not cross the Bridge."

In modern times, Carmine de Sapio did much to reform the autocratic system—and cause his own downfall —by bringing about the direct election of district leaders by the RANK AND FILE. His successors have tried to stress the name "New York County Democratic Organization," as if Tammany were not the name of the club. Cartoonists, however, have too much invested in the tiger to let it die. But now the tiger, as drawn on most editorial pages, has lost much of its ferocity and usually appears battered and bandaged, but still alive.

See SACHEM; PAPER TIGER.

TANTAMOUNT TO ELECTION
as much as elected.

There must be an unwritten law prohibiting the use of the following: "Nomination in that solidly partisan district is the *equivalent* of election," or "being nominated there is as much as being elected." Equivalent to, as much as, the same as, equal to, amounts to—all are crushed under

the heel of the overwhelming political cliché, "tantamount to election."

Once the tanta is mounted, Election Day is a formality; the political pundit's favorite bromide rides triumphantly into the jungle of jargon. An amusing election-night parlor game is to count the number of times "tantamount to election" is used on television, a competition more rewarding to the viewer than seeing who calls the winners first on the basis of the fewest returns.

Only ridicule can break up such a rigidly stereotyped phrase; for the foreseeable future, "tantamount" will remain as close to "election" as "unmitigated" remains to "gall."

TAPS AND BUGS   electronic
eavesdropping equipment.

A "tap," short for "wiretap," means an intercept placed on a telephone; a "bug" is a tiny transmitter designed to send conversations to a receiver elsewhere. To be "wired" means to be outfitted with a "bug" so as to transmit a conversation to a receiver out of sight. Confusion is caused when a "bug" is used in a "tap"—by placing a transmitter in a telephone, the conversation is effectively tapped, though no wire intercept is made.

"To have a tap in" does not necessarily mean to have a wiretap monitoring somebody; frequently the phrase means to have nonelectronic access to a leaker, the meaning taken from the way sap is tapped from a tree.

Lexicographer Peter Tamony found an early use of the word in Civil War literature, referring to a telegraph wire. "Tapping the wires at Lebanon Junction," ran an account of Morgan's raid of 1863, "we learned from intercepted despatches that the garrison at Louisville was much alarmed, and in expectation of immediate attack."

In 1878, two years after Alexander Graham Bell invented the telephone, George B. Preston warned: "The observations made in the course of these experiments convinced those present that the telephone presents facilities for the dangerous practice of tapping the wire, which may make it useful or dangerous, according as it is used for proper or dangerous purposes."

Mr. Tamony writes: "Telephone wiretapping, according to the New York police, dates from 1895 when a former employee of the N.Y. Telephone company walked into headquarters to suggest the possibilities of such information gathering and surveillance. However, another story bases such methods from a chance discovery of the 'Extension telephone' in a home by a telephone company employee in 1909, this man becoming the 'King of the Wiretappers' in the service of the U.S. government from 1920 to 1949. During World War I, eavesdropping was widely encouraged, the government tapping thousands of lines from a central office switchboard set up in the N.Y. Customs House. Whenever a suspected alien lifted his receiver a light flashed, and a stenographer recorded the conversation."

The author, whose home telephone was tapped on White House orders by the FBI in 1969, later obtained the order from one agent to another for "technical surveillance," which was the government euphemism for wiretapping. Searching for earlier political use, the author was directed to William Roscoe Thayer's biography of Theodore Roosevelt, written in 1919, in the section about the Republican convention in Chicago in 1912: "Roosevelt had not intended to appear at the Convention, but when he

discovered that the long-distance telephone from Chicago to Oyster Bay, by which his managers conferred with him, was being tapped, he changed his mind."

The term "bugged," in the sense of "electronically overheard," came into use in the twenties. In A. J. Pollock's *The Underworld Speaks* (San Francisco, 1935) an entry reads: "Bugged, a room in which a dictaphone has been installed by the police." Speculates Mr. Tamony: "As anything that impeded a criminal process was a nuisance, a *bugbear,* calculated to drive a burglar crazy, or bugs, these perhaps are the basis of the allusion to sound detection and wiring."

For a different etymology of BUG, see that entry.

TARIFFS, *see* KENNEDY ROUND.

TASK FORCE committee given a military name to make it sound vigorous.

The appointment of a committee has long been an effective political gambit to avoid direct action, but many people began to bridle at the word—"another committee" became a derisive term implying delay, unfiled reports, and meandering discussion leading up blind alleys.

Television commentator Richard Harkness took note of this prevalent attitude in 1960. "When it comes to facing up to serious problems," he wrote, "each candidate will pledge to appoint a committee. And what is a committee? A group of the unwilling, picked from the unfit, to do the unnecessary. But it all sounds great in a campaign speech." See BLUE RIBBON PANEL.

John F. Kennedy fulfilled the promises to appoint committees, but he avoided the static word. Within two weeks after his election, he dictated a memorandum to his aides on Latin America ("Who should chair the task force—what about Berle?") and Africa ("We should set up a similar task force . . .") and foreign aid ("We should set up a task force on the distribution of our agricultural surpluses abroad . . .").

In 1960, as "task force" reached full flower, two linguistics professors discussed the matter in an issue of *American Speech.* Acheson L. Hench of the University of Virginia revealed a usage that he had cherished for eleven years waiting for the phrase to mature: a clipping from the March 1, 1949, *Richmond* (Va.) *Times Dispatch:* "The work stoppage [the strike of garbage and trash collectors] resulted from an attempt by the city to try out a 'task force' system of collections. Under this plan, workers are assigned a certain route to be covered each day. When they complete their route, they can go home, regardless of how long it has taken . . . if they fail to get over the entire route in one regular work day, they must catch up the next day. The 'task force' system was to have been tried by 21 collectors in South Richmond . . ."

Professor Thomas Pyles, now of Northwestern, performed a linguistic feat by using twelve space-age clichés in a single intelligible sentence: *"Task force* and *breakthrough* are attractive additions to the vocabulary of those who are geared to the space age, who spearhead drives, set target dates, make spot checks, give rundowns and fill-ins—in short, of those who take an overall view instead of merely a comprehensive one, and who give the rest of us the advantage of their thinking on whatever is truly meaningful in the American way of life."

In the Justice Department, a committee of lawyers set up in a region to combat organized crime is called a "strike force"—like "task force," a naval term.

TAX AND TAX, *see* **SPEND AND SPEND.**

TAX REVOLT a movement to roll back rapidly increasing property taxes; more generally, an uprising of middle-class taxpayers against the rise in the cost of government.

Who shall be taxed how much has always been a most sensitive political subject. Liberals, sensing voter discontent about the rise in taxes in the seventies, concentrated on the unfairness of the tax system: "tax inequities." In this way, they sought to channel the resentment along populist lines: the reason our tax system is "a disgrace to the human race," as candidate Jimmy Carter put it, was that rich people were getting through the tax "loopholes" and the average man had to pay the rich man's share.

The phrase "taxpayer's revolt" was originally popularized around this unfairness idea. In 1968 Joseph Barr —longtime Undersecretary of the Treasury, appointed to the top job in President Johnson's final months in office—created a stir by testifying to Congress that more than 240 people who earned over a quarter-million dollars were paying no taxes, thanks to the "loopholes" (otherwise called incentives) in the tax system. He predicted that resentment at this kind of inequity would cause a "taxpayer's revolt."

The Nixon Administration, in its 1969 tax-reform act, worked out a "minimum tax" schedule that made it difficult for anyone to completely avoid tax payments, but the stress on unfairness was continued by Democratic candidates George McGovern in 1972 and Jimmy Carter in 1976 (see **THREE-MARTINI LUNCH**).

However, what ultimatedly caused the "tax revolt" of 1978 was not resentment at unfairness so much as anger by middle-class taxpayers at the rising level of taxation. Many felt their taxes provided too much welfare for the nonworking, and too much work for "bureaucrats."

"Tax-bracket creep" was one element: with a DOUBLE DIGIT inflation, these middle-income taxpayers found themselves pushed into higher tax brackets on the same purchasing power. In the state of California, soaring property taxes were the trigger: as property assessments rose, many retired homeowners—whose income was fixed, or who were living on savings, the value of which was eroding —were forced to move to cheaper neighborhoods, which seemed to them the antithesis of the American dream.

A movement to lower the tax rates substantially and permanently had been brewing in the mid-seventies. Arthur Laffer, a USC economist, interested Congressman Jack Kemp (Rep-N.Y.) and others in the "Laffer curve," a chart showing the relationship between tax rates and revenue production: it was his idea that the current high tax rates depressed incentive and growth, and lowered revenues—defeating its own purpose. This apporach provided the philosophical framework to a drive to cut tax rates that would otherwise be suspect as "irresponsible."

In June of 1978, despite the united opposition of California Governor Edmund G. Brown and most of the press and political leadership in that state, "Proposition 13"—the Jarvis-Gann initiative to reduce property taxes to 1 percent of market value— passed by a 2-to-1 landslide. Howard Jarvis, a veteran tax lobbyist, ap-peared on the cover of *Time*, and both *Time* and *Newsweek* featured the same phrase on their covers: "Tax Revolt!"

"The cry of pain from voters," grumbled the *New York Times* editorially, "has made tax cutting a new political credo. And the theory offered by the Laffer Curve makes the idea even more seductive . . . unfortunately, with inflation running close to 10 percent, the Federal Government cannot afford to cut taxes . . ."

Which was the way of FISCAL RESPONSIBILITY: holding down the deficits by maintaining tax rates? Or cutting taxes on the theory that this would ultimatley increase revenues, an anomaly that had taken place in the early sixties? In the "tax revolt" (the preferred shortening of "taxpayer's revolt"), liberals, worried about a cut in services to the poor, were surprised to find some NEW CONSERVATIVES willing to take the chance of high short-term deficits. They suspected rightly that the conservatives would call for a cut in government spending if the deficit stayed too high too long.

Thus the original "revolt" over tax *unfairness* never took place; instead, the voters in California rebelled against the *levels* of taxation. Many political leaders saw this as evidence that voters wanted to SEND THEM A MESSAGE: more than tax reform, what was wanted was tax reduction.

TAX SHARING collection of revenues by the federal government, returned directly to the state governments without federal control of state expenditures.

Grants-in-aid from the federal government to the states include close supervision of spending. The special attraction to states of *tax sharing* is that it eliminates federal control of the way federally collected money is spent, while removing from states the political stigma of tax collection.

Walter Heller, first Kennedy's and then Johnson's chairman of the Council of Economic Advisers, began to promote the plan in 1964. As the economy produced greater tax revenues, he reasoned, the extra money could be used for increased federal spending (and further undesirable centralization) *or* tax reduction (not likely) *or* reduction of the national debt (deflationary and least likely of all). A fourth alternative could be the return of a portion of the federal tax revenues to the states for expenditures as they saw fit.

Heller took as his text a White House press release promising exploration of new "methods of channeling federal revenues to states and localities which will reinforce their independence while enlarging their capacity to serve their citizens."

Expanding on this theme, Heller held: "Federal grants to serve highly specialized objectives have proliferated in recent years. And once established, they do not yield gracefully to change or abolition. Unless this trend is reversed, federal aids may weave a web of particularism, complexity, and federal direction which will significantly inhibit a state's freedom of movement. The picture of Gulliver and the Lilliputians comes to mind."

After flirting with the idea as part of his CREATIVE FEDERALISM, President Johnson backed away from tax sharing, partly because of the growing needs of the war in Vietnam, partly because Heller's TRIAL BALLOON had drawn fire from some liberals. Leon Keyserling (like most economists, he called the plan *revenue sharing*) pointed out: "The more we become *one* nation rather than *fifty* states, the more our economic and so-

cial problems require national treatment."

Republicans in Congress and in the state capitols loved the idea and took it to heart. They pointed to the cost efficiency of collection, and more important to the renewal of supervision of spending by "government closest to the people"—i.e., the states and localities, where Republicans traditionally fared better than on the national level.

Richard Nixon preferred the term "revenue sharing" and made it the keystone of his "New American Revolution"—the method by which he proposed to "reverse the flow of power in this country."

In his 1973 budget message, he wrote: "Revenue sharing has been debated at length. . . . The states and cities urgently require this aid; individual Americans need it for everything from improved law enforcement to tax relief." Democrats in Congress, seeing this as a diminution of their power, refused to share the President's enthusiasm, and passed a bill for a limited amount of string-free aid to states.

TEACH-IN, *see* **SIT-IN.**

TECHNOCRAT a scientist or engineer in a position of power, making policy in areas that appear too difficult for the laymen to judge.

"How unlike Stalin and Khrushchev," wrote the *Saturday Evening Post* during Alexei Kosygin's first visit to the U.S. in 1967, "is the quiet, rather dour technocrat Kosygin."

Technocracy was a movement that enjoyed a brief vogue in California early in the Depression. Coined in 1919 by William Henry Smythe in a call for a rule by technicians, it was popularized by disciples of Thorstein Veblen, using his 1921 book, *The En-*

gineers and the Price System, as their guide. The movement urged that government be placed in the hands of scientists and engineers ("But Hoover was an engineer" was one criticism); the end of the profit system; the application of all modern techniques and discoveries to the alleviation of human want; a working-age span from twenty-five years to forty-five years; and a work year of 132 hours.

Historian Robert Glass Cleland described technocracy as "a strange mixture, so far as the layman is qualified to judge, of scientific principles, mumbo jumbo, and skillful publicity." Its immediate successor was "Utopianism," which Cleland called "a goulash of technocracy, State Socialism, the Ku Klux Klan, Populism, Pacifism, Evangelism and Voodoo." (Slogans for these kinds of goulash were "End Poverty in California" and "Thirty Dollars Every Thursday.")

After a period of disuse, "technocrat" came back into use in the fifties to describe members of the MILITARY-INDUSTRIAL COMPLEX who deal with the expenditures of huge sums for weapons systems. The newer use of the word is simply a shortening of "technical bureaucrat," or administrator of scientific programs for industry and government. As with most words ending in -crat, it is mildly pejorative: though *democrat* is good, *autocrat, aristocrat, bureaucrat* (see BUREAUCRACY), and *technocrat* are suspect.

The underlying suspicion of technocrats was expressed by Harold Macmillan in 1950: "Fearing the weakness of democracy men have often sought safety in technocrats. There is nothing new in this. It is as old as Plato. But frankly the idea is not attractive to the British. . . . We have not overthrown the divine right of kings to fall down before the divine right of experts."

See NEW CLASS.

TELL IT LIKE IT IS   an exhortation by student demonstrators and crowds to their leaders, demanding an articulation of the audience's own feelings.

Evidence of the New Left's faith in "participatory democracy" (or fetish of leadership-rejection) is that its most popular battle cry was directed not from speaker to crowd, but from crowd to speaker. Though this is hardly new—"GIVE 'EM HELL, HARRY!" was one precursor—it indicates a rare and powerful two-way communication between spokesman and group. In Arab countries, demonstrations have long been conducted in a singsong, speaker-shouts, crowd-shouts-back fashion. In his MARTIN, BARTON AND FISH speech, FDR encouraged the crowd to anticipate repetition of the slogan and join in. But rarely in U.S. politics has the rank and file been so much an organized, disciplined, practiced part of a demonstration as in the civil rights and commingled New Left movement, with its chanting, clapping, "Jim, Crow, [*clap, clap*] Must, Go!" This participation has extended to speech-listening, where the listener encourages the speaker with approving shouts.

Alert cartoonists and writers in 1967 picked up the expression and used or parodied it. A cartoon in the *New York Times Book Review* showed a long-haired, "with-it" teen-ager calling to his balding, bespectacled father sitting at a typewriter: "Write it like it is, Pop!"

Profilist Thomas B. Morgan, writing in *Life* about playwright Edward Albee, concluded: "One can only hope that one day—perhaps even next season—he will find a new spark that will enable him once again to tell it like it is."

Grammarians would render the slogan "Tell it the way it is," or "Tell it as it is," but standard usage was dealt a near-fatal blow in the U.S. by the R. J. Reynolds Tobacco Company's slogan, "Winston Tastes Good Like a Cigarette Should."

The expression began to fade in the late sixties, to be replaced by "Right on!"

TENNIS SHOES, *see* **LITTLE OLD LADIES IN TENNIS SHOES.**

TERRORISM persuasion by fear; the intimidation of society by a small group, using as its weapon that society's repugnance at the murder of innocents.

Terrorisme may have originated with the Jacobins of the French Revolution. *Le Néologiste Français* (published in 1796) claimed that the extremists had coined the term about themselves and used it proudly, but soon after the "reign of terror," the word was a term of abuse with a connotation of criminality. In 1795 British statesman Edmund Burke wrote of "thousands of those hell hounds called terrorists" that afflicted the French people.

Although it temporarily had a secondary meaning of ALARMIST, the word "terrorist" traveled from the particular Jacobins to a system using fear of sudden and unexpectable violence to coerce others into obedience, or—in modern times—to trigger such official repression as to encourage revolution.

The names of sects employing terrorism have become synonyms for violence or irrationality. In A.D. 70, the *zealots* in Palestine had a group called the "sicarii" who attacked crowds on holidays; in the eleventh century, the *assassins* roamed Persia and Syria, killing political leaders systematically, always with a dagger as a part of a sacramental act; in the nineteenth century, the *thugs* in India always strangled their political victims with a silk tie.

In his book *Terrorism* (1977), Walter Laqueur focused on the dilemma that faces the targets of political fear: "The debate on whether or not one should compromise with terrorists has lasted a long time. Concessions may be advisable in some exceptional cases; consistent conciliation of terrorism on the other hand is bound to claim a higher toll in human life in the long run than resisting it . . . societies facing a determined terrorist onslaught will opt for a hard-line policy in any case." The unanswerable question that faces all students of terrorism: What to do when a terrorist group builds or acquires a nuclear weapon, and the means of its delivery?

The American use of the word was traced by Sperber and Trittschuh to an *Atlantic Monthly* in 1858: "Every form of terrorism [in Kansas], to which tyrants all alike instinctively resort to disarm resistance to their will, was launched at the property, the lives, and the happiness of the defenseless settlers." In 1868 *Harper's Weekly* headed an article about Democratic tactics to win Southern elections as "Political terrorism."

The words that describe terrorists reflect the bias of the describer. A *bomb thrower,* once a description of the bearded, wild-eyed anarchists of the 1890s, is now a term of amused contempt; a *partisan* connotes an irregular army unit, with a positive connotation lingering from the anti-Nazi partisans of Yugoslavia; a *guerrilla* is also positive, a hit-and-run defender of land against an invader, with the word used in Wellington's dispatches from the Peninsula campaign; *commando* is usually a self-description by a force striking in secret, and though it dates to the eighteenth century, is colored by its use for shock troops in Great Britain in World War II; *skyjacker* is an American neologism based on "hijacker," and is usually taken to mean a single deranged person unless further modified; *freedom fighter* is the most laudatory of descriptions, with a value judgment clear in the name, coined in a John Lehmann poem of 1942: "Their freedom-fighters staining red the snow."

Only the appellation *terrorist* is rejected by users of terror; the word is unqualifiedly negative, even though the philosophy can be construed to be —in the words of Wilhelm Weitling, the first German Communist— "founding the kingdom of heaven by unleashing the forces of hell."

TESTIMONIAL DINNERS, *see* **RUBBER-CHICKEN CIRCUIT.**

THAT MAN IN THE WHITE HOUSE a denunciation of Franklin Roosevelt by those too furious with him to even mention his name; now, an exasperated reference to any President.

FDR, hailed by Democrats in 1936 as "The Gallant Leader" and "The Gideon of Democracy," was called by Republicans "The New Deal Caesar," "The Raw Dealocrat," "The American Dictator," "The Feather-Duster of Dutchess County," "Kangaroosevelt," "Franklin Deficit Roosevelt," and most often "That Man in the White House."

Frank Sullivan, collecting clichés for *The New Yorker* in the early days of the New Deal, headed his list with "That Madman in the White House" and "That Fellow Down in Washington," who was admonished "You can't spend your way out of a Depression" and "Our children's children will be paying." Jokes of the time were "There's only six Dwarfs now . . . Dopey's in the White House" and "Why is a WPA worker like King Solomon? . . . He takes his pick and goes to bed."

Many commuter lines had what some of their riders called "Assassination Specials"; Robert Bendiner reported: ". . . the President of the United States was referred to by the kindlier passengers as 'That Man,' a designation useful for those who didn't want to be nasty in front of children and who couldn't bear to pronounce the dread name." When Elsa Maxwell threw a "Pet Hates Ball," guests were warned not to come dressed as "that man" with a cigarette holder because the ball would be jammed with imitation Roosevelts.

Like many epithets, it was soon adopted in an affectionate manner by the target's supporters. When Bronx Democratic leader Ed Flynn accepted the post of national chairman, he went home to break the news to his wife that they would have to move to Washington. "That silly grin on your face," Mrs. Flynn said to him before he said anything, "tells me 'that man' has talked you into it."

The phrase did not vanish with Roosevelt. It is now used occasionally to refer to any President who must accept criticism with the job. Political scientist Richard Neustadt wrote in 1960 that the public's "unreality" was an unseen enemy of the prestige and power of any president: "the groundless hopes, the unexpected happenings, the unaccepted outcomes that members of their public feel in daily life and relate, somehow, anyhow, to That Man in the White House."

See TRAITOR TO HIS CLASS.

THE MAN WHO the nominee; the person proposed for a nomination.

Speculation about a party designee usually includes the phrase "Who will be 'the man who' "? The phrase is taken from bombastic nomination speeches; since the speaker knows that the signal for a demonstration will be mention of the name of the man he is proposing, he usually refrains from giving the signal until the end of his speech. Throughout the nominating speech, of course, the audience knows who "the man who" is.

Until 1876, nominations at national political conventions were mercifully brief: in the 1860 Republican convention, Abraham Lincoln was put in nomination by Norman B. Judd of Illinois with a single sentence.

The oratorical dam burst in 1876 with the nomination of James G. Blaine by the Republicans. Robert G. Ingersoll of Illinois gave Blaine the title of "The Plumed Knight" in this classic "man-who":

Our country . . . asks for a man who has the audacity of genius; asks for a man who is the grandest combination of heart, conscience and brain beneath her flag. . . .

Like an armed warrior, like a plumed knight, James G. Blaine marched down the halls of the American Congress and threw his shining lance full and fair against the brazen foreheads of the defamers of our country and the maligners of his honor. . . .

Gentlemen of the convention . . . Illinois nominates for the next president of the United States that prince of parliamentarians, that leader of leaders, James G. Blaine.

"The Man" (without the who) is a reference of blacks to white men; of staffers to their leader; and in Washington, D.C., of politicians to the President.

THE SPEECH the standard stump speech developed during a campaign, compressing all the best issues and punch lines into a single adaptable package.

When *the* speech begins, reporters roll up their eyes and put away their pencils; they have heard it a hundred times. It contains the applause-pulling and laugh-getting lines of a dozen other speeches made in the same campaign by the same candidate. The difference is that it is not a television speech, with the necessity for new material; it is this particular candidate's particular gospel, refined to a rhythm comfortable for him, edited by practice and crowd reaction, punching away at the issues with pet phrases ("that do-nothing Eightieth Congress. . . . I think we have to get America moving again . . . that's your money he's spending, not his . . . the brotherhood of Man and the Fatherhood of God . . .").

A half-dozen writers may write speeches, but nobody, not even the candidate, writes what politicians call *the* speech. It seems to evolve by itself, and is carried around like sourdough to mix in with local jokes, timely references to newsbreaks and deferences to local party politicians.

When a candidate does not have his own *the* speech by the end of a campaign, he has not figured out in his own mind what the campaign was really all about.

THINKING ABOUT THE UNTHINKABLE, *see* UNTHINKABLE THOUGHTS.

THINK PIECE, *see* **BACK-GROUNDER; DOPE STORY; THUMBSUCKER.**

THINK TANK the brain; or a group of advisers; or, specifically, a research organization developing plans and projects for government and defense-connected industries.

Harry Truman, on his eightieth birthday, in 1964, used the phrase in its original sense of "brain," hoping to live until ninety, but only "if the old think tank is working."

The phrase enjoyed a brief period as substitute for **BRAIN TRUST** as politicians turned to colleges for **TASK FORCES** of academicians to provide new approaches to solving new and old problems. This meaning was superseded with the emergence of the RAND Corporation, the Hudson Institute, and similar institutions, where physical and social scientists can exercise and socialize in pleasant surroundings while doing profound research and planning on government or commercial assignments.

RAND, an acronym for "Research and Development," was set up in 1946 by Air Force General "Hap" Arnold. (Some say the name came from "random sample," which the firm used in its early research days.) He recognized the need for scientists to work in civilian surroundings, but wanted to keep their brainpower available to the military establishment. "Observers impressed with the high-level intellectual atmosphere at RAND," *Ramparts* magazine editor Sol Stern wrote, "have often referred to the Corporation as 'a university without students.' It would be more accurate to say that RAND, like other think tanks, has become a kind of halfway house between the university and the Department of Defense."

In a week-long series of articles on

"U.S. Think Tanks: A $2 Billion Industry," *New York Times* reporter Richard Reeves wrote in 1967:

> The work of think tanks is often similar to work done by universities, industrial research-and-development departments and management consultants. Although the term is used arbitrarily, the think tanks have one thing in common: all are groups of men with impressive credentials who conduct inter-disciplinary research.

In politics as well as science, the necessity for solitude and time to figure out plans and programs in the midst of hectic campaigns is always a problem, and many politicians envy the scientists at "think tanks" their reflective opportunity. When Senator David Hill of New York was told that Democratic candidate William Jennings Bryan was making up to sixteen campaign speeches a day, he wondered pointedly: "When does he think?"

See **SCENARIO**.

THIRD-PARTY MOVEMENT a bolter's extreme.

Third parties engender no warmth in the hearts of most professional politicians. Thomas E. Dewey, who had his troubles first with the American Labor party and then with the Liberal party, both exclusively New York organizations, said that such sectional parties "have proved to be a menace to responsible government elsewhere." On the national scene, however, Dewey found occasional justification for third parties. Historian Richard Hofstadter noted that their principal role is to provide ideas when the two major parties have stagnated. "Third parties," he wrote, "are like bees: Once they have stung, they die."

The **POPULISTS**, most successful of

the third parties, expressed a radical, primarily rural, revolt against the uncontrolled power of industry in general and the railroad in particular. They won twenty-two electoral votes in 1892 but they, together with such parts of their platform as unlimited coinage of silver (cheap money) and avowed enmity to unfeeling business interests, were ultimately absorbed by the Democrats.

The income tax and the direct election of senators were Populist ideas; each came to pass a generation after the party died. Their influence in the West lingered among the Republicans as well, leading to the Progressive revolt against Eastern-dominated, Republican conservatism. The break came in the Progressive "Bull Moose" campaign of 1912: Theodore Roosevelt's stand at ARMAGEDDON divided Republicans and elected Woodrow Wilson.

Progressivism was the watchword again when liberals, disgusted with a contest in which both major parties seemed to vie as to which was the more conservative, scored some minimal success with Senator Robert La Follette of Wisconsin as their candidate. See DON'T WASTE YOUR VOTE.

In 1948 a potpourri of liberals, radicals, and disguised Communists again went to the people, headed by former Vice President Henry Wallace, who told his followers, "When the old parties rot, the people have a right to be heard through a new party."

In that same campaign there was still another party, the States Rights Democrats. They hoped that Governor Strom Thurmond of South Carolina, calling for racial segregation and political conservatism, could win enough support to throw the final presidential selection into the House of Representatives where, on a state-by-state count, the South might make its views dominate. This happened in 1824, denying Andrew Jackson the White House despite his plurality; the idea occurred in 1968 to George Wallace as well.

There is always a core around which a third-party movement can gather support. Those fearful of change or dissatisfied with its pace often agree with cockroach critic archy, of Don Marquis' *archy and mehitabel,* who answered the Announcer's question "Do you think the time is ripe for launching a third national political party in America?" with "It is more than ripe it is rotten."

In 1968, Alabama's George Wallace achieved 9 percent of the vote, making his 1972 plans a concern to both parties. (See SEND THEM A MESSAGE.) Such was the likelihood of his third-party campaign continuing, before an assassination attempt crippled him, that other splinter movements in the early seventies were automatically called "fourth parties."

See BOLT; SPLINTER PARTY.

THIRD-RATE BURGLARY, see **NOBODY DROWNED AT WATERGATE.**

THIRD TERM, see **VOICE FROM THE SEWER; SMOKE SCREEN.**

THIRD WORLD originally, nations—usually underdeveloped—which were not aligned diplomatically with the "free world" of Western democracies or the "Communist world"; now, the Arab–African–Latin American–Indian bloc, with which the People's Republic of China identifies.

The phrase was originally French (*tiers monde),* in use to describe the neutralists (see NEUTRALISM) in the

Cold War since the late forties. As the *Barnhart Dictionary of New English Since 1963* points out, the reason for the archaic *tiers,* rather than the modern French *troisième,* is that the phrase is patterned after *tiers état,* or "Third Estate" (the commoners, who often fought the first and second estates, the king and clergy). See FOURTH ESTATE. The idea behind "third world" was that it would represent the common man, standing independent of the first and second worlds of established power.

The phrase came into U.S. use in the sixties. "The students, following the gospel of Marcuse, look to the Third World," wrote Philip Shabecoff in the *New York Times Magazine* in a typical late-sixties usage, "to Fidel Castro and Ho Chi Minh, for salvation." "Third Worlders" were Africans, Asians, or Arabs.

However, with the oil-price increases of the mid-seventies, some third-world countries—Nigeria, Venezuela, Saudi Arabia—became far more wealthy, and lost some popular support among liberals in the U.S. In addition, when the "Group of 77" (as 126 nations in the UN called themselves) demanded a "new world economic order"—in effect, a redistribution of wealth from HAVE to HAVE-NOT NATIONS—and topped that with a UN vote equating Zionism with RACISM, the third world became a more pejorative label in the U.S.

As may be expected from the analogy of "fourth estate," a "fourth world" will be coined, but this could be either on political or economic lines.

THOSE WHO   the amorphous armies of the vaguely venal; a rhetorical device that enables an attacker to ostentatiously avoid naming names.

"There are those who say . . ." This frequently employed technique in political discourse enables a speaker to lump together moderate adversaries with extremists, thereby discrediting the moderates; and to characterize a opposing position in its most easily attackable terms.

"Those who" are never right; they are often dangerous, if unwitting, tools of sinister forces; and they are always triumphed over. Their only supporters are "some," as in "Some say . . ."

See STRAWMAN.

THOUSAND DAYS   phrase associated with the length of the Kennedy Administration, from January 20, 1961, to November 22, 1963, or 1,037 days.

The phrase, taken from Kennedy's inaugural address, was quoted five days after his assassination by President Johnson before a joint session of Congress:

> On the twentieth day of January in 1961, John F. Kennedy told his countrymen that our national work would not be finished "in the first thousand days, nor in the life of this Administration, nor even perhaps in our lifetime on this planet. But," he said, "let us begin."
> Today, in this moment of new resolve, I would say to all my fellow Americans, let us continue.

Johnson dropped a "one" in quoting Kennedy, probably for rhetorical cause. Kennedy used "one thousand days" to compare with "one hundred days" as follows:

"All this will not be finished in the first one hundred days. Nor will it be finished in the first one thousand days . . ."

Arthur Schlesinger, Jr., chose *A Thousand Days* for the title of his book on the Kennedy Administration which, along with Ted Sorensen's *Kennedy,* provided much of the source material about the language of the Kennedy years in this book.

See HUNDRED DAYS; "LET US CONTINUE."

THOUSAND PERCENT less than total support; fulsome verbal backing as abandonment is being planned.

As Senator George McGovern's 1972 presidential campaign got under way, the secret mental health record of his running mate, Senator Thomas Eagleton, was revealed: three hospital stays for exhaustion and depression, complete with shock therapy. Senator McGovern at first backed his colleague, who had not told him of this vulnerability, but then—while professing "a thousand percent" support —was accused of undercutting him with hints to the press that he wished Senator Eagleton would voluntarily remove himself from the ticket.

In *Grassroots,* his memoirs that appeared in early 1978, Senator McGovern gave his account of the key phrase of the episode: "Carl Leubsdorf of the Associated Press tracked me down on a tennis court and asked me what I thought the public reaction to Eagleton's disclosure would be. I answered truthfully, and I thought, harmlessly, by saying, 'We'll have to wait and see.' The Leubsdorf story was filed accurately enough, but the headline on the story in some papers was typified by this one: MCGOVERN RECONSIDERING EAGLETON DECISION. "Gary Hart [then McGovern's campaign manager, later a senator] called me from Washington in distress about what appeared to be a weakening of our public position. . . . I angrily called [press secretary] Dick Dougherty and ordered him to tell the press that the Leubsdorf story was false and that I was backing Eagleton 'a thousand percent.' "

The Democratic nominee reported that he privately cautioned Senator Eagleton on the phone that he might have to reconsider, but "to my amazement, I was to learn that almost as soon as our conversation ended, Tom went out of his San Francisco motel and told the press corps, 'McGovern still backs Eagleton one thousand percent.' "

McGovern told the press corps traveling with him at the Sylvan Lake Lodge in the Black Hills of South Dakota a story different from Eagleton's: ". . . as calmly as I could, [I] let the journalists traveling with me know that I was reviewing the situation. . . . The press reaction astounded me. The reporters saw my forewarning as a stab in Tom Eagleton's back. They concluded that while having stated publicly a few days earlier that I was 1,000 percent for Eagleton, I was using them to force Eagleton off the ticket without confronting him face to face. . . . they were unaware of my effort to reach Eagleton that evening . . ."

Since that time, the expression "one thousand percent"—a tenfold emphasis of Theodore Roosevelt's "one hundred percent American"— has been treated with skepticism and used only in irony, accompanied by comments like "With friends like these, who needs enemies?"

See LANDSLIDE.

THOU SHALT NOT STEAL convention battle cry of 1912 and 1952, directed at candidates named Taft.

"From the outset," said Theodore Roosevelt's campaign manager, Senator Joseph Dixon of Montana, "the scheme to renominate Taft was a scheme to steal the nomination." As most state conventions in 1912 went for President William Howard Taft over former President Roosevelt, Dixon cried foul. "You will become a deliberate receiver of stolen goods," he charged in an open letter. At the convention, the national committee leaned hard toward Taft whenever there was a contested delegation: 164 Taft delegates were seated to 19 for Roosevelt in contests. "A fraud," said Roosevelt, "as vulgar, as brazen and as cynically open as any ever committed by the Tweed regime . . ." He labeled them "stolen delegates" and thundered the Biblical commandment: "Thou shalt not steal!"

It didn't work. Taft got the nomination, Teddy formed a third party to stand at ARMAGEDDON and industrialist Chauncey Depew correctly sized up the situation: "The only question now is which corpse gets the most flowers." Democrat Woodrow Wilson won.

Forty years later, the commandment worked. In the 1952 Eisenhower-Taft clash, the balance of power was held by the Southern delegations whose election was contested. Eisenhower's manager Henry Cabot Lodge said: "In the interest of fair play and decency, we will support at the opening session a resolution to amend the rules and to bar these contested delegates from voting to seat themselves or other contested delegations—regardless of whether they are for us or for Senator Taft."

The "fair play" resolution and "Thou shalt not steal" charge gave the Eisenhower forces their moral issue; the General was quoted as growling about "cattle rustlers."

Stephen Hess wrote: "There was a grand irony in charging the two Tafts, William Howard and his son Robert, both with trying to steal presidential nominations. Bob had been called 'Mr. Integrity,' and it was certainly an inherited characteristic. Yet at the 1912 convention and forty years later their opponents contended that the Tafts had secured Southern delegates by foul means."

Politicians are continually on the lookout for slight shadings of immorality by the opposition. Often a public that will shrug off major blunders or serious breaches of morality will become infuriated by a small trick. Winston Churchill, speaking in the House of Commons on the conciliation of South Africa in 1906, put it this way: "In dealing with nationalities, nothing is more fatal than a dodge. Wrongs will be forgiven, sufferings and losses will be forgiven or forgotten, battles will be remembered only as they recall the martial virtues of the combatants; but anything like a trick, will always rankle."

THREE-EYE LEAGUE a high-status club that can be joined by any politician willing to tour Ireland, Italy, and Israel.

In many big cities, the three largest —or at least most active—ethnic groups are the Irish, Italians, and Jews. In the fifties, so many urban political figures made the new Grand Tour that it gained the "Three-Eye" label.

In baseball, the Three-Eye League was a decidedly minor league made up of teams in Illinois, Indiana, and Iowa; it came to typify "bush league" and was spoken of as a kind of Siberia for pitchers who could not find the plate. But in urban politics, a man who hits well in the Three-Eye League belongs on the All-Star team.

THREE-MARTINI LUNCH symbol of tax unfairness.

In the keynote speech at the Democratic National Convention in Miami

Beach on July 11, 1972, Florida Governor Reubin Askew zinged the "system" that has "forgotten the average man or woman in America today. What can we expect them to think," he asked rhetorically, "when the business lunch of steak and martinis is tax-deductible, but the workingman's lunch of salami and cheese is not?" The line by speechwriter Roland Page was little noticed at the time, but was destined for two revivals.

George McGovern, who became the 1972 Democratic nominee, picked up the "martini lunch" in his campaign and improved it: "The rich businessman can deduct his three-martini lunch, but you can't take off the price of a baloney sandwich." The applause-getting line became a part of THE SPEECH, but it was lost in the debacle of his "THOUSAND PERCENT support" for a running mate he was in the process of dropping, in a campaign that was lost before it began.

The line survived the McGovern campaign. The picture of the FAT CAT imbibing while the workingman paid appealed to the POPULISM of Jimmy Carter. As he began his 21-month trek to the 1976 nomination, Carter took the line as his own, beginning with "expense-account lunch" and then adding the "martini" (a gin-and-vermouth cocktail which derives its name from an Italian vermouth). Candidate Carter called such a tax system "a disgrace to the human race," which had a nice rhyme; after Carter's victory in November, Senator Edward Kennedy of Massachusetts added: "There are few more vivid symbols of the disgrace of our current tax laws than the martini lunch."

Finally a counterattack began, not from the expected source of wealthy, inebriated martini-lunchers, but from the Hotel and Restaurant Employees and Bartenders Union (AFL–CIO), which issued a press release in 1977 with this lead: "Martini lunches make an appealing villain, but the martinis are made by bartenders and the meals served are served by waiters after being prepared by chefs."

When President Carter floated a trial balloon of tax reform in which only half of a business luncheon or similar entertainment could be deducted, *Newsweek* columnist George F. Will pointed to the irony of the union opposition: "So what is intended as an attack on privilege is opposed by the proletariat." As for himself, the conservative writer argued, "the tax subsidy for the 'Martini lunches' is a defect in the nation's moral system."

NEOCONSERVATIVE Irving Kristol disagreed: in the *Wall Street Journal* on October 18, 1977, he wrote: "Senator McGovern, in the 1972 campaign, tried—and failed—to make an issue out of the 'two-martini lunch' . . . apparently, President Carter is convinced that the Senator underestimated the seriousness of the situation . . . if you spend all your time worrying whether or not a business executive is getting a tax-free martini with his lunch, you might very well fail to pay due attention to the obvious—that is, encouraging businessmen to make profits."

Despite the catchiness of the martini-lunch phrase, it was not tax "reform" that most voters wanted, but tax reduction. Resentment in the late seventies was directed not at the rich businessman, but at the tax-guzzling bureaucracy. See TAX REVOLT.

The use of libations to loosen up a tough customer has another term, coined on the analogy of "hard sell" in the late fifties: "wet sell," defined in the *Polyglot Dictionary* as "a business deal facilitated by alcohol."

The other use of a cocktail in political rhetoric is a standard gibe at the sitting President's economic policy: "Recipe for a Johnson (or Nixon, Ford, or Carter) cocktail: economy on the rocks." For more on the metaphoric use of delicatessen meats, see BALONEY and SALAMI TACTICS.

THROTTLEBOTTOM caricature of a useless, bumbling Vice President.

From the 1931 Kaufman-Ryskind-Gershwin musical satire, *Of Thee I Sing,* where Vice President Alexander Throttlebottom, played by Victor Moore, had to join a guided tour to get into the White House. Little-known Charles Curtis was Hoover's Vice President when this show was written.

The vice presidency has taken its share of abuse. John Adams said: "My country has in its wisdom contrived for me the most insignificant office that ever the invention of man contrived or his imagination conceived. . . . Today I am nothing, but tomorrow I may be everything."

He may be sure of being ridiculed. In November of 1977 *New Times* magazine headlined an item about Vice President Walter Mondale with this pun: "Throttlebottoming out."

For other assessments, see VEEP; DEAD END, POLITICAL; STEPPING-STONE; HEARTBEAT AWAY FROM THE PRESIDENCY.

THROW AWAY YOUR VOTE, *see* **DON'T WASTE YOUR VOTE.**

THUMBSUCKER political reporter's term for an analytical story; a think piece.

From time to time in the early seventies, Don Oberdorfer of the *Washington Post* would call this writer at the White House and begin the conversation with "I'm doing a thumbsucker for tomorrow."

The term is currently limited to journalists' argot, and because of its similarity to an obscene word, may not cross over to general use, as has a related term, DOPE STORY.

In December 1977 "The Ear," a gossip column in the *Washington Star,* ran this item about *New York Times* reporter James Wooten: "Jim will become a kind of Haynes Johnson, if you get Ear's meaning. (Say Thumb Suckers if you're in the biz . . .)." The meaning was that Wooten might write fewer hard-news stories and more stories with a sociological bent, which sometimes require more thought and introspection.

Reporters and editors use the term with derision, to mean the opposite of "well researched," as in this letter from John Sweet, publisher of *U.S. News & World Report* in its January 2, 1978, issue, promoting the cover article: " 'Life in the 80s'—see page 75—is not one of those 'thumb sucker' articles consisting of opinions from futurists, gathered over THREE-MARTINI LUNCHES . . ."

In current usage, a *background piece* provides general information, not to be confused with the story that results from a BACKGROUNDER, which a reporter calls a *dope story* and a SOURCE calls a *plant;* a *dope story* is an analytical piece that can make news; a *think piece* or *thumbsucker* is an attempt at PUNDITRY.

THUNDER ON THE LEFT liberal objections.

"An end to the Vietnam War would change the situation drastically," wrote Louis Heren in the *Times* of London in 1968. "Much of the thunder from the left would die away, and the right, as represented by Mr. George Wallace, would be more clearly identified as anti-racist."

The phrase harkens to days of fierce liberalism, first in England and then in the U.S.; currently it is used mainly in an ironic sense, as if the rumbling were remote.

The phrase was the title of a book by Christopher Morley in 1925 and was thus popularized. Professor Irwin Stark of City College of New York directed the author to its origin in *The Dangers of This Mortall Life,* by Sir Eustace Peachtree, who was said to have flourished about 1640: "Among the notionable dictes of antique Rome was the fancy that when men heard thunder on the left the gods had somewhat of special advertisement to impart. Then did the prudent pause and lay down their affaires to study what ómen Jove intended."

One might have thought that such a gentleman as Sir Eustace Peachtree had existed, since the source given was *Bartlett's Familiar Quotations* (11th and 12th editions). However, "Kit" Morley liked an occasional practical joke, and the "quotation" placed in *Bartlett's*—which Morley helped edit—was a hoax. It is no longer in recent editions, which is a pity, since it added a human element to a compilation of quotations.

On the analogy of Morley's title, "thunder on the right" is occasionally used to describe conservative mutterings. When *Time* wrote a piece on this writer in 1977, calling attention to his interest in wordplay as well as his right-wing espousals, the headline was "Pun-der on the Right."

TICKET   the slate of candidates, running as a team.

"The old ticket forever!" wrote Benjamin Franklin's daughter Sarah in 1766, her usage duly noted by Webster in 1879. ". . . its usage in this sense dates back to early colonial times," Charles Ledyard Norton wrote in 1890, "since Mrs. Bache (*née* Franklin) would not have used the word in this sense had not its meaning been popularly recognized."

Tickets discussed elsewhere in this book include BALANCED TICKET, with hopefully broad-based appeal; SPLIT TICKET, a voter selection, as from a Chinese menu, of "one from column A, one from column B." Al Smith joked about being able to win on a LAUNDRY TICKET, while politicians are only half in jest about their imaginary, unbeatable DREAM TICKET. A predecessor to split ticket was *mixed ticket,* now obsolete; *scratched ticket,* where a name was erased on a paper ballot, was made obsolete by the voting machine.

Political regulars prefer the "straight ticket," which in voting-machine times became "vote row A all the way." The practice was being described as "straight" over a century ago. "Old Henry," wrote *Harper's* in January 1860, "generally votes a 'straight ticket' . . ." Lord Bryce, an English observer of American politics, used a variant form in his 1888 *American Commonwealth*: "The electors . . . give little thought to the personal qualifications of the candidates, and vote the 'straight-out ticket.' "

Harry Truman used the word to stretch a historical point: "Lincoln had dropped Hannibal Hamlin of Maine because he wanted a Union ticket. Lincoln was elected in 1864 on the American Union ticket and not on the Republican ticket." (To err is Truman: Lincoln was elected in 1864 on the National Union ticket.)

At one time, ticket was synonymous with ballot; voters cast their tickets, or written slips of paper. This sense has been preserved in the current political phrase, *to have the tick-*

ets, meaning to have enough votes to win.

TICK-TOCK   journalists' argot for a story detailing the chronology leading up to a major announcement or event.

"I'm doing a tick-tock on the new economic policy," Henry Hubbard, White House correspondent for *Newsweek,* told the writer after the President had frozen wages and prices on August 15, 1971.

A tick-tock (the metaphor, obviously, of a clock moving toward a fateful hour) is often written with boldface dates indicating significant meetings or preliminary events, and is more reportorial than a THINK PIECE or THUMBSUCKER.

Another term especially associated with newsmagazines is "violin piece," which is the lead story in the magazine that sets the tone of the week. Usage: "What's the violin this week?" "The economy," or "The isolation of the President." A purple-prose assessment of the national mood once led newsmagazines in the thirties as if to the accompaniment of a violin; this has been modified in recent times to a general story that is intended to capture the significant trend of the week. Though the style is less ornate, the term lingers on.

TILT   lean toward, give preferred treatment to.

"Tilt toward Pakistan." Columnist Jack Anderson reported in 1971 that Henry Kissinger had passed on this advice from Richard Nixon at a National Security Council meeting on the India-Pakistan dispute about Bangladesh. Mr. Nixon wanted to rebuke the neutralist Indian government and help Mohammed Yahya Khan in Pakistan, who was helping him to arrange his trip to China.

"Tilt" was a favorite Nixon locution, referring not to the warning flashed when a pinball machine is tampered with, but to the angle of "slant." ("A few individuals think and speak for themselves," wrote Hiram Haydn in the *American Scholar* in 1946, "a few newspapers refuse to tilt their headlines and news stories to satisfy their advertisers' slanted views . . .")

After the widely noted Anderson quotation, the word gained in favor. "With all its reins on the bureaucrat," wrote Leslie Gelb and Morton Halperin in *Harper's* in June 1972, "the new system did not prevent part of the bureaucracy from tilting the 'wrong way' [meaning against the President, as revealed in the Anderson papers] in the recent India-Pakistan crisis."

"Tilt" has a purpose: it is crisper than "lean toward," and less pejorative than "slant." Its adoption as part of the diplomatic lingo was evident in this use by Harvard professor Jerome Alan Cohen in a *Foreign Affairs* article in 1976: "Or do the realities of world politics say that the United States should 'lean to one side'—that of Peking? . . . If so, how, and to what extent, should such a de facto tilt be carried out?"

Wags sometimes refer to any hotel in Pisa, Italy, as "the tiltin' Hilton."

TIMBER, PRESIDENTIAL a man who could be THE MAN WHO; one who has the background, personality, and voter appeal to "go all the way" to the White House.

The metaphor originated with Sir Francis Bacon, whose "Essay on Goodness," written in 1612, was about men whose nature was the opposite of goodness, in whom there was a "natural malignity." "Such dispositions are the very errors of human nature, and yet they are the fittest timber to make great politics of." He compared these warped men to "knee timber," wood that has grown crooked and has been cut so as to form an angle "that is good for ships that are ordained to be tossed, but not for building houses that shall stand firm."

Political uses of the metaphor in the U.S. go back as far as 1833. The *Cleveland Plain Dealer* grumbled in 1880 that "the situation now so chaotic arises from the fact that there is a superabundance of timber."

Finley Peter Dunne's Mr. Dooley (see DOOLEY, MR.) offered his friend Hennessey this advice: "If ye say about a man that he's good prisidintial timber he'll buy ye a dhrink. If ye say he's good vice-presidintial timber ye mane that he isn't good enough to be cut up into shingles, an' ye'd better be careful."

The qualities that make a man's timber "presidential" include the timbre of his voice and the warmth of his smile; courage (his timbers cannot be shivered); either a proven record of vote-getting power or a powerful vote in the opinion polls; age between forty and sixty; a power base in a major state or national renown; nothing in his record that would permanently alienate a major group or region; and AVAILABILITY. The qualities that make a good president—judgment, intelligence, decisiveness, character— are not always the qualities that make good presidential timber. In that regard, Bacon's point remains a good definition: presidential timber is that which best resists twists and strain— "ordained to be tossed"—but not necessarily to support weight.

TIME FOR A CHANGE appeal to unrest and dissatisfaction; Republi-

can slogan in 1944, 1948, and finally —successfully—in 1952.

Thomas E. Dewey said in San Francisco, September 21, 1944: "That's why it's time for a change." In 1946, a better slogan—"HAD ENOUGH?"—came on the Republican scene, and "Time for a Change" became a subsidiary slogan in the campaign of 1948. Dewey's running mate, Earl Warren, modified it further in his own speeches, predicting that the American people would turn to the Republicans "not because they want a change, but because they want a chance."

By 1952 the Democrats had been in power for twenty consecutive years. Long before, Democrat Grover Cleveland had made a similar point about long Republican rule: "Parties may be so long in power, and may become so arrogant and careless of the interests of the people, as to grow heedless of their responsibility to their masters." The *New York Times* editorialized in 1952: "The Republicans have pegged their campaign largely on one theme—that it's time for a change because of the 'top to bottom MESS IN WASHINGTON.' "

Democratic candidate Adlai Stevenson, whose grandfather—Cleveland's running mate—had exploited the desire for new faces, felt the pull of the appeal, and fought directly against the phrase: "As divided, as silent as both wings of the Republican Party are on major objectives, on policies to guide the nation, they have wholeheartedly united on one profound proposition: 'It's time for a change.' . . . They talk of change. These days they do little else but talk of change. But where were the Republicans when the great changes of these twenty years were made? I'll tell you where they were. They were trying to stop the changes."

The desire for a "new face," a "fresh approach," is strong; counterbalancing it is another human feeling, a resistance to make changes in high places illustrated by phrases like "The Devil we know" and "DON'T CHANGE HORSES." In the *British General Election of 1964*, D. E. Butler and Anthony King wrote: "Yet perhaps the most important issue of all was one that scarcely figured in the manifestos, television broadcasts or speeches —the feeling that it was time for a change. . . . If the feeling did exist, it could not be argued with: it could only be exorcised, or displaced by another, more powerful feeling. 'The issue at this election,' as one Conservative put it privately, 'is time for a change versus fear of change. Who wins will depend on which feeling is stronger.' " See SELLING CANDIDATES LIKE SOAP.

TIN BOX, *see* **LITTLE TIN BOX.**

TINHORN POLITICIAN, *see* **TWO-BIT POLITICIAN.**

TITULAR LEADER the most recently defeated presidential candidate of the party out of power; leader in name, not necessarily in fact.

Both Thomas E. Dewey and Adlai Stevenson, "titular leaders" of their parties for eight years, felt ambivalent about the phrase. Dewey wrote in 1950: "Who speaks for the party out of power? It has its last nominee for President who is called the 'Titular Head of the Party.' I have held that title in my party now for nearly six years and I still have some doubts about what it means except that I am the last, duly nominated spokesman for my party."

Stevenson said in 1956:

The titular leader has no clear and defined authority within his party. He has no party office, no staff, no funds, nor is there any system of consultation whereby he may be advised of party policy and through which he may help to shape that policy. There are no devices such as the British have developed through which he can communicate directly and responsibly with the leaders of the party in power. Yet he is generally deemed the leading spokesman of his party.

Because there is no "leader of the opposition" in America as in great Britain, the defeated candidate is often challenged by the wing of the party that felt it could have done better. A year after Willkie's defeat in 1940, Senator Robert A. Taft said that Willkie could not "speak for the Republican party," because there was "no justification in precedent or principle for the view that a defeated candidate for President is the titular leader of the party."

The titular leader, however, does carry a special responsibility to oppose the incumbents. In the late thirties, Republican candidate Alf Landon told Republican Minority Leader Joe Martin that Roosevelt had offered him the post of Secretary of War. "I advised him not to accept," wrote Martin. "He was, after all, the titular head of the Republican Party, and I felt it would be damaging to the Party for him to enter Roosevelt's Cabinet at a time when we were coming up to a convention and a campaign."

Does a titular leader have any special advantage in recapturing a nomination? Probably not. Wendell Willkie, defeated in the primaries of 1944, dropped out of the race. Thomas E. Dewey lost to Harold Stassen in Wisconsin and Nebraska in 1948, but was able to win in Oregon and go into the convention as the favorite. Adlai Stevenson in 1956 started to play the same reluctant role that had been so successful for him in 1952, but soon discovered—after primary losses in New Hampshire and Minnesota—that he needed some victories to capture the nomination. He dropped his reluctance, campaigned in Oregon, Florida, and California, and won those primaries and the nomination.

The role of the titular leader, never really defined, is what the man makes it. William Jennings Bryan, who seemed to be a born titular leader, made much of the position and became Woodrow Wilson's Secretary of State. Alfred E. Smith was an outspoken anti-Republican voice between 1928 and 1932 until he found himself losing the mantle of leadership to Franklin Roosevelt. Dewey was the titular leader most responsible for the choice of his successor, fighting for Eisenhower and defeating his archrival, Robert A. Taft. Richard Nixon was campaigning for governor of California in the midst of his titular leadership and did not really speak for the party; oddly, he assumed that role in the 1966 off-year elections in the midst of Barry Goldwater's titular leadership.

The word has a built-in derogation: titular means "holding the title"—nominal, or "in name only."

TO ERR IS TRUMAN, *see* RED HERRING.

TOKENISM   resistance to change by dint of symbolic acceptance; lip service; yielding to the principle but not the practice.

Newsweek reported in 1963:
... for every Western Electric, Lockheed, or R. J. Reynolds making sincere desegregation efforts, there is another firm—more likely several others—practicing   "tokenism." "There are a lot of showcase compa-

nies which say 'Look, there's our Negro over there,' " reports Atlanta's Noyes Collinson, an executive of the American Friends Service Committee.

Negro leaders hurl the tokenism charge at all the steel, auto and textile giants, at the airlines and most banks and utilities, and at the communications industry.

Writing in 1964, Professor Alan Westin pointed out that during 1963 in the eleven Southern states, Negro school enrollment was 2,840,452; of those, only 12,868 were registered in schools that also had white students, with Texas accounting for more than half the tiny percentage. "It was against this backdrop of wholesale noncompliance and 'tokenism' in the Old South and a seeming halt to the process of integration in the border states that the Negro community looked at school integration as the 1963 school year came to a close."

In the rhetoric of racial resistance, *gradualism* proceeds WITH ALL DELIBERATE SPEED with emphasis on the deliberate; *massive resistance,* a play on Gandhi's "passive resistance," is outright opposition to any form of desegregation; and *tokenism* tries to preserve the pattern of segregation by pretending to let it win. To civil rights advocates, gradualism delays, massive resistance denies, and tokenism deceives.

TOMMING, *see* UNCLE TOM.

TOO LITTLE AND TOO LATE a criticism of unpreparedness and inadequacy.

"Too Late" was the caption of a famous 1885 *Punch* cartoon showing the belatedly dispatched relief column reaching Khartoum two days after the death of General "Chinese"

Gordon at the hands of the African Mahdi.

The addition of "too little" to the words made a phrase both balanced and pointed. Professor Allan Nevins of Columbia coined it in an article titled "Germany Disturbs the Peace" in the May 1935 *Current History*: "The former allies have blundered in the past by offering Germany too little, and offering even that too late, until finally Nazi Germany has become a menace to all mankind."

The phrase was sharpened and popularized by David Lloyd George, who had served as Great Britain's Prime Minister during World War I. On the day after the fall of Finland—March 13, 1940—the seventy-seven-year-old statesman told the House of Commons: "It is the old trouble—too late. Too late with Czechoslovakia, too late with Poland, certainly too late with Finland. It is always too late, or too little, or both."

Throughout the early part of World War II, the phrase was used to deride Allied defeats and lack of preparation. Toward the end of the war, "enough and on time" was used to explain the reason for Allied successes.

After the war, the phrase was used by an "out" party to attack policy on the grounds of inadequacy, which is a political attack permitting little counterattack. John F. Kennedy, campaigning in 1960, called an Eisenhower embargo on shipments to Cuba "too little and too late," suggesting that the U.S. also "attempt to strengthen the non-Batista democratic anti-Castro forces in exile. . . ." In his memoirs of the Kennedy Administration, Ted Sorensen used the phrase in its current generic sense: "Kennedy's error in 1960 on the 'MISSILE GAP' had been the result of the public's being in-

formed too little and too late—even after the facts were certain—about a danger which he had in good faith overstated."

The danger of delayed decision was expressed in different words by Defense Secretary Charles E. Wilson early in the Eisenhower Administration. "I have so many people in my department," he said sadly, "who keep putting off decisions until the only thing left to do is the wrong thing."

New York State Controller Arthur Levitt said in 1967 regarding a $2.5 billion transportation bond issue: "Too much, too soon" (the title of a 1957 autobiography by Diana Barrymore). The possibilities of this phrase are not yet exhausted. "Too much, too late" was never tried by opponents of bombing North Vietnam, and a use may even be found for "too little, too soon."

TOO OLD TO CRY, *see* **CONCESSION SPEECH.**

TOO PROUD TO FIGHT a high-minded Wilsonian defense of neutrality that helped unite his opposition.

A British ship, the *Lusitania*, was sunk with many Americans aboard on May 7, 1915, by a German submarine. Three days later, clinging to his "mediator nation" philosophy, President Wilson said to a group of newly naturalized citizens: "The example of America must be the example not merely of peace because it will not fight, but of peace because peace is the healing and elevating influence of the world and strife is not. There is such a thing as a man being too proud to fight. There is such a thing as a nation being so right that it does not need to convince others by force that it is right . . ."

The "too proud to fight" phrase was used as a gibe at Wilson until his policy changed and he toured the country urging preparedness for war. Years later, *Nation* editor Oswald Garrison Villard claimed authorship: "I supplied the President through Tumulty with a phrase which brought down upon him a storm of abuse and denunciation. The words 'too proud to fight' were mine."

But neither the phrase nor the criticism of it died. In 1961, former Congresswoman and Ambassador Clare Boothe Luce quoted Wilson's statement as an example of how not to keep the peace:

This was certainly a statement which the embattled French and British heard with dismay and contempt and bitterness. How can a man be proud not to fight while his friends are being killed and even conquered in a war they did not start? America was not too proud to sell guns, make loans, ship supplies to the Allied side, and to heap abuse on Kaiser Bill—a procedure which American morality permitted us nevertheless to call "neutrality," since neutrality also consisted entirely in not joining the fighting until "war came."

The phrase, however, had its defenders later in the decade. Some used it to justify a U.S. withdrawal from Southeast Asia. A quite different use was made of it in 1967 by Florida Governor Claude R. Kirk in giving awards to young blacks who helped "cool" a race riot in Tampa before any lives were lost: "Half a century ago, an American President was vilified for suggesting that there are occasions when courageous men should be 'too proud to fight.'

"Negro leaders in Tampa last week showed they were too proud—too conscious of their real responsibility —to allow the hoodlums to take over, to allow vandals to loot and burn and terrorize their neighbors under a false cover of racial tension."

TOPIC A   the subject at the tip of everybody's tongue; a continuing news story that currently gets top coverage.

The expression appeared in the late fifties and was formalized by the *New York Herald Tribune,* which headed the lead item in its front-page news summary "Topic A."

A politician ignores Topic A at the peril of being ignored himself. In current usage, PARAMOUNT ISSUE is synonymous with—though more sedate than—*burning question:* both must be addressed by both parties in depth. GUT ISSUE is an underlying social phenomenon, like a religious or racial issue, and need never be addressed head-on. *Topic A* is the event or running story that draws attention that day or week, generating arguments, cartoons, and jokes, and requires some attention from a public figure who cannot appear out of touch.

TORCH HAS BEEN PASSED
an allusion to a new generation, or at least the transfer of responsibility to a more vigorous group.

"Let the word go forth from this time and place," said John F. Kennedy at his inaugural, "to friend and foe alike, that the torch has been passed to a new generation of Americans . . ."

The torch is a favorite political symbol. In 1555, just before being burned at the stake for heresy, English prelate Hugh Latimer said, "Be of good cheer, brother, we shall this day kindle such a torch in England as, I trust in God, shall never be extinguished."

The passing of the torch, perhaps

derived from the passing of a baton in relay races, was popularized in a sentimental World War I poem by John McCrae:

Take up our quarrel with the foe:
To you from failing hands we throw
The torch; be yours to hold it high.
If ye break faith with us who die
We shall not sleep, though poppies grow
In Flanders fields.

An incendiary speaker is called a *firebrand*; the statue in New York harbor holds the *torch of liberty*; a rejected lover *carries the torch*; and the liberation of North Africa in World War II was *Operation Torch*.

TOTALITARIAN highly centralized government, permeating all aspects of the society it controls, repressing internal opposition and promoting a fear and awe of the leadership.

"Police state" is a popular derogatory synonym for totalitarian government, popularized during the era of Nazi Germany and Fascist Italy.

"Totalitarian" is to the free world vocabulary what "imperialist" is to Communist terminology. Walt Whitman Rostow, later an adviser to the Johnson Administration, wrote in 1952:

A totalitarian regime . . . can be defined as a state in which the potentialities for control over society by governmental authority are exploited to the limit of available modern techniques—where no significant effort is made to achieve the compromise between the sanctity of the individual and the exigencies of efficient communal life; where the moral weakness of men in the administration of concentrated power is ignored; where the aspiration toward a higher degree of democratic quality is not recognized as a good; and where, conversely, the extreme

authority of concentrated power is projected as an intrinsic virtue.

Existentialist philosopher Karl Jaspers gave this view in 1961:

The totalitarian world is weak at home and strong abroad. At home it can maintain its rule only by terror, but abroad, on the soil of the free world, it can utilize the rules of this world to carry on propaganda and to form subversive organizations with immense resources by centrally planned and directed totalitarian methods. The free world can meet this propaganda only with its own spiritual power, with the ethos of its principle, which will eventually let the propaganda machine idle without effect. With subversive organizations—that incipient formation of a totalitarian state within the free state—it must cope by vigilance and police action under law. It must not resort to totalitarian methods, for if it did, it would destroy its own essence.

In 1975, French philosopher-columnist Jean-François Revel wrote *The Totalitarian Temptation*, challenging the argument of EUROCOMMUNISTS that they offered "Communism with a human face." He used the example provided by Alexander Solzhenitsyn (see GULAG) to show that severe repression was part of the essence of Communism.

Friendly dictators are considered *paternalistic;* totalitarian regimes necessary to the defense of the free world are called *authoritarian*.

TOOTH FAIRY, *see* **SANTA CLAUS, NOBODY SHOOTS AT.**

TOTAL WAR wars involving a general mobilization, destruction of the opposition's productive capacity; a war carried "home" to the enemy.

The phrase was popularized by a book, *Der totale Krieg,* by Nazi General Erich Ludendorff in 1935. The aging general, who was the chief German strategist in World War I, stressed the need to mobilize the economy of a nation behind a war effort. The German word for this mobilization was *Wehrwirtschaft,* or war economy, based on rearmament that would prepare an economy for the strain of war.

"Total," therefore, did not mean "more ferocious than usual"; it meant the addition of economic and psychological warfare to what had once been a strictly military affair. During World War II, its meaning changed to "all-out effort" and the destruction of civilian population centers.

In current usage, *total war* is sometimes used as a contrast to LIMITED WAR, though it is more often replaced by *all-out* or *atomic war,* and *World War III.*

Total, however, has become a favorite oratorical word for politicians favoring "total commitment," "total involvement," "bold new total approaches to problems which must be viewed in their totality."

In the seventies the word was turned into a verb to mean "destroy completely"—as: "In the crash, my car was totalled."

TOUGH-MINDED AND TENDER-MINDED, *see* DOVES.

TRADE-OFF   compromise; the tension that exists between divergent but mutually necessary elements, such as target date and cost.

The word was a favorite of the NEW ECONOMICS and an explanation by Walter Heller is included in that entry. The delicate-balance meaning is limited to the fields of economy and defense, however. To politicians, the word is used as BARGAINING CHIP, an expendable person or issue that can be used to close a negotiation (or make a distasteful deal more palatable by using it as a "sweetener").

In the sense of political compromise, the word is not new. John Gunther reported that Republicans in 1940 planned to use the youthful Thomas E. Dewey in a cavalier fashion: " 'The original plan,' a Republican leader is supposed to have said, 'was to use him as a STALKING HORSE and trade him off later.' "

TRAINED SEALS, *see* RUBBER STAMP.

TRAINS RAN ON TIME   a defense of the Fascist "corporate state" on the basis of its efficiency; now only used derisively.

Whenever a government or political organization abridges personal liberties—giving as its reason the need for "master planning" or "efficiency"—the mid-thirties expression is recalled: "But you have to admit that Mussolini made the Italian trains run on time."

Writing about Boss Ed Crump of Tennessee in 1947, John Gunther made the point vividly:

> Of course the boss has given Memphis first-class government—in some respects. But almost all the creditable items are the equivalent of Mussolini making the trains in Italy "run on time." Perhaps they did run on time, and a good thing too. But at what sacrifice?—at what cost to things much more important? Mr. Crump has made Memphis a "clean" enough city. But it is a community that has not really functioned as a democracy for more than a quarter of a century; a whole generation has grown up without fulfilling the first and simplest duty of citizenship, that of exercising political choice.

TRAITOR TO HIS CLASS epithet applied to Franklin Roosevelt.

"His background belied his political philosophy," wrote White House correspondent Charles Hurd. "On several occasions he laughed rather grimly at the comment that he was 'a traitor to his class.' "

Roosevelt's "class" included ancestors dating back two hundred years in America; he was educated at Groton and Harvard, and lived like a country squire in fashionable Hyde Park, New York. In the twenties and early thirties, millionaires and men of high social standing were not identified with liberal positions or considered "men of the people," a situation since rectified. At the time of FDR's election to the presidency, he was probably the wealthiest person ever to hold that office.

Roosevelt's New Deal programs were especially startling to those fellow-patricians who felt he would be "reasonable" once elected; indeed, his pre-election speeches laid heavy stress on budget balancing and efficiency in government. For an idea of the depth of antipathy FDR inspired among members of his "class", see THAT MAN IN THE WHITE HOUSE.

FDR led the way for other men of wealth in politics, particularly in New York State. Herbert Lehman of the banking family, Averell Harriman of the railroad family, Nelson Rockefeller of the oil and banking family, and Robert Kennedy of the Kennedy family have since held high office in New York.

Sir Denis Brogan showed a variation of class distinctions in the U.S. in this way: "There is the famous story of a lively discussion in a smart New York club in which FDR was attacked as being 'a traitor to his class.' A member who was the head of a very old, distinguished and, more important, rich family (he is the father of the present junior Senator from Rhode Island) protested. 'The President is not a traitor to your class; he doesn't belong to it. You are business men. He is a gentleman.' "

TRIAL BALLOON a testing of public reaction by suggestion of an idea through another person, causing no embarrassment to the author if the reaction is not good.

The idea of placing a political toe in the water—with no commitment to plunge in—by the use of NOT FOR ATTRIBUTION stories to reporters was developed by Theodore Roosevelt. Quincy Howe wrote: "He also originated the 'trial-balloon' technique and gave favored correspondents 'OFF-THE-RECORD' statements that they attributed to 'AUTHORITATIVE SOURCES.' If the statement caught on, Roosevelt would make it his own. If it fell flat, he would drop it."

Pointing out that Teddy Roosevelt had ordered the first White House press room installed (after he noticed a group of rain-soaked newsmen standing disconsolately at the gate), AP correspondent Jack Bell observed: "Roosevelt was a great man for trial balloons. He tried out some of his ideas on the reporters. If they backfired, he denied everything and denounced the newsmen for printing what he had told them."

Another White House correspondent—Charles Hurd—recalled the use made of the technique by Teddy's cousin, Franklin Roosevelt:

Roosevelt showed himself to be the master of the "trial balloon." A trial balloon is a politician's idea launched for public reaction before he commits himself. By this means, much background, argument, good and bad reaction can be studied. ... The trial balloons and other techniques quickly won Roosevelt a reputation—not bothersome at all to him—of being less consistent than some other political leaders. He would blithely shift any course of action, if the public reacted negatively.

Reporters are not the only medium of the trial balloon. Minor officials, major party spokesmen, even university professors may be used by accomplished ballooners to float out an idea. The balloonee—the spokesman or reporter—always denies that he is being used in that manner, always righteously, often rightly. Walter Heller refused to concede that his plan of TAX SHARING was a Johnson trial balloon. It may not have been so motivated, but the criticism it engendered from liberals, among other things, caused the President to back away from it, making the Heller proposal a trial balloon, intended or not.

"When I made the speech on 'Old Myths and New Realities'" (see GRAND DESIGN), wrote Senator J. William Fulbright, "many persons immediately assumed that it was a 'trial balloon' inspired by the White House. It was not."

An alternative to the trial balloon is "putting a ball in the air" which differs in that the ballooner admits to being the source. Dean Acheson (then Truman's Undersecretary of State) made a probing address in 1947 that indicated a direction that led to the Marshall Plan, and carefully got White House clearance. "I wanted everyone to understand," said Acheson some years later, "that I was putting a ball in the air and that we had all better be prepared to field it when it came down, because if it just landed, plunk! on the ground, it would be a very bad thing."

The derivation may not be as obvious as it seems. A trial balloon is a balloon put up to test the direction and velocity of the wind in balloon ascensions and kite-flying contests. Both kites and balloons, however, have speculative and fraudulent connotations in their history, and like LAME DUCK might be a political borrowing from business. "Ballooning a stock" meant promoting its rise by spreading false information, a technique now described as "touting"; this was also described at one time as "kite-flying." Issuing a check with no money yet in the bank to cover it is still called "kiting a check." It could be that the speculative meaning was helped into politics by its financial usage.

The phrase may be of French origin. In *Great Englishmen of the Sixteenth Century,* S. Lee wrote in 1907: "Bacon set forth these views as mere *balloons d'essai,* as straws to show him which way the wind blew."

For methods of launching trial balloons, see LEAK; BACKGROUNDER; NOT FOR ATTRIBUTION; DOPE STORY.

TRIAL HEAT   a mock election by poll of a limited number of candidates.

This is a poll that asks: "Supposing the election were being held today; of the following candidates, which one would you vote for?" It differs from DEPTH POLLING, and many other more useful "issues" polls.

A trial heat, or *mano a mano* survey (expression taken from the bullfight ring) is the poll most interesting to the public, most gossiped about, and often least useful to professional politicians. It indicates only where one stands on a given day; it does not indicate what to do or in what direction public opinion is likely to go or what issues are growing in importance. However, the trial heat may be devastating in a CAN'T WIN campaign, convincing delegates to switch to another candidate who runs better in a trial heat against an incumbent.

In current use, a *trial heat* is between candidates of opposing parties; a *preference poll* is among candidates of a single party. The candidate leading the preference poll is not necessarily the strongest in the trial heat; Taft was preferred by Republicans in 1952 who were swayed by Eisenhower's power in the trial heats.

In racing and track sports, a trial heat is often an elimination of competitors before a major race; this is not its political meaning, which is why it is confused with preference poll.

See POLLSTER.

TRICKLE-DOWN THEORY
idea that aid to the prosperity of large corporations will "trickle down" to employees and irrigate the economy.

William Jennings Bryan drew the metaphor, if not the phrase, in his "Cross of Gold" speech in 1896: "There are two ideas of government. There are those who believe that, if you will only legislate to make the well-to-do prosperous, their prosperity will leak through on those below. The Democratic idea, however, has been that if you legislate to make the masses prosperous, their prosperity will find its way up through every class which rests upon them."

At the 1975 Gridiron Dinner, a newsman impersonating presidential press secretary Ron Nessen led a group of cheerleaders serenading President Gerald Ford with this spoof of "Buckle Down, Winsocki":

Trickle down, Winsocki, trickle down,
You can win, Winsocki, if you trickle down,
Give a tax rebate
To the highest rate,

Let it gravitate
And trickle down.

In the campaign of 1932, Herbert Hoover argued that public relief measures proposed by some Democrats were "playing politics with human misery" and that his program was aimed at restoring prosperity to corporations and banks which would in turn reinvigorate the economy. The Democrats derided this as a "trickle-down theory" aimed at "feeding the sparrows by feeding the horses."

The opposition theory retained water as the metaphor in the phrase PUMP PRIMING.

In current use, Republicans—twice stung by the phrase—shy away from it. Robert Donovan reported that in an Eisenhower cabinet meeting in 1954, "this attitude refuted charges that Republicans were bound to the 'trickle down' theory of economics— the theory of helping the few at the top in expectation that the benefits will then seep down to the rest of the people."

See PARTY OF THE PEOPLE.

TRIGGER-HAPPY   inclined to a panicky decision on war; bellicose.

Barry Goldwater, tagged as "trigger-happy" early in his primary campaign against Nelson Rockefeller in 1964, heard the identification reiterated by the Scranton forces at the convention, and could not shake it throughout the general election campaign. His use of DEFOLIATE and stress on "victory" were turned into issues that pictured him as an irresponsible candidate who "shot from the hip" and whose election would plunge the country into nuclear war.

The Democratic advertising agency, Doyle Dane Bernbach Inc., produced two commercials so extreme that they were quickly withdrawn. One pictured a hand reaching toward a nuclear button (see FINGER ON THE BUTTON). Another, which became known as the "daisy spot," showed a little girl pulling the petals off a daisy, with a voice of doom in the background counting down the firing of a missile with each petal pulled.

"Finally," wrote Theodore White, "there was the hazard of the bomb, the 'trigger issue,' which Goldwater must somehow erase or neutralize, as Kennedy had neutralized the issue of religion in 1960. Yet here again the candidate seemed so stunned, so shocked by the attack on him as a killer, that he could not clear his mind to guide a counter-attack."

Goldwater characterized this as "the warmonger charge" but Democrats did not need to use the word warmonger (see -MONGER); trigger-happy was good enough. Art Buchwald wrote a column long after the election about how happy he was that Goldwater had not been elected, because of all the escalation that would have resulted. He then proceeded to list all Johnson's escalating decisions. In this vein, economist Pierre Rinfret told a group of economists in 1966 of the lady who said, "They told me if I voted for Goldwater, we'd be at war in six months, and by golly, I voted for Goldwater and we were."

The compound adjective made a brief political appearance in the previous campaign. When Richard Nixon made clear he would defend the islands of Quemoy and Matsu off the shore of mainland China—an outpost of the Chiang Kai-shek forces in Taiwan—John F. Kennedy called this position "trigger-happy." Ted Sorensen, in retrospect, called this one of the rare occasions Kennedy "stepped over the borders of fair comment."

The Western allusion made its first political appearance in 1904 as "hair-

trigger," to describe Teddy Roosevelt's impulsiveness. Roosevelt himself used the phrase in 1908, predicting a "hair-trigger convention." The word submerged for many years until it was reactivated during World War II.

At that time there were a rash of "happy's." The original, *slap-happy,* or dizzy, intoxicated, was closely akin to punch-drunk. The first variations appeared in 1940 ("I'm *snap-happy* since I discovered Kleenex cleans the . . . lens of my camera"), *power-happy* for power-crazed, *footlight-happy* for stage-struck, etc. The military applications were legion: *stripe-happy, bomb-happy, flak-happy,* and in a *Life* magazine of November 1, 1943: "Cadets are taught here to be 'trigger happy': to shoot at anything any time." As can be seen, the adjective "happy" is like an unstable chemical ready to form a compound with anything. When it joins with a noun, it transforms the noun into a hyphenated adjective, useful information for grammar-happy readers.

TRIPWIRE   the presence of troops in an area as hostages to peace, an attack on whom would automatically trigger military involvement of the nation from which the token force is drawn.

The expression took on its strategic sense early in the COLD WAR, in connection with the garrison of U.S. troops in Berlin. The troops were placed in that four-power city, an island surrounded by East Germany, not to make a serious defense in case of attack but to provide the "tripwire," or national commitment to come to their rescue or avenge their loss.

Later the word was used in NATO terminology, to justify the presence of 300,000 American armed forces in

Europe: not that this force would stop a Soviet offensive to seize Europe, but it would trigger U.S. nuclear response. In PENTAGONESE, this is part of "automaticism," a technique that removes the possibility of a craven response and thus contributes to a DETERRENT.

The term is based on military tactics: a device, strung low along the ground, to be tripped over by an advancing scout which sets off a signal or an explosion.

TROIKA in diplomacy, an executive committee of three—one from each differing camp, the other neutral; in economics, the President's three leading economic advisers.

At a General Assembly session in New York in the fall of 1960, Nikita S. Khrushchev proposed that the office of Secretary-General of the United Nations be replaced by a trio of Secretaries-General, one each for the Communist, capitalist, and NEUTRALIST states.

The Soviet Premier's proposal followed action by the United Nations in the Congo which angered the Russians. Since all decisions by the troika would have had to be unanimous, it was quite clear that its aim was to make effective action by the international organization unlikely. John F. Kennedy said of the proposal at the time that it would "entrench the COLD WAR in the headquarters of peace."

The proposal was directed against the Secretary-General of the time, Dag Hammarskjöld. Khrushchev called Hammarskjöld a "nice man" but, unfortunately, the representative of "the imperialist nations." At this session Khrushchev took off a shoe and pounded it on his desk.

The word was adopted in the sixties to describe a committee of Adminis-tration economic officials: the Chairman of the Council of Economic Advisers, the Director of the Office of Management and Budget, and the Secretary of the Treasury. When joined by the Chairman of the Federal Reserve Board, they become the QUADRIAD.

The word is Russian; it means a sled which is pulled by three horses. Since its UN introduction, it has come to mean any political triumvirate, although a three-sided entity containing more than three men, such as the Pay Board set up in late 1971, is called "tripartite."

TROLLOPE PLOY, *see* **PLOY.**

TROOPS party workers, or those volunteers willing to ring doorbells.

Primary *campaigns* are decided by the *regular* organization's ability to "turn out the *troops*"; the opposing *camp* sets up a *cadre* of *volunteers* who are expected to turn out *troops* of their own. The italicized terms are MILITARY METAPHORS; *troops* is a term gaining preference over *workers,* possibly because of Communist use of the latter.

"Troops" is a collective plural noun from *troupe,* used as "The troops are getting restless." Similarly, a *cohort* was originally a group of soldiers, but now means a single ally or crony.

Although "troops" is mainly used to mean low-level workers, it means all supporters in a campaign. David Broder, writing about the political experts gathering around Governor Ronald Reagan in 1967, headlined his column with a military triple metaphor: "Gunning for a Draft: The Reagan Troops."

See PARTY FAITHFUL.

TROT OUT THE GHOSTS

speechwriters' term for reference to the past luminaries of the speaker's party and to the past "failures" of the opposition party.

"I stand in direct succession to Woodrow Wilson and Franklin Roosevelt and Harry Truman," candidate John F. Kennedy said often in a version of THE SPEECH. "Mr. Nixon, the Republican leader, stands in direct succession to McKinley, to Coolidge, to Hoover, to Landon and to Dewey." He did not mention Eisenhower.

Republican reference to "the party of Lincoln" is another example of "trotting out the ghosts," although constant quotation of Lincoln by Adlai Stevenson and John Kennedy has resulted in watering down of Lincoln's Republican identification, an erosion which Republicans combat each year at their Lincoln Day dinners.

A good example of "trotting out the ghosts" was Warren G. Harding's 1912 nomination of William Howard Taft; the future President's speech was, in his words, "glorying in retrospection." He hailed Taft as one "as wise and patient as Abraham Lincoln, as modest and dauntless as Ulysses S. Grant, as temperate and peace-loving as Rutherford B. Hayes, as patriotic and intellectual as James A. Garfield, as courtly and generous as Chester A. Arthur, as learned in the law as Benjamin Harrison, as sympathetic and brave as William McKinley, as progressive as his predecessor."

Harding did not mention the name of "his predecessor" because he was Theodore Roosevelt, who was running against Taft for the nomination. Harding feared that that particular ghost was too lively to trot out.

TRUE BELIEVER

used in friendly fashion, a loyalist and comrade in arms; used by a political opponent, a fanatic.

In current political usage, "true believer" is most often applied to conservatives, as one who holds firmly to the articles of faith and considers any compromise of them for political gain to be an abandonment of basic principles. The most frequently used charge by a true believer is SELLOUT.

The term is applied to any hardline group. "To the pragmatists such as Chou En-lai," editorialized the *New York Times* in October, 1971, "the invitation to the American President was an opportunity to advance China's prestige on the world scene and to deter the preventive war advocates in Moscow. But to the true believers in Peking, the invitation must have seemed a sellout of all China's proclaimed revolutionary principles —as reprehensible in the eyes of those fanatics as was Nikita Khrushchev's visit to the United States in 1959 as President Eisenhower's guest."

But the expression need not reflect either fanaticism or tough-mindedness; a certain affection for steadfastness can be seen in the use of the phrase as the title of a 1953 book by longshoreman-philosopher Eric Hoffer, and in the *Wall Street Journal*'s farewell to Hubert Humphrey on January 16, 1978: "Last of the True Believers?"

The origin is in the Koran, written in the seventh century: "O true believers, take your necessary precautions against your enemies, and either go forth to war in separate parties, or go forth all together in a body."

See IDEOLOGY; LITMUS-TEST ISSUE.

TRUMAN DOCTRINE, see DOCTRINES.

"TRUTH-IN" CONSTRUCTION
a device to build persuasion into the generic name of legislation.

"Truth in Packaging" legislation caused running controversy in the early sixties. Proponents held that the public needed to be protected from misleading claims on packages of goods, especially regarding weight and bulk; opponents felt such restraints were captious, unnecessary, and a step toward government control of all advertising.

"Truth in Lending" followed, with proponents seeking to force banks, loan companies, and all suppliers of credit to show borrowers exactly how much the interest charges would add to costs.

The technique of slipping a message in a name (see RIGHT TO WORK) did not begin with truth in packaging. Early New Deal legislation included an attempted reform of the Wall Street community. "Undiscriminating people," wrote Raymond Moley, "described the securities bill [of 1933] as the 'Truth in Securities Act.' . . . But as the year passed, even Roosevelt realized that the Act in its existing form was unworkable . . ." This led to the Securities Act of 1934, and the Securities and Exchange Commission. This act continued to be called "Truth in Securities" throughout the thirties, though the designation is no longer current.

Columnist Max Lerner wrote in 1939:

> In meeting the propaganda danger, something like the SEC pattern would be the most effective procedure. We have a Truth in Securities Act to make sure that there is no rigging of the stock market . . . are we to have nothing to protect us against the infinitely more dangerous advertising of anti-labor, anti-democratic, anti-Semitic lies?

I know that liberals will immediately say: Why could not a Truth in Opinion Act be used against the left as well as the right? The answer is that it is already in use against the left.

TRUTH SQUAD a team of officials, usually congressmen, organized to harass an opposition candidate by following close on his heels with refutations.

The phrase has a built-in advantage, implying what the opposition leader says is not true. The technique is useful and growing, since it makes the opposition more careful in its charges and gets newspaper space with "the last word" after a candidate has left a city.

John F. Kennedy was dogged by a "truth squad" headed by Republican Senator Hugh Scott of Pennsylvania in the 1960 campaign. Toward the end of the campaign, he used them as a foil: "Now we have five days before this campaign is over. I cannot predict what is going to happen. The 'truth squad' has been ditched. They told the truth once and they don't let them travel around anymore."

The term may have had its origin in the Agriculture Department's so-called Poison Squad at the turn of the century. The department's Chief Chemist, Dr. Harvey W. Wiley, had collected a group of young scientists so dedicated to the fight for good food-and-drug legislation that they won the nickname by actually testing adulterated foods on themselves. Their efforts and the publicity about the adulteration of food—and particularly meat—led to the Pure Food Bill of 1906.

Its early use as a political technique was in 1919, when a group of Republican congressmen dogged Woodrow Wilson's steps as he tried to sell the idea of the League of Nations to the American people.

The best squelch was Adlai Stevenson's, who said of a Republican squad following him around in 1956: "A truth squad bears the same relationship to 'truth' as a Fire Department does to 'fire.' "

TUESDAY LUNCH, *see* **WEDNESDAY CLUB.**

TURNAROUNDS creating a phrase by reversing the construction of a famous saying.

Franklin Roosevelt in 1932 said that the aim of the national economy "should not be the survival of the fittest," but rather "the fitting of as many human beings as possible into the scheme of surviving."

"It has been said of the world's history hitherto," said Abraham Lincoln, "that might makes right. It is for us and for our time to reverse the maxim, and to say that right makes might." He liked that turnaround, using it again in his 1860 Cooper Union speech: "Let us have faith that right makes might, and in that faith let us to the end dare to do our duty as we understand it."

Turnarounds are not to be confused with *parallel constructions,* often created for purposes of ridicule: G. K. Chesterton undermined "my country, right or wrong" with "my mother, drunk or sober" and anti-Goldwater partisans paralleled "In Your Heart You Know He's Right" with "In Your Guts You Know He's Nuts."

President James Buchanan, never noted for his wit, provided a classic turnaround in 1858, after an off-year setback at the polls: "We have met the enemy and we are theirs." (Cartoonist Walt Kelly, in "Pogo," also played with Captain Oliver Perry's line: "We have met the enemy and he is us.")

See Fitzgerald's use under SPOILS SYSTEM, and "shoo-out" under SHOO-IN.

TURNIP DAY, *see* **DO-NOTHING CONGRESS.**

TURNOUT the number of voters on Election Day; also, the size of a partisan crowd.

Lip service is always given to the advisability of getting everyone to come to the polls. Franklin D. Roosevelt on election eve in 1940 said on the radio: "Last Saturday night, I said that freedom of speech is of no use to the man who has nothing to say and that freedom of worship is of no use to the man who has lost his God. And tonight I should like to add that a free election is of no use to the man who is too indifferent to vote . . ."

But what the working politician really means is the need for his own side to turn out the vote. The importance of doing so may have been illustrated by the rueful remark of Archibald Crossley, one of the many incorrect pollsters in the 1948 Truman-Dewey contest, who said later, "The result clearly showed what happens when one party gets out its vote and the other does not." (For a contrary opinion, see Samuel Lubell's comment under STAY-AT-HOMES.)

Systematic party efforts at turnout probably started with Aaron Burr and his Tammany Hall organization in 1800. Using a card index of the voters, members of the Society of Tammany made sure that all the FAITHFUL went to the polls.

According to columnist Leonard Lyons, President Johnson was touched by the huge crowd which greeted him at the airport in Seoul, Korea. Johnson said he had asked his host how large the crowd was and the President of Korea replied, "Two million, two million people"—and then continued earnestly, "I'm sorry, President Johnson, but that's all the people I have."

The word has been exported. In the South Vietnamese election of 1967, civilian candidate Tran Van Huong nodded approvingly at a crowd that had come to hear him speak and told a reporter, "If everywhere we go from now on, the publicity and the turnout are as good, I am satisfied."

Not everyone is impressed by the need to turn out the vote. There was, for instance, the little old lady, quoted by comedian Jack Paar, who firmly stated, "I never vote. It only encourages them."

TWEEDLEDUM AND TWEED-LEDEE literary characters used to attack the similarity of the two parties by those who claim to see not a DIME'S WORTH OF DIFFERENCE.

The twinlike characters popularized by Lewis Carroll in 1869 were injected into American political discourse by cartoonist Thomas Nast throughout the 1870s as he caricatured the characters chosen by "Boss" Tweed of Tammany. Long after Nast, the useful device has been brought into political play.

"There is little doubt," wrote Clinton Rossiter in 1960, "that many voters see nothing to choose between the Tweedledumism of the Democrats and Tweedledeeism of the Republicans. Lacking any third choice, they fail to choose at all."

As a Republican candidate attacked by disappointed conservatives as being a "me-tooer" (see ME TOO), Thomas E. Dewey wrote:

> It is only necessary to compare the platforms of both parties in a normal presidential year to find how

similar they are. This similarity is highly objectionable to a vociferous few. They rail at both parties, saying they represent nothing but a choice between Tweedledee and Tweedledum. . . . These impractical theorists with a "passion for neatness" demand that our parties be sharply divided, one against the other, in interest, membership, and doctrine. They want to drive all moderates and liberals out of the Republican party and then have the remainder join forces with the conservative groups of the South. Then they would have everything very neatly arranged, indeed. The Democratic party would be the liberal-to-radical party. The Republican party would be the conservative-to-reactionary party. The results would be neatly arranged too. The Republicans would lose every election and the Democrats would win every election.

Tweedledum and Tweedledee are generally assumed to be creations of Lewis Carroll; in his *Through the Looking Glass,* they sing the ditty "The Walrus and the Carpenter." Carroll took them from John Byrom's satire about bickering schools of musicians in the 1750s whose real difference was negligible. The best-known Byrom verse:

> *Some say compared to Bononcini*
> *That Mynheer Handel's but a ninny;*
> *Others aver that he to Handel*
> *Is scarcely fit to hold a candle.*
> *Strange all this difference should be*
> *'Twixt tweedle-dum and tweedle-dee.*

TWEED RING, *see* **TAMMANY TIGER.**

TWENTY YEARS OF TREASON an extreme version of the SOFT ON COMMUNISM charge, referring to the period (1932–52) in which Democrats occupied the White House.

In early 1954 Senator Joseph

McCarthy made a series of speeches arranged by the Republican National Committee in nine cities, giving them the title "Twenty Years of Treason." In Charleston, W. Va., he stated the theme: "The issue between the Republicans and Democrats is clearly drawn. It has been deliberately drawn by those who have been in charge of twenty years of treason."

"Dwight Eisenhower," wrote Robert Donovan, "was quick to proclaim his belief in the loyalty of Democrats in disassociating himself from McCarthy's claim that the Roosevelt and Truman administrations represented 'twenty years of treason.' " As the senator demanded information from Administration appointees in hearings, the White House bluntly stated that its rights "cannot be usurped by any individual who may seek to set himself above the laws of our land." The use of "individual" rather than "man" or "person" or even "anyone" is pure Eisenhower style, indicating that he personally composed or edited the statement.

Senator McCarthy promptly amended his phrase, referring to "the evidence of treason that has been growing over the past twenty—[*pause*] —twenty-one years."

The phrase is used today mainly in recollections of the McCarthy era, though as late as 1960 the Bulletin of the John Birch Society held that the "key" to the advance of world Communism was "treason right within our government and the place to find it is right in Washington."

If this be demagoguery, some made the most of it. The combination of alliteration and neat packaging of the combined Roosevelt-Truman Administrations made "twenty years of treason" a well-turned catch phrase.

The construction, however, predated McCarthy. In Great Britain, Labour party spokesmen since the end of World War II have hammered at the Conservatives for "thirteen wasted years," blaming the nation's ills on thirteen consecutive years of Conservative domination. Though Labour governments had twice won power in the postwar period, Harold Wilson returned to the theme in 1966 as he led the Labour party's campaign for re-election: "We have been brought to the brink because for thirteen years British industry has lost ground in the world."

This, in turn, was preceded by a 1936 Republican convention key-note address punctuated with "three long years!" This slogan threatened to become effective until FDR flattened it with his own account of the Harding-Coolidge-Hoover era: "Nine mocking years with the golden calf and three long years of the scourge . . . nine crazy years at the ticker and three long years in the breadline!"

TWISTING SLOWLY, SLOWLY IN THE WIND left exposed to political attack; abandoned.

The phrase was made a part of the political vocabulary in 1973 by White House Domestic Council director John Ehrlichman, who reports to this lexicographer on its origin: " 'Twisting slowly' is on a recording I made of a phone talk with [John] Dean re [FBI Acting Director] Pat Gray. RN [Richard Nixon] had decided to withdraw his nomination but no one had told Gray, and Pat was going back to the Judiciary Committee and taking punishment day after day. He was a corpse hanging there and RN hadn't yet cut him down for a decent burial. It seemed an apt description."

The nice overkill of the word— treating an undefended aide as a corpse dangling in the breeze—is in the grand tradition of political hyperbole, and has been used frequently since, especially regarding confirmation hearings.

The phrase has an ancient "hanging" connotation: in his 1785 edition of *A Dictionary of the Vulgar Tongue,* Captain Frances Grose lists "twisted" as "executed, hanged" and there is another reference to that lugubrious meaning in the *New Canting Dictionary* (1725). Slang expert Stuart Berg Flexner, in a letter to the author, suggests: "I find that the trapdoor scaffold and the hangman's knot weren't accepted before the 19th century, meaning that before this late date victims suffered slow strangulation while out there kicking and twisting at the end of the rope."

The most vivid fictional use of the metaphor (and perhaps Ehrlichman's unconscious source) was in the concluding paragraph of *Brave New World*, written in 1932 by novelist Aldous Huxley: "Just under the crown of the arch dangled a pair of feet . . . Slowly, very slowly, like two unhurried compass needles, the feet turned towards the right; north, northeast, east, south-east, south, south-south-west; then paused, and, after a few seconds, turned as unhurriedly back towards the left. South-south-west, south, south-east, east . . ."

The Ehrlichman phrase will probably become fixed in the political lexicon more securely than most other WATERGATE WORDS. In 1976 the British publication *The Economist* explained how Hua Kuo-feng's rise led to the downfall of Chiang Ching, widow of Chairman Mao Tse-tung, and titled the story: "How Hua Left Mrs. Mao Twisting in the Wind."

TWISTING THE LION'S TAIL speeches originally aimed at nineteenth-century Irish voters; now, any attack on the British government.

Early written references are few, though *Harper's Weekly* in 1872 ran a cartoon showing President Grant with his foot on the British lion's tail. Later, in 1889, Theodore Roosevelt wrote that "just at present our statesmen seem inclined to abandon the tail of the lion and instead we are plucking vigorously at the caudal feathers of that delightful war-fowl, the German eagle—a cousin of our own bald-headed bird of prey" (see BALD EAGLE).

Carl Schurz indicated in 1898 that the phrase was already familiar when he wrote: ". . . for the present attitude of Great Britain will no longer permit the American demagogue to seek popularity by twisting the British Lion's tail."

The phrase remains current as the act becomes more frequent.

TWO-BIT POLITICIAN a cheap politician, often used in conjunction with "tinhorn gambler," with adjectives interchangeable.

"Tinhorn politician" was an epithet coined by William Allen White in an *Emporia* (Kansas) *Gazette* editorial on October 25, 1901. "Tinhorn gambler" has been traced back to an 1885 issue of the *New Mexican Review:* "We have been greatly annoyed of late by a lot of tin horn gamblers and prostitutes."

New York Mayor Fiorello La Guardia lumped both usages together in frequent blasts at the "tinhorn gamblers and two-bit politicians." Former Tammany leader Edward Costikyan wrote in 1966: "La Guardia fortified the anti-political-leader bias of the good-government tradition. His tirades against 'tinhorn gamblers' and 'two-bit politicians' deepened the public association between politicians and evildoers. In retrospect, his administration became a myth—a myth which equated good government with the absence of political leaders in government . . ."

An obvious derivation might appear to be from a cheap, or tin, noisemaker—hence, noisy politician of a low variety. However, historian George Willison offers a more plausible explanation in discussing gambling ethics of the early West in *Here They Found Gold:* "Chuck-a-luck operators shake their dice in a small churn-like affair of metal—hence the expression 'tinhorn gambler,' for the game is rather looked down on as one for 'chubbers' and chuck-a-luck gamblers are never admitted within the aristocratic circle of faro-dealers."

TWO CARS IN EVERY GARAGE, *see* CHICKEN IN EVERY POT.

TWO MINUTES TO MIDNIGHT, *see* DOOMSDAY MACHINE.

TWO-PARTY SYSTEM in American thinking, happy medium between one-party control and a profusion of splinter parties; something most U.S. politicians speak of with reverence.

"I think it is very important that we have a two-party country," President Lyndon Johnson joked at a press conference in 1964. "I am a fellow that likes small parties, and the Republican party is about the size I like."

The two-party system, a practice seldom found outside the U.S. and Great Britain, is a phrase difficult to find in early writings about government, but there are plenty of strong opinions about the general idea. Warnings against parties in general range from George Washington's "The spirit of party serves always to distract the public councils, and en-

feeble the public administration" (1796) to Nikita Khrushchev "After the liquidation of classes we have a monolithic society. Therefore, why found another party? That would be like voluntarily letting someone put a flea in your shirt" (1957).

Most of the comments about the division of political activity by parties, gleefully quoted today by those who plead for more BIPARTISANSHIP in foreign policy and urban affairs, are based on ideological division (as in England and France) rather than administrative division (as in the U.S.). Joseph Addison wrote about a philosophical split in *The Spectator* in 1711: "There can not be a greater judgment befall a country than such a dreadful spirit of division as rends a government into two distinct people, and makes them greater strangers and more averse to one another than if they were actually two different nations." The wrench of ideological faction concerned Thomas Jefferson in 1789: "If I could not go to Heaven but with a party I would not go there at all."

The early defenders of the two-party system also spoke mostly of ideological division. "Party divisions," wrote Edmund Burke in 1769, "whether on the whole operating for good or evil, are things inseparable from free government." Horace Walpole wrote in 1760 that "A nation without parties is soon a nation without curiosity," and Disraeli in 1864 held that "Party is organized opinion."

Another reason given for the two-party system was the inherent cleansing process of having INS AND OUTS. Congressman, later autocratic Speaker, Thomas B. Reed put it bluntly in 1880: "The best system is to have one party govern and the other party watch." The "watching," in its active sense, meant keeping it honest and responsive; competition for office bred new programs and advances.

The ideological differences within each major U.S. party are greater than the difference between the parties, despite attempts to delineate fundamental schisms of beliefs. Democratic orators have tried to separate themselves—the PARTY OF THE PEOPLE—from the "party of the SPECIAL INTERESTS"; the Republicans have countered with variations of their platform of 1908: "The trend of Democracy is toward Socialism, while the Republican party stands for a wise and regulated individualism. Socialism would destroy wealth; Republicanism would prevent its abuse."

There is undoubtedly a general difference in the approach, appeal, and personality of the two U.S. parties, but the "two-party system" is more of a means to political power and administration than a means to social revolution. In this sense, the system is much the same as our "adversary system" of criminal justice, in which the truth is expected to win in fair competition.

Coalition is always a danger to the two-party system. FDR's war cabinet brought in Republicans Stimson and Knox; Churchill's deputy was his archrival, Clement Attlee. Wendell Willkie, in his LOYAL OPPOSITION speech, drew the line: "We, who stand ready to serve our country behind our Commander in Chief, nevertheless retain the right, and I will say the duty, to debate the course of our government. Ours is a two-party system. Should we ever permit one party to dominate our lives entirely, democracy would collapse and we would have dictatorship."

To most Americans, the two-party system is a contrasting phrase for *one-party rule* or *single-party domination.* It ranks with FREE ENTERPRISE, the AMERICAN WAY OF LIFE, CHECKS AND BALANCES, and the AMERICAN DREAM as an unassailable political phrase.

Whenever one party wins a particularly lopsided victory, as in 1936, 1964, and 1972, fears are expressed about the future of the system. Politicians worry about the U.S. adopting a configuration of power such as that in Japan's Diet in most of the postwar period, which Yale professor Warren M. Tsuneishi called "the one-and-one-half party system" characterized by "a dominant party that monopolizes power and alone knows how to govern while opposed by a permanent minority group that at times seems 'positively afraid of power.'" Somehow, in the U.S., the pendulum has always managed to swing back.

A left-handed but intensely practical reason for attaching oneself to one of two parties was given by George Savile, Marquess of Halifax, in 1690: "If there are two parties a man ought to adhere to that which he disliketh least, though in the whole he doth not approve it; for whilst he doth not list himself in one or the other party, he is looked upon as such a straggler that he is fallen upon by both."

See ME TOO; TWEEDLEDUM AND TWEEDLEDEE; PARTISAN; PARTY LOYALTY.

UGLY AMERICANS American diplomats and businessmen abroad who undercut foreign policy with their pomposity, high living, and lack of communication with the great majority of natives.

The phrase was taken from Eugene Burdick and William Lederer's *The Ugly American,* a group of related fictional stories about U.S. businessmen and officials in Southeast Asia.

In the book, the "ugly American" was a man who embodied just the opposite of what the phrase has come to mean. He was a hard-working, compassionate American who helped to overcome the ill will caused by other characters in the book. "Ugly" referred to his physical appearance. However, since the novel attacked those Americans who caused resentment by their isolation and greed, the word "ugly" has come to be applied to the villains of the piece.

Graham Greene titled a subsequent book *The Quiet American*; Victor Lasky wrote about blunders in Soviet diplomacy in *The Ugly Russians.*

New York Times correspondent Michael Kaufman wrote from Africa in July 1978: " 'The Ugly Nigerian' has become a cliché in parts of Africa . . . as in the case of the stereotyped American, the newer epithet is the product as much of admiration and envy as of contempt."

UMBRELLA SYMBOL APPEASEMENT, from the umbrella carried by British Prime Minister Neville Chamberlain on his return from the Munich Conference (see MUNICH, ANOTHER).

A character of Fred Allen's radio program in the thirties who was afflicted with amnesia and trying—by the slow process of elimination—to figure out who he was, said, "I don't have an umbrella—so I can't be Neville Chamberlain."

The continuing close identification with Chamberlain, appeasement, and umbrellas is illustrated in this passage from historian Eric Goldman's *The Crucial Decade* about Eisenhower's arrival at an airport: "When the President's plane, the Columbine III, neared the Washington airport, a summer shower was spattering the Capital. Vice-President Richard Nixon issued an instruction to the officials going out to the airport. No umbrellas, the Vice-President said, because people might be reminded of Prime Minister Neville Chamberlain coming back with his umbrella from the Munich appeasement of Hitler."

In the final days before the Democratic nomination in 1960, columnists Rowland Evans and Robert Novak claimed that candidate Lyndon Johnson joined the attack on Joseph P. Kennedy, his rival's father, recalling the former ambassador's reputation for appeasement. "On the very day of the balloting, July 14," they wrote,

"Johnson took up the cry: 'I wasn't any Chamberlain-umbrella policy man. I never thought Hitler was right.' "

The umbrella has other political symbolic meanings as well. A presidential program can be an umbrella under which congressional candidates scurry before an election. Not surprisingly, the symbol can be extended from mild protection to military preparedness to pessimism. "The American people," wrote Al Smith in 1931, "never carry an umbrella. They prepare to walk in eternal sunshine."

For other symbols in politics, see CIGARETTE-HOLDER SYMBOL.

UN-AMERICAN not conforming to the ideology or sharing the same values as the particular American using the term.

The word "American," as used in the term "un-American," describes neither a man's nationality (he is a U.S. citizen) nor his point of origin (he comes from the Western Hemisphere). American in this sense is short for AMERICANISM, a creed based on economic opportunity, political freedom, and social mobility.

The Fourth of July is not a national holiday hailing the birth of a nation, like Bastille Day in France; it is more of a commemoration of the realization of an ideology, comparable to the Communist May Day.

One who is "un-American" does not, in the accuser's opinion, share that ideology. "This concept of 'un-American activities,' as far as I know, does not have its counterpart in other countries," wrote Berkeley professor Seymour Martin Lipset. "American patriotism is allegiance to values, to a creed, not solely to a nation. An American political leader could not say, as Winston Churchill did in 1940, that the English Communist Party was composed of Englishmen, and he did not fear an Englishman . . . this emphasis on ideological conformity to presumably common political values . . . legitimatizes the hunt for 'un-Americans' in our midst."

The word might have had its origin in the aristocratic point of view of Alexander Hamilton, alluded to in this 1880 letter by President James Garfield: "More than a hundred years ago, a young student of Columbia College was arguing the ideas of the American Revolution and American Union against the un-American loyalty to monarchy of his college president and professors."

The word gained political popularity in a reaction against the American, or KNOW NOTHING, party in the mid-nineteenth century. The anti-Catholic, anti-Semitic, anti-foreign philosophy of the "Sams," styled as American, naturally drew a blast as anti-American, or un-American, as in this 1844 pamphlet: "Misguided men assuming the title Native American, but un-American at heart, breathing destruction on those not born here, denouncing a whole religious community and all professing a particular faith, have been joined with the Whigs."

Republican William Seward added a few years later: ". . . every thing is un-American which makes a distinction of whatever kind, in this country, between the native born American and him whose lot is directed to be cast here by an overruling Providence . . ."

In its early use, then, the word meant "intolerant"; this usage continues today as a second meaning of the word, as intolerant not of religion or race but of dissent or any form of radicalism.

After the collapse of the Know-

Nothings, *un-American* took on its antiradical, antinonconformist coloration. The *New York Times* complained in 1870 that the *New York Tribune* "stigmatizes its opponent as false to his party, or as 'un-American' —its two favorite and well-worn labels."

The Democratic platform of 1896 held gold bimetallism to be "not only un-American, but anti-American"; soon afterward editor William Allen White began a generation-long campaign against Bryan's "un-American doctrine of state paternalism." Third-party candidate Robert La Follette in 1924 stressed his movement's moderation: "We are unalterably opposed to any class government, whether it be the existing dictatorship of plutocracy or the dictatorship of the proletariat. Both are essentially undemocratic and un-American."

The word gained its greatest prominence in the late thirties as the name of a congressional committee, nicknamed by its initials in the sixties, HUAC. *The New Yorker* commented in 1948:

> One questionable thing about the House Committee on un-American Activities is its name. . . . The word "un-American," besides beginning with a small letter and gradually working up to a capital, is essentially a foolish, bad word, hardly worth the little hyphen it needs to hold it together. Literally, nothing in this country can be said to be un-American. "Un" means "not," and anything that happens within our borders is American, no matter what its nature, no matter how far off the beam it may be.

The word is used as an epithet casting the man attacked outside the pale of common values; its use, however, carries the built-in boomerang of indicating the user to be intolerant of dissent.

UNCERTAIN TRUMPET, *see* **MUSICAL METAPHORS.**

UNCLE SAM   symbol for the collective citizenry of the U.S.

In the minds of most Americans, Uncle Sam is a stern-looking man on a World War I recruiting poster by James Montgomery Flagg pointing his finger directly at the viewer and saying: "I want YOU for the U.S. Army."

He was created in the War of 1812. The first written record of his appearance is in the *Troy* (N.Y.) *Post,* September 3, 1813: "'Loss upon loss,' and 'no ill luck stir[r]ing but what lights upon Uncle Sam's shoulders,' exclaim the Government editors, in every part of the Country. . . . This cant name for our government has got almost as current as 'John Bull.' The letters U.S. on the government waggons &c are supposed to have given rise to it." (John Bull had a more specific genesis in a 1712 satire by Dr. John Arbuthnot, and is now the cartoonists' symbol—along with a lion— of Great Britain.)

Forst's *Naval History of the United States* relates that a government inspector of provisions in Troy, New York, named Samuel Wilson was the original Uncle Sam. He was supposed to have been given the nickname during the War of 1812 by workmen in the military stores handling casks labeled "E.A.—U.S.," with Elbert Anderson the name of the contractor. The story is not substantiated.

Charles Ledyard Norton wrote in 1890: "Uncle Sam is for Americans what John Bull is for the English, save that he is always pictorially represented in exaggerated and impossible habiliments, such as might be worn on the stage by a burlesque actor, and with a personality to match, while the typical John Bull takes life seriously in sober garb, like a 'fine old English gentleman.' "

There is, however, a tradition of taking advantage of Uncle Sam. In current usage, when Uncle Sam is being described as one unduly taken advantage of, he becomes *Uncle Sugar*. To European debtor nations in the 1920s, U.S. stood for *Uncle Shylock*, demanding his pound of flesh. Individual Americans were known for a time as BROTHER JONATHAN; members of the Know-Nothing party, styled the "American" party, were known as "Sams" after the Uncle Sam symbol.

There may be some Uncle Sam connection with a small boy's demand that another quit a fight by "saying uncle"; at any rate, when a politician talks about *going to Uncle*, he means going to the federal government for aid.

UNCLE TOM a subservient Negro; as an "ism," inadequate militancy on civil rights; verb form, "tomming."

Time magazine in 1963 defined the most recent usage of "Uncle Tom" as "one who warns against violence in civil rights demonstrations." A subsequent definition by Alex Haley, in the March 1, 1964, *New York Times Magazine*, is broader: "Uncle Tom: A Negro accused by another of comporting himself among white people in a manner which the accuser interprets as servile or cowardly; or a Negro who other Negroes feel has betrayed, or sullied, in any way, a dignified, militant, forthright Negro image."

The usage in this sense is at least a generation old. In 1943 Roi Ottley wrote in *New World A-Coming:* "These Southern leaders, sometimes called 'Uncle Toms' by the more radical Negroes, apparently have not

made up their minds which way to turn in the present crisis."

By the mid-1960s "Uncle Tom" was one of the worst names a Negro could direct at another, and posed a danger to any Negro speaking out for moderation (see BLACK POWER). In 1963, when President Kennedy sent the 88th Congress a far-reaching civil rights bill, a "Community Relations Service" was incorporated to work with local communities. In naming this service, Ted Sorensen wrote, "Negro Congressmen had urged that the words 'mediation' and 'conciliation' had an 'Uncle Tom' air about them and should be stricken from the title."

The largest-circulation Negro magazine, *Ebony,* made this comparison: "Not unlike those Jews who actively helped their exterminators, are the Uncle Toms who collaborate with white racists by playing the roles of apologist and informer.... Such duplicity and complacency, coupled with the old custom of adjusting to a position of inferiority rather than insisting upon his constitutional rights, would have led the Negro to his Buchenwald, had he not learned the prudence—and the power—of positive resistance."

Origin of the phrase, obviously, was Harriet Beecher Stowe's 1852 novel *Uncle Tom's Cabin,* which did more than any other book of the period to dramatize the evils of slavery and became an abolitionists' bible. In 1853 the *New York Tribune* reported the European reception of the Stowe book: "Europe has achieved the luxury of a new sensation in the reception and digestion of Mrs. Stowe's great work.... Even our Diplomacy stands aghast at the rushing, swelling flood of Uncle Tomism which is now sweeping over the continent."

The original Uncle Tom was said to

have been a slave subsequently ordained as the Rev. J. Henson and presented to Queen Victoria in 1876. A variety of usages of the phrase followed: among them Uncle Tomtitude, Uncle Tomized, and Uncle Tomific.

It was not, until the civil rights movement gained new momentum in this century that the meaning of Uncle Tom changed from "long-suffering but heroic" to "subservient and not militant enough."

Today some blacks feel that the use of "Uncle" and "Aunt" has often been a racial slight by whites reluctant to give older Negroes the titles of "Mr." or "Mrs." Some commercial trade names using avuncular titles—like "Aunt Jemima Pancake Mix" and "Uncle Ben's Rice"—have avoided criticism by changing the picture of their characters to appear slimmer and more attractive, less the stereotype of the "Mammy" or "Uncle Tom."

The name Tom has been used as a generic slight throughout the history of the English language. Tom Fool (leading to tomfoolery) and Tom Farthing were early English dunces; a famous midget was named Tom Thumb, and *tommyrot, tomcat,* and *tomboy* are still in use.

During the MARCH ON WASHINGTON in August 1963 a favorite song was "Keep On a-Walkin' " with its final verse:

> *Ain't gonna let no Uncle Tom,*
> *Lawdy, turn me 'round, turn*
> *me 'round, turn me 'round,*
> *Ain't gonna let no Uncle Tom,*
> *Lawdy, turn me 'round,*
> *Keep on a-walkin' (yea!)*
> *Keep on a-talkin' (yea!)*
> *Marchin' on to Freedom land.*

A recent synonym for Uncle Tom is "Oreo," the trade name of a cookie that is black on the outside and white in the middle. Similarly, "Toms" among American Indians have been called "apple"—red outside, white inside.

As might be expected, feminists refer to women who cater to male chauvinism as "Aunt Toms."

UNCOMMITTED NATIONS, *see* **THIRD WORLD; NEUTRALIST.**

UNDERGROUND PRESS, *see* **SAMIZDAT.**

UNFINISHED BUSINESS reason usually given, after much public soul-searching, for running again.

No man ever runs again because he likes the job, because he couldn't make as much in private industry, because he enjoys the play of power, because retirement would be boring or because he owes too many people too many favors.

On the contrary, reassuming the burdens of office is a great personal sacrifice. His neglected family will gamely go along with his decision because the country, state, or assembly district must come first. The crushing demands of the job must be faced again for another term because the party and the nation needs him.

Why does he do it? Why does he hang on grimly to the onerous torch rather than pass it on to the next generation of grasping, ambitious, inexperienced Young Turks who are eager to get their hands on it? The standard reason: "unfinished business."

Any number of quotations from Presidents who chose to run again could be used here, but Harry Truman phrased it in its classic form:

> The compelling motive in my decision to run for the Presidency in 1948 was the same as it had been in

1944. There was still "unfinished business" confronting the most successful fifteen years of Democratic administration in the history of the country. . . . I also felt, without undue ego, that this was no time for a new and inexperienced hand to take over the government and risk the interruption of our domestic program and put a dangerous strain on our delicately balanced foreign policy.

UNFLAPPABLE calm in a crisis; unmoved by furor.

The sobriquet "unflappable Mac" was applied to Harold Macmillan, British Foreign Minister and Prime Minister (1957–63). For a time spanning the Suez crisis to the Profumo affair he retained his reputation for imperturbability in the face of political storms. In 1967 Mayor Jerome Cavanagh of Detroit was described by the *New York Times* in a profile during the racial riots in his city as "unflappable."

The opening lines from Kipling's "If" describe the unflappable man:

> *If you can keep your head
> when all about you
> Are losing theirs and blaming
> it on you . . .*

A commentary on this poem appeared in the form of signs put up in offices by advertising executives in the early sixties: "If you can keep your head when all about you are losing theirs—perhaps you don't understand the gravity of the situation."

Flap, according to H. L. Mencken, originated with British aviators in World War I as a word for air raid. The mental picture of the flapping wings of birds when frightened is apt; a political flap is a minor crisis, with assurances by professionals that "this, too, shall pass." "Flapdoodle,"

or nonsense, can be traced back to the American Civil War.

A frequently used synonym for "flap" is *brouhaha,* a fifteenth-century French word for "commotion" or "hubbub" which was introduced into English letters by Oliver Wendell Holmes Sr. in 1890. The probable origin of brouhaha is the Hebrew *baruch habba,* "blessed be he who enters," exclaimed noisily by actors playing priests disguised as devils in early French farce.

For the causes of flaps, see FLAK and FALLOUT.

UNGOVERNABLE what pessimists consider every major U.S. city to be.

"Is New York City ungovernable?" was a question often asked in the late sixties when strikes, smog, congestion, and a general malaise afflicted the city dweller. The word was probably first used by CBS commentator Eric Sevareid.

"Ungovernable" soon became an urban affairs cliché, trotted out in think pieces following each new strike by public employees, along with "crisis of the cities," the title of a series by the *New York Herald Tribune* in the early sixties.

"Governance," another word from the same French root, sprouted in academia and became a vogue-word substitute for "government" or "governing."

UNHOLY ALLIANCE attack phrase on any political agreement, especially when disparate elements find themselves in opposition to the same thing.

"Unholy alliance" was Franklin Roosevelt's characterization of the groups backing Wendell Willkie in the 1940 presidential campaign. Both John L. Lewis, head of the United

Mine Workers, and the American Communist party opposed Roosevelt for different reasons; he skillfully used their support of Willkie as a KISS OF DEATH. Wrote Samuel Rosenman: "The President, who for years had been called by political enemies a Communist or a tool of the Communists, was now able to turn the tables on his Republican adversary, and attack the alliance of the Communists, the dictatorial labor leader Lewis, and the old-guard reactionary Republican leaders. This opportunity was unique in his political experience, and he cheerfully took full advantage of it." FDR warned:

There is something very ominous in this combination . . . within the Republican Party between the extreme reactionary and the extreme radical elements of this country. . . . We all know the story of the unfortunate chameleon which turned brown when placed on a brown rug, and turned red when placed on a red rug, but who died a tragic death when they put him on a Scotch plaid. We all know what would happen to Government if it tried to fulfill all the secret understandings and promises made between the conflicting groups which are now backing the Republican Party.

Bernard Schwartz was an energetic counsel for a House subcommittee investigating the Federal Communications Commission in 1958. When he appeared overzealous to members of the subcommittee, he was fired. His subsequent statement illustrates the current usage of the word: "I accuse the majority of this subcommittee, in order to further their own partisan interests, of joining an unholy alliance between business and the White House to obtain a WHITEWASH."

All "unholy" alliances are based on the "Holy Alliance" signed by the kings of Russia, Prussia, and Austria in Paris in 1815.

See STRANGE BEDFELLOWS; COALITION.

UNION, *see* STATE OF THE UNION.

UNITED NATIONS   international organization of member states; name coined by FDR.

Samuel Rosenman wrote of the bathroom agreement that named the world body:

He [FDR] was also pleased—and proud—that it was he who had suggested the phrase "United Nations" to Churchill. Churchill, in public utterances, had referred to them as "Allied Nations" and "Associated Nations." The President thought of "United Nations," not as an analogy to "United States," but rather as expressive of the fact that the Allies were united in a common purpose. Having hit upon that phrase one day, he immediately had someone wheel him right into Churchill's room, interrupting the Churchillian bath, and the two agreed then and there upon the name. The same name was used three years later to designate the formal worldwide entity, the United Nations Organization.

The British Prime Minister confirmed this in his war memoirs: "The President has chosen the title 'United Nations' for all the Powers now working together. This is much better than 'Alliance,' which places him in constitutional difficulties, or 'Associated Powers,' which is flat."

Ironically, it was another American President, Woodrow Wilson, who chose "covenant" rather than "agreement" or "treaty" in the "Covenant of the League of Nations"; he felt that the Old Testament word, recalling God's covenant with

Abraham, added a necessary solemnity.

UNITED STATES OF AMERICA

coinage attributed to pamphleteer Thomas Paine.

Claims a biographer, in *Tom Paine, America's Godfather:* "To Paine also belongs the honor of naming our country the 'United States of America.' He was the first to use the name in print, and it was his own creation." Soon after the Declaration of Independence, Paine brandished the title at Lord Howe. "The United States of America," he wrote in the second issue of *The Crisis,* "will sound as pompously in the world or in history as The Kingdom of Great Britain." ("Pompous" then meant "important," rather than the present meaning, "self-important.")

The naming was authoritative. The Articles of Confederation begin: "Article I. The style of this confederacy shall be, 'THE UNITED STATES OF AMERICA.' "

In current usage, it is referred to as the U.S., which is often written as US. The use of all three initials seems corny, as in "the good old U.S.A." It is known familiarly as UNCLE SAM and Uncle Sugar.

UNITED WE STAND an early

U.S. motto that never quite made it to official status.

John Dickenson wrote "The Patriot's Appeal" in 1776:

> Then join hand in hand, brave
> Americans all—
> By uniting we stand, by dividing
> we fall.

The State of Kentucky sharpened it to "United we stand; divided we fall" and adopted it as its state motto in 1792. But the U.S. had adopted another motto in 1777—"E Pluribus Unum" (From Many, One) first found on the title page of the *Gentleman's Miscellany* in January 1692— and "united we stand" was blocked, though many Americans still think it is the translation for *E Pluribus Unum.*

Salmon P. Chase, Lincoln's Secretary of the Treasury, placed "In God We Trust" on coins to go with "E Pluribus Unum" and "Liberty," crowding the coin so that there was obviously no space left for "United We Stand." The rear of the Great Seal, published on every dollar bill, contains some Latin slogans not known to one American in a million. "Annuit Coeptis" means "He [God] has favored our undertakings" (from Vergil's *Aeneid,* Book IX, verse 625), and "Novus Ordo Seclorum" means "A new order of the ages" (from Vergil's fourth *Eclogue*). Both mottoes were proposed by Charles Thomson, Secretary of Congress, in a report adopted by the Continental Congress on June 20, 1782. Why? Edwin S. Costrell, chief of the Historical Division of the U.S. Department of State, informs the author: "In response to your query 'why they appear on the Seal,' I can only conjecture that Thomson, in proposing the mottoes, and the Congress, in adopting them, considered them to be appropriate."

"United we stand, divided we fall" combines two old concepts. "Union is Strength" is an old English proverb; the idea is expressed in Shakespeare's *King John:* "This union shall do more than battery can/To our fast-closed gates." "Divide and conquer" (in the original "divide and reign,") has a record at least as old as 1633.

"America the Beautiful" is more singable than "The Star-Spangled Banner," which, however, remains the national anthem. Similarly, "United we stand" is stronger and more intelligible than any Latin motto, including the sacrosanct "E Pluribus Unum"; unfortunately, its supporters have been divided.

UNLEASH CHIANG a Republican promise to remove restraints on Chiang Kai-shek's Taiwan forces which it was felt might intimidate Communist China; promise was kept, but China was not intimidated.

In the late forties and early fifties, there was a strong feeling in the U.S. that the "let the dust settle" policy had caused the free world to "lose" China to Communism. To add insult to injury, the anti-Communist Chinese forces on Formosa were being held back from launching an invasion of their homeland.

John Foster Dulles, first Dewey's and then Eisenhower's chief foreign policy adviser, was the American most associated with a promise to "unleash Chiang." When he became President, Eisenhower redeemed the Republican pledge with this statement:

> In June, 1950, following the aggressive attack on the Republic of Korea, the United States Seventh Fleet was instructed both to prevent attack upon Formosa and also to insure that Formosa should not be used as a base of operations against the Chinese Communist mainland. . . . I am . . . issuing instructions that the Seventh Fleet no longer be employed to shield Communist China. Permit me to make crystal clear this order implies no aggressive intent on our part. But we certainly have no obligation to protect a nation fighting us in Korea.

In fact, the Seventh Fleet had been protecting Formosa (now Taiwan) from invasion by China, and not vice versa. The purpose of the removal of the "shield" was to put Communist China on notice that the U.S. might

have a surprise in store, and to require deployment of defense forces opposite Formosa on the mainland. But when years slipped by and no action was taken by Chiang's forces—nor was any permitted by the U.S.—the phrase boomeranged, and became a derisive term for foreign policy bluffing.

When the offshore islands of Quemoy and Matsu were bombarded early in 1955, the Administration took a deliberately vague posture, indicating the U.S. would come to their defense if they were considered necessary to the defense of Formosa. At the same time, a promise was extracted from the Nationalists not to invade the mainland without first informing the U.S. Critics called this "re-leashing Chiang." After the 1972 signing of the Shanghai Communique between the U.S. and the People's Republic of China, the phrase was used only in ironic recollection.

The phrase was and is associated with Secretary of State Dulles, usually critically. Writing about "journalese" in the *Dictionary of Contemporary American Usage,* Bergen and Cornelia Evans wrote in 1957: "Certain pompous phrases must remain permanently set up in type: *bipartisan foreign policy, act of overt aggression . . . titular head of the party, diplomat without portfolio . . . policy of containment.* But to assume such inflated terminology is confined to newspapers is to be as ignorant as unjust. It was not some petty, pretentious scribbler who invented *massive retaliation* and *agonizing reappraisal* or spoke of *unleashing* Chiang Kai-shek." The Evanses left out LIBERATION OF CAPTIVE PEOPLES and BRINKMANSHIP in the last grouping, and a less colorful successor to Dulles, Dean Rusk, popularized EYEBALL TO EYEBALL.

The "unleash" metaphor was used

successfully by British MP, later Prime Minister, Harold Macmillan in 1945: he advocated "the unleashing of production" after the war, playing further on the canine image by urging the Labour party to "let sleeping dogmas lie."

UNPACK punch line of a religious-racial issue joke.

Threats of rampant popery in the U.S. if Catholic Al Smith were elected in 1928 led to this gag: When Smith lost to Hoover, he was said to have sent a one-word wire to the Pope in the Vatican: "Unpack."

When a Catholic finally was elected, in 1960, he took a strong position against federal aid to parochial schools. John F. Kennedy, proposing an education bill to Congress, knew it would cause some anger in Catholic circles. He turned around the old Smith joke: "As all of you know, some circles invented the myth that after Al Smith's defeat in 1928, he sent a one-word telegram to the Pope: 'Unpack.' After my press conference on the school bill, I received a one-word wire from the Pope: 'Pack.' "

After Kennedy was assassinated, blacks were worried about the Administration of Texan Lyndon Johnson. After his first speech to the joint session of Congress on November 27, 1963, in which he called for civil rights legislation, black comedian Dick Gregory revived the gag: "Twenty million of us unpacked our bags."

UN-POOR, UN-YOUNG, UN-BLACK, *see* **MIDDLE AMERICA.**

UNTHINKABLE THOUGHTS proposals too mind-boggling to discuss; phrase used by those who want to advance schemes that shatter shibboleths.

The word became agitated in political parlance by nuclear physicist Herman Kahn, who wrote *On Thermonuclear War* in 1959. James Newman in *Scientific American* magazine attacked Kahn's character as well as style of writing in a vitriolic review calling his book "a moral tract on how to justify mass murder." The reviewer's lead was memorable: *"Is there really a Herman Kahn? It's hard to believe. Doubts cross one's mind almost from the first page of this deplorable book: no one could write like this; no one could think like this. Perhaps the whole thing is a staff hoax in bad taste."*

Perturbed about the violence of the reviewer's onslaught, Kahn wrote the editor of *Scientific American,* Dennis Flanagan, asking him to consider a rebuttal entitled "Thinking about the Unthinkable." Flanagan replied: "I do not think there is much point in thinking about the unthinkable; surely it is more profitable to think about the thinkable . . . nuclear war is unthinkable. I should prefer to devote my thoughts to how nuclear war can be prevented."

Kahn—there really is one, he works for the Hudson Institute THINK TANK in New York—wrote a 1962 book, entitled, oddly enough, *Thinking about the Unthinkable.* He made his point in this manner:

It is characteristic of our times that many intelligent and sincere people are willing to argue that it is immoral to think and even more immoral to write in detail about having to fight a thermonuclear war. . . . In a sense we are acting like those ancient kings who punished messengers who brought them bad news. . . . In our times, thermonuclear war may seem unthinkable, immoral, insane, hideous, or highly unlikely, but it is not impossible. To act intelligently we must learn as much as we can about the risks. We may thereby be able better to avoid nuclear war.

Senate Foreign Relations Committee chairman J. William Fulbright further popularized the term in 1964:

It is within our ability, and unquestionably in our interests, to cut loose from established myths and to start thinking some "unthinkable thoughts"—about the cold war and East-West relations, about the underdeveloped countries and particularly those in Latin America, about the changing nature of the Chinese Communist threat in Asia, and about the festering war in Vietnam. . . . The Soviet Union is of course one of the users of the Panama Canal, albeit a minor one, and this fact suggests an "unthinkable thought": the possibility of Soviet participation in a consortium constituted to build and operate a new Central American canal. I am not advocating Soviet participation, but neither do I think it must be ruled out as "unthinkable."

Technically, "unthinkable" should be limited to such metaphysical concepts as infinity and the nature of God, but in current usage it is synonymous with "inconceivable" with a pinch of condemnation added.

A recent usage by columnist Meg Greenfield in *Newsweek* (May 8, 1978) brings the phrase closer to the purely political arena. " 'Thinking about the unthinkable'—the old nuclear strategist's phrase—has a new meaning in Washington these days," she wrote. "It means thinking about the possibility that the Senate will reject the SALT agreement Jimmy Carter brings home."

UP TO SPEED   familiar with the latest details; *au courant;* briefed

and ready to answer questions.

A newly appointed cabinet officer is brought "up to speed" by the permanent bureaucracy before his confirmation hearings; a White House aide who has been on vacation or working on a special assignment must be brought "up to speed" by his colleagues when he returns; a President, preparing for a press conference, needs to be brought "up to speed" on a variety of topics that have not been the focus of recent attention.

This phrase was made part of Washington parlance by White House aides with advertising backgrounds in the sixties. One origin is said to be in radio, referring to the need to bring an electrical transcription up to a certain number of revolutions per minute on a turntable before turning up the sound for broadcast, to avoid jarring listeners with a "wow" sound. In television, it was defined in the *1955 Television Dictionary/Handbook for Sponsors* as "Time when the camera and sound mechanisms are ready for filming and moving at the same speed."

The opposite of being "up to speed" is, curiously, *out of pocket,* a phrase that used to mean "unreimbursed," but in the seventies has come to mean *out of touch,* or in its most extreme form, *out to lunch.* A related term, from moviemaker's lingo, is *off my screen*—that is, beyond my ken. A synonym for "up to speed," in its sense of being ready to go, with all in agreement, is *on all fours.*

UTOPIANISM, *see* **TECHNOCRAT; WAR TO END WARS.**

VAST WASTELAND   a criticism of television programming; a gloomy description about the results of any unfulfilled effort.

Newton Minow, a law partner of Adlai Stevenson's appointed by John F. Kennedy to be chairman of the Federal Communications Commission, astounded a National Association of Broadcasters audience in 1961. He said that if anyone watched television from morning to night, "I can assure you that you will observe a vast wasteland."

Minow's use of the phrase was taken up immediately because (1) it was directed to an audience in the communications field; (2) that audience is notorious for self-flagellation on artistic grounds while it increases earnings on mediocre programs; and (3) previous phrases of criticism—"boob tube," "idiot box," and "videot"—were too frivolous or severe. Minow's phrase combined a proper forum with, perhaps, a fitting literary source—poet T. S. Eliot's *The Waste Land.*

Joseph P. Kennedy told Minow that "this was the best speech since January 20 [the inaugural address]—give 'em hell—hit 'em again." President Kennedy let Minow take the lead on the subject of television programming. At a press conference July 24, 1962, Kennedy was asked if the introduction of the Telstar communications satellite meant that "the U.S.

networks should make a greater effort to do something about the 'vast wasteland?' " Kennedy evaded the question: "I'm going to leave Mr. Minow to argue the wasteland issue, I think."

In 1952 Minow's associate Adlai Stevenson quoted an unnamed "famous American critic" as saying that "the South was the wasteland of the mind." The phrase continues to be used in this general sense, usually recalling the description of television. Former President Eisenhower called President Kennedy's economic program in 1963 "fiscal recklessness" that would lead not to "a free country with bright opportunities but a vast wasteland of debt and financial chaos."

VEEP   affectionate nickname for the Vice President.

Senate Majority Leader Alben Barkley of Kentucky was a popular choice for Truman's Vice President in 1948, after Justice William O. Douglas turned down the nomination. At that time, more and more corporate Vice Presidents were becoming known as "VPs," and the familiar form "veep"—to describe an informal-minded man—was natural.

Barkley's successor, Richard Nixon, sidestepped the title: "I think *veep* was a term of affection applied to Mr. Barkley and should go out with him." Barkley then appropriated the acronym for a television series, *Meet the Veep.*

Writing about acronyms for *American Speech* magazine in 1955, Temple University's S. V. Baum predicted: "It is a near certainty that *veep* will pass out of general use and will eventually fall into linguistic obsolescence." Its use did decline for a time, but it remains a useful alternative to VP for headline writers and political punsters. *Newsweek,* in a 1967 article on candidates for the Republican vice-presidential nomination, said that Governors Love, Kirk, and Chafee and Senators Tower and Javits were entries in "The Veepstakes."

VESTED INTERESTS the wealthy; the powerful; the privileged class; the Establishment.

Great Britain's policy in the nineteenth century was reputed to have been that a great power had only interests, never friends. The interests—*vested, special, predatory,* and *sinister*—have made no new friends since.

Vested (from its meaning of clothed) legally means a consummated right. The term "vested rights" was used in a political sense by English essayist and historian Thomas Babington Macaulay in 1857: "On one side is a statesman preaching patience, respect for vested rights. . . . On the other side is a demagogue ranting about the tyranny of capitalists. . . . Which of the two candidates is likely to be preferred by a workingman who hears his children cry for bread?"

Economists had an affinity for the phrase. American economist and politician Henry George, who died of apoplexy while running for mayor of New York City in 1897, probably coined the term "vested interests" in urging a single tax on landowners. Es-

sayist Agnes Repplier wrote at the turn of the century that "A world of vested interests is not a world which welcomes the disruptive force of candor." British economist John Maynard Keynes wrote in 1947, in his *General Theory:* "I am sure that the power of vested interests is vastly exaggerated compared with the gradual encroachment of ideas . . . it is ideas, not vested interests, which are dangerous for good or evil." Walter Heller, leading Kennedy-Johnson economic adviser, used the phrase in 1966: "As a statesman, a President has a vital, not to say vested, interest on behalf of the nation, in prosperity and rapid growth."

The "interest" half of the phrase is more interesting. English philosopher Jeremy Bentham became suspicious of the "sinister interests" early in the nineteenth century. Prime Minister William Gladstone said, "The interests are always awake while the country often slumbers and sleeps." In 1883 Joseph Chamberlain, defending English radicalism, said that "private interests are like a disciplined regiment while the public good was defended by an unorganized mob."

"The Interests," wrote H. L. Mencken, ". . . were first heard of during the Bryan saturnalia of vituperation at the end of the Nineteenth Century." William Jennings Bryan called them "the predatory interests" in his three campaigns; Robert La Follette attacked "special privilege" at the same time, and the two expressions merged with Theodore Roosevelt's attack on SPECIAL INTERESTS."

Roosevelt, who attacked President Taft as "a tool of the interests," left no group out, hitting equally at "the big special interests and the little special interests." The man who benefited by the Roosevelt-Taft split, Woodrow Wilson, was not above adopting the magic "radical" word: "The business of government is to organize the common interest against the special interests."

Because the word "interest" had a progressive-populist-radical tradition, Republicans as a rule stayed away from it. But Wendell Willkie, campaigning in 1940 first for the nomination and then against FDR, used it in both directions. First, he charged that the Republican Old Guard was "corrupted by vested interests in its own ranks and by reactionary forces. It forgot its own liberal tradition." After he became the nominee, he gave it a new twist in a "petition" to FDR: "Give up this vested interest that you have in the depression, open your eyes to the future, help us to build a New World."

More than anyone else in modern times, Harry Truman revived the battle cry. He declared in several campaigns that the task of the Democratic party was to take government out of the hands of "the special interests" and return it to "the people"; in 1948, he dipped into Robert La Follette's vocabulary to specify a portion of those interests as "gluttons of privilege."

Politicians know that attacking "interests" has become a cliché, but there continues a certain STEMWINDING affection for the word, especially by Democrats. It has been spoofed: Victor Aloysius ("Just Call Me Vic") Meyers, Lieutenant Governor of California during World War II, told reporters: "Habitually I go without a vest so that I can't be accused of standing for the vested interests."

See PUBLIC INTEREST, CONVENIENCE AND INTEREST.

VETO, *see* POCKET VETO; ONE-HOUSE VETO.

VICE PRESIDENCY, *see* VEEP; THROTTLEBOTTOM; STEPPINGSTONE; RUNNING MATE; DEAD END, POLITICAL; HEARTBEAT AWAY FROM THE PRESIDENCY.

VICTORY HAS A THOUSAND FATHERS expression made famous by President John F. Kennedy in 1961 as he assumed responsibility for the BAY OF PIGS FIASCO: "Victory has a thousand fathers, but defeat is an orphan."

When Kennedy was asked the source of this expression, he told an aide, "Oh, I don't know; it's just an old saying." *Bartlett's Quotations* cites a 1942 use by Count Galleazo Ciano, in *The Ciano Diaries,* "As always, victory finds a hundred fathers but defeat is an orphan."

It had been reported earlier. N.Y.C. Transit Commissioner John J. Gilhooley heard Philippines Ambassador Carlos Romulo use this expression to describe the Korean conflict to Secretary of State John Foster Dulles on an airplane en route to a CIO convention in 1953.

Phrase watcher Paul Hoffman informs the author that the phrase, in its entirety, and used just as President Kennedy used it, "is spoken by the character portraying Field Marshal von Rundstedt in the film *The Desert Fox* (1951)."

In 1968 Florida Governor Claude Kirk told a Ripon, Wisconsin, audience that the war in Vietnam was "the first in which defeat has a thousand fathers and victory is an orphan."

VICUÑA COAT, *see* INFLUENCE PEDDLER; I NEED HIM; ABOMINABLE NO-MAN.

VIETNAMIZATION a plan for the extrication of U.S. ground forces from Vietnam, with the concurrent build-up of South Vietnamese forces, so as to provide the South Vietnamese people with what President Nixon called "a reasonable chance for survival."

The predecessor word, used in the later stages of the Johnson Administration by both Democrats and Republicans, was the awkward "de-Americanization." In 1968, however, this began to be replaced by newsmen and American officials in Saigon with "Vietnamization."

In a dispatch from Saigon to the *Los Angeles Times* by correspondent Robert Elegant on February 16, 1969, a distinction was drawn: "In Washington the fashionable term is 'de-Americanizing' the Vietnam war. In Saigon, men talk of 'Vietnamizing' the allied military machine. The two efforts must obviously go hand-in-hand. The semantic difference is slight, but the actual difference is great. Washington is primarily concerned with reducing the American commitment—with regard to developments on the battlefield and in Paris. For reasons equally apparent, both Americans and Vietnamese in Saigon are primarily concerned with building an effective native military force to cope with Communist forces when the American presence is greatly reduced—and eventually removed."

The word was popularized in the U.S. by Secretary of Defense Melvin Laird. He first used it in verb form on *Meet the Press,* March 23, 1969:

"I believe that we can move toward Vietnamizing the war by the program that I outlined to the Armed Services Committee on Wednesday, by modernizing the forces of the South Vietnamese on a realistic basis."

In his November 3 SILENT MAJOR-ITY speech, President Nixon gave the word the presidential imprimatur: "The Vietnamization Plan was launched following Secretary Laird's visit to Vietnam in March. Under the plan, I ordered first a substantial increase in the training and equipment of South Vietnamese forces." He described "our plan for Vietnamization . . . a plan in which we will withdraw all of our forces from Vietnam on a schedule in accordance with our program, as the South Vietnamese become strong enough to defend their own freedom."

President Thieu did not like the word. On November 15 he publicly urged the Vietnamese media to avoid using the term because he felt it gave credence to North Vietnamese charges that the U.S. was turning the fighting over to "puppet, mercenary troops." But he did not offer an alternative phrase, and Vietnamization had already taken hold.

The "-ization" construction had been used in diplomacy before. "Balkanization" was used to mean the breakup of an empire into small, usually ineffective, states. The West German newspaper *Die Zeit* used it in a modern context in 1968: "After the Second World War, we witnessed the Communization of the Balkans. Today we witness the Balkanization of Communism."

Americanization never before had a diplomatic meaning; it was used to refer to the assimilation of immigrants, and in the sixties the book and motion picture called *The Americanization of Emily* used the word in a more general way. The de-Americanization word was a new formulation of the LET ASIANS FIGHT ASIANS idea, sterilized by the mouth-filling nature of the word.

"-ize" can be used linguistically for good or evil. A word like "modern-ize" transforms an adjective into a needed verb, but a word like "finalize" is a pretentious substitute for "finish." "In the early stages of finalization" is bureaucratese for "not finished yet."

"Normalization" became popular in the diplomatic lexicon in 1971, popularized by Henry Kissinger and usually referring to relations between the U.S. and mainland China. A bland, unexciting word was required here, and "normalization" is so bland as to be tranquilizing. ("Tranquilize" is a pretentious word for "calm.") See WINDING DOWN; VIETNAM LINGO.

VIETNAM LINGO words and phrases left over from the Vietnam war, now only used bitterly or ironically, usually to derogate political and military hawkishness.

Washington writer and futurologist Paul Dickson ran down a farrago of these expressions in a *New York Times* Op-Ed piece in 1972: "Many of the words and terms of the war are by now so completely debunked and abused that if they were not so laden with tragedy they would be funny. Among them: 'pacification,' 'light at the end of the tunnel,' 'body count,' 'free-fire zone,' 'hearts and minds of the people' . . . 'kill ration' . . . 'search and destroy' . . ." (See VIETNAMIZATION; PACIFICATION; HACK IT; WINDING DOWN.)

In the investigation of the destruction of the village of My Lai, the term "waste" to mean "kill" was used by Lieutenant William Calley. Linguist Mario Pei traced the use of the word in the *Modern Age* quarterly review:

> *To lay waste* goes back to Middle English, and there is an antiquated legal use of *to waste* (to do away with) in the sense of to destroy property (but not human life). From 1689 on we find *to waste* (to do away

with) used in connection with such impersonal things as sin and sorrow. Shakespeare comes a shade closer to the modern usage in 'Would he were wasted, marrow, bones and all.' Wentworth and Flexner's *Dictionary of American Slang* informs us that the verbal use of *waste* originated with teenage gangs, becoming current in the 1950's in the sense of to defeat decisively, to destroy. This is still not the precise counterpart of 'We were ordered to waste all the villagers,' and it is possible that this ultimate semantic shift originated in Vietnam."

A reprise of these terms by war correspondent Homer Bigart in the *New Republic* in 1977 shows how they are used in bitter hindsight today, with an interesting twist to "waste":

> Let us rejoice over the demise of some dreary slogans associated with the Vietnam conflict. For the next imbroglio a whole new set of incantations are needed. Our leaders no longer can tell us to get out there and fight to keep the dominoes from falling. Nobody will profess to see the light at the end of the tunnel. There will be no more crusades to win the hearts and minds of people and save them from agression. One term— "waste"—is not easily shelved. GIs in Vietnam used it as a synonym for kill. When a man was killed he was wasted. A chillingly appropriate term for the 46,229 Americans who fell in action in the Indochina War.

VIETNIK, *see* -NIK SUFFIX.

VIOLIN PIECE, *see* TICK-TOCK.

VISION OF AMERICA the kind of society a leader is required to hope for; once an uplifting and inspiring part of any campaign, now considered a cliché.

Among speechwriters, the **"I SEE"** construction has a revered place in political oratory. When candidate

Jimmy Carter was asked what his vision of America was, he turned to writer Patrick Anderson in the summer of 1976 to produce the appropriate speech. Mr. Anderson provided a draft with "I see" at the beginning of many sentences of its peroration, in the grand tradition, which Mr. Carter used effectively; when it was pointed out by the author that the technique was time-honored, there was some consternation at Carter headquarters, which wanted its candidate to be antipolitical, and the phraseology was dropped.

In *New York* magazine on October 25, 1976, "Adam Smith" (George Goodman) showed how the phrase had become a cliché by capitalizing it: "In the age of instantaneous transmission, these surveys will have been well-studied by the candidates, who will emphasize right and wrong in the Vision of America."

The following week, columnist Russell Baker wrote in the *New York Times Magazine:* "So I decided to vote for President Ford because he had a vision of America. Then a ghostwriter who specializes in composing vision-of-America speeches for politicians explained that this was baloney because Mr. Ford had never been anywhere in America except Grand Rapids, Capitol Hill and the Burning Tree Golf Club, and what's more, nobody had a vision of America anymore, even the ghostwriters who specialized in vision-of-America speeches."

But even thus lampooned, the phrase lives on: in September 1977 Carter pollster Pat Caddell was reported by *Time* to believe "The President needs to spell out more clearly the vision he has for America . . ."

VITAL CENTER, *see* **CENTRIST.**

VOICE FROM THE SEWER any anonymous, disembodied voice in a crowd that seeks to stampede or heckle; particularly, the unidentified voice at a hidden microphone that reassured the 1940 Democratic convention.

Senate Majority Leader Alben Barkley electrified the convention audience with a message from President Roosevelt that at first seemed like a warning not to nominate him for a third term: "The President has never had, and has not today, any desire or purpose to continue in the office of President, to be a candidate for that office, or to be nominated by the convention for that office. He wishes in all earnestness and sincerity to make it clear that all of the delegates to this convention are free to vote for any candidate."

Stunned silence followed. Then a voice on the loudspeaker began the chant, "We want Roosevelt!" and the "draft" began. It turned out that the "voice from the sewer," as it was called, was a member of Chicago Mayor Edward J. Kelley's organization, primed to begin the chant immediately after the Barkley bombshell.

See SPONTANEOUS DEMONSTRATION.

VOICE OF THE PEOPLE, *see* **VOX POPULI.**

VOLUNTEERS unpaid political workers, enthusiastic and vital to a campaign, or a method of committing troops without officially entering a war.

The Eisenhower "volunteers" and CITIZENS COMMITTEE gave pep, sparkle, panache, and a sense of idealistic purpose to the Republican campaign of 1952. See AMATEURS; BANDWAGON. In 1960 the President wondered aloud to Sherman Adams, "What happened to all those fine young people with stars in their eyes who sailed balloons and rang doorbells for us in 1952?"

Adlai Stevenson also attracted a devoted group of volunteers in his 1952 campaign, but by 1956 the ranks of the starry-eyed had dwindled for him as well. Volunteers are attracted mainly by personal CHARISMA and partially by a desire to participate in the fun of a campaign, very little by any expectation of appointive office.

Direct-mail advertising of candidates almost always carries a "volunteer card." (Check one: I will (a) address envelopes (b) hold a coffee klatsch for the candidate in my home (c) canvass my building (d) contribute funds (e) participate in a telephone solicitation.) The "pull" on these cards indicates to the managers what kind of campaign organization they can expect.

Many volunteers come to a headquarters once, get bored if given an assignment they consider beneath their talents, and disappear; others amaze a campaign staff with a zeal that can never really be purchased. Alexis de Toqueville noted it in *Democracy in America:* "I have often admired the extreme skill with which the inhabitants of the United States succeed in proposing a common object for the exertions of a great many men and inducing them voluntarily to pursue it . . ."

In its international warfare meaning, the word was popularized in the Spanish Civil War. German and Italian troops were dispatched to General Francisco Franco by Hitler and Mussolini under the guise of "volunteers." Foreign nationals supporting Loyalist forces were also called volunteers, but quotation marks did not appear around the word because it was felt in the U.S. that they were genuine idealists, not troops serving the disguised interests of their respective countries.

When the Chinese Communists decided to enter the Korean War, they reused this technique and term, which has since become a standard method of intervention, along with "military advisers."

VOTE EARLY AND OFTEN an election day greeting by politicians.

This is the sort of line that is ordinarily lost in the mists of election time, but historian James Morgan found the originator in his 1926 book of biographies: the jokester was John Van Buren, New York lawyer, who was the son of President Martin Van Buren.

VOTE FRAUD, *see* **BALLOT-BOX STUFFING; CEMETERY VOTE.**

VOTE OF CONFIDENCE legislative reassurance; more generally, any expression of support.

The phrase originated in the British Parliament, where it is a division of the House of Commons in which the government tests its strength. Members of the majority party must vote with their party; if enough defect to lose a vote, the government is expected to call for a general election.

Conversely, if a motion of no confidence is introduced by the opposition in the House of Commons and passes, the result is called a *vote of censure* (although it contains the words "no confidence," it is not referred to as a *vote of no confidence,* except in America); in that case, the government is "upset" or "falls," and an election is called.

When criticism of the conduct of the war rose in 1942, Prime Minister Winston Churchill asked for a vote of confidence, calling the procedure "thoroughly normal, constitutional, and democratic"; after three days of debate, the motion was carried 464 to 1. In effect, Churchill brought the criticism to a head and then mustered support for his policies.

In the U.S., there is no such formal method of saying, "There may be sniping, but when the chips are down, we have a majority." As used in this country, the phrase means some voter expression, such as a special local election or a referendum, that is interpreted as a renewed MANDATE; or a re-election, which is called "a vote of confidence for his policies," or any pat on the back from a group of supporters. *Newsweek* reported in 1967 that a group of anti-Reagan voters in California had hopes of forcing a "recall" election: "They want to make him face an embarrassing 'vote of confidence.'"

VOX POPULI . . . vox Dei. "The voice of the people is the voice of God."

The phrase is attributed to Alcuin, in an epistle to Charlemagne, around the year 800. It was used as the text of a sermon by Walter Reynolds, Archbishop of Canterbury, early in the fourteenth century at the coronation of Edward III; the "voice of the people," through the nobles, had dethroned Edward II.

The thought is beautiful and universal; the Japanese language has a parallel proverb: "Heaven has no mouth but it talks through the people." However, the phrase has been used to justify the bending of leadership to the popular will, and in that sense has been attacked, for instance by:

Alexander Hamilton, who said in a speech to the Federal Convention in 1787: "The voice of the people has been said to be the voice of God; and, however generally this maxim has been quoted and believed, it is not true to fact. The people are turbulent and changing; they seldom judge or determine right."

Theodore Roosevelt, who said: "It may be that the voice of the people is the voice of God in fifty-one cases out of a hundred; but in the remaining forty-nine it is quite as likely to be the voice of the devil, or what is still worse, the voice of a fool."

General William Tecumseh Sherman, who wrote in a letter to his wife in 1863: "Vox populi, vox humbug."

Walter Lippmann, who in 1925 gave the phrase a narrower meaning: "I have conceived public opinion to be, not the voice of God, nor the voice of society, but the voice of the interested spectators of action."

Dwight Eisenhower, who, after viewing the film in Paris of Tex McCrary's Madison Square Garden rally of 15,000 people urging him to come home and run in 1952, yelling "We Like Ike!" found the voice unclear: "Even though we agree with the old proverb, 'The voice of the people is the voice of God,' it is not always easy to determine just what that voice is saying. I continue to get letters from certain of my friends who are almost as violent in their urgent recommendations that I do not make an early visit home as those who believe that I should come."

The phrase has been used as a barb (Abraham Lincoln was called "Fox populi" by *Vanity Fair*), as the title of a radio show ("Vox Pop") and as doggerel in the presidential campaign of 1920:

Cox or Harding, Harding or Cox?
You tell us, populi, you got the vox.

WAFFLE to straddle or refuse to commit; to use **WEASEL WORDS.**

At the time of the Israeli-Arab war in 1967, U.S. Secretary of State Dean Rusk evaded a question from Senator John Sherman Cooper (R-Ky.) regarding a declaration of intent to keep open the Gulf of Aqaba to all international shipping. Rusk said, "That matter has not been finally decided. There are some plusses and minuses. At the present time, no, I cannot give you a final answer."

A dispatch by Chalmers Roberts of the *Los Angeles Times-Washington Post* syndicate commented, "That sort of response led Senators and Representatives to tell reporters afterwards that Rusk had waffled about supporting Israel. One said, 'They just walked around it.' "

Suddenly the rare verb found new admirers. C. L. Sulzberger of the *New York Times* wrote on June 11, 1967: "The United States can claim no credit for Israel's swift victory, but the fact of that victory was of strategic benefit to us although our role was confined to waffling."

Newsweek's July 19 issue, written a week before, reported that "many Jews felt that Israel had been forced to go to war because of waffling by the Administration . . ."

In a letter dated June 13 to the *Times* of London, Desmond Donnelly, a Labour Member of Parliament, demanded: "Are the Western powers going to act about the Arab refugees or continue to waffle?"

It seemed as if journalism had been taken over by a chef who had over-ordered waffle mix and told his waiters, "Push waffles." Occasionally when a bellwether reporter uses an out-of-the-ordinary word in a particular context, there follows a brief flurry of usage by other commentators and soon the word returns to limbo.

The word is derived from *waff*, a Scottish word for wave, and its dictionary definition is "to flutter or flap like a clumsy bird." Another possible derivation is from *waff*, to bark and snarl, or to talk foolishly. It does not seem likely to come from the noun "waffle," from wafer, an indented cake baked in a waffle iron, though the crisscrossed pattern may give an indication of uncertainty.

In its political use, to *waffle* is synonymous with the verb to *fudge,* which appears also to be taken from the name of a food—in this case a candy—but actually comes from to *fudge,* to succeed. In Washington, the State Department is called "the fudge factory." Former President Gerald Ford, in a December 1977 breakfast meeting with reporters, was asked about the change in President Carter's position on the Panama Canal, and replied with candor, "I think we both fudged a little on Panama in the campaign." That was a far cry from his charge about Carter in the 1976 campaign: "He wavers, he wanders, he wiggles and he waffles, and he shouldn't be President of the United States."

WAGING PEACE Eisenhower's phrase showing the new nature of foreign relations; it means ideological competition without warfare; no "war" but also no real "peace."

Dwight Eisenhower used the phrase as the title of a volume of his memoirs: he followed *Mandate for Change* with *Waging the Peace*.

The technique of substituting the word "peace" for the word "war" is frequently used, often effectively. When the stock market booming in a wartime economy gets news of the likelihood of peace, any market drop is termed a "peace scare"; opponents of the U.S. effort in Vietnam have been called "peacemongers."

In 1946 Ely Culbertson wrote: "God and the politicians willing, the United States can declare peace on the world, and win it." This continued a linguistic tradition popularized by Napoleon in 1802, who said after the signing of the Treaty of Amiens, "What a beautiful fix we are in now: peace has been declared!"

WALKING-AROUND MONEY cash payoffs to precinct workers.

Campaign managers searching for a euphemism to gently describe payments to doorbell-ringing volunteers came up with "walking-around money" at a date uncertain; the phrase was popularized in the early sixties. Managers often feel that a precinct captain should have a few dollars in his pocket to pay for a babysitter, or buy a potential voter a drink, or pay a parking fine; thus, the cash is distributed for these "anticipated expenses." In fact, rarely are the expenses used other than as recompense for the captain's time, but the phrase is as common as "miscellaneous" on political expense accounts.

On June 16, 1976, the *Washington Post* editorial wondered "how much of the $40,000 [spent to defeat Democratic Senator Joseph Tydings in 1970] was spent for 'walking-around money' in Baltimore City on election day."

Sometimes the practice is called "street money." The Associated Press reported on August 9, 1976: "The Jimmy Carter campaign gave donations to black ministers who supported him in the California primary and paid out other 'street money' that was not properly accounted for, the *Los Angeles Times* said in its Sunday editions." The *New York Times* correspondent covering the same story, Charles Mohr, wrote: ". . . the use of subcontractors, or neighborhood leaders, who are given 'walking around money' is an established part of political life in some cities."

Michael Kiernan of the *Washington Star* wrote on September 13 of that year—with the street-money issue raised in the post-Watergate morality—that

walking-around money . . . is the phrase used to describe the money political candidates give Baltimore political clubs just prior to a city election for all sorts of purposes— like canvassing, poll-watching, the printing of ballots and getting out the vote. Some purists in Baltimore insist the term only should be applied to money spent by political clubs in showing a candidate around a ward or precinct. It is "mingling money," as one Baltimore politician put it this week. The other expenditures more properly are called "election day expenses."

Whatever the proper definition, Jack Pollack gets the drift. "Oh, I know what you mean. You give a guy a $50 bill before the election and he does a chore for you. So what?"

The phrase is usually hyphenated; in pronunciation, the *g* in "walking" is always clipped.

WALKING BACK THE CAT retreating from a negotiating position.

Foreign service officers use this diplomatic slang, which is similar to the "down off the mountaintop" expression of labor leaders faced with the need to reduce demands. (See MOUNTAINTOP.)

When President Carter's chief armaments negotiator, Paul Warnke, was criticized for making an unrevealed concession to the Soviets in strategic arms limitation talks, columnists Rowland Evans and Robert Novak wrote on April 29, 1977: "The 600-kilometer mystery, therefore, raises suspicions that Paul Warnke will begin 'walking back the cat' on the Carter SALT package, unless checked by the President himself."

WALL, POLITICAL USE OF the Berlin Wall was erected August 13, 1961, after the rate of refugees arriving in West Berlin had reached 300 per day. The Western powers in Berlin, caught unaware, decided not to react and the Wall became a *de facto* part of the joint occupation of the former German capital. Some propaganda advantage was sought by naming it "The Wall of Shame," and visiting politicians on NONPOLITICAL TRIPS made it a standard part of their itinerary, posing for pictures looking sternly across the barbed wire atop the concrete blocks.

Walls and similar obstructions (see IRON CURTAIN and for the opposite, BRIDGE BUILDING) have always been a useful political metaphor, often in regard to tariffs. Thomas Jefferson spoke of the need for "a wall of separation between church and state." John F. Kennedy, the day before his assassination, used a wall to draw an excellent word picture: "This nation has tossed its cap over the wall of space—and we have no choice but to follow it. . . . With the help of all those who labor in the space endeavor, with the help and support of all Americans, we will climb this wall with safety and with speed—and we shall then explore the wonders on the other side."

In the Nixon presidency, H. R. Haldeman and John Ehrlichman—because of their Germanic names and assignment to restrain access to the President—became known as "The Berlin Wall."

See STONEWALL.

WAR CLOUDS metaphor (approaching cliché) about an approaching storm.

"A cloud hangs over your heads and ours," Richard Henry Lee, of the Continental Congress, told the people of Great Britain in 1775. "Ere this reaches you, it may probably burst upon us . . . let us entreat Heaven to avert our ruin and the destruction that threatens our friends, brethren, and countrymen on the other side of the Atlantic."

"As the war clouds gather, far across the sea," are the opening words of the verse to Irving Berlin's "God Bless America." Dwight Eisenhower used it uncharacteristically in describing the arms race: "Under a cloud of war, it was humanity hanging from a cross of iron."

The metaphor could use a good rest. For too long, clouds of suspicion have led to storms of criticism, and war clouds to mushroom clouds.

WARD HEELER   hack, hanger-on, hangdog politician.

"As the crowd dispersed into the corridor," the *New York Times* wrote in 1876, "a gentleman happened to say that the gang in the room was composed of Tammany 'heelers', when a Tammany retainer taking umbrage at the epithet knocked the gentleman down."

The gentleman deserved it; "heeler" comes from the way a dog is "brought to heel" to follow its master closely. In 1912 Herbert Croly wrote of Mark Hanna: "He used to go to the businessmen of his ward, and try to persuade them . . . that they, the taxpayers, and not the wardheelers, should rule the city."

"Ward" is still used in many cities as a political subdivision; ward heeler was preceded by "ward politician," which can be traced to Washington Irving's *Salmagundi* in 1807: "He, however, maintained as mysterious a countenance as a Seventh Ward politician."

The word still has sting to reformers; to regulars, a ward heeler is a term of fond condescension. Occasionally the ward heeler will have defenders, such as Boss Martin Lomasney of Boston: "I think that there's got to be in every ward somebody that any bloke can come to—no matter what he's done—and get help. Help, none of your law and justice, but help."

WAR-GAMING WORDS, *see* **FAIL-SAFE; INFRASTRUCTURE; MEASURED RESPONSE; OPTIONS; OVERKILL; PACIFICATION; PENTAGONESE; PREVENTIVE WAR; SCENARIO; SALT (LEXICON).**

WAR HAWKS   bellicose statesmen; an early American phrase that was replaced by "jingoist" and later reappeared as "hawk." See **DOVES, JINGOISM.**

"In a contest between a hawk and dove," wrote Senator J. William Fulbright, "the hawk has a great advantage, not because it is a better bird but because it is a bigger bird with lethal talons and a highly developed will to use them." The senator also wrote: "The agitation of the 'war hawks' of 1812, and of the Committee on the Conduct of the War in the 1860s, and the neutrality legislation of the 1930s are among the more striking instances which may be cited from the past of the Congress either forcing or binding the hands of the executive."

"War hawk" was a coinage of Thomas Jefferson in 1798 ("as for Jefferson," wrote H. L. Mencken, "he produced two of the best bugaboos of all time in his *war hawks* and *monocrats*"). Wrote Jefferson to James Madison on April 26, 1798: "At present, the war hawks talk of septemberizing, deportation, and the examples for quelling sedition set by the French executive." The phrase was originally applied to those Federalists who wished to bring on a war with France. In 1810 the epithet—along with "war dogs"—was revived by Jeffersonian Republican John Randolph against the "war Republicans," who were accused of seeking a renewal of war with England to expand into Canada and take Florida from Spain, Britain's ally. The group included Senators Johnson, Calhoun, Lowndes, Cheves, Grundy, and Porter, led by House Speaker Henry Clay. Clay was "the" War Hawk; later in life he was to become known as the Great Pacificator (see **CAN'T-WIN TECHNIQUE**). The war hawks succeeded in bringing on the War of 1812. Recent scholarship indicates

that patriotism—i.e., resentment at
British interference with American
rights—rather than expansionism
motivated the war hawks.

Some will find comfort in the fact
that the American bald eagle is a species of hawk; others will point out
that its close relation is the vulture.

WAR HORSE a veteran campaigner who has had a battle-scarred
career in politics.

Samuel Medary, a leading Ohio editor in the mid-nineteenth century,
who is credited with the coinage of
"Fifty-Four Forty or Fight," was
nicknamed "The War Horse of Democracy."

This MILITARY METAPHOR comes
from the charger used in battle.
"[Thou] didst pick up Andrew Jackson," wrote Herman Melville in *Moby
Dick*, "[and] didst hurl him upon a
war-horse." Confederate soldiers
called Generals Lee "Mas' Bob,"
Johnston "Old Joe," and Longstreet
"the War Horse."

In the vote-as-you-shot, BLOODY
SHIRT politics of Reconstruction, the
war horses had an edge. In time the
phrase came to be an affectionate, occasionally contemptuous name for a
veteran politician. "There poured
into the city by every train," wrote
the *Weekly New Mexican Review* in
1885, ". . . democratic 'war horses'
from the four corners of New Mexico."

"War horse" is in current use,
though not as frequent as its synonym, WHEEL HORSE.

**WAR OF NATIONAL LIBERA-
TION** Communist terminology
for a "just war" against "colonial"
powers, started by a faction within
the country and possibly assisted by a
Communist neighbor.

Nikita Khrushchev, in a January 6,

1961, speech in Moscow, stated:
"Liberation wars will continue to
exist as long as imperialism exists, as
long as colonialism exists. These are
revolutionary wars. Such wars are not
only admissible but inevitable. . . .
The Communists fully support such
just wars and march in the front rank
with the peoples waging liberation
struggles."

The party line did not end with
Khrushchev's fall. In 1967 Alexei
Kosygin said: "We [the Soviet lead-
ers] believe that national liberation
wars are just wars and that they will
continue as long as there is national
oppression by imperialist powers.
Take Southern Rhodesia. There will
be a national liberation war there."

The "war of national liberation" is
an extension of the FIFTH COLUMN
technique in an era where fear of
atomic warfare causes nations to limit
their warfare. The phrase does not
mean "popular uprising" to Western
minds; it means deliberate Communist subversion and attempted takeover of a state with local guerrillas
supported from outside.

Obviously the meaning of the
phrase depends on who is using it.
Abraham Lincoln illustrated this dilemma in 1864: "The shepherd drives
the wolf from the sheep's throat, for
which the sheep thanks the shepherd
as his liberator, while the wolf denounces him for the same act as the
destroyer of liberty."

In that manner, a Soviet leader
could substitute "Soviet Union" for
"United States" in the following
statement by Harry Truman in 1947,
and find it perfectly consistent: "I believe it must be the policy of the
United States to support free peoples
who are resisting attempted subjugation by armed minorities or by outside pressure."

The phrase itself was not born in

the cold war. MUGWUMP statesman Carl Schurz, opposing the annexation of Hawaii and the Philippines in 1889, reminded President McKinley that the American people who went to war against Spain over Cuba "were indeed willing to wage a war of liberation, but would not have consented to a war of conquest."

WAR OF NERVES in political terms, psychological pressure; in diplomacy, threats, and feints to the point of terrorization.

Adolf Hitler dissected the theory in *Mein Kampf:* "At a given sign it unleashes a veritable barrage of lies and slanders against whatever adversary seems most dangerous, until the nerves of the attacked persons break down. . . . This is a tactic based on precise calculation of all human weaknesses, and its result will lead to success with almost mathematical certainty . . ."

Before Bernard Baruch's use of COLD WAR filled the need for a new phrase, "war of nerves" was used by world leaders to describe the tension building between the Soviet Union and the West. In 1946, upon receipt of George Kennan's CONTAINMENT memorandum (see MR. X), Secretary of State James Byrnes stated that "we must not conduct a war of nerves to achieve strategic ends" and indicated that the Soviets should not conduct one either. Harold Macmillan, worried about what he called the "cordon sanitaire" of satellites in Eastern Europe, in 1947 warned Parliament that the situation was "only a war of nerves, but a war of nerves may be very dangerous."

On a personal level, some reporters said that a war of nerves was conducted against Justice Felix Frankfurter to get him to resign from the Supreme Court bench in 1953. *The Nation* wrote:

> Sen. William Knowland is said to have demanded, as his price for accepting the truce in Korea . . . the appointment of Governor Warren to the first Supreme Court vacancy. . . . Recently a curious war of nerves has been launched to induce Justice Frankfurter to resign. It has taken the form of stories that his letter of resignation is on the President's desk, pointed inquiries about his health, a drumbeat insistence in the gossip columns . . .

Frankfurter sent word to Warren through one of the badgering newsmen, Clint Mosher of the *San Francisco Examiner:* "Tell him I would not want it on my conscience that I had kept him off the Supreme Court." Warren did get the next available seat, but it was not Frankfurter's, who remained on the court for a decade, outlasting five other justices in that time.

A more modern term, with a military ring, is "psywar" or "psychological warfare" (see PROPAGANDA); its practitioners are called "psyops."

WAR ON POVERTY President Lyndon Johnson's catch phrase for his domestic social welfare program, reminiscent of FDR's ONE THIRD OF A NATION.

England's Edmund Burke foresaw the need and the probable reaction. "Government is a contrivance of human wisdom to provide for human *wants,*" he wrote after the French Revolution. Later, he added, "and having looked to Government for bread, on the very first scarcity they will turn and bite the hand that fed them."

In the U.S., *Progress and Poverty* by economist Henry George (see VESTED INTERESTS), published in 1879, was one of the biggest nonfiction best sellers of the times.

Herbert Hoover, who earned a reputation after World War I as a man concerned with the relief of suffering, said in 1928: "We in America today are nearer to the final triumph over poverty than ever before in the history of any land." The stock-market crash came one year later, and newsman Elmer Davis called 1930 "the Second Year of the Abolition of Poverty."

It was not until the early sixties, however, that governmental action to alleviate poverty found its slogan. Three books paved the way: John Galbraith's *The Affluent Society* (see AFFLUENT SOCIETY) in 1958, with a provocative chapter on "The New Position of Poverty"; a study directed by economist Leon Keyserling in 1962 called "Poverty and Deprivation in the U.S.—The Plight of Two-Fifths of the Nation"; and most important, *The Other America* (1962), a passionate book by Michael Harrington showing how poverty haunts our otherwise affluent society, and translating the statistics into bitter, human terms.

Campaigning in 1960, John F. Kennedy had been impressed by the extent of poverty in West Virginia and elsewhere in Appalachia and used the phrase that was to be the Johnson battle cry: "The war against poverty and degradation is not yet over . . ." A year earlier Dwight Eisenhower in New Delhi had called for "a successful war against hunger— the sort of war that dignifies and exalts human beings."

President Johnson, in his first address to a joint session of Congress five days after the Kennedy assassination, promised to "carry on the fight against poverty." In a meeting of his staff going over the State of the Union message a month later, he said he was worried about the word "poverty." "It's not poverty," he said, "it's wastage of resources and human lives"— but nobody came up with a better word, so the President agreed to call it a "poverty" program.

In that speech, the phrase became his own: "Unfortunately many Americans live on the outskirts of hope, some because of their poverty and some because of their color, and all too many because of both. Our task is to help replace their despair with unconditional war on poverty in America . . ."

By 1966 the phrase was open to attack. Republicans pointed out waste and inefficiency in local programs, and pledged to "take the profit out of poverty." In an economic context, Richard Nixon said the President's unwillingness to cut nondefense spending amounted to "a war on prosperity."

Soon many programs became "wars." Every racketeering crackdown became a "war on crime," even education programs were labeled "wars on ignorance." One sloganeer, who refused to let his candidate name a highway safety program a "war on roadhogs," declared he would start a war of his own—"A WAR TO END 'WARS.' "

WAR PARTY desperation charge against the Democrats; like DEPRESSION PARTY against Republicans, considered a low blow.

"He kept us out of war" was the proud Democratic slogan in 1916, re-electing Wilson. "I hate war" was a familiar Franklin Roosevelt line in 1939. By the time of the Vietnam war —the fourth in this century entered under Democratic Administrations— Democrats were understandably touchy about the charge of being the "war party."

Not surprising, then, is the emphasis by Democratic candidates on peace, paralleling the emphasis of Republicans on prosperity. Wrote former Eisenhower speechwriter Emmet Hughes about the 1952 campaign: ". . . the irony was this: each party recognized that its popular strength was plainly greater in the sphere where its public record was plainly weaker. Democrats feared popular distrust of their foreign policies as deeply as Republicans feared popular distrust of their domestic policies. Each was haunted by its own caricature—the Democrats as 'the Party of War,' the Republicans as 'the Party of Depression.' "

WAR TO END WARS an idealistic World War I slogan, now used only cynically.

Like MAKE THE WORLD SAFE FOR DEMOCRACY, this phrase is associated with Woodrow Wilson and the disillusionment following World War I.

The phrase was not Wilson's. *The War That Will End War* was the title of a 1914 book by English author H. G. Wells; in *Portraits from Memory*, in 1956, Bertrand Russell recalled that it was Wells who popularized the phrase.

When Neville Chamberlain returned from Munich (see MUNICH, ANOTHER) with what he called "PEACE FOR OUR TIME," *The Nation* headlined its issue: "A Peace to End Peace." That phrase had been applied before to the Treaty of Versailles.

The phrase has a steady current use. In 1967, Walter Lippmann described Secretary of State Dean Rusk in *Newsweek* as "one of the few surviving TRUE BELIEVERS among statesmen, in the great Utopian Delusion which has been employed so extensively by propagandists ever since

it was fabricated in the first world war. The delusion is that whatever war we are fighting is a war to end war. Anyone with experience and some toughness of mind knows from the history of the past 50 years that these wars which are supposed to end wars have never, in fact, ended wars. The historical record is quite plain: on the contrary, each of the wars to end wars has set the stage for the next war."

Richard Nixon, in the peroration of his November 3, 1969, SILENT MAJORITY speech, recognized the grandiose nature of the promise and set more realistic sights: "Tonight I do not tell you that the war in Vietnam is the war to end wars. But I do say this: I have initiated a plan which will end this war in a way that will bring us closer to that great goal to which Woodrow Wilson and every American President in our history has been dedicated—the goal of a just and lasting peace . . ."

See FULL GENERATION OF PEACE.

WARTS AND ALL, *see* IMAGE.

WASP White Anglo-Saxon Protestant: an ethnic group.

By the time the expression "WASP" came to be used, White Anglo-Saxon Protestants were no longer the majority of Americans. In urban politics, ticket-balancing to attract the votes of minority groups—Catholics, Jews, Irish, Germans, Puerto Ricans, or blacks—has become accepted. In some circles, WASP is used to connote snobbish patrician types, but politicians use it affectionately in the big cities.

Richard Scammon and Ben Wattenberg wrote in 1965:

Some day someone will write an inspiring piece about one of America's greatest and most colorful minority groups. They came here on crowded ships, were resented by the natives and had to struggle mightily for every advance they made against a hostile environment. Despite these handicaps, despite even a skin color different from the native Americans, this hardy group prospered and, in prospering, helped build the nation. . . . The only thing different about the group is that it is the one traditionally viewed as the "American majority." For the minority group described is of course the "White Anglo-Saxon Protestant," further qualified today as "native-born of native parentage." The key point is that neither the WASP-NN, nor any solidified ethnic or religious group constitutes an "American majority."

The facts are that about one American in ten is nonwhite; one in six is foreign-born or has a foreign-born parent; one in four is a Catholic; and two out of three are *not* of Anglo-Saxon descent.

Accused of being "waspish" toward the press in 1971, Herbert Stein, newly appointed chairman of the Council of Economic Advisers, said, "I'm not waspish, I'm Jewish."

WASTE, *see* **VIETNAM LINGO.**

WASTELAND, *see* **VAST WASTE-LAND.**

WATCHDOG COMMITTEE a committee that "probes" waste in government operations, or overseas expenditures in agencies like the Central Intelligency Agency or the Atomic Energy Commission.

The "watchdogs of the Treasury," a usage traced back to 1827, were originally those trying to hold down government spending; the meaning today has narrowed to trying to cut waste out of specific areas of spending.

In the earlier sense, Representative William S. Holman of Indiana was given the sobriquet "The Watchdog of the Treasury" in the mid-nineteenth century, along with his earlier nickname "The Great Objector" (to appropriations bills in the House).

In the current sense, Senator Lyndon Johnson headed the Defense Preparedness Subcommittee of the Senate Armed Services Committee in 1951, investigating the conduct of the Korean conflict. The same kind of work made Senator Harry Truman famous during World War II. Economic journalist Eliot Janeway wrote a glowing account of "Johnson of the 'Watchdog Committee' " in the *New York Times Magazine* in 1951, and *Newsweek* put Johnson on its cover with the caption "Watchdog in Chief."

See OVERSIGHT.

WATCHFUL WAITING diplomatic restraint, or a justification for inaction.

President Woodrow Wilson did not want to be drawn into a war with Mexico in 1913. "We shall not," he told Congress, "I believe, be obliged to alter our policy of watchful waiting." President Victoriano Huerta had seized power, murdered the previous president, and provoked an incident by arresting a group of U.S. Marines. Wilson sent in troops that took Veracruz.

The phrase had been used by President Grover Cleveland in a letter in 1893 criticizing the U.S. seizure of Hawaii: "There seemed to arise . . . the precise opportunity for which he was watchfully waiting . . ."

The "watchful" gives purpose to the "waiting," like a cat on a stakeout in front of a mousehole. The phrase is current. The *New York Times* editorialized in 1967: "The United States has an embassy in Port-au-Prince. Its policy is to adopt a 'correct attitude' toward the Duvalier Government. It watches and it waits."

The predecessor phrase was "masterly inactivity" by Sir James Mackintosh (1765–1832), who was also the espouser of "disciplined inaction": "The Commons, faithful to their system, remained in a wise and masterly inactivity."

In opposition to the look-before-you-leap school is the he-who-hesitates-is-lost school, whose favorite recent derogation has been "Let the dust settle," a 1950s condemnation of U.S. China policy, which, its critics felt, permitted Mao Tse-tung's Communists to take over mainland China.

WATER'S EDGE   where partisan politics, in the interests of national foreign policy, supposedly stops.

Democratic Majority Leader Lyndon Johnson viewed the election in 1956 of a Democratic Congress and a Republican President as an affirmation of the principles of the bipartisanship he had been talking about since 1952. According to Arthur Krock, "As defined by Lyndon Johnson, . . . these principles were: Partisan politics stops 'at the water's edge.' The only test of all legislation is whether 'it is good for the country.' "

In 1964, harking back to his Majority Leader's role, President Johnson repeated one of his favorite phrases: "I took the position that politics stopped at the water's edge. We had but one President and Commander-in-Chief."

The phrase is most frequently used in connection with "BIPARTISAN foreign policy." The architect of the policy, Senator Arthur Vandenberg, used it in his own 1950 definition to a constituent: "To me 'bipartisan for-

eign policy' means a mutual effort under our indispensable two-party system to unite our official voice at the water's edge . . ."

"What mainly stops at the water's edge," countered historian James MacGregor Burns, "is not party politics in general but congressional party politics in particular. The real 'UNHOLY ALLIANCE' to a good congressional Republican is the historic coalition between the internationalists in both parties."

Describing Harry Truman, Richard Neustadt wrote: "He played 'Chief of State' like a gracious host, 'Chief of Party' like an organization politician, 'Chief of Foreign Policy' like a career official anxious to obey his own injunction that 'politics stops at the water's edge.' "

Describing Woodrow Wilson, Winston Churchill sidestepped the use of a cliché by substituting other words: "He did not truly divine the instinct of the American people. First and foremost, all through and last, he was a party man. The spacious philanthropy which he exhaled upon Europe stopped quite sharply at the coasts of his own country."

WATERGATE WORDS   "Watergate," like "Teapot Dome," means everything associated with a scandal that became a national trauma.

"Watergate" means a place: the hotel–offices–apartment-house complex in Washington D.C., facing the Potomac, named after the dockside facility that once occupied the site, into which the "waterbugs" stole to plant a BUG in the offices of the Democratic National Committee.

"Watergate" means a time: the period from June 17, 1972, when the "break-in" was considered merely a madcap "caper," to the near-impeachment, resignation and pardon of President Nixon, and then back in time to the start of eavesdropping in his Administration by the **PLUMBERS.**

And Watergate means a mood: a time of revulsion against the **ENEMIES LISTS** and the **LAUNDERING** of campaign contributions, of diehards who protested "double standards" and "ex post facto morality," of tips from "*Deep Throat*," of condemnation of the men of **CREEP** who "shredded" and **DEEP-SIXED** evidence in a **COVER-UP.**

"Watergate" came to mean a drama on the grandest scale: of a search for the **SMOKING GUN** by the "straight arrows," of the **FIRESTORM** that followed the **SATURDAY NIGHT MASSACRE** of the "good guys," of the **STONEWALLING** about **DIRTY TRICKS** and "White House horrors" by the **BIG ENCHILADA,** of plans to "paper the file" by "team players" who had not been brought **UP TO SPEED,** of the **RATFUCKING** of the "black advance," of legalese like "misprision of a felony" and **EXECUTIVE PRIVILEGE,** of a "sinister force" known only as the **OVAL OFFICE** capable of producing an 18½-minute **GAP.**

After the "stroking" had failed, after the **HANGING TOUGH** and the "limited modified hangout route" had led nowhere, the men who had maneuvered themselves between a rock and a hard place found themselves **TWISTING SLOWLY, SLOWLY IN THE WIND.** A few instant revisionists with the best anti-Nixonian credentials observed that more than a few "abuses of power" had been perpetrated in the name of civil liberty, and that **NOBODY DROWNED AT WATERGATE,** but that a perspective on the "long national nightmare" was too soon **AT THIS POINT IN TIME.**

WATERSHED ELECTION a campaign that decides the course of politics for decades; one that is especially memorable, or that proves to be a dividing line between historical periods.

California Lieutenant Governor Robert Finch said in 1967: "The Nixon-Kennedy campaign of 1960 will prove to be the great watershed election of this century."

The word "watershed" is only beginning to enter dictionaries in its new meaning. The literal meaning is a water-storage area making the surrounding region fertile, or providing a city with its water supply. A second meaning is "dividing line" as between drainage areas. The political meaning comes from both the nourishing meaning (of the vital water-holding uplands) and the epochal meaning (a line between two areas, or a moment between two eras).

The political meaning emerges in these examples. Biographer Leo Katcher: "The University of California was one of the great watersheds of experience for Earl Warren." *Times* of London headline, 1965: "Parliament at a Watershed." Treasury Secretary Douglas Dillon, describing 1961–64 as "a watershed in the development of American economic policy." Author Theodore White: "The great revolutionary in the flow of ideas proved to be John Fitzgerald Kennedy.... He was the watershed."

The word crested in the late sixties. Here are three examples from the *New York Times* taken from a three-month period in 1967: "The Cuban confrontation," wrote C. L. Sulzberger, "was a historic watershed but the U.S. didn't gain much from it save prestige ..." A dispatch from Tokyo quoted visiting Richard M. Nixon as praising the new political and economic leadership of Japan and describing that country as "at a watershed." And Henry Steele Commager, Amherst professor of history, wrote: "In the great watershed of the eighteen-nineties we found ourselves, somewhat to our own surprise, a world power."

In 1968 this writer suggested to candidate Richard Nixon that he adopt the word to describe the forthcoming election, which he did in several speeches. However, in 1969, when *Newsweek* described a conference on Midway Island about Vietnam as "a watershed in the quagmire," editorial writer Meg Greenfield of the *Washington Post* proceeded to blast the shed out of the water: ". . . I have also become an incurable, even obsessive collector of printed watersheds, of which I believe I now have the best collection in town —watersheds perching on escalation ladders, watersheds embedded in arms spirals, watersheds wrapped (like chicken livers, perhaps) in an enigma. It is not, however, an expression that I would dare to use myself. I came to that drainage basin two years ago and paddled left, into the sunset."

Miss Greenfield's sandbagging of the watershed flood was widely hailed. "In terms of getting things done," she wrote in a follow-up article, "a number of MOVERS AND SHAKERS stepped forward to reveal their sympathy. . . . for instance, a principal presidential speechwriter (who had done invaluable pioneer work on the subject in his political lexicon), sent a letter to say that 'watershed' deserved all the opprobrium we could heap upon it, and he added that the term had long since been dropped from the presidential vocabulary. From the Executive Offices, no less, of Encyclopaedia Britannica came a heartrending executive vow

'never again to drown in a sea of watersheds.' . . . And, finally, it can be reliably reported that the Secretary of State acknowledged having seized upon this frail document in support of his own lonely battle to rid the State Department's prose of its embarrassment of watersheds . . ."

However, two leading political figures—Dr. Henry Kissinger and then Senate Majority Leader Mike Mansfield—had used the word in the interim. "I was still prepared to issue a rather favorable report," continued Miss Greenfield, "speaking harshly only to these two offenders. I was only dissuaded from doing so by a sharp-eyed colleague, who asked how I would explain exactly whom I spoke for at *The Washington Post,* which had only recently hailed the Apollo moon adventure as—yes—'a watershed' in history in space . . . I would be less than candid if I did not report that, at the present time, there is no light at the end of the watershed."

WAVE OF THE FUTURE admiring description of totalitarianism; a phrase used today only to be denied or derogated.

In 1940, poet Anne Morrow Lindbergh, influenced by her isolationist husband Charles Lindbergh, wrote a long essay published as a book with the title *The Wave of the Future,* which many readers took to be an apologia for Fascism.

Working on Roosevelt's third inaugural address, speechwriter Robert Sherwood said to the President, "I certainly wish we could use that terrible phrase, 'the wave of the future.' " Samuel Rosenman recollects FDR calmly saying, "Why not?" and dictating the following: "There are men who believe that democracy, as a form of government and a frame of life, is limited or measured by a kind of mystical and artificial fate—that, for some unexplained reason, tyranny and slavery have become the surging wave of the future—and that freedom is an ebbing tide. But we Americans know that this is not true."

A few months later Interior Secretary Harold Ickes castigated what he called "the wavers of the future" at an "I Am an American Day" rally in New York's Central Park:

> For years we have been told that we are beaten, decayed, and that no part of the world belongs to us any longer. Some amongst us have fallen for this carefully pickled tripe . . . this calculated poison. Some amongst us have begun to preach that the "wave of the future" has passed over us and left us a wet, dead fish.
>
> Americans, with the aid of our brave allies—yes, let's call them "allies"—the British, can and will build the only future worth having. I mean a future, not of concentration camps, not of physical torture and mental straitjackets, not of sawdust bread or sawdust Caesars—I mean a future when free men will live free lives in dignity and in security. This tide of the future, the democratic future, is ours.

The same technique of setting up "wave of the future" as a kind of strawman phrase, and then knocking it down, has been used often since. The change in the past generation has been to identify Communism rather than Fascism as the "waver." President John Kennedy, speaking to students at the Berkeley campus of the University of California, said: "No one can doubt that the wave of the future is not the conquest of the world by a single dogmatic creed but the liberation of the diverse energies of free nations and free men."

In the 1968 campaign Richard Nixon found a sure-fire applause line in "the wave of crime must not become the wave of the future."

The word "future" was given a bad name not only by the Lindbergh use, but by a 1920s comment of author Lincoln Steffens about the Soviet Union: "I have been over into the future, and it works."

The undulation of the sea, in use politically as GROUNDSWELL, was best used metaphorically by Ralph Waldo Emerson in his essay "On Self-Reliance": "Society is a wave. The wave moves onward, but the water of which it is composed does not. . . . The persons who make up a nation today, next year die, and their experiences with them."

WAXWORKS   dais guests at a political dinner.

"It's a pleasure to be back up here as a member of the waxworks," defeated senatorial candidate Bernard Shanley told a New Jersey political dinner in 1968.

The reference is to Madame (Marie) Tussaud's Exhibition, a wax museum in Paris during the Reign of Terror which moved to London and became a landmark with its lifelike representations of historical figures.

People who sit on daises, even when thoroughly bored, must appear friendly and interested. The resulting expression is a frozen or waxen smile which, when strung out in a line of twenty people, makes "waxworks" an apt description. See RUBBER-CHICKEN CIRCUIT.

WEANED ON A PICKLE, *see* **MAN ON THE WEDDING CAKE.**

WE ARE ALL   declaration of membership in a group that becomes highly quotable when expressed by an unlikely source.

The first well-known use was unifying rather than surprising. "We have called by different names brethren of the same principle," said Thomas Jefferson in his first inaugural address. "We are all Republicans, we are all Federalists."

When the Prince of Wales (later Edward VII) used it in an 1895 speech in England, it startled the world: "We are all Socialists now-a-days." (Sir Denis Brogan credited this line to Sir William Harcourt.)

And conservative economist Milton Friedman put the NEW ECONOMICS over the top when *Time* magazine put his remark on its cover in 1965: "We are all Keynesians now." Liberal economist Walter Heller commented a year later: "When Milton Friedman, the chief guardian of the laissez-faire tradition in American economics, said not long ago, 'We are all Keynesians now,' the profession said 'Amen.'" Overlooked was the second half of Friedman's remark: "—and there are no longer any Keynesians."

"We are all guilty" was described in 1969 by linguist Mario Pei as "perhaps the most ingenious of all Communistic slogans created to demoralize us by giving us collective and inherited guilt as a substitute for individual responsibility."

WEASEL WORDS   ambiguous speech; deliberately fuzzy phraseology.

"One of our defects as a nation," said Theodore Roosevelt in 1916, "is a tendency to use what have been called weasel words." He had popularized the phrase as President, and gave this example of what he meant: "You can have universal training, or you can have voluntary training, but when you use the word voluntary to qualify the word universal, you are using a weasel word; it has sucked all the meaning out of universal. The words flatly contradict one another." (The origin of that metaphor can be found in Shakespeare's *As You Like It,* Act II, Scene 5, when "the melancholy Jaques" asks Lord Amiens to continue his singing: "I can suck melancholy out of a song, as a weasel sucks eggs.")

Author Stewart Chaplin explained the phrase in an article about political platforms in a 1900 issue of *Century* magazine: ". . . weasel words are words that suck all the life out of the words next to them, just as a weasel sucks an egg and leaves the shell. If you heft the egg afterward it's as light as a feather, and not very filling when you're hungry; but a basketful of them would make quite a show, and would bamboozle the unwary."

President Franklin D. Roosevelt, according to speechwriter Samuel Rosenman, "was extremely impatient with some of the drafts that came over from the State Department during those years, and with some of the suggested corrections in the drafts he had sent over to them for consideration. He felt that they were too apt to use 'weasel words' (a favored phrase he had borrowed from Theodore Roosevelt); that they made too many reservations and were too diplomatically reserved."

Editor William Allen White, writing about the direct quality of Wendell Willkie in 1940, thought the Republican candidate was making headway because "The American people are tired of the smoothy in politics—even if he is honest. They don't like the oleaginous weasel words with which so many politicians grease their way back when they venture upon a dangerous salient of honesty."

The colloquial verb "to weasel" means to renege on a promise, usually for some cowardly reason. The *Dictionary of American Slang* points out that the prison term "weasel" refers to an informer, adding that "applied to small, thin males, the word retains its physical connotation." Why the weasel has acquired a cowardly reputation is not known; it is a bold, vicious little beast that kills more than it can eat; in snowy areas, it acquires a white coat and enters judicial metaphors as "ermine."

President Nixon, in a meeting with Chinese Premier Chou En-lai in Peking in 1972, first used the word in high-level international diplomacy (and, ironically, presaged the use of COVER-UP in the same sentence): "The conventional way to handle a meeting at the summit like this, while the whole world is watching is to have meetings for several days, which we will have, to have discussions and discover differences, which we will do, and then put out a weasel-worded communiqué covering up the problems." Nixon then disclaimed such intention.

President Eisenhower wrote to Ambassador to Italy Clare Boothe Luce in 1953: "I assure you first that, so far as I know, we have no intention of weaseling on our October 8th decision on Trieste." In that statement, "so far as I know" are weasel words.

See REPORTEDLY; WAFFLE.

WEDNESDAY CLUB the best-known of the many luncheon groups of legislators in Washington; more of a real club, but far less than a center of power as the Senate's INNER CLUB.

The Wednesday Club is a group of Republican moderates; the Marching and Chowder Society is a more conservative group of MOVERS AND SHAKERS in which then Republican House leader Gerald Ford was prominent; similar groups meeting in Washington include the S.O.S. (Save Our Souls), the Sundowners (older members), and A-Corns. In New York, a widely diverse group of leaders in business, the professions, and the arts calls itself "the Wednesday Ten."

The "Tuesday Lunch" was a Johnson Administration addition. "Every week at the White House," wrote the *New York Post* in 1967, "President Johnson and three of his top officials —Robert McNamara, Dean Rusk, Walt Whitman Rostow—get together for a solemn occasion that has come to be known as the Tuesday Lunch."

English slang authorities trace "Blue Monday" to the sadness of children returning to school after a happy weekend, and "Black Friday" to mid-nineteenth century financial panics.

WELFARE REFORM, *see* **WORKFARE.**

WELFARE STATE government that provides economic protection for all its citizens; this is done, say its critics, at the price of individual liberty and removes incentives needed for economic growth.

When British politician Edward Hallett Carr said in 1948, "Let us substitute welfare for wealth as our governing purpose," linguistics expert Simeon Potter delightedly pointed out that the word "wealth" had returned to its original meaning: "weal," "well-being," and "welfare."

The welfare state, publicized by *New Republic* editor Herbert Croly at the turn of the century, had often been applied to the government of Sweden, and after World War II, particularly to Great Britain. Conservatives in England, accepting many social security programs short of nationalization, often reacted bitterly. In 1951 a reader of *Picture Post* urged Prime Minister Clement Attlee to dismiss "everyone who used the term 'welfare state,' because 'nobody is very well, and the state of the fare is rotten.' "

The phrase had a competitor at the start. *The Servile State* was the title of a 1913 book by Hilaire Belloc, which he defined as "that arrangement of society in which so considerable a number of the families and individuals are constrained by positive law to labor for the advantage of other families and individuals as to stamp the whole community with the mark of such labor." But statism was not ripe for an attack phrase so early; the welfare state triumphed as a proud assertion at first, and later became an epithet.

Current use in the U.S. is as an attack phrase. Those who urge more social welfare legislation rarely use the term; those who oppose it use "welfare state" as synonymous with CREEPING SOCIALISM. The use of "state" in the sense of "society" has a totalitarian connotation: "police state," "garrison state," "corporate state," "state socialism."

The fire is not only directed at left-wingers. The *Chicago Tribune* said of Eisenhower's 1955 State of the Union message: "Welfare statism and a tender if meddlesome solicitude for every fancied want of a once self-reliant citizenry were pyramided and compounded in this message." See WORK-FARE.

Welfare—the word without the "state"—has had a curious history. It began as a cousin of its turnaround "farewell," and was used by Shakespeare politically in *Henry VI*, as Warwick advised "study for the people's welfare." In the U.S. the word first appeared in its aid-to-people sense in a 1904 *Century* magazine article about "the welfare manager . . . is a recognized intermediary between the employers and employees of mercantile houses and manufacturing plants." Lexicographer of Americanisms Mitford Mathews found a citation from a year later in the *Westminster Gazette:* "The home of the 'welfare policy' is the city of Dayton, Ohio." British etymologist Sir Ernest Weekly explained: *"Welfare,* as in 'child welfare,' 'welfare centre,' and so forth, was first used in this special sense in Ohio in 1904."

The name of an island next to Manhattan, in the East River, gives a clue to the fortunes of the word in recent years. Blackwell's Island, the site of a prison, was renamed Welfare Island in the thirties, as some of its facilities were turned to other than penal use. In the seventies, when housing developers wanted to rent out apartments on the island, they insisted on a name change—"welfare" was too evocative of charity and the poor. It is now Roosevelt Island.

WELTANSCHAUUNG world view.

The use of foreign words for political concepts or practices is usually regarded as pretentious by politicians. News magazines may write of a candidate's "apparat" being concerned with REALPOLITIK but neither of the words is in the spoken tongue.

Joseph Alsop, wrote Douglass Cater in *The Fourth Branch of Government,* "can claim to have a reasoned *Weltanschauung."* Thermonuclear thinker Herman Kahn counters his critics by saying that "often the reluctance to think about these problems is not caused by the advocacy of any particular *Weltanschauung.* Rather it is based on nothing sounder that a supernatural fear of the magical power of words . . ."

Other German words used tangentially in politics are *Zeitgeist* (spirit of the age), *Schadenfreude* (the guilty pleasure one feels at the sufferings of friends), *Weltschmerz* (world-weariness), and *Fingerspitzengefühl* (a "feel" for nuances).

WE POLKED YOU IN 1844, WE'LL PIERCE YOU IN 1852, *see* SLOGAN; DARK HORSE.

WE SHALL OVERCOME   civil rights chant of the early sixties.

More than any other song, "We Shall Overcome" was the anthem of the civil rights movement led by the "moderates"; it was one of the highlights of the 1963 March on Washington and was sung in front of the Lincoln Memorial.

Arthur Schlesinger, Jr., called the tune "an old Baptist hymn," John Anthony Scott in *The Ballad of America* called it "an old spiritual," pointing out that it originated among the coal miners of West Virginia in the early New Deal days. Stevenson's *MacMillan Book of Quotations* credits the tune to Mrs. Zilphia Horton, who conducted a folk school in Tennessee in the 1940s, and additional verses to folk singers Pete Seeger, Frank Hamilton, and Guy Carawan in 1962.

The words are familiar to every civil rights marcher:

We shall end Jim Crow, we shall end Jim Crow,
We shall end Jim Crow some day, some day;
Oh, deep in my heart, I know that I do believe
We shall end Jim Crow some day.
We shall overcome, we shall overcome,
We shall overcome some day, some day;
Oh, deep in my heart, I know that I do believe
We shall overcome some day.

President Johnson chose it as his text in a speech to a joint session of Congress in 1965, urging them to adopt a voting rights bill: "It is not just Negroes but really it is all of us who must overcome the crippling legacy of bigotry and injustice. And we shall overcome . . . these enemies, too, poverty, disease, and ignorance, we shall overcome."

WE WILL BURY YOU   a truculent, offhand remark by a Russian leader that was blown up into a dire threat by Westerners.

"Whether you like it or not," Nikita Khrushchev told Western diplomats at a Kremlin reception in November 1956, "history is on our side. We will bury you."

He chose the wrong word. In context, he appears to have meant "outstrip," "beat," or "leave you far behind." The reaction to the word he chose, however, was shock and anger: "bury" was a word too close to death. Two years later *Pravda* quoted the Soviet leader in a kind of retraction: "My life would be too short to bury every one of you if this were to occur to me. . . . I said that in the course of historical progress and in the historical sense, capitalism would be buried and communism would come to replace capitalism."

On a trip to the U.S. in 1959, the Russian Premier was angered by Los Angeles Mayor Norris Poulson's hometown grandstanding ("You shall not bury us . . . if challenged, we shall fight to the death") and spelled out the evolutionary character of the burial. "The words 'We will bury capitalism' should not be taken literally as indicating what is done by ordinary gravediggers who carry a spade and dig graves and bury the dead. What I had in mind was the outlook for the development of human society. Socialism will inevitably succeed capitalism."

But Khrushchev was never able to inter the statement. After a while, he took it philosophically. To a group of Westerners in the audience in Yugoslavia, he remarked, "I once said, 'We will bury you,' and I got into trouble with it. Of course we will not bury you with a shovel. Your own working class will bury you."

Six months later, in his first State of the Union message, Lyndon Johnson made a point of it again. "We intend to bury no one—and we do not intend to be buried."

WHAT'S GOOD FOR GENERAL MOTORS . . . is good for the country. A misquotation used to show the supposed big-business bias of the Eisenhower Administration.

Charles E. Wilson, called "Engine Charlie" to distinguish him from the former head of General Electric, Charles E. ("Electric Charlie") Wilson, gave a fairly innocent answer to a question posed by a senator at the hearing before approval of his nomination for Secretary of Defense: ". . . if a situation did arise where you had to make a decision which was extremely adverse to the interests of your stock and General Motors Corporation, or any of these other companies, or extremely adverse to the company, in the interests of the United States Government, could you make that decision?"

Mr. Wilson: "Yes, sir, I could. I cannot conceive of one because for years I thought what was good for our country was good for General Motors, and vice versa. The difference did not exist. Our country is too big. It goes with the welfare of the country. Our contribution to the nation is considerable."

As Eisenhower put it in his memoirs: "This was interpreted and broadcast—it still is—in the form of 'What is good for General Motors is good for the country,' and of course

the breast-beaters had a field day."

The construction has become locked into the political lexicon, taking many forms. In 1970 President Nixon told black leader Whitney Young, Jr., shortly before his death: "To paraphrase a former Defense Secretary, what's good for the Urban League is good for the country."

See BIRD DOG . . . KENNEL DOG.

WHEELHORSE dependable party man; a regular.

A wheelhorse in a team is one that bears the most weight; hitched between the shafts, he pulls more of a load than the leader. Like WAR HORSE, the phrase has been used politically for over a century; the *Marion* (Ohio) *Eagle* wrote in 1848 about Lewis Cass that he "has been the very wheel horse on which the party has relied to carry through all their great measures."

Historian Eric Goldman, writing about the struggle to find a vice-presidential nominee for Harry Truman in 1948: "Finally a sacrificial victim was found—the faithful party wheelhorse Alben Barkley."

John F. Kennedy used the word in 1960, discussing his early days as a congressman: "We were just worms over in the House—nobody paid much attention to us nationally. And I had come back from the service, not as a Democratic wheelhorse who came up through the ranks. I came in sort of sideways."

WHEELS WITHIN WHEELS the minutiae of government; the infinitely detailed workings that a leader must not concern himself with, at the peril of wasting the time needed for broad policy.

Wendell L. Willkie, defeated Republican nominee in 1940, gave this phrase political context in a 1943 *Reader's Digest* article titled: "Better Management, Please, Mr. President!" Willkie held that Roosevelt was too "zealous for the accumulation of power and loath to disburse it," and pointed out that the presidency of the United States "is not a small-claims court." His main point was stated in these terms:

> The President's desk is cluttered and his mind distracted by his concern with the wheels within wheels, the foremen and the subforemen of our gigantic Federal machine. He is his own supervisor and trouble shooter. Broken parts are brought to him for patching and he undertakes to patch them. Bruised feelings are brought for his treatment and he sets about anointing them.
>
> No man could do all these things well. No President should try.

The phrase probably comes from the Bible, Ezekiel 1:16: ". . . Their work was as it were a wheel in the middle of a wheel." The expression was used in Shaftesbury's *Characters* in 1709: "Thus we have Wheels within Wheels. And in some national constitutions . . . we have one Empire within another."

Other uses of the word "wheel" in American slang often applied to politics are *big wheel,* a derogatory term for a man of authority and power, probably derived from "the man at the wheel" or baseball's "side-wheeler," a left-handed sidearm pitcher; and *wheeler-dealer,* one who acts independently, ruthlessly, and often unethically, probably derived from gambling's roulette wheel (wheeler) and card shark (dealer).

WHIP a party leader, chosen in caucus, who makes certain that members are present for important votes, and vote the way the leadership wants.

The *party whip* must be tough and tactful; he is expected to turn out every member on crucial party-line votes. In recent years in the U.S., the whip's job is considered the best STEPPINGSTONE to party congressional leadership. (Mike Mansfield, party whip under Lyndon Johnson, became Majority Leader of the Senate when Johnson was elected Vice President.) Robert Byrd, who defeated Edward Kennedy in a struggle for party whip, succeeded Mansfield.

The word comes from "whipper-in," a man assigned to keep the hounds from straying in a fox hunt, and was turned into a political word in England in the eighteenth century. Benjamin Disraeli said the Government Chief Whip's office required "consummate knowledge of human nature, the most amiable flexibility, and complete self-control."

In England, a *documentary whip* is a weekly agenda sent to Members of Parliament, with attendance requirements underlined. Sir Wilfred Lawson explained that a one-line whip meant "you ought to attend"; a two-line whip meant "you should attend"; a three-line whip meant "you must attend"; and a four-line whip "stay away at your peril."

The official name of the party whip in the U.S. is *assistant floor leader.* Its original whipping-in meaning is illustrated in an observation made by General Maxwell Taylor, who explained the relationship of the Chairman of the Joint Chiefs of Staff to the other chiefs of staff: "a sort of party whip, charged with conveying the official line to the chiefs."

WHIPSAW to accept money from both sides in a dispute.

In lumbering, a whipsaw—operated by two men—cuts both ways; in poker, two players in collusion bid up the pot to cheat a third; in the business of bribery, a legislator will whipsaw two opposing crooked lobbyists by accepting money for a "fix" from both and then delivering for only one.

Charles Ledyard Norton suggested in 1890 that the term originated in the New York State Legislature (cradle of LULUS). An old Albany joke concerns a grafting boss who called two "fixers" into his office and said, "One of you paid me two thousand dollars to get this bill passed. The other paid me one thousand to get it killed. I want to be fair. How about the second guy paying me another thousand—making two even from each—and we'll debate the bill on its merits?"

WHIRLWIND CAMPAIGN a busy campaign, usually of short duration.

This is a DISASTER METAPHOR that began in the Harrison–Van Buren campaign of 1840. A campaign that "spreads like a prairie fire" was already a political expression, and whirlwind—occasionally the result of a prairie fire—was a natural extension. "The prairies are on fire," wrote the *Annals of Cleveland* in 1840, "and the whirlwind they create will be felt east of the mountains . . ."

In 1896 the *Review of Reviews* reported that William McKinley's FRONT-PORCH CAMPAIGN speeches were carefully prepared in advance, "punctuated with statistics and precise statements of fact which a 'whirlwind campaign' from a platform would not allow."

The phrase is in current use, but is beginning to appear quaint, a prelude to obsolescence.

WHISPERING CAMPAIGN word of foul mouth; a slander about a candidate's sex life, drinking habits, or possible mental or physical disability.

"Where there is whispering there is lying" is an English proverb traced back to 1678; John Randolph, fighting the WAR HAWKS in 1811, said his opponents' plan was "to assail me by every species of calumny and whisper, but Parthian-like never to show their faces or give battle on fixed ground."

The phrase "whispering campaign" was popularized in the presidential campaign of 1928. In an Edwin Marcus cartoon in the *New York Times,* a bigot with a rifle labeled "whispering campaign" was shown hiding behind a large jug labeled "prohibition issue," taking aim at candidate Al Smith. The anti-Catholic rumors (see UNPACK) undoubtedly harmed his candidacy, though he was beaten more by general prosperity and the prohibition issue. After the campaign, Smith wrote: "I was probably the outstanding victim of the last half-century of a whispering campaign."

Reporter Elliot Bell, later head of McGraw-Hill, wrote of a similar campaign attacking Franklin Roosevelt as "mentally deranged" in the early New Deal days. "It came out in the course of a Senate investigation that an obscure and misguided publicity man had conceived the idea of undermining the President by a whispering campaign to the effect that his mind was unbalanced."

John F. Kennedy in 1960 suffered from a whispering campaign—in no way connected with his Catholicism —about his back ailment. Before the convention the "Addison's disease" charge was talked about; it turned out to be largely true, but is still classified as a whispering campaign, indicating the meaning comes from the method of dissemination rather than the content. See SMEAR; ROOR-BACK.

WHISTLEBLOWER a government employee who "goes public" with complaints of mismanagement or corruption in his agency.

On June 13, 1977, the Institute for Policy Studies in Washington called together a "conference on whistle-blowing," to focus "on government harassment of workers who publicly disclose mismanagement, illegality and other wrongdoing by agency heads."

In December of that year, *Village Voice* writers James Ridgeway and Alexander Cockburn used the expression in print: "Then there is the case of whistle-blower Dr. J. Anthony Morris. He has long argued against government inoculation programs (including the swine-flu-shot fiasco). Morris recently lost his case in the Civil Service Commission . . ."

The best-known whistleblower (the hyphen is being lost as the word becames better known) is Air Force cost expert Ernest Fitzgerald. During the 1976 campaign, candidate Jimmy Carter said "the Fitzgerald case, where a dedicated civil servant was fired from the Defense Department for reporting cost overruns, must never be repeated." Fitzgerald, who did get a job within government, has not since been one of its most trusted insiders.

The activity can be a reason for, or an excuse for, being fired. After widespread firings at the CIA in late 1977, John Kendall of the *Los Angeles Times* wrote on January 2, 1978, of one of those dismissed: "For half his career he says he considered himself a 'whistle blower' who tried to correct perceived faults in the CIA's domestic operations." When the CIA retorted that the man had been fired for insubordination, the ex-employee said, he "became a 'whistleblower' to correct [abuses] with full realization he was harming his career."

"Whistleblower" has a positive connotation (contrary to its predecessor slang term, "whistler," for police informer); the phrase portrays a public servant risking his job by publicly blowing a whistle to call attention to a crime. A related term is "leaker" (see LEAK; PLUMBER), which connotes stealthiness in exposure, and describes an employee not willing to risk dismissal by becoming known as a SOURCE.

WHISTLESTOPPING going to the people by railroad train with a series of short, ad-lib speeches in small communities.

The *Jackson* (Tennessee) *Sun* gave the background of the word in 1952:

> A "whistle-stop," in railroad terms, is a community too small to enjoy a regular scheduled service. Customarily, the passenger trains whiz right by. But if there are passengers to be discharged, shortly before the train approaches the station, the conductor signifies that fact by pulling the signal cord. The engineer responds with two toots of the whistle. Naturally enough, such unscheduled pauses became known as "whistle-stops." The communities were "whistle-stop towns," shortened in the course of time to "whistle-stops."

President Harry Truman discovered a gift for ad-libbing speeches in May 1948. "My first formal experience at extemporaneous speaking had come just a few weeks before I opened the whistle-stop tour in June. After reading an address to the American Society of Newspaper Editors in April, I decided to talk 'off the cuff' on American relations with Russia. When I finished my remarks about thirty minutes later, I was surprised to get the most enthusiastic applause . . ."

Truman made an old-fashioned back-of-the-platform railroad tour of the nation, ad-libbing seventy-one out of seventy-six speeches. Senator Robert A. Taft, speaking to the Union League Club in Philadelphia, derided the spectacle of an American President "black-guarding Congress at whistlestops all across the country."

Taft had blundered; "whistlestop" was an insult to a town, nearly as bad as calling its residents "hicks." Railroad men had stopped calling small stations whistlestops years ago, preferring "flag stop" or "flag station" so as not to offend the citizens of small towns. The Democratic National Committee wired the mayors of thirty-five cities through which Truman had passed asking if they agreed with Taft's slur on their civic importance. "Very poor taste," said the mayor of Gary, Indiana; "Must have the wrong city," replied the mayor of Eugene, Oregon. (For another Republican train disaster, see "idiot engineer" under BLOOPER.)

Truman said later about the word "whistlestop": "You know, that phrase was invented by Senator Taft on October 8, 1948. The Republicans were trying to make fun of my efforts to take the issues in that campaign directly to the people all over the country."

An AP reporter showed how the word had become locked into politics in this 1952 lead: "Whistlestopper Harry S. Truman lent a hand to Adlai Stevenson here Saturday in the biggest 'whistlestop' of them all." The reference was to New York City.

In the 1976 campaign President Gerald Ford hired a riverboat to cruise into the heart of Jimmy Carter strength in the South; it was called "the whistlefloat." Evidently any conveyance used by a candidate to reach small towns can be described as a whistle-whatever.

WHITE BACKLASH, see BACKLASH.

WHITE HATS   GOOD GUYS.

Liberal members of Washington's permanent establishment differentiated between Nixon Administration officials in this Western-movie metaphor, where heroes wear white hats and villains wear black.

White-hat status was given Robert Finch, Leonard Garment, Elliot Richardson, Peter Flanigan, Henry Kissinger, George Shultz, and Peter Peterson, among others; viewed as "black hats" by liberal hostesses were John Mitchell, H. R. Haldeman, Murray Chotiner, Charles Colson, and anyone associated with the Vice President.

The phrase was given currency in the late sixties by TV commentator and hostess Barbara Howar, who once invited this writer to a party with the admonition: "Wear your white hat."

The white hat has an ancient political history. In fourteenth-century Flanders, the badge of the democratic party, led by Ghent brewer Jacob von Artevelde, was the white hat. In England, during the administrations of the Duke of Wellington and Robert Peel, radical protesters wore the white hat as a form of derision.

The metaphor lends itself to cartoon treatment. On the cover of the *National Journal* for December 17, 1977, a group of black-hatted cloak-and-dagger types are shown marching into the office of reform-minded Director of Central Intelligence Stansfield Turner, and then marching out wearing white hats.

In India, as in the U.S., the white hat is a symbol of political purity. "Before the last few shifts of the sands of Indian politics," wrote *New York Times* correspondent William Borders from New Delhi in 1978, "it was possible to identify Congress Party members by their starchy white 'Gandhi caps,' named after Mohandas K. Gandhi, the independence hero. But now the caps are worn on all sides . . ."

See BLACK HATS.

WHITE HOUSE   the metaphoric center of executive power; or the place where the President of the U.S. is at any moment; or the Executive Mansion in Washington, D.C.

The White House, in its figurative and most often used sense, is the presidency. "A White House spokesman" is a presidential spokesman. The "White House Office" includes staffers who do not have a pass to get into the President's house.

To Americans, it combines the tradition of Buckingham Palace with the working center of power at 10 Downing Street. Its symbolism is evident in this mid-sixties use by *Ebony* magazine: "There is a joke going the rounds about a telephone conversation between Martin Luther King and John F. Kennedy. Says the President: 'Yes, Dr. King. I know, Dr. King. I understand, Dr. King. But Dr. King —it has always been known as the White House!' "

The second sense of the usage, as a dateline, was also described by Eisenhower: "The dateline 'White House' carries a meaning far broader than a mere structure or location; the White House, in newspaper stories, always means the President's headquarters, all the time, even when dispatches identify it as the 'Summer' or the 'Vacation' [or 'western'] White House."

As a specific house, it was known as the Executive Mansion (which is its formal title) until its destruction by the British in 1814, when it was rebuilt and painted white and became known informally as the White House. Theodore Roosevelt changed the stationery from "Executive Mansion" to "The White House," formalizing the name.

As a place to live, its prisonlike, goldfish-bowl, transient nature gets complaints from its residents. Harry Truman called it "a big white jail"; Theodore Roosevelt said, "You don't live there, you're only Exhibit A to the country." And when a senator joked to Calvin Coolidge, "I wonder who lives there," the President replied, "Nobody. They just come and go."

In calibrating power, the OVAL OFFICE gets the most attention; then the West Wing, and finally the most general, the White House. Carter presidential aide Hamilton Jordan informed the author that when they place phone calls, there is little of the imperious "The White House is on the line"; in fact, he reported that Attorney General Griffin Bell likes to say, "The White House is a building. Don't tell me 'the White House' is calling—I work for the President."

WHITE MAN'S WAR, *see* **RICH MAN'S WAR, POOR MAN'S FIGHT.**

WHITE PAPER   a statement of official government policy with background documentation.

In the U.S., a "blue book" is a directory of the social elite; in England, it is an extended explanation of government policy, bound in blue covers. See RED TAPE. "White Paper" was the English terminology for a report too short to be bound as a blue book, and that phrase was adopted in the U.S.

American political usage leans harder on the background than the policy. (Sorensen: "All the economists in government were to pull together a 'Fact Book' or 'White Paper' on steel to be widely distributed.") Also, "black book" is a new variation. (*Wall Street Journal,* 1967: "Israel published a 'black book' charging that Soviet propaganda paved the way for justifying an Arab attack on Israel.")

In current use, a *White Paper* (usually capitalized) is an official statement with the government rationale; a POSITION PAPER is an unofficial document that can be synonymous with *aide-mémoire* in diplomacy, or may mean a candidate's stand with background; a *blue book* is limited to Great Britain and means a lengthy statement of policy, a *black book* is a documented charge or attacking brief, and the *black briefing book* is the loose-leaf notebook the President of the U.S. studies before press conferences.

WHITE POWER STRUCTURE
American society, as viewed by the black militant, conspiring to retain "Establishment" control and excluding Negroes.

The phrase was introduced by black intellectuals early in the more militant phase of the civil rights movement, with or without the word "white." Barbara Brandt of SNCC used it typically in 1965: "In trying to become part of the power structure, he [the Negro] is forced to lose his militancy; he forgets the people he should be fighting for. He has been taken over by the system."

Theodore White, in *The Making of the President 1964,* gave this definition:

The term "power structure" when translated down to the level of the street becomes the term "whitey"— and "whitey" in the Negro ghetto is as contemptuous a word as "nigger" is in a Southern village. . . . Translated out to where it reaches juvenile hoodlums in the streets, it lifts from them the responsibility for anything —"whitey" made it this way, so "whitey" has got to fix it. . . . The dogma requires Negro leaders, too, to denounce the entire power structure; it forbids them to recognize its awkward, ponderous but sincere effort to wipe out prejudice. They must stand by and watch rioting and looting—and explain to their children and followers that it is wrongful, yet that the power structure caused it.

WHITE RACISM, *see* RACISM.

WHITEWASH, *see* SMEAR; WITCH HUNT.

WHITEY, *see* WHITE POWER STRUCTURE; CHARLIE.

WHIZ KIDS
the relatively young executive team skilled in the most modern management methods, brought to the Defense Department in 1961 by Secretary Robert McNamara.

McNamara, then forty-five, was a member of the original "Whiz Kids" at the Ford Motor Company, one of ten Army Air Force statistical-control experts who came to Ford in a group in 1946 (Arjay Miller, later Ford president, was also a member).

The Ford nickname was picked up by Pentagon officials who resented what they felt was high-handed, ruthless administration by youthful civilians who relied too heavily on "thinking machines."

Meanwhile, back at Ford, *Fortune* magazine reported in 1966: "There's another generation of Whiz Kids at Ford—they're young, unabashedly brainy, boundlessly aggressive, open to new ideas—and they don't want to be called 'Whiz Kids.'"

The McNamara group at the Pentagon often relied on PERT—the Program Evaluation and Review Technique—a computerized decision-indicating method of pointing to the "critical path" that will most efficiently produce a new weapons system. Their espousal of this advanced technique reinforced the "Whiz Kid" image of them held by some military planners.

The word "whiz" came into American slang about 1880 as a short form of "wizard"; the phrase grew out of "The Quiz Kids," a radio program of the forties featuring brilliant youngsters.

"Whiz Kids" was probably first applied to the University of Illinois basketball team in the late 1940s.

WHO GETS WHAT, WHEN, AND HOW   a frequent definition of politics, stressing its less spiritual rewards.

The phrase was coined by political scientist Harold Lasswell in 1936, as *who gets what, when, how.* The *Political Primer for All Americans* (1944) added an introspective word to the definition: "Politics is the science of how who gets what, when and why."

"The structure of coalition politics," wrote James MacGregor Burns in 1963, "is inevitably the structure of 'who gets what, when and how' in American national politics. As the Madisonian system in being, it is also the structure of slowdown and stalemate in American Government."

Burns was using the old definition in the sense of a division of the power of the executive; in most uses, it is a division of the spoils, such as "slicing the pie" or "divvying up the melon."

For a more frequent and more charitable definition of politics, see ART OF THE POSSIBLE. For the less uplifting side, see SPOILS SYSTEM and PATRONAGE.

WHOLE HOG, *see* **DYED-IN-THE-WOOL.**

WHO'S POLK? *see* **DARK HORSE.**

WIN-ABILITY, *see* **CAN'T WIN.**

WINDFALL PROFITS   a sudden financial bonanza to a private firm or individual caused by a change in government policy.

In October 1976 President Jimmy Carter laced into the opponents of his energy program as "war profiteers" whose "windfall profits" constituted the "biggest ripoff in our history."

The word "windfall," in its sense of an unexpected gift, such as a piece of fruit blown off a tree, has been in the language since the mid-sixteenth century. It was applied politically by Franklin Roosevelt in a message to Congress accompanying the 1936 Revenue Bill; the Supreme Court, in January of that year, had held a processing tax provision of the Agricultural Adjustment Act unconstitutional, and FDR's message was drawn to deny to processors a "windfall" from the tax they had already collected: "The first relates to the taxation of what may well be termed a 'windfall' received by certain taxpayers," wrote President Roosevelt on March 3, 1936. Supporting the Administration bill, Representative John McCormack of Massachusetts said on the House floor that "the tax on unjust enrichment" amounted to a "windfall."

An "excess profits tax" was used in World War I; it is still the formal name for the "windfall profits tax," which remains polemical.

Modifiers for profits have turned from "healthy" or "surging" to "swollen" and "obscene." These last two are recognized as judgmental, while "windfall" is taken to be descriptive of something unexpected and unfair.

WINDING DOWN   de-escalating; causing to come to an end gradually.

This was one of the oddest terms to come out of the war in Vietnam, and the author is unable to determine first usage or even the reasons for its use.

The verb "to wind" is most often followed by "up" in the sense of "to conclude"; the noun "windup" means "conclusion." Therefore, the process of VIETNAMIZATION could logically be called "the winding up of the war in Vietnam." But the term that came into use in 1969, and was elevated to cliché status in 1970, was "winding down the war."

The metaphor appears to be that of a clock, which is wound up by hand and—in the process of doing its job—runs down, or may be said to "wind down." Unwind has a modern meaning of "relax." The trouble with the metaphor in this case is that "winding down" has a passive connotation—that is, one may permit a clock to wind itself down, but no action is taken to remove the tension in the mainspring. However, the term is used here in an active sense.

William Zinsser, in the May 21, 1971, issue of *Life* magazine, had some fun with the phrase: "I submit that if science tells us anything, it tells us that man can only wind things *up.* Indeed, in the long and restless search of *Homo sapiens* for mastery of his physical environment, one invention that continues to elude him is the downwinder . . ."

Whatever the source, the term has come to mean the deliberate, steady pursuit of a policy to reduce the intensity of a war, in the hopes of an honorable extrication, and is used in defense of that policy, not to attack it.

WINDS OF CHANGE   a fundamental shift in power or policy; an inexorable current not under control of leaders.

The phrase was popularized in its present context by British Prime Minister Harold Macmillan in an address to the South African Parliament, February 4, 1960, speaking about the future of Africa: "The wind of change is blowing through the Continent. Whether we like it or not, this growth of national consciousness is a political fact."

In an editorial, the *Christian Science Monitor* later congratulated Macmillan (see UNFLAPPABLE) on coining an excellent expression, and pointed to *The Libation-bearers,* written by Aeschylus in 458 B.C.: "Zeus at last may cause our ill winds to change."

As with most memorable phrases, a long history can be traced, which does not detract from the ring of originality. Of course nothing is more changeable than the direction of the wind, but the use of the simple metaphor in the turmoil of African affairs was apt.

An early use of changing winds can be found in *Sweet William's Farewell to Black-Eyed Susan* by English poet John Gay (1685–1732):

We only part to meet again.
Change, as ye list, ye winds; my heart shall be
The faithful compass that still points to thee.

Typical use of the wind metaphor in modern times was by Indian Prime

Minister Jawaharlal Nehru in 1947: "The masses are awake and they demand their heritage. Strong winds are blowing all over Asia. Let us not be afraid of them but rather welcome them for only with their help can we build the new Asia of our dreams."

And John Gunther wrote of the Mormon community in Utah in 1947: ". . . the astringent winds of a new world, which bewilder the older believers, are beating mercilessly at the pillar they drove into the desert."

"Windy," of course, is slang for long-winded, and is related to "full of hot air." "Winds of doctrine" was used by Milton in *Areopagitica* (1644): "Though all the winds of doctrine were let loose to play upon the earth, so Truth be in the field, we do injuriously, by licensing and prohibiting, to misdoubt her strength."

George Santayana used *Winds of Doctrine* as the title of a book in 1913. In 1934 British Prime Minister Stanley Baldwin said: "There is a wind of nationalism and freedom blowing around the world."

When Harold Macmillan came to titling his own memoirs in 1966, he accepted the editing of common usage that changed his "wind of change" to "winds" and called his book *The Winds of Change.*

WINNING, *see* **CAN'T-WIN TECHNIQUE; NO-WIN POLICY; NO SUBSTITUTE FOR VICTORY; ZERO-SUM GAME;** and the saying under **PROVERBS, POLITICAL** that goes "Show me a good loser and I'll show you a loser."

WINNING THE PEACE only victory promise possible in **LIMITED WARS**.

When it became apparent in the late sixties that the cost of victory in South Vietnam would be too high, political emphasis in the U.S. shifted to an honorable settlement. Thus, in the 1968 primary campaign, Richard Nixon pledged to "end the war and win the peace," which caused supporters of George Romney to demand that Nixon make public a "secret plan to end the war."

The use of the word "win" appealed to those who were distressed at a no-win strategy (see **NO-WIN POLICY**) and disturbed those who feared that military victory was Nixon's objective. As President, Nixon held to the policy, and occasionally the rhetoric, of "winning a peace"—through a withdrawal that will give the South Vietnamese "a reasonable chance of survival as a free people."

The phrase is based on the time-honored device of military terms to describe peace (see **WAGING PEACE**) and is taken directly from Will Rogers' aphorism: "The United States has never lost a war or won a peace." See **NEVER LOST A WAR.**

WIRETAP, *see* **TAPS AND BUGS.**

WITCH HUNT investigation characterized by hysteria.

Woodrow Wilson's Attorney General, A. Mitchell Palmer, led what was called a "Red hunt" just after World War I, finding "Communists under every bed."

The phrase "witch hunt"—an allusion to the Salem, Massachusetts, witch trials in the seventeenth century—is now applied to investigations considered to be motivated by a desire to capitalize on a popular fear. One of Eisenhower's campaign pledges made on the eve of election in 1952 was that we would engage in no "witch hunts or **CHARACTER ASSASSINATION**," adding he would strive to "prevent infiltration of Communists and **FELLOW TRAVELERS**" into government that straddled the "McCarthy issue."

A *witch hunt*—an attack phrase on an attack—is the opposite of a *whitewash* (see SMEAR), which is an attack on an exoneration. A witch hunt is a FISHING EXPEDITION with a vengeance.

Controller of the Currency John Heimann, in describing the ground rules for a 1977 investigation by his office, showed a nice understanding of the Scylla and Charybdis of probes when he told his employees: "I want this to be neither a whitewash nor a witch hunt."

WITH ALL DELIBERATE SPEED
the operative phrase in the U.S. Supreme Court decision striking down segregation in schools. See SEPARATE BUT EQUAL.

On May 17, 1954, in *Brown* v. *Board of Education*, the Supreme Court directed public schools throughout the U.S. to integrate; a year later, on May 31, 1955, another unanimous Court directed that this be done "with all deliberate speed."

The question was soon raised: How speedy is "deliberate"? The Court obviously chose the phrase so as to give some flexibility to the lower courts in determining compliance, and the phrase became the center of legal controversy for the next decade. In 1964, writing for the majority in a decision ordering reopening of Virginia schools that closed rather than integrate, Hugo Black stated: "There has been entirely too much deliberation and not enough speed. The time for mere 'deliberate speed' has run out . . ."

The phrase can be found in a poem by Francis Thompson, "The Hound of Heaven," written in 1893: "But with unhurrying chase/And unperturbed pace/Deliberate speed, majestic instancy . . ."

The Supreme Court, however, probably chose the phrase from a 1912 decision by Justice Oliver Wendell Holmes, in the case of *Virginia* v. *West Virginia:* ". . . a State cannot be expected to move with the celerity of a private business man; it is enough it proceeds, in the language of the English Chancery, with all deliberate speed."

Drawing on Holmes, Justice Felix Frankfurter used the phrase five times in cases preceding the desegregation decisions. Although scholars assume Justice Holmes knew what he was talking about in attributing the phrase to English Chancery practice, diligent research has failed to come up with a single quotable instance of its use.

The most fascinating clue was found in a letter to his publisher from George Gordon, Lord Byron, dated April 6, 1819. The poet had often been threatened with Chancery Court action, and in *Don Juan* wrote that his hero was "sole heir to a Chancery suit." Writing to publisher John Murray, he complained of a previous exhaustion that obliged him to "reform my 'way of life' which was conducting me from the 'yellow leaf' to the ground with all deliberate speed." Certainty in phrase detection is rare; it can only be assumed that Bryon drew the phrase from his Chancery experience.

The more familiar Chancery phrase was "all convenient speed," which can also be found in Shakespeare's *The Merchant of Venice.* Just before Shylock's trial, Portia sends Balthasar to consult a lawyer and her messenger replies "Madame, I go with all convenient speed." Robert Browning used this, as did Abraham Lincoln ("with all convenient dispatch"). Lincoln approached this thought from another angle in 1861 when asked if he favored the immediate emancipation of the slaves. "It will do no good," he replied, "to go ahead any faster than the country will follow. . . . You know the old Latin motto, *festina lente.*" That motto, a frequent saying of Augustus Caesar, means "make haste slowly."

For much of the above information the writer is indebted to Justice Potter Stewart and to Professor Alwin Thaler of the University of Tennessee.

"Deliberate speed" is almost an oxymoron, a phrase or epigram built on the jarring juxtaposition of opposites, like "thunderous silence" or "cruel kindness." It does not qualify as a full-fledged oxymoron (a word that columnist William Buckley Jr. uses because it sounds like an insult) for the reason that it is possible to have a "speedy deliberation." See LOYAL OPPOSITION.

WOMEN'S LIB   a movement promoting equal rights for women, more militant than similar women's rights and women's suffrage movements in the past.

Betty Friedan, whose 1963 book, *The Feminine Mystique,* focused on the emptiness in the lives of suburban women, tells the author that the phrase originated with the women of Students for a Democratic Society in the late sixties. Feminist editor Gloria Steinem, in response to the author's query, confirms this:

> As far as I know, Women's Liberation is a phrase that sprang from the women of SNCC and the women of SDS . . . I think I first heard it early in 1967. Those women were very active. They went to jail with the men, demonstrated with the men, and earned Ph.D.'s with the men. Yet, when they got back to their organizational meetings they were supposed to make coffee, not revolutionary policy. This made it

very clear to them that the revolution they were fighting was not necessarily going to benefit the other half of the human race.

Shortening the phrase to Women's Lib is a bit of ridicule perpetrated by the press. Would you say Black Lib? Puerto Rican Lib? I doubt it. The cavalier shortening is a kind of put-down in itself. Because of this, and because of the vast enlargement of the numbers of women involved, women now tend to say "Women's Movement" rather than Women's Liberation.

In either case, the phrase indicates a large umbrella movement, comprised of hundreds of local or national organizations, plus consciousness-changing among many, many women who belong to no organizations at all. In that sense, I suppose it's comparable to "Civil Rights Movement" as a phrase."

In its unshortened form, Women's Liberation is considered appropriate by many of its leaders. Kate Millet, who wrote *Sexual Politics* in 1970, says "Women's Liberation is my life."

The attack phrases of the movement are "male chauvinist" (for origin of chauvinist, see SUPERPATRIOTS) and SEXISM. *Time* magazine wrote in 1970: "Sexism was the sin of one professor who admitted at a San Francisco meeting of the staid Modern Language Association that, all things considered, he would look at a girl's legs when considering her for a teaching post. 'You bastard, you bastard!' one girl screamed (s.o.b. is out in the best feminist lexicons)."

At a Washington dinner party, this writer made a passing reference to "Women's Lip" which was quoted in the *Washington Post* and triggered a fusillade of irate letters, causing him to be considerably less flippant in subsequent treatment of the Women's Liberation movement. See MACHISMO; CONSCIOUSNESS-RAISING.

WORKERS, *see* **TROOPS, VOL-UNTEERS.**

WORK ETHIC the idea that work in itself is good for a person, molding character and inspiring a quality of thrift and an understanding of values.

In *The Protestant Ethic and the Spirit of Capitalism* (1904), Max Weber pointed to a paradox: although the pursuit of money was once regarded as unworthy of a Christian, and the possession of riches seen long ago as evidence of selfishness, in modern times religion has endowed material success with the aura of godliness. Calvinism's themes of hard work and personal asceticism led to the accumulation of fortunes, which was considered the mark of a good man—thus, went Weber's thesis, "the Puritan stood at the cradle of economic man," providing "good conscience in money making."

At its coinage, then, the Protestant ethic (later Puritan ethic, or work ethic) was intended to be a term of derogation by its author. It has since gained in stature and is now a compliment, politically popularized in a Labor Day speech by Richard Nixon in 1972.

President Nixon was impressed with a memorandum entitled "The Problem of the Blue-Collar Worker," written in 1970 by Assistant Secretary of Labor Jerome Rosow. Inflation and the cost of family education had driven up these workers' cost of living at a time when their income was topping out, the memo showed, and white-collar work had been glamorized while blue-collar jobs were denigrated as menial.

This writer, then a White House speechwriter, was assigned a speech on the "dignity of work" to reassure these lower-middle-class ETHNICS

that their work was respectable and respected, and—in retrospect—to exploit a resentment at "the greening of America" that put too great a stress on youth and intellectual endeavors while patronizing the calloused hand.

A speech was drafted on the work ethic; the President removed references to "Protestant" and broadcast the speech on radio with some pride: "As the name implies, the work ethic holds that labor is good in itself; that a man or woman at work not only makes a contribution to his fellow man, but becomes a better person by virtue of the act of working. The work ethic is ingrained in the American character. That is why most of us consider it immoral to be lazy or slothful—even if a person is well off enough not to work." Here the President wrote in: "—or can avoid work by going on welfare."

Columnist Max Lerner, with an eye for sociology in politics, noted: "President Nixon's Labor Day sermonette on the work ethic was addressed not only to the traditional audience of union members but also to the South and Midwest, where the language of the work ethic is politically warming, and to the whole middle class which feels that honest work has gone down the drain."

The phrase is in current use, although it occasions this riposte to politicians who evoke it: "What are you doing about people who have the work ethic but who cannot find jobs?"

WORKFARE conservative label for welfare reform, stressing an intent to "get people off welfare rolls and onto payrolls."

In the late spring of 1969, the Nixon Administration's plan for the overhaul of the welfare system was at an impasse: counselors Arthur Burns and Daniel P. Moynihan differed on the need for a work requirement. George Shultz, then Labor Secretary, came up with a solution that was not a compromise, but a fresh approach: supplementing the incomes of the working poor, to provide an incentive to move from welfare to work.

Inside the government, the plan was originally called Family Security, but that was too much like Social Security; "Fair Share" was proposed, but that sounded to conservative members of the Administration too much like FAIR DEAL or share-the-wealth. At a cabinet meeting at Camp David, President Nixon directed some of the discussion of the plan to its name, because he had already decided on substance and wanted its opponents to get their licks in somewhere. Family Assistance Plan was decided upon, despite this writer's concern about the initials sounding like an expression of a cartoon character named Major Hoople.

However, in his nationwide television address on August 8, 1969, the President tried out a new word: "In the final analysis, we cannot talk our way out of poverty; we cannot legislate our way out of poverty; but this Nation can work its way out of poverty. What America needs now is not more welfare, but more 'workfare.' " In his message to the Congress three days later, he used the term again: "This would be the effect of the transformation of welfare into 'workfare,' a new work-rewarding program . . ."

The emphasis on the work requirement—called "the conservative rhetoric"—was said to offend many liberals who ordinarily might be expected to support the program. Whether the rhetoric was the cause, or a resentment that this major social legislation should be credited to a longtime political adversary underlay it, the welfare reform legislation bogged down in a combination of conservative opposition and liberal lack of enthusiasm.

Welfare, as a word, has fallen far from its heights as one of the basic national purposes described in the Constitution: "to promote the general welfare." Today, recipients and taxpayers alike characterize it as "the welfare mess," the "archaic welfare system" and the "welfare quagmire." See WELFARE STATE.

"Work," on the other hand, is doing better all the time, despite the efforts to change "workers" into "employees" and ultimately to bloodless "personnel." However, demonstration organizer Abbie Hoffman called work "the only dirty four-letter word in the English language."

WORLD OPINION the moral force, real or imagined, of the anticipated reaction of uncommitted nations, or of leaders not firmly aligned with any international power group.

The idea is rooted in the Declaration of Independence: ". . . a decent Respect to the Opinions of Mankind requires that they should declare the causes which impel them to the Separation. . . . To prove this, let Facts be submitted to a candid World."

The phrase was probably written by Thomas Jefferson, who used it later: "The good opinion of mankind, like the lever of Archimedes with the given fulcrum, moves the world."

Daniel Webster, speaking to the House of Representatives on January 19, 1823, about the Greek revolution, gave the phrase its moral overtones: "Moral causes come into consideration, in proportion as the progress of knowledge is advanced; and the *public opinion* of the civilized world is rapidly gaining an ascendancy over mere brutal force."

After Jefferson, the phrase was most closely associated with President Woodrow Wilson, who used it in his PEACE WITHOUT VICTORY address early in 1917: "The present war must first be ended; but we owe it to candor and to a just regard for the opinion of mankind to say that, so far as our participation in guarantees of future peace is concerned, it makes a great deal of difference in what way and upon what terms it is ended." In his speech, Wilson used "mankind" as in the Declaration of Independence. Thirteen months earlier, in a letter to Colonel House, he wrote: "If either party to the present war will let us say to the other that they are willing to discuss peace on such terms, it will clearly be our duty to use our utmost *moral* force to oblige the other to parley, and I do not see how they could stand in the *opinion of the world* if they refused."

Dwight Eisenhower, in his SPIRIT OF GENEVA speech in 1955, gave a quasi-legal standing to world opinion: "The case of the several leading nations on both sides is on trial before the bar of world opinion."

As can be seen, many political leaders have made obeisances to "the opinion of mankind" and "world opinion" (which is now more frequently used than the Jeffersonian phrase). In practice, however, the requirements of national policy have often led to decisions contrary to the "dictates" of world opinion. Who, after all, forms world opinion? In most cases, the phrase is used to mean its effect on the "uncommitted nations" of the THIRD WORLD and other neutralist forces in Western nations. Not all of these, however, feel bound by world opinion themselves: India's takeover of Portuguese Goa, an enclave on its coast, flew in the face of world opinion—at least in Western eyes—but accomplished what India's

leaders felt was an important national goal.

South Carolina Congressman Mendel Rivers, chairman of the House Armed Services Committee, urged in September 1966 that the U.S. "flatten Hanoi if necessary" and "let world opinion go fly a kite." This was generally regarded as a hard-line extreme.

Ralph Waldo Emerson suggested a kind of compromise in 1841: "It is easy in the world to live after the world's opinion; it is easy in solitude to live after our own; but the great man is he who in the midst of the crowd keeps with perfect sweetness the independence of solitude."

WORLD POLICEMAN, *see* **POLICEMAN OF THE WORLD.**

WORLD VIEW, *see* **WELTANSCHAUUNG.**

WORST OF BOTH WORLDS, *see* **INFLATION.**

WRAP-UP, *see* **ADVANCE MAN.**

WRITE-IN a vote requiring the voter's "writing-in" of the candidate's name, rather than marking a ballot or pulling a lever next to a printed name.

Politicians go to great lengths to make voting easier for the voter. Party symbols (see PARTY EMBLEMS) appear above the line to reassure the nearly illiterate; parties jockey for the first line or column, as if the inside track provides greater speed; "sample ballots" are distributed as literature, with a large arrow pointing to the candidate's name and the rest of the ballot screened with a dull gray overlay. Accordingly, a "write-in"— where the voter has to work, rather than react—is given little chance of winning.

On primaries, however, a successful write-in campaign occasionally comes to pass. In 1964 in New Hampshire, a late-starting, enthusiastic campaign for former Senator Henry Cabot Lodge upset the well-financed campaigns of Barry Goldwater and Nelson Rockefeller.

Dwight Eisenhower recalled the Minnesota primary of 1952, which gave a big boost to his candidacy: "The effort to promote a write-in vote had, as with the Madison Square Garden meeting, been opposed by persons who, while participating in the effort to make me a candidate, believed that any write-in effort was doomed to miserable failure and would have a depressing effect." For the result, see POLITICAL MIRACLE.

WRONG WAR a criticism of military strategy.

President Harry Truman and General Douglas MacArthur clashed in 1951 over the strategic course to take in Korea. As 200,000 Chinese Communist VOLUNTEERS swarmed across the Yalu River to retake North Korea, MacArthur wanted to strike back at China's PRIVILEGED SANCTUARIES in force, but the President restrained him. General Omar Bradley, Chairman of the Joint Chiefs of Staff, supported Truman's position before Congress, calling the MacArthur strategy "the wrong war, at the wrong place and at the wrong time, and with the wrong enemy." See NO SUBSTITUTE FOR VICTORY.

Critics of a "land war in Asia" have often termed this kind of involvement "the wrong war," though no "air war in Asia" is ever posed as "the right war." Benjamin Franklin said, "There never was a good war or a bad peace," and educator Charles Eliot Norton, denouncing the Spanish-American War in 1898, said, "If a war be undertaken for the most righteous end, before the resources of peace have been tried and proved vain to secure it, that war has no defense, it is a national crime." The antonym to "wrong war" is "just war"; see WAR OF NATIONAL LIBERATION.

President Johnson used the same construction in a different way, as he appointed Negro Thurgood Marshall to the U.S. Supreme Court in 1967: "I believe it is the right thing to do, the right time to do it, the right man and the right place."

YAHOO   a political brute.

Senator Herbert Lehman of New York walked down the Senate aisle to confront Senator Joseph McCarthy, who told him, "Go back to your seat, old man." Wrote Stewart Alsop in his 1968 book *The Center:* "Thus old Senator Lehman's back, waddling off in retreat, seemed to symbolize the final defeat of decency and the triumph of the yahoos."

In 1970 a reader of the *Washington Post* wrote the editor: "Justice Douglas makes a perfect target for the KNOW-NOTHINGS overrunning Washington. . . , The Yahoos are on the loose. Who is to stop them?"

In 1978, as Washington social pages reported blunders by "the Georgians" on the staff of President Carter, Meg Greenfield wrote in *Newsweek:* "There are far too many Carter Administration Georgians in town who do not play the bumpkin game to lend credibility to the notion that the principal tension here is between a stuffy, decrepit Establishment and a bunch of bare-chested, peanut-feeding Yahoos."

The word comes from Jonathan Swift's *Gulliver's Travels,* written in 1726, coined by him to describe a race of brutes in the form of men who are slaves to the noble breed of "houyhnhnm," highly intelligent horses. It has also been used as a cheer, similar to "yippee" and "hooray," and the two senses com-

bined in Yates's *The Rock Ahead* (1868), describing "a dam low-bred lot, yahooin' all over the place."

The trend is against capitalization in modern political use, which applies the word almost exclusively to anti-intellectual right wingers (see RED-NECK; DINOSAUR WING).

YALTA, *see* MUNICH, AN-OTHER; OPEN COVENANTS.

YARDSTICKS, *see* GUIDELINES.

YELLOW DOG DEMOCRAT
an unswerving party loyalist; used only as a compliment.

A yellow dog is a cur. In labor terminology, a "yellow dog contract" is an agreement signed by employees not to join a union.

But the yellow dog has taken on a different political coloration as a Southern regionalism. When Senator Tom Heflin of Alabama refused to support fellow Democrat Al Smith in the 1928 election and bolted to Herbert Hoover, other Alabamans who disagreed with Heflin popularized the line "I'd vote for a yellow dog if he ran on the Democratic ticket."

This was hardly complimentary to Smith, but it did illustrate the lengths to which some Southern Democrats would go in supporting the ticket.

The phrase is in active use in the Deep South, as an admiring description of a fellow REGULAR. See BRASS COLLAR DEMOCRAT.

YES, BUT one who supports a principle but refuses to support its implementation; more a straggler than a follower.

This was a coinage of Franklin D. Roosevelt's, when he was under fire in 1937 for trying to PURGE the Democratic party of its conservative members. Writes Samuel Rosenman: "He invented a new word to describe the Congressman who publicly approved a progressive objective but who always found something wrong with any specific proposal to gain that objective—'a yes-but' fellow."

In 1952 Adlai Stevenson, a close student of Rooseveltian phrases, blasted his opposition in these terms: "The Republicans have a 'me, too' candidate running on a 'yes, but' platform, advised by a 'has been' staff . . ."

The phrase, while never as popular as ME TOO, remains alive. Columnist Flora Lewis, writing with prescience of possible successors to Charles de Gaulle in 1967: "Emerging from the shadow of de Gaulle is . . . the lean, eager face of Valéry Giscard d'Estaing, who says 'yes, but' to de Gaullism to separate his profile from the crowd."

YOU CAN'T BEAT SOMEBODY WITH NOBODY proverb used when an "out" party is jubilant over the "in" party's unpopularity, and then is faced with the task of finding a well-known candidate. See INS AND OUTS.

Historian Mark Sullivan wrote in 1930: "When, finally, [Theodore] Roosevelt put his mind upon selecting his successor . . . he was moved by the axiom of practical politics which says, 'You can't beat somebody with no-

body.' " The proverb was current at the turn of the century, and is often attributed to "Uncle Joe" Cannon, House Speaker from 1903 to 1911.

Its origin may be in a Lincoln anecdote, taken from Carl Sandburg's writings, related by Everett McKinley Dirksen on the floor of the Senate:

> When I think of all the comments by persons who seem to think they are better able to do this job in the defense field than is the President of the United States, I think of the Committee on the Conduct of the War, which was established away back in the Civil War days. . . . On that committee there was a man named Benjamin Wade, from Ohio. He started out as a canal driver and as a mule skinner. Then he became a teacher, as I recall, and then a lawyer. That qualified him to conduct a war. He marched down to the White House, shook his finger at Lincoln, and said, "You have to fire General McClellan." Lincoln said, "Well, whom shall I use to replace him?" And Wade said, "Anybody." Lincoln, out of his majestic concepts, said, "I cannot fight a war with anybody; I must have somebody."

> Away back in those days we had a little of the same attitude which is now apparent.

See PROVERBS AND AXIOMS, POLITICAL.

YOU CAN'T FIGHT CITY HALL, *see* GO FIGHT CITY HALL.

YOU NEVER HAD IT SO GOOD slogan of "In" party stressing prosperity.

"You Never Had It So Good" was the Democratic party slogan in the 1952 Stevenson campaign against Eisenhower. See $K_1 C_2$. Those "madly for Adlai" were not enthusiastic about the slogan, since it appeared as a weak defense against the MESS IN WASHINGTON. Arthur Schlesinger,

Jr., writing in 1965, tried to dissociate Stevenson from it: "In the last days of Truman the party motto had been, 'You never had it so good.' The essence of the party appeal was not to demand exertions but to promise benefits. Stevenson changed all that."

In 1955 the British Conservative party did better with the slogan. The official Tory campaign theme was "Conservative Freedom Works" but the unofficial battle cry was taken from the American campaign three years earlier. British author John Montgomery wrote in his book *The Fifties:* "Mr. Harold Macmillan's statement, that the British people had 'never had it so good,' attracted wide attention. It was, however, only a half-truth. It failed to convince many housewives, struggling against the rising prices of food and other essentials, or brides, or business girls striving to furnish homes, or youngsters attempting to save to get married."

Whenever any political leader asks voters to count their blessings, the criticism heightens, with "You never had it so good" now turned into an attack phrase. Lyndon Johnson in 1967 set forth some of the things that were right about America: "We produce more goods, we transport more goods and we use more goods than anyone in the world. We own almost a third of the world's railroad tracks. We own almost two-thirds of the world's automobiles. We own half the trucks in the world. And although we have only about 6 per cent of the population in the world, we have half its wealth."

Columnist James Reston commented: "This, of course, is the old doctrine of 'you-never-had-it-so-good.' . . . The Johnson theme will probably do all right, especially since the Republicans have renewed their old game of self-destruction. It is the

poor voters who are in trouble, for they are about to be overwhelmed by all the accumulated political rubbish of the centuries."

YOUNG TURKS   insurgents; restive elements within a party seeking control or at least a voice; usually, not always, comparatively young.

The Young Turks were the reformers of the Ottoman Empire, a revolutionary group that seized power in 1908 from the aging sultans; in 1922 the House of Osman gave up and the Young Turks—middle-aged by then —set up a republic.

The name was used to describe a group of Republican senators in 1929 who broke with their leadership over tariff legislation. Wrote *Time* magazine at the time: "Spectators of the Senate tariff war last week gasped with surprise at the sight of a trim new regiment marching briskly and in close order out of the Republican redoubts. These new Republican warriors were called the Young Turks, a band of about 20 who had mutinied against the feeble leadership of the OLD GUARD. For Senators they were young men (average age: 56). As legislative legionnaires they were mostly rookies serving their first Senate enlistment."

Today the phrase is used to describe any faction impatient with delay or defeat, seeking action. Party regulars use it patronizingly, but those so labeled do not resent it. The phrase has been eclipsed in recent years by ANGRY YOUNG MEN.

During the Bermuda Conference of 1953, Winston Churchill digressed from the agenda to discuss imperialism with Dwight Eisenhower, expressing his doubts about the wisdom of self-government for peoples not yet ready for it. When the American President disagreed with a portion of the Prime Minister's argument, Churchill smiled and said, "You're just like the Young Turks in my government."

YOUR HOME IS YOUR CASTLE

a slogan appealing to whites opposed to residential integration.

George Mahoney, perennial candidate for statewide office in Maryland, used this slogan in his 1966 campaign. It was picked up by Louise Day Hicks, candidate for mayor of Boston in 1967; both campaigns lost.

"Your Home Is Your Castle—Protect It" was regarded as a CODE WORD phrase by most analysts, playing on the prejudices of voters concerned with property values in their neighborhoods if blacks moved in.

The phrase "a man's home is his castle" is taken from a proverb and was codified in English law by Sir Edward Coke in 1604: "For a man's house is his castle, *et domus sua cuique tutissimum refugium.* . . . Resolved: The house of every man is his castle, and if thieves come to a man's house to rob or murder, and the owner or his servants kill any of the thieves in defence of himself and his house, it is no felony and he lose nothing . . ."

In recent usage, the proverb has been more the property of opponents of desegregation than of the "gun lobby."

ZERO-BASE BUDGETING starting a budget from scratch every year, challenging all assumptions of allocations; a management technique intended to improve efficiency.

Peter A. Pyhrr, manager, Staff Control, of Texas Instruments in Dallas, wrote an article in the *Harvard Business Review* (November-December 1970) coining the phrase and describing the technique. He began by quoting a speech made on December 2, 1969, by Dr. Arthur Burns, then counselor to the President: "Customarily, the officials in charge of an established program have to justify only the increase which they seek above last year's appropriation. In other words, what they are already spending is usually accepted as necessary, without examination. Substantial savings could undoubtedly be realized if every agency . . . made a case for its entire appropriation request every year, just as if its program or programs were entirely new."

Commented Mr. Pyhrr: "Burns was advocating that government agencies start from ground zero, as it were, with each year's budget and present their requests for appropriations in such a fashion that all funds can be allocated on the basis of cost/benefit or some similar kind of evaluative analysis."

The use of the "ground zero" metaphor was in error: "ground zero" refers to that area on the ground directly below an atomic explosion, the epicenter from which the distance from the middle is measured, and does not imply getting to the bottom of things. But the phrase and the article caught the eye of management-conscious Governor Jimmy Carter of Georgia, who hired Mr. Pyhrr to come to Atlanta and try out his ideas.

During the 1976 campaign Mr. Carter used the phrase frequently, as evidence of his managerial know-how. When in office—on April 28, 1977—President Carter described it this way: "We have a means now to put into effect a new budgeting system called zero-base budgeting, that will let us go deep within the government as the 1979 Fiscal year budget is prepared to eliminate unnecessary programs and to re-examine those things that are now accepted as impervious to criticism and scrutiny and analysis, and to bring them to the surface and look them over again and see which ones need to be continued, which ones enhanced, which ones reduced or abolished."

Mr. Carter's Office of Media Liaison defined it in these words: "In zero-base budgeting, the budget process for all federal agencies start from zero—no funding at all. The agencies must build their budget each year from the ground up, insuring that spending is as economical as possible."

The technique has been criticized,

more for presuming to be new than for its basic idea; in an article in the *Wall Street Journal* on April 27, 1977, Harvard Business School professor Robert Anthony held: "Under the term 'management by objectives' this idea has been common in industry and in certain parts of the government for years . . . so, even though zero-base budgeting is a fraud, and even though the good parts of it are not new, experienced budget people should not let the phrase make them nauseous. [*sic*]. They should disregard the rhetoric and latch on to the term as a way of accomplishing what really needs to be accomplished anyway."

See SUNSET LAWS.

ZERO-SUM GAME   in politics or diplomacy, a confrontation in which a face-saving way out is impossible, and one side wins what the other side loses.

In game theory, pioneered by Professors John von Neumann and Oskar Morgenstern, a game in which the interests of the two players are diametrically opposed is called "zero-sum"—that is, the sum of the winnings is always zero, with one player winning what the other loses. A non-zero-sum game is one in which both sides can both win or lose—for example, in a labor-management negotiation, if no agreement is reached and a disruptive strike ensues, both sides have lost. In a successful peace negotiation, considering the savings of not fighting a war, both sides have won.

Game theory is closely studied by national security strategists, and a confrontation to be avoided at all costs is often referred to as a "zero-sum game," which is a form of NO-WIN POLICY.

ZINGER   a barb; or, a punch line; or, a stirring conclusion to a speech.

"Zing" is a word with many slang meanings, from "punch" to "liveliness." ("It don't mean a thing if you ain't got that zing.") In politics, a "zinger" is a verbal jab at an opponent, often on the light side, well short of a denunciation, or "blast." Common usage in this sense: "Give him a zinger and see how he reacts."

"Zing" also has a verb form. The Spring 1978 catalogue for Arlington House publishers advertised *The Power of the Positive Woman,* by Phyllis Schlafly, with this line: "The nation's leading ERA [Equal Rights Amendment] opponent zings Womens' Lib and the ERA in her first book on women." The verb "to zing" describes criticism less forceful than a related slang verb, "to zap," from a Johnny Hart comic strip, "B.C.," which is usually accompanied by a bolt of lightning.

Speechwriters use zinger in another sense, that of a moment of uplift or poignancy in a speech, or a punch line likely to trigger applause. When a zinger comes at the end of a speech or line of thought, it is called a "snapper," (from "to snap out of it"). See PERORATION.

ZOO PLANE   the least desirable campaign transportation; airborne home of the scorned ANIMALS of television technology.

Late in most presidential campaigns, the candidate's aircraft has room only for a press "pool"—that handful of reporters who stay close to "the Man" while staying in touch with the accompanying press plane, which lands first at campaign stops to report the arrival and swell the crowd. Often a second press plane is needed to accommodate photographers, television crews, and reporters from less prestigious publications or from local stations.

Jules Witcover, then a *Washington Post* reporter, wrote in 1973 about a Republican observer who was discovered on a Democratic campaign plane: "Given campaign press credentials as a representative of the Women's News Service and a freelance book writer, she was shunted to the 'zoo plane'—the No. 2 plane in the McGovern entourage. It was so named by reporters because it mostly carried TV cameramen and technicians—'the animals' in the quasi-affectionate, quasi-snobbish parlance of political campaigns."

The author first heard the expression in the campaign of 1968, when Republican press aide Ronald Ziegler said jokingly to a critical "pool" reporter: "You'll never get off the zoo plane after this."

Bibliography and Research

In the beginning are the words.

Which words make up the current political lexicon? To find out, the lexicographer must survey much of the writing and speaking in the field today with an eye and an ear for the current, the clichéd, and the colorful.

The technique is to make the words come to him. A reading plan comes first, to be certain all periods are covered in books on history and biography, weighted to this century, and heavily weighted to the last five presidential administrations. This chronology is then crosshatched by reading on a subject: books and guides to politics on the precinct level, on foreign policy, on defense, on national conventions. Collections of quotations come next, dictionaries of slang, and the other dictionaries on government and politics that have been written over the years. And all the while, the daily newspapers and weekly news magazines and Sunday afternoon television panel shows must be culled, especially the syndicated political columnists to whom the political language is second nature.

The lexicographer selects a book in his plan, trains his eye to look for catch phrases, and begins scanning. In a book on the Truman Administration he runs across a phrase—RED HERRING, for example—and makes out a 5 × 7 index card for it, noting the title and page of the book that refers to it. After a hundred books and a thousand newspaper columns, he has about 2,000 of those index cards. Reading the *Oxford Book of English Proverbs,* he comes to an 1890 political use of the phrase as well as a sixteenth-century use from John Heywood's proverbs; a bell rings, and a check is made to see if he already has that card. He has; there are three other notations on that entry already, all in current use.

Three hundred books and uncounted columns later, the card file begins to say something. There are not that many more cards—perhaps 2,500 in all—but some have a dozen notations and others only the one that caused the card to be made out. Two possibilities arise: either many of the cards contain words that do not belong in a current dictionary or something is wrong with the reading plan.

This is where political experience is useful. He knows the word LIGHTWEIGHT is current and active, because he uses it himself and has heard it often; a single notation on the card means more digging is needed. On the other hand, a single notation on *janissary,* which he does not hear or use himself, is a good indication that the word deserves only a passing reference under HENCHMAN or a mention that BRAIN TRUST was once labeled the "janissariat." Perhaps it's worth a cross reference; perhaps it should be lumped in with an entry on "OBSOLETE TERMS" or perhaps forgotten.

At this stage the file of terms can be edited to about 1,600 words, phrases, and slogans. Some will be added (CRUNCH and TAX REVOLT come toward the end) and others deleted ("amen corner" isn't current enough and "honkie" is not primarily political) but this is the size of the current political vocabulary, according to the lexicographer's standards.

By this time, the lexicographer no longer has the remotest idea what the little squiggles on the index cards refer to. The bibliography code indicates that *Sor/-Dec* is *Decision Making in the White House* by Ted Sorensen, but he does not remember anything about what was in that book on that page that made him write down that notation. Going back to RED HERRING, an average entry, this is what the card looks like:

Tru Ad 385, 6	Stone 317
Truman 242	Eng Prov 309, 510
Goldman Cru 225	DAPT 363
Hess 324	Cater 4th 37
Phillips 228	Krock 150, 164
Donovan 180	W. Johnson 285
Bart 92a	Dict Origins 291

This means the books that will help with this entry are: Barton J. Bernstein and Allen J. Matusow, *The Truman Administration;* Harry S. Truman, *Years of Trial and Hope;* Eric F. Goldman, *The Crucial Decade—and After;* Stephen Hess, *America's Political Dynasties;* Cabell Phillips, *The Truman Presidency;* Robert J. Donovan, *The Inside Story;* John Bartlett, *Familiar Quotations;* Irving Stone, *They Also Ran;* William George Smith and Janet E. Heseltine, *Oxford Dictionary of English Proverbs;* Sperber and Trittschuh, *American Political Terms: An Historical Dictionary;* Douglass Cater, *The Fourth Branch of Government;* Arthur Krock, *In the Nation: 1932–1966;* Walter Johnson, *1600 Pennsylvania Avenue;* William and Mary Morris, *Dictionary of Word and Phrase Origins.*

With the aid of four paperweights, two heavy rulers, one cracked binding, and by laying some books across portions of others, he can see all the results of the book research on that entry. Meanwhile, back in the filing cabinet, he has a file folder that corresponds to each one of the active index cards, containing the pages torn out of magazines and newspapers and the little notes made from television programs. These are spread out on the floor.

The building of an entry begins. Suddenly a word or phrase takes shape, differences in usage and meaning appear, and a small version of the "great conversation" Mortimer Adler wrote about in his Syntopicon can be heard.

And the holes show up. Everything but the actual coinage or the most famous use is there, or the uses in print do not jibe with the use the lexicographer knows (*graveyard* is a political secret, not just a dead end); or, the sources show meaning, coinage, and development, with a good quotation about the subject—but no usage in the past few years that includes the phrase itself. The lexicographer goes back to the books a second time to fill the holes.

For the Johnson years, the behind-the-scenes memoirs are not yet available, of course, but the best books to date for phrase-detecting are *Lyndon B. Johnson: The Exercise of Power* by Evans and Novak; *The Johnson Treatment* by Jack Bell; collections of speeches and press conference transcripts. For the Kennedy era, Schlesinger's *A Thousand Days* and Sorensen's *Kennedy* are quoted extensively throughout this book; backup sources were Roger Hilsman's *To Move a Nation,* Pierre Salinger's *With Kennedy,* and Bill Adler's series of "Kennedy Wit" books.

Eisenhower's memoirs are an excellent source for phrases; Robert Donovan's *Eisenhower: The Inside Story,* Sherman Adams' memoirs, and Emmet John Hughes's unfriendly *The Ordeal of Power* were helpful. Truman's memoirs sparkle with turns of phrase, backed up by Cabell Phillips' *The Truman Presidency* and Eric Goldman's *The Crucial Decade—And After.*

The Roosevelt years offer the widest choice of materials for phrase-detecting; the best are Samuel Rosenman's *Working with Roosevelt* and Raymond Moley's *The First New Deal.*

Among books of quotations, H. L. Mencken's *New Dictionary of Quotations* is by far the most helpful in this area, though many entries were "hidden" under what, for political phrase selection, were the wrong headings. Bartlett's *Familiar Quotations* is weak on contemporary quotations, though its index of first lines is superb for finding derivations; Bergen Evans' *Dictionary of Quotations* has an even better index. George Seldes' *The Great Quotations* leans hard on the unpopular and offbeat thinkers, usefully supplementing Bartlett, and the compiler went to the trouble of contacting many of his sources for clarification. James Simpson's *Contemporary Quotations* is necessary for the past decade's words of wisdom, and the *Home Book of American Quotations* usefully groups follow-up comments under the original quotation.

All quotation books, however, have a habit of establishing "first use" that is often undercut by the *Dictionary of American English* and Mathews' *Dictionary of Americanisms,* as well as by *American Speech,* a quarterly publication whose forty years of back issues were made available to me by Random House. These publications take scholarly delight in finding earlier uses of famous phrases and, therefore, most entries in this dictionary speak of "popularized by" rather than "coined by."

Political dictionaries were started by—or perhaps popularized by—Charles Ledyard Norton, whose *Political Americanisms,* published in 1890, is a charming, personal survey of the political language of his day. Since then, political dictionaries have been more descriptive of the terms of government (amendment, lobby, legislator) and the terms of history (Monroe Doctrine, XYZ Incident, Marshall Plan) with a few of the classics of political language sprinkled in *(logrolling, pork barrel, caucus).*

The breakthrough in the field of the language of politics was in 1962, with Hans Sperber and Travis Trittschuh's dictionary, *American Political Terms,* the work cited most often herein. There is about a 20 percent overlap in terms covered by that book and this; however, their emphasis is philological and historical, whereas this book stresses current political usage. But this dictionary draws heavily on what they modestly termed their "bagful of seeds."

Political columnists in newspapers use political phrases so habitually that they do not always realize they are using them, resulting in occasional "triples"—three unrelated political terms or metaphors in a single sentence that still makes sense, at least to users of the insider's lingo. A good example can be found in the TROOPS entry.

Of past PUNDITS (a *Time* popularization), Walter Lippmann, coiner of ATLANTIC COMMUNITY and popularizer of Swope's COLD WAR, the Alsops, who brought out EGGHEAD and PECKING ORDER, and Arthur Krock, the self-described "wag" who inflicted GOVERNMENT BY CRONY on Harry Truman, lead the phrase usage field because of their span of years writing about events of the

day. David Broder, Evans and Novak, James Reston (STONEWALL, FOGGY BOT-
TOM), and Joseph Kraft (MIDDLE AMERICA) bid fair to catch up in the future.

Time, Newsweek, the *New Republic,* and London's *Economist* are on the
lookout for neologisms, *U.S. News & World Report* and *The Nation* less so; the
New York Times' editorial and weekly review pages make frequent efforts to
straighten out the confusion in some political words (they were unsuccessful with
"de-escalate"). Two quarterlies, *Foreign Policy* and *Foreign Affairs,* are filled with
the latest diplomatic and war-gaming usages, as is the weekly bulletin put out by
the U.S. Department of State.

But the books, magazines, and newspapers do not fill up all the gaps in the
research. One entry in five required a letter to a source; amazingly, out of 250
letters written to people who were "there" at phrase coinages, the author received
some 150 useful replies. Some, like SNAKE IN THE TUNNEL, found the coiner.
Sargent Shriver wrote to say he was sorry about not knowing the origin of PEACE
CORPS, but Hubert Humphrey and General James Gavin contributed what they
knew, and the reader can now watch the phrase develop. Alf Landon, queried
about NEW FRONTIER, had a Kansas University professor look up his use of the
phrase in 1936 and passed it along; Mrs. Herbert Bayard Swope, a month before
her death, turned over a file of correspondence by her husband detailing the origin
of COLD WAR.

The earlier the Administration, the more willing were the participants to reply
for quotation. My acknowledgment to Professor Raymond Moley and Judge
Samuel Rosenman was expressed in the foreword; Elizabeth B. Drewry at the
Roosevelt Library in Hyde Park offers prompt and thorough help to any historian. The Library of Congress is set up to aid government officials and not the
general public, but after a certain amount of badgering, contacts can be made;
the entries on WINDFALL; HILL, THE; and UNITED WE STAND are better for them.
The Pentagon threw up its hands at the origin of *escalate,* but an official at Health,
Education and Welfare opened a fascinating trail to the origin of MEDICARE.

Since the author worked on Eisenhower, Rockefeller, and Nixon campaigns,
some speechwriters and aides of those men were available for checking origins
and usages by telephone; in some instances, like KITCHEN DEBATE, SPONTANE-
OUS DEMONSTRATION, HOOPLA, WORKFARE, WORK ETHIC, NATTERING NABOBS
OF NEGATIVISM, BLACK CAPITALISM and FIELD EXPEDIENT, he was present and
could write from personal experience. Officials of the Kennedy Administration
were understandably more cautious, requesting anonymity in many cases, but
were helpful nonetheless. When the lexicographer wrote Dean Rusk for verification of a coinage, he received a reply from the special assistant to the Secretary
of State, Ernest K. Lindley; a quick follow-up resulted in a horse's-mouth definition of *Lindley Rule* (see NOT FOR ATTRIBUTION).

At this point the words are selected, the research is done, and mail is coming
in filling up the holes. In the course of six months a first draft of the entries is
written, as more newspaper notations are added to the card file. A danger arises:
this is a history book, and the lexicographer no professional historian; at the same
time it is a dictionary dealing with etymology as well as current use, and the
lexicographer is not a linguistics expert. In a book of this type and length, the
possibility for errors in history and in linguistics is enormous. The saving grace
in the lexicographer being a practicing politician and public relations man is,
presumably, a "feel" for current usage and familiarity with the techniques and

catchwords of persuasion—but that is still no answer to the danger of error.

To minimize the risk, four lines of defense were drawn. The first was linguistic: a team of Random House editors, fresh from the triumph of the unabridged *Random House Dictionary of the English Language,* reviewed every etymological statement and commented on every decision on grammar, spelling, punctuation, and capitalization in the first edition. The author did not agree with every one of their suggestions, and thus retains responsibility for the decisions made, but at least he has been guided to the point where he can defend his position. Linguistics is not mathematics; a layman can argue with an expert. For an amusing example of this editing, see MISHMASH.

The second line of defense was historical. A Columbia University history professor went through the first draft for errors and came up with a remarkable series of instances in which men were quoted saying things years after they had died. With some heat, the lexicographer rechecked his source books; occasionally he had incorrectly transcribed a date, but more often the sources were wrong. Nobody is to be trusted. Samuel Maverick is identified in at least five reliable history books as a Boston innkeeper, but he was probably not; this dictionary may pass along some errors, and make some new ones of its own, but not for lack of trying to comb them out.

The third defense was political, as sections of the dictionary's early draft were placed with several political speechwriters and campaign managers, with particular query made about definitions. In this way, a geographical and political bias was adjusted and shadings of meanings added in many cases.

The final reading has a purpose of cross-fertilization. By this time the lexicographer is familiar with the individual words and proceeds to tie the dictionary together with cross-references and horizontal entries like MILITARY METAPHORS, DISASTER METAPHORS, SPORTS METAPHORS, RELIGIOUS METAPHORS, and WAR-GAMING WORDS.

Then come the corrections from readers. Between editions of this dictionary, the lexicographer has been blessed with studious emendations, irate straightenings-out, and scornful "any-idiot-knows" from people who have taken the trouble to cull this material and participate in its improvement. In addition, as a *New York Times* columnist stationed in Washington during my present incarnation, I have been exposed to some of the phrasemakers of the phrases herein, and they have not hesitated to claim credit or direct blame.

The bibliography that follows is the one that appeared in the first edition; each book contains at least five, and as many as a hundred, notations on the index cards. I have not brought the bibliography up to date because the emphasis in recent years has been on phrases found not in books, but in newspapers and magazines and on television, which are a couple of years ahead of most books when it comes to neologisms.

Bibliography

Adams, Sherman. *First-Hand Report.* New York: Harper & Bros., 1961.

Adler, Bill. *The Kennedy Wit.* New York: Citadel Press, 1964.

————. *More Kennedy Wit.* New York: Citadel Press, 1965.

————. *Presidential Wit.* New York: Trident Press, Inc., 1966.

————. *The Washington Wits.* New York: Macmillan Co., 1967.

Allen, Frederick Lewis. *Only Yesterday.* New York: Bantam Books, Inc., 1939.

Allibone, S. Austin (ed.). *Prose Quotations.* Philadelphia: J. B. Lippincott Co., 1875.

American Speech. New York: Columbia University Press.

Bain, Richard C. *Convention Decisions and Voting Records.* Washington: Brookings Institution, 1960.

Baker, Russell. *Baker's Dozen.* New York: The New York Times, 1964.

Barch, Oscar T., Jr. *A History of the United States Since 1945.* New York: Dell Publishing Co., 1965.

Barnett, A. B. (ed.). *Quotations from Chairman Mao Tse-Tung.* New York: Bantam Books, Inc., 1967.

Bartlett, John *Familiar Quotations.* Boston: Little, Brown and Co., 1955.

Beer, Samuel H. *Modern British Politics.* London: Faber & Faber, Ltd., 1965.

Bell, Daniel (ed.). *The Radical Right.* New York: Doubleday & Co., Inc., 1964.

Bell, Jack. *The Johnson Treatment.* New York: Harper & Row, 1964.

Bendiner, Robert. *Just Around the Corner.* New York: Harper & Row, Inc., 1967.

Benedict, Stewart H. (ed.). *Famous American Speeches.* New York: Dell Publishing Co., 1967.

Bernstein, Barton J. and Matusow, Allen J. *The Truman Administration.* New York: Harper & Row, Inc., 1966.

Bohle, Bruce (ed.). *The Home Book of American Quotations.* New York: Dodd, Mead & Co., 1967.

Boorstin, Daniel J. *An American Primer.* Chicago: University of Chicago Press, 1966.

Brewer's Dictionary of Phrase and Fable. New York: Harper & Row, 1965.

Burns, James MacGregor. *The Deadlock of Democracy.* Englewood Cliffs, New Jersey: Prentice-Hall, Inc., 1963.

————. *Roosevelt: The Lion and the Fox.* New York: Harcourt, Brace & World, Inc., 1956.

Butler, D. E. and King, Anthony. *The British General Election of 1966.* New York: Macmillan Co., 1966.

Cater, Douglass. *The Fourth Branch of Government.* New York: Vintage Books, 1965.

————. *Power in Washington.* New York: Vintage Books, 1964.

Christensen, A. N. and Kirkpatrick, E. M. *Running the Country.* New York: Henry Holt & Co., 1946.

Churchill, Winston. *Sir Winston Churchill—A Self Portrait.* London: Eyre & Spottiswoode, 1954.

Chute, William J. (ed.). *The American Scene: 1860 to the Present.* New York: Bantam Books Inc., 1966.

Coit, Margaret L. *Mr. Baruch.* Boston: Houghton Mifflin Co., 1957.

Connable, Alfred and Silverfarb, Edward. *Tigers of Tammany.* New York: Holt, Rinehart & Winston, Inc., 1967.

Copeland, Lewis and Lamn, Lawrence. *The World's Great Speeches*. New York: Dover Publications, Inc., 1958.

Cornuelle, Richard C. *Reclaiming the American Dream*. New York: Random House, Inc., 1965.

Costikyan, Edward N. *Behind Closed Doors*. New York: Harcourt, Brace & World, Inc., 1966.

Craigie, Sir William and Hulbert, James R. (eds.). *A Dictionary of American English*, Vols. I, III, IV. Chicago: University of Chicago Press, 1938.

Crawford, Kenneth G. *The Pressure Boys*. New York: Julian Messner, Inc., 1939.

Curtis, Michael (ed.). *The Nature of Politics*. New York: The Hearst Corp., 1962.

Daniels, Jonathan. *The Time Between the Wars*. New York: Doubleday & Co., Inc., 1966.

David, Paul; Goldman, Ralph; Bain, Richard C. *The Politics of National Party Conventions*. New York: Vintage Books, 1960.

Davidoss, Henry (ed.). *The Pocket Book of Quotations*. New York: Pocket Books, Inc., 1951.

Davis, Kenneth S. *A Prophet in His Own Country*. New York: Doubleday & Co., Inc., 1957.

Dewey, Thomas E. *Thomas E. Dewey on the Two Party System*, ed. John A. Wells. New York: Doubleday & Co., Inc., 1966.

Dialect Notes. University of Alabama Press.

DiSalle, Michael V. *Second Choice*. New York: Hawthorn Books, Inc., 1966.

Donovan, Robert J. *Eisenhower: The Inside Story*. New York: Harper & Bros., 1956.

Dunne, Finley Peter. *The World of Mr. Dooley*, ed. Louis Filler. New York: Harper & Bros., 1956.

Eisenhower, Dwight D. *Peace with Justice*. New York: Columbia University Press, 1961.

Evans, Rowland and Novak, Robert. *Lyndon B. Johnson: The Exercise of Power*. New York: New American Library, 1966.

Faber, Harold (ed.). *The New York Times Election Handbook 1964*. New York: McGraw-Hill Book Co., Inc., 1964.

Fay, Gerard (ed.). *The Bedside Guardian 14* (Selections 1964–65). London: Collins Clear-Type Press, 1965.

Felknor, Bruce L. *Dirty Politics*. New York: W. W. Norton & Co., Inc., 1966.

Filler, Louis (ed.). *The President Speaks*. New York: G. P. Putnam's Sons, 1964.

Fine, Sidney. *Recent America*. New York: Macmillan Co., 1962.

Flynn, Edward J. *You're the Boss*. New York: Viking Press, 1947.

Foreign Affairs, Vol. XLV (Nos. 1, 2, 3). New York: Council on Foreign Relations, Inc.

Fowler, H. W. *Modern English Usage* (2nd ed.). Oxford: Clarendon Press, 1965.

Fulbright, J. William. *The Arrogance of Power*. New York: Random House, Inc., 1966.

———. *Old Myths and New Realities*. New York: Random House, Inc., 1964.

Funk, Wilfred. *Word Origins*. New York: Grosset & Dunlap, Inc., 1950.

Galbraith, John Kenneth. *The Affluent Society*. New York: New American Library, Inc., 1958.

Garret, Charles. *The La Guardia Years*. New Brunswick, N.J.: Rutgers University Press, 1961.

Gilder, George and Chapman, Bruce K. *The Party That Lost Its Head*. New York: Alfred A. Knopf, Inc., 1966.

Goldman, Eric F. *The Crucial Decade— And After*. New York: Vintage Books, 1960.

———. *Rendezvous With Destiny*. New York: Vintage Books, 1952.

Gunther, John. *Inside USA*. New York: Harper & Bros., 1947.

Hadley, Arthur T. *Power's Human Face*. New York: William Morrow & Co., Inc., 1965.

Harris, Leon A. *The Fine Art of Political Wit*. New York: E. P. Dutton & Co., Inc., 1966.

Heller, Walter W. *New Dimensions of Political Economy*. Cambridge: Harvard University Press, 1966.

Hess, Stephen. *America's Political Dynas-*

ties. New York: Doubleday & Co., Inc., 1966.

Hibbitt, George W. (ed.). *The Dolphin Book of Speeches.* New York: Doubleday & Co., Inc., 1965.

Hilsman, Roger. *To Move a Nation.* New York: Doubleday & Co., Inc., 1967.

Hofstadter, Richard. *The Age of Reform.* New York: Vintage Books, 1955.

———. *The American Political Tradition.* New York: Vintage Books, 1948.

———. *Great Issues in American History,* Vols. I–II. New York: Vintage Books, 1958.

Holt, Sol. *The Dictionary of American Government.* New York: Macfadden-Bartell Books, 1964.

Horowitz, Irving Louis (ed.). *C. Wright Mills.* New York: Ballantine Books, Inc., 1963.

Howe, Quincy. *A World History of Our Own Times.* New York: Simon and Schuster, 1949.

Hughes, Emmet John. *The Ordeal of Power.* New York: Atheneum, 1963.

Hurd, Charles (ed.). *A Treasury of Great American Quotations.* New York: Hawthorn Books, Inc., 1964.

———. *When the New Deal Was Young and Gay.* New York: Hawthorn Books, Inc., 1965.

Ike, Nobutaka. *Japanese Politics.* London: Eyre & Spottiswoode, 1958.

Jacobs, Paul and Landau, Saul. *The New Radicals.* New York: Vintage Books, 1966.

Jennings, Sir Ivor. *Party Politics.* 3 vols. London: Cambridge University Press, 1961.

Johnson, Lyndon B. *A Time for Action.* New York: Atheneum, 1964.

Johnson, Walter. *1600 Pennsylvania Avenue.* Boston: Little, Brown and Co., 1963.

Josephson, Matthew. *The Politicos.* New York: Harcourt, Brace & World, Inc., 1938.

Kahn, E. J., Jr. *The World of Swope.* New York: Simon and Schuster, Inc., 1965.

Kahn, Herman. *Thinking About the Unthinkable.* New York: Avon Books, 1962.

Kane, Joseph Nathan. *Facts About the President.* New York: Pocket Books, Inc., 1959.

Kaplan, Donald M. and Schwerner, Armand. *The Domesday Dictionary,* ed. Louise Kaplan. London: Jonathan Cape, 1964.

Katcher, Leo. *Earl Warren: A Political Biography.* New York: McGraw-Hill Book Co., Inc., 1967.

Kennedy, John F. *Profiles in Courage.* New York: Harper & Row, Inc., 1964.

Kirwan, Michael J. *How to Succeed in Politics.* New York: Macfadden-Bartell Books, 1964.

Krock, Arthur. *In the Nation: 1932–1966.* New York: McGraw-Hill Book Co., Inc., 1966.

Laski, Harold. *Introduction to Politics.* London: Unwin Books, 1961.

Leech, Margaret. *In the Days of McKinley.* New York: Harper & Row, 1959.

Lorant, Stefan. *The Presidency.* New York: Macmillan Co., 1951.

Lubell, Samuel. *The Future of American Politics.* New York: Harper & Bros., 1951.

Luce, Robert B. (ed.). *The Faces of Five Decades.* (Selections from *The New Republic.*) New York: Simon and Schuster, Inc., 1964.

Martin, Joe. *My First Fifty Years in Politics.* New York: McGraw-Hill Book Co., Inc., 1960.

Mathews, Mitford M. (ed.). *A Dictionary of Americanisms.* Chicago: University of Chicago Press, 1951.

McCarthy, Eugene J. *The Crescent Dictionary of American Politics.* New York: Macmillan Co., 1962.

McElroy, Robert. *Grover Cleveland,* Vols. I & II. New York: Harper & Bros., 1923.

Mencken, H. L. *The American Language.* New York: Alfred A. Knopf, 1962.

———. *A New Dictionary of Quotations.* New York: Alfred A. Knopf, Inc., 1966.

Meyerson, Maxwell. *Memorable Quotations of John F. Kennedy.* New York: Thomas Y. Crowell Co., 1965.

Minney, R. J. *No. 10 Downing Street.* Boston: Little, Brown & Co., 1963.

Moley, Raymond. *The First New Deal.*

New York: Harcourt, Brace & World, Inc., 1966.

Montgomery, Hugh and Cambray, Philip G. *A Dictionary of Political Phrases & Allusions.* London: Swan Sonnenschein & Co., 1906.

Montgomery, John. *The Fifties.* London: George Allen and Unwin, Ltd., 1965.

Morris, Richard B. (ed.). *Encyclopedia of American History.* New York: Harper & Bros., 1953.

Morris, William and Mary. *Dictionary of Word & Phrase Origins.* New York: Harper & Row, 1962.

Morison, Samuel Eliot. *The Oxford History of the American People.* New York: Oxford University Press, 1965.

Neustadt, Richard E. *Presidential Power.* New York: Signet Books, 1960.

Nixon, Richard M. *Six Crises.* New York: Doubleday & Co., Inc., 1962.

Norton, Charles Ledyard. *Political Americanisms.* New York: Longmans, Green & Co., 1890.

Nye, Russell B. *Midwestern Progressive Politics.* New York: Harper & Row, Inc., 1959.

The Oxford Dictionary of Quotations. New York: Oxford University Press, 1955.

Padover, Saul K. (ed.). *Thomas Jefferson on Democracy.* New York: New American Library, Inc., 1939.

Parks, E. Taylor and Parks, Lois F. *Memorable Quotations of Franklin D. Roosevelt.* New York: Thomas Y. Crowell Co., 1965.

Partridge, Eric. *Usage and Abusage.* Baltimore: Penguin Books, 1947.

Pei, Mario. *Language of the Specialists.* New York: Funk & Wagnalls Co., Inc., 1966.

Phillips, Cabell. *The Truman Presidency.* New York: Macmillan Co., 1966.

Plano, Jack and Greenburg, Milton. *The American Political Dictionary.* New York: Holt, Rinehart & Winston, Inc., 1965.

Potter, Simeon. *Our Language.* Baltimore: Penguin Books, 1967.

Pringle, Henry F. *Theodore Roosevelt.* New York: Harcourt, Brace & World, Inc., 1931.

Pyles, Thomas. *Words & Ways of American English.* New York: Random House, Inc., 1952.

Raymond, Jack. *Power at the Pentagon.* New York: Harper & Row, Inc., 1964.

Reed, Thomas B. (ed.). *Modern Eloquence,* Vols. VI, IX–XIII. Philadelphia: John D. Morris & Co., 1903.

Riordon, William L. *Plunkitt of Tammany Hall.* New York: E. P. Dutton & Co., Inc., 1963.

Rosenau, James N. (ed.). *The Roosevelt Treasury.* New York: Doubleday & Co., Inc., 1951.

Rosenman, Samuel I. *Working with Roosevelt.* New York: Harper & Bros., 1952.

Rossiter, Clinton and Lare, James (eds.). *The Essential Lippman.* New York: Vintage Books, 1965.

Rossiter, Clinton. *Parties and Politics in America.* New York: New American Library, 1964.

Salinger, Pierre. *With Kennedy.* New York: Doubleday & Co., Inc., 1966.

Sampson, Anthony. *Macmillan.* London: The Penguin Press, 1967.

Schlesinger, Arthur M., Jr. *The Crisis of the Old Order.* Boston: Houghton Mifflin Co., 1957.

————. *A Thousand Days.* Boston: Houghton Mifflin Co., 1965.

Scott, John Anthony. *The Ballad of America.* New York: Bantam Books, Inc., 1966.

Seldes, George (ed.). *The Great Quotations.* New York: Lyle Stuart, 1966.

Shirer, William L. *The Rise and Fall of the Third Reich.* New York: Simon and Schuster, Inc., 1960.

Simpson, James B. (ed.). *Contemporary Quotations.* New York: Thomas Y. Crowell Co., 1964.

Smith, Edward Conrad and Zurcher, Arnold John (eds.). *Dictionary of American Politics.* New York: Barnes & Noble, Inc., 1966.

Smith, Alfred E. *Progressive Democracy: Addresses and State Papers of Alfred E. Smith,* compiled by H. Moskowitz. New York: Harcourt, Brace & Co., 1928.

Smith, William Gene and Hesiltine, Janet

E. (eds.). *Oxford Dictionary of English Proverbs.* London: Oxford University Press.

Sorensen, Theodore C. *Kennedy.* New York: Harper & Row, Inc., 1965.

Sperber, Hans and Trittschuh, Travis. *American Political Terms.* Detroit: Wayne State University Press, 1962.

Stevenson, Adlai E. *Major Campaign Speeches of Adlai E. Stevenson.* New York: Random House, Inc., 1953.

Stoddard, Henry L. *It Costs to Be President.* New York: Harper & Bros., 1938.

Stone, Irving. *They Also Ran.* New York: Doubleday & Co., Inc., 1943.

Sullivan, Mark. *Our Times.* Vol. III. New York: Charles Scribner's Sons, 1930.

Swanberg, W. A. *Citizen Hearst.* New York: Charles Scribner's Sons, 1961.

Tanzer, Lester. *The Kennedy Circle.* Washington: Luce, 1961.

Time Capsule/1929. New York: Time Incorporated, 1967.

Tourtellot, Arthur Bernon. *The Presidents on the Presidency.* New York: Doubleday & Co., Inc., 1964.

Truman, Harry S. *Years of Trial and Hope.* New York: New American Library, 1956.

Tsuneishi, Warren M. *Japanese Political Style.* New York: Harper & Row, Inc., 1966.

Viorst, Milton. *The Great Documents of Western Civilization.* New York: Bantam Books, Inc., 1965.

Vietnam Day Committee. *We Accuse.* Berkeley: Diablo Press, 1965.

Wattenberg, Ben J. with Scammon, Richard D. *This USA.* New York: Doubleday & Co., Inc., 1965.

Weisbord, Marvin R. *Campaigning for President.* New York: Washington Square Press, Inc., 1966.

Werth, Alexander. *De Gaulle.* Middlesex: Penguin Books, 1965.

Westin, Alan F. (ed.). *Freedom Now.* New York: Basic Books, Inc., 1964.

Whalen, Richard J. *The Founding Father.* New York: New American Library, 1964.

White, F. Clifton. *Suite 3505.* New Rochelle: Arlington House, 1967.

White, Theodore H. *The Making of the President 1960.* New York: Pocket Books, Inc., 1961.

White, Theodore H. *The Making of the President 1964.* New York: New American Library, 1966.

White, Wilbur W. *White's Political Dictionary.* New York: World Publishing Co., 1947.

Wilding, Norman and Laundy, Philip. *An Encyclopedia of Parliament.* London: Cassell & Co. Ltd., 1958.

Index

ABOUT THE AUTHOR

WILLIAM SAFIRE is a man of many careers. He began
as a reporter for a column in the *New York Herald Tribune*
(see JOURNALESE), was a television producer (see MEDIA
EVENT) and a public relations executive (see FLACK),
worked as a senior speechwriter in the Nixon White
House (see WORDSMITH) and escaped in time to become
a columnist for the *New York Times* (see PUNDIT).

Along the way, he has been an historian (*Before the
Fall: An Inside View of the Pre-Watergate White House*)
and a best-selling novelist (*Full Disclosure*). In 1978 he
was awarded the Pulitzer Prize for Commentary.

To these careers, add lexicographer: the unifying thread
in Safire's life has been a fascination with words, and his
insider's status in so many fields makes his work a diction-
ary-reader's delight.